FINANCIAL ACCOUNTING

Text and Problems

PROF. JAWAHAR LAL

Ex–Head, Department of Commerce

Ex–Dean, Faculty of Commerce and Business
Delhi School of Economics
University of Delhi
Delhi - 110007

&

DR. SEEMA SRIVASTAVA

Assistant Professor
Department of Commerce

Motilal Nehru College (Day)
University of Delhi
New Delhi - 110021

Himalaya Publishing House

ISO 9001 : 2015 CERTIFIED

© **Authors**

No part of this publication may be reproduced, stored in a retrieval system, or transmitted in any form or by any means, electronic, mechanical, photocopying, recording and/or otherwise without the prior written permission of the publisher.

First Edition : 2012
Edition : 2020
Edition : 2025
Edition : 2026

Published by : Mrs. Meena Pandey
for **Himalaya Publishing House Pvt. Ltd.,**
Vishal Industrial Estate, 1st Floor, Office No. 63/64,
Bhandup Village Road, Subhash Nagar (Opp. CEAT Tyres),
Nahur (W), Mumbai - 400 078. **Phone:** 022-35131464/65/66/67
E-mail: himpub@bharatmail.co.in; **Website:** www.himpub.com

Branch Offices :

New Delhi : "Pooja Apartments", 4-B, Murari Lal Street, Ansari Road, Darya Ganj, New Delhi - 110 002. Phone: 011-23270392, 23278631; Fax: 011-23256286

Nagpur : Kundanlal Chandak Industrial Estate, Ghat Road, Nagpur - 440 018. Mobile: 09325409992, 09325908881

Bengaluru : Plot No. 91-33, 2nd Main Road, Seshadripuram, Behind Nataraja Theatre, Bengaluru - 560 020. Phone: 080-41138821; Mobile: 09379847017, 09379847005

Hyderabad : No. 3-4-184, Lingampally, Besides Raghavendra Swamy Matham, Kachiguda, Hyderabad - 500 027. Phone: 040-27560041, 27550139

Chennai : No. 34/44, Motilal Street, T. Nagar, Chennai - 600 017. Mobile: 09380460419

Pune : "Laksha" Apartment, First Floor, No. 527, Mehunpura, Shaniwarpeth (Near Prabhat Theatre), Pune - 411 030. Phone: 020-24496323, 24496333; Mobile: 09370579333

Cuttack : Plot No 5F-755/4, Sector-9, CDA Markat Nagar, Cuttack - 753 014, Odisha. Mobile: 09338746007

Kolkata : 3, S.M. Bose Road, Near Gate No. 5, Agarpara Railway Station, North 24 Parganas, West Bengal - 700109. Mobile: 09674536325

DTP by : Twinkle Graphics, Shalimar Bagh, Delhi-110088

Printed at : Trinity Academy, Mumbai. On behalf of HPH.

PREFACE

Accounting, as a discipline, is accepted as the information system and the language of business with the objective of providing details and communicating useful information about an organization. Today, understanding this information system and this language has become more important than it was earlier. This will make accounting more purposeful and more realiable as a discipline–as a branch of knowledge.

In accounting, the discussion and the subject of financial accounting comes first because the structure of financial accounting underlies and guides, to some extent, all accounting. Financial Accounting uses some basic concepts and principles, describes a set of relationships among the different elements of the accounting system and the financial statements and a set of rules and guidlines for applying concepts and principles to specific business situations. There is a need to understand financial accounting to understand a business and its activities. To achieve such an understanding, we need a text which can discuss the subject in a clear, accurate and logical manner and which is easy to use by both the teachers and students. The present text has been written with the primary objective of providing a coprehensive, useful flexible and well presented text to serve the complete needs of B.Com (Hons.) students of University of Delhi and other Indian Universities.

ORGANIZATION OF THE TOPICS

The text is divided into four parts.

Part I provides an overview of financial accounting and discusses Financial Accounting: Nature and Scope; Basic Accounting Concepts and Financial Statements and Accounting Standards.

Part II titled 'Recording of Transactions and Preparation of Final Accounts' deals with the Accounting Framework and Transaction Analysis, Accounting Process : Journalization, Cash Book and Subsidiary Books, Ledger Posting and Trial Balance, Preparation of Final Accounts of Non-Corporate Business Entitles.

Part III titled as 'Income Measurement' discusses some accounting topics relating to measurement of income such as Business Income, Revenue Recognitions, Depreciation Accounting and Inventory Valuation.

Part IV focuses on financial accounting system followed by some organizations. This part covers Final Accounts of Not-For-Profit Organizations; Single Entry System; Accounting for Hire Purchase and Instalment Transactions; Branch Accounting; Dissolution of Partnership Firm.

CHAPTER ORGANIZATION

Each chapter in the text has the following features :

1. Each chapter begins with a set of learning objectives focused on the major issues covered in the chapter.
2. The coverage in the chapters concisely addresses more substantive and representative topics for commercial and industrial enterprises.
3. The book has more–and better–solved practical problems than the competitors.
4. Chapters conclude with assignment material, short- answer theory questions, long-answer theory questions and practical problems (relating to relevant chapters). These

end-of-chatper materials cover full spectrum of the chapter text, test understanding of the chapter contents and tie directly with the text in terminology, setup and difficulty level.

5. All the theory questions which have come in B.Com. (Hons.), examinations of University of Delhi have been included in the book.
6. The solved practical problems and unsolved practical problems given in the text have been taken from B. Com. (Hons.) examinations of Univesity of Delhi, CA (Professional Competence Course Examination), I.C.W.A. (Intermediate) examinations.

END OF BOOK MATERIAL

An Appexdix containing objective-type questions along with the answers has been given at the end of the book to help students assess understanding of the financial accounting knowlwdge. The objective-type questions given are True/False Questions, Multiple Choice Questions and Fill in the Blank Questions.

PRACTICAL PROBLEMS AND SOLUTIONS MANUAL

Problems and Solutions Manual, as a supplement to the text, provide complete problems and solutions to all the practical problems contained in the following chapters of the book.

- **Accounting Process III :** Completion of the Accounting Cycle, Preparation of Final Accounts of Non-Corporate Business Entitles
- Depreciation Accounting
- Inventory Valuation
- Final Accounts of Not-for-Profit Organizations.
- Single Entry System
- Accounting for Hire Purchase and Instalment Transactions
- Branch Accounting
- Dissolution of Partnership Firm

We believe that the book has a coverage that is sufficiently complete and self-contained and well suited to B.Com. (Hons.) of University of Delhi and other Indian Universities. We hope that students pursuing B.Com. (Hons.) in University of Delhi and other Indian Universities will find this book highly useful and friendly to study.

We thank many colleagues and friends who have provided help in the course of completing this project.

We appreciate very much the valuable help provided by Dr. Bibhoo Prasad Sahoo, (S.G.T.B. Khalsa College), Dr. Shivani Abrol (Zakir Hussain College), Dr. Ranu Gupta (Jesus and Merry College), Dr. Shalini Gupta (Saheed Bhagat Singh College) and Ms. Sucheta Gauba (Laxmi Bai College) of University of Delhi in completing this book.

We are also grateful to our family – Pratibha, Sanjay, Ashish, Rajnish, Anupriya, Akshita, Siddharth, Anirudh – for their moral support and understanding in the course of completing this book.

We welcome suggestions to further improve the quality of the book.

PROF. JAWAHAR LAL
DR. SEEMA SRIVASTAVA

CONTENTS

Part II

RECORDING OF TRANSACTIONS AND PREPARATION OF FINAL ACCOUNTS

Part III

INCOME MEASUREMENT

Part IV

FINANCIAL ACCOUNTING SYSTEMS

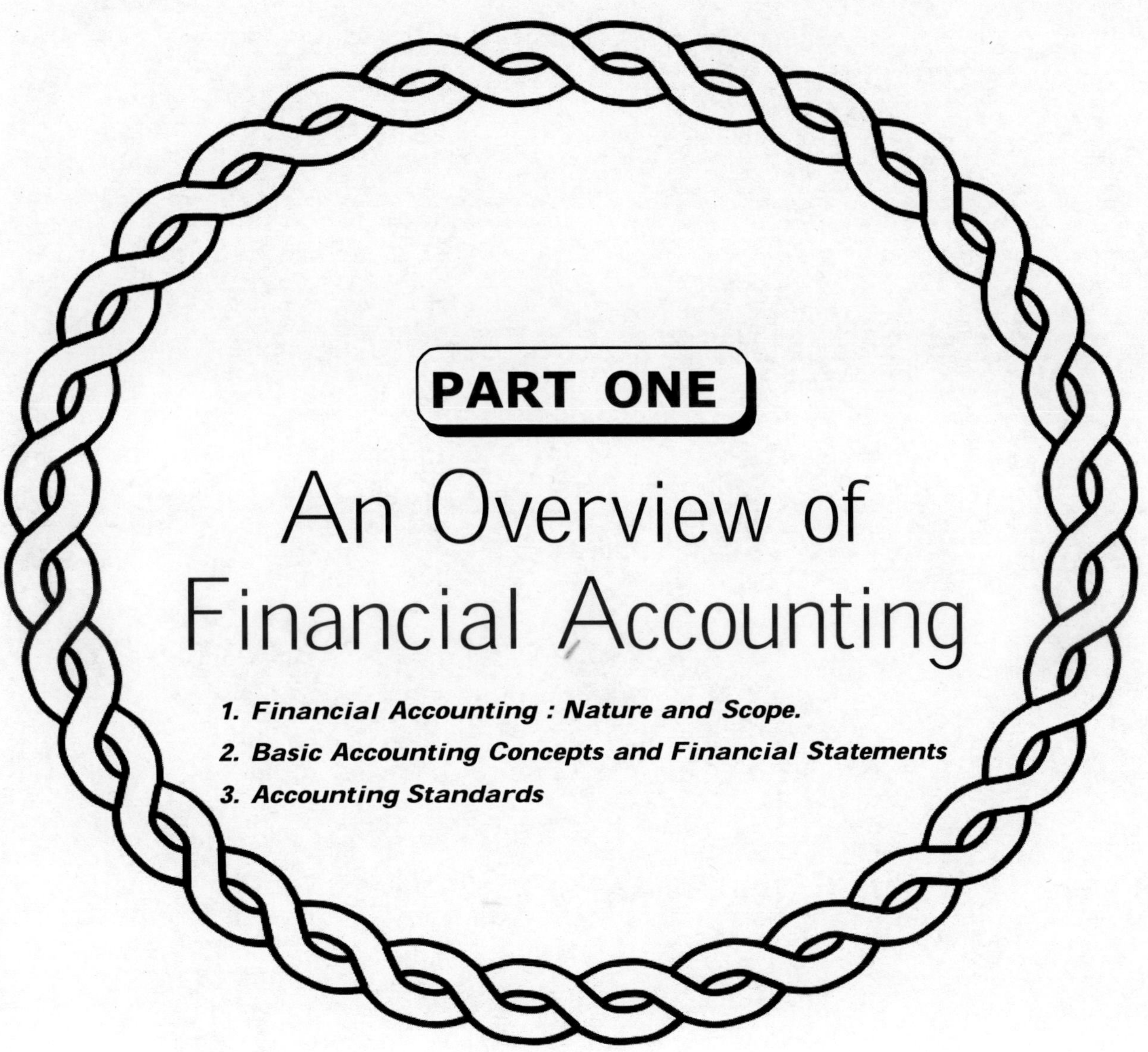

PART ONE

An Overview of Financial Accounting

1. *Financial Accounting : Nature and Scope.*
2. *Basic Accounting Concepts and Financial Statements*
3. *Accounting Standards*

CHAPTER 1

Financial Accounting : Nature and Scope

Learning Objectives

After studying this chapter, you should be able to :

1. *Describe the evolution of accounting.*
2. *Define accounting.*
3. *Distinguish between accounting and book keeping.*
4. *Explain the role of accounting as an information system.*
5. *Understand accounting as a language of business.*
6. *Identify different users of accounting.*
7. *Explain the advantages of accounting.*
8. *Evaluate the scope of financial accounting and management accounting.*

EVOLUTION OF ACCOUNTING

Accounting has evolved in a manner similar to law, medicine and most other fields of human activity, in response to the social and economic needs of society. Book-keeping and accounting did not emerge as chance phenomena, but as a pragmatic response to a specific world need.[1] This is true not only of the days of Paciolo[2] but also important for present-day accounting survival. Sieveking one of the few historians who have paid attention to the subject, says that book-keeping developed as a direct response to the establishment of partnership on a large scale.

For centuries after the system of double-entry book-keeping appeared, accounting was practised without a uniform methodology or any form of theory. It was only during the 19th century that a distinct move from book-keeping to accounting—a move from relatively simple recording and analysis of transactions towards a comprehensive accounting information system—was effected. The close of 19th century was marked by the most extraordinary expansion of business.

Company form of organisation, a phenomenon which was becoming increasingly common in business, world, grew at a great speed. Books about business transactions were written, conventions were followed and accounting was recognised as a system of analysing and maintaining records of business transactions.

In part, the new significance of accounting gained recognition because of separation between ownership and control and also due to diversification in ownership. The increased reliance on capital as a factor of production necessitated extensive record-keeping, and finally, in the 19th century a theoretical framework began to evolve. This framework or methodology provided a technical means to measure, evaluate, and communicate information of economic and financial nature.

Modern business is marked by continuity, a never-ending flow of economic activities. Therefore, accounting has grown to meet a social requirement and to guide the business and industry accordingly. Accounting is moving away from its traditional procedural base, encompassing record-keeping and such related work as the preparation of budgets and final accounts, towards the adoption of a role which emphasizes its social importance. Welsch and Anthony[3] comment :

"The growth of business organizations in size, particularly publicly-held corporations, has brought pressure from stock-holders, potential investors, creditors, governmental agencies, and the public at large, for increased financial disclosure. The public's right to know more about organizations that directly and indirectly affect them (whether or not they are shareholders) is being increasingly recognised as essential. An open society is one that has high degree of freedom at the individual level and typically evidences an effective commitment to measuring the quality of life attained. These characteristics make it essential that the members of that society be provided adequate, understandable, and dependable financial information from the major institutions that comprise it".

Profit calculation is no longer a simple comparison of financial values at the beginning and end of a transaction or series of transactions. It is now related to a complex set of allocations and valuations pertaining to the operational activities of a business enterprise. The concept of accountancy or accounting has broadened to include description of the recording, processing, classifying, evaluating, interpreting and supplying of economic–financial information for presentation of financial statements and decision-making purposes.

Further refinements in cost and management accounting followed later on in the 20th century along with large-scale production and high-capital investment. These developments created a need to allocate costs correctly over the units of production, and also to provide a measure of productivity and efficiency. Thereafter, cost accounting evolved naturally to meet recognized managerial requirements of pricing and costing for competitive purposes, and towards determining and setting forth of operational information for decision-making purposes.

Traditionally, governmental accounting was linked to taxation and revenue control, and to the recoding of, and accountability for, receipts and expenditures. Development in budgeting in the 20th century created a much larger scope for government accounting. The national budget became a managerial and policy-making instrument and developed into a mechanism for the forward planning of receipts and expenditures. Budgeting has now developed to form one of the bases of—and is closely associated with—economic planning and programming.

The use of enterprise accounting for the purpose of macro (economic or national) accounting is largely a recent development. For purposes of economic policy and economic planning, the national data—to a large extend derived from commercial data—have assumed greater significance. This, in turn, has given rise to the concept of macro accounting which has presented the professional with a new sphere of operation and perspective. Macro accounting has particular importance in helping build the bridge between economics and accounting, and thus offers accounting a significant scope to make a contribution towards macro economic policy.[4]

Accounting, thus, has gone through many phases—simple double-entry book-keeping, enterprise, government and cost and management accounting, and recently, social accounting. These phases have largely been a product of changing economic and social environments. As business and society have become more complex over the years, accounting has developed new concepts and techniques to meet the ever increasing needs for financial information.

DEFINITION OF ACCOUNTING

What is accounting? This basic question has never been answered precisely and many definitions of the term are available.

Back in 1941, the Committee on Terminology of the American Institute of Certified Public Accounts (AICPA) formulated the following definition,[5] which was widely quoted for many years :

"Accounting is the art of recording, classifying and summarising in a significant manner, and in terms of money, transactions and events which are, in part at least, of a financial character, and interpreting the results thereof".

In 1966, The American Accounting Association (AAA), in order to emphasise the broader perspective of accounting, provided the following definition of accounting.[6]

> "Accounting is the process of identifying, measuring and communicating economic information to permit informed judgements and decisions by users of the information".

In 1970, the AICPA of the USA defined accounting with reference to the concept of information :[7]

> "Accounting is a service activity. Its function is to provide quantitative information, primarily financial in nature, and about economic activities, that is intended to be useful in making economic decisions".

The term, 'quantitative information' used in the above definition is wider in scope than financial or economic information. Both the definitions, AAA (1966), and AICPA (1970) emphasise on using the information for the purposes of decision-making.

Modern accounting, therefore, is not merely concerned with record-keeping but also with a whole range of activities involving planning, control, decision-making, problem solving, performance measurement and evaluation, coordinating and directing, auditing, tax determination and planning, cost and management accounting.

The managers within an organization and interested outside parties use accounting information in making decisions that effect the organization. Today's accounting focusses on the ultimate needs of those, who use accounting information, whether these users are inside or outside the business itself.

Others have also given their definitions of accounting, but none has succeeded in clearly establishing the nature and scope of accounting. Each definition has merit in that it describes essentially what accountants do, but the boundaries are fuzzy[8]. Of the several available definitions of accounting, the one developed by American Accounting Association is perhaps the best because of its focus on accounting as an aid to decision-making[9].

ACCOUNTING AND BOOK-KEEPING

Book-keeping should be distinguished from accounting which has been defined earlier. Book-keeping is a process of accounting concerned merely with recording transactions and keeping records. Book-keeping is a small and simple part of accounting. It is mechanical and repetitive while dealing with business transactions.

As business transactions are observed and measured by the accountant, their effects are measured and recorded sequentially in a journal. The journal tells the accountant which accounts have been affected and which need to be updated. Temporary accounts are usually established to keep track of details of transactions that affect a business firm and owners equity. At the end of each accounting period, the length of which is determined by the needs or interests of managers or owners, the accountant may adjust the balances in some accounts before summarizing the effects of entries in temporary accounts on net profit. Information in the temporary accounts is used to prepare Income Statement and Balance Sheet. This exercise, repeated each accounting period, is known as the book-keeping and book-keeping cycle.

Accounting, on the other hand, aims at designing a satisfactory information system which may fulfil informational needs of different users and decision-makers. Accounting primarily focusses on measurement, analysis, interpretation and use of information. It highlights the relevance and relationship of the information produced by the accounting process and effects of different accounting alternatives. Accounting includes budgeting, strategic planning, cost analysis, auditing, income-tax preparation, performance measurement, evaluation, control, preparing managerial reports for decision-making etc.

ACCOUNTING AS AN INFORMATION SYSTEM

The term 'system' may be defined as a set of elements which operate together in order to attain a goal. A system does not consist of random sets of elements but elements which may be identified as belonging together because of a common goal. A system contains three activities (*i*) input, (*ii*) processing of input, and (*iii*) output.

Accounting comprises a series of linked activities. These accounting activities form a progression of steps, beginning with observing, then collecting, recording, analysing, and finally communicating information to users. As an information system, accounting links an information source or transmitter (generally the accountant), a channel of communication (generally the financial statements) and a set of receivers (external users). When accounting is looked upon as a process of communication, it is defined as "the process of encoding observations in the language of the accounting system, of manipulating the signs and statements of the systems and decoding and transmitting the result[10].

Figure 1.1, displays how accounting as an information system aids business and economic decisions made by user-decision-makers. In this service activity, as shown in Fig. 1.1., accounting assumes a link between business activities and transactions and the decision makers. First, accounting measures business activities and transactions through recording data. Second, the recorded data is processed and stored until needed. Processing can be done in such a manner or format as to become useful information. Alternatively, sometimes, the processed data are further processed or prepared to provide the required information to the user. Thirdly, processed and prepared information is communicated to users and decision makers in the forms of financial statements, other statements, reports, etc. In this accounting system, business transactions and activities are the input and statements and reports generated for the decision makers comprises the output.

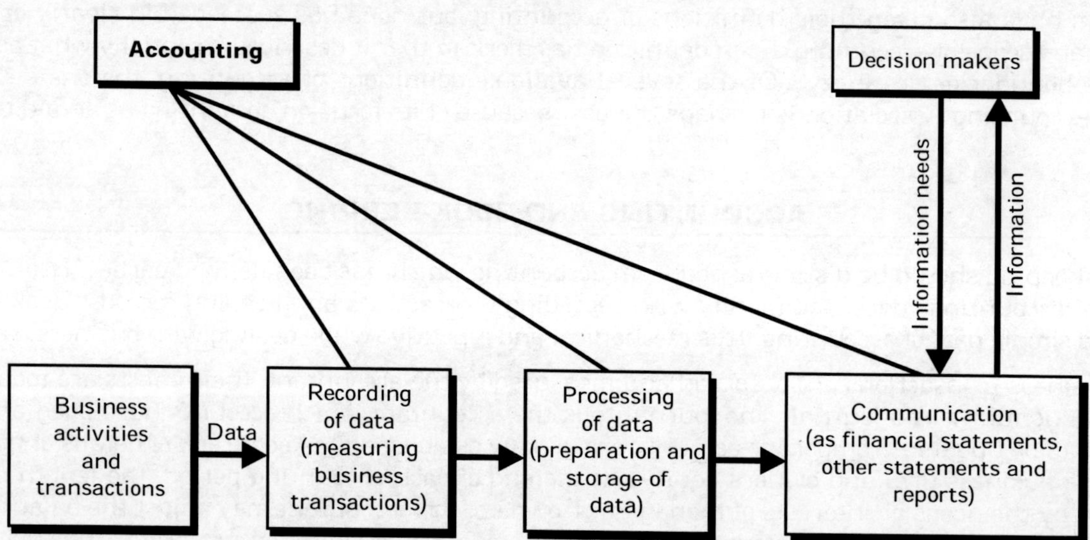

Fig. 1.1 Accounting as an information system in business and economic decision-making.

ACCOUNTING AS A LANGUAGE

Accounting is often called the 'language of business'. It is one means of communicating information about a business. As a new language is to be learnt to converse and communicate, so also accounting is to be learnt and practised to communicate *vis-a-vis* business events. For instance. Yuji Ijiri[11] observes.

> "As the language of business, accounting has many things in common with other languages. The various business activities of a firm are reported in accounting statements using accounting language, just as news events are reported in newspapers, in English or another Language. To express an event in accounting or in English we must follow certain rules. Without following certain rules diligently, not only does one run the risk of being misunderstood but also risks a penalty for misrepresentation, lying or perjury. Comparability of statements is essential to the effective functioning of a language whether it is in English or in accounting. At the same time, language has to be flexible to adapt to a changing environment".

There are important similarities between a language and accounting. A language broadly has two components : (*i*) symbols, and (*ii*) rules to make it purposeful. Symbols are the meaningful units or words identifiable in any language, known as linguistic objects and which are used to convey particular meaning or concepts. The arrangement of symbols in a systematic manner becomes a language. The rules which influence the usage and pattern of the symbols are known as the grammar of the language or grammatical rules.

In accounting too, there are two components : (*i*) symbols, and (*ii*) grammatical rules. In accounting, numerals and words and debits and credits are accepted as symbols which are unique to the accounting discipline. The grammatical rules in accounting refer to the general set of procedures followed to create all manner of financial data for business. Anthony and Reece[12] draw the following parallel between accounting and language :

> "Accounting... resembles a language in that some of its rules are definite whereas others are not. Accountants differ as to how a given event should be reported, just as grammarians differ as to many matters of sentence structure, punctuation and choice of words. Nevertheless, just as many practices are clearly poor English (language), many practices are definitely poor accounting. Languages evolve and change in response to the changing needs of society, and so does accounting".

USERS OF ACCOUNTING INFORMATION

Accounting provides useful information about the activities of an entity to various individuals or groups for their use in making informed judgements and decisions. The following are the users of accounting information :

1. **Management :** Management is a group of people who are responsible for using the resources and managing the affairs of an entity to achieve certain predetermined goals and objectives. Managers perform many managerial functions such as planning, controlling, directing, measuring, evaluating and taking corrective action. Business managers need to decide continuously what to do, how to do it and whether the actual results tally the original plans and targets. Accounting provides timely and useful information to the management for planning, control, performance measurement, decision making and for performing many activities and functions in the company. Thus, management is one of the most important users of accounting information and a major function of accounting is to provide useful information to the managers and management.

2. **Investors :** The providers of risk capital and their advisors are concerned with the risk inherent in, and return, provided by their investments. They need information to help them determine whether they should buy, hold or sell. Shareholders are also interested in information which enables them to assess the ability of the enterprise to pay dividends.

3. **Employees :** Employees and their representative groups are interested in information about the stability and profitability of their employers. They are also interested in information which enables them to assess the ability of the enterprise to provide remuneration, retirement benefits and employment opportunities.

4. **Lenders :** Lenders are interested in information that enables them to determine whether their loans, and the interest attaching to them, will be paid when due.

5. **Suppliers and Others Trade Creditors :** Suppliers and other creditors are interested in information that enables them to determine whether amounts owing to them will be paid when due. Trade creditors are likely to be interested in an enterprise over a shorter period than lenders unless they are dependent upon the continuation of the enterprise as a major customer.

6. **Customers :** Customers have an interest in information about the continuance of an enterprise, especially when they have a long-term involvement with, or are dependent on, the enterprise.

7. **Governments and their Agencies :** Governments and their agencies are interested in the allocation of resources and, therefore, the activities of enterprises. They also require information in order to regulate the activities of enterprises, determine taxation policies and as the basis for national income and similar statistics.

8. **Public :** Enterprises affect members of the public in a variety of ways. For examples, enterprises may make a substantial contribution to the local economy in many ways including the number of people they employ and their partronage of local suppliers. Financial statements may assist the public by providing information about the trends and recent developments in the prosperity of the enterprise and the range of its activities.

ACCOUNTING SYSTEMS

An accounting system consists of the personnel, procedures, technology, and records used by an organization (1) to develop accounting information and (2) to communicate this information to decision makers. The design and capabilities of these systems vary greatly from one organization to another. In small businesses, accounting systems may consist of little more than a cash register, a cheque book, and income tax preparation. In large businesses, accounting systems include computers, highly trained personnel, and accounting reports that affect the daily operations of every department. But in every case, the basic purpose of the accounting system remains the same : *to meet the organization's needs for information as efficiently as possible.*[13]

Many factors affect the structure of the accounting system within a particular organization. Among the most important are (1) a business firm's *needs for accounting information* and (2) the *resources available* for operation of the system.

ADVANTAGES OF ACCOUNTING

Accounting and information generated in this has significant utility in evaluating the performance of an organization, predicting its future prospects and growth and helping many users and user groups in making sound decisions in their economic objectives. More specifically the following are the advantages associated with accounting and accounting statements.

1. **Determination of Business Performance and Financial Position :** The most important benefit of accounting is to provide help in ascertaining the results of operation and financial position. Income statement determines the results of operation and balance sheet ascertains financial position of a business enterprise. Both the statements—income statement and balance sheet—are central features of accounting. These two statements assists in judging the accountability of management and how effectively management is able to utilise the resources entrusted to it.

2. **Economic Decisions Making :** The two important economic decisions that external users usually make are (*a*) security investment (*b*) credit decision. Sound economic decisions require assessment of impact of current business activities and developments on the earning power of a company. Both economic decisions require detailed information to determine benefits (to be received) in lieu of sacrifices (resources given). Information about economic resources and obligations of a business enterprise is also needed to form judgements about the ability of the enterprise to survive, to adapt, to grow, and to prosper amid changing economic conditions. In this task, accounting can provide information important in evaluating the strength and weakness of an enterprises and its ability to meet its commitments. It can supply information about transactions within the business and factors outside the company such as taxation policy, trade restrictions, technological changes, market potentialities etc., which affect the earning power of a business enterprise.

3. **Employee Decisions :** Employee decisions may be based on perceptions of a company's economic status acquired through financial statements. In particular, prospective and present employees may

use the accounting reports to assess risk and growth potential of a company and therefore, job security and future promotional possibilities. Labour unions and individual employees may use financial statement data as a basis for making contractual wage and employment benefit demands.

4. **Customer Decisions :** The data presented in financial statements prepared in accounting may affect the decision of a company's customers and hence have economic consequences. Customers, like employees, may use financial statement data to predict the likehood and/or timing of a firm going bankrupt or being unable to meet its commitments. This information may be important in estimating the value of a warranty or in predicting the availability of supporting services or continuing supplies of goods over an extended period of time.

5. **Manager's Decisions :** The accounting data in financial reports may have economic effects through its impact on the behaviour of the managers and owners of business enterprises. The inclusion of accounting numbers in management compensation schemes or the fear of market misinterpretation of accounting reports may influence a manager's operating and financing decisions. Shareholders prefer accounting procedures that mirror economic events as closely as possible. However, shareholders also must be concerned that the managers might manipulate the reported data to increase their compensation. Therefore, shareholders, like creditors and union leaders, also want numbers that are reliable and objectively determined.

KINDS OF ACCOUNTING

There are four kinds of accounting :

1. **Financial Accounting :** Financial accounting is used by profit-making entities and is based on Generally Accepted Accounting Principles (GAAP). It aims to provide information to investors, creditors, suppliers, employees, managers, government and regulatory authorities and general public for helping them in making economic decisions about a business enterprise. The end product of financial accounting is three primary financial statements—income statement, balance sheet, cash flow statement. Financial accounting uses double entry accounting system in measuring, describing and communicating financial data to users.

2. **Not-for-Profit Accounting :** Many economic entities do not have profit as an objective. Municipalities, clubs etc., simply receive money from service fees, membership fees, donations, subscriptions, taxes (in case of municipalities) and allocate it to address needs. For example, a city allocates funds to a police department to ensure public safety. The process of recording these fund inflows and outflows and reporting them to the public is called **not-for-profit accounting.**

3. **Cost and Management Accounting :** Managers need *internal information systems* to generate timely and accurate information that helps them plan and operate efficiently on a day-to-day basis. To guide their decisions, managers rely to some extent on the information produced by the financial accounting system. However, more important to such decisions is information that is not available to the public and is produced strictly for management's own use. Such information is referred to as **cost** and **management accounting** information.

4. **Tax Accounting :** The area of accounting devoted to understanding and applying the tax law is known as **tax accounting.** Tax law is extremely detailed and complicated.

   An important distinction should be made between the net income resulting from applying income tax laws (called *taxable income*) and the income that results from financial accounting (called *net income*). Financial accounting income, or net income, is determined by applying financial accounting principles and procedures, which differ in many ways from the income tax laws. As a result, net income is not necessarily equal to taxable income.

REFERENCES

1. Maurice Moonitz and A.C. Littleton, *Significant Accounting Essays,* Prentice-Hall, 1965. p. 12.
2. Francisan Monk, Paciolo, is looked upon as the father of modern accounting. His Summa, published in 1494, comprised the first text reference on book-keeping, Later book-keeping spread throughout the world through a series of paciolo imitations.
3. Glenn A. Welsch and Robert N. Anthony, *Fundamentals of Financial Accounting,* Richard D. Irwin, 1971, p. 19.
4. Dr. Adolf J.H. Enthoven, *Accounting Education in Economic Development,* North-Holland Publishing Co., 1981, p. 11.
5. Accounting Terminology Bulletin No.1; *Review and Resume,* AICPA, 1953, para 9.
6. American Accounting Association, *A Statement of Basic Accounting Theory,* 1966, p.1.
7. Accounting Principles Board, Statement No.4, *Basic Concepts and Accounting Principles Underlying Financial Statement of Business Enterprises,* 1970, para 40.
8. "A good definition, besides providing a description so that people have an understanding of what the object is, should establish clear-cut boundaries. Any object that falls within the boundaries of the set is identified as a member of the set and any object that falls outside is then not a member of the set". Vernon Kam, *Accounting Theory,* John-Wiley and Sons, 1990. p. 33.
9. Robert N. Anthony and James S. Reece, *Accounting Principles,* Richard D. Irwin 1991, p. 8.
10. R.J. Chambers, *Accounting Evaluation and Economic Behaviour,* Scholars Book Company, 1974, p. 184.
11. Yuji Ijiri, *Theory of Accounting Measurement,* Accounting Research Study No. 10. AAA, 1975, p. 14.
12. Robert N. Anthony and James S. Reece, *Accounting Principle,* Richard D. Irwin, 1991, p. 14.
13. Jane R. Williams, Susan F. Haka and Mark S. Bettner, *Financial and Management Accounting,* McGraw Hill, 2005, p. 6.

ASSIGNMENT MATERIAL

Note : The Objective–Type Questions (True/False, Multiple Choice Questions etc.) have been given in the Appendix at the end of the book.

SHORT ANSWER THEORY QUESTIONS

1. Write a note on purposes of accounting.
2. Explain objectives of financial statements.
3. Define accounting.
4. Distinguish between accounting and book-keeping.
5. Write a note on accounting as an information system.
6. In what way accounting is treated as a language of business?
7. Explain management and investors as users of accounting information.
8. Write a note on the users of accounting information.
9. Explain briefly the concept of accounting system.
10. What groups besides managers, investors and creditors use accounting information?
11. Explain briefly different kinds of accounting.

LONG ANSWER THEORY QUESTIONS

1. Define accounting and explain the steps in the accounting process.
2. Describe the real nature of accounting. Why accounting has been called the language of business?
3. Trace the evolution of accounting.
4. Critically evaluate two definitions of accounting.
5. Explain accounting as an information system.
6. Discuss accounting as language of business.
7. Explain different users of accounting information.
8. Discuss advantages associated with accounting.
9. Examine the utility of accounting as a discipline.
10. What is the scope of financial accounting?
11. Discuss four kinds of accounting.
12. What are the objectives of accounting, financial accounting and management accounting?
13. Which decision-makers use accounting information?
14. What objectives does management seek to achieve by using accounting information?
15. Why are investors and creditors interested in the financial statements of a business enterprise?
16. "Accounting is an information system." Explain this statement.
17. List and briefly describe the main audiences for financial accounting information.
18. Accounting is said to be the language of business. What does it try to communicate and how?

CHAPTER 2

Basic Accounting Concepts and Financial Statements

Learning Objectives

After studying this chapter, you should be able to :

1. *Define Postulates, Assumptions, Concepts, Principles and Convention.*
2. *Explain basic accounting concepts such as entity, going concern, money measurement, accounting period, cost, dual-aspect, conservatism, matching, realization, consistency, materiality, full disclosure.*
3. *Understand Generally Accepted Accounting Principles (GAAP).*
4. *Understand briefly the nature of three basic financial statements—profit and loss account, balance sheet, cash flow statement.*
5. *Have a view of actual financial statements constituting profit and loss account, balance sheet. cash flow statement.*
6. *Explain briefly elements of financial statements—assets and liabilities.*
7. *Discuss qualitative characteristics of financial statement information such as relevance, reliability, understandability, comparability, neutrality, timeliness, verifiability.*

POSTULATES, ASSUMPTION, CONCEPTS, PRINCIPLES AND CONVENTIONS

Terms such as postulates, assumptions, concepts, principles and convention (and others such as procedures, rules) are widely used, but with no general agreement as to their precise meaning. Often, what is referred to as 'Postulate's' or 'Assumptions' by some writers, are termed as 'Concepts' or 'Principles' by others and vice-versa. Similarly, what are understood by some as Accounting Conventions', are forcefully recognised as 'Accounting Principles' or 'Accounting Concepts' and vice versa. Thus, it can be observed that finding a precise terminology has always been one of the most difficult task in accounting. Further, the lack of agreement about precise meaning has affected, to some extent, the attempts made towards developing a theory for financial accounting.

The purpose of this chapter is not to engage the readers in a debate of suitable terminology but to explain something which are widely accepted as of greatest importance and widest applicability, whether as postulates, assumptions, concepts, principles or convention. But before this, an attempt has been made to define the terms postulates, assumptions, concepts, principles and conventions.

Postulates

Accounting postulates are basic assumptions which are generally accepted as self-evident truths in accounting. Postulates are established or general truths which do not require any evidence to prove them. They are the propositions taken for granted.

American Institute of Certified Public Accountants (US) observes :

"Postulates are few in number and are the basic assumptions on which principles rest. They necessarily are derived from the economic and political environment and from the modes of thought and customs of all segments of the business community. The profession, however, should make clear their understanding and interpretation of what they are, to provide a meaningful foundation for the formulation of principles and the development of rules or other guides for the application of principles in specific situations."[1]

According to Kohler[2]

"The truth of a postulate, like that of other assumptions, is taken for granted as something generally admitted as self-evident...Postulates are chosen for their convenience and fruitfulness in organising and promoting inquiry or useful action. Postulates may be expected to change as activities within the field are modified, and as the public interest in the field alter its views concerning the value of the field to society."

Assumptions

Assumptions in accounting are considered and accepted as postulates. There is a wider consensus that both postulates and assumptions carry the same meaning and importance in the accounting context. Assumptions are premises, self-evident truths, statements accepted without proof as a basis for a line of reasoning or course of action. Applicability and utility of assumptions are deemed to be self-evident and consequences associated with applying assumptions justify their exploration and use.

Concepts

Accounting concepts are also self-evident statements or truths. Accounting concepts are so basic that accept them as valid without any questioning. Accounting concepts provide the conceptual guidelines for application in the financial accounting process, *i.e.* for recording, measurement, analysis and communication of information about an organisation. These concepts provide help in resolving future accounting issues on a permanent or a longer basis, rather than trying to deal with each issue on an *ad-hoc* basis. The concepts are important because they (*a*) help explain the 'why' of accounting (*b*) provide guidance when new accounting situations are encountered, and (*c*) significantly reduce the need to memorise accounting procedures when learning about accounting.[3]

Principles

Accounting principles are general decision rules derived from the accounting concepts. According to AICPA (US), a principles means "a general law or rule adopted or professed as a guide to action : a settled ground or basis of conduct or practice". Accounting principles are characterised as 'how to apply' concepts. Anthony and Reece[4] comment:

"Accounting principles are man-made. Unlike the principles of physics, chemistry and other natural science, accounting principles were not deducted from basic axioms, nor can they be verified by observation and experiment. Instead, they have evolved. This evolutionary process is going on constantly; accounting principles are not eternal truths".

A principle is an explanation concisely farmed in words to compress an important relationship among accounting ideas into a few words. Principles are concise explanations. Accounting principles do not suggest exactly as to how each transaction will be recorded. This is the reason that accounting practices differ from one enterprise to another. The differences in accounting practices is also due to the fact that GAAP provides flexibility in the recording and reporting of business transactions.

Accounting principles influence the development of accounting techniques which are specific rules to record specific transactions and events in an organisation.

Convention

Convention is referred to as a statement or a rule of practice adopted by common consent, express or implied. It can be distinguished from an Assumption, Axiom or Postulate in that it need not represent what is the thought to be self-evident truth[5]. For example, it is a convention (established by long usage) that debits are placed on the left hand side of a 'T' account and credits on the right hand side. The opposite would be an equally useful convention.

A convention may be said to exist when it is known that an alternative equally logical rule or procedure is available but is not used because of considerations of habit, cost, time or convenience. Convention dictates many of the activities in accounting such as measures of materiality, the style and content of financial statements. Modified conventions emerge in the world of accounting from time-to-time. They are generally attributed to the growth of the public interest in the improvement of financial reporting.

BASIC ACCOUNTING CONCEPTS

Accounting principles are built on a foundation of a few basic concepts. These concepts are so basic that most preparers of financial statements do not consciously think of them. As stated earlier, they are regarded as self-evident. Some accounting researchers and theorists argue that certain of the present accounting concepts are wrong and should be changed. Nevertheless, in order to understand accounting as it now exists, one must understand the underlying concepts currently used.

Basic accounting concepts discussed herein may not be identical to those listed by other authors or groups. However, these are the concepts that are widely accepted and used in practice by preparers of financial statements and by auditor while verifying such statements. The basic accounting concepts are as follows :

1. Entity Concept : The entity concept assumes that the financial statements and other accounting information are for the specific business enterprise which is distinct from its owners. Consequently, the analysis of business transactions involving costs and revenue is expressed in terms of the changes in the firm's financial conditions. Similarly, the assets and liabilities devoted to business activities are entity assets and liabilities. The transactions of the enterprise are to reported rather than the transaction of the enterprise's owners. This concept, therefore, enables the accountant to distinguish between personal and business transactions. The concept applies to sole proprietorship, partnership, companies, and small and large enterprise. It may also apply to a segment of a firm, such as division, or several firms, such as when inter-related firms are consolidated.

2. Going Concern Concept : A business entity is viewed as continuing in operation in the absence of evidence to the contrary* Because of the relative permanence of enterprises, financial accounting is formulated assuming that the business will continue to operate for an indefinitely long period in the future.

The going-concern concept justifies the valuation of assets on a non-liquidation basis and it calls for the use of historical cost for many valuations. Also, the fixed assets and intangibles are amortised over their useful life rather than over a shorter period in expectations of early liquidation.

The going-concern concept leads to the proposition that individual financial statements are part of a continuous, inter-related series of statements. This further implies that data communicated are tentative and that current statements should disclose adjustments to past year statements revealed by more recent developments.

3. Money Measurement Concept : A unit of exchange and measurement is necessary to account for the transactions of business enterprises in a uniform manner. The common denominator chosen in accounting is the monetary unit. Money is the common denominator in terms of which the exchangeability of goods and services, including labour, natural resources and capital are measured. Money measurement concept holds that accounting is a measurement and communication process of the activities of the firm that are measurable in monetary terms. Obviously, financial statements should indicate the money used.

Money Measurement concept implies two limitations of accounting. First, accounting is limited to the production of information expressed in terms of a monetary unit : it does not record and communicate other

* A related proposition is that if liquidation appears imminent, financial information may be prepared on the assumption that liquidation will take place.

relevant but non-monetary information. Secondly, the monetary measurement concept concerns the limitations of the monetary unit itself as a unit of measure. The primary characteristics of the monetary unit – purchasing power, or the quantity of goods or services that money can acquire – is of concern. Traditionally, financial accounting has dealt with this problem by stating that this concept assumes either that the purchasing power of the monetary unit is stable over time or that the changes in prices are not significant. While still accepted for current financial reporting, the stable monetary unit concept is the object of continuous and persistent criticism.

4. Accounting Period Concept : Financial accounting provides information about the economic activities of an enterprise for specified time periods that are shorter than the life of the enterprise. Normally, the time periods are of equal length to facilitate comparison.

The time period is identified in the financial statements. The time periods are usually of twelve months. Some times quarterly or half-yearly statements are also issued. These are considered interim and different from annual statements. For managerial use, statements covering shorter periods such as a month or a week may also be prepared.

5. Cost Concept : The cost concept requires that assets be recorded at the exchange price, *i.e.*, acquisition cost or historical cost. Historical cost is recognised as the appropriate valuation basis for recognition of the acquisition of all goods and services, expenses, costs and equities. For accounting purposes, business transactions are normally measured in terms of the actual prices or costs at the time the transaction occurs, *i.e.* financial accounting measurements are primarily based on exchange prices at which economic resources and obligations are exchanged. Thus, the amounts at which assets are listed in the accounts of a firm do not indicate what the assets could be sold for.

The historical cost concept implies that since the business is not going to sell its asset as such there is little point in revaluing assets to reflect current values. In addition, for practical reasons, the accountant prefers the reporting of actual costs to market values which are difficult to verify.

6. Dual-Aspect Concept : This concept lies at the heart of the whole accounting process. The accountant records events affecting the wealth of a particular entity. The question is — which aspect of this wealth are important? Since an accounting entity is an artificial creation, it is essential to know to whom its resources belong to or what purpose they serve. It is also important to know what kind of resources it controls. *e.g.* cash, buildings or land. Accounts recording systems have therefore been developed so as to show two main things : (*a*) the source of wealth and (*b*) the form it takes.

Suppose Mr. X decides to establish a business and transfers A 1,00,000 from his private bank account to a separate business account. He might record this event as follows :

Business Entity Records

Liabilities	*Assets*
Source of wealth	Form of wealth
X's capital A 1,00,000	Cash at bank A 1,00,000

Clearly, the source of wealth must be numerically equal to the form of wealth. Since they are simply different aspects of the same thing, *i.e.* in the form of an equation: S (sources) must equal F (forms).

Moreover, any transaction or event affecting the wealth of entity must have two aspects recorded in order to maintain the equality of both sides of the accounting equation. If business has acquired an asset, it must have resulted in one of the following:

(*a*) Some other asset has been given up.

(*b*) The obligation to pay for it has arisen.

(*c*) There has been a profit, leading to an increase in the amount that the business owes to the proprietor.

(*d*) The proprietor has contributed money for the acquisition of asset.

This does not mean that a transaction will affect both the source and form of wealth. There are four categories of events affecting the accounting equation:

(*a*) Both, sources and forms of wealth, increase by the same amount.

(*b*) Both, sources and forms of wealth, decrease by the same amount.

(*c*) Some forms of wealth increase while others decrease without any change in the source of wealth.

(*d*) Some sources of wealth increase while others decrease without any change in the form in which wealth is held.

The example given above illustrates category (*a*) since the commencing transaction for the entity results in the source of wealth, and form of wealth, cash, both increasing from zero to A 1,00,000. By contrast, X might decide to withdraw A 20,000 cash from the business. Then financial position of business entity would result in.

Liabilities	*Assets*
Source of wealth	Form of wealth
X's capital A 80,000	Cash A 80,000

It is essential to appreciate why both sides of the equation decrease. By taking out cash, X automatically reduces his supply of private finance to the business by the same amount.

Suppose now that Mr. X buys stocks of goods for A 30,000 with the available cash. His supply of capital does not change, but the composition of the business assets does.

Source of Wealth		*Form of Wealth*	
X's capital	A 80,000	Stock	A 30,000
		Cash	A 50,000
	A 80,000		**A 80,000**

The two aspects of this transaction are not in the same direction but compensatory, an increase in stocks of setting a decrease in cash. Similarly, sources of wealth also may be affected by a transaction. Thus, if X gives his son Y, a A 20,000 share in the business by transferring part of his own interest, the effect is as follows:

Source of Wealth		*Form of Wealth*	
X's capital	A 60,000	Stocks	A 30,000
Y's capital	A 20,000	Cash	A 50,000
	A 80,000		**A 80,000**

If however, X gives Y A 20,000 in cash privately and Y then puts it into the business, both sides of equation would be affected. Y's capital of A 20,000 being balanced by an extra A 20,000 in cash, X's capital remaining at A 80,000.

7. Accrual Concept : According to Financial Accounting Standards Boards (US): "Accrual accounting attempts to record the financial effects on an enterprise of transactions and other events and circumstances that have cash consequences for the enterprise in the periods in which those transactions, events and circumstances occur rather than only in the periods in which cash is received or paid by the enterprise. Accrual accounting is concerned with the process by which cash expended on resources and activities is returned as more (or perhaps less) cash to the enterprise, not just with the beginning and end of that process. It recognizes that the buying, producing, selling and other operations of an enterprise during a period, as well as other events that effect enterprise performance often do not coincide with the cash receipts and payments of the periods".

Realization concept and matching concept are central to accrual accounting. Accrual accounting measures income for a period as the difference between the revenues recognized in that period and the expenses that are matched with those revenues. Under accrual accounting the period's revenues generally are not the same as the period's cash receipts from customers, and the period's expenses generally are not the same as the period's cash disbursements.

Cash-Basis Accounting : Under cash basis accounting, sales are not recorded until the period in which they are received in cash. Similarly, costs are deducted from sales in the period in which they are paid for cash disbursements. Thus, neither the realization nor matching concept applies in cash-basis accounting.

In practice, "pure" cash-basis accounting is rare. This is because a pure cash-basis approach would require treating the acquisition of inventories as a reduction in profit when the acquisition costs are paid rather than when the inventories are sold. Similarly, costs of acquiring items of plant and equipment would be treated as profit reductions when paid in cash rather than in the later periods when these long-lived items are used. Clearly, such a pure cash-basis approach would result in balance sheets and income statements that would be of limited usefulness. Thus, what is commonly called *cash-basis accounting* is actually a mixture of cash basis for some items (especially sales and period costs) and accrual basis for other items (especially product costs and long-lived assets.) This mixture is also sometimes called **modified cash-basis accounting** to distinguish it from a pure cash-basis method.[6]

Cash-basis accounting is seen most often in small firms that provide services and therefore do not have significant amounts of inventories. Examples include restaurants, beauty parlors and barber shops, and income tax preparation firms. Since most of these establishments do not extend credit to their customers, cash-basis profit may not differ dramatically from accrual-basis income. Nevertheless, cash-basis accounting is *not* permitted by GAAP for any type of business entity.

8. Conservatism* Concept : This principles is often described as "anticipate no profit, and provide for all possible losses". This characterisation might be viewed as the reactive version of the minimax managerial philosophy, *i.e.* minimise the chance of maximum losses. The concept of accounting conservatism suggest that when and where uncertainly and risk exposure so warrant, accounting takes a wary and watchful stance until the appearance of evidence to the contrary. Accounting conservatism does not mean intentionally understating income and assets, it applies only to situations in which there are reasonable doubts. For example, inventories are valued at the lower ends of cost or market value.

In its application to the income statement, conservatism encourages the recognition of all losses that have occurred or are likely to occur but does not acknowledge gains until actually realised. The early amortisation of intangible assets and the restrictions against recording appreciation of assets have also, at least to some extent, been motivated by conservatism. Failure to recognise revenue until a sale has taken place is still another manifestation of conservatism.

9. Matching Concept : The matching concept in financial accounting is the process of matching (relating) accomplishments or revenues (as measured by the selling prices of goods and services delivered) with efforts or expenses (as measured by the cost of goods and services used) to a particular period for which the income is being determined. This concept emphasises which items of cost are expenses in a given accounting period. That is, costs are reported as expenses in the accounting period in which the revenue associated with those costs is reported. For example, when the sales value of some goods is reported as revenue in a year, the cost of those goods would be reported as an expenses in the same year.

Matching concepts needs to be fulfilled only after realisation concept has been completed by the accountant: first revenues are measured in accordance with the realisation concept and then costs are associated with these revenues. *Costs are, matched with revenues, not the other way around.* The matching process, therefore, requires cost allocation which is significant in historical cost accounting. Past (historical)

* According to some writers 'prudence' is a better word than conservatism, Uncertainties inevitably surround many transactions and this should be recognized by exercising prudence in preparing financial statements. Prodence does not, however, justify the creaction of secret or hidden reserves.

costs are examined and are subjected to a procedure whereby elements of cost regarded as having expired service potential are allocated or matched against relevant revenues. The remaining elements of costs which are regarded as continuing to have future service potential are carried forward in the historical balance sheet and are termed as assets. *Thus, the balance sheet is nothing more than a report of unallocated past costs waiting expiry of their estimated future service potential before being matched with suitable revenues.*

10. Realization or Recognition Concept : The realization or recognition concept indicates the amount of revenue that should be recognised from a given sale. Realization rules help the accountant in determining that a revenue or expense has occurred, so that it can be measured, recorded, and reported in financial reports.

Realization refers to inflows of cash or claims to cash (*e.g.,* accounts receivable) arising from the sale of goods or services. Thus, if a customer buys A 500 worth of items at a grocery store, paying cash, the store realizes A 500 from the sale. If a clothing store sells a suit for A 3000, the purchaser agreeing to pay within 30 days, the store realizes A 3000 (in receivables) from the sale, *provided* that the purchaser has a good credit record so that payment is reasonably certain (conservatism concept).

The realization concept states that the amount recognized as revenue is the amount that is reasonably certain to be realized – that is, that customers are reasonably certain to pay. Of course, there is room for differences in judgment as to how certain "reasonably certain" is. However, the concept does clearly allow for the amount of revenue recognized to be less than the selling price of the goods and services sold.[7] The obvious situation is the sale of merchandise at a discount – at an amount less than its normal selling price. In such cases, revenue is recorded at the lower amount, not the normal price.

11. Consistency Concept : This concept requires that once an organization has decided on one method, it should use the same method for all subsequent transactions and events of the same nature unless it has sound reasons to change methods. If accounting methods are frequently changed, comparison of financial statements for one period with those of another period would be difficult. The consistent use of accounting methods and procedures over time will check the distortion of profit and loss account and the balance sheet and the possible manipulation of these statements. Consistency is necessary to help external users in comparing financial statements of a given firm over time and in making sound economics decisions.

12. Materiality Concept : In law there is a doctrine called *de minimis non curat lex,* which means that the court will not consider trivial matters. Similarly, the accountant does not attempt to record events so insignificant that the work of recording them is not justified by the usefulness of the results.

Materiality concept implies that the transactions and events that have immaterial or insignificant effects should not be recorded and reported in the financial statements. It is argued that the recording of insignificant events cannot be justified in terms of its subsequent poor utility to users. For example, conceptually, a brand-new pad of paper is an asset of the entity. Every time someone writes on a page of the pad, part of this asset is used up, and retained earnings decreases correspondingly. Theoretically, it would be possible to ascertain the number of partly used pads that are owned by the entity at the end of the accounting period and to show this amount as an asset. But the cost of such an effort would obviously be unwarranted, and no accountant would attempt to do this. Accountants take the simpler, even though less exact, course of action and treat the asset as being used up (expensed) either at the time the pads were purchased or at the time they were issued from supplies inventory to the user.

Unfortunately, there is no agreement on the meaning of materiality and the exact line separating material events from immaterial events. The decision depends on judgment and common sense. It is for the preparer of accounts to interpret what is and what is not material. Probably the materiality of an event or transaction can be decided in terms of its impact on the financial position, results of operations, changes in the financial position of an organization and on evaluation or decisions made by users.

13. Full Disclosure Concept : The full disclosure concept requires that a business enterprise should provide all relevant information to external users for the purpose of sound economic decisions. This concept implies that no information of substance or of interest to the average investors will be omitted or concealed from an entity's financial statements.

GENERALLY ACCEPTED ACCOUNTING PRINCIPLES (GAAP)

Financial accounting follows a set of ground rules or accounting principles in presenting financial information which are known as Generally Accepted Accounting Principles (GAAP). In fact, to be useful, financial accounting information should be collected, classified, summarised and reported objectively. Those who use such information and rely on such data have a right to be assured that the data are reliable, free from bias and inconsistencies, whether delibrate or otherwise. For this reason, financial accounting depends on certain guidelines or standards that have proved useful over the years in accounting and reporting information. In this task, GAAP plays a vital role and financial accounting information can be meaningful only when prepared according to some agreed upon standards and procedures, *i.e.,* Generally Accepted Accounting Principles.

Accounting Principles Board[8] of the USA observes :

"Generally Accepted Accounting Principles incorporate the consensus at a particular times as to which economic resources and obligations should be recorded as assets and liabilities by financial accounting, which changes in assets and liabilities should be recorded, when these changes are to be recorded, how the assets and liabilities and changes in them should be measured, what information should be disclosed and which financial statements should be prepared".

GAAP are simply guides to action and may change over time. They are not immutable laws like those in the physical science. Sometimes specific principles must be altered or new principles must be formulated to fit changed economic circumstances or changes in business practices. Accounting principles originate from problem situations such as changes in the law, tax regulations, new business organizational arrangements, or new financing or ownership techniques.

Certain accounting techniques or procedures are tried in response to the effect such problems have on financial reports. Through comparative use and analysis, one or more of these techniques are judged most suitable, obtain substantial authoritative support and are then considered a generally accepted accounting principle.[9]

Walgenbach, et al. comment

> "Because no basic natural accounting law exists, accounting principles have developed on the basis of their usefulness. Consequently, the growth of accounting is more closely related to experience and practice than to the foundation provided by ultimate law. As such, accounting principles tend to envolve rather than be discovered, to be flexible rather than precise and to be subject to regular evaluation rather than be ultimate or final".

In India, organizations such as the Accounting Standards Board (ASB), Institute of Chartered Accountants of India, Department of Corporate Affairs (Government of India), Securities and Exchange Board of India (SEBI), Institute of Costs and Works Accountants of India, Institute of Company Secretaries, Stock Exchanges, and the literature each of these publishes, are instrumental in the development of most accounting principles. In the US, financial Accounting Standards Board (FASB), American Institute of Certified Public Accountants (AICPA). Securities and Exchange Commission (SEC), Internal Revenue Service and the American Accounting Association are instrumental in the formulation of accounting principles. At the international level, International Accounting Standards Board (IASB) has taken upon the responsibility of formulating accounting principles for use by all the countries of the world.

BASIC FINANCIAL STATEMENTS

The end product of the financial accounting process is a set of reports that are called financial statements. The nature and format of financial statements are derived directly from the basic accounting framework and the accounting equation. Generally, Accepted Accounting Principles (GAAP) require that three such reports be prepared and these three reports constitute the financial statements.

1. Profit and Loss Account
2. Balance Sheet (a statement of financial position)
3. Cash Flow Statement

1. Profit and Loss Account

Profit and loss account, also known as income statement, presents the results of operations of a business enterprise for a period of time. This statement shows net profit or net income of an entity for a period of time. Net profit or income is the difference between revenues and expenses. The profit and loss account indicates how successful a business enterprise has been in achieving its profit goal for a given time span. It also gives the sources and amounts of revenues earned and the different types and amounts of expenses. Net profit indicates an enterprise's accomplishments (revenues) in relation to the efforts required (expenses) in pursuing its operating activities. When expenses exceed revenues for a period, a business enterprise incurs a net loss.

2. Balance Sheet

Balance sheet shows the financial position of a business on a certain date. For this reason, it is often called the statement of financial position. Balance sheet indicates the investing and financing activities of a business enterprise at a point of time and shows a firm's assets, liabilities and equity capital usually at the close of the last day of a month or a year. Assets are economic resources and provide future benefits to a firm such as cash, inventories, building, plant, patent, goodwill, etc. Liabilities are outsiders' claims on the assets of a business enterprise such as creditors, accounts payables, salaries payable, income-tax payable, debentures. Liabilities include shareholders equity as well which is in the forms of ordinary shares, preference shares, retained earnings. Shareholders equity is the shareholders' or owners' claim on the assets of a firm. The shareholders' claims are only residual, *i.e.,* shareholders have claims against the assets of a company only after all creditors' claims have been met.

3. Cash Flow Statement

Cash flow statement summarises the flow of cash in and out of the firm over a period of time. It focusses on various items which bring out changes in the cash balance between two balance sheet dates. Cash flow statement covers all items which increase or decrease the cash of a business enterprise. In USA, UK and other countries, statement of cash flows is legally required to be prepared by companies alongwith income statement and balance sheet. In India also, cash flow statement is required to be given in published company annual reports by the Indian companies whose securities are listed on the Stock Exchanges.

Figure 2.1 summarises the information provided by the financial statements.

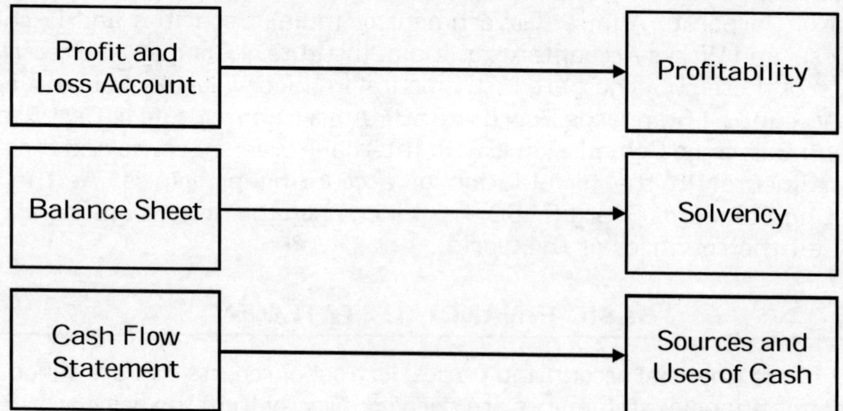

Fig. 2.1. Information provided by the financial statements.

Most reports, in any field, can be classified into one of two categories : (1) **stock,** or **status, reports** and (2) **flow reports.** The amount of water in a reservoir at a given moment of time is a measure of stock, whereas the amount of water that moves through the reservoir in a day is a measure of flow. Reports of stocks are always as of a specified *instant* in time; reports of flow always cover a specified *period* of time. Reports of stocks are like snapshots; reports of flows are more like motion pictures. One of the accounting reports, the balance sheet, is a report of stock. It shows information about the resources and obligations of an organization at a specified moment of time. The other two reports, the income statement and the cash flow statement, are reports of flows. They report activities of the organization for a period of time, such as a quarter or a year.[10]

ILLUSTRATION OF ACTUAL FINANCIAL STATEMENTS

Although financial statements are prepared in many different formats and may use account classifications that differ substantially, a reader of financial reports who understands the basic accounting equation can usually figure out how to read the financial reports of an organization regardless of the particular reporting scheme that the organization has chosen. The financial statements of the Hindustan Unilever Ltd., for the year 2009-10 provide an illustration of the relationship between the accounting equation and a set of financial reports. The Profit and Loss Account (See Exhibit 2.1) measures how net income were affected by operations before the payment of cash dividends. The balance sheet (See Exhibit 2.2) illustrates the basic equality between assets and liabilities. The cash flows statement (See Exhibit 2.3) shows why the amount of cash and cash equivalents changed because of operating, investing, and financing activities.

Exhibit 2.1

Profit and Loss Account

For the year ended 31st March, 2010

Figures in brackets represent deductions

A Crores

		12 Months Ended 31st March, 2010	15 months Ended 31st March, 2009
Income			
Sales (Net of excise)		17,523.80	20,239.33
Other Income (Current year : net of Mark to Market Loss)		349.64	589.72
Total		**17,873.44**	**20.829.05**
Expenditure			
Operating Expenses		(14,975.36)	(17,583.31)
Depreciation		(184.03)	(195.30)
Interest		(6.98)	(25.32)
Total		**(15,166.37)**	**(17,803.93)**
Profit before Taxation and Exceptional/ Extraordinary Items		**2,707.07**	**3,025.12**
Taxation for the year	- current tax	(626.23)	(535.86)
	- deferred tax	(22.13)	(0.02)
	- Fringe benefit tax	–	(37.06)
Taxation adjustments of previous years (net)		43.97	48.53
PROFIT AFTER TAXATION AND BEFORE EXCEPTIONAL/EXTRAORDINARY ITEMS		**2,102.68**	**2,500.71**
Exceptional/Extraordinary items (net of tax)		99.35	(4.26)

	2010	2009
NET PROFIT	**2,202.03**	**2,496.45**
Balance brought forward	531.66	197.50
Profit and loss Balance of Bon Limited	(55.33)	
Available for distribution	**2,678.36**	**2,693.95**
Dividends :		
On equity shares :		
Interim - A 3.00 per share - declared on 31st October, 2009 (2009 : A 3.50 per share)	(654.35)	(762.56)
(includes A 0.08 crores on Final Dividend for 2009)		
Final - A 3.50 per share - Proposed (2009: A 4.00 per share)	(763.59)	(871.95)
Tax on distributed profits (includes A 0.01 crores on Final Divided for 2009)	(238.03)	(277.78)
Transfer to General Reserve	(220.20)	(250.00)
Balance carried forward	**802.19**	**531.66**
Earnings per share (A) **- Basic (Face Value of A 1 each)**	11.46	10.10
- Diluted (Face value of A 1 each)	11.44	10.08

Source : Hindustan Unilever Ltd., Annual Report, 25th May, 2010, p. 64

Exhibit 2.2
Balance Sheet
As at 31st March, 2010

Figures in brackets represent deductions

A Crores

		As at 31st March 2010		**As at 31st March, 2009**
Sources of Funds				
Shareholder's funds				
Capital		218.17		217.99
Reserves and surplus		2,365.35		1,843.52
		2,583.52		2,061.51
Loan funds				
Secured loans	-		144.65	
Unsecured loans	-	-	277.29	421.94
		2,583.52		**2,483.45**
APPLICATION OF FUNDS				
Fixed Assets				
Gross block	3,581.96		2,881.73	
Depreciation and impairment loss	(1,419.85)		(1,274.95)	
Net Block	2,162.11		1,606.78	
Capital work-in-progress	273.96	2,436.07	472.06	2,078.84
Investments		1,264.08		332.62
Deferred Tax				
Deferred Tax Assets	451.13		439.09	
Deferred Tax Liabilities	(202.31)	248.82	(184.26)	254.83

Current assets, loans and advances				
Inventories	2,179.93		2,528.86	
Sundry debtors	678.44		536.89	
Cash and bank balances	1,892.21		1,777.35	
Other current assets	16.62		15.74	
Loans and advances	600.56		742.12	
	5,367.76		**5,600.96**	
Current Liabilities and provisions				
Liabilities	(5,291.66)		(4,255.82)	
Provisions	(1,441.55)		(1,527.98)	
	(6,733.21)		**(5,783.80)**	
Net current assets		(1,365.45)		(182.84)
		2,583.52		**2,483.45**

Source : Hindustan Unilever Ltd., Annual Report, 25th May 2010, p. 65.

Exhibit 2.3
Cash Flow Statement
for the year ended 31st March, 2010

Figures in brackets represent deductions
A Crores

		12 Months Ended 31st March, 2010	**15 Months Ended 31st March, 2009**
A. Cash Flow from Operating Activities :			
Profit before taxation and exceptional/ extra-ordinary items		2,707.07	3,025.12
Adjustments for :			
Depreciation	184.03		195.30
Surplus on disposal of investments (net)	(19.54)		(53.90)
Reversal of provision for diminution in value of investments, net of cost over fair value of current investments (net)	–		(3.09) –
Deficit on disposal of fixed assets (net)	7.19		9.27
Interest income	(93.91)		(80.94)
Dividend income	(34.65)		(70.71)
Interest expenditure	6.98		25.32
		50.10	**21.25**
Operating Profit before Working Capital Changes		2,757.17	3,046.37
Adjustments for :			
Trade and other Receivables	(16.12)		(151.88)
Inventories	348.92		(575.25)
Trade Payables and other Liabilities	1,096.14		398.21
		1,428.94	**(328.92)**
Cash generated from operations		4,186.11	2,717.45
Taxes paid (net of refunds)		(661.74)	(633.65)

Cash flow before exceptional/extraordinary items	**3,524.37**	**2,083.80**
Exceptional :		
Compensation paid under voluntary separation schemes and amount paid for an industrial dispute relating to a closed factory	(84.97)	(35.99)
Transitional cost due to consolidation of offices/factories	(6.65)	(16.41)
Amounts paid for other restructuring activities	(0.38)	(4.24)
Extraordinary :		
Consideration received on disposal of Bertolli brand	–	1.50
Net Cash from Operating Activities.........A	**3,432.37**	**2,028.66**
B. CASH FLOW FROM INVESTING ACTIVITIES :		
Purchase of fixed assets	(570.08)	(636.13)
Sale of fixed assets	13.27	6.64
Purchase of investments	(6,128.94)	(12,482.27)
Investment in subsidiary company	(5.15)	(0.68)
Sale of investments	5,207.15	13,649.75
Interest received	96.55	77.59
Dividend received	34.65	70.71
Cash flow before exceptional/extra-ordinary items	**(1,352.55)**	**685.61**
Exceptional :		
Consideration received on disposal of unused land and building (including residential properties)	100.77	172.20
Consideration received on disposal of a long term investment	91.13	20.38
Consideration received on sale of a business to a subsidiary (including non-compete fees)	3.30	–
Consideration received on disposal of a subsidiary	19.89	–
Net Cash (used in)/from investing Activities........B	**(1,137.46)**	**878.19**
C. CASH FLOW FROM FINANCING ACTIVITIES :		
Dividends paid	(1,523.27)	(1,435.96)
Tax on distributed profits	(259.39)	(240.61)
Interest paid	(6.98)	(25.32)
Bank overdrafts, etc., (net)	(49.37)	(37.99)
Proceeds from borrowings	–	1,280.86
Proceeds from share allotment under Employee Stock option scheme	31.27	38.12
Repayments of borrowings	(372.58)	(909.46)
Net Cash used in Financing Activities........C	**(2,180.32)**	**(1,330.36)**
Net Increase in Cash and Cash equivalents. (A+B+C)	114.59	1,576.49
Cash and Cash equivalents as at 1st April, (Opening Balance)	1,777,35	200.86
Cash and Cash equivalents as at 1st April, 2009 of Bon Ltd. (Refer note 12 to profit and loss account)	0.27	–
Cash and Cash equivalents as at period end (Closing Balance)	1,892.21	1,777,35

Source : Hindustan Unilever Ltd., Annual Report, 25th May, 2010, p. 67.

ELEMENTS OF FINANCIAL STATEMENTS

The financial statements exhibited suggest that broadly the following are the elements that are found in every set of financial reports.

1. Assets
2. Liabilities
3. Revenues
4. Expenses
5. Gains and Losses

The elements Assets and Liabilities have been briefly reviewed herein. Revenue, Expenses, gains and losses have been explained in Chapter 10.

ASSETS

Different assets possessed by a business enterprise appear on the balance sheet. These assets are classified as follows :

1. **Fixed Assets :** Fixed assets are tangible assets and refer to a firm's property, plant and equipment. Fixed assets are assets held with the intention of being used for the purpose of producing or providing goods or services and is not held for sale in the normal course of business.
2. **Investments :** Investments are created by a firm through purchase of shares and other securities. Investment by a firm can be made for long term or short term.
3. **Intangible Assets :** Intangible assets do not have physical substance but they are the resources that benefit an enterprise's operations. Intangible assets provide exclusive rights or privileges to the owner. Examples are patents, copyrights, trademarks. Some intangible assets arise from the creation of a business enterprise—organization costs or reflect a firm's ability to generate above normal earnings—that is goodwill.
4. **Current Assets :** Current assets include cash and assets that will be converted into cash or used up during the normal operating cycle of the business or one year, whichever is longer. Examples are debtors, closing stocks, marketable securities, besides the cash.

LIABILITIES

Liabilities may be defined as currently existing obligations which a business enterprise intends to meet at some time in future. Such obligations arise from legal or managerial considerations and impose restriction on the use of assets by the enterprise for its own purposes. Liabilities are obligations resulting from past transactions that require the firm to pay money, provide goods, or perform services in the future. The existence of a past transaction is an important element in the definition of liabilities. According to Institute of Chartered Accountants of India, liability is "the financial obligation of an enterprise other than owners' funds".[11]

Liabilities are generally classified as follows :

1. Current Liabilities
2. Long Term Liabilities

Current Liabilities

Current liabilities are those that will be paid from among the assets listed as current assets. Current liabilities are debtor obligations payable within one year of the balance sheet date.

Current liabilities can be divided into two main groups based on the means by which their values are determined. These groups include (A) Liabilities with specific values usually determined from contracts and

(B) Liabilities whose values must be estimated. Some liabilities falling under these two categories are as follows :

1. **Accounts Payable :** Trade accounts payable are debts owed to trade creditors. They normally arise from the purchase of goods or services.
2. **Bills (Notes) Payable :** Although bills payable may arise from the same sources as trade accounts payable, they are evidenced by negotiable instruments and therefore should be reported separately. The maturity date of these bills may extend from a few days to year and they may be either interest bearing or non-interest bearing.
3. **Interest Payable :** Interest payable is typically the result of an accrual and is recorded at the end of each accounting period. Interest payable on different types of items is usually reported as a single item.
4. **Wages and Salary Payable :** A liability for unpaid wages and salaries is created when employees are paid at fixed intervals that do not coincide with the balance sheet date. Unclaimed wages that have not been paid to employees because of failure to claim their earnings should be included in salaries and wages payable.
5. **Current Portion of Long-term Debt :** Current liabilities usually include that portion of long term debt which becomes payable within the next year.
6. **Advance from Customers :** Money received in advance from customers create a liability for the future delivery of goods or services. The advances are initially recorded as liabilities and are then transferred from liability account to revenue account when the goods or services are delivered.

Long-Term Liabilities

Long-term liabilities are those liabilities that are not due during the next year or during the normal operating cycle. That is, long-term liabilities become due after one year and are the liabilities which are not classified as current liabilities. Long-term liabilities are often incurred when assets are purchased, large amounts are borrowed for replacement, expansion purposes etc. Example of long-term liabilities are debentures and bonds, mortgages, long-term notes payable, other long-term obligations.

Contingent Liabilities

A contingent liability is not a legal or effective liability, rather it is a potential future liability. The amount of a contingent liability may be known or estimated. Contingent liabilities are those which will arise in the future only on the occurrence of a specified event. Although they are based on past contractual obligations, they are conditional rather than certain liabilities.

Owner's Equity

Equity is a residual claim—a claim to the assets remaining after the debts to creditors have been discharged. Equity is the residual interest in the assets of an entity that remains after deducting its liabilities. In other words, ownership equity is the excess of total assets over total liabilities. It represents the book value of the owner's interest in the business enterprise.

QUALITATIVE CHARACTERISTICS OF FINANCIAL STATEMENT INFORMATION

The qualitative characteristics are attributes that improve the usefulness of information provided in financial statements. The characteristics make information a desirable commodity and guide the selection of preferred accounting policies and methods from among available alternatives.

The qualitative characteristics that have been found possessing wider acceptance and recognition in accounting literature are as follows :

1. Relevance

Relevance is closely and directly related to the concept of useful information. Relevance implies that all those items of information should be reported that may aid the users in making decisions and/or predictions. In general, information that is given greater weight in decision-making is more relevant.

2. Reliability

To be useful, the information must be reliable, that is to say, they must be free from material error and bias. The information provided are not likely to be reliable unless:

(*a*) Transactions and events reported are faithfully represented.

(*b*) Transactions and events are reported in terms of their substance and economic reality, not merely on the basis of their legal form. This principle is called the principle of 'substance over form'.

(*c*) The reporting of transactions and events are neutral, *i.e.,* free from bias.

(*d*) Prudence is exercised in reporting uncertain outcome of transactions or events.

3. Understandability

Understandability is the quality of information that enables users to perceive its significance. The benefits of information may be increased by making it more understandable and hence useful to a wider circle of users. Presenting information which can be understood only by sophisticated users and not by others, creates a bias which is inconsistent with the standard of adequate disclosure. Thus, understandable financial accounting information presents data that can be understood by users of the information and is expressed in a form and with terminology adopted to the user's range of understanding.

4. Comparability

Economic decision requires making choice among possible courses of actions. In making decisions, the decision-maker will make comparisons among alternatives, which is facilitated by financial information. Comparability implies to have like things reported in a similar fashion and unlike things reported differently.

Comparable financial accounting information presents similarities and differences that arise from basic similarities and differences in the enterprise or enterprises and their transactions, and not merely from difference in financial accounting treatment. Information, if comparable, will assist the decision-maker to determine relative financial strengths and weaknesses and prospects for the future, between two or more firms or between periods in a single firm.

5. Neutrality

Neutrality is also known as the quality of 'freedom from bias' or objectivity. Neutrality means that, in formulating or implementing standards, the primary concern should be the relevance and reliability of the information that results, not the effect that the new rule may have on a particular interest or user(s). A neutral choice between accounting alternatives is free from bias towards a predetermined result. The objectives of (general purpose) financial reporting serve many different information users who have diverse interests, and no one predetermined result is likely to suit all user' interests and purposes. Therefore, accounting facts and accounting practices should be impartially determined and reported with no objective of purposeful bias towards any user or user group. If there is no bias in selection of accounting information reported, it cannot be said to favour one set of interests over another. It may, in fact, favour certain interests, but only because the information points that way.

6. Timeliness

Timeliness means having information available to decision-makers before it loses its capacity to influence decisions. Timeliness is an ancillary aspect of relevance. If information is either not available when it is needed or becomes available long after the reported events then it has no value for future action, it lacks relevance and is of little or no use. Timeliness alone cannot make information relevant, but a lack of timeliness can rob information of relevance it might otherwise have.

7. Verifiability

The quality of verifiability contributes to the usefulness of accounting information because the purpose of verification is to provide a significant degree of assurance that accounting measures represent, what they purport to represent. Verification does not guarantee the suitability of method used, much less the correctness of the resulting measure. It does convey some assurance that the measurement rule used, whatever it was, was applied carefully and without personal bias on the part of the measurer.

REFERENCES

1. American Institute of Certified Public Accountants, *The Basic Postulates of Accounting.* Accounting Research Study No. 1, AICPA, 1961, p. 7.
2. Eric L. Kohler, A Dictionary for Accountants, Prentice Hall, 1983, p. 361.
3. Glewn A. Welsch and Daniel G. Short, Fundamentals of Financial Accounting, Irwin 1987, p. 144.
4. Robert N. Anthony and James S. Reece, Accounting Principles, Irwin, 1991, p. 15.
5. R.H. Parker, MacMillan Dictionary of Accounting, MacMillan, 1984, p. 46.
6. Robert N. Anthony, David F. Hawkins and Kenneth A. Merchant, Accounting, Text and Cases, McGraw Hill, 2008, p. 68.
7. Robert N. Anthony, Davit F. Hawkins and Kenneth A. Merchant, Accounting, Text and Cases, McGrawHill, 2008, p. 56.
8. Accounting Principles Board, Statement No. 4, AICPA, 1970.
9. Paul H. Walgenbach, Ernst I, Hanson and Norman E. Dittrich, *Financial Accounting, An Introduction,* Harcourt Brace Jovanovich, 1988, p. 443.
10. Robert N. Anthony, David F. Hawkins, Kenneth A. Merchant, Accounting, Text and Cases, McGrawHill, 2008, p. 12.
11. The Institute of Chartered Accountants of India, Guidance Note on Terms used in Financial Statements, ICAI, September, 1983, p. 19.

ASSIGNMENT MATERIAL

Note : The Objective Type Questions (True/False, Multiple Choice Questions etc.) have been given in the Appendix at the end of the book.

SHORT-ANSWER THEORY QUESTIONS

1. "Accounting Principles become Generally Accepted Accounting Principle (GAAP) when they satisfy certain norms." What are those norms? Explain.
2. Explain any four of the following concepts/conventions with suitable examples.

   (*a*) Money Measurement (*b*) Consistency
   (*c*) Going Concern (*d*) Disclosure
   (*e*) Conservatism

3. Briefly explain the following :

   (*a*) Consistency (*b*) Realisation concept
   (*c*) Materiality (*d*) Going Concern

4. Explain matching concept and realisation concept.
5. Distinguish between Accrual Basis of Accounting and Cash Basis of Accounting.
6. Explain Going Concern concept and Realisation concept.
7. Write notes on :
   (*i*) Money Measurement Concept.
   (*ii*) Business Entity Concept
8. Explain the following :
   Dual Aspect Concept and Conservatism.
9. Distinguish between Accrual Basis of Accounting and Cash Basis of Accounting.
10. Write Short notes on :
    (*i*) Money Measurement Concept
    (*ii*) Convention of Full Disclosure
11. Write notes on
    (*i*) Business Entity Concept. (*ii*) Consistency
12. Recognising that the values of land have been increasing in the recent years, Anil, owner of Anil Construction Ltd. increased the balance sheet amount of land from 50 lacs Rupees to 6 Crore Rupees. Explain the Accounting concept which has been violated.
13. Briefly explain :
    (*i*) Going Concern Concept (*ii*) Conservatism
14. Define the following terms :
    (*a*) Postulates (*b*) Assumptions
    (*c*) Concepts (*d*) Principles
    (*e*) Convention
15. Distinguish between Accounting Concepts and Accounting Principles.
16. What is a Realization or Recognition Concept?
17. What are the constraints in Materiality Concept?
18. Explain the concept of Generally Accepted Accounting Principles (GAAP).
19. What are fundamental Accounting Assumptions as per AS1 (India).
20. Explain Contingent Liabilities.
21. What are the basic financial statements?
22. Write notes on :
    (*a*) Cash Basis and Accrual basis of Accounting
    (*b*) Meaning and Importance of Convention of Consistency
    (*c*) Concept of Historical Cost and its Importance.
    (*d*) Money Measurement Concept [*B.Com.(Hons.), Delhi University, 2005, 2006*]
23. Explain Money Measurement concept of Accounting. [*B.Com.(Hons.), Delhi University, 2007*]
24. Explain the Relevance of Disclosure Principle in Accounting.
    [*B.Com.(Hons.), Delhi University, 2009*]
25. What is a contingent Liability? Give three examples of Contingent Liability.
    [*B.Com.(Hons.), Delhi University, 2010*]
26. Write notes on :
    (*a*) Profit and Loss Account

(b) Balance Sheet
(c) Cash Flow Statement

27. Identify elements of financial statements.
28. Explain briefly different types of assets.
29. Write a note on current liabilities and long-term liabilities.
30. What is a contingent liabilities?
31. Write notes on the following qualities :
    (a) Relevance (b) Reliability
    (c) Understandability (d) Comparability
    (e) Timeliness
32. What are different areas in Accounting where different Accounting policies are encountered.
33. A company charges to expense all items (appearing like assets) that costs A 1000 or less. Which concept supports this policy?
34. Certain generally accepted accounting principles or concepts have been violated in each of the situations described below:

    Indicate for each situation which concept or principle has been violated.
    (a) When the Alpha company acquired its branch office building for A 50,000, the total amount of cash outlay was recorded as rent expense.
    (b) The personal automobile of Rajiv Dhawan, major shareholder of a company, is listed among the company assets.
    (c) Land acquired at a cost of A 25 lakhs in 2005 is upto 45 lakhs
    (d) Equipment acquired on January 15, for A 70,00,000 is recorded on December 31 balance sheet at A 84,00,000 Mr. Ashok Johnson, the managing director of the company explains that since at the date of acquisition, the consumer price index was 100 and had increased to 120 by year-end, the appropriate value for financial statement presentation would accordingly be A 84,00,000.
    (e) A calculator purchased in early March for A 1150 can be purchased at year-end for A 925. The company has used the later value on the balance sheet date.
    (f) Land bought on July 1 for A 5,15,000 is valued on the December 31 balance sheet at A 7,05,000, a value obtained by considering recent land sales in the vicinity.
    (g) A lawnmower used by Mr. Rakesh, the managing director of the company, for his residence is included among the December 31 assets of the company.

LONG ANSWER THEORY QUESTIONS

1. Write a note on the convention of conservatism. Does it lead to understatement of income?
2. Distinguish between Postulates, Concepts, Principles and Convention.
3. Explain the following accounting terms:
    (a) Entity Concept (b) Going-Concern Concept
    (c) Dual-aspect Concept (d) Matching Concept
    (e) Accrual Concept (f) Cost Concept
4. Explain the significance of separate entity postulate in recording transactions and events of an entity.
5. Why is the Going-Concern postulate central to accounting practice?

6. What limitations does the money measurement concept impose on accounting?
7. "Many important events that influence the prospects for the entity are not recorded in the financial records". Comment and give examples.
8. Would an account record the personal assets and liabilities of the owners in the account of the business. Explain.
9. "It is not important to know when cash is received and when payment is made". Comment.
10. Financial statements are prepared using generally accepted accounting principles. What does this term mean? Why are these principles necessary?
11. Discuss the utility of three primary financial statements.
12. Explain different types of assets that appear on the balance sheet of a business enterprise.
13. Discuss current and long-term liabilities.
14. Discuss qualitative characteristics of financial statement information.
15. Explain the following qualities of accounting information.
    (*a*) Relevance (*b*) Reliability
    (*c*) Understandability (*d*) Comparability
16. Discuss the nature of income statement and balance sheet. What information is generally found in these two statements?
17. Explain limitations of Financial Statements. [*B.Com.(Hons.), Delhi University, 2007*]

CHAPTER 3

Accounting Standards

Learning Objectives

After studying this chapter, you should be able to :

1. *Define accounting standard.*
2. *Explain benefits of accounting standards.*
3. *Understand status of accounting standard in India.*
4. *Discuss compliance with accounting standards in India.*
5. *Explain AS1 disclosure of accounting policies.*

Definition of Accounting Standard

The use of world 'Standard' in accounting literature is of a recent origin. What is described as 'standard' today, used to be generally known as 'principles; a few years ago. The British introduced the term 'standards' in place of 'principles' when they set up their Accounting Standards Steering Committee at the end of 1969, and the Americans adopted the same term ('standard') in 1973, when the Accounting Principles Board was wound up and the Financial Accounting Standards Board was created. In India, this term has mainly become popular since the formation of Accounting Standards Board (ASB) in April 1977 by the Institute of Chartered Accountants of India.

The term 'Accounting Standard' may be defined as written statements issued from time-to- time by institutions of the accounting profession or institutions in which it has sufficient involvement and which are established expressly for this purpose. They are written documents, policy documents issued by expert accounting body or by Government or other regulatory body covering the aspects of recognition, measurement, treatment, presentation and disclosure of accounting transaction in the financial statement.

The objective of accounting standards is to standardize the diverse accounting policies and practices with a view to eliminate to the extent possible the non-comparability of financial statements and increase relevance and reliability of financial statements.

Accounting standards mainly deal with financial measurements and disclosures used in producing a set of fairly presented financial statements. In this respect, accounting standards can be thought of as a system of measurements and disclosure. They also draw the boundaries within which acceptable conduct lies and in that and many other respects, they are similar in nature to laws.

BENEFITS OF ACCOUNTING STANDARDS

The benefits of accounting standards may be listed as follows :

1. To Improve the Relevance and Objectivity of Financial Statements : Financial statements of business enterprises are used by a diverse group of users for making sound economic decision. The users are shareholders (existing and potential), trade creditors, customers, suppliers, employees, taxation authorities and other interested parties. It is necessary, therefore, that the financial statements the users use and upon which they rely, present a fair picture of the position and progress of the enterprises. It is the function of accounting (and auditing) standards to create this general sense of confidence by providing a framework within which credible financial statements can be produced. Accounting standards are required to meet a basic need of managers, investors and creditors to compare results and financial conditions of different segments of firms, different periods of a firm, different firms and different industries. In the absence of standards, there would be no incentives to encourage an enterprise to conform to any particular model for the sake of comparison. Thus, the main aim of accounting standards is to protect users' interest by providing them with information in which they can have confidence.

2. Benefits to Accounting Profession : Preparers and auditors, with the passage of time and changing climate of opinion, have to work in an environment where they face the threat of stern sanctions and a bad name to their professions. These result partly from changed penalties and remedies available under the company law and partly from the greater willingness of aggrieved parties to take their causes before the courts. The risk of these developments are considerable to auditors whether in terms of uncovered financial exposure to liability or adverse effects on professional reputation resulting from unfavourable publicity.

Particularly dangerous are causes of undetected fraud, and audited accounts, which are held to be misleading due to insufficient disclosure or use of inappropriate accounting principles. Given the increasing risks, the accounting profession realised that it needed to have the accounting standards for their own benefits.

3. Determining Business Performance : Accounting standards facilitate in determining specific corporate accountability and regulation of the company. They help in assessing managerial skill in maintaining and improving the profitability of the company, depicting the progress of the company, its solvency and liquidity.

Generally they are important factors in assessing the effectiveness of management's performance of its duties and leadership. Standards aim to ensure consistency and comparability in place of (imposed) uniformity in financial reporting to permit better comparisons in profitability, financial position, future prospects and other performance indicators associated with different business firms.

ACCOUNTING STANDARDS IN INDIA

The Institute of Chartered Accounts of India constituted the Accounting Standard Board (ASB) in April 1977, recognising the need to harmonise the diverse accounting policies and practice in India and keeping in view the international development in the field of accounting. The ASB is entrusted with the following functions :

1. To formulate accounting standards which may be established by the council of ICAI in India. While formulating standards, the ASB is required to take into consideration the applicable laws, customs and usages and business environment; it is also required to give due consideration to International Accounting Standards Issued by IASC (now IASB) and to integrate them, to the extent possible, in the light of the conditions and practices prevailing in India.
2. To propagate the Accounting Standards and persuade the concerned parties to adopt them in the preparation and presentation of financial statements.
3. To issue guidance notes on the Accounting Standards and give clarifications on issues arising therefrom.
4. To review the accounting standards at periodic intervals.

The date from which a particular standard will come to effect, as well as the class of enterprises to which it will apply, will also be specified by the Institute. Unless otherwise stated, no standard will have retrospective application. Normally, before formulating the standards, ASB will hold discussions with the representatives of the government, public sector undertakings, industry and other organizations, for ascertaining their views. An exposure draft of the proposed standards will be prepared and issued for comments by members of the institute and the public at large. After considering the comments received, the draft of the proposed standard will be finalised by ASB and submitted to the council which will study it, modify it if necessary and issue it under its own authority.

ACCOUNTING STANDARDS ISSUED BY ASB (INDIA)

The Institute of Chartered Accountants of India has issued so far 32 Accounting Standards. They are displayed in Exhibit 3.1.

Exhibit 3.1
Status of the Accounting Standards issued by the Institute of Chartered Accountants of India

Number of the Accounting Standards (AS)	*Title of the Accounting Standard*	*Date from which Mandatory (Accounting periods commencing on or after)*
1	*2*	*3*
AS - 1	Disclosure of Accounting Policies	01.04.1993
AS - 2 (Revised)	Valuation of Inventories	01.04.1999
AS - 3 (Revised)	Cash Flow Statement	01.04.2001
AS - 4 (Revised)	Contingencies and Events occurring after the Balance Sheet Date	01.04.1998
AS - 5 (Revised)	Net Profit or Loss for the Period. Prior Period items and Changes in Accounting Policies	01.04.1996
AS - 6 (Revised)	Depreciation Accounting	01.04.1995
AS - 7 (Revised)	Accounting for Construction Contracts	01.04.2003
AS - 8	Withdrawn and included in AS-26	
AS - 9	Revenue Recognition	01.04.1993
AS - 10	Accounting for Fixed Assets	01.04.1993
AS - 11 (Revised)	The Effects of Changes in Foreign Exchange Rates (Revised 2003)	01.04.2004
AS - 12	Accounting for Govt. Grants	01.04.1994
AS - 13	Accounting for Investments	01.04.1995
AS - 14	Accounting for Amalgamations	01.04.1995
AS - 15	Accounting for Retirement Benefits in the Financial Statements of Employers	01.04.1995
AS - 16	Borrowing Costs	01.04.2000
AS - 17	Segment Reporting	01.04.2001
AS - 18	Related Party Disclosures	01.4.2001
AS - 19	Leases	01.04.2001
AS - 20	Earning Per Share	01.04.2001
AS - 21	Consolidated Financial Statement	01.04.2001
AS - 22	Accounting for Taxes on Income	01.04.2001
AS - 23	Accounting for Investment in Associates in Consolidated Financial Statements	01.04.2002

1	*2*	*3*
AS - 24	Discontinuing Operations	01.04.2004
AS - 25	Interim Financial Reporting	01.04.2002
AS - 26	Intangible Assets	01.04.2003
AS - 27	Financial Reporting of Interests in Joint Venture	01.04.2002
AS - 28	Impairment of Assets	01.04.2004
AS - 29	Provisions, Contingent Liabilities and Contingent Assets	01.04.2004
AS - 30	Financial Instruments : Recognition and Measurement and Limited Revision to AS-2, AS-11 (Revised 2003), AS-21, AS-23, AS-26, AS-27, AS-28.	01.04.2011
AS-31	Financial Instruments–Presentation	01.04.2011
AS-32	Financial Instruments Disclosures	01.04.2011

In addition to these standards, the Institute of Chartered Accountants of India has issued statements, Guidance Notes and opinions which seek to bring about uniformity in corporate accounting and reporting practices.

COMPLIANCE WITH ACCOUNTING STANDARDS

Compliance with accounting standards has been made mandatory, Sub-section (3A) to section 211 (Inserted by the Companies Amendment Act, 1999) requires that every profit and loss account and balance sheet shall comply with the accounting standards. Accounting standards means the standards of accounting recommended by the Institute of Chartered Accountants of India (ICAI) and prescribed by the Central Government in consolation with the National Advisory Committee on Accounting Standards (NACAS) constituted under sub-section 210A(1).

Until the Central Government proscribes accounting standards under the section, accounting standards issued by the ICAI shall be deemed to be the accounting standards.

As per newly inserted clause 50 of the Listing Agreement it is mandatory for the companies listed in a recognized stock exchange to comply with all applicable accounting standards in the preparation and presentation financial statements.

(*i*) *Establishment of NACAS* : Section 210A (inserted *vide* the Companies Amendment Act, 1999) discusses about the establishment of the NACAS. The Central Government is empowered by the virtue of the provision of section 210A(1) to establish NACAS which would advise the Central Government on the formulation and laying down of accounting policies and accounting standards for adoption by companies or class of companies under the Act. The NACAS shall give its recommendation to the Central Government on such matters of accounting policies and standards and auditing as may be referred to it for advice from time-to time.

The ICAI is free to set Accounting Standards as it has been doing since 1977. For the purpose of the Companies Act, the Central Government enjoys the authority to prescribe such accounting standards which are recommended by the ICAI. While prescribing any accounting standard, the Central Government may consult the NACAS.

(*ii*) *Deviation from Accounting Standards* : Sub-section (3B) to section 211 requires that in case the profit and loss account and balance sheet of a company do not comply with the requirements of the accounting standards, disclosure should be made stating :

⇨ Deviations from the accounting standards;

- ⇨ The reasons for such deviation; and
- ⇨ The financial effect, if any, arising due to such deviation.

The disclosure requirement as stated in section 211 (3A) will bring transparency but such deviations may be material enough to affect the truth and fairness of the financial statements. Accordingly, it is necessary for the statutory auditors to give negative report in case truth and fairness of the financial statements are violated by virtue of such deviations. This needs a change in the auditors reporting norm.

(*iii*) *Duties of the statutory auditors with regard to mandatory accounting standards*: The statutory auditors are required to make qualification in their report in case any item is treated differently from the prescribed treatment in the relevant accounting standard. However, while qualifying they should consider the materiality of the relevant item.

In case of non-disclosure of significant accounting policies the auditors are required to specify the fact in their report. The ICAI suggests that it should be in the following lines :

"The company has disclosed those accounting policies the disclosure of which is required by the Companies Act, 1956. Other significant accounting policies, *viz.,* those relating to method of accounting followed for recognizing revenue of the long term construction contracts and recognition of warranty expenses have not been disclosed nor have all the policies been disclosed at one place, which is contrary to Accounting Standard-1 "Disclosure of Accounting Policies" issued by the ICAI."

Similarly, an auditor is required to specify the fact in case a non-corporate body prepares financial statements on cash basis. The ICAI suggests that specifying the fact is sufficient and the auditors may state that accounts give true and fair view on the cash basis if it is so.

The newly inserted sub-section (3) of section 227 requires the auditors to report whether, in his opinion, the profit and loss account and balance sheet comply with the accounting standards referred to in section 211(3C).

(*iv*) *Income-tax Act, 1961* : Pursuant to an amendment to the Income-tax Act, 1961 in 1995, it has been provided that the Central Government may notify in the official Gazette from time-to-time accounting standards to be followed by any class of assesses or in respect of any class of income. Two accounting standards, *viz.,* (1) Disclosure of Accounting Policies and (2) Disclosure of Prior Period and Extraordinary items and changes in accounting policies have been issued. These standards are more or less in conformity with the parallel standards issued by the ICAI. The main reason advanced for the necessity for the amendment of the Income-tax Act was the belief that the standards issued by the ICAI permitted alternative treatment in various situations. ICAI has already initiated action to reduce the alternatives.

The RBI as a regulatory authority also issues directions to banks and financial institutions as also to Non-Banking Finance Companies (NBFCs) on the manner in which certain accounting matters should be dealt with.

An equally significant development is the establishment by the Securities and Exchange Board of India (SEBI) of a Standing Committee on Accounting Standards. This committee monitors the existence of relevant accounting standards and their harmonization with the corresponding International Accounting Standards. It mandates the adherence to the standards and enforces the same through the listing agreements between the companies and stock exchanges. Therefore, atleast in so far as listed companies are concerned, a better enforcement mechanism has been put in place.

AS-1 : DISCLOSURE OF ACCOUNTING POLICIES

The Institute of Chartered Accountants of India (ICAI) issued AS-1 titled 'Disclosure of Accounting Policies' in November 1979. This standard is now mandatory and deals with the disclosure of significant accounting policies followed in preparing and presenting Financial Statements.

In General, accounting policies are not at present regularly and fully disclosed in all financial statements. Many enterprises include in the Notes on the Accounts, description of some of the significant accounting policies.

Even among the few enterprises that presently include in their annual reports a separate statement of accounting policies, considerable variation exists. The statement of accounting policies form part of the accounts in some cases while in others it is given as supplementary information.

The purpose of AS-1 is to promote better understanding of financial statements by establishing through an accounting standard the disclosure of significant accounting policies and the manner in which accounting policies are disclosed in the financial statements. Such disclosure would also facilitate a more meaningful comparison between financial statements of different enterprises.

AS-1 contains explanations on following points :

Fundamental Accounting Assumptions

1. Certain fundamental accounting assumptions underlie the preparation and presentation of financial statements. They are usually not specifically stated because their acceptance and use are assumed. Disclosure is necessary if they are not followed.

The following have been generally accepted as fundamental accounting assumption:

(*a*) *Going Concern* : The enterprise is normally viewed as a going concern, that is, as continuing in operation for the foreseeable future. It is assumed that the enterprise has neither the intention nor the necessity of liquidation or of courtailing materially the scale of the operations.

(*b*) *Consistency* : It is assumed that accounting policies are consistent from one period to another.

(*c*) *Accrual* : Revenues and costs are accrued, that is, recognised as they are earned or incurred (and not as money is received or paid) and recorded in the financial statements of the periods to which they relate. (The considerations affecting the process of matching costs with revenues under the accrual assumption are not dealt with in this statement).

2. Nature of Accounting Policies

(*i*) The accounting policies refer to the specific accounting principles and the methods of applying those principles adopted by the enterprise in the preparation and presentation of financial statements.

(*ii*) There is no single list of accounting policies which are applicable to all circumstances. The differing circumstances in which enterprises operate in a situation of diverse and complex economic activity make alternative accounting principles and methods of applying those principles acceptable. The choice of the appropriate accounting principles and the methods of applying those principles in the specified circumstances of each enterprise calls for considerable judgement by the management of the enterprise.

(*iii*) The various statements of the Institute of Chartered Accountants of India combined with the efforts of government and other regularity agencies and progressive managements have reduced in recent years the number of acceptable alternatives particularly in the case of corporate enterprises. While continuing efforts in this regard in future are likely to reduce the number still further, the availability of alternative accounting principles and methods of applying these principles is not likely to be eliminated altogether in view of the differing circumstances faced by the enterprises.

3. Areas in which differing accounting policies are encounted

The following are examples of the areas in which different accounting policies may be adopted by different enterprises.

- Method of depreciation, depletion and amortisation

- Treatment of expenditure during construction
- Conversion of translation of foreign currency items
- Valuation of inventories
- Treatment of goodwill
- Valuation of investments
- Treatment of retirement benefits
- Recognition of profit on long-term contracts
- Valuation of fixed assets
- Treatment of contingent liabilities

The above list of examples is not intended to be exhaustive.

4. Considerations in the Selection of Accounting Policies

The primary consideration in the selection of accounting policies by an enterprise is that the financial statements prepared and presented on the basis of such accounting policies should represent a true and fair view of the state of affairs of the enterprise as at the balance sheet date and of the profit or loss for the period ended on that date.

For this purpose, the major considerations governing the selection and application of accounting policies are :

(*a*) *Prudence* : In view of the uncertainty attached to future events, profits are not anticipated but recognized only when realised though not necessarily in cash. Provision is made for all known liabilities and losses even though the amount cannot be determined with certainty and represents only a best estimate in the light of available information.

(*b*) *Substance over Form* : The accounting treatment and presentation in financial statements of transactions and events should be governed by their substance and not merely by the legal form.

(*c*) *Materiality* : Financial statements should disclose all "material" items, *i.e.,* items the knowledge of which might influence the decisions of the user of the financial statements

5. Disclosure of Accounting Policies

(*i*) To ensure proper understanding of financial statements, it is necessary that all significant accounting policies adopted in the preparation and presentation of financial statements should be disclosed.

(*ii*) Such disclosure should form part of the financial statements.

(*iii*) It would be helpful to the reader of financial statements if they are all disclosed as such in one place instead of being scattered over several statements, schedules and notes.

(*iv*) Examples of matters in respect of which disclosure of accounting policies adopted will be required are contained in point No.3. This list of examples is not, however, intended to be exhaustive.

(*v*) Any change in an accounting policy which has a material effect should be disclosed. The amount by which any item in the financial statements is affected by such change should also be disclosed to the extent ascertainable. Where such amount is not ascertainable, wholly or in part, the fact should be indicated. If a change is made in the accounting policies which has no material effect on the financial statements for the current period but which is reasonably expected to have a material effect in later periods, the fact of such change should be appropriately disclosed in the period in which the change is adopted.

(*vi*) Disclosure of accounting policies or of changes therein cannot remedy a wrong or inappropriate treatment of the item in the accounts.

6. Accounting Standard in AS-1

(*i*) All significant accounting policies adopted in the preparation and presentation of financial statements should be disclosed.

(*ii*) The disclosure of the significant accounting policies as such should form part of the financial statements and the significant accounting policies should normally be disclosed in one place.

(*iii*) Any change in the accounting policies which has material effect in the current period or which is reasonably expected to have a material effect in later periods should be disclosed. In the case of a change in accounting policies which has a material effect in the current period, the amount by which any item in the financial statements is affected by such change should also be disclosed to the extent ascertainable. Where such amount is not ascertainable, wholly or in part, the fact should be indicated.

(*iv*) If the fundamental accounting assumptions, *viz.*, Going Concern, Consistency and Accrual are followed in financial statements, specific disclosure is not required. If a fundamental accounting assumption is not followed, the fact should be disclosed.

INTERNATIONAL FINANCIAL REPORTING STANDARDS (IFRSs)

Accounting standards issued by the international accounting body, International Accounting Standards Board (IASB), set up in 2001, are known as International Financial Reporting Standards (IFRSs). Earlier, such accounting standards were issued by International Accounting Standards Committee (IASC) which was formed in 1973 through an agreement made by professional accountancy bodies from Australia, Canada, France, Germany, Ireland, Japan, Maxico. Netherlands, UK and USA. In 2001, the IASB replaced IASC as standard setter body at the international level.

The objectives of the IASB stated in its Constitution (2000) are :

(*a*) to develop in the public interest, a single set of high-quality, understandable and enforceable global accounting standards that require high quality, transparent and comparable information in financial statements and other financial reporting to help participants in the world's capital markets and other users make economic decisions;

(*b*) to promote the use and rigorous application of those standards; and

(*c*) to bring about convergence of national accounting standards and International Accounting Standards to high-quality solutions.

In developing international accounting standards known as IFRSs, the IASB follows the following procedures :

1. The IASC board selects a topic and assigns it to a steering committee which is made of four representatives, at least one of which is a board member and at least one of which is from a developing country.
2. The steering committee studies the issues involved and presents to the board a point outline on the topic.
3. The board gives its comments to the steering committee which then prepares a preliminary draft of the proposed standard.
4. The board reviews preliminary draft of the new standard and then circulates it among all the member bodies for their comments.
5. Based on these comments, the steering committee prepares a revised draft and a final exposure draft is submitted to the board for approval.
6. If approved by a two-third vote of the board, the exposure draft will be sent to IASB members. The exposure draft is published in all member countries and world-wide public comments are invited from all interested parties, both professional and non-professional.

7. At the conclusion of the exposure period, usually six months, the comments submitted are considered by the steering committee, and then a final standard is drafted.
8. The steering committee submits the revised draft of the final standard to the board for its approval; and if approved by at least 8 of the 14 members of the board, it will be issued as a new IFRSs.

The old IASC called its standards International Accounting Standards. The new name for standards issued by the IASB is International Financial Reporting Standards (IFRSs). In one of its earliest action, the IASB voted to make clear that the IASs issued by the former IASC continue with full force and effect unless and until the IASB amends or replaces them. The IASB announced that the term 'IFRS' should be understood to include IAS. Consistent with that announcement, the term IFRS is used to refer to the entire body of IASB standards, including the old IASs and interpretations. However, the old IASs have not been renumbered. They remain outstanding until replaced by an IFRS. The IASB has amended some of the old IASs without replacing them, in which case they keep their old IAS number.

From its inception in 1973 until it was reorganised into the International Accounting Standards Board (IASB) in early 2001, the IASC developed 41 standards, known as International Accounting Standards. Many of those were revised one or more times over the year. Several were superseded or merged in with other standards. Since 2001, the IASB has revised a number of the IASs and has begun a second series of standards known as International Financial Reporting Standards (IFRSs) starting again with number 1.

ASSIGNMENT MATERIAL

Note : The Objectives Type Questions (True/False, Multiple Choice Questions, etc.) have been given in the Appendix at the end of the book.

SHORT ANSWER THEORY QUESTIONS

1. Refine accounting standards.
2. What is the importance of accounting standards?
3. What is ASB?
4. How many standards have been issued so far by ASB (India).
5. Write a note on compliance with accounting standards.
6. What is the duty of Statutory auditors with regard to mandatory accounting standards?
7. What are fundamental assumptions in AS1?
8. List the areas in which different accounting policies are found.
9. What are the considerations in the selection of accounting policies?
10. What are the suggestions given in AS1 on disclosure of accounting policies?

LONG-ANSWER THEORY QUESTIONS

1. Discuss AS1 relating to disclosure of accounting policies.
   [*B.Com.(Hons.), Delhi University, 2006, 2007*]
2. Define accounting standards. What are its advantages?
3. Explain developments in accounting standards setting in India.
4. What are the Provisions about compliance with accounting standards in India?

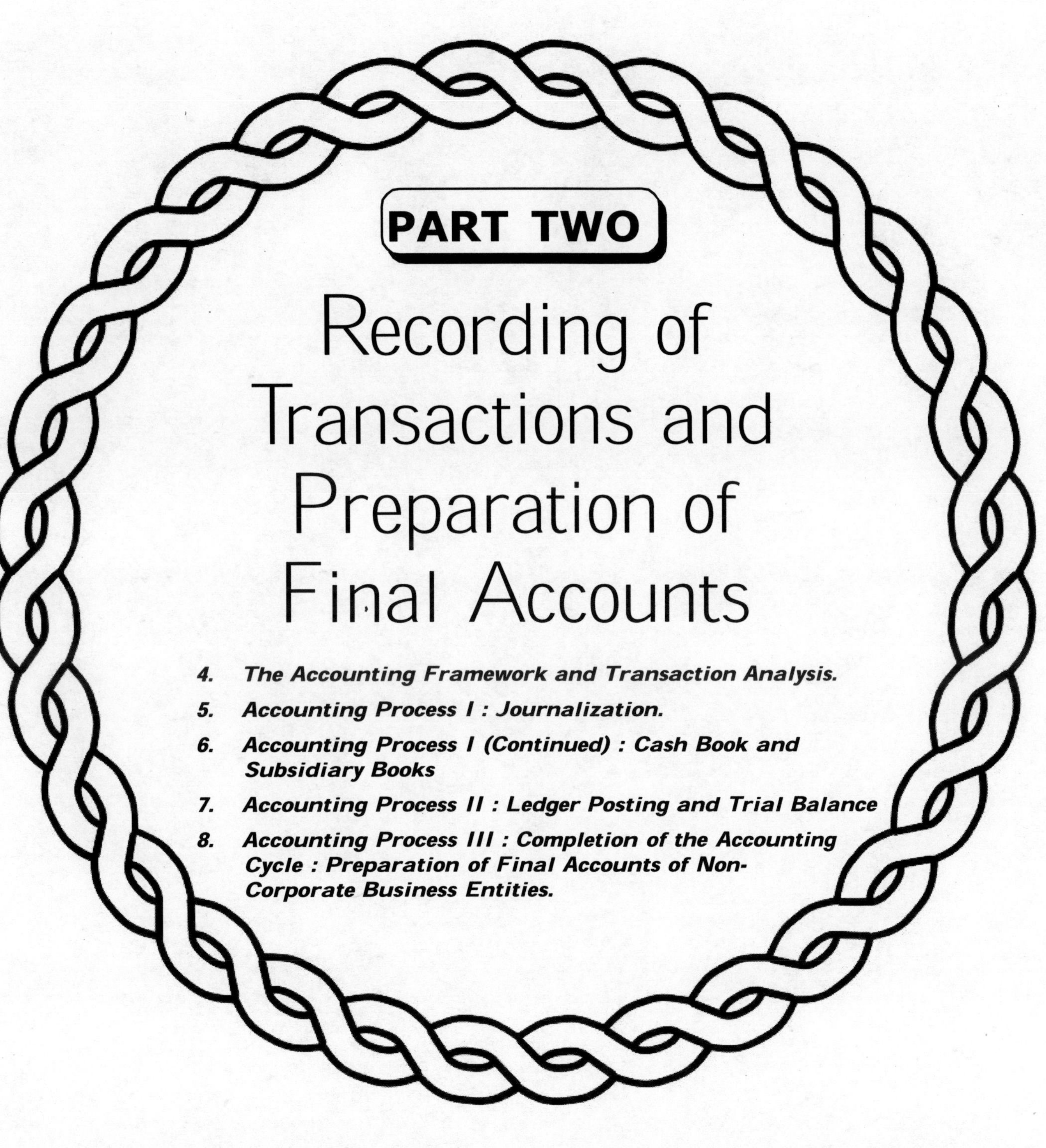

PART TWO

Recording of Transactions and Preparation of Final Accounts

CHAPTER 4

The Accounting Framework and Transaction Analysis

Learning Objectives

After studying this chapter, you should be able to :

1. *Explain Basic Accounting Equation.*
2. *Discuss the effects of Financial Transaction on Accounting Equation.*
3. *Understand Transaction Analysis with illustrations.*

BASIC ACCOUNTING EQUATION

The end result of the accounting process for a business entity is the financial statements such as balance sheet, profit and loss account, statement of changes in financial position. These statements are presented in condensed (highly summarised) form and cannot be prepared until the financial transactions of the business entity have been recorded, classified and summarised. The framework of the financial statements and the elements shown in these statements rests on important and basic relationship, referred to as basic or fundamental accounting framework, basic accounting equation. This basic equation is expressed by the balance sheet equation, and therefore, is known as the balance sheet equation also. The accounting equation is written as follows :

Sources of Funds = Uses of Funds

Or

Equities = Assets

Or

Proprietor's Equity (Capital) + Outside Liability = Assets

The above accounting framework or equation rests on two premises. The first is the idea that it is possible to distinguish an *accounting entity*—the person or organization for which a set of accounts is kept—from other persons or organizations that are associated with it. The second premise is that for any accounting entity, the resources available will be exactly equal to the resources provided by creditors and owners. This second assumption in usually called the *accounting equation.*

The accounting processes of observing, measuring, and reporting are always carried out with an eye to maintaining this fundamental equality of assets and equities, i.e. accounting equation.

The above accounting equation signifies that assets of a business are always equal to the total of outside liabilities and proprietor's equity. It means that the accounting equation should always be in balance. This fundamental equality is always true because the left side of the equation is simply another view of the right side. This is because whatever funds are raised by the business, either through capital or business operations or from outsider, will be tied up in one or other form of uses (assets). Assets represent resources owned by the business entity; equity represents the claims of those who supplied the assets. Thus, the fundamental accounting equation emphasises accounting equivalence or duality concept *i.e.,* each financial transaction has a dual nature and affects both the assets and liabilities side of the balance sheet.

Algebraically the equations can be expressed as :

$$A = L + P$$

where A = Assets

L = Outside Liabilities

P = Proprietor's Equity

The above equation can also be expressed as :

$$P = A - L \quad ...(1)$$

$$L = A - P \quad ...(2)$$

$$A - L - P = \text{Zero} \quad ...(3)$$

Effects of Financial Transactions on Accounting Equation

Every business transaction can be analysed by or expressed in terms of its effect on the balance sheet equation. A business transaction results into a change in all or any of the components of the equation. Whatever may be the change, the Accounting Equation remains in balance. Different types of business transactions may result into a maximum of nine possible effect combinations on the components of accounting equation.

These nine possible combinations of changes or effects are :

(*i*) Increase in one asset; decrease in another asset.

(*ii*) Increase in one liability; decrease in another liability.

(*iii*) Increase in one item of proprietor's equity; decrease in another item of proprietor's equity.

(*iv*) Increase in one item of proprietor's equity, decrease in liability.

(*v*) Increase in a liability; decrease in proprietor's equity.

(*vi*) Increase in asset; Increase in liability.

(*vii*) Increase in asset; increase in proprietor's equity.

(*viii*) Decrease in asset; decrease in liability.

(*ix*) Decrease in asset; decrease in proprietor's equity.

TRANSACTION ANALYSIS

Determining the effect of a business transaction on assets, liabilities and equities of the accounting equation is called transaction analysis. A transaction analysis shows increases and decreases in the assets, liabilities or proprietor's equity of a business entity. Where these effects are presented in an account form, they are shown by a simultaneous debit and credit in the relevant accounts of assets, liabilities and/or equities.

Some illustrations are given to explain the transaction analysis and the effects of business transactions on the accounting equation.

Example 1

Transaction 1

X starts business and invests A 1,00,000 as his capital. *(Amt. in A)*

Assets		*= Liabilities + Proprietor's equity*	
	Cash	= –	X's Capital
Effect of transaction	1,00,000	= –	1,00,000
	1,00,000	= –	1,00,000

Transaction 2

On April 2, the firm purchases furniture for A 40,000 for cash.

Assets		*= Liabilities + Proprietor's equity*	
Cash + Furniture		= –	X' Capital
Old Balance	1,00,000	= –	1,00,000
Effect of Transaction	– 40,000 + 40,000	= –	1,00,000
New Balance	60,000 + 40,000	= –	1,00,000

Transaction 3

On April 3, the firm purchases merchandise (goods) costing A 30,000 for cash.

Assets		*= Liabilities + Proprietor's equity*	
Cash + Furniture		= –	X' Capital
Cash + Furniture + Merchandise		= –	X' capital a/c
Old Balance			
	60,000 + 40,000	= –	1,00,000
Effect of Transaction			
	– 30,000 + 30,000	= –	1,00,000
New Balance	30,000 + 40,000 + 30,000	= –	1,00,000

Transaction 4

On April 4, the firm purchases merchandise costing A 40,000 on credit.

Assets		*= Liabilities + Proprietor's equity*	
Cash + Furniture		= –	X' Capital
Cash + Furniture + Merchandise		= Creditors	+ X's capital
Old Balance	30,000 + 40,000 + 30,000	= –	+ 1,00,000
Effect of Transaction	+ 40,000	= + 40,000	
New Balance	30,000 + 40,000 + 70,000	= 40,000 + 1,00,000	

Transaction 5

On April 6, the firm sells merchandise for A 30,000 on credit to Mr. A, costing A 20,000.

Assets		*= Liabilities + Proprietor's equity*	
Cash + Debtors + Merchandise + Furniture		= Creditors + X's capital + Surplus Profit	
Old Balance	30,000 + – + 70,000 + 40,000	= 40,000 + 1,00,000	
Effect of Transactions + 30,000 – 20,000		= –	10,000
New Balance 30,000 + 30,000 + 50,000 + 40,000 = 40,000 + 1,00,000 + 10,000			

Transaction 6

On April 15, the firm receives A 20,000 cash from Debtors.

Assets		*= Liabilities + Proprietor's equity*	
Cash + Debtors + Merchandise + Furniture		= Creditor + X's Cap + surplus profit	
Old Balance	30,000 + 30,000 + 50,000 + 40,000	= 40,000 + 1,00,000 + 10,000	
Effect of Transaction + 20,000 – 20,000	= –	–	–
New Balance 50,000 + 10,000 + 50,000 + 40,000 = 40,000 + 1,00,000 + 10,000			

Transaction 7

On April 16, the firm pays A 40,000 to its creditors.

Assets		*= Liabilities + Proprietor's equity*	
Cash + Debtors + Merchandise + Furniture= Creditors + X's capital + Surplus/Profit			
Old Balance	50,000 + 10,000 + 50,000 + 40,000	= 40,000 + 1,00,000 + 10,000	
Effect of Transaction – 40,000	– – –	= 40,000	– –
New Balance 10,000 + 10,000 + 50,000 + 40,000 = 1,00,000 + 10,000			

Transaction 8

On April 17, the firm pays A 2,000 as rent.

Assets		*= Liabilities + Proprietor's equity*	
Cash + Debtors + Merchandise + Furniture = Creditors + X's Cap + Surplus/Profit			
Old Balance	10,000 + 10,000 + 50,000 + 40,000 =	+ 1,00,000 + 10,000	
Effect of Transaction – 2,000		=	– 2000
New Balance 8,000 + 10,000 + 50,000 + 40,000 = 1,00,000			+ 8,000

Profit & Loss A/C
for the year ending ....

	A		A
To Purchases a/c	30,000	By Sales a/c	30,000
To Purchases a/c	40,000	By Closing Stock	50,000
To G/P c/d	10,000		
	80,000		80,000
To Rent a/c	2,000	By Gross profit b/d	10,000
To Net Profit	8,000		
	10,000		10,000

Balance Sheet
as on ....

Liabilities	A	*Assets*	A
Capital	1,00,000	Cash	8,000
		Furniture	40,000
Profit	8,000	Debtors	10,000
		Closing Stock (*Merchandise*)	50,000
	1,08,000		1,08,000

Example 2

Shows the Accounting equation on the basis of the following transactions :

(*i*) X started business with cash A 1,00,000

(*ii*) Purchases goods on credit from Mohan A 40,000

(*iii*) Sold goods for cash A 26,000 (Cost A 22,000)

Solution

	Assets		*= Liabilities + Proprietor's Equity*	
1.	X started business with cash	bank + Goods A 1,00,000 + 0	= Creditors 0	+ Capital + A 1,00,000
	Beginning Equation	1,00,000 + 0	= 0	+ A 1,00,000
2.	Purchased goods on Credit from Mohan	(+) 40,000	= (+) 40,000	
	New Equation	1,00,000 + 40,000	= 40,000	+ 1,00,000
3.	Sold goods for cash A 26,000 (cost A 22,000)	(+) 26,000 (–) 22,000	=	+ 4,000
	Ending Equation	1,26,000 + 18,000	= 40,000	+ 1,04,000

Example 3

On January 1, 2012, a company Super Consultants India Ltd. was incorporated. The following transactions occurred during January 2012.

January

1. Business was started with capital of A 1,00,000 cash.
4. Equipment was rented (and paid) for the month at a cost of A 12,000.
8. Paper stationery purchased on credit A 8,000.
15. The company charged A 30,000 as consulting fees from the customers during January. This amount is due to be received next month.
20. Miscellaneous expenses of A 6,000 were paid.
29. Land was purchased by borrowing A 4,00,000 from a bank. The loan is due to be repaid in five years. Interest payments are due at the end of each month beginning July 31.
30. Salaries of A 7,000 for the month were paid.
31. Lesson fees were billed to customers in the amount of A 28,000. (They are due to be received next month).

Prepare a summary of the preceding transactions. Determine balances after each transaction to show that the basic equation is in balance.

Prepare an income statement, a statement of retained earnings, balance sheet for January 2012.

Solution

Super Consultants India Ltd.
Summary of Transaction
January 2012

(Amount in A)

Date	*Cash +*	*Assets Accounts receivables*	*+ Land*	*=*	*Liabilities + Equity = A/Cs payables*	*+ Loan*	*Capital*	*+ Profit or Retained Earning*
1	1,00,000			=			1,00,000	
4	– 12,000							– 12,000
	88,000			=	+ 8,000		1,00,000	– 12,000
8								– 8,000
	88,000				800		1,00,000	– 20,000
15		+ 30,000						+ 30,000
	88,000	30,000		=	8,000		1,00,000	+ 10,000
20								
	– 6,000							– 6,000
	82,000	30,000		=	8,000		1,00,000	+ 4,000
29			+4,00,000	=		+ 4,00,000		
	82,000	30,000	4,00,000	=	8,000	4,00,000	1,00,000	4,000
30								
	– 7,000							– 7,000

31	75,000	30,000	4,00,000	= 8,000	4,00,000	1,00,000	– 3,000
		+ 28,000					+ 28,000
	75,000	58,000	4,00,000	= 8,000	4,00,000	1,00,000	25,000

Income Statement for the Month Ended January 31, 2012

Revenue		*(A)*
	Consulting Fees	30,000
	Lesson Fees	28,000
	Total Revenues	58,000
Less :	Expenses :	
	Rent Expense	12,000
	Paper & Stationery	8,000
	Salaries	7,000
	Misc. Expenses	6,000
		33,000
	Net Income	25,000

Statement of Retained Earnings

	Retained earnings as on January 1	NIL
Add :	Net Income for January 2012	A 25,000
	Total	25,000
Less =	dividends	NIL
	Retained earnings, January 31	25,000

Balance Sheet as on January 31, 2012

Liabilities	*A*	*Assets*	*A*
Capital	1,00,000	Cash	75,000
retained earnings	25,000	Accounts Receivable	58,000
Accounts payables	8,000	Land	4,00,000
Loan	4,00,000		
	5,33,000		5,33,000

Example 4

Prove that accounting equation is satisfied in all of the following transactions of Mr. X.

(*i*) Commenced business with cash – A 80,000

(*ii*) Purchased goods for cash – A 40,000 and on credit A 30,000

(*iii*) Sold goods for cash – A 40,000 costing A 25,000

(*iv*) Paid salary – A 2,000 and salary outstanding A 1,000.

(*v*) Bought Scooter for personal use for cash at A 20,000

Solution

(Amount in A)

Transaction	*Cash*	*Assets = Liabilities + Owners Equity* Goods	= Creditors	+ Salary outstanding	+ Capital
(*i*) X commenced business with cash, beginning equation	80,000		=		80,000
(*ii*) Purchased goods for cash and on credit	– 40,000	+ 70,000	= 30,000		
(*iii*) Sold goods for cash (A 40,000) costing A 25,000	40,000	– 25,000	= – –		+ 15000
New Equation	80,000	+ 45,000	= 30,000	–	+ 95000
(*iv*) Paid salary of A 2,000 and salary outstanding is A 1,000	– 2,000	–	–	+ 1,000	– 3,000
New Equation	78,000	+ 45,000	= 30,000	1,000	+ 92,000
(*v*) Bought scooter for personal	– 20,000				– 20,000
use for cash Ending equation	58,000	+ 45,000	= 30,000	+ 1,000	+ 72,000

Example 5

Show the accounting equation on the basis of the following transactions :

		(A)
(*i*)	Y started business with cash	90,000
(*ii*)	Purchased good on credit	50,000
(*iii*)	Purchased furniture for cash	10,000
(*iv*)	Sold goods costing A 20,000 for	40,000
(*v*)	Sold goods costing A 20,000 on credit for	42,000
(*vi*)	Bought goods worth A 20,000. (A 15,000 paid in cash and balance on credit)	
(*vii*)	Drawn for personal use	5,000
(*viii*)	Paid as rent	1,000
(*ix*)	Paid for salaries	3,000
(*x*)	Paid for creditors	40,000
(*xi*)	Received from debtors	12,000

Solution

(Amount in A)

Transaction	*Assets =* Cash	+ Goods	+ Debtors	+ Furniture	*Liabilities + Owners Equity* = Creditors	+ Y's Capital
1. Y started business with cash Beginning equation	90,000				=	90,000

2.	Purchased goods on credit	–	+ 50,000	+ –	+ –	=	50,000	+ –
	New Equation	90,000	+ 50,000	+ –	+ –	=	50,000	+ 90,000
3.	Purchased furniture for cash	– 10,000	+ –	+ – +	10,000	=	–	+ –
	New Equation	80,000	+ 50,000	+ – +	10,000	=	50,000	+90,000
4.	Sold goods costing A 20,000 for A 40,000	+ 40,000	– 20,000	+ – +	–	=	– +	20,000
	New equation	1,20,00	+ 30,000	+ – +	10,000	=	50,000	+1,10,100
5.	Sold goods costing A 20,000 on credit A 42,000 on credit	–	–20,000	+ 42,000		=	– +	22,000
	New equation	1,20,000	+10,000	+ 42,000	+ 10,000	=	50,000	+1,32,000
6.	Bought goods worth A 20,000 (A 15,000 paid in cash, balance on credit	– 15,000	+ 20,000	+ – +	–	=	+ 5,000	+ –
	New equation	1,05,000	+30,000	+ 42,000	+ 10,000	=	55,000	+ 1,32,000
7.	Drew for personal use	– 5,000	+	– +	– + –	=	– –	– 5,000
	New equation	1,00,000	+30,000	+ 42,000	+ 10,000	=	55,000	+ 1,27,000
8.	Paid as rent	– 1,000	+	– +	– + –	=	–	– 1,000
	New equation	99,000	+ 30,000	+ 42,000	+ 10,000	=	55,000	+ 1,26,000
9.	Paid for salaries	– 3,000	+ – +	– +	–	=	–	– 3,000
	New equation	96,000	+ 30,000	+ 42,000	+ 10,000	=	55,000	+ 1,23,000
10.	Paid to creditors	– 40,000	+ – +	– +	–	=	– 40,000	+ –
	New equation	56,000	+ 30,000	+ 42,000	+ 10,000	=	15,000	+ 1,23,000
11.	Received from Debtors	+ 12,000	+ –	– 12,000	+ –	=	–	+ –
	Ending equation	68,000	+ 30,000	+ 30,000	+ 10,000	=	15,000	+ 1,23,000

Example 6

Show the accounting equation on the basis of the following transactions and present a balance sheet on the basis of the ending equation.

		A
(*i*)	Mohan commence business with cash	70,000
(*ii*)	Purchased goods on credit	14,000
(*ii*)	Withdrew for private use	3,000
(*iv*)	Goods purchased for cash	10,000
(*v*)	Paid wages	2,000
(*vi*)	Paid to creditors	10,000
(*vii*)	Sold goods, on credit (Cost price - A 10,000)	15,000
(*viii*)	Sold goods for cash (Cost price - A 3,000)	6,000
(*ix*)	Purchased furniture for cash	2,000

Solution

(*Amount in A*)

Transaction	*Assets =*					*Liabilities + Owners Equity*	
	Cash +	*Goods +*	*Debtors +*	*Furniture*	*=*	*Creditors +*	*Mohan's Capital*
1. Mohan commenced Business with cash	70,000 + –	+ –	+ –		=	– +	70,000
Beginning equation	70,000 + –		+ –		=	– +	70,000
2. Purchased goods on credit		+ 14,000	+ –	+ –	=	14,000	+ –
New Equation	70,000	+ 14,000	+ – + –		=	14,000	+ 70,000
3. Withdrawn for private use	– 3,000	+ –	+ –	+ –	=	– –	– 3,000
New Equation	67,000	+14,000	+ –	=		14,000	+ 67,000
4. Goods purchased for cash	– 10,000	+ 10,000	+ –	+ –	=	– +	–
New Equation	57,000	+ 24,000	+ –	+ –	=	14,000	+ 67,000
5. Paid wages	– 2,000	+ –	+ –	+ –	=	14,000	+ – 2,000
New Equation	55,000	+ 24,000	–	–	=	14,000	+ 65,000
6. Paid to creditors	– 10,000	+ –	+ –	+	=	–10,000	+ –
New Equation	45,000	+ 24,000	+ –	+ –	=	4,000	+ 65,000
7. Sold goods on credit for A 15,000 (Cost A 10,000)	–	– 10,000	+15,000	= –	=	–	+ 5,000
New Equation	45,000	+ 14,000	+ 15,000	+ –	=	4,000	+70,000
8. Sold goods for cash A 6,000 costing A 3,000	+ 6,000	– 3,000	+ –	+ –	=	–	+ 3,000
New Equation	51,000	+ 11,000	+ 15,000	+	=	4,000	+ 73,000
9. Purchased furniture for cash	– 2,000	+ –	+ –	+ 2,000	=	–	+ –
Ending Equation	49,000	+ 11,000	+15,000	+ 2,000	=	4,000	+ 73,000

Balance Sheet

As on ....

Liabilities	*A*	*Assets*	*A*
Creditor	4,000	Cash	49,000
Mohan's capital	73,000	Goods	11,000
		Debtors	15,000
		Furniture	2,000
	77,000		77,000

ASSIGNMENT MATERIAL

Note : The Objective Type Questions (True/False, Multiple Choice Questions etc.) have been given in the Appendix at the end of the book.

SHORT ANSWER THEORY QUESTIONS

1. Write notes on Accounting equation.
2. What is Basic Accounting Framework?
3. What are the assumptions in Accounting Framework?
4. List some assets and liabilities.
5. Explain the effect of financial transactions on Accounting Equation.
6. What is a Transaction Analysis.
7. What is the fundamental accounting equation? Express it in two different forms.
8. What are the two classification of equities in a balance sheet?
9. What do you understand by transaction analysis? Illustrate.
10. Each business transaction has two elements, Explain.
11. Indicate whether each of the following would increase, decrease or have no effect on owners equity :
    (*a*) Purchased supplies for cash
    (*b*) Withdrew supplies for personal use
    (*c*) Paid salaries
    (*d*) Purchased equipment for cash
    (*e*) Invested cash in business
    (*f*) Rendered service to customers, on account
    (*g*) Rendered service to customers, for cash
12. Give one suitable transaction that would result into each of the following :
    (*i*) Increase in an asset and decrease in another asset
    (*ii*) Increase in one liability and decrease in another liability
    (*iii*) Increase in liability and decrease in proprietor's equity
    (*iv*) Increase in one asset and increase in liability

LONG ANSWER THEORY QUESTIONS

1. What is an accounting equation? Explain with suitable examples.
2. "All transactions are subject to accounting equation." Comment on this statement.
3. Give the example of different transactions which may influence assets, liabilities and owner's funds.
4. "Assets and liabilities both are claims, one in favour of business, the other against business". Explain this statement.
5. Explain with examples as to how accounting equation is not influenced by occurrence of some transactions.
6. Discuss nine possible effect combinations on the accounting equation.

PRACTICAL PROBLEMS

1. Show the Accounting Equation on the basis of the following transactions :

		(A)
1.	Ravi started business with cash	40,000
2.	Purchased goods on credit	10,000
3.	Received commission	250
4.	Paid rent	1,000
5.	Purchased goods for cash	14,000
6.	Withdrew cash for private use	1,500
7.	Sold goods on credit (Cost price A 15,000)	20,000
8.	Purchased furniture for cash	3,000
9.	Paid to creditors	7,500

[***Ans :*** Assets A 45,250; Liabilities A 2,500; Capital A 42,750]

2. Show the Accounting Equation on the basis of the following transactions :

		(A)
1.	Mohan commenced business with cash	15,000
2.	He purchased goods on credit	5,000
3.	He sold goods for cash (costing A 2,500) for	3,000
4.	Purchased furniture for cash	1,500
5.	Sold goods to Rakesh on credit (costing A 400) for	500
6.	Paid salaries	250
7.	Received cash from Rakesh	500
8.	Withdrew cash for private use	1,200
9.	Received rent from tenants	1,500
10.	Purchased goods from Mukesh for cash	500

[***Ans :*** Assets A 20,650; Liabilities A 5,000; Capital A 15,650]

3. Prove that the accounting equation is satisfied in all the following transactions :
   1. Started business with cash A 1,20,000
   2. Purchased a typewriter for cash for A 8,000 for office use
   3. Purchased goods for A 50,000 for cash
   4. Purchased goods for A 40,000 on credit
   5. Goods costing A 60,000 sold for A 80,000 on credit
   6. Paid for rent A 1,500 and for salaries A 2,000
   7. Received A 800 for commission
   8. Withdrew for private use A 5,000 in cash

[***Ans :*** Assets A 1,72,300; Liabilities A 40,000; Capital A 1,32,300]

4. Develop accounting Equation for the following transactions :

		(A)
1.	Rohit started business with cash	1,50,000
2.	He Purchased goods from Ram on credit	50,000

3.	Paid carriage	500
4.	Sold goods for (profit A 3,000)	9,000
5.	Received security deposits from tenants	1,500
6.	Invested in shares (personal)	50,000
7.	Introduced fresh capital	25,000
8.	Goods destroyed by fire	2,500

[***Ans :*** Assets A 1,76,500; Liabilities A 51,500; Capital A 1,25,000]

5. Prakesh started a business with a cash investment of A 70,000. Following transactions took place :
   1. Paid three months advance rent for office accommodation A 4,200
   2. Bought office car A 42,000
   3. Purchased office furniture A 14,000
   4. Bought office type-writer from Alpine Supply Company A 6,000.
   5. Sold extra office furniture at cost to Ajay for A 2,000. Ajay paid A 1,200 in cash and accepted a bill at three months for the balance.
   6. Ajay paid the amount of the bill at maturity and Prakash paid half the amount he owed to Alpine Supply Company.
   7. Collected A 1,20,000 as commission.
   8. Paid telephone bill amounting to A 300.

   Develop Accounting Equation.

CHAPTER 5

Accounting Process - I : Journalization

Learning Objectives

After studying this chapter, you should be able to :

1. *Understand the nature of Journal.*
2. *Define the term 'Account' and know the features of an account.*
3. *Explain rules of Debit and Credit with examples.*
4. *Discuss different types of accounts.*
5. *Demonstrate journal entries with some examples.*

The financial accounting systems have two major components. One of these, called the journal, is a sequential listing of events that have had a measurable effect on an organization's economic condition. The journal is, in effect, a diary of the economic events that have taken place on a day-to-day basis. The second component, called accounts, consists of summaries by categories of all events that have occurred during a period or since the formation of the entity. A complete set of accounts is called a ledger. A set of accounts for assets, liabilities, and owners' equity is called a general ledger. The purpose of this chapter is to illustrate briefly the nature of a journal and accounts and to describe some of the conventions used in maintaining them.

The development of electronic media, such as computers, has drastically changed the way records are kept in most organizations. The introduction of new technologies, however, has not displaced the terminology and basic record-keeping functions of the double-entry system originally developed before the end of the 15th century.

The Journal

The journal is a sequential record of events and their effects on the entity. The double-entry system is a means of ensuring that the accounting equation *i.e.,* assets = liabilities remains in balance. Entries are made in the journal using this system. It is labeled double entry because there will always be at least two parts to the entry. For example, if an asset increases, something else must occur to keep the equation in balance (such as an equity increase or another asset decrease).

In journal, one line has a different margin than the other. This left-versus-right format is a conventional way of describing whether these accounts have increased or decreased. Convention dictates that all lines with left margins are presented first with all indented lines following in each individual journal entry.

There are some important characteristics of almost all journals. Each event is dated. Where a date is not shown, it is presumed to be the same as that of the preceding entry. A description is included giving details about classifications that are increased or decreased. Finally, the amount of increase or decrease is listed in two columns labelled debit (dr.) or credit (cr.). The words debit and credit in accounting have no meaning other than left and right, and no attempt should be made to relate the meaning of these two words in other contexts to the way in which they are used in accounting records.

A journal may contain other information as well, in parentheses which allows a reader to understand more quickly the journal entry.

JOURNALIZING THE TRANSACTIONS

Recording the dual aspects of a transaction is known as journalizing. Normally, in a business it is impossible to record every transaction as a journal entry. Hence, special journals such as purchases book, sales book etc., are used. Only certain special transactions are recorded in the journal book. However, for a clear understanding of the readers, the journal entries for various transactions are explained below. Let us apply the rules of debit and credit for a few sample transactions after ascertaining dual aspects.

Transaction	*Aspects*	*Account Debited*	*Reason for The debit*	*Account Credited*	*Reason for the credit*
(1)	(2)	(3)	(4)	(5)	(6)
ABC Ltd. received A 5,000 from Gupta & Co.	Aspect 1 Cash of A 5,000 is received. Aspect 2 The amount is given by Gupta & Co.	Cash A/c	Cash A/c is a real A/c The rule of 'Debit what comes in' applies	Gupta & Co.	Gupta & Co. A/c is a personal A/c. The rule of 'credit the giver' applies.
PQR Ltd. purchased A 6,000 worth of goods from X Co.	Aspect 1 Goods worth A 6,000 is received Aspect 2. The goods are supplied by X Co.	Purchases A/c	Purchase A/c is a real A/c. The rule of 'Debit What comes in' applies	X Co. A/c	X Co. A/c a personal A/c. The rule of 'credit the giver' applies
XYZ Ltd. paid the salaries of A 15,500 to its staff for the month through bank transfer.	Aspect 1. payment of an expense of A 15,500 Aspect 2. Balance balance is reduced by A 15,500.	Salaries A/c.	Salaries A/c is a nominal A/c. The rule of 'Debit all expenses' applies.		Bank A/c is a Real A/c the rule of 'credit what goes out' applies

THE ACCOUNT

The account is the basic building block of any accounting system. An account is a standardised format used to maintain separate record and to accumulate data for each of the individual items in order to facilitate the preparation of periodic financial statements and to provide a continuous check on the accuracy of the recording of transactions. An account exists, therefore, for each asset, liability, owner capital, revenue and expense item. The account is used to record increases and decreases in these items (asset, liability, owner capital, revenue and expense) resulting from business transactions. No entry is made in the account until a record has been made in the journal and every entry in the journals results in a change in the status of two or more accounts. The account (of an item) shows the following things :

1. The account title, which is the name of a particular accounting element, such as Cash Account.
2. A place to record increases in the monetary amounts in the account.

3. A place to record decreases in the monetary amounts in the account.
4. Dates and descriptive notations.
5. Cross-references to other accounting records.

To illustrate the nature of the account, an example of Cash Account is given below:

Cash Account

Debit *Credit*

Date	*Parti-culars*	*Ledger Folio*	*Amount (A)*	*Date*	*Parti-culars*		*Ledger Folio*	*Amount (A)*
2012				**2012**				
Jan. 1	To balance b/d		50,000	Jan. 12	By	Salaries		11,000
Jan. 15	To Debtors		21,000	Jan. 27	By	Rent		17,000
Jan. 25	To sales		35,000	Jan. 31	By	Balance c/d		78,000
Total :			1,06,000	Total :				1,06,000
Feb. 1	To Balance b/d		78,000					

On the left side of the Cash Account, there are three accounting entries, one representing the beginning balance and the other two entries representing increases to this account. On the right side there are three accounting entries, two entries representing decreases to this account and the third entry representing the closing balance. The left-side entries begins with the prefix "to" and right-side entries begins with the prefix "by". One may notice that the total of the left side of the cash account is A 1,06,000 and the total of the right side is A 28,000. The net difference between increases and decreases in the cash account is an increase and that is why the balance of A 78,000 is located on the increases in cash side. In the account plus (+) and minus (–) signs are not needed. Of course, total decreases in cash could not have exceeded total increases; as we cannot spend more cash than we have. The balance in an account is the difference between increases and decreases. The cash account (or any other account) thus, shows the four money elements :

1. Beginning balance
2. Increases or additions
3. Decreases or deductions
4. Closing balance

The form of the account looks like the letter T. For this reason it is referred to as a T-Account. The T-Account form is used by accountants for preparing accounts, actual record keeping, analysis of accounting problems and by accounting teachers for teaching accounting.

DEBIT AND CREDIT

As stated earlier, accounts are prepared to provide help in the preparation of financial statements and to check the correctness of transactions recorded by a business enterprise. It is obvious that the financial statements can be prepared only after accounts for different elements (transactions) have been prepared which have to be reported on the financial statements.

Checking the accuracy of recorded transactions and the accounting system is done in terms of basic accounting equation (discussed in the previous chapter) and rules of debit and credit.

The terms debit and credit are used to describe the left-hand and the right-hand sides of an account, as shown below. The verb to "debit" means to make entry in the left-hand side of an account and the verb to "credit" means to make an entry in the right-hand-side of an account. The terms debit and credit have no other meaning in accounting.

(Any Type of Account)

Debit	*Credit*
Always the left-side	Always the right side

The abbreviations Dr. and Cr. are used in place of Debit and Credit. An entry made on the left-hand side is a debit to the account and entry recorded on the right-hand side is a credit to the account. About the debit and credit, a writer has commented in the following manner :

"When the book lies open in front of you and you look at the book (not the book at you) then the side where you have your heart is the left or Debit side. The side away from your heart is the right side and is called Credit".[1]

All accounts show entries recording increases and deceases. In some accounts (such as Cash Account illustrated earlier), increases are recorded on the left-hand side (Debit side) of the account and decreases are recorded on the right-hand side (credit side) of the account. In other accounts, the reverse is true. It means debits and credits by themselves do not indicate increases or decreases. Reference must be made to a specific account to determine if the debits or credits represent increases or decreases.

The five major categories of accounts are illustrated below showing debits and credits related to increases or decreases.

1. Asset Accounts

Debit Side	*Credit Side*
Shows increases Normal Balance-Debit	Shows Decreases

2. Liabilities Account

Debit Side	*Credit Side*
Shows decreases	Shows increases Normal balance-credit

3. Owners' Equity Account

Debit Side	*Credit Side*
Shows decreases	Shows increases Normal balance-Credit

4. Revenue Account

Debit Side	*Credit Side*
Shows decreases	Shows increases Normal balance-Credit

5. Expenses Account

Debit Side	*Credit Side*
Shows Increases Normal balance-Debit	Shows decreases

Normal balance refers to positive balance of an account. For any account, generally speaking the total of the increases to the account exceeds the total of the decreases to the account. The resulting balance is a positive balance rather than a negative balance. For example, a typical asset account (such as plant Account) have total debits in excess of total credits and consequently have a normal debit balance. After observing the above five types of account, the following inferences are drawn :

1. Debit is always the left-side of all account, and credit is always the right-side of the account.
2. Increases in assets and expenses accounts are always debit entries.
3. Increases in liabilities, Owner's equity and revenue accounts are always credit entries.
4. Decreases are always recorded on the side opposite increases.
5. The normal balance of any account is on the side on which increases are recorded.
6. Assets and expense accounts normally have debit balances. The liabilities, owners' equity and revenue accounts generally have credit balances.

It should be understood that all the above types of accounts are part of the basic balance sheet equation, Assets = Liabilities + Owners Equity. That is, each financial transaction has two parts. For example, if an asset is increased, then, if the balance sheet equation is to remain in balance, something else must happen, namely one of the following :

1. Another asset must decrease, or
2. A liability must increase, or
3. Owners' equity must increase.

In all the above situations, debit will always equal the credit and the basic balance sheet equation will remain in balance.

Illustration of Debit and Credit Rules and Recording of Transactions in the Accounts

The following illustration are taken to explain the application of debit and credit rules (entries) in the various accounts, using T accounts for simplicity and understanding. Prior to making debit and credit entries, a transaction should be analysed to determine which accounts must be increased or decreased. After this has been determined, the rules of debit and credit are applied to record the appropriate increases and decreases to the accounts.

Transactions 1

Ashok invested A 80,000 of his funds in a new business entitled Alpha Co. Ltd.

Asset (increase)

(Amount in A)

Debit	*Cash A/c*	*Credit*
(1) 80,000		

Equity (increase)

Debit	*Capital A/c*	*Credit*
	(1)	80,000

This transaction increases both the assets and equities of the firm. According to rules of debit and credit, debits will increase assets and credits will increase equity accounts of the firm.

Transaction 2

Alpha Co. Ltd., purchased the following assets for cash : Supplies A 9,000, office equipment A 7,000, Tools A 6,000.

Assets (increases)
Supplies A/c

Debit	*Credit*
(2) 9,000	

Office Equipment A/c

Debit	*Credit*
(2) 7,000	

Tools A/c

Debit	*Credit*
(2) 6,000	

Assets (decrease)
Cash A/c

Debit	*Credit*
(1) 80,000	(2) 22,000

Three assets-supplies, office equipment and tools are purchased by the firm in cash, reducing the asset cash by A 22,000. Assets are increased by debits and reduced by credits. Therefore, the three asset account– supplies, office equipment and tools are debited, each for its respective amount and cash is credited for the total of A 22,000.

Transaction 3

Alpha Co., acquired land for A 75,000 for storing purposes, paying A 15,000 in cash and issuing bills payable for the difference.

Asset (Increase, Decrease)
Cash A/c

Debit		*Credit*
(1)	80,000	(2) 22,000 (3) 15,000

Land A/c

Debit		*Credit*
(3)	75,000	

Liability (Increases)
Account Payable A/c

Debit	*Credit*
	(3) 60,000

The asset land account is debited by A 75,000 (increases) and the asset cash account is credited by A 15,000 (decrease). Bills payable account is credited by A 60,000 (increase in liabilities). This transaction shows that increases in assets are recorded by debits, decreases in assets by credits and increases in liabilities by credits.

Transaction 4

Alpha Co. paid A 12,000 for three months' rent in advance.

Asset (increase)

Debit	*Prepaid Rent A/c*	*Credit*
(4)	12,000	

Asset (decrease)

Debit	*Cash A/c*	*Credit*
(1)	80,000	(2) 22,000
		(3) 15,000
		(4) 12,000

Rent paid in advance (or any expense paid in advance) is an asset or resource having future economic benefit as it gives right to the firm to occupy the rented property. As increases in assets are recorded by debits and decreases in assets are recorded by credits, prepaid rent is debited for A 12,000 and cash is credited for A 12,000.

Transaction 5

Alpha Co. received A 9,500 as payment for consultancy services rendered by the firm to the customers.

Assets (Increase)

Debit	*Cash A/c*	*Credit*
(1)	80,000	(2) 22,000
		(3) 15,000
(5)	9,500	(4) 12,000

Equity (Increases)

Debit	*Consultancy Services A/c*	*Credit*
		(5) 9,500

This transaction increases the asset cash and equity of the firm by the revenue received for services rendered. Assets are increased by debits and revenues are increased by credits. Therefore, a debit of A 9,500 to cash and a credit of A 9,500 to Receipts for consultancy services are made to record the transaction.

Transaction 6

Alpha Co., rendered consultancy services to its customers for A 13,500 on credit and the customers will pay later.

Assets (Increases)

Debit	*Account Receivable*	*Credit*
(6) 13,500		

Equity (Increases)

Debit	*Consultancy Services*	*Credit*
		(5) 9,500
		(6) 13,500

The firm has given consultancy services to the customers who will pay in future. Since the services has been completed, revenue is earned. A future economic benefit has been received and therefore an asset account - Accounts Receivable - is created in exchange for the services rendered. Assets are increased by debits. Revenues are increased by credits.

Transaction 7

Alpha Co. paid A 12,000 for the land earlier purchased on credit for A 60,000.

Assets (Decrease)

Debit	*Cash A/c*	*Credit*
(1) 80,000		(2) 22,000
(5) 9,500		(3) 15,000
		(4) 12,000
		(7) 12,000

Liabilities (Decrease)

Debit	*Accounts Payable A/c*	*Credit*
(7) 12,000		(3) 60,000

The asset cash and liability bills payable are reduced by A 12,000 each by this transaction. Assets are decreased by credits; liabilities are decreased by debits.

Transaction 8

Additional tools are purchased on credit, for A 1,500.

Assets (Increase)

Debit	*Tools A/c*	*Credit*
(2) 6,000		
(8) 1,500		

Debit	*Accounts Payable A/c*	*Credit*
		(8) 15,000

This transaction increases the asset Tools and the liability Accounts Payable each by A 1,500. Assets are increased by debits. Liabilities are increased by credits.

Transaction 9

Alpha Co. paid utilities expense of A 1,000.

Assets (Decrease)

Debit	*Cash A/c*	*Credit*
(1) 80,000		(2) 22,000
(5) 9,500		(3) 15,000
		(4) 12,000
		(7) 12,000
		(9) 1,000

A separate expense account is created for each expense item. This transaction increases the utility Expense and reduces the asset cash by A 1,000. Expenses are increased by debits and assets are decreased by credits.

Transaction 10

Alpha Co., received A 7,500 in cash from customers for whom consultancy services was earlier rendered (transaction 6).

Asset (Increase)

Debit	*Cash A/c*	*Credit*
(1) 80,000 (5) 9,500 (10) 7,500		(2) 22,000 (3) 15,000 (4) 12,000 (7) 12,000 (9) 1,000

Asset (Decrease)

Debit	*Accounts Receivable*	*Credit*
(6) 13,500		(10) 7,500

Payments by customers reduce the asset accounts receivable and increase the asset cash. Assets are increased by debits and decreased by credits.

Transaction 11

Depreciation of A 7,500 is recorded on the office equipment.

Assets (Decrease)

Debit	*Depreciation*	*Credit*
		(12) 7,500

Debit	*Equity (decrease)*	*Credit*
(12) 7,500		

Depreciation expense is recorded by increasing an expense and reducing an asset. The reduction of the asset is accomplished by the use of a contra-asset account. Expenses are increased by debits. Assets are reduced by credits.

Transaction 12

Ashok withdrew A 2,000 from the firm for personal use.

Assets (Decrease)

Debit	*Cash A/c*	*Credit*
(1) 80,000 (5) 9,500 (10) 7,500		(2) 22,000 (3) 15,000 (4) 12,000 (7) 12,000 (9) 1,000 (12) 2,000

Equity (Decrease)

Debit	*Drawing A/c*	*Credit*
(12) 2,000		

This transaction reduces cash and decreases equity of the firm by A 2,000. Assets are reduced by credits and liabilities are reduced by debits. For withdrawals made by the proprietor, a separate account - Drawing Account - is opened. Drawing is a contra account because its balance represents a reduction of equity (capital) account. Debiting the drawing account to reflect the reduction in owner's equity has the same effect as debiting the owner's capital account directly because, at the end of the period, after net profit is added to the owner's capital account, the debit balance in the drawing account is deducted to arrive at the ending amount of owner's capital.

Transaction 13

A 4,000 of the prepaid rent (A 12,000) had expired; as mentioned in transaction 4.

Assets (Decrease)

Debit	*Prepaid Rent A/c*	*Credit*
(4) 12,000		(13) 4,000

Equity (Decreases)

Debit	*Rent Expense A/c*	*Credit*
(13) 4,000		

In transaction 4 the firm paid A 12,000 for three months' rent in advance. At the end of one month. A 4,000 rent has expired and no longer represents an asset. Assets are decreased by credits and liability is decreased by debits. Expenses reduce the equity of the firm.

TYPES OF ACCOUNTS

The accounts maintained by a business organization are classified into three types as shown in the following figure.

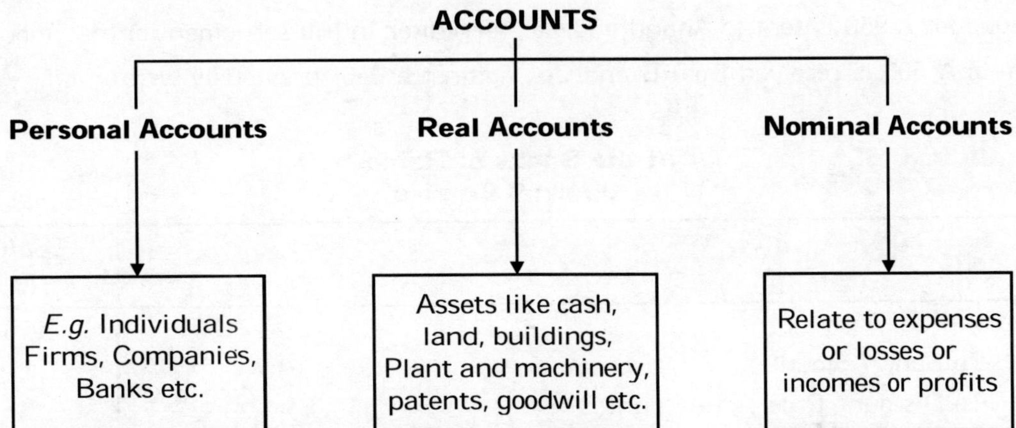

Personal Account : It deals with accounts of individuals like creditors, debtors, bank etc. It shows the balance due to these individuals or due from them on a particular date.

Real Account : It represents assets like plant and machinery, land and buildings, goodwill etc. As on a particular date, this account shows the worth of the asset.

Nominal Account : It consists of different types of expenses or incomes or loss or profit. These accounts show the amount of income earned or expenses incurred for a particular period say a month, a year etc.

Example 1

Journalise the following transactions in the books of Ramesh :

(*i*) Started business with A 10,00,000/-, out of which A 1,00,000 was borrowed from ICICI as loan.

(*ii*) Machinery purchased for A 4,00,000/- on credit and Furniture purchased for A 1,50,000 on cash.

(*iii*) Deposited cash in Vijaya Bank Current A/c A 2,50,000/-.

[*I.C.W.A., Foundation, June, 2010*]

Solution

In the Book of Ramesh

(*i*)	Cash A/c	Dr.	10,00,000	
	To Capital			9,00,000
	To Loan from ICICI			10,00,000
	(Started business with 10,00,000)			
(*ii*)	Machinery A/c	Dr.	4,00,000	
	To Supplier A/c			4,00,000
	(Machinery purchased)			
	Furniture A/c	Dr.	1,50,000	
	To Cash A/c			1,50,000
	(Furniture purchased)			
(*iii*)	Vijaya Bank A/c	Dr.	2,50,000	
	To Cash			2,50,000
	(Cash deposited)			

Example 2

Journalise the following transactions in the books of Ramesh :

(*a*) A cheque for A 950 is sent to Anand and Co., a creditor in full settlement of the amount due A 975.

(*b*) A sum of A 500 is received from B and Co., against a debt previously written off.

Solution

In the Books of Ramesh
Journal Entries

			Debit (*A*)	*Credit* (*A*)
(*a*)	Anand and Co. Account	Dr.	975	
	To Bank Account			950
	To Discount Received Account			25
	(Account settled and discounted earned)			
(*b*)	Cash Account	Dr.	500	
	To Bad Debts Recovered Account			500
	(Recovery of debts previously written off as bad)			

Example 3

Journalise the following transactions :

(*i*) Depreciate furniture purchased for A 10,000 @ 10% per annum for 3 months.

(*ii*) Received from Murthy A 1,950 in full settlement of his account for A 2,000.

Solution.

Journal Entries

			Debit (*A*)	*Credit* (*A*)
(*i*)	Depreciation Account	Dr.	250	
	To Furniture Account			250
	(Depreciation charged on furniture @10% on A 10,000 for 3 months)			
(*ii*)	Cash Account	Dr.	1,950	
	Discount Allowed Account	Dr.	50	
	To Murthy			2,000
	(Received A 1,950 from Murthy in full settlement of A 2,000)			

Example 4

Journalise the following transactions in the books of Om Prakash :

(*a*) Om Prakash sold goods to Chowdhary for A 750 against a cheque.

(*b*) Received as commission A 400.

(*c*) Bank paid A 300 directly for insurance premium of Basu.

(*d*) Cash deposited into bank A 5,000.

(*e*) Withdrawn cash from bank for personal expenses A 850.

Solution.

In the Books of Om Prakash
Journal Entries

			Debit (*A*)	*Credit* (*A*)
(*a*)	Bank Account	Dr.	750	
	To Sales Account			750
	(Goods sold against cheque)			
(*b*)	Cash Account	Dr.	400	
	To Commission Account			400
	(Commission received in Cash)			
(*c*)	Drawings Account	Dr.	300	
	To Bank Account			300
	(Payment of Insurance premium of Basu)			

(*d*)	Bank Account	Dr.	5,000	
	To Cash Account			5,000
	(Cash deposited into bank)			
(*e*)	Drawings Account	Dr.	850	
	To Bank Account			850
	(Cash withdrawn for personal expenses)			

Example 5

Pass the necessary journal entries for the following :

(*i*) A fire occurred on 15 March 2012 and stock of A 25,000 was destroyed. The Insurance Company accepted a claim for A 22,000.

(*ii*) Wages A 450 were paid for erection of plant.

Solution.

Journal Entries

			Debit (*A*)	Credit (*A*)
(*i*)	Insurance Company Account	Dr.	22,000	
	Profit and Loss Account	Dr.	3,000	
	To Trading Account			25,000
	(The loss by fire not admitted by insurance company transferred to profit and loss account)			
(*ii*)	Plant Account	Dr.	450	
	To Cash Account			450
	(Wages paid for erection of plant debited to plant account)			
	Or			
	(*a*) Wages Account	Dr.	450	
	To Cash Account			450
	(*b*) Plant Account	Dr.	450	
	To Wages Account			450

Example 6

Journalise the following :

(*i*) Machine with original cost of A 3,000 was sold A 4,300. Depreciation provision to date was A 300. A 30 were paid for removing the machine from the plant. A 43 were paid commission to the selling agent.

(*ii*) Paid Mukund A 325 for goods bought from him last month for 340 in full settlement.

Solution.

Journal Entries

			Debit (A)	Credit (A)
(*i*)	Cash Account **(4,300 – 30 – 43)**	Dr.	4,227	
	Provision for Depreciation Account		300	
	To Machine Account			3,000
	To Profit and Loss Account			1,527
	(Profit on sale of machine transferred to profit and loss account)			
(*ii*)	Mukund	Dr.	340	
	To Cash Account			325
	To Discount Received Account			15

Example 7

Journalise the following transactions in the books of Manoj.

(*a*) Issued a cheque in favour of M/s Karanvir Timber Company on account of the purchase of timber of A 75,000.

(*b*) Paid A 2,500 in cash for installation of a machinery.

(*c*) Timber sold costing A 60,000 to Kalu Ram at an invoice price 10% above cost less 5% trade discount.

(*d*) Paid A 500 to repair second hand furniture.

Solution.

In the Books of Shri Manoj
Journal Entries

			Debit (A)	Credit (A)
(*a*)	Purchases Account	Dr.	75,000	
	To Bank Account			75,000
	(Bought Goods by Cheque)			
(*b*)	Machinery Account	Dr.	2,500	
	To Cash Account			2,500
	(Cash paid for installation capitalised)			
(*c*)	Kulu Ram	Dr.	62,700	
	To Sales Account			62,700
	(Sale of timber to Kalu Ram)			
(*d*)	Furniture Account	Dr.	500	
	To Cash Account			500
	(Payment made for repair of second hand furniture added to the cost of furniture)			
	Or			

Repair A/c	Dr.	500	
To Cash Account			500
(Repair done on furniture)			
Hint : Sale price has been calculated as :			
Cost	60,000		
Add : Profit @ 10%	6,000		
	66,000		
Less : Trade discount @ 5%	3,300		
Sale price	62,700		
Trade discount is not recorded			

Example 8

Journalise the following transactions in the books of Shri Shiv Kumar Gupta

2012		(A)
Jan. 1	Commenced business with	50,000
Jan. 2	Goods purchased for cash	30,000
Jan. 3	Paid freight	2,000
Jan. 7	Goods sold to Rajani Kant on credit	13,000
Jan. 8	Paid for stationery	1,000
Jan. 9	Paid for Rent	5,000
Jan. 10	Cash received from Mohan Das	15,400
	Allowed him discount	600
Jan. 17	Paid Premium	4,000
Jan. 19	Paid Postage	100
Jan. 20	Rakesh was declared insolvent, fifty paise in the rupees was received from his estate, total debt being A 10,000	
Jan. 29	Paid for Salaries	8,000

Solution.

Journal

Date	*Particulars*	*L.F.*	*Dr. Amount*	*Cr. Amount*
2012				
Jan. 1	Cash A/c Dr.		50,000	
	To Capital A/c			50,000
	(Started business with A 50,000)			
Jan. 2	Purchases A/c Dr.		30,000	
	To Cash			30,000
	(Being the amount of Cash purchases)			
Jan. 3	Freight A/c Dr.		2,000	
	To Cash			2,000
	(Being the payment for freight)			

Jan. 7	Rajani Kant	Dr.	13,000	
	To Sales, A/c			13,000
	(Being the sale of Goods on credit)			
Jan. 8	Stationery A/c	Dr.	1,000	
	To Cash A/c			1,000
	(Being the amount of stationery paid)			
Jan. 9	Rent A/c	Dr.	5,000	
	To Cash A/c			5,000
	(Being the amount of rent paid)			
Jan. 10	Cash A/c	Dr.	15,400	
	Discount A/c	Dr.	600	
	To Mohan Das			16,000
	(Being cash received from Mohan Das)			
Jan 17	Premium A/c	Dr.	4,000	
	To Cash			4,000
	(Being the payment for premium)			
Jan 19	Postage A/c	Dr.	100	
	To Cash			100
	(Being the payment for postage)			
Jan 20	Cash A/c	Dr.	5,000	
	Bad Debts A/c	Dr.	5,000	
	To Rakesh			10,000
	(Being the recovery of 50 paise in the rupee from Rakesh, total debt being A 10,000)			
Jan 29	Salaries A/c	Dr.	8,000	
	To Cash			8,000
	Being the payment for salaries)			
	Total		**1,39,100**	**1,39,100**

Example 9

Journalise the following transaction :

2012		(*A*)
July 1	X started business with cash	80,000
July 3	Goods purchased for cash	30,000
July 5	Goods purchased from A	5,000
July 7	Goods sold for cash	10,000
July 10	Goods sold to P	30,000
July 12	Cash paid to A	3,000
July 15	Cash received from P	10,000
July 21	Paid for wages	1,500

July 25	Purchased furniture from Sunil Kumar for cash	5,000
July 28	Paid rent	5,000
July 31	Paid for salaries	2,000

Solution.

Journal

Date	*Particulars*	*L.F.*	*Dr. Amount*	*Cr. Amount*
2012				
July 1	Cash A/c	Dr.	80,000	
	To Capital a/c			80,000
	(Started business with cash)			
July 3	Purchases a/c	Dr.	30,000	
	To Cash			30,000
	(Being the purchase of goods for cash)			
July 5	Purchases a/c	Dr.	5,000	
	To A			5,000
	(Being goods purchased from A)			
July 7	Cash a/c	Dr.	10,000	
	To Sales a/c			10,000
	(Being goods sold on cash)			
July 10	P	Dr.	30,000	
	To Sales a/c			30,000
	(Being goods sold to P)			
July 12	A	Dr.	3,000	
	To cash a/c			3,000
	(Being cash paid to A)			
July 15	Cash a/c	Dr.	10,000	
	To P			10,000
	(Being cash received from P)			
July 21	Wages a/c	Dr.	1,500	
	To cash a/c			1,500
	(Being wages paid)			
July 25	Furniture a/c	Dr.	5,000	
	To cash a/c			5,000
	(Being furniture purchased from Sunil Kumar)			
July 28	Rent a/c	Dr.	5,000	
	To Cash			5,000
	(Being rent paid)			
July 31	Salaries a/c Dr.	2,000		
	To Cash		2,000	
	(Being salaries paid)			

Example 10

Journalise the following transactions in the books of Khanu and Co.

2012		(A)
Jan. 2	Started business with	8,00,000
Jan. 3	Bought furniture for	1,20,000
Jan. 6	Bought stationery for	5,000
Jan. 7	Purchased goods for cash at	2,00,000
Jan. 9	Sold goods for cash worth	50,000
Jan. 11	Sold to R Desai goods worth	1,00,000
Jan. 14	Bought goods from Mundra Bros at	80,000
Jan. 18	Paid office cleaning charges for	1,500
Jan. 20	Bought goods from Hari worth	1,00,000
Jan. 22	Sold to Sharma and Co. goods worth	60,000
Jan. 24	Received from R Desai	50,000
Jan. 25	Paid to Hari	90,000
Jan. 28	Bought typewriter for	80,000
Jan. 31	Paid house rent	7,500
Jan. 31	Paid light charges	5,000
Jan. 31	Paid salary amounting to	50,000
Jan. 31	Received commission	15,000

Solution.

Journal

Date	*Particulars*	*L.F.*	*Dr. Amount*	*Cr. Amount*
2012				
Jan 2	Cash	Dr.	8,00,000	
	To capital a/c			8,00,000
	(Started business with A 8,00,000)			
Jan 3	Furniture a/c	Dr.	1,20,000	
	To cash			1,20,000
	(Purchased furniture)			
Jan 6	Stationery a/c	Dr.	5,000	
	To cash			5,000
	(Purchased stationery)			
Jan 7	Purchases a/c	Dr.	2,00,000	
	To cash a/c			2,00,000
	(Being the purchase of goods)			
Jan 9	Cash a/c	Dr.	50,000	
	To cash a/c			50,000
	(Being the sale of goods)			

Date	Particulars		Dr. (Rs.)	Cr. (Rs.)
Jan 11	R. Desai	Dr.	1,00,000	
	To sales a/c			1,00,000
	(Being the sale of goods to R. Desai)			
Jan 14	Purchases a/c	Dr.	80,000	
	To Mundra Brothers			80,000
	(Being the purchases of goods from Mundra Bros.)			
Jan 18	Office cleaning charges a/c	Dr.	1,500	
	To cash			1,500
	(Being the office cleaning charges paid)			
Jan 20	Purchases a/c	Dr.	1,00,000	
	To Hari			1,00,000
	(Being the purchase of goods)			
Jan 22	Sharma and Co.	Dr.	60,000	
	To sales a/c			60,000
	(Being the sale of goods)			
Jan 24	Cash a/c	Dr.	50,000	
	To R. Desai			50,000
	(Being amount received from R. Desai)			
Jan 25	Hari	Dr.	90,000	
	To Cash a/c			90,000
	(Being the amount paid to Hari)			
Jan 28	Typewriter a/c	Dr.	80,000	
	To cash a/c			80,000
	(Being the purchase of typewriter)			
Jan 31	Rent a/c	Dr.	7,500	
	Lighting a/c	Dr.	5,000	
	Salary a/c	Dr.	50,000	
	To cash			62,500
	(Being the payment made for rent lighting and salary)			
Jan 31	Cash a/c	Dr.	15,000	
	To Commission A/c			15,000
	(Being the amount of commission received)			

REFERENCE

1. Paul H. Walgenbach, Ernest I. Hanson and Norman E., Dittrich, Financial Accounting, Harcourt Brace Jovanovich, 1988, p. 42.

ASSIGNMENT MATERIAL

Note : The Objective-Type Questions (True/False, Multiple Choice Questions etc.) have been given in the Appendix at the end of the book.

SHORT-ANSWER THEORY QUESTIONS

1. Distinguish between Journal and Ledger.
2. Explain Journal Proper.
3. Write a note on 'Journal'.
4. Define the term 'Account'.
5. Explain the term 'Debit' and 'Credit'.
6. What are different types of accounts.

LONG ANSWER THEORY QUESTIONS

1. What is Journal? What is the purpose of preparing Journal?
2. What are the rules for Journalising the transaction?
3. Explain the nature of an Account. What information is found in an Account?
4. Give the rules of Debit and Credit with suitable examples.
5. Discuss different types of accounts.
6. Explain the nature of an account. What information is recorded in an account? Illustrate with an example.
7. What are the rules of debit and credit for different accounts?
8. Debits and credits are used to increase and decrease in accounts. How is it possible for one of these items, say, debits, to be able to both increase and decrease accounts?
9. What are normal balances? How are they determined.
10. Identify the following as asset, liability, owner's equity, revenue or expense accounts and indicate whether a debit entry or credit entry increases the balance of the account.

    Accounts receivable — Accounts payable
    Cash — Professional fees
    Owner's capital — Advertising expense
    Supplies on hand — Plant
    Owners' drawings
11. What is justification for using a separate owner's drawing account?
12. "During the year the total owner's equity of Alpha Co., increased from A 1,00,000 to A 1,50,000. Therefore, the annual earnings must have been A 50,000". Is this statement necessarily true? Explain.
13. "Every journal entry made to the journal in a financial accounting system must have atleast one debit and one credit" Do you agree or not, explain.
14. What do debits and credits mean in different types of accounts.

15. What is an account? How would you classify different accounts maintained by a business enterprise?
16. "All transactions have double aspects". Comment giving examples.
17. What is double entry system? What are its benefits? Give examples.
18. Indicate the nature (debit or credit) of normal balance in the following accounts :
    (*i*) Personal Accounts of Debtor
    (*ii*) Furniture a/c
    (*iii*) Merchandise a/c
    (*iv*) Salaries a/c
    (*v*) Rent payable a/c
    (*vi*) Bills payable a/c

PRACTICAL PROBLEMS

1. Journalise the following transactions in the books of Hari.

2012		*A*
April 1	Hari started business with cash	60,00,000
April 2	Purchased furniture for cash	10,00,000
April 4	Purchased goods for cash	25,00,000
April 5	Bought goods from Kamlesh	1,50,000
April 6	Sold goods for cash	36,00,000
April 8	Sold good to Ram	30,00,000
April 10	Paid cash to Kamal	15,00,000
April 14	Received cash from Ram	18,00,000
April 16	Purchased goods from Sohan	6,00,000
April 18	Purchased goods from Sohan for cash	8,00,000
April 20	Paid rent for the office	1,00,000
April 26	Received commission	75,000
April 27	Paid Salary to Gopal	1,20,000
April 28	Received cash from Ram	12,00,000
April 29	Withdrew cash from office for personal use	4,00,000
April 30	Wages paid	7,20,000

2. Journalise the following transaction in the books of Sumit :

2012		*A*
Jan. 1	Sumit started business with cash	10,00,000
Jan. 2	Paid into bank	6,00,000
Jan. 3	Bought goods from Mohan on credit	2,00,000
Jan. 4	Purchased furniture	20,000

	Purchased adding machine	80,000
	Purchased typewriter	60,000
Jan. 6	Paid for postage	1,500
Jan. 8	Sold goods for cash	40,000
Jan. 9	Sold goods on credit to Mahesh & Co.	1,00,000
Jan. 15	Paid to Mohan	1,95,000
	Discount allowed by them	5,000
Jan. 25	Sold goods to Ray & Co.	56,000
Jan. 26	Received cheque from Mahesh & Co. in full settlement of amount due to them	97,500
Jan. 31	Paid for electric charge	1,000
	Paid rent by cheque	20,000

3. Record the following transactions :
    1. Gee commences business with a capital of A 25,00,000 trading under the name of Jain General Store.
    2. Paid into State Bank of India A 5,00,000.
    3. Bought goods from Chander for A 10,00,000.
    4. Bought furniture from Sharda and Co. for A 3,00,000.
    5. Sold goods to Paras for A 50,000.
    6. Received a sum of A 1,00,000 being rent for the portion of a building let out.
    7. Gee contracted with Deep Construction Co., for the renovation of the building at an estimated cost of A 5,00,000.
    8. Bought Shares in Siyaram Ltd., for A 5,00,000.
    9. Paid Gee's life insurance premium A 15,000.
    10. Bank collected dividends on our investments A 50,000.
4. Journalise the following :
    1. Bought goods from Kapil for A 40,000 at a trade discount of 10% and cash discount of 2%, paid 60% of the amount immediately.
    2. Received a cheque from *Y* for A 8,000, this cheque was deposited into bank the next day.
    3. Cheque received from *Y* was dishounoured.
    4. Old newspapers sold A 50.
    5. Purchased goods from *X* and paid by cheque A 7,000.
    6. Sold half of the above goods to *P* at a profit of 30% on cost.
5. Journalise the following transaction :

2012

Jan. 1	Mohan Bros, commenced business with capital of A 50,000 and goods worth A 30,000.
Jan. 11	Sold old machinery to Nathu for A 2,500.
Jan. 15	Goods worth A 5,000 given as charity.
Jan. 20	Proprietor withdrew for private use A 2,000 from office and A 3,000 from Bank.

Jan. 25 Cash purchases were of A 10,000, Cash Sales of A 8,000.

Jan. 30 Rent due has been decided to pay in the next accounting year amounting to A 1,000. Interest on capital A 500.

6. Journalise the following transactions :

   1. Amit is declared insolvent, Received from his official Receiver a first and final composition of 60 paise in the rupee on a debt of A 4,000.
   2. Paid A 250 in cash as wages on installation of a machine.
   3. Provide 10% depreciation on furniture costing A 5,000.
   4. Sold goods to Manu list price A 4,000, trade discount 10% and cash discount 5%. He paid the amount on the same day and availed the cash discount.
   5. Out of rent paid this year, A 1,000 is related to next year.

7. Journalise the transactions :

   1. Goods for A 2,500 were given away as charity.
   2. Goods worth A 2,500 were distributed as free samples.
   3. Goods worth A 5,000 and cash A 4,00 were stolen by an employee.
   4. Goods worth A 1,000 were destroyed by fire. Half of money received from Insurance Co.
   5. Interest charged on drawings @5% when total drawings were A 10,000.

CHAPTER 6

Accounting Process - I (*Continued*) : Cash Book and Subsidiary Books

Learning Objectives

After studying this chapter, you should be able to :

1. *Explain the nature of Cash Book, Petty Cash Book.*
2. *Discuss different types of special journals or subsidiary books such as Purchase Book, Purchase Return Book, Sales Book, Sales Return Book. Bills Receivable Book, Bills Payable Book, Journal Proper.*

CASH BOOK

Cash Book records all receipts of and payments in cash. Usually, the deposits into bank accounts maintained by a business firm, withdrawals from such accounts and cheque payments are also recorded in the Cash Book. Sometimes a separate book for recording receipts and payments by cheques/DDs etc., is kept, known as the Bank Book. A Cash Book which is used to record both cash and bank transactions is referred to as a Two-column Cash Book. The format of this cash book is given below :

Cash Book of Ramesh & Co.

Dr. *Cr.*

Date	*Receipts*	*Cash* (₹)	*Bank* (₹)	*Date*	*Payments*	*Cash* (₹)	*Bank* (₹)
2012				**2012**			
April 1	To Balance b/d	1,500	13,000	April 2	By Wages	50	
6	To Sales	800		5	By Electricity		400
7	To Arvind Co.		2,000	8	By Plumbing repairs	400	
11	To Bela Corp.		2,350	15	By Y Ltd.		10,800
20	To Sales	500		30	By balance c/d	2,350	6,150
		2,800	17,350			2,800	17,350

Cash Discounts

Sometimes, in order to encourage early payments due from customers, a company may offer a certain percentage of the amount as a discount. For example, if a customer owes the company ₹ 1,000 the company may allow 2% discount if the payment is made before a certain date. In such a case, the customer would pay an actual cash of ₹ 980 only (₹ 1000-2% of ₹ 1,000) and ₹ 20 would be treated as discount expense by the company. In the same way, a company might be given some discounts by its creditors for early payment of the amounts payable by it. A cash discount may be distinguished from a trade discount which is given on the invoice price, especially when orders for large quantities are placed. The trade discount is therefore reflected as a reduction in the sale price itself.

A Cash Book can also be used to record the Cash discounts that are allowed to customers for prompt payments and the cash discounts that are received on payments made to suppliers within a stipulated time period. Since discounts will be allowed to customers at the time of receipt of money and received from suppliers at the time of payment of dues, it is convenient to maintain the column for discounts allowed on the receipts side of the Cash book and the column for discount received on the payments side. A Cash book in which the cash and bank transactions and the details of cash discounts are recorded is referred to as a Three-column Cash Book. An illustrative format of this type of Cash Book is given below :

Cash Book of Ramesh & Co.

Dr. *Cr.*

Date	*Receipts*	*Discount*	*Cash*	*Bank*	*Date*	*Payment*	*Discount*	*Cash*	*Bank*
2012					**2012**				
April 1	To balance b/d		1,500	13,000	April 2	By Wages		50	
6	To Sales		800		5	By Electricity			400
7	To Arvind Co.	50		2,000	8	By Plumbing repairs		400	
11	To Bela Corp.	60		2,350	15	By Y Ltd.	150		10,800
20	To Sales		500		30	By Balance c/d		2,350	6,150
		110	2,800	17,350			150	2,800	17,350

The Cash Book normally also carries Columns for Cash Memo No., Ledger Folio, Vouchers No. etc.

The unique feature of the Cash Book is that it performs the functions of a Journal and the General Ledger with regard to the Cash and Bank transactions. In other words, Cash Book is the book of first entry for all such transactions and the ledger accounts for cash in hand and cash at bank will not be maintained in the General Ledger.

Petty Cash Book

When the petty cash fund is operated as an imprest fund, the recording of the petty expenses paid will be made in the petty cash book. This would also avoid recording too many small value transactions in the main cash book. The petty cash book would contain a number of analytical columns for grouping the various expenses under a few classifications which would facilitate subsequent posting into the General Ledger. A specimen petty cash book is given below :

Analytical Petty Cash Book of Ramesh & Co.

Amt. Recd.	*Date*	*Particulars*	*Total Amount*	*Postage & Stationery*	*Car-riage*	*Travel-ling*	*Sundary Exp.*
A			*A*	*A*	*A*	*A*	*A*
2012							
3,000	April, 1	To bank a/c (cheque encashed)					
	April 7	By postal stamps	800	800			
	April 10	By Stationery	320	320			
	April 15	By Carriage	160		160		
	April 20	By Auto fare of salesman	200			200	

	April 22	By Telegram	50	50			
	April 27	By tea to customers	150				150
	April 30	By stationery	360	360			
		Total	2040	1530	160	200	150
	April 30	By balance c/d	960				
3000			3000				
2012							
960	May 1	To Balance b/d					
2040	May 1	To Bank a/c (Cheque encashed)					

The Imprest System

When an analytical petty cash book is maintained for recording the petty expenses, it will be practically more convenient to consider the petty cash as a separate account and take cheques issued for the petty cash imprest as a debit to petty cash account and all petty expenses paid as credits in petty cash account. The journal entries in the months of April and May, 2012 in the books of Ramesh & Co. will be as follows :

April, 1	Petty Cash Account	Dr.	3,000	
	To Bank Account			3,000
	(being the imprest amount released for petty expenses)			
April, 30	Postage and Stationery A/c	Dr.	1,530	
	Carriage Account	Dr.	160	
	Travelling Expenses Account	Dr.	200	
	Sundry Expenses Account	Dr.	150	
	To Petty Cash Account			2040
	(being the petty expenses incurred during April)			
May, 1	Petty Cash Account	Dr.	2,040	
	To Bank Account			2,040
	(being the reimbursement of petty expenses)			

If credit for all the expenses is also given in the Cash Account (or Bank A/c) then the Cash A/c will be understated (due to two credits-one in respect of release of imprest and the other in respect of actual expenses), and to counter balance the understatement, the balance in Petty Cash Account must be added to that of the Cash Account.

SPECIAL JOURNALS OR SUBSIDIARY BOOKS

The entries made in Journal, discussed in previous chapter, are general in character; many accounting systems use forms that are quite different. When a large number of entries of the same type is to be made in the journal, often a special journal will be established to simplify the clerical task involved in making that group of entries. In some cases, a variety of journals may be used to take advantage of special characteristics of the accounting task in a particular firm or situation. Such special journals are knows as subsidiary books or subsidiary ledgers. Rather than maintain a separate account in the general ledger for each customer or creditor, subsidiary books or ledgers are established that relate in total to an account maintained in the general ledger of the accounting system. When a subsidiary ledger is used, the total of all debits and credits in the subsidiary ledger will be equal to the total amounts listed in the control account in the general ledger.

It is not necessary for an organization to adopt all possible forms of journals or ledgers or subsidiary books and the ways in which they are used. The design of an effective accounting record system depends upon the comprehension and ingenuity of the accountant and the needs of the business and its managers, who must develop and adopt an effective accounting system. The following subsidiary books may constitute the special journals or subsidiary ledgers for an enterprise.

(*i*) Purchase Book
(*ii*) Purchase Returns Book
(*iii*) Sales Book
(*iv*) Sales Returns Book
(*v*) Bills Receivable Book
(*vi*) Bills Payable Book
(*vii*) Journal Proper.

Specimen formats of these books and brief explanations regarding their use are given in the following sections.

Purchases Book

Also known as the Purchases Journal, this book is used to record credit purchases of goods only. The term 'goods' covers only those items procured by the business for resale.

Purchase Book of Johnson Co.

Date	*Name of Supplier*	*Ledger Folio*	*Inward Invoice No.*	*Amount A*
2012				
April 12	Y Limited		3,354	10.95,000
12	Sharp Enterprises		401	2,70,000
20	Best and Company		5,542	3,90,000
	Total			17,55,000

Purchase Returns Book

This subsidiary book is used to record the goods purchased on credit and sent back to suppliers as they are found not conforming to specifications or for any other reason.

Purchase Returns Book of Johnson Co.

Date	*Name of Supplier*	*Ledger Folio*	*Debit Note No.*	*Amount A*
2012				
April 15	Sharp Enterprises		80	1,00,000
25	Best and Company		81	90,000
	Total			1,90,000

Sales Book

Also known as the Sales Journal, this subsidiary book is used to record all sale of goods on credit.

Sales Book of Johnson Co.

Date	*Name of Customer*	*Ledger Folio*	*Outward Invoice No.*	*Amount A*
2012				
April 3	Beta Corporation		1001	2,41,000
5	Zeta Company		1002	3,94,000
6	Quality Dealers		1003	4,90,000
15	Sooraj Traders		1004	1,80,000
25	Star Enterprises		1005	19,50,000
	Total			32,55,000

Sales Returns Book

This book is used to record the transactions relating to goods sold on credit and received back from the customers as not conforming to the specifications or for any other reason.

Sales Returns Book of Johnson Co.

Date	*Name of Customer*	*Ledger Folio*	*Credit Note No.*	*Amount A*
2012				
April 10	Zeta Company		10	54,000
27	Star Enterprises		11	2,00,000
	Total			2,54,000

Bills Receivable Book

The Bills Receivable of an enterprise consist of all Promissory Notes given or Bills of Exchange accepted by customers in respect of amounts due from them. The Bills Receivable Book is used to record all such Promissory Notes given or such bills of Exchange accepted by customers.

Bills Receivable Book of Johnson Co.

Date	*From whom recd.*	*Acceptor*	*Date of Bills*	*Term*	*Date of Maturity*	*Where Payable*	*Amnt. A*	*How disposed*
April 12	Quality Dealers	Quality Dealers	8.4.12	90 days	10.7.12	Bank of India Bombay	4,90,000	Discounted on 20.4.2012
18	Sooraj Traders	Sooraj Traders	16.4.12	60 days	10.6.12	Union Bank of Bombay	1,80,000	
							6,70,000	

Bills Payable Book

The Bills Payables consist of all promissory Notes given or Bills of Exchange accepted by the business in respect of amounts owing to its supplies. The Bills Payable Book is used to record all such Promissory Notes given or Bills of Exchange accepted by the business.

Bills Payable Book of Johnson Co.

Date	*Name of the the drawer*	*Payee*	*Date of bill*	*Term*	*Date of maturity*	*Where payable*	*Amount A*	*Remark*
2012								
Apr. 25	Best & Co.	Best & Co.	25.4.2012	90 days	27.7.2012	Canara Bank Bombay	3,00,000	

Journal Proper

This Book is used to record all transactions which cannot be included in the cash book or any of the other six subsidiary books discussed above. The transactions that will be recorded in Journal Proper are, purchase or sale of fixed assets and investments on credit, adjusting entries, rectification entries etc.

Journal Proper of Johnson Co.

Date	*Particulars*	*Ref.*	*Ledger Folio*	*Debit A*	*Credit A*
2012					
April 10	Furniture and Fittings A/c	Dr.		4,00,000	
	To Furniture Mart A/c				4,00,000
	(Being the purchase of Furniture on credit)				
30	Repairs to Machinery A/c	Dr.		5,00,000	
	To Machinery A/c				5,00,000
	(Being the rectification of a wrong posting of a repair expense to asset A/c)				

Example 1

From the following transactions of M/s J. Choudhary, write up his cash book (three column form, bringing down the balance as on May 31, 2012.

May 1	Balance at Bank	1,50,000
May 2	Drew from bank for office use	50,000
May 3	Bought office furniture for cash	32,000
May 8	Paid wages in cash	15,000
May 14	Drew from bank from office use	25,000
May 16	Sold goods for cash	22,000
May 19	Received a cheque from B. Batiwala & Co. in settlement of their account of A 75,000 less 5 percent	
May 23	Bought goods for cash	45,000
May 25	Drew cheque for self	40,000
May 31	Paid Agrawal's account A 40,000 by cheque less 21/2 percent.	

Solution.

Cash Book

Date	*Particulars*	*L.F.*	*Dis.* A	*Cash* A	*Bank* A	*Date*	*Particulars*	*L.F.*	*Dis.* A	*Cash* A	*Bank* A
2012						**2012**					
May						May					
1	To Balance b/d				1,50,000	2	By Cash A/c	C			
50,000											
2	To Bank A/c	C		50,000		3	By Furniture A/c			32,000	
14	To Bank A/c	C		25,000		8	By Wages A/c			15,000	
16	To Sales A/c			22,000		14	By Cash A/c				25,000
19	To Batiwala & Co.		3,750		71,250	23	By Purchases A/c			45,000	
						25	By Drawing A/c				40,000
						31	By Agarwala		1,000		39,000
						31	By balance c/d			5,000	67,250
			3,750	97,000	2,21,250				1,000	97000	2,21,250
June 1	To Balance b/d			5,000	67,250						

Example 2

Enter the following transactions in the purchase day book.

January 2012

Jan. 2 Bought of G Saha and Co., 60 yards of long cloth @ A 140 per yard.

Jan. 8 Purchased from B Chandra & Co. piece goods for A 20,000.

Jan. 16 Purchased from A Basu & Co., 100 yards of shirting @ A 300 per yard less trade discount @ 2%.

Jan. 28 Bought of S.K. Sarkar and Sons, 200 yards of terycot a A 1,200 per yard less 2½ percent trade discount.

Solution.

Purchase Book

Date	*Particulars*	*L.F.*	*Details* A	*Amount* A
2012	G. Saha			
Jan. 2	60 yds of longcloth @ A 140 per yard			8,400
Jan. 8	B. Chandra & Co. piece Goods			20,000
Jan. 16	A Basu & Co., 100 yards of shirting @ A 300 per yard		30,000	
	Less trade discount @ 2%		600	
				29,400
Jan. 28	SK. Sarkar & Sons 200 yards of terycot @ A 1,200 per yard		2,40,000	
	Less trade discount @ 2½%		6,000	2,34,000
	Total			2,91,800

Example 3

Prepare a sales day book from the following transactions.

2012

July 2 Sold to Nilima, spices worth A 80,000 less 10% trade discount.

July 4 Sold to Sadhana, sugar worth A 40,000, extra charges A 1,000

July 5 Sold to Mohan, wheat worth A 20,000 forwarding expenses A 1,500

Solution.

Sales Book

Date	*Particulars*	*L.F.*	*Details*	*Amount* A
2012				
July 2	Nilima			
	Spices		80,000	
	Less : trade discount 10%		8,000	72,000
	(Sales of spices to Nilima worth A 80,000 less 10% trade discount)			
July 4	Sadhana			
	Sugar		40,000	
	Add : Extra Charge		1,000	41,000
	(Sale of sugar worth A 40,000 to Sadhna, extra charges being A 1,000)			
July 5	Mohan			
	Wheat		20,000	
	Add : Forwarding charges		1,500	21,500
	(Sale of wheat to Mohan for A 20,000 forwarding charges being A 1,500)			
	Total			1,34,500

Example 4

Prepare the sales day book from the following transaction 2012.

Feb. 1 Sold goods to Ram, 200 meters cloth @ A 100 per meter less trade discount 7%.

Feb. 3 Sold to Rahim, 500 meters cloth @ A 200 per meter less trade discount 5% packing charges A 3,000.

Feb. 4 Sold to Shyam, 2,000 meteres cloth @ A 200 per meter less trade discount 5% other charges made of A 2,500.

Feb. 7 Sold to Jadu, 300 meteres cloth @ A 250 per meter less trade discount of 10%.

Solution.

Sales Book

Date	*Particulars*	*Details*	*Amount* A
2012	Ram		
Feb. 1	200 meters cloth @ A 100	20,000	
	Per meter less trade discount 7%	1400	18,600
Feb. 3	Rahim		
	500 meters cloth @ A 200 per	1,00,000	
	meter less trade discount 5%	5,000	
		95,000	
	Add : Packing charges	3,000	98,000
Feb. 4	Shyam		
	2000 meters cloth @ A 200 per meter	4,00,000	
	less trade discount 5%	20,000	
		3,80,000	
	Add : Other charges	2,500	3,82,500
Feb. 7	Jadu		
	300 meters cloth @ A 250 per meter	75,000	
	Less : trade discount 10%	7,500	67,500
	Total		5,66,600

Example 5

Prepare purchase returns book (returns outward) from the following particulars.

2012

July 1 Returned to Sumit Prakesh 50 m of cloth @ A 20.

July 15 Bharat Kumar & Sons 10 sarees @ A 300.

July 20 Prem Chandra 200 m of cloth @ A 70.

July 31 Bihari Brothers 100 m of cloth @ A 100.

Solution.

Purchase Returns Book

Date	*Particulars*	*Details*	*Amount* A
2012			
July 1	Sumit Prakesh 50 m of cloth @ A 20.		1000
July 15	Bharat Kumar & Sons of 10 Sarees @ A 300.		3,000
July 20	Prem Chandara 200 m of cloth @ A 70		14,000
July 31	Bihari Brothers 100 m of cloth @ A 100		10,000
			28,000

Example 6

Enter the following transactions in the appropriate book.

2012

Aug. 1 Returned to us by Harish Gupta & Co. 200 bags coffee @ A 100.

Aug. 17 Returned by Bipin Pal & Brothers, 300 chests tea @ A 70 per chest.

Aug. 31 Returned by Bhagwan Das 50 tins of ghee @ A 1,000 per tin.

Solution.

Returns Inwards Book

Date	*Particulars*	*Details*	*Amount* *A*
2012			
Aug. 1	Harish Gupta & Co.		
	200 bags coffee @ A 100		20,000
Aug 17	Bipin Pal & Broths		
	300 chests tea @ A 70 per chest		21,000
Aug. 31	Bhagwan Das		
	50 tins of ghee @ A 1,000 per tin		50,000
	Total		91,000

Example 7

Prepare a Cash Book from the following transactions :

2012		*A*
Jan. 1	Cash in hand	1,000
Jan. 1	Cash at bank	15,000
Jan. 3	Received from Mohan	12,850
	and allowed him Discount	150
Jan. 4	Cash Sales	20,000
Jan. 5	Paid for Rent	4,000
Jan. 6	Cash purchasing	26,000
Jan. 7	Paid to Harish by Cheque	10,000
Jan. 8	Stationery purchased	2,000
Jan. 9	Goods sold for cash	25,000
Jan. 10	Paid salary	6,000
Jan. 12	Paid to Ram Prakesh	20,500
	Discount allowed by him	500
Jan. 15	Cash Sales	10,000
Jan. 16	Received a cheque from Prem Das and allowed discount A 400	15,600
Jan. 22	Paid charity	1,000
Jan. 25	Paid to travelling expenses	3,000
Jan. 29	Paid into Bank	5,000

Solution

Cash Book

Date 2012	Particulars	L.F.	Discount	Cash (A)	Bank (A)	Date 2012	Particulars	L.F.	Dis (A)	Cash (A)	Bank (A)
Jan. 1	To Bal. b/d	—	—	1,000	15,000	Jan. 5	By Rent	—	—	4,000	
Jan. 3	To Mohan	—	150	12,850	—	Jan. 6	By Purchase	—	—	26,000	
Jan. 4	To Sales	—	—	20,000	—	Jan. 7	By Harish	—	—	—	10,000
Jan. 9	To Sales	—	—	25,000	—	Jan. 8	By Stationary	—	—	2,000	—
Jan. 15	To Sales	—	—	10,000	—	Jan. 10	By Salary	—	—	6,000	—
Jan. 16	To Prem Dass	—	400	—	15,600	Jan. 12	By Ram Prakesh	—	500	20,500	
Jan. 29	To cash	—	—	C	5,000	Jan. 22	By Charity	—	—	1,000	
						Jan. 25	By Travelling	—	—	3,000	
						Jan. 29	By Bank	—	—	5,000	
						Jan. 31	By Bal c/d	—	—	1,350	25,600
	Total		550	68,850	35,600		Total		500	68,850	35,600
Feb. 1	To Bal b/d			1,350	25,600						

Example 8

Write out an analytical petty cash book from the following transactions :

2012

Aug.	1	Issued a cheque of A 10,000 to the petty cashier.
Aug.	2	Paid electricity charges A 325.
Aug.	4	Paid telephone charges A 250.
Aug.	8	Paid for printing A 375.
Aug.	15	Paid for stationery A 600.
Aug.	20	Purchased post cards A 300.

Solution.

Petty Cash Book

Receipts	*Date*	*Voucher Particulars*	*Total*	*Elect.*	*Telp.*	*Printing*	*Stat.*	*Post Cards*
	2012							
10,000	Aug. 1	To Cash						
	Aug. 2	By Electricity charges	325	325				
	Aug. 4	By Telep charges	250		250			
	Aug. 8	By Printing	375			375		
	Aug. 15	By Stationery	600				600	
	Aug 20	By Post Card	300					300
			1,850	325	250	375	600	300
		By Balance c/d	8,150					
10,000			10,000					
8,150		By Balance b/d						
1,850		To cash						

ASSIGNMENT MATERIAL

Note : The Objective – Type Questions (True/False, Multiple Choice Questions etc.) have been given in the Appendix at the end of the book.

SHORT-ANSWER THEORY QUESTIONS

1. Write note on Imprest System of Petty Cash.
2. What are subsidiary books and what are its advantages?
3. Write short notes on special purpose Subsidiary Books.
4. Distinguish between Trade Discount and Cash Discount.
5. What is Cash Discount?
6. Write a note on Cash Book.
7. What is Imprest System?

8. What is the utility of special Journals.
9. Write notes on :
   (*a*) Purchases Book (*b*) Sales Book (*c*) Journal Proper

LONG ANSWER QUESTIONS

1. Explain the nature of Cash Book giving suitable examples.
2. What are the purposes of Subsidiary Books? What subsidiary books are generally maintained in a business enterprise?
3. What is Journal Proper. Give an example of Journal Proper.
4. What is importance of Purchases Book and Sales Book. Give specimen of Purchases Book and Sales Book.
5. List the various subsidiary books.
   What is the purpose of each subsidiary book. Give specimen of purchase book and sales book and enter four imaginary transactions therein.
6. What is a cash book? How is it balanced?
7. What is contra entry? How are contra entries recognised?
8. What is the imprest system of petty cash? What are its advantages?
9. "The cash book generally shows a debit balance". Comment.
10. What is petty Cash Book? How will you maintain the petty Cash Book on imprest system?
11. What do you mean by 'balancing of account'? What are the two types of balances?

PRACTICAL PROBLEMS

1. Gopi commenced business on 1st April, 2012 with A 4,00,000 as capital. He had the following cash transactions. Prepare double-column cash book.

2012

April 1	Purchased furniture and paid cash	50,000
April 1	Purchased goods	60,000
April 4	Sold goods for cash	30,000
April 5	Purchased goods	40,000
April 5	Paid cash to Ram Mohan	1,12,000
April 5	He allowed discount	2,000
April 6	Received cash from Krishna and Co.	1,20,000
	Allowed discount	4,000
April 7	Paid for petty expenses	3,000
April 8	Cash Purchase	30,000
April 9	Cash Sales	40,000
April 11	Received from Mohan Bros.	1,20,000
April 13	Paid for type writer	1,60,000
April 15	Paid for telephone	40,000
April 15	Paid Ali and Sons	80,000
	They allowed discount	1,600

[***Ans.*** Cash Balance A 1,35,000]

2. Prepare a three-column Cash Book.

2012		A
June 1	Cash Balance	1,00,000
	Bank Balance	3,50,000
June 5	Cash received from sale of shares	11,00,000
June 6	Paid into Bank	10,00,000
June 7	Paid Jyoti by cheque	2,50,000
June 9	Paid wages in cash	60,000
June 20	Received from Tareen by a cheque and sent to bank	1,20,000
June 21	Drawn from Bank	1,00,000
June 29	Paid office salaries in cash	80,000
June 30	Sold goods for cash and banked the same	1,60,000
	Paid rent by cheque	20,000
	Paid into Bank	1,50,000

[***Ans.*** Cash Balance A 10,000; Bank Balance A 14,10,000]

3. Prepare three column Cash Book :

2012		A
April 1	Cash in hand A 80,000 and at Bank A 5,00,000	
April 4	Discounted a bill for A 5,00,000 at 1% through bank	
April 5	Bought goods by cheque	4,00,000
April 8	Bought goods by cash	10,000
April 10	Paid by cheque for a bill drawn upon us	3,00,000
April 12	Paid trade expenses	5,000
April 17	Paid into bank	50,000
April 18	Jai who owned us A 10,000 became bankrupt and paid us 50 p. in a rupees	
April 20	Received A 5,000 from Rajan and allowed him discount A 100.	
April 21	Paid A 12,500 to Ashu and he allowed us discount A 250	
April 22	Received a bill of exchange from Ram and deposited the same into Bank	1,20,000
April 24	Withdrew from Bank	10,000
April 25	Withdrew from Bank for private expenses	5,000
April 26	Sold goods for cash	5,000
April 27	Received a cheque for goods sold	4,50,000
April 28	Received payment of a loan of A 1,50,000 and deposited out of it A 1,25,000 in the bank	

[***Ans.*** Cash Balance A 52,500; Bank Balance A 10,25,000]

4. From the following transactions prepare three column Cash Book :

2012		A
May 1	Cash in hand	4,80,000
May 2	Bank Overdraft	30,40,000
May 2	Fresh Capital introduced	20,00,000
May 3	Deposited into Bank	15,00,000
May 5	An amount of A 4,20,000 due from Asha written off as bad debts in the previous year, now recovered.	
May 6	Withdrew from bank for the payment of life Insurance premium	3,00,000
May 8	Received a cheque from Manu for A 6,00,000 and deposited the same into bank.	
May 10	Sold goods to Vijay on credit.	30,00,000
May 12	Received a cheque for A 28,00,000 from Vijay in full settlement.	
May 15	Cheque received from Vijay sent to Bank.	
May 18	Vijay's cheque returned by Bank dishonoured. Bank charged A 2,500 on this cheque.	
May 19	Received a cheque of A 6,80,000 from Vipin which was endorsed to Amarpal on the same day.	
May 25	Withdrew cash from Bank A 5,00,000 for paying gift to his daughter on her birthday.	
May 26	Bought goods from Garg General Store for A 10,00,000 on credit and they allowed us trade discount of 25%.	
May 28	Paid to Garg General Store in cash in full settlement.	7,00,000
May 28	Sale of old machinery, payment received in cash A 7,70,000	
May 30	Paid salary by cheque A 1,50,000. Paid rent in cash A 2,20,000.	
May 31	Paid into Current Account the entire balance after retaining A 5,00,000 at office.	

[***Ans.*** Cash Balance (Dr.) A 5,00,000; Bank Overdraft A 11,42,500].

Petty Cash Book

5. Prepare the columer Petty Cash Book of Sanjay Ltd., for the month of January 2012 under the imprest system. The petty cash limit fixed was A 2,500 and the cashier draws money under imprest petty cash system as and when the balance available with him is below A 500. Petty cash transactions for the month of January 2012 given below :

Jan. 1	Opening balance	2,500
2	Paid towards conveyance charges	420
3	Purchase of stationery	830
5	Wages to Sweeper	210
7	Paid towards conveyance charges	620
8	Postage stamps purchased	1,100
11	Wages to Sweeper	420
14	Telegram charges paid	95
16	Conveyance charges paid	225

20	Wages to Sweeper	490
20	Postage stamps purchased	810
23	Telegram charges	140
26	Entertainment expenses	313
26	Wages to Sweeper	630
27	Taxi charges paid	276
28	Postage stamps purchased	360
31	Entertainment expenses	270
31	Wages to Sweeper	420

6. Prepare Petty Cash Book from the following :

June 1	Received from Cashier A 1,500 as petty Cash	
2	Postages	A 90
3	Travelling	60
4	Cleaning	75
7	Petrol for Van	110
8	Travelling	125
9	Stationery	85
11	Cleaning	90
14	Postage	25
15	Travelling	40
18	Stationery	45
18	Cleaning	115
20	Postage	65
24	Delivery van service	220
26	Petrol	90
27	Cleaning	105
29	Postage	25
30	Petrol	140

7. Prepare a Purchase Book from the following transactions :

2012

June 5 Bought of Kishan and Co. Agra :
20 quintal Sugar @ A 1,200 per quintal.
40 bags Rice each containing one quintal @ A 1,500 per quintal Trade Discount 15%.

June 10 Purchased from Chadha and Sons, Mathura :
Desi Ghee 20 tins, each containing 16 Kg, @ A 120 per kg.
Kerosene Oil, 1,000 litre @ A 6 per litre.
Trade Discount 10%.

June 14 Purchased from Sunil Kumar, Delhi :
Wheat 30 quintals @ A 500 per quintal; Gram 20 quintals @ A 1,200 per quintal, Rice 10 quintals, @ A 1,400 per quintal Cartage and other expenses paid in cash A 700.

June 20 Purchased for cash from Roop Chand, Delhi :
50 Bales of Cotton @ A 1,500 per bale.

June 25 Bought Furniture for office use from Furniture House, Meerut on Credit :
20 Godrej Chairs @ A 300 per chair.
2 Godrej Tables @ A 1,600 per Table.

[***Ans.*** Total of purchases Book A 1,64,360]

8. Enter the following transactions in Sales Book of M/s Mira Lal and Sons, Calcutta:

2012

May 5 Sold to Sudesh Stationery House, Calcutta;
100 Dozen Pencils @ A 20 per dozen.
40 Dozen Pens @ A 5 per pen.
Trade Discount 10%

May 8 Sold to Kapur Stationery Shop, Indore;
20 Dozen Note Books @ A 60 per dozen.
30 Gross Rubbers @ A 10 per dozen.

May 20 Sold old newspapers for A 300

May 24 Sold to Jain Stationery House, Lucknow for Cash;
50 dozen Pencils @ A 22 per dozen.

May 28 Sold to Ghulam Ali and Sons, Agra;
20 Ream of Paper @ A 80 per Ream, discount 15%.

May 31 Sold old furniture to Kamal Nath and Co., Alipur on credit A 2,200

[***Ans.*** Total of Sales Book A 10,120]

9. Prepare Purchases and Sales Book in the books of Deep Book Depot from the following transactions :

Jan. 1 Bought of Sunil, Bombay on credit.
200 copies Physics by Resnick Holidey @ A 750
200 copies Mathematics without Fears by N. Arora @ A 500

Jan. 2 Sold to Shri Ram
48 copies Physics @ A 750
50 copies Mathematics without Fears @ A 500

Jan. 8 Bought of Sultan Chand, Delhi
80 copies Economics by K.K. Dewet @ A 1000
Less 15% Trade Discount

Jan. 12 Sold to Sexena Bros.
40 copies Economics @ A 1000

Jan. 18 Sold to Kalicharan
40 copies Physics @ A 750

Jan. 22 Bought of Rahul
200 copies M.S.L.C Arithmetic @ A 400
Less Trade Discount 20%

Jan. 25	Bought of Hari Ram, Delhi on Credit 100 copies History of England @ A 500 Less 15% Trade Discount
Jan. 31	Sold to Arun 50 copies M.S.L.C., Arithmetic @ A 400.

10. Prepare Returns Inward and Returns Outward Books from the following :

2012	
Jan. 3	Returned to Lakhani 50 pairs of chappals being not up to the approval sample @ A 42 per pair. *Less :* Trade Discount 20%
Jan. 10	Murari and Co., Fatehpuri, returned to us : 10 pairs of shoes for being defective @ A 120 per pair *Less :* Trade Discount 10%
Jan. 15	Returned to Balaji Shoe Co. 20 pairs of ladies chappals @ A 36 per pair *Less* 15%.
Jan. 22	Pratik and Sons, Roop Nagar returned to us : 50 pairs of Shoes @ A 150 per pair.
Jan. 27	Manas Shoe Co., Model Town, returned to us : 20 pairs of Sandal @ A 85 per pair.
Jan. 31	Returned to Bata Shoe Co. Defective shoes worth A 1,200.

[***Ans.*** Returns Outward Book A 3,492; Returned Inward Book A 10,280]

CHAPTER 7

Accounting Process - II : Ledger Posting and Trial Balance

Learning Objectives

After studying this chapter, you should be able to :

1. *Define Ledger.*
2. *Understand rules of posting.*
3. *Discuss objectives and limitations of Trial Balance.*
4. *Identify errors disclosed and not disclosed by Trial Balance.*
5. *Explain Suspense Account.*
6. *Understand the procedure of making rectification entries.*

LEDGER

An accounting system typically contains a large number of accounts. Collectively these individual accounts are contained in a record known as the ledger. A ledger is simply the grouping of the accounts that are used to prepare financial statements for a business. It contains a classified summary of all transactions recorded in the cash book and journal. The transactions recorded in a ledger are derived from either the cash book or the journal. A ledger account is summary device and it is shaped like the letter 'T' and called a 'T' account. Ledger is a principal book of an enterprise though it is not an independent record. It contains all the accounts in which all the business transactions pertaining to a business enterprise are recorded. The main function of the ledger is to classify and summarise all the items appearing in journal and other books of original entry under appropriate accounts so that at the end of the accounting period, each account contains the entire information of all transactions relating to it.

Relationship between Journal and Ledger

Journal and ledger are the most important books maintained in an enterprise. They are closely interrelated. Business transactions are recorded first in Journal and other books of original entry and then from these books they are transferred to Ledger. Journal records transactions in a chronological order while the ledger records the transactions in a classified form. Journal, being the book of original entry is more reliable as compared to ledger.

A journal is not useful in answering a question such as, what is the balance of cash at a certain date? This question is answered by referring to the ledger, which summarises the cumulative effect of recorded transactions in separate accounts. This is accomplished by transferring or posting information from the journal into appropriate accounts in the ledger.

POSTING

Posting is a process of transferring debits and credits from the Journal and other books of original entry to their respective accounts in the ledger. The aim of posting is to make a classified and summarised record of business transactions in appropriate accounts.

Rules Regarding Posting

The following rules are observed while posting/transferring the transactions in the ledger.

1. Separate accounts should be opened in the ledger for posting the different transactions recorded in the book of original entry.
2. All the transactions pertaining to one account should be posted in the same account.
3. Two aspects of the business transaction namely—debit aspect and credit aspect—should be posted on the debit side and credit side of the account respectively.

POSTING OF DIFFERENT SUBSIDIARY BOOKS

Cash Book

Rules regarding posting of cash book are given below :

(*i*) Transactions recorded on the debit side of Cash Book are posted on the credit side of accounts opened in the ledger.

(*ii*) Transactions recorded on the credit side of the cash book are posted on the debit side of different accounts in the ledger.

(*iii*) Contra entries appearing in the cash book are not posted.

(*iv*) Totals of discount columns of the cash book are posted in the discount account opened in the ledger. Debit side total is posted on the debit side and credit side total is posted on the credit side of the discount account.

(*v*) Balance in the cash column and bank column of the cash book is not posed anywhere. It is shown on the asset side of the Balance Sheet.

Petty Cash Book

Transaction recorded in the Petty Cash Book are posted on the debit side of the accounts opened for the purpose. Balance of Petty Cash Book is not posted anywhere. It is shown on the asset side of Balance Sheet.

Purchase Book

In Purchases Books, credit purchases of goods in which the enterprises deals, are recorded. Accounts of all those persons who have supplied goods are to be opened and credited with the amount of purchases made from them. Total of purchases book is to be posted on the debit side of purchases account. This is illustrated below :

Harish Jain, Delhi

Dr. ₹	₹ *Cr.*
	[20.5.2012 By purchases A/c 10,000]

Summant Prasad

Dr. ₹	₹ *Cr.*
	[31.5.2012 By purchases A/c 20,000]

Purchase A/c

Dr. *A*	*A* *Cr.*
[01.6.2012 To Sundaries A/c 30,000]	

PURCHASES RETURN BOOK

Purchases Return Book, also called Returns Outward Book, records returns of purchase made to suppliers. Personal accounts of all those persons to whom goods have been returned are debited and total of purchase returns book is credited to purchases returns account as illustrated below :

Harish Jain, Delhi

Dr.	*Cr.*
15.7.2012 To Purchase Returns A/c 1,000	01.7.2012 By Purchases A/c 10,000

Summant Prasad

Dr.	*Cr.*
20.6.2012 To Purchase Return A/c 3,000	31.5.2012 By Purchases 20,000

Purchases Returns A/c

Dr.	*Cr.*
31.7.2012	By Sundries 4,000

SALES BOOK

Sales Book records all credit sales. While posting Sales Book to ledger, personal accounts of the customers are opened and debited by the amount of sales made to them. Total of Sales Book is credited to Sales account. This is illustrated below :

Ram Prasad

Dr.			*Cr.*
[2.7.2012	To Sales A/c	15,000]	

Devi Prasad

Dr.			*Cr.*
[25.6.2012	To Sales A/c	20,000]	

Sales A/c

Dr.			*Cr.*
	[15.7.2012	By Sundriues	35,000]

SALES RETURNS BOOK/RETURNS INWARD BOOK

When goods are returned by customers, they are recorded in sales returns book/returns inward book. While posting Sales Returns book to Ledger, personal accounts of the customers are credited and total of Sales Returns Book is debited to Sales Returns A/c. This is illustrated below :

Ram Prasad

Dr.	*Cr.*
02.7.2012 To Sales A/c 15,000	14.7.2012 By Sales returns A/c 4,000

Devi Prasad

Dr.				*Cr.*
25.6.2012	To Sales A/c 20,000		10.7.2012	By Sales return A/c 4,000

Sales Return A/c

Dr.		*Cr.*
15.7.2012	To Sundried 8,000	

BILLS RECEIVABLE BOOK

In bills receivable book, bills received by the enterprises are recorded. While posting Bills receivable book, personal accounts of the persons giving the bills are credited. Total of Bills Receivable book is debited to Bills Receivable A/c.

Sunder Kumar

Dr.			*Cr.*
	July 10 2012	By B/R A/c	10,000

Suresh Chander

Dr.			*Cr.*
	July 7 2012	By B/R	15,000

Bills Receivable A/c

Dr.			*Cr.*
15.7.2012	To Sundries	25,000	

BILLS PAYABLE BOOK

The enterprises may accept so many bills in the business. Acceptances given are recorded in Bills Payable Book. While posting Bills Payable Book acceptances given are debited to the personal accounts of the persons to whom they have been given and total of Bills Payable Book is posted to the credit side of Bills Payable A/c. This is illustrated below :

Ram Prasad

Dr.			*Cr.*
02.7.2012	To B/P A/c	8,000	

Chandra Mohan

Dr.			*Cr.*
10.7.2012	To B/P	A/c 7,000	

Bills Payable A/c

Dr.			*Cr.*
	15.7.2012	By Sundries	15,000

POSTING OF JOURNAL

When we journalise a transaction we write out in the journal as to which account is to be debited and which account is to be credited. The same information is transferred to ledger in the two concerned accounts. This is illustrated below :

Furniture A/c	Dr.	70,000	
To Jain & Co.			70,000
(Being furniture bought from Jain & Co. on credit)			
Depreciation A/c	Dr.	7,000	
To Furniture A/c			7,000
(Being depreciation on furniture)			

Furniture A/c

Dr.			*Cr.*
To Jain & Co.	70,000	By Depreciation A/c	7,000

Depreciation A/c

Dr.			*Cr.*
To Furniture A/c	7,000		

Jain & Co.

Dr.			*Cr.*
		By Furniture A/c	70,000

BALANCING OF AN ACCOUNT

Balancing of an account implies a process of ascertaining the net balance of an account after considering and comparing the total of both sides-*viz* debit and credit side. The balance is put on the side which is smaller and the two totals-debits side and credit side are made equal. Against the balance is reference is put that it has been carried forward (c/f) or carried down (c/d). The balance of an account will be termed as debit balance if the total of debit side is greater than the total of credit side. On the other hand, if total of credit side is greater than total of debit side, balance will be a credit balance. This is illustrated below :

Mohan

		A			*A*
05.5.2012	To B/R A/c	7,000	01.5.2012	By Purchase A/c	15,000
06.5.2012	To Purchases	2,000	16.5.2012	By Purchases A/c	25,000
17.5.2012	To Bank A/c	15,000			
31.5.2012	To Balance c/d	16,000			
		40,000			40,000
			01.6.2012	By balance b/d	16,000

Furniture A/c

01.5.2012	To Bank A/c	16,000	31.5.2012	By balance c/d	16,000
		16,000			16,000
01.6.2012	To balance b/d	16,000			

TRIAL BALANCE

When all accounts of the ledger are in balance, a Trial Balance is prepared. A Trial Balance is a listing of all the accounts and their respective balances. Trial Balance is a statement of debit balances and credit balance extracted from ledger accounts on a particular date. A Trial Balance, is thus, a summary of all the Ledger Balances outstanding as on a particular date.

Proforma of a Trial Balance is as follows :

Trial Balance as at ....

Ledger Accounts	Debit Balance	Credit Balance

It must be stated here that total of debit balance column must be equal to total of credit balances column. This is so because under double entry system, for each item of debit there is a corresponding credit and secondly all the transactions recorded in the books of original entry are transferred to ledger.

Objectives of Preparing a Trial Balance

The following are the objectives of preparing a Trial Balance :

1. To check the arithmetical accuracy of accounting entries posted in the ledger. When the trial balance tallies, it is an indication of the fact that ledger accounts are arithmetically accurate. It also indicates that :
   (*i*) For each transactions, the debits and credits were recorded in equal amounts.
   (*ii*) The balance (debit balances and credit balances) for each account was calculated correctly.
   (*iii*) The balances of the various debit and credit accounts have been correctly added together to arrive at the total equality of the debit and credits. Of course there may be certain errors in the books of accounts inspite of the agreement of Trial Balance. These have been discussed later in this chapter.
2. To Provide a Basis for Financial Statements : Trial Balance is a first step towards preparation of financial statements of an organisation. If trial balance is not prepared, it will be impossible to prepare the financial statement.
3. Trial Balance serves as a summary of all the ledger accounts and provides a complete picture of each account in the ledger.

LIMITATIONS OF TRIAL BALANCE

The Trial Balance is prepared to ensure the arithmetical accuracy of the ledger of a business and also to ensure that for every debit entry, a credit of an equal amount has been recorded. Thus, a trial balance in which the total of the debits does not equal the total of credits can be taken as an evidence for the existence of some errors in the records. On the other hand, a trial balance in which the total of the debits equal the total of credits is not a conclusive proof of the accuracy of the records. Certain errors may not effect the agreement of a trial balance as the erroneous entries may not violate the dual aspect concept. It means that even if the Trial Balance agrees, steps should be taken to ensure that the records are free from errors.

To understand the nature of errors and their rectification we may classify them into (*i*) errors disclosed by a Trial Balance and (*ii*) errors not disclosed by a Trial Balance.

Errors Disclosed by a Trial Balance

The errors which cause a mismatch in the trial balance totals are frequently referred to as errors disclosed in a Trial Balance. However, the mismatch does not automatically point to the actual errors. It is only the diligence and ingenuity of the person preparing the accounts which would help in the location of the errors.

The various errors which would cause a mismatch in the trial balance totals are as follows:

(*i*) *Wrong totalling in a subsidiary book :* For example, if the total of the purchase for a month is stuck as A 26,150 instead of A 26,250 then the debit in the purchases account would be A 26,150 (as the total from the subsidiary book will be posted to the debit of the purchase account). The total of the credits posted in the individual suppliers A/c would be A 26,250 and in the Trial Balance the total credits will exceed total debits by A 100.

(*ii*) *Wrong calculation of balances in a ledger account :* For example, if the debit balance in the furniture A/c has been taken as A 5,650 instead of A 5,850, then the Trial Balance will show the total credits exceeding the total debits by A 200.

(*iii*) *Partial omission of an entry :* If the debit or credit aspect of a transaction has been omitted to be recorded, the Trial Balance will disagree. For example, if a cash sales of A 800 is omitted to be recorded in the Sales A/c, then the total debits will exceed the total credits by A 800.

(*iv*) *Posting an aspect of a transaction more than once :* For example, if an amount of A 2,000 paid to XY Limited has been posted to the debit of XY Limited A/c twice, then the debits will exceed the credits by A 2,000.

(*v*) *Debit entries wrongly recorded as credit entries or vice-versa :* for example, if an amount of A 3,500 received from Z is posted to the credits of Z's A/c, then the debits will exceed the credits by A 7,000.

(*vi*) *Errors in totalling the debit column or the credit column of the Trial Balance :* Obviously, if a total mistake occurs while casting either the debit side or credit side of the Trial Balance, it will not tally.

(*vii*) *Balance of ledger accounts are wrongly transferred to the trial balance :* For example, the balance of A 46,945 in the Plant and Machinery A/c is transferred to the trial balance as A 46,495. This will cause the credits to exceed the debit by A 450.

(*viii*) *Omitting to include an account's balance in the trial balance :* When an account which is outstanding in the ledger account is omitted to be included in the trial balance, it will not tally.

SUSPENSE ACCOUNT

When a combination of the various errors mentioned above have been committed, the mismatch in the totals of the Trial Balance will be totally different for the amounts of the individual transactions and only through scrutiny and checking of the books of accounts will help in detecting the errors. Sometimes, when the Trial Balance disagrees and sufficient time is not available to scrutinize the books, the accountant will include 'Suspense A/c' in the Trial Balance to make it agree and proceed with the preparation of Profit and Loss A/c' and Balance Sheet. For instance, if the totals of the credits in a Trial Balance exceeds the debits by A 2,550 then a suspense A/c with a debit balance of 2,550 will be included in the Trial Balance. At a later date, the books may be scrutinised to detect the errors and the rectification entries passed to clear the balance in the Suspense A/c.

Errors not Disclosed by Trial Balance

Even though a trial balance may be in agreement, certain errors might have been committed while recording the transactions. Such errors are referred to as errors not disclosed by Trial Balance. The errors which will not cause a mismatch in the totals of a Trial Balance are as follows :

(*a*) *Omission of the recording of a transaction from the books of accounts :* If the withdrawal of goods worth A 1,200 by the proprietor is omitted to be recorded in the books, the Trial Balance will still agree as both the debit and credit aspects have been omitted to be recorded.

(*b*) *Recording a transaction at an amount which is totally different from the actual amount :* If the purchases of goods worth A 7,500 is recorded in the Purchase Book as A 5,700, the error will not cause the trial balance to disagree.

(*c*) *Compensating errors :* These are quite difficult to detect. If a cash discount of A 215 allowed to a customer has been posted to the credit of his account as A 251 and a cash sale of A 2,851 has been posted to sales account as A 2,815, then the excess credit caused by the first error would be exactly compensated by the lower credit recorded by the second error and the trial balance will be in agreement.

(*d*) *Posting of an aspect of a transaction on the correct side of wrong account :* If the amount of A 800 received from MN Ltd. a debtor, is posted to the credit of NM Ltd. A/c, also a debtor, the Trial Balance totals will still agree, because both are debit accounts and the total effect is the same.

(*e*) *Recording both aspects of a transaction more than once in the books of accounts :* If a sales of A 3,500 made to PQR Ltd., is entered in the Sales Book twice, the error will not cause a mismatch in the totals of Trial Balance.

(*f*) *Errors of principle :* If the machinery A/c is debited for an amount of repair charges incurred for the machinery, the error will not be disclosed by the Trial Balance. This is because both machinery A/c and repairs A/c are debit A/cs and it is a question of principle that repairs charges should not be debited to the machinery A/c. Hence, the total effect will be the same and therefore the Trial Balance will tally.

Example 1

During January 2012, Anil Kumar transacted the following business. You are required to make journal entries for the transactions and prepare cash book and other necessary ledger accounts based on the journal entries.

		A
January 2012		
1.	Commenced business with cash	20,000
2.	Purchased goods on credit from Shyam	15,000
3.	Purchased goods for cash	500
4.	Paid Gopal an advance for goods ordered	1,000
5.	Received cash from Murthy as advance for goods ordered by him	1,500
6.	Purchased furniture for office use for cash	1,000
7.	Paid wages	250
8.	Received commission (in cash)	300
9.	Goods returned to Shyam	100
10.	Goods sold to Kamal	5,000
11.	Paid for postage and telegrams	100
12.	Goods returned by Kamal	250
15.	Paid for Stationery	100
18.	Paid into bank	250
20.	Goods sold for cash	375
22.	Bought goods for cash	500
25.	Paid salaries	350
28.	Paid rent	250
31.	Drew cash for personal use	500

Journal Entries

Date	*Particulars*		*Debit (A)*	*Credit (A)*
2012				
Jan.1	Cash Account	Dr.	20,000	
	To capital account			20,000
	(Being the cash brought into business as capital)			

Date	Particulars		Dr.	Cr.
Jan.2	Purchases account	Dr.	15,000	
	To Shyam's account			15,000
	(Being the goods purchased on credit)			
Jan. 3	Purchase account	Dr.	500	
	To Cash account			500
	(Being the goods purchased for cash)			
Jan. 4	Gopal account	Dr.	1,000	
	To cash account			1,000
	(Being the amount paid to Gopal)			
Jan. 5	Cash account	Dr.	1,500	
	To Murthy account			1,500
	(Being the cash received from Murthy)			
Jan. 6	Furniture account	Dr.	1,000	
	To cash account			1,000
	(Being the furniture purchased for office use for cash)			
Jan. 7	Wages account	Dr.	250	
	To cash account			250
	(Being the wages paid)			
Jan. 8	Cash Account	Dr.	300	
	To Commission received A/c			300
	(Being the commission received)			
Jan. 9	Shyam account	Dr.	100	
	To purchase returns account			100
	(Being goods returned to Shyam)			
Jan. 10	Kamal account	Dr.	5,000	
	To sales account			5,000
	(Being goods sold to Kamal on credit)			
Jan. 11	Postage and telegram account	Dr.	100	
	To cash account			100
	(Being the amount paid for postage & telegram)			
Jan. 12	Sales returns account	Dr.	250	
	To Kamal account			250
	(Being the goods returned by Kamal)			
Jan. 15	Stationery account	Dr.	100	
	To cash account			100
	(Being the amount paid for stationery)			
Jan. 18	Bank account	Dr.	250	
	To cash account			250
	(Being the amount deposited into the bank)			
Jan. 20	Cash account	Dr.	375	
	To sales account			375
	(Being the goods sold for cash)			

Jan. 22	Purchase account	Dr.	500	
	To cash account			500
	(Being the goods purchased for cash)			
Jan. 25	Salaries account	Dr.	350	
	To cash account			350
	(Being the amount paid as salaries)			
Jan. 28	Rent account	Dr.	250	
	To Cash account			250
	(Being the rent paid)			
Jan 31	Drawings account	Dr.	500	
	To cash account			500
	(Being the cash drawn for personal use)			

LEDGER ACCOUNTS

Cash Book

Dr. *Cr.*

Date	*Receipts*	*Ledger Folio*	*Cash (A)*	*Bank (A)*	*Date*	*Payments*	*Ledger Folio*	*Cash (A)*	*Bank (A)*
2012					**2012**				
Jan. 1	To capital A/c		20,000		Jan. 3	By purchase A/c		500	
Jan. 5	To Murthy A/c		1,500		Jan. 4	By Gopal A/c		1,000	
Jan. 8	To commission A/c		300		Jan. 6	By Furniture A/c		1,000	
Jan. 18	To cash A/c	C		250	Jan. 7	By wages A/c		250	
Jan. 20	To sales A/c		375		Jan. 12	By postage & telegrams		100	
					Jan. 15	By stationery A/c		100	
					Jan. 18	By bank A/c	C	250	
					Jan. 22	By purchase A/c		500	
					Jan. 25	By salaries A/c		350	
					Jan 28	By rent A/c		250	
					Jan. 31	By drawing A/c		500	
					Jan. 31	By balance c/d		17,375	250
			22,175	250				22,175	250

Note : The letter 'C' in the Ledger Folio column denotes a contra entry. This is an entry for which the debit and credit aspects are found in the cash book itself.

Purchase Book

Dr.

Date	*Name of Supplier*	*Ledger Folio*	*Inward Invoice No.*	*Amount (A)*
2012				
Jan.2	Shyam			15,000
			Total	15,000

Purchaser Returns Book

Dr. *Cr.*

Date	*Name of Supplier*	*Ledger Folio*	*Debit Note No.*	*Amount* (A)
2012				
Jan. 9	Shyam			100
			Total	100

Sales Book

Date	*Customer* (A)	*Invoice No.*	*Amount*
2012			
Jan. 10	Kamal		5,000
		Total	5,000

Sales Return Book

Dr. *Cr.*

Date	*Name of Supplier*	*Ledger Folio*	*Outward Invoice No.*	*Amount* (A)
2012				
Jan. 12	Kamal			250
			Total	250

General Ledger

Capital Account

2012		(A)	**2012**		(A)
Jan. 31	To balance c/d	20,000	Jan. 1	By cash A/c	20,000
		20,000			20,000
			Feb. 1	By Balance b/d	20,000

Shyam' Account

2012		(A)	**2012**		(A)
Jan. 9	To Purchase returns	100	Jan. 2	By Purchase A/c	15,000
Jan. 31	To Balance c/d	14,900			
		15,000			15,000
			Feb. 1	By Balance b/d	14,900

Purchases Account

Dr. *Cr.*

2012		(A)	**2012**		(A)
Jan. 2	To Shyam A/c	15,000	Jan. 31	By Balance c/d	16,000
Jan. 3	To Cash	500			
Jan. 22	To Cash	500			
		16,000			16,000
Feb. 1	By balance b/d	16,000			16,000

Sales Account

Dr. | | | | | *Cr.*

2012		(A)	2012		(A)
Jan. 31	To balance c/d	5,375	Jan. 10	By Kamal A/c	5,000
			Jan. 20	By cash	375
		5,375			5,375
			Feb. 1	By balance b/d	5,375

Purchase Returns Accounts

2012		(A)	2012		(A)
Jan.31	To Balance c/d	100	Jan.9	By Shyam A/c	100
		100			100
			Feb.1	By balance b/d	100

Sales Returns Account

2012		(A)	2012		(A)
Jan. 12	To Kamal A/c	250	Jan.31	By balance c/d	250
		250			250
Feb.1	To balance b/d	250			

Gopal's Accounts

2012		(A)	2012		(A)
Jan.4	To cash A/c	1,000	Jan.31	By balance c/d	1,000
		1,000			1,000
Feb.1	To balance b/d	1,000			

Wages Account

2012		(A)	2012		(A)
Jan. 7	To cash A/c	250	Jan. 31	By balance c/d	250
		250			250
Feb.1	To balance b/d	250			

Commission Received Account

2012		(A)	2012		(A)
Jan.31	To balance c/d	300	Jan.8	By cash A/c	300
		300			300
			Feb.1	By balance b/d	300

Kamal's Account

Dr.					*Cr.*
2012		(*A*)	**2012**		(*A*)
Jan.10	To sales A/c	5,000	Jan.12	By sales returns	250
		5,000	Jan.31	By balance c.d	4,750
Feb.1	To balance b/d	4,750			5,000

Postage and Telegrams Account

Dr.					*Cr.*
2012		(*A*)	**2012**		(*A*)
Jan.11	To cash A/c	100	Jan.31	By balance c/d	100
		100			100
Feb.1	To balance b/d	100			

Stationery Account

Dr.					*Cr.*
2012		(*A*)	**2012**		(*A*)
Jan.15	To cash A/c	100	Jan.31	By balance c/d	100
		100			100
Feb.1	To balance b/d	100			

Salaries Account

Dr.					*Cr.*
2012		(*A*)	**2012**		(*A*)
Jan.25	To cash A/c	350	Jan.31	By balance c/d	350
		350			350
Feb.1	To balance b/d	350			

Rent Account

Dr.					*Cr.*
2012		(*A*)	**2012**		(*A*)
Jan. 28	To cash A/c	250	Jan.31	By balance c/d	250
		250			250
Feb.1	To balance b/d	250			

Drawing Account

Dr.					*Cr.*
2012		(*A*)	**2012**		(*A*)
Jan.31	To cash A/c	500	Jan.31	By balance c/d	500
		500			500
Feb.1	To balance b/d	500			

Murthy's Account

Dr.					Cr.
2012		(A)	**2012**		(A)
Jan.31	To balance c/d	1,500	Jan.5	By cash A/c	1,500
		1,500			1,500
			Feb.1	To balance b/d	1,500

Furniture Account

Dr.					Cr.
2012		(A)	**2012**		(A)
Jan.6	To cash A/c	1,000	Jan.3	By balance c/d	1,000
		1,000			1,000
Feb.1	To balance b/d	1,000			

Example 2

Record the following transactions in the purchase day book and show the ledger postings.

(*a*) 16.10.2012 Purchase 480 kg butter from M/s. Dairy Product Co. @ A 78 per kg less 15%.

(*b*) 20.12.2012 Purchased 56 kg ghee from Bharat Vegetable Products @ A 120 per kg less 17.5%.

(*c*) 22.10.2012 Purchased 46 kg butter from Bazaar Milk Cooperative @ A 100 kg less 10%.

Solution

Purchase Book

Date	*Particulars*	*LF*	*Debit* (*A*)	*Credit* (*A*)
2012				
	M/s Dairy Products Co.			
Oct.16	480 kg Butter @ 78 per kg.		37,440	
	Less : discount 15%		5,616	31,824
Oct.20	Bharat Vegetable products			
	56 kg ghee @ A 120		6,720	
	Less : discount 17.5%		1,176	5,544
Oct.22	Bazar Milk Coop. Ltd.			
	46 kg Butter @ 100 per kg		4600	
	Less : discount 10%		460	3,940
		Total		41,308

Ledger

M/s Dairy Products Co.

Date	*Particulars*	*Amt.*	*Date*	*Particulars*	*Amount*
			2012		
			Oct. 16	By purchases A/c	31,824

M/s Bharat Vegetable Products

2012			
Oct. 20		By Purchases A/c	5,544
Bow bazaar Milk coop. Ltd.			
2012			
Oct. 22		By Purchases A/c	3,940

Purchase A/c

2012		
Oct. 31	To Sundries	41,308

Example 3

From the following, prepare return books, and show the ledger.

March 2012

5	Returned 10 shirts to Kundu Bros. @ A 50 each less 10% trade discount
8	Kamal & Co., returned goods worth A 1,500.
9	Returned goods to A Roy, A 750
12	Returned 60 packing boxes, A 50 each, to J Roy
14	S. Das returned 20 baba suits @ A 120 each
15	Received return of blouse 30 piece @ A 70 each from Silk House.

Solution

Returns Inward Book

Date	*Particulars*	*L.f.*	*Details*	*Total (A)*
2012	Kamal & Co.			
Mar. 8	Goods returned			1,500.00
Mar. 14	S. Das			2,400.00
	20 baba suits @ 120			
Mar. 15	Silk House			
	30 Blouse piece @ A 70			2,100.00
			Total	6000.00

Returns Outward Book

Date	*Particulars*	*L.f.*	*Details*	*Total (A)*
Mar. 5	Kundu Brothers			
	10 Shirts @ A 50			500
	Less : 10% trade discount			50
				450
Mar. 9	A Roy			
	Goods returned			750
	J. Roy			
Mar. 12	60 packing boxes @ A 50 each			3,000

Ledger

Date	Particulars	L.F.	Amount	Date	Particulars	L.F.	Amount
				2012	Kamal & Co.		
				March 8	By returns inward A/c		1,500
					S. Das & Co.		
				March 14	By returns inward A/c		2,400
					Silk House		
				March 15	By returns inward A/c		2,100

Returns Inward A/c

Date	Particulars	Amount
2012		
Mar. 31	To Sundries	6000

Kundu Bros.

Date	Particulars	L.F.	Amount	Date	Particulars	L.F.	Amount
Mar.5	To returns Outwards		450.00				
					A. Roy		
Mar.9	To returns Outwards A/c		750.00				
					J. Roy		
Mar.12	To returns Outward A/c		3,000.00				

Returns Outward A/c

Date	Particulars	Amount
2012		
Mar. 31	By Sundries	4,200

Example 4

From the following information, prepare a suitable Cash Book :

April 2012		(A)
1.	Cash at hand	2,200
2.	Cash at Bank	8,700
3.	Bought goods from Rahim	7,300
4.	Cash Sales banked	5,500
8.	Sold goods to Das	8,200
9.	Received cheque in full settlement of Das's A/c	8,000
10.	Paid to settle Rahim's A/c	7,000
12.	Purchased office furniture by cheque	3,500
13.	Bought goods from P.K. Ghosh	10,400

15.	Paid carriages	200
18.	Bank collected dividend	500
20.	Withdrawn from bank	2,000
25.	Paid wages	1,500
27.	Paid to P.K. Ghosh by cheque	1,000

Show also the Ledger accounts that will be prepared from the cash book.

Solution

Cash Book

Date	*Particular L.F.*	*Dis-count (A)*	*Cash (A)*	*Bank (A)*	*Date*	*Particulars L.F.*	*Dis-count (A)*	*Cash (A)*	*Bank (A)*
2012					**2012**				
April 1	To balance b/d		2,200	8,700	April 10	By Rahim A/c	300	–	7,000
April 4	To Sales A/c			5,500	April 12	By furnitureA/c			3,500
April 9	The Das	200		8,000	April 15	By carriage A/c		200	
April 8	To dividend A/c			500	April 20	By cash A/c C			2,000
April 20	The bank A/c C		2,000						
					April 25	By wages A/c		1,500	
					April 27	By P.K. Ghosh			1,000
					April 30	By balance c/d		2,500	9,200
		200	4,200	22,700			300	4,200	22,700
May, 1	To balance b/d		2,500	9,200					

Ledger

Sales A/c

Date	*Particulars*	*L.F.*	*Amount*	*Date*	*Particulars*	*L.F.*	*Amount*
2012				**2012**			
				April 4	By bank A/c		5,500
			Das A/c				
April 8	To sales A/c		8,200	April 9	By bank A/c		8,000
				April 9	By discount A/c		200
			8,200				8,200
			Rahim's A/c				
April 10	To bank A/c		7,000	April 2	By purchase A/c		7,300
	To discount A/c		300				
			7,300				7,300
			Furniture A/c				
April 12	To bank A/c		3,500				
			Carriage A/c				
April 15	To cash A/c		200				

			Wages A/c				
April 25	To cash A/c		1,500				
			P.K. Ghosh				
April 27	To bank A/c		1,000				

Dividend A/c

			April 18	By bank A/c	A 500

Discount Allowed A/c

April 9	To Das	A 200			

Discount Received A/c

			April 2	By Rahim	A 1,300

Note :

1. Contra entries are not posted to ledger.
2. Purchases from Rahim and Sales to Das will be posted from purchases book and sales book, respectively.

Example 5

The following were the transactions of a firm dealing in furniture :

March 2012		(*A*)
1	Started business with cash	2,00,000
	Bank	8,00,000
	Furniture (goods)	5,00,000
3	Bought furniture from Ratan Bros.	2,00,000
4	Bought furniture for the office	1,00,000
6	Sold furniture of J. Mitra	2,00,000
8	Bought furniture	1,80,000
10	Returned furniture to Ratan Bros.	5,000
12	J. Mitra returned furniture	20,000
14	Paid taxi fare	1,000
15	Sold to J. Kabiraj furniture for A 50,000 *Less* trade discount @ 10%	
17	Received commission from J. Das	1,500
18	Paid to Ratan Bros by cheque	1,00,000
19	Sent to bank	20,000
20	Received a cheque of A 42,500 from J. Kabiraj in full settlement of his account	
22	Received a cheque of A 50,000 from J. Mitra and deposited the same into bank.	
23	Loan to Naren	15,000
24	J. Mitra cheque dishonoured	
25	Furniture taken away for personal use	40,000

26	Received interest	1,000
27	Received dividend	2,500
29	Paid for postage stamps	500
30	Paid house rent by cheque	10,000
31	Cash withdrawn from bank	2,00,000
31	Paid salary	30,000
31	Paid for taxes	15,000

Journalise the above transaction in the books of the firm and show the ledger posting. Also prepare a trial balance as on March 31, 2012.

Solution

Journal

Date	*Particulars*	*LF*	*Debit (A)*	*Credit (A)*
2012				
Mar.1	Cash A/c	Dr.	2,00,000	
	Bank A/c	Dr.	8,00,000	
	Stock A/c	Dr.	5,00,000	
	To capital A/c			15,00,000
	(Brought into the business as capital)			
Mar.3	Purchases A/c	Dr.	2,00,000	
	To Ratan Bros			2,00,000
	(Being the purchase of goods (furniture)			
Mar.4	Furniture A/c	Dr.	1,00,000	
	To Bank A/c			1,00,000
	(Being the purchase of furniture for office)			
Mar.6	J Mitra	Dr.	2,00,000	
	To Sales A/c			2,00,000
	(Being the sale of goods (furniture) to J. Mitra)			
Mar.8	Purchase A/c	Dr.	1,80,000	
	To Bank A/c			1,80,000
	(Being the purchase of goods)			
Mar. 10	Ratan Bros		5,000	
	To Returns outward A/c			5,000
	(Being goods (furniture returned to Ratan Bros)			
Mar.12	Returns inwards A/c	Dr.	20,000	
	To J. Mitra			20,000
	(Goods returned by Mitra)			
Mar.14	Conveyance A/c	Dr.	1,000	
	To Cash A/c			1,000
	(Being the payment of Taxi Fare)			

Date	Particulars	LF	Debit (A)	Credit (A)
Mar.15	J. Kabiraj	Dr.	45,000	
	To Sales A/c			45,000
	(Being the sale of goods worth A 50,000 to J. Kabiraj, trade discount being 10%)			
Mar.17	Bank A/c	Dr.	1,500	
	To Commission			1,500
	(Received commission from J. Das)			
Mar.18	Ratan Bros	Dr.	1,00,000	
	To Bank A/c			1,00,000
	(Being payment made to Ratan Bros.)			
Mar.19	Bank A/c	Dr.	20,000	
	To Cash A/c			20,000
	(Being money sent to Bank)			
Mar.20	Bank A/c	Dr.	42,500	
	Discount A/c	Dr.	2,500	
	To Kabiraj			45,000
	(Being a cheque for A 42,500 received from J. Kabiraj in full settlement of this account)			
Mar.22	Bank A/c	Dr.	50,000	
	To J. Mitra			50,000
	(Being cheque received from J. Mitra)			
Mar.23	Loan to Naren A/c	Dr.	15,000	
	To Bank A/c			15,000
	(Money given to Naren)			
Mar.24	J. Mitra	Dr.	50,000	
	To Bank A/c			50,000
	(Being the cheque of J. Mitra dishonoured)			
Mar.25	Drawing A/c	Dr.	40,000	
	To Purchases A/c			40,000
	(Being goods (furniture) taken for personal use)			
Mar.26	Bank A/c	Dr.	1,000	
	To Interest A/c			1,000
	(Being interest received)			
Mar.27	Bank A/c	Dr.	2,500	
	To dividend A/c			2,500
	(Being the amount of dividend received)			
Mar.29	Postage A/c		500	
	To cash A/c			500
	Payment for postage stamps)			

Date	Particulars	LF	Debit (A)	Credit (A)
Mar.30	Rent A/c	Dr.	10,000	
	To Bank A/c			10,000
	(Being the payments of house rent)			
Mar.31	Cash A/c	Dr.	2,00,000	
	To Bank A/c			2,00,000
	(Cash withdrawn from bank)			
Mar.31	Salary A/c	Dr.	30,000	
	Tax A/c	Dr.	15,000	
	To Cash A/c			45,000
	(Being the payment for salary and taxes)			

Ledger

Cash A/c

Date	Particulars	L.F.	Amount (A)	Date	Particulars	L.F.	Amount (A)
2012				**2012**			
Mar. 1	To Capital A/c		2,00,000	Mar.14	By Conveyance A/c		1,000
Mar. 31	To Bank A/c		2,00,000	Mar.19	By Bank		20,000
				Mar.29	By Postage		500
				Mar.31	By Salary A/c		30,000
				Mar.31	By Taxes A/c		15,000
				Mar.31	By Balance c/d		3,33,500
			4,00,000				4,00,000
April 1	To balance b/d		3,33,500				

Bank A/c

Date	Particulars	L.F.	Amount (A)	Date	Particulars	L.F.	Amount (A)
2012				**2012**			
Mar.1	To Capital A/c		8,00,000	Mar.5	By Furniture		1,00,000
Mar.17	To Commission A/c		1,500	Mar.8	By Purchase		1,80,000
Mar.19	To Cash A/c		20,000	Mar.18	By Ratan Bros		1,00,000
Mar.20	To J. Kabiraj		42,500	Mar.23	By Loan to Naren		15,000
Mar.22	To J. Mitra		50,000	Mar.24	By J. Mitra		50,000
Mar.26	To Interest A/c		1,000	Mar.30	By Rent A/c		10,000
Mar.27	To divident A/c		2,500	Mar.31	By Cash A/c		2,00,000
				Mar.31	By balance c/d		2,62,500
			9,17,500				9,17,500
April 1	To balance b/d		2,62,500				

Capital A/c

2012		(A)	2012		(A)
Mar.31	To balance c/d	15,00,000	Mar.1	By Cash	2,00,000
				By Bank	8,00,000
				By Stock	5,00,000
		15,00,000			15,00,000
			April 1	By balance b/d	15,00,000

Stock A/c

2012		(A)	2012		(A)
Mar. 1	To Capital A/c	5,00,000	Mar.25	By Drawings A/c	40,000
			Mar.31	By balance c/d	4,60,000
		5,00,000			5,00,000
April 1	To balance b/d	4,60,000			

Purchase A/c

2012		(A)	2012		(A)
Mar.3	To Ratan Bros.	2,00,000	Mar.31	By balance c/d	3,80,000
Mar.8	To Bank A/c	1,80,000			
		3,80,000			3,80,000
April 1	To Balance b/d	3,80,000			

Ratan A/c

2012		(A)	2012		(A)
Mar.10	To Returns outward A/c	5,000	Mar.3	By Purchase A/c	2,00,000
Mar.18	To Bank A/c	1,00,000			
Mar.31	To Balance c/d	95,000			
		2,00,000			2,00,000
			April 1	By Balance b/d	95,000

Furniture A/c

2012		(A)	2012		(A)
Mar.5	To Bank	1,00,000	Mar.31	By Balance c/d	1,00,000
April 1	To Balance b/d	1,00,000			

J. Mitra

2012		(A)	2012		(A)
Mar.6	To Sales A/c	2,00,000	Mar.12	By Returns Inward A/c	20,000
Mar.24	To Bank A/c	50,000	Mar.22	By Bank A/c	50,000
			Mar.31	By Balance c/d	1,80,000
		2,50,000			2,50,000
April 1	To Balance b/d	1,80,000			

Sales A/c

2012		(A)	2012		(A)
Mar.31	To Balance c/d	2,45,000	Mar.6	By Mitra	2,00,000
			Mar.15	By J. Kabiraj	45,000
		2,45,000			2,45,000
			April 1	By Balance b/d	2,45,000

Returns Outward A/c

2012		(A)	2012		(A)
Mar.31	To Balance c/d	5,000	Mar.10	By Ratan Bros.	5,000
		5,000			5,000
			April, 1	By Balance b/d	5,000

Returns Inward A/c

2012		(A)	2012		(A)
Mar.12	To J. Mitra	20,000	Mar.31	By Balance c/d	20,000
April 1	To Balance b/d	20,000			

Conveyance A/c

2012		(A)	2012		(A)
Mar.10	To Cash A/c	1,000	Mar.31	By Balance c/d	1,000
April 1	To Balance b/d	1,000			

J. Kabiraj

2012		(A)	2012		(A)
Mar.15	To Sales A/c	45,000	Mar.20	By Bank A/c	42,500
			Mar.20	By Discount A/c	2,500
		45,000			45,000

Commission A/c

2012		(A)	2012		(A)
Mar.31	To Balance c/d	1,500	Mar.17	By Bank A/c	1,500
			April 1	By Balance b/d	1,500

Discount Allowed A/c

2012		(A)	2012		(A)
Mar.20	To J. Kabiraj	2,500	Mar.31	By Balance c/d	2,500
April 1	To Balance b/d	2,500			

Loan to Naren A/c

2012		(A)	2012		(A)
Mar.23	To Bank A/c	15,000	Mar.31	By Balance c/d	15,000
April 1	To Balance b/d	15,000			

Drawings A/c

2012		(A)	2012		(A)
Mar.25	To Purchases A/c	40,000	Mar.31	By Balance c/d	40,000
April 1	To Balance b/d	40,000			

Interest A/c

2012		(A)	2012		(A)
Mar.31	To Balance c/d	1,000	Mar.26	By Bank	1,000
			April 1	By Balance b/d	1,000

Dividend A/c

2012		(A)	2012		(A)
Mar.31	To Balance c/d	2,500	Mar.27	By Bank	2,500
			April 1	By Balance b/d	2,500

Postage A/c

2012		(A)	2012		(A)
Mar.29	To Cash A/c	500	Mar.31	By Balance c/d	500
Mar.31	To Balance b/d	500			

Rent A/c

2012		(A)	2012		(A)
Mar.30	To Bank A/c	10,000	Mar.31	By Balance c/d	10,000
April 1	To Balance b/d	10,000			

Salary A/c

2012		(A)	2012		(A)
Mar.31	To Cash A/c	30,000	Mar.31	By Balance c/d	30,000
April 1	To Balance b/d	30,000			

Taxes A/c

2012		(A)	2012		(A)
Mar.31	To Cash A/c	15,000	Mar.31	By Balance c/d	15,000
April 1	To Balance b/d	15,000			

Trial Balance as on March 31, 2012

Particular	*Dr. Balance* (A)	*Cr. Balance* (A)
Cash A/c	3,33,500	
Bank A/c	2,62,500	
Capital A/c		15,00,000
Stock A/c	4,60,000	
Purchase A/c	3,80,000	

Ratan Bros.		95,000
Furniture A/c	1,00,000	
J. Mitra	1,80,000	
Salary A/c	30,000	
Sales A/c		2,45,000
Returns Outward A/c		5,000
Returns Inward A/c	20,000	
Conveyance A/c	1,000	
Commission A/c		1,500
Discount A/c	2,500	
Loan to Naren A/c	15,000	
Drawings A/c	40,000	
Interest A/c		1,000
Dividend A/c		2,500
Postage A/c	500	
Rent A/c	10,000	
Taxes A/c	15,000	
Total	18,50,000	18,50,000

Example 6

The balance sheet of a company as on March 31, 2012 is given below :

	(A)	*(A)*
Cash	21,000	
Accounts Receivable	45,000	
Inventory	5,000	
Prepaid Rent	1,000	
Accounts Payable		12,500
Share Capital		50,000
Profit & Loss Account		9,500
Total	72,000	72,000

Following is the summary of transactions that occurred during April

(*a*) Collections of accounts receivable A 44,000.

(*b*) Payments of accounts payable A 12,000.

(*c*) Acquisition of inventory on credit A 40,000.

(*d*) Inventory costing A 35,000 was sold on credit for A 42,500.

(*e*) Recognition of rent expense for April A 500.

(*f*) Wages paid in cash for April A 4,000.

(*g*) Dividends declared and disbursed to shareholders in April A 9,000.

Prepare all ledger accounts after including the opening balances as on March 31, 2012.

Ledger Accounts

Cash A/c

Dr. Cr.

Date	Particular	A		Particular	A
Jan. 28	To cash A/c	250	Jan.31	By balance c/d	250
01.4.2012	To Balance b/d	21,000	1.4.2012	By A/c payable	12,000
	To A/c receivable	44,000		By Wages	4,000
				By Dividents	9,000
				By Balance c/d	40,000
	Total	65,000			65,000

Inventory A/c

Dr. Cr.

Date	Particular	A		Particular	A
01.4.2012	To Balance b/d	5,000	April	By Customers A/c	35,000
	To Supplier	40,000		By Balance c/d	10,000
	Total	45,000			45,000

Account Payable A/c

Dr. Cr.

Date	Particular	A		Particular	A
2012			**2012**		
April	To Cash	12,000	01.4.2012	By Balance b/d	12,500
	Balance c/d	40,500	April	By Inventory	40,000
	Total	52,500			52,500

Profit & Loss A/c

Dr. Cr.

Date	Particular	A		Particular	A
2012			**2012**		
April	To Rent Expenses	500	01.4.2012	By Balance b/d	9,500
	To Dividends	9,000		By Customers A/c	7,500
	To Balance c/d	3,500			
	Total	17,000			17,000

Accounts Receivable A/c

Dr. Cr.

Date	Particular	A		Particular	A
2012			**2012**		
01.4.2012	To Balance b/d	45,000	April	By Cash	44,000
	To Inventory A/c	35,000		By Balance c/d	43,500
	To P&L A/c	7,500			
	Total	87,500			87,500

Wages A/c

Dr. *Cr.*

Date	*Particular*	*A*		*Particular*	*A*
2012			**2012**		
April 2012	To Cash	4,000	01.4.2012	By P & L A/c	4,000
	Total	4,000			4,000

Prepaid Rent A/c

Dr. *Cr.*

Date	*Particular*	*A*		*Particular*	*A*
01.4.2012	To Balance b/d	1,000	30.4.2012	By Rent A/c	500
				By Balance c/d	500
	Total	1,000			1,000

Share Capital A/c

Dr. *Cr.*

Date	*Particular*	*A*		*Particular*	*A*
30.4.2012	To Balance c/d	50,000	01.4.2012	By Balance b/d	50,000
	Total	50,000			50,000

Rent Expenses A/c

Dr. *Cr.*

Date	*Particular*	*A*		*Particular*	*A*
April	To Prepaid A/c	500	April	By P & L A/c	500
	Total	500			500

Dividend A/c

Dr. *Cr.*

Date	*Particular*	*A*		*Particular*	*A*
April 1	To Cash A/c	9,000	April 30	By P & L A/c	9,000
		9,000			9,000

Trial Balance as on April 30, 2012

Particular	*Amount (A)*	*Amount (A)*
Cash	40,000	
Accounts Receivable	43,500	
Inventory	10,000	
Prepaid Rent	500	
Accounts Payable		40,500
Share Capital		50,000
Profit & Loss Account		3,500
	94,000	94,000

Example 7

The accountant of a business from wrongly prepared the following the trial balance. You are required to draw-up a trial balance correctly stating reasons in brief.

S.No.	*Head of Accounts*	*Debit Balance (A)*	*Credit Balance (A)*
1.	Capital		60,000
2.	Stock at commencement	5,000	
3.	Discount allowed		500
4.	Commission received		700
5.	Fixed Assets		60,000
6.	Sales	85,000	
7.	Purchase		45,000
8.	Return Outwards		1,000
9.	Returns Inwards	2,000	
10.	Carriage Inwards		600
11.	Carriage Outwards		700
12.	Wages and Salary	25,000	
13.	Bills Receivable	7,000	
14.	Debtors	9,000	
15.	Bills Payable		7,000
16.	Rent	3,000	
17.	Interest Paid		2,000
18.	Cash	800	
19.	Creditors	6,900	
20.	Stock at the end	33,800	
	Total	1,77,500	1,77,500

Solution

Trial Balance as on..........

S.No.	*Head of Accounts*	*Debit Balance (A)*	*Credit Balance (A)*
1.	Capital		60,000
2.	Stock at commencement	5,000	
3.	Discount allowed	500	
4.	Commission received		700
5.	Fixed Assets	60,000	
6.	Sales		85,000
7.	Purchase	45,000	
8.	Return Outwards		1,000
9.	Returns Inwards	2,000	

10.	Carriage Inwards	600	
11.	Carriage Outwards	700	
12.	Wages and Salary	25,000	
13.	Bills Receivable	7,000	
14.	Debtors	9,000	
15.	Bills Payable		7,000
16.	Rent	3,000	
17.	Interest Paid	2,000	
18.	Cash	800	
19.	Creditors		6,900
	Total	1,60,600	1,60,600

Reasons

1. Discount allowed is an expenses and therefore it has a debit balance.
2. Fixed assets always reflect debit balance, because assets coming in are debited.
3. Sales has credit balance.
4. Purchases has a debit balance.
5. Carriage inwards is an expense and has a debit balance.
6. Carriage outwards is an expense and has a debit balance.
7. Interest paid is an expense and has a debit balance.
8. Creditor is a liability and has a credit balance.
9. Closing stock is not an account, so it cannot have any balance, and consequently, if does not find a place in the trial balance. Only when closing stock is adjusted against purchases, it appears in the trial balance.

Example 8

An accountant who finds his Trial balance not agreeing opens a Suspense Account and rectifies the following errors :

(*i*) A cheque A 750 received for loss of stock by fire had been deposited in the proprietor's Private Bank Account.

(*ii*) An item of purchase of A 151 was entered in the purchase book as A 15 and posted to the supplier's account A 51.

(*iii*) A sales return of A 500 was not entered in the financial accounts though it was duly taken in the stock book.

(*iv*) An amount of A 300 was received in full settlement from a customer after he was allowed a discount of A 50 but while writing the books, the amount received was entered in the discount column and discount allowed in the amount column.

(*v*) Bills receivable from Mr. A of A 1,000 was posted to the credit of bills payable account and also credited to the account of Mr.A.

Show the suspense account and find out the opening balance.

Solution

		LF	Debit (A)	Credit (A)
(*i*)	Drawing A/c	Dr.	750	
	To Loss of stock A/c			750
	(Being the rectification of a cheque wrongly passed to proprietor's Private Bank A/c			
(*ii*)	Purchase A/c	Dr.	136	
	To Supplier's personal A/c			100
	To Suspense A/c			36
	(Being the rectification of understanding of purchases amount in Purchases Book and Supplier's A/c)			
(*iii*)	Sales Return A/c	Dr.	500	
	To Customer's A/c			500
	(Being the sales return transaction omitted to be recorded in books)			
(*iv*)	Bank A/c	Dr.	250	
	To Discount Allowed A/c			250
	(Being the amount received from a customer wrongly entered in discount allowed column)			
(*v*)	Bills Payable A/c	Dr.	1,000	
	Bills Receivable A/c	Dr.	1,000	
	To Suspense A/c			
	(Being Bill Received from Mr.A wrongly posted to Bills Payable A/c and on credit ride of Mr. A's A/c)			

Suspense A/c

Particular	*A*	*Particular*	*A*
To Balance (Different transferred to trial balance)	2,036	By Purchases	36
		By Bills Payable	1,000
		By Bills Receivable	1,000
Total	2,036		2,036

Example 9

The credit column of a Trial Balance as on 31st March, 2012 is short by A 3,800.

On 01.04.2012 the following errors were discovered.

(*i*) A credit item of A 9,300 has been debited to the personal account of Raman as A 3,900.

(*ii*) A 7,500 written off as depreciation on plant and machinery account has not been debited to depreciation account.

(*iii*) A discount of A 4,500 allowed to Nataraj and Sons has been credited to them as A 5,400.

(*iv*) The total of Sales Returns Book has been undercast by A 1,000.

Pass the rectification entries. Assume that the difference in Trial Balance is taken to a suspense account. You need not show the suspense account.

Solution

Sl.No.	*Particulars*	*LF*	*Debit (A)*	*Credit (A)*
(*i*)	Suspense A/c	Dr.	13,200	
	To Raman A/c			13,200
	(Being the rectification of a credit item of A 9300 wrongly debited as A 3900)			
(*ii*)	Depreciation A/c	Dr.	7,500	
	To Suspense A/c			7,500
	(Being the rectification of omission of posting to depreciation A/c)			
(*iii*)	Natraj & Sons A/c	Dr.	900	
	To Suspense A/c			900
	(Being the rectification of discount allowed of A 4500 credited as A 5400)			
(*iv*)	Sales Returns A/c	Dr.	1,000	
	To Suspense A/c			1,000
	(Being the rectification of undercasting of the Sales Returns Book.)			

Example 10

Give the correct journal entries for the following :

(*a*) Cost of repairing one machine, *i.e.,* A 100 has been charged to machinery account.

(*b*) A 50 paid to S. Roy in settlement of his account has been posted to the debit of purchase account.

(*c*) Goods sold on credit of A 200 to B. Bose have been posted to the debit of general charges account.

(*d*) A 250 received from B.K. Ghose has been credited to account of K.B. Ghose.

(*e*) Wages account includes A 1,500 being wages paid to workmen engaged in construction work of the firm's new building.

Solution

Sl.No.	*Particulars*	*LF*	*Debit (A)*	*Credit (A)*
(*a*)	Repairs A/c	Dr.	100	
	To Machinery A/c			100
	(Being the amount for repairs wrongly charged to machinery A/c now rectified)			

	Particulars	LF	Debit	Credit
(*b*)	S. Roy Dr.	50		
	To Purchase A/c			50
	(Being the payment to S.Roy wrongly debited to purchases A/c, recitified)			
(*c*)	B.Bose Dr.	200		
	To General charges A/c			200
	(Being the credit sale to B. Bose wrongly debited to general charges, now rectified)			
(*d*)	K.B. Ghosh	Dr.	250	
	To B.K. Ghosh			250
	(Being A 250 received from B.K. Ghosh wrongly credited to K.B. Ghosh, now rectified)			
(*e*)	Building A/c	Dr.	1,500	
	To wages A/c			1,500
	(Being the payment of wages for construction building debited to wages A/c, now rectified)			

Example 11

Rectify the following errors :

1. Wages paid to the workers (A 250) for repairing the building have been debited to wages A/c.
2. A sum of A 65 spent for repairing office furniture has been debited to furniture A/c.
3. Purchase of typewriter for A 800 has been passed through the day book.
4. A 75 paid as the examination fees of the proprietor's son has been posted to general expenses A/c.
5. Stock of goods valued at A 950 donated to ND fund has been posted to general expenses A/c.
6. A 5,400 received from M. Mehta were posted to the debit side of his account.
7. A 1,000 being purchases return were posted to the purchase A/c.
8. Discount of A 2,000 received was posted to the debit of discount A/c.
9. A 3,740 paid for repairs to motor car were debited to motor car A/c as A 1,740.

Solution

Journal

Sl.No.	*Particulars*	*LF*	*Debit (A)*	*Credit (A)*
1.	Repairs A/c	Dr.	250	
	To Wages A/c			250
	(Being the amount of wages paid for repairs wrongly debited to wages A/c, now rectified)			
2.	Repairs A/c	Dr.	65	
	To Furniture A/c			65

No.	Particulars		Dr.	Cr.
	(Being the sum spent for repair of office furniture wrongly debited to furniture A/c, now rectified)			
3.	Typewriter A/c	Dr.	800	
	To Purchase A/c			800
	(Being the purchase of typewriter wrongly passed through day book, now rectified)			
4.	Drawing A/c	Dr.	75	
	To General Expenses A/c			75
	(Being the payment of examination fees of the proprietors son wrongly debited to general expenses, now rectified)			
5.	Donations A/c	Dr.	950	
	To General Expenses A/c			950
	(Being the stock of goods donated to ND Funds wrongly debited to general expenses, now rectified)			
6.	Suspense A/c	Dr.	10,800	
	To M. Mehta A/c			10,800
	(Being the receipt of A 5,400 from M. Mehra wrongly debited to his account, now rectified)			
7.	Suspense A/c	Dr.	2,000	
	To Purchase Return A/c			1,000
	To Purchase A/c			1,000
	(Being the amount of purchase returns wrongly debited to purchase now rectified)			
8.	Suspense A/c	Dr.	4,000	
	To Discount A/c			4,000
	(Being the discount of A 2,000 was debited to discount A/c, now rectified)			
9.	Repairs A/c	Dr.	3,740	
	To Motor Car A/c			1,740
	To Suspense A/c			2,000
	(Being the payment of A 3,740 for repairs to motorcar wrongly debited to motorcar as A 1,740, now rectified)			

Example 12

The account of a business firm prepared the trial balance and the total of debits equalled the total of credits. However, some of the errors subsequently discovered were as follows :

(*i*) The sales day book was overcast by A 2,500.

(*ii*) Machinery maintenance expenditure of A 17,500 had been debited to machinery A/c.

(*iii*) A Purchase Return of A 2,000 had been posted to the credit of the supplier account.

(*iv*) An amount of A 10,000 received from a customer had been omitted to be posted to the customer's account.

(*v*) The purchases day book was undercast by A 500.

After correcting the above errors the suspense account would have e balance of :

(*a*) A 2,050 (Debit) (*b*) A 3,000 (Credit)

(*c*) Nil (*d*) A 3,000 (Debit)

(*e*) None of the above.

Solution

Suspense A/c

Particular	*A*	*Particular*	*A*
To customer A/c	10,000	By Sales A/c	2,500
		By Supplier A/c	4,000
		By Purchase A/c	500
		By Bal. c/d	3,000
Total	10,000		10,000

Example 13

This trial balance of M/s P.M. Kashyap as on 31st March 2012 did not tally. The difference of A 15,000 was transferred to the credit of suspense A/c. After the completion of final accounts, the following errors were discovered.

(*a*) Total of Sales figure was taken as A 56,000 instead of 65,000.

(*b*) The total of purchases Returns book was under cast by A 100.

(*c*) Sale of old furniture for A 900 was wrongly entered in machinery A/c.

(*d*) A credit purchase of A 5,000 made from Mr. Y was recorded in purchases book but was not posted in Y's account.

(*e*) A 1,000 received from A was posted to the credit of B.

(*f*) A credit sale of A 2,000 made to Mr. S was recorded twice in his account.

(*g*) Wages amounting to A 1,000 were paid on 20th March, 2012. They were recorded in Cash Book but were not recorded in the wages A/c.

Give Journal entries to record the above transactions and prepare the suspense A/c.

Solution

Sl.No.	*Particulars*	*LF*	*Debit (A)*	*Credit (A)*
(*a*)	Suspense A/c	Dr.	9,000	
	To Sales A/c			9,000
	(Being the sales figure undercast by A 9,000)			
(*b*)	Suspense A/c	Dr.	100	
	To Purchase Returns A/c			100
	(Being the total of purchases returns under cast by A 100)			

(*c*)	Machinery A/c	Dr.	900	
	To Furniture			900
	(Being the sale of old furniture wrongly entered in Machinery A/c)			
(*d*)	Suspense A/c	Dr.	5,000	
	To Y		5,000	
	(Being the credit purchase of A 5,000 made from Y not recorded in his account earlier)			
(*e*)	B Dr.	1,000		
	To A		1,000	
	(Being the wrong credit given to B now rectified)			
(*f*)	Suspense A/c	Dr.	2,000	
	To S		2,000	
	(Being the entry for rectifying the error of debiting S twice)			
(*g*)	Wages A/c	Dr.	1,000	
	To Suspense A/c			1,000
	(Being the amount of wages not recorded earlier)			

Suspense A/c

Particular	*A*	*Particular*	*A*
To Sales A/c	9,000	By Balanced B/d	15,100
To Purchase returns A/c	100	By Wages A/c	1,000
To Y	5,000		
To S	2,000		
Total	16,000		16,000

ASSIGNMENT MATERIAL

Note : The objective-Type Questions (True/False, Multiple Choice Questions etc.) have been given in the Appendix at the end of the book.

SHORT ANSWER THEORY QUESTIONS

1. Explain procedure of posting.
2, Distinguish between (*i*) errors of omission and Errors of Commission; and (*ii*) Trial Balance and Balance Sheet.
3. Explain method of preparing Trial Balance.
4. Explain Contra Entry.
5. What is a Ledger?
6. What are the rules regarding posting.

7. What is balancing of an account?
8. What is Trial Balance?
9. Define Suspense Account.

LONG ANSWER THEORY QUESTIONS

1. Explain the terms Ledger and Trial Balance. What are the reasons for preparing a Trial Balance?
2. What is Trial Balance? What are the objectives of preparing a Trial Balance?
3. "A Trial Balance is list showing all account titles in the Ledger and the total of debits and credits in each account." Do you agree with this statement? Why or why not?
4. What type of errors could cause a Trial Balance not to balance?
5. A Trial Balance may be in balance but the accounts may be incorrect. How is this possible?
6. "If a Trial Balance tallies it can be concluded that there are no errors in the books of accounts." Comment.
7. Explain the errors which effect the agreement of Trial Balance.
8. Explain the errors which are not disclosed in spite of the agreement of a Trial Balance.
9. How would you post the transactions recorded in the following books :
   (*i*) Purchases Books (*ii*) Sales Book
   (*iii*) Journal (*iv*) Bills Receivable Books
   (*v*) Bills Payable Book
10. Listed below are the total debits and credits from three trial balances that do not balance. For each case, indicate the type of error you would initially attempt to locate.

	Debit Total	*Credit Total*
(*a*)	A 25,500	A 25,400
(*b*)	A 43,470	A 43,230
(*c*)	A 80,614	A 80,974

11. A number of events common to the accounting function of a business entity are presented below. Prepare a list of these events as they would occur in their logical order.
    (*a*) Determining Ledger Account Balances
    (*b*) Analysing the transaction
    (*c*) Preparing a Balance Sheet
    (*d*) Preparing a Trial Balance
    (*e*) Occurrence of a Business Transaction
    (*f*) Posting from the Journal to the Ledger
    (*g*) Preparing Profit and Loss Account
    (*h*) Journalising Transactions
12. Explain the stages involved in the preparation of Trial Balance.
13. Explain the procedure of rectifying the errors.
14. What error can be disclosed by a Trial Balance?
15. Discuss errors which are not disclosed by Trial Balance.

PRACTICAL PROBLEMS

1. Give Journal Entries to rectify the following errors :
   (*i*) An account of A 4,000 spent for the extension of machinery has been debited to wages A/c.
   (*ii*) A 150 paid as cartage for the newly purchased furniture posted to cartage A/c.
   (*iii*) A builder's bill for A 6,000 for erection of a small cycle shed was debited to repairs A/c.
   (*iv*) A cheque A 2,000 received from Ashok was dishonoured and had been posted to the debit side of 'Allowance A/c'.
   (*v*) A 1,000 paid for the newly purchased 'cooler' posted to 'purchase account'.
2. There was a difference of A 725 in a Trial Balance. It has been transferred to credit side of Suspense A/c. Later on following errors were discovered. Pass the rectifying entries and prepare Suspense A/c.;
   (*a*) A amount of A 375 has been posted in the debit side of commission account instead of A 275.
   (*b*) Goods of A 200 purchased from Depak have been posted to his account as A 250.
   (*c*) Total of Sales Returns Book was overcast by A 475.
   (*d*) A credit amount of A 50 was posted as A 150 to the debit side of a personal account.
   (*e*) Goods of A 300 were sold to Nitin, but it was recorded in Purchase Book.
3. Pass rectification entries for the following transaction :
   (*i*) A bill of exchange (received from Preeti) for A 3,000 had been returned by the bank with whom, it had been discounted, as dishonoured and had been credited to Bank A/c and debited to Bill Receivable A/c.
   (*ii*) A purchase of goods from Anku amounting to A 300 has been wrongly passed through the Sales Book.
   (*iii*) On 31st Dec., 2012 goods of the value of A 200 were returned by Gopi Chand and were taken into stock on the same date, but no entry was passed in the books.
   (*iv*) An amount of A 2,000 due from Deepak, which has been written off as a Bad debt in a previous year, was unexpectedly recovered and has been posted to the personal account of Deepak.
   (*v*) A cheque of A 500 received from Manish was dishonoured and had been posted to the debit side of Sales Returns Account.
   (*vi*) A Bill Receivable of A 400 received from Ram was passed through the Bills Payable Book.
   (*vii*) A 480 paid for wages to workman for making showcases had been charged to wages A/c.
   (*viii*) A 5,000 paid for the purchase of a Motor cycle for the proprietor had been charged to miscellaneous expenses A/c.
   (*ix*) *X* was paid cash A 5,000 but *Y* was debited by A 5,000.
   (*x*) Purchases Returns Book was carried forward as A 132 instead of 123.
4. The books of a private firm have been posted upto 31st December, 2012, how would you correct the following errors which were subsequently found therein :
   (*i*) An amount of A 1,000 received from Motilal on 1st January, 2013 had been entered in the Cash Book as having been received on 31st December, 2012.
   (*ii*) A 750 paid for the purchase of a consumable durable for one of the partners has been charged to General Expenses A/c.
   (*iii*) An addition in the returns Inward Book has been cast A 100 short.
   (*iv*) A cheque of A 200 drawn for Petty Cash Account in the Ledger.

(*v*) A 150 appearing in the discount column on the credit side of the Cash Book, had not been posted to a personal account.

5. The accountant of a firm finds that the Trial Balance as on 31st December, 2012 is out by an excess debit of A 566. He placed the amount in the Suspense A/c. In the first week of January, 2013, he discovered the following errors. Pass Journal Entries necessary to rectify these errors and show the Suspense A/c., as it would appear at the end of the week. Do you have any comment to make?

   (*a*) Cash paid to Amar Nath, A 150, was posted on the credit of Amar Singh's Account as A 114.

   (*b*) Discount allowed by Jones A 10, was not entered in the Cash Book, but Jones stands debited correctly.

   (*c*) No entry was made for goods worth A 80 taken away by proprietor for personal use.

   (*d*) A 1,000 received from Jhaveri Bros., for interest on loan advanced to them were recorded in the Cash Book. But the entry was not posted in the Ledger.

   (*e*) The total of Returns Outward Book was short by A 200.

   [***Hint*** *:* At the end of the week, the Suspense A/c will indicate a debit balance of A 380. It means that there are still some errors left undetected, due to which Trial Balance will not tally].

CHAPTER 8

Accounting Process - III : Completion of the Accounting Cycle : Preparation of Final Accounts of Non-Corporate Business Entities

Learning Objectives

After studying this chapter, you should be able to:

1. *Understand the procedure of preparing final accounts—Trading and Profit and Loss Account and Balance Sheet.*
2. *Explain the nature of adjustment entries.*
3. *Discuss different types of adjustment entries.*
4. *Know closing entries and their importance in the preparation of financial statements.*
5. *Explain Capital Receipts, Capital Expenditures, Revenue Receipts and Revenue Expenditures.*
6. *Understand arrangement of assets and liability items on the balance sheet.*
7. *Explain limitations of Balance Sheet.*
8. *Know the concept of Provisions, Contingent Liabilities and Contingent Assets.*
9. *Illustrate preparation of Adjustment Entries Accounts, Trading and Profit and Loss Account and Balance Sheet.*

PREPARATION OF FINANCIAL STATEMENTS : PROFIT AND LOSS ACCOUNT AND BALANCE SHEET

Trial Balance is first step towards preparation of financial statements—namely Trading and Profit and Loss Account and Balance Sheet. Trading and Profit and Loss Account are prepared in order to determine the income earned or loss incurred during the accounting period. Balance Sheet indicates the financial position of the enterprise. However, before preparing trading account, profit and loss account and balance sheet, certain adjustment entries are required.

ADJUSTMENT ENTRIES

As stated earlier, financial accounting uses accrual basis of accounting which is supported by Generally Accepted Accounting Principles (GAAP). Under accrual basis of accounting.

1. Revenue are recognised when earned, without regard to the timing of cash receipts.
2. Expenses are recognised either; (*a*) in the period in which related revenues are recognised or; (*b*) when incurred, without regard to the timing of cash disbursements.

When the accrual basis of accounting is used, adjusting entries are required at the end of the period to record any previously unrecognised changes in assets, liabilities, revenues, or expenses. Adjusting entries are

are made to modify certain account balances at the end of the accounting period so that they will reflect fairly the situation at the end of the period. Adjusting entries can be referred to as internal transactions, distinct from external transactions which are between a business entity and the parties external to the entity. It should be noted that the external (exchange) transactions are already found recorded in the accounting records and different ledger accounts.

The following are a few examples of situations where adjusting entries are needed and the accountant has to process these additional information before preparing the financial statements on the basis of trial balance :

(*a*) The accountant may know (or be instructed by the Accounts Manager) that the depreciation on building is to be charged at the rate of 10%.

(*b*) The accountant would ascertain that the salary of some workers for March is unpaid at the end of the month.

(*c*) The accountant is informed by the store-keeper that the goods lying unsold in the store (representing closing stock) is worth A 17,000 at cost.

(*d*) The accountant knows or is informed that the loan of A 2,00,000 was taken at an interest of 12% per annum. He also knows that the interest accrued for March is unpaid as on March 31, since there is no ledger account for any interest paid.

(*e*) The accountant knows that the insurance premium was paid on October 1, Last year for the whole year whereas the accounts are being prepared for 31 March next year.

(*f*) The accountant is informed that A 50,000 may not be collected from PQR Company owing to some technical dispute.

Thus, if profit and loss Account is to report a realistic net profit (or net loss) based on accrual accounting, all revenues earned during the period and all expenses incurred must be shown. Therefore, revenues and costs must be properly matched or aligned for the reporting period in question, popularly known as matching concept in the accounting literature.

Generally, four general types of adjustment (adjustment entries) are needed at the end of the accounting period prior to the preparation of financial statements :

1. Reflecting unrecorded revenue earned during the accounting period.
2. Reflecting unrecorded expenses incurred during the accounting period.
3. Reflecting or aligning recorded costs with the appropriate accounting periods *i.e.,* considering expenditures benefiting more than one accounting period.
4. Reflecting or aligning recorded revenue with the appropriate accounting periods *i.e.,* considering revenues received in advance.

Adjustment in the first two categories—unrecorded revenues and unrecorded expenses–are referred to as accruals such as salaries and wages incurred but not paid, interest earned but not received. Adjustments in the last two categories–reflecting recorded costs and revenues with the appropriate periods–are referred to as deferrals such as prepaid expenses, unearned revenue and depreciation.

Adjustment Entries have the following features :

1. Every adjusting entry affects both the profit and loss account and the balance sheet.
2. Adjusting entries do not directly affect the cash account.
3. They are generally recorded at the end of the accounting period.
4. A profit and loss account balance (revenue or expense) is changed.

5. A balance sheet account balance (asset or liability) is changed.

TYPES OF ADJUSTMENT ENTRIES

The different items or situations which are subject to adjustment entries before preparing financial statements are explained below :

Closing Inventory

Under the periodic verification method, the closing inventory of every item is arrived at by physically counting the inventory available and assigning a value to the same. In concerns adopting the periodic verification method, the value of closing inventory will be brought into the books of accounts through the following journal entry :

Closing inventory A/c Dr.

To Trading A/c

While the closing inventory appears on the credit side of the trading account to reduce the cost of goods sold, it also appears as an asset in the Balance Sheet.

Outstanding or Accrued Expense

The nominal accounts record the actual expense paid during the accounting period. However, prior to the preparation of the financial statements, it must be ensured that all expenses which have fallen due to be paid but which have not been paid during the accounting period are also brought into the books to help in the proper matching of revenues and expenses. For example, ABC Trading Company had the practice of paying the salaries of the employees on 4th of the subsequent month. During the financial year ending 31st March, 2012 the salaries account shows a debit balance of A 55,000. The salaries of A 6,000 pertaining to March 2012 were paid on 4th April, 2012. While preparing the financial statements for the year ending 31st march, 2012, the salaries of A 6,000 of March must also be included. This is done with the following adjusting journal entry.

Salaries A/c Dr. 6,000

To Outstanding Salaries A/c 6,000

The above journal entry increase the salaries to the correct amount of A 61,000 and the outstanding salaries of A 6,000 will be shown as a liability in the Balance Sheet.

The adjusting journal entry to record any outstanding accrued expense is

Expense A/c Dr.

To Outstanding Expense A/c

While the amount of expense taken from the Trial Balance will be increased by the amount outstanding and shown in the trading and Profit and Loss Account, the actual amount outstanding will be a shown as a liability in the Balance Sheet.

In the subsequent accounting period, the outstanding expense liability will be transferred to the expense or nominal account and will be setoff by the entry of actual payments when it is made.

Prepaid Expense

Certain expenses paid may relate to more than one accounting period. In such cases, it is necessary to identify that portion of the expenditure for which the benefit is yet to be received by the concern and treat that part of the expenditure as prepaid.

ABC Trading Company took an insurance cover for all assets against fire on 1st October 2011 and paid the annual premium of A 2,400 on the same day. Since the benefit of the entire expenditure will expire only on 30th September, 2012, it is necessary to recognise this aspect while preparing the financial statements as on 31st March, 2012.

The amount of expense prepaid on 1st October 2011 = (1/2 × 2,400 = A 1,200)

The adjusting entry to record the prepaid insurance is

Prepaid Insurance A/c Dr.	1,200
To Insurance A/c	1,200

This ensures that the insurance expense is reported at the correct figure of A 1,200 in the profit and loss account and the prepaid amount is shown as an Asset in the balance sheet.

The journal entry to record any prepaid expense is,

Prepaid Expense A/c Dr.

To Expense A/c

In the subsequent accounting period, the balance in the prepaid expense account will be transferred back to the expense account.

Outstanding Income

Outstanding income is that amount of income which is earned and due and therefore receivable but not yet received. A business firm or a person has a legal right and enforceable claim to receive it immediately from the other party. If a portion of an income has not yet been received or is outstanding at the end of the accounting period, then the outstanding amount must be brought into books. It is added to income in profit and loss account and is shown as asset on balance sheet when accounts are finalised on the date of accounting period end.

Assume, ABC Trading Company have not received the due interest of A 35,000 during the accounting period ending 31st March 2012. However, while preparing the financial statements for the year ending 31st March 2012 the interest revenue to be recognised is the amount of A 35,000.

The following adjusting entry will bring into books the amount of outstanding interest:

Outstanding Interest A/c Dr.	35,000
To Interest Received A/c	35,000

While the interest received and due but not received are shown in the profit and loss account, the outstanding interest will be listed as an asset in the Balance Sheet.

In the subsequent accounting period, the amount in the outstanding interest A/c will be transferred to interest received A/c and the actual receipt of the interest will offset the former transfer entry.

To record any outstanding income in the books of accounts, the journal entry is :

Outstanding Income A/c Dr.

To Income A/c

Accrued Income

Accrued income is that income which is earned but not yet due and therefore not receivable on the date of period end. Accrued income is the amount earned in an accounting period but for which the firm or person has no legal right or enforceable claim to receive it immediately from the other party. It becomes due due to passage of time and at the date of accounting has been partly performed and are not yet receivable (payable). Assume, a person gets his salary (becomes due to be paid) on 10th of next month regularly and therefore his salary, say for the month of March 2012, is accrued income on the date of period end i.e., March

31, 2012 if accounts are prepared and finalised on March 31, 2012. The person cannot force the other party to pay salary by March 31 although the income (salary) has been earned; however it is not yet due to receive.

To take another example, a business firm has invested Rs. 5 crores in 15% bond on January 1, 2011. Interest is payable half yearly on June 30 and December 31 every year. Accounts are finalised on March 31 every year. In this case, if the firm has not received interest due half yearly on December 31 and has not received even upto March 31, 2012 next year, this interest for the period July to December 2011 is an example of outstanding income (interest) on the date of period end i.e., March 31. However, interest for three months January to March 31, 2012 is accrued interest (income) on the date of the period end i.e., March 31, 2012. This accrued interest for three months (January to March 2012) has been earned but is not receivable by March 31 and therefore the firm has no legal right or enforceable claim to force the other party to pay by March 31 the interest due from January to March 2012. However, the firm in case of outstanding interest (income) (*i.e.,* interest due from July to December 2011 and yet not received) has legal right and enforceable claim to force the other party to pay this period interest immediately.

Accrued income like outstanding income, is added to income in the profit and loss account and is an asset to be shown on the asset side of balance sheet on the date of period end *i.e.,* March 31, 2012.

It is significant to observe that the accounting treatment of outstanding income and accrued income is the same. However, both differ in nature and concept.

Income Received in Advance

While preparing the financial statements, adjustments may be necessary in respect of any income received in advance.

Law publications has received subscriptions amounting to A 50,000 during the financial year ending 31st December, 2011, out of this A 2,500 represent subscriptions relating to the next financial year.

The entry to adjust for the income received in advance will be,

Subscriptions A/c Dr.	2,500
To Subscriptions received in Advance	2,500

With the posting of the above journal entry, the subscriptions account will be shown in the profit and loss account at the credit figure of A 47,500 and in the balance sheet, the subscriptions received in advance as liability. Any income received in advance is a liability as benefits are yet to be conferred to the person from whom the amount has been received. The journal entry to record the adjustment of any income received in advance is :

Income A/c Dr.

To Income Received in Advance A/c

Depreciation

Depreciation is the acquisition cost of an asset (less the expected salvage value) spread over the economic life of that asset. The purpose of charging depreciation over the economic life of the asset is to match the cost of the asset over the period for which revenue is earned by using the asset.

There are two methods of recording depreciation. Under the first method, the asset account is directly credited for the depreciation and the written down value is readily ascertained. The journal entry to record depreciation under the method is :

Depreciation A/c Dr.

To Asset A/c

Under the second method, the depreciation charged is credited to a depreciation provision A/c and the written down value of the asset is shown in the balance sheet by deducting the provision from the original cost of the asset. The journal entry recorded under this method is:

Depreciation A/c Dr.

To Depreciation Provision A/c

Balance in Depreciation is transferred to Profit and Loss account. The accounting entry is as under :

Profit and Loss A/c Dr.

To Depreciation A/c

Depreciation provision account, if opened, will be shown by way of deduction from the relevant Asset A/c in the Balance Sheet.

Loss of Stock-in-Trade

If stock-in-trade is lost due to fire or theft and the firm has insured the stock-in-trade, then the loss can be made good fully or partly by the insurance company. The loss will be treated in financial statements as follows :

(*a*) When the claim on account of loss of stock is fully recoverable from the insurance company, the journal entry will be as follows :

Insurance Claim A/c Dr.

To Trading A/c

Insurance claim is an asset and will be shown as an asset in the Balance Sheet until actually received in cash.

(*b*) When the claim on account of loss of stock is partly accepted by the insurance company, the journal entry will be :

Insurance Claim A/c Dr. [by the claim accepted by the insurance company]

Profit and Loss A/c Dr. [by the amount not recoverable from insurance company]

To Trading A/c

(*c*) When stock is uninsured, nothing is recoverable from the insurance company, the journal entry will be :

Profit and Loss A/c Dr.

To Trading A/c

Therefore, trading account is always credited with gross amount of stock lost by fire or theft.

Interest on Loans or Deposits

If the trial balance includes loan account (Cr.) or deposit account (Dr.) carrying certain rate of interest and rate of interest is given, then it is necessary to calculate interest at the rate given. If the interest account does not appear then the complete interest is treated as outstanding. But if interest account appears, then it should be compared with the amount arrived at after the calculation. The difference between the two figures is treated as interest paid or outstanding. This should be brought into final account by making adjustment entry. Interest on deposits (Dr.) not received becomes accrued and should be brought in the final account by making adjustment entry.

Manager's Commission on Net Profit

Sometimes, the manager of a business may be given a commission based on a fixed percentage of the net profits earned by the business. In such a case, the total net profits are calculated and then the percentage of the commission is applied. Suppose, the net profits after taking into account all expenses except commission are A 2,00,000 and the manager is to be given a commission of 5% on the net profits before charging such commission. His commission will be A 2, 00, 000 $\frac{5}{100}$ or A 10,000. The journal entry for this commission is:

Profit and Loss A/c	Dr.	10,000
To Outstanding Manager's Commission A/c		A 10,000

Outstanding Manager's Commission is shown on the debit side of Profit and Loss Account and as a liability on the liabilities side of the Balance Sheet.

If the commission to manager is to be paid on net profit *after* charging such commission. It will be calculated using the following formula :

$$\frac{\%\ \text{Commission}}{100 \quad \%\ \text{Commission}} \quad \text{Net profits before commission.}$$

Taking the above figures, the commission in this case will be :

$$\frac{5}{100 \quad 5} \quad 2{,}00{,}000 \quad \frac{5}{105} \quad 2{,}00{,}000$$

= A 9523.8

Withdrawal of Goods by the Proprietor

When the proprietor withdraws some goods from the business for his personal use or consumption, the withdrawals of such goods is recorded at cost price. The adjustment entry passed for this purpose is :

Proprietor's Drawings or Capital A/c	Dr.
To Purchases A/c	

Thus, the goods so taken are deducted from purchases on the debit side of the trading account and included in Proprietor's Drawings account or deducted from capital on the liabilities side of the Balance Sheet.

Provision for Bad Debts, Cash Discounts Payable and Cash Discounts Receivable

Bad Debts

The sales revenue recorded in the books of accounts of an organisation represent the amount realised or to be realised from the sale of goods. When goods are sold on credit it may sometimes happen that even though customers bought them with every intention of paying for them, due to certain subsequent change in circumstances, they may not be able to fulfil their obligations. For instance, if a customer, subsequent to the date of credit sales, is declared an insolvent and his estate cannot pay anything towards satisfaction of the amount due from him, then logically, the entry passed at the time of sale should be removed by reversing it, as the situation is similar to the sale not having taken place. In practice, however, instead, of reversing the previous entry, the amount which cannot be recovered is considered as a loss called 'Bad Debts'.

Example

ABC Ltd., had debtors outstanding to the extent of A 75,000/- as on 31st March 2011 Mr. *X*, who owned A 1,500/- to the company has been adjudged insolvent and his estate is unable to pay anything.

The journal entry to record the above loss would be :

Bad Debts A/c	Dr.	1,500	
To X A/c	Cr.		1,500

Now that the sales account remains unchanged. However, in the income statement, while sales revenue will appear at the full figure, the bad debts will appear as a loss and thus the reduction in the amount realised will be accounted for. The Account Receivable account will also appear in the Balance Sheet at the realisable value of A 73,500.

The journal entry for recording Bed Debts is :

Bad Debts A/c Dr.

To Accounts Receivable A/c

Provision for Bad and Doubtful Debts

We have already seen that according to the realisation concept, the amount to be recognised as revenue is the amount that is reasonably certain to be realised. When there is possibility that all the sales revenue may not be realised in the future due to occurrence of bad debts, the sales revenue, then in the income statement should reflect this position. However, in practice, the sales revenue is shown as the gross figure and any possible loss due to bad debts is shown as an expense.

When bad debts are expected to occur in the future, (*a*) the exact amount of loss may not be known and (*b*) a particular debtor's account cannot be identified to write off the expected loss or even if the debtor's account can be identified, a reduction in claim can be given effect to only when it becomes certain. To circumvent these problems usually, a provision is made for the expected bad debts loss out of profits of the current year. This reduces the profit and hence the income statement conforms to the realisation principle and also prevents an estimated portion of profits from being distributed to the proprietors. The provision in this context means any amount retained by providing for any known decline in value of assets of which the amount cannot be determined with substantial accuracy. For creating the provision for bad and doubtful debts, the journal entry is,

Profit and Loss A/c Dr.

To Provision for Bad Debts A/c

Example

The Accounts Receivable of PQR Ltd. was A 1,50,000/- as on 31st March, 2012. It was estimated that A 5,000/- of the amount due may turn out to be uncollectable during the forthcoming year.

For creation of the provision the journal entry will be,

Profit and Loss A/c	Dr.	5,000	
To Provision for Bad Debts A/c			5,000

While the amount of the possible loss will appear on the debit side of the profit and loss account, the provision created, though a liability will be shown as a deduction from Accounts Receivable on the asset side of balance sheet. This would ensure that the current asset is shown at the realizable value.

Balance Sheet of PQR Ltd., as on 31.3.2012

Liabilities	*Assets*	*A*	*A*
	Accounts Receivable	1,50,000	
	Less : Provision for Bed Debts	5,000	1,45,000

Estimating Bad and Doubtful Debts

Any one of the following methods may be used to estimate the amount of possible bad debts.

1. Bad debts may be estimated as a percentage of total sales during the year. This method can be used only when there are no cash sales or such sales are negligible.
2. Bad debts may be estimated as a percentage of credit sales.
3. Estimate bad beats as a percentage of receivable outstanding at the end of the accounting period.

The percentage used will be based on the judgement of the management and the past experience with regard to bad debts. Another logical way to estimate bad debts would be to draw up an aging schedule for the outstanding debtors and apply different percentage for amounts outstanding for various lengths of time.

Treatment of Bad Debts when a Provision for Bad Debts Exists

Let us extend the example of PQR Ltd., to the financial year ending 31st March 2012.

The following details are available.

Bad Debts during the year	A 3,500
Accounts Receivable as on 31.3.2012	A 1,70,000

PQR Ltd., would like a maintain the provision at 5% of Sundry Debtors.

The Accounts Receivable of A 1,70,000 as on 31.3.2012 is after account for the bad debts of A 3,500/-. When bad debts occurred, the following entry would have been passed.

Bad Debts A/c	Dr.	A 3,500/-
To Sundry Debtors A/c		A 3,500/-

Since provision for bad debts to the extent of A 5,000/- already exists, the actual bad debts of A 3,500/- will be transferred at the end of the year to this provision account and not to the profit and loss account.

The entry for the transfer will be :

Provision for the Bad Debts A/c	Dr.	A 3,500
To Bad Debts A/c		A 3,500

At this point the provision A/c will appear as under :

Provision for Bad Debts A/c

31.3.2012	*A*	*01.4.2011*	*A*
To Bad Debts A/c	3,500	By Balance b/d	5,000

Since the provision has been utilised to the extent of A 3,500/-, only A 1,500/- is left for setting off any bad debts in the forthcoming year. However, PQR Ltd., wishes to maintain the provision at 5% on debtors. So, the balance required in the provision account as on 31.3.2012 is,

$$1,70,000 \quad \frac{5}{10} \quad A\ 8,500$$

To bring up the provision to the required balance a further appropriation of A 7,000 (A 8,500 – A 1,500) will have to be made from the profits and loss account. Entry will be,

Profit and Loss A/c	Dr.	7,000
To Provision for Bad Debts A/c		7,000

The provision account after posting this entry will appear as follows :

Provision for Bad Debts A/c

Dr. Cr.

	A		A
31.03.2012		01.4.2011	
To Bad Debts	3,500	By Balance b/d	5,000
31.3.2012		31.3.2012	
To Balance c/d	8,500	By Profit and Loss A/c	7,000
	12,000		12,000

The balance sheet will again show the Accounts Receivable at their realisable value.

Balance Sheet of PQR Ltd., as on 31.3.2012

Liabilities	*Assets*	A	A
	Accounts Receivable	1,70,000	
	Less : Provision for Bad Debts	8.500	1,61,500

We will extend the above example to yet another financial year.

The following details are available for the year ending 31.3.2013.

Bad Debts during the year	1,000
Sundry Debtors as on 31.3.2013	1,10,000

PQR Ltd., would like to maintain the provision for bad debts as 5% of debtors.

As in the previous year, the total bad debts will be transferred to the provision for bad debts.

Provision for Bad Debts A/c	Dr.	1,000
To Bad Debts A/c		1,000

The provision account after the above transfer will appear as follows :

Provision for Bads Debts A/c

Dr. Cr.

	A		A
31.3.2013		01.4.2012	
To Bad Debts A/c	1,000	By Balance b/d	8,500

The provision required on the closing debtors will be,

(5 × 100) × 1,10,000 = A 5,500

The opening provision of A 8,500/- has been utilised only to the extent of A 1,000 and therefore, A 7,500/- is the amount available for further appropriation. Since the balance to be carried forward to the next accounting year is only A 5,500/- a sum of A 2,000/- (7,500/- less 5,500/-) can be transferred back to Profit and Loss A/c., as excess provision which is not required to be carried forward. So, to retain a balance of A 5,500/ in the provision account, the journal entry will be

Provision for Bad Debts A/c	Dr.	2,000
To Profit and Loss A/c		2,000

Provision for Bad Debts A/c

Dr. *Cr.*

		A			A
31.3.2013	To Bad Debts A/c	1.000	01.4.2012	By Balance b/d	8,500
31.3.2013	To Profit & Loss A/c	2.000			
31.3.2013	To Balance c/d	5,500			
		8,500			8,500

The balance sheet will show the realisable value of sundry debtors.

Balance Sheet of PQR Ltd., as on 31.3.2013

Liabilities	*Assets*	A	A
	Accounts Receivable	1,10,000	
	Less : Provision for Bad Debts	5,500	1,04,500

Recovery for Bad Debts Written Off

Sometimes, an amount written off as bad debts may be subsequently recovered. Any such recovery must be treated as a windfall and transferred to the profit and loss A/c as a gain.

The journal entries will be :

At the time of receipt of the amount

Bank A/c or Cash A/c Dr.

To Bad Debts Recovered A/c

At the end of the financial year,

Bed Debts Recovered A/c Dr.

To Profit and Loss A/c

Provision for Discounts on Accounts Receivable

The organizations which allow the facility of making payments before the due date and enable their debtors to avail of cash discounts, must take into account the possible amount of discounts that may be allowed on closing debtors in the forthcoming year. This is necessary to show the closing debtors at their realisable value.

The principles for creation and maintenance of the provisions for discounts on debtors are the same as those discussed in the section on non-provision for bad debts. The only additional point to be noted is that discounts will be estimated on debts considered goods *i.e.,* closing sundry debtors minus provision for bad debts.

The illustrations given here in clearly explains the methods of maintaining a provision for discounts on debtors. The following details are available for M. Limited.

Year Ending

	31.3.2011 A	*31.3.2012* A	*31.3.2013* A
Accounts Receivable	5,00,000	4,50,000	6,00,00
Discounts		1,000	800

While the company maintains 5% provision for bad debts, it would like to maintain 3% provision for discounts beginning from 31.3.2011.

The entries in the provision for discounts on receivable and the relevant extracts from the balance sheets are shown below :

Provision for Discounts on Accounts Receivable A/c

Dr.			Cr.
	A		A
31.3.2011		31.3.2011	
To Balance c/d	14,250	By Profit and Loss A/c	14,250
	14,250		14,250
31.3.2012		01.4.2011	
To Discount Allowed	1,000	By Balance b/d	14,250
To Profit and Loss A/c	425		
To Balance c/d	12,825		
	14,250		14,250
31.3.2013		01.4.2012	
To Discounts Allowed	8,000	By Balance c/d	12,825
To Balance c/d	17,100	By Profit and Loss A/c	12,275
Total	25,100		25,100

Working Note

31.3.2011

Accounts Receivables	5,00,000
Less : Provision for Bad Debts at 5%	25,000
Debts considered Goods	4,75,000
Provision for discounts on Account Receivable = (3/100) × 4,75,000/-	14,250
31.3.2012	
Accounts Receivable	4,50,000
Less : Provision for Bad Debts at 5%	22,500
Debts considered good	4,27,500
Provision for discount on Account Receivable = (3/100) × 4,27,500/-	12,825
Opening Balance of Provision	14,250
Less : Discounts allowed during the year	1,000
	13,250

Since provision to be carried forward is only A 12,825 an amount of A 425 would be transferred to Profit and Loss A/c as excess provision.

31.3.2013

Accounts Receivable	6,00,000
Less : Provision for Debts at 5%	30,000
Debts considered goods	5,70,000
Provision for discounts on Receivable = (3/100) × 5,70,000	17,100

Opening Balance of Provision	12,825
Less : Discounts allowed	8,000
	4,825

Additional amount to be transferred from
Profit and Loss A/c (17,100 – 4,825) = 12,275

Balance Sheet of M. Ltd., as on 31.3.2011

Assets	*A*	*A*
Accounts Receivable	5,00,000	
Less : Provision for Bad Debts	25,000	
	4,75,000	
Less : Provision for Discounts	14,250	4,60,750

Balance Sheet of M. Ltd., as on 31.3.2012

Assets	*A*	*A*
Accounts Receivable	4,50,000	
Less : Provision for Bad Debts	22,500	
	4,27,500	
Less : Provision for discounts	12,825	4,14,675

Balance Sheet of M. Ltd., as on 31.3.2013

Assets	*A*	*A*
Accounts Receivable	6,00,000	
Less : Provision for Bad Debts	30,000	
	5,70,000	
Less: Provision for Discounts	17,100	5,52,900

Reserve for Discounts on Accounts Payable

Organizations may like to show the sundry creditors in the balance sheet at the net payable value by estimating in advance the amount of cash discounts that may be received at the time of settlement amounts due. This is usually done by creating a reserve for discounts on creditors and then transferring the discounts received to such reserve. Since, income in respect of discounts receivable is recognised in advance, the journal entry for creating the reserve will be :

Reserve for Discount on Accounts Payable A/c Dr.

To Profit and Loss A/c

The following illustration explains the mechanics of maintaining the reserve for discount on creditors.

The following details are available from the books of R. Limited.

Year Ending

	31.3.2011 *A*	*31.3.2012* *A*	*31.3.2013* *A*
Accounts Receivable	2,00,000	3,25,000	2,75,00
Discounts Received		3,200	900

R. Limited would like to maintain a reserve for discount on Accounts Payable at 2% beginning from 31.3.2011.

The reserve account and the relevant extracts from the balance sheet are shown below:

Reserve for Discounts on Accounts Payable A/c

Dr.			*Cr.*
	A		*A*
31.3.2011		31.3.2011	
To Profit and Loss A/c	4,400	By Balance c/d	4,400
	4,400		4,400
01.4.2011		31.3.2012	
To Balance b/d	4,400	By Discounts Received A/c	3,200
31.3.2012			
To Profit and Loss A/c	5,300	By Balance c/d	6,500
	9,700		9,700
01.4.2013		31.3.2013	
To Balance b/d	6,500	By Discounts Received A/c	900
		By Profit and Loss A/c	100
		By Balance c/d	5,500
	6,500		6,500

Working Notes

31.3.2011	
Accounts Payable	2,20,000
Reserve for Discounts on Accounts Payable at 2%	4,400
31.3.2012	
Accounts Payable	3,25,000
Reserve for Discounts at 2%	6,500
Opening Balance of Reserve	4,400
Less : Discounts Received	3,200
	1,200
Additional reserve required = 6,500 – 1,200 =	5,300
31.3.2013	
Accounts Payable	2,75,000
Reserve for Discounts at 2%	5,500
Opening Balance of Reserve	6,500
Less : Discounts Received	900
	5,600

Since the available reserve exceeds the amount to be carried forward, the amount of excess – A 100 will be transferred to the profit and loss account to off–set the income taken in excess in the previous year.

Balance Sheet of R. Limited as on 31.3.2011

Liabilities	A		*Assets*	A
Accounts Payable	2,20,000			
Less : Reserve for Discounts	4,400	2,15,600		

Balance Sheet of R. Limited as on 31.3.2012

Liabilities	A		*Assets*	A
Accounts Payable	3,25,000			
Less : Reserve for Discounts	6,500	3,18,500		

Balance Sheet of R. Limited as on 31.3.2013

Liabilities	A		*Assets*	A
Accounts Payable	2,75,000			
Less : Reserve for Discounts	5,500	2,69,500		

CLOSING ENTRIES

The accounting treatment of the adjustments to be given effect to the various accounts for the preparation of financial statements have been discussed above. The next stage in the preparation of financial statements is the recording of the closing journal entries for the drawing up of the trading and profit and loss accounts. While the balance sheet is a mere listing of the assets and liabilities, the trading and profit and loss account are prepared in the form of ledger accounts and postings can be made into such accounts only if they have been entered in the book of prime entry of Journal. The trading and profit and loss accounts are nominal accounts and all expenses and incomes are transferred to this account. While expenses are shown on the debit side, the incomes are posted on the credit side.

Entries for the Preparation of Trading Account

(*i*) The purchases and sales returns must be transferred to the purchases and sales accounts respectively so that the net purchases and net sales can be determined. The entries for the transfer of returns are,

Purchases Returns A/c Dr.

To Purchases A/c

Sales A/c Dr.

To Sales Returns A/c

(*ii*) For the transfer of opening stock, purchases and other direct expenses such as carriage inwards, wages etc., the entry is

Trading A/c Dr.

To Opening Stock A/c

To Purchase A/c

To Direct Expenses A/c

(*iii*) For the transfer of net sales to trading account, the entry is,

Sales A/c Dr.

To Trading A/c

(*iv*) The balance in the trading account is known and the gross profit/loss is determined. For transferring the gross profit and gross loss to profit and loss account, the entry is :

(*a*) In case of gross profit

Trading A/c Dr.

To Profit and Loss A/c

(*b*) In case of gross loss

Profit and Loss A/c Dr.

To Trading A/c

Entries for Preparation of Profit and Loss Account

(*i*) For transfer of all expenses, other than direct expenses, to profit and loss account the entry is,

Profit and Loss A/c Dr.

To Expenses A/c

(*ii*) For transfer of all income, other than sales and related income, to profit and loss account the entry is,

Income A/c Dr.

To Profit and Loss A/c

(*iii*) The credit balance in the profit and loss account represents the net profit earned and belongs to the proprietors. The entry for the transfer of net profit is,

Profit and Loss A/c Dr.

To Capital A/c

The debit balance in profit and loss account represent the net loss. The entry for the transfer of net loss is

Capital A/c Dr.

To Profit and Loss A/c

Adjustments in the Capital Account

The capital account of the proprietor as shown in the balance sheet should reveal the net amount owing to him by the business as on the closing date. The opening balance of the capital account must be adjusted for :

(*i*) Drawings

(*ii*) Net Profit earned during the year/Net loss occurred during the year

(*iii*) Salary, if any, due to the proprietor

(*iv*) Interest on capital, if any, due to the proprietor

(*v*) Interest on drawings, if any, due from the proprietor

We have already seen the entry needed to transfer the net profit/net loss to the capital account. The entries for the other adjustments will be as under :

For Transfer of drawings,

Capital A/c Dr.

To Drawings A/c

For providing for salary payable to proprietor

Proprietor's Salary A/c Dr.

To Capital A/c

The Proprietor's salary will be shown as an expenses in the profit and loss account.

For interest on capital

Interest on Capital A/c Dr.

To Capital A/c

The interest on capital will be shown as an expenses in the profit and loss account.

For interest on drawings,

Capital A/c Dr.

To Interest on Drawings A/c

The interest on drawings will be shown as an income in the profit and loss account.

While the entries for the adjustment of drawings and net profit/net loss in the capital account are in the nature of closing entries, all other items will be entered in the capital account only with the help of adjusting entries.

With the completion of the posting of adjusting and closing entries in the general ledger, balances will exist only for the assets, liabilities and capital account. These balances will be carried forward to the next accounting period. At the beginning of the subsequent accounting period, when a new general ledger is brought into use, the opening assets and liabilities will be brought into the ledger through an opening journal entry.

The opening journal entry is,

Assets A/c Dr.

To Liabilities A/c

To Capital A/c

CAPITAL AND REVENUE—RECEIPTS AND EXPENDITURES

After explaining the adjusting and closing entries, it would be appropriate to discuss separately the different types of receipts and expenditures whose understanding are useful while preparing the financial statement of a business enterprises.

Expenditure

Expenditure can be classified into three categories :

1. **Capital Expenditure :** It means an expenditure which has been incurred for the purpose of acquiring an asset to be held in business on long term basis which results in increasing the earning capacity of the business. Some examples of capital expenditure are :

   (*a*) Expenditure incurred on the purchase of furniture, plant, copyright, patents, goodwill etc.

   (*b*) Expenditure incurred in increasing the capacity or efficiency of a fixed asset.

(*c*) Expenditure incurred on purchase of shares and debentures of other companies for a long duration.

2. **Revenue Expenditure :** Expenditure incurred in running the business is termed as revenue expenditure. Examples of revenue expenditure are rent, salaries, office expenses, cost of manufacturing and selling the product, repairs, depreciation etc.

Difference Between Capital Expenditure and Revenue Expenditure

The following are the differences between capital and revenue expenditures :

(*i*) Capital expenditures are incurred to acquire fixed assets whereas revenue expenditures are incurred for running the business.

(*ii*) Capital expenditures provide benefits to a firm for more than one accounting year. However, revenue expenditures are meant to provide benefit only in current accounting period.

(*iii*) Capital expenditures aim to enhance the earning capacity of the business through acquisition of fixed assets and increasing the firm capacity. Revenue expenditures focus at maintaining the existing earning capacity.

(*iv*) Capital expenditures are of non-recurring nature. But revenue expenditures are of recurring nature.

(*v*) Capital expenditures may be incurred before the start of the business. However, revenue expenditures are incurred only after the start of the business.

(*vi*) There is no matching between capital expenditures and capital receipts. But matching between revenue receipts and revenue expenditures is always attempted under matching concept.

(*vii*) Capital Expenditure is capitalised while Revenue Expenditure is transferred to the Trading or Profit and Loss Account. In other words, Capital expenditure enter into the Balance Sheet and revenue expenditure enter into the Trading and Profit and Loss Account.

3. **Deferred Revenue Expenditure :** It is that revenue expenditure which is incurred in one accounting period but the benefit of which is available in future periods. Deferred revenue expenditure is also referred to as capitalised revenue expenditure.

According to Guidance Note issued by Institute of Chartered Accountants of India on terms used in financial statements, "deferred revenue expenditure is that expenditure for which payment has been made or a liability incurred but which is carried forward on the presumption that it will be of benefit over a subsequent period or periods". Sometimes, revenue expenditure incurred during the year is very large and it is expected to benefit not only the current year but also subsequent period or periods. As the benefit from this accrues in future periods also, it is not charged to profit and loss account of the current year and it is capitalized. Therefore, it is termed as Capitalized Revenue Expenditure or deferred revenue expenditure. It is written off over a number of years, usually three to five years. Heavy amounts spent on advertising, amount spent on formation of business, development costs in mines and plantations, discount on debentures in limited companies, market research, cost of experiments etc. are normally spread over a period of 3 to 5 years. Another possibility is that heavy losses due to fire, theft, earthquake etc. are not charged to profit and loss account of the current year but spread over a number of years, and that is why it is also called deferred revenue expenditure. A part of deferred revenue expenditure to be written off in a particular accounting year is treated as an expense and transferred to profit and loss account. The portion of the deferred revenue expenditure not written off at the end of the period (and to be written off in the subsequent accounting years) is recorded on assets side of the balance sheet.

Receipts

Receipts are of two types : Capital Receipts and Revenue Receipts.

1. **Capital Receipts :** Capital receipts consist of payments made to the enterprises either by share holders, or by proprietors of business, receipts from sale of fixed assets of a business or loan raised.

   It may be noted here that capital receipt is different from capital profit. For example if the price of machinery costing A 20,000/- is sold for A 21,000/-, there is a capital receipt of A 21,000/- but capital profit is only A 1,000/-. Suppose the same machinery is sold for A 15,000/- then there is a capital receipt of A 15,000/- but there is a capital loss of A 5,000/-

2. **Revenue Receipts :** Any receipt which is not a capital receipt is termed as revenue receipt. Examples of revenue receipts are (*i*) Amount from sale of goods (*ii*) Amount received from rendering services to other parties, interest received, commission received.

   Capital receipts and Capital expenditure is not shown in Trading and Profit and Loss A/c. It is only revenue receipts and revenue expenditure of the current year which are shown in trading and profit and loss account. It may also be noted that capital profit is transferred to Capital Reserve whereas capital loss is charged to profit and loss account of the same year or over a few years in case it occurs in the course of purchase and sale of goods and services and are included in the Profit and Loss A/c., in the year in which they occur.

PREPARING TRADING A/C AND PROFIT AND LOSS ACCOUNT

From the given Trial Balance we can prepare a Profit and Loss Account to determine the profit and loss made by a business organization during a particular period. At the time of preparation of profit and loss account the following may be kept in mind.

All expenses are debited to Profit and Loss A/c

All incomes are credited to Profit and Loss A/c

Balance, if any would be the profit/loss

Further, we may have to give special treatment to adjustment entries also (discussed in detail earlier in the chapter).

In the case of companies the profit is credited to Reserves Account and net loss is debited to Reserves Account in the Balance Sheet. In the case of sole trader and partnership, the net profit is credited to capital account and net loss debited to capital account.

Sometimes, it is possible to first determine the gross profit (arising out of trading operations) and then deduct all administrative and selling expenses from gross profit to determine the net profit. Whether or not a separate Trading Account is prepared to determine gross profit or loss, the Net Profit/Loss remains the same.

It is necessary to emphasis here that Profit and Loss Account (including Trading Account) is prepared on 'Accrual Basis'. In other words all expenses incurred and due are debited to Profit and Loss Account whether they are actually paid for or not. Similarly all incomes earned and due are credited to profit and loss account whether they are actually received or not.

Note that there is no hard and fast rule about segregation of expenses between Trading Account and Profit and Loss Account. The decision about expenses going to Trading A/c and Profit and Loss A/c is based on generally accepted accounting principles. However, in specific circumstances, it may become necessary to adopt a flexible approach. The question of segregation of expenses does not arise where only the Profit and Loss Account is prepared without a separate Trading Account.

Profit and Loss Account may be prepared in the 'T' form or in the vertical form. If the profit and loss is prepared in the vertical form, the revenue are shown first and all expenses are shown as a deduction from the total revenues. A sample of vertical format is shown below:

Profit and Loss Account of ....
for the year ended

Revenue

Sales

Other (Dividends, Interest etc.)

Expenses

Raw Materials Cost

Employee's Remuneration and Benefits

Other Expenses

Depreciation

Profit before Interest

Interest

Profit before Taxation

Income Tax

Net Profit available for appropriation

Appropriation

Interim dividend

Proposed final dividend

Transfer to General Reserve

DIFFERENCE BETWEEN TRADING ACCOUNT AND PROFIT AND LOSS ACCOUNT

The following are the differences between Trading Account and Profit and Loss Account.

Basis	*Trading Account*	*Profit and Loss Account*
1. Purpose	Its purpose is to ascertain gross profit	Its purpose is to ascertain net profit
2. Focus	It aims to focus on highlighting manifacturing efficiency	Its focus is on highlighting overall profitability.
3. Inclusion of Items	The items in this account mainly relate to producing activity undertaken in the factory such as raw materials purchases, wages, other direct expenses necessary for manufacturing. It also shows opening stock, closing stock and sale of finished goods.	This account includes many indirect expenses such as administrative costs, selling and distribution costs, office costs and similar other expenses.
4. Balance Amount	It is transferred to Profit and Loss Account.	The balance in this account is transferred to capital account in Balance Sheet.

PREPARING BALANCE SHEET

What is Balance Sheet?

A balance sheet, also commonly referred to as a statement of financial position, is a statement of assets and liabilities of business enterprises at a particular date. The balance sheet summarises and reveals the financial position of an enterprises on a particular date, by showing what is owns and what it owes. Because the balance sheet is a snap shot as of an instant in time, it is status report rather than flow report.

The balance sheet is a fundamental or first accounting statement in the sense that every accounting transaction can be analysed in terms of its dual impact on the balance Sheet. Moreover, most often, revenues and expenses are defined in terms of changes in assets and liabilities. Thus, a thorough understanding of the nature and measurement of assets and liabilities is needed to understand net income and its components. A Balance Sheet has no debit and credit side. It is a prepared on a particular date and as such, it shows the assets and liabilities of a business enterprises on that date. Even a single transaction will cause a change in the assets and liabilities of the enterprises as shown in the Balance Sheet. Therefore, it is true only for the date on which it has been prepared. It is called Balance Sheet because it is actually a sheet containing balances of ledger accounts which have not been closed by transfer to trading and profit and loss A/c.

The balance sheet is also called a statement of sources of funds (*i.e.,* liabilities or obligations) and utilisation of funds (i.e. assets or resources). The financial position of an enterprise includes its economic resources (assets), economic obligations (liabilities), owner's equity and their relationship to each other on a particular date. The balance sheet reveals an enterprise's resource structure (major classes and amounts of assets) and its financial structure (major classes and amounts of liabilities and equity). The balance sheet is a detailed summary of the basic accounting equation (which must always remain in balance) :

Assets = Liabilities + Owner's Equity

The proper heading of a balance sheet consists of (*a*) the name of organization, (*b*) the title of the statement, and (*c*) the date for which the statement is prepared.

It should be understood that the balance sheet does not aim to show the value of an enterprise. Together with other financial statements and other information, however, it provides information that is useful to external users who desire to make their own estimates of a company's value. More specifically, the Balance Sheet helps in assessing the solvency (liquidity), financial structure and operating capability of a business enterprise.

To sum up, while preparing Trading A/c and Profit and Loss Account and Balance Sheet, the following important points should be noted :

(*i*) Start with a tallied Trial Balance. It provides the arithmetical accuracy of entries made in the books namely Cash Book, Journal and Ledger. However, there are certain errors which are not disclosed by a Trial Balance.

(*ii*) On account of certain errors if the Trial Balance is not tallied, the Suspense Account is opened with the difference of two sides and the same is inserted on the side having difference. If Suspense Account shows :

(*a*) Debit Balance, record on the Asset side of Balance Sheet.

(*b*) Credit Balance, record on the liabilities side of Balance Sheet.

The Suspense Account is closed after rectifying the errors. Real and Personal Accounts items alone are taken to Balance Sheet.

(*iii*) Adjustments given at the end of a trial balance should be given double-entry effect. Otherwise accounts will not be complete. The balance sheet will not tally.

The treatment of adjustments for expenses and incomes in balance sheet is :

(*a*) Outstanding liabilities for expenses shown on liabilities side;

(*b*) Prepaid expenses shown on asset side;

(c) Income received in advance shown on liabilities side;

(d) Income earned but not received, shown on assets side.

(e) Fixed assets are recorded at cost minus depreciation.

(f) Closing stock recorded at cost price or Net realisable value price whichever is less.

Profit and Loss Account may be divided into three components.

Trading Account	To reflect gross profit or loss arising out of trading and manufacturing operations.
Profit and Loss Account	To reflect the net profit or loss of the entire business after duly accounting for all adminis-trative and selling expenses.
Profit and Loss Appropriation Account	To reflect the various appropriations made out of disposable profits like dividends, transfer to reserves etc.

Profit and loss account is prepared for an accounting period. On the other hand a balance sheet is prepared as on a particular day (usually the last day of the accounting period).

ARRANGEMENT OF ASSETS AND LIABILITY ITEMS ON THE BALANCE SHEET

In the case of a company, The Companies Act 1956 provides that balance sheet should be prepared as per schedule VI given therein and assets and liabilities should be written in the sequence (or order) shown in the Schedule. However, in the case of sole proprietorship, and partnership, no rule is provided for recording assets and liabilities on the balance sheet.

Generally, assets and liabilities on a balance sheet may be written on :

(a) Liquidity basis and

(b) Fixity basis

Liquidity basis is that basis where assets and liabilities are arranged according to their realisability and payment preference. Fixity basis is the basis when Assets and Liabilities are arranged in the order of permanence. Proforma of balance sheet on liquidity basis and fixity basis are given below :

Proforma of a Balance Sheet (in order of Liquidity/Liquidity Basis)

Balance Sheet as at..........................

Liabilities			*Assets*
Current Liabilities :		**Current Assets :**	
Bank Overdraft	–	Cash in Hand	–
Outstanding Expenses	–	Cash at Bank	–
Bills Payable	–	Prepaid Expenses	–
Sundry Creditors	–	Sundry Debtors	–
Income Received in Advance	–	Accrued Income	–
		Bills Receivable	–
		Stock (closing)	–

Liabilities		Assets	
Fixed or Non-Current Liabilities :		**Non-Current Assets (Fixed Assets) :**	
Loan	–	Investment	–
Capital	–	Furniture and Fixture	–
Opening Balance	–	Plant and Machinery	–
Add : Net Profit (less Loss)	–	Loose Tools	–
Less : Drawing	–	Building	–
		Land	–
		Goodwill	–

Proforma of Balance Sheet
(In order of Permanence/Fixity Basis)

Balance Sheet as at........................

Liabilities		*Assets*	
Capital :		**Non-Current Assets/Fixed Assets :**	
Opening Balance	–	Goodwill	–
Add : Net Profit (Less Loss)	–	Land	–
Less : Drawings	–	Building	
		Plant and Machinery	–
Non-Current/Fixed Liabilities		Loose Tools	–
		Furniture and Fixture	–
Loan	–	Investments	–
Current Liabilities :		**Current Assets :**	
Income Received in Advance	–	Stock (Closing)	–
		Accrued Income	–
Sundry Creditors	–	Sundry Debtors	–
Bills Payable	–	Prepaid Expenses	–
Outstanding Expenses	–	Bills Receivable	–
Bank Overdraft	–	Cash at Bank	–
		Cash in Hand	

ADJUSTMENT ITEMS

Treatment of various types of items that require adjustments for the preparation of Balance Sheet are given as under :

Items	*Adjusting Entry*	*Treatment in Balance Sheet*
1. Outstanding expenses	Expenses A/c Dr. To Outstanding Exp., A/c.	Shown on the Liabilities side
2. Prepaid Expenses	Prepaid Expenses A/c Dr. To Expenses A/c.	Shown on the Asset side
3. Closing Stock	Closing Stock Dr. To Trading A/c	Shown on the Asset Side
4. Accrued Income	Accrued Income A/c Dr. To Income A/c	Shown on the Asset Side

Items	Adjusting Entry	Treatment in Balance Sheet
5. Depreciation	(*a*) Depreciation A/c. Dr. To Assets A/c (*b*) Depreciation A/c. Dr. To Provision for depreciation A/c	Shown by way of deduction from the value of the Asset on the Asset side
6. Income Received in Advance	Income A/c Dr. To Income Received in Advance A/c	Shown on the Liabilities side
7. Provision for Bad Debts	Profit and Loss A/c. Dr. To Provision for Bad Debts	Deducted from Sundry Debtors on the Assets side
8. Provision for Discount	Profit and Loss A/c Dr. To Provision for Discount on Debtors	Deducted from Sundry Debtors on the Asset side
9. Reserve for Discount on Creditors	Reserve for Discount on Creditors A/c Dr. To Profit and Loss A/c	Shown by way of deduction from Sundry Creditors.

LIMITATIONS OF BALANCE SHEET

A balance sheet contains useful information about liquidity, operating capability and financial flexibility of an enterprise and thus, is very useful to external users and others in making sound investment decisions. However, inspite of being a useful financial statement, it has some limitations.

Balance Sheet is considered to be a static document and it reflects the position of the concern at a given date. The real position of the concern may be changing day-to-day and the same is not depicted in Balance Sheet.

Balance Sheet is not a valuation statement. The values shown in it are not real values of Assets. Thus, the exact position of the business cannot be gauged from balance sheet.

A Balance Sheet is prepared based on certain accounting policies. Such policies relate to inventory valuation (*i.e.,* closing stock), depreciation etc. Inventory may be valued using several methods like First-in-First Out (FIFO), Last-in-First-Out (LIFO), weighted average cost etc. Similarly, depreciation may be provided using straight line method or written down value method. The management may select accounting policies which may not reflect real financial position.

Similarly, accounting policies may differ from company to company in respect of accounting for prepaid expenses, prior period adjustments, classification between revenue and capital expenditure, writing-off preliminary expenses etc. These may affect the comparability of financial statements among the business enterprises.

Management may follow accounting procedures and treatments which may result into window dressing of Balance Sheets with a view to forecast a better picture to shareholders, bankers and financial institutions. Window-dressing is accomplished in general ways, say, by not making adequate provisions (though prudence would require them) for expenses and potential losses, by recognizing income even before its actual accrual, by suppressing vital information, etc.

PROVISIONS, CONTINGENT LIABILITIES AND CONTINGENT ASSETS

Provisions

Provision is a liability, which can be measured only by using a substantial degree of estimation.

In order to become provision there must be a liability. A liability is present obligation of the enterprise arising from past events, the settlement of which is expected to result in an outflow from the enterprise of resources implying economic benefits.

The characteristics of provision are as under :

- Provision is a liability.
- A Liability is a present obligation, not future obligation.
- Settlement of liability should result in an outflow from enterprise of resources.
- Liability is a result of obligating event.

Contingent Liabilities

As per the Accounting Standard 29, a contingent liability is a possible obligation that arises from past event and existence of which will be confirmed only by the occurrence or non-occurrence of one or more uncertain future events not wholly within the control of the enterprises.

To be called contingent liability, the following conditions must be fulfilled—

(*i*) Possible obligation is as a result of past event.

(*ii*) Existence of possible obligation creating contingent liability is confirmed only by the occurrence or non-occurrence of future event.

(*iii*) Future event is not wholly within the control of the enterprises.

Contingent Assets

As per AS-29, contingent asset is a possible asset that arises from past events the existence of which will be confirmed only by the occurrence or non-occurrence of one or more uncertain future events not wholly within control of the enterprise.

To be called a 'Contingent Asset', the following conditions must be fulfilled—

(*i*) Possible asset as a result of past events.

(*ii*) Existence of contingent assets is to be confirmed by occurrence and non-occurrence of one or more future events.

(*iii*) Future event is not wholly within the control of the enterprise.

Example

Reliance Industries Ltd., has filed the damages case of A 5 crores against X Ltd., for not supplying the quantity and quality of raw materials as per order, chances of winnning the case by the Reliance Industries Ltd., is probable.

To test the event for contingent asset it should satisfy the following conditions :

(*a*) Possible assets as a result of past events—possible assets are A 5 crores because if Reliance Industries wins the case, it will get A 5 crores.

(*b*) As a result of past event–for non-supply of raw materials as per order.

(*c*) Existence will be confirmed by the future event–court order.

(*d*) Future event not controlled–Reliance Industries Ltd., cannot control the court order.

Hence, suit for A 5 crore damages is contingent asset for Reliance Industries Ltd.

DISTINCTION BETWEEN TRIAL BALANCE AND BALANCE SHEET

The following are the differences between trial balance and balance sheet.

Basis	*Balance Sheet*	*Trial Balance*
1. Objective	The objective of balance sheet is to show financial position of a business firm.	It is prepared to check the arithmetical accuracy of business transactions.
2. Structure	Balance sheet has two sides : one side displays asset and the other liabilities	It has two columns : one column shows debit balances and the other credit balances.
3. Subject matter	Balance Sheet shows only personal and real accounts of asset and liability items.	All the accounts resulting from journalization and ledger posting are found in trials balance
4. Preparation	Balance sheet is prepared generally at the end of an accounting year.	A trial balance is prepared whenever desired, say every month.
5. Focal point	Balance sheet indicates business performance and liquidity and net worth of a business firm.	Trial Balance has no objective of indicating performance, liquidity or net worth of a business enterprise.
6. Essentiality	Balance sheet is a basic and legally required statement to be prepared	Trial balance is not considered financial statement and is not legally required. However, by nature and importance it is an indispensable document.
7. Relationship	Balance Sheet is related with profit and loss account and is prepared after Profit & Loss account.	Profit and Loss account is prepared with the help of trial balance.
8. Adjustment items	Balance sheet is prepared considering adjustment items.	Trial balance is prepared without any consideration of adjustment items.

Example 1

Find out the missing figure :

Opening	A	50,000
Closing Stock	A	70,000
Sales	A	5,60,000
Carriage Inward	A	10,000
Purchases		**?**
Gross Profit	A	25% on Sales

Solution

Purchases are calculated as balancing figure of the Trading A/c prepared as under :

Trading Account

Dr. *Cr.*

Particulars	*Amount (A)*	*Particulars*	*Amount (A)*
31.03.2012		01.4.2011	
To Opening Stock	50,000	By Sales	5,60,000
To Purchases (*Bal.Fig.)*	4,30,000	By Closing Stock	70,000
To Carriage Inward	10,000		

To Gross Profit $\frac{25}{100}$ 5, 60, 000	1,40,000		
	6,30,000		6,30,000

Ans. : Purchases A 4,30,000

Example 2

From the following particulars, calculate :

(*i*) Cash paid to sundry creditors during the year.

(*ii*) Cash received from sundry debtors during the year.

	(*A*)
Opening creditors	20,600
Closing creditors	34,800
Opening debtors	66,400
Closing debtors	37,400
Opening stock	50,000
Closing stock	40,000
Purchased during the year	1,40,000
Discount allowed by creditors	800
Discount allowed to customers	1,000
Bills payable issued to creditors	20,000
Bills receivable received from customers	35,000
Bills receivable dishonoured	2,000

The rate of gross profit is 25% on selling prices. Of the total sales, A 35,000 were for cash.

Solution.

(*i*) Sundry Creditors Account

Dr. *Cr.*

Particulars	*Amount (A)*	*Particulars*	*Amount (A)*
To Discount	800	By Balance b/d	20,600
To Bills Payable	20,000	By Purchases A/c	1,40,000
To Cash A/c (Bal. Figure)	1,05,000		
To Balance c/d	34,800		
	1,60,600		1,60,600
Cash Paid to Creditors	1,05,000		

(ii) Sundry Debtors Account

Dr. Cr.

Particulars	Amount (A)	Particulars	Amount (A)
To Balance b/d	66,400	By Discount A/c	1,000
To Credit Sales*	1,65,000	By Bills Receivable A/c	35,000
To Bills Receivable A/c	2,000	By Cash A/c	1,60,000
(Dishonoured)		By Balance c/d	37,400
	2,33,400		2,33,400

***Calculation of Credit Sales**

	A
Opening Stock	50,000
Add : Purchases	1,40,000
	1,90,000
Less : Closing Stock	40,000
	1,50,000
Add : Gross Profit (25% on selling price or 33½ on cost)	50,000
Total Sales	2,00,000
Less : Cash Sales	35,000
Credit Sales	1,65,000

Example 3

On 1st January, 2011 the reserve for Doubtful Debts account showed a balance of A 10,000. During the year the bad debts written off amounted to A 10,000/- and the Sundry Debtors at the end stood at A 2,40,000/- on which the provision for doubtful debts was to be 5%.

During 2012 the bad debts written off amounted to A 4,000/- and the closing balance of debtors was A 1,40,000/-. The concern continued to provide for doubtful debts at 5% on closing balance of debtors.

Show the provisions for doubtful debts account for 2011 and 2012. All bad debts written off are adjusted through the Provision Account.

Solution

Provision for Doubtful Debts A/c

Date	Particulars	Amount (A)	Date	Particulars	Amount (A)
Dec.31			Jan.1		
2011	To Bad Debts written off	10,000	2011	By Balance (given)	10,000
Dec.31	To Balance (Closing)	12,000	Dec.31	By Profit and Loss A/c	12,000
	(5/100 × 2,40,000)			(Bal. Fig.)	
		22,000			22,000
2012			2012		
Dec.31	To Bad Debts	4,000	Jan.1	By Balance b/d	12,000
Dec.31	To Balance (Closing)	7,000			

	(5/100 × 1,40,000)				
Dec.31	To PandL A/c (Bal.Fig)	1,000			
		12,000			12,000

Example 4

There were A 2,500 bad debts during the year ended 31st March, 2012. An amount of A 3,000 for provision of bad debts is brought forward from last year. During the year ended at 31st March, 2012 provision of A 1,750/- was made for bad and doubtful debts. Prepare bad debts account and provision for bad and doubtful debts account.

Solution

Bad Debt A/c

Date	*Particulars*	*Amount (A)*	*Date*	*Particulars*	*Amount (A)*
2012			**2012**		
Mar.31	To Balance (Given)	2,500	Mar.31	By Provision for Bad Debts	2,500
		2,500			2,500

Provision for Bad and Doubtful Debts A/c

Date	*Particulars*	*Amount (A)*	*Date*	*Particulars*	*Amount (A)*
2012			Apr.2011	By Balance b/d	3,000
Mar.31	To Bad Debts	2,500	2012	By P and L A/c	1,250
Mar.31	To Balance (Closing)	1,750	Mar. 31	(Bal. Fig)	
		4,250			4,250

Example 5

The following figures appear in the books of a firm :

Provision for doubtful debts on 01.01.2012	A 6,500
Bad debts written off during the year	A 4,000

Sundry Debtors on 31.12.2012 A 75,000. Of the sundry debtors A 2,000 was bad and the provision for doubtful debts was to be maintained at 5% on sundry debtors. Pass Journal entries.

Solution

Journal Entries

S.No.	*Particulars*	*Dr. Amount (A)*	*Cr. Amount (A)*
1.	Bad Debts A/c Dr.	4,000	
	To Sundry Debtors A/c		4,000
	(Being bad debts provided on debtors)		
2.	Provision for bad and Doubtful Debts A/c Dr.	4,000	
	To Bad Debts A/c		4,000
	(Being bad debts transferred)		

3.	Profit and Loss A/c Dr. To Provision for Doubtful Debts A/c (Being provision on debtors transferred to P and L A/c.)	3,650	3,650
4.	Provision for Bad and Doubtful Debts A/c Dr. To Profit and Loss A/c (Being amount transferred to P and L A/c and Provision for doubtful debts)	1,150	1,150

Example 6

The following balances appear in the trial balance of Joshi and Co., relating to the accounts for the year ending December 31, 2012.

Wages A/c	A 30,000
Salaries A/c	A 40,000
Rent A/c	A 5,000
Advertising A/c	A 17,000

It is found that following adjustments have not been made in the books.

1.	Wages due but not paid	A 3,000
2.	Salaries paid in advance	A 2,000
3.	Unpaid Rent	A 1,000
4.	Advertising expenses not recorded in the books	A 2,000

You are required to pass necessary journal entries to adjust these items. Also show how these items would appear in trading and profit and loss accounts and Balance Sheet.

Solution

Journal Entries

S.No.	*Particulars*		*Dr. Amount (A)*	*Cr. Amount (A)*
1.	Wages A/c To Outstanding Wages A/c (Being the amount of outstanding wages)	Dr.	3,000	3,000
2.	Prepaid Salaries A/c Salaries A/c (Being the salaries paid in advance)	Dr.	2,000	2,000
3.	Rent A/c To Outstanding Rent A/c (Being the amount of rent outstanding)	Dr.	1,000	1,000
4.	Advertising A/c To Outstanding Advertising A/c (Being the amount of Advertising Outstanding)	Dr.	2,000 2,000	

Profit and Loss Account
For the year ended Dec. 31, 2012

		Amount A		Amount A
Wages	30,000			
Add : Outstanding	3,000	33,000		
Salaries	40,000			
Less : Paid in advance	2,000	38,000		
Rent	5,000			
Add : Unpaid	1,000	6,000		
Advertising	17,000			
Add : Unpaid	2,000	19,000		

Balance Sheet
As on 31 Dec., 2012

Liabilities	(*A*)	*Assets*	(*A*)
Outstanding Expenses :		Prepaid Expenses :	
Wages	3,000	Salaries	2,000
Rent	1,000		
Advertising	2,000		

Example 7

In a firm a shortage of stock has arisen during the year ended September 20, 2012. The firm gathers the following information :

Opening Stock	=	A 87,500
Purchases	=	A 2,87,500
Closing Stock (on physical verification)	=	A 50,000

The goods are sold at a uniform mark-up of 20 per cent on selling price. The following details regarding Sundry Debtors are available :

Balance as on 01.10.2012	30,000
Balance as on 30.09.2013	27,500
Cash and Cheques received from customers in the year	3,90,000
Sales Returns	12,500

Find out the shortage of stock.

Solution

Sundry Debtors A/c

Dr. **(*Amount in A*)** *Cr.*

Particulars	(*A*)	*Particulars*	(*A*)
To Balance b/d	30,000	By Sales Returns	12,500
To Sales (Balancing Fig.)	4,00,000	By Cash and Bank	3,90,000
		By Balanced c/d	27,500
	4,30,000		4,30,000

Memorandum Trading Account

Particulars	*(A)*	*Particulars*	*(A)*
To Opening Stock	87,500	By Sales	4,00,000
To Purchase	2,87,500	By Closing Stock	55,000
To Gross Profit	80,000		
@ 20% of A 4,00,000			
	4,55,000		4,55,000
Closing Stock	55,000		
Less: Physical Stock	50,000		
Shortage of Stock	5,000		

Example 8

The stock held by a firm at their godown were completely damaged by fire on February 1, 2013

The books of accounts, show the following information :

	(A)
Sales - year ended December 31, 2012	2,00,000
Sales - January 2013	50,000
Purchases - year ended December, 2012	1,25,000
Purchases - January 2013	20,000
Stocks - 01.01.2012	37,500
Stocks - 31.12.2012	25,000

Taking the gross profit ratio to be constant from 2012 to January, 2013 ascertain the insurance claim for inventory.

Solution

Workings

Gross Profit for the year ended December 31, 2012 = A 2,00,000 + 25,000 – (1,25,000 + 37,500) = A 62,500

Gross Profit margin (ratio) = $\frac{62,500 \quad 100}{2,00,000}$ 31.25%

Gross Profit earned during Jan. 2013 = A 50,000 × 31.25% = A 15,625

Value of Closing Stock as on Jan. 31, 2013 = A (25,000 + 20,000 + 15,625 – 50,000)

= A 10,625

Ans. : A 10,625.

Example 9

From the following particulars, ascertain the amount of credit sales and credit purchases for the year ended 31st March, 2006 :

	A
Total Creditors 1.4.2005	4,00,000
Total Debtors 1.4.2005	7,00,000
Cash received from customers	14,50,000
Received for Bills Receivable	80,000
Paid to Sundry Creditors	5,60,000
Bills Payable met	1,20,000
Discount allowed to customers	20,000
Discount earned	10,000
Sales Returns	60,000
Purchases Returns	80,000
Bad debts	30,000
Total Creditors 31.3.2006	9,20,000
Total Debtors 31.3.2006	8,80,000
Bills Receivables 1.4.2005	60,000
Bills Payable 1.4.2005	1,40,000
Bills Receivable 31.3.2006	1,80,000
Bills Payable 31.3.2006	1,00,000

Solution

Total Debtors Account

Dr. *Cr.*

Date	*Particulars*	*Amount (A)*	*Date*	*Particulars*	*Amount (A)*
01.4.05	To Balance b/d	7,00,000		By Cash A/c	14,50,000
	To Sales (Credit)			By Discount allowed A/c	20,000
	(Bal. Fig.)	19,40,000		By Sales Returns A/c	60,000
				By Bad Debts	30,000
				By Bills Receivable A/c*	2,00,000
			31.3.06	By Balance b/d	8,80,000
		26,40,000			26,40,000

*Bills receivable received from sundry debtors during the year have been found out by preparing Bills Receivable Accounts, which is as follows :

Bills Receivable Account

Dr. *Cr.*

Date	*Particulars*	*Amount (A)*	*Date*	*Particulars*	*Amount (A)*
1.4.05	To Balance b/d	60,000		By Cash A/c	80,000
	To Total Debtors A/c	2,00,000	31.3.06	By Balance c/d	1,80,000
	(Bal. Fig.)				
		2,60,000			2,60,000

Total Creditors Account

Dr. Cr.

Date	Particulars	Amount (A)	Date	Particulars	Amount (A)
	To Cash A/c	5,60,000	1.4.05	By Balance b/d	4,00,000
	To Discount A/c	10,000		By Purchases (Credit) (Bal. Fig.)	12,50,000
	To Purchases Returns	80,000			
	To Bills Payable A/c* (accepted during the year)	80,000			
31.3.06	To Balance c/d	9,20,000			
		16,50,000			16,50,000

*Bills payable accepted and given to creditors during the year have been computed by preparing Bills Payable A/c which is as given below :

Bills Payable A/c

Dr. Cr.

Date	Particulars	Amount (A)	Date	Particulars	Amount (A)
	To Cash A/c	1,20,000	1.4.05	By Balance b/d	1,40,000
31.3.06	To Balance c/d	1,00,000		By Total Creditors A/c (Bills Payable accepted during the year) (Bal. Fig)	80,000
		2,20,000			2,20,000

Example 10

From the Trial Balance of 31.3.2001 and additional information given, prepare Trading and Profit and Loss Account and Balance Sheet as on 31.03.2001 :

Trial Balance

Particulars	Dr. Amount (A)	Cr. Amount (A)
Capital	–	4,00,000
Drawings	50,000	–
Opening Stock	75,000	–
Purchases	4,20,000	–
Sundry Creditors	–	75,000
Sundry Debtors	1,20,000	–
Sales	–	8,10,000
Discounts	16,000	18,000

Commissions	12,000	14,000
Returns	16,000	20,000
Salaries	1,20,000	–
Rent, Rates and Taxes	40,000	–
Postage, Telegrams and Telephone	25,000	–
Loan	–	3,10,000
Interest	20,000	–
Furniture	3,50,000	–
Brand Names and Designs (Patents)	60,000	–
Advertisement	1,00,000	–
Cash in Hand	1,50,000	
Cash in Bank	63,000	
Frieght Inward	20,000	
Duty Drawbacks (Income)	–	10,000
	16,57,000	16,57,000

Other Information

(*i*) Closing Stock A 1,70,000.

(*ii*) Sales included Sales Tax A 50,000

(*iii*) Depreciate Furniture @ 10%

(*iv*) Write-off Brand Names and Designs @ 20%.

(*v*) Advertisement to be written-off in 5 years.

(*vi*) Salaries outstanding A 12,000 and Salaries paid in Advance A 10,000

Solution

Trading and Profit and Loss Account
for the year ended 31.3.2001

Dr. *Cr.*

Particulars		*Amount (A)*	*Particulars*		*Amount (A)*
To Opening Stock		75,000	**By Sales**	8,10,000	
To Purchases	4,20,000		*Less:* Returns	16,000	
Add: Freight Inward	20,000			7,94,000	
	4,40,000		*Less:* Sales tax	50,000	7,44,000
Less: Returns	20,000		By Closing Stock		1,70,000
	4,20,000				
Less: Duty Drawback*	10,000	4,10,000			
To Gross Profit transferred		4,29,000			
		9,14,000			9,14,000

To Salaries	1,20,000		By Gross Profit	4,29,000
Add: Outstanding	12,000		By Discount Received	18,000
	1,32,000		By Commission Received	14,000
Less : Paid in Advance	10,000	1,22,000		
To Rent, Rates and Taxes		40,000		
To Postage, Telegrams and Telephone		25,000		
To Discount allowed		16,000		
To Commission allowed		12,000		
To Interest		20,000		
To Depreciation on Furniture		35,000		
To Amortization of Brand Names and Designs		12,000		
To Amortization of Advertisement (1/5 of A 1,00,000)		20,000		
To Net Profit Transferred to Capital A/c		1,59,000		
		4,61,000		4,61,000

Balance Sheet as on 31st March, 2001

Liabilities		*Amount (A)*	*Assets*		*Amount (A)*
Capital	4,00,000		Furniture	3,50,000	
Add: Net Profit	1,59,000		*Less:* Depreciation	35,000	3,15,000
	5,59,000		Brand Names and Design	60,000	
Less : Drawings	50,000	5,09,000	*Less :* Amortization	12,000	48,000
Loan		3,10,000	Advertisement	1,00,000	
Sundry Creditors		75,000	*Less :* Amortization	20,000	80,000
Outstanding Salaries		12,000	Closing Stock		1,70,000
Provision for Sales-tax Liability		50,000	Sundry Debtors		1,20,000
			Prepaid Salaries		10,000
			Cash in Bank		63,000
			Cash in Hand		1,50,000
		9,56,000			9,56,000

Duty Drawback : This is paid to exporter as an incentive. It is duty levied on purchases and is returned subsequently. This can be treated as income or alternatively can be deducted from purchases.

Example 11

From the following Trial Balance of Shishir, you are required to prepare Final Accounts for the year ended 31 March, 2003 after making the necessary adjustments.

Particulars	*Dr. Amount (A)*	*Cr. Amount (A)*
Capital and Drawings Accounts	10,000	2,00,000
Freehold Property	60,000	–
Plant and Machinery	1,00,000	–
Salaries	14,000	–
Printing and Stationery	2,000	–
Furniture and Fixtures	4,000	–
Discount	1,500	
Bills Payable	–	5,700
Debtors and Creditors	25,000	40,000
Insurance	3,000	–
Bad Debts	600	–
Office Rent	2,600	–
Loose Tools	2,000	–
Provision for Doubtful Debts	–	4,800
Loan to Sudhir @ 10% on 1st October, 2002	40,000	–
Interest on loan to Sudhir	–	1,000
Cash at Bank	25,000	–
Cash in Hand	10,500	–
Stock – 31st March, 2003	74,000	–
Trading Profits	–	1,17,200
Outstanding Wages on 31st March, 2003	–	500
Insurance Claim received for Loss of Goods	–	5,000
Total	3,74,200	3,74,200

Adjustments

(*i*) Outstanding Salaries A 700.

(*ii*) Prepaid Insurance A 400.

(*iii*) Value of Loose Tools on 31st March, 2003 – A 1,500.

(*iv*) A new machinery was purchased on credit and installed on 31st December, 2002 costing A 15,000. No entry for the same has yet been made in the books.

(*v*) Depreciate (on closing Balance) – Plant and Machinery at 10 per cent, Furniture and Fixtures at 5 per cent.

(*vi*) The provision for doubtful debts is to be maintained at 5 per cent on debtors.

Solution

Profit and Loss Account of Mr. Shishir
for the year ending 31.3.2003

Dr. Particulars		Amount (A)	Particulars		*Cr.* Amount (A)
To Salaries	14,000		By Trading A/c		
Add : Outstanding	700	14,700	(Trading Profit)		1,17,200
To Printing and Stationery		2,000	By Interest on loan	1,000	
To Discount		1,500	*Add* : Accrued	1,000	2,000
To Insurance	3,000		By Insurance Claim Received		5,000
Less : Prepaid	400	2,600	By Provision for Doubtful		
To Bad Debts		600	Debts (31.03.2002)	4,800	
To Office Rent		2,600	*Less* : Provision required		
To Depreciation on :			(5% of A 25,000)	1,250	3,550
Loose Tools	500				
Plant Machinery	11,500				
[1,15,000 × 10/100]					
Furniture and Fixtures	200	12,200			
[4000 × 5/100]					
To Net Profit transferred		91,550			
		1,27,750			1,27,750

Balance Sheet as at 31st March, 2003

Liabilities		Amount (A)	Assets		Amount (A)
Capital	2,00,000		Freehold Property		60,000
Add : Net Profit	91,550		Plant and Machinery	1,00,000	
	2,91,550		Additions	15,000	
				1,15,000	
Less : Drawings	10,000	2,81,550	*Less* : Depreciation	11,500	1,03,500
Bills Payable		5,700	Furniture and Fixtures	4,000	
Creditors		40,000	*Less* : Depreciation	200	3,800
Creditors for Machinery		15,000	Loose Tools	2,000	
			Less : Depreciation	500	1500
Outstanding Wages		500	Debtors	25,000	
Outstanding Salaries		700	*Less* : Provision	1,250	23,750
			Loan to Sudhir	40,000	
			Add : Interest Accrued	1,000	41,000
			Cash at Bank		25,000
			Cash in Hand		10,500
			Stock		74,000
			Prepaid Insurance		400
		3,43,450			3,43,450

Example 12

The following balances were taken from the books of Shri Ram Prasad on 31st March 2003.

	(A)		(A)
Capital Account	1,00,000	Rent (Cr.	2,100
Drawings	17,600	Railway freight and other	
Purchases	80,000	expenses on goods sold	16,940
Sales	1,40,370	Carriage Inwards	2,310
Purchase Returns	2,820	Office Expenses	1,340
Opening Stock	11,460	Printing and Stationery	660
Bad Debts	1,400	Postage and Telegrams	820
Bad Debts Provision		Sundry Debtors	62,070
(Ist April, 2002)	3,240	Sundry Creditors	18,920
Rates and Insurance	1,300	Cash at Bank	12,400
Discount (Cr.)	190	Cash in Hand	2,210
Bills Receivable	1,240	Office Furniture	3,500
Sales Returns	4,240	Salary and Commission	9,870
Wages	6,280	Additions to Buildings	7,000
Buildings	25,000		

Prepare Trading, Profit and Loss Account for the year ending 31st March 2003 and Balance Sheet as on 31st March, 2003, after keeping in view these adjustments :

1. Depreciate Old Building @ 2½ % and New Addition to Building @ 2% and office furniture @ 5%.
2. Write off further Bad debts A 570.
3. Increase the Bad Debts Provision to 6% of Debtors.
4. On 31st March, 2003 A 570 was outstanding for salaries.
5. Rent receivable A 200.
6. Interest on Capital at 5%.
7. On 31st March, 2003 stock is valued at A 14,290.
8. Unexpired insurance A 240.

Solution

Trading and Profit and Loss Account
for the year ending 31st March, 2003

Dr. *Cr.*

Particulars		*Amount* (A)	*Particulars*		*Amount* (A)
To Opening Stock		11,460	By Sales	1,40,370	
To Purchase	80,000		*Less* : Returns	4,240	1,36,130
Less : Returns	2,820	77,180	By Gross Profit		14,290
To Wages		6,280			
To Carriage Inwards		2,310			
To Gross Profit c/d		53,190			
		1,50,420			1,50,420

Particulars		Amount (A)	Particulars		Amount (A)
To Salaries and Commission	9,870		By Gross Profit b/d		53,190
Add : Salary outstanding	570	10,440	By Rent	2,100	
To Rates and Insurance	1,300		*Add*: Rent Receivable	200	2,300
Less : Unexpired insurance	240	1,060	By Discount		190
To Railway Freight and other Expenses on sales		16,940			
To Office Expenses		1,340			
To Printing and Stationery		660			
To Postage and Telegrams		820			
To Bad debts	1,400				
Add : Further Bad Debts	570				
Add : Provision for Bad debts	3,690				
	5,660				
Less : Old Provision	3,240	2,420			
To Interest on Capital		5,000			
To Depreciation :					
Building (625 + 140)	765				
Office Furniture	175	940			
To Net Profit transferred to Capital A/c		16,060			
		55,680			55,680

Balance Sheet
as at 31st March, 2003

Liabilities		Amount (A)	Assets		Amount (A)
Creditors		18,920	Cash in hand		2,210
Salaries Outstanding		570	Cash at Bank		12,400
Capital	1,00,000		Bills Receivable		1,240
Add : Interest on Capital	5,000		Debtors	62,070	
Add : Net Profit	16,060		*Less* : Further Bad Debts	570	
	1,21,060			61,500	
Less : Drawings	17,600	1,03,460	*Less* : Provision	3,690	57,810
			Closing stock		14,290
			Accrued Rent		200
			Unexpired Insurance		240

Liabilities	Amount (A)	Assets		Amount (A)
		Office Furniture	3,500	
		Less : Depreciation	175	3,325
		Building	25,000	
		Add : Additions	7,000	
			32,000	
		Less : Depreciation	765	31,253
	1,22,950			1,22,950

Example 13

From the following balances taken from the ledgers of Krishna on 31st March, 2005, prepare the Trading and profit and Loss Account for the year ending 31st March, 2005 and the Balance Sheet on that date :

Particulars	Amount (A)	Particulars	Amount (A)
Sundry Creditors	19,000	Bad Debts	100
Building	15,000	Loan from Ram	2,500
Income Tax	1,025	Sundry Debtors	9,500
Loose Tools	1,000	Investments	6,500
Cash at bank	16,200	Bad Debts reserve	1,600
Sundry Expenses	1,990	Rent and Rates	850
Bank Interest (Credit)	75	Furniture	3,000
Purchases	1,57,000	Stock (01.4.2004)	27,350
Wages	10,000	Capital	47,390
Carriage Inwards	1,120	Discount Allowed	630
Sales	1,85,000	Discount Received	535
Motor Van	12,500	Drawings	2,000
Cash in hand	335	Bills Payable	10,000

Adjustments

(*i*) Write off further A 300 as bad debts and create a provision for bad debts at 20% on debtors.

(*ii*) Dividend accrued and due on investments is A 135. Rates paid in advance A 100 and wages owing A 450.

(*iii*) On 31.3.2005 stock was valued at A 15,000 and loose tools were valued at A 800.

(*iv*) Write off 5% for depreciation on buildings and 40% on motor van.

(*v*) Provide for interest at 12% p.a. due on loan taken on 01.6.2004.

(*vi*) Manager is entitled to a commission of 5% on net profits after charging his commission.

Solution

Trading and Profit and Loss Account
for the year ending 31st March, 2005

Dr. *Cr.*

Particulars		*Amount (A)*	*Particulars*	*Amount (A)*
To Opening Stock		27,350	By Sales	1,85,000
To Purchases		1,57,000	By Closing Stock	15,000
To Wages	10,000			
Add : Outstanding	450	10,450		
To Carriage Inwards		1,120		
To Gross Profit c/d		4,080		
		2,00,000		2,00,000
To Sundry Expenses		1,990	By Gross Profit b/d	4,080
To Outstanding Interest			By Discount Received	535
on loan from Ram		250	By Dividend Accrued	135
Rs. 2, 500 $\frac{10}{12}$ $\frac{12}{100}$			By Bank Interest	75
To Bad Debts	100		By Net Loss (T/f to Capital A/c)	5,385
Add : Further Bad Debts	300			
Add : Provision for Bad Debts (New)	1,840			
	2,240			
Less : Old Bad Debts Reserve	1,600	640		
To Rent and Rates	850			
Less : Prepaid Rates	100	750		
To Discount Allowed		630		
To Depreciation :				
Loose Tools	200			
Buildings	750			
Motor Van	5,000	5,950		
		10,210		10,210

Balance Sheet *as on 31st March, 2005*

Liabilities		*Amount (A)*	*Assets*		*Amount (A)*
Sundry Creditors		19,000	Cash in Hand		335
Loan from Ram	2,500		Cash at Bank		16,200
Add : o/s Interest	250	2,750	Sundry Debtors	9,500	
Bills Payable		10,000	*Less* : Further Bad Debts	300	
Wages Outstanding		450		9,200	
Capital	47,390				
Less :			*Less* : New Provision	1,840	7,360
Income Tax	1,025		Closing Stock		15,000

Liabilities			Amount (A)	Assets		Amount (A)
Drawings		2,000		Investments		6,500
Net Loss	5,385	8,410	38,980	Dividend Accrued		135
				Loose Tools	1,000	
				Less : Depreciation	200	800
				Motor Van	12,500	
				Less : Depreciation	5,000	7,500
				Furniture		3,000
				Building	15,000	
				Less : Depreciation	750	14,250
				Rate Prepaid		100
			71,180			71,180

Note : As there is net loss, the manager is not entitled to commission.

Example 14

From the following Trial Balance of a trader on March 31st, 2005, prepare Trading and profit and Loss Account for the year ending 31st March, 2005 and Balance Sheet as at that date after giving effect to the undermentioned adjustments :

Debit Balances	Amount (A)	Credit Balances	Amount (A)
Drawings	6,000	Bank Overdraft	25,000
Wages	15,500	Interest on Investment	5,800
Stock	12,800	Bills Payable	4,600
Loan to X	4,000	Interest on Loan to X	320
Rent	5,000	Capital	1,00,000
General Expenses	1,480	Reserve for Bad and doubtful	
Investments	60,000	debts	250
Purchases	1,60,000	Sales	2,30,000
Frieght Carriage	2,100	Sundry Creditors	12,590
Goodwill	40,000		
Bills receivable	6,200		
Rates and Taxes	1,800		
Sales Returns	2,100		
Insurance	900		
Cash and Bank Balance	3,700		
Postage and Telegram	3,800		
Land and Buildings	25,000		
Plant and Machinery	10,000		
Sundry Debtors	16,500		
Packing Charges	400		
Bad Debts	1,280		
	3,78,560		3,78,560

Adjustments

(*i*) Closing Stock as on 31.3.2005—A 16,000.

(*ii*) Goods worth A 700 were sent on 25.3.2005 as "Sale on Approval Basis" for A 800 and the approval was not received before the end of the month.

(*iii*) 20% of the Goodwill is to be written off.

(*iv*) Further bad debts were estimated at A 350. Increase reserve for bad debts to the extent of A 1,500.

(*v*) Depreciate Land and Building by 3% and Plant and Machinery by 10%.

(*vi*) Goods worth A 800 were distributed as free samples.

Solution

Trading and Profit and Loss Account
for the year ending 31st March, 2005

Dr. Particulars		Amount (A)	Particulars		*Cr.* Amount (A)
To Opening Stock		12,800	By Sales	2,30,000	
To Purchases	1,60,000		*Less* : On Approval	800	
Less : Samples	800	1,59,200		2,29,200	
To Freight and Carriage		2,100	*Less* Returns	2,100	2,27,700
To Wages		15,500	By Stock at the end	16,000	
To Gross Profit c/d		54,200	*Add* : On Approval	700	16,700
		2,43,800			2,43,800
To Free Samples		800	By Gross Profit b/d		54,200
To Rent		5,000	By Interest on Investment		5,800
To General Expenses		1,480	By Interest on Loan		320
To Rates and Taxes		1,800			
To Insurance		900			
To Postage and Telegram		3,800			
To Packing Charges		400			
To Bad Debts	1,280				
Add : Further bad debts	350				
Reserve (New)	1,500				
	3,130				
Less : Reserve for Bad and Doubtful debts (old)	250	2,880			
To Goodwill written off		8,000			
To Depreciation on :					
Land and Buildings	750				
Plant and Machinery	1,000	1,750			
To Net Profit c/d		33,510			
		60,320			60,320

Balance Sheet as on 31st March, 2005

Liabilities		*Amount (A)*	*Assets*		*Amount (A)*
Capital	1,00,000		Goodwill	40,000	
Add : Net Profit	33,510		*Less* : w/o	8,000	32,000
	1,33,510		Land and Building	25,000	
Less : Drawings	6,000	1,27,510	*Less* : Depreciation	750	24,250
Bank Overdraft		25,000	Plant and Machinery	10,000	
Bills Payable		4,600	*Less* : Depreciation	1,000	9,000
Sundry Creditors		12,590	Investments		60,000
			Stock at the end		16,700
			Bills Receivable		6,200
			Sundry Debtors	16,500	
			Less : Sent on Approval	800	
				15,700	
			Less : Further bad debts	350	
				15,350	
			Less : Reserve for doubtful debts	1,500	13,850
			Cash and Bank		3,700
			Loan to X		4,000
		1,69,700			1,69,700

Example 15

Given below is the Trial Balance of Mr. Alok, a trader, as on 31.3.2006 :

Particulars	*Dr. Amount (A)*	*Cr. Amount (A)*
Cash in Hand	5,000	–
Land and Building	80,000	
Plant and Machinery	50,000	
Debtors and Creditors	25,000	40,000
Stock on 1.4.2005	10,000	
15% Investment on 1.4.2005	20,000	
Purchases and Sales	95,000	1,90,000
Bank Overdraft		20,000
Wages	28,000	
Salaries	16,000	
Rent, Rates and Taxes	15,000	
Bad Debts	6,000	
Drawings	5,000	
Bills Receivable and Bills Payable	15,000	21,000
Carriage Inwards	6,000	
Custom Duty and Purchases	16,000	
Life Insurance Premium	4,000	

Particulars	Dr. Amount (A)	Cr. Amount (A)
Advertisement	30,000	
Provision for Doubtful Debts		2,000
Interest on investment		2,000
Trade Expenses	11,000	
Furniture	20,000	
Sales Tax Payable		25,000
Capital		1,57,000
	4,57,000	4,57,000

Additional Information

(*i*) Stock on 31.03.2006 was valued at A 40,000

(*ii*) Included in Debtors are A 8,000 due from Ram and included in Creditors are A 6,000 due to Ram.

(*iii*) Bills Receivable include a bill of A 5,000 received from Varun, which has been dishonored.

(*iv*) Sales include A 5,000 for the goods sold on approval basis. Gods are sold at a profit of 25% on cost. Approval was not received upto 31.3.2006.

(*v*) Wages include A 5,000 spent on the erection of machinery.

(*vi*) Advertisement includes A 20,000 spent at the time of launching a new product. It is the policy of the business to write off such expenses in 5 years.

(*vii*) Create a provision for doubtful debts at 5% on debtors.

(*viii*) Prepaid taxes amounted to A 2,000.

(*ix*) Depreciate machinery by 10%.

Prepare Trading and Profit & Loss Account for the year ended 31st March, 2006 and a Balance Sheet on that date.

Solution

Trading and Profit & Loss Account for the year ending on 31.3.2005

Debit *Credit*

Particulars		*Amount* (A)	*Particulars*		*Amount* (A)
To Opening Stock		10,000	By Sales	1,90,000	
To Purchases		95,000	*Less* : Sales on approval	5,000	1,85,000
To Wages	28,000		By Closing Stock	40,000	
Less : For Erection of machinery (capitalised)	5,000	23,000	*Add* : Cost of Goods sold on approval*	4,000	44,000
To Carriage Inwards		6,000			
To Custom Duty on Purchases		16,000			
To Gross Profit c/d		79,000			
		2,29,000			2,29,000
To Salaries		16,000	By Gross Profit b/d		79,000
To Rent, Rates & Taxes	15,000		By Interest on investments	2,000	

Particulars		Amount (A)	*Particulars*		Amount (A)
Less : Prepaid	2,000	13,000	*Add* : Accrued interest	1,000	3,000
To Bad Debts	6,000				
Add : Provision for					
Doubtful Debts (New)*	950				
	6,950				
Less : Provision for					
Doubtful Debts (Old)	2,000	4,950			
To Advertisement	30,000				
Less : Carried forward	16,000	14,000			
To Trade expenses		11,000			
To Depreciation on machines		5,500			
To Net Profit transferred		17,550			
		82,000			82,000

Balance Sheet of Mr. Alok as on 31st March, 2006

Liabilities		Amount (A)	*Assets*		Amount (A)
Capital	1,57,000		Land and Buildings		80,000
Add : Net Profit	17,550		Plant and Machinery	50,000	
	1,74,550		*Add* : Wages	5,000	
Less : Life Insurance				55,000	
Premium	4,000		*Less* : Depreciation	5,500	49,500
	1,70,550		Furniture		20,000
Less : Drawings	5,000	1,65,550	Stock at the end		
Creditors	40,000		A [40,000 + 4,000]		44,000
Less : Due to Ram	6,000	34,000	15% Investment	20,000	
Bank Overdraft		20,000	*Add* : Accrued interest	1,000	21,000
Bills Payable		21,000	Bills Receivable	15,000	
Sales Tax Payable		25,000	*Less* : Dishonoured	5,000	10,000
			Debtors	25,000	
			Less : Sale on approval	5,000	
				20,000	
			Less : Due from Ram	6,000	
				14,000	
			Add : Varun (for Bill		
			Dishonoured	5,000	
				19,000	
			Less : Provision for		
			Doubtful Debts	950	18,050
			Cash in Hand		5,000
			Prepaid taxes		2,000
			Advertisement Account (Deferred)	16,000	
		2,65,550			2,65,550

*1 Less the Cost = A 100; Profit = A 25; Selling Price = A 125

Cost of goods sold on approval = A 5,000 × 100/125 = A 4,000

*2 Debtors	25,000
Less : Due from Ram	(6,000)
Less : Sale on Approval	(5,000)
Add : Varun for Bill Dishonoured	5,000
	19,000

5% of A 19,000 = A 950

Example 16

Mr. Ajay Kumar, a shopkeeper, had prepared the following trial balance from his ledger as on 31st March, 2006:

Particulars	*Dr. Amount (A)*	*Cr. Amount (A)*
Purchase and Sales	6,20,000	8,30,000
Cash in Hand	4,200	
Cash at Bank	24,000	
Stock of goods on 1.4.2005	1,00,000	
Capital Account		5,77,200
Drawings	8,000	
Salaries	64,000	
Postage and telephones	23,000	
Salesmen's commission	70,000	
Insurance	18,000	
Advertising	34,000	
Furniture	44,000	
Printing and Stationery	6,000	
Motor Car	96,000	
Bad Debts	4,000	
Cash Discount	8,000	
General Expenses	60,000	
Carriage Inwards	20,000	
Carriage Outwards	44,000	
Wages	40,000	
Debtors and Creditors	2,00,000	80,000
	14,87,200	14,87,200

You are required to prepare Trading and Profit & Loss Account for the year ended 31st March, 2006 and Balance Sheet as on that date. You are also given the following information:

(*i*) Stock on 31.3.2006 was A 1,45,000

(*ii*) Mr. Ajay Kumar had withdrawn goods worth A 5,000 during the year.

(*iii*) Purchases include purchase of furniture worth A 10,000

(*iv*) Debtors are bad to the extent of A 5,000

(*v*) Creditors include a balance of A 4,000 to the credit of Mr. Vijay in respect of which it has been decided and settled with the party to pay only A 1,000.

(*vi*) Sales include goods worth A 15,000 sent to Ram & Co. on approval and remain unsold as on 31.3.2006. The cost of the goods was A 10,000.

(*vii*) Provision for Bad Debts is to be created at 5% on Sundry Debtors.

(*viii*) Depreciate Furniture by 15% and Motor Car by 20%

(*ix*) The salesman are entitled to a commission of 10% on total sales.

Solution

Trading and Profit & Loss Account
for the year ending 31.3.2006

Particulars		*Amount (A)*	*Particulars*		*Amount (A)*
To Opening Stock		1,00,000	By Sales	8,30,000	
To Purchases	6,20,000		Less : Goods sent on		
Less : Drawings	5,000		approval	15,000	8,15,000.
	6,15,000		By Closing Stock	1,45,000	
Less : Furniture	10,000	6,05,000	*Add* : Cost of Goods		
To Carriage Inwards		20,000	sent on approval	10,000	1,55,000
To Wages		40,000			
To Gross Profit b/d		2,05,000			
		9,70,000			9,70,000
To Salaries		64,000	By Gross Profit b/d		2,05,000
To Postage & telephones		23,000	By Creditors		3,000
To Salesmen' Commission	70,000		By Net Loss transferred		1,75,800
Add : Outstanding	11,500	81,500	to Capital A/c		
To Insurance		18,000			
To Advertising		34,000			
To Printing & Stationery		6,000			
To Bad Debts	4,000				
Add : Further Bad Debts	5,000				
Add : Provision for Bad Debts*	9,000	18,000			
To Cash Discount		8,000			
To General Expenses		60,000			
To Carriage Outwards		44,000			
To Depreciation on :					
Furniture	8,100				
Motor car	19,200	27,300			
		383,800			3,83,800

Balance Sheet as at 31.03.2006

Liabilities		Amount (A)	Assets		Amount (A)
Drawings	2,000		Investments		6,500
Creditors [A 80,000 – A 3,000]		77,000	Cash in Hand		4,200
Outstanding Commission		11,500	Cash at Bank		24,000
Capital	5,77,200		Stock A [1,45,000 + 10,000]		1,55,000
Less : Drawings			Debtors	2,00,000	
A [8,000 + 5000]	13,000		*Less* : Sale on approval	15,000	
	5,54,200			1,85,000	
Less : Net Loss	1,75,800	3,88,400	*Less* : Further Bad debts	5,000	
				1,80,000	
			Less : Provision for Bad debts	9,000	1,71,000
			Furniture	44,000	
			(+) Purchases	10,000	
				54,000	
			(–) Depreciation	8,100	45,900
			Motor Car	96,000	
			(–) Depreciation	19,200	76,800
		4,76,900			4,76,900

Working Notes

* Outstanding Commission = [10% of (A 8,30,000 – A 15,000)] – A 70,000
= A 81,500 – A 70,000 = A 11,500

* Provision for Bad Debts = 5% of [Debtors – (Further Bad Debts + Sales on approval)]
= 5% of A [2,00,000 – (5,000 + 15,000)]
= 5% of A [1,80,000]
= A 9,000

Examples 17

The following is the Trial Balance of Mr. Ram Lal as at 31st December, 2006 :

Particulars	*Dr. Amount (A)*	*Cr. Amount (A)*
Ram Lal's Capital	–	86,690
Stock on 1.1.2006	46,800	–
Purchases and Sales	3,21,700	3,89,600
Returns	8,600	5,800
Freight and Carriage	18,600	–

Particulars	Dr. Amount (A)	Cr. Amount (A)
Rent and Taxes	5,700	–
Salaries and Wages	9,300	–
Sundry Debtorsand Creditors	24,000	14,800
Bank loan @ 6% p.a.	–	20,000
Bank Interest on loan	900	–
Printing and Advertising	14,600	–
Miscellaneous Income	–	250
Cash at Bank	8,000	–
Discount	1,800	4,190
Furniture and Fittings	5,000	–
General Expenses	11,450	–
Insurance	1,300	–
Postage and Telegrams	2,330	–
Cash in Hand	380	–
Travelling expenses	870	–
Drawings	40,000	
	5,21,330	5,21,330

The following adjustments should be made :

(*i*) Included amongst the Debtors is A 3,000 due from Suresh Kumar and included among the creditors A 1,000 due to him.

(*ii*) Provision for Bad and Doubtful Debts be created at 5% and Reserve for Discount @ 2% on Sundry Debtors.

(*iii*) Depreciate Furniture and Fittings by 10%.

(*iv*) Personal Purchases amounting to A 600 had been included in the Purchases Day Book.

(*v*) Interest on Bank Loan shall be provided for the whole year.

(*vi*) One quarter of the amount of Printing and Advertising is to be carried forward to next year.

(*vii*) Credit purchase invoice amounting to A 400 had been omitted from the books.

(*viii*) Stock on 31st December, 2006 was A 78,600.

Prepare Trading and Profit & Loss Account for the year ended 31st December, 2006 and Balance Sheet as on the date.

Solution

Trading and Profit & Loss Account
for the year ending 31st December, 2006

Particulars		Amount (A)	Particulars	Amount (A)
To Opening Stock		46,800	By Sales	3,89,600
To Purchases	3,21,700		*Less* : Returns	8,600
Less : Returns	(5,800)			3,81,000

Particulars		Amount (A)	Particulars	Amount (A)
Drawings	(600)		By Cl.Stock	78,600
Add : Omitted	400	3,15,700		
To Freight & Carriage		18,600		
To Gross Profit		78,500		
		4,59,600		4,59,600
To Rent & Taxes		5,700	By Gross Profit	78,500
To Salaries & Wages		9,300	By Discount	4,190
To Intt. on loan (900 + 300)		1,200	By Mis. Income	250
To Printing and Stationary (14,600 – 3650)		10,950		
To Discount		1,800		
To Gen. Expenses		11,450		
To Insurance		1,300		
To Purchase & Telegrams		2,330		
To Travelling Exp.		870		
To Provision for B/D		1,150		
To Provision for Discount		437		
To Depreciation on furniture		500		
To Net Profit		35,953		
		82,940		82,940

Balance Sheet
as on 31st December, 2006

Liabilities		Amount (A)	Assets		Amount (A)
Capital	86,690		Furniture	5,000	
Add : N.P.	35,953		*Less* : Depreciation	500	4,500
	1,22,643		Debtors (24,000 – 1,000 – 1150 – 437)		21,413
Less : Drawings	40,600	82,043	Prepaid expense		3,650
Creditors (14,800 – 1,000 + 400)		14,200	Stock		78,600
Loan (20,000 + 300)		20,300	Bank		8,000
			Cash		380
		1,16,543			1,16,543

Example 18

From the following Trial Balance and Information, prepare Trading and Profit & Loss Account of Mr. Rishabh for the year ended 31st March, 2007 and a Balance Sheet as on that date.

Particulars	Dr. Amount (A)	Cr. Amount (A)
Capital		1,00,000
Drawings	12,000	

Particulars	*Dr. Amount (A)*	*Cr. Amount (A)*
Land and Building	90,000	
Plant & Machinery	20,000	
Furniture	5,000	
Sales		1,40,000
Returns Outward		6,000
Debtors	18,400	
Loan from Gajanand on 1.7.2006 @ 6% p.a.		30,000
Purchases	80,000	
Returns Inward	5,000	
Carriage	10,000	
Sundry Expenses	600	
Printing & Stationery	500	
Insurance Expenses	1,000	
Provision for bad and doubtful debts		1,000
Provision for Discount on Debtors		380
Bad Debts	400	
Opening Stock on 01.4.2006	21,300	
Salaries and Wages	18,500	
Creditors		12,000
Trade Expenses	800	
Cash at Bank	4,600	
Cash in Hand	1,280	
	2,89,380	2,89,380

Additional Information

(*i*) Value of Closing Stock on 31.3.2007 was A 27,300.

(*ii*) Fire occurred on 23rd March, 2007 and A 10,000 worth of general goods were destroyed. The Insurance company accepted claim for A 6,000 only and paid the claim money on 10th April, 2007.

(*iii*) Bad Debts amounting to A 400 are to be written off. Provisions for bad and doubtful debts is to be made at 5% and for discount at 2% on debtors. Make a provision of 2% on creditors for discount.

(*iv*) Received A 6,000 worth of goods on 27th March, 2007 but the Invoice of purchases was not recorded in Purchase Book.

(*v*) Rishabh took away goods worth A 2,000 for personal use but no record was made thereof.

(*vi*) Charge depreciation at 2% on Land and Building, 20% on Plant and Machinery and 5% on furniture.

(*vii*) Insurance prepaid amounts to A 200.

Solution

Trading and Profit & Loss A/c
for the Year ending 31st March, 2007

Dr. Particulars		Amount (A)	Particulars		*Cr.* Amount (A)
To Opening Stock		21,300	By Sales	1,40,000	
To Purchases	80,000		*Less* : Returns	5,000	1,35,000
Less : Returns Outward	6,000		By Loss by fire		10,000
	74,000		By Closing Stock		27,300
Less : Drawings	2,000				
	72,000				
Add : Omitted	6,000	78,000			
To Carriage		10,000			
To Gross Profit c/d		63,000			
		1,72,300			1,72,300
To Interest on Loan			By Gross Profit b/d		63,000
– Outstanding			By Provision for Discount on		
(30,000 × 6/100 × 9/12)		1,350	Debtors (old)	380	
To Sundry Expenses		600	*Less* : Provision for Discount		
To Printing & Stationery		500	on Debtors (New)	342	38
To Insurance	1,000		By Provision for Discount on		
Less : Prepaid	200	800	Creditors		360
To Salaries and Wages		18,500			
To Trade Expenses		800			
To Loss by Fire	10,000				
Less : Insurance claim	6,000	4,000			
To Depreciation on :					
Land & Building	1,800				
Plant & Machinery	4,000				
Furniture	250	6,050			
To Provision for Bad					
& Doubtful Debts (New)					
5/100[18,400 – 400]	900				
Add : Bad Debts	400				
Add : Further Bad Debts	400				
	1,700				
Less : Provision for Bad					
& Doubtful Debts	1,000	700			
To Net Profit T/f					
To Capital Account		30,098			
		63,398			63,398

Balance Sheet as on 31st March, 2007

Liabilities		*Amount (A)*	*Assets*		*Amount (A)*
Creditors	12,000		Cash in Hand		1,280
Add : Omitted Purchases	6,000		Cash at Bank		4,600
	18,000		Prepaid Insurance		200
Less : Provision for			Closing Stock		27,300
for Discount	360	17,640	Insurance Company		6,000
6% Loan from Gajanand		30,000	Debtors	18,400	
Interest Accrued on Loan		1,350	*Less* : Further Bad Debts	400	
				18,000	
Capital	1,00,000		*Less* : Provision for		
Add : Net Profit	30,098		doubtful debts	900	
	1,30,098			17,100	
Less : Drawings	14,000		*Less* Provision for		
(12,000 + 2,000)		1,16,098	Discount	342	16758
		Furniture	5,000		
			Less : Depreciations	250	4,750
			Land & Buildings	90,000	
			Less : Depreciations	1,800	88,200
			Plant & Machinery	20,000	
			Less : Depreciation	4,000	16,000
		1,65,088			1,65,088

Example 19

On 31st March 2008 the following Trial Balance was prepared from the books of Mr. Maneet :

Particulars	*Dr. Amount (A)*	*Cr. Amount (A)*
Debtors and Creditors	30,600	10,000
Bills Receivable	5,000	–
Plant and Machinery	75,000	–
Purchases (Adjusted)	1,90,000	–
Capital Account	–	70,000
Freehold Premises	50,000	–
Salaries	21,000	–
Wages	24,400	–
Postage and Stationery	1,750	–
Carriage in	1,750	–
Carriage out	1,000	–
Bad debts	950	
Bad debts provision	–	350
Office charges	1,500	–

Particulars	Dr. Amount (A)	Cr. Amount (A)
Cash at Bank	5,300	–
Cash in Hand	800	–
Bills payable	–	7,000
General Reserve	–	20,000
Sales	–	3,31,700
Closing stock	30,000	–
	4,39,050	4,39,050

The following adjustments are required :

(*a*) Manpreet gets a salary of A 12,000 p.a.

(*b*) Allows interest on capital @ 10% p.a.

(*c*) Bad debts provision is 2½% on Debtors.

(*d*) 10% of net profit to be carried to General Reserve

(*e*) It was discovered in April 2007 that the stock as on 31st March, 2007 were overcast by A 1,000. However no entry was passed in April 2007.

(*f*) Depreciate Plant and Machinery @ 10% and Freehold Premises @ 2% p.a. Prepare the Trading and Profit and Loss Account of the firm for the year ended 31st March, 2008 and a Balance Sheet as at the date.

Solution

Trading and Profit and Loss Account
for the year ended 31st March 2008

Particulars		Amount (A)	Particulars	Amount (A)
To Purchases (Adjusted)	1,90,000		By Sales	3,31,700
Less : Over Valued Stock	1,000	1,89,000		
To Wages		24,400		
To Carriage Inwards		1,750		
To Gross Profit c/d		1,16,550		
		3,31,700		3,31,700
To Salaries		21,000	By Gross Profit b/d	1,16,550
To Salary to Maneet		12,000		
To Interest on Capital 10% of 69,000 [70,000 – 1000]		6900		
To Postage & Stationery		1,750		
To Carriage Outward		1,000		
To Bad Debts	950			
Add : Provision for Doubtful Debts	765			
	1,715			

Particulars		*Amount (A)*	*Particulars*	*Amount (A)*
Less : Provision for Doubtful Debts (Existing)	350	1365		
To Office Charges		1,500		
To Depreciation on :				
Plant & Machinery	7,500			
Freehold Promises	1,000	8,500		
To General Reserve (10% of A 62535)		6,254		
To Net Profit transferred to Maneet's Capital A/c [62535 – 6254]		56,281		
		56,281		
		1,16,550		1,16,550

Balance Sheet as at 31st March, 2008

Liabilities		*Amount (A)*	*Assets*		*Amount (A)*
Capital	70,000		Debtors	30,600	
Less : Over Valued Stock	1,000		*Less* : Provision	765	29,835
	69,000		Plant and Machinery	75,000	
Add : Salaries	12,000		*Less* : Depreciation	7,500	67,500
Net Profit	56,281		Freehold Premises	50,000	
Interest on Capital	6,900	1,44,181	*Less* : Depreciation	1,000	49,000
General Reserve	20,000		Bills Receivable		5,000
Addition	6,254	26,254	Cash in Hand		800
Creditors		10,000	Cash at Bank		5,300
Bills Payable		7,000	Closing Stock		30,000
		1,87,435			1,87,435

Example 20

Given below is the Trial Balance of Mr. Ramesh as on 31st December, 2009 :

Particulars	*Dr. Amount (A)*	*Cr. Amount (A)*
Land and Buildings	1,20,000	
Office Machinery	70,000	
Furniture and Fittings	20,000	
Stock on 1-1-2009	16,000	
Purchases and Sales	90,000	2,20,000

Particulars	Dr. Amount (A)	Cr. Amount (A)
Salaries	20,000	
Bad Debts	10,000	
Debtors and Creditors	35,000	40,000
Sales Tax	10,000	
Rent, Rates and Taxes	15,000	
Advertisement	18,000	
Drawings	5,000	
Loan to Ashok @ 16% p.a. on 1-7-2009	20,000	
Wages	33,000	
Interest on Loan to Ashok	–	1,000
Bills Receivables	10,000	
Trade Mark	8,000	
Discount	1,000	
Wages Payable	–	2,000
Capital	–	1,98,000
Bank Overdraft	–	40,000
	5,01,000	5,01,000

Additional Information

(*i*) The value of stock on 31-12-2009, A 30,000.

(*ii*) Sales include, A 5,000 for the goods sold on approved to Hemant. Goods are sold at a profit of 25% on cost. Approval was not received till 31st December.

(*iii*) Furniture purchased during the year for A 5,000 was wrongly debited to Purchase Book.

(*iv*) A cheque of A 8,000 received from customers was deposited in the bank in the last week of December. It was reported to have been dishonoured.

(*v*) Free samples worth A 4,000 were distributed during the year.

(*vi*) Write off further bad debts A 2,000. Also create a provision for doubtful debts at 10% on debtors.

(*vii*) Depreciate furniture by 10% and office machinery by 5%.

Prepare Trading and Profit & Loss Account for the year ended 31st December, 2009 and a Balance Sheet as on that date.

Solution

Trading and Profit & Loss Account
for the year ended 31st December, 2009

Dr. Cr.

Particulars		*Amount (A)*	*Particulars*		*Amount (A)*
To Opening Stock		16,000	By Sales	2,20,000	
To Purchases	90,000		*Less* : Sale on approval	5,000	
Less: Trfd. to Furniture A/c	5,000			2,15,000	
	85,000		*Less* : Sales Tax	10,000	2,05,000

Particulars		Amount (A)	Particulars		Amount (A)
Less : Free Samples	4,000	81,000	By Closing Stock		30,000
To Wages		33,000	By Stock with Customers		4,000
To Gross Profit c/d		1,09,000	(at cost)		
		2,39,000			2,39,000
To Salaries		20,000	By Gross Profit b/d		1,09,000
To Bad Debts	10,000		By Interest on Loan to		
Add : Further Bad Debts	2,000		Ashok	1,000	
Add : Provision for Doubtful Debts (New)	3,600	15,600	*Add* : Accrued Interest	600	1,600
To Rent, Rates and Taxes		15,000			
To Advertisement		18,000			
To Discount		1,000			
To Free Samples		4,000			
To Depreciation on Furniture		2,500			
To Dep. on Office Machinery		3,500			
To Net Profit transferred to Capital A/c		31,000			
		1,10,600			1,10,600

Balance Sheet as at 31st December, 2009

Liabilities		Amount (A)	Assets		Amount (A)
Capital	1,98,000		Land & Building		1,20,000
Add : Net Profit	31,000		Office Machinery	70,000	
	2,29,000		*Less* : Depreciation	3,500	66,500
Less : Drawings	5,000	2,24,000	Furniture & Fittings	20,000	
Creditors		40,000	*Add* : Trsf. from Purchase	5,000	
Wages Payable		2,000		25,000	
Bank Overdraft	40,000		Less : Depreciation	2,500	22,500
Add : Dishonour of			Loan to Ashok		20,000
Cheque	8,000	48,000	Bills Receivable		10,000
			Trade Mark		8,000
			Debtors	35,000	
			Less : Sale on Approval	5,000	
				30,000	
			Less : Further Bad Debts	2,000	
				28,000	
			Add : Cheque Dishonoured	8,000	
				36,000	

Liabilities	Amount (A)	Assets		Amount (A)
		Less : Provision for		
		Doubtful Debts	3,600	32,400
		Accrued Interest		600
		Closing Stock		30,000
		Stock with Customers		4,000
	3,14,000			3,14,000

Example 21

The following is the trial balance of a trader as on 31.3.2009 :

Particulars	Dr. Amount (A)	Cr. Amount (A)
Cash in hand	8,000	
Land and Building	40,000	
Plant and Machinery	20,000	
Debtors and Creditors	25,000	60,000
Stock 1.4.08	10,000	
15% investment 1.4.08	20,000	
Purchases and Sales	95,000	1,90,000
Bills Payable and Bills Receivable	15,000	21,000
Wages	8,000	
Salaries	16,000	
Rent and Rates	15,000	
Drawings	5,000	
Carriage outward	6,000	
Customes duty on purchase	16,000	
Customs duty payable		25,000
Fire Insurance Premium	15,000	
Advertisement	20,000	
Provision for bad debt		2,000
Bad debts	6,000	
Interest		2,000
Furniture	20,000	
Capital		60,000
	3,60,000	3,60,000

Additional Information to be Adjusted

(*i*) Stock on 31st March 2009 was valued at Rs. 60,000.

(*ii*) Bill receivable includes a bill of Rs. 4,000 which has become bad.

(*iii*) Sale also includes sale of furniture on 1.4.08 for rs. 10,000 (Book value Rs. 12,000).

(*iv*) Wages include Rs. 6,000 spent on erection of machine on 1.4.08.

(*v*) Depreciate machinery by 10%, furniture by 20%.

(*vi*) Appreciate building by 10%.

(*vii*) Interest includes Rs. 200 received from a debtor for late payment and balance for investment.

(*viii*) Bad debts recovered Rs. 500 were taken as receipt from debtors.

Prepare Trading and Profit and Loss Account for the year ending 31.3.09 and a Balance Sheet as on that date.

Solution

Trading and Profit and Loss A/c for the Year Ending 31.3.2009

Dr. *Cr.*

Particulars		*Amount* (*A*)	*Particulars*		*Amount* (*A*)
To Opening Stock		10,000	By sales	1,90,000	
To Purchases		95,000	*Less :* Furniture	10,000	1,80,000
To Wages	8,000				
Less : Wages on machines	6,000	2,000	By Closing Stock		60,000
To Customduty		16,000			
To G/P c/d		1,17,000			
		2,40,000			2,40,000
To Salaries		16,000	By G/P b/d		1,17,000
To Rent and Rates		15,000	By Bad Debts		
To Carriage outward		6,000	recovered		500
To Five insurance		15,000	By Building A/c		4,000
To Advertisement		20,000	(10% of A 40,000)		
To Bad debts	6,000		By Interest for late		200
Add : B/R bad	4,000		payment		
	10,000		By Interest on investments		
Less : Old provision	2,000	8,000	(2,000 – 200)	1800	
To loss on sale of furniture		2,000	*Add :* Outstanding	1200	3,000
(12,000 – 10,000)					
To Dep. on machinery		2,600			
(10% of 20,000 + 6,000)					
To Dep. on furniture		1,600			
(20% of A 8,000)					
To net profit		38,500			
		1,24,700			1,24,700

Balance Sheet as on 31.3.2009

Liabilities		*Amount (A)*	*Assets*		*Amount (A)*
DCapital	60,000		Cash in hand		80,000
Add : Net Profit	38,500		Land and Building	40,000	
	98,500		*Add :* 10%	4,000	44,000
Less : Drawings	5,000		Plant and Machinery	20,000	
		93,500	*Add :* Wages	6,000	
Creditors		60,000		26,000	
Bills Payable		21,000	*Less :* Dep.	2,600	23,400
Custom duty payable		25,000	Furniture	20,000	
			Less : Sale	12,000	
				8,000	
			Less : Dep.	1,600	6,400
			Debtors	25,000	
			Add : Bad debts recovered	500	25,500
			Investment		20,000
			O/S interest on investment		1,200
			Bills Receivable	15,000	
			Less : Bad debts	4,000	11,000
			Closing stock		60,000
		1,99,500			1,99,500

Example 22

From the following Trial Balance of Shri Ganesh prepare Trading and Profit & Loss A/c for the year ending 31st Dec., 2007 and Balance Sheet as on that date after taking into consideration the adjustments given at the end of the Trial Balance.

Trial Balance as on 31.12.07

Dr. *Cr.*

Particulars	*Dr. Amount (A)*	*Cr. Amount (A)*
Sales		7,40,000
Purchase (adjusted)	6,99,200	–
Wages	900	–
Capital A/c	–	48,500
National Insurance	300	–
Carriage in	400	–
Carriage out	500	–
Lighting	600	–
Rates and Insurance (including premium of A 300 p.a. paid upto 30th June, 2008)	400	–
Stock at 31-12-07	61,250	–

Particulars	*Dr. Amount (A)*	*Cr. Amount (A)*
Cash in hand and at bank	1,750	–
Discount earned	–	600
Buildings	30,000	–
Discount allowed	100	–
Debtors and Creditors	6,000	20,000
Furniture	8,000	–
Dividends received	–	300
	8,09,400	8,09,400

Adjustments

(*i*) National Insurance balance also include employer's contribution A 150 Wages are shown 'net' after deducting national insurance contribution borne by the employees.

(*ii*) Owing to the nature of employment, some employees are housed in the building of the business. The rental value of such portion is assessed at A 500.

(*iii*) Sales as shown in the trial balance sheet include the sale of old furniture (effected half way through the year) realising A 200. The book value of the furniture at the commencement of the period was A 300. The depreciation has been written off at 20% p.a.

(*iv*) The manager is to get a commission of 1/5 on the net profits after charging his commission but before considering income from dividend.

(*v*) Depreciate building by 5%.

Solution

Trading and Profit & Loss Account
for the year ended 31st Dec. 2007

Dr. *Cr.*

Particulars		*Amount (A)*	*Particulars*		*Amount (A)*
To Purchases (Adjusted)		6,99,200	By Sales	7,40,000	
To Wages	900		*Less* : Sale of furniture	200	7,39,800
Add : Employees contribution to National Insurance	150				
Add : Rental value of building	500	1,550			
To Carriage in		400			
To Gross Profit c/d		38,650			
		7,39,800			7,39,800
To National Insurance (Employer's contribution)		150	By Gross Profit b/d		38,650
			By Discount earned		600
To Carriage out		500	By Dividend received		300
To Rates and Insurance	400		By Rental value of building		
Less : Prepaid	150	250	occupied by employees		500

Particulars		*Amount (A)*	*Particulars*	*Amount (A)*
To Lighting		600		
To Discount allowed		100		
To Loss on Sale of furniture		70		
To Depreciation :				
(*i*) Building	1,500			
(*ii*) Furniture	1,570	3070		
To Manager's Commission		5,835		
To Net Profit		29,475		
		40,050		40,050

Balance Sheet of Shri Ganesh
as on 31st December, 2007

Liabilities		*Amount (A)*	*Assets*		*Amount (A)*
Sundry Creditors		20,000	Cash in hand and at bank		1,750
Manager's Commission due		5,835	Sundry Debtors		6,000
Capital	48,500		Closing Stock		61,250
Add : Net Profit	29,475	77,975	Prepaid Insurance		150
			Furniture	8,000	
			Less : Book value of furniture sold	300	
				7,700	
			Less : Depreciation	1,540	6,160
			Building	30,000	
			Less : Depreciation	1,500	28,500
		1,03,810			1,03,810

Working Notes

1 Employees contribution to National Insurance and rental value of building occupied by workers are part of gross wages.

2 Calculation of depreciation on furniture and loss on sale of furniture

		A
(*a*)	Furniture sold : Book Value at the beginning	300
	Less : Depreciation for 6 months [A 300 × 20/100 × 6/12]	30
		270
	Less : Selling Price	200
	Loss on Sale of furniture	70
(*b*)	Furniture in hand	7,700
	[A 8,000 – A 300 (Book Value of furniture sold)]	
	Depreciation 20% of A 7,700	1,540

Add : 6 months depreciation on furniture sold (*a*)	30
Total Depreciation on furniture	1,570

3 **Calculation of Manager's Commission**

Net Profit before dividend income

= A [38,650 + 600 + 500 – 150 – 500 – 250 – 600 – 100 – 70 – 3,070] = A 35,010

Manager's Commission = A 35,010 × 20/120 = A 5,835

Example 23

The following balances are available from the books of Abhishek as on 31.12-2004 and 31.12.2005 :

	31.12.2004 *(A)*	*31.12.2005* *(A)*
Building	60,000	60,000
Equipments	1,20,000	1,34,000
Furniture	10,000	10,000
Debtors	?	48,000
Creditors	32,000	?
Stock	?	34,000
Bank Loan	20,000	16,000
Cash	32,000	22,000

The transactions of Abhishek during the year ended 31.12.2005 were the following:

Collection from Debtors A 1,86,000; Payment to creditors A 1,22,000; Cash purchases A 32,000; Expenses A 20,000; Sale of an equipment (book value A 10,000) A 6,000 on January 1, 2005; Drawing A 20,000; Purchase of an equipment on July 1, 2005.

Cash sales amounted to 10% of total sales. Credit sales amounted to A 1,80,000. Credit purchases were 80% of total purchases. Abhishek sells goods at cost plus $33\frac{3}{1}\%$. His Suppliers allowed him discount A 2,000.

Equipments and furniture are to be depreciated by 10% p.a. and building by 2% p.a.

Prepare the Trading and Profit & Loss Account for the year ended 31.12.2005 and a Balance Sheet as on that date. [*B.Com (Hons.), Delhi University 2006*]

Solution

Trading and Profit & Loss Account
for the year ended 31st March 2005

Dr. *Cr.*

Expenditure		*Amount* *(A)*	*Income*		*Amount* *(A)*
To Opening Stock		24,000	By Sales :		
To Purchases : Cash	32,000		Cash	20,000	
Credit	1,28,000	1,60,000	Credit	1,80,000	2,00,000
To Gross Profit c/d		50,000	By Closing Stock		34,000
		2,34,000			2,34,000

Expenditure		Amount (A)	Income	Amount (A)
To Expenses		20,000	By Gross Profit b/d	50,000
To Loss on Sale of Equipment		4,000	By Discount Received	2,000
To Depreciation :				
Building	1,200			
Furniture	1,000			
Equipment	12,200	14,400		
To Net Profit transferred to Capital Account		13,600		
		52,000		52,000

Balance Sheet
as on 31st December, 2005

Liabilities		Amount (A)	Assets		Amount (A)
Capital	2,48,000		Building	60,000	
Add: Net Profit	13,600		*Less:* Depreciation	1,200	58,800
	2,61,600		Equipments	1,34,000	
Less: Drawings	20,000	2,41,600	*Less:* Depreciation	12,200	1,21,800
Creditors		36,000	Furniture	10,000	
Bank Loan		16,000	*Less:* Depreciation	1,000	9,000
			Debtors		48,000
			Stock		34,000
			Cash		22,000
		2,93,600			2,93,600

Working Notes :

(*i*) Credit purchase is 80% of total purchases. So cash purchase is 20% of total purchases. Thus credit purchase is 80 ÷ 20 of cash purchase, *i.e.,* A 32, 000 $\frac{80}{20}$ A 1,28,000.

Total purchases – A 1,28,000 (Credit) + A 32,000 (Cash) = A 1,60,000

(*ii*) Cash sales is 10% of the total sales, so credit sale is 90% of the total sales. Thus cash sales is 10 ÷ 90 of credit sales, *i.e.,* A 1, 80, 000 $\frac{10}{90}$ A 20, 000.

Total Sales = A 1,80,000 (Credit) + A 20,000 (Cash) = A 2,00,000

(*iii*) Opening Stock = Cost of goods sold + Closing Stock – Purchases

= A 1,50,000 + A 34,000 – A 1,60,000

= A 24,000

(*iv*) **Calculation of cost of goods sold :**

Let the Cost = A 100

Profit = $33\frac{1}{3}$

Sales = A $133\frac{1}{3}$ or A $\frac{400}{3}$

When sales are A $\frac{400}{3}$, then cost = A 100

When sales are A 1, then cost $\frac{100 \quad 3}{400}$ or $\frac{300}{400}$

When sales are A 2,00,000, then cost $2,00,000 \quad \frac{300}{400}$ A 1,50,000

(*v*) **Loss on sale of equipment has been calculated as under :**

	A
Book value on 1.1.2005	10,000
Less: Sale price	6,000
Loss on sale	4,000

(*vi*) **Depreciation on Equipment:**

	A
On A 1,10,000 (1,20,000 – 10,000) = $1,10,000 \quad \frac{10}{100}$	11,000
On A 24,000 (A 1,34,000 – A 1,10,000) = $24,000 \quad \frac{6}{12} \quad \frac{10}{100}$	1,200
To be charged to Profit & Loss Account	12,200

(*vii*) **Calculation of Opening Capital :**

Balance Sheet
as on 31st December, 2004

Liabilities	*Amount (A)*	*Assets*	*Amount (A)*
Creditors	32,000	Building	60,000
Bank Loan	20,000	Equipments	1,20,000
Capital (*Bal. figure*)	2,48,000	Furniture	10,000
		Debtors	54,000
		Stock	24,000
		Cash	32,000
	3,00,000		3,00,000

Example 24

The following is the Trial Balance of Ms. AJIT Traders as at 31st March, 2011 :

Trial Balance as on 31.12.07

Dr. *Cr.*

Particulars	*Dr. Amount (A)*	*Cr. Amount (A)*
Drawing and Capitals	19,000	65,690
Stock 1st April, 2010	46,800	–
Purchases and Sales	3,21,700	3,89,600
Returns	8,600	5,800
Debtors and Creditors	24,000	14,800
Discount	1,800	4,110
Bank Loan @ 14% p.a.	—	20,000
Carriage Inward	19,600	
Rent and Taxes	9,300	
Salaries & Wages	4,000	
Printing & Stationery	8,700	
Interest on Bank Loan	1,100	
Travelling Expenses	870	
Postage & Telephone	2,000	
Insurance	6,400	
General Expenses	12,750	
Furniture	5,000	
Cash Balance	380	
Bank Balance	8,000	
	5,00,000	5,00,000

Adjustments :

(*i*) Closing stock on 31.3.2011 was A 78,600.

(*ii*) Credit purchases A 400 have not been entered in the Books.

(*iii*) Printing and stationery amounting to A 3,600 is to be carried forwards

(*iv*) Interest on Bank Loan shall be provided for whole year.

(*v*) Personal purchases of proprietor amounting to A 600 have been recorded in purchase Day Book.

(*vi*) Depreciate furniture by 10%.

(*vii*) Provision for Bad & Doubtful Debts to be created @ 5% on Debtors and 2% for Discount on Debtors.

(*viii*) Included among Debtors A 3,000 due from him and included among creditor A 1,000 due to him.

Prepare Trading, Profit & Loss A/c for the year ending 31st March, 2011 and a Balance Sheet as on that date. [*B.Com. (Hons.), Delhi University, Nov. 2011*]

Solution

Trading and Profit & Loss Account
for the year ended 31st March 2011

Dr. | *Cr.*

Particulars		*Amount (A)*	*Particulars*		*Amount (A)*
To Opening stock		46,800	By Sales	3,89,600	
To Purchases	3,21,700		*Less:* Returns	8,600	3,81,000
Add: Credit Purchases	400		By Closing Stock		78,600
	3,22,100				
Less: Drawing	600				
	3,21,500				
Less: Returns	5,800	3,15,700			
To Carriage Inward		19,600			
To Gross profit C/d.		77,500			
		4,59,600			4,59,600
To Rent and Taxes		9,300	By G/P b/d		77,500
To Salary & Wages		4,000	By Discount		4,110
To Printing Stationery	87,00				
Less : Prepaid	3,600	5,100			
To Int. on Bank Loan	1,100				
Add : Outstanding	1,700	2,800			
To Travelling exp.		870			
To Discount		1,800			
To Dep. on Furniture		500			
To General expenses		12,750			
To Postage and telephone		2,000			
To Insurance		6,400			
To Provision for bad debts. (5% of Rs. 23,000)		1,150			
To Provision for discount on Creditors (2% of Rs. 21,850)		437			
To Net Profit		34,503			
		81,610			81,610

Balance Sheet
as on 31st March, 2011

Liabilities		*Amount (A)*	*Assets*		*Amount (A)*
Capital	65,690		Cash in hand		380
Add: Net Profit	34,503		Cash at bank		8,000
	1,00,193		Furniture	5,000	
Less: Drawings	19,600	80,593	*Less:* Depreciation	500	4,500

(19,000 + 600)				
Bank Loan	20,000	Closing Stock		78,600
Interest on Bank Loan	1,700	Printing & Stationery		3,600
Creditors (14,800+400–1,000)	14,200	Debtors	24,000	
		Less: Creditors	1,000	
			23,000	
		Less: Provision for bad. debt	1,150	
			21,850	
		Less: Provision for discount	437	21,413
	1,16,493			1,16,493

Working Notes

Provision for Bad Debts : Debtors include a debtor from whom A 3,000 is due, but he is also a creditor to whom A 1,000 is due. Therefore

Provision for bad debts = (A 24,000 – A, 1,000) × 5%

= A 1,150

Provision for discount on debtors = 2% (23,000 – 1,150)

= A 437

Creditors = A. 14,800 – A 1,000 + Credit purchases A 400

= A 14,200

Example 25

From the following Trial Balance as on 31.3.06, you are requested to prepare Trading and Profit & Loss A/c, for the year ended 31.3.06 and a Balance Sheet as on that date after making necessary adjustments.

Particulars	*Dr. Amount (A)*	*Cr. Amount (A)*
Sundry Debtors/Creditors	5,00,000	2,00,000
Outstanding liability for expenses	55,000	–
Wages	1,00,000	–
Carriage Outward	1,10,000	–
Carriage Inward	50,000	–
General Expenses	70,000	–
Cash Discount	20,000	–
Bad Debts	10,000	–
Motor Car	2,40,000	–
Printing Stationery	15,000	–
Furniture & Fittings	1,10,000	–
Advertisement	85,000	–
Insurance	45,000	–
Salesman's Commission	87,500	–
Postage and Telephone	57,500	–
Salaries	1,60,000	–

Particulars	*Dr. Amount (A)*	*Cr. Amount (A)*
Rates and Taxes	25,000	–
Capital A/c and Drawings	20,000	14,43,000
Purchases/Sales	15,50,000	19,87,500
Stock on 01.4.2005	2,50,000	–
Cash at bank	60,000	–
Cash in hand	10,500	–
	36,30,500	36,30,500

The following adjustments are to be made :

(*a*) Stock on 31.3.06 was valued at A 7,25,000.

(*b*) A provision for Doubtful Debts is to be created to the extent of 5 per cent on Sundry Debtors.

(*c*) Depreciate Furniture and Fittings by 10%, Motor car by 20%.

(*d*) The proprietor had withdrawn goods worth A 25,000 during the year.

(*e*) Sales include goods worth A 75,000 sent out to C on approval and remain unsold on 31.3.06. The cost of the goods was A 50,000.

(*f*) The salesmen were entitled to a commission of 5% on total sales.

(*g*) Debtors include A 25,000 bad debts.

(*h*) Printing and Stationery expenses of A 55,000 relating to 2004-2005 had not been provided in that year but was paid in 2005-06 by debiting outstanding liabilities.

(*i*) Purchases include purchase of furniture worth A 50,000.

Solution

Trading and Profit & Loss A/c
for the year ended 31st March, 2006

Dr. *Cr.*

Particulars		*Amount (A)*	*Particulars*		*Amount (A)*
To Opening Stock		2,50,000	By Sales	19,87,500	
To Purchases	15,50,000		*Less* : Good sent on		
Less : Drawings	25,000		approval (at		
Less : Purchase of			selling price)	75,000	19,12,500
Furniture	50,000	14,75,000	By Closing Stock	7,25,000	
To Wages		1,00,000	*Add* : Stock on		
To Carriage Inwards		50,000	approval (at cost)	50,000	7,75,000
To Gross Profit c/d		8,12,500			26,87,500
		26,87,500			
To Salaries		1,60,000	By Gross Profit b/d		8,12,500
To Postage & Telephone		57,500			
To Insurance		45,000			
To Rates & Taxes		25,000			
To General Expenses		70,000			
To Printing & Stationery		15,000			

Particulars		Amount (A)	Particulars	Amount (A)
To Depreciation :				
On existing furniture	11,000			
On additional Furniture	5,000			
On Motor Car	48,000	64,000		
To Saleman Commission	87,500			
Add : Outstanding Comm.				
(5% of A 19,12,500 – 87,500)				
(A 95,625 – 87,500)	8,125	95,625		
To Advertisement		85,000		
To Carriage Outward		1,10,000		
To Bad Debts	10,000			
3*Add* : Further Bad Debts	25,000			
Add : Required Provision for Doubtful Debts				
(5% of A 4,00,000)	20,000	55,000		
To Cash Discount		20,000		
To Net profit T/f to Capital A/c		10,375		
		8,12,500		8,12,500

Balance Sheet
as on 31st March, 2006

Liabilities		Amount (A)	Assets		Amount (A)
Salesmen Comm. outstanding		8,125	Furniture & Fittings	1,10,000	
Sundry Creditors		2,00,000	*Add* : Addition during the year	50,000	
Capital	14,43,000				1,60,000
Add : Net Profit	10,375				
	14,53,375		*Less* : Depreciation	16,000	1,44,000
Less : Drawings			Motor Car	2,40,000	
(A 20,000 + 25,000)	45,000		*Less* : Depreciation	48,000	1,92,000
	14,08,375		Closing Stock	7,25,000	
			Add : Stock on Approval	50,000	7,75,000
Less : Printing &			Sundry Debtors	5,00,000	
Stationery of last year	55,000	13,53,375	*Less* : Goods sent on approval	75,000	
				4,25,000	
			Less : Bad Debts	25,000	

Liabilities	Amount (A)	Assets		Amount (A)
			4,00,000	
		Less : Provision for		
		Doubtful Debts	20,000	3,80,000
		Cash at Bank		60,000
		Cash in Hand		10,500
	15,61,500			15,61,500

Example 26

The following is the Trial balance of Mr. 'A' as on 31st March 2008. You are required to prepare the Trading and Profit & Loss Account for the year ended 31st march, 2008 and balance Sheet as on that date after making the necessary adjustments :

Particulars	Dr. Amount (A)	Cr. Amount (A)
Stock 01.4.2007	5,50,000	–
Purchases and Sales	19,25,000	29,35,000
Wages and Salaries	1,25,000	–
Discount	–	2,000
Carriage Inward	40,000	–
Bill Receivable and Bill Payable	2,25,000	1,85,000
Insurance	35,000	–
Debtors and Creditors	15,00,000	9,32,500
Consignor's Balance (01.4.2007)	–	4,00,000
Capital	–	8,95,000
Commission	40,000	–
Cash sent to Consignor	8,00,000	–
Interest	35,000	–
Trade Expenses	34,500	–
Furniture (1.4.2007)	60,000	–
Consignment Sales	–	6,40,000
Cash in Hand and at bank	4,22,500	–
Rent and Taxes	1,27,500	–
Sale of Furniture (31.3.2008)	–	10,000
Charges paid against Consignment	80,000	–
	59,99,500	59,99,500

Adjustment

Stock on 31st March, 2008 was valued at A 8,00,000 (including stock of stationery A 800).

(*ii*) Bill Receivable include a dishonoured bill of A 8,000.

(*iii*) Trade Expenses include payment for stationery of A 22,500.

(*iv*) Stock in the beginning include stock of stationery A 1,800.

(*v*) Furniture sold was appearing in the balance Sheet on 31 st march, 2007 at A13,000.

(*vi*) Creditors at the end include creditors for stationery A 3,000 for credit purchases.

(*vii*) Commission receivable on sale of consignment is A 40,000.

(*viii*) Stationery A 2,000 was consumed by Mr. 'A'.

(*ix*) Make provision for bad and doubtful debts at 5% on debtors.

(*x*) Depreciate furniture at 10% p.a. [*CA, Nov., 2003*]

Solution

Trading and Profit & Loss A/c of Mr. A
for the year ended 31st March, 2008

Dr. *Cr.*

Particulars		*Amount (A)*	*Particulars*		*Amount (A)*
To Opening Stock	5,50,000		By Sales		29,35,000
Less : Stock of			By Closing Stock	8,00,000	
stationery	1,800	5,48,200	*Less :* Stock of stationery	800	7,99,200
To Purchases	19,25,000				
Less : Stationery	3,000	19,22,000			
To Wages and Salaries		1,25,000			
Carriage Inward		40,000			
To Gross profit c/d		10,99,000			
		37,34,200			37,34,200
To Insurance		35,000	By Gross profit		10,99,000
To Commission		40,000	By Discount		2,000
To Interest		35,000	By Commission from consignment		
To Rent & Taxes		1,27,500	business		40,000
To Trade Expenses	34,500				
Less : Stationery	22,500	12,000			
To Stationery consumed		24,500			
To Provision for Doubtful Debts		75,400			
To Loss on Sale of Furniture		1,700			
To Depreciation on Furniture		6,000			
To Net profit T/f to Capital A/c		7,83,900			
		11,41,000			11,41,000

Balance Sheet of Mr. A
as at 31st March, 2008

Particulars		*Amount (A)*	*Particulars*		*Amount (A)*
Capital	8,95,000		Furniture	60,000	
Add : Net Profit of current year	7,83,900		*Less* : FurnitureSold (WDV)	11,700	
	16,78,900			48,300	
Less : Drawings	2,000	16,76,900	*Less* : Depreciation	6,000	42,300
Consignor's Balance		1,20,000	Debtors	15,00,000	
Creditors for goods		9,29,500	*Add* : Bill Receivable dishonoured	8,000	
Creditors for Stationery		3,000		15,08,000	
Bills Payable		1,85,000	*Less* : Provision for bad & doubtful debts	75,400	14,32,600
			Bill Receivable	2,25,000	
			Less : Bill receivable dishounoured	8,000	2,17,000
			Closing Stock		7,99,200
			Stock of Stationery		800
			Cash in hand & at Bank		4,22,500
		29,14,400			29,14,400

Working Note

(*i*) Consignor's A/c

Cash	8,00,000	Balance b/d	4,00,000
Charges	80,000	Consignment Sales	6,40,000
Commission	40,000		
Balance c/d	1,20,000		
	10,40,000		10,40,000

(*ii*) Furniture : Loss on Sale of Furniture :

Cost 31.3.2007	A 13,000
Depreciation 10%	1,300
W.D.V.	11,700
Sold on 31.3.2008	10,000
Loss on Sale of Furniture	1,700

(*iii*) Stationery A/c

Balance b/d	1,800	Drawing	2,000
Cash Purchases	22,500	Profit & Loss A/c (Bal. Fig for stationery consumed)	24,500
Credit Purchases	3,000	Balance c/d	800
	27,300		27,300

Example 27

From the following balances and information, prepare Trading and Profit & Loss Account of Mr. X for the year ended 31st March, 2008 and a Balance Sheet as on that date :

Particulars	*Dr. Amount (A)*	*Cr. Amount (A)*
X's Capital Account	–	10,000
Plant and machinery	3,600	–
Depreciation on Plant and Machinery	400	–
Repairs to Plant	520	–
Wages	5,400	–
Salaries	2,100	–
Income-tax of Mr. X	100	–
Cash in Hand and at Bank	400	–
Land and Building	14,900	–
Depreciation on Building	500	–
Purchases	25,000	–
Purchases Return	–	300
Sales	–	49,800
Bank Overdraft	–	760
Accrued Income	300	–
Salaries Outstanding	–	400
Bills Receivable	3,000	–
Provision for Bad Bedts	–	1,000
Bills Payable	–	1,600
Bad Debts	200	–
Discount on Purchases	–	708
Debtors	7,000	–
Creditors	–	6,252
Opening Stock	7,400	–
	70,820	70,820

Additional Information

(*i*) Stock on 31 st March, 2008 was A 6,000.

(*ii*) Write off further A 600 for Bad Debts and maintain a provision for Bad Debts at 5% on Debtors.

(*iii*) Goods costing A 1,000 were sent to customer for A 1,200 on 30th March, 2008 on sale or return basis. This was recorded as actual sales.

(*iv*) A 240 paid as rent of the office were debited to landlord account and were included in the list of debtors.

(*v*) General manager is to be given commission at 10% of net profit after charging the commission of the Works manager and his own.

(*vi*) Works Manager is to be given commission at 12% of net profit before charging the commission of General manager and his own. [*CA*]

Solution

Trading and Profit & Loss A/c
for the year ended 31st march, 2008

Dr.					*Cr.*
Liabilities		Amount (A)	*Assets*		Amount (A)
To Opening Stock		7,400	By Sales	49,800	
To Purchases	25,000		*Less* : Sale on Approval	1,200	48,600
Less : Returns	300	24,700	Basis		
To Wages		5,400			
To Gross Profit c/d		18,100	By Closing Stock	6,000	
			Add : Stock with Customer		
			(at cost)	1,000	7,000
		55,600			55,600
To Repairs to Plant		520	By Gross Profit b/d		18,100
To Salaries		2,100	By Discount on Purchases		708
To Rent		240	By Provision for Bad Debts		752
To Bad Debts (200 + 600)		800	(1,000–248)		
To Depreciation on :					
Plant & Machinery	400				
Building	500	900			
To Commission to :					
Works manager		1,800			
General manager		1,200			
To Net Profit		12,000			
		19,500			19,500

Balance Sheet as at 31st March, 2008

Liabilities		Amount (A)	*Assets*		Amount (A)
Capital A/c	10,000		Land & Building		14,900
Less : Income Tax	100		Plant & Machinery		3,600
	9,900		Stock in Hand	6,000	
Add : Net Profit	12,000	21,900	*Add* : Stock with Customer	1,000	7,000
Bank Overdraft		760	Debtors	4,960	
Bills Payable		1,600	*Less* : Provision for Bad Debts	248	4,712
Sundry Creditors		6,252	Bills Receivable		3,000
Salaries Outstanding		400	Accrued Income		300
Outstanding Commission			Cash In Hand and at Bank		400
Works Manager	1,800				
General Manager	1,200	3,000			
		33,912			33,912

Work Notes

		(A)	(A)
(1)	Debtors as per Trial Balance		7,000
	Less : Debtors on account of goods sold on approval basis	1,200	
	Landlord Account wrongly taken as debtor	240	1,440
			5,560
	Less : Bad Debts written off		600
			4,960

Provision for Bad Debts required (Closing Balance) :

5% on Debtors A 4,960 = A 248

(2) Calculation of Commission of Works manager :

12% of A 15,000 = A 1,800

Calculation of Commission of Works Manager :

10/110 × A 13,200 (15,000 – 1,800) = A 1,200

(3) As discount on purchases is appearing in the Trial Balance, it can be safely assumed that it is a cash discount. Alternatively, it may be assumed that it is trade discount which has been wrongly recorded in the books. In that case, it should be shown as deduction from purchases in the Trading Account.

Example 28

From the following particulars for the year ending 31st March, 2008 of M/s. ABC Company prepare Trading and Profit and Loss Account and Balance Sheet on that date :

Stock (1.4.2007)	23,200	Advertisement	15,950
Capital (1-4-2007)	1,45,000	Apprenticeship premium	3,480
Purchases	58,000	Bill Receivable	10,150
Sales	2,32,000	Bill Payable	7,250
Office Expenses	23,345	Sundry Debtors	58,000
Return Inward	4,350	Plants and Machinery	13,050
Interest on Loan	870	Sundry Creditors	45,820
Return Outward	1,160	Loan (Dr.), @ 10% on 1.4.2007	14,500
Drawings	8,700	Investment	8,700
Wages	20,010	Cash at Bank	10,150
Land and Building	1,59,500	Cash in hand	725
Furniture and Fixtures	7,250	Stock (31-3-2008)	20,300

Adjustments

(*i*) Interest on capital to be allowed at 5% for the year.

(*ii*) Interest on drawings to be charged to him as ascertained for the year A 232.

(*iii*) Apprenticeship premium is for three year received in advance on 1st April, 2007.

(*iv*) Stock valued at A 8,700 destroyed by fire on 25-3-2008, but the insurance company admitted a claim of A 5,800 only to be paid in the year 2009.

(*v*) A 14,500 out of advertisement expenses are to be carried forward.

(*vi*) The manager is entitled to commission of 10% at the net profit calculated after charging such commission.

(*vii*) The stock includes material worth A 2,900 for which bill had not been received and therefore, not yet accounted for [*CA December, 2002*]

Solution

Trading Account for the year ended 31-3-2008

Dr. *Cr.*

Liabilities		*Amount* (*A*)	*Assets*		*Amount* (*A*)
To Opening Stock		23,200	By Sales	2,32,000	
To Purchases	58,000		*Less* : Return inward	4,350	2,27,650
Less : Return outward	1,160		By Closing Stock		20,300
	58,840				
Add : Unrecorded purchases	2,900				
	59,740				
Less : Loss of stock by fire	8,700	51,040			
To Wages		20,010			
To Profit and Loss A/c (Gross Profit)		1,53,700			
		2,47,950			2,47,950

Alternatively, loss of stock by fire may be shown on credit side of trading account.

Profit and Loss Account for the year ended 31.03.2008

Dr. *Cr.*

Liabilities		*Amount* (*A*)	*Assets*		*Amount* (*A*)
To Loss of stock by fire (8,700 - 5,800)		2,900	By Trading A/c (Gross Profit)		1,53,700
			By Interesting on drawings		232
To Office expenses		23,345	By Interest on loan	870	
Advertisement	15,950	1,450	Add : Accrued interest	580	1,450
Less : Carried forward	14,500	1,450	(1,450 - 870)		
			By Apprenticeship premium	3,480	
To Interest on capital			*Less* : Received in advance		
(5% on A 1,45,000)		7,250	(2/3 × A 3,480)	2,320	1,160
To Manager's commission					
(10/110 × A 1,21,597)		11,054			
To Capital A/c (Net profit)		1,10,543			
		1,56,542			1,56,542

Balance Sheet as on 31-3-2008

Liabilities		*Amount (A)*	*Assets*		*Amount (A)*
Capital	1,45,000		Land and building		1,59,500
Add : Interest on capital	7,250		Plant and Machinery		13,050
Profit	1,10,543		Furniture and fixtures		7,250
	2,62,793		Investment		8,700
Less : Drawings	8,700		Bills receivable		10,150
Interest on drawings	232	2,53,861	Sundry debtors		58,000
Sundry creditors	45,820		Insurance claim		5,800
Add : Unrecorded	2,900	48,720	Loan	14,500	
purchases			*Add* : Accrued interest	580	15,080
Bills payable		7,250	Advertisement (not written off)		14,500
Manager's commission payable		11,054	Closing Stock		20.300
Apprenticeship premium received			Cash at Bank		10,150
in advance		2,320	Cash In Hand		725
		3,23,205			3,23,205

ASSIGNMENT MATERIAL

Note : The objective - Type Questions (True / False, Multiple Choice Questions etc.) have been given in the Appendix at the end of the book.

SHORT ANSWER THEORY QUESTIONS

1. Explain objectives and limitations of financial statements.
2. Distinguish between deferred revenue expenses and prepaid expenses.
3. Answer the following :
   (*i*) The proprietor has withdrawn some goods from the business for his personal use. Is it compulsory to record it in the books of the firm? Give reasoning.
   (*ii*) The life of business is assumed to be indefinite (going concern concept), yet companies prepare their accounts annually. What is the basis?
   (*iii*) You started a business on 1st April, 2004 (financial year close on 31st March, 2005). Salaries for March, 2005 were paid on 7th April, 2005. Monthly salaries bill amounts to A one lac How much amount would be shown in 2004-05 P&L A/c and on what basis?
4. Explain deferred revenue expenditure.
5. Write notes on contingent liability.
6. Explain capital expenses and revenue expenses.
7. Distinguish between capital receipts and revenue receipts.
8. Distinguish between capital expenditure and revenue expenditure.
9. Distinguish between reserves and provisions.
10. Write notes on limitations of financial statements.

11. Distinguish between accrued income and outstanding income.
12. What are adjustment entries?
13. Write notes on :
    (*a*) Outstanding expense
    (*b*) Accrued income
    (*c*) Depreciation
    (*d*) Loss of stock in trade
    (*e*) Manager's commission on net profit

    How are these treated in final accounts?
14. What is provision for bad and doubtful debts?
15. What are closing entries?
16. Distinguish between capital expenditure and revenue expenditures.
17. How are assets and liability items are arranged on the balance sheet?
18. Define contigent liabilities and contingent assets.
19. Explain the concept of deferred revenue expenditure by giving suitable examples. How is it different from capital expenditure? [*B.Com.(Hons.), Delhi University, 2011*]
20. Distinguish between capital expenditure and revenue expenditure. [*B.Com.(Hons.) Delhi University, 2009*]
21. Write a note on Accrued Income and outstanding income. [*B.Com.(Hons.) Delhi University, 2005*]
22. **Comment in brief on the following naming the principles of accounting on which these statement are based:**
    (*i*) Balance sheet is not valuation statement.
    (*ii*) Advance received from a supplier is not taken as income or sales.
    (*iii*) Calibre or quality of management team is not directly disclosed on the Balance Sheet. [*B.Com.(Hons.) Delhi University, 2008*]
23. What is a contingent liability? Give three examples of contingent liability. [*B.Com.(Hons.) Delhi University, 2010*]
24. State with reasons whether the following items are Capital expenditure or Revenue expenditure.
    (*i*) A factory building was constructed at a cost A 15,00,000. A sum of A 64,000 were incurred for the construction of the temporary huts for storing building materials.
    (*ii*) A 5,000 paid for removal of stock to a new site.
    (*iii*) Expenses incurred in connection with obtaining a licence to start the business were A 15,000.
25. State which item of expenditure would be charged to capital and which to revenue:
    (*i*) Freight and cartage on the new machine A 150, erection charges A 200.
    (*ii*) Fixtures of the book value of A 1,500 were sold off at A 600.
    (*iii*) A sum of A 1,100 was spent on painting the factory.

Answer :

(*i*) The expenditure incurred by way of freight and carriage on the new machine A 150 and erection charges A 200 are both of **capital nature.**

(*ii*) The loss suffered on sale of fixture amount to (1,500 – 600) A 900 should be taken as **revenue** loss.

(*iii*) The painting charges are for maintenance of a capital asset, hence they are of a **revenue** nature.

26. The drama club in Indian School of Drama, New Delhi has made certain purchases to improve their organization. As specified in the club rules, the treasurer regards all consumable and breakable items as revenue expenditures. Which of the following item would you regard as capital and which as revenue expenditure :

(*i*) Erection of a theatre for club use.

(*ii*) Make – up for the next presentation

(*iii*) Membership fee for Indian Drama Association

(*iv*) Stage fittings, wings and pillars.

(*v*) Flash powder for special effects.

(*vi*) Purchases of spotlights and dimmers.

(*vii*) A club minibus for outside performance.

(*viii*) Crockery for refreshment service.

(*ix*) Bar stocks.

(*x*) Tickets for next performance. (*C.A.*)

Answer :

(*i*) It is **Capital expenditure** since it will provide benefit for more than one accounting year.

(*ii*) It is Revenue expenditure as the make-up expenses are incurred for the services for one day at the most.

(*iii*) In the absence of specific information, it may be presumed that it is an annual expenditure and therefore, **revenue expenditure**.

(*iv*) It is **capital expenditure** since the benefits would accrue for long time.

(*v*) It is **revenue expenditure** since it is a regular or recurring expense.

(*vi*) It is **capital expenditure** as the spot lights and dimmers would be used for longer duration.

(*vii*) It is **capital expenditure** as mini bus would remain in use for many years.

(*viii*) It is **capital expenditure** since crockery can be used for more than one accounting year.

(*ix*) It is **revenue** expenditure as expenses on bar stock is regular and routine.

(*x*) It is revenue expenditure because expenses associated with it are of frequent nature.

27. State with reasons, how you would classify the following items of expenditure :

(*i*) Overhauling expenses of A 25,000 for the engine of a Motor Car to get better fuel efficiency.

(*ii*) Inauguration expenses of A 25 lakhs incurred on the opening of a new manufacturing unit in an existing business.

(*iii*) Compensation of A 2.5 crores paid to workers who opted for voluntary retirement. (*C.A.*)

Answer :

(*i*) It is a capital expenditure because it will help to increase the capacity of vehicle.

(*ii*) Such expenditures do not create any tangible asset nor do they increase the efficiency of the factory and therefore is revenue expenditure.

(*iii*) Basically it is a revenue expenditure. However since the amount involved is considerable, it may be preferably treated as Deferred Revenue Expenditure.

LONG ANSWER THEORY QUESTIONS

1. What basis of accounting is required by Generally Accepted Accounting Principles for the profit and loss account and balance sheet.
2. Explain the basic difference between accrual basis accounting and cash basis accounting. Which of the two is required by Generally Accepted Accounting Principles?
3. What are adjusting entries. Why are they needed for preparing financial statements?
4. List different types of adjusting entries.
5. What are prepaid expenses and unearned revenues?
6. What are accrued expenses and accrued revenues. Give an example of an adjustment to record each of the these items.
7. At the end of an accounting period, certain accounts are adjusted. Why?
8. Explain the difference between deferrals and accruals as classification of adjusting entries.
9. "The net income of a business entity is determined by measuring the amount of revenue generated and subtracting expenses incurred, appropriately measured. As a consequence, the resulting difference, net profit, is a precise measure of operating performance for the period under consideration." Comment.
10. What is a trading account? What are its purposes?
11. What are the objectives of preparing profit and loss account?
12. Give a specimen of trading, profit and loss account, using imaginary figures.
13. What is a balance sheet? What are its characteristics?
14. Explain the rationale behind preparing a balance sheet. What are its limitation?
15. Explain the linkage between trial balance, profit and loss account and balance sheet.
16. A company balance sheet is a major financial statement. What information does it contain?
17. What are the purposes behind a balance sheet?
18. List the major sections (and the components of each section) of a balance sheet.
19. How will you deal with the following in the final accounts :
    (*a*) Loss of stock-in-trade
    (*b*) Manager's commission on net profit.
    (*c*) Withdrawal of goods by proprietor
    (*d*) Provision for bad and doubtful debts
20. Discuss capital expenditures and revenue expenditures and bring out differences between them.
21. Explain the nature of balance sheet and its limitations.
22. Write explanatory notes on :
    (*a*) Provisions
    (*b*) Contingent liabilities
    (*c*) Contingent assets.

PRACTICAL PROBLEMS

1. The provision for Doubtful Debts A/c shows a balance of A 5,000 on 1st January, 2009. The Bad Debts during the year 2009 amounted to A 3,000. The Sundry Debtors on 31st December, 2009 are A 50,000. On 31st December, 20007, there is an additional Bad Debts of A 3,000. Create a new provision for Bad Debts @ 10% on debtors.

You are required to show how the different items will appear in the firm's Profit and Loss A/c and Balance Sheet. [***Ans.*** Amount transferred to Profit and Loss A/c A 5,700]

2. From the following particulars prepare provision for doubtful debts account and bad debts account.

2012	Jan. 1	Provision for Doubtful Debts	A 2,500
	Dec. 31	Bad Debts	A 1,870
		Debtors	A 20,000

Make provision for bad debts at 5% on debtors.

[***Ans.*** Balance in Provision for Doubtful A/c A 1,000]

3. From the following figures, you are required to show :
   (*a*) Provision for doubtful debts account
   (*b*) Bad Debts account
   (*c*) Profit and Loss account

Provision for Doubtful Debts 1.4.2011	A 1,000
Provision for Doubtful Debts 31.3.2012	A 2000
Debts Written off in 2011-12	A 1,200

4. A company has a bad debts provision of A 20,000. The amount of debtors at the end of the year amounted to A 3,20,000 out of these A 2,60,000 are good debtors and A 60,000 is doubtful on which a provision of 40 percent to be made. Show as these items will appear in the books.

[***Ans.*** Amount in P&L A/c A 4000]

5. The following balances appeared in the trial balance of X on December 31, 2012.

Debtors	A 1,00,000
Bad Debts	A 5,000
Provision for bad debts (1.1.2012)	A 6,000

It was found that bad debts worth A 3,000 were not recorded in the books till Dec. 31, 2012. It was decided that a provision for bad debts equal to 8 percent on the closing debtors will be adequate. You are required to prepare bad debts accounts and provision for bad debts account. Also show how these items would appear in profit and loss account and balance sheet.

[***Ans.*** Amount transferred to Profit and Loss A/c A 9760].

6. A firm had the following balances on April 1, 2012

Provision for doubtful debts	A 6,500
Provision for discount on debtors	A 3,200
Reserve for discount on creditors	A 4,800

During the year ended March 31, 2013, bad debts amounted to A 4,500, discounts allowed were A 15,800 and discount received were A 9,700. During the year 2013-14, bad debts amounting to A 2,300 were written off while discount allowed and received were A 12,500 and A 8,900 respectively. Sundry debtors were A 1,50,000 on 31.3.2013 and A 90,000 on 31.3.2014. Sundry creditors were A 1,05,000 and A 1,26,000 on 31.03.2013 and 31.03.2014 respectively. It is the firm's policy to maintain a provision of 5 percent against bad and doubtful debts and 3 percent for discount on debtors and reserve of 2 percent on creditors. Show the necessary accounts for the year 2012-13 and 2013-14.

7. A company maintains its Reserve for bad debts @ 5% and reserve for discount on Debtors @ 2%. You are given the following details :

	2011 (A)	2012 (A)
Bad Debts	1,600	3,000
Discount allowed	2,400	1,000
Recovery of Bad Debts written off in earlier Years	1,000	600

Sundry Debtors (before writing off bad debts and discount) amounted to A 1,20,000 on December 31, 2011 and A 90,000 on December, 31, 2012.

On January 1, 2011 reserve for bad debts and reserve for discount on debtors had balances of A 900 and A 1,600, respectively. Show the reserve for bad debts account and reserve for discount on debtors Account for 2011 and 2012.

8. On 31.12.2012 the following Trial Balance was prepared from the books of Raju :

	Dr. (A)	*Cr.* (A)
Sundry Debtors	50,600	
Sundry Creditors	–	10,000
Bills Receivable	5,000	–
Plant & Machinery	75,000	–
Purchases	90,000	–
Capital	–	70,000
Freehold Premises	50,000	–
Salaries	11,000	–
Wages	14,400	–
Postage and Stationery	750	–
Carriage In	750	–
Carriage Out	1,000	–
Bad Debts	950	–
Bad Debts Provisions	–	350
General Charges	1,500	–
Cash at Bank	5,300	–
Cash in Hand	800	–
Bills Payable	–	5,000
Reserve	–	20,000
Sales	–	2,31,700
Closing Stock	30,000	–
Total :	3,37,050	3,37,050

The following adjustments are required :

(*i*) Raju gets a salary of A 9,000 p.a.

(*ii*) Allow 5% interest on capital.

(*iii*) Bad Debts provision to be adjusted to 2½% on sundry debtors.

(*iv*) 2½% of the net profit to be credited to Reserve.

(*v*) It was discovered in January 2012 that stock sheets as on 31.12.2011 were overcast by A 1,000

You are required to prepare Trading and Profit and Loss account for the year ended 31st December, 2012 and a Balance Sheet as at that date.

[***Ans.*** G/P A 1,27,550, Net Profit A 98,935, B/S total A 2,16,435.]

9. From the following Trial Balance prepare Trading and Profit and Loss Account for the year ended 31st December, 2012 and Balance Sheet as on that date :

	Dr.(A)	*Cr.*(A)
Drawings	10,000	–
Stock on 1,1,2012	46,000	–
Purchases and Purchases Returns	1,50,200	600
Cash in Hand	3,400	–
Bank Balance	22,660	–
Freehold Premises	38,600	–
Trade Expenses	840	–
Printing, Stationery and Advertising	1,640	–
Professional Charges	280	–
Commission Received	–	3,300
Investments as on 1st Jan. @ 10%	4,000	–
Interest on above	–	200
Sundry Debtors and Creditors	36,000	29,000
Wages	25,000	–
Salaries	14,000	–
Capital	–	1,14,000
Income Tax	1,600	–
Discount allowed and Received	6,300	4,600
Sales Returns and Sales	550	2,08,950
Bills Receivable / Bills Payable	3,200	10,000
Office Furniture	3,050	–
Rent, Rates and Insurance	4,000	–
Bad Debts Provision	–	670
Total	3,71,320	3,71,320

Adjustments

(*a*) Provide for wages A 5,000.

(*b*) Write Off 5% depreciation on freehold premises and 10% on office furniture.

(*c*) Insurance to the extent of A 200 relates to 2013.

(*d*) Stock on 31.12.2012 is A 5,20,000.

(*e*) Charge interest on capital 5% and on drawings A 300.

(*f*) Further bad debts are A 1,000.

(*g*) Provide for doubtful debts @ 5% on sundry debtors.

(*h*) Make provision for discount on debtors and reserve for discount on creditors @ 2%.

[***Ans.*** G/P A 34,800; N/P A 4840, B/S total 1,57,660]

10. From the following Trial Balance of Shri Chandershekar, prepare Trading and Profit and Loss Account for the year 31st March, 2013 and Balance Sheet as on that date after taking into account the adjustments given at the bottom of the trial balance.

Debit Balance	*Dr.* (A)	*Credit Balance*	*Cr.* (A)
Chandershekar's Drawings	4,500	Chandershekar's Capital	24,000
Purchases	20,000	Sales	30,500
Returns Inwards	1,500	Discount	1,900
Stock (1.4.2012)	8,000	Sundry Creditors	10,000
Salary	4,200	Bills Payable	2,500
Wages	1,200		
Rent	350		
Bad Debts	400		
Dicounts	700		
Sundry Debtors	14,000		
Cash in Hand	260		
Cash at Bank	5,940		
Insurance	400		
Trade Expenses	300		
Printing	150		
Furniture	2,000		
Machinery	5,000		
Total	68,900		68,900

Adjustments

(*a*) Closing stock was valued at A 7,000.

(*b*) Insurance was prepaid to the extent of A 60.

(*c*) Outstanding liabilities were : Salary A 200, Wages A 200.

(*d*) Make provision for doubtful debts at 5% on sundry debtors.

(*e*) Calculate Interest on Capital at 5% p.a..

(*f*) Depreciate machinery at 5% and Furniture at 10%.

(*g*) Provide for discount on creditors at 1%.

[***Ans.*** G/P A 6,600, Net Loss A 390; B/S Total A 33,110]

11. The following Trial Balance was extracted from the books of Mr. X as on 31st December, 2012.

Debit Balance :	Dr. A		
Plant and Machinery	20,000	Opening Stock	34,200
Manufacturing Wages	34,500	Motor Car	12,000
Salaries	15,850	Sales Return	3,100
Furniture	10,000	Purchases	1,02,000
Freight on Purchases	1,860	Bad Debts	1,400
Freight on Sales	2,140		
Building	24,000	Interest and Bank Charges	400
Manufacturing Expenses	9,500	Cash at Bank	4,200

Insurance and Tax	4,250	Cash in Hand	1,120
Goodwill	25,000	**Credit Balances :**	
General Expenses	8,200	Capital Account	80,000
Factory Fuel and Power	1,280	Sundry Creditors	44,560
Sundry Debtors	78,200	Bank Loan	15,000
Factory Lighting	950	Purchases returns	1,740
		Sales	2,50,850
		Reserve for Bad Debts	2,000

Prepare Trading and Profit and Loss Account for the year ended 31st December, 2012 and the balance sheet as on that date taking into consideration the following information :

(*a*) Stock in hand on 31st December, 2012 was valued at A 30,500.

(*b*) Depreciate Plant and Machinery by 10% Furniture by 5% and Motor car by A 1,000.

(*c*) Bring provision for Bad debts to 5%, on Sundry Debtors.

(*d*) A commission of 1% on the gross profit is to be provided for Works Manager.

(*e*) A commission of 2% (two percent) on net profit (after charging the Works Manager commission but before charging General Managers Commission) is to be paid to the General Manager.

[***Ans.*** G/P A 95,700, N/P A 55,951, B/S Total A 1,97,610]

12. From the following Trial Balance prepare Trading, Profit & Loss Account and Balance Sheet as on 31st December 2012.

Capital	*Dr.* (*A*)	*Cr.* (*A*)
Capital	–	25,000
Loans	–	5,000
Sales	–	35,000
Account Payable	–	4,000
Bills Payable	–	5,000
Purchase Returns	–	2,000
Dividends Received	–	3,000
Plant & Machinery	13,000	–
Buildings	17,000	–
Receivable	9,650	–
Purchases	18,000	–
Discount Allowed	1,200	–
Wages	7,000	–
Salaries	3,000	–
Travelling Expenses	750	–
Freight	200	–
Insurance	300	–
Commission paid	100	–

Capital	*Dr.* *(A)*	*Cr.* *(A)*
Cash in Hand	100	–
Bank	1,600	–
Repairs	500	–
Interest on Loans	600	–
Opening Inventory	6,000	–
	79,000	79,000

Additional Data

(*a*) Closing Inventory A 8,000.

(*b*) Depreciation on Plant and Machinery at 15% and 10% on Building.

(*c*) Provision for doubtful Receivable A 500.

(*d*) Insurance prepaid A 50.

(*e*) Outstanding rent A 100.

[***Ans.*** G/P A 14,000; N/P A 6150; B/S Total A 45,250]

13. The following is the Trial Balance of Raman Traders as on 31st December, 2013.

Dr.	*Amount (A)*	*Cr.*	*Amount (A)*
Cash in Hand	1,500	Sales	2,50,000
Cash at Bank	3,000	Returns Outwards	2,000
Purchases	1,10,000	Capital	56,000
Returns Inwards	1,500	Account Payable	30,000
Wages	20,000		
Power and Fuel	8,000		
Carriage Outwards	6,000		
Carriage Inwards	5,000		
Opening Inventory	6,000		
Land	10,000		
Building	80,000		
Machinery	30,000		
Patents	15,000		
Salaries	12,000		
Sundry Expenses	6,000		
Insurance	1,000		
Drawings	8,000		
Accounts Receivable	15,000		
Total	3,38,000		3,38,000

You are required to prepare Trading and Profit & Loss Account for the year ended 31.12.2013 and Balance Sheet as at 31.12.2013. Adjustments to be made are given below :

1. Closing Inventory as at 31.12.2013, A 20,000.
2. Provision for bad and doubtful receivable at 5% on debtors.
3. Outstanding Salary A 5,000 outstanding wages A 3,000.
4. Depreciation 10% on all assets.

[***Ans.*** G/P A 1,18,500; N/P A 75,250; B/S Total A 1,61,250]

14. The following is the Trial Balance of Kamal Enterprises for the year ended 31st December, 2012. You are required to prepare a Profit & Loss Account and Balance Sheet after taking into account the adjustments given below :

Dr.	*Amount (A)*	*Cr.*	*Amount (A)*
Cash in Hand	500	Sales	1,50,300
Cash at Bank	1,200	Purchase Returns	5,000
Office Furniture	6,000	Accounts Payable	12,000
Accounts Receivable	15,000	Bills Payable	8,000
Commissions	1,200	Discount Receivable	1,000
Bills Receivable	3,500	Dividend Received	2,000
Power and Fuel	6,000	Rent Receivable	3,500
Plant & Machinery	24,000	Capital	27,000
Office Expenses	2,000		
Carriage Inwards	1,200		
Carriage Outwards	3,500		
Rent, Rates & Taxes	1,700		
Leasehold Premises	25,000		
Wages	30,000		
Salaries	7,000		
Opening Inventory	12,000		
Sales Returns	2,000		
Purchases	60,000		
Drawings	7,000		
	2,08,000		2,08,000

Adjustments

1. Closing Inventory as on 31.12.2012 A 18,000.
2. Depreciate Plant and Machinery at 10%.
3. Salaries outstanding A 1,000, Power and Fuel outstanding A 2,000.
4. A 5,000 was spent on Plant and machinery but wrongly included in wages.
5. Provide for bad and doubtful debts for A 1,500.
6. Discount earned but not received A 100.
7. Commission due but not recorded A 200.
8. Rent received includes A 500 received in advance.

[***Ans.*** G/P A 1,66,300; N/P A 50,200; B/S Total A 93,900]

15. The following is the Trial Balance of Rajan Jewellers as on December 31, 2013.

Dr.	*Amount (A)*	*Cr.*	*Amount (A)*
Opening Inventory	72,000	Capital	5,00,000
Purchases	2,25,000	Sales	3,50,000
Furniture	15,000	Purchase Returns	1,800
Motor Car	30,000	Murthy	32,000
Buildings	4,25,800	Vardan	24,000
Gangappa	12,000	Commission	7,500
Gorishankar	20,000		
Methews	18,000		
Advertisement	22,000		
Repairs and Maintenance	13,000		
General Expenses	16,000		
Insurance	7,000		
Cash in hand	3,500		
Cash at Bank	6,000		
Salaries	30,000		
	9,15,300		9,15,300

Notes

To arrive at Accounts Receivable and Accounts Payable you have to add necessary ledger accounts. You are required to draft Profit & Loss Account and Balance Sheet as on 31st December, 2013.

1. Closing Inventory as at 31.12.2013 A 80,000.
2. Interest on Capital at 6%.
3. Prepaid advertisement A 2,000.
4. Goods used for domestic purposes A 1,800.
5. Outstanding Salaries A 3,000.
6. Depreciation on Building at 5%, Furniture 5% and Motor Car at 10%.

[***Ans.*** G/P A 1,36,600; N/P A 60; B/S Total A 5,87,260]

16. On March 31, 2012 the following Trial Balance was extracted from the books of W. Brothers :

Particulars	*Dr. Amount (A)*	*Cr. Amount (A)*
Capital A/c	–	1,00,000
Plant & Machinery	1,00,000	–
Sales	–	4,07,000
Purchases	2,60,000	–
Return	6,000	5,750
Opening Stocks	40,000	–
Discounts	350	–
Bank Charges	75	–
S. Debtors	45,000	–

Particulars	Dr. Amount (A)	Cr. Amount (A)
S. Creditors	–	35,000
Salaries	26,800	–
Wages	30,000	–
Carriage	1,950	–
Bad Debts Provision	–	1,325
Rent, Rates & Taxes	10,000	–
Advertising	2,000	–
Cash in Hand	900	–
Cash at Bank	6,000	–
Furniture & Fitting	20,000	–
	5,49,075	5,49,075

You are required to prepare final accounts for the year ended 31st March, 2012 and the Balance Sheet as on the date. The following adjustments are required :

1. Closing Stock A 35,000.
2. Depreciation on Plant and machinery @ 15% p.a., and on furniture and fittings @10% p.a., to be provided.
3. Bad Debts provision to be adjusted to A 500.
4. Interest on Capital to be allowed at 10% p.a.
5. 15% of the profit remaining after charging interest on capital to be carried to General Reserve.

[***Ans.*** G/P A 1,09,800; N/P A 37,740; B/S Total A 1,89,400]

17. Prepare Trading and Profit & Loss Account and Balance Sheet as on 31st March 2013 from the following balance :

	Amount (A)
M. Mirza's Capital A/c	1,19,400
M. Mirza's Drawings A/c	10,550
Sundry Creditors	59,630
15% Loan A/c (Cr.)	20,000
Cash in Hand	3,030
Cash at Bank	18,970
Sundry Debtors (Including Badri Das for Dishonoured bill of A 1,000)	62,000
Bills Receivable	9,500
Provision for doubtful Debts	2,500
Fixtures & Fittings	8,970
Plant & Machinery	28,800
Stocks, April 1, 2012	89,680
Purchases	2,56,590
Manufacturing Wages	40,970
Sales	3,56,430

	Amount (A)
Returns Inwards	2,780
Salaries	11,000
Rent & Taxes	5,620
Interest and Discount (Debit)	5,870
Travelling Expenses	1,880
Repairs and Renewals	3,370
Insurance (Including Premium of A 300 p.a. Paid upto Sept, 30, 2013)	400
Bad Debts	3,620
Commission Received	5,640

Stocks in hand on March 31, 2013 was A 1,28,960. Write off half of Badri Das's dishonoured bill. Create a provision of 5% on Sundry Debtors. Charge 10% interest on Capital. Manufacturing Wages include A 1,200 for erection of new machinery purchased last year. Depreciate Plant and Machinery by 15% and Fixtures and Fittings by 10% per annum. Commission earned but not received amount to A 600. Interest on loan for the last two months is not paid. [***Ans.*** G/P A 96,570; N/P A 52,313; B/S Total A 2,53,233]

18. The following is the Trial Balance extracted from the books of Akhilesh as on 30 September, 2012.

Particulars	*Dr. Amount (A)*	*Cr. Amount (A)*
Capital Account	–	1,00,000
Plant & Machinery	78,000	–
Furniture	2,000	–
Purchases and Sales	60,000	1,27,000
Returns	1,000	750
Opening Stock	30,000	–
Discount	425	800
Sundry Debtors/Creditors	45,000	25,000
Salaries	7,550	–
Manufacturing wages	10,000	–
Carriage outwards	1,200	–
Provision for doubtful debts	–	525
Rent, rates, Taxes	10,000	–
Advertisements	2,000	–
Cash	6,900	–
	2,54,075	2,54,075

Prepare trading and profit and loss Account for the year ended 30 September 2012 and a balance sheet on that date after taking into account the following adjustments:

(*a*) Closing stock was valued at A 34,220.

(*b*) Provision for doubtful debts is to be kept at A 500.

(c) Depreciate plant and machinery @ 10% p.a.

(d) The proprietor has taken goods worth A 5,000 for personal use and additionally distributed goods worth A 1,000 as samples.

(e) Purchase of furniture A 920 has been passed through purchases book.

[***Ans.*** G/P A 67,890; N/P A 38,740; B/S Total A 1,58,740]

19. From the following Trial Balance extracted from the books of Mr. Nair. Prepare a Trading and Profit and Loss Account for the year ended 31st December 2012 and a Balance Sheet as on that date :

Particulars	*Dr. Amount (A)*	*Cr. Amount (A)*
Nair's Capital A/c	–	1,80,000
Nair's Drawings A/c	12,960	–
Land	50,000	–
Plant and machinery	28,540	–
Furniture	2,500	–
Carriage inwards	8,740	–
Wages (Manufacturing)	42,940	–
Salaries	9,340	–
Bad Debts provision	–	3,940
Sales	–	182,460
Sales Return	3,520	–
Bank Charges	280	–
Coal, Gas and Water	1,440	–
Rates & Taxes	1,680	–
Discount Account (balance)	–	240
Purchases (Adjusted)	61,460	–
Bills receivable	2,540	–
Trade expenses	3,980	–
Sundry debtors	75,600	–
Sundry creditors	–	24,340
Stock, 31st December 2012	58,780	–
Apprentice premium	–	2,000
Fire Insurance	980	–
Cash at bank	26,000	–
Cash in hand	1,280	–
Bad Debts	420	–
	3,92,980	3,92,980

Charge depreciation on Land at 2½%, on Plant and Machinery at 10% and on Furniture at 10%. Make a provision of 5% on the sundry debtors for bad Debts. The bank has intimated that cheque for A 800 received from a customer has been dishonoured. The customer is in difficulties and it is expected that he would be able to pay 60% of the claims on him.

Carry forward the following unexpired amounts :

Fire insurance A 250; Rates and Taxes A 480; Apprentice premium A 800. Trade expenses amounting to A 430 have not yet been paid. Wages include A 500 spent on the installation of new machinery on 1st January 2012. Allow 5 percent interest on capital but not on drawings.

[***Ans.*** G/P A 64,860; N/P A 36,356; B/S Total A 2,37,966.]

20. From the following Trial Balance and other information prepare Profit & Loss Account for the year ended 31st march, 2012 and a Balance Sheet on that date :

Particulars	*Dr. Amount (A)*	*Cr. Amount (A)*
Aprna Capital Account	–	10,00,000
Withdrawls of Goods for personal use	1,000	–
Balance at bank	1,76,000	–
Motor vehicle	1,50,000	–
Debtors and creditors	2,94,000	2,30,000
Printing and stationery	6,600	–
Gross Profit	–	5,71,400
Provision for doubtful debts	–	5,000
Bad Debts	11,400	–
Freehold Premises	8,00,000	–
Repairs to premises	47,600	–
General reserve	–	2,00,000
Proprietor Remuneration	20,000	–
Stock	2,80,000	–
Delivery Expenses	99,000	–
Administrative Expenses	1,31,400	–
Rates and Taxes	15,000	–
Drawings	1,00,000	–
Unpaid Wages	–	1,600
Last Year Profit & Loss account Balance	–	1,24,000
	21,32,000	21,32,000

Adjustments

(*i*) Depreciation on Motor Vehicles @50%.

(*ii*) Creditors include a claim for damages of A 25,000 and which was settled by paying A 15,000.

(*iii*) Rates paid in advance A 3,000.

(*iv*) Provision for bad debts is to be reduced to A 3,500.

(*v*) The item of repairs to premises includes A 20,000 for acquisition of capital asset.

(*vi*) Stock of stationery in hand on 31 March, 2012 is A 2,200.

[***Ans.*** N/P A 3,26,100; B/S Total 16,26,700]

21. From the following figures extracted from the books of Mohan, you are required to prepare a trading account and profit and loss account for the year ended 31st March, 2012 and a Balance Sheet as on that date after making the necessary adjustments.

	Amount (A'000)
Mohan's Capital	22,880
Mohan's Drawings	1,320
Plant and machinery	9,900
Freehold Property	6,600
Purchases	11,000
Returns Outwards	110
Salaries	1,320
Office-Expenses	715
Office furniture	550
Discount (Dr.)	132
Sundry debtors	2,926
Loan to Krishna @ 10% per annum, Balance on 1st April, 2011	4,400
Cash at bank	2,926
Bills Payable	550
Stock on 1st April, 2011	3,850
Wages	3,520
Sundry Creditors	4,400
Gas and fuel	297
Bad debts	66
Freight	990
Loose Tools on 1st April, 2011	220
Factory Lighting	286
Provision for doubtful debts	88
Interest on loan to Krishan	110
Cash in Hand	264
Sales	23,144

Adjustments

(*i*) Stock on 31st March, 2012 was valued at A 7,260 thousand.

(*ii*) Depreciate Plant & Machinery by 33 1/3% Furniture by 10% and freehold property by 5%.

(*iii*) Loose Tools were valued at A 176 thousand on 31st March, 2012.

(*iv*) Of the sundry debtors A 6 thousand are bad and should be written off. Maintain a provision of 5% on sundry debtors for doubtful debts.

[CA]

[***Ans.*** G/P A 10,571; N/P A 4,985; B/S Total A 31,495]

22. The following is the schedule of balances on 31st March, 2012, extracted from the books of Dinesh :

Particulars	*Dr. Amount (A)*	*Cr. Amount (A)*
Cash in Hand	1,400	–
Cash at Bank	2,600	–
Sundry Debtors	86,000	–
Stock as on 1st April, 2011	62,000	–
Furniture and Fixtures	21,400	–
Office Equipments	16,000	–
Buildings	60,000	–
Motor car	20,000	–
Sundry Creditors	–	43,000
Loan	–	30,000
Provision for Bad Debts	–	3,000
Purchases	1,40,000	–
Purchases Return	–	2,600
Sales	–	2,30,000
Sales Return	4,200	–
Salaries	11,000	–
Rent for godown	5,500	–
Interest of Loan	2,700	–
Rates and Taxes	2,100	–
Discount Allowed to Debtors	2,400	–
Discount received from creditors	–	1,600
Freight on Purchases	1,200	–
Carriage Outwards	2,000	–
Drawings	12,000	–
Printing and Stationery	1,800	–
Electric Charges	2,200	–
Insurance Premium	5,500	–
General Office Expenses	3,000	–
Bad Debts	2,000	–
Bank Charges	1,600	–
Motor Car Expenses	3,600	–
Capital Account	–	1,62,000
	4,72,200	4,72,200

Prepare the Trading and Profit & Loss Account for the year ended 31st march, 2012 and the Balance Sheet as on that date after making the following adjustments :

(*i*) Provide Depreciation on—

(*a*) Building @5%

(*b*) Furniture and Fixture @10%.

(c) Office equipments @15% and

(d) Motor Car @20%.

(ii) Value of Stock at the close of the year was A 44,000.

(iii) Provision for bad debts is to be maintained at 5% of sundry debtors.

(iv) Insurance premium includes A 4,000 paid towards proprietor's life insurance policy and the balance of the insurance charges covers the period from 1st July, 2011 to 30th June 2012. [*CA*]

[***Ans.*** G/P A 69,200; N/P A 16,935; B/S Total A 2,35,935]

23. Mr. Neel had prepared the following Trial Balance from his Ledger as on 31st March, 2012.

Particulars	*Dr. Amount (A)*	*Cr. Amount (A)*
Stock as on 1st April, 2011	5,00,000	–
Purchases and Returns	31,00,000	45,000
Sales and Returns	55,000	41,50,000
Cash in Hand	2,50,000	–
Cash at Bank	5,00,000	–
Trader's Capital	–	22,59,200
Rates and Taxes	50,000	–
Drawings	45,000	–
Salaries	95,000	–
Postage & Telegram	1,05,000	–
Insurance	90,000	–
Salesman Commission	78,000	–
Printing and Stationery	95,500	–
Advertisement	1,70,000	–
Furniture and Fittings	5,50,000	–
Motor Car	48,000	–
Discounts	50,000	75,000
General Expense	65,700	–
Carriage Inward	10,000	–
Carriage Outward	22,000	–
Wages	50,000	–
Sundry Debtors/Creditors	10,00,000	4,00,000
Total	69,29,200	69,29,200

You are required to prepare Trading and Profit & Loss Account for the year ended on 31st March, 2012 and Balance Sheet as on that date after making the necessary adjustments.

You are provided with the following information :

(i) Closing Stock as on 31 st March, 2012 A 1,45,000.

(ii) Neel had withdrawn goods worth A 50,000 during the year.

(iii) Purchases include Purchase of furniture worth A 1,00,000.

(iv) Debtors include A 50,000 bad debts.

(v) Sales include goods worth A 1,50,000 sent out to NN & Co., on approval and remained unsold as on 31st March, 2012. The cost of the goods was A 1,00,000.

(*vi*) Provision for Bad Debts is to be created at 5% of Sundry Debtors.

(*vii*) Depreciate Furniture and Fittings by 10% and Motor Car by 20%.

(*viii*) The salesman is entitled to a commission of 10% on total sales. [*CA 2004*]

[***Ans.*** G/P A 7,25,000; Net Loss A 5,02,300; B/S Total A 23,78,400]

24. The following are the balances as at 31st March, 2012 extracted from the books of Mr. XYZ.

Particulars	*Amount (A)*	*Particulars*	*Amount (A)*
Plant & Machinery	19,550	Bad Debts recovered	450
Furniture & Fittings	10,250	Salaries	22,550
Bank Overdraft	80,000	Salaries payable	2,450
Capital Account	65,000	Prepaid Rent	300
Drawings	8,000	Rent	4,300
Purchases	1,60,000	Carriage Inward	1,125
Opening Stock	32,250	Carriage Outward	1,350
Wages	12,165	Sales	2,15,300
Provision for doubtful bedts	3,200	Advertisement Expenses	3,350
Provision for Discount on Debtors	1,375	Printing and Stationery	1,250
Sundry Debtors	1,20,000	Cash in Hand	1,450
Sundry Creditors	47,500	Cash at Bank	3,125
Bad Debts	1,100	Office Expenses	10,160
		Interest paid on Loan	3,000

Additional Information

1. Purchases include sales return of A 2,575 and sales include purchases return of A 1,725.
2. Goods withdrawn by Mr. XYZ for own consumption A 3,500 included in purchases.
3. Wages paid in the month of April for installation of plant and machinery amounting to A 450 were included in wages account.
4. Free samples distributed for publicity costing A 825.
5. Create a provision for doubtful debts @5% and provision for discount on debtors @2.5%.
6. Depreciation is to be provided on plant and machinery @15% p.a., and on furniture and fitting @10% p.a.,
7. Bank overdraft is secured against hypothecation of stock. Bank overdraft outstanding as on 31.3.2012 has been considered as 80% of real value of stock (deducting 20% as margin) and after adjusting the marginal value 80% of the same has been allowed to draw as overdraft. Prepare Final Accounts. [*CA*]

[***Ans.*** G/P A 1,39,535, N/P A 83,800; B/S Total A 2,67,250.]

25. From the following Trial Balance of Shri Shivam as on 31st march, 2012, You are required to prepare a Trading and profit & Loss Account for the year ended 31st march, 2012 and Balance Sheet as on that date, after making the necessary adjustments as mentioned hereunder :

Particulars	*Dr. Amount (A)*	*Cr. Amount (A)*
Shivam's Capital	–	1,60,000
Shivam's Drawings	24,000	–
Furniture and Fixtures	8,000	–

Particulars	*Dr. Amount (A)*	*Cr. Amount (A)*
Plant & Machinery	60,000	–
Patents (Ten years from 01.4.2011)	40,000	–
Stock on 1.4.2011	40,000	–
Purchases	1,70,000	–
Salaries	14,800	–
Wages	30,000	–
Sundry Debtors	20,400	–
Sales	–	2,64,000
Cash in Hand	13,250	–
Land	28,350	–
Loan from Shyam (at 6% from 01.10.2011)	–	20,000
Postage and Fax	3,000	–
Rent, Rates and Taxes	7,200	–
Bad Debts	800	–
Sundry Creditors	–	24,000
Discount	–	1,200
Carriage Inward	400	–
Interest on Loan	300	–
Insurance	1,600	–
Travelling Expenses	1,000	–
Sundry Expenses	600	–
Cash at Bank	20,500	–
Bank Overdraft	–	15,000
Total	4,84,200	4,84,200

Adjustments

(*i*) Stock as on 31.3.2012 is valued at A 30,000.

(*ii*) A new machine was installed on 1st April, 2011 for A 3,000. No entry in this respect was passed in the books. Wages of A 1,000 paid for installing the machine were debited to Wages Account.

(*iii*) Of the sundry debtors, A 200 are bad and are to be written off. You are required to maintain a provision for doubtful debts @ 5% on debtors and provision for discount on debtors @2%.

(*iv*) Goods costing A 2,000 were given away as free samples for publicity.

(*v*) Depreciate Plant & Machinery at 20% per annum and Furniture and Fixtures at 10% per annum.

(*vi*) On 01.4.2011, Machinery of the value of A 10,000 was destroyed by fire and the insurance claim settled at A 8,000 was credited to Machinery Account.

(*vii*) Goods costing A 1,000 were sent to a customer for A 1,200 on 30th March 2012 on sale or return basis. This was recorded as actual sales. [*CA 2005*]

[***Ans.*** G/P A 56,400; N/P A 5,289; B/S Total A 2,03,589]

26. Shri Patit Bansali submitted to you the following Trial Balance, which he has not been able to agree. Rewrite the Trial Balance and prepare Trading and Profit & Loss Account for the year 31.12.2012 and a Balance Sheet as on that date after giving effect to the undermentioned adjustments :

Particulars	*Dr. Amount (A)*	*Cr. Amount (A)*
Capital	–	16,000
Opening Stock	17,500	–
Closing Stock	–	18,790
Drawings	3,305	–
Return Inward	–	550
Carriage Inward	1,240	–
Deposit with *X*		1,400
Return Outward	840	–
Carriage Outward	–	725
Rent Paid	800	–
Rent Outstanding	150	–
Purchases	13,000	–
Sundry Debtors	5,000	–
Sundry Creditors	–	4,000
Furniture	–	29,000
Sales	–	29,000
Wages	850	–
Cash	1,370	–
Goodwill	1,800	–
Advertisement	950	–
	48,305	70465

Adjustments

1. Write off A 600 as Bad Debts and make Reserve for Bad Debts on Sundry Debtors at 5%.
2. Stock valued at A 2,000 was destroyed by fire on 25 December, 2012 but Insurance Company admitted a claim for A 1,500 only and paid the sum in January, 2013.
3. Depreciate Furniture by 10%. [C.A.]

Ans. Correct Total of Trial Balance A 49,990; G/P A 17,490; N/P A 13,545; Total of B/S Total A 30,390.

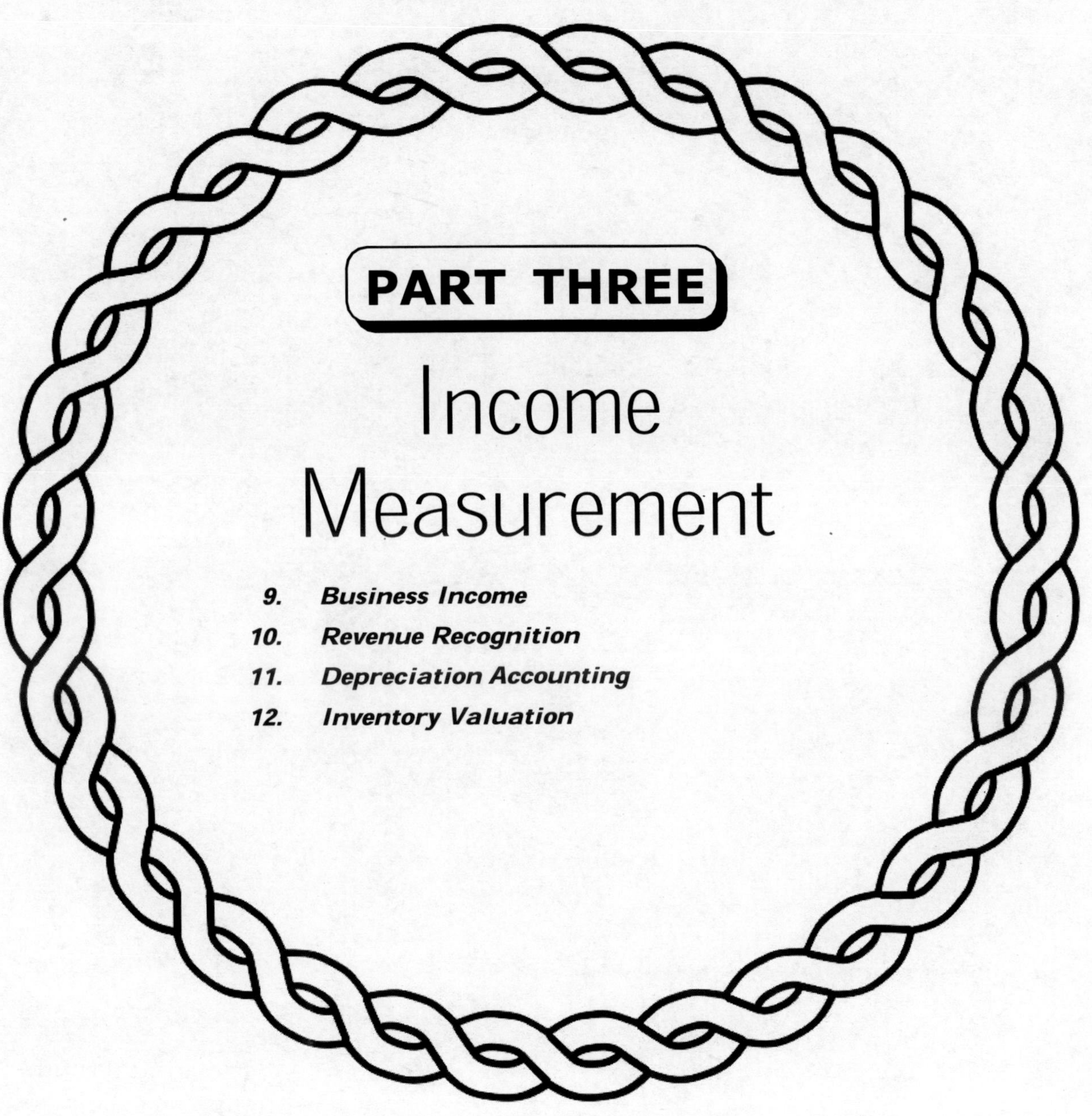

PART THREE

Income Measurement

CHAPTER 9

Business Income

Learning Objectives

After studying this chapter, you should be able to:

1. *Understand relevance of income measurement.*
2. *Explain business income (Accounting income) — its meaning, procedure of computing, advantages and limitations.*
3. *Understand economic income and its differences with business income.*

RELEVANCE OF INCOME MEASUREMENT

The measurement of income occupies a central position in accounting. Income measurement is probably the most important objective and function of accounting, accounting concepts, principles and procedures used by a business enterprise. The following are some of the major areas where income information is practically useful :

(*i*) **Income as a guide to dividend and retention policy :** Income information determines as to how much of a business enterprise's periodic income can be distributed to its owners and how much shall be retained to maintain or expand its activities. The income is the maximum amount which can be distributed as dividends and retained for expansion. However, because of the differences in accrual accounting and cash accounting income, a firm may not distribute the total income as dividends.

(*ii*) **Income as a measure of managerial efficiency :** Income is regarded as an indicator of management's effectiveness in utilising the resources belonging to the external users. Income tends to provide the basic standard by which success is measured.

(*iii*) **Income as a guide to future predictions :** Income helps in predicting the future income and future economic events of a business enterprise as current income acts to influence future expectations. It helps in evaluating the worth of future investments while making investment decisions.

(*iv*) **Income as a means of determining tax :** Income figure determines the tax liability of a business enterprise. How tax is determined is important to management and investors both. The taxation authorities generally accept accounting income as a basis of assessing the tax.

(*v*) **Income as a guide to creditworthiness and other economic decisions :** Credit grantors — individuals and institutional both — require evidence of sound financial status before advancing loans to business enterprises. Income — current and future both — is a relevant data to determine a concern's ability to repay loans and other liabilities at maturity.

DIFFERENT CONCEPTS OF INCOME MEASUREMENT

Measuring periodic income of a business has been a debatable issue among the theorists, researchers, accounting bodies, accounting educators and practitioners. Accordingly, many concepts and approaches have emerged which aim to determine net income of a business for an accounting period. The different concepts of income measurement have led to different types of income which can be measured for a business enterprise.

The different concepts of income measurement or different types of income are as follows :

1. Business Income or Accounting Concept of Income.
2. Economic Income (or Economic Concept of Income).

BUSINESS INCOME

Business income, often referred to as accounting income or conventional income is measured in accordance with generally accepted accounting principles. The profit and loss account or income statement determines the net income or operating performance of a business enterprise for some particular period of time. Income is determined by following income statement approach, *i.e.,* by comparing sales revenue and costs related to the sales revenue. Net income is determined as follows :

Revenue – Expenses = Net Income

The net income defined as the difference between revenue and expenses determine the business income of an enterprise. Under the income statement approach, expenses are matched with the revenues and the income statement is the most significant financial statement to measure income of a business enterprise. Thus, business income of an entity represents the difference between the realised revenues arising from the transactions of the period and the corresponding historical costs. It is the increase in the resources of a business (or other) entity which results from the operations of the enterprise. In other words, accounting or business income is the net increase in owner's equity resulting from the operations of a company. It should be distinguished from the capital contributed to the entity. Income is a net concept; it consists of the revenue generated by the business, less losses and less expired costs that contribute to the production of revenue.

Procedure of Computing Business Income

The procedure for computing business income may be summarised as follows :

(*i*) **Defining the particular accounting period :** Business income refers to the financial performance of the firm for a definite period. The commonly accepted accounting period is either the calendar or natural business year.

(*ii*) **Identify revenues of the accounting period selected :** Business income requires the definition, measurement, and recognition of revenues. In general, realisation principle is used for recognition of revenues and consequently for the recognition of income. Revenue is the aggregate of value received in exchange for the goods and services of an enterprise. Sale of goods is the commonest form of revenue. In accordance with realisation principle, the accountant does not consider changes in value until they have crystallised following a transaction.

(*iii*) **Identifying costs corresponding to revenue earned :** Business concept of income is based on the historical cost concept. Income for an accounting period considers only those costs which have become expenses, *i.e.,* those costs which have been applied against revenue. Those costs which have not yet expired or been utilised in connection with the realisation of revenue are not the costs to be used in computing accounting income. Such costs are assets and appear on the balance sheet. Prepaid expenses, inventories, and plant thus represent examples of deferred unallocated costs.

(*iv*) **Matching Principle :** Traditional accounting or business income is expressed as a matching of revenue and expenditure transactions, and results in a series of residuals for balance sheet purposes. Matching principle requires that revenues which are recognised through the application of the realisation principle are then related to (or matched with) relevant and appropriate historical costs. The cost elements regarded as having expired service potential are allocated or matched against relevant revenues. The remaining elements of costs which are regarded as continuing to have future service potential are carried forward in the traditional balance sheet and are termed as assets.

Arguments in Favour of Business Income

1. Business income has the benefit of a sound, factual and objective transaction base. It has stood the test of time and therefore is used by the universal accounting community.
2. Another argument in favour of historical cost-based income is that it is based on actual and factual transactions which may be verified.
3. Business income is very useful in judging the past performance and decisions of management. Also it is useful for control purposes and for making management accountable to shareholders for the use of resources entrusted to it.
4. Income based on historical cost is the least costly because it minimises potential doubts about information reliability, and time and efforts in preparing the information.
5. In times of inflation, which is now a usual feature, alternative income measurement approaches as compared to business income could give lower operating income, lower rates of return which could lower share prices of a business firm.

Limitations of Business Income

Despite of accounting income being useful in many respects, it has certain limitations :

Firstly, the historical cost concept and realisation principle conceal essential information about unrealised income since it is not reported under historical accounting. Unrealised income results from holding assets, which should be reported to provide useful information about a business and its profitability and financial position. Business income does not report current values; balance sheet is merely a statement of unallocated cost balances and is not a value statement.

Secondly, validity of business income depends on measurement – process and the measurement process depends on the soundness of the judgements involved in revenue recognition and cost allocation and related matching between the two. There is a great deal of flexibility and subjectivity involved in choosing accounting principles in assigning cost and revenue items to specific time periods and using matching concept.

Thirdly, the traditional accounting income is based upon historical cost principle and conventions which may be severally criticised, *e.g.,* lack of useful contemporary valuations in times of price level changes, inconsistencies in the measurement of periodic income of different firms and even between different years for the same firm due to generally accepted accounting principles. Thus, business income could be misleading, misunderstood and irrelevant to users for making investment decisions.

ECONOMIC INCOME

The economic concept of income is based on Hick's concept (1946) of income defined as follows :

"... the maximum value which he can consume during a week, and still expect to be as well-off at the end of the week as he was at the beginning.

Hicks presented his concept of "well offness" as the basis for a rough approximation of personal income. According to Hicks, income is the maximum which can be consumed by a person in a defined period without impairing his "well offness" as it existed at the beginning of the period. "Well offness" is equivalent to wealth or capital. Hick's concept of personal income was subsequently adopted in accounting to define business profit. Economic income of an enterprise is the maximum amount which a firm can distribute to shareholders during a period and still be as well off at the end of the period as at the beginning.

Economic income results from changes in the value of assets and liabilities at the beginning and at the end of the accounting period., If closing values are more than the beginning values, the surplus resulting is known as net profit under economic concept of income. In the reverse situation, there will be net loss. There is no matching of revenues and expenses in economic income. Further, the economic income recognises holding gains due to changes in the value of assets possessed by a firm and considers it as a component of net income. Economic income does not consider realisation principle in income measurement. It follows balance sheet approach to determine net income where as business income adopts income statement approach to ascertain net income of a business firm.

ASSIGNMENT MATERIAL

Note : The Objective Type Questions (True / False, Multiple Choice Questions etc.) have been given in the Appendix at the end of the book.

SHORT ANSWER THEORY QUESTIONS

1. What is income measurement?
2. What are the benefits associated with income determination?
3. Explain business income.
4. Explain economic income.
5. How is business income determined?
6. Distinguish between business income and economic income.

LONG ANSWER THEORY QUESTIONS

1. Discuss the objectives of income measurement.
2. Define business income. How is it determined?
3. Explain advantages and limitations of business income.
4. Distinguish between business income and economic income.
5. Explain accounting income and economic income. Which concept is more useful and why?

   [*B.Com.(Hons.), Delhi University, 2008*]

CHAPTER 10

Revenue Recognition

Learning Objectives

After studying this chapter, you should be able to:

1. *Understand concept of revenue.*
2. *Explain revenue recognition criteria as per AS9.*
3. *Explain the meaning of expenses, gains and losses.*

REVENUE

Broader Concept of Revenue

The broad or comprehensive concept of revenue includes all of the proceeds from business and investment activities. This view accepts revenues as all changes in the net assets resulting from ordinary activities (or revenue producing activities) and other gains or losses resulting from the sale of fixed assets and investments. The broader view is taken by AICPA (USA) when it defines revenues as follows :

"Revenue results from the sale of goods and the rendering of services and is measured by the charge made to customers, clients or tenants for goods and services furnished to them. It also includes gains from the sale or exchange of assets (other than stock in trade), interest and dividends earned on investments, and other increases in the owners equity except those arising from the capital contributions and capital, adjustments."

Narrower Concept of Revenue

The narrower concept considers revenues resulting from the primary or normal activities of a business entity and thus the narrower view of the revenues excludes investment income and gains and losses on the disposal of fixed assets. The Institute of Chartered Accountants of India (ICAI) defines revenue in its Accounting Standards (AS) No. 9 as following, taking a narrower view.

"Revenue is the gross inflow of cash, receivables or other consideration arising in the ordinary activities of an enterprise from the sale of goods, from the rendering of services, and from the use by others of enterprise resources yielding interest, royalties and dividends. Revenue is measured by the charges made to customers or clients for goods supplied and services rendered to them and by the charges and rewards arising from the use of resources by them. In an agency relationship, the revenue is the amount of commission and not the gross inflow of cash, receivables or other consideration."

The FASB (USA) also takes a narrower view while defining revenues:

"Revenue are inflows or other enhancements of assets of an entity or settlements of its liabilities (or combination of both) during a period from delivery or producing goods, rendering services, or other activities that constitute the entity's ongoing major or central operations."

Taking a narrower concept of revenues, the following items are not included within the definition of revenue:

(*a*) Realised gains resulting from the disposal of, and unrealised gains resulting from the holding of non-current assets, *e.g.*, fixed assets;

(*b*) Unrealised holding gains resulting from the change in value of current assets, and the natural increase in the herds and agricultural and forest products;

(*c*) Realised or unrealised gains resulting from changes in foreign exchange rates and adjustments arising on the translation of foreign currency financial statements;

(*d*) Realised gains resulting from the discharge of an obligation at less than its carrying amount;

(*e*) Unrealised gains resulting from the restatement of the carrying amount of an obligation.

Thus, revenue does not include all recognised increases in assets or decreases in liabilities. Receipts of the proceeds of a cash sale is revenue under generally accepted accounting principles because the net result of the sale is a change in owner's equity. On the other hand, receipts of proceeds of a loan, investment by owners or receipt of an asset purchased for cash, income on investments, gains on the sale of fixed assets are not revenues, as per the accounting standard issued by the ICAI.

The second narrower interpretation of revenues is more appropriate and useful to the external user and other decision-makers as revenues are defined in terms of primary activities and operations of a firm which are truly income-generating business activities.

REVENUE RECOGNITION CRITERIA AS PER AS9

Accountants always debate and have problems as to when during the operating cycle can revenue be recorded as earned. For this, some criteria have been developed which are called 'Revenue Recognition Criteria.' AS-9 'Revenue Recognition' contains the following criteria for revenue recognition.

1. **Revenue Recognised at the Point of Sale :** With limited exceptions, revenue is recognised at the point of sale. Generally Accepted Accounting Principles, require the recognition of revenue in the accounting period in which the sale occurs. Throughout the operating cycle, the business enterprise works for the eventual sale of the goods and collection of the sales price. The enterprise's earning process should be substantially complete before revenue is recorded.

   Also, the revenue should be realised before it is recorded in the accounts. Realised means the goods or services are exchanged for cash or claims to cash. It is at the point of sale, that the two important conditions for revenue recognition are met—at that time the revenue is both earned and realised.

   Revenue for goods is not recognised when a firm receives sales order. Even though in some businesses the amount of income that will be earned can be realiably estimated at that time, there is no performance until the goods have been sold. A key point for determining when to recognise revenues from a transaction involving the sale of goods is that the seller has transferred the property in the goods to the buyer for a price. The transfer of property in goods, in most cases results in or coincides with the transfer of significant risk and rewards of ownership to the buyer. However, there may be situations where transfer of property in goods does not coincide with the transfer of significant risk and rewards of ownership. Rvenue in such situation is recognised at the time of transfer of significant risk and rewards of ownership to the buyer. Such cases may arise where delivery has been delayed through the fault of either the buyer or the seller and the goods are at the risk of the party at fault as regards any loss which might not have occurred but for such fault. Further, sometimes, the parties may agree that the risk will pass at a time different from the time when ownership passes.

2. **Revenue Recognition in Sale of Services :** In transaction involving sale or rendering of services, revenues are usually recognised as the services are performed. For services, providing the service is the act of performance. For example, a real estate broker should record sale commission or brokerages as revenues when the real estate transaction is consummated. Revenues from renting hotel rooms are recognised each day the room is rented. Revenues from maintenance contracts are recognised in each month covered by the contract. Revenues from repairing an automobile will be recognised when the repairs have been fully completed. In the repair of automobile, revenues are not recognised in case of partial repairs, because the service is to provide a completed repair job.

3. **Revenue Recognition in Construction Work :** Some transactions may involve long term constructions and projects that may extend over several years. Examples are construction of roads, dams, large office buildings, bridges, ships, aircrafts, etc. In all such projects, the customer usually provides the product or project specifications. The long term construction contract has provisions for predetermined amounts the customer must pay at different points and stages of work or suggest a formula that will determine customer payments within the actual project costs plus a reasonable profit.

   In construction projects, revenues are recognised by the (*i*) Percentage-completion method or (*ii*) Completed Contract method.

   (*i*) **Percentage-Completion Method :** The percentage-completion method simply allocates the estimated total gross profit on contract among the several accounting periods involved in proportion to the estimated percentage of the contract completed each period. To use this method we must have a reasonably accurate and reliable procedure for estimating periodic progress on the contract. Most often, estimates of the percentage of contract completion are tied to the proportion of total costs incurred. If the income earned by the work done in the period can be reliably estimated, then revenue is appropriately recognised in each such period. This method of revenue recognition is called the percentage-completion method because the amount of revenue is related to the percentage of the total project work that was performed in the period.

   The percentage-completion method is most often used when the production cycle is long, the work is done under contracts with specific clients or customers, and adequate data on progress are available. The contracts provide a basis on which to estimate the amount of cash to be collected after all production work has been completed; if the progress percentage data are valid, they provide assurance that the work done to date is readily measurable, the revenue recognition criteria are satisfied at the time of production as long as reliable progress percentage data are available.

   The percentage-completion method recognises net revenue (profit) prior to realisation. It is accepted in order to permit the reporting of profit on a yearly basis by those entities involved in long-term construction projects. It is significant to note that the matching process normally entails first identifying revenues of a given period and then matching certain costs against them to obtain net income or profit. That is, revenues are identified as the independent variable and costs, the dependent. But the percentage-completion method reverses the procedure by identifying the costs incurred in a given period as the independent variable and then matching future revenue to them.

Income Effects of Percentage-Completion Method

Percentage–completion method has two effects. First, it leads to earlier recognition of revenue. Investors and external users my be informed more promptly of changes in volume of business activity or in the profit rate. Second, this method is likely to report smoother income stream in long-cycle operations. Income smoothing is said to occur when a business enterprise selects from among acceptable alternative accounting methods to achieve income results that are relatively stable (*i.e.,* smooth) over time.

(*ii*) **Completed Contract Method :** Performance consists of the execution of a single act. Alternatively services are performed in more than a single act, and the services yet to be performed are so significant in realtion to the transaction taken as a whole that performance cannot be deemed to have been completed until the execution of those acts. The completed contract method is relevant to those patterns of performance and accordingly revenue is recognised when the sole or final act takes place and the service becomes chargeable. As an alternative to percentage-completion method, the completed contract method may be used to account for long-term construction projects. This method recognises revenues upon final approval of the project by the customer, *i.e.,* in effect at delivery.

The completed contract method would be suitable for an entity engaged in many long term projects some of which are completed each year. It should also be used in reference to the percentage-completion method in cases in which reasonable estimates of future costs cannot be done.

Under the completed contract method cost incurred on a project are treated as assets and held in an asset account (Work in Progress Account) till the period in which revenue is recognised.

An example is taken here to illustrate the percentage-completion method and completed contract method. Assume the following data about a contract to be completed within three years.

Year	*Project*	*Payments*	*Work*	*Percentage Completion Method*			*Complete contract method*		
	cost A	*Received from customer A*	*Completed %*	*Revenues A*	*Expenses A*	*Income A*	*Revenues A*	*Expenses A*	*Income A*
2010	80,000	60,000	20	90,000	80,000	10,000	—	—	—
2011	2,00,000	2,05,000	70	2,25,000	2,00,000	25,000	—	—	—
2012	1,20,000	1,85,000	100	1,35,000	1,20,000	15,000	4,50,000	4,00,000	50,000
	4,00,000	4,50,000	—	4,50,000	4,00,000	50,000	4,50,000	4,00,000	50,000

In the above example, 20 per cent, 50 per cent and 30 per cent of the project work was completed in the year 2010, 2011 and 2012 respectively. Revenues for different years under the percentage-completion method has been calculated taking into account total contract price or project revenue and percentage of work performed each year, shown as follows :

Revenue : Total contract price × percentage of work completed.

2010 : 4,50,000 × 20% = A 90,000

2011 : 4,50,000 × 50% = A 2,25,000

2012 : 4,50,000 × 30% = A 1,35,000

It can be noticed that both the methods report the same total income over the entire three-year period. But, in percentage-completion method, the total income A 4,50,000 is allocated to each of the three years – 2010, A 90,000, 2011 A 2,25,000, 2012 A 1,35,000. Also the total payments received from the customer each year do not become revenue and are not relevant as well in determining the amount of revenue recognised each year under the two methods.

4. **Revenue Recognition in Instalment Credit Sales :** Many business and merchandising firms sell goods on instalment basis wherein the customer pays a certain amount as instalment on the dates of instalment. In instalment sales, revenue is not recognised at the point of sale. The reason is that the amount of income cannot be reliably measured at the point of sale if customers do not pay the future instalments. Therefore, in this case, revenue is recognised when the instalment payments are received.

   Under the instalment method, the instalment payment received is considered as revenue and a proportionate part of the cost of sales becomes costs in the same period. The cost of the product is allocated by the ratio, cash collected during the period divided by total sales price (total cash expected). A more conservative view is sometimes taken for recognising revenue in the instalment method, which is known as the cost recovery method. In the cost recovery method, all cash collections until all costs are recovered are mere return of costs of product. Therefore, no income is reported until the instalment payments have recovered the total costs of sales; thereafter any additional cash received is income. The instalment method is more popular than the cost recovery method.

5. **Revenue Recognition Using Production Method :** In some cases, the amount of income that can be earned can be reliably measured as soon as the production is over. For instance, in case of certain grains and other crops, the government announces the price at which the farmers can sell their products. In such cases, although no sales has taken place, revenue can be reliably estimated at the point when the crops have been harvested. Therefore, revenue can also be recognised at the time of harvest. The ICAI (India) in its Accounting Standard No. 9, states :

   "At certain stages in specific industries, such as when agricultural crops have been harvested or mineral ores have been extracted, performance may be substantially complete prior to the execution of the transaction generating revenue. In such cases, when sale is assured under forward contract or a government guarantee or where market exists and there is a negligible risk of failure to sell, the goods involved are often valued at net realisable value. Such amounts while not revenue, are sometimes recognised in the statement of profit and loss and appropriately described."

6. **Revenue Recognition when a firm receives interest, royalties and dividends :** A firm may allow others to use its resources and thereby can receive :

(*i*) Interest

(*ii*) Royalties and

(*iii*) Dividents

(*a*) Interest are charges for the use of cash resources or amounts due to the enterprises;

(*b*) Royalties are charges for the use of such assets as known-how, patents, trade marks and copyrights;

(*c*) Dividends are rewards from the holding of investments in shares.

Interest accrues, in most circumstances, on the time basis determined by the amount outstanding and the rate applicable. Usually, discount or premium on debt securities held is treated as though it were accruing over the period to maturity. Royalties accrue in accordance with the terms of the relevant agreement and are usually recognised on that basis unless, having regard to the substance of the transactions, it is more appropriate to recognise revenue on some other systematic and rational basis.

Dividends from investments in shares are not recognised in the statement of profit and loss until a right to receive payment is established.

When interest, royalties and dividends from foreign countries require exchange permission and uncertainty in remittance is anticipated, revenue recognition may need to be postponed.

7. **Money Received or Amounts paid in Advance :** Sometimes money is received or amounts are billed in advance of the delivery of goods or rendering of services, *i.e.,* before revenue is to be recognised, *e.g.,* rents or amount of magazine subscriptions received in advance. Such items are rightly not treated as revenue of the period in which they are received but as revenue of the future period or periods in which they are earned. These amounts are carried as 'unearned revenue', *i.e.,* liabilities, until the earning process is complete. In the future periods when these amounts are recognised as revenues, it results in recording a decrease in a liability rather than an increase in an asset.

EXPENSES

Expenses are the monetary amount of resources used up or expended by an entity during a period to earn revenues. Expenses are essentially cost incurred in the process of earning revenues through the using or consuming of goods and services. Expenses represent actual or expected cash outflows (or the equivalent) that have occurred or will eventuate as a result of the enterprise's ongoing major or central operations during the period. The expenses may be incurred in one period and payment made in another period.

Categories of Expenses

Important classes of expense are :

(*i*) Cost of assets used to produce revenue (for examples, cost of goods sold, selling and administrative expenses and interest expenses).

(*ii*) Expenses from non-reciprocal transfers and casualties (for example, taxes, fires and theft).

(*iii*) Cost of assets other than products (for example, plant and equipment or investments in other companies) disposed of.

(*iv*) Costs incurred in unsuccessful efforts.

Expenses do not include repayments of borrowing, expenditures to acquire assets, distributions to owners, or adjustments of expenses of prior periods. Sales discounts and bad debts have been treated conventionally as expenses.

GAINS AND LOSSES

Gains are defined as increase in net assets other than from revenues or from changes in capital. Gains are increases in equity (net assets) from peripheral or incidental transactions of an entity and from all other transactions and other events and circumstances affecting the entity during a period except those that result from revenues or investment by owners. Losses are decreases in equity (net assets) from peripheral or incidental transactions of an entity and from all other transactions and other events and circumstances affecting the entity during a period except those that result from expenses or distribution to owners. Gains and losses represent favourable and unfavourable events not directly related to the normal revenue producing activities of the enterprise. Revenue and expenses from other than sale of products, merchandise, or services such as disposition of assets may be separated from other revenue and expenses and the net effects disclosed as gains or losses.

ASSIGNMENT MATERIAL

Note : The Objective Type Question (True/False Qustions, Multiple choice Questions etc.) have been given in the Appendix at the end of the Book.

SHORT ANSWER THEORY QUESTIONS

1. Define revenue.
2. What are the rules regarding revenue recognition in construction work.
3. Explain revenue recognition in instalment credit sales.
4. Define expenses.
5. Define gains and losses.
6. "Revenue is recognized when a sale transaction is made or when services are rendered." State three exceptions to this rule. [*B.Com. (Hons.), Delhi University, 2005*]

LONG ANSWER THEORY QUESTIONS

1. What is revenue? Discuss recognition criteria as per AS9.
2. Explain the concept of expenses, gains and losses.

CHAPTER 11

Depreciation Accounting

Learning Objectives

After studying this chapter, you should be able to :

1. *Identify long-term assets.*
2. *Define depreciation.*
3. *Explain the causes for depreciation.*
4. *Discuss the factors for computing depreciation.*
5. *Understand the need for depreciation.*
6. *Discuss Straight Line and Diminishing Balance Methods of depreciation along with their advantages and disadvantages.*
7. *Distinguish between Straight Line Method and Diminishing Balance Method.*
8. *Understand Provision for Depreciation Account and Asset Disposal Account.*
9. *Explain provisions of AS6 on change in depreciation method.*

LONG-TERM ASSETS

This chapter discusses the accounting problems related to the use of long-term assets whose benefits to a firm extend over many accounting periods, specially the problem of depreciation accounting.

Before taking up depreciation, it should be understood that the costs relating to the use of long-term assets should be properly calculated and matched against the revenue earned so that periodic net income can be determined. These use costs or expenses or periodic write-offs are known by different names for different category of assets as shown here :

Types of Long-term Assets	*Term of expenses for write-off or use costs*
1. Tangible assets :	
(*i*) Land	None
(*ii*) Plant, building, equipment tools, furniture, vehicles	Depreciation
(*iii*) Natural resources such as oil, timber, coal, ore, mineral deposits	Depletion
2. Intangible assets such as patent, copyrights, trade marks, goodwill.	Amortisation

Among the above assets, land is a tangible asset that has an indefinite or unlimited useful life. Therefore, it is not subject to depreciation or periodic write-off to expenses.

Depletion is the name of expenses or write-off in the case of natural resources. Depletion refers to the systematic and rational allocation of the acquisition cost of natural resources to future periods in which the use of those natural resources contributes to revenue. Natural resources are exhausted or used up through mining, cutting, pumping, etc.

The term amortisation is used in case of intangible assets. Amortisation refers to the systematic and rational allocation of the acquisition cost of intangible assets to future periods in which the benefits contribute to revenue. It is the periodic write-off to expenses of the intangible asset's cost over its expected useful life.

The term depreciation refers to periodic allocation of the acquisition cost of a tangible long-term asset over its useful life. Depreciation has been discussed in detail later.

NATURE OF DEPRECIATION

As stated earlier, depreciation is a term applicable in case of plant, building, equipment, furniture, fixtures, vehicles, tools. These long-term or fixed assets have a limited useful life, *i.e.* they will provide service to the entity (in the form of helping in the generation of revenue) over a limited number of future accounting periods. Depreciation implies allocating the cost of a tangible fixed or long-term asset over its useful life. Depreciation makes a part of the cost of asset chargeable as an expense in profit and loss account of the accounting periods in which the asset has helped in earning revenue.

Thus, allocating the capitalised cost of an asset into expense for different accounting periods is known as depreciation.

The Institute of Chartered Accountants of India (ICAI) defines depreciation as follows:

"Depreciation is a measure of the wearing out, consumption or other loss of value of depreciable asset arising from use, effluxion of time or obsolescence through technology and market changes. Depreciation is allocated so as to charge a fair proportion of the depreciable amount in each accounting period during the expected useful life of the asset. Depreciation includes amortisation of assets whose useful life is pre-determined."

SSAP 12 of the UK also defines the depreciation in the same manner.

"Depreciation is the measure of the wearing out, consumption or other loss of value of a fixed asset whether arising from use, effluxion of time or obsolescence through technology and market changes."

International Accounting Standards Board (IASB) defines this terms as follows :

"Depreciation is the allocation of the depreciable amount of an asset over its estimated useful life. Depreciation for the accounting period is charged to income either directly or indirectly."

Depreciation accounting is based on the matching concept wherein an attempt is made to match a part of acquisition cost of an asset (shown as depreciation expense) with the revenue generated by the use of such asset. To determine the amount of depreciation, three items are needed : (*i*) actual acquisition cost, (*ii*) estimated net residual value, and (*iii*) estimated useful life. Of these three items, two are estimates, residual value and useful life. Due to this, it can be said that the amount of depreciation recorded in an accounting period is only an estimate. To take an example, assume an asset was purchased for A 10,00,000 and it has a life of 10 years. At the end of 10 years, the asset can be sold for A 1,00,000. It means that decline in value of A 9,00,000 (A 10,00,000 – A 1,00,000) is an expense for generating the revenue realised during the ten-year period that the asset was used. Therefore, in order to determine correct net income figure, A 9,00,000 of expense shall be allocated to these periods and matched against the revenue. Failure to do so would overstate income for these periods. Depreciation expense for each accounting year can be determined as follows:

Acquisition cost	A 10,00,000
Less : Salvage or residual value	A 1,00,000
Amount to be depreciated over useful life	A 9,00,000
Estimated useful life	A 10 years
Annual depreciation expense A $\frac{9,00,000}{10 \text{ years}}$ =	A 90,000

CAUSES FOR DEPRECIATION

Depreciation implies a decline in the service potential of an asset and the decline in the service potential makes the asset have only a limited useful life. Unless the asset should eventually be retired from its planned use, there is no cause for depreciation. For example, services provided by land do not decrease over time, therefore, land is not depreciated and all costs are recovered when the land is sold.

There are many factors that cause decline in the service potential or economic utility of asset, and hence, become the causes of depreciation. However, the major causes are physical deterioration and obsolescence.

Physical deterioration of the asset results from use and physical factors such as normal wear and tear, chemical action such as rust, effects of wind and rain. To some extent, maintenance and repairs may partially check or offset deterioration. Therefore, while estimating the useful life and salvage value of the asset, a given level of maintenance is assumed. However, this does not eliminate the need for depreciation.

Obsolescence is another important cause for depreciation. Obsolescence is non-physical factor and means becoming out-of-date. With fast-changing technology as well as fast-changing demands, machinery and even buildings often become obsolete before they wear out. Inventions may result in new processes that reduce the unit cost of production to the point where continued operation of old equipment is not economical. Firms replace computers that work as well as when they were purchased because new, smaller computers occupy less space and compute faster.

It should also be noted that replacing the asset is not essential to the existence of depreciation. Depreciation is the expiration or disappearance of service potential from the time the plant asset is put into use until the time it is retired from service. Whether or not the asset is replaced does not effect the amount or treatment of its depreciation.

FACTORS AFFECTING THE COMPUTATION OF DEPRECIATION

The computation of depreciation for an accounting period depends on the following factors :

1. Depreciable Assets : Depreciable assets are assets which :

(*i*) Are expected to be used during more than one accounting period;

(*ii*) have a limited useful life; and

(*iii*) are held by an enterprise for use in the production or supply of goods and services, for rental to others, or for administrative purposes and not for the purpose of sale in the ordinary course of business.

2. Useful Life : Useful life is either :

(*i*) the period over which a depreciable asset is expected to be used by the enterprises; or

(*ii*) the number of production or similar units expected to be obtained from the use of the asset by the enterprise.

The useful life of a depreciable asset is shorter than its physical life and is :

(*i*) pre-determined by legal or contractual limits, such as the expiry dates;

(*ii*) directly governed by extraction or consumption;

(*iii*) dependent on the extent of use and physical deterioration on account of wear and tear which again depends on operational factors, such as, the number of shifts for which the asset is to be used, repair and maintenance policy of the enterprise, etc;

(*iv*) reduced by obsolescence arising from such factors as :

(*a*) technological changes;

(*b*) improvement in production methods;

(*c*) change in market demand for the product or service output of the asset;

(*d*) legal or other restrictions.

Estimation of the useful life of a depreciable asset or a group of similar depreciable assets is a matter of judgement ordinarily based on experience with similar types of assets. For an asset using new technology or used in the production of a new product or in the provision of a new service with which there is little experience, estimation of the useful life is more difficult but is nevertheless required.

3. Depreciable Amount : Depreciable amount of a depreciable asset is its historic cost, or other amount substituted for historic cost in the financial statements, less the estimated residual value.

4. Residual Value : The residual value of an asset is often insignificant and can be ignored in the calculation of the depreciable amount. If the residual value is likely to be significant, it is estimated at the date of acquisition, or the date of any subsequent revaluation of the asset, on the basis of the realisable value prevailing at the date for similar assets which have reached the end of their useful lives and have operated under conditions similar to those in which the asset will be used. The gross residual value in all cases is reduced by the expected costs of disposal at the end of the useful life of the asset.

DEPRECIATION IS A PROCESS OF ALLOCATION, NOT OF VALUATION

The Statement that 'depreciation is a process of allocation not of valuation' is found in the following definition of AICPA (USA):

"Depreciation accounting is a system of accounting which aims to distribute the cost ... of tangible capital assets, less salvage (if any) over the estimated useful life of the unit in a systematic and rational manner. It is a process of allocation, not of valuation."

Allocation Process

Allocation in accounting refers to the process of partitioning a set or an amount and the assignment of resulting subsets or amounts to separate periods of time or classifications. Depreciation accounting attempts to allocate in a rational and systematic manner the difference between acquisition cost and estimated salvage value over the estimated useful life of the asset. The main emphasis in depreciation accounting is on the computation of periodic charge to be allocated as an expense and to be matched with revenues reported in each period. Depreciation considers the original cost as deferred expenses and the original cost is charged against the profit of the various periods by allocating it over a given period in a systematic manner. Depreciation does not refer to physical deterioration of an asset or decrease in market value of an asset over time. If it is so, then it can be claimed that periodic repairs and sound maintenance policy may keep buildings and equipment in good running order or as good as new and thus physical deterioration can be stopped or checked. However, every building or machine at sometime has to be discarded and replaced. The need for depreciation is not eliminated by repairs and depreciation does not depend on physical deterioration alone or no physical deterioration. Similarly, depreciation process is not affected by what happens to the price level in general or to the price of asset in particular. It is related to the income statement which shows the net income after accounting for depreciation. Depreciation is simply the allocation of the cost of a plant asset to the periods that benefit from the services of the asset.

Depreciation not a Valuation Process

Depreciation is not a process of valuation. The valuation concept consider depreciation as the decline in the value of the asset over a period of time. It requires the valuation of assets at two points of time and assuming decline in value, the amount of depreciation is determined as the difference between the value of asset at the beginning and at the end of an accounting period. However, depreciation does not arise due to decline in value during that period, but rather from the process of ensuring a return of capital invested.

A depreciation problem will exist whenever (1) funds are invested in services to be rendered by a plant asset, and (2) at some date in the future, the asset must be retired from service with a residual value less than its original cost.

The valuation concept is related to the balance sheet which aims to reflect the values of different assets at a particular date or point in time.

The valuation concept implies that depreciation should reflect the decreases in value of the asset over a period of time. The term value means (1) market value (2) value to the owner. The valuation concept would provide a very unsatisfactory basis for distributing the depreciation charges. Decline in the value of asset with time is likely to be unequal and would make net income comparison difficult and unreliable. When the value of the new asset increases, it is not brought into accounting records because the increase in value may not be permanent and also no profit (due to increase in value of asset) should be taken into account unless they are realised. Further, even if the market value of a plant or building increases, depreciation should be recorded as a result of allocation. Eventually, the building will wear out, the plant will lose its utility or become obsolete regardless of interim fluctuations in market value.

NEED FOR DEPRECIATION

The need for charging a reasonable amount of depreciation over the estimated useful life of the asset arises for the following purposes :

1. To Ascertain the Correct Income : The basic need of depreciation is to ascertain the true income. If depreciation is ignored, the loss that is occurring in respect of fixed assets will be ignored. The loss will suddenly loom large when the asset become useless or valueless. From another angle, when goods are produced it involves use of fixed assets–the reduction in their value should be treated as element of cost of production of goods. Therefore, depreciation should be debited to P&L A/c before profit is ascertained.

2. To Show the Asset at its Proper Value : In the absence of depreciation charge, the asset will be shown at its acquisition cost every year in the balance sheet. If depreciation is not allowed, the Balance Sheet would fail to show the true financial position. Therefore, depreciation must be accounted for in order to present the assets at their proper value.

3. To Maintain the Capital Invested : Depreciation helps to maintain the capital invested in the asset intact in the business so that it can be reinvested in the profit earning process.

4. To Retain Fund for Replacement : The other need for depreciation is to retain funds for replacement of assets. The amount debited in P&L A/c are retained in the business. These are available for replacement of the assets when its life is over.

5. To Allocate the Cost of Fixed Asset to Product : The business firms, to find out the accurate cost of production, requires to allocate the cost of fixed asset to product.

6. To Compute Tax Liability : In such a case the rate of depreciation is influenced by tax laws.

METHODS OF DEPRECIATION

There are different methods for allocating costs of fixed depreciable assets. Such allocation has a direct effect on the determination of net income because depreciation expense is a necessary charge.

There are two basic methods of depreciation :

1. Straight Line Method
2. Diminishing Balance Method

1. Straight Line Method : This method assumes that depreciation is a function of time rather than use. This method is based on the assumption that each accounting period receives same benefits from using the assets. It allocates an equal amount of depreciation in each accounting periods of the service life of the assets. Therefore, it is called Straight Line Method.

The formula for calculating depreciation charge for each accounting period is

$$\text{Annual Depreciation} = \frac{\text{Acquisition cost} - \text{Estimated scrap value}}{\text{Estimated Life in Years}}$$

Advantages

(*i*) It is simple in use.

(*ii*) It realistically matches cost and revenue and determine income of each period easily.

(*iii*) There is no change either in the rate or the amount of depreciation over the useful life of the assets. Such a procedure provides for improved comparability.

Disadvantages

(*i*) It ignores the cost of capital.

(*ii*) It is based on the wrong assumption of equal utility of the assets during the useful life.

(*iii*) It is also wrong to consider depreciation as a function of time rather than use.

(*iv*) The maintenance of asset is generally costly in the later years with the result that deductions from the revenue would be greater in later years than in the earlier years.

JOURNAL ENTRIES UNDER STRAIGHT LINE METHOD

Illustration

On 1st April 2011 a firm purchased a firm machine for A 8,00,000 and spent A 2,00,000 on its and installation. The residual value at the end of its expected useful life of 4 years is estimated at A 4,00,000. On 30th September 2013 this machine is sold for A 5,00,000 Depreciation is to be provided according to Straight Line Method.

Make journal entries to record the above transaction under straight line method of depreciation.

Journal Entries

Date	*Particulars*		*L.F.*	*Debit (A)*	*Credit(A)*
1.4.2011	Machinery A/c	Dr.		8,00,000	
	To Bank A/c				8,00,000
	(Being the machinery purchased)				
1.4.2011	Machinery A/c	Dr.		2,00,000	
	To Bank A/c				2,00,000
	(Being installation charges paid)				
31.03.2012	Depreciation A/c	Dr.		1,50,000	
	To Machinery A/c				1,50,000
	(Being the depreciation provided)				
31.3.2012	Profit and Loss A/c	Dr.		1,50,000	
	To Depreciation A/c				1,50,000
	(Being the transfer of Depreciation A/c)				
31.3.2013	Depreciation A/c	Dr.		1,50,000	
	To Machinery A/c				1,50,000

	(Being the depreciation provided)			
31.3.2013	Profit and Loss A/c	Dr.	1,50,000	
	To Depreciation A/c			1,50,000
	(Being the transfer of Depreciation A/c)			
30.9.13	Depreciation A/c	Dr.	75,000	
	To Machinery A/c			75,000
	(Being the depreciation provided)			
30.9.2013	Bank A/c	Dr.	5,00,000	
	To Machinery A/c			5,00,000
	(Being the Machinery sold)			
30.9.2013	Profit and Loss A/c	Dr.	1,25,000	
	To Machinery A/c			1,25,000
	(Being the transfer of loss on sale of machinery)			
31.3.2014	Profit and Loss A/c	Dr.	75,000	
	To Depreciation A/c			75,000
	(Being the transfer of depreciation A/c)			

Example 1

A firm bought a plant for A 4,00,000 on 1.1.2012 and its useful life was estimated to be 10 years. Its scrap value at the end of period was A 40,000. Find out amount of depreciation by straight line method.

Solution

$$\text{Annual Depreciation} = \frac{\text{Cost} - \text{Estimated Scrap Value}}{\text{Expected Life in Years}}$$

$$= \text{A}\frac{4,00,000 - 40,000}{10 \text{ years}} = \text{A } 36,000$$

Example 2

ABC Ltd. acquires a machine on 1st July 2012 at a cost of A 2,80,000 and spent A 20,000 on its installation. The firm writes off depreciation at 10% of the original cost every year. The books are closed on 31st December every year. Prepare machinery A/c for 3 years.

Solution

Machinery A/c

Dr. *Cr.*

Date	*Particulars*	*A*	*Date*	*Particulars*	*A*
2012	To Bank	2,80,000	**2012**	By Depreciation A/c	15,000
July 1	To Bank	20,000	Dec. 31	By Balance c/d	2,85,000
	(installation Exps.)				
		3,00,000			3,00,000
2013			**2013**		
Jan. 1	To balance b/d	2,85,000	Dec. 31	By Depreciation A/c	30,000
			Dec. 31	By balance c/d	2,55,000
		2,85,000			2,85,000

2014				**2014**	
Jan. 1	To balance b/d	2,55,000	Dec. 31	By Depreciation A/c	30,000
			Dec. 31	By balance c/d	2,25,000
		2,55,000			2,55,000

Sale of Asset : If the asset is disposed of in the middle of the year, the amount realised should be credited to the asset a/c for the time it has been in use. Any balance left in the account of asset will be profit or loss and should be transferred to P&L a/c.

Example 3

Z Ltd. purchased machine for A 200,000 on 1.1.2011. The machine is depreciated at 10% p.a. on the original cost. On 1.7.2013 the machine was sold for A 1,20,000. Prepare Machining A/c, assuming the books are closed on 31st December every year.

Solution

Machinery A/c

Dr. *Cr.*

Date	*Particulars*	*A*	*Date*	*Particulars*	*A*
2011			**2011**		
Jan. 1	To Bank	2,00,000	Dec. 31	By Depreciation A/c	20,000
			Dec. 31	By Balance c/d	1,80,000
		2,00,000			2,00,000
2012			**2012**		
Jan. 1	To balance b/d	1,80,000	Dec. 31	By Depreciation A/c	20,000
			Dec. 31	By balance c/d	1,60,000
		1,80,000			1,80,000
2013			**2013**		
Jan. 1	To balance b/d	1,60,000	July 1	By Depreciation A/c	10,000
			July 1	By Bank	1,20,000
				By P&L A/c (loss)	30,000
		1,60,000			1,60,000

2. Diminishing Balance Method

Under this method, a fixed percentage is applied to book value of the assets (cost of assets). In other words, the depreciation is calculated on the reducing balance (assets cost–depreciation) and not on the original cost. The procedure is that depreciation calculated is deducted from the cost of assets and balance known as the written down value. The written down value at the end of the estimated useful life of the assets should equal the estimated salvage or scrap value.

Under diminishing balance method, the amount of depreciation is based on written down value of the asset. Therefore, it is also referred to as 'Written Down Value Method'. Another term used for this method is 'Reducing Instalment Method' because the amount of depreciation does not remain same every year but keeps on decreasing from year to year.

Formula for calculating rate of depreciation is as follows :

$$\text{Rate of Depreciation} = \left[1 - \sqrt[n]{\frac{\text{Residual Value}}{\text{Cost of Asset}}}\right] \times 100$$

where n = Number of years of asset life.

For example, if cost is A 10,00,000; residual value is A 64,000 and life is 3 years then the rate of depreciation $= \left[1 - \sqrt[3]{\frac{64,000}{10,00,000}}\right] \times 100 = 60\%$

Advantages

1. It is easy to use.
2. There is same weightage, in totality, on profit and loss A/c, of depreciation.
3. It facilitates replacement of fixed assets as it makes more funds available at an early stage.
4. This method is permissible under the Income Tax Act.
5. The higher depreciation is charged in the earlier years when the machine is most efficient compared to later years.

Disadvantages

1. Under this method, value of asset can never be zero.
2. It is difficult to calculate proper rate of depreciation.
3. There is no provision of interest on capital invested in use of assets.

JOURNAL ENTRIES UNDER DIMINISHING BALANCE METHOD

Illustration

On 1st April 2011, a firm purchased a machine for A 8,00,000 and spent A 2,00,000 on its installation. On 30th September 2013, this machine is sold for A 5,00,000. Depreciation is to be provided @ 20% p.a. according to Diminishing Balance Method.

Make journal entries to record the above transactions under diminishing balance method.

Journal Entries

Date	*Particulars*		*L.F.*	*Debit (A)*	*Credit(A)*
1.4.2011	Machinery A/c	Dr.		8,00,000	
	To Bank A/c				8,00,000
	(Being the machinery purchased)				
1.4.2011	Machinery A/c	Dr.		2,00,000	
	To Bank A/c				2,00,000
	(Being the installation charges paid)				
31.3.2012	Depreciation A/c	Dr.		2,00,000	
	To Machinery A/c				2,00,000
	(Being the depreciation provided)				
31.3.2012	Profit and Loss A/c	Dr.		2,00,000	
	To Depreciation A/c				2,00,000
	(Being the transfer of Depreciation A/c)				

Date	Particulars		L.F.	Dr.	Cr.
31.3.2013	Depreciation A/c	Dr.		1,60,000	
	To Machinery A/c				1,60,000
	(Being the depreciation provided)				
31.3.2013	Profit and Loss A/c	Dr.		1,60,000	
	To Depreciation A/c				1,60,000
	(Being the transfer of Depreciation A/c)				
30.9.2013	Depreciation A/c	Dr.		64,000	
	To Machinery A/c				64,000
	(Being the depreciation provided)				
30.9.2013	Bank A/c	Dr.		5,00,000	
	To Machinery A/c				5,00,000
	(Being the Machinery sold)				
30.9.2013	Profit and Loss A/c	Dr.		76,000	
	To Machinery A/c				76,000
	(Being the transfer of loss on sale of Machinery)				
31.3.2014	Profit and Loss A/c	Dr.		64,000	
	To Depreciation A/c				64,000
	(Being the transfer of Depreciation A/c)				

Differences between Straight Line Method and Diminishing Balance Method

The following are the differences between the above two methods of depreciation.

Straight Line Method	*Diminishing Balance Method*
1. Depreciation is calculated at a fixed percentage or rate on the original cost of the fixed asset.	1. Depreciation is calculated at a fixed percentage or rate on written down value of the fixed asset.
2. The amount of depreciation remains fixed from year to year.	2. The amount of depreciation keeps on decreasing from year to year.
3. At the end of life of fixed asset, the written down value becomes equal to residual (scrap) value, if any, or zero.	3. At the end of useful life of the asset, the written down value never becomes zero.
4. Rate of depreciation can be calculated easily.	4. Calculation of rate of depreciation is very difficult and involves the use of logarithm tables.
5. It is suitable for assets in which the repair charges are less and the possibility of obsolescence is less and expiration of cost depends upon time period involved.	5. It is suitable for assets which are affected by technological changes, require more repairs with the passage of time etc.
6. The effect on profit and loss account is greater in later years because the repair charges increase while the depreciation amount is same.	6. The effect on profit and loss due to depreciation and repair is almost same in all the years (early years and later years) of the asset. The reason is that under this method more depreciation is charged in the beginning and lower depreciation later. Further less repair is required in the beginning and more repair later. Thus, the total effect on income state-ment will be the equal.
7. This method is not accepted under Income Tax Law.	7. This method is recognised under Income Tax Law.

Opening 'Provision for Depreciation Account'

For recording depreciation, sometimes, provision for depreciation account is opened. In this case, depreciation is credited to the Provision for Depreciation Account and as a result, the Respective Asset Account appears at its Original Cost. When the asset is sold or discarded, Asset Disposal Account is prepared to ascertain profit or loss.

The following journal entries are made when Provision for Depreciation Account is introduced.

(*i*) For providing Depreciation	Depreciation A/c	Dr.
	To Provision for Depreciation A/c	
(*ii*) For closure of Depreciation A/c	Profit and Loss A/c	Dr.
	To Depreciation A/c	

Opening of Asset Disposal Account

Sometimes, a separate account referred to as Asset Disposal Account is opened. In this case, the book value of the asset sold is transferred to Asset Disposal Account. The following journal entries are made in case Asset Disposal Account is introduced.

(*i*) Asset Disposal A/c Dr.

To Asset A/c

The amount of depreciation provided on the asset sold from the date of purchase to the date of sale is transferred from the 'Provision for Depreciation Account' to the 'Asset Disposal Account', the entry being :

Provision for Depreciation A/c Dr.

To Asset Disposal A/c

(*ii*) When cash is realised on sale of asset, it is credited to Asset Disposal A/c; entry being:

Bank A/c Dr.

To Asset Disposal A/c

(*iii*) Loss on disposal is transferred to Profit and Loss Account by passing the following entry :

Profit and Loss A/c Dr.

To Asset Disposal A/c

(*iv*) Profit on disposal is transferred by reversing the above entry, *i.e.*,

Asset Disposal A/c Dr.

To Profit and Loss A/c

Profit on disposal represents excess depreciation provided in the past years now credited back to profit and loss account, whereas loss on disposal represents depreciation not provided for in the earlier years.

AS 6 ON DEPRECIATION

The ICAI has issued (revised) accounting standard in August 1994 on depreciation and this has been made mandatory in respect of accounts for periods commencing on or after 1.4.1995. This standard deals with depreciation accounting and applies to all depreciable assets, except the following items to which special considerations apply :

(*i*) forests, plantations and similar regenerative natural resources;

(*ii*) wasting assets including expenditure on the exploration for and extraction of minerals, oils, natural gas and similar non-regenerative resources;

(*iii*) expenditure on research and development;

(*iv*) goodwill;

(*v*) livestock.

This standard also does not apply to land unless it has a limited useful life for the enterprise.

CHANGE IN DEPRECIATION METHOD

The depreciation method selected should be applied consistently from the period to period. According to ICAI's AS 6, a change from one method of providing depreciation to another should be made only if the adoption of the new method is required by statute or for compliance with an accounting standard or if it is considered that the change would result in a more appropriate preparation or presentation of the financial statements of the enterprise. When such a change in the method of depreciation is made, the unamortised depreciable amount of the asset is charged to revenue over the remaining useful life by applying the new method.

When there is change from one method of depreciation to another, the unamortised cost of the asset should be written off over the remaining useful life on the new basis commencing with the period in which the change in made. The effect should be disclosed in the year of change, if material.

Procedure to be followed in case of change in method—

(*i*) Depreciation should be recomputed applying the new method from the date of its acquisition/installation till the date of change of method.

(*ii*) Difference between the total depreciation under the new method and accumulated depreciation under the old method till the date of change may be surplus/deficiency.

(*iii*) Such resultant surplus is credited to profit and loss account under the head "Depreciation written back".

(*iv*) Such resultant deficiency is charged to profit and loss account.

Such change of depreciation method should be treated as change in accounting policy and its effect should be quantified and disclosed.

Change in Estimated Useful Life

When there is change in estimated useful life of assets, outstanding depreciable amount on the date of change in estimated useful life of asset should be allocated over the revised remaining useful life of assets.

Change in Historical Cost

(*i*) Increase/decrease in amount of historical cost is added/deducted from the outstanding written down value on the date of change.

(*ii*) Depreciation on the revised WDV will be provided prospectively over the remaining useful life of the asset.

(*iii*) Change in historical cost may be due to exchange variation on long-term foreign liability, price adjustment and change in duties etc.

Example 4

Y Ltd. Co. purchased a machine costing A 3,00,000 on 1 Jan. 2012. The depreciation is to be charged at 20% p.a. on Diminishing Balance method.

Write up Machinery A/c for first four years.

Solution

Machinery A/c

Dr. *Cr.*

2012		(A)	2012		(A)
Jan.1	To Bank	3,00,000	Dec. 31	By Depreciation	60,000
			Dec. 31	By Balance c/d	2,40,000
		3,00,000			3,00,000
2013			**2013**		
Jan. 1	To Balance	2,40,000	Dec. 31	By Depreciation	48,000
			Dec. 31	By Balance c/d	1,92,000
		2,40,000			2,40,000
2014			2014		
Jan. 1	To Balance b/d	1,92,000	Dec. 31	By Depreciation	38,400
			Dec. 31	By Balance c/d	1,53,600
		1,92,000			1,92,000
2015			**2015**		
Jan. 1	To Balance b/d	1,53,600	Dec. 31	By Depreciation	30,720
			Dec. 31	By Balance c/d	1,22,880
		1,53,600			1,53,600

Example 5

A machine is purchased for A 3,00,000 and its estimated useful life is 3 years with scrap value A 30,000. It is decided to depreciate the machine by diminishing balance method. Find out the rate of depreciation p.a.

Solution

S : A 30,000 C = A 3,00,000 n = 3

$$r = 1 - n\sqrt{\frac{S}{C}} = 1 - 3\sqrt{\frac{30,000}{3,00,000}}$$

$$= 1 - 3\sqrt{\frac{1}{10}}$$

$$= \frac{1-(1)1/3}{10}$$

$$= \frac{1-1}{2.154}$$

= 1.0 – .464

= .536

= 53.6%

Example 6

A Company had bought machinery for A 2,00,000 including a boiler worth A 20,000. The machinery Account had been credited for depreciation on the reducing instalment system for the past four years at the rate of 10 per cent. During the fifth year, the boiler became useless on account of damage to some of its vital parts. The damaged boiler is sold in the very beginning of the fifth year for A 4,000. Write up the Machinery Account for all these five year.

Solution

Machinery Account

Dr. *Cr.*

Date	*Particulars*	*A*	*Date*	*Particulars*	*A*
1st year	To Bank A/c	2,00,000	1st year	By Depreciation A/c	20,000
				By Balance c/d	1,80,000
		2,00,000			2,00,000
2nd year	To Balance b/d	1,80,000	2nd year	By Depreciation A/c	18,000
				By Balance c/d	1,62,000
		1,80,000			1,80,000
3rd year	To Balance b/d	1,62,000	3rd year	By Depreciation A/c	16,200
				By Balance c/d	1,45,800
		1,62,000			1,62,000
4th year	To Balance b/d	1,45,800	4th year	By Depreciation A/c	14,580
				By Balance c/d	1,31,220
		1,45,800			1,45,800
5th year	To Balance b/d	1,31,220	5th year	By Bank-Sale	4,000
				By P&L A/c*	9,122
				(Loss on Sale of boiler)	
				By Dep. A/c*	11,810
				By Balance c/d	1,06,288
	Total	1,31,220			1,31,220

Working Notes

* Loss on Sale :

Cost of boiler	20,000
Less : Depreciation for four years	
(A 2,000 + A 1,800 + A 1,620 + A 1,458)	6,878
Book Value at the beginning of 5th year	13,122
Less : Sale Proceeds	4,000
Loss on Sale of boiler	9,122

* *Depreciation for 5th year :*

Balance of remaining machinery at the beginning of 5th year

= A 1,31,220 – A 13,122

= A 1,18,098

Hence, Depreciation for the 5th year @ 10%

= A 11,810 (to the nearest rupee)

Example 7

A transport company purchases 5 Trucks at A 2,00,000 each on 1 April 2008. The company writes off depreciation @ 20% per annum on original cost and observes calendar year as its accounting year. On 1 October 2010 one of the trucks is involved in an accident and is completely destroyed. Insurance company pays A 90,000 in full settlement of the claim. On the same day the company purchases a truck for A 1,00,000 and spends A 20,000 on its overhauling. Prepare Truck Account for three years ending on 31 December 2010.

[B.Com. (Hons.) Delhi University]

Solution.

Truck Account

	A		A
1 April 2008		31 December 2008	
Bank Account	10,00,000	Depreciation Account	1,50,000
		Balance c/d	8,50,000
	10,00,000		10,00,000
1 January 2009		31 December 2009	
Balance b/d	8,50,000	Depreciation Account	2,00,000
		Balance c/d	6,50,000
	8,50,000		8,50,000
1 January 2010		31 October 2010	
Balance b/d	6,50,000	Depreciation Account	30,000
1 October 2010		(20% on A 2,00,000 for 9 months)	
Cash (1,00,000 + 20,000)	1,20,000	Insurance Company	90,000
		Profit and Loss Account	10,000
		31 December 2010	
		Depreciation Account	1,60,000
		Depreciation Account	6,000
		(20% on A 1,20,000 for 3 months)	
		Balance c/d	4,74,000
	7,70,000		7,70,000

Example 8

On 1st April, 2000, a firm purchased a machinery for A 2,00,000. On 1st October, 2000, additional machinery costing A 1,00,000 was purchased. On 1st October, 2001, the machinery purchased on 1st April, 2000 was sold for A 90,000. On 1st October, 2002 new machinery was purchased for A 2,50,000, while the machinery purchased on 1st October, 2000 was sold for A 85,000 on the same day.

The firm provides depreciation on its machinery @ 10% per annum on original cost. It closes its books of accounts on 31st March every year. Show machinery account for three accounting years ending 31st March, 2003.

Solution

Machinery Account

Dr. *Cr.*

Date	*Particulars*	A	*Date*	*Particulars*		A
2000			**2001**			
April 1	To Bank A/c	2,00,000	Mar. 31	By Dep. a/c A 2,00,000		
Oct. 1	To Bank A/c	1,00,000		@ 10%	20,000	
				A 1,00,000 @ 10%		
				for 6 months	5,000	25,000
				By Balance c/d		2,75,000
		3,00,000				3,00,000
2001			**2001**			
April 1	To Balance b/d	2,75,000	Oct. 1	By Bank A/c (Sale)		90,000
				By Dep. A/c A 2,00,000		
				@ 10% for 6 months		10,000
				By Profit and Loss A/c		80,000
				(Loss on Sale*)		
			2002			
			Mar. 31	By Dep. A/c A 1,00,000		
				@ 10%		10,000
				By Balance c/d		85,000
		2,75,000				2,75,000
2002			**2002**			
April 1	To Balance b/d	85,000	Oct. 1	By Bank A/c		85,000
Oct. 1	To Bank A/c	2,50,000		By Dep. A/c		
	To Profit and Loss		2003	A 1,00,000		
	A/c		Mar. 31	@ 10% for 6 months		5,000
	(Gain on Sale)	5,000		By Dep. A/c Rs/ 2,50,000		
				@ 10% for 6 months		12,500
				By Balance c/d		2,37,500
		3,40,000				3,40,000

Working Notes

* Calculation of Loss on Sale of Machinery purchased on 1st April 2000	A
Cost	2,00,000
Less : Depreciation [1.4.2000 – 31.3.2001]	20,000
	1,80,000
Less : Depreciation [1.4.2001 – 30.9.2001]	10,000
	1,70,000
Less : Sale Proceeds	90,000
Loss	– 80,000

* *Calculation of Profit on Sale of Machinery purchased on 1st October 2000*

		A	A
Cost			1,00,000
Less : Depreciation		A	
	[1.10.2000 – 31.3.2001]	5,000	
	[1.4.2001 – 31.3.2002]	10,000	
	[1.4.2002 – 30.9.2002]	5,000	20,000
	Book Value on 1.10.2002		80,000
	Sale Proceeds		85,000
∴ Profit on Sale of Machinery (A 85,000 – A 80,000)			+ 5,000

Example 9

Mr. X purchased a second hand machinery on 1.2.2003 for A 50,000; paid A 11,000 for its over-hauling and A 5,000 for its installation which was completed by 31.3.2003. The company provides depreciation on its machinery at 15% on diminishing balance method from the date it was put to use and closes its books on 31st December every year. On 1.10.2004, a repair work was carried out on the machine and A 5,000 were paid for the same. The machine was sold on 31.10.2005, for a sum of A 11,000 and an amount of A 1,000 was paid as dismantling charges.

Prepare machinery account from 2003 to 2005.

Solution

Machinery Account

Dr. *Cr.*

Date	*Particulars*	A	*Date*	*Particulars*	A
2003			**2003**		
Feb. 1	To Bank A/c	50,000	Dec. 31	By Depreciation	
Mar. 31	To Bank A/c	16,000		A/c (15% on 66,000)	7,425
	[A 11,000 +			for 9 months	
	A 5,000]			By Balance c/d	58,575
		66,000			66,000
2004			**2004**		
Jan. 1	To Balance b/d	58,575	Dec. 31	By Depreciation	
				A/c (15% on	8,786
				A 55,875)	
				By Balance c/d	49,789
		58,575			58,575
2005			**2005**		
Jan. 1	To Balance b/d	49,789	Oct. 31	By Depreciation A/c	
				(15% on A 49,789	6,223
				for 10 months)	
				By Bank A/c	10,000
				By Profit and Loss A/c	
				(Loss) (Balance Fig.)	33,566
		49,789			49,789

Working Note

- * Repair cost is not capitalised since it is a routine expense and it does not increase the capacity of the machine.
- * Cost of dismantling has been deducted from the sale price for calculating loss on sale of machine.

Example 10

Rama Motors Limited purchased a machinery for A 15,00,000 on April 1, 2002. On October 1, 2003 another machinery was purchased for A 6,00,000. On October 1, 2004 a new machine was purchased for A 4,50,000.

Depreciation at 20% per annum on the diminishing value basis was accumulated in Provision for Depreciation Account.

On January 1, 2006, machine no. 2 (purchased on October 1, 2003) was damaged and had to be replaced by a new machine costing A 7,50,000. It was expected that damaged machine will fetch A 33,000 but it was insured and an insurance claim for A 3,72,000 was admitted by the insurers.

Show for the year ending 31st March, 2006 the Machinery Account, Provision for Depreciation Account and Machinery Disposal Account.

Solution

Machinery Account

Dr. *Cr.*

Date	*Particulars*	*A*	*Date*	*Particulars*	*A*
2005			**2006**		
April 21	To Balance b/d*	25,50,000	Jan. 1	By Machine Disposal A/c (Cost of damaged machine)	6,00,000
2006					
Jan. 1	To Bank A/c	7,50,000	Mar. 31	By Balance c/d	27,00,000
		33,00,000			33,00,000

Provision for Depreciation A/c

Dr. *Cr.*

Date	*Particulars*	*A*	*Date*	*Particulars*	*A*
2006			**2005**		
Jan. 1	Machinery Disposal* A/c (Accumulated depreciation on damaged machine)	1,68,000	Apr. 1	By Balance b/d*	9,45,000
			2006		
			Mar. 31	By Depreciation A/c*	2,72,100
Mar. 31	To Balance c/d	10,49,100			
		12,17,100			12,17,100
			2006		
			Apr. 1	By Balance b/d	10,49,100

Machinery Disposal A/c

Dr. *Cr.*

Date	*Particulars*	*A*	*Date*	*Particulars*	*A*
2006			**2006**		
Jan. 1	To Machinery A/c	6,00,000	Jan. 1	By Provision for Depreciation A/c*	1,68,000
			Jan. 1	By Insurers (Insurance claim admitted)	3,72,000
			Jan. 1	By Depreciation A/c on A 4,32,000 for 9 months [20/100 (6,00,000 – 1,68,000 × 9/12]	64,800
Mar. 31	To Profit and Loss A/c (Transfer of profit on disposal)	37,800	Mar. 31	By Balance c/d (Estimated value)	33,000
		6,37,800			6,37,800

Working Notes

* *Calculation of balance of Provision for Depreciation Account as on 1st April 2005*

	A	A
Cost of three machines (A 15,00,000 + A 6,00,000 + A 4,50,000)		25,50,000
Cost of machine No. 1	15,00,000	
Less : Depreciation @ 20%		
for machine No. 1 year (2002-2003)	3,00,000	
	12,00,000	
Add : Cost of Machine No. 2 (1.10.2003)	6,00,000	
		18,00,000
Less : Depreciation for the year 2003-04 :	A	
On Machine No. 1 for full year [A 12,00,000 × 20/100]	2,40,000	
On machine No. 2 for 6 months [A 6,00,000 × 20/100 × 6/12]	60,000	3,00,000
		15,00,000
Add : Cost of Machine No. 3 (1.10.2004)		4,50,000
		19,50,000
Less : Depreciation for the year (2004-05)		
On machines No. 1 and 2 for full year [A 15,00,000 × 20/100]	3,00,000	

On machine No. 3 for 6 month		
[4,50,000 × 20/100 × 6/12]	45,000	3,45,000
Written down value of all the machine taken		16,05,000
together [A 1950,000 – A 3,45,000]		
Balance of Provision for Depreciation Account		
[A 25,50,000 – A 16,05,000]		9,45,000

* *Accumulated depreciation on damaged machine :*

	A
Depreciation on A 6,00,000 for six months during the year (2003-04)	
[A 6,00,000 × 20/100 × 6/12]	60,000
Add : Depreciation on A 6,00,000 – A 60,000 *i.e.,* on A 5,40,000	
for the year (2004 – 05) [*i.e.,* A 5,40,000 × 20/100]	1,08,000
	1,68,000

* *Calculation of depreciation to be provided on March 31, 2006*

		A
Written Down Value of Machines No. 1, 2 and 3 on 1st April 2005*	16,05,000	
Less : Written Down Value of Machine No. 2 on 1st April 2005		
[A 6,00,000 – A 1,68,000 (Accumulated Dep. on damaged machine)	4,32,000	
Written Down Value of Machines No. 1 and 3		11,73,000
Depreciation on Machines No. 1 and 3 for full year		
[A 11,73,000 × 20/100]		2,34,600
Depreciation on Machine No. 4 for 3 months		
[A 7,50,000 × 20/100 × 3/12]		37,500
		2,72,100

Example 11

A company provides depreciation on Plant and Machinery at 20% per annum on reducing balance method. On April 1st, 2006, the balance of Plant and Machinery Account was A 5,00,000. It was discovered in 2006-07 that :

(*i*) A 25,000 being repairs to machinery incurred on June 30th, 2004 had been capitalised.

(*ii*) A 50,000 being cost of a machine purchased on October 1st, 2003 had been treated as ordinary goods.

Management wants to correct the mistakes while preparing accounts for the year ending March 31st, 2007. A plant that costed A 40,000 on September 30th, 2005 was scrapped and replaced with a modern plant on 31st December, 2006 by spending A 60,000.

Calculate the amount of depreciation for the year ended March 31st, 2007. Also prepare machinery Account upto March 31st, 2007.

Solution

Working Notes

(*i*) **Effect of repairs capitalised :** A 25,000 on June 30th, 2004

		A	A
	Depreciation charged for 9 months A 3,750		
	Remaining amount = 25,000 – 3,750	21,250	on 1.4.2005
	Depreciation for 2005-06	4,250	
		17,000	on 1.4.2006
(*ii*)	**Machine to be capitalised**		
	Purchased on 1.10.2003	50,000	
	Less : Depreciation for 6 months	5,000	
	W.D.V. as on 1.4.2004	45,000	
	Less : Depreciation for 2004-05	9,000	
		36,000	
	Less : Depreciation for 2005-06	7,200	
	W.D.V. as on 1.4.2006	28,800	
(*iii*)	**Plant Scrapped**		
	Cost as on 30.9.2005	40,000	
	Less : Depreciation for 2005-06	4,000	
		36,000	
	Depreciation upto 31st December, 2006	5,400	
	Loss on abandonment	30,600	
(*iv*)	**Depreciation for 2006-07**		
(*a*)	On [A 5,00,000 + 28,800 – 17,000 – 36,000] @ 20%		A 95,160
(*b*)	On A 60,000 for 3 months		3,000
			98,160

Plant and Machinery Account

Dr. *Cr.*

Date	*Particulars*	*A*	*Date*	*Particulars*	*A*
1.4.06	To Balance b/d	5,00,000	31.12.06	By Depreciation	5,400
1.4.06	To Profit and Loss A/c	11,800	31.12.06	By Profit and Loss A/c	30,600
31.12.06	To Bank	60,000	31.3.07	By Depreciation	98,160
			31.3.07	By Balance c/d	4,37,640
		5,71,800			5,71,800
1.4.07	To Balance b/d	4,37,640			

Example 12

On 1-2-2006, Mr. X purchased a second hand machinery for A 50,000, paid A 11,000 for its overhauling and A 5,000 for its installation which was completed on 31.3.2006. On 1.10.2007 a repair work was carried out on the machine and A 5,000 were spent for the same. The machine was sold on 31.10.2008 for a sum of A 21,000 and an amount of A 1,000 was paid as dismantling charges. The company provides depreciation on its machinery at 20% on diminishing balance method and closes its books on 31st December every year.

Prepare machinery account from 2006 to 2008.

Solution

Machinery Account

Dr. *Cr.*

Date	*Particulars*	A	*Date*	*Particulars*	A
1.2.06	To Bank A/c	66,000	31.12.06	By Depreciation A/c	
	[A 50,000 + 11,000			[A 66,000 × 20/100	
	+ A 5,000]			× 9/12]	9,900
				By Balance c/d	56,100
		66,000			66,000
1.1.07	To Balance b/d	56,100	31.12.07	By Depreciation A/c	
				[A 56,100 × 20/100]	11,220
				By Balance c/d	44,880
		56,100			56,100
1.1.08	To Balance b/d	44,880	31.10.08	By Depreciation A/c	7,480
31.10.08	To Bank A/c	1,000		[44,880 × 10/12	
	[Dismantling Charges]			× 20/100]	
			31.10.08	By Bank A/c	21,000
				By Profit and Loss A/c	17,400
				(Loss on Sale) (*Bal. Fig.*)	
		45,880			45,880

Notes

1. Installation charges are always capitalised, overhauling and repair charges on the second hand machine incurred are capitalised before the machine is put to use. However, all such charges after the installation of machine are treated as revenue charges and hence not capitalised.
2. Dismantling expenses are debited to Machinery Account. Alternatively, these expenses may be deducted out of the sale proceeds of the machine disposed off.

Example 13

A Co. charged depreciation @ 20% on written down value. Machinery costing A 1,00,000. A 40,000 and A 30,000 were purchased on 1.1.2000, 1.7.2001 and 1.10.2002 respectively. On 1.10.2003, machinery purchased on 1.7.2001 was damaged and replaced by a new machine costing A 50,000. The damaged machinery was insured and an insurance claim of A 24,800 (after adjustment of value of scrap) was admitted by the Insurance Co. The scrap was sold for A 2,200.

Show Machinery Account, Accumulated Depreciation Account and Machinery Account for the year 2003.

Solution

Machinery Account

Dr. *Cr.*

Date	Particulars	A	Date	Particulars	A
1.1.03	To Balance b/d (1,00,000 + 40,000 + 30,000)	1,70,000	1.10.03	By Machinery Disposal A/c	40,000
				By Balance c/d	1,80,000
1.10.03	To Bank A/c	50,000			
		2,20,000			2,20,000

Accumulated Depreciation Account

Dr. *Cr.*

Date	Particulars	A	Date	Particulars	A
1.10.03	To Machinery Disposal A/c	15,520	1.1.03	By Balance b/d	61,500
			1.10.03	By Depreciation A/c	4,320
31.12.03	To Balance c/d	68,740	31.12.03	By Depreciation a/c (A 10,240 + A 5,700 + A 2,500)	18,440
		84,260			84,260

Machinery Disposal Account

Dr. *Cr.*

Date	Particulars	A	Date	Particulars	A
1.10.03	To Machinery A/c	40,000	1.10.03	By Accumulated Depreciation A/c	15,520
	To profit and Loss A/c (*Balancing Figure*)	2,520		By Cash A/c	2,200
				By Insurance Co. A/c	24,800
		42,520			42,520

Working Notes

*1. Calculation of Depreciation on Machinery

Date of Purchase	*1.1.2000* A	*1.7.2001* A	*1.10.2002* A	*1.10.2003* A
Cost of Machinery	1,00,000	40,000	30,000	50,000
Depreciation for 2000	20,000	—	—	—
WDV on 1.1.2001	80,000			
Depreciation for 2001	16,000	4,000	—	—
WDV on 1.1.2002	64,000	36,000	—	—
Depreciation for 2002	12,800	7,200	1,500 (3 months)	—
WDV on 1.1.2003	51,200	28,800	28,500	—
Depreciation for 2003	10,240	4,320 (9 months)	5,700	2,500 (3 months)

2. *Balance of Accumulated Depreciation Account on 1.12003*

   = (A 20,000 + A 16,000 + 12,800) + (A 4,000 + A 7,200) + A 1,500

   = A 61,500

3. *Accumulated Depreciation on Machinery sold*

   = A 4,000 + A 7,200 + A 4,320 = A 15,520.

Example 14

A machine is purchased for A 1,60,000 on 16.6.2003. The company took delivery on 27.06.2003 incurring A 2,500 for transportation. The machine was installed on 15.7.2003 spending A 2,000 for wages and A 1,000 for consultancy fees. Trial run was conducted on 15.11.2003 spending A 2,500. The machine was put to use on 1.1.2004. Useful life of the machine was expected to be 5 years and scrap value at the end was expected to be A 12,000. The firm follows straight line method of depreciation.

Show Machinery Account and Provision for Depreciation account assuming that machine realised A 13,000 at the end of 5 years. The accounts are closed on 31st December each year.

Solution

Machinery Account

Dr. *Cr.*

Date	*Particulars*	*A*	*Date*	*Particulars*	*A*
16.6.03	To Bank A/c	1,60,000	31.12.03	By Balance c/d	1,68,000
27.6.03	To Bank A/c	2,500			
15.7.03	To Bank A/c	3,000			
	(2,000 + 1,000)				
15.11.03	To Bank A/c (Cost)	2,500			
		1,68,000			1,68,000
1.1.04	To Balance b/d	1,68,000	31.12.04	By Balance c/d	1,68,000
1.1.05	To Balance b/d	1,68,000	31.12.05	By Balance c/d	1,68,000
1.1.06	To Balance b/d	1,68,000	31.12.06	By Balance c/d	1,68,000
1.1.07	To Balance b/d	1,68,000	31.12.07	By Balance c/d	1,68,000
1.1.08	To Balance b/d	1,68,000	31.12.08	By Provision for	1,56,000
31.12.08	To Profit and Loss A/c	1,000		Depreciation A/c	
	(Profit)			By Bank	13,000
		1,69,000			1,69,000

Provision for Depreciation Account

Dr. *Cr.*

Date	*Particulars*	*A*	*Date*	*Particulars*	*A*
31.12.04	To Balance c/d	31,200	31.12.04	By Profit and Loss A/c	31,200
			1.1.2005	By Balance b/d	31,200
31.12.05	To Balance c/d	62,400	31.12.05	By Profit and Loss A/d	31,200
		62,400			62,400
			1.12006	By Balance b/d	62,400
31.12.06	To Balance c/d	93,600	31.12.06	By Profit and Loss A/c	31,200

		93,600			93,600
			1.1.2007	By Balance b/d	93,600
31.12.07	To Balance c/d	1,24,800	31.12.07	By Profit and Loss A/c	31,200
		1,24,800			1,24,800
			1.1.2008	By Balance b/d	1,24,800
31.12.08	To Balance c/d	1,56,000	31.12.08	By Profit and Loss A/c	31,200
		1,56,000			1,56,000

Notes

1. *Calculation of Annual Depreciation*

	A
Cost of machine including expenses incurred before the machine is put to use	1,68,000
Less : Scrap Value	12,000
Depreciable Cost	1,56,000

Depreciation per year on straight line method = A 1,56,000/5 = A 31,200.

2. The machinery is put to use on 1.1.2004. Hence, depreciation will be charged from this date.

Example 15

A, who closes his books on 30 June every year, operates his factory with two machines purchased from B under an arrangement by which at the end of three years B allows him 20 per cent per annum of the cost price as an **exchange** for a new model. A provides depreciation at the rate of 30 per cent per annum of original cost for each of the first two years and 20 per cent per annum for the third years. The following payments to B have been recorded since A commenced business on 1 July 2001 :

		(A)
On 1 July, 2001	Purchase of Machine A	2,000
On 1 July, 2002	Purchase of Machine B	3,000
On 30 June, 2004	On purchase of Machine C in exchange for machine A	3,600

On 31 December 2004, A purchased from B a new model (Machine D) which would do the work of two machines. The cost was A 5,000 and B allowed A 3,000 for Machine B and C in part exchange.

You are required to prepare Plant Account for four years upto 31 December 2001 in the books of A, open a separate account for Depreciation Provisions and show the balances on these accounts carried down as on 30 June every year and on 31 December 2004. Also prepare Plant Disposal Account clearly differentiating between depreciation and loss on sale. [*B.Com (Hons.) Delhi University*]

Solution

Mr. A

Plant & Machinery Account

	A		A
1 July 2001		**30 June 2002**	
Bank **(Machine A)**	2,000	Balance c/d	2,000
1 July, 2002		**30th June, 2003**	
Balance b/d	2,000	Balance c/d	5,000
Bank **(Machine B)**	3,000		
	5,000		5,000

1 July, 2003		**30th June, 2004**	
Balance b/d	5,000	Machinery Disposal Account	2,000
Vendor **(Machine C)**	4,000	Balance c/d	7,000
(3,600 + 400)			
	9,000		9,000
1 July, 2004		**31 Dec. 2004**	
Balance b/d	7,000	Machinery Disposal Account	7,000
Vendor **(Machine D)**	5,000	**(Machinery B & C)**	
(2,000 + 3,000)		30 June 2005	
		balance c/d	5,000
	12,000		12,000
1 July, 2005			
Balance b/d	5,000		

Provision for Depreciation on Machinery Account

	A		A
30 June 2002		**30 June 2002**	
Balance c/d	600	Depreciation Account	600
	600		600
30 June 2003		**1 July, 2002**	
Balance c/d	2,100	Balance b/d	600
		30 June, 2003	
		Depreciation Account (600 + 900)	1,500
	2,100		2,100
30 June, 2004		**1 July, 2003**	
Machinery Disposal Account	1,600	Balance b/d	2,100
Balance c/d	1,800	**30 June, 2004**	
		Depreciation Account (400 + 900)	1,300
	3,400		3,400
31 December 2004		**1 July, 2004**	
Machinery Disposal		Balance b/d	1,800
Account	2,700	**31 December, 2004**	
		Depreciation Account (300 + 600)	900
	2,700		2,700

Machinery Disposal Account (30 June, 2004 For Plant A)

2004		**2004**	
30 June		**30 June**	
Plant Account	2,000	Provision for Depreciation	1,600
		Vendor **(exchange value)**	400
	2,000		2,000

Machinery Disposal Account (31 Dec., 2004 For Plants B & C)

2004		**2004**	
31 December		**31 December**	
Plant & Machinery Account	7,000	Provision for Depreciation	2,700
		Vendor **(exchange value)**	3,000
		Profit and Loss Account **(Loss)**	1,300
	7,000		7,000

Example 16

A limited company purchased on 1st January, 1998 a second-hand plant for A 12,000 and immediately spent A 8,000 on its overhauling. On 1st July in the same year additional plant costing A 10,000 is purchased. On 1st July, 2000 the plant purchased on 1st January, 1998 having become obsolete is sold for A 4,000 and on the same date fresh plant is purchased at a cost of A 24,000.

Depreciation is provided @ 10% per annum on original cost on 31st December every year. In 2001, however the company changes the method of providing depreciation and adopts the method of writing off 15% per annum on the diminishing balance method.

Show the Plant Account from 1998 to 2001.

Plant Account

Dr. *Cr.*

Date	*Particulars*	*A*	*Date*	*Particulars*	*A*
1998			**1998**		
	To Bank A/c	20,000		By Depreciation A/c	
Jan. 1	A (12,000 + 8,000)		Dec. 31	A (2,000 + 500)	2,500
July 1	To Bank A/c	10,000		By Balance c/d	27,500
		30,000			30,000
1999			**1999**		
Jan. 1	To Balance b/d	27,500	Dec. 31	By Depreciation A/c	3,000
				By Balance c/d	24,500
		27,500			27,500
2000			**2000**		
Jan. 1	To Balance b/d	24,500	July 1	By Bank A/c	4,000
July 1	To Bank A/c	24,000		By Depreciation A/c	1,000
				By Profit and Loss A/c Loss*	11,000
				A (20,000–5,000–4,000)	
			Dec. 31	By Depreciation A/c	2,200
				A (1,000 + 1,200)	
				By Balance c/d	30,300
		48,500			48,500

2001			**2001**		
Jan. 1	To Balance b/d	30,300	Dec. 31	By Profit and Loss A/c* (Additional Depreciation)	1,416
				By Depreciation A/c (15% on A 28,884)	4,332
				By Balance c/d	24,552
		30,300			30,300
2002					
Jan. 1	To Balance b/d	24,552			

Working Notes

*1 *Computation of Loss on Sale of Machinery on 1.7.2000*

	A
Cost of machinery sold (as on 1.1.98)	20,000
Less : Depreciation @10% p.a. for 2½ years on original cost	5,000
Book value as on 1.7.2000	15,000
Less : Realised Value	4,000
Loss on Sale of Machinery	11,000

*2 *Computation of Depreciation on change of method on additional plant :*

	S.L.M. @ 10% A	*W.D.V. @15%* A
Cost of machinery in use on 1.7.1998	10,000	10,000
Less : Depreciation for 1998	500	750
Book Value on 1.1.1999	9,500	9,250
Less : Depreciation for 1999	1,000	1,387
Book Value on 1.1.2000	8,500	7,863
Add : Addition to Machinery on 1.7.2000	24,000	24,000
	32,500	31,863
Less : Depreciation	2,200	2,979
Book value on 1.1.2001	30,300	28,884

∴ Additional Depreciation A (30,300 – 28,884) = A 1,416

W.D.V. of machinery as per new method on 1.1.2001 = A 28,884.

Example 17

On January 1, 2001 X Ltd. purchased a machine for A 58,000 and spent A 2,000 on its erection. On July 1,2001, and additional machine costing A 20,000 was purchased. On July 1,2003 the machine purchased on 1.1.2001 was sold for A 28,600 and on the same date a new machine was purchased at a cost of A 40,000. Depreciation was provided for annually on December 31, at the rate of 10% p.a. on written down value of the machinery. In 2004 the company decided to change the method of depreciation from Written Down Value Method to Straight Line Method @5% p.a. with effect from 1st Jan. 2001. Prepare the Machinery Account for the four calender years.

Solution

Dr. *Cr.*

Date	*Particulars*	A	*Date*	*Particulars*	A
D					
1.1.01	To Bank A/c	58,000	31.12.01	By Depreciation A/c	7,000
1.1.01	To Bank A/c (erection charges)	2,000		By Balance c/d	73,000
1.7.01	To Bank A/c	20,000			
		80,000			80,000
1.1.02	To Balance b/d	73,000	31.12.02	By Depreciation A/c	7,300
				By Balance c/d	65,700
		73,000			73,000
1.1.03	To Balance b/d	65,700	1.7.03	By Bank A/c	28,600
1.7.03	To Bank A/c	40,000	1.7.03	By Depreciation A/c (on Machinery sold)	2,430
			1.7.03	By Profit and Loss A/c	17,570
			31.12.03	By Depreciation A/c	3,710
			31.12.03	By Balance c/d	53,390
		1,05,700			1,05,700
1.1.04	To Balance b/d	53,390	31.12.04	By Depreciation A/c	3,000
31.12.04	To P and L A/c* (Depreciation written back on account of change from WDV Method to Straight Line Method)	3,110		By Balance c/d	53,500
		56,500			56,500

Working Notes

*1 *Calculation of Short/Excess Depreciation on Existing Machines*

Year A	*Machine* B	*Cost* C	*WDV as on 1.1.04* D	*Dep. Under WDV* E = C – D	*Dep. Under SLM* F
2001	II	20,000	(20,000 × 95/100 × 90/100 × 90/100) = 15,390	4,610	(20,000 × 5% × 2½ = 2,500
2003	III	40,000	(40,000 × 95/100) = 38,000	2,000	(40,000×5%×½=1,000
		60,000	53,390	6,610	3,500

Excess Depreciation provided = Depreciation under Old Method
– Depreciation under New Method
= A 6,610 – A 3,500 = A 3,110.

Example 18

The Plant and Machinery Account of a company had a debit balance of A 1,47,390 on April 1,2006. The company was incorporated in April, 2003 and has been following the practice of charging full year's depreciation every year on Diminishing Balance System @ 15%. In 2006 it was, however, decided to change the method from Diminishing Balance to Straight Line with retrospective effect from April, 2003 and to give effect to the change while preparing the final accounts for the year ending 31st March, 2007, the rate of depreciation remaining same as before.

In 2006-07, new machinery was purchased at a cost of A 50,000. All the other machines were acquired in 2003-04.

Show the Plant and Machinery Account from 2003-04 to 2006-07.

Solution

Dr. Cr.

Date	Particulars	A	Date	Particulars	A
1.4.03	To Bank A/c*	2,40,000	31.3.04	By Depreciation A/c [15/100 × A 2,40,000]	36,000
				By Balance c/d	2,04,000
		2,40,000			2,40,000
1.4.04	To Balance b/d	2,04,000	31.3.05	By Depreciation A/c [15/100 × A 2,04,000]	30,600
				By Balance c/d	1,73,400
		2,04,000			2,04,000
1.04.05	To Balance b/d	1,73,400	31.3.06	By Depreciation A/c [15/100 × A 1,73,400]	26,010
				By Balance c/d	1,47,390
		1,73,400			1,73,400
1.4.06	To Balance b/d	1,47,390	1.4.06	By Profit and Loss A/c* (Additional Depreciation)	15,390
	To Bank	50,000	31.3.07	By Depreciation A/c*	43,500
				By Balance c/d	1,38,500
		1,97,390			1,97,390

Working Notes

*1. Calculation of Cost Price of Plant on 1st April 2003 :

	A
Let Cost Price on 1st April 2003	100.00
Less : Depreciation (2003-04) [15% of A 100.00]	15.00
	85.00
Less : Depreciation (2004-05) [15% of A 85.00]	12.750
	72.250
Less : Depreciation (2005-06) [15% of A 72.250]	(approx.) 10.828
	61.412

$$\text{Cost Price on 1st April 2003} = \frac{100}{61.412} \times \text{A } 147390 = \text{A } 2,40,000 \text{ (approx)}$$

*2. *Calculation of Depreciation :*

	S.L.M.	*D.B.M.*
	A	*A*
Cost (1.4.2003)	2,40,000	2,40,000
Less : Depreciation (2003-04)	36,000	36,000
	2,04,000	2,04,000
Less : Depreciation (2004-05)	36,000	30,600
	1,68,000	1,73,400
Less : Depreciation (2005-06)	36,000	26,010
	1,32,000	1,47,390

Difference on Account of change in method of Depreciation :

(A 1,47,390 – A 1,32,000) = A 15,390

∴ Additional Depreciation to be transferred to P & L A/c = A 15,390

*3. *Calculation of Depreciation for 2006-07*

	A
On Old Machinery	36,000
On New Machinery [@ 15% of A 50,000]	7,500
	43,500

Example 19

M/s Hot and Cold commenced business on 1st April, 2002 when they purchased a new machinery costing A 8,00,000. On 1st October, 2003, they purchased another machinery for A 6,00,000 and again on 1st July, 2006, machinery costing A 15,00,000 was purchased. They adopted a policy of charging @20% p.a. on diminishing balance basis.

On April 1st, 2006, they, however, changed the method of providing depreciation and adopted the method of writing-off the machinery account at 15% p.a. under straight line method with retrospective effect from 1st April, 2002, the adjustment being made in the accounts for the year ended 31st March, 2007.

Show the Machinery Account for the year ending 31st March, 2007.

Solution

Dr. *Cr.*

Date	*Particulars*	*A*	*Date*	*Particulars*	*A*
2002 April 1	To Bank	8,00,000	2003 Mar. 31	By Depreciation	1,60,000
				By Balance c/d	6,40,000
		8,00,000			8,00,000
2003			2004		
April 1	To Balance b/d	6,40,000	Mar. 31	By Depreciation	1,88,000
Oct. 1	To Bank	6,00,000		By Balance c/d	10,52,000
		12,40,000			12,40,000
2004			2005		
April	To Balance b/d	10,52,000	Mar. 31	By Depreciation	2,10,400
				By Balance c/d	8,41,600
		10,52,000			10,52,000

2005			2006		
April 1	To Balance b/d	8,41,600		By Depreciation	1,68,320
				By Balance c/d	6,73,280
		8,41,600			8,41,600
2006			2007		
April 1	To Balance b/d	6,73,280	Mar. 31	By Depreciation	3,78,750
July 1	To Bank	15,00,000		By Balance c/d	18,16,250
2007 Mar. 31	To Profit and Loss A/c (Depreciation written back)	21,720			
		21,95,000			21,95,000

Working Notes

Machine No. 1

Depreciation for 4 years :	SLM	4,80,000
	WDV	4,72,320
Depreciation to be charged		7,680

Machine No. 2

Depreciation for 2½ years :	SLM	2,25,000
	WDV	2,54,400
Depreciation to be written back		29,400
Result : Depreciation to be written back in 2006-07		21,720

Example 20

A Company had a balance of A 4,05,000 on 1st January, 2003 in its Machinery account. 10% per annum depreciation was charged by diminishing balance method. On 1st July, 2003, the company sold a part of machinery for A 87,500, which was purchased on 1st January, 2001 for A 1,20,000 as a part of it become useless, and on the same date *i.e.* on 1st July, 2003, the company purchased a new machine for A 2,50,000. On 31st December, 2003, the Directors of the company decided to adopt the fixed instalment method of depreciation from 1st January, 2001 instead of diminishing balance method. The rate of depreciation will remain the same.

Prepare Machinery account in the books of Company for the year ending 2003.[*C.A.* (*PE-1*) *Nov. 2004*]

Dr. **Machinery Account** *Cr.*

Date	*Particulars*	*A*	*Date*	*Particulars*	*A*
1.1.03	To Balance b/d		1.7.03	By Cash A/c	87,500
	(I) 97,200 (W.N.1)		1.7.03	By Depreciation A/c (W.N. 1)	4,860
	(II) 3,07,800	4,05,000	1.7.03	By Profit and Loss A/c (W.N.1)	
1.7.03	To Cash A/c (III)	2,50,000		(Loss on Sale)	4,840
			31.12.03	By Profit and Loss A/c (W.N.3) (Additional Depreciation)	3,800
			31.12.03	By Depreciation A/c	
				(II) 38,000 (W.N. 3)	
				(III) 12,500	50,500
			31.12.03	By Balance c/d	5,05,500
		6,55,000			6,55,000

Working Notes

1. *Calculation of written down value (W.D.V.) of machinery on 1-7-2003 and Loss on its sale :*

	A
Cost of machine on 1.1.2001	1,20,000
Less : Depreciation @ 10% for 2001	12,000
W.D.V. on 1.1.2002	1,08,000
Less : Depreciation @ 10% for 2002	10,800
W.D.V. on 1.1.2003	97,200
Less : Depreciation @ 10% for 6 months	4,860
W.D.V. on 1.7.2003	92,340
Less : Amount received from sale	87,500
Loss on sale	4,840

2. *Calculation of book value of unsold machine on 1.1.2001*

If A 97,200 is the W.D.V. on 1.1.2003 then cost	1,20,000
If A 3,07,800 is the W.D.V. on 1.1.2003 then cost	1,20,000 × 3,07,800/97,200
	= 3,80,000

3. *Calculation of additional depreciation because of change in method of depreciation:*

	Fixed Instalment Method (A)	*Diminishing Balance Method (A)*
Cost of machine on 1.1.2001	3,80,000	3,80,000
Less : Depreciation @ 10% p.a.	38,000	38,000
W.D.V. on 1.1.2002	3,42,000	3,42,000
Less : Depreciation @ 10% p.a.	38,000	34,200
W.D.V. on 1.1.2003	3,04,000	3,07,800
Additional depreciation to be charged.		
Value as per old method		3,07,800
Less : Value as per new method		3,04,000
Difference		3,800

Example 21

Jindal Manufacturing Ltd. which depreciate its machinery at 10% on diminishing balance method had on 1 January 2002 A 19,72,000 to the debit of machinery account. During the year 2002, part of the machinery purchased on 1 January 2000 for A 10,80,000 was sold for A 10,45,000 on 1 July 2002 and a new machinery at a cost of A 11,50,000 was purchased and installed on the same date, installation charges being A 80,000. The company wanted to change its method of depreciation from diminishing balance method to straight line method with effect from 1 January 2000 and adjust the difference before 31 December 2002, the rate of depreciation remains the same as before. Show the Machinery Account and ascertain the amount chargeable to Profit and Loss Account and depreciation or obsolescence loss in the year.

Machinery Account

	A		A
1.1.2002		**1.7.2002**	
Balance b/d	19,72,000	Bank Account	10,45,000
1.7.2002		**31.12.2002**	
Bank Account	12,30,000	Profit and Loss Account	13,546

(11,50,000 + 80,000)		**(Additional Depreciation) (ii)**	
Profit and Loss Account **(ii)**	2,13,940	Depreciation Account **(iii)**	2,40,697
		Balance c/d	21,16,697
	34,15,940		34,15,940

Working Notes

(i) Calculation of Profit on Sale of Machinery

Cost of machinery sold on 1.1.2000		10,80,000
Less : Depreciation for 2,000 @ 10% on Diminishing Balance Method		1,08,000
		9,72,000
Less : Depreciation for 2001 @ 10% on Diminishing Balance Method		97,200
		8,74,800
Less : Depreciation for 6 months @ 10%		43,740
		8,31,060
Add : Profit (10,45,000 – 83,160)		2,13,940
Sale Price		**10,45,000**

***(ii)* Calculation of Additional Depreciation**

Cost of Machinery on 1.1.2002		
$19,72,000 \quad \frac{100}{90} \quad \frac{100}{90}$		24,34,568
Less : Cost of machinery sold		10,80,000
		13,54,568
Depreciation on Rs. 13,54,568 at 10% p.a. on original cost for two years		2,70,914
Less : Depreciation on diminishing balance basis :		
Depreciation for 2001	1,35,457	
Depreciation for 2002	1,21,911	2,57,368
		13,546

***(iii)* Depreciation for 2002**

On machinery sold	43,740
On Rs. 13,54,568 for one year @ 10% p.a.	1,35,457
On Rs. 12,30,000 **(new machine)** @ 10% p.a. for 6 months	61,500
	2,40,697

Example 22

A firm purchased on 1 January, 1996, certain machinery for A 19,40,000 and spent A 60,000 on its erection. On 1 July in the same year additional machinery costing A 10,00,000 was acquired. On 1 July, 1998 the machinery purchased on 1 January, 1996 having become obsolete was auctioned for A 8,00,000 and on the same date fresh machine was purchased at a cost of A 15,00,000.

Depreciation was provided for annually on 31 December at the rate of 10% per annum on the original cost of the asset. In 1999 however, the firm changed this method of providing depreciation and adopted the method of writing off 20% on the written down value.

Give the machinery Account as it would stand at the end of each year from 1996 to 2000.

[C.A. (Foundation)]

Solution

Machinery Account

Dr. *Cr.*

Date	*Particulars*	A	*Date*	*Particulars*	A
1.1.1996	To Bank Account (19,40,000 + 60,000)	20,00,000	31.12.96	By Depreciation A/c (2,00,000 + 50,000)	2,50,000
1.7.1996	To Bank Account	10,00,000		By Balance c/d	27,50,000
		30,00,000			30,00,000
1.1.1997	To Balance b/d	27,50,000	31.12.97	By Depreciation Account (2,00,000 + 1,00,000)	3,00,000
				By Balance c/d	24,50,000
		27,50,000			27,50,000
1.1.1998	To Balance b/d	24,50,000	1.7.98	By Depreciation Account	1,00,000
1.7.1998	To Bank Account	15,00,000		By Bank A/c	8,00,000
				By Profit and Loss Account	7,00,000
			31.12.98	By Depreciation Account (1,00,000 + 75,000)	1,75,000
				By Balance c/d (6,00,000 + 11,40,000)	21,75,000
		39,50,000			39,50,000
1.1.1999	To Balance b/d	21,75,000	31.12.99	By Depreciation Account (1,50,000 + 2,85,000)	4,35,000
				By Balance c/d (6,00,000 + 11,40,000)	17,40,000
		21,75,000			21,75,000
1.1.2000	To Balance b/d	17,40,000	31.12.00	By Depreciation Account (1,20,000 + 2,28,000)	3,48,000
				By Balance c/d (4,80,000 + 9,12,000)	13,92,000
		17,40,000			17,40,000

Loss on sale of machinery has been calculated as under :

	A
Cost of Machine	20,00,000
Less : Depreciation for 2½ years @ 10% on S.L.M. basis	5,00,000
	15,00,000
Less : Sale price	8,00,000
Loss on sale	7,00,000

Example 23

On 1st January, 2004, R and Co. purchased machinery for A 74,000 and spent A 4,000 on its repair and A 2,000 on its installation. On 1st January, 2005 the firm purchased another machinery for A 20,000. On 1st July, 2006 the machinery purchased on 1st January, 2004 was sold for A 56,000 and on the same date a new machinery was purchased for A 50,000. On 1st July, 2007, the machinery purchased on 1st January, 2005 was sold for A 4,000. In 2004 depreciation was charged at the rate of 10% per annum on original cost of assets. From 2005, it decided to write off depreciation at the rate of 15% per annum on Written Down Value Method with retrospective effect. Show the machinery Account for 4 years starting from 2004.

Solution

Machinery Account

Dr. *Cr.*

Date	*Particulars*	*A*	*Date*	*Particulars*		*A*
2004			**2004**			
Jan. 1	To Bank A/c	74,000	Dec. 31	By Depreciation A/c		8,000
	To Bank A/c (Repair)	4,000		[A 80,000 × 10/100]		
	To Bank A/c	2,000		By Balance c/d		72,000
	(installation)					
		80,000				80,000
2005			**2005**			
Jan. 1	To Balance b/d M_1	72,000	Dec. 31	By Profit and Loss A/c		
Jan. 1	To Bank A/c (M_2)	20,000		(Adjustment of		
				Depreciation)		4,000
				By Depreciation A/c		
				M_1 [68,000 × 15/100]		10,200
				M_2 [20,000 × 15/100]		3,000
				By Balance c/d		
				M_1 [68,000 – 10,200]		57,800
				M_2 [20,000 – 3,000]		17,000
		92,000				92,000
2006			**2006**			
Jan. 1	To Balance b/d		July 1	By Bank A/c (Sale)		56,000
	M_1		57,800			
	M_2		17,000			
July 1	To Profit and Loss A/c					
	(Profit) Note-1)	2,535				
July 1	To Bank A/c (M_3)	50,000	Dec. 31	By Depreciation A/c		
				M_1 (Note-1)	4,335	
				M_2 (17,000 × 15/100)	2,550	
				M_3 (50,000 × 15/100		
				× 6/12]	3,750	10,635
				By Balance c/d		
				M_2 (17,000 – 2,550)		14,450
				M_3 (50,000 – 3,750)		46,250
		1,27,335				1,27,335

2007			2007			
Jan. 1	To Balance b/d		July. 1	By Bank A/c		4,000
	(M_2)	14,450		By Profit and Loss A/c		
	(M_3)	46,250		(*Loss*-Note 2)		9,366
			Dec. 31	By Depreciation A/c		
				M_2 (Note-2)	1,084	
				M_2 (46,250 × 15/100)	6,938	8,022
				By Balance c/d		
				M_2 (46,250 – 6,938)		39,312
		60,700				60,700

Working Notes

1. *Calculation of Profit/Loss on sale of Machinery (M_1)*

	A
Cost of Machine on Jan. 1, 2004	80,000
Less : Depreciation for 2004 [80,000 × 15/100]	12,000
Book value on Jan. 1, 2005	68,000
Less : Depreciation for 2005 [68,000 × 15/100]	10,200
Book Value on Jan. 1, 2006	57,800
Less : Depreciation for 2006 [57,800 × 15/100 × 6/12]	4,335
Book Value on 1st July, 2006	53,465
Profit on sale (Balancing Figure)	2,535
Sale Proceeds	56,000

2. *Calculation of Profit/Loss on sale of machinery (M_2)*

Book value of Machinery (M_2) on 1.1.2007	14,450
Less : Depreciation for 2007 (14,450 × 15/100 × 6/12)	1,084
Book value on 1.7.2007	13,366
Less : Sale proceeds	4,000
Loss on Sale of Machinery	9,366

Example 24

X Ltd. commenced business on 1.1.2002, when the company purchased plant and equipment for A 7,00,000. It adopted a policy of :

(*a*) Charging depreciation at 15% p.a. on diminishing balance basis and

(*b*) Charging full year's depreciation on additions.

Over the years, its purchases of plant have been : on 1.8.2003 A 1,50,000 and on 30.9.2006 A 2,00,000.

On 1.1.2006, it was decided to change the method and rate of depreciation to 10% p.a. on straight line basis with retrospective effect from 1.1.2002, the adjustment being made in the accounts for the year ending 31.12.2006. Calculate the difference in depreciation to be adjusted in the Plant and Equipment Account on 1.1.2006 and show the ledger account for the year 2006. [*B.Com. (Hons.), Delhi University, 2007, 2009*]

Solution

Plant and Equipment Account

Dr. *Cr.*

Date	*Particulars*	*A*	*Date*	*Particulars*	*A*
1.1.06	Balance b/d	4,57,523	31.12.06	Depreciation	1,05,000
	Profit and Loss Account	67,477		Balance c/d	6,20,000
1.9.06	Bank Account	2,00,000			
		7,25,000			7,25,000

Working Notes

Calculation of Depreciation on Diminishing Balance Method

	Particulars	*Bank Value (A)*
1.	Cost of Plant and Equipment on 1.1.2002	7,00,000
	Less : Depreciation @ 15% (2002)	1,05,000
		5,95,000
	Less : Depreciation # 15% (2003)	89,250
		5,05,750
	Less : Depreciation @ 15% (2004)	75,863
		4,29,887
	Less : Depreciation @ 15% (2005)	64,483
		3,65,404
II.	Cost of Plant and Equipment	1,50,000
	Less : Depreciation @ 15% (2003)	22,500
		1,27,500
	Less : Depreciation @ 15% (2004)	19,125
		1,08,375
	Less : Depreciation @ 18% (2005)	16,256
		92,119
	Opening Balance on 1.1.2006	
I.	Plant and Equipment Account	3,65,404
II	Plant and Equipment Account	92,119
		4,57,523

Calculation of Depreciation on Straight Line Method

	Particulars	*Bank Value (A)*
I.	Cost of Plant and Equipment	7,00,000
	Less : Depreciation for 2002, 2003, 2004 and 2005 @ 10%	2,80,000
		4,20,000
II.	Cost of Machine	1,50,000
	Depreciation for 2003, 2004 and 2005 @ 10%	45,000
		1,05,000
	Opening Balance on Straight Line = (4,20,000 + 1,05,000)	5,25,000

Calculation of Difference Due to Change of Method

Particulars	*Bank Value (A)*
Opening Balance on the Basis of Straight Line Method	
= (4,20,000 + 1,05,000)	5,25,000
Less : Opening Balance (1.1.2006) on Diminishing Balance Method	
(3,65,404 + 92,119)	4,57,523
To be adjusted in Profit and Loss Account	67,477
Depreciation for 2006 on Straight Line Basis	
10% of A 10,50,000 (7,00,000 + 2,00,000 + 1,50,000)	1,05,000

Example 25

The book value of plant and machinery on 1.1.2004 was A 2,00,000. New machinery for A 10,000 was purchased on 1.10.2004 and for A 20,000 on 1.7.2005. On 1.4.2006, a machine whose book value had been A 30,000 on 1.1.2004 was sold for A 16,000. Depreciation had been charged at 10% per annum since 2004 on straight line method. It was decided in 2006 that depreciation @20% p.a. on diminishing balance method should be charged with retrospective effect since 1.1.2004. Show Plant and Machinery Account upto 31.12.2006. give detailed workings.

Plant and Machinery Account

Dr. *Cr.*

Date	*Particulars*	*A*	*Date*	*Particulars*		*A*
1.1.04	To Balance b/d (M_1)	2,00,000	31.12.04	By Depreciation A/c		
31.10.04	To Bank A/c (M_2)	10,000		M_1	20,000	
				M_2	250	
				[10,000 × 10/100		
				× 3/12]		20,250
				By Balance c/d		
				M_1 [2,00,000 – 20,000]		1,80,000
				M_2 [10,000 – 250]		9,750
		2,10,000				2,10,000
1.1.05	To Balance b/d		31.12.05	By Depreciation A/c		
	(M_1)	1,80,000		M_1	20,000	
	(M_2)	9,750		M_2	1,000	
				M_3	1,000	
				[20,000 × 10/100 × 6/12]	22,000	
31.7.05	To Bank A/c (M_3)	20,000		By Balance c/d		
				M_1 (1,80,000 – 20,000)		1,60,000
				M_2 (9,750 – 1,000)		8,750
				M_3 (20,000 – 1,000)		19,000
		2,09,750				2,09,750
1.1.06	To Balance b/d		1.4.06	By Bank A/c		16,000
	(M_1)	1,60,000		By Depreciation A/c		750
				(For 3 months)		

(M$_2$)	8,750		By Profit and Loss A/c (Loss on Sale) (Note-1)	7,250
(M$_3$)	19,000	31.12.06	By Profit and Loss A/c (Additional Depreciation)	29,350
			By Depreciation A/c	
			M$_1$ 21,760	
			M$_2$ 1,520	
			M$_3$ 3,600	26,880
			By Balance c/d	1,07,520
	1,87,750			1,87,750

Working Notes

1. *Calculation of Profit/Loss on sale Machinery*

		A
Book value on 1.1.2004		3,000
Less : Depreciation for 2004	3,000	
Depreciation for 2005	3,000	
Depreciation for 2006 (3 Months)	750	6,750
Book value on the date of sale		23,250
Less : Sale Price		16,000
Loss on Sale		7,250

2. *Calculation of Additional Depreciation due to Change of Method :*

	Machine I A	*Machine II* A	*Machine III* A	*Total* A
1. Depreciation on Straight Line Method (S.L.M.)				
@ 10% p.a. for 2004				
(M$_1$) 10/100 [2,00,000 – 30,000]	17,000			
(M$_2$) 10/100 × 10,000 × 3/12		250	—	17,250
For 2005				
(M$_1$) 10/100 × 1,70,000	17,000			
(M$_2$) 10/100 × 10,000		1,000		
(M$_3$) 10/100 × 20,000 × 6/12			1,000	19,000
Total Depreciation for 2004 & 2005				36,250 (A)
2. Depreciation on Diminishing Balance Method (W.D.V.)				
at 20% p.a.				
for 2004				
(M$_1$) 20/100 × 1,70,000	34,000			

Particulars				
(M_2) 20/100 × 10,000 × 3/12		500	—	34,500
for 2005				
(M_1) 20/100 [1,70,000 – 34,000]	27,200			
(M_2) 20/100 [10,000 – 500]		1,900		
(M_3) 20/100 × 20,000 × 6/12			2,000	31,100
Total Depreciation (2004 and 2005)				65,600(B)

Additional Depreciation due to Change of Method = B – A = A 65,600 – A 36,250

= A 29,350

3. *Depreciation to be charged on 31st Dec. 2006 as per new method :*

(M_1) = 20/100 (1,70,000 – 34,000 – 27,200)

= 20/100 × A 1,08,800 = A 21,760

(M_2) = 20/100 [10,000 – 500 – 1,900]

= 20/100 × A 7,600 = A 1,520

(M_3) = 20/100 × [20,000 – 2,000] = A 3,600

Example 26

Mayur Traders, which depreciates its machinery at 10% p.a. according to Diminishing balance method, had on 1.1.2009 A 4,86,000 balance in Machinery Account. Part of the machinery purchased on 1.1.2007 for A 60,000 was sold for A 40,000 on 1st July, 2009 and a new machinery at a cost of A 70,000 was purchased and installed on the same date, installation charges being A 5,000.

Mayur Traders wanted to change its method of depreciation on 1.1.2009 from Diminishing balance method to Straight line method with effect from 1.1.2007. The rate of depreciation remains the same as before.

Show Machinery Account for the year 2009. Also show your workings clearly.

[*B.Com.(Hons.), Delhi University, 2010*]

Solution

Machinery Account

Dr. *Cr.*

Date	*Particulars*	*A*	*Date*	*Particulars*	*A*
1.1.09	To balance b/d	4,86,000	1.7.09	By Bank A/c	40,000
1.7.09	To Bank A/c A (70,000 + 5,000)	75,000		By Depreciation A/c (on machine sold)	3,000
				By Profit & Loss A/c (Loss on Sale)*1	5,600
			31.12.09	By Profit & Loss A/c (Additional Dep.)*2	5,400
				By Depreciation A/c	57,750
				By Balance c/d	4,49,250
		5,61,000			5,61,000

Working Notes

1. Calculation of Loss on Sale of Machinery :

		(A)
	Cost of Machinery sold as on 1.1.07	60,000
Loss :	Depreciation for 2007	6,000
	Book Value on 1.1.2008	54,000
Less :	Depreciation for 2008	5,400
	Book Value on 1.1.2009	48,600
Less :	Depreciation for half year upto 1st July, 2009 as per SLM	
	A 60,000 $\frac{10}{100}$ $\frac{6}{12}$	3,000
	Book Value on the date of Sale (1.7.09)	45,600
Less :	Realised Value	40,000
	Loss on Sale of Machinery	5,600

*2 **Calculation of Additional Depreciation :**

Cost of Machinery on 1.1.2007 = A 4,86,000 $\frac{100}{81}$ 6,00,000

Book value on 1.1.2007, excluding the machinary sold = (A 6,00,000 – A 60,000) = A 5,40,000

Calculation of Depreciation under Straight Line Method (SLM) and Diminishing Balance Method or Written-down Value (WDV) Method :

		WDV (A)	*SLM (A)*
	Book Value on 1.1.2007 excluding the machinery sold = (A 6,00,000 – A 60,000)	5,40,000	5,40,000
Less :	Depreciation for 2007	54,000	54,000
	Book Value on 1.1.2008	4,86,000	4,86,000
Less :	Depreciation for 2008	48,600	54,000
	Book Value on 1.1.2009	4,37,400	4,32,000

	A
Depreciation for 2 years (2008 & 2009) by SLM (A 54,000 + A 54,000)	= 1,08,000
Depreciation for 2 years (2008 & 2009) by WDV (A 54,000 + A 48,600)	= 1,02,600
Additional depreciation to be charged to Profit and Loss A/c due to change in method :	5,400

*3 **Depreciation charged for 2009 :**

On A 5,40,000 @ 10% on SLM	54,000
On Machinery purchased on 1st July 2009 for 6 months @ 10% p.a.	
(A 75,000 $\frac{10}{100}$ $\frac{6}{12}$]	3,750
	57,750

Example 27

ABC Ltd. purchased on 1st October 2004, a machinery for A 4,50,000 and spent A 10,000 on freight and transit insurance. On 25th December, 2004, it further spent 40,000 on its erection. The machinery was put to use on 1.1.2005. On 1st July 2005, it purchased another machinery for A 1,00,000. During the year 2006, it spent A 10,000 for repairs on 1.4.2006.

However, on 1.4.2007, a part of the machinery purchased on 1.10.2004 costing A 2,00,000 was sold for A 1,50,000. On 1,10,2007 it purchased another machinery for A 3,00,000.

On 1st July, 2008, however, machinery purchased on 1st July, 2005 was sold for A 65,000. Depreciation was charged by the firm @ 10% p.a. by written down value method. During the year 2008, ABC Ltd. decided to change the method of providing depreciation and adopted the Straight Line Method of charging depreciation @ 10% p.a. Prepare Machinery Account as per the provisions of AS-6 upto the year ending 31.12.2008.

[B.Com.(Hons.), Delhi University, 2011]

Solution

In the Books of ABC Ltd.
Machinery Account

Dr. *Cr.*

Date	*Particulars*	*A*	*Date*	*Particulars*	*A*
1.1.05	Balance b/d.	5,00,000	31.12.05	Depreciation : (50,000 + 5,000)	55,000
1.7.05	Bank	1,00,000		Balance c/d	5,45,000
		6,00,000			6,00,000
1.1.06			31.12.06		
	Balance b/d	5,45,000		Depreciation	54,500
				Balance c/d	4,90,500
		5,45,000			5,45,000
1.1.07	Balance t/d	4,90,500		Bank Account (Sale price)	1,50,000
1.10.07	Bank Account	3,00,000		Depreciation (for 3 months)	4,050
				Profit and Loss A/c (Loss on sale)	7,950
				Depreciation	40,350
				Balance c/d	5,88,150
		7,90,500			7,90,500
1.1.08			**1.7.08**		
	Balance b/d	5,88,150		Bank (sale price)	65,000
				Depreciation (for 6 months)	3,847
				Profit and Loss A/c	8,103
			31.12.08	Profit and Loss A/c (Additional Depreciation)	8,700
				Depreciation (30,000 + 30,000)	60,000
				Balance c/d	4,42,500
		5,88,150			5,88,150

Example 28

Ahaan Ltd. which depreciates its machinery at 10% on Diminishing Balance Method, had on 1st April, 2010 A 9,72,000 to the debit of Machinery Account. During the year 2010-11, the machinery purchased on 1st April, 2008 for A 80,000 was sold for A 45,000 on 1st October, 2010 and a new machinery at a cost of A 1,50,000 was purchased and installed on the same date, installation charges being A 8,000. The company wants to change its method of depreciation from Diminishing Balance Method to Straight Line Method with effect from 1st April, 2008 and adjust the difference in the accounts for the year 2010-11. The rate of depreciation remains the same as before.

Show the Machinery Account and Machinery Disposal Account for the year 2010-11.

[*B.Com.(Hons.), Delhi University, Nov. 2011*]

Solution

Machinery Account

Dr. *Cr.*

Date	*Particulars*	*A*	*Date*	*Particulars*	*A*
1.4.10	Balance b/d	9,72,000	1.10.10	By Depreciation Account (6 months)	3,240
1.10.10	Bank Account (1,50,000 + 8,000)	1,58,000		By Bank	45,000
				By Profit and Loss A/c	16,560
			31.3.11	Profit and Loss A/c (Extra Depreciation)	11,200
				By Depreciation (1,12,000 + 7,900)	1,19,900
				Balance c/d	9,34,100
		11,30,000			11,30,000

Working Notes

1. Calculation on Loss on Sale

	(A)
Cost 1.4.2008	80,000
Less : Depreciation for 2008-09 @ 10%	8,000
	72,000
Less : Depreciation for 2009-10 @ 10%	7,200
	64,800
Less : Depreciation for 6 months in 2011 @ 10%	3,240
	61,560
Less : Sale price	45,000
Loss on Sale	16,560

2. Calculation of Book value on 1.4.2008

	(A)
Suppose the book value	100
Less : Depreciation for 2008	10
	90
Less : Depreciation for 2009	9
	81

If book value is Rs. 81 in 2009, the book value in 2008 = 100

If book value is 9,72,000 in 2009 the book value on 1.1.2008

$$\frac{100 \quad 9,72,000}{81}$$ 12,00,000

Less : Book value of the asset sold	80,000
	11,20,000

3. Calculation of Extra Depreciation

	WDV (A)	*SLM (A)*
Cost	11,20,000	11,20,000
Less : Depreciation for 2008-09	1,12,000	1,12,000
	10,08,000	10,08,000
Less : Depreciation for 2009-10	1,00,800	1,12,000
	9,07,200	8,96,000
Total Depreciation	2,12,800	2,24,000

Extra Depreciation = 2,24,000 – 2,12,800 = 11,200

4. Depreciation for 2010-11

On A 11,20,000 @ 10%	1,12,000
On A 1,58,000 for 6 months @ 10%	7,900
	1,19,900

Machinery Disposal Account

	A		A
1.10.10		**1.10.10**	
To Machinery A/c	64,800	By Bank Account	45,000
		By Depreciation (6 months)	3,240
		By Profit & Loss Account (Loss on sale)	16,560
	64,800		64,800

A 64,800 = Depreciation (6 months) A 3,240 + sale amount A 45,000 + Loss on sale A 16,560

A 64,800 = A 64,800

ASSIGNMENT MATERIAL

Note : The Objective type Questions (True/False, Multiple Choice Questions etc.) have been given in the Appendix at the end of the book.

SHORT ANSWER THEORY QUESTIONS

1. Distinguish between Straight Line and Diminishing Balance as a method of providing depreciation.
2. Write short notes on Change of method of depreciation as per AS6.
3. Define Depreciation.
4. What are the causes for Depreciation?
5. What are the factors that cause Depreciation?
6. Explain Straight Line Method of Depreciation.
7. What is Diminishing Balance Method?

8. Distinguish between Straight Line and Diminishing Balance methods of Depreciation.
9. What is Provision for Depreciation Account?
10. What are the provisions under AS6 on change in depreciation method.
11. What is the need for Depreciation?
12. Comment on salient features of AS-6 relating to depreciation accounting. *[B.Com.(Hons.) Delhi University, 2005, 2006, 2007]*
13. Specify causes of depreciation. *[B.Com.(Hons.) Delhi University, 2007]*
14. "Depreciation accounting, is a process of allocation and not of valuation." Comment. *[B.Com.(Hons.) Delhi University, 2011]*

LONG-ANSWER THEORY QUESTIONS

1. Explain the concept of Depreciation. What are the reasons for charging depreciation?
2. What are the factors considered for computing depreciation?
3. Discuss the meaning of Straight Line and Diminishing Balance Methods of Depreciation. What are their advantages and disadvantages.
4. Bring out the differences between Straight Line Method and Diminishing Balance Method of Depreciation.
5. Discuss the guidelines given in AS6 with regard to depreciation.
6. Discuss the nature and need for providing depreciation. *[B.Com.(Hons.) Delhi University, 2005]*
7. Define depreciation. What are the contributory factors for decline in the value of fixed assets. *[B.Com.(Hons.) Delhi University, 2010]*
8. List three major types of long-term (fixed) assets, present examples of each and indicate for each type the term that denotes the periodic write off to expense.
9. In what way is land different from other long-term assets.
10. In computing depreciation, what factors or values must be known or estimated. Identify and explain the nature of each.
11. Which of the following qualities are characteristic of plant assets?
    (*a*) Intangible
    (*b*) Tangible
    (*c*) Capable of repeated use in the operation of the business.
    (*d*) Held for sale in the normal course of business.
    (*e*) Used continuously in the operations of the business.
    (*f*) Long-lived.
12. Explain why the recognition of depreciation expenses is necessary to match revenues and expenses properly.
13. Explain the nature of depreciation.
14. What kind of a depreciation expense pattern is provided under the straight-line method? When would its use be appropriate?
15. How is disposal of fixed assets treated in accounting?
16. A company purchased a building five years ago. The market value of the building is now greater than it was when the building was purchased. Should the company stop depreciating the building?
17. "Replacing the asset is not essential to the existence of depreciation. Depreciation is the expiration or disappearance of service potential from the time an asset is put into use until the time it is retired from service." Explain.

18. Why does an accountant provide for depreciation when he measures profit?
19. Contrast straight-line depreciation with diminishing balance method in terms of the effect of each on reported net income.
20. Explain how charging depreciation affect :
    (*a*) the income statement, and
    (*b*) the balance sheet.
21. The manager of an electricity company stated that since its transmission lines are kept in good condition by regular repairs and maintenance and their efficiency remains constant, the lines do not depreciate. Do you agree with this statement?

PRACTICAL PROBLEMS

1. On 1st Jan. 2009, a company purchased a machine costing A 5,00,000. Its estimated working life is 20 years at the end of which it will fetch A 20,000. Additions are made on 1 Jan 2010 and 1 July 2011 to the value of A 80,000 (scrap value A 4000) and A 40,000 (scrap value A 2,000) respectively.

   The life of both the new machines is 20 years. Show machine a/c for first four years.

   [***Ans.:*** Final balance in Machine A/c A 5,09,750]

2. Rubal Ltd. purchased a machine costing A 3,00,000 on 1st April 2000 and an additional machine on 1 Oct. 2000 costing A 2,00,000 and on 1 July 2001 costing A 1,00,000.

   On 1 Jan. 2002, one third of Machine purchased on 1 April 2000 was sold at A 30,000.

   Prepare machine A/c for 3 years, it is given that depreciation is charged @ 10% p.a. on straight line method. [***Ans.:*** Final balance in machine A/c A 3,85,000]

3. On 1st Jan. 2000, Asha Ltd. purchased machinery for A 12,00,000 and on 30 June 2001, one more machine of worth A 2,00,000. On 31 March 2002, one of the original machinery which had cost A 50,000 was found to have become obsolete and was sold as scrap for A 7,000. It was replaced on that date by a new machine costing A 80,000. Depreciation is to be provided @ 15% p.a. on W.D.V. method. Accounts are closed on 31 December every year. Show machinery A/c for 3 years.

   [***Ans.:*** Final balance in Machinery A/c A 9,34,500]

4. On July 1, 2007, Gopal Ltd purchased second hand machine A 20,000 and spent A 3000 on reconditioning and installing. On Jan. 1, 2008 the firm purchased new machine worth A 12,000. On June 30, 2009 the machine purchased on January 1,2008 was sold for A 8000. On July 1, 2009 fresh machine was purchased on installment basis, payment for this machine was to made as follows.

   July 1, 2009 A 5000, June 2010, A 6,000, June 30, 2011, A 5500.

   Payment in 2010, 2011 include interest A 1000 and A 500 respectively.

   The Company writes off depreciation @ 10% p.a. on original cost. The A/c are closed every year on 31 March. Show the machine A/c for 3 years. [***Ans.:*** Final balance in Machine A/c A 30,550]

5. *X* Ltd. which depreciates its machinery at 10% p.a. under the diminishing balance method, had on 1st January 2003, A 9,72,000 to the debit of Machinery Account. During the year 2003, a part of the machinery purchased on 1st January 2001 for A 80,000 was sold for A 45,000 on 1st July 2003 and a new machinery at a cost of A 1,50,000 was purchased and installed on the same date, installation charges being A 8,000. No depreciation is to be charged on assets sold during the year of disposal. Except the first purchase of machinery on 1st January 2001, no other purchase was made during 2001 and 2002. Show the Machinery Account from 1st January 2001 to 31st December 2003.

   [***Ans. :*** Final balance in Machinery A/c A 9,66,580]

6. On 1 April, 1999, Moon Ltd. purchased a plant for A 10,00,000. On 1 October, 1999, an additional plant was purchased costing A 5,00,000. On 1 October, 2,000, the plant purchased on 1 April, 1999 was sold off for A 4,00,000. On 1 October, 2001, a new plant was purchased for A 12,00,000 and the plant purchased on 1 October, 1999 was sold for A 4,20,000 on the same date. Depreciation is to be provided at 10% per annum on the written down value on 31 March every year. Prepare the plant account for three years ended 31 March, 2002.

[*C.S. (Foundation)*]

[***Ans. :*** Balance in Plant Account A 11,40,000]

7. Naresh commenced business in March 2000. He acquired some machines for A 2,00,000 on April 1,2000. He acquired another machine for A 50,000 on March 1,2002. He sold machines, original cost of which was A 60,000 for A 35,000 on October 31.2001. Assuming depreciation @ 15% under WDV basis, compute the depreciation for the year ended March 31, 2001 and March 31, 2002.

(*C.A.P.E. May 2003; Adapted*)

[***Ans.*** : Final balance in Machinery A/c A 1,50,525]

8. Metropal Ltd. acquired a machine for A 5,40,000 on 1st April 2011. Depreciation was to be charged at 20% p.a. on straight line method. During 2013-14, a modification was made to improve its technical reliability at a cost of A 50,000 which it was considered would extend the useful life of the machine for two years. At the same time an important component of the machine was replaced at a cost of A 10,000 because of excessive wear and tear. Routine maintenance during the said accounting period cost A 7,500. Show the Machinery Account, Provision for Depreciation on Machinery Account and the charge to Profit and Loss Account for the year ending 31st March 2014 only assuming that the company follows a policy of charging full year's depreciation on additions.

[***Ans.:*** Balance in Provision for Depreciation A/c A 2,92,800]

9. A business enterprise which depreciates the machines @ 25% p.a. on the reducing balance method, provides you the following particulars :

Cost on 31.12.2002 A 2,46,000. Provision for Depreciation (on 31.12.2002) A 1,24,000. No amounts being charged in the year of sale but full charge is being made for the years during which addition is made. On 1.7.2004, one new machine was purchased for A 24,000 and old machinery purchased on 1.7.2001 for A 20,000 was discarded but could not be sold immediately. However, it was expected to realise A 5,000 for the same.

Prepare (*a*) Machinery Account. (*b*) Provision for Depreciation Account, and (*c*) Machinery Disposal Account for the years 2003 and 2004.

[***Ans.:*** Balance in Provision for Depreciation A/c A 169,703.
Balance in Disposal A/c A 5,000]

CHANGE IN DEPRECIATION METHOD

10. *Y* Ltd. company purchased a second hand machinery on 1st January 2009 for A 3,70,000 and immediately spent A 20,000 on its repairs and A 10,000 for installation. On 1 July 2010, it purchased another machine for A 1,00,000.

On 1 July 2011, it sold off the first machine for A 2,50,000 and bought another for A 3,00,000 Depreciation was provided on the machine @ 10% on original cost annually on 31 December. With effect from 1st Jan. 2012, the company changed the method of providing Depreciation and adopted the W.D.V. method and rate of Depreciation was 15% p.a.

Prepare machinery A/c for 4 years. [***Ans.:*** Balance in machinery A/c A 3,14,500]

11. ABC Ltd. purchased second hand machinery on 1st April 2006 for A 3,70,000 and installed it at a cost of A 30,000. On 1st Oct 2007 it purchased another machinery for A 1,00,000 and on 1st Oct. 1998, it sold off the first machine purchased in 2006, for A 2,80,000.

On the same date it purchased a machinery for A 2,50,000. On 1st Oct. 2009, the second machinery purchased for A 1,00,000 was sold off for A 20,000.

In the beginning depreciation was provided on Machinery at rate of 10% p.a. on the original cost each year on 31st March. From the year 2007-2008, however, the company changed the method of providing depreciation and adopted the written down value method, the rate of Depreciation being 15%.

Give machinery A/c for the period 2006-2010. [***Ans.:*** Balance in Machinery A/c A 1,96,562]

12. General Manufacturers had a debit of balance of A 8,00,000 in their machinery account on 1.1.2000. The concern was charging depreciation @15% p.a. on diminishing balance. On 31.3.2000, a part of the machinery purchased on 1.1.1997 at a cost of A 70,000 was sold for A 45,000. New machinery was purchased for A 80,000 on 1.7.2000 and A 6,700 was spent for installation. On 31.12.2000 the concern decided to change the depreciation method from diminishing balance method to straight-line method. It was also decided to charge depreciation @10% p.a. under the new method. Prepare machinery account for the year 2000.

    [***Ans.:*** Profit on sale of machinery A 3,623; Balance in Machinery A/c A 8,21,164]

13. Hanuman Enterprises purchased on 1.4.2011 certain machinery for A 72,800 and paid A 2,200 on its installation. On 1.10.2011 another machinery for A 25,000 was acquired. On 1.4.2012, the first machinery was sold at A 50,000 and on the same date a fresh machinery was purchased at a cost of A 45,000. Depreciation was annually provided on 31st March at 10% p.a. on written down value. On 1.4.2013, however, the firm decided to change the method of providing depreciation and adopted the method of providing depreciation @ 10% p.a. on the original cost, with retrospective effect.

    Ascertain the value of machinery as on 31.3.2014. *[C.A. (Foundation) November 1999]*

    [***Ans.:*** Balance in Machinery A/c, Machine II A 18,750; Machine III A 36,000]

14. *X* Ltd. purchased on 1st January 2011 certain machinery for A 1,94,000 and spent A 6,000 on its erection. On 1st July 2011 additional machinery costing A 1,00,000 was purchased. On 1st July 2013 the machinery purchased on 1st January 2011 having become obsolete was auctioned for A 1,00,000 and on the same date, new machinery was purchased at a cost of A 1,50,000. Depreciation was provided for annually on 31st December at the rate of 10% per annum on the original cost of the machinery. No depreciation need to be provided when a machinery is sold or auctioned, for that part of the year in which sale or auction took place. In 2014 however, *X* Ltd. changed this method of providing depreciation and adopted the method of writing off 15% p.a. on the written down value on the balance as appeared in machinery account on 1.1.2014. Show the machinery account for the calender years 2011 to 2014. [***Ans.:*** Balance Machine II A 56,807; Machine III A 1,17,938]

15. Deva Ltd., charged depreciation on its plant and machinery @ 10% per annum on the diminishing balance method. On 31 March 2005, the company decides to adopt straight line method of charging depreciation with retrospective effect from 1 April, 2001 the rate of depreciation being 15%. On 1st April, 2004, the plant and machinery account stood in the books at A 2,91,600. On 1 July, 2004 a sum of A 65,000 was realised by selling a machine cost of which on 1 April, 2001 was A 90,000. On 1 January, 2005, a new machine was acquired at a cost of A 1,50,000. *[C.S. (Foundation)]*

    [***Ans.:*** Profit on sale of machine A 1,030; Additional depreciation A 55,490;
    Depreciation on 31 March 2005 for 2004-2005 A 52,125 (46,500 + 5,625);
    Balance at the end A 2,68,375]

16. A company purchased second hand machinery on 1st January, 2000 for A 3,00,000, subsequent to which A 60,000 and A 40,000 were spent on its repairs and installation, respectively. On 1st July, 2001 another machinery was purchased for A 2,60,000. On 1st July, 2002, the first machinery having become outdated was auctioned for A 3,00,000 and on the same date, another machinery was purchased for A 2,50,000.

    On 1st July, 2003, the second machinery was also sold off and it fetched A 2,30,000.

Depreciation was provided on machinery @ 10% on the original cost annually on 31st December, under the Fixed Instalment method. From 1st January, 2002, the method of providing depreciation was changed to Reducing Balance method, the rate being 15% p.a.

You are required to prepare the following accounts in the books of the company :

(*i*) Machinery Account for the years ending 2000 to 2003.

(*ii*) Machinery Disposal Account. [*C.A.; P.E., Nov. 2005*]

[***Ans.***: Balance in Machinery A/c Machine II, A 15,330; Machine III, A 34,690]

17. Green Channel Co. purchased a second-hand machine on 1st January, 2000 for A 1,60,000. Overhauling and erection charges amounted to A 40,000.

Another machine was purchased for A 80,000 on 1st July, 2000.

On 1st July, 2002, the machine installed on 1st January, 2000 was sold for A 1,00,000. On the same date another machine was purchased for A 30,000 and was installed on 30th September, 2002.

Under the existing practice the company provides depreciation @10% p.a. on original cost. However, from the year 2003, it decided to adopt WDV method and to charge depreciation @ 15% p.a. This change was to be made with retrospective effect.

Prepare Machinery Account in the book of Green Channel Co. from the years 2000 to 2003.

[*B.Com. (Hons.), Delhi University, 2006*]

[***Ans.***: Balance in Machinery A/c A 69,989, Additional depreciation to be charged A 6,910]

18. ABC Ltd. purchased on 1 Jan. 1998 second hand plant for A 30,000 and immediately spent A 20,000 in overhauling it. On 1 July, 1998 additional machinery at cost of A 25,000 was purchased. On 1 July 2000, the plant purchased on 1 Jan. 1998 became obsolete and was sold for A 10,000. On that date new machinery was purchased at a cost of A 60,000.

Depreciation was provided at 10% p.a. on the original cost of the asset. In 2001 the company changed this method of providing depreciation to 15% p.a. W.D.V. with retrospective effect. Show Plant and Machinery Accoûnt and Provision for Depreciation Account for the years 1998-2001.

[***Ans.***: Balance in Machinery A/c A 85,000; Balance for depreciation A/c A 23,623]

19. M/s. S.S. Traders commenced business on 1st January, 2005, when they purchased machinery of Rs. 7,00,000. They adopted a policy of

(*i*) charging depreciation at 15% p.a. on diminishing balance basis, and

(*ii*) charging full year's depreciation on additions made during the year. Over the year, the purchases of machinery have been : 10

Date	A
1.8.2006	1,50,000
30.9.2008	2,00,000

On 1st January 2008, it was decided to change the method of depreciation and rate of depreciation to 10% on straight line basis with retrospective effect from 1.1.2005, the adjustment being made in the accounts for the year ending 31st December, 2008.

Prepare Machinery Account and Provision for Depreciation Account for the year 2008.

[*B.Com.(Hons.), Delhi University, 2009*]

[***Ans.***: Excess depreciation already charged and to be written back A 71,738]

CHAPTER 12

Inventory Valuation

Learning Objectives

After studying this chapter, you should be able to:

1. *Explain the meaning of inventory.*
2. *Discuss the need for inventory and objectives of inventory measurement.*
3. *Explain inventory costing methods – FIFO, LIFO, Weighted Average.*
4. *Explain AS2 on inventory valuation.*
5. *Discuss inventory system – perpetual inventory system and periodic inventory system.*

MEANING OF INVENTORY

Inventory includes tangible property that (*i*) is held for sale in the normal course of business or (*ii*) will be used in producing goods or services for sale. Inventories are current assets and reported on the balance sheet and as current assets they can be used or converted into cash within one year or within the next operating cycle of the business, whichever is longer. The Institute of Chartered Accountants of India in its Accounting Standard No. 2 defines inventory as :

"Tangible property held (*i*) for sale in the ordinary course of business or (*ii*) in the process of production for such sale, or (*iii*) for consumption in the production of goods or service for sale, including maintenance, supplies and consumables other than machinery spares."

Inventories are kept by manufacturing firms and merchandising (retailing) firms. For merchandising firms, inventories are often the largest or most valuable current asset. The types of inventory usually held by these two kinds of enterprise are as follows :

(A) Manufacturing Enterprises

(*i*) Finished Goods Inventory – goods produced, completed and kept ready for sale.

(*ii*) Work in Process Invtentory – goods in the process of being produced but not yet completed as finished goods. When completed, work in process inventory becomes finished goods inventory.

(*iii*) Raw Materials Inventory – Items purchased or acquired for using in making finished goods. Such items are known as raw materials inventory until used. When raw materials are used, they become the part of the work in process inventory. (Work in process includes cost such as raw materials, direct labour and factory overhead).

(B) Merchandising Enterprises

In merchandising or retailing firms, inventory consists of goods (generally known as merchandise) held for resale in the normal course of business. The goods are acquired in a finished condition and are ready for sale without further processing.

NEED FOR INVENTORIES

Inventory is one of the major problems that accountants face today. It is difficult to value it in terms of cash. It is almost impossible to assess its value in terms of future profits. The basic reason for holding inventories is that it is physically impossible and economically impractical for each inventory item to arrive exactly where it is needed and exactly when it is needed.

Inventory is not purchased as investment or to hold or to realise a gain from possession but rather to sell and realise a gain from resale. In fact, each purchase of saleable goods is in anticipation of the very next sale. Inventory should be considered as an investment and should compete for funds with other investments contemplated by the business firm. Inventory represents type of business insurance which assures the company that it will not have to close down due to shortages of saleable goods. Inventory is a variable cost insurance. That is the cost of this insurance will vary in the same direction as the value of sales. As the sales increase the company will find it necessary to maintain a larger and larger inventory to meet the expanded sale volume. The variable cost, the increased capital investment, necessary to maintain the continuing operations should not be deferred and charged against later revenues but rather should be charged against the current period of which it is a direct factor.

It is often claimed that, for seasonal industries, it is advisable to have adequate opening inventories. If attractive quantity discounts are available, a business enterprise may prefer to buy in excess of its current sales requirements and can build up additional inventories. Many firms—especially those that sell in seasonal markets—buy in excess of their needs when supply prices are favourable. They store the goods and can then maintain sales during a period of unfavourable supply prices.

OBJECTIVES OF INVENTORY MEASUREMENT

The following are the objectives of inventory valuation :

(*i*) Determination of Income : The measurement of inventory has a significant effect on income determination and financial position of a business enterprise. The American Institute of Certified Public Accountants (USA) states :

"A major objective of accounting for inventories is the proper determination of income through the process of matching appropriate costs against revenues."

It is significant to observe that a direct relationship exists between costs of goods sold and closing inventory. Costs of goods sold is measured by deducting closing inventory from cost of goods available for sale. Because of these relationships, it may be said that the higher the cost of closing inventory, the lower the cost of goods sold will be and the higher the resulfing net income. On the contrary, the lower the value of closing inventory, the higher the cost of goods sold and the lower the net income. Items which are not in the closing inventory are considered as sold and become the part of cost of goods sold. In this way, measurement of closing inventory influences the income statements (through influencing cost of goods, and net income) and balance sheet because inventory appears as current assets on the balance sheet. Also, closing inventory influences net income of not only the current period but it also influences the net income of the next accounting period because closing inventory of the current period becomes the opening inventory for the next period and thus becomes cost of goods sold.

Since closing inventory determines cost of goods sold, the most common objective of inventory measurement is the attempt to match costs with related revenues in order to compute net income within the traditional accounting structure. The expression matching costs against revenues means determining what portion of the cost of goods available for sale should be as cost of the period and deducted from the revenue of the current period and what portion should be carried (as inventory) to be matched against the revenue of the following period.

Other things remaining the same, *i.e.,* if all other items appearing on an income statement are constant and also income tax rates do not change, any change in the amount of closing inventory will bring similar change in the amount of reported net income. This is illustrated in the following data taken to explain this situation.

Effect of Inventory Value on Net Income

(A in Lakhs)

Date	Situations A	B	C	D
Sale	50	50	50	50
Opening inventory	6	6	6	6
Purchases	40	40	40	40
Goods available for sale	46	46	46	46
Closing inventory	8	10	12	14
Cost of goods sold	36	36	34	32
Net Income	12	14	16	18

In the above example, it can be noted that in all four situations, (*A, B, C, D*) sale, opening inventory, purchases are identical. As the value of closing inventory changes among the four situations, net income also changes, to the extent the closing inventory increases or decreases. For instance, closing inventory increases by ***A*** 2 Lakhs from situations A to B, from B to C, C to D, so net income also goes up by ***A*** 2 lakhs.

(*ii*) **Determination of Financial Position :** A second objective of inventory measurement is to state the fair value of inventory which appears as current assets on the balance sheet. This, alongwith other assets, reflect the value of assets to the firm and in turn, the financial position of a business enterprise.

(*iii*) **Prediction of Cash Flow :** Further, the value of inventory will help permit inventory and other users to predict the future cash flows of the firm. This can be accomplished from two points of view. First, the amount of inventory resources available will support the inflow of cash through their sale in the ordinary course of business. Second, the amount of inventory resources available will, under normal circumstances, have an effect on the amount of cash required during the subsequent period to acquire the merchandise that will be sold during the period.

INVENTORY COSTING METHODS

The pricing or costing of inventory is one of the most interesting and most widely debated problems in accounting. Generally, inventories are priced at their cost in conformity with the cost concept.

The cost of inventory, as per the above definition and in practice as well, includes the following costs :

(*i*) Invoice price less cash discounts;

(*ii*) Freight or transportation, insurance including insurance in transit and;

(*iv*) Applicable taxes and tariffs

Other costs such as those for purchasing, receiving and storage should theoetically be included in inventory cost. In practice, however, it is so difficult to allocate these costs to specific inventory items and also sometimes these costs are often not material in amount that they are in most cases considered expenses of the accounting period instead of an inventory cost.

Two terms—goods flow and cost flow—are useful in considering the problems of pricing inventories under fluctuating prices. Goods flow refers to the actual physical movement of goods in the firm's operations. Cost flow is the real or assumed association of costs with goods either sold or in inventory. The assumed cost flow may or may not be the same as the actual goods flow. Though this statement or practice may appear strange, there is nothing wrong or illegal about this practice. Generally accepted accounting principles (GAAP) accept the use of an assumed cost flow that does not reflect the real physical movement of goods. In fact, the assumption about the cost flow is more important to goods flow as the former helps in determining net income which is the major objective of inventory valuation.

The following methods of inventory princing, each based on a different assumption of cost flow have been discussed here.

1. First-in, First-out (FIFO).
2. Last-in, First-out (LIFO)
3. Weighted Average

FIRST-IN, FIRST-OUT (FIFO)

The FIFO method follows the principle that materials received first are issued first. After the first lot or batch of materials purchased in exhausted, the next lot is taken up for supply. It does not suggest, however, that the same lot will be issued from stores. Sometimes, all materials are tagged with their arrival date and issued in date order especially with stocks that deteriorate. The inventory is priced at the latest costs.

Advantages

A good system of inventory management requires that oldest units should be sold or used first and inventory should consist of the latest purchases. This is found in the FIFO method of costing. Under the FIFO method, management has little or no control over the selection of units in order to influence recorded profit. Valuation of inventory and cost of goods manufactured are consistent and realistic. Besides, the FIFO method is easy to understand and operate.

Disadvantages

The objectives of matching current cost with current revenues is not achieved under the FIFO method. If the prices of materials are rising rapidly, the current production cost may be understated. If the sales price is fixed, then sales revenue may not produce enough income to cover the purchase of raw materials. The valuation of inventory in terms of current cost depends on the frequency of price changes and the stock turnover. In case stocks turnover rapidly, the inventory valuations will reflect current prices. There are other limitations under the FIFO method. FIFO costing is improper if many lots are purchased during the period at different prices. This method overstates profit especially with high inflation. It does not consider the cost of replacing used materials, a situation created by high inflation.

The FIFO method is suitable where (*i*) the size and cost of raw materials units are lorge, (*ii*) materials are easily identified as belonging to a particular purchased lot, and (*iii*) not more than two or three different receipts of the materials are on hand at one time.

Example 1. The following is a summary of the receipts and issue of materials in a facrtory during January.

January	
1	Opening balance 500 units @ A 25 per unit
3	Issue 70 units
4	Issue 100 units
8	Issue 80 units
13	Received from supplier 200 units @ A 24.50 per unit
14	Returns to store 15 units @ A 24 per unit.
16	Issue 180 units
20	Received from supplied 240 units @ A 24.75 per unit
24	Issue 304 units
25	Received from supplier 320 units @ A 24.00 per units
26	Issue 112 units
27	Returned to store 12 untis @ A 24.50 per unit
28	Received from supplier 100 units @ A 25 per unit

Work out on the basis of First-in, First-out. It is revealed that on the 15th there was a shortage of five units and another on the 27th of eight units.

Solution

Stores Ledger Account (FIFO)

	Receipts			*Issue*			*Stock*		
Date	*Qty.*	*Rate*	*Amt.*	*Qty.*	*Rate*	*Amt.*	*Qty.*	*Rate*	*Amt.*
Jan.									
1	–	–	–	–	–	–	500	25.00	12,500
3	–	–	–	70	25	1,750	430	–	10,750
4	–	–	–	100	25	2,500	330	–	8,250
8	–	–	–	80	25	2,000	250	–	6,250
13	200	24.500	4,900	–	–	–	250	25.00	6,250
	Refund						200	24.50	4,900
14	15	24.00	36	–	–	–	250	25.00	6,250
							200	24.50	4,900
							15	24.00	360
15	–	–	Shortage	5	25	125	245	25.00	6,125
							200	24.00	4,900
							15	24.00	360
16	–	–	–	180	25	4,500	65	25.00	1,625
							200	24.00	4,900
							15	24.50	360
20	240	24.75	5,940	–	–	–	65	25.00	1,625
							200	24.50	4,900
							15	24.00	360
							240	24.75	5,940
24	–	–	–	65	25.00	1,625			
				200	24.50	4,900			
				15	24.00	360			
				24	24.75	594	216	24.75	5,346
25	320	24.00	7.680	–	–	–	216	24.75	5,346
							320	24.50	7,680
26	–	–	–	112	24.75	2,772	104	24.75	2,574
							320	24.00	7,680
27	12	24.50	294	–	–	–	104	24.75	2,574
							320	24.00	7,680
	–	–	–	–	–	–	12	24.50	294
27	–	–	Shortage	8	24.75	198	96	24.75	12,376
							320	24.00	7,680
	–	–	–	–	–	–	12	24.50	294
28	100	25.00	2,500	–	–	–	96	24.75	2,376
							320	24.00	7,680
							12	24.50	294
							100	25.00	2,500

Closing stock 528 units = Rs. 12,850.

LAST-IN, FIRST-OUT (LIFO)

The LIFO method of costing and inventory valuation is based on the principle that materials entering production are the most recently purchased. The method assumes that the most recent cost, generally the replacement cost is the most significant in matching cost with revenue in the income determination. The cost of the last lot of materials received is used to price materials issued until the lot is exhausted, then the next lot pricing is used, and so on through successive lots.

Advantages

1. It provides a better matching of current costs with current revenues.
2. It results in real income in times of rising prices, by maintaining net income at a lower level than other costing methods.
3. In industries subject to sharp materials price fluctuations, the method minimises unrealised inventory gains and losses and tends to stabilise reported operating profits. Income is reported only when it is available for distribution as dividends or for other purposes.
4. Probably the most important arguments in favour of LIFO is its role in tax saving. It is generally considered a cheap form of tax avoidance by business firms. By valuing inventory at beginning-of-period prices and calculating cost of sales at the current prices, the firm creates secret reserves which are not taxed. As long as prices and inventory levels do not decline, this benefit remains and in this case the tax saving is permanent. However, if the tax rates go up in the meantime, the so-called tax saving will be eliminated by higher tax rates.
5. LIFO produces an income statement which shows correct profit or losses and financial position. It correlates current cost and sales, and income statements show the result of operation, excluding profits or losses due to changing price level.

Disadvantages

The following are the limitations of the LIFO method of costing :

1. Inventory valuations do not reflect the current prices and therefore are useless in the context of current conditions.
2. The argument that LIFO should be used for matching current costs with current revenue, is not sound. The most recent purchase costs are matched against the revenues of the current period. However, unless both purchases and sales occur regularly in even quantities, the revenues will not be matched with the current costs at the time of sale. When purchases are irregular and unrelated to the timing of sales, the matching is illogical and unsystematic, particulary if prices and costs are changing rapidly.
3. The profit of a firm can be manipulated with the LIFO method in operation. By timing purchases, a company can cause higher or lower costs to flow into the income statement, thus increasing or decreasing reported net income at will.
4. Another limitation which also results from LIFO's lowering of the earnings figure is the effect it will have on existing bonus and profit sharing plans. Employees and managers who are interested in the growth of these plans may have difficulty in understanding a drop in the benefits which were created wholly or partially by an accounting change.

During a period of rising costs, LIFO produces the desirable effect of reducing taxable income and tax liability; thereby conserving cash. On the other hand, it also affects the profit reported in the financial statements.

Example 2

Prepare a stores ledger account from the following transactions under the LIFO method.

Jan. 1	Received 1,000 units @	A 1.00 per unit

10	Received 260 units @	A 1.05 per unit
20	Issue 700 units	
Feb. 4	Received 400 units @	A 1.15 per unit
21	Received 300 units @	A 1.25 per unit
March 16	Issue 620 units	
April 12	Issued 240 units	
May 10	Received 500 units @	A 1.10 per unit
25	Issued 380 units	

Solution

Stores Ledger Account (LIFO)

	Receipts			*Issue*			*Stock*		
Date	*Qty.*	*Rate*	*Amt.*	*Qty.*	*Rate*	*Amt.*	*Qty.*	*Rate*	*Amt.*
Jan.									
1	1,000	1.00	1,000	–	–	–	1,000	1.00	1,000
10	260	1.05	273	–	–		1,260		1,273
20	–	–	–	260	1.05	273	560		560
				440	1.00	440			
Feb.									
4	400	1.15	460	–	–	–	960		1,020
21	300	1.25	375	–	–	–	1,260		1,395
March									
16	–	–	–	300	1.25	375	640		652
				320	1.15	368			
April									
12	–	–	–	80	1.15	92	400		400
				160	1.00	160			
May									
10	500	1.10	550	–			900		950
25	–	–	–	380	1.10	418	520		532

The closing Stock consists of

120 units at A 1.10 = 132

400 units at Re. 1.00 = 400

A 532

WEIGHTED AVERAGE

Under this method, issue of materials is priced at the average cost price of the materials in hand, a new average being computed whenever materials are received. In this method, total quantities and total cost are considered while computing the average price and not the total of rates divided by total number of rates as in simple average. The weighted average is calculated each time a purchase is made. The quantity bought is added to the stock in hand, and the revised balance is then divided into the new cash value of the stock. The effect of early price is thus eliminated. This method avoids fluctuations in price and reduces the number of calculations to be made, as each issue is charged at the same price until a fresh purchase necessitates the computations of a new average. It gives an acceptable figure for stock values.

Advantages

The following are the advantages of the weighted average method:

1. The method is logical and consistent as it absorbs cost while determining the average for pricing material issues.
2. The changes in the prices of materials do not affect much the materials issues and stock.
3. The method follows the concept of total stock and total valuation.
4. Both cost of materials issued and in stock tend to reflect actual costs.

Disadvantages

However, the weighted average method has the following disadvantages:

1. Simplicity and convenience are lost when there is too much change in the prices of materials.
2. An average price is not based on actual price incurred, and therefore is not realistic. It follows only arithmetical convenience.

Example 3

From the following information prepare a stores ledger account using weighted average method.

		Rate per unit (A)
2012		
Jan. 1	Received 500 units	20
10	Received 300 units	24
15	Issued 700 units	–
20	Received 400 units	28
25	Issued 300 units	–
27	Received 500 units	22
31	Issued 200 units	–

Solution

	Receipts			*Issue*			*Stock*		
Date	*Qty.*	*Rate*	*Amt.*	*Qty.*	*Rate*	*Amt.*	*Qty.*	*Rate*	*Amt.*
2012									
Jan. 1	500	20	10,000	—	—	—	500	20	10,000
10	300	24	7,200				800	21.50	17,200
15	—	—	—	700	21.50	15,050	100		2,150
20	400	28	11,200	—	—	—	500	26.70	13,350
25	—	—	—	300	26.70	8,010	200		5,340
27	500	22	11,000	—	—	—	700		16,340
31	—	—	—	200	23.34	4,668	500		11,672

AS-2 ON INVENTORY VALUATION

AS-2 has advocated to value inventories at the lower of historical cost and net realisable value. It comments :

"Inventories are held in the expectation of deriving revenue directly or indirectly from their sale or use. In order to determine the results of a business for a given period, it is necessary to carry forward the cost related to inventories until the inventories are sold or consumed. However, if there is no reasonable expectation that net realisable value would cover the cost incurred (as a result, for example, of deterioration, obsolescence or a change in demand), it is necessary that cost which cannot be recovered should be charged against the revenue of the current period. Therefore, inventories are normally stated at the lower of historical cost and net realisable value."

According to AS-2:

1. **Historical cost** represents an appropriate combination of the
   (*a*) cost of purchase;
   (*b*) cost of conversion; and
   (*c*) other cost incurrend in the normal course of business in bringing the inventories upto their present location and condition.
2. **Cost of Purchase** consists of the purchase price including duties and taxes, freight inwards and other expenditure directly attributable to acquisition, less trade discounts, rebates, duty drawbacks and subsidies, in the year in which they are accounted, whether immediate or deferred, in respect of such purchase.
3. **Cost of Conversion consists of**
   (*i*) costs which are specifically attributable to units of production, *i.e.*, direct labour, direct expenses and sub-contracted work; and
   (*ii*) production overheads, ascertained in accordance with either the direct costing or absorption costing method.

Production overheads exclude expenses which relate to general administration, finance, selling and distribution.

AS-2 has suggested to apply different cost formula for determination of historical cost which are listed below :

Several different formulae with widely effects are in current use for the purpose of assigning costs, including the following:

(*a*) First in First out (FIFO)
(*b*) Average cost
(*c*) Last in first out (LIFO)
(*d*) Base stock
(*e*) Specific identification
(*f*) Standard cost
(*g*) Adjusted selling price (also called retail inventory method)
(*h*) Latest purchase price.

Valuation of Inventories Below Historical Cost

AS-2 'Valuation of Inventories' has the following guidelines regarding valuation of inventories below historical cost.

1. The historical cost of inventories may at times not be realised, *e.g.,* if their selling prices have significantly declined, or if they become wolly or partially obsolete, or if the quantity of inventories is so large that it is unlikely to be sold/utilised within the normal turnover period and there exists a genuine risk of physical deterioration, obsolescence or loss on disposal. In such circumstances, it becomes necessary to write down the inventory to 'net realisable value', in accordance with the principle of conservatism which required that current assets should not carried in the financial statement in excess of amounts expected to be realised in the ordinary course of business.

2. Comparison of the historical cost and the net realisable value can be made separately in respect of each item of inventory or for groups of similar (or interchangeable) items. However, to compare the aggregate of the net realisable value of all dissimilar and non-interchangeable items in a class of business, or all the inventories of an enterprise on an overall basis, with the aggregate of the cost of all those items is not prudent because it amounts to setting off loss against unrealised profit.
3. Normal quantity of materials and other supplies held for use in production are not written down below historical cost if the finished goods are expected to be sold at or above historical cost.
4. Inventory of maintenance supplies and consumable stores is ordinarily valued at cost. In appropriate circumstances, this is valued at below cost.
5. Inventory of by products is valued at lower of cost and net realisable value. Where cost of the by–product cannot be separately determined, it is valued at net realisable value. Inventory of non-reusahle waste is also valued at net realisable value. Inventory of reusable waste is valued on the following basis:
   (*i*) Where facilities (either in house or external) exist for reprocessing of such wastes, and such facilities are being used for reprocessing, the stock of waste is valued at the raw material cost less reprocessing cost.
   (*ii*) Where reprocessing facilities are not available, the inventory is valued at 'net realisable value.'
6. In computing the cost of purchase of raw materials consumed and the cost of conversion, the value of by-products and/or waste is deducted.
7. Inventories are normally classified in the financial statements as under
   (*i*) Raw materials and components
   (*ii*) Work-in-process
   (*iii*) Finished goods
   (*iv*) Stores and spares

ICAI's Guidelines on Inventory valuation and disclosure

The Institute of Chartered Accountants of India in its AS-2 'Valuation of Inventories' (June 1981) has listed the following guidelines :

1. Subject to the exceptions stated in pares 6.1 to 6.4 inventories should be valued at lower of historical cost and net realisable value.
2. For the purpose of comparing historical cost with net realisable value each item in the inventory may be dealt with separately, or similar items may be dealt with as a group.
3. The historical cost of inventories should normally be determined by using FIFO formulae.
   3.1 The specific identification method may be used for inventories of items that are not ordinarily interchangeable or for goods manufactured and earmarked for a specific purpose.
   3.2 The adjusted selling price may be used in retail business or in businesses where the inventory comprises items the individual cost of which are not readily ascertainable.
   3.3 The standard cost method of valuing inventories may be used if the results approximate consistently the resuls that would be obtained in accordance with paragraph 3.1.
   3.4 The base stock method may be used in exceptional circumstances only.
4. The historical cost of manufactured inventories may be arrived at on the basis of either direct costing or absorption costing. Where absorption costing has been used, the allocation of fixed costs of inventories should be based on the normal level of production.
5. Overheads other then production overheads should be included as part of the inventory cost only to the extent that they clearly relate to putting the inventories in their present location and condition.

6. 6.1 Inventory of consumable stores and maintenance supplies should ordinarily be valued at cost. In appropriate circumstances, however, this may be valued at below cost.

   6.2 Inventory of by-products should be valued at lower of cost and net realisable value. Where cost of the by-product cannot be separately determined, it should be valued at net realisable value.

   6.3 Inventory of reusable waste should be valued at raw material cost less reprocessing cost where facilities for reprocessing exits.

   6.4 Inventory of non-reusable waste or inventory of reusable waste for which facilities for reprocessing do not exist should be valued at net realisable value.

7. The accounting policy adopted for valuation of inventories, including the cost formulae used should be disclosed in the financial statements. Where the base stock method is used, the difference between the value at which it is carried and the value by applying the method at which stock in excess of the base stock is valued should be disclosed.

8. Consistency is generally accepted as a fundamental accounting assumption. Therefore, any change in the accounting policy relating to inventories (including the basis of comparison of historical cost with net realisable value and the cost formulae used) which has a material effect in the current period or which is reasonably expected to have a material effect in later periods should be disclosed. In the case of a change in accounting policy which has material effect in the current period, the amount by which any items in the financial statement is affected by such change should also be disclosed to the extent ascertainable. Where such amount is not ascertainable, wholly or in part, the fact should be indicated.

INVENTORY SYSTEMS

There are two principal ways of accounting for inventories :

Perpetual Inventory System

The perpetual inventory method requires a continuous record of addition to or reduction in material, work-in-progress and cost of goods sold on a day-to-day basis. Such a record facilitates managerial control and preparation of interim financial statements. Physical inventory counts are usually taken at least once a year in order to check the validity of the accounting records. The perpetual inventory system may give such additional information as goods ordered, expected delivery date and units costs. Usually, these records are maintained on a quantity basis but values can be included. It is an essential feature of the perpetual inventory method that items of stock are checked periodically, normally at least once or twice each year. This ensures that the stock records tally with the physical stocks, which is vital if the control procedure is to function properly.

The perpetual inventory method has the following advantages :

1. The stock-taking task which is long and costly is avoided under this method. On the other hand, the inventory of different items of materials in accordance with the stores ledger can be promptly prepared for the preparation of the income statement and balance sheet at interim periods if required without a physical inventory being taken.
2. Management may be informed daily of number of units and the value of each kind of material on hand – information which tends to eliminate delays and stoppage in production.
3. The investment in materials and supplies may be kept at the lowest point in conformity with operating requirements.
4. A system of internal check is always in operation and the activities of different departments, such as purchasing, stores and production are continuously checked against each other. This results into detailed and reliable checks on the stores also.
5. It is not necessary to stop production so as to carry out a complete physical stock-taking.

6. Perpetual inventory records provide details about materials cost for individual products, jobs, processes, production orders or departments. These information are helpful to management in exercising control over costs.
7. Discrepancies and errors are promptly discovered and localised and remedial action can be taken to avoid their occurrence in the future.
8. This method has a moral effect on the staff, makes them disciplined and careful and acts as a check against dishonest actions.
9. The disadvantages of excessive stock are avoided, such as loss of interest on capital invested in stock, loss through deterioration, risk of obsolescence.

Periodic Inventory System

Under the periodic method, the entire book inventory is verified at a given date by an actual count of materials on hand. This physical inventory is usually taken near the end of the accounting period. Some firms even suspend plant operations when this is done. This method provides for the recording of purchases, purchase returns and purchase allowances on a daily basis but does not provide for a continuous inventory or for a daily computation of the goods sold. At the end of each accounting period, a physical count is made of the quantity of goods on hand and the value of inventory is determined by using an inventory pricing method (FIFO, LIFO or Average Cost) and attaching costs to units counted. The cost of goods sold is computed by deducting closing inventory from the sum of opening inventory and purchases made during the current period. It is assumed that goods not on hand at the end of accounting period have been sold. There is no system and accounting for shrinkage, losses, theft and waste throughout the accounting period and they can be discovered only after the end of the period.

Taking a physical inventory at the year end is an important task in the periodic inventory system. It must be ensured that all items have been counted accurately. Counting procedures usually involves teams of people assigned to specific sections of the factory and to inventory storage areas. Large items are counted individually, while small items may be weight-counted. Counted items are tagged to prevent double counting and information from the tags concerning each item's description and quantity is recorded on the inventory sheet.

DIFFERENCE BETWEEN PERPETUAL INVENTORY AND PERIODIC INVENTORY SYSTEM

The following are the differences between perpetual inventory system and periodic inventory system.

Basis	*Perpetual Inventory System*	*Periodic Inventory System*
1. Determining Inventory	Inventory is ascertained on the basis of accounting records.	Inventory is ascertained by taking actual physical count.
2. Valuation of Inventory	Invetory is calculated as a residual figure as follows : Closing Inventory = Opening Inventory + Purchases – Cost of Goods Sold.	Inventory is directly calculated by applying the method of valuation of inventories at the end of the period.
3. Ascertainment of cost of goods sold	Cost of Goods Sold is direcly calculated by applying the method of valuation of inventories.	Cost of Goods Sold is calculated as a residual figure as follows: Cost of Goods Sold = Opening Inventory + Purchases – closing Inventory.
4. Stock taking	It does not require closing down of work for Stock taking.	It requires, closing down of work for stock taking.
5. Stock Checking	It facilitates the continuous stock checking	It does not facilitate the continuous stock checking
6. Quality of the system	It is elaborate and expensive.	It is simple and inexpensive.

7. Use of Inventory methods	The method of valuation (*e.g., FIFO/LIFO/* Weighted Average) is applied on continuous basis during the accounting period to ascertain the cost of goods sold.	The method of valuation (*e.g.*, FIFO/LIFO/ Weighted Average) is applied only once at the end of the accounting period to ascertain the cost of Closing Inventory.
8. Lost Goods	The cost of closing Inventory includes cost of lost goods (if any).	Cost of Goods sold includes cost of lost goods (if any).

Example 4. From the following information find out the value of stock as on 31.3.2012 according to AS-2:

(*i*) Cost of physical stock on 31.3.2012 was A 2,00,000.

(*ii*) Cost of stock held as consignee was A 40,000.

(*iii*) Stock was expected to realise the normal selling price of 150% of cost except for the following goods;

1. Goods costing A 10,000 were damaged and an expenditure of 10% of normal selling price was necessary to realise the cost.
2. Goods costing A 20,000 were damaged beyond repair and were expected to realise A 5,000 only.

[*B.Com.(Hons.) Delhi University, 2008*]

Solution. **Valuation of Stock as on 31.3.2012**

		(A)
Physical Stock as on 31.3.2012		2,00,000
Less : Stock held as consignee		40,000
Cost of Stock		1,60,000
Less : Reduction in value due to valuation at below cost:		
(*i*) Repairable Damaged Goods (10% of 150% of A 10,000)	1,500	
(*ii*) Non-Repairable Damaged Goods (A 20,000 – A 5,000)	15,000	16,500
Value of stock		1,43,500

Example 5. The following are the details of S Ltd. :

1.1.2006	Opening Stock	NIL
1.1.2006	Purchases	100 units @ A 30 per unit
15.1.2006	Issued for consumption	50 units
1.2.2006	Purchases	200 units @ A 40 per unit
15.2.2006	Issued for consumption	100 units
20.2.2006	Issued for consumption	100 units
1.3.2006	Purchases	150 units @ A 50 per unit
15.3.2006	Issued for consumption	100 units

Find out the value of stock as on 31.3.2006 if the company follows :

(*a*) First in first out;

(*b*) Weighted average basis. [*B.Com.(Hons.), Delhi University, 2007*]

Solution. (*a*) First-in-First-out basis :

Store Ledger

	Receipts			*Issue*			*Stock*		
Date	*Units*	*Rate (A)*	*Amt. (A)*	*Units*	*Rate (A)*	*Amt. (A)*	*Units*	*Rate (A)*	*Amt. (A)*
1.1.2006	Balance						NIL		

	100	30	3,000				100	30	3,000
15.1.2006				50	30	1,500	50	30	1,500
1.2.2006	200	40	8,000				50 200	30 40	1,500 8,000
15.2.2006				50 50	30 40	1,500 2,000	150	40	6,000
20.2.2006				100	40	4,000	50	40	2,000
1.3.2006	150	50	7,500				50 150	40 50	2,000 7,500
15.3.2006				50 50	40 50	2,000 2,500	100	50	5,000

Closing Stock = 100 units @ A 50 = A **5,000**

(*b*) Weighted average basis

Store Ledger

	Receipts			Issue			Stock		
Date	*Units*	*Rate (A)*	*Amt. (A)*	*Units*	*Rate (A)*	*Amt. (A)*	*Units*	*Rate (A)*	*Amt. (A)*
1.1.2006	Balance						NIL		
1.1.2006	100	30	3,000				100	30	3,000
15.1.2006				50	30	1,500	50	30	1,500
1.2.2006	200	40	8,000				250	38*1	9,500
15.2.2006				100	38	3,800	150	38	5,700
20.2.2006				100	38	3,800	50	38	1,900
1.3.2006	150	50	7,500				200	47*2	9,400
15.3.2006				100	40	4,700	100	47	4,700

Closing Stock = 100 units @ A 47 = A **4,700**

Working Notes :

$$*1 \quad \frac{50 \quad \text{Rs. } 30 \qquad 200 \quad \text{Rs. } 40}{50 \quad 200} \quad \text{Rs. } 38.$$

$$*2 \quad \frac{50 \quad \text{Rs. } 38 \qquad 150 \quad \text{Rs. } 50}{50 \quad 150} \quad \text{Rs. } 47.$$

Example 6

A company started its business on 1st January, 2008. It purchased and used raw material during the year 2008 as stated below :

January	10	800 kgs @ A 62 per kg.
February	28	1,200 kgs @ A 57 per kg.
March	10	Issued 1,000 kgs.
March	26	Issued 500 kgs.
May	20	900 kgs @ A 65 per kg.
June	28	Issued 600 kgs.

Calculate the value of closing stock of raw materials on June 30 according to

(*i*) Last in First out basis, and

(*ii*) Weighted average basis, using perpetual inventory system. [*B.Com.(Hons.) Delhi University, 2009*]

Solution

Valuation of Closing Stock of Raw Materials (LIFO)

	Receipts			Issue			Balance		
Date 2008	*Units kgs.*	*Rate (A)*	*Value (A)*	*Units kgs.*	*Rate (A)*	*Value (A)*	*Units kgs.*	*Rate (A)*	*Value (A)*
Jan 10	800	62	49,600	—	—	—	800	62	49,600
							800	62	49,600
Feb. 28	1,200	57	68,400	—	—	—	1,200	57	68,400
Mar. 10	—	—	—	1,000	57	57,100	800	62	49,600
							200	57	11,400
Mar. 26				200	57	11,400			
				300	62	18,600	500	62	31,000
May 20	900	65	58,500				500	62	31,000
							900	65	58,500
							500	62	31,000
June 28	—	—	—	600	65	39,000	300	65	19,500

Value of Closing Stock = A 31,000 + A 19,500 = A **50,500**

Valuation of Closing Stock of Raw Materials (Weighted Average)

	Receipts			Issue			Balance		
Date 2008	*Units kgs.*	*Rate (A)*	*Value (A)*	*Units kgs.*	*Rate (A)*	*Value (A)*	*Units kgs.*	*Rate (A)*	*Value (A)*
Jan 10	800	62	49,600	—	—	—	800	62	49,600
Feb. 28	1,200	57	68,400	—	—	—	2,000*	59**	1,18,000
Mar. 10	—	—	—	1,000	59	59,100	1,000	59	59,000
Mar. 26	—	—	—	500	59	29,500	500	59	29,500
May 20	900	65	58,500	—	—	—	1,400	62.86	88,004
June 28	—	—	—	600	62.86	37,716	800	62.86	50,288

Value of Closing Stock = A 50,288

*[1] Total Units = 800 + 1,200 = 2,000 kgs

*[2] Weighted average = A 1,18,000 / 2,000 units = A 59

Example 7

The following are the details of material of Sai Mills :

1.1.2009	Opening Stock	100 units @ *A* 25 per unit
1.1.2009	Purchases	200 units @ *A* 30 per unit
15.1.2009	Issued for consumption	100 units
1.2.2009	Purchases	400 units @ *A* 40 per unit

15.2.2009	Issued for consumption	200 units
20.2.2009	Issued for consumption	200 units
1.3.2009	Purchases	300 units @ *A* 50 per unit
15.3.2009	Issued for consumption	200 units

Find out the cost of closing stock as on 31.3.2009 according to :

(*i*) First in first out basis, and

(*ii*) Weighted average price basis, using perpetual inventory system. Also calculate cost of closing inventory on LIFO basis under periodic system. [*B.Com.(Hons.), Delhi University, 2010*]

Solution. (*i*)

Stores Ledger (FIFO : Perpetual)

	Received			*Issued*			*Balance*		
Date	*Units*	*Rate (A)*	*Amt. (A)*	*Units*	*Rate (A)*	*Amt. (A)*	*Units*	*Rate (A)*	*Amt. (A)*
1.1.09							100	25	2,500
1.1.09	200	30	6,000				100 200	25 30	2,500 6,000
15.1.09				100	25	2,500	200	30	6,000
1.2.09	400	40	16,000				200 400	30 40	6,000 16,000
15.2.09				200	30	6,000	400	40	16,000
20.2.09				200	40	8,000	200	40	8,000
1.3.09	300	50	15,000				200 300	40 50	8,000 15,000
15.3.09				200	40	8,000	300	50	15,000

Value of Closing Stock : 300 units @ A 50 = A 15,000

(*ii*) **Stores Ledger (Weighted Average : Perpetual)**

	Received			*Issued*			*Balance*		
Date	*Units*	*Rate (A)*	*Amt. (A)*	*Units*	*Rate (A)*	*Amt. (A)*	*Units*	*Rate (A)*	*Amt. (A)*
1.1.09							100	25	2,500
1.1.09	200	30	6,000				300	28.33*	8,500
15.1.09				100	28.33	2,833	200	28.33	5,667
1.2.09	400	40	16,000				600	36.11	21.667
15.2.09				200	36.11	7,222	400	36.11	14,445
20.2.09				200	36.11	7,222	200	36.11	7,223
1.3.09	300	50	15,000				500	44.45	22,223
15.3.09				200	44.45	8,890	300	44.45	13,333

* Issue Price (Weighted Average) $\frac{8,500}{300}$ A 28.33

Value of Closing Stock : 300 units @ A 44.45 = A 13,333

Value of Closing Inventories on LIFO basis under periodic system :

Stock of mateirals (units) = (Op. Stock + Purchases) – (Issued for consumption)

= (100 + 200 + 400 + 300) – (100 + 200 + 200 + 200)

= (1,000 – 700 = 300 units

Cost of Closing Inventory (material)

= 100 units @ A 25 = A 2,500

= 200 units @ A 30 = A 6,000

A 8,500

Example 8

X who was closing his books on 31.3.2011 failed to take the actual Stock which he did only on 9th April, when it was ascertained by him to be worth Rs. 2,50,000.

It was found that sales are entered in the sales book on the same day of despatch and return inwards in the returns book as and when the goods are received back. Purchases are entered in the purchases day book once the invoices are received.

It was found that sales beween 31st March and 9th April as per the sales day book are *A* 17,200. Purchases between 31st March and 9th April as per purchases day book are *A* 1,200 out of these goods amounting to *A* 500 were not received until after the stock was taken.

Goods invoice during the month of March, but goods received only on 4th April, amounted to *A* 1,000 Rate of gross profit is 33–1/3% on cost.

Required : Ascertain the value of physical stock as on 31.3.2011. [*C.A. (Foundation) May 1996*]

Solution

Statement of Valuation of Physical Stock as on 31st March 2011

				(A)
A.	Value of Stock as on 9th April			2,50,000
B.	*Add:*	Cost of sales during the intervening period :		
		Sales made between 31st March and 9th April	17,200	
	Less :	Gross profit @ 25% on sales	4,300	12,900
C.	*Less :*	Purchases actually received during the intervening period :		
		Purchases from 1st April to 9th April	1,200	
	Less :	Goods not received upto 9th April	500	700
D.	*Less :*	Purchases during March received on 4th April		1,000
E.	Value of Physical stock as on 31st March (A + B – C – D)			2,61,200

Example 9

From the following information, ascertain the value of stock as on 31.3.2012 :

	(A)
Value of Stock on 1.4.2011	70,000
Purchases during the period from 1.4.2011 to 31.3.2012	3,46,000
Manufacturing expenses during the above period	70,000
Sales during the same period	5,22,000

At the time of valuing stock on 31.3.2011, a sum of A 6,000 was written off a particular item which was originally purchased for A 20,000 and was sold for A 16,000. But for the other transactions the gross profit earned during the year was 25% on cost. *[C.A. (Foundation) May 1997]*

Solution

Statement Showing the Valuation of Closing Stock as at 31st March 2012

			(A)
A.	Normal Sales [A 5,22,000 – A 16,000]		5,06,000
B.	*Less:* Gross Profit @ 20% on Sales		1,01,200
C.	Cost of Goods Sold		4,04,800
D.	*Less :* Opening stock of Normal Goods [A 70,000 – A 14,000]	56,000	
	Purchases	3,46,000	
	Manufacturing Expenses	70,000	4,72,000
E.	Value of Stock as on 31.3.2012		67,200

ASSIGNMENT MATERIAL

Note : The Objective Type Questions (True/False Qustions, Multiple Choice Questions etc.) have been given in the Appendix at the end of the Book.

SHORT ANSWER THEORY QUESTIONS

1. What is Inventory?
2. What is the need for inventories in a manufacturing enterprises?
3. Explain the need for inventory valuation.
4. Explain FIFO as a method of inventory valuation.
5. Disccuss LIFO as a method of inventory valuation.
6. Write a note on weighted average method of costing inventory.
7. Explain briefly the main features of AS-2 on Inventory Valuation.
8. Write a note on perpetual inventory system.
9. What is a periodic inventory system?

LONG ANSWER THEORY QUESTIONS

1. Define inventory. Why does a business enterprise need inventories?
2. Discuss the objectives of inventory measurement.
3. Discuss the following methods of inventory costing alongwith their advantages and disadvantages.
   (*i*) First-in-first-out (FIFO)
   (*ii*) Last-in, First-out (LIFO)
   (*iii*) Weighted Average
4. Explain fully provisions of AS-2 on Inventory Valuation.
5. Discuss perpetual inventory system. What are its merits and demerits.
6. Discuss fully periodic inventory system.
7. Compare perpetual and perpetual inventory system. Which one is better and why?

8. Explain briefly the salient features of Accounting Standard-2 (AS-2) as recommended by ICAI.
[*B.Com.(Hons.), Delhi University, 2006*]
9. Distinguish between Periodic and perpetual system of inventory valuation.
[*B.Com.(Hons.), Delhi University, 2007, 2009*]

PRACTICAL PROBLEMS

1. The following details are extracted from the production unit of a manufacturing company.

1.1.2011	Opening Stock	NIL
1.1.2011	Purchases 100 units @ *A* 30 per unit	
15.1.2011	Issued for consumption	50 units
1.2.2011	Purchases 200 units @ *A* 40 per unit	
15.2.2011	Issued for consumption	100 units
20.2.2011	Issued for consumption 100 units	
1.3.2011	Purchase 150 units @ *A* 50 per unit	
15.3.2011	Issued for consumption 100 units	

Compute the Value of Stock as on 31.3.2011 Based on LIFO.

Ans. : Value of Closing stock, 100 units, A 4,000

2. From the following particulars for the month of March, 2012, find out the cost of inventory on 31 March 2012 under perpetual inventory system using FIFO method of pricing issue of materials:

Date		*Particulars*	*Quantity (kg.)*	*Rate per Kg. (A)*
2012				
March	1	Opening inventory	400	100
March	4	Purchases of material	2,000	140
March	8	Issue of material	1,600	—
March	15	Purchase of material	1,000	160
March	24	Issue of material	200	—
March	26	Purchase of material	300	180
March	28	Issue of Material	360	—

Also show cost of different issues. [*C.S. (Foundation) June 2002*]

Ans. : Cost of inventory A 2,47,600

3. A company purchased raw materials during the month of March, 2011 as stated below :

March 02	—	1,600 units @ *A* 60 per unit
March 08	—	2,400 units @ *A* 55 per unit
March 11	—	5,000 units @ *A* 57 per unit
March 19	—	6,000 units @ *A* 54 per unit
March 23	—	3,000 units @ *A* 58 per unit
March 30	—	2,000 units @ *A* 63 per unit

While preparing the final accounts on 31 March, 2011, the company had 2,600 units of raw materials in the godown.

You are required to calculate the value of closing stock of raw materials according to

(*i*) First in first out method; and

(*ii*) Weighted average price method [*C.S. (Foundation) Dec. 2004*]

Ans. : Value of Closing Stock, FIFO A 1,60,800

Weighted Average A 1,47,810.

4. A company, started on 1 January 2011 purchased raw material during 2011 as started below :

January 2	800 kg.	@ *A* 62 per kg.
February 26	1,200 kg.	@ *A* 57 per kg.
April 13	2,500 kg.	@ *A* 59 per kg.
July 10	3,000 kg.	@ *A* 56 per kg.
September 18	1,500 kg.	@ *A* 60 per kg.
November 29	1,000 kg.	@ *A* 65 per kg.

While preparing its final accounts on 31 December 2011 the company had 1,300 kg of raw material in its godown.

Required Calculate the values of closing stock of raw materials according to :

(*i*) 'First in First out' basis,

(*ii*) 'Last in First out' basis, and

(*iii*) 'Weighted Average' basis. [*B.Com. (Hons.), Delhi University*]

Ans. : (*i*) FIFO, A 83,000; (*ii*) LIFO, A 78,100; (*iii*) Weighted Average A 76,505.

5. From the following data, calculate the value of closing inventory according to FIFO and LIFO on 31 March 2011 using :

(*i*) Periodic inventory system, and

(*ii*) Perpetual inventory system.

March 1	Stock in hand 400 units @ A 7.50 each
Purchases :	
March 5	600 units @ *A* 8 each
March 15	500 units @ *A* 9 each
March 25	400 units @ *A* 8.50 each
March 30	300 units @ *A* 9.50 each
Issue :	
March 3	300 units
March 10	500 units
March 17	400 units
March 26	500 units
March 31	200 units

[*B.Com.(Hons.), Delhi University*]

Ans. : (*i*) Periodic system, FIFO, *A* 2,850; (*ii*) LIFO, *A* 2,250;
(*iii*) Perpetual system, FIFO *A* 2,850; LIFO *A* 2,500.

6. Calculate cost of goods sold, value of closing stock and profit under LIFO method of stock valuation from the following information :

1 January 2012	Stock 200 units at *A* 60 each
16 January 2012	Bought 240 units at *A* 80 each
3 February 2012	Bought 220 units at *A* 100 each
21 February 2012	Bought 280 units at *A* 20 each
During March 2012,	800 units were sold at *A* 160 each.

[*B.Com. (Hons.), Delhi University*]

Ans. : Cost of Goods sold *A* 78,400; Closing stock *A* 8,400; Profit *A* 49,600.

7. Johnson Co. Limited purchased goods at the cost of *A* 40 lakhs in October 2009. Till March 2010, 75% of the stocks were sold. The company wants to disclose closing stock at *A* 10 lakhs.

The expected sale value is *A* 11 lakhs and a commission at 10% on sale is payable to the agent. Advise, what is the correct closing stock to be disclosed as at 31.3.2010? [*C.A. Foundation*]

Ans. : *A* 9,90,000.

8. Following information are available from the books of accounts of ABC Co. for the year 2011-12 :

	A
Purchases during the year	28,200
Stock on 1.4.2011	5,960
Sales during the year	31,610

At the time of valuation of stock for 2011-12 a part of the stock costing *A* 1,800 was recorded in the books for *A* 1,560; one-third of these goods were sold during the year for *A* 610.

Required Find out the value of the stock as on 31st March 2012 assuming that firm makes 25% profit on cost. [*B.Com., Delhi-2000*]

Ans. : *A* 8,840

9. Mr. Vijay's financial year ends on 30th June 2011, but actual stock is not taken until the following 8th July when it is ascertained at *A* 74,250.

You find that :

(*a*) Sales are entered in the sales book on the same day as despatched and returns inward in the return inward book the day the goods are received back.

(*b*) Purchases are entered in the purchases day book as the invoices are received.

(*c*) Sales between 30th June and 8th July as per the sales day book and cash book are Rs. 86,000.

(*d*) Purchases between 30th June and 8th July as per the purchases day book are Rs. 6,600 but, of these goods amounting to *A* 600 are not received until after the stock was taken.

(*e*) Goods invoiced during the June (before 30th June) but not received until after 30th June amounted to Rs. 5,000 of which Rs. 3,500 worth are received between 30th June and 8th July.

(*f*) Rate of Gross Profit is 33 1/3% on cost.

Ascertain the value of Stock on 30th June 2011. [*B.Com., Delhi University*]

Ans. : *A* 1,34,250.

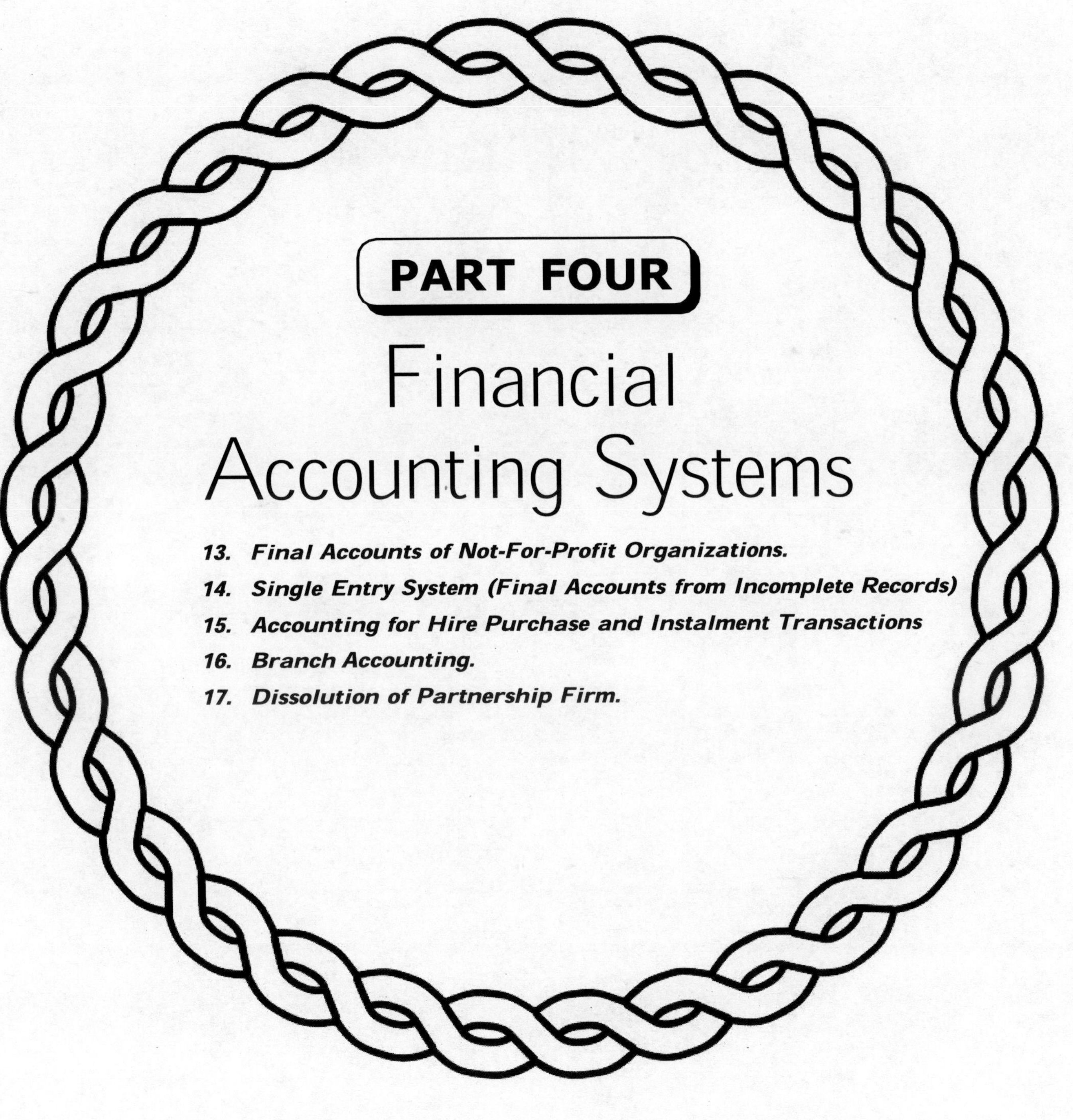

PART FOUR

Financial Accounting Systems

13. *Final Accounts of Not-For-Profit Organizations.*
14. *Single Entry System (Final Accounts from Incomplete Records)*
15. *Accounting for Hire Purchase and Instalment Transactions*
16. *Branch Accounting.*
17. *Dissolution of Partnership Firm.*

CHAPTER 13

Final Accounts of Not-For-Profit Organizations

Learning Objectives

After studying this chapter, you should be able to :

1. *Explain the concept of Not-For-Profit Organizations.*
2. *Discuss the preparation of Income and Expenditure Account, Receipts and Payments Accounts, Balance Sheet.*
3. *Distinguish between Receipts and Payments Accounts and Income and Expenditure Account.*
4. *Explain the treatment of special items applicable to Not-for-Profit Organizations.*

CONCEPT OF NOT-FOR-PROFIT ORGANIZATIONS

In the previous chapter, we have discussed the preparation of Final Accounts *i.e.,* Profit and Loss A/c and the Balance Sheet. These Final Accounts are prepared by profit-making organizations *i.e.,* those organization whose main objective is to earn profit. They earn profit by selling goods or services to the customers. The business is conducted keeping in mind only one main goal which is maximization of profit. But there are some organizations which are formed not to earn profit but to serve the society at large. These organizations are called Not-for-Profit Organizations, such as Charitable Institutions, Sports Clubs, Hospitals, Educational Institutions etc. Although the objective of these organizations is not to earn profit but still the manner in which funds are obtained and are utilised in these concerns, has to be accounted for. Accounting for Not-For-Profit Organization is done by preparing three accounts :

1. Income and Expenditure Account.
2. Receipts and Payments Account.
3. Balance Sheet.

These organizations collect funds from its members in the form of subscriptions, donations and grants. These funds are utilized to achieve the objective set by individual Not-For-Profit Organizations.

ACCOUNTS PREPARED BY NOT-FOR-PROFIT ORGANIZATIONS

Income and Expenditure Account

Every non-profit organization has to prepare Income and Expenditure A/c at the end of financial year. This account is prepared in the same manner as Profit and Loss A/c. It is a nominal A/c and all items of revenue nature appear in this account. While preparing Income and Expenditure A/c, expenses of the organization are shown on the debit side and Income on the credit side. Both the sides are then totalled and balance calculated. If incomes are more than expenses the balance is termed as surplus. If expenses are more than incomes then the balance is termed as deficit. The surplus of non-profit making organizations is not meant for distribution, but are re-invested in the organization to achieve the objectives for which organization is formed.

Income and Expenditure A/c is based on Accrual concept of accounting. It records only those Expenses and Incomes which relates to current year. Therefore, adjustment is required for prepaid expenses, outstanding expenses, accrued income and unearned income.

A specimen of Income and Expenditure account is given in Exhibit 13.1.

Income and Expenditure Account for the Year Ending

Expenditure	(*A*)	*Income*	(*A*)
1. Expenses Account (e.g. salaries) Total salaries paid during the year. *Add :* Outstanding at the end *Less :* Outstanding in the beginning (or actual amount of last year paid) *Add :* Advance paid for the salaries last year. *Less :* Advance paid for the salaries in the current year. **Salaries for the year.** 2. Loss on the sale of an asset : Book value of the asset sold *Less :* Sale price Net loss on sale 3. Expenses for specific purpose : (*e.g.,* tournament) Expenses paid *Less :* Collection 4. **Net expenses on specific item** 5. Depreciation 6. **Expenses on consumable material (*e.g.,* stationery) :** Opening stock of stationery *Add :* Purchases during the year *Less :* Creditors for stationery in the beginning *Add :* Creditors for stationery for the current year *Add :* Advance payments for stationery last year *Less :* Advance payment for stationery in the current year *Less :* Stock of stationery at the end. **Value of stationery actually consumed.** 7. Other expenses and losses after necessary adjustments. 8. Excess of Income over Expenditure to be added to the Capital Fund in the Balance Sheet **(Balancing Figure)**		1. Profit on sale of asset : Sale price of the asset *Less :* Book value of the asset sold **Net profit on sale** 2. Receipts for specific items : (tournament) *Less :* Amount spent **Net income on specific item** 3. **Income Account (*e.g., subscriptions*):** Total amount of subscriptions received during the year. *Add :* Outstanding at the end *Less :* Outstanding in the beginning (or actual amount of the last year received this year) *Add :* Advance received last year. *Less :* Advance received this year **Current year's subscriptions** 4. Other income and gains with adjustment 5. Excess of Expenditure over Income to be deducted from the Capital Fund in the balance sheet (Balancing Figure).	

Exhibit 13.1 : Specimen of Income and Expenditure Account.

Receipts and Payments Account

Every Not-For-Profit organization has to prepare Receipts and Payments Account also at the end of financial year. It is a real account, where, summary of all cash transactions which occurred in the financial year are recorded. This account is prepared in 'T' form, where cash receipts are entered on the debit side and cash payments on the credit side. If the organization has cash and bank balance of previous year then it is shown on the debit side as opening balance and then transactions are recorded in chronological order. Unlike Income and Expenditure Account it shows items of revenue nature as well as capital nature. Also, it records all cash receipts and payments whether it is of previous year, current year or of next accounting year. Since, it records cash transactions only, therefore, non-cash items like depreciation does not appear in Receipts and Payments Account.

A specimen of Receipts and Payments Account is given in Exhibit 13.2.

Receipts Capital and Revenue	(*A*)	*Payments* Capital and Revenue	(*A*)
I. Balance b/d (opening balance)		**I. Revenue Payments**	
1. Cash in hand		1. Prizes paid	
2. Cash at Bank		2. Entertainment expenses	
II. Revenue Receipts		3. Printing and stationery	
3. Subscriptions		4. Newspapers and periodicals	
4. General donations		5. Postages	
5. Proceeds from entertainments		6. Honorarium paid to secretary and others.	
6. Interest or dividends on general investments		7. Insurance, rent, salaries.	
7. Sale of old newspapers, waste papers etc.		8. Advertisement	
8. Miscellaneous receipts		9. Audit fees	
III. Capital Receipts		10. Telephone, electricity charges	
9. Legacies		11. Gardening	
10. Sale of office furniture		12. Up-keep of lawns	
11. Sale of sports equipment		13. Municipal taxes	
12. Donations for special purposes, *e.g.,* building, prizes etc.		14. Charity	
13. Membership fees		15. Printing expenses	
14. Sale of investments		**II. Capital Payments**	
15. Endowment fund receipts		16. Building construction	
16. Receipts on account of special funds *e.g.,* Prize fund, Tournament fund.		17. Books	
17. Interest on specific fund investments		18. Sports equipment	
18. Entrance fees.		19. Cost of leasehold	
IV. Balance c/d (Bank Overdraft)		20. Investments	
		21. Advance for purchase of buildings.	
		22. Government's loan	
		23. Furniture	
		III. Balance c/d (closing balance).	
		24. Cash in hand	
		25. Cash at Bank	

Exhibit 13.2 : Specimen of Receipts and Payments Accounts.

Balance Sheet

The third statement required is the balance Sheet of the financial year. Most of the items in the balance sheet is the same as found in Balance Sheet of Profit-making organizations. Not-For-Profit Organizations does not issue shares to its members. Contribution received from the members of the organization are shown in the Balance Sheet on the Liability side as 'Fund'. If the organization receive donations from non-members then the amount received is added to the fund. The surplus or deficit calculated while preparing Income and Expenditure A/c., is adjusted in fund, *i.e.,* surplus is added to the fund and deficit is deducted from the fund.

Actual Accounts of a Real Non-Profit Organization

To illustrate actual accounts prepared by a real Non-Profit organization, the accounts prepared by the Institute of Cost and Works Accountants of India, has been displayed in Exhibit 13.3.

THE INSTITUTE OF COST AND WORKS ACCOUNTANTS OF INDIA

Balance Sheet as at 31st March. 2011.

Last year 2009-2010 A	*Particulars*	*This Year 2010–2011* *A*	*A*
	Institute Fund :		
738,121,402	General Fund		1,185,508,498
5,913,533	Employees, Gratuity Fund		4,987,633
2,616,686	Employees' Benevolent Fund		2,629,577
4,035,430	Misc. Prize Fund		4,198,641
94,924,690	Other Fund		77,920,743
845,611,741	**Total**		**1,275,245,092**
	Represented By :		
	Fixed Assets :		
212,902,869	(a) Gross Block	279,960,020	
102,918,641	(*b*) Less Depreciation	122,360,772	
109,984,228	(*c*) NetBlock		157,599,248
5,119,134	Capital Work in Progress		13,186,429
98,111	Investment		98,100
818,554,076	Current Assets	1,155,057,209	
20,270,929	Loans & Advances	57,233,568	
838, 825, 005		1,212,290,777	
109,676,410	*Less :* Current Liabilities & Provisions	109,228,717	
729,148,595	**Net Current Assets**		1,103,062,060
1,261,673	Miscellaneous Expenditure (to the extent not written off)		1,299,255
845,611,741	**Total**		**1,275,245,092**
	Notes to Accounts		
	Schedules from part of the Accounts		

THE INSTITUTE OF COST AND WORKS ACCOUNTANTS OF INDIA

Income and Expenditure Account for the year ended 31st March, 2011

Last year 2009-2010 A	*Particulars*	*This Year 2010–2011 A*
	Income :	
15,479,090	Membership & Other Fees	17,287,212
520,721,975	Tuition & other Fees	648,399,322
75,012,230	Examination & Other Fees	103, 595, 569
30,533,692	Continuing Education Programme Receipt	34,564,283
7,821,938	National Award and Convention Receipt	14,363,771
814,415	Journal Subscription	930,500
109,550	Advertisement for Journal	298,816
986,692	Rent Receipt	1,183,474
801,911	Sale of Publication	402,593
44,119,582	Interest	54,617,116
5,695,717	Other Income	9,036,002
702,096,792	**Total**	**884,678,658**
	Expenditure :	
132,242,813	Establishment	140,482,513
61,232,144	Office Expenses	69,147,468
365,306	Audit Fees	494,255
205,566	Internal Audit Fees	322,593
8,131,915	Travelling & Conveyance	10,580,339
28,221,328	Examination Expenses	38,409,503
16,973,011	Council & Committee Meeting Expenses	19,631,150
1,013,453	Election Expenses incl. Tribunal	1,013,453
5,430,937	Journal Expenses	7,076,113
1,516,073	Membership Subscription to Foreign Bodies	1,692,980
1,710,695	Conference & Meeting International	2,593,769
24,058,081	Continuing Education Programme Expenses	25,987,865
4,543,329	National Award for Cost Excellence Expenses	16,915,627
21,327,967	Professional Development Expenses	9,231,634
69,392,717	Coaching Expenses	85,282,158
26,038,275	Study Materials & Prospectus Consumed	30,207,314
199,468	Publication Stock Consumed	241,982
1,616,613	Non Moving Stock Written Off	610,814
806,491	Sundry Debtors – Written Off	1,343,079
18,477,898	Depreciation	20,903,318
423,504,080	**Total**	**482,167,927**
278,592,712	**Balance being excess of Income over Expenditure c/d**	**402,510,731**
1,262,652	Prior Period Adjustment	364,286
279,855,364	**Balance being surplus of Income over Expenditure transferred to General Fund**	**402,875,017**
	Notes to Accounts	

Source : Annual Report and Audited Accounts, The Institute of Cost and Works Accountants of India, The Management Accountants, April 2012, pp.478–480

TREATMENT OF SPECIAL ITEMS

1. *Subscription* : Subscription is the amount which is paid by the members to the non-profit making organizations. This amount is generally paid on yearly basis. It is a major source of income of non-profit making organization which is utilised to run the organization. Since, it is an income, the amount received as 'Subscription' is entered on the Receipts side of Receipts and Payment A/c., and on the Income side of Income and Expenditure A/c. Sometimes, members may give subscription of previous year or of next year in the current year. Then, adjustments have to be done in accounts by following the accrual basis of Accounting. Treatment of subscriptions are explained through some illustrations here.

Illustration

If subscription received relates to current year only.

United Sports Club has received A 5,000 as Annual Subscription for the year 2011-12. Financial year of the club ends on 31st March every year.

Since, this amount relates to one financial year only, the entry will be as follows :

Receipts and Payment A/c

Dr. *Cr.*

Receipt	*(A)*	*Payment*	*(A)*
To Subscription	5,000		

Income and Expenditure A/c

Expenditure	*(A)*	*Income*	*(A)*
		By Subscription	5,000

Illustration

If subscription received relates to previous year and next year. For example, Hope Education Society consists of 50 members paying Annual Subscription of A 500 each. The society has received subscription from 40 members in the current year. Also, 5 members who have not paid subscription in the previous year have paid subscription in the current year. Out of 40 members who have paid subscription in the current year 3 members have paid subscription of next year. Current financial year of the Society is 2010-11. The necessary entries are as follows :

Receipts and Payment A/c

Dr. *Cr.*

Receipt	*(A)*		*Payment*	*(A)*
To Subscription				
2009-10	2,500			
2010-11	20,000			
2011-12	1,500	24,000		

Income and Expenditure A/c

Dr. *Cr.*

Expenditure	*(A)*	*Income*		*(A)*
		By Subscription 20,000		
		Add : O/s	5,000	25,000

Balance Sheet

Liabilities	*(A)*	*Assets*	*(A)*
Subscription received in advance	1,500	Subscription outstanding	5000

2. Donations : Donations might ionalionalionalhave been raised for meeting some revenue or capital expenditures. If donation is received to meet revenue expenditure, it is credited directly to the Income and Expenditure Account. The other donations, where the donors have declared their specific intention, are credited to special fund account or in its absence, to the capital fund account. This donation is capitalised and is entered on the liability side of Balance Sheet. If any investments are purchased out of a special fund or an asset is acquired therefrom, these are disclosed separately. Any income received from such investments or any donations collected for a special purpose are credited to an account indicating the purpose and correspondingly the expenditure incurred in carrying out the purpose of the fund is debited to this account. On no account any such expense is charged to the Income and Expenditure Account. The term "Fund" is strictly applicable to the amounts collected for a special purpose when these are invested, e.g., Scholarship Fund, Prize Fund etc. In other cases, when the amounts collected are not invested in securities or assets distinguishable from those belonging to the institution, the word "Account" is more appropriate *e.g.,* Building Account, Tournament Account etc.

Further, if the donation is for general purpose then the treatment will depend on the amount received. If the amount is large then it is capitalised and entered on the liability side of the Balance Sheet. If the amount is small then, it is entered on the Income side of Income and Expenditure Account.

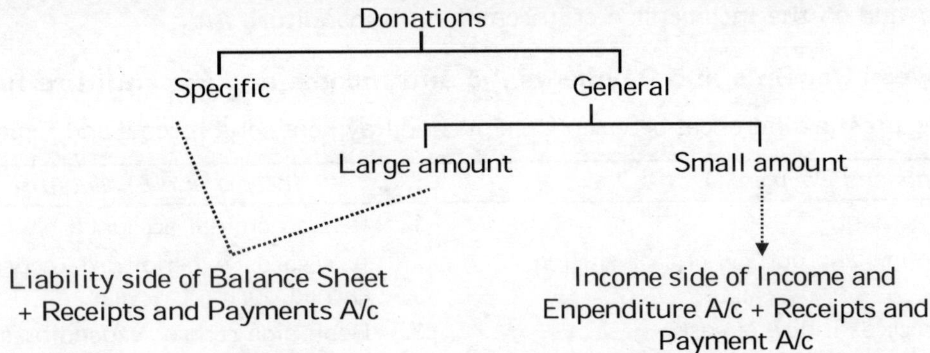

When the organization receives General Donation then the donation will come into the category of large amount or small amount, will depend on members discretion. Limit of small amount have not been specified by law.

3. Legacy : Legacy is also a donation. The only difference is that, it is given as per will of the dead person. The classification and treatment is same as of donations.

4. Entrance Fees : Whenever a new member joins a non-profit making organizations, he pays a fees at the time of joining, this is called Entrance Fees. This fees is paid once in a life-time. The treatment of Entrance fees in accounts can be done in two ways :

(*i*) It may be capitalised and then it is entered on the liability side of the Balance Sheet. (Capital Receipt)

(*ii*) It may be treated as Income and is entered on the Income side of Income and Expenditure A/c (revenue Receipt)

The treatment of Entrance Fees will be decided by the members of the organization.

Note : In the absence of any information, students while answering a question, should themselves decide and mention it in foot note accordingly.

5. Life-Membership Fees : When the member intends to be a member of non-profit making organization throughout his life, then fees paid in lumpsum by the member is called Life-Membership Fees. Since, this fees is paid once hence, it is treated as capital receipt and is transferred to liability side of the Balance Sheet.

Another treatment of this item is to write-off a certain portion of amount every year and show it on the income side of Income and Expenditure A/c., till the total amount received is expired.

6. Honorarium : Sometimes Non-Profit making organizations may invite outsiders for special type of services. Payment made to such persons is called Honorarium'. This amount is shown on the expenditure side of 'Income and Expenditure A/c'.

7. Endowment Fund : When a donor gives a property to Not-For-Profit making organizations which will provide a regular source of income to the organization, then it is called 'Endowment Fund'. The value of the property received is entered on the Receipt side of 'Receipts and Payment A/c., in the year of receipt and then, also entered on the liability side of the Balance Sheet. This amount will continue to appear in the Balance Sheet in coming year till the properly remains with the organization.

8. Grants from Govt. and other Institutions : When the Government or other Institutions give grant to Not-for profit organizations, the treatment of grant will depend on the purpose for which grant is given. If grant is given for maintenance, then it is entered on the Receipt side of 'Receipt and Payment A/c' and also on the Income side of Income and Expenditure A/c *i.e.,* it is treated as revenue receipt. However, if the grant is given for some specific purpose then it is entered on the Liability side of Balance Sheet *i.e.,* it is treated as 'Capital Receipt'.

9. Sale of Old Newspapers : The amount received from sale of old newspaper is entered on the Receipt side of Receipt and Payment A/c and on the Income side of Income and Expenditure A/c.

10. Sale of Assets : The amount received from Sale of Assets is entered on the Receipt side of 'Receipt and Payment A/c' and on the Income side of 'Income and Expenditure A/c'.

Difference Between Receipts and Payments A/c and Income and Expenditure A/c

The following are the differences between Receipts and Payments and Income and Expenditure Account.

Receipts and Payment A/c	*Income and Expenditure A/c*
1. It is a real account.	1. It is a nominal account.
2. It records inflow and outflow of cash during the year.	2. It records expenditure incurred and revenue earned during the year.
3. Debit side records inflow of cash.	3. Debit side records expenditure incurred.
4. Credit side records outflow of cash.	4. Credit side records income earned.
5. It records items of capital and revenue nature both.	5. It records item of Revenue nature only.
6. It records all cash transactions whether they relate to previous year, current year or next year.	6. It records only those transactions which relates to current year. It is based on accrual concept of accounting.
7. It starts with the opening balance of cash in hand on the Dr. side.	7. There is no opening balance in the beginning.
8. Closing balance depicts cash in hand at the end.	8. Closing balance shows excess of income over expenditure or excess of expenditure over income
9. Non-cash items are not recorded.	9. Non-cash items are recorded.
10. It is summary of cash transactions.	10. It shows the net result of operations during a year.
11. Preparation of Balance Sheet is not compulsory after preparing this account.	11. Preparation of Balance Sheet is essential after preparing this account.
12. Balance at the end becomes the opening balance of next year.	12. Balance at the end is adjusted in the Balance Sheet of current year.

Fund Based Accounting

Fund based accounting essentially involves preparation of financial statements fund-wise. Not-for-profit organizations, particularly educational institutions, sometimes maintain separate account or fund for any specific activities of the organization such as sports prizes, refreshments, and in that cases presentation of information in Financial Statements is made fund wise. In such cases, contribution and donations for income from and expenses on those activities are not recorded in Income and Expenditure account but are directly adjusted in Specific Fund Account.

TYPES OF NUMERICAL PROBLEMS TO BE SOLVED.

The following types of practical problems may relate to Not-for-Profit organizations.

1. Preparation of Income and Expenditure Account and closing Balance Sheet when Receipts and Payments Account and some additional information are given.
2. Preparation of Receipts and Payments Account when Income and Expenditure Account and some additional information are given.
3. Preparation of Balance Sheet (Closing) when Receipts and Payments account and Income and Expenditure and some additional information are given.
4. Preparation of Receipts and Payments account and Balance Sheet (closing) when Income and Expenditure account and some additional information are given.

Besides the above, opening balance sheet, if required, may need to be prepared to find out opening capital or any other asset or liability items.

Example 1

Calculate the amount of stationery consumed during the calendar year 2007 :

	A
Stock of stationary as on January 1, 2007	3,000
Creditors for stationery on January 1, 2007	2,000
Advance paid for stationery carried from 2006	200
Amount paid for stationery during the year	10,800
Stock of stationery on December 31, 2007	500
Creditors for stationery for December 31, 2007	1,300
Advance paid for stationery on December 31, 2007	1,300

[*B.Com.(Hons.) Delhi University*]

Solution

Calculation of Stationery Consumed in 2007

	A
Opening Stock on 1.1.2007	3,000
Add : Amount paid in 2007	10,800
	13,800
Less : Creditors for stationery on 1.1.2007	2,000
	11,800
Add : Advance paid carried forward from 2006	200
	12,000
Less : Advance paid on 31.12.2007	1,300

	10,700
Add : Creditors for stationery on 31.12.2007	1,300
	12,000
Less : Stock on 31.12.2007	500
	11,500

Example 2

From the following information, calculate the amount of subscriptions received in advance during 2008-09 :

(*i*) Subscriptions received during the year 2008-09, A 52,500.

(*ii*) There were 200 members each paying subscription at the rate of A 250 p.a.

(*iii*) Some members have paid their annual subscription in advance during the year.

(*iv*) As on 1 April 2008, no subscription had been received in advance but subscriptions were outstanding to the extent of Rs. 1,000 as on 31 March 2008.

(*v*) Subscriptions accrued as on 31 March 2009 Rs. 1,500. [*B.Com.(Hons.), Delhi University*]

Solution

Subscriptions Account

	(*A*)		(*A*)
1.4.2008		1.4.2008	
Balance b/d	1,000	balance b/d	NIL
Income and Expenditure		Cash	52,500
Account (200 × 250)	50,000	31.3.09	
31.3.09		Balance c/d	1,500
Balance c/d			
(Balancing figure)	3,000		
	54,000		54,000

Example 3

From the following particulars, prepare Income and Expenditure Account :

		A
(*i*)	Fees collected, including A 80,000 on account of the previous year.	3,80,000
(*ii*)	Fees for the year outstanding	10,000
(*iii*)	Salary paid including A 8,000 on account of the previous year	98,000
(*iv*)	Salary outstanding at the end of the year	9,000
(*v*)	Entertainment Expenses	3,000
(*vi*)	Tournament Expenses	42,000
(*vii*)	Meeting Expenses	18,000
(*viii*)	Travelling Expenses	6,000
(*ix*)	Purchase of Books and Periodicals (including A 18,000 for purchase of books)	28,000
(*x*)	Rent paid	17,000
(*xi*)	Advertising Expenses	15,500
(*xii*)	Postage and Stationery	4,500
(*xiii*)	Donations received (50% of which is to be capitablised)	25,000

Solution.

Income and Expenditure Account
for the year ending on ......

Expenditure		(A)	*Income*		(A)
To salaries paid	98,000		By Fees received	3,80,000	
Less : O/S for Previous year	8,000		*Less* : O/S for Previous Year	80,000	
	90,000			3,00,000	
Add : O/S for Current year	9,000	99,000	*Add* : O/S for Current year	10,000	3,10,000
To Entertainment Expenses		3,000	By Donations [50% of A 25,000]		12,500
To Tournament Expenses		42,000			
To Match Expenses		6,000			
To Travelling Expenses		18,000			
To Periodical A [28,000 – 18,000]		10,000			
To Rent		17,000			
To Advertisement		15,500			
To Postage and Stationery		4,500			
To Excess of Income over Expenditure		1,07,500			
		3,22,500			3,22,500

Example 4

Show what amount will appear in Income & Expenditure A/c for the year ending 31.3.08 and Balance Sheet as at that date in each of the following cases :

Case (*i*) — Prize fund as at 31.3.2007 A 12,000. Donations for prizes received during the year 2007-08 A 2,800; Prize awarded A 2,000; 10% prize fund investments as at 31.3.2007 A 12,000. Interest received on prize fund investments A 600.

Case (*ii*) — Stock of stationery on 31.3.07 A 3,000. Creditors of stationery on 31.3.07 A 2,000; advance paid for stationery carried forward from 2006-07 A 200; Amount paid for stationery during the year 2007-08 A 10,800, Stock of stationery on 31.3.08 A 500, creditors for stationery on 31.3.08 A 1,300 and advance paid for stationery on 31.3.08 A 300.

Case (*iii*) — Subscription outstanding as on 31.3.07 A 2,000, subscription received in advance on 31.3.07 A 3,000. Amount of subscription received during 2007-08 A 35,000 out of which A 1,500 related to 2006-07 and A 800 related to 2008-09. On 31.3.08 subscription oustanding for 2007-08 amounted to A 1,300.

[*B.Com.(Hons.) Delhi University, 2008*]

Solution

Case (*i*)

Balance Sheet (only Relevant Items)
as at 31st March, 2008

Liabilities		(A)	*Assets*	(A)
Prize fund	12,000		Prize fund investments	12,000
Add : Donations for Prize	2,800		Accrued interest on	

Interest received on prize fund investments	600		Prize fund*	600
Accrued interest*	600			
	16,000			
Less : Prize awarded	2,000	14,000		

Working Notes

	(A)
* Yearly interest on prize fund investment [10% of Rs. 12,000]	1,200
Less : Interest received during the year	600
Accrued interest but not received	600

Case (*ii*)

Creditors for Stationery Accounts

Dr. *Cr.*

Particulars	(*A*)	*Particulars*	(*A*)
To Balance b/d	200	By Balance b/d	2,000
To Bank A/c	10,800	By Stock of Stationery A/c	10,000
To Balance c/d	1,300	(Credit Purchases)* *(Balancing Figure)*	
		By Balance c/d	300
	12,300		12,300

Stock of Stationery Account

Dr. *Cr.*

Particulars	(*A*)	*Particulars*	(*A*)
To Balance b/d	3,000	By Income & Expenditure A/c	12,500
To Creditors for Stock of Stationery (Transfer)*	10,000	(Stationery consumed) (*Balancing Figure*)	
		By Balance c/d	500
	13,000		13,000

An extract of Income and Expenditure Account for the year ending on 31st March, 2008

Dr. *Cr.*

Expenditure	(*A*)	*Income*	(*A*)
To Stationery Consumed	12,500		

An extract of Balance Sheet as at 31st March 2008

Liabilities	(A)	*Assets*		(A)
Creditors for Stationery	1,300	Advance for Stationery (Prepaid)		300
		Stock of Stationery		500

Case (*iii*)

Subscription A/c

Dr. *Cr.*

Particulars	(A)	*Particulars*		(A)
To Outstanding Subscription A/c	2,000	By Advance Subscription A/c		3,000
To Income & Expenditure A/c	37,000	By Bank A/c		35,000
(*Balancing Figure*)		By Outstanding Subscription A/c		
To Advance Subscription	800	2006-07 (2,000 – 1,500)	500	
(2008-09)		2007-08	1,300	1,800
	39,800			39,800

An extract of Income and Expenditure Account for the year ended 31st March, 2008

Expendigure	(A)	*Income*	(A)
		By Subscription A/c	37,000

An extract of Balance Sheet as at 31st March, 2008

Liabilities	(A)	*Assets*		(A)
Subscription Received in Advance	800	Subscription Outstanding		
		2006-07	500	
		2007-08	1,300	1,800

Example 5

From the following particulars relating to Excel Hospital prepare :

(*i*) Receipts & Payments Account for the year ended 31 March, 2006; &

(*ii*) Balance Sheet as on March 31, 2005

Income and Expenditure Account for the year ended 31 March, 2006

Expenditure	(A)	*Income*		(A)
Medicines used	29,980	Subscriptions		56,000
Honorarium to visiting doctors	12,000	Donations		9,500
Salaries	27,500	Interest on Investments @ 11% p.a.		11,000
Printing & Stationery	1,100	Income from film show—		
Electricity and Water	475	Proceeds	11,450	

Rent	6,000	*Less* : Expenses	780	10,670
Depreciation on:				
Furniture and Fixtures	2,100			
Equipment	3,250			
Surplus	4,765			
	87,170			87,170

Additional Information

		31.3.2005	31.3.2006
(*i*)	Subscriptions due	120	160
(*ii*)	Subscriptions Received in Advance	64	100
(*iii*)	Electricity and Water Bills unpaid	92	115
(*iv*)	Stock of Medicines	7,820	9,750
(*v*)	Estimated value of Equipment	11,600	13,900
(*vi*)	Furniture & Fixtures (Cost *Less* Depreciation)	21,000	18,900
(*vii*)	Land	—	10,000
(*viii*)	Interest accrued on Investments in 11% Debentures Costing A 1,02,500	3,750	3,750
(*ix*)	Cash in hand	340	160
(*x*)	Cash at Bank	9,000	?

[*B.Com. (Hons.) Delhi University, 2001*]

Solution

Excel Hospital Receipts and Payments Account for the Year Ending 31 December, 2006

Receipts		(*A*)	*Payments*	(*A*)
Balance b/d : Cash	340		Film show expenses	780
Bank	9,000	9,340	Medicines purchases	31,910
Subscriptions	56,000		(29,980 + 9,750 – 7,820)	
Add : due (2005)	120		Honoraium to visiting doctors	12,000
	56,120		Salaries	27,500
Less : due (2006)	160		Printing and Stationery	1,100
	55,960		electricity and water	452
Add : Advance (2007)	100		(475 + 92 – 115)	
	56,060		Rent	6,000
			Land	10,000
Less :Advance received in 2005	64	55,996	Purchase of equipment	5,550
Donations		9,500	(13,900 + 3,250 – 11,600)	
Interest on Investments	11,000		Balance c/d :	
Less: due (2006)	3,750		Cash	160

	7,250		Bank (Balancing Figure)	1,834
Add : due (2007)	3,750	11,000		
Proceeds of film show		11,450		
		97,286		97,286

Balance Sheet as at 31 December 2005

Liabilities	*(A)*	*Assets*	*(A)*
Subscriptions received in advance	64	Equipment	11,600
Outstanding electricity bill	92	Furniture and Fixtures	21,000
Capital Fund	1,55,974	Stock of medicines	7,820
(Balancing Figure)		Investments	1,02,500
		(Face value 1,00,000)	
		Cash in hand	340
		Cash at Bank	9,000
		Subscriptions due	120
		Accrued interest	3,750
	1,56,130		1,56,130

Balance Sheet as at 31 December, 2006

Liabilities		*(A)*	*Assets*	*(A)*
Subscriptions received in advance		100	Equipment	13,900
			Furniture and fixtures	18,900
Outstanding electricity bill		115	Land	10,000
Capital Fund	1,55,974		Stock of medicines	9,750
Add : Surplus	4,765	1,60,739	Investments	
			(Face value Rs. 1,00,000)	1,02,500
			Subscriptions due	160
			Accrued interest	3,750
			Cash in hand	160
			Cash at Bank	1,834
		1,60,954		1,60,954

Example 6

Prepare Receipts and Payments Account of Tina Social Club for the year ending 31 March 2006 and also the Balance Sheet as on that dates from the following :

Income and Expenditure Account for Year ending 31 March, 2006

Expenditure	*(A)*	*Income*	*(A)*
Salaries	29,500	Interest	10,000
Stationery	5,000	Donations	15,000
Taxes and Rent	2,500	Susbcriptions	25,000
Insurance	1,200	Miscellaneous Receipts	300
Other Expenses	1,800		

Depreciation :				
Properties	3,750			
Furniture	120			
Books	100	3,970		
Surplus		6,330		
		50,300		50,300

Other Informations

	31.3.05 (A)	*31.3.06 (A)*
Cash in hand and at Bank	?	23,700
Investments in Share and Debentures (face value A 3,00,000)	2,80,000	2,80,000
Subscriptions outstanding	7,000	10,000
Subscription received in advance	1,200	1,600
Salaries outstanding	500	1,000
Furniture	2,000	1,980
Properties	3,00,000	2,96,250
Interest on Investments accrued	1,000	1,000
Books	3,500	3,900
Stationery payment due	200	300
Stock of Stationery	1,000	800

[*B.Com.(Hons.), Delhi University, 2000*]

Solution

Tina Social Club

Receipts and Payment Account for the Year Ending 31 March 2006

Receipts	*(A)*	*Payments*	*(A)*
Balance b/d	15,800	Salaries	29,000
(Balancing Figure)		Stationery	4,700
Subscriptions	22,400	Taxes and Rent	2,500
Interest	10,000	Insurance	1,200
Donation	15,000	Other Expenses	1,800
Miscellaneous Receipts	300	Purchase of Furniture	100
		Purchase of Books	500
		Balance c/d	23,700
	63,500		63,500

Balance Sheet as at 31 March 2005

Liabilities	*(A)*	*Assets*	*(A)*
Subscriptions received in advance	1,200	Cash and Bank Balance	15,800
		Shares and Debentures	2,80,000
Outstanding Salary	500	(Face Value 3,00,000)	
Outstanding Stationery expenses	200	Subscription due	7,000

		Furniture	2,000
Capital Fund	6,08,400	Properties	3,00,000
(Balancing Figure)		Investments	1,000
		Books	3,500
		Stock of Stationery	1,000
	6,10,300		6,10,300

Balance Sheet as at 31 March 2006

Liabilities	(*A*)	*Assets*		(*A*)
Capital fund	6,08,400	Cash and Bank Balance		23,700
		Subscriptions Due		10,000
Add : Surplus	6,330	Stock of stationery		800
	6,14,730	Shares and Debentures		2,80,000
Subscriptions Received in advance	1,600	(Face Value 3,00,000)		
		Investments		1,000
Oustanding Salary	1,000	Books	3,500	
Outstanding Stationery Expenses	300	*Add :* Purchases	500	
			4,000	
		Less : Depreciation	100	3,900
		Furniture	2,000	
		Add : Purchases	100	
			2,100	
		Less : Depreciation	120	1,980
		Properties	3,00,000	
		Less : Depreciation	3,750	2,96,250
	6,17,630			6,17,630

Working Notes

*	Subscriptions Received in cash during 2005-06		*A*
	Subscription Income for 2005-06		25,000
	Add : Subscription outstanding on 31.3.2005		7,000
	Subscription received in advance on 31.3.06		1,600
			33,600
	Less : Outstanding on 31.3.06	10,000	
	Received in Advance on 31.3.05	1,200	11,200
			22,400
(*ii*)	Payment of salaries in cash during 2005-06		
	Salary expenditure for 2005-06		29,500
	Add : Outstanding salaries on 31.3.05		500
			30,000
	Less : Outstanding salaries on 31.3.06		1,000
			29,000

(*iii*) Payments for stationery in cash during 2005-06		
Stationery expenditure for 2005-06		5,000
Add : Outstanding expenses on stationery on 31.3.05		200
Stock at the end		800
		6,000
Less : Outstanding expenses on 31.3.06	300	
Stock in the beginning	1,000	1,300
		4,700
(*iv*) Purchases of furniture in cash during 2005-06		
Book value of furniture on 31.3.06		1,980
Add : Depreciation		120
		2,100
Less : Book value of Furniture on 31.3.05		2,000
		100
(*v*) Purchases of books in cash during 2005-06		
Book Value of books on 31.3.06		3,900
Add : Depreciation		100
		4,000
Less : Book value on 31.3.05		3,500
		500

Example 7

Following is the Receipts and Payments Account of India Medical Society for the year ended March 31, 1998 :

Receipts and Payments Account
for the Year ended on 31st March, 1998

Receipts	*(A)*	*Payments*	*(A)*
To Balance b/d	7,000	By Medicine Suppliers	30,000
Tu Subscriptions	50,000	By Honorarium to Doctors	10,000
To Donations	14,500	By Salaries	30,000
To Interest on Investments		By Sundry Expenses	2,000
(@10% p.a. for the year)	10,000	By Equipments	12,000
To Charity Show Proceeds	15,000	By Charity Show Expenses	4,000
		By Balance c/d	8,500
	96,500		96,500

Additional Information :

	1.4.1997 (A)	*31.3.1998 (A)*
(*a*) Subscriptions in arrears	Nil	2,000
(*b*) Stock of Medicines	10,000	15,000

(*c*) Medicine Suppliers (Cr.)	8,000	12,000
(*d*) Value of Equipments	23,000	30,000
(*e*) Value of Buildings	50,000	47,500

Donations are not received for any specific purpose.

You are required to prepare :

(*a*) Income and Expenditure Account for the year ended on March 31, 1998; and (*b*) Balance Sheet as on that date.

Show your workings. [*B.Com. (Hons), Delhi University, 2000*]

Solution

Balance Sheet of India Medical Society
as on 31.3.1997

Liabilities	(*A*)	*Assets*	(*A*)
Due to Medicine Suppliers	8,000	Cash in hand	7,000
Accumulated Capital Fund	1,82,000	Investments	1,00,000
		Equipments	23,000
		Subscriptions in Arrear	Nil
		Stock of Medicines	10,000
		Buildings	50,000
	1,90,000		1,90,000

Income and Expenditure A/c of India Medical Society
for the year ending on 31.3.98

Liabilities		(*A*)	*Assets*		(*A*)
To Medicines : Paid	30,000		By Subscriptions Received	50,000	
+ Stock from last year	10,000		+ Still in Arrers	2,000	52,000
	40,000		By Donations		14,500
— Unused this year	15,000		By Interest on Investments		10,000
	25,000		By Charity Show Proceeds		15,000
— Paid for Last Year	8,000				
	17,000				
+ Due this year	12,000	29,000			
To Honorarium to Doctors		10,000			
To Salaries		30,000			
To Sundry Expenses		2,000			
To Depreciation on Equipments		5,000			
To Depreciation on Buildings		2,500			
To Charity Show Expenses		4,000			
To Surplus		9,000			
		91,500			91,500

Balance Sheet of India Medical Society
as on 31.3.98

Liabilities		(A)	Assets		(A)
Accumulated Capital Fund			Investments		1,00,000
As on 1.4.1997	1,82,000		Equipments :		
+ Surplus	9,000	1,91,000	As on 1.4.1997	23,000	
Due to Medicine Suppliers		12,000	+ Purchases	12,000	
				35,000	
			– Depreciation*2	5,000	30,000
			Cash in hand		8,500
			Subscription in Arrers		2,000
			Stock of Medicines		15,000
			Buildings		
			As on 1.4.1997	50,000	
			– Depreciation*2	2,500	47,500
		2,03,000			2,03,000

Working Notes

*1 Investments should be $\frac{100}{10}$ 10, 000 *i.e.*, A 1,00,000 and should be brought forward from last year.

*2 Depreciation are the balancing figures.

*3 Accumulated Capital Funds as on 1.4.97 is the balancing figure of the last year's Balance Sheet.

Exmaple 8

From the following Trial Balance and other information given below for a school, prepare Income and Expenditure A/c for the year ended 31st Dec., 2000 and a Balance Sheet as on 31.12.2000 :

Debit Balances	(A)	*Credit Balances*	(A)
Building	2,50,000	Admission Fees	5,000
Furniture	40,000	Tuition Fees received	2,00,000
Library Books	60,000	Creditors for supplies	6,000
Investments @ 9%	2,00,000	Rent for the school hall	4,000
Salaries	2,00,000	Misc. Receipts	12,000
Stationery	15,000	Govt. Grant	1,40,000
General Expenses	8,000	General Fund	4,00,000
Sports Expenses	6,000	Donation for Library Books	25,000
Cash at Bank	20,000	Sale of Old Furniture	8,000
Cash in hand	1,000		
	8,00,000		8,00,000

Fees yet to be received for the year are A 10,000. Salaries yet to be paid amount to Rs. 12,000. Furniture costing Rs. 15,000 was purchased on 1.7.2000. The book-value of the furniture sold was A 20,000 on 1.1.2000. Depreciation is to be charged @ 10% p.a. on Furniture, 15% p.a. on Library Books and 5% p.a. on Building. Give working notes. [*B.Com.(Hons.), Delhi University, 2005*]

Solution

Income and Expenditure A/c
for the year ending 31 December, 2000

Expenditure		*(A)*	*Income*		*(A)*
To Loss on Sale of Furniture			By Admission Fees		5,000
(A 20,000 – A 8,000)		12,000	By Tuition Fees	2,00,000	
To Depreciation on Furniture*1		1,250	*Add :* Outstanding	10,000	2,10,000
To Salaries	2,00,000		By Rent for the School Hall		4,000
Add : Outstanding	12,000	2,12,000	By Misc. Receipts		12,000
To Stationery		15,000	By Govt. Grant		1,40,000
To General Expenses		8,000	By Interest on Investment accrued		18,000
To Sports Expenses		6,000	(Rs. 2,00,000 × 9/100)		
To Depreciation on Library Books (15% on A 60,000)		9,000			
To Depreciation on Building (5% on A 2,50,000)		12,500			
To Excess of Income over Expenditure		1,13,250			
		3,89,000			3,89,000

Assumptions :

1. It is assumed that Furniture was sold on 1.1.2000.
2. It is assumed that the school is a Government aided school. Hence Government grant is a regular feature. Otherwise the Government grant should be capitalised.

Working Notes

*1 Depreciation on furniture has been calculated as follows :

	(A)
Balance in Furniture Account on 1.1.2000	40,000
Less : Book value of Furniture sold	20,000
	20,000
∴ Depreciation on A 5,000 @ 10% for one year	500
Depreciation on A 15,000 @ 15% for 6 months	750
	1,250

Balance Sheet
as on 31st December, 2000

Liabilities		*(A)*	*Assets*		*(A)*
Creditors for supplies		6,000	Building	2,50,000	
General Fund	4,00,000		*Less :* Depreciation	12,500	2,37,500
Add : Surplus	1,13,250	5,13,250	Furniture		
Donation for Library Books		25,000	(A 40,000 – A 20,000)	20,000	
Outstanding Salaries		12,000	*Less :* Depreciation	1,250	18,750
			Library Books	60,000	
			Less : Depreciation	9,000	51,000

		Investments	2,00,000
		Accrued Interest	18,000
		Cash at Bank	20,000
		Cash in hand	1,000
		Outstanding Fees	10,000
	5,56,250		5,56,250

Exmaple 9

Delhi Sports Club gives you the following information :

Income and Expenditure A/c
for the year ended 31st December, 2000

Expenditure	*(A)*	*Income*		*(A)*
To Coach Remuneration	9,000	By Subscription		50,000
To Staff Salaries	12,000	By Bar Receipts	12,000	
To Ground Rent	6,000	*Less:* Exp.	10,000	2,000
To Repairs	6,500	By Rent of Hall		6,000
To Sundry Expenses	3,500	By Sale of used kits		2,000
To Ground Maintenance	9,000			
To Depreciation on Furniture	1,500			
To Surplus	12,500			
	60,000			60,000

Balance Sheet as on 31.12.1999

Liabilities	*(A)*	*Assets*	*(A)*
Capital Fund	44,000	Furniture	21,000
Subscription received in advance	4,000	Subscription in Arrear	6,000
Sundry Expenses o/s	1,500	Cash in hand	5,000
Staff Salaries o/s	2,000	Fixed Deposits	22,500
Ground Rent o/s	3,000		
	54,500		54,500

Balance Sheet as on 31.12.2000

Liabilities	*(A)*	*Assets*	*(A)*
Capital Fund	62,500	Furniture	19,500
Subscription received in advance	3,000	Subscription in Arrear	8,000
Sundry Expenses o/s	1,000	Cash in hand	4,000
Staff Salaries o/s	3,000	Fixed Deposit	30,000
Ground Rent o/s	2,000	Cash at Bank	10,000
	71,500		71,500

Increase in capital fund was due to receipt of entrance fees of Rs. 6,000 in the year ended 31st December 2,000. Prepare Receipts and Payments Account of Delhi Sports Club for the year ended 31st December, 2000.

[*B.Com.(Hons.), Delhi University, 2005*]

Solution

Receipts and Payments Account of Delhi Sports Club
for the year ended 31st December, 2000

Expenditure	*(A)*	*Income*		*(A)*
To cash in hand on 1st Jan. 2000	5,000	By Coach Remuneration		9,000
To Subscription*[1]	47,000	By Staff Salaries*[2]		11,000
To Bar/Receipts	12,000	By Ground Rent*[3]		7,000
To Rent of Hall	6,000	By Repairs		6,500
To Sale of used kits	2,000	By Sundry Expenses*[4]		4,000
To Entrance Fees	6,000	By Ground Maintenance		9,000
		By Bar Expenses		10,000
		By Fixed Deposits		7,500
		By Balancs c/d :		
		Cash	4,000	
		Bank	10,000	14,000
	78,000			78,000

Working Notes

*[1] **Subscription received :**

		(A)
Income on account of subscription		50,000
Add : Subscription in Arrear 31.12.1999		6,000
Subscription received in Advance 31.12.2000		3,000
		59,000
Less : Subscription in Arrear 31.12.2000	8,000	
Subscription received in Advance 31.12.1999	4,000	12,000
		47,000

*[2] **Staff Salaries paid :**

	(A)
Year's expenditure on staff salaries	12,000
Add : Staff Salaries outstanding 31.12.1999	2,000
	14,000
Less : Staff Salaries outstanding 31.12.2000	3,000
	11,000

*[3] **Ground Rent :**

	(A)
Year's expenditure on Ground Rent	6,000
Add : Ground Rent outstanding 31.12.1999	3,000
	9,000
Less : Ground Rent outstanding 31.12.2000	2,000
	7,000

*[4] **Sundry Expenses Paid :**

	(A)
Year's expenditure on Sundry Expenses	3,500
Add : Sundry Expenses outstanding 31.12.1999	1,500
	5,000
Less : Sundry Expenses outstanding 31.12.2000	1,000
	4,000

Exmaple 10

Following is the Income and Expenditure A/c of C.P. Club for the year ending 31st March, 2005 :

Expenditure	*(A)*	*Income*	*(A)*
To Salaries	77,750	By Subscription	2,25,000
To Stationary	6,250	By Donations	37,500
To Postage	4,000	By Govt. Grant	25,000
To Sundry Expenses	23,500	By Int. on Fixed Deposit	4,000
To Repairs	18,000		
To Sports Expenses	9,000		
To Pool Expenses	10,000		
To Affiliation Fee	2,500		
To Electricity	16,250		
To Billiard Room Expenses	6,250		
To Magazines	7,000		
To Audit fee	1,250		
To Depreciation on :			
Equipment	5,000		
Building	12,500		
Furniture	2,250		
To Surplus	90,000		
	2,91,500		2,91,500

The above account is prepared after considering the information given below :

	As at 1.4.04 *(A)*	*As at 31.3.05* *(A)*
Building	5,00,000	5,50,000
Sports Ground	5,00,000	5,00,000
Sports Equipment	30,000	45,000
Furniture	25,000	30,000
10% Fixed Deposit	40,000	40,000
Savings Bank Account	—	1,25,000
Subscription due	25,000	10,000
Subscription received in advance	15,000	5,000
Audit fee due	1,000	1,250
Affiliation fee paid in advance	–	1,250
Cash in hand	6,250	?

You are required to prepare :

(*i*) Receipts and Payments A/c for the year ending March 31, 2005; and

(*ii*) Balance Sheet as at 31.3.05.

Show all workings [*B.Com. (Hons.), Delhi University, 2006*]

Solution

Receipts and Payments Account
for the Year ending March 31, 2005

Receipts		(A)	*Payments*		(A)
To Balance b/d		6,250	By Salaries		77,750
To Subscription	2,25,000		By Stationery		6,250
Add : Outstanding (2004)	25,000		By Postage		4,000
	2,50,000		By Sundry Expenses		23,500
Less : Outstanding (2005)	10,000		By Repairs		18,000
	2,40,000		By Sports Expenses		9,000
Add : Received in Advance			By Pool Expenses		10,000
(2005)	5,000		By Affiliation fee	2,500	
	2,45,000		*Addl.* Advance (2005)	1,250	3,750
Less : Received in Advance			By Electricity Charges		16,250
(2004)	15,000	2,30,000	By Billiard Room Expenses		6,250
To Donations		37,500	By Magazines		7,000
To Government Grant		25,000	By Audit fee	1,250	
To Interest on Fixed Deposit		4,000	*Add :* Outstanding (2004)	1,000	
To Balance c/d (Bal. Figure)		94,750		2,250	
			Less : Outstanding (2005)	1,250	1,000
			By Equipment purchased :		
			[45,000 + 5,000 – 30,000]		20,000
			By Building		
			[5,50,000 + 12,500 – 5,00,000]		62,500
			By Furniture		
			[30,000 + 2,250 – 25,000]		7,250
			By Deposit in Savings Bank		1,25,000
		3,97,500			3,97,500

Balance Sheet
as at 31st March, 2004

Liabilities	(A)	*Assets*	(A)
Subscription received in advance	15,000	Buildings	5,00,000
Audit fee outstanding	1,000	Sports Ground	5,00,000
Capital Fund (Bal. Figure)	11,10,250	Sports Equipment	30,000
		Furniture	25,000
		10% Fixed Deposit	40,000
		Subscription Due	25,000
		Cash in hand	6,250
	11,26,250		11,26,250

Balance Sheet
as on 31st March, 2005

Liabilities		*(A)*	*Assets*	*(A)*
Subscription Received in Advance		5,000	Subscription Due	10,000
Audit fee due		1,250	Sports Equipment	45,000
Bank Overdraft		94,750	Buildings	5,50,000
Capital Fund	11,10,250		Furniture	30,000
Add : Surplus	90,000	12,00,250	Sports Ground	5,00,000
			Fixed Deposit	40,000
			Savings Bank Account	1,25,000
			Affiliation fee paid in Advance	1,250
		13,01,250		13,01,250

Exmaple 11

A club gives you the following Receipts and Payments Account for the year ended 31st March, 2006 :

Receipts and Payments Account

Receipts	*(A)*	*Payments*	*(A)*
To Balance b/d	4,820	By Salaries	12,000
To Subscriptions	28,600	By Rent	6,000
To Miscellaneous income	700	By Electricity	1,220
To Interest on fixed depisit	2,000	By Liberary books	1,000
		By Magazine and Newspapers	2,170
		By Sundry Expenses	10,280
		By Sports Equipment	1,000
		By Balance c/d	2,450
	36,120		36,120

Additional Information :

	31.3.2005 *(A)*	*31.3.2006* *(A)*
Outstanding salaries	710	170
Outstanding for electricity bill	864	973
Fixed deposit with bank at 10%	20,000	20,000
Outstanding for magazines and newspapers	226	340
Interest accrued on fixed deposit	500	500
Subscription receivable	1,263	1,575
Prepaid sundry expenses	417	620
Furniture	9,600	?
Sports equipment	7,200	?
Library books	5,000	5,250

Charge depreciation on furniture and sports equipments at 10% and 20% per annum respectively inclusive of additions. The library books are revaluated at the end of every year and the value at the end of 31st March, 2006 as stated above was A 5,250.

You are required to prepare the Income and Expenditure Account for the year ended 31st March, 2006 and the Balance Sheet as at that date. *[B.Com (Hons.), Delhi University, 2006]*

Solution

Income and Expenditure A/c
for the Year ending March 31, 2005

Expenditure		*(A)*	*Income*		*(A)*
To salaries	12,000		By Subscriptions	28,600	
Add : Outstanding (06)	170		*Add :* Outstanding on 31.3.06	1,575	
	12,170			30,175	
Less : Outstanding (05)	710	11,460	*Less :* Outstanding on 31.2.05	1,263	28,912
To Rent		6,000	By Miscellaneous Income		700
To Electricity	1,220		By Interest on Fixed Deposit	2,000	
Add : Oustanding (06)	973		*Add :* Accrued (06)	500	
	2,193			2,500	
Less : Outstanding (05)	864	1,329	*Less :* Accrued (05)	500	2,000
To Magazines and Newspapers	2,170		By Deficit		2,888
Add : Outstanding (06)	340				
	2,510				
Less : Outstanding (05)	226	2,284			
To Sundry Expenses	10,280				
Add : Prepaid (05)	417				
	10,697				
Less : Prepaid (06)	620	10,077			
To Depreciation on:					
Library books					
[5,000 + 1,000 – 5,250]		750			
Sports Equipment					
[20% of Rs. 8,200]		1,640			
Furniture [10% of A 9,600]		960			
		34,500			34,500

Balance Sheet
as at 31st March, 2006

Liabilities		*(A)*	*Assets*		*(A)*
Outstanding Salaries		170	Cash in Hand		2,450
Outstanding for electricity bill		973	Prepaid Expenses		620
Outstanding for magazines			Subscription Receivable		1,575
and newspapers		340	Fixed Deposit		20,000
Capital Fund*[1]	47,000		Interest Receivable		500
Less : Deficit	2,888	44,112	Furniture	9,600	
			Less : Depreciation	960	8,640
			Sports Equipment [7,200+1,000]	8,200	
			Less : Depreciation	1,640	6,560
			Library Books [5,000+1,000–750]		5,250
		45,595			45,595

Working Notes

*1

Balance Sheet
As at 31st March, 2005

Liabilities	*(A)*	*Assets*	*(A)*
Outstanding salaries	710	Cash in Hand	4,820
Outstanding for electricity Bill	864	Accrued Bank Interest	500
Outstanding for magazines & newspapers	226	Subscription Receivable	1,263
Capital Fund (Bal. Figures)	47,000	Fixed Deposit with Bank	20,000
		Prepaid Expenses	417
		Furniture	9,600
		Sports Equipment	7,200
		Library books	5,000
	48,800		48,800

Exmaple 12

The following balances are obtained from the books of Kanpur Cricket Club :

Items	*31.3.2006* (A)	*31.3.2007* (A)
Building	80,000	85,500
Furniture	40,000	30,600
Advance subscription	1,500	1,000
Arrears of subscription	3,000	5,000
Prepaid Expenses	800	1,000
Outstanding expenses	3,000	1,200
Sports equipment	24,000	21,600
Investments	—	12,000
Books	15,000	16,200
Cash	16,000	17,100

Consider the following information relevant to the year 2006–07 :

(*i*) Depreciation provided for the year :

Building A 4,500; Furniture A 3,400; Sports equipment A 5,400; Books A 1,800.

(*ii*) Some old furniture standing in the books for A 6,000 on 1st April, 2006 was sold for A 4,000 on the same date.

(*iii*) The club had 310 members on 31st March, 2006 as per the Register of Members. No fresh members were admitted during the year but 10 members left the club on 1st October, 2006.

(*iv*) Subscription payable A 15 per month.

(*v*) Donation received A 5,000 has been capitalised.

(*vi*) Considerable expenses were paid during the year.

Required : Show the Receipts and Payment Account, the Income and Expenditure Account for the year ended 31st March, 2007 and Balance Sheet as at 31st March, 2007.

[B.Com. (Hons.), Delhi University, 2007]

Solution

Kanpur Cricket Club.
Receipts and Payments Account
for the year ended 31st March, 2007

Particulars	*(A)*	*Parciculars*	*(A)*
To Balance b/d	16,000	By Building*3	10,000
To Sale of Furniture*3	4,000	By Sports Equipment*4	3,000
To subscription*1	52,400	By Books*5	3,000
To Donations	5,000	By Investment*6	12,000
		By Expenses (Bal. Fig.)	32,300
		By Balance c/d	17,100
	77,400		77,400

Income and Expenditure Account
for the year ended 31st March, 2007

Particulars		*(A)*	*Parciculars*	*(A)*
To Expenses*7		30,300	By Subscription*1	54,900
To Loss on sale of furniture [A 6,000 – A 4,000]		2,000		
To Depreciation on:				
Building	4,500			
Furniture	3,400			
Sports Equipment	5,400			
Books	1,800	15,100		
To Excess of Income over Expenditure (Surplus)		7,500		
		54,900		54,900

Balance Sheet of Kanpur Cricket Club
as on 31st March, 2007

Liabilities		*(A)*	*Assets*	*(A)*
Capital fund :			Building	85,500
Opening Balance*7	1,74,300		Furniture	30,600
Add : Surplus	7,500		Sports Equipment	21,600
Donation	5,000	1,86,800	Books	16,200
Advance Subscription		1,000	Investment	12,000
Outstanding Expenses		1,200	Arrears of Subscription	5,000
			Prepaid Expenses	1,000
			Cash	17,100
		1,89,000		1,89,000

Working Notes

*1 **Calculation of Susbcription due and received.**

There were 310 members as on 31.3.2006 and 10 members left the club on 1.10.2006. Therefore, the number of members at the end of the year *i.e.,* 31.3.07 will be 310 – 10 = 300.

Total amount of subscription for the year 2006-07 is as under :	(A)
300 members @ A 15 per month for the whole year [300 × A 15 × 12]	= 54,000
10 members @ A 15 per month for 6 months [10 × A 15 × 6]	= 900
	54,900

Subscription received can be ascertained by preparing the Subscription Account as under :

Subscription Account

Particulars	*(A)*	*Particulars*	*(A)*
To Outstanding Subscription (Opening Balance)	3,000	By Advace Subscription (Opening Balance)	1,500
To Income and expenditure A/c (as above)	54,900	By Receipts and Payment A/c (Bal. Fig.)	52,400
to Advance Subscription (Closing Balance)	1,000	By Outstanding Subscription (Closing Bal.)	5,000
	58,900		58,900

*2

Building Account

Particulars	*(A)*	*Particulars*	*(A)*
To Balance b/d.	80,000	By Depreciation A/c	4,500
To Bank A/c (Purchase (Balance Fig.)	10,000	By Balance c/d	85,500
	90,000		90,000

*3

Furniture Account

Particulars	*(A)*	*Particulars*	*(A)*
To Balance b/d	40,000	By Bank A/c (Sale)	4,000
		By Income & Expenditure A/c (Loss)	2,000
		By Depreciation	3,400
		By Balance c/d	30,600
	40,000		40,000

*4

Sports Equipment Account

Particulars	*(A)*	*Particulars*	*(A)*
To Balance b/d	24,000	By Depreciation A/c	5,400
To Bank A/c (Purchase (Balance Fig.)	3,000	By Balance c/d	21,600
	27,000		27,000

*5

Books Account

Particulars	*(A)*	*Particulars*	*(A)*
To Balance b/d	15,000	By Depreciation A/c	1,800
To Bank A/c (Purchase) Balance Fig.)	3,000	By Balance c/d	16,200
	18,000		18,000

*6

Investment Account

Particulars	*(A)*	*Particulars*	*(A)*
To Bank A/c	12,000	By Balance c/d	12,000
	12,000		12,000

*7

Expenses Account

Particulars	(A)	*Particulars*	(A)
To Prepaid Expenses (Opening)	800	By Outstanding Expenses (Opening)	3,000
To Receipts and Payments A/c (Balance of Receipts & Payments A/c)	32,300	By Income and Expenditure A/c (*Balancing Figure*)	30,300
To Outstanding Expenses (Closing)	1,200	By Prepaid Expenses (Closing)	1,000
	34,300		34,300

*8

Balance Sheet of Kanpur Cricket Club as at 1.4.2006

Liabilities	(A)	*Assets*	(A)
Subscription Received in Advance	1,500	Building	80,000
Outstanding Expenses	3,000	Furniture	40,000
Capital Fund (Balance Figure)	1,74,300	Sports Equipment	24,000
		Books	15,000
		Arrears of Subscription	3,000
		Cash	16,000
		Prepaid Expenses	800
	1,78,800		1,78,000

Exmaple 13

The following is the Receipts and Payments Account of a Sports Club for the year ended 31st December, 2008.

Receipts	(A)	*Payments*	(A)
To Balance b/d	7,500	By Salaries	14,000
To Subscriptions (including A 2,000 for the year 2007)	40,000	By Match Expenses	28,000
		By 12% Investment on 1.1.2008	40,000
To Donations	15,000	By Sports Materials	15,000
To Life Membership Fees	35,000	By Printing & Stationery	12,000
To Sale of Furniture at book value	5,000	By Honorarium	5,000
To Entrance Fees	10,000	By Furniture	15,000
To Interest on 10% Investments for full year	20,000	By Magazines & Journals	10,000
		By Books	35,000
To Match Fund	40,000	By Municipal Taxes	6,000
To Donation for Building Fund	45,000	By Balance c/d	40,000
To Sale of Newspapers	2,500		
	2,20,000		2,20,000

Additional Information :

(*i*) The position of the Club on Jauary 1, 2008 was as follows :

	(A)
Subscriptions due	3,000
Furniture	10,000
Books	20,000
Building	1,25,000
Stock of Sport Materials	4,500
Creditors for Printing	2,500

(*ii*) The Club has 1,000 members each paying an annual subscription of A 50. 20 members paid their subscription in advance in 2007. In the year 2008, subscription was received in advance from 15 members.

(*iii*) Municipal Taxes are paid every year on 1st April.

(*iv*) One member donated a Billiard Table worth A 50,000.

(*v*) Books were worth A 46,000 on 31st December, 2008 and stock of sports materials on that date amounted to A 4,000.

(*vi*) 12% investments include Rs. 30,000 invested from donations received for building fund.

Prepare Income and Expenditure Account for the year ended 31st December 2008 and a Balance Sheet as on that date. [*B.Com.(Hons.), Delhi University, 2009*]

Solution

Income and Expenditure Account
for the year ended 31st December, 2008

Expenditure		*(A)*	*Income*			*(A)*
To Salaries		14,000	By Susbcriptions		40,000	
To Sports Materials :			*Add :* Advance Received			
Opening Stock	4,500		(2007)	1,000		
Add : Purchases	15,000		Outstanding (2008)	11,750*[1]	12,750	
	19,500				52,750	
Less : Closing Stock	4,000	15,500	*Less :* Outstanding (2007)	2000		
To Printing & Stationery	12,000		Received in Advance (2008)	750	2,750	50,000
Less : Outstanding for 2007	2,500	9,500	By Donations			15,000
To Honorarium		5,000	By Interest on 10% Investments			20,000
To Magazines and Journals		10,000	By Sale of Newspapers (Old)			2,500
To Depreciation on Books [20,000 + 35,000 – 46,000]		9,000	By Accrued Interest on 12% Investment [10,000 × 12/100]*[2]			1,200
To Municipal Taxes	6,000					
Add : Prepaid (2007)	1,500					
	7,500					
Less : Prepaid (2008)	1,500	6,000				
To Surplus (*i.e.*, excess of Income over Expenditure)		19,700				
		88,700				88,700

Balance Sheet as on 31st December, 2008

Liabilities		*(A)*	*Assets*		*(A)*
Subscriptions Received in Advance		750	Building		1,25,000
Match Fund	40,000		Furniture	10,000	
Less : Match Expenses	28,000	12,000	Addition	15,000	
Donation for Billard Table		50,000		25,000	
Donation for Building Fund	45,000		*Less :* Sold	5,000	20,000
Add: Accrued Interest [30,000 × 12/100]	3,600	48,600	Books (20,000 + 35,000 – 9,000)		46,000
			Stock of Sports Materials		4,000

Capital Fund*3	3,68,000		10% Investments		2,00,000
Add : Surplus	19,700		12% Investments		40,000
Life Membership Fees	35,000		Accrued Interest on 12% Investments		4,800
Entrance Fees	10,000	4,32,700	Billiard Table		50,000
			Prepaid Municipal Taxes		1,500
			Subscriptions Outstanding		
			2007 (3000 – 2000)	1,000	
			2008	11,750	12,750
			Cash in hand		40,000
		5,44,050			5,44,050

Working Notes

*1

Subscription Account (2008)

Particulars	(A)	Particulars	(A)
To Subscriptions Due A/c	3,000	By Subscriptions Received in Advance A/c (20 × 50), 2007	1,000
To Income & Expenditure A/c (1000 × 50)	50,000	By Receipts & Paymets A/c	40,000
To Subscriptions Received in Advance (50 × 15)*2 for 2008	750	By Subscriptions Due : 2007 (3,000 – 2,000)	1,000
		2008 (Balancing Figure)	11,750
	53,750		53,750

*2

12% Investment on 1.1.2008 : A 40,000

[Includes A 30,000 invested from donations received for building, so interest of this (30,000 × 12/100 = A 3,600) should be credited to Building Fund]

[Remaining Investment (A 40,000 – 30,000 = A 10,000) is general investment, so interest on 12% investment (10,000 × 12/100 = A 1,200) is treated as income and credited to Income and Expenditure A/c]

*3

Balance Sheet as on 31st December, 2007

Liabilities	(A)	Assets	(A)
Creditors for Printing	2,500	Cash in Hand	7,500
Subscriptions Received in Advance (20 × 50)	1,000	Prepaid Municipal Taxes	1,500
		Subscriptions Outstanding	3,000
Capital Fund (Balancing Figure)	3,68,000	Furniture	10,000
		Books	20,000
		Building	1,25,000
		10% Investments (A 20,000 × 100/10)	2,00,000
		Stock of Sports Material	4,500
	3,71,500		3,71,500

Exmaple 14

From the following Income and Expenditure Account of Mayur Club for the year ended 31st December, 2009, prepare Receipts and Payments Account for the year ended 31st December, 2009 and a Balance Sheet as on that date.

Income and Expenditure Account
for the year ended 31.12.2009

Expenditure	*(A)*	*Income*	*(A)*
To Salaries	48,000	By Subscriptions	1,56,000
To Stationery	3,200	By Donations	16,000
To Postage & Telephone	6,400	By Billiard Room Collections	14,000
To Rates and Taxes	12,000	By Entrance Fees	24,000
To Repairs	16,000	By Interest from Investments	5,400
To Table Tennis Balls	2,400		
To Printing of Magazines	4,000		
To Electricity Charges	12,000		
To Billiard Room Expenses	6,000		
To Upkeep of Ground	18,800		
To Depreciation on Assets	4,000		
To Excess of Income over Expenditure	82,600		
	2,15,400		2,15,400

Additional Information :

	As on 1.1.2009 *(A)*	*31.12.2009* *(A)*
Fixed Assets	96,000	64,000
Investments	54,000	94,000
Cash at Bank	3,600	?
Subscriptions Outstanding	6,000	10,000
Subscriptions received in advance	12,000	20,000
Expenses Outstanding :		
Stationery	1,200	800
Telephone	600	400
Electricity	1,400	600

[*B.Com.(Hons.), Delhi University, 2010*]

Solution

Receipts and Payments Account
for the year ended 31st December, 2009

Receipts			*(A)*	*Payments*		*(A)*
To Balance b/d				By Salaries		48,000
Cash at Bank			3,600	By Stationery	3,200	
To Subscriptions		1,56,000		*Add :* Outstanding ('08)	1,200	
Add : Subscriptions					4,400	
Outstanding ('08)	6,000			*Less :* Outstanding ('09)	800	3,600
Subscription recd. in				By Postage & Telephone	6,400	
advance ('09)	20,000	26,000		*Add :* Outstanding ('08)	600	
		1,82,000			7,000	

Less : Subscriptions				*Less :* Outstanding ('09)	400	6,600
Outstanding ('09)	10,000			By Rates & Taxes		12,000
Subscription recd. in				By Repairs		16,000
advance ('09)	12,000	22,000	1,60,000	By Table Tennis Balls		2,400
To Donations			16,000	By Printing of Magazines		4,000
				By Electricity Charges	12,000	
To Billiard Room Collections			14,000	*Add :* Outstanding ('08)	1,400	
To Entrance Fees			24,000		13,400	
To Interest from Investments			5,400	*Less :* Outstanding ('09)	600	12,800
To Sale of Fixed Assets*2			28,000	*b/f*		1,05,400
				By Billiard Room Expenses		6,000
				By Upkeep of Ground		18,800
				By Investments		40,000
				By Balance c/d : Cash at Bank		80,000
			2,51,000			2,51,000

Balance Sheet as on 31st December 2009

Liabilities		*(A)*	*Assets*		*(A)*
Capital Fund*1	1,44,400		Fixed Assets		64,000
Add: Surplus	82,600	2,27,000	Investments	54,000	
Subscription received in advance		20,000	*Add :* Addition	40,000	94,000
Creditors for Stationery		800	Cash at Bank		80,800
Telephone Bill Outstanding		400	Subscriptions Outstanding		10,000
Electricity Bill Outstanding		600			
		2,48,800			2,48,800

Working Notes

*1 **Calculation of Capital Fund as on 1.1.2009 :**

Balance Sheet as at 1.1.09

Liabilities		*(A)*	*Assets*	*(A)*
Susbcriptions received in advance		12,000	Fixed Assets	96,000
Expenses Outstanding :			Investments	54,000
Stationery	1,200		Cash at Bank	3,600
Telephone	600		Subscriptions Outstanding	6,000
Electricity	1,400	3,200		
Capital Fund (Bal. Figure)		1,44,400		
		1,59,600		1,59,600

*2

Fixed Assets Account

Particulars	*(A)*	*Particulars*	*(A)*
To Balance b/d	96,000	By Depreciation A/c	4,000
		By Bank A/c (Sale) (Bal. Figure)	28,000
		By Balance c/d	64,000
	96,000		96,000

Exmaple 15

The following particulars relate to Ganeev Sports Club :

Income and Exnpenditure Account
for the year ending on 31st March, 2011

Expenditure	*(A)*	*Income*	*(A)*
To Secretary's Salary	15,000	By Entrance Fees	1,05,000
To Printing and Stationery	22,000	By Subscriptions	1,56,000
To Advertising	16,000	By Rent	28,000
To Audit Fees	5,000	By Interest on Investments	12,000
To Fire Insurance	10,000		
To Depreciation :			
Sports Equipments	90,000		
Furniture	5,000		
To Surplus	1,38,000		
	3,01,000		3,01,000

Receipts and Payments Account
for the year ending on 31st March, 2011

Receipts	*(A)*	*Payments*	*(A)*
To Balance b/d.	42,000	By Secretary's Salary	10,000
To Entrance Fee		By Printing and Stationery	26,000
2010	10,000	By Advertising	16,000
2011	1,00,000	By Fire Insurance	12,000
To Subscriptions :		By 12% Investments	
2010	6,000	(purchased on 1.10.2011)	2,00,000
2011	1,50,000	By Furniture	20,000
2012	4,000	By Balance c/d	58,000
To Rent received	24,000		
To Interest received	6,000		
	3,42,000		3,42,000

The assets as on 31st March, 2010 included Club Grounds and Pavilion A 4,40,000, Sports Equipments A 2,50,000 and Furniture and Fixtures A 40,000. Subscriptions in arears on that date were A 8,000. Subscriptions received in advance on that date were A 2,000. Creditors for Printing and Stationery on that date were A 5,000. Prepare the Balance Sheet as on 31.3.2010 and 31.3.2011. [*B.Com. (Hons.), Delhi University, Nov. 2011*]

Solution

Balance Sheet as on 31st March, 2010

Liabilities	*(A)*	*Assets*	*(A)*
Advance Subscription	2,000	Cash in hand	42,000
Creditors (Stationery & Printing)	5,000	Subscriptions outstanding	8,000
Capital (Balancing Figure)	7,83,000	Entrance fees Outstanding	10,000
		Furniture & Fixtures	40,000
		Sports Equipment	2,50,000
		Grounds & Pavilion	4,40,000
	7,90,000		7,90,000

Balance Sheet as on 31st March, 2011

Liabilities		*(A)*	*Assets*		*(A)*
Capital	7,83,000		Cash		58,000
Add : Net Profit	1,38,000		O/s Subscriptions :		
		9,21,000	2009-10	2000	
Advance Subscription		4,000	2010-11	4000	6,000
O/s Secretary Salary		5,000	Entrance fees o/s		
Creditors (Printing & Stationery)		1,000	(1,05,000 – 1,00,000)		5,000
O/s. Audit fees		5,000	Accrued Rent(28,000 – 24,000)		4,000
			Prepaid Fire insurance		
			(12,000 – 10,000)		2,000
			Investment		2,00,000
			Sports equipment	2,50,000	
			Less : Depreciation	90,000	1,60,000
			Furniture & Fixtures		55,000
			(40,000 + 20,000 – 5,000)		
			Ground Pavilion		4,40,000
			Accrued Interest		6,000
		9,36,000			9,36,000

Example 16

A summary of Receipts and Payments of Medical Aid Society for the year ended 31.12.2008 is given below :

Particulars	*(A)*	*Particulars*	*(A)*
To Balance (1.1.2008)	70,000	By Payment for Medicines	3,00,000
To Subscriptions	5,00,000	By Honorarium to doctors	1,00,000
To Donations	1,45,000	By Salaries	2,75,000
To Interest on Investments		By Sundry Expenses	5,000
@ 7% p.a.	70,000	By Equipment Purchased	1,50,000
To Charity show proceeds	1,00,000	By Charity show expenses	10,000
		By Balance (31.12.2008)	45,000
	8,85,000		8,85,000

Additions Information

	Amount in A	
	01.1.2008	***31.12.2008***
Subscriptions Due	5,000	10,000
Subscriptions received in advance	10,000	5,000
Stock of Medicines	1,00,000	1,50,000
Amount due to Medicine Suppliers	80,000	1,20,000
Value of Equipments	2,10,000	3,00,000
Value of Buildings	4,00,000	3,80,000

You are required to prepare Income and Expenditure Account for the year ended 31st December, 2008 and the Balance Sheet as on that date.

Solution

Medical Aid Society Income and Expenditure Account for the year ended 31st December, 2008

Dr. *Cr.*

Expenditure	*(A)*	*Income*	*(A)*
To Medicine Consumed (Note 4)	2,90,000	By Subscription (Note 2)	5,10,000
To Honorarium to Doctors	1,00,000	By Interest on Investment	70,000
To Salaries	2,75,000	By Charity Show Proceeds	1,00,000
To Sundry Expenses	5,000	By Deficit *i.e.,* Excess of	
To Charity Show Expenses	10,000	Expenditure over	
To Depreciation on :		Income	80,000
Equipment (Note 6)	60,000		
Building (4,00,000 – 3,80,000)	20,000		
	7,60,000		7,60,000

Balance Sheet *as at 31st December 2008*

Liabilities		*(A)*	*Assets*		*(A)*
Subscription Received			Cash at Bank		45,000
in Advance		5,000	Subscription Due		10,000
			Stock of Medicines		1,50,000
Creditors for medicines		1,20,000	Investments		10,00,000
			Buildings	4,00,000	
Capital Fund (Note 1)	16,95,000		*Less* : Depreciation	20,000	3,80,000
Add : Donations	1,45,000		Equipments	2,10,000	
	18,40,000		*Add* : Purchased	1,50,000	
Less : Deficit	80,000	17,60,000		3,60,000	3,00,000
			Less : Dep. (Note 6)	60,000	
		18,85,000			18,85,000

Working Note

(*i*) Calculation of Capital Fund :

Balance Sheet *as at 1st Jan 2008*

Liabilities	*(A)*	*Assets*	*(A)*
Subscription received in Advance	10,000	Cash at bank	70,000
Creditors for Medicines	80,000	Subscription Due	5,000
(Amount due to Medicine Suppliers)		Stock of Medicines	1,00,000
		Equipment	2,10,000
Capital Fund (Bal. Fig.)	16,95,000	Building	4,00,000
		Investments (Note 5)	10,00,000
	17,85,000		17,85,000

(*ii*) *Subscription Income for 2008* *A*

(*ii*)	Subscription received during the year		5,00,000
	Add : Subscription Due (31.12.08)	10,000	
	Subscription Received in Advance (01.1.08)	10,000	20,000
			5,20,000
	Less : Subscription Due (01.1.08)	5,000	
	Subscription Received in Advance (31.12.08)	5,000	10,000
	Subscription Income for 2008		5,10,000

(*iii*) Creditors for Medicines A/c

Dr. *Cr.*

Date	*Particulars*	*L.F.*	*Amount (A)*	*Date*	*Particulars*	*L.F.*	*Amount (A)*
2012				**2012**			
	To Bank A/c (Payment)		3,00,000	01.1.08	By Balance b/d		80,000
					By Purchase of		
31.12.08	To Balance c/d		1,20,000		Medicines (Bal. Fig.)		3,40,000
			4,20,000				4,20,000

(*iv*) **Medicines Consumed during 2008**

= Opening Stock + Purchases – Closing Stock

= A 1,00,000 + A 3,40,000 (Note 3) – A A 1,50,000

= A 2,90,000

(*v*) Interest on investment received A 70,000 in 2008 indicates that there were investments at the beginning of 2008. The rate of interest is 7%. So, the value of investment = 100/7 × A 70,000 = A 10,00,000

(*vi*) **Equipment A/c**

Particulars	*(A)*	*Particulars*	*(A)*
To Balance b/d	2,10,000	By Income and Expenditure A/c	
To Bank A/c (Purchased)	1,50,000	(Depreciation)	60,000
		By Balance c/d	3,00,000
		(Bal. Fig.)	
	3,60,000		3,60,000

Example 17

Given below is the Receipts and Payments Account of ABC Club :

Receipts and Payments A/c
for the year ended 31st December, 2008

Particulars		*(A)*	*Particulars*	*(A)*
Balance			Salary of Secretary	3,600
Cash	60		Honorarium	450
Bank	3,000	3,060	Wages	2,400

Subscription (including subscription for 2007 A 1,050)	9,000	Charities	2,000
		Printing and Stationery	300
		Postage	100
Sale of old furniture on 1st Jan, 2008	750	Rent and Taxes	1,200
		Upkeep of Land	500
Sale of Old Newspaper	50	Sports Material	2,500
Legacies	3,000	Balance c/d	14,850
Interest on Investment (Cost A 20,000)	1,200		
Endowment Fund	10,000		
Proceeds of concerts	800		
Advertisement	40		
	27,900		27,900

Assets and Liabilities as on 31st Dec., 2007 and 31st December, 2008 are as follows :

	31.12.2007	***31.12.2008***
Subscription in Arrear	200	450
Subscription in advance	300	600
Furniture	2,000	1,080

Depreciation was 10% p.a.,, on the furniture left after selling a part of it. It was decided that half of legacies may be capitalised.

Prepare Income and Expenditure account for the year ending 31st December, 2008 and Balance Sheet as on that date.

Solution

Income and Expenditure A/c
for the year ending 31st December, 2008

Dr. *Cr.*

Expenditure	*(A)*	*Income*		*(A)*
To Salary	3,600	By Subscriptions	9,000	
To Honorarium	450	*Less* : for 2007	150	
To Wages	2,400		8,850	
To Charities	2,000	*Less* : Received in advance in 2008	600	
To Printing and Stationery	300			
To Postage	100		8,250	
To Rent and Taxes	1,200	*Add* : Received in Advance in 2007	300	
To Upkeep of Land	500			
To Depreciation on : Furniture (Note 1)	120		8,550	
To Loss on Sale of Furniture (Note 1)	50	*Add* : Outstanding for 2008	450	9,000
		By Sale of Old Newspaper		50
To Sports materials	2,500	By Interest on Investment		1,200
		By Legacies	3,000	

		Less : Capitalised	1,500	1,500
		By Proceeds of concerts		800
		By Advertisement		40
		By Excess of Expenditure over Income		630
.	13,220			13,200

Balance Sheet
as at 31st December, 2008

Liabilities		*(A)*	*Assets*		*(A)*
Capital Fund (Note 2)	24,960		Furniture	2,000	
Less : Excess of			*Less* : Sold	800	
Expenditure over income	630			1,200	
	24,330		*Less* : Depreciation	120	1,080
Add : Legacies	1,500	25,830	Investments		20,000
Endowment Fund		10,000	Subscription Due:		
Subscription received			For 2007	50	
in Advance		600	For 2008	450	500
			Cash in Hand		14,850
		36,430			36,430

***Working Notes* :**

(*i*) *Calculation of loss on sale of furniture*

	A
Depreciated value of furniture on Dec. 31, 2008	1,080
The value before depreciation would be $= \frac{100}{90} \times$ A 1,080	1,200
The total value of Furniture on Jan.1, 2008	2,000
Less : Book value of Furniture left after sale	1,200
Cost of Furniture Sold	800
Less : Sale Price of Furniture	750
Loss on Sale of Furniture	50

(*ii*) *Calculation of Capital Fund as on Jan.1, 2008*

Balance Sheet *as at January 1, 2008*

Dr. *Cr.*

Liabilities	*(A)*	*Assets*	*(A)*
Subscription Received in Advance	300	Cash in Hand	60
Capital Fund		Cash at Bank	3,000
(Bal. Figure)	24,960	Subscription in arrear	200
		Furniture	2,000
		Investments	20,000
	25,260		25,260

Example 18

How will you deal with the following cases while preparing final accounts of Sports Club as on 31st December 2007?

(*i*) Extract of Trial Balances as on 31st December, 2007

Particulars	*Debit (A)*	*Credit (A)*
Match Fund	–	20,000
Match Fund Investment	18,000	–
Match Fund Bank Balance	875	–
Match Fund Investment Interest	–	720
Match Expenses	1,250	–

(*ii*) Balance Sheet as on 1st January, 2007

Liabilities	*(A)*	*Assets*	*(A)*
Creditors for Sports Material	15,000	Sports Material	20,000

Receipts and Payments A/c
for the year ended 31st December, 2007

Receipts	*(A)*	*Payments*	*(A)*
Sports material		Sports Material	3,50,000
(Sale of old material)	9,000		

Sports material on hand on 31st December, 2007 was A 55,000.

(*iii*)

	A
Subscription received during 2007	2,50,000
Subscription outstanding on 31.12.2006	50,000
Subscription outstanding on 31.12.2007	1,00,000
Subscription received in advance on 31.12.2006	75,000
Subscription received in advance on 31.12.2007	50,000

Solution

(*i*) Balance Sheet as on 31st December, 2007

Liabilities		*(A)*	*Assets*	*(A)*
Match Fund	20,000		Match Fund Bank Balance	875
Add : Match Fund			Match Fund Investment	18,000
Investment Interest	720			
	20,720			
Less : Match Expenses	1,250	19,470		

(ii) **Income and Expenditure A/c**
for the year ended 31st December, 2007

Dr. Cr.

Expenditure	*(A)*	*Income*	*(A)*
To Sports Material (Consumed) (Note 1 and 2)	3,00,000	By Sale of Old Sports material	9,000

Balance Sheet as on 31st December, 2007

Liabilities	*(A)*	*Assets*	*(A)*
		Sports Material	55,000

Note (*i*)

Creditors for Sports Material A/c

Dr. Cr.

Particulars	*(A)*	*Particulars*	*(A)*
To Bank A/c	3,50,000	By Balance b/d	15,000
		By Purchases A/c (Bal. Fig.)	3,35,000
	3,50,000		3,50,000

(*ii*) *Calculations of Sports Material consumed during the year* :

	A
Opening Stock of Sports material	20,000
Add : Purchases of Sports Material (Note-1)	3,35,000
	3,55,000
Less : Closing Stock of Sports Material	55,000
Sports Material consumed during the year	3,00,000

(*iii*) **Income and Expenditure A/c**
for the year ended 31st December, 2007

Expenditure	*(A)*	*Income*	*(A)*
		By Subscription (Note)	3,25,000

Balance Sheet As on 31st December, 2007

Liabilities	*(A)*	*Assets*	*(A)*
Subscription Received in advance	50,000	Subscription Outstanding	1,00,000

Note : Calculation of Subscription Income for 2007

		A
Subscription received during 2007		2,50,000
Add : Subscription in outstanding on 31.12.2007	1,00,000	
Subscription received in advance on 31.12.2006	75,000	1,75,000
		4,25,000
Less : Subscription outstanding on 31.12.2006	50,000	
Subscription received in advance on 31.12.2007	50,000	1,00,000
Subscription income for 2007, to be credited to Income and Expenditure A/c		3,25,000

Example 19

From the following information relating to Dwarka Sports Club, prepare the Balance Sheet as on 01.1.2007 and on 31.12.2007 :

(*i*) Assets on 01.1.2007 are–Club grounds and building A 5,00,000; Sports equipment A 3,00,00; Furniture A 70,000; Subscription in arrears on that date A 10,000. Creditors for stationery A 5,000.

(*ii*) Receipts and Payments Account for the year ending 31st December, 2007.

Dr. *Cr.*

Particulars	(*A*)	*Particulars*	(*A*)
Balance b/d	50,000	Printing and Stationery	30,000
Subscriptions :		Salaries	1,10,000
2006	9,000	Advertising	20,000
2007	1,80,000	Fire Insurance	15,000
2008	5,000	Furniture	20,000
Sale of old newspapers	3,000	Investments	1,80,000
Rent Received	22,000	Balance c/d	14,000
Entrance Fees	1,20,000		
	3,89,000		3,89,000

(*iii*) Income and Expenditure Account for the year ending 31st December, 2007

Dr. *Cr.*

Particulars	(*A*)	*Particulars*	(*A*)
Salaries	1,20,000	Subscriptions	1,90,000
Printing and Stationery	28,000	Entrance Fees	1,20,000
Audit Fees	5,000	Rent Received	24,000
Advertising	20,000	Sale of old newspapers	3,000
Fire Insurance	12,000		
Depreciation :			
On Sports Equipment	60,000		
On Furniture	8,000		
Excess of Income			
Over Expenditure	84,000		
	3,37,000		3,37,000

Solution

Balance Sheet as on 1.1.2007

Liabilities	(*A*)	*Assets*	(*A*)
Creditors for Stationery	5,000	Club grounds and Building	5,00,000
Capital Fund		Sports Equipment	3,00,000
(*Balancing Figure*)	9,25,000	Furniture	70,000
		Subscription in Arrears	10,000
		Cash in Hand	50,000
	9,30,000		9,30,000

Balance Sheet as on 31.12.2007

Liabilities		(A)	*Assets*		(A)
Creditors for Stationery		3,000	Club grounds and Building		5,00,000
Outstanding Salary		10,000	Sports	3,00,000	
(A 1,20,000 – A 1,00,000)			*Less* : Depreciation	60,000	2,40,000
Outstanding Audit Fees		5,000	Furniture	70,000	
Subscription Received			Addition	20,000	
in Advance (2008)		5,000		90,000	
Capital Fund	9,25,000		*Less* : Depreciation	8,000	82,000
Add : Surplus	84,000	10,09,000	Subscription in Arrears :		
			2006 (10,000 – 9,000)		1,000
			2007 (1,90,000 – 1,80,000)		10,000
			Cash in Hand		14,000
			Rent Receivable		
			(24,000 – 22,000)		2,000
			Prepaid Fire Insurance		3,000
			Investments		1,80,000
		10,32,000			10,32,000

Creditors for Stationery A/c

Dr. *Cr.*

Receipts	(A)	*Payments*	(A)
To Bank a/c	30,000	By Balance b/d	5,000
To Balance c/d	3,000	By Purchase	28,000
	33,000		33,000

Example 20

The following are Income and Expenditure Account for the year ending 31st December, 2009 and Balance Sheet as on 1st January and additional information of a club.

Income and Expenditure Account
For the year 31st December, 2009

Dr. *Cr.*

Expenditure	(A)	*Income*	(A)
To Salaries	6,000	By Subscription	11,280
To Rent	1,320	By Entrance Fee	720
To Travelling Expenses	60	By Donation	1,200
To Printing and Stationery	120	By Interest	600
To General Expenses	180		
To Equipment used	3,000		
To Surplus	3,120		
	13,800		13,800

Balance Sheet as on 1st January, 2009 :

Liabilities	*(A)*	*Assets*	*(A)*
Capital Fund	20,700	Furniture	4,000
Rent outstanding	120	Building	8,000
Salaries outstanding	780	Investment	6,000
		Sports Equip.	1,200
		Bank	1,680
		Accrued Interest	120
		Subscription Due	600
	21,600		21,600

Additional Information (Balance as on 31st December, 2009) :

Subscription receivable was	960
Salaries outstanding was	480
Rent outstanding was	240
Sports equipment was	3,000

Prepare Receipts and Payments Account for the year ending 31st Dec., 2009 and a Balance Sheet as on 31st Dec., 2009.

Solution

Receipts and Payments A/c for the Year ending 31.12.2009

Dr. *Cr.*

Receipts		*(A)*	*Payments*		*(A)*
To Bank b/d		1,680	By Salaries	6,000	
To Subscription	11,280		*Add :* O/S 2008	780	
Add : O/S 2008	600			6,780	
	11,880		*Less :* O/S 2009	480	6,300
Less : O/S 2009	960	10,920	By Rent	1,320	
To Entrance fees		720	*Add :* O/S 2008	120	
To Donation		1,200		1,440	
To Interest	600		*Less :* O/S 2009	240	1,200
Add : O/S 2008	120		By Travelling Expenses		60
		720	By Printing and Stationery		120
			By General Expenses		180
			By Sports equipment used	3,000	
			closing balance	3,000	
				6,000	
			Less : Opening Balance	1,200	4,800
			By Bank A/c c/d		2,580
		15,240			15,240

Balance Sheet as on 31.12.2009

Liabilities		(A)	*Assets*	(A)
Capital Fund	20,700		Bank	2,580
Add : Surplus	3,120	23,820	Investments	6,000
O/s Salaries		480	Building	8,000
O/s Rent		240	Furniture	4,000
			Sports equipment	3,000
			Subscription due	960
		24,540		24,540

Example 21

Summary of Receipts and Payments of Bombay Medical Aid Society for the year ended 31.12.2006 is as follows :

Opening cash balance in hand as on 01.1.2006 : A 8,000; Subscriptions A 50,000; Donation A 15,000; Interest on Investment @ 9% p.a. A 9,000; Charity show collection A 12,500. Payments for Medicine supply A 30,000; Honorarium to Doctor A 10,000; Salaries A 28,000; Sundry Expenses A 1,000; Equipment purchase A 15,000 and Charity show expenses A 1,500.

Additional Information :

	01.1.2006	31.12.2006
	(A)	(A)
Subscription due	1,500	2,200
Subscriptions received in advance	1,200	700
Stock of medicine	10,000	15,000
Amount due for Medicine Supply	9,000	13,000
Value of Equipment	21,000	30,000
Value of Building	50,000	48,000

Prepare Receipts and Payments Account and Income and Expenditure Account for the year ended on 31.12.2006. Also prepare Balance Sheet as on 31.12.2005 and 31.12.2006.

Solution

Receipts and Payments A/c of Bombay Medical Aid Society for the year ended 31st December, 2006

Dr. *Cr.*

Receipts	(A)	*Payments*	(A)
To cash in Hand (Opening)	8,000	By Medicine Supply	30,000
To Subscription	50,000	By Honorarium to Doctor	10,000
To Donations	15,000	By Salaries	28,000
To Interest on Investments	9,000	By Sundry Expenses	1,000
To Charity show collections	12,500	By Purchase of Equipment	15,000
		By Charity show Expenses	1,500
		By Cash in Hand (closing) (*Balancing Figure*)	9,000
	94,500		94,500

Income and Expenditure A/c of Bombay Medical Aid Society for the year ended 31st December, 2006

Dr.					Cr.
Expenditure		*(A)*	*Income*		*(A)*
To Medicine consumed (Notes 2 and 3)		29,000	By Subscription (Note-1)		51,200
To Honorarium to Doctor		10,000	By Donation		15,000
To Salaries		28,000	By Interest on Investments		9,000
To Sundry Expenses		1,000	By Profit on Charity show :		
To Depreciation on			Show Collection	12,500	
Equipment (Note-4)	6,000		*Less* : Show Expenses	1,500	11,000
Building (Note-5)	2,000	8,000			
To Surplus-Excess of Income over Expenditure		10,200			
		86,200			86,200

Balance Sheet of Bombay Medical Aid Society as on 31st December, 2005

Liabilities	*(A)*	*Assets*	*(A)*
Capital Fund (Bal. Fig.)	1,80,000	Building	50,000
Subscription received in advance	1,200	Equipment	21,000
Amount due for Medicine supply	9,000	Stock of Medicine	10,000
		Investments [A 9,000 × 100/9]	1,00,000
		Subscription due	1,500
		Cash in Hand	8,000
	1,90,500		1,90,500

Balance Sheet of Bombay Medical Aid Society *as on 31st December, 2006*

Liabilities		*(A)*	*Assets*		*(A)*
Capital Fund :			Building	50,000	
Opening Balance	1,80,300		*Less* : Depreciation	2,000	48,000
Add : Surplus	10,200	1,90,500	Equipment	21,000	
			Add : Purchase	15,000	
				36,000	
Subscription received in advance		700	*Less* : Depreciation	6,000	30,000
			Stock of Medicine		15,000
Amount due for medicine supply		13,000	Investments		1,00,000
			Subscription Due		2,200
			Cash in Hand		9,000
		2,04,200			2,04,200

Working Notes

Subscription Account

Particulars	(*A*)	*Particulars*	(*A*)
To Outstanding Subscription A/c (Opening)	1,500	By Advance Subscription A/c (Opening)	1,200
To Income and Expenditure A/c (Balance Fig.)	51,200	By Bank A/c	50,000
		By Outstanding Subscription A/c (End)	2,200
To Advance Subscription A/c (End)	700		
	53,400		53,400

Alternatively

		A
Subscription received during the year 2006		50,000
Add : Subscription due (31.12.2006)	2,200	
Subscription received in advance (1.1.2006)	1,200	3,400
		53,400
Less : Subscription Due (1.1.2006)	1,500	
Subscription received in advance (31.12.2006)	700	2,200
Amount of subscription to be credited to Income and Expenditure Account		51,200

Creditors for Medicine A/c

Dr. *Cr.*

Particulars	(*A*)	*Particulars*	(*A*)
To Bank A/c	30,000	By Balance b/d	9,000
To Balance c/d	13,000	By Credit Purchase (Bal. Fig.)	34,000
	43,000		43,000

Stock of Medicine Account

Particulars	(*A*)	*Particulars*	(*A*)
Balance b/d	10,000	By Income and Expenditure A/c (*Bal. Fig.* Medicine consumed)	29,000
Purchases (Note-2)	34,000		
		By Balance c/d	15,000
	44,000		44,000

Equipment A/c

Particulars	(*A*)	*Particulars*	(*A*)
To Balance b/d	21,000	By Depreciation A/c	6,000
To Bank A/c (Purchase)	15,000	By Balance c/d	30,000
	36,000		36,000

Building A/c

Particulars	(A)	Particulars	(A)
To Balance b/d	50,000	By Depreciation A/.c	2,000
		By Balance c/d	48,000
	50,000		50,000

Example 22

Given below is the Receipts and Payments Account of a "Residents Welfare Association"—Sports Club for the year ending 31.12.2006 :

Receipts and Payments A/c

Receipts	(A)	Payments	(A)
Balance b/d	2,100	Purchase of sports material	7,000
Subscription (including		Stationery	5,700
A 1,000 for 2005 and		Salaries	7,000
A 1,500 for 2007	18,000	Honorarium	3,000
Life Membership Fees	9,000	Upkeep of ground	2,600
Lagacies	2,000	Application Fees	2,000
Entrance Fees	4,000	Refreshments	1,400
Donations for building Fund	10,000	Tournament Expenses	6,000
Tournament Fund	8,000	Match Expenses	1,000
Hire of Club Hall	5,000	10% Investment	
Sale of old Bats and Balls etc.	500	(on 01.7.2006)	12,000
Sale of old Furniture	700	Furniture (part payment)	5,000
		Balance c/d	6,600
	59,300		59,300

Additional Information :

	01.1.2006	31.12.2006
	A	*A*
Subscription due	1,400	2,400
Subscription received in advance	–	1,500
Audit Fees outstanding	–	1,000
Creditors for stationery	600	500
Stock of Stationery	–	800
Stock of sports material	1,100	1,500
Building	40,000	40,000

Furniture was sold on 01.1.2006 at its book value. On the same date furniture A 8,000 was purchased. Depreciation is to be charged at 10% p.a.

Prepare Income and Expenditure Account for the year ended 31.12.2006 and Balance Sheet as on the date.

Solution

Income and Expenditure A/c
for the year ending 31st Dec., 2006

Dr. Expenditure	(A)	Income	(A) *Cr.*
To Sports Material A/.c (Note 4)	6,100	By Subscription A/c (Note 4)	17,500
To Stationery (Notes 2 and3)	4,800	By Hire of Club Hall	5,000
To Salaries	7,000	By Accrued Interest A/c	
To Honorarium	3,000	(Interest on Investment) [A 12,000 10/100 × 6/12]	600
To Upkeep of ground	2,600	By Entrance Fee	4,000
To Application Fees	2,000	By Deficit *i.e.,* excess of	
To Refreshments	1,400	Expenditure over Income	2,600
To Match Expenses	1,000		
To Depreciation on Furniture (Note 5)	800		
To Audit Fees outstanding	1,000		
	29,700		29,700

Balance Sheet as on 31.12.2006

Liabilities		(A)	*Assets*		(A)
Subscription received			Cash in Hand		6,600
in advance		1,500	Subscription Due		2,400
Audit Fee outstanding		1,000	Stock of Stationery		800
Creditors for Stationery		500	Stock of Sports Material		1,500
Creditors for Furniture		3,000	10% Investment		12,000
[8,000 – 5,000]			Accrued Interest on Investment		600
Tournament Fund	8,000		Building		40,000
Less : Tournament			Furniture	8,000	
Expenses	6,000	2,000	*Less* : Depreciation	800	7,200
Donation for Building Fund		10,000			
Capital Fund :					
Opening Balance					
(Note 6)	44,700				
Add : Life Membership					
Fee	9,000				
Lagacies	2,000				
	55,700				
Less : Deficit	2,600	53,100			
		71,100			71,100

Working Notes

(*i*) Sports Material A/c

Dr. *Cr.*

Particulars	(*A*)	*Particulars*	(*A*)
To Balance b/d	1,100	By Bank A/c (Sale of Old bats	
To Bank A/c(Purchasese)	7,000	and balls etc.)	500
		By Income and Expenditure A/c	6,100
		(Bal. Fig : used)	
		By Balance c/d	1,500
	8,100		8,100

(*ii*) Creditors for Stationery A/c

Dr. *Cr.*

Particulars	(*A*)	*Particulars*	(*A*)
To Bank A/c	5,700	By Balance b/d	600
To Balance c/d	500	By Stock of Stationery	5,600
		(Bal. Fig.)	
	6,200		6,200

(*iii*) Stock of Stationery A/c

Dr. *Cr.*

Particulars	(*A*)	*Particulars*	(*A*)
To Creditors for Stationery A/c	5,600	By Income and Expenditure A/c	4,800
(Purchase)		(*Bal. Fig* : Used)	
		By Balance c/d	800
	5,600		5,600

(*iv*) Subscription A/c

Dr. *Cr.*

Particulars	(*A*)	*Particulars*	(*A*)
To Subscription Due (Opening)	1,400	By Bank A/c	18,000
To Income and Expenditure A/c	17,500		
(*Bal. Fig.*)			
To Subscription Received		By Subscription Due (end)	2,400
in advance (Closing)	1,500	[For 2005 : A 400	
		for 2006 : A 2,000]	
	20,400		20,400

(_v_) Furniture A/c

Dr. *Cr.*

Particulars	(*A*)	*Particulars*	(*A*)
To Balance b/d (Opening)	700	By Bank A/c (Sales)	700
To Bank A/c (Purchases)	8,000	By Depreciation A/c	
		[A 8,000 × 10/100]	800
		By Balance c/d	7,200
	8,700		8,700

There is neither profit nor loss on sale of furniture because it was sold at its book value.

(_vi_) Balance Sheet as at 01.1.2006

Particulars	(*A*)	*Particulars*	(*A*)
Creditors for Stationery	600	Cash	2,100
Capital (*Bal. Fig.*)	44,700	Subscription Due	1,400
		Stock of Sports Material	1,100
		Building	40,000
		Furniture	700
	45,300		45,300

Example 23

The following is the Income and Expenditure Account of a Charitable Hospital for the year ending 31.12.2006 :

Dr. *Cr.*

Expenditure		(*A*)	*Income*	(*A*)
Salaries		2,35,000	Subscriptions	2,20,000
Diet Expenses		20,000	Donations	40,000
Rent and Rates		5,000	Interest on Investment	
Insurance		2,000	for full year @5% p.a.	90,000
Office Expenses		8,000	Miscellaneous Receipts	6,000
Surgery and				
Dispensary Expenses		10,000		
Depreciation :				
Building	37,500			
Furniture	1,200			
Instruments	8,000	46,700		
Surplus of Income				
over Expenditure		29,300		
		3,56,000		3,56,000

Other information supplied to you are as under :

	31.12.2005	31.12.2006
	A	*A*
Cash in Hand	2,000	1,500
Cash at Bank	54,000	?
Building	7,50,000	?
Furniture	20,000	?
Instruments	35,000	?
Subscription Outstanding	15,000	45,000
Subscription received in advance	6,000	8,000
Salaries Outstanding	18,000	20,000

Instruments purchased during the year 2006 were A 5,000.

You are required to prepare the Receipts and Payments Account of the Hospital for the year ended 31st December, 2006 and the Balance Sheet as on that date. Submit your working clearly.

Solution

Receipts and Payment A/c
For the year ending on 31st Dec., 2006

Dr. *Cr.*

Receipts		*(A)*	*Particulars*		*(A)*
To Balance b/d			By Salaries	2,35,000	
Cash	2,000		*Add* : Outstanding (2005)		
Bank	54,000	56,000		18,000	
To Subscription	2,20,000			2,53,000	
Add : Outstanding (2005)	15,000		*Less* : Outstanding (2006)		
	2,35,000			20,000	2,33,000
Less : Outstanding (2006)	45,000		By Diet Expenses		20,000
	1,90,000		By Rent and Rates		5,000
Add : Advance(2006)	8,000		By Insurance		2,000
	1,98,000		By Office Expenses		8,000
Less : Advance (2005)	6,000	1,92,000	By Instruments		5,000
To Donations		40,000	By Surgery and Dispensary Exp.		10,000
To Interest on Investment		90,000	By Balance c/d		
			Cash	1,500	
			Bank (*Bal. Fig.*)	99,500	1,01,000
		3,84,000		3,84,000	

Balance Sheet as at 31st Dec., 2006

Liabilities		*(A)*	*Assets*		*(A)*
Capital Fund (Note)	26,52,000		Building	7,50,000	
Add : Surplus	29,300	26,81,300	*Less* : Depreciation	37,500	7,12,500
Subscription received in Advance		8,000	Furniture	20,000	
Outstanding Salary		20,000	*Less* : Depreciation	1,200	18,800
			Instruments	35,000	
			Add : Purchased	5,000	
				40,000	
			Less : Depreciation	8,000	32,000
			Investment		18,00,000
			Subscription Outstanding		45,000
			Cash in Hand		1,500
			Cash at Bank		99,500
		27,09,300			27,09,300

Working Notes

Calculations of Capital Fund as at 31st Dec., 2005.

Balance Sheet as at 31st Dec., 2005

Liabilities	*(A)*	*Assets*	*(A)*
Subscription Received in Advance	6,000	Cash in Hand	2,000
Salaries Outstanding	18,000	Cash at Bank	54,000
Capital Fund (*Bal. Fig.*)	25,52,000	Building	7,50,000
		Furniture	20,000
		Instruments	35,000
		Subscription Outstanding	15,000
		Investments [A 90,000 × 100/5]	18,00,000
	26,76,000		26,76,000

Example 24

The following is the Income and Expenditure Account of ABC Club for the year ended on 31st March, 2004 :

Liabilities	*(A)*	*Assets*	*(A)*
Salaries	24,000	Subscription	78,000
Stationery	1,600	Donation	8,000
Postage and Telephone	3,200	Billiard Table Collection	7,000
Rates and Taxes	6,000	Profit on Annual Meet	12,000
Repairs	8,000	Income from Investment	2,700
Table Tennis Balls	1,200		

Printing of Souvenir	2,000		
Electricity Charges	6,000		
Billiard Room Expenses	3,000		
Miscellaneous Expenses	9,400		
Depreciation of Club Assets	2,000		
Surplus	41,300		
	1,07,700		1,07,700

The following information are available :

	01.04.03	31.03.04
	A	A
Club Assets	48,000	52,000
Outstanding Subscription	3,000	5,000
Advance Subscription	6,000	10,000
Expenses O/S :		
Stationery	600	400
Telephone	300	200
Electricity	700	300
Cash at Bank	1,800	?
Investment	27,000	47,000

Prepare Receipts and Payments Account for the year ended on 31st March, 2004 and Draw a Balance Sheet as at 31st march, 2004.

Solution

ABC Club
Receipts and Payments A/c
for the year ended 31st March, 2004

Dr. *Cr.*

Receipts	(*A*)	*Payments*	(*A*)
To Bank Balance b/d	1,800	By Salaries	24,000
To Subscription *2	80,000	By Stationery*3	1,800
To Donations	8,000	By Postage and Telephone*	3,300
To Billiard Table Collection	7,000	By Rates and Taxes	6,000
To Annual Meet (Profit)	12,000	By Repairs	8,000
To Income from Investment	2,700	By Table Tennis Balls	1,200
		By Printing of Souvenir	2,000
		By Electricity *5	6,400
		By Billiard Room Expenses	3,000
		By Misc. Expenses	9,400
		By Investment	20,000
		By Club Assets	6,000
		By Bank Balance c/d (*Bal. Figure*)	20,400
	1,11,500		1,11,500

Balance Sheet as on 31st March, 2004

Liabilities		(A)	*Assets*		(A)
Capital Fund*1	72,200		Club Assets	48,000	
Add : Surplus	41,300	1,13,500	Additions	6,000	
Subscription Received in Advance		10,000		54,000	
Expenses O/S :			*Less* : Depreciation	2,000	52,000
Stationery	400		Subscription receivable		5,000
Telephone	200		Investment		47,000
Electricity	300	900	Cash at Bank		20,400
		1,24,400			1,24,400

Working Notes

*1 *Calculation of Capital Fund* :

Balance Sheet as on 31st March, 2003

Liabilities		(A)	*Assets*	(A)
Subscription Received in advance		6,000	Club assets	48,000
			Investments	27,000
Outstanding Expenses :			Subscription Receivable	3,000
Stationery	600		Cash	1,800
Telephone	300			
Electricity	700	1,600		
Capital Fund (*Bal. Fig.*)		72,200		
		79,800		79,800

*2 *Subscription Received* :

		A
As per Income and Expenditure A/c		78,000
Add : Received in Advance 31.3.04		10,000
Received for 01.4.03		3,000
		91,000
Less : Outstanding Subscription 31.3.04	5,000	
advance Subscription 01.4.03	6,000	11,000
		80,000

*3 *Stationery*

As per Income and Expenditure A/c	1,600
Add : Payment for 2002-03	600
	2,200
Less : Outstanding for 2003-04	400
	1,800

*4	*Postage and Telephone*	
	As per Income and Expenditure A/c	3,200
	Add : Paid for 2002-03	300
		3,500
	Less : Outstanding for 2003-04	200
		3,300
*5	*Electricity Charges*	
	As per Income and Expenditure A/c	6,000
	Add : Paid for 2002-03	700
		6,700
	Less : Outstanding for 2003-04	300
		6,400

Example 25

Following are the Receipts and Payments and Income and Expenditure Account of Delhi Club for the year ending 31st March, 2004.

Receipts and Payments A/c
for the year ending 31st March, 2004

Liabilities		*(A)*	*Assets*	*(A)*
Balance b/d		1,000	Ground Maintenance	1,200
Subscription			Salary and Honorarium	
2002-03	400		(Including Salary of	
2003-04	10,300		02-03 A 700)	1,800
2004-05	500	11,200	Water and Electricity	350
Lagacy		800	Books out of Donation	3,000
Donation for Library		7,000	Fixed Deposit out of Donation	4,000
Match Fund		3,300	Match Expenses	2,200
Sale of Furniture		500	Crockery	1,000
			Food	2,000
			Entertainment	2,000
			Sports Materials	2,000
			Balance c/d	4,250
		23,800		23,800

Income and Expenditure A/c
for the year ending 31st March, 2004

Expenditure	*(A)*	*Income*	*(A)*
Ground Maintenance	1,200	Subscription	10,400
Salary and Honorarium	1,800		
Entertainment	2,000		
Loss on Sale of Furniture	300		

Electricity and Water	350		
Sports Material used			
75% of Total Stock in			
Hand during the year	2,010		
Food consumed			
80% of Total Stock			
in Hand	1,500		
Excess of Income over			
Expenditure	1,240		
	10,400		10,400

Additional Information :

(*a*) Subscription outstanding on 31.3.03 A 550 estimated at A 500.

(*b*) Subscription outstanding on 31.3.04 A 120.

(*c*) Furniture on 31.3.03 A 3,000.

(*d*) Crockery on 31.3.04 A 2,500.

You are required to prepare Balance Sheet as on 01.4.03 and 31st March, 2004.

Solution

Balance Sheet as on 1st April, 2003

Liabilities	*(A)*	*Assets*	*(A)*
Salary and Honorarium o/s	700	Cash in Hand	1,000
Capital Fund		Subscription outstanding	500
(Balance Figure)	5,980	Furniture	3,000
		Crockery*[1]	1,500
		Sports Materials*[2]	680
	6,680		6,680

Balance Sheet as on 31st March, 2004

Liabilities		*(A)*	*Assets*		*(A)*
Match Fund	3,300		Cash in Hand		4,250
Less : Match Expenses	2,200	1,100	Subscription outstanding		
Subscription Received			2002-03		
in Advance		500	[550 - 50 - 400]	100	
Legacy		800	2003-04		
Donation for Library		7,000	[120 - 20		
Outstanding Salary and Honorarium		700	(over estimated)]	100	200
			Furniture	3,000	
Capital Fund	5,980		*Less* : Sold (Book Value)		

Add : Excess of Income over Expenditure	1,240	7,220	[500 + 300 (Loss)]	800	2,200
			Crockery		2,500
			Stock of Food*3		375
			Sports Material*2		670
			Fixed Deposit		4,000
			Books		3,000
			Prepaid for Food*3		125
		17,320			17,320

Working Notes

		A
*1	Crockery on 31st March, 2004	2,500
	Less : Purchased during the year	1,000
	Balance of Crockery as on 1st April, 2003	1,500
*2	Sports Materials used = 75% of Total	
	Hence, Material available $= \frac{100}{75} \times 2,010$	2,680
	Less : Purchased during the year	2,000
	Balance of Sports material on 1st April, 2004	680
	Balance of Sports material on 31st March, 2005	(2,680 – 2,010) = 670
*3	Food : Total Stock $= \frac{100}{80} \times 1,500$	1,875
	Payments during the year	2,000
	Prepaid on 31.3.2004	125
	Stock of food as on 31st March, 2004 = (1,875 – 1,500) = A 375	
*4	Difference of subscription outstanding and estimated A 50 (A 550 – A 500) is written off	

Example 26

From the following Receipts and Payments Account of 'Free Legal Aid Society' for the year 2001-02 (ending 31.3.2002) and information, prepare Income and Expenditure Account for the year and Balance Sheet as at 31st March, 2002 :

Liabilities	*(A)*	*Assets*	*(A)*
To Balance	14,000	By Salaries of Office Staff	60,000
To Subscriptions	1,00,000	By Honorarium (Legal Advisors)	30,000
To Donations	29,000	By Sundry Expenses	3,000
To Interest on Investments		By Stationery	5,000
(10% p.a.)	40,000	By Court Fee Stamps	10,000
To Charity Show Receipts	20,000	By Typewriters	20,000
		By Charity Show Expenses	5,000
		By Cash in Hand	70,000
	2,03,000		2,03,000

Addition Information as on :

	01.4.2001 A	31.3.2002 A
Subscription due	1,000	2,000
Subscription received in advance	2,000	1,000
Stock of Court Fee Stamps	4,000	6,000
Value of Office Equipment (Typewriters)	42,000	60,000
Value of Buildings	80,000	72,000

Solution

Income and Expenditure A/c
for the year ending on 31st march, 2002

Dr. *Cr.*

Expenditure		*(A)*	*Income*	*(A)*
To Salaries of Office Staff		60,000	By Subscriptions	1,02,000
To Honararium (Legal Advisors)		30,000	By Donations	29,000
To Sundry Expenses		3,000	By Interest on Investment	40,000
To Stationary		5,000	By Charity Show Receipts	20,000
To Court Fee Stamps :				
Opening Stock	4,000			
Add : Purchases	10,000			
	14,000			
Less : Closing Stock	6,000	8,000		
To Depreciation on Typewriters				
[42,000 + 20,000 – 6,000]		2,000		
To Charity Show Expenses		5,000		
To Depreciation on Building		8,000		
[80,000 – 72,000]				
To Surplus transferred to				
Capital Fund		70,000		
		1,91,000		1,91,000

Balance Sheet as at 31st March, 2002

Liabilities		*(A)*	*Assets*	*(A)*
Subscription received in advance		1,000	Cash in Hand	70,000
Capital Fund	5,39,000		Subscription due	2,000
Add : Surplus	70,000	6,09,000	Stock of Court Fee stamps	6,000
			Office Equipment (Typewriters)	60,000
			Investments	4,00,000
			Buildings	72,000
		6,10,000		6,10,000

Work Notes

Balance Sheet as at 31st March, 2001

Liabilities	*(A)*	*Assets*	*(A)*
Subscription received in Advance	2,000	Cash in Hand	14,000
		Subscription due	1,000
Capital Fund (*Bal. Fig.*)	5,39,000	Investments (A 40,000 × 100/10)	4,00,000
		Office Equipment	42,000
		Stock of Court fee Stamps	4,000
		Building	80,000
	5,41,000		5,41,000

Subscription A/c

Dr. *Cr.*

Liabilities	*(A)*	*Assets*	*(A)*
To Subscription Due A/c (in the beginning)	1,000	By Advance Subscription A/c (in the beginning)	2,000
To Income and Exp. (*Bal. Fig.*)	1,02,000	By Bank	1,00,000
To Advance Subscription A/c (at the end)	1,000	By Subscription Due A/c (at the end)	2,000
	1,04,000		1,04,000

Example 27

The following particulars are related to a Sports Club :

Income and Expenditure A/c
for the year ending 31st March, 2004

Dr. *Cr.*

Liabilities	*(A)*	*Assets*	*(A)*
To Salaries	11,500	By Entrance Fees	10,500
To Printing and Stationery	2,200	By Subscription	25,600
To Advertising	1,600	By Rent	4,000
To Audit Fees	500		
To Fire Insurance	1,000		
To Depreciation on Sports Equipments	9,000		
To Surplus	14,300		
	40,100		40,100

Receipts and Payments A/c
for the year ending 31st March, 2004

Dr. *Cr.*

Liabilities	*(A)*	*Assets*	*(A)*
To Balance b/d	4,200	By Salaries	11,000
To Entrance Fees	10,500	By Printing and Stationery	2,600
To Subscriptions :		By Advertising	1,600
2002-03	600	By Fire Insurance	1,200
2003-04	25,000	By Investments	20,000
2004-05	400	By Balance c/d	7,800
To Rent received	3,500		
	44,200		44,200

The assets on 1st April, 2003 included Club Grounds and Pavilion 44,000; Sports Equipment A 25,000 and Furniture and Fixtures A 4,000. Subscriptions in arrear on that date were A 800. Prepare Balance Sheet of Sports Club as on 31st March 2004.

Solution

Balance Sheet of Sports Club
for the year ending on 31st March, 2004

Liabilities		*(A)*	*Assets*		*(A)*
Outstanding Salary		500	Prepaid Fire Insurance		
Outstanding Audit Fees		500	[A 1,200 – A 1,000]		200
Subscriptions Received			Club Ground and Pavilion		44,000
in advance		400	Sports Equipment		
Capital Fund*1	77,600		A (25,000 – 9,000)		16,000
(Working)			Investments		20,000
Add : Surplus	14,300	91,900	Subscriptions in Arrear :		
			2003 A [800 – 600]	200	
			2004		
			[25,600 – 25,000]	600	800
			Furniture and Fixtures		4,000
			Accrued Rent		
			A (4,000 – 3,500)		500
			Cash in Hand		7,800
		93,300			93,300

Working Note* $_1$

Balance Sheet as at March 31. 2003

Liabilities	*(A)*	*Assets*	*(A)*
Outstanding for Stationery	400	Club Grounds and Pavilion	44,000
[A 2,600 – 2,200]		Sports Equipment	25,000

		Furniture and fixtures	4,000
Capital Fund		Subscriptions in arrear	800
(*Balancing Figure*)	77,600	Cash in Hand	4,200
	78,000		78,000

Example 28

The Receipts and Payments Account of Delhi Football Club for the year ending 31st March, 2001 was as under :

Dr. *Cr.*

Liabilities	*(A)*	*Assets*	*(A)*
To Balance b/d (01.4.2000).	48,000	By Purchase of Balls	80,000
To Subscriptions Received	2,46,000	By Tournament Fees	10,000
To Interest	2,000	By Affiliation Fees	2,000
To Sale of Furniture	10,000	By Rent of Playground	5,000
To Donations for Club Building	60,000	By Refreshment Expenses	4,000
		By Investment	1,00,000
		By Salaries	12,000
		By Miscellaneous Expenses	8,000
		By Balance c/d (31.3.01)	1,15,000
	3,66,000		3,66,000

Prepare Club's Income and Expenditure Account for the year ending 31st March, 2001 and a Balance Sheet as on that date, after taking the following information into account :

(*i*) Subscriptions received include A 10,000 for the year 1999-2000 and A 8,000 for the year 2001-2002, A 16,000 are still outstanding as subscriptions for the year 2000-2001.

(*ii*) The book-value of furniture sold was A 14,000.

(*iii*) Interest earned but not received amounted to A 500.

(*iv*) Rent of playground due but not paid for the current year amounted to A 6,000, A 1,000 was paid for the year 1999-2000.

(*v*) Stock of balls on 31st March, 2001 was A 4,000.

(*vi*) Salary outstanding for the year 2000-01, A 5000.

Solution

Income and Expenditure A/c of Delhi Foot Ball Club
for the year ending on 31st March, 2001

Dr. *Cr.*

Liabilities		*(A)*	*Assets*		*(A)*
To Balls	80,000		By Subscriptions	2,46,000	
Less : Closing Stock	4,000	76,000	*Less* : Outstanding (1999-2000)	10,000	
To Tournament fees		10,000		2,36,000	

To Affiliation Fees		2,000			
To Rent of Playground	5,000		*Less* : Received in		
Add : Outstanding	6,000		advance for 2001-02	8,000	
	11,000			2,28,000	
Less : Paid for last year	1,000	10,000	*Add* : Outstanding		
To Refreshment Expenses		4,000	(2000-2001)	16,000	2,44,000
To Travelling Expenses		30,000	By Interest	2,000	
To Salaries	12,000		*Add* : Accrued Interest	500	2,500
Add : Outstanding	5,000	17,000			
To Miscellaneous Expenses		8,000			
To Loss on Sale of Furniture					
A (14,000 – 10,000)		4,000			
To Excess of Income Over					
Expenditure		85,500			
		2,46,500			2,46,500

Balance Sheet of Delhi Foot Ball Club
as on 31st March, 2001

Liabilities		*(A)*	*Assets*	*(A)*
Building Fund		60,000	Investment	1,00,000
Subscription Received		8,000	Cash/Bank Balance	1,15,000
in advance			Subscriptions Due	16,000
Rent of Playground due but			(for 2000-01)	
not paid		6,000	Interest due but not received	500
Salary unpaid		5,000	Stock of Balls	4,000
Capital Fund*1				
Opening Balance	71,000			
Add : Surplus	85,500	1,56,500		
		2,35,500		2,35,500

***Working Note* *1**

Balance Sheet of Delhi Foot Ball Club
as on 1st April, 2000

Liabilities	*(A)*	*Assets*	*(A)*
Rent of Playground unpaid	1,000	Cash/Bank	48,000
Capital Fund (*Bal. Fig.*)	71,000	Subscriptions Due	10,000

		Furniture	14,000
	72,000		72,000

Example 29

The Receipts and Payments Account and the Income and Expenditure Account of a club for the year ended 31st march, 2000 were as follows :

Receipts and Payments A/c

Dr. *Cr.*

Receipts		*(A)*	*Payments*	*(A)*
To Cash at bank on 1st			By Books	30,000
April, 1999		15,000	By Stationery	2,400
To Subscriptions :			By Salary	33,000
for 1998-99	6,000		By Water and Electricity	3,900
For 1999-2000	43,000		Balance on 31.3.2000	22,200
For 2000-2001	500	49,500		
To Interest on Investments		10,000		
To Rent Received		12,000		
To Special Donation		5,000		
		91,500		91,500

Income and Expenditure A/c

Dr. *Cr.*

Expenditure		*(A)*	*Income*	*(A)*
To Stationery		2,100	By Subscriptions	48,000
To Salary		136,000	By Interest	10,000
To Water and Electricity		4,100	By Rent	12,000
To Depreciation on :				
Buildings	5,000			
Books	7,000			
Furniture	1,000	13,000		
To Surplus		14,800		
		70,000		70,000

On 31st March, 1999, the Club's assets included Building A 1,00,000, Books A 40,000, Furniture A 10,000; 10% Investments A 1,00,000 (Bought at par), Stock of Stationery A 500, Subscriptions due A 6,500; Interest accrued A 5,000; Rent receivable A 1,000. There were no liabilities on that date.

Prepare Balance Sheet as on 31st March, 1999 and on 31st March, 2000.

Solution

Balance Sheet as on 31st March, 1999

Liabilities	*(A)*	*Assets*	*(A)*
Capital (*Bal. Fig.*)	2,78,000	Cash at Bank	15,000
		Subscriptions Due	6,500
		Interest Accrued	5,000
		Rent Receivable	1,000
		Stock of Stationery	500
		10% Investments	1,00,000
		Furniture	10,000
		Books	40,000
		Building	1,00,000
	2,78,000		2,78,000

Balance Sheet as on 31st March, 2000

Liabilities		*(A)*	*Assets*		*(A)*
Subscription Received in Advance		500	Cash at bank		22,200
			Subscription Due :		
Outstanding Water			1998-99		500
and Electricity Bills		200	1999-2000		5,000
Salaries Outstanding		3,000	Accrued Interest		5,000
Capital	2,78,000		Books	40,000	
Surplus	14,800	2,92,800	*Add* : Purchases	30,000	
Special Donation		5,000		70,000	
			Less : Depreciation	7,000	63,000
			Buildings	1,00,000	
			Less : Depreciation	5,000	95,000
			Furniture	10,000	
			Less :Depreciation	1,000	9,000
			Stock of Stationery	500	
			Add : Purchases	2,400	
				2,900	
			Less : Stationery consumed	2,100	800
			Rent Receivable		1,000
			Investments		1,00,000
		3,01,500			3,01,500

Example 30

From the following particulars relating to Mother Teresa Charitable Trust Hospital prepare Receipts and Payments Account for the year ended 1st March, 2000 and a Balance Sheet as on that date :

Income and Expenditure A/c
for the year ended 1st March, 2000

Dr. *Cr.*

Liabilities	*(A)*	*Assets*		*(A)*
To Medicines used	1,49,900	By Subscription		2,80,000
To Honorarium to Doctors	60,000	By Donations		47,500
To Salaries	1,37,500	By Interest on Investments		
To Printing and Stationery	5,500	at 11% p.a.		55,000
To Electricity and Water	2,375	By Proceeds from		
To Rent	30,000	Charity Show	57,250	
To Depreciation on Furniture	10,500	*Less* : Expenses	3,900	53,350
To Depreciation on Equipment	16,250			
To Surplus	23,825			
	4,35,850			4,35,850

Additional Information

		31.3.1999	*31.3.2000*
		A	A
(*i*)	Subscription	600	800
(*ii*)	Subscription received in advance	320	500
(*iii*)	Electricity and Water outstanding	460	575
(*iv*)	Stock of Medicines	39,100	48,750
(*v*)	Estimated value of Equipment	58,000	69,500
(*vi*)	Furniture (Cost less Depreciation)	1,05,000	94,500
(*vii*)	Land	–	50,000
(*viii*)	Interest accrued on investments in 11% Bonds costing A 5,12,500 (Face Value A 5,00,000)	13,750	13,750
(*ix*)	Cash in Hand	1,700	800
(*x*)	Cash at Bank	45,000	?

Solution

Receipts and Payments A/c
for the year ended 31st March, 2000

Dr. *Cr.*

Receipts		(*A*)	*Payments*		(*A*)
To Balance b/d :			By Land		50,000
Cash	1,700		By Medicines*1		1,59,550
Bank	45,000	46,700	By Honorarium to Doctors		60,000
To Subscription*4		2,79,980	By Salaries		1,37,500
To Donations		47,500	By Printing and Stationery		5,500
To Interest on Investments			By Electricity and Water*2		2,260
	55,000		By Rent		30,000
Add : O/s 1998-99	13,750		By Equipments*3		27,750
Less : O/s 1999-2000	13,750	55,000	By Charity Show Expenses		3,900
To Proceeds from Charity Show		57,250	By Balance c/d		
			Cash	800	
			Bank	9,170	9,970
		4,86,430			4,86,430

Balance Sheet as on 31st March, 2000

Receipts		(*A*)	*Payments*	(*A*)
Capital Fund	7,74,870		Subscription Due	800
Add : Surplus	23,825	7,98,695	Stock of Medicines	48,750
Subscription received in Advance		500	Equipment	69,500
Outstanding Electricity			Furniture	94,500
and Water Bill		575	Land	50,000
			Accrued Interest	13,750
			Investment at Cost	5,12,500
			Cash in Hand	800
			Bank Balance	9,170
		7,99,770		7,99,770

Balance Sheet as on 31st March, 1999

Liabilities	(*A*)	*Assets*	(*A*)
Subscription in Advance	320	Subscription Due	600
Outstanding Electricity		Stock of Medicines	39,100
and Water Bill	460	Equipment	58,000
Capital Fund	7,74,870	Furniture	1,05,000
(Balancing Figure)		11% Investments	5,12,500

		Accrued Interest	13,750
		Cash in Hand	1,700
		Cash at bank	45,000
	7,75,650		7,75,650

Working Notes

*1	*Purchase of Medicines*	A
	Medicines used as Per Income and Expenditure A/c	1,49,900
Less :	Opening Stock	39,100
		1,10,800
Add :	Stock at the end	48,750
		1,59,500
*2	*Payment for Electricity and Water*	A
	Expenses as per Income and Expenditure A/c	2,375
Add :	Paid for last year (1999)	460
		2,835
Less :	Outstanding for current year (2000)	575
		2,260
*3	*Purchase of Equipment*	A
	Balance at the end	69,500
Add :	Depreciation	16,250
		85,750
Less :	Balance in the beginning	58,000
		27,750
*4	*Subscription received in Current Year*	A
	Subscription as per Income and Expenditure A/c	2,80,000
Add :	Received for last year	600
		2,80,600
Less :	Outstanding for current year	800
		2,79,800
Add :	Received in advance in the current year	500
		2,80,300
Less :	Received in Advance last year	320
		2,79,980

Example 31

The following is the Receipts and Payment Account of Free Aid Medical Society for the year ended 31.3.2000.

Receipts and Payments A/c
for the year ending 31st march, 2000

Dr. *Cr.*

Receipts	*(A)*	*Payments*	*(A)*
To Balance b/d	14,000	By Payment for Medicine	60,000
To Subscriptions	1,00,000	By Honorarium to Doctors	20,000
To Donations	29,000	By Salaries	55,000
To Interest on Investments		By Sundry Expenses	1,000
at 7% for the year	14,000	By Equipment Purchased	30,000
To Charity Show		By Charity show expenses	2,000
collections	20,000	By Balance c/d	9,000
	1,77,000		1,77,000

***Additional Information*:**

		On 01.4.1999	*On* 31.3.2000
(*a*)	Subscription due	1,000	2,000
(*b*)	Subscription received in advance	2,000	1,000
(*c*)	Medicine Stock	20,000	30,000
(*d*)	Creditors for medicine	16,000	24,000
(*e*)	Equipments	42,000	60,000
(*f*)	Buildings	80,000	76,000

You are required to prepare Income and Expenditure Account for the year ended 31.3.2000 and Balance Sheet as at that date.

Solution

Free Aid Medical Society's
Income and Expenditure A/c
for the year ended 31.3.2000

Dr. *Cr.*

Expenditure		*(A)*	*Income*		*(A)*
To Medicine*1		58,000	By Subscription	1,00,000	
To Honorarium to Doctors		20,000	*Add* : Due on 31.3.2000	2,000	
To Salaries		55,000	Advance 01.4.99	2,000	
To Sundry Expenses		1,000		1,04,000	
To Depreciation on :			*Less* : Due on 01.4.99	1,000	
Equipments*2	12,000			1,03,000	
Building	4,000	16,000	Adv : 31.3.2000	1,000	1,02,000
A [80,000 – 76,000]			By Donations		29,000
To Charity Show Expenses		2,000	By Interest on Investments		14,000
To Surplus Excess of Income			By Charity Show Collections		20,000
over expenditure		13,000			
		1,65,000			1,65,000

Balance Sheet as on 31.3.2000

Dr. *Cr.*

Liabilities		*(A)*	*Assets*	*(A)*
Capital Fund*4	3,39,000		Buildings	76,000
Add : Surplus	13,000	3,52,000	Equipments	60,000
Subscription received			Investments*3	2,00,000
in advance		1,000	Medicine Stock	30,000
Creditors for medicine		24,000	Subscription due	2,000
			Cash in Hand	9,000
		3,77,000		3,77,000

Working Note

*1 **Creditors for Medicine A/c**

Dr. *Cr.*

Particulars	*(A)*	*Particulars*	*(A)*
To Bank A/c	60,000	By Balance b/d	16,000
To Balance c/d	24,000	By Purchases (Bal. Figure)	68,000
	84,000		84,000

Medicine Consumed = Opening Stock + Purchase – Closing Stock
= A 20,000 + A 68,000 – 30,000 = A 58,000

*2 **Equipments A/c**

Dr. *Cr.*

Particulars	*(A)*	*Particulars*	*(A)*
To Balance b/d	42,000	By Income and Expenditure	12,000
To Bank (Purchases)	30,000	(Depreciation)	
		By Balance c/d (*Bal. Fig.*)	60,000
	72,000		72,000

*3 **Calculation of Investments**

Interest is received at 7% p.a., for full year = A 14,000

$\therefore$ Interest A 14,000 $\times \frac{100}{7}$ = A 2,00,000

*4 **Calculation of Capital Funds as on 01.4.1999**

Balance Sheet as on 01.4.1999

Dr. *Cr.*

Liabilities	*(A)*	*Assets*	*(A)*
Creditors for Medicine	16,000	Buildings	80,000
Subscription received in		Equipments	42,000
Advance	2,000	Medicine Stock	20,000

Capital Fund	3,39,000	Subscription due	1,000
(Balance Figure)		Investments	2,00,000
		Cash in Hand	14,000
	3,57,000		3,57,000

Example 32

Following is the Receipts and Payments Account of Mayur Club for the year ended 31st March, 2008 :

Receipts	*Amount* *A*	*Payments*	*Amount* *A*
Opening balance (1.4.2007)			
Cash on hand	39,100	Sports materials	3,04,500
Cash at bank	50,000	Salaries	3,15,000
Receipts :		Equipment purchased on 1.10.2007	60,000
Subscriptions		Bank fixed deposits on 31.3.2008	1,50,000
For the year 2006-07	18,000	Rent	1,48,500
For the year 2007-8	9,63,000	Ground maintenance	22,120
For the year 2008-09	4,500	Insurance	38,400
Interest on bank Fixed deposits @ 10%	45,000	Stationery	3,450
		Sundry expenses	5,880
		Closing balance as on 31.3.2008	
		Cash on hand	31,750
		Cash at bank	40,000
	11,19,600		11,19,600

Following additional information is provided to you :

(*i*) The club has 220 members. The annual subscription is A 4,500 per member.

(*ii*) Depreciation to be provided on furniture at 10% p.a. and on sports equipment at 15% p.a.

(*iii*) On 31st March, 2008, stock of sports material in hand (after members use during the year) is valued at A 78,000 and stock of stationery at A 3,150. Rent for 1 month is outstanding. Unexpired insurance amounts to A 9,600.

(*iv*) On 31st March, 2007 the club had the following assets :

Furniture	A	2,70,000
Sports equipment	A	1,80,000
Bank fixed deposit	A	4,50,000
Stock of stationery	A	1,500
Stock of sports material	A	73,500
Unexpired insurance	A	8,400
Subscription in arrear	A	22,500

Note : There was no liability on 31.3.2007

You are required to prepare :

(*i*) Income and Expenditure Account; and

(*ii*) Balance Sheet as at 31st March, 2008. [*CA, Professional Competence Examination, May 2008*]

Solution

Mayur Club
Income and Expenditure Account for the Year Ended 31.3.2008

Expenditure		*Amount* A	*Income*	*Amount* A
To Sports Material used			By Subscription (W.N.2)	9,90,000
Opening stock	73,500		By Interest on fixed deposit	45,000
Add : Purchases	3,04,500			
	3,78,000			
Less : Closing stock	78,000	3,00,000		
To Salaries		3,15,000		
To Rent	1,48,500			
Add : Outstanding (W.N.6)	13,500	1,62,000		
To Ground maintenance		22,120		
To Insurance	38,400			
Less : Unexpired on 31.3.08	9,600			
	28,800			
Add : Unexpired on 1.4.07	8,400	37,200		
To Stationery used				
Opening stock	1,500			
Add : Purchases	3,450			
	4,950			
Less : Closing Stock	3,150	1,800		
To Sundry expenses		5,880		
To Depreciation on				
Furniture	27,000			
Sports equipment	31,500	58,500		
To Excess of income over expenditure		1,32,500		
		10,35,000		10,35,000

Balance Sheet As At 31st March, 2008

Expenditure		*Amount* A	*Assets*		*Amount* A
Capital Fund :			Equipments Opening balance	1,80,000	
Opening balance (W.N. 1)	10,95,000		*Add :* Addition	60,000	
Add : Excess of income				2,40,000	
Expenditure	1,32,500	12,27,500	*Less :* Depreciation (W.N.5)	31,500	2,08,500
Rent outstanding (W.N.6)		13,500	Furniture :	2,70,000	
			Less : Dep.	27,000	2,43,000

Subscription received in advance for 2008-09	4,500			
		Sports material		78,000
		Stock of stationery		3,150
		Fixed deposit in bank (4,50,000 + 1,50,000)		6,00,000
		Subscription in arrears :		
		For 2006-07 (W.N.3)	4,500	
		For 2007-08 (W.N.4)	27,000	31,500
		Prepaid insurance (unexpired)		9,600
		Cash on hand		31,750
		Cash at bank		40,000
	12,45,000			12,45,500

Working Notes

1. Balance Sheet As At 31st March, 2007

Expenditure	*Amount* A	*Assets*	*Amount* A
Capital fund (Bal. fig.)	10,95,000	Sports equipment	1,80,000
		Furniture	2,70,000
		Sports materials	73,500
		Stock of stationery	1,500
		Fixed deposits in bank	4,50,000
		Subscription in arrears	22,500
		Prepaid insurance (unexpired)	8,400
		Cash on hand	39,100
		Cash at bank	50,000
	10,95,000		10,95,000

2. **Income on account of subscription**

220 members @ A 4,500 each	9,90,000

3. **Subscription still in arrears of 2006-2007**

Opening balance of subscription in arrears (as on 1.4.2007)	22,500
Less : Arrears subscription of 2006-07 received during the year 2007-08	18,000
Subscription of 2006-07 still in arrears as on 31.3.2008	4,500

4. **Subscription in arrear on 31.3.2008**

Subscription for the year 2007-08	9,90,000
Less : Subscription received for the year	9,63,000
Subscription in arrears for 2007-08	27,000

5. **Depreciation on sports equipment**

On A 1,80,000 @ 15% for full year	27,000
On A 60,000 @ 15% for 6 months	4,500
Total	31,500

6. **Outstanding rent of 2007-2008**

Outstanding rent $= \frac{\text{Rs. } 1,48,500}{11 \text{ months}} \times 1 \text{ month}$ 13,500

Example 33

Following is the Receipt and Payments account of Nanoo Club for the year ended 31st March, 2009 :

Receipts	*Amount* A	*Payments*	*Amount* A
Opening balance :		Salaries	1,20,000
Cash	10,000	Creditors	15,20,000
Bank	3,850	Printing and stationery	70,000
Subscription received	2,02,750	Postage	40,000
Entrance donation	1,00,000	Telephone and fax	52,000
Interest received	58,000	Repairs and maintenance	48,000
Sale of fixed assets	8,000	Glass and table linen	12,000
Miscellaneous income	9,000	Crockery and cutlery	14,000
Receipts at coffee room	10,70,000	Garden upkeep	8,000
Wines and spirits	5,10,000	Membership fees	4,000
Swimming pool	80,000	Insurance	5,000
Tennis court	1,02,000	Electricity	28,000
		Closing balance :	
		Cash	8,000
		Bank	2,24,600
	21,53,600		21,53,600

Following additional information is provided to you :

(*i*) Assets and liabilities as on 31.3.2008 were as follows :

Fixed Assets	5,00,000
Stock	3,80,000
Investment in 12% Government securities	5,00,000
Outstanding subscription	12,000
Gratuity fund	1,50,000
Prepaid insurance	1,000
Sundry creditors	1,12,000
Subscription received in advance	15,000
Entrance donation received pending membership	1,00,000

(*ii*) Subscription received in advance as on 31.3.09 was A 18,000.

(*iii*) Outstanding subscription as on 31.3.09 was A 7,000.

(*iv*) Outstanding expenses as on 31.3.09 are :

Salaries	A	8,000
Electricity	A	15,000

(*v*) 50% of the entrance donation was to be capitalized. There was no pending membership as on 31.3.09.

(*vi*) The cost of assets sold as on 1.4.08 was A 10,000.

(*vii*) Depreciation was provided @ 10% p.a. on fixed assets on written down value basis.

(*viii*) A sum of A 20,000 received in October, 2008 as entrance donation from an applicant was to be refunded, as he has not fulfilled the requisite membership qualification. The refund was made on 3.6.09.

(*ix*) Purchases made during the year 2008-09 amounted to A 15,00,000.

(*x*) The value of closing stock as on 31.3.09 was A 2,10,000.

(*xi*) The Club as a matter of policy charges off to Income and Expenditure account, all purchases made on account of crockery, cutlery, glass and linen in the year of purchase.

You are required to prepare :

(*i*) Income and Expenditure account for the year ended 31st March, 2009.

(*ii*) Balance Sheet as on 31st March, 2009. [*CA, Professional Competence Examination June 2009*]

Solution

Income and Expenditure Account of Nanoo Club
for the Year Ended 31st March, 2009

Expenditure	*Amount* A	*Income*	*Amount* A
To Salaries (W.N. 8)	1,28,000	By Subscriptions (W.N.2)	1,94,750
To Printing and stationery	70,000	By Entrance donation (W.N. 3)	90,000
To Postage	40,000	By Interest (W.N.4)	60,000
To Telephone and Fax	52,000	By Miscellaneous income	9,000
To Repairs and maintenance	48,000	By Profit from operations (W.N. 6)	92,000
To Glass and table linen	12,000	By Excess of expenditure over	
To Crockery and cutlery	14,000	income transferred to capital	
To Garden upkeep	8,000	find (deficit)	30,250
To Membership fees	4,000		
To Insurance (W.N.5)	6,000		
To Electricity charges (W.N. 8)	43.000		
To Loss on sale of assets (10,000 – 8,000)	2,000		
To Depreciation (W.N.9)	49,000		
	4,76,000		4,76,000

Balance Sheet of Nanoo Club as on 31st March, 2009

Liabilities	*(A)*	*Assets*	*(A)*
Capital Fund (W.N. 10)	10,89,600	Fixed assets (W.N.9)	4,41,000
Gratuity fund	1,50,000	Stock	2,10,000
Sundry creditors (W.N.7)	92,000	Investments in 12%	
Subscription received in advance	18,000	Government securities	5,00,000
Entrance donation refundable	20,000	Subscription outstanding	7,000
Outstanding salary	8,000	Interest accrued (W.N. 4)	2,000
Outstanding electricity charges	15,000	Bank	2,24,600
		Cash	8,000
	13,92,600		13,92,600

Working Notes

1. **Opening Balance Sheet as on 1st April, 2008**

Liabilities	*Amount* A	*Assets*	*Amount* A
Capital fund (Bal. fig.)	10,29,850	Fixed assets	5,00,000
Sundry creditors	1,12,000	Stock	3,80,000
Subscription received in advance	15,000	Investment in 12% Government securities	5,00,000
Entrance donation received in advance (pending membership)	1,00,000	Subscription outstanding	12,000
		Prepaid insurance	1,000
Gratuity fund	1,50,000	Cash	10,000
		Bank	3,850
	14,06,850		14,06,850

2. **Subscription**

Subscription received during the year	2,02,750
Add : Outstanding subscription on 31.3.2009	7,000
Add : Received in advance as on 1.4.2008	15,000
	2,24,750
Less : Outstanding subscription as on 1.4.2008	(12,000)
Less : Received in advance as on 31.3.2009	(18,000)
	1,94,750

3. **Entrance Donation**

Entrance Donation received during the year	1,00,000
Add : Received in Advance as on 1.4.2008	1,00,000
	2,00,000
Less : Refundable to Ineligible Member	20,000
	1,80,000
Less : 50% Capitalized	90,000
	90,000

4. **Interest Received :** Interest on A 5,00,000 @ 12% p.a. 60,000

Less : Interest received during the year	58,000
Interest accrued as on 31.3.2009	2,000
Interest credited to Income and Expenditure A/c	60,000

5. **Insurance**

Insurance paid during the year	5,000
Add : Prepaid Insurance as on 1.4.2008	1,000
	6,000

6. **Profit from Operations**

Cost of goods sold

Opening Stock as on 1.4.2008	3,80,000
Add : Purchases	15,00,000
	18,80,000
Less : Closing Stock	2,10,000
Cost of Goods Sold (A)	16,70,000
Receipts from operations	
Receipts from Coffee Room	10,70,000
Receipts from Wines and Sprits	5,10,000
Receipts from Swimming Pool	80,000
Receipts from Tennis Court	1,02,000
Total of Receipts (B)	17,62,000
Profit from Operations (B-A)	92,000

7. **Sundry Creditors**

Opening Balance as on 1.4.2008	1,12,000
Add : Purchases made during the year	15,00,000
	16,12,000
Less : Payment made during the year	15,20,000
Closing Balance as on 31.3.2009	92,000

8. (a) **Salary**

Salary paid as on 31.3.2009	1,20,000
Add : Outstanding Salary as on 31.3.2009	1,28,000
	8,000
(*b*) **Electricity Charges :** Electricity paid during the year 2008-09	28,000
Add : Outstanding Electricity charges as on 31.3.2009	43,000
	15,000

9. **Fixed Assets**

Fixed Assets as per Trial Balance	5,00,000
Less : W.D.V. of Assets sold	10,000
	4,90,000
Less : Depreciation @ 10% on A 4,90,000	49,000
Fixed Assets as on 31.3.2009	4,41,000

10. **Capital Fund**

Capital fund as on 31.3.2008	10,29,850
Add : Entrance donation capitalized	90,000
	11,19,850
Less : Deficit	30,250
	10,89,600

Example 34

The following (*i*) Receipts and Payments Account for 2009-10; (*ii*) Balance Sheet as on 31st March, 2009 and other information are given by the Shiva City College :

(*i*) **Receipts and Payments Account for the Year Ended 31st March, 2009**

Receipts	*Amount* A	*Payments*	*Amount* A
To Opening Balance	6,00,000	By Salary & Allowances	21,15,000
To Tuition Fees	18,00,000	By Provident Fund Contribution	1,66,200
To Grant	9,00,000	By Printing & Stationery	51,000
To Interest on Bank FD	9,000	By Books for Library	78,000
To Hall Rent	30,000	By Postage & Telegram	15,000
		By Newspapers	9,000
		By Laboratory Equipments	29,400
		By Telephone Expenses	25,000
		By Repairs for Building	32,000
		By Misc. Charges	18,000
		By Audit Fee	10,000
		By Creditors for outstanding	21,000
		By Bank Fixed Deposit	4,00,000
		By Closing Balances	3,69,400
	33,39,000		33,39,000

(*ii*) **Balance Sheet as on 31st March, 2009**

Liabilities	*Amount* A	*Assets*	*Amount* A
Outstanding Exp.	21,000	Cash and Bank	6,00,000
Building Fund	18,00,000	Furniture	10,50,000
Scholarship Fund	3,00,000	Land and Building	48,00,000
General Reserves	15,00,000	Tuition Fee (Outstanding)	66,000
Capital Fund	39,15,000	Library Books	7,20,000
		Fixed Deposit in Bank	3,00,000
	75,36,000		75,36,000

(*iii*) Other information :

1. It was ascertained that A 1,70,000 was outstanding by way of tuition fees on 31.03.2010.
2. The creditors outstanding for library books amounted to A 30,000 at the end of the financial year 2009-10.
3. Outstanding salaries were A 90,000 as on 31.3.10.
4. Depreciation to be charged : Land and Building at 5%, Furniture at 10%, and Library Books at 20%. You are required to prepare for Shiva City College;

(*a*) Income and Expenditure Account for the year ended 31st March, 2010.

(*b*) Balance Sheet as on 31st March, 2010. [*I.C.W.A., Inter, Dec. 2010*]

Solution

Income and Expenditure Account of Shiva City College for the Year Ended 31st March, 2010

Expenditure		*Amount* A	*Income*	*Amount* A
To Salary & Allowances (21,15,000 + 90,000)		22,05,000	By Tuition fee (18,00,000 – 66,000 + 1,70,000)	19,04,000
To P.F. Contribution		1,66,200	By Grant	9,00,000
To Printing & Stationery		51,000	By Interest on F.D.	9,000
To Postage & Telegram		15,000	By Hall Rent	30,000
To News Papers		9,000	By Excess of Expenditure over income	1,98,800
To Telephone Expenses		25,000		
To Repair for Building		32,000		
To Misc. Charges		18,000		
To Audit Fee		10,000		
To Depreciation :				
Land & Building	2,40,000			
Furniture	1,05,000			
Library Books	1,65,600	5,10,600		
		30,41,800		30,41,800

Balance Sheet of Shiva City College as on 31st March, 2009

Liabilities		*Amount* A	*Assets*	*Amount* A
Capital Fund:	39,15,000		Land & Building (48,00,000 – 2,40,000)	45,60,000
Less : Excess of Exp. over income	1,98,800	37,16,200	Furniture (10,50,000 – 1,05,000)	9,45,000
Building Fund		18,00,000	Library Books (7,20,000 + 1,08,000 – 1,65,600)	6,62,400
Scholarship Fund		3,00,000		
General Reserve		15,00,000	Laboratory Equipments	29,400
Outstanding salary		90,000	Fixed Deposit in Bank (3,00,000 + 4,00,000)	7,00,000
Creditors for Library Books		30,000	Outstanding Tuition Fee	1,70,000
			Cash and Bank	3,69,400
		74,36,200		74,36,200

Working Notes :

1. Addition in Library Books during the year A 78,000 (Paid) + A 30,000 (Outstanding) = A 1,08,000.
2. Laboratory Equipment is treated Capital in nature.

Example 35

The following is the Income and Expenditure Account of Rising Sun Club for the year ended 31.12.2010.

Expenditure	*A*	*Income*	*A*
To Printing & Stationery	3,200	By Entrance Fees	3,000
To Interest & Bank Charges	1,100	By Subscription :	80,200
To Annual Dinner Expenses	18,400	By Annual Dinner Receipt	15,000
To General Expenses	6,400	By Profit on Annual Sports	18,300
To Salaries	52,500		
To Audit Fees	3,200		
To Honorarium to Secretary	15,000		
To Depreciation on Sports Equipments	4,000		
To Surplus (being the excess of income over expenditure)	12,700		
	1,16,500		1,16,500

The following adjustments were made to prepare the accounts :

	(A)
Subscription outstanding on 01.01.10	4,000
Subscription outstanding on 31.12.10	6,300
Subscription received in advance on 31.12.09	5,600
Subscription received during the year	3,400
Salaries outstanding on 31.12.09	5,200
Salaries outstanding on 31.12.10	6,800

General expenses include insurance prepaid to the extent of A 800; Audit fees is due for the year 2010. Audit fees paid in 2010 A 2,800 for 2009.

The Club has the following assets :

	(A)
Football Ground	1,80,000
Sports Equipments on 01.01.2010	35,000

Sports Equipments on 31.12.2010, such sports equipments after depreciation amounted to37,000

The club had taken a loan of A 30,000 from a bank a few year back which remain outstanding on 31.12.10. On 31.12.10 the cash in hand amounted to A 20,000.

Prepare the Receipts and Payments Account for the year ended 31.12.10 and Balance Sheet as on that date. [*I.C.W.A., Intermediate, June 2011*]

Solution

Receipts and Payment Account for the Year Ended 31.12.2010

Receipt	*A*	*Payment*	*A*
To Balance b/d. (Bal. Fig.)	12,600	By Salaries	50,900
Subscription	75,700	General Exp. (6,400 + 800)	7,200
Entrance Fees	3,000	Audit Fees (2009)	2,800

Receipts from Annual Dinner	15,000	Sports Equipments	6,000
Profits on Sports	18,300	Hon. to Secretary	15,000
		Printing & Stationery	3,200
		Dinner Expenses	18,400
		Interest & Bank Charges	1,100
		Balance c/d	20,000
	1,24,600		1,24,600

Balance Sheet as on 31.12.2010

Liabilities		*A*	*Assets*		*A*
Capital Fund	1,88,000		Football Ground		1,80,000
Add Surplus	12,700	2,00,700	Sports Equipments	35,000	
				6,000	
Bank Loan		30,000		41,000	
Outstanding salaries		6,800	Less depreciation	4,000	37,000
Outstanding Audit Fees		3,200	Accrued Subscription		6,300
Pre-received subscription		3,400	Prepaid insurance		800
			Cash		20,000
		2,44,100			2,44,100

Working Notes **:**

		A	*A*
1.	Subscription receivable (Op. Balance)	4,000	
	Add : Income & Expenses (income for the year)	80,200	
	Add : Subscription received in advance (cl.)	3,400	87,600
	Less : Subscription in advance (Op. Bal.)	5,600	
	Less : Subscription receivable (Cl)	6,300	
			11,900
	Subscription received during the year in cashg		75,700
2.	Sports Equipments		
	Closing Balance	37,000	
	Add : Depreciation	4,000	41,000
	Less : Opening Balance		35,000
	Cash Purchase		6,000
3.	Salaries :		
	Oustanding Salary (01.01.10)	5,200	
	Income & Expenditure (Given)	52,500	
		57,700	
	Less : Outstanding Salary (31.12.10)	6,800	
	Salaries paid in cash	50,900	

4. Balance Sheet as on 01.01.10.

	(A)		(A)
Capital fund	1,88,000	Football Ground	1,80,000
Bank Loan	30,000	Sports Equipments	35,000
Advance Subscription	5,600	Outstanding, Subscription	4,000
Outstanding Salaries	5,200		
Outstanding Audit Fees	2,800	Cash in hand	13,600
	2,31,600		2,31,600

Note : While solving this problem it has been assumed that the figure of A 3,400 as "Subscription received during the year" in the question is actually "Subscription received during the year in advance".

ASSIGNMENT MATERIAL

Note : The objective type questions (True/False, Multiple Choice Questions etc.) have been given in the Appendix at the end of the book.

SHORT ANSWER THEORY QUESTIONS

1. Distinguish between Receipts and Payments Account and Income and Expenditure account.
2. What is Not for profit organizations?
3. What is an Income and Expenditure account?
4. Write a note on Receipts and Payments Account.
5. How are the following items treated?
   (*i*) Subscription
   (*ii*) Donation
6. What is endowment fund?
7. What is fund based accounting?

LONG ANSWER THEORY QUESTIONS

1. Explain the accounting system used in profit making and Not for Profit Organizations.
2. Discuss the financial statements prepared by Not for Profit Organizations.
3. Explain the treatment of the following items in the final accounts of Not for Profit Organization :
   (*i*) Donation
   (*ii*) Subscription
   (*iii*) Entrance fees
   (*iv*) Life membership fees.

PRACTICAL PROBLEMS

1. Prepare the "Subscriptions Account" from the following items for the year ending 31 March 2003 :

		A
(*i*)	Subscriptions in arrears on 31 March 2002	500
(*ii*)	Subscriptions received in advance at 31 March 2002 for 2002-03	1,100

(*iii*) Total Subscriptions received during 2002-03 35,400
(including A 400 for 2001-02, A 1,200 for 2003-04 and A 300 for 2004-05)

(*iv*) Subscriptions outstanding for 2002-03 400

[*B.Com. (Hons.) Delhi University*]

Ans. Balance A 1,500

2. (*a*) How will you deal with the following case while preparing final accounts of a non-profit organization.

	01.1.1998 (*A*)	*31.12.1998* (*A*)
Stock of Stationery	600	100
Creditors for Stationery	400	260
Advance paid for stationery	40	60

Amount paid for Stationery during 1998 was A 2,160.

(*b*) There were 450 members in a club each paying an annual subscription of A 50. A 500 were in arrears as on 31st December, 1998 Subscription received during 1999 were A 22,300 including A 450 for 1998 and A 750 for the year 2000. Calculate the amount of subscription in arrears as on 31st December, 1999 by preparing Subscription Account.

Ans. (*a*) Stationery used during the year A 2,500
(*b*) A 1,400.

3. From the following particulars, prepare income and expenditure account :

		A
(*i*)	Fees collected, including A 80,000 on account of the previous year	3,80,000
(*ii*)	Fees for the year outstanding	10,000
(*iii*)	Salary paid, including A 3,000 on account of the previous year	28,000
(*iv*)	Salary outstanding at the end of the year	1,000
(*v*)	Entertainment expenses	3,000
(*vi*)	Tournament expenses	12,000
(*vii*)	Meeting expenses	18,000
(*viii*)	Travelling expenses	6,000
(*ix*)	Purchase of books and periodicals, including A 19,000 for purchase of books	29,000
(*x*)	Rent	10,000
(*xi*)	Postage, telegrams ad telephones	15,000
(*xii*)	Printing and stationery	4,000
(*xiii*)	Donations received	20,000

[*Company Secretary, Foundations*]

Ans. Excess of income over expenditure A 2,26,000.

4. From the following information available for the records of the Indian Sports Association, prepare Income and Expenditure Account for the year ended 31st March 2004.

	A		*A*
Subscription Received	25,000	Tournament Fees Received	25,000
Upkeep of playground	3,000	Tournament Prizes Awarded	7,000
Entrance Fees Received	8,000	Stock of Refreshment (1.4.2003)	540

Rent Paid	1,200	Purchases of Canteen Stores and Refreshments	8,460
Salaries and Wages	3,200		
Travelling Expenses	900	Cash and Bank Balances	47,000
Stock of Equipment (1.4.2003)	9,000	Tournament Fund	10,000
Tournament Expenses	14,000	General Fund	30,000
Printing and Stationery	3,000	Subscription Arrears	14,000
General Charges	6,000	Creditors for Expenses	3,300

Information

(*a*) Equipment is to be valued on the basis of Revaluation at the end of year. The Committee of Management has decided to have the equipment valued at 85% of its book value on 1.4.2003.

(*b*) Subscriptions in arrears as on 31.3.2004 were as follows :

For 2001-2002 A 2,000, For 2002-2003 A 3,000, For 2003-2004, A 13,000. During the year, arrears of subscriptions totalling A 9,000 relating to earlier periods had been collected.

(*c*) Donations of A 11,000 include A 4,000 received on account of Tournament account.

(*d*) 25% of the Entrance fees has to be capitalised.

(*e*) Stock of Refreshment as on 31.3.2004 was as follows :

Value of Provision, Stores etc. A 2,000. Value of Eatable and perishables A 500. Value of water bottles, cigarettes etc. A 300..

The Committee of Management decides to adhere to the scheme of valuation of these items as hitherto followed, *viz.*,

(*i*) to value provisions and stores at cost;

(*ii*) the stock of perishables and eatables on the basis of realised sales proceeds on the subsequent day to the closing of accounts; and

(*iii*) water bottles and cigarettes at 80% of their purchase price.

Sales of eatable and perishables on 1 April 2004 amounted to A 275.

(*f*) The Association had printed its annual report for 2002 – 2003 and the bill due from the printers is for A 500. Another bill for the brochure brought out for tournament is also pending for settlement and is for A 1,200. [*CA, Foundation*]

Ans. Excess of Income over Expenditure A 16,365.

5. From the following Receipts and Payments Account of Delhi Club and additional information, prepare an Income and Expenditure Account for the year ending 31 March 2006 :

Receipts and Payment Account for 2005-06

	(A)		*(A)*
Cash in hand 1.4.2005	10,200	Purchase of Balls	65,000
Cash at Bank as per Bank Pass Book	30,000	Tournament Fees	10,000
Subscriptions	2,45,000	Affiliation fees for 5 years	2,000
Interest on investments	1,800	Rent of Playground	6,000
Sales of Tickets for Variety Programme	20,000	Variety Programme (expenses)	15,000
Sale of Furniture on 30.9.2005	9,000	Refreshment expenses	4,000
Donations for Club Building	50,000	Travelling expenses	20,000
Legacy	11,000	Furniture bought on 1.10.2005	5,000

		Repairs to Building	5,000
		Advance paid to contractor for Pavilion Building	50,000
		Salary	15,000
		Telephone Bill	1,500
		Miscellaneous expenses (including Honorarium of Rs. 3,000)	8,000
		12% Investments (Face value A 1,70,000)	1,50,000
		Bought on 31.12.2005	
		Cash in hand 31.3.06	8,500
		Balance in the Bank as per Pass Book on 31.3.2006	12,000
	3,77,000		3,77,000

Additional Information

(*i*) Subscriptions received include A 9,000 outstanding subscriptions of the year 2004-05. Subscriptions for the year 2005-06 amounting to A 16,000 are still outstanding. Some members have paid subscriptions for the year 2006-07 amounting to A 8,000 which is included in the subscriptions received.

(*ii*) Face value of 12% Investments on 31 March 2005 was A 15,000 (cost price Rs. 12,000).

(*iii*) Book value of furniture sold on 1 April 2005 was A 12,000 depreciation being 20% p.a. Provide depreciation on new furniture at the same rate.

(*iv*) Telephone bill for one quarter is outstanding, the amount outtanding being A 300. The charge for each quarter is same both for 2004-05 and 2005-06.

(*v*) Unpresented cheques for repairs to building being A 4,000 for 2004-05 and A 12,000 for 2005-06.

(*vi*) Stock of Balls with the club on 31 March 2006 amounted to Rs. 6,000.

[*B.Com. (Hons.) Delhi University, 1993*]

Ans. Surplus A 1,15,800.

6. From the following Receipts and Payments Account, prepare the Income and Expenditure Account for the year 31st December 2011 :

Receipts	*A*	*Payments*	*A*
To Balance b/d	10,000	By Rent (including A 1,500 for 2010)	6,000
To Entrance Fees :		By Insurance Premium	6,000
2010	1,000	(including A 1,500 for 2012)	
2011	5,000	By sports Materials	5,000
To Subscriptions :		By Sports Equipment	6,000
2010	1,000	(Purchased on 31.12.2011)	
2011	9,000	By 8% Fixed Deposits	12,000
2012	500	(made on 1.7.2011)	
To Life Membership Subscription	2,000	By Tournament Expenses	1,000
To Donations	12,000	By Purchase of books	2,000
To Donation for Tournament	5,000	By Postage Stamps	500
To Subscription for Governor's Party	1,500	By Printing and Stationery	1,500

To Interest on 8% Fixed Deposit	240	By Newspapers and Periodicals	2,000
To Sale of Old Sports Materials	30	By Balance c/d	6,000
To Sale of Old Sports Equipment (Books Value A 120)	50		
To Locker Rents (including A 60 for 2010)	500		
To Sale of Old Newspapers and Periodicals	180		
	48,000		48,000

[*CA, Foundation*]

Ans. Excess of Income over Expenditure A 9060.

7. Prepare Receipts and Payments Account and Income and Expenditure Account of Rakhi (India) club for the year ended 31st March 2003, from the following particulars:

	A
Subscriptions collected (including A 4,000 for 2001)	30,000
Donation received (not to be capitalised)	2,000
Subscription outstanding at the end of the year	6,000
Rent paid	1,800
Purchase of furniture (life 10 years) at the beginning of the year	1,000
Purchase of sport equipments	2,500
Purchase of magazines and newspapers	1,200
Sale of all old furniture at the beginning of the year (book value A 300)	500
Opening cash balance and the bank balance	6,800
Investments purchased	4,000
Interest on investments received	1,000
Bank charges	20
Postage, telegrams and telephones	1,800
Printing and stationery (one bill of A 300 for last year)	1,000
Printer's bill not yet paid	500
Entrance fees (50% to be capitalised)	1,400
Legacies received (to be capitalised)	2,000
Honorary Secretary's Allowances (including A 200 for the last year)	1,800
Outstanding Allowances (honorary Secretary)	300

[*CA, Foundation*]

Ans. Receipts and payments A/c balance A 28,580; Excess of income over expenditure A 27,880.

8. Given below is the Receipts and Payments Account of the National Club for the year ended 31 March 1994 :

Receipts	*A*	*Payments*	*A*
Balance b/d	10,250	Salaries	6,000
Subscriptions :		General expenses	800
1992 – 93	400	Entertainment programme	

1993 – 94	20,500	Expenses	4,500
1994 – 95	600	Newspapers	1,500
Donations	5,400	Charity	3,500
Proceeds of entertainment		Investment (Govt. Bonds)	20,000
Programme	9,500	Municipal taxes	500
Sale of waste papers	450	Electricity charges	1,400
		Balance c/d	8,900
	47,100		47,100

Prepare the club's income and expenditure account for the year ended 31 march 1994 and the balance sheet as on that date, after taking the following information into account :

(*a*) There are 500 members paying an annual subscription of A 50 each; A 500 is still in arrear for 1992-93.

(*b*) Municipal taxes amounting to A 400 per annum have been paid up to 30 June 1994 and A 500 for salaries are outstanding.

(*c*) Buildings stand in the books at A 50,000 and it is required to write off depreciation at 5 per cent per annum.

(*d*) 6 per cent per annum interest is accrued on government bonds for 5 months.

Ans. Surplus A 19,750; Balance Sheet total A 82,000.

9. Following is the Receipts and Payments Account of Diamond Literary Club for the year ended on 31 March 1996 :

	(A)		*(A)*
Cash at Bank	12,500	Salaries	2,500
Subscriptions	52,500	Printing and Stationery	1,250
Annual Day Receipts	26,800	Annual Day Expenses	2,500
Mushaira Receipts	22,000	Telephone Charges	2,500
Dividend Receipts	2,000	Sundry expenses	2,000
		Investments in Shares	75,000
		Postage and Telegrams	2,250
		Building and Maintenance	6,000
		Rent of Theatre	10,000
		Cash at Bank	11,800
	1,15,800		1,15,800

Additional Information

(*i*) On 1 April 1995, Buildings stood in the books at A 50,000 and Investments in Shares at A 5,000. Buildings are subject to depreciation @ 5% p.a.

(*ii*) There are 200 members paying subscription at the rate of A 250 per annum each. Some members have paid their annual subscription in advance during the year.

(*iii*) As on 1 April 1995, no subscription had been received but subscriptions were outstanding to the extent of A 1,000 as at 31 March 1995. Subscription accrued as on 31 March 1996 was A 1,500.

(*iv*) Postage stamps worth A 250 were in stock with Secretary as on 1 April 1995 and as on 31 March 1996, they were valued at A 150.

(*v*) Telephone charges paid in advance were A 300.

You are required to prepare Income and Expenditure Account for the year ended on 31 March 1996 and the Balance Sheet as at that date.

Ans. Excess of Income over Expenditure A 69,500; Balance Sheet total A 1,41,250.

10. From the following particulars relating to a Charitable Hospital, prepare Income and Expenditure Account for the year ended 31 December 1999 and a Balance Sheet as at that date :

Receipts and Payments Account
for the Year Ended 31st December 1999

	(A)		(A)
Balance b/d	7,130	Debtors's Honorarium	9,000
Subscriptions	47,996	Suppliers of Medicines	30,590
Donations	4,500	Petty Expenses	461
Legacies	10,000	Salaries	27,500
Interest on Investments		Equipment Purchased	15,000
@ 10% for full year	7,000	Expenses on Charity Show	2,750
Proceeds from Charity Show	10,450	Balance c/d	1,775
	87,076		87,076

Additional Information

	1.1.1999 A	31.12.1999 A
Subscriptions Due	650	800
Subscriptions Received in Advance	254	300
Stock of Medicines	8,910	9,800
Suppliers of Medicines	4,000	2,500
Outstanding Salaries	3,600	4,800
Equipment	21,200	31,600
Buildings (Cost less Depreciation)	90,000	81,000

Ans. Excess of Expenditure over Income A 12,661, B/S total A 1,94,975.

11. The following is the Receipts and Payments Account of a cultural society for the year ended 31 December 1999 :

Receipts	A	*Payments*	A
Cash in hand, 1 January	1,500	Bank Overdraft, 1 January	3,100
Subscriptions : 1998	200	Investments in Securities	3,000
1999	16,200	Furniture	1,450
2000	250	Salary	6,200
Entertainment Proceeds	2,000	Printing and Stationery	890
Entrance Fees	670	Entertainment Expenses	1,710
Interest on securities	480	Sundry Expenses	1,420
Sale of old Chairs	120	Balance on 31.12.1999 :	
(Book Value-Nil)		Cash	550
		Bank	3,100
	21,420		21,420

You are required to prepare income and expenditure account of cultural society for the year ended 31 December 1999 and a balance sheet as on that date after considering the following :

(*i*) The society has 1,800 members each paying annual fees of A 10. Subscriptions amounting to A 90 were still in arrears for the year 1998.

(*ii*) Stock of stationery on 31 December 1998 was A 125 and on 31 December 1999 was A 87.

(*iii*) Entrance fees are to be capitalised.

(*iv*) Salary of A 550 for December 1999 is outstanding. Expenses accrued on 31 December 1998 were A 132. The society had paid A 500 in 1998 for telephone charges out of which A 125 related to the year 1999.

(*v*) On 31 December 1998, premises stood in the books at A 24,500 and investments at A 6,500.

(*vi*) Depreciate fixed assets by 5%.

Ans. Excess of Income over Expenditure A 8501; Balance Sheet total A 39,779.

12. The following is the Receipts and Payments Account of Mehruli Club for the year ended 31 December 2011 :

Receipts		A	*Payments*	A
Cash in hand (1.1.2011)		3,500	Bank overdraft (1.1.2011)	1,800
Subscriptions :			Salaries	6,700
2010	4,000		Printing and Stationery	500
2011	22,000		Furniture	10,000
2012	1,000	27,000	Investment in Securities	15,000
Income from Entertainment		2,300	Balance on 31.12.2011 :	
Entrance Fee		4,500	Cash in hand	1,700
Interest on Securities		5,600	Cash at Bank	9,000
Sale of old Furniture		1,800		
(Book value 1,500)				
		44,700		44,700

Prepare Income and Expenditure Account for the year ended 31 December 2011 and the Balance Sheet as on that date having due regard to the following additional information :

(*i*) The Club has 250 members paying an annual subscription of A 100 each.

(*ii*) Salary of A 500 was outstanding on 1.1.2011 and A 600 are still payable for the year 2011.

(*iii*) The Club had furniture A 26,500, Building A 50,000 and Investments A 70,000 as on 1.1.2011.

(*iv*) Depreciate Building and Furniture by 5% of their closing balances. [*C.A.* (*Entrance*)]

Ans. Surplus A 21,650; Capital Fund A 1,51,700; Balance Sheet total A 1,79,450.

13. From the following Receipts and Payments A/c of Mumbai Club, prepare Income and Expenditure A/c for the year ended 31.12.2012 and its Balance Sheet as on that date:

Dr. *Cr.*

Receipts	A	*Payments*	A
Cash in Hand	4,000	Salary	2,000
Cash at Bank	10,000	Repair Expenses	500
Donations	5,000	Purchase of Furniture	6,000
Subscriptions	12,000	Misc. Expenses	500
Entrance Fees	1,000	Purchases of Investments	6,000

Interest on Investments	100	Insurance Premium	200
Interest Received from Bank	400	Billiard Table	8,000
Sale of old newspaper	150	Paper, Ink, etc.	150
Sale of Drama Tickets	1,050	Drama Expenses	500
		Cash in Hand	2,650
		Cash at Bank	7,200
	33,700		33,700

Information

1. Subscription in arrear for 2012 A 900 and subscriptions in advance for 2012 A 350.
2. Insurance Premium Outstanding A 40.
3. Miscellaneous expenses prepaid A 90.
4. 50% of donation is to be capitalised.
5. Entrance fees are to be treated as revenue income.
6. 8% interest has accrued on investment for five months.
7. Billiard table costing A 30,000 was purchased during the last year and A 22,000 were paid for it. [*C.A.*]

Ans. Excess of Income over Expenditure A 14,150; Balance Sheet total A 53,040.

14. The following was the Receipts and Payments account of Exe Club for the year ended Dec. 31, 2012 :

Dr. *Cr.*

Receipts	*A*	*Payments*	*A*
Cash in hand	100	Groundsman's Fee	750
Balance at Bank as per Pass Book:		Mowing Machine	1,500
Deposit Account	2,230	Rent of Ground	250
Current Account	600	Cost of Tea	250
Bank Interest	30	Fares	400
Donations and Subscriptions	2,600	Printing and Office Expenses	280
Receipts from Tea	300	Repairs to Equipment	500
Contribution to fares	100	Honoraria to Secretary	
Sale of Equipment (at book value)	80	and Treasurer for year 2011	400
Net proceeds of Variety Entertainment	780	Balance at Bank as per Pass Book:	
Donation for forthcoming	1,000	Deposit Account	3,090
Tournament		Current Account	150
		Cash in hand	250
	7,820		7,820

You are given the following additional information :

	1.1.2012	31.12.2012
Subscriptions Due	150	100
Amount due for printing etc.	100	80
Cheques unpresented being payment for repairs	300	260
Estimated value of machinery and equipment	800	1,750
Interest not yet entered in the Pass Book		20

Bonus to Groundsman	300

For the year ended Dec. 31,2012, the honoraria to the Secretary and Treasurer are to be increased by a total of A 200.

Prepare the Income and Expenditure Account for 2012 and the Balance Sheet as at 31.12-2012.
[*C.A. Adapted*]

Ans. Excess of income over expenditure A 40; Balance Sheet total A 5210.

15. Excellent Library Society showed the following position on 31st December 2001 :

Dr. *Cr.*

Liabilities	*(A)*	*Assets*	*(A)*
Capital Fund	7,93,000	Electrical Fittings	1,50,000
Expenses due	7,000	Furniture	50,000
		Books	4,00,000
		Investments as Securities	1,50,000
		Cash at Bank	25,000
		Cash in Hand	25,000
	8,00,000		8,00,000

The Receipts and Payments Account for the year ending on 31st December 2002 is given below :

Dr. *Cr.*

Receipts		A	*Payments*	A
To Balance b/d			By Electric Charges	7,200
Cash at Bank	25,000		By Postage and Stationery	5,000
Cash on Hand	25,000	50,000	By Telephone Charges	5,000
To Entrance Fees		30,000	By Books purchases (on 1.1.2002)	60,000
To Membership Subscription		2,00,000	By Outstanding Expenses Paid	7,000
To Sale Proceeds of Old Papers		1,500	By Rent Account	88,000
To Hire of Lecture Hall		20,000	By Investment in Securities	40,000
To Interest on Securities		8,000	By Salaries	66,000
			By Balance c/d	
			Cash at Bank	20,000
			Cash in Hand	11,300
		3,09,500		3,09,500

You are required to prepare Income and Expenditure Account for the year ending 31.12.2002 and a Balance Sheet as on that date after making the following adjustments:

(*a*) Membership subscriptions included A 10,000 received in advance,

(*b*) Provide for Outstanding Rent A 4,000 and Salaries A 3,000,

(*c*) Books to be depreciated @ 10% including additions. Electrical Fittings and Furniture are also to be depreciated at the same rate,

(*d*) 75% of the Entrance fees is to be capitalised,

(*e*) Interest on Securities is to be calculated @ 5% p.a. including purchases of investments made on 1.7.2002 for A 40,000. [*C.A. (Foundation) May 2002*]

Ans. Excess of expenditure over income A 16,700. Balance Sheet total A 8,15,800.

16. The following is the receipts and payments account of a charitable hospital for the year ended 31 March 2012.

Dr. *Cr.*

Receipts	*A*	*Payments*	*A*
Balance b/f :		Medicines	1,500
Cash in hand	50	Honorarium to Doctors	500
Cash at Bank	300	Salaries	1,375
Subscriptions	2,500	Sundry expenses	25
Donations	725	Equipments purchased	750
Interest for full year		Charity show expenses	50
On investments @ 7%		Balance c/f :	
Per annum	350	Cash in hand	25
Charity show receipts	500	Cash at bank	200
	4,425		4,425

Additional Information

	31.3.2011 (A `000)	*31.3.2012 (A `000)*
Subscriptions outstanding	25	50
Subscriptions received in advance	50	25
Stock of medicines	500	750
Amounts due to suppliers of medicines	400	600
Value of equipments	1,050	1,500
Value of buildings	2,000	1,900

You are required to prepare income and expenditure account for the year ended 31 March, 2012 and the balance sheet as on that date. [*C.S.* (*Foundation*)]

Ans. Excess of income over expenditure A 3,25,000; Total of Balance Sheet A 94,25,000.

17. The Accountant of Diana Club furnishes you the following Receipts and Payments account for the year ending 30th September, 2012

Dr. *Cr.*

Receipts	*Amount A*	*Payments*	*Amount A*
Opening balance		Honoraria to secretary	9,600
Cash and bank	16,760	Misc. expenses	3,060
Subscriptions	21,420	Rates and taxes	2,520
Sale of old newspapers	4,800	Groundman's wages	1,680
Entertainment fees	8,540	Printing and stationery	940
Bank interest	460	Telephone expenses	4,780
Bar receipts	14,900	Payment for bar purchases	11,540
		Repairs	640
		New car (Less-sale proceeds of old car A 6,000)	25,200
		Closing Balance :	
		Cash and bank	6,920
	66,880		66,880

Additional Information

		1.10.2011	30.9.2012
(*i*)	Subscriptions Due (not received)	2,400	1,960
(*ii*)	Cheques issued, but not presented for payment of printing	180	60
(*iii*)	Club premises at cost	58,000	–
(*iv*)	Depreciation on club premises provided so far	37,600	–
(*v*)	Car at cost	24,380	–
(*vi*)	Depreciation on car	20,580	–
(*vii*)	Value of Bar stock	1,420	1,740
(*viii*)	Amount unpaid for bar purchases	1,180	860

(*ix*) Depreciation is to be provided @ 5% p.a. on the written down value of the club premises and @ 15% p.a. on car for the whole year.

You are required to prepare an Income and Expenditure account of Diana Club for the year ending 30th September, 2012 and Balance Sheet as on that date. [*CAPEI Nov. 2004*]

Ans. Excess of Income over Expenditure A 12060, Balance Sheet total A 56,520.

18. From the following Income and Expenditure Account and Balance Sheet of a Club, prepare Receipts and Payments Account for the year ending 31 March 2012 :

Income and Expenditure Account
For the Year Ending 31 March 2012

Dr. *Cr.*

Expenditure	*Amount A*	*Income*	*Amount A*
Upkeep of Ground	10,000	Subscriptions	17,320
Printing	1,000	Sale of old Newspapers	160
Salaries	12,000	Lectures	2,500
Depreciation	1,000	Entrance Fees	1,300
Rent	1,200	Miscellaneous Income	1,100
		Deficit	2,820
	25,200		25,200

Balance Sheet as on 31 march 2012

Liabilities		*Amount A*	*Assets*	*Amount A*
Subscription in Advance		100	Furniture	9,000
Prize Fund	25,000		Ground and Building	47,000
Add : Interest	1,000		Prizes Fund Investments	20,000
	26,000		Subscriptions Receivable	700
Less : Prizes	2,000	24,000	Cash in hand	2,300
Accumulated surplus	56,420			
Add : Entrance Fees	1,300			
	57,720			
Less : Deficit	2,820	54,900		
		79,000		79,000

The other relevant information is given below ;

(*i*) Upkeep of ground A 600 and Printing A 240 were paid for the year ending 31 March 2011.

(*ii*) Subscriptions outstanding for 2010-11 were A 800 and that for 2011-12 were A 700.

(*iii*) Subscriptions received in advance during 2010-11 were shown at A 200 and that for 2011-12 at A 100. **Ans.** Receipts and Payments A/c Balance A 2300.

19. The following is the Income and Expenditure Account of a charitable hospital for the year 2005 :

Dr. *Cr.*

Expenditure		*Amount* A	*Income*	*Amount* A
Salaries		23,500	Subscriptions	22,000
Diet expenses		2,000	Donations	4,000
Rent		500	Interest on investments	
Insurance		200	for one year @ 5%	9,000
Office expenses		800	Miscellaneous receipts	600
Surgery and Dispensary expenses		1,000		
Depreciation on :				
Building	3,750			
Furniture	120			
Instruments	800	4,670		
Surplus		2,930		
		35,600		35,600

Additional Information

	A
Cash in hand on 31.12.2004	200
Cash at bank on 31.12.2004	5,400
Building on 31.12.2004	75,000
Furniture on 31.12.2004	2,000
Instruments on 31.12.2004	3,500
Subscriptions outstanding on 31.12.2004	1,500
Salaries outstanding on 31.12.2004	1.800
Subscriptions received in advance on 31.12.2004	600
Subscription received in advance on 31.12.2005	800
Subscriptions outstanding on 31.12.2005	4,500
Salaries outstanding on 31.12.2005	2,000
Instruments purchased during the year	500
Cash in hand on 31.12.2005	150

You are required to prepare the Receipts and Payments Account for 2005 and a Balance Sheet of the hospital as at 31 December 2005. Also show your workings.

Ans. Cash at Bank on 31.12.2005 – A 9,950; Capital Fund on 31.12.2004 – A 2,65,200; Balance Sheet totals on 31.12.2004 – A 2,67,600 and on 31.12.2005 – A 2,70,930.

20. The income and expenditure account of Bharat Club for the year ended 31 March, 2000 was as follows :

Dr. *Cr.*

Expenditure	*Amount* A	*Income*	*Amount* A
Salaries	1,20,000	Subscriptions	1,70,000
Printing	6,000	Entrance fees	4,000
Postage	500	Contribution for dinner	36,000
Telephone	1,500		
General expenses	12,000		
Interest charges	5,500		
Audit fees	2,500		
Annual dinner expenses	25,000		
Depreciation on sports equipment	7,000		
Surplus	30,000		
	2,10,000		2,10,000

The income and expenditure account has been prepared after taking into consideration the following information :

	As on 31.3.1999 A	*As on 31.3.2000* A
Subscriptions outstanding	16,000	18,000
Subscriptions received in advance	13,000	8,400
Salaries outstanding	6,000	8,000
Audit fees outstanding	2,000	2,500
Buildings	1,90,000	1,90,000
Sports equipment	52,000	63,000

During the year 1998-99, the Bharat Club raised a bank loan of A 30,000 which was outstanding on 31 March, 2000 also. Cash in hand on 31 March, 2000 was A 28,500.

Prepare the receipts and payments account of the Bharat Club for the year ended 31 March, 2000 and the balance sheet as on that date.

Ans. Cash in hand A 28,500; total of Balance Sheet A 2,99,500.

21. From the following Income and Expenditure Account of Diamond Club for the year ended on march 31, 1998 and its Balance Sheet as on March 31, 1997, prepare Receipts and Payments Account for the year ended on March 31, 1998 and a Balance Sheet as at that date :

Income and Expenditure Account
for the Year Ending 31 March 1998

Dr. *Cr.*

Expenditure	*Amount* A	*Income*	*Amount* A
Salaries	50,000	Subscriptions	94,000
Rent	11,000	Entrance Fees	6,000
Travelling Expenses	1,000	Donations	10,000

Printing and Stationery	1,000	Interest	5,000
General Charges	1,500		
Periodicals	500		
Surplus	50,000		
	1,15,000		1,15,000

Balance Sheet as at 31 March 1997

Liabilities	*Amount* A	*Assets*	*Amount* A
Outstandings :		Furniture	40,000
Rent	1,000	Sports Equipments	20,000
Salaries	6,500	Investments	1,00,000
Accumulated Fund	1,72,500	Subscription Receivable	5,000
		Interest Receivable	1,000
		Bank Balance	14,000
	1,80,000		1,80,000

Other Information as on 31 March, 1998 :

Subscription Receivable A 8,000, Salaries Outstanding A 4,000; Rent Outstanding A 2,000.

Ans. Receipts and Payments A/c Balance A 60,500; Balance Sheet total A 2,28,500.

22. The Charitable Dispensary of Agra had the following Balance Sheet on 31st December, 2008.

Balance Sheet as at December 31,2008

Liabilities		*Amount* A	*Assets*	*Amount* A
Salaries payable		3,000	Cash	1,500
Subscriptions received in Advance		500	Equipment	8,000
Capital Fund :			Stock of Medicines	1,600
As on 1.1.2008	11,200		Furniture and Fittings	6,000
Add : Life Membership	2,500		Subscription Due and Receivable	2,000
Surplus	1,900	15,600		
		19,100		19,100

The accompanying Income and Expenditure Account was the following :

Income and Expenditure Account
for the Year Ended December 31, 2008

Dr. *Cr.*

Expenditure	*Amount* A	*Income*	*Amount* A
Salaries	35,000	Entrance Fees	300
Cost of Medicines used	6,700	Subscriptions	36,100
Depreciation of equipment	600	Miscellaneous Receipts	150

Miscellaneous Expenses	1,500	Profit on Sale of Old Furniture (Book value A 1,500)	200
Surplus	1,900	Grant from Municipal Corporation	8,950
	45,700		45,700

You learn that on 31st December, 2007 equipment stood at A 6,000 subscription due and receivable totalled A 2,500 where subscription already received for 2008 were A 700. Stock of medicines on December 31, 2007 was A 1,100.

Prepare the Receipts and Payments Account of the Dispensary for 2008. [*C.A.*]

Ans. Receipts and Payments A/c Balance A 1500.

23. Following is the Income and Expenditure Account of Victoria Club for the year ending 31st March 2008 :

Dr. *Cr.*

Expenditure		*Amount* A	*Income*		*Amount* A
Salaries and Wages		19,000	Subscription		30,000
Misc. Expenses (including insurance)		2,000	Entrance Fees received		1,000
Audit fees		1,000	Annual Sports Income		
Chief Executives' Honorarium		4,000	Receipts	6,000	
Printing and Stationery		1,800	*Less :* Expenses	3,000	3,000
Annual day Celebration Expenses	6,000				
Less : Donation	4,000	2,000			
Interest on Bank loan		600			
Depreciation on Sports Equipment		1,200			
Excess of Income over Expenditure		2,400			
		34,000			34,000

Additional Information

	31.3.2007	31.3.2008
(*i*) Subscription outstanding	2,400	3,000
(*ii*) Subscription received in advance	1,800	1,080
(*iii*) Salaries outstanding	1,600	1,800
(*iv*) Sports equipment (after deducting depreciation)	10,400	10,800
(*v*) Prepaid Insurance	–	240
(*vi*) Cash in Hand	?	6,400
(*vii*) The Club owned a Sports' ground of A 40,000		
(*viii*) The Club took a loan of A 8,000 from a bank during the year 2006-07, which was not paid on 2007-08.		
(*ix*) Audit fee of 2007-08 was outstanding, but Audit fees of A 800 for 2006-07 was paid in 2007-08.		

Prepare Receipts and Payments Account for the year ending 31st March, 2008 and a Balance Sheet on that date. [*CAPEI May 2006*]

Ans. Receipts and Payments A/c Balance A 6,400 Balance Sheet total 60,440.

24. The following the Income and Expenditure Account of Delhi Youth Club for the year ended 31st March, 2008 :

Income and Expenditure Account for the Year Ended 31st March, 2008

Dr. *Cr.*

Expenditure	*Amount* A	*Income*	*Amount* A
Salaries	19,500	Subscription	68,000
Rent	4,500	Donation	5,000
Printing	750		
Insurance	500		
Audit Fees	750		
Games and Sports	3,500		
Subscriptions written off	350		
Misc. Expenses	14,500		
Loss on Sale of Furniture	2,500		
Depreciation :			
Sports Equipment	6,000		
Furniture	3,100		
Excess of Income over expenditure	17,050		
	73,000		73,000

Additional Information

	31.3.2007 A	*31.3.2008* A
Subscriptions in arrears	2,600	3,700
Advance Subscriptions	1,000	1,500
Outstanding expenses :		
Rent	500	800
Salaries	1,200	350
Audit Fees	500	750
Sports Equipment *less* depreciation	25,000	24,000
Furniture *less* depreciation	30,000	27,900
Prepaid Insurance	—	150

Book value of furniture sold is A 7,000. Entrance fees capitalised A 4,000. On 1st April, 2007, there was no cash in hand but Bank Overdraft for A 15,000. On 31st March, 2008, Cash in hand amounted to A 850 and the rest was Bank Balance.

Prepare the Receipts and Payments Account of the Club for the year ended 31st March, 2008. [*C.A.*]

Ans. Receipts and Payments A/c Bank Balance A 7250.

25. The Receipts and Payments account of Trustwell Club prepared on 31st March, 2008 is as follows :

Receipts and Payments Account

Dr. *Cr.*

Receipts		*Amount* A	*Payments*	*Amount* A
Balance b/d		450	Expenses (including payment for sports material A 2,700)	6,300
Annual Income from Subscription	4,590		Loss on Sale of Furniture (cost price A 450)	180
Add : Outstanding of last year received this year	180		Balance c/d	90,450
	4,770			
Less : Prepaid of last year	90	4,680		
Other fees		1,800		
Donation for Building		90,000		
		96,930		96,930

Additional Information

Trustwell Club had balance as on 1.4.2007 : Furniture A 1,800; Investment at 5% A 27,000; Sports material A 6,660; Balances as on 31.3.2008 : Subscription outstanding A 270; Subscription received in advance A 90; Stock of sports material A 1,800.

Do you agree with above Receipts and Payment account? If not, prepare correct Receipts and Payments account and Income and Expenditure account for the year ended 31st March, 2008 and Balance Sheet on that date. [*C.A.(PE-1)–May, 2003*]

Ans. Receipts and Payments A/c balance A 90,720, Excess of Expenditure over Income A 3600; Balance Sheet total A 1,22,490.

26. The following are the receipts and payments account and income and expenditure account of a club for the year ending 31st March 2008 :

Receipts and Payments Account
for the Year Ended on 31.3.2008

Dr. *Cr.*

Expenditure	*Amount* A	*Income*	*Amount* A
Balance	7,600	Salaries	4,800
Entrance fees	5,200	Insurance	1,000
Subscription (including for 2005-06 A 1,500)	17,000	Rates and Taxes	1,400
		Addition to library on 31.3.2008	2,500
Sale of old Newspapers	120	Payments of creditors of last year	1,300
Rent of Hall (Library) (including A 700 for 2006-07)	2,080	Postage	100
		Repairs	500
Entertainment show	6,000	Printing and Stationery	800
Sale of old furniture	300	Electricity Installation expenses	9,000
		Sundry expenses (including outstanding)	4,300
		Balance c/d	12,600
	38,300		38,300

Income and Expenditure Account
for the Year Ended on 31.3.2008

Expenditure	*(A)*	*Income*	*(A)*
Salaries	4,800	Entrance Fees	5,200
Rates and Taxes	1,400	Subscription	17,700
Insurance	650	Rent of library hall	2,130
Repair	500	Sale of old newspapers	120
Printing and stationery	800	Entertainment show	6000
Postage	100		
Sundry expenses	1,900		
Depreciation : Building @ 5%	700		
Library books @10%	3,370		
Investment @5%	500		
Loss on sale of furniture	50		
Surplus	16,380		
	31,150		31,150

The club sold all its furniture during the year. Prepare opening and closing balance sheet of the club,

Ans. Balance Sheet total (closing) A 80,530; capital fund A 64,150.

27. Novel Education Society supplied the following information :

Income and Expenditure Account
for the Year Ended 31st March, 2008

Dr. *Cr.*

Expenditure	*Amount (A '000)*	*Income*	*Amount (A '000)*
Salaries	830	Subscriptions	4,780
Scholarships	4,130	Government grant	530
Rent	280	Proceeds of tickets for	
General expenses	310	entertainment	830
Audit fees	60	Advertisement in Souvenir	510
Printing tickets and souvenir	150	Interest on bank fixed deposits	150
Cost of entertainment	350	(for full year @ 6% per annum)	
Loss on sale of furniture (book value, A 80,000)	30		
Depreciation on furniture	60		
Surplus, *i.e.*, excess of income over expenditure	600		
	6,800		6,800

Receipts and Payments Account
for the Year Ended 31st March, 2008

Expenditure	*(A)*	*Income*	*(A)*
Balance b/f	380	Salaries	940
Subscriptions	4,600	Scholarships	4,010

Government grant	530	Rent	260
Sale of tickets	830	General expenses	310
Advertisements in souvenir	460	Printing of tickets and souvenir	120
Interest on bank fixed deposits	100	Cost of entertainment	350
Sale of furniture	50	Furniture	200
		Balance c/f	760
	6,950		6,950

On 31st March, 2007, subscriptions due were A 1,50,000, furniture on that date was A 6,00,000. Prepare balance sheets as at 31st March, 2007 and 31st March 2008.[*C.A. Foundation June 2005]*

Ans. Balance Sheet total (closing) A 4350. Capital fund A 3520.

28. The following is the Receipts and Payments Account of Delhi Football Association for the first year ending 31 December 2007 :

Receipts and Payments Account

Dr. *Cr.*

Receipts	*Amount* A	*Payments*	*Amount* A
Donations	50,000	Pavilion Offices (constructed)	40,000
Reserve Fund (Life membership fees and entrance fees received)	4,000	Expenses in connection with matches	900
		Furniture	2,100
Receipts from football matches	8,000	Investment at cost	16,000
Revenue Receipts		*Revenue Payments*	
Subscriptions	5,200	Salaries	1,800
Locker Rents	50	Wages	600
Interest on Securities	240	Insurance	350
Sundries	350	Telephone	250
		Electricity	110
		Sundry expenses	210
		Balance in hand	5,520
	67,840		67,840

Additional Information

(*i*) Subscriptions outstanding for 2007 are A 250.

(*ii*) Salaries unpaid for 2007 are A 170.

(*iii*) Wages unpaid for 2007 are A 90.

(*iv*) Outstanding bills for sundry expenses are A 40.

(*v*) Donations received have to be capitalised.

Prepare from the details given above, an Income and Expenditure Account for the year ended 31.12.2007 and the Balance Sheet of the Association as on 31.12.2007.

Hint : As the revenue receipts and revenue payments have been separately given, match receipts and expenses would be taken direct to the Balance Sheet. [*C.A. (Entrance), November, 2007*]

Ans. Surplus A 2,470; B/s total A 63,870.

29. A club gives you the following Receipts and Payments Account for the year ended 31 March, 2008 :

Receipts and Payments Account

Dr. *Cr.*

Receipts	*(A)*	*Payments*	*(A)*
Balance b/d	4,820	Salaries	12,000
Subscriptions	28,600	Rent and electricity	7,220
Miscellaneous Income	700	Library Books	1,000
Interest on fixed deposit	2,000	Magazines and newspapers	2,172
		Sundry expenses	10,278
		Sports eqipments	1,000
		Balance c/d	2,450
	36,120		36,120

Figures of other assets and liabilities :

	31.3.2007 A	*31.3.2008* A
Outstanding salaries	710	170
Outstanding rent and electricity	864	973
Outstanding for magazines and newspapers	226	340
Fixed deposit (10%) with bank	20,000	20,000
Interest accrued thereon	500	500
Subscriptions receivable	1,263	1,575
Prepaid expenses	417	620
Furniture	9,600	
Sports equipments	7,200	
Library Books	5,000	

The closing values of furtniture and sports equipments are to be determined after charging depreciation at 10% and 20% p.a. respectively inclusive of additions, if any, during the year. The library books are revalued at the end of every year and the value at the end of March 31, 2008 was A 5,250.

Required :

(*i*) Balance Sheet as at 31.3.2007

(*ii*) Income and Expenditure Account for the year ended on March 31, 2008.

(*iii*) Balance Sheet as at 31.3.2008. [*C.A. (Entrance)*]

Ans. Excess of Expenditure over Income A 2,888; B/s total A 45,595.

30. The following is the Receipts and Payments Account of an Amusement Club :

Receipts and Payments Account for the year ended 31 December 2008.

Receipts		*(A)*	*Payments*	*(A)*
Balance b/d :			Salary of Secretary	3,600
Cash	60		Honorarium	450
Bank	3,000	3,060	Wages	2,400
Subscriptions (including			Charities	2,000
Subscription for 2007 A 150)		9,000	Printing and Stationery	300

Sale of Old Furniture on Jan. 1, 2008	750	Postage	100
		Rent and Taxes	1,200
Sale of Newspapers	50	Upkeep of the Land	500
Legacies	3,000	Sports Materials	2,500
Interest on Investments (Cost of Investments A 20,000)	1,200	Balance c/d	14,850
Endowment Fund Receipts	10,000		
Proceeds of Concerts	800		
Advertisement in the Year Book	40		
	27,900		27,900

Current assets and liabilities as on December 31, 2007 and 2008 were as follows :

	31.12.2007 A	*31.12.2008* A
Subscriptions in Arrears	200	450
Subscriptions in Advance	300	600
Furniture	2,000	1,080

Depreciation was 10% p.a. on the furniture left after selling a part of it. It was decided that half of the legacies may be capitalised.

Prepare Income and Expenditure Account and the Balance Sheet as on that date.

[*B.Com.(Hons.) Delhi University*]

Ans. Excess of Expenditure over Income A 680; B/s total A 36,380.

31. The following informations were obtained from the books of Delhi Club as on 31.3.2006, at the end of the first year of the Club. You are required to prepare Receipts and Payments Account, Income and Expenditure Account for the year ended 31.3.2006 and a balance Sheet as at 31.3.2006.

(*i*) Donations received for Building and Library Room A 2,00,000.

(*ii*) Other revenue income and actual receipts.

	Revenue Income (A)	*Actual Receipts (A)*
Entrance Fees	17,000	17,000
Subscriptions	20,000	19,000
Locker Rents	600	600
Sundry Income	1,600	1,060
Refreshment Account	—	16,000

(*iii*) Other revenue expenditure and actual payments :

	Revenue Expenditure (A)	*Actual Payments (A)*
Land (cost A 10,000)	—	10,000
Furniture (cost A 1,46,000)	—	1,30,000
Salaries	5,000	4,800
Maintenance of Playgrounds	2,000	1,000
Rent	8,000	8,000
Refreshment Account	—	8,000

Donations to the extent of A 25,000 were utilised for the purchase of Library Books, balance was still unutilised. In order to keep if safe, 9% Govt. Bonds of A 1,60,000 were purchased on 31.3.2006. Remaining amount was put in the Bank on 31.3.2006 under the term deposit. Depreciation at 10% p.a. was to be provided for the whole year on furniture and library books.

[*CA, Foundation*]

Ans. Surplus A 15,100; B/s total A 3,40,440

32. The following particulars relate to Mumbai Sports Club :

Income and Expenditure Account
for the year ended 31 March 2007.

Dr. *Cr.*

Expenditure	*Amount* A	*Income*	*Amount* A
Salaries	60,000	Admission Fees	1,50,000
Printing and Stationery	25,000	Subscriptions	2,50,000
Advertising	10,000	Rent	48,000
Insurance Charges	9,000		
Electricity Charges	5,000		
Depreciation on Sports Equipment	1,20,000		
Surplus	2,19,000		
	4,48,000		4,48,000

Receipts and Payments Account
for the year ended 31 March 2007.

Dr. *Cr.*

Receipts		*Amount* A	*Payments*	*Amount* A
Balance b/d		50,000	Salary (including paid in advance)	75,000
Admission Fees :			Printing and Stationery	25,000
2006-2007	25,000		Advertising	10,000
2007-2008	1,35,000	1,60,000	Insurance (including prepaid)	12,000
Subscriptions :			Electricity Charges	5,000
2005-06	10,000		Sports Equipment	2,00,000
2006-07	2,30,000		Balance c/d	1,79,000
2007-08	20,000	2,60,000		
Rent		36,000		
		5,06,000		5,06,000

Further on 1 April 2006, the Club had the following assets :

(*i*) Land and Building A 6,00,000

(*ii*) Furniture A 45,000

(*iii*) Sports Equipments A 3,00,000

(*iv*) Subscriptions for 2005-06 A 12,000

Subscriptions for 2006-07 received in advance were A 8,000. Outstanding salary was A 6,000. Admission fees received in advance for 2006-07 were A 1,25,000.

Prepare the opening and closing balance sheets. [*C.A. Intermediate*]

Ans. Capital A 8,68,000; B/s Total A 12,42,000.

CHAPTER 14

Single Entry System
(Final Accounts from Incomplete Records)

Learning Objectives

After studying this chapter, you should be able to :

1. *Define single entry system.*
2. *Identify features of single entry system.*
3. *Discuss advantages and disadvantages of single entry system.*
4. *Distinguish between double entry system and single entry system.*
5. *Explain the methods of ascertaining profit under single entry system – Statement of Affairs Method, Conversion Method.*

MEANING OF SINGLE ENTRY SYSTEM

It is difficult to define single entry system because, in fact, there exists no system like single entry system. Broadly speaking, it is a defective double entry system. Any system that falls short of complete double entry method is called single entry system.

Accounting records maintained on the basis of double entry system of book-keeping have a special feature *i.e.,* every transaction has two aspects, debit and credit. The meaning of single entry system emerges from this feature of double entry system. Single entry system is that system where complete double entry system is not followed for maintaining books of accounts. Under this system, sometimes both aspects of a transaction is recorded, sometimes only one aspect of a transaction is recorded and sometimes transaction is not recorded at all in the books of accounts. The owner of a business firm records only those transactions which are important from his point of view. Generally, record of cash, accounts receivable, accounts payable and taxes paid may be maintained under this system. Only those transactions are important which affects personal accounts. Nominal account which relates to revenues, expenses, gains and losses and real account which relates to assets and liabilities of a business firm are totally ignored. Since, all transactions are not recorded, hence single entry system is also called accounting from Incomplete Records.

To conclude, single entry system may be defined as a system which does not strictly conform to the double entry system of book keeping. Under this system what is found in practice is an intermixture of single entry, double entry and no entry.

FEATURES OF SINGLE ENTRY SYSTEM

The following are the features of Single Entry System.

1. The method of recording business transactions is unsystematic and unscientific. Recording is done, according to convenience and information needs of business.
2. There is no uniformity in maintenance of records under single entry system by different organisations.
3. There is generally no systematic record of real and personal accounts, only a record is kept for cash transactions which mixes up business and personal transactions.

4. Rules of double entry system are not followed in single entry system.
5. Single entry system is less expensive since time and labour involved in maintaining accounting records is less in comparison to double entry system.
6. This system can be used by sole traders and partnership firms to some extent but not used by corporate organizations.
7. Profit and financial position can not be determined accurately under single entry system.

Advantages

The following are the advantages of single entry system.

1. Single entry system is suitable in those enterprises where business is done on a small scale.
2. To maintain records by single entry system, well qualified staff is not required and hence, this system is not expensive.

Disadvantages

The following are the disadvantages of single entry system.

1. Under this system accounting is done from incomplete records and hence, is unreliable.
2. Arithmetical accuracy of the records cannot be checked because both aspects of transactions are not recorded in some cases, hence, trial balance cannot be prepared.
3. Entries relating to nominal account and real account are not done. Therefore, it is not possible to maintain profit and loss account and balance sheet.
4. Statements prepared under financial accounting helps manager to take decision for the future. Preparation of financial statements with accuracy is not possible under single entry system. Hence, it is difficult for managers to take decision for future.
5. Control function also becomes difficult due to unavailability of complete and reliable data.
6. Under single entry system it is difficult to detect fraud and thefts.
7. This system is not recognised by Accounting and Legal Authorities.

DIFFERENCE BETWEEN DOUBLE ENTRY SYSTEM AND SINGLE ENTRY SYSTEM

The following are the differences between double entry system and single entry system.

Double Entry System	*Single Entry System*
1. In this systems both aspect of a transaction is recorded.	1. In this system for some transaction both aspects are recorded, for some only one aspect is recorded and some transactions are not recorded in books of accounts.
2. Arithmetical accuracy of transactions can be checked by preparing trial balance	2. Arithmetical accuracy of transactions cannot be checked as Trial Balance cannot be prepared.
3. Profit and Loss Account and the Balance Sheet can be prepared as under this system personal, nominal account and real account is maintained.	3. Profit and Loss Account and Balance Sheet cannot be prepared as only personal account is maintained in this system.
4. Under this system, all transactions are recorded. Therefore, accounts and statements prepared are reliable.	4. In this system all transactions are not recorded; statements are prepared from incomplete records hence, they are unreliable.
5. This system is suitable for small as well as large business enterprises.	5. This system is suitable only for small business enterprises.
6. This system is expensive as well qualified trained staff is required to maintain records.	6. This system is less expensive as well qualified trained staff is not required.

Double Entry System	*Single Entry System*
7. This system is recognised by accounting and legal bodies.	7. This system is not recognised by accounting and legal bodies.
8. Double entry system help managers to perform planning and control functions.	8. Single entry system cannot help managers to perform planning and control functions.
9. Theft and errors can be detected easily.	9. Theft and errors cannot be detected.
10. Financial statements are comparable between two or more firms as recording of transactions is done on the basis of rules and regulations.	10. Financial statements results cannot be compared as no rules and regulations are followed to record the transactions.

METHODS OF ASCERTAINMENT OF PROFIT

In single entry system, profit or loss is ascertained and financial position of business firms can be determined using the following two methods.

I Statement of Affairs Method (or Pure Single Entry System)

II Conversion Method (or Quasi Single Entry System)

I. STATEMENT OF AFFAIRS METHOD

Under this method, statement of affairs is prepared in the beginning and the end of the year, to calculate capital in the beginning and at the end of the year respectively. Statement of affairs lists assets on right hand side, liabilities on the left hand side and the excess of assets over liabilities is assumed to be capital and recorded on left hand side so that total assets are equal to liabilities plus capital. It should be noted that complete information about assets and liabilities is not available from accounting records and some of these assets and liabilities are estimated. Proforma of a Statement of Affairs is as follows :

Statement of Affairs as on .....

Liabilities	*(A)*	*Assets*	*(A)*
Creditors		Cash	
Bills payable		Bank	
Outstanding expenses		Debtors	
Unearned income		Bills receivable	
Loans		Stock	
Capital (*Balancing Figure)*		Prepaid expenses	
		Accrued income	
		Fixed assets	

To prepare final accounts, two statements of Affairs are prepared, one at the beginning of year and other at the end of the year. If capital (which we derive as balancing figure) at the end is more than the capital at the beginning, the difference will represent the amount of profit. If capital at the end is less than the capital at the beginning, the difference will represent the amount of loss.

In order to calculate profit and loss by this method two items must be adjusted to calculate profit & loss which are as follows :

(*i*) **Capital Invested during the Accounting Period :** If fresh capital is introduced during the accounting period, then capital is increased to that extent. To calculate profit or loss, fresh capital introduced must be deducted from the capital at the end.

(*ii*) **Drawings :** If the proprietor had withdrawn some amount for personal use, then capital decreases to that extent. To calculate profit or loss drawings must be added back to the capital at the end.

Thus, Profit or Loss = (Capital at the end + Drawing – Additional capital introduced) – Capital at the beginning.

Illustration

Rakesh maintains his book on the basis of Single Entry System. On 1st Jan. 2010 his position was as follows :

	(A)
Cash in hand	1,000
Cash at Bank	15,000
Stock in trade	1,00,000
Sundry Debtors	42,500
Furniture	9,000
Machinery	75,000
Sundry Creditors	1,10,000

On 31st December 2010, his financial position was as follows

	(A)
Cash in hand	1,500
Cash at Bank	10,000
Machinery	1,35,000
Furniture	7,500
Sundry Debtors	70,000
Stock in trade	95,000
Sundry Creditors	1,45,000

During the year Rakesh introduced fresh capital of A 25,000 and withdrew A 45,000 for his personal use.

Prepare a statement showing the profit or loss made by him during 2010.

Solution

Statement of Affairs as at 1st Jan. 2010

Liabilities	*(A)*	*Assets*	*(A)*
Sundry Creditors	1,10,000	Cash in hand	1,000
Capital (Bal. Fig.)	1,32,500	Cash at Bank	15,000
		Sundry Debtors	42,500
		Stock in trade	1,00,000
		Furniture	9,000
		Machinery	75,000
	2,42,500		2,42,500

Statement of Affairs as at 31st Dec. 2010

Liabilities	*(A)*	*Assets*	*(A)*
Sundry Creditors	1,45,000	Cash in Hand	1,500
Capital (*Bal. Fig.*)	1,74,000	Cash at Bank	10,000
		Sundry Debtors	70,000
		Stock in trade	95,000
		Furniture	7,500
		Machinery	1,35,000
	3,19,000		3,19,000

Statement of profit for the year ending 31st Dec. 2010.

	(A)
Capital as at 31st Dec. 2010	1,74,000
Add : Drawing during the year	45,000
	2,19,000
Less : Capital Introduced during the year	25,000
	1,94,000
Less : Capital as at 1st Jan. 2010	1,32,500
Net Profit during the year	61,500

DIFFERENCE BETWEEN STATEMENT OF AFFAIRS AND BALANCE SHEET

As discussed earlier, in Single entry system we cannot prepare a Balance Sheet because in this system transactions relating to Real A/c are not recorded which are the basis of preparing a Balance Sheet. Still in order to have an idea of financial position of a business, a statement similar to a Balance Sheet is prepared which is called "Statement of Affairs".

Following are the points of difference between Statement of Affairs and a Balance Sheet.

Statement of Affairs	*Balance Sheet*
1. It is prepared under the single entry system.	1. It is prepared under double entry system.
2. In order to equal both sides of statement of affairs capital as a balancing figure has to be calculated.	2. Total of both sides of balance sheet equal automatically on its own.
3. Final account are prepared from transaction recorded, estimates and sometimes from memory.	3. It is prepared from the data available from the accounts books only.
4. It is prepared on the basis of incomplete information and other sources which are not reliable.	4. All transactions are recorded in accounts books which can be verified by vouchers which are reliable.

II. CONVERSION METHOD

Single entry system is not helpful in preparing trial balance at the end of the accounting period. Therefore, final accounts or financial statements can not be prepared from incomplete records, unless steps are taken to complete the records. Under conversion method, cash account, debtors accounts, creditors account etc. are examined and an attempt is made to complete double entry by making posting/entries into unposted ledger accounts.

If a particular account is not found in books, a new account is opened and necessary posting is done. After completing records on the basis of double entry from incomplete records, trial balance is extracted and, then, final accounts are prepared. This is the reason that this method is also called conversion of single entry into double entry system or preparation of final accounts from incomplete records.

In reality, conversion involves completion of ledger books, preparation of a trial balance and, then financial statements. However, this procedure of conversion is generally not followed because of time and labour involved in the lengthy process of conversion and due to the absence of detailed information. To solve examination problems significant missing information required for completion of trading account, profit and loss account and balance sheet is calculated from whatever information is given in the question. After calculating significant information missing in the question, final accounts are prepared.

The following procedure should be followed under conversion method to prepare final accounts *i.e.*, trading account, profit and loss account and balance sheet.

(*i*) Prepare Cash and Bank Summary (if not available in proper form with both sides tallied) to ascertain missing information (such as opening and closing balance, cash sales/cash purchases, drawings.)

(*ii*) Prepare Total Debtors Account to ascertain the missing information (such as opening/closing balance, credit sales, collection, B/R drawn).

(*iii*) Prepare Bills Receivable Account to ascertain the missing information (such as opening/closing balance, B/R drawn, B/R collection).

(*iv*) Prepare Total Creditors Account to ascertain the missing information (such as opening / closing balance, credit purchases, payment made, B/P accepted).

(*v*) Prepare Bills Payable Account to ascertain the missing information (such as opening/closing balance, B/P accepted, B/P discharged).

(*vi*) Prepare Stock Account to ascertain the missing information (such as opening stock/closing stock, total purchases, cost of goods sold, shortage).

(*vii*) Prepare Revenue Expenses Account to ascertain the missing information (such as opening/closing balance of outstanding/prepaid expenses, expenses paid, current year's expenses).

(*viii*) Prepare Revenue Income Account to ascertain the missing information (such as opening/closing balance of accrued/unaccrued income, Income received, current year's income).

(*ix*) Prepare Fixed Asset Account to ascertain the missing information (such as opening/closing balance, purchases/sale, depreciation provided, profit/loss on sale).

(*x*) Ascertain Opening Capital by preparing Statement of Affairs at the beginning of the accounting period.

(*xi*) Prepare Trial Balance to check the arithmetical accuracy.

(*xii*) Prepare Trading and Profit and Loss Account and the Balance Sheet.

Specimen of some accounts are given here to understand the items which appear in these accounts.

Dr. *Total Debtors A/c* *Cr.*

To Balance b/d (Debtors in the beginning) To Sales A/c (Credit Sales) To Bills Receivable A/c (Bill dishonoured)		By Cash or Bank A/c (Amount received from debtors) By Bills receivable A/c (Bills drawn on debtors) By Sales Return A/c By Discount Allowed A/c By Bad Debts A/c	

		By Balance c/d (Debtors at the end of the year)	

Dr.	*Total Creditors A/c*		Cr.
To Cash A/c or Bank A/c (Amount paid to creditors) To Bills Receivable A/c (for B/R endorsed) To Bills payable A/c (Bills accepted) To Purchases Return A/c To Discount Received A/c To Balance c/d (Creditors at the end)		By Balance b/d (Creditors in the beginning) By Purchases A/c (Credit purchases) By Bills Payable A/c (Bills Payable disonoured)	

Dr.	*Bills Receivable A/c*		Cr.
To Balance b/d (Balance in the beginning) To Debtors A/c (Bills drawn during the year)		By Bank A/c & Discount A/c (for Discounting of Bills) By creditors A/c (B/R endorsed to creditors) By Cash A/c (B/R encashed on due date) By Debtors A/c (B/R dishonoured) By Balance c/d (B/R at the end)	

Dr.	*Bills Payable A/c*		Cr.
To Cash A/c (B/P paid on due dates) To Creditors A/c (B/P Dishonoured)		By Balance b/d (B/P in the beginning) By Creditors A/c (Bills accepted during the year)	

Example 1

	(A)
Find out the profit of Mr. A from the following information :	
Capital at the beginning of the year	20,00,000
Drawing made by Mr. A	2,00,000

Capital at the end of the year 25,00,000

Additional capital introduced during the year 1,00,000

[C.A., November, 2009]

Solution

Statement showing profit earned by Mr. A during the year

	(A)
Capital at the end of the year	25,00,000
Add : Drawings	2,00,000
	27,00,000
Less : Additional capital introduced during the year	(1,00,000)
	26,00,000
Less : Capital at the beginning of the year	20,00,000
Profit earned during the year	6,00,000

Example 2

A trader purchased goods of A 1,70,000. The opening stock of inventory prior to the said purchase was A 30,000. His sales was A 2,10,000. Find out the closing stock of inventory if the gross profit margin is 25% on cost.

[C.A. November, 2009]

Solution

Calculation of closing stock.

Cost of goods sold = Sales – Gross Profit

$= \text{A } 2{,}10{,}000 - (\text{A } 2{,}10{,}000 \times \frac{25}{125})$

= A 1,68,000

Closing Stock = Opening Stock + Purchases – Cost of goods sold

= A 30,000 + A 1,70,000 – A 1,68,000

= A 32,000.

Example 3

Rashid and Co. keeps his book on single entry system, his position on 1st January 2011 was as follows :

Cash in hand A 200, Cash at Bank A 3,000; Stock in trade A 20,000, sundry debtors A 8,500; furniture A 1,800; machinery A 15,000; sundry creditors A 22,000.

On 31st December 2011 the financial position was as follows :

Cash in hand A 300; cash at bank A 2,000; machinery A 27,000; furniture A 1,500; sundry debtors A 14,000; stock in trade A 19,000; sundry creditors A 29,000.

During the year Rashid introduced a new capital of A 5,000 and withdrew for his personal expenditure A 9,000.

From the above figure, prepare a statement showing the profit or loss made by him during 2011.

Solution

Rashid & Co.
Statement of Affairs as at 1st January 2011

Liabilities	*(A)*	*Assets*	*(A)*
Sundry creditors	22,000	Cash in Hand	200
Capital (balancing figure*)	26,500	Cash at Bank	3,000
		Sundry debtors	8,500
		Stock in trade	20,000
		Furniture	1,800
		Machinery	15,000
	48,500		48,500

*48,500 – 22,000

Rashid & Co.
Statement of Affairs as at 31st December, 2011

Liabilities	*(A)*	*Assets*	*(A)*
Sundry creditors	29,000	Cash in Hand	300
Capital (balancing figure)	34,800	Cash at Bank	2,000
		Sundry debtors	14,000
		Stock in trade	19,000
		Furniture	1,500
		Machinery	27,000
	63,800		63,800

Statement of Profit for the Year ending 31st December 2011

	(A)
Capital as at 31st December 2011	34,800
Add : Drawings during the year	9,000
	43,800
Less : Capital introduced during the year	5,000
	38,800
Less : Capital as at 1st January, 2011	26,500
Net Profit during the year	12,300

Example 4

Tridepa does not maintain complete double entry books of accounts. From the following details determine profit for the year and a statement of affairs as at the end of the year. A 1,000 (cost) Furniture was sold for A 5,000 on 1.1.2008. 10% depreciation is to be charged on furniture. Drawing are A 1,000 per month and additional capital introduced amounted to A 2,000.

	1.1.2008 (A)	31.12.2008 (A)
Stock	40,000	60,000
Debtors	30,000	40,000
Cash	2,000	1,000
Bank	10,000	5,000 (Overdraft)
Creditors	15,000	25,000
Outstanding Expenses	5,000	8,000
Furniture (Cost)	3,000	2,000

Bank balance on 1.1.2008 is as per cash book, but the bank balance on 31.12.2008 is as per bank pass book. A 2,000 cheques drawn in December 2008 have not been encashed within the year.

[*B.Com. (Hons.) Delhi University*]

Solution

Tridepa
Statement of Affairs

Liabilities	*1.1.08 (A)*	*31.12.08 (A)*	*Assets*	*1.1.08 (A)*	*31.12.08 (A)*
			Stock	40,000	60,000
Creditors	15,000	25,000	Debtors	30,000	40,000
Outstanding Expenses	5,000	8,000	Cash	2,000	1,000
Bank Overdraft as			Bank	10,000	
Per Cash Book (5,000 + 2,000)	–	7,000	Furniture	3,000	2,000
Capital (Balancing Figure)	65,000	63,000			
	85,000	1,03,000		85,000	1,03,000

Statement of Profit and Loss (2008)

Capital at the end (31.12.2008)	63,000
Add : Drawings	12,000
	75,000
Less : Additional Capital	2,000
	73,000
Less : Capital in the beginning (1.1.2008)	65,000
Gross Profit	**8,000**
Less : Profit on sale of furniture	4,000
	4,000
Less : Depreciation on furniture (10% on A 2,000)	200
Operating Profit	**3,800**
Add : Profit on sale of furniture	4,000
Net Profit	7,800

Example 5

Mr. Ashok owns a general store in Delhi and does not maintain his accounts on Double Entry System. His assets and liabilities on 1st April 2011 were as follows :

Bills payable A 2,000, Creditors A 3,310. Stock and Debtors A 18,600, Banks and Cash Balance A 6,710 and Machine A 15,000. His position as on 31st March 2012 was as follows :

Machine A 15,000. Debtors A 9,320, Motor Cycle A 12,000, Cash in hand A 3,000. Bank Balance as per Bank statement A 5,930, Stock A 13,400 and Creditors A 8,700.

During the year he had withdrawn A 4,500 for household requirements and a motor-cycle was purchased for business use. A cheque of A 700 issued in March 2012 was not presented on 31st March 2012.

Required : Ascertain the amount of profit of the trader for the year ending 31st March 2012 after making following adjustments :

(*a*) Write off A 400 as bad debts and provide 5% provisions for doubtful debts.

(*b*) Provide 8% depreciation on Machine and 10% on Motor-Cycle [*B.Com.(Hons.) Delhi*]

Solution

Statement of Profit Earned During the Year 2011-12

	(A)	(A)
A. Closing Capital		49,250
B. *Add :* Drawings		4,500
C. Adjusted Closing Capital		53,700
D. *Less :* Opening Capital		35,000
E. Profit subject to adjustments		18,750
F. Adjustments :		
Depreciation on machines	1,200	
Depreciation on Motor Cycle	1,200	
Bad Debts	400	
Provision for Doubtful Debts	446	3,246
G. Net Profit		15,504

Working Notes :

(i) Statement of Affairs as on 1.4.2011

Liabilities	(A)	*Assets*	(A)
Bills Payable	2,000	Stock and Debtors	18,600
Creditors	3,310	Cash and Bank Balance	6,710
Capital (Balancing figure)	35,000	Machines	15,000
	40,310		40,310

Dr. **(i) Statement of Affairs as on 31.3.2012** Cr.

Liabilities	*(A)*	*Assets*	*(A)*
Creditors	8,700	Machines	15,000
Capitals (Balancing figure)	49,250	Motor Cycle	12,000
		Stocks	13,400
		Debtors	9,320
		Cash in hand	3,000
		Bank Balance [A 5,930 – A 700]	5,230
	57,950		57,950

Example 6

A, B and C were in partnership, and towards the end of year 2012 most of their books and records were destroyed in a fire. The Balance Sheet as on 31st December 2011 was as follows :

Liabilities	*(A)*	*Assets*	*(A)*
Creditors	55,000	Cash	24,000
Capitals :		Debtors	36,000
A	45,000	Stock	65,000
B	30,000	Machinery	14,400
C	15,000	Fixture and Fittings	6,000
Current Accounts :		Advance Payments	350
A	1,450	Current Account—C	1,700
B	1,000		
	1,47,450		1,47,450

The partner's drawing during year 2012 were:

A. A 14,000; B: A 10,000 and C : A 6,500. A introduced A 15,000 as additional Capital in July 2012. On 31st December 2012 the cash was A 32,000, Debtors A 40,250, Stock A 59,000, Advanced Payments A 250 and Creditors A 45,400, Machinery is to be depreciated by 10% p.a. and Fixtures and Fittings at 7½%, 5% interest is to be allowed on capitals. No interest is to be charged on drawings. The partners share profits in the proportions of 3 : 2 : 1.

Required : Prepare a Statement showing the net trading profit for the year 2012 and the division of the same between partners, together with the Balance Sheet as on 31st December 2012.

[B.Com. (Hons.) Delhi 2001]

Solution

Statement Showing the Net Profit for the Year 2012

	(A)
A. Closing Net Balance of Current Accounts at the end	1,500
B. *Add :* Drawing during the year [A 14,000 + A 10,000 + A 6,500]	30,500
C. Adjusted Closing Balance [A + B]	32,000

D.	*Less :* Opening Net Balance of Current Accounts [A 1,450 + A 1,000 – A 1,700]		750
E.	Profit subject to adjustments :		31,250
F.	Adjustments :		
	Depreciation on Machinery @ 10%	1,440	
	Depreciation on Fixtures and Fittings @ 7.5%	450	1,890
G.	Net Operating Profit		29,360
H.	*Less :* Interest as Capital		
	A. [45,000 × 5% × 1] + [15,000 × 5% × 6/12]	2,625	
	B. [30,000 × 5% × 1]	1,500	
	C. [15,000 × 5% × 1]	750	4,875
I.	Net Profit [*G – H*]		24,485

Balance Sheet as at 31st December 2012

Liabilities	*(A)*	*Assets*		*(A)*
Creditors	45,400	Cash		32,000
Capitals :		Debtors		40,250
A	60,000	Stock		59,000
B	30,000	Advance Payments		250
C	15,000	Machinery	14,400	
Current Accounts :		*Less :* Depreciation	1,400	12,960
A	2,317	Fixture and Fittings	6,000	
B	662	*Less :* Depreciation	450	5,550
		Current Account : C		3,369
	1,53,379			1,53,379

Working Notes :

(*i*) Statement of Affairs as at 31st December 2012

Liabilities	*(A)*	*Assets*	*(A)*
Creditors	45,400	Cash	32,000
Capitals :		Debtors	40,250
A	60,000	Stock	59,000
B	30,000	Advance Payments	250
C	15,000	Machinery	14,400
Current Accounts :	1,500	Fixture and Fittings	6,000
	1,51,900		1,51,900

Dr. **(*i*) Current Accounts of Partners** Cr.

Particulars	A (A)	B (A)	C (A)	Particulars	A (A)	B (A)	C (A)
To Balance b/d	—	—	1,700	By Balance b/d	1,450	1,000	—
To Cash A/c	14,000	10,000	6,500	By Interest on Capitals	2,625	1,500	750
To Balance c/d	2,317	662		By Profit	12,242	8,161	4,081
				By Balance c/d	—	—	3,369
	16,317	10,662	8,200		16,317	10,662	8,200

Example 7

Preeti and Kareena are equal partners in a business in which the books are maintained using single entry system. On 1 April, 2009, their statement of affairs was as under :

Liabilities		*(A)*	*Assets*	*(A)*
Bills payable		12,400	Cash in hand	540
Sundry creditors		40,000	Cash at Bank	27,760
Capital accounts :			Bills receivable	9,200
Preeti	1,60,000		Sundry Debtors	67,600
Kareena	1,60,000	3,20,000	Stock	97,300
			Furniture and Fixtures	10,000
			Plant and Machinery	1,60,000
		3,72,400		3,72,400

On 31 March, 2010, following was the state of affairs :

Cash in hand A 800; cash at bank A 31,600; sundry creditors A 42,400; stock A 1,33,400; sundry debtors A 60,600; bills payable A 13,200; bills receivable A 17,600. Plan and machinery and furniture and fixtures are to be depreciated by 10%.

Ascertain the profit for the year ended 31 March, 2010, and draw up the statement of affairs as on that date, showing the accounts of the partners in detail, assuming Preeti withdrew A 30,000 and Kareena withdrew A 26,000 during the year. *[C.S. (Foundation) December 2000]*

Solution

Statement of Affairs of Preeti and Kareena as on 31 March, 2010

	(A)		*(A)*
Creditors	42,400	Cash in hand	800
Bills Payable	13,200	Cash at Bank	31,600
Combined Capital	3,58,400	Stock	1,33,400
(Balancing Figure)		Sundry Debtors	60,600
		Bills Receivable	17,600
		Furniture and Fixtures	10,000
		Plant and Machinery	1,60,000
	4,14,000		4,14,000

Statement of Profit (2009-10)

		(A)	(A)
(i) Combined Capital as at 31 March, 2009			3,58,000
Add : Drawings :			
	Preeti	30.,000	
	Kareena	26,000	56,000
			4,14,400
Less : Combined Capital as on 31 March 2009			
	Preeti	1,60,000	
	Kareena	1,60,000	3,20,000
Gross (or Trading) Profit			94,400
Less : Depreciation :			
	Furniture and Fixtures	1,000	
	Plant and Machinery	16,000	17,000
Net Profit			77,400
Each Partner gets : 77,400 ÷ 2 = A 38,700			

Statement of Affairs as on 31 March, 2010

Particulars		(A)	*Particulars*		(A)
Sundry Creditors		42,400	Cash in hand		800
Bills payable		13,200	Cash at Bank		31,600
Preeti's Capital	1,60,000		Stock		1,33,400
Less : Drawing	30,000		Sundry Debtors		60,600
	1,30,000		Bills Receivable		17,600
Add : Net Profit	38,700	1,68,700	Furniture and Fixtures	10,000	
Kareena's Capital	1,60,000		*Less :* Depreciation	1,000	9,000
Less : Drawing	26,000				
	1,34,000		Plant and Machinery	1,60,000	
Add : Net Profit	38,700	1,72,700	*Less :* Depreciation	16,000	1,44,000
		3,97,000			3,97,000

Example 8

In a concern, the opening provision for doubtful debts in A 51,000. During the year a sum of A 10,000 was written off as bad debt. The closing balance of sundry debtors amounts to A 6,30,000. It was decided that 10% of the debtors is to be maintained as provision. Calculate the closing balance towards provision for doubtful debts and pass journal entry for giving effect to the provision maintained. [*C.A., May, 2008*]

Solution

Closing balance of Sundry Debtors	A 6,30,000
Closing Provision for doubtful debts to be maintained @ 10%	A 63,000
Less : Opening Provision for doubtful debts	A 51,000
Additional provision to be maintained	A 12,000

Journal Entry

	(A)	(A)
Profit and Loss A/c	12,000	
To Provision for doubtful debts		12,000
(Being additional provision on doubtful debts maintained @ 10%		

Example 9

A company sold 25% of the goods on cash basis and the balance on credit basis. Debtors are allowed 2 months credit and their balance as on 31.3.2008 is A 1,40,000. Assume that the sale is uniform through out the year. Calculate the total sales of the company for the year ended 31.3.2008. [*C.A. May, 2008*]

Solution

Debtors as on 31.3.2008	A 1,40,000
Credit period allowed	2 months
i.e., Debtors as on 31.3.2008 is standing for credit sales of February and March 2008	
Credit sales per month	A 1,40,000/2
	A 70,000
Credit sales for the year 2007-2008	A 70,000 × 12
	A 8,40,000
Add : Cash sales 8,40,000 × $\frac{25}{75}$	A 2,80,000
Total sales of the company for the year ended 31.3.2008	A 11,20,000

Example 10

From the following information find out the opening balance of debtors and closing balance of creditors :

Opening Balance	
Debtors	?
Creditors	36,000
Bills Receivable	35,000
Bills Payable	26,000
Closing Balances :	
Bills Receivable	34,000
Bills Payable	23,000
Debtors	45,000
Creditor	?
Transaction During the year :	
Total Sales	8,00,000
Cash Sales	3,93,000

Total Purchases	5,00,000
Cash purchases	2,00,000
Discount Allowed	2,000
Discount Received	1,000
Payable to Creditors	1,47,000
Received from Debtors	2,90,000
Bills Receivable encashed at the time of maturity	1,00,000
Bills Receivable dishonoured at the time of maturity	10,000
Bills Payable paid	1,43,000
Bills Payable dishonoured	10,000

[*B.Com.(Hons.), Delhi University*]

Solution

Dr. *Total Debtors A/c* *Cr.*

	(A)		(A)
To Balance b/d	29,000	By Cash A/c	2,90,000
(Balancing figure)		By Bills Receivable A/c	1,09,000
To Sales A/c		(from B/R A/c)	
(8,00,000--3,93,000)	4,07,000	By Discount A/c	2,000
To Bills Receivable A/c	10,000	By Balance c/d	45,000
	4,46,000		4,46,000

Dr. *Bills Receivable A/c* *Cr.*

	(A)		(A)
To Balance b/d	35,000	By Cash A/c	1,00,000
To Debtors A/c	1,09,000	By Debtors A/c	10,000
(*balancing figure* being bills		By Balance c/d	34,000
drawn on debtors)			
	1,44,000		1,44,000

Dr. *Total Creditors A/c* *Cr.*

	(A)		(A)
To Cash A/c	1,47,000	By Balance b/d	36,000
To Bills Payable A/c (from B/P A/c)	1,50,000	By Purchases A/c (5,00,000–2,00,000)	3,00,000
To Discount A/c	1,000	By Bills Payable A/c	10,000
To Balance c/d			
(*balancing figure*)	48,000		
	3,46,000		3,46,000

Dr.	Bills Payable A/c		Cr.
	(A)		(A)
To Cash A/c	1,43,000	By Balance b/d	26,000
To Creditors A/c	10,000	By Creditors A/c	1,50,000
To Balance c/d	23,000	(*balancing figure* being bills accepted)	
	1,76,000		1,76,000

Example 11

P and Q are in partnership sharing profits in the ratio of 3 : 2 respectively. They maintain their books of accounts on single entry system. Taking into account the following information, you are required to prepare trading and profit and loss Account for the year ended 31.3.2003 and their balance sheet as at that date.

Analysis of Cash Book for the Year

	(A)
Bank Balance as on 1.4.2002	40,000
P's Drawing	95,000
Q's Drawings	80,000
Paid to trade creditors	3,00,000
Paid against bills payable	80,000
Wages	1,10,000
Salaries	1,50,000
Other trade expenses	1,32,550
Received from trade debtors	4,56,000
Received against bills receivable	80,450
Received from cash sales	3,58,100
Cash in hand on 31.03.2003	2,000
There was no cash in hand on 1.4.2002	

The respective capitals of P and Q on 1.4.2002 were A 8,00,000 and A 2,00,000. Particulars of other assets and liabilities are as follows :

	1.4.2002 (A)	*31.3.2003* (A)
Stock on hand	2,98,000	3,50,000
Trade Debtors	2,50,000	1,93,550
Trade Creditors	2,20,000	70,000
Bills Receivable	50,000	70,000
Bills Payable	30,000	—
Business Premises	5,00,000	5,00,000
Office Furniture	1,12,000	1,12,000

Interest on drawings was agreed as A 3,500 for P and A 3,000 for Q. Interest on capital is to be allowed at 10%. Q is also to be credited with a commission of 6% on the net profit remaining after charging such commission. Allow 5% depreciation on premises and furniture. Also create a provision for bad debts amounting to A 13,250. [*B.Com. (Hons.) Delhi, 2003*]

Solution

Trading and Profit and Loss Account for the year ended 31.3.2003

		(A)			(A)
To Opening Stock		2,98,000	By Sales : Cash	3,58,000	
To Purchases		2,00,000	Credit	5,00,000	8,58,100
To Wages		1,10,000	By Closing Stock		3,50,000
To Gross Profit c/d		6,00,100			
		12,08,100			12,08,100
To Salaries		1,50,000	By Gross Profit b/d		6,00,100
To Trade Expenses		1,32,550			
To Provision for Doubtful Debts		13,250			
To Depreciation on					
Furniture		5,600			
Premises		25,000			
To Net Profit c/d		2,73,700			
		6,00,100			6,00,100
To P's Commission [6/106 × 2,73,700]		15,492	By Net Profit b/d		2,73,700
To Interest on Capital			By Interest on drawings :		
P		80,000	P		3,500
Q		20,000	Q		3,000
To Capital A/cs : (Profit)					
P(3/5)	98,825				
Q(2/5)	65,883	1,64,708			
		2,80,200			2,80,200

Note : As commissioned is based on profit, it is calculated on the basis of profit before appropriations. Calculations of commission based on profit after considering interest on capital and interest on drawings does not appeal as appropriations deal with allocation of profit. However, the amount of commission, if based on profit after interest on capital and interest on drawings, will be A 10,200 (6/106 × 1,80,200).

Balance Sheet as on 31.3.2003

Liabilities	(A)	*Assets*		(A)
Bank overdraft	15,000	Debtors	1,93,550	
Creditors	70,000	*Less :* Provision	13,250	1,80,300
Capital Accounts : P	8,95,817	Stock		3,50,000
Q	2,02,883	Bill Receivable		70,000

		Furniture	1,12,000	
		Less : Depreciation	5,600	1,06,400
		Premises	5,00,000	
		Less : Depreciation	25,000	4,75,000
	11,83,700			11,83,700

Working Notes **:**

Partner's Capital Accounts

	P	Q		P	Q
To Drawings	95,000	80,000	By balance b/d	8,00,000	2,00,000
To Interest on Drawings	3,500	3,000	By Interest on Capital	80,000	20,000
To Balance c/d	8,95,817	2,02,883	By Commission	15,492	—
			By Profit and Loss Appropriation (Profit)	98,825	65,883
	9,94,317	2,85,883		9,94,317	2,85,883

Total Debtors A/c

	(*A*)		(*A*)
To Balance b/d	2,50,000	By Cash	4,56,000
To Sales (*balancing figure)*	5,0,000	By B/R	1,00,450
		By Balance c/d	1,93,550
	7,50,000		7,50,000

Total Creditors A/c

	(*A*)		(*A*)
To Cash	3,00,000	By Balance b/d	2,20,000
To B/P	50,000	By Purchases	2,00,000
To Balance c/d	70,000	(*balancing figure*)	
	4.20,000		4,20,000

Bills Receivable A/c

	(*A*)		(*A*)
To Balance b/d	50,000	By Cash	80,450
To Debtors (*balancing figure)*	1,00,450	By Balance c/d	70,000
	1,50,450		1,50,450

Bills Payable A/c

	(*A*)		(*A*)
To Cash	80,000	By Balance b/d	30,000
		By Creditors (*balancing figure*)	50,000
	80,000		80,000

Cash and Bank A/c

	(A)		(A)
To Balance b/d : Cash	—	By Drawing (P + Q)	1,75,000
Bank	40,000	By Creditors	3,00,000
To Debtors	4,56,000	By B/P	80,000
To B/R	80,450	By Wages	1,10,000
To Sales	3,58,100	By Salaries	1,50,000
To Balance c/d : Bank		By Trade expenses	1,32,550
(*balancing figure*)	15,000	By Balance c/d : Cash	2,000
	9,49,550		9,49,550

Example 12

Abhay is diamond merchant. He follows the practice of paying creditors for goods purchased through his bank account and making payments in cash on all nominal accounts. X had not kept his books on the double-entry principles nor had he balanced his three-columnar cash book. However, the following information has been extracted from X's accounting records :

Particulars	*1 Jan. 2009 (A)*	*31 Dec. 2009 (A)*
Cash in hand	30	50
Cash at Bank	1,000	1,500
Sundry Debtors	1,750	2,500
Sundry Creditors	3,410	3,750
Investments	6,250	6,250
Stock	2,500	1,870

Transactions during the year 2009 were as follows :	
Salaries Paid	1,500
General Expenses Paid	3,500
Payment for Stationery	870
Payment of Rent and Rates	700
Lighting Charges Paid	250
Cash Receipts from Debtors	31,250
Payments to Creditors through Bank and of Trade Expenses in Cash	20,000
Payment into Bank : Business	18.750
Payment into Bank : Additional Capital	250
Payment from Bank Account : Personal	3,250
Cash Payment : Personal	910
Stock taken for Personal use	140

You are required to prepare Trading and Profit and Loss Account for the year ended 31 December, 2009 and Balance Sheet of X on 31st December, 2009. [*B.Com. (Hons.) Delhi 1995*]

Solution

Statement of Affairs as on 1.1.2009

Liabilities	(*A*)	*Assets*	(*A*)
Creditors	3,410	Cash in hand	30
Capital (*Balancing Figure)*	8,120	Cash at Bank	1,000
Sundry Debtors	1,750		
Investments	6,250		
Stock	2,500		
	11,530		11,530

Total Debtors Account

Particulars	(*A*)	*Particulars*	(*A*)
Balance b/d	1,750	Cash Account	31,250
Sales Account	32,000	Balance c/d	2,500
	33,750		33,750

Total Creditors Account

Particulars	(*A*)	*Particulars*	(*A*)
Bank Account	15,250	Balance b/d	3,410
Balance c/d	3,750	Purchases Account	15,590
	19,000		19,000

Cash Book with Bank Column

	Office (*A*)	Bank (*A*)		Office (*A*)	Bank (*A*)
Balance	30	1,000	Salaries	1,500	—
Debtors	31,250	—	General Expenses	3,500	—
Cash (C)	—	18,750	Stationery	870	—
X's Capital Account	—	250	Rent and Taxes	700	—
Lighting Charges	250	—			
			Sundry Creditors **(Balancing Figure)**		**15,250**
			Trade Expenses (20,000–15,250)	4,750	—
			Bank (C)	18,750	—
			Drawings	910	3,250
			Balance c/d	50	1,500
	31,280	20,000		31,280	20,000

Trading and Profit and Loss Account
For the Year Ending on 31 December 2009

Particulars		*(A)*	*Particulars*	*(A)*
Opening Stock		2,500	Sales	32,000
Purchases	15,590		Stock at the end	1,870
Less : Drawings	140	15,450		
Gross Profit c/d		15,920		
		33,870		33,870
Salaries		1,500	Gross Profit b/d	15,920
General Expenses		3,500		
Stationery		870		
Rent and Rates		700		
Lighting Charges		250		
Trade Expenses		4,750		
Net Profit transferred to X's Capital Account		4,350		
		15,920		15,920

Balance Sheet of X as on 31 December 2009

Liabilities		*(A)*	*Assets*	*(A)*
Capital	8,120		Cash in hand	50
Additions	250		Cash at Bank	1,500
Net Profit	4,350		Sundry Debtors	2,500
	12,720		Investments	6,250
Less : Drawings	4,300	8,420	Stock	1,870
Sundry Creditors		3,750		
		12,170		12,170

Example 13

Mr. X keeps his books according to Single Entry System. From the following, prepare Trading and Profit & Loss A/c for the year ended 31.3.2000 together with a Balance Sheet as on that date.

Cash Book shows the following :

	(A)
Interest Charges	100
Personal Drawings	2,000
Salaries	8,500
Business Expenses	7,900
Payment to Creditors	15,000
Balance at Bank as on 31.3.2000	2,425
Cash in hand as on 31.3.2000	75
Cash from Debtors	25,000
Cash Sales	15,000

Further details are :

	As on 1.4.1999 *(A)*	AS on 31.3.2000 *(A)*
Stock in Hand	9,000	10,220
Creditors	8,000	5,500
Debtors	22,000	30,000
Furniture	1,000	1,000
Office premises	15,000	15,000

Provide 5% interest p.a. on the capital of X as on 1.4.1999. Provide A 1,500 for doubtful debts. Provide 5% depreciation on all fixed assets. [*B.Com. (Hons.) Delhi University, 2005*]

Solution

Trading and Profit and Loss Account of Mr. X for the Year Ending March 31, 2000

Particulars	*(A)*	*Particulars*	*(A)*
To Stock	9,000	By Sales*₂	48,000
To Purchases	12,500	By Stock	10,220
To Gross Profit c/d	36,720		
	58,220		58,220
To Interest	100	By Gross Profit b/d	36,720
To Salaries	8,500		
To Business Expenses	7,900		
To Provision for Doubtful Debts	1,500		
To Interest on Capital	1,750		
To Depreciation : Furniture	50		
Premises	750		
To Net Profit transferred to Capital A/c	16,170		
	36,720		36,720

Balance Sheet of Mr. X as on March 31,2000

Liability		*(A)*	*Assets*		*(A)*
Capital*₃	35,000		Premises	15,000	
Add : Interest on Capital	1,750		*Less:* Depreciation	750	14,250
Net Profit	16,170		Furniture	1,000	
	52,920		*Less :* Depreciation	50	950
Less : Drawings	2,000	50,920	Stock in hand		10,220
Creditors		5,500	Debtors	30,000	
			Less : Provision for doubtful debts	1,500	28,500
			Cash at Bank		2,425
			Cash in hand		75
		56,420			56,420

Working Notes **:**

Total Creditors Account*$_1$

Particulars	*(A)*	*Particulars*	*(A)*
To Cash	15,000	By Balance b/d	8,000
To Balance c/d	5,500	By Purchases (Balancing Fig.)	12,500
	20,500		20,500

Total Debtors Account*[1]

Particulars	*(A)*	*Particulars*	*(A)*
To Balance b/d	22,000	By Cash	25,000
To Sales (*balancing figures)*	33,000	By Balance c/d	30,000
	55,000		55,000

Total Sales = Cash sales + *Credit Sales* = A 15,000 + A 33,000 = A 48,000.

Balance Sheet, as on April 1, 1999

Particulars	*(A)*	*Particulars*	*(A)*
Capital (Balancing Figure)	35,000	Stock-in-hand	9,000
Bank Overdraft*$_4$	4,000	Debtors	22,000
Creditors	8,000	Furniture	1,000
		Office Premises	15,000
	47,000		47,000

Cash Book

Date	*Particulars*	*Amount (A)*	*Date*	*Particulars*	*Amount (A)*
31.3.00	To Debtors	25,000	1.4.99	By Balance b/d.*	4,000
	To Sales	15,000		(Balancing Figure)	
			31.3.00	By Interest	100
				By Drawings	2,000
				By Salaries	8,500
				By Business Expenses	7,900
				By Creditors	15,000
				By Balance c/d :	
				Bank	2,425
				Cash	75
		40,000			40,000

Example 14

A Submits to you the following figures relating to his business in respect of the year, ending 31st December, 2001. You are required to prepare a Trading and Profit and Loss Account for the year ended, and a Balance Sheet as at 31st December, 2001. Any difference in the cash balance is assumed to be drawings:

	(A)
Cash paid into bank	1,50,000
Private dividends paid into bank	2,000
Private payment out of Bank	26,000
Payments for goods out of Bank	1,22,000
Cash received from debtors	2,50,000
Payments for goods by cash and cheques	1,60,000
Wages	40,000
Delivery Expenses	7,000
Rents and Rates	2,000
Lighting and heating	1,000
General Expenses	4,600

The Assets and liabilities are as follows

Assets and Liabilities	*1 January, 2001 (A)*	*31 December, 2001 (A)*
Stock	20,000	15,000
Bank Balance	8,000	12,000
Cash in hand	300	400
Trade Debtors	14,000	20,000
Trade Creditors	27,300	30,000
Investments	50,000	50,000

[*B.Com. (Hons.), Delhi University*]

Solution

Sundry Debtors A/c

	(A)		*(A)*
To Balance b/d	14,000	By Cash A/c	2,50,000
To Sales A/c (*balancing figure*)	2,56,000	By Balance c/d	20,000
	2,70,000		2,70,000

Sundry Creditors A/c

	(A)		*(A)*
To Bank A/c	1,22,000	By Balance b/d	27,300
To Cash A/c	38,000	By Purchases A/c (*Balancing figure*)	1,62,700
To Balance c/d	30,000		
	1,90,000		1,90,000

Cash Book

	Cash	Bank		Cash	Bank(*A*)
To Balance b/d	300	8,000	By Bank A/c	1,50,000	
To Debtors A/c	2,50,000		By Creditors A/c	38,000	1,22,000
To Cash A/c		1,50,000	By Wages A/c	40,000	
To Dividend A/c		2,000	By Delivery Expenses A/c	7,000	
			By Rent and Rates A/c	2,000	
			By General Expenses A/c	4,600	
			By Lighting & Heating A/c	1,000	
			By Drawing A/c (*Balancing Figure*)	7,300	26,000
			By Balance c/d	400	12,000
	2,50,300	1,60,000		2,50,300	1,60,000

Trading & Profit & Loss A/c for the year ended 31.12.2001

	(*A*)		(*A*)
To Opening Stock A/c	20,000	By Sales A/c	2,56,000
To Purchases A/c	1,62,700	By Closing Stock A/c	15,000
To Wages A/c	40,000		
To Gross Profit	48,300		
	2,71,000		2,71,000
To Rent & Rates A/c	2,000	By Gross Profit	48,300
To Light & Heating A/c	1,000		
To Delivery Expenses A/c	7,000		
To General Expenses A/c	4,600		
To Net Profit	33,700		
	48,300		48,300

Statement of Affairs

Liabilities		1.1.2001	31.12.2001	*Assets*	1.1.2001	31.12.2001
Creditors		27,300	30,000	Cash	300	400
Capital (*balancing Figure)*		65,000		Bank	8,000	12,000
	65,000			Debtors	14,000	20,000
Add : Net Profit	33,700			Stock	20,000	15,000
Dividend	2,000			Investment	50,000	50,000
Less : Drawings	(33,300)		67,400			
		92,300	97,400		92,300	97,400

Example 15

Suhani does not maintain regular books but keeps only a memoranda of her transactions. She furnishes the following information for the year ended 31st March, 2006 :

	(A)
Total collections from Debtors	58,000
Cash Sales	7,400
Cash received on maturity of Bills Receivable	20,000
Salaries paid	9,800
Wages	3,160
Bills Payable matured	28,600
Cash paid to creditors	29,400
Office Expenses	1,600
Drawings	9,000
Investment at par (9% Govt. Loan on October 1, 2005)	2,000

Summary of remaining Transactions :

Sales (credit)	81,400
Discount to Debtors	400
Purchases	60,000
Discount earned	200
Bills Receivable received	21,800
Bills Payable accepted	30,000
Stock of goods on 31st March, 2006	10,600

Other balances as submitted by Suhani as on 1 April, 2005 are given below :

Bank overdraft	1,000
Creditors	7,200
Bills Payable	3,200
Cash in hand	140
Bills Receivable	5,000
Debtors	7,800
Stock of Goods	15,060
Plant and Machinery	9,400
Land and Building	14,000

Provide depreciation on Plant and Machinery at 10%, and on Land and Building at 5%. Make a provision for doubtful debts at 5% on debtors.

You are required to prepare :

(*a*) Trading and Profit & Loss Account for the year ended on 31 March, 2006

(*b*) The balance Sheet as at 31 March, 2006

Show all working clearly. *[B.Com.(Hons.), Delhi University, 2006]*

Solution

Trading and Profit & Loss Account
for the year ending 31 March, 2006

Particulars	(*A*)	*Particulars*		(*A*)
To Opening Stock	15,060	By Sales :		
To Purchases	60,000	Cash	7,400	
To Wages	3,160	Credit	81,400	88,800
To Gross Profit c/d	21,180	By Closing Stock		10,600
	99,400			99,400
To Salaries	9,800	By Gross Profit b/d		21,180
To Office Expenses	1,600	By Interest on Investments		90
To Discount Allowed	400	By Discount Received		200
To Dep. on Plant & Machinery	940			
To Dep. on Land and Building	700			
To Prov. for Doubtful Debts	450			
To Net Profit transferred to Capital Account	7,580			
	21,470			21,470

Balance Sheet
As at 31 March 2006

Liabilities		(*A*)	*Assets*		(*A*)
Capital*[1]	40,000		Investments	2,000	
Add : Net Profit	7,580		Interest due	90	2,090
	47,580		Stock at the end		10,600
Less : Drawings	9,000	38,580	Plant and Machinery	9,400	
Creditors*[4]		7,600	*Less* : Depreciation	940	8,460
Bills Payable*[5]		4,600	Land and Buildings	14,000	
			Less : Depreciation	700	13,300
			Bills Receivable*[3]		6,800
			Debtors*[2]	9,000	
			Less : Provision	450	8,550
			Cash in hand*[6]		980
		50,780			50,780

Working Notes **:**

*[1]

Statement of Affairs
As at 31st March, 2005

Liabilities	(*A*)	*Assets*	(*A*)
Bank overdraft	1,000	Cash in hand	140
Creditors	7,200	Bills Receivable	5,000

Bills Payable	3,200	Stock	15,060
Capital (*balancing figure*)	40,000	Debtors	7,800
		Plant and Machinery	9,400
		Land and Building	14,000
	51,400		51,400

*2

Total Debtors Account

Particulars	(*A*)	*Particulars*	(*A*)
To Balance b/d	7,800	By Cash A/c	58,000
To Credit Sales	81,400	By Discount Allowed	400
		By Bills Receivable	21,800
		By Balance c/d (*Balancing Figures*)	9,000
	89,200		89,200

*3

Bills Receivable Account

Particulars	(*A*)	*Particulars*	(*A*)
To Balance b/d	5,000	By Cash A/c	20,000
To Debtors	21,800	By Balance c/d (*balancing figure)*	6,800
	26,800		26,800

*4

Total Creditors Account

Particulars	(*A*)	*Particulars*	(*A*)
To Cash A/c	29,400	By Balance b/d	7,200
To Discount Received	200	By Credit purchases	60,000
To Bills Payable	30,000		
To Balance c/d (*Bal. figure)*	7,600		
	67,200		67,200

*5

Bills Payable Account

Particulars	(*A*)	*Particulars*	(*A*)
To Cash A/c	28,600	By Balance b/d	3,200
To Balance c/d	4,600	By Creditor	30,000
	33,200		33,200

*2

Cash Account

Particulars	(*A*)	*Particulars*	(*A*)
To Balance b/d	140	By Wages	3,160
To Debtors	58,000	By Salaries	9,800
To Sales	7,400	By Bills Payable	28,600

To Bills Receivable	20,000	By Creditors	29,400
		By office Expenses	1,600
		By Drawings	9,000
		By Investments	2,000
		By Bank Overdraft	1,000
		By Balance c/d (*Balancing figure*)	980
	85,540		85,540

Example 16

The following facts have been ascertained from the records of C who maintains his books of accounts under the single entry system :

Receipts for the year ended 31.3.2006 :

From sundry debtors A 88,125; Cash Sales A 20,625; Paid in by the proprietor A 12,500

Payments made during the year ended 31.3.2006 :

New plant purchased A 3,125; Drawing A 7,500; Wages A 33,625; Salaries A 5,625; Interest paid A 375; Telephone A 625; Rent A 6,000; Light and Power (Direct) A 2,375; Sundry Expenses A 10,625; Sundry creditors A 38,125.

It may be noted that he banks all receipts and makes all payments only by means of cheques.

Assets and Liabilities :	*As at 31.3.05* (*A*)	*As at 31.3.06* (*A*)
Sundry Creditors	12,625	12,000
Sundry Debtors	18,750	30,625
Bank	3,125	?
Stock	31,250	15,625
Plant	37,500	36,575

From the above data prepare the Trading and Profit & Loss A/c for the year ended 31.3.06 and Balance Sheet as on that date.
[*B.Com. (Hons.) Delhi University 2007*]

Solution

Trading and Profit & Loss Account
for the year ended 31st March, 2006

Particulars	(*A*)	*Particulars*		(*A*)
To Opening Stock	31,250	By Sales :		
To Purchases*2	37,500	Cash	20,625	
To Wages	33,625	Credit*2	1,00,000	1,20,625
To Light & Power	2,375	By Closing Stock		15,625
To Gross Profit c/d	31,500			
	1,36,250			1,36,250
To Salaries	5,625	By Gross Profit b/d		31,500

To Interest	375		
To Telephone Charges	625		
To Rent	6,000		
To Sundry Expenses	10,625		
To Depreciation on Plant*3	4,050		
To Net Profit transferred to Capital Account	4,200		
	31,500		31,500

Balance Sheet
as on 31st March, 2006

liabilities		(A)	*Assets*		(A)
Sundry Creditors		12,000	Cash at Bank*4		16,375
Capital*5	78,000		Sundry Debtors		30,625
Add : Net Profit	4,200		Closing Stock		15,625
Capital Introduced	12,500		Plant	37,500	
	94,700		*Add :* Addition	3,125	
Less : Drawings	7,500	87,200		40,625	
			Less : Depreciation*3	4,050	36,575
		99,200			99,200

***Working Notes* :**

*1 **Calculation of Credit Purchases :**

Sundry Creditors Account

Particulars	(A)	*Particulars*	(A)
To Bank	38,125	By Balance b/d	12,625
To Balance c/d	12,000	By Credit Purchases (*balancing figure*)	37,500
	50,125		50,125

*2 **Calculation of Credit Sales :**

Sundry Debtors Accounts

Particulars	(A)	*Particulars*	(A)
To Balance b/d	18,750	By Bank A/c	88,125
To Credit Sales (*Balancing Figure*)	1,00,000	By Balance c/d	30,625
	1,18,750		1,18,750

*3 **Calculation of Depreciation**

Plant as on 31.3.2500	37,500
Add : Plant purchased during the year	3,125
	40,625
Less : Plant as on 31.3.2006	36,575
Depreciation for the year	4,050

*4 **Calculation of Bank Balance as on 31.3.2006**

Bank Account

Particulars	(A)	Particulars	(A)
To Balance b/d	3,125	By Plant purchased	3,125
To Sundry Debtors	88,125	By Drawings	7,500
To Cash Sales	20,625	By Wages	33,625
To Capital A/c	12,500	By Salaries	5,625
(Additional Capital introduced)		By Interest	375
		By Telephone charges	625
		By Rent	6,000
		By Light and Power	2,375
		By Sundry Expenses	10,625
		By Sundry Creditor	38,125
		By Balance c/d (*Balancing Figure*)	16,375
	1,24,375		1,24,375

*5 **Calculation of Capital as on 31.3.2005**

Statement of Affairs as on 31.3.2005

Liabilities	(A)	Assets	(A)
Sundry Creditors	12,625	Cash at Bank	3,125
Capital (*Balancing Figure*	78,000	Stock	31,250
		Sundry Debtors	18,750
		Plant	37,500
	90,625		90,625

Example 17

Mr. X does not keep complete records of his business but gives you the following information :

His assets on 31st March, 2007 consisted of :

Machineries A 1,50,000; Furniture A 60,000; Motor Car A 40,000; Stock in trade A 50,000; Debtors A 80,000; Cash in hand A 12,000 and Cash at Bank A 30,000; Creditors on that date amounted to A 1,20,000.

On further information received, you come to know that;

(*i*) On 1 October, 2006 he purchased a new machinery costing A 50,000.

(*ii*) Sales are made for cash as well as on credit. There are no cash purchases.

He always sells his goods at cost plus 25%. Cash sales for the year were accounted for A 80,000.

(*iii*) During the year collection from Debtors amounted to A 5,00,000 and a sum of A 4,25,000 was paid to creditor

(*iv*) He obtained a bank loan for A 50,000 on 1st April, 2006, the entire amount was repaid in February, 2007 with interest A 2,500.

(*v*) On 1st November, 2006 his Life Insurance Policy for A 50,000 became matured and the same was invested in the business. He drawings were A 2,500 per month all throughout the year.

(*vi*) On 1st April, 2006 he had A 1,500 as cash in hand and balance at bank for A 40,000. Debtors and creditors on that date amounted to A 60,000 and A 90,000 respectively.

(*vii*) Provide depreciation on Machineries @ 15% p.a. Furniture @ 10% p.a. and on Motor Car at 20% p.a.

Prepare a Trading and Profit & Loss Account for the year ended 31st March, 2007 and a Balance Sheet as on that date. [*B.Com. (Hons.), Delhi University, 2007*]

Solution

Trading and Profit & Loss Account
for the year ended 31st March, 2007

Particulars		(*A*)	*Particulars*		(*A*)
To Opening Stock (*Bal. Fig.*)		75,000	By Sales:		
To Purchases*[2]		4,55,000	Cash	80,000	
To Gross Profit c/d*[5]			Credit*[3]	5,20,000	6,00,000
(20% on Sales)		1,20,000	By Closing Stock		50,000
		6,50,000			6,50,000
To Depreciation :			By Gross Profit b/d		1,20,000
Furniture	6,000		By Net Loss		37,250
Motor Car	8,000				
Machineries*[6]	18,750	32,750			
To Interest on Bank loan		2,500			
To General Expenses*[5]		1,22,000			
		1,57,250			1,57,250

Balance Sheet
as at 31st March, 2007

Particulars		(*A*)	*Particulars*		(*A*)
Creditors		1,20,000	Machineries	1,50,000	
Capital*[1]	2,86,500		*Less* : Depreciation	18,750	1,31,250
Add : Capital Introduced	50,000		Furniture	60,000	
	3,36,500		*Less* : Depreciation	6,000	54,000
Less : Drawings	30,000		Motor Car	40,000	
	3,06,500		*Less* : Depreciation	8,000	32,000
Less : Net Loss	37,250	2,69,250	Stock in trade		50,000
			Debtors		80,000
			Cash		12,000
			Bank Balance		30,000
		3,89,250			3,89,250

***Working Notes* :**

*1

Balance Sheet
As at 31st March, 2006

Liabilities	(A)	*Assets*	(A)
Creditors	90,000	Cash	1,500
Capital (*Bal. Fig.*)	2,86,500	Bank	40,000
		Debtors	60,000
		Stock in trade	75,000
		Machineries	1,00,000
		Furniture	60,000
		Motor Car	40,000
	3,76,500		3,76,500

*2

Total Creditors Account

Particulars	(A)	*Particulars*	(A)
To Cash	4,25,000	By Balance b/d	90,000
To Balance c/d	1,20,000	By Purchases (*Bal. Fig.*)	4,55,000
	5,45,000		5,45,000

*3

Total Debtors Account

Particulars	(A)	*Particulars*	(A)
To Balance b/d	60,000	By Cash	5,00,000
To Sales (Credit) (*Bal. Fig.*)	5,20,000	By Balance c/d	80,000
	5,80,000		5,80,000

*4 Credit Sale during the year = A 5,20,000

Cash Sale = A 80,000

A 6,00,000

Gross Profit @ 25% at cost = A 6,00,000 $\frac{25}{125}$ A 1,20,000

*5 *Dr.* **Cash and Bank Account** *Cr.*

Particulars		(A)	*Particulars*		(A)
To balance b/d :			By Creditors		4,25,000
Cash	1,500		By Machineries		50,000
Bank	40,000	41,500	By Interest on loan		2,500
To Sales		80,000	By Bank loan		50,000
To Debtors		5,00,000	By Drawings		30,000
To Bank Loan		50,000	By Expenses (*Bal. Fig.*)		1,22,000
To Life Insurance Policy (Capital)		50,000	By Balance c/d :		
			Cash	12,000	
			Bank	30,000	
					42,000
		7,21,500			7,21,500

*4 Depreciation on Machineries :

15% on A 1,00,000 for full year = A 15,000

15% on A 50,000 for 6 months = A 3,750

18,750

Example 18

From the following information of M/s Kapil Brothers, prepare Trading and Profit & Loss Account for the year ended 31st March, 2008 and the Balance Sheet as on that date :

Liabilities and Assets	*31.03.2007* *(A)*	*31.3.2008* *(A)*
Motor Car	90,000	90,000
Stock	70,000	90,000
Furniture	10,000	10,000
Debtors	62,000	46,000
Creditors	60,000	?
Bank	9,000	16,000

The following further information is also available :

(*i*) M/s. Kapil Brothers purchases goods for resale from manufacturers who allow discount of 3% on goods purchased in excess of A 5,00,000 in a year. The discount for the year ended 31st March, 2008 was A 12,480.

(*ii*) All goods are sold at a gross profit margin of 30% on selling price.

(*iii*) Bank statements for the year reveal the following payments :

	(A)
Creditors	9,03,520
Salaries	60,000
Car Expenses	23,000
Rent	30,000
Printing & Stationery	6,400
Rates and Taxes	3,000
Carriage Outward	18,600
Travelling Expenses	14,900
Bought Delivery Van	1,70,000
Misc. Expenses	9,580
Drawings	50,000

Depreciation on Car and Delivery Van @ 20% and Furniture @ 10% is to be provided on balances as on 31.3.2008. [*B.Com. (Hons.), Delhi University, 2009*]

Solution

Working Notes :

*1 Calculation of Purchases on the basis of discount received.

Purchases in excess of A 5,00,000 = $\frac{12480}{3}$ 100 = A 4,16,000

Total Purchases = A 5,00,000 + A 4,16,000 = A 9,16,000

*2 Calculation of Sales

Cost of Goods Sold = Opening Stock + Purchases – Closing Stock

= A 70,000 + A 9,16,000 – A 90,000

= A 8,96,000

Goods Profit margin of 30% on Selling Price

Let the Selling Price = A 100

Gross Profit = A 30

Cost of Good Sold = 100 – 30 = A 70

When Cost of goods sold is A 70, Selling Price = A 100

When cost of goods, sold is A 8,96,000, Selling Price = $\frac{100}{70}$ A 8,96,000

= A 12,80,000

*3

Total Creditors Account

Particulars	(*A*)	*Particulars*	(*A*)
To Bank A/c	9,03,520	By Balance b/d	60,000
To Discount A/c	12,480	By Purchases*1	9,16,000
To Balance c/d (*Balancing Figure*)	60,000		
	9,76,000		9,76,000

*4

Total Debtors Account

Particulars	(*A*)	*Particulars*	(*A*)
To Bank b/d	62,000	By Bank A/c*5	12,96,000
To Sales*2	12,80,000	By Balance c/d	46,000
	13,42,000		13,42,000

*5

Bank Account

Particulars	(*A*)	*Particulars*	(*A*)
To Balance b/d	9,000	By Creditors	9,03,520
To Debtors (*Balancing Figure*)	12,96,000	By Salaries	60,000
		By Car Expenses	23,000
		By Rent	30,000
		By Printing & Stationery	6,400
		By Rates & Taxes	3,000
		By Carriage Outward	18,600
		By Travelling Expenses	14,900
		By Delivery Van	1,70,000
		By Misc. Expenses	9,580
		By Drawings	50,000
		By Balance c/d	16,000
	13,05,000		13,05,000

Statement of Affairs (as on 1.4.2007)

Particulars	(A)	*Particulars*	(A)
Creditors	60,000	Cash at Bank	9,000
Capital (*Balancing Figure*)	1,81,000	Motor Car	90,000
		Stock	70,000
		Furniture	10,000
		Debtors	62,000
	2,41,000		2,41,000

Kapil Brothers
Trading and Profit & Loss Account
for the Year ended 31st March, 2008

Particulars		(A)	*Particulars*	(A)
To Opening Stock		70,000	By Sales	12,80,000
To Purchases		9,16,000	By Closing Stock	90,000
To Gross Profit c/d		3,84,000		
		13,70,000		13,70,000
To Salaries		60,000	By Gross Profit b/d	3,84,000
To Car Expenses		23,000	By Discount Received	12,480
To Rent		30,000		
To Printing & Stationery		6,400		
To Rates & Taxes		3,000		
To Carriage Outward		18,600		
To Travelling Expenses		14,900		
To Misc. Expenses		9,580		
To Depreciation on :				
Car	18,000			
Delivery Van	34,000			
Furniture	1,000	53,000		
To Net Profit Transferred To Capital Account		1,78,000		
		3,96,480		3,96,480

Balance Sheet as on 31st March, 2008

Particulars		(A)	*Particulars*		(A)
To Creditor		60,000	Motor Car	90,000	
Capital*6	1,81,000		*Less :* Depreciation	18,000	72,000
Add : Net Profit	1,78,000		Delivery Van	1,70,000	
	3,59,000		*Less :* Depreciation	34,000	1,36,000
Less : Drawings	50,000	3,09,000	Furniture	10,000	
			Less : Depreciation	1,000	9,000

		Stock	90,000
		Debtors	46,000
		Bank	16,000
	3,69,000		3,69,000

Example 19

A trader keeps his book of account under Single Entry System. On 31st March, 2009, his Statement of Affairs stood as follows :

Liabilities	(A)	*Assets*	(A)
Capital	2,50,000	Furniture (Cost A 1,50,000)	1,00,000
Trade Creditors	5,80,000	Stock	6,10,000
Bills Payable	1,25,000	Trade Debtors	1,48,000
Outstanding Expenses	45,000	Bills Receivable	60,000
		Unexpired Insurance	2,000
		Cash and Bank	80,000
	10,00,000		10,00,000

The following was the summary of Cash Book for the year ended 31st March. 2010 :

Receipts	(A)	*Payment*	(A)
To Balance b/d	80,000	By Trade Creditors	75,07,000
To Cash Sales	73,80,000	By Bills Payable	8,15,000
To Receipts from Trade Debtors	15,10,000	By Sundry Expenses	6,20,700
To Receipt from Bills Receivable	3,40,000	By Drawings	2,40,000
		By Balance c/d	1,27,300
	93,10,000		93,10,000

Discount allowed to trade debtors and received from trade creditors amounted to A 36,000 and A 28,000 respectively. Bills endorsed amounted to A 15,000. Annual Fire Insurance premium of A 6,000 was paid every year on 1st August for renewal of the policy. Furniture was subject to depreciation @ 15% per annum on reducing balance.

You are also informed about the following balances as on 31st March, 2010

	(A)
Stock	6,50,000
Trade Debtors	1,52,000
Bills Receivables	75,000
Bills Payable	1,40,000
Outstanding Expenses	5,000

The trader maintains a gross profit of 10% on sales.

Prepare Trading and Profit & Loss Account for the year ended 31st March, 2010 and Balance Sheet as on that date. [*B.Com. (Hons.), Delhi University, 2010*]

Solution

Trading and Profit & Loss Account
for the year ended 31st March, 2010.

Liabilities		*(A)*	*Assets*		*(A)*
To Opening Stock		6,10,000	By Sales :		
To Purchases (*Bal. Fig.*)		84,10,000	Cash	73,80,000	
To Gross Profit c/d			Credit*1	19,20,000	93,00,000
(10% of A 93,00,000)		9,30,000	By Closing Stock		6,50,000
		99,50,000			99,50,000
To Sundry Expenses	6,20,700		By Gross Profit b/d		9,30,000
–O/s 2009	45,000		By Discount Received		28,000
	5,75,700				
+ Prepaid 2009 (Ins.)	2,000				
	5,77,700				
+ O/s 2010	5,000				
	5,82,700				
– Prepaid 2010 (Ins.)	2,000	5,80,700			
To Discount Allowed		36,000			
To Depreciation on Furniture		15,000			
To Net Profit Transferred to Capital A/c		3,26,300			
		9,58,000			9,58,000

Balance Sheet as at 31st March, 2010

Liabilities		*(A)*	*Assets*		*(A)*
Capital	2,50,000		Furniture	1,00,000	
Add : Net Profit	3,26,300		*Less :* Depreciation	15,000	85,000
	5,76,300		Stock		6,50,000
Less : Drawings	2,40,000	3,36,300	Trade Debtors		1,52,000
Creditors		6,10,000	Bills Receivable		75,000
Bills Payable		1,40,000	Unexpired Insurance		2,000
Outstanding Expenses		5,000	Bank		1,27,300
		10,91,300			10,91,300

Working Notes **:**

*1

Total Debtors Account

Particulars	*(A)*	*Particulars*	*(A)*
To Balance b/d	1,48,000	By Bank A/c	15,10,000
To Sales (Credit) (*Bal. Fig.*)	19,20,000	By Bills Receivable A/c*2	3,70,000
		By Discount A/c	36,000
		By Balance c/d	1,52,000
	20,68,000		20,68,000

*2

Bills Receivable Account

Particulars	*(A)*	*Particulars*	*(A)*
To Balance b/d	60,000	By Bank A/c	3,40,000
To Debtors A/c (*Bal. Fig.*)	3,70,000	By Creditors A/c	15,000
		By Balance c/d	75,000
	4,30,000		4,30,000

*3

Total Creditors Account

Particulars	*(A)*	*Particulars*	*(A)*
To Bank A/c	75,07,000	By balance b/d	5,80,000
To Bills Payable *4	8,30,000	By Purchase A/c	84,10,000
To Discount A/c	28,000	(From Trading A/c)	
To Bills Receivable A/c	15,000		
To Balance c/d	6,10,000		
	89,90,000		89,90,000

*4

Bills Payable Account

Particulars	*(A)*	*Particulars*	*(A)*
To Bank A/c	8,15,000	By Balance b/d	1,25,000
To Balance c/d	1,40,000	By Creditors A/c (*Bal. Fig.*)	8,30,000
	9,55,000		9,55,000

Example 20

From the following particulars, prepare a Trading and Profit & Loss Account and Balance Sheet on 31st March, 2011 :

(i) Assets and Liabilities	*1.4.2010* *(A)*	*31.3.2011* *(A)*
Furniture	8,000	9,000
Stock	10,000	9,000
Debtors	20,000	?
Creditors	14,000	18,000
Expenses Outstanding	2,200	2,000
Bank	1,800	1,225

(ii) Receipts and Payments during the year.

	(A)
Receipt from Debtors	1,17,000
Payment to Creditors	78,400
Payment of Freight Inward	6,000
Purchase of Furniture	1,800
Payment of Expenses	29,000
Miscellaneous Receipts	5,000

(*iii*) Goods costing A 2,000 were used as advertising materials.

(*iv*) Goods are sold to show profit $33\frac{1}{3}$% on sales.

(*v*) Difference in Bank, if any, is to be treated as drawing or introduction of capital by the proprietor.

[*B.Com. (Hons.), Delhi University, Nov. 2011*]

Solution

Dr. **Bank Account** Cr.

	(A)		(A)
To Balance b/d	1,800	By Creditors	78,400
To Debtors	1,17,000	By Freight	6,000
To Receipts	5,000	By Furniture	1,800
		By Expenses	29,000
		By Drawings (*balancing figure)*	7,375
		By Balance c/d	1,225
	1,23,800		1,23,800

Dr. **Debtors Account** Cr.

	(A)		(A)
To Balance b/d	20,000	By Cash	1,17,000
To Sales	1,31,100	By Balance c/d (*Balancing Figure)*	34,100
	1,51,100		1,51,100

Dr. **Creditors Account** Cr.

	(A)		(A)
To Cash A/c	78,400	By Balance b/d	14,000
To balance c/d	18,000	By Purchases (*Balancing Figure*)	82,400
	96,400		96,400

Dr. **Opening Balance Sheet** Cr.

Liabilities	(A)	*Assets*	(A)
Creditors	14,000	Furniture	8,000
Outstanding expenses	2,200	Stock	10,000
Capital (*balancing figure)*	23,600	Debtors	20,000
		Bank	1,800
	39,800		39,800

Calculations of Sales

Opening Stock	10,000
Add : Purchases (78,400 + 2,000 advertising materials)	80,400
Freight	6,000
	96,400

Less : Closing Stock	9,000
Cost of goods sold	87,400
Add : Profit (50% on cost or $33\frac{1}{3}$% on sales)	43,700
Sales	1,31,100

Dr. **Trading and Profit & Loss Account for the year ending 31 March, 2011** *Cr.*

		(A)		(A)
To Opening stock		10,000	By Sales	1,31,100
To Purchases	82,400		By Closing Stock	9,000
Less : Advertising Material	2,000	80,400		
To Freight		6,000		
To Gross Profit		43,700		
		1,40,100		1,40,100
To Sundry Expenses	29,000		By G/P	43,700
Add : Current O/s	2,000		By Misc. Receipts	5,000
	31,000			
Less : Previous O/s	2,200	28,800		
To Depreciation on Furniture (8,000 + 1,800 – 9,000)		800		
To Advertising Materials		2,000		
To Net Profit		17,100		
		48,700		48,700

Balance Sheet as at 31 March, 2011

Liabilities		(A)	*Assets*	(A)
Capital	23,600		Cash at Bank	1,225
Add : Net Profit	17,100		Debtors	34,100
	40,700		Closing Stock	9,000
Less : Drawing	7,375	33,325	Furniture	9,000
Creditors		18,000		
Outstanding Expenses		2,000		
		53,325		53,325

Example 21

Mr. Anand commenced business on 1st January, 2007 with a capital of A 45, 000. He immediately purchased furniture for A 24,000. During the year he received from his uncle a gift of A 3,000 and he borrowed from his father a sum of A 5,000. He had withdrawn A 600 per month for his household expenses. He had no bank account and all dealing were in cash. He did not maintain any books but the following information is given :

	(A)
Sales (including cash sales 30,000)	10,00,000
Purchases (including cash purchases 10,000)	75,000
Carriage inwards	700
Wages	300
Discount allowed to Debtors	800
Salaries	6,200
Band debts written-off	1,500
Trade expenses	1,200
Advertisements	2,200

He used goods worth 1,300 for personal purposes and paid A 500 to his son for examination and college fees. On 31st December, 2007 his debtors were worth A 21,000 and creditors A 15,000. Stock-in-trade was valued at A 10,000. Furniture to be depreciated by 10% p.a. Prepare Trading and Profit and Loss Account for the year ended 31st December, 2007 and Balance Sheet as at 31st December, 2007.

[*B.Com. (Hons.), Delhi University, 2011*]

Solution

Cash Account

Particulars	(A)	*Particulars*	(A)
Anand's Capital Account	45,000	Furniture	24,000
Anand's Capital Account (Gift)	3,000	Drawings	7,200
Loan from father	5,000	Drawings	500
Sales	30,000	Purchases	10,000
Debtors	46,700	Carriage	700
		Wages	300
		Salaries	6,200
		Trade expenses	1,200
		Advertisement	2,200
		Creditors	50,000
		Balance c/d	27,400
	1,29,700		1,29,700

Trading and Profit and Loss Account
For the Year Ending on 31, December, 2007

Particulars		(A)	*Particulars*	(A)
Purchases	75,000		Sales	1,00,000
Less : Drawings	1,300	73,700	Stock at the end	10,000
Carriage		700		
Wages		300		
Gross Profit c/d		35,300		
		1,10,000		1,10,000

Particulars	*(A)*	*Particulars*	*(A)*
Salaries	6,200	By G/P b/d	35,300
Trade Expenses	1,200		
Advertisement	2,200		
Discount Allowed	800		
Bad Debts	1,500		
Depreciation on furniture	2,400		
Net Profit transferred to Anand Capital Account	21,000		
	35,300		35,300

Balance Sheet As on 31 December, 2007

Liabilities	*(A)*	*Assets*	*(A)*
Anand's Capital Account	45,000	Furniture	24,000
Add : Net Profit	21,000	*Less :* Depreciation	2,400
Add : Gift	3,000		21,600
	69,000	Debtors	21,000
Less : Drawings	9,000	Cash	27,400
	60,000	Stock	10,000
Creditors	15,000		
Loan from father	5,000		
	80,000		80,000

Example 22

Mr. *Y* keeps his books under single entry system. On 31st March, 2006 his Balance Sheet was as follows:

Liabilities	*(A)*	*Assets*	*(A)*
Capital of Mr. Y	4,50,000	Fixed assets	2,25,000
Creditors	8,70,000	Stock	9,15,000
Bills payable	1,87,500	Debtors	2,22,000
Expenses outstanding	67,500	Bills receivable	90,000
		Prepaid insurance	3,000
		Cash/Bank balance	1,20,000
	15,75,000		15,75,000

(*i*) Following are the summary of cash and bank transactions for the year ended 31st March, 2007 :

	(A)
Cash sales	1,10,70,000
Collection from debtors	22,65,000
Payments to creditors	1,12,60,500
Paid for bills payable	12,22,500
Sundry expenses paid	9,31,050
Drawings for domestic expenses by Mr. *Y*	3,60,000
Cash and bank balance as on 31.3.2007	1,90,590

(*ii*) Following further details are furnished :

	(A)
Gross profit on sales @ 10%	
Bills receivable from debtors during the year	6,52,500
Discount allowed to debtors	54,000
Discount received from creditors	42,000
Bills receivable endorsed to creditors	22,500
Annual fire insurance premium paid (This is paid on 1st August every year)	9,000
Depreciate fixed assets @ 10%	

(*iii*) Balances as on 31.3.2007 are given below :

	(A)
Stock in hand	9,75,000
Debtors	2,28,000
Bills receivable	2,10,000
Bills payable	2,10,000
Outstanding expenses	7,500

Prepare Trading, Profit and Loss Account for the year ended 31st March, 2007 and Balance Sheet on that date. [*C.A., May, 2007*]

Solution

Trading and Profit and Loss Account of Mr. *Y* for the year 31.3.2007

Particulars	*(A)*	*Particulars*		*(A)*
To Opening stock	9,15,000	By Sales : Cash	1,10,70,000	
To Purchases (W.N.5)	1,27,02,750	Credit (W.N.2)	29,77,500	1,40,47,500
To Gross profit	14,04,750	By closing stock		9,75,000
	1,50,22,500			1,50,22,500
To Expenses (W.N. 6)	8,71,050	By Gross profit		14,04,750
To Discount allowed	54,000	By Discount received		42,000
To Depreciation	22,500			
To Net profit	4,99,200			
	14,46,750			14,46,750

Balance Sheet of Mr. *Y*
as on 31st March, 2007

Liabilities		*(A)*	*Assets*		*(A)*
Capital	4,50,000		Fixed assets	2,25,000	
Add : Net profit	4,99,200		*Less :* Depreciation	22,500	2,02,500
	9,49,200		Stock		9,75,000
Less : Drawings	3,60,000	5,89,200	Debtors		2,28,000
Bills payable		2,10,000	Bills receivable		2,10,000
Creditors		10,02,750	Prepaid insurance		3,000
Outstanding expenses		7,500	Cash on hand/bank		1,90,950
		18,09,450			18,09,450

***Working Notes* :**

Bills Receivable Account

	(A)		(A)
To Balance b/d	90,000	By Cash (Balancing figure)	5,10,000
To Debtors	6,52,500	By Creditors (Bills endorsed)	22,500
		By Balance c/d	2,10,000
	7,42,500		7,42,500

Debtors Account

	(A)		(A)
To Balance b/d	2,22,000	By Cash / Bank	22,65,000
To Credit Sales (Balancing Figure)	29,77,500	By Discount allowed	54,000
		By Bills receivable	6,52,500
		By Balance c/d	2,28,000
	31,99,500		31,99,500

Bills Payable Account

	(A)		(A)
To Bank	12,22,500	By Balance b/d	1,87,500
Tp Balance c/d	2,10,000	By Creditor (Balancing figure)	12,45,000
	14,32,500		14,32,500

Creditors Account

	(A)		(A)
To Cash/Bank	1,12,60,500	By Balance b/d	8,70,000
To Discount	42,000	By Purchases	1,27,02,750
To B/R endorsed	22,500		
To B/P	12,45,000		
To Balance c/d (Balancing figure)	10,02,750		
	1,35,72,750		1,35,72,750

Stock Account

	(A)		(A)
To Balance b/d	9,15,000	By Cost of goods sold	1,26,42,750
To Purchases (Balancing figure)	1,27,02,750	(A 1,40,47,500 × 90%)	
		By Balance c/d	9,75,000
	1,36,17,750		1,36,17,750

Expenses for the year ended 31st March, 2007

	(A)
Expenses paid during the year	9,31,050
Add : Outstanding expenses as on 31.3.2007	7,500
	9,38,550

Less : Outstanding expenses as on 1.4.2006	67,500
	8,71,050
Add : Prepaid Insurance as on 1.4.2006	3,000
	8,74,050
Less : Prepaid Insurance as on 31.3.2007 (9,00 × 4/12)	3,000
Expenses shown in the profit and loss account for the year ended 31.3.2007	8,71,050

Example 23

'A' and 'B' are in partnership sharing profit and losses equally. They keep their books by single entry system. The following balances are available from their books as on 31.3.2006 and 31.3.2007,

Particulars	*31.3.2006 (A)*	*31.3.2007 (A)*
Building	1,50,000	1,50,000
Equipments	2,40,000	2,72,000
Furniture	25,000	25,000
Debtors	?	1,00,000
Creditors	65,000	?
Stock	?	70,000
Bank loan	45,000	35,000
Cash	60,000	?

The transactions during the year ended 31.3.2007 were the following :

Particulars	*(A)*
Collection from debtors	3,80,000
Payment to creditors	2,50,000
Cash purchases	65,000
Expenses paid	40,000
Drawings by 'A'	30,000

On 1.4.2006 an equipment of book value A 20,000 was sold for A 15,000. On 1.10.2006, some equipments were purchased.

Cash sales amounted to 10% of sales.

Credit sales amounted to A 4,50,000.

Credit purchases were 80% of total purchases.

The firm sells goods at cost plus 25%.

Discount allowed A 5,500 during the year.

Discount earned A 4,800 during the year.

Outstanding expenses A 3,000 as on 31.3.2007.

Capital of 'A' as on 31.3.2006 was A 15,000 more than the capital of 'B', equipments and furniture to be depreciated at 10% p.a. and building @2% p.a.

You are required to prepare :

(*i*) Trading and Profit and Loss account for the year ended 31.3.2007 and

(*ii*) The Balance Sheet as on that date. [*C.A. PE II Nov. 2007*]

Solution

Trading and Profit and Loss A/c for the year ended 31.3.2007

Liabilities		*(A)*	*Particulars*		*(A)*
To Opening stock (W.N. 3)		1,45,000	By Sales-Cash (W.N. 1)	50,000	
To Purchases-Cash	65,000		Credit	4,50,000	5,00,000
Credit W.N.2)	2,60,000	3,25,000	By Closing stock		70,000
To Gross profit c/d		1,00,000			
		5,70,000			5,70,000
To Loss on sale of equipment					
(20,000-15,000)		5,000	By Gross profit b/d		1,00,000
To Depreciation :			By Discount received		4,800
Building	3,000				
Furniture	2,500				
Equipment (W.N. 4)	24,600	30,100			
To Expenses paid	40,000				
Add : Outstanding expenses	3,000	43,000			
To Discount allowed		5,500			
To Net profit transferred to :					
A's capital A/c	10,600				
B's capital A/c	10,600	21,200			
		1,04,800			1,04,800

Balance Sheet as on 31.3.2007

Liabilities		*(A)*	*Assets*		*(A)*
A's capital (W.N. 7)	2,80,250		Building	1,50,000	
Less : Drawings	30,000		*Less :* Depreciation	3,000	1,47,000
	2,50,250		Equipments	2,72,000	
Add : Net profit	10,600	2,60,850	*Less :* Depreciation	24,600	2,47,400
B's capital (W.N. 7)	2,65,250		Furniture	25,000	
Add : Net profit	10,600	2,75,850	*Less :* Depreciation	2,500	22,500
Sundry creditors (W.N. 5)		70,200	Debtors		1,00,000
Bank loan		35,000	Stock		70,000
Outstanding expenses		3,000	Cash balance (W.N. 8)		58, 000
		6,44,900			6,44,900

Working Notes :

1. *Calculation of total sales and cost of goods sold*

   Cash sales = 10% of total sales

   Credit sales = 90% of total sales = A 4,50,000

   $$\text{Total sales} = \frac{4,50,000}{90} \quad 100 \quad 5,00,000$$

   Cash sales = 10% of 5,00,000 = A 50,000

2. *Calculation of total purchases and credit purchases*

Cash purchases = A 65,000

Credit purchases = 80% of total purchases

Cash purchases = 20% of total purchases

Total purchases = $\frac{65,000}{20}$ 100 A 3,25,000

Credit purchases = 3.25.000 – 65,000 = A 2,60,000

3. *Calculation of opening stock*

Stock Account

Particulars	*(A)*	*Particulars*	*(A)*
To Balance b/d (Bal. Fig.)	1,45,000	By Cost of goods sold	
		$\frac{5,00,000}{125} \times 100$	4,00,000
To total purchases (W.N. 2)	3,25,000	By balance c/d	70,000
	4,70,000		4,70,000

4. *Purchase of equipment and depreciation on equipment*

Equipment Account

Particulars	*(A)*	*Particulars*	*(A)*
To balance b/d	2,40,000	By cash-equipment sold	15,000
To cash-purchase (bal. fig.)	52,000	By profit and loss accounts	
		(Loss on sale)	5,000
		By balance c/d	2,72,000
	2,92,000		2,92,000

Depreciation on equipment :

@ 10% p.a. on A 2,20,000 (i.e. A 2,40,000 – A 20,000) = 22,000

@ 10% p.a. on A 52,000 for 6 months (*i.e.* during the year) = 2,600

24,600

5. *Calculation of closing balance of creditors*

Creditors Account

Particulars	*(A)*	*Particulars*	*(A)*
To Cash	2,50,000	By Balance b/d	65,000
To Discount received	4,800	By Credit purchases (W.N. 2)	2,60,000
To Balance c/d (Bal. Fig.)	70,200		
	3,25,000		3,25,000

6. *Calculation of opening balance of debtors*

Debtors Account

Particulars	*(A)*	*Particulars*	*(A)*
To Balance b/d (Bal. Fig.)	35,500	By Cash	3,80,000
To Sales (Credit)	4,50,000	By Discount allowed	5,500
		By Balance c/d	1,00,000
	4,85,500		4,85,500

7. *Calculation of capital accounts of A and B as on 31.3.2006*

Balance Sheet as on 31.3.2006

Liabilities	*(A)*	*Assets*	*(A)*
Combined Capital Accounts of A and B (Bal. Fig.)	5,45,500	Building	1,50,000
Creditors	65,000	Equipments	2,40,000
Bank Loan	45,000	Furniture	25,000
		Debtors (W.N. 6)	35,500
		Stock (W.N. 3)	1,45,000
		Cash balance	60,000
	6,55,500		6,55,500

	(A)
Combined Capitals of A and B	5,45,500
Less : Difference in capitals of A and B	15,000
	5,30,500

A's Capital as on 31.3.2006 $\frac{5,30,500}{2}$ = A 2,65,250

B's Capital as on 31.3.2006 $\frac{5,30,500}{2}$ = A 2,65,250

8. **Cash Account**

Particulars	*(A)*	*Particulars*	*(A)*
To Balance b/d	60,000	By Creditors	2,50,000
To Debtors	3,80,000	By Purchases	65,000
To Equipment (sales)	15,000	By Expenses	40,000
To Cash sales (W.N. 1)	50,000	By A's drawings	30,000
		By Bank loan paid (45,000–35,000)	10,000
		By Equipment purchased (W.N. 4)	52,000
		By Balance c/d (bal. fig.)	58,000
	5,05,000		5,05,000

Example 24

The books of Mr. *Z* showed the following information :

	1.1.2007 (A)	31.12.2007 (A)
Bank balance	–	50,000
Debtors	–	87,500
Creditors	–	46,000
Stock	50,000	62,500
Fixed assets	7,500	9,000

The following are the details of the bank transactions :

	(A)
Receipt from customers	3,40,000
Payments to creditors	2,80,000
Capital brought in	5,000
Sale of fixed assets	1,750
Expenses paid	49,250
Drawings	25,000
Purchase of fixed assets	5,000

Other information :

(*i*) Cost of goods sold (A) 2,60,000

(*ii*) Gross profit 25% on cost of goods sold

(*iii*) Book value of assets sold 2,500

Prepare Trading, Profit and Loss account for the year ended 31.12.2007 and Balance Sheet as at 31.12.2007.

Solution

Trading and Profit and Loss Account for the year ended 31.12.2007

Liabilities	*(R)*	*Assets*	*(R)*
To Opening stock	50,000	By Sales (W.N. 8)	3,25,000
To Purchases (W.N. 7)	2,72,500	By Closing Stock	62,500
To Gross profit (W.N. 6)	65,000		
	3,87,500		3,87,500
To Expenses	49,250	By Gross profit	65,000
To Loss on sale of fixed asset	750		
To Depreciation on fixed assets	1,000		
To Net Profit	14,000		
	65,000		65,000

Balance Sheet as at 31.12.2007

Liabilities		(R)	*Assets*	(R)
Capital as on 1.1.2007	1,69,000		Fixed Assets	9,000
Add : Net profit	14,000		Debtors	87,500
Additional capital	5,000		Stock	62,500
	1,88,000		Bank	50,000
Less : Drawings	25,000	1,63,000		
Creditors		46,000		
		2,09,000		2,09,000

Working Notes :

Balance Sheet as at 1.1.2007

Liabilities	(A)	*Assets*	(A)
Capital (Bal. fig.)	1,69,000	Fixed Assets	7,500
Creditors	53,500	Debtors	1,02,500
		Stock	50,000
		Bank Balance	62,500
	2,22,500		2,22,500

Bank account

Liabilities	(A)	*Assets*	(A)
To Balance b/d (bal. fig.)	62,500	By Creditors	2,80,000
To Debtors	3,40,000	By Expenses	49,250
To Capital	5,000	By Drawings	25,000
To Fixed Assets	1,750	By Assets (purchased)	5,000
		By Balance c/d	50,000
	4,09,250		4,09,250

Debtors account

Liabilities	(A)	*Assets*	(A)
To Balance b/d (Bal. Fig.)	1,02,500	By Bank	3,40,000
To Sales (W.N. 8)	3,25,000	By Balance c/d	87,500
	4,27,500		4,27,500

Creditors account

Liabilities	(A)	*Assets*	(A)
To Bank	2,80,000	By Balance b/d (bal. fig.)	53,500
To Balance c/d	46,000	By Purchases (W.N. 7)	2,72,500
	3,26,000		3,26,000

Fixed Assets account

Liabilities	(A)	*Assets*	(A)
To Balance b/d	7,500	By Bank (sale)	1,750
To Bank	5,000	By Profit and Loss A/c (loss on sale)	750
		By Depreciation (bal. fig.)	1,000
		By Balance c/d	9,000
	12,500		12,500

6. Gross profit = A 2,60,000 × 25% = A 65,000.
7. Cost of goods sold = Opening stock + Purchases – Closing stock

   (A) 2,60,000 = A 50,000 + Purchases – A 62,500

   Purchases = A 2,72,500.
8. Sales = Cost of goods sold + gross profit

   = A 2,60,000 + A 65,000

   = A 3,25,000.

Example 25

Following is the Balance Sheet of Mr. Ram, a small trader, as on 31 March, 2008 :

Liabilities	(A)	*Assets*	(A)
Creditors	1,00,000	Cash	10,000
Capital	4,00,000	Bank	20,000
		Stock	80,000
		Debtors	1,00,000
		Fixed Assets	2,90,000
	5,00,000		5,00,000

A fire occurred on the night of 31 March, 2009, destroying the accounting records as well as the closing cash of the trader. However, the following information was available :

(*i*) Debtors and creditors as on 31 March, 2009 showed an increase of 20% as compared to 31 March, 2008.

(*ii*) Credit period :

Debtors : 1 months

Creditors : 2 months

(*iii*) Stock was maintained at the same level throughout the year.

(*iv*) Cash sales constituted at 20% of the total sales.

(*v*) All purchases were on credit basis only.

(*vi*) Current ratio on 31 March, 2009 was exactly 2.

(*vii*) Total expenses excluding depreciation for the year amounted to A 5,00,000.

(*viii*) Depreciation was provided @ 10% on the closing book value of fixed assets.

(*ix*) Bank and cash transactions for the financial year 2008-09 were as under :

(*a*) Payment to creditors included A 1,00,000 by cash.

(*b*) Received from debtors included A 11,80,000 by way of cheques.

(*c*) Cash deposited into the Bank A 2,40,000.

(*d*) Personal drawings from Bank A 1,00,000.

(*e*) Fixed assets purchased and paid by cheques A 4,50,000.

(*f*) Assume that cash destroyed by fire is written off in the Profit and Loss account.

You are required to prepare :

(*i*) Trading and Profit and Loss account of Shri Ram for the year ended 31 March, 2009.

(*ii*) A Balance Sheet as at that date. [*C.A., June, 2009*]

Solution

Trading and Profit and Loss Account
for the year ended 31.3.2009

Particulars	(*R*)	*Particulars*		(*R*)
To Opening stock	80,000	By Sales (W.N. 2) :		
To Purchases (W.N. 1)	7,20,000	Cash	3,60,000	
To Gross profit	10,80,000	Credit	14,40,000	18,00,000
		By closing stock		80,000
	18,80,000			18,80,000
To Expenses	5,00,000	By Gross profit		10,80,000
To Loss of cash by fire	20,000			
To Depreciation	74,000			
To Net profit transferred to Capital A/c	4,86,000			
	10,80,000			10,80,000

Balance Sheet as on 31.3.2009

Liabilities		(*R*)	*Assets*		(*R*)
Creditors		1,20,000	Cash at bank (W.N. 3)		40,000
Capital	4,00,000		Debtors		1,20,000
Add : Net profit			Stock		80,000
during the year	4,86,000				
	8,86,000		Fixed assets	2,90,000	
Less : Drawings	1,00,000	7,86,000	During the year	4,50,000	
				7,40,000	
			Less : Depreciation	74,000	6,66,000
		9,06,000			9,06,000

Working Notes

1. *Calculation of creditors as on 31.3.2009 and credit purchase for 2008-2009*

Creditors = Previous year creditors + 20% increase

= 1,00,000 + 20,000

= A 1,20,000

Credit purchases = Creditors at the end × $\frac{12}{2}$

= 1,20,000 × $\frac{12}{2}$ = A 7,20,000

2. *Calculation of Debtors as on 31.3.2009 and Cash and Credit Sales for 2008-09*

Debtors on 31.3.2009 = Debtors on 31.3.2008 + 20% Increase

= 1,00,000 + 20,000

= A 1,20,000

Credit sales for 2008-09 = Debtors at the end (i.e. one month credit) × 12

= A 1,20,000 × 12 = A 14,40,000

Total sales = A 14,40,000 × $\frac{100}{80}$ A 18,00,000

Cash sales = Total sales – Credit sales

= A 18,00,000 – A 14,40,000

= A 3,60,000

3. *Cash and Bank Balance as on 31.3.2009*

Current ratio = 2

Current ratio $\frac{\text{Current assets}}{\text{Current liabilities}}$ $\frac{2}{1}$

Current assets = Current liabilities × 2

Current assets = 1,20,000 × 2 = 2,40,000

Cash and bank balance = Current assets – (Debtors + Stock)

Cash and bank balance = 2,40,000 – (1,20,000 + 80,000)

Cash and bank balance = 2,40,000 – 2,00,000 = A 40,000

Cash Account

	(R)		(R)
To Balance b/d	10,000	By Creditors A/c	1,00,000
To Sales A/c	3,60,000	By Bank A/c	2,40,000
To Debtors A/c (W.N. 6)	2,40,000	By Expenses A/c	2,50,000
		(5,00,000 – 2,50,000)	
		By Loss by fire (bal. fig.)	20,000
	6,10,000		6,10,000

Bank Account

	(R)		(R)
To Balance b/d	20,000	By Creditors A/c (W.N. 7)	6,00,000
To Debtors A/c	11,80,000	By Fixed assets A/c	4,50,000
To Cash A/c	2,40,000	By Drawings	1,00,000
		By Expenses (bal. fig.)	2,50,000
		By Balance c/d	40,000
	14,40,000		14,40,000

Debtors Account

	(R)		(R)
To Balance b/d	1,00,000	By Bank	11,80,000
To Sales	14,40,000	By Cash (bal. fig.)	2,40,000
		By Balance c/d	1,20,000[1]
	15,40,000		15,40,000

Creditors Account

	(R)		(R)
To Cash A/c	1,00,000	By Balance b/d	1,00,000
To Bank (bal. fig.)	6,00,000	By Purchases A/c	7,20,000
To Balance c/d	1,20,000[2]		
	8,20,000		8,20,000

[1] Debtors on 31.3.2009 = Debtors on 31.3.2008 × 120% i.e., 1,00,000 × 120% = A 1,20,000.

[2] Creditors on 31.3.2009 = Creditors on 31.3.2008 × 120% i.e., 1,00,000 × 120% = A 1,20,000.

ASSIGNMENT MATERIAL

Note : The Objective–Type Questions (True/False, Multiple Choice Questions etc.) have been given in the Appendix at the end of the book.

SHORT ANSWER THEORY QUESTIONS

1. Define Single Entry System.
2. What are the features of Single Entry System.
3. Write a note on advantages of single entry system.
4. Discuss the disadvantages of single entry system.
5. Distinguish between single entry system and double entry system.
6. What is a Statement of Affairs method?
7. Distinguish between a Statement of Affairs and a Balance Sheet?
8. What is conversion method?
9. What are the limitations of incomplete records? [*B.Com.(Hons.), Delhi University, 2007*]
10. What are the limitations of single entry system. [*B.Com.(Hons.), Delhi University, 2011*]

LONG ANSWER THEORY QUESTIONS

1. Define single entry system. What are its advantages and disadvantages.
2. Distinguish between the followings :
   (*i*) Single Entry System and Double Entry System.
   (*ii*) Statement of affairs and balance sheet.
3. Explain how profit is determined under statement of affair method.
4. Explain how profit is determined under conversion method.

PRACTICAL PROBLEMS

1. Calculate the capital of Mr. Ashok as at 31st March 2012 from the following information :

	(A)		(A)
Cash on hand	10,000	Bank overdraft	20,000
Creditors	30,000	Debtors	40,000
Bills Receivable	50,000	Bills Payable	60,000
Outstanding Salaries	10,000	Prepaid Rent	10,000
Loans and Advances (Dr.)	1,00,000	Loan (Cr.)	80,000
Land and Building	1,30,000	Stock in trade	60,000

Ans. A 2,00,000

2. Mr. Gupta keeps his account on single entry system. He wants to know the results of his business on 31 December 2012 and for that following information is available :

Particulars	*31.12.2011 (A)*	*31.12.2012 (A)*
Cash in hand	1,50,000	1,75,000
Bank Balance	7,50,000	8,00,000
Furniture	1,00,000	1,00,000
Stock	5,00,000	6,50,000
Creditors	3,50,000	4,00,000
Debtors	2,50,000	3,00,000

During the year he had withdrawn A 50,000 for his personal use and invested A 25,000 as additional capital.

Required : Calculate his profit for the year ended 31st December 2012.

Ans. A 4,75,000

3. A, B and C were in partnership sharing profit and losses in the ratio of 3 : 2 : 1. At the end of the accounting year 2001, most of their books and record were destroyed in a fire. However, following information could be gathered from the records :

Balance Sheet as at January 1, 2001

Liabilities		(A)	*Assets*	(A)
Creditors		10,000	Cash	8,000
Capital Accounts :			Debtors	15,000
A	30,000		Stock	12,000
B	30,000		Fixed Assets	55,000
C	20,000	80,000		
		90,000		90,000

(*b*) Balance on 31.12.2001 : Cash A 7,000, Debtors A 18,000, Stock A 18,000 and Creditors A 4,000.

(*c*) Partners are entitled to 18% interest on Capital.

(*d*) Depreciation is charged on fixed assets @ 10% p.a.

(*e*) Drawings made by the partners during the year 2001 were as follows :

A – A 2,000; B – A 5,000 and C – A 4,000

12% interest on drawings is charged on total drawings made during any year.

You are required to show :

(*a*) Calculation of profit.

(*b*) The distribution of profit earned during 2001.

(*c*) Capital accounts of partner

(*d*) Balance sheet as at 31.12.2001 [*B.Com. (Hons.) Delhi University*]

Ans. Profit A 6,420; B/s Total A 92,500.

4. Johnson keeps his books by the Single Entry method. His position on 31st December 2011 and on 31st December 2012 are as follows :

Particulars	*31.12.2011 (A)*	*31.12.2012 (A)*
Cash in hand	3,000	2,000
Cash at Bank	25,000	28,000
Debtors	18,000	25,000
Stock	29,000	31,000
Furniture	5,000	6,000
Machinery	5,000	5,000
Creditors for Goods	18,000	25,000
Expenses outstanding	1,500	—
Prepaid Insurance	—	400

On 1st October 2011 Johnson introduced A 5,000 as further capital in the business and withdrew on the same date A 2,000 for personal use.

Depreciation is to be calculated on machinery at 10% p.a. A provision for doubtful debts is to be created on sundry debtors at 5%. Goods taken for personal use amounted to A 1,500. Also provide interest on capital at 10% p.a.

Required : Prepare the necessary statement showing the profit or loss made by him during the year ending 31st December 2012. [*B.Com. (Hons.), Delhi University*]

Ans. Loss A 3,150

5. Raj Kumar keeps his books on the single entry system. His statement of assets and liabilities as at 31 December 2008 is as follows :

Liabilities	*(A)*	*Assets*	*(A)*
Sundry Creditors	65,000	Land and Building	20,000
Loan from Money Lender	56,600	Furniture and Fixture	3,000
Outstanding Liabilities	13,400	Plant and Machinery	55,000
		Stock	9,200
		Sundry Debtors	75,500
		Cash	8,300

His drawings during the year amounted to A 3,000. Land and Building are to be depreciated by 2%; Furniture and Fixtures by 5% and Plant and Machinery by 10%. Sundry Debtors are to be reduced by 2%. He has used A 800 worth of Stock of his business for private purposes. During the year 2008, he sold some of his household furniture for A 1,000 and put this into his business bank account, His capital at the beginning of the year was A 30,000. Draw up the statement of profit and loss for the year ended 31.12.2008. [*B.Com. (Hons.) Delhi University*]

Ans. Net Profit : A 1,240.

6. Mr. Narayan could not keep complete records. He furnishes you the following information for the year 2011-12.

(*a*) Particulars of Assets and Liabilities

Particulars	*1.4.2011 (A)*	*31.3.2012 (A)*
Stock in trade	37,400	46,800
Sundry Debtors	24,000	28,000
Sundry Creditors	18,000	3,000
Bills Receivable	8,000	10,000
Bills Payable	2,000	400
Furniture and Fixture	1,200	1,200
Buildings	24,000	24,000
Bank Balance	8,700	1,660 (Cr)

Information : He sold his private investment of A 4,000 at 25% premium and brought this money into his business. His drawings were A 1,000 p.m.; Stock costing A 3,000 was taken by Mr. Narayan for his personal use. A provision @ 10% is required for doubtful debts and depreciation @ 5% p.a. is to be written-off and fixtures and buildings. A 6,000 is outstanding for wages and A 2,400 for salaries, prepaid insurance amounted to A 400, outstanding legal expenses are A 1,400.

Required : From the above particulars, find out by Statement of Affairs method, the Profit or Loss made by Mr. Narayan during 2011–12. Also prepare his Balance Sheet as at 31st March 2012.

7. Prepare necessary statements showing profit (or loss) made during the year 2001 and the balance sheet as at December 31, 2001 from the following information :

	1.1.2001 (A)	*31.12.2001 (A)*
Cash	5,000	6,000
Bank	15,000	18,000
Debtors	10,000	8,000
Stock	8,000	12,000
Furniture	12,000	12,000
Creditors	4,000	6,000

During the year, the proprietor introduced A 4,000 as further capital in the business. He has withdrawn cash A 20,000 out of which he spent A 15,000 on 1.7.2001 for purchase of a scooter for business use. Calculate net profit after making following adjustments :

(*a*) Depreciate furniture @ 10% p.a.

(*b*) Depreciate scooter @ 20% p.a.

(*c*) Create provision for doubtful debts @ 5% of debtors balance as on 31.12.2001, and

(*d*) Provide interest on capital in the beginning of the year @ 18%.

Ans. Profit A 8,620; B/s Total A 67,900.

8. From the following information supplied by Mr. X. calculated total sales :

	(A)
Capital in the beginning	1,20,000
Cash in hand in the beginning	40,000
B/R in the beginning	7,800
Debtors (opening)	30,800
Cash received from Y as loan	10,000
Cash received from Debtors	70,000
B/R encashed during the year	20,900
Bad Debts written off	2,800
Returns outward	10,000
Credit purchases	1,50,000
Cash paid to suppliers	30,000
Returns inward	8,700
B/R dishonoured	1,800
B/R at the end of the year	6,000
Debtors at the end of the year	25,500
Cash Sales	40,900
Cash received from a customer whose account closed last year because of his insolvency	500

[*B.Com. (Hons.) Delhi University 1999*]

Ans. A 1,27,500

9. Ashima runs a retail food store but does not keep proper accounts. A summary of her bank account for the year ended 31 October, 2001 was as follows :

	(A)
Receipts	
Balance in hand : 1 November, 2000	20,850
Cash Sales	3,16,300
Legacy paid into Business	4,000
Payment :	
Trade creditors (Goods for resale)	2,96,000
Purchase of fitting and fixtures	2,500
Rates	6,000
Light and heat	2,900
Sundry Expenses	1,200

The following information is also available.

(*i*) All takings have been paid into the bank with the exception of A 1,000 per week which Ashima has withdrawn for private purposes and A 500 per week which she pays to a part-time assistant.

(*ii*) Ashima's assets and liabilities (other than her bank balance) on 1 November, 2000 were as follows : Premises A 3,50,000; Fixtures and Fittings A 27,500; Vehicles A 60,000; Sundry Expenses occured A 250; Stock A 15,000 and Creditors A 9,000.

(*iii*) On 31st October 2001, stock in hand was valued at A 18,000 and creditors were A 7,500. There is an electricity bill of A 900 outstanding and rates have been prepaid by A 500.

(*iv*) Fixed assets have been purchased as per bank account and depreciation is to be written off as follows :

Fitting and Fixtures @ 10% of the book value at 31st October, 2001; motor vehicles @ 25% of the book value at 31st October, 2001.

(*v*) During the year, Ashima has taken goods costing A 7,500 for her own use. No payment has been made for these goods.

Prepare trading and profit and loss account for the year ending 31st October, 2001 and a balance sheet as at that date. Give detailed workings. [*B.Com. (Hons.) Delhi*]

Ans. Profit A 56,050; B/S Total A 4,73,050.

10. Manju commenced business as a cloth merchant with A 40,000 on 1.1.2008. On the same day, she purchased furniture for cash A 12,000. The books are maintained by single entry system. From the following particulars : (*i*) Ascertain the cash in hand on 31.12.2008; (*ii*) Prepare a Trading and Profit and Loss Account for the year ending 31.12.2008; and (*iii*) a Balance Sheet on that date.

	(A)
Sales (including cash sales of A 28,000)	68,000
Purchases (including cash purchases of A 16,000)	60,000
Manju's drawings	4,800
Salaries to Staff	8,000
Bad debts written off	2,000
Business expenses	2,800
Stock (31.12.2008)	26,000
Sundry Debtors (31.12.2008)	20,800
Sundry Creditors (31.12.2008)	14,400

Manju took cloth worth A 2,000 for her son and gave A 800 cash to her daughter for school fee but omitted to record these transactions in her books. Provide depreciation on furniture at 10% p.a. [*B.Com. (Hons.) Delhi*]

Ans. Profit A 22,000; B/S Total A 68,800

11. Bose supplied the following information about his business to you :

Assets and Liabilities	*1.4.2006 (A)*	*31.3.2007 (A)*
Sundry Debtors	1,81,000	1,93,000
Stock	1,50,000	1,40,000
Machinery	2,50,000	?
Furniture	40,000	?
Sundry creditors	1,10,000	1,25,000

Summary of cash book for the year ended 31 March, 2007 is as follows :

Receipts	*(A)*	*Payments*	*(A)*
Opening balance	5,000	Payments to creditors	3,50,000
Cash sales	61,000	Wages	1,60,000
Receipts from Debtors	7,53,000	Salaries	1,50,000
Miscellaneous receipts	2,000	Drawings	40,000
Loan from Dass @ 9% per annum (taken on 1.10.2006)	1,00,000	Sundry Office Expenses	1,10,000
		Machinery purchased (on 1.10.2003)	95,000
		Closing balance	16,000
	9,21,000		9,21,000

Discount allowed totalled A 7,000 and discount received was A 4,000. Bad debts written off were A 8,000. Depreciation was written off on furniture @ 5% per annum and machinery @ 10% per annum under the straight line method of depreciation. The office expenses included A 5,000 paid as insurance premium for the year ending 30 June, 2007. Wages amounting to A 20,000 were still due on 31 March, 2007.

Prepare trading and profit and loss account for the year ended 31 March, 2007, and the balance sheet as on that date. [*C.S. (Foundation) June 2004*]

Ans. Profit A 31,750; B/s Total A 7,03,500

12. Following information is available from incomplete records kept by Mr. X :

	April 1, 2011 *(A)*	*March 31, 2012* *(A)*
Cash	1,000	?
Bank	32,500	?
Debtors	73,600	82,500
Stock	91,000	92,600
Furniture	42,500	42,500
Creditors	45,400	52,600
Analysis of pass book reveals the following :		
Cash Sales (Payment received by cheque)	67,300	
Received from Debtors	3,26,500	
Additional Capital Introduced	3,500	
Payment to Creditors	2,16,000	
Business Expenses	83,500	
Personal Expenses	46,000	
Income Tax	12,300	

In addition, cash sales, cash purchases and cash expenses amounted to A 12,500, A 3,800 and A 8,100 respectively.

Prepare final accounts as on March 31, 2012 after taking into account the following :

(*i*) Depreciation on furniture A 2,500.

(*ii*) Bad Debts not recorded A 3,500

(*iii*) Outstanding Expenses A 700. [*C.A., Foundation*]

Ans. Profit A 91,500; B/s Total A 2,85,200

13. Mr. Ramamurthy has a small trading business for which the following procedures are followed:

1. All collections are deposited with the bank each day.
2. All payments except petty expenses are made by cheque.
3. To meet petty expenses, a cheque of A 500 is withdrawn from the bank on the 1st day of each month.
4. Mr. Ramamurthy makes personal drawings from the bank.
5. The assets and liabilities are as under :

	Opening *(A)*	*Closing* *(A)*
Cash in hand	320	200

Bank	2,500	5,000 (bank overdraft)
Debtors	20,000	30,000
Creditors	20,000	30,000
Stock	10,000	30,000

Payment to creditors during the year A 20,000. Sales made during the year A 30,000. Mr. Ramamurthy spent A 200 from the office cash for his personal expenses. Prepare final Accounts. *[C.A. Adapted]*

Ans. Profit A 14,080; Balance Sheet Total A 60,200

14. The Balance Sheet of C. Raja as on 31.12.2008 was as follows :

Liabilities	*(A)*	*Assets*	*(A)*
Creditors	36,050	Freehold premises	78,000
Capital	1,67,700	Plant and Machinery	21,000
		Furniture and fittings	10,200
		Stock	43,800
		Debtors	49,100
		Cash	1,650
	2,03,750		2,03,750

Raja maintained only a cash book and a ledger. The summary of his receipt and payments for the year ended 31 December 2009 is given below :

Receipts	*(A)*	*Payments*	*(A)*
Cash Sales	93,150	Cash purchases	25,000
Cash received from credit sales	2,13,800	Creditors for goods purchased	1,72,700
Capital introduced	10,000	Wages	37,150
		General expenses	31,350
		Addition to Plant and Machinery	6,400
		Addition to Furniture	1,600
		Drawings	26,800

As on 31.12.2009 the amount due from Debtors was A 45,900 and the amount due to Creditors was A 40,800; liability for expenses was A 2,550 and the value of stock was A 42,700 as on that date. You are required to prepare the Trading and Profit and Loss Account of C. Raja for the year ending 31 December 2009 and a Balance Sheet as on that date after making adjustments in respect of followings :

(*i*) Depreciation at 10% is to be provided on plant and machinery and on furniture and fittings;

(*ii*) A 7,500 to be provided for bad debts.

(*iii*) Goods supplied to the proprietor for his private purpose A 1,900 was included in the Debtor's balance as on 31.12.2009.

(*iv*) Sales returns amounted to A 6,600. *[I.C.W.A. (Inter)]*

Ans. Profit A 17,730; Balance Sheet total A 2,10,080.

15. From the following particulars furnished by Shri Ramji, Prepare Trading and Profit and Loss Account for the year ended 31.3.2007. Also draft his Balance Sheet as at 31.3.2007 :

	1.4.2006 (A)	31.3.2007 (A)
Creditors	3,15,400	2,48,000
Expenses outstanding	12,000	6,600
Fixed assets (includes Machinery)	2,32,200	2,40,800
Stock in hand	1,60,800	2,22,400
Cash in hand	59,200	24,000
Cash at Bank	80,000	1,37,600
Sundry Debtors	3,30,600	?

Details of the year's transactions are as follows :

	(A)
Cash and discounts credited to debtors	12,80,000
Returns from Debtors	29,000
Bad Debts	8,400
Sales (Both Cash and Credit)	14,36,200
Discount allowed by creditors	14,000
Returns to creditors	8,000
Capital introduced by Cheque	1,70,000
Collection from debtors (Deposited into Bank after receiving cash)	12,50,000
Cash purchases	20,600
Expenses paid by cash	1,91,400
Drawings by Cheque	8,600
Machinery acquired by Cheque	63,600
Cash deposited into Bank	1,00,000
Cash withdrawn from bank	1,84,800
Casl Sales	92,000
Payment to creditors by Cheque	12,05,400

Note : *Ramji has not sold any Fixed Asset during the year.* [*CA, November 2005*]

Ans. Profit A 30,800; Balance Sheet total A 9,82,200.

16. Purnima and Kusum are in partnership sharing profit in the ratio of 3 : 2 respectively. They maintain their books of account on single entry system. Taking into account the following information also, you are required to prepare Trading and Profit & Loss Account for the year ended 31 March 2007 and their Balance Sheet as at that date.

Analysis of Cash Book for the Year

	(A)
Bank balance as on 1 April, 2006	40,000
Purnima's Drawings	95,000
Kusum's Drawings	80,000
Paid to Trade Creditors	3,00,000
Paid against bills Payable	80,000
Wages	1,10,000

Salaries	1,50,000
Other Trade Expenses	1,32,550
Received from Trade Debtors	4,56,000
Received against Bills Receivable	80,450
Received from Cash Sales	3,58,100
Cash in hand on 31st March, 2007	2,000

There was no cash in hand on 1 April, 2006.

The respective capitals of Purnima and Kusum on 1 April, 2006 were A 8,00,000 and A 2,00,000. Particulars of other assets and liabilities are as follows :

	1.4.2006 *(A)*	*31.3.2007* *(A)*
Stock on Hand	2,98,000	3,50,000
Trade Debtors	2,50,000	1,93,550
Trade Creditors	2,20,000	70,000
Bills Receivable	50,000	70,000
Bills Payable	30,000	—
Business Premises	5,00,000	5,00,000
Office Furniture	1,12,000	1,12,000

Interest on drawings was agreed as A 3,500 for Purnima and A 3,000 for Kusum. Interest on capital is to be allowed at 10%. Kusum is also to be credited with a commission of 6% on the net profit remaining after charging such commission. Allow 5% depreciation on premises and furniture. Also create a provision for bad debts amounting to A 13,250. [*B.Com. (Hons.) Delhi 2003*]

Ans. Profit A 1,70,000; Balance Sheet Total A 11,83,700.

17. The following information relates to the business of Mr. Shiv Kumar, who request you to prepare a Trading and Profit & Loss Account for the year ended 31 March, 2008 and a Balance Sheet as on that date :

	Balance as on 31.3.2007 *(A)*	*Balance as on 31.3.2008* *(A)*
Building	3,20,000	3,60,000
Furniture	60,000	68,000
Motor Car	80,000	80,000
Stocks	—	40,000
Bills Payable	28,000	16,000
Cash and Bank balances	1,80,000	1,04,000
Sundry Debtors	1,60,000	—
Bills Receivable	32,000	28,000
Sundry Creditors	1,20,000	—

(*b*) Cash transactions during the year included the following besides certain other items :

	(A)		(A)
Sale of Old papers and miscellaneous income	20,000	Cash Purchases	48,000
		Payment to creditors	1,84,000
Miscellaneous Trade expenses (including Salaries etc.)	80,000	Cash Sales	80,000
Collection from debtors	2,00,000		

(*c*) Other information :

(*i*) Bills receivable drawn during the year amount to A 20,000 and Bills payable accepted A 16,000.

(*ii*) Some items of old furniture, whose written down value on 31 March, 2007 was A 20,000 was sold on 30 September, 2007 for A 8,000. Depreciation is to be provided on Building and Furniture @ 10% p.a. and on motorcar @ 20% p.a. Depreciation on sale of furniture to be provided for 6 months and for additions to Building for whole year.

(*iii*) Of the Debtors, a sum of A 8,000 should be written off as Bad Debt and a reserve for doubtful debts is to be provided @ 2%.

(*iv*) Mr. Shivkumar has been maintaining a steady gross profit rate of 30% on turnover.

(*v*) Outstanding salary on 31 March, 2007 was A 8,000 and on 31 March, 2008 was A 10,000. Profit & Loss Account had a credit balance of A 40,000.

(*vi*) 20% of total Sales and total purchases are to be treated as for cash.

(*vii*) Additions in Furniture Account took place in the beginning of the year and there was no opening provisions for doubtful debts.

[*C.A., P.E. (Examination II) November 2003*]

Ans. Profit A 5,040; Balance Sheet total A 8,68,160.

CHAPTER 15

Accounting for Hire Purchase and Instalment Transactions

Learning Objectives

After studying this chapter, you should be able to :

1. *Explain the meaning of Hire Purchase System.*
2. *Recognise some important terms used in Hire Purchase Agreement.*
3. *Distinguish between Hire Purchase System and Instalment System.*
4. *Understand the way interest is calculated.*
5. *Discuss the Cash Price Method (Full Cash Price Method, Down Payment/Accrual Method) Accounting for Hire Purchase.*
6. *Understand Debtor System and Stock and Debtor System accounting for Hire Purchase.*
7. *Explain the concept of lease and their types – finance lease and operating lease.*

MEANING OF HIRE PURCHASE SYSTEM

The hire purchase system is regulated by the Hire Purchase Act 1972. This Act defines a hire purchase as "an agreement under which goods are let on hire and the hirer has an option to purchase them in accordance with the terms of the agreement and includes an agreement under which

1. The owner delivers possession of goods thereof to a person on condition that such person pays the agreed amount in periodic instalments.
2. The property in the goods is to pass to such person on the payment of the last instalment.
3. Such person has a right to terminate the agreement at any time before the property passes to the purchaser.

Thus, Hire Purchase transaction involves an agreement between Hire Vendor and Hire Purchaser whereby hire vendor gives the delivery of goods to hire purchaser on signing of an agreement and after down payment. The hire purchaser undertakes to pay the balance amount in agreed number of instalments together with interest. The ownership of goods shall be transferred from hire vendor to hire purchaser only when all the agreed number of instalments have been paid by the purchaser or when the last instalment is paid. Hire Vendor has the right to repossess the goods on the failure to pay any instalment by hire purchaser.

Hire Purchase is financial facilities, which allow a business to use an asset over a fixed period, in return of regular payments. Many kinds of business assets are suitable for financing using hire purchase including :

- Plant & Machinery
- Cars
- Commercial Vehicles
- Agricultural Equipment
- Computers including Software packages
- Office Equipment

Important Terms used in Hire Purchase Agreement

(*a*) ***Hire Vendor*** **:** The one who sells goods under hire purchase agreement.

(*b*) ***Hirer*****:** Also known as hire purchaser, the person who purchases goods under hire purchase agreement.

(*c*) ***Cash Price*** **:** It is actual price of goods charged under normal cash sale or the price at which the goods may be purchased by hirer for cash.

(*d*) ***Down Payment*** **:** Down payment is an initial payment payable by the hirer at the time of entering into a hire purchase agreement.

(*e*) ***Hire Purchase Price*** **:** It is total amount payable under the terms of hire purchase agreement in the form of down payment and installments

Hire Purchase Price = Down Payment + Instalments

Since, instalments are spread over a longer period, the seller charges interest and it is included in the aforesaid instalments. Hence instalments include payment towards cash price financed and interest on the amount financed.

Hire-Purchase Price = Cash Price + Interest

(*f*) ***Hire Charges*****:** Hire purchase charges are the difference between hire purchase price and cash price.

Hire Purchase System *Vs* Instalment System

Hire Purchase System differs from Instalment System in the following ways :

Hire Purchase System	*Instalment System*
1. It is a contract of hire.	1. It is a contract of sale.
2. It is governed by Hire Purchase Act 1972.	2. It is governed by Sales of Goods Act 1930.
3. Price is paid by purchaser through instalment which is treated as hire.	3. Every instalments is treated as part of price.
4. The property in goods (ownership) is transferred from vendor to purchaser only when the last instalment is paid.	4. The title of goods (ownership) passes immediately as in the case of usual sale.
5. The purchaser cannot transfer or temper the goods until he pays final instalment.	5. The buyer has right to sell, transfer or dispose off the goods at any time.
6. The seller may take possession of the goods back if the hirer is in default.	6. The seller can only sue for price if the buyer is in default. He cannot take possession of the goods.
7. The purchaser has the right to terminate the agreement at any time before the property so passes	7. The buyer has no right to terminate the agreement and return goods.

CALCULATION OF INTEREST

The hire purchase price consists of (*a*) Payment towards cash price; (*b*) Interest. The interest is charged on the unpaid cash price, which decreases with every instalment paid.

On the basis of information given in a particular situation, problems of calculation of interest can be classified as the following :

Case 1 : Given : Rate of interest, Total Cash price and Hire Purchase Price

(Unequal instalments) : On 01.4.2008, *R* Purchased a computer from *C* Ltd., on hire purchase basis. The cash price of computer is A 80,000 payable A 20,000 as cash down and three instalments of A 23,000, A 22,000 and A 21,000 on 31st March 2009, 2010 and 2011 respectively. Interest is charged @ 5% p.a.. Calculate the amount of interest paid by buyer to seller every year.

Solution

		A
	Total Cash Price	80,000
Less :	Down Payment	20,000
		60,000
Add :	Interest on A 60,000 @ 5% p.a. for one year	3,000
		63,000
Less :	First Instalment	23,000
		40,000
Add :	Interest on A 40,000 @ 5% p.a. for one year	2,000
		42,000
Less :	Second Instalment	22,000
		20,000
Add :	Interest (*Balance Figure*)	1,000
		21,000
Less :	Third Instalment	21,000

(Equal Instalments) : On 1st Jan 2008, Vee Kay Enterprises purchased a Printing Machine on hire purchase system from Modern Machinery Company. The payment was to be made as A 20,000 down and balance in three equal annual instalments of A 30,000 each payable on 31st December every year. The vendors company charged interest @ 5% p.a.. The cash down value of machine was A 1,01,697. Calculate the interest on three instalments.

Solution

		A
	Cash Price	1,01,697
Less :	down Payment	20,000
		81,697
Add :	Interest on A 81,697 @ 5% p.a. for one year	4,085
		85,782
Less :	1st Instalment	30,000
		55,782
Add :	Interest on A 55,782 @ 5% p.a. for one year	2,789
		58,571
Less :	IInd Instalment	30,000
		28,571
Add :	Interest on A 28,571 @ 5% p.a. for one year (*Balance Fig.*)	1,429
		30,000
Less :	IIIrd Instalment	30,000
		—

Case 2 : Given : Rate of Interest and Instalments

On 1st April 2006, Mr. Shyam purchased Machinery from M/s Navya Enterprises on hire purchase basis. The term of payments being A 10,000 down A 29,500 at the end of 2006, A 20,200 at the end of year 2007, A 13,300 by the end of year 2008 and A 14,700 at the end of 2009. Interest is charged @ 5% p.a.

Solution

In this type of question we should start calculation of interest from last instalment, since last instalment includes cash payment of last instalment and interest towards that pending instalment only.

Suppose, Cash Price instalment	= A	100
Interest @ 5%	= A	5
Hire Purchase instalment	= A	105
So, interest on Hire Purchase instalment is	=	5/105

Year	*Instalment* A	*Amount Outstanding (A)*	*Interest* A	*Cash Price* A
2009	14,700	14,700	$14{,}700 \ \frac{5}{105}$ = 700	14,700 – 700 = 14,000
2008	13,300	13,300 + 14,000 = 27,300	$27{,}300 \ \frac{5}{105}$ = 1,300	13,300 – 1.300 = 12,000
2007	20,200	20,200 + 12,000 + 14,000 = 46,200	$46{,}200 \ \frac{5}{105}$ = 2,200	20,200 – 2,200 = 18,000
2006	29,500	29,500 + 18,000 + 12,000 + 14,000 = 73,500	$73{,}500 \ \frac{5}{105}$ = 3,500	29,500 – 3,500 = 26,000
Down Payment	10,000	–	–	10,000
	Hire Purch. Price = *A 87,700*	–	Total Interest = A 7,700	Total Cash Price = *A 80,000*

Raj purchases an air conditioner on the hire purchase system. He pays A 7,000 down and A 6,000 at the end of 2 years, 4 years and 6 years. Interest is charged by the vendor @ 10% at 2 yearly rate on the unpaid balance. Calculate interest paid with each instalment.

Solution

Suppose, Cash Price =	A 100
Interest @ 10% p.a. for 2 years	20
Hire purchase instalment	120

Interest on hire purchase instalment = 20/120

Year	*Instalment* A	*Amount Outstanding (A)*	*Interest* A	*Cash Price* A
End of 6th Year	6,000	6,000 = 1,000	$6{,}000 \ \frac{20}{120}$ = 5,000	6,000 – 1,000

End of 4th Year	6,000 = 11,000	6,000 + 5,000 = 1,833	11,000 $\frac{20}{120}$ = 4,167	6,000 – 1,833
End of 2nd year	6,000 + 5,000 = 15,167	6,000 + 4,167 = 2,528	15,167 $\frac{20}{120}$ = 3,472	6,000 – 2,528
Down Payment	7,000	–	–	7,000
	Hire Purchase Price = A 25,000	–	Total Interest = A 5,361	Total Cash Price = A 19,639

Note : If interest is charged @ 10% p.a. at yearly rate. Then

	A	
Suppose Cash Price be	100	
Add : Interest @ 10% p.a. for 1 year	10	
	110	
Add : Interest @ 10% p.a. for 1 year	11	(10% of 110)
Hire Purchase Instalment	121	

Interest on hire purchase instalments = 21/121

Case 3 : Given : Rate of interest and instalments (Annuity Method)

Annuity means a series of equal payments at fixed intervals. Annuity table is used to find out the present value of annuity for a number of years at a certain rate of interest.

(Equal Instalments) : Suresh purchases a computer from M/s Software. The term of payment being A 12,000 annually for 3 years. The rate of interest charged is 5% p.a. Calculate cash price of computer with the help of annuity tables.

Solution

Annuity table shows present value of annuity of A 1 @5% p.a. interest for three years is A 2.7233.

Cash price of Computer = 12,000 × 2.7233

= A 32,680

(Unequal instalments) : Sunita purchased machinery by paying A 10,000 down A 15,000 at the end of 1st year, 12,000 at the end of 2nd year and A 10,000 at the end of 3rd year. Rate of interest charged is 5% p.a. Calculate cash price with the help of annuity tables.

Solution

Annuity table shows that present value of one rupee for 1, 2 and 3 year at 5% interest is 0.9529, 0.9070 & 0.8639 respectively.

Cash Price of Machinery = Down Payment + (First instalment × PV of annuity) + (Second Instalment × PV of annuity) + (Third instalment × PV of annuity)

= 10,000 + (15,000 × 0.9529) + (12,000 × 0.9070) + (10,000 × 0.8639)

= A 10,000 + 14,294 + 10,884 + 8,639 = A 43,817

Case 4 : Given : Cash Price and Rate of Interest

On 1st Jan. 2009, *N* Ltd., purchased a machine costing A 80,000 from *Z* Ltd. on hire purchase basis. The terms of payment being A 20,000 down and balance in 3 annual instalments of A 20,000 each together with interest @ 10% p.a. Calculate the hire purchase price of machine.

Solution

	A
Total Cash Price	80,000
Less : Down payment	20,000
	60,000
Add : Interest @ 10% on 60,000 for 1 year	6,000
	66,000
Less : 1st instalment (20,000 + 6,000)	26,000
	40,000
Add : Interest @ 10% on 40,000 for 1 year	4,000
	44,000
Less : 2nd instalment (20,000 + 4,000)	24,000
	20,000
Add : Interest @ 10% on 20,000 for 1 year	2,000
	22,000
Less : 3rd instalment (20,000 + 2,000)	22,000
	—

Total Hire Purchase Price = Down payment + First instalment + Second Instalment + Third Instalment

= 20,000 + 26,000 + 24,000 + 22,000

= A 92,000

Case 5 : Given : Total Cash Price and Hire Purchase Price

Harshal purchases a refrigerator on hire purchase basis. The cash price of refrigerator is A 30,000. The terms of payment being A 4,000 down and balance in 3 equal instalments of A 10,000 each, payable on 31st March every year. Calculate amount of interest included in each of the annual instalment.

Solution

Cash Price = A 30,000

Hire Purchase Price = Down payment + Total Amount of instalments

= 4,000 + 10,000 × 3

= 4,000 + 30,000

= A 34,000

Total Interest = Hire purchase price – Cash price

= (34,000 – 30,000)

= A 4,000

When rate of interest is not given, the amount of total interest is apportioned in the ratio of amount outstanding at the end of each year.

Year	*Amount outstanding at the end of year* A	*Ratio*	*Interest Apportioned* A
I	30,000	3	$\frac{3}{6}$ 4,000 2,000
II	20,000	2	$\frac{2}{6}$ 4,000 1,333
III	10,000	1	$\frac{1}{6}$ 4,000 667
		6	A 4,000

ACCOUNTING FOR HIRE PURCHASE

The following are the methods of recording hire-purchase transaction:

I Method : Cash Price Method

This method is based on the following :

1. Full Cash Price
2. Down Payment/Accrual Method

II Method

It includes the following Methods :

1. Debtor System/Method
2. Stock & Debtor System/Method

METHOD I

Cash Price Method

The accounting entries of the hire purchase transaction under the two methods of cash price method are discussed below :

1. *Full Cash Price Method* : The asset is recorded at full cash price.

The following journal entries will be passed :

In Books of Hire Purchaser

First Year

(*i*) *On purchases of the Asset*

Asset on Hire Purchase A/c Dr. With full cash price
To Hire Vendors A/c of Asset

(*ii*) On making down payment on delivery

Hire Vendor's A/c Dr. With amount of
To Bank/Cash A/c down payment

(*iii*) For interest due on instalment

Interest on Hire Purchase A/c	Dr.	with amount of
To Hire Vendor's A/c		interest due

(*iv*) On payment of Hire Purchase Instalment

Hire Vendor's A/c	Dr.	with amount of
To Cash/Bank A/c		instalment

(*v*) For depreciation charged on the Asset

Depreciation A/c	Dr.
To Asset on Hire Purchase	

(*vi*) For transfer of interest

Profit & Loss A/c	Dr.
To Interest on Hire Purchase A/c	

(*vii*) For transfer of depreciation

Profit & Loss A/c	Dr.
To Depreciation A/c	

or

Profit & Loss A/c	Dr.
To Interest on Hire Purchase A/c	
To Depreciation A/c	

Second and subsequent years entries (*iii*), (*iv*), (*v*), (*vi*) and (*vii*) will be repeated with their respective amount of interest and depreciation provided.

In the Books of Hire Vendor

First Year

(*i*) On Sale of asset under Hire Purchase

Hire Purchaser's A/c	Dr.	With total cash
To Hire Purchase Sale A/c		price of asset

(*ii*) On receiving down payment

Cash/Bank A/c	Dr.	With amount of
To Hire Purchaser's A/c		down payment

(*iii*) For interest due on instalment

Hire Purchaser's A/c	Dr.	With amount of
To Interest on Hire Purchase Sales A/c		interest

(*iv*) On receipt of hire purchase instalment

Cash/Bank A/c	Dr.	With amount of
To Hire Purchaser's A/c		instalment

(*v*) For transfer of interest

Interest on Hire Purchase Sales A/c	Dr.
To Profit & Loss A/c	

Second and subsequent Years entries (*iii*), (*iv*), and (*v*) will be repeated with their respective amount of interest and depreciation provided.

2. Down Payment/Accrual Method : When asset is recorded at cash actually paid, the following journal entries will be passed :

In the books of Hire Purchaser

First Year

(*i*) On Purchase of the Asset

Asset on Hire Purchase A/c Dr. With down payment being due
 To Hire Vendor's A/c

(*ii*) On making down payment on delivery of asset

Hire Vendor's A/c Dr. With the amount of down payment
 To Cash/Bank A/c

(*iii*) When instalment becoming due

Asset on Hire Purchase A/c Dr. With the amount of part of cash Price

Interest on Hire Purchase A/c Dr. With the amount of interest

To Hire Vendor's A/c

(*iv*) On payment of instalment

Hire Vendor's A/c Dr. With the amount of instalment
 To Cash/Bank A/c

(*v*) For Depreciation charged on asset

Depreciation A/c Dr.
 To Asset on Hire Purchase A/c

(Depreciation is always charged on the total cash price of the asset and not on the debit balance shown by the asset account)

(*vi*) For transfer of Interest and depreciation

Profit & Loss A/c Dr.
 To Depreciation A/c
 To Interest on Hire Purchase A/c

Second and subsequent year's entries (*iii*), (*iv*), (*v*) and (*vi*) will be repeated with their respective amount of interest and depreciation provided.

In the Books of Hire Vendor

There is no change in the accounting treatment in the books of hire vendor under accrual system.

DEFAULT AND REPOSSESSION

When a hire purchaser makes default and fails to pay instalments, the hire vendor has the right to take back the goods under hire purchase agreement. In case of non-payment of instalments by the purchaser, the hire vender not only re-possess goods but also forfeits the amount of instalments already received, thus treating the instalments already paid as hire charges. There are two cases.

(*i*) ***Full Repossession* :** When the hire vendor takes back all the goods sold to hire purchaser.

(*ii*) ***Partial Repossession* :** In such a case, the hire vendor takes the possession of only some of the total assets sold to hire purchaser and balance of goods are retained by hire purchaser.

ACCOUNTING TREATMENT IN CASE OF FULL REPOSSESSION

In the Books of Hire Purchaser

When the goods are repossessed by the hire vendor, then the hire purchaser closes both Hire Vendor Account and Asset on Hire Purchaser Account on the date of default by making the following entries.

(*i*)	Hire Vendor's A/c To Asset on Hire Purchase A/c	Dr.	(With amount outstanding)

(*ii*) Any balance left in the asset account is transferred to profit & loss account.

Profit & Loss A/c To Asset on Hire Purchase A/c	Dr.	(With Balance Figure)

In the Books of Hire Vendor

On the date of default the hire vendor closes hire purchaser account by transferring the balance to Goods Repossessed Account.

Goods Repossessed A/c To Hire Purchase' A/c	Dr.	(with balance outstanding)

The newly opened Goods Repossessed Account is further debited with expenses incurred on the repair of goods repossessed and credited with cash received from resale of goods. Any balance left in goods repossession account, being profit or loss on resale, is transferred to Profit and loss Account.

(*a*)	Good Repossessed A/c To Cash A/c	Dr.	(with amount of expenses)
(*b*)	Cash A/c To Good Repossessed A/c	Dr.	(With resale price)
(*c*)	Profit & Loss A/c To Goods Repossessed A/c	Dr.	(With amount of loss)
	or		
	Goods Repossessed A/c To Profit & Loss A/c	Dr.	(With amount of Profit)

ACCOUNTING TREATMENTS IN CASE OF PARTIAL REPOSSESSION

In partial repossession, only some of the total assets sold to hire purchaser are repossessed and balance of goods are retained by hire purchaser.

All the journals entries are same as in case of full repossession except the following difference. In case of default *i.e.,* in case of non-payment of instalments, goods on hire purchase are divided into parts :

- Goods retained with hire purchaser
- Goods repossessed by vendor

Goods retained with hire purchaser are valued at cost less normal rate of depreciation to the date and shown as closing balance of the asset on hire purchase account in the books of hire vendor. Goods taken back by hire vendor are valued at agreed price. Agreed price can be calculated on either of the following basis :

(*i*) Goods repossessed may be valued on the basis of enhanced rate of depreciation *i.e.,* agreed value of goods repossessed is calculated after charging rate of depreciation higher than normal rate applied by hire purchaser.

(*ii*) Any amount determined by mutual agreement between hire purchaser and hire vendor may be taken as agreed value.

(*iii*) Agreed value may also be taken as a certain percentage of cash price or hire purchase price.

The hire purchaser does not close the account of hire vendor and hire vendor does not close the account of hire purchaser in their respective books. However, following entries are made.

In Books of Hire Purchaser

(*a*) Hire Vendor's A/c Dr. (With agreed value)
    To Asset on Hire Purchase A/c

The balance of vendor's account is carried forward to next period.

(*b*) Value of goods retained by the purchaser is shown as closing balance in the goods on hire purchase account and balance is transferred to profit and loss account.

Profit & Loss A/c Dr.
    To Asset on Hire Purchase A/c

In the Books of Hire Vendor

Goods Repossessed A/c Dr. (With agreed amount)
    To Hire Purchaser's A/c

The balance of hire purchaser's account will be carried forward to next year.

However, all the entries relating to repairs and resale of goods repossessed will be same as in case of full repossessions.

METHOD II

---

3. Debtor System/Method (Also known as Hire Purchase Trading Account Method)

Sometimes, business sells goods both on cash basis and hire purchase basis. When numerous items of the small value such as cycles, fans, radios, TV etc., are sold on hire purchase basis involving many transactions during an accounting year, it becomes very difficult to maintain separate accounts for each customer, calculation of interest and profit & Loss. It will involve lot of cost, efforts and time. Under such circumstances, Hire Purchase Trading account is adopted. For keeping records of hire purchase method transactions a separate book called Hire Purchase Register or Hire Purchase Sales book is maintained to record date of contract, name of hire purchaser, cost price, hire purchase price, down payment, number of instalments and amount of each instalment with dates when they become due. At the end of the year, profit or loss on hire purchase is calculated by extracting the following information from accounting records :

1. Cost of goods sold on hire purchase.
2. Total cash received from hire purchase customer (down payment + instalments) during the year.
3. Instalments due but not paid by the hire purchase customer.
4. Instalments not yet due. It is also known as stock lying with hire purchase customers.

Hire purchase Trading Account may either be prepared at cost or at hire purchase price.

(*i*) Hire Purchase Trading Account at Cost : Under this method all transaction are recorded at cost. The following entries will be made in this method.

1. For recording opening balances.

Hire Purchase Trading A/c	Dr.	
To Stock with HP Customers A/c / Instalments Not Due A/c		Cost Price
To Instalments Due A/c		Hire Purchase Price

2. For goods sold on hire purchase basis during the year

Hire Purchase Trading A/c	Dr.	Cost Price
To Goods sold on Hire Purchase A/c		

3. On receipt of cash from HP customers including cash down

Bank/Cash A/c	Dr.	Down payment and instalments received
To Hire Purchase Trading A/c		

4. On repossession of goods due to non-payment of instalment due

Goods Repossessed A/c	Dr.	with agreed or estimated value
To Hire Purchase Trading A/c		

5. For recording closing balances

Instalment Due A/c	Dr.	Hire Purchase Price
Stock with HP customer A/c/ Instalment No Due A/c	Dr.	Cost Price
To Hire Purchases Trading A/c		

6. In case of Profit

Hire Purchase Trading A/c	Dr.	Profit
To Profit & Loss A/c		

7. In case of loss

Profit & Loss A/c	Dr.	Loss
To Hire Purchase Trading A/c		

Hire Purchase Trading A/c (At Cost)

Balance b/d		Cash Received from HP	–
Stock with HP customer (at cost)	–	Customer	–
Instalment Due (at HP Price)	–	Goods Repossessed (Agreed value)	
Goods Sold on HP basis (Cost)*	–	Balance c/d	
Profit & Loss A/c (Profit)	–	Stock with HP customer (at cost)	–
(*Balancing Figure*)	–	Instalment Due (at HP Price)	
		Profit & Loss A/c (Loss)	
		(*Balancing Figure*)	

* Cost of Goods sold on HP is arrived as :

Stock at shop in the beginning (at cost)

Add : Purchases during the year

Less : Stock at shop at the end.

(*ii*) Hire Purchase Trading Account (At selling price)

The entries are same as in Hire Purchase Trading A/c at cost, but for elimination of profit margin from opening stock with HP customer, goods sold on hire purchase and closing stock with HP Customer, the following additional entries are made :

(*i*) For adjusting/removing loading on Goods sold on HP basis

Goods Sold on HP A/c Dr.

To Hire Purchase Trading A/c
(With profit element)

(*ii*) For adjusting/removing loading on opening stock with HP customer
Stock Reserve A/c Dr.
To Hire Purchase Trading A/c
(With profit element)

(*iii*) For adjusting/removing loading on closing stock with HP customer
Hire Purchase Trading A/c Dr.
To Stock Reserve A/c
(With profit element)

Proforma
Hire Purchase Trading A/c
(At Selling Price)

Dr.			*Cr.*
Stock with HP Customers in the beginning	HPP	Cash Received during the year	–
Instalment Due in the beginning	HPP	Goods Repossessed from defaulting customers (valued at)	Agreed Value
Goods sold on HP basis during the year	HPP		
Stock Reserve Account (loading on closing stock)	Profit Element	Stock Reserve Account (loading on opening stock)	Profit Element
Hire Purchase Expenses		Goods sold on HP basis (loading on goods sold on HP)	Profit Element
Profit & Loss Account (Profit) (Balancing Figure)		Stock with HP customer at the end	HPP
		Instalment Due at the end	HPP
		Profit & Loss Account (Loss) (Balancing Figure)	

Calculation of Missing Figures

In most of practical problems, information which is required for the preparation of Hire Purchase Trading Account such as opening or closing balance of stock with HP customers or instalment not due or instalment due, cash received from customers or any other figure is missing. For calculation of these missing figures, we prepare the following three accounts :

1. Shop Stock Account (Always at cost price).
2. Stock with the Hire Purchase Customers/Instalment. Not due Account. (Always at HPP).
3. Instalment Due Account. (Always at HPP).

First Account

Shop Stock A/c (At cost price)

Dr.			*Cr.*
Balance b/d (Opening Stock)	–	Stock with HP customer (Being goods sold at hire purchase at cost)	Cost
Purchases	–	Balance c/d (Closing Stock)	–

Second Account

Stock with HP Customer A/c (At HPP)

Dr.			*Cr.*
Balance b/d		Instalment Due A/c (Being instalments due during the year)	–
Shop Stock A/c	–		
Goods sold to HP Customer (Transfer from Shop Stock A/c)	(Cost+Profit)	Balance c/d	–

Third Account

Instalments Due A/c (At HPP)

Dr.			*Cr.*
Balance b/d	–	Cash Received	–
Stock with HP customer (Instalment due, transfer from Stock with HP customer A/c)	–	Goods Respossessed	–
		Balance c/d	–

4. Stock and Debtor System/Method : This is an alternative method of calculating profit or loss on hire purchase transactions. Under this method, in addition to the three ledger accounts namely Shop Stock Account, Instalment Not Due A/c and Instalment Due A/c, Hire Purchase Adjustment Account is prepared (instead of Hire Purchase Trading A/c) for calculation of Profit or Loss on hire purchase transactions. Goods Repossessed A/c should also be prepared, if goods have been repossessed.

The following journal entries are made under this method :

(*i*) When goods are purchased

Shop Stock A/c	Dr.	(Cost Price)
To Purchases A/c		

(*ii*) When goods are sold on Hire Purchase

Hire Purchase Stock A/c	Dr.	HP Price
To Shop Stock A/c		Cost
To Hire Purchases Adjustment A/c		Loading

(*iii*) When Instalments become due

Instalment Due A/c Dr.

Hire Purchase Debtors A/c Dr. HP Price

To Hire Purchase Stock A/c

(*iv*) When cash is received from Hire Purchase Debtors

Cash A/c Dr.

To Instalment Due/Hire Purchase Debtors A/c

(*v*) When goods are repossessed on default

Goods Repossessed A/c Dr. Estimated/Agreed Value

HP Adjustment A/c Dr. Loss on Repossession

To Hire Purchase Debtors A/c Total Instalments Due

(*vi*) For reserve on opening Stock with Hire Purchase Customers

Stock reserve A/c Dr. Loaded Price

To Hire Purchase Adjustment A/c

(*vii*) For Reserve on closing stock on hire purchase

Hire Purchase Adjustment A/c Dr. Loaded price

To Stock Revenue A/c

(*viii*) For Profit on Hire Purchase

Hire Purchase Adjustment A/c Dr. Profit

To Profit & Loss A/c

or

For loss on Hire Purchase

Profit & Loss A/c Dr. Loss

To Hire Purchase Adjustment A/c

Hire Purchase Adjustment A/c

Dr. *Cr.*

Particulars	*A*	*Particulars*	*A*
Stock Reserve Account (Loading on closing stock)	–	Stock Reserve Account (Loading on opening Stock)	–
Loss on Goods Repossessed	–	Goods sold on HP Basis/Hire Purchase Stock Account (Load)	–
		Profit on Repossession	
Hire Purchase Expenses	–	Profit & Loss A/c (Loss) (*Balancing Figure*)	
Profit & Loss A/c (Profit) (*Balancing Figure*)	–		

Example 1

Ram & Co., acquired a motor lorry on hire-purchase basis. It has to make cash down payment of A 1,00,000 at the beginning. The payments to be made subsequently are A 2,63,000; A 1,85,000 and A 1,14,000 at the end of first year, second year and third year respectively. Interest charged is @ 14% per annum. Calculate the cost price of motor lorry and interest paid in each instalment.

[*C.A., Professional Competence Examination, May, 2008*]

Solution

Calculation of Cost price and Total Interest to be Paid on Motor Lorry

No. of Instalment	*Amount due at the time of Instalment*	*Interest on Cumulative Instalment*	*Cash Price in each instalment*
III	1,14,000	1,14,000 $\frac{14}{114}$ 14,000	1,00,000
II	1,85,000	2,85,000 * $\frac{14}{114}$ 35,000	1,50,000
I	2,63,000	5,13,000 * * $\frac{14}{114}$ 63,000	2,00,000
Cash down payment			1,00,000
Total		1,12,000	5,50,000

* 1,00,000 + 1,85,000 = 2,85,000

** 2,63,000 + 1,50,000 + 1,00,000 = 5,13,000

Example 2

Mr. *X* purchased a machine on hire purchase system. He made cash payment of A 30,000 and the balance was payable in 5 annual instalments of A 60,000 each. The cash price of the machine is A 3,00,000. Assume that the purchase was made on 1st April and the annual instalments are payable on 31st march of every year. Calculate the amount of interest for each year.

[*C.A., Professional Competence Examination, November, 2009*]

Solution

Hire Purchase = Total of all Instalments + Down Payment

= (5 × 60,000) + 30,000 = Rs 3,30,000

Total Interest = H.P. Price – Cash Price

= A 30,000 – A 3,00,000

= A 30,000

Statement Showing Calculation of Interest for Each Year

Year	*Interest (A)*
I	A 30,000 × $\frac{5}{15}$ = 10,000
II	A 30,000 × $\frac{4}{15}$ = 8,000
III	A 30,000 × $\frac{3}{15}$ = 6,000
IV	A 30,000 × $\frac{2}{15}$ = 4,000
V	A 30,000 × $\frac{1}{15}$ = 2,000
	30,000

Example 3

A Ltd., purchased a machine on hire-purchase system from *B*. Ltd., on 1st Jan, 2002, paying immediately A 20,000 and agreeing to pay three instalments of A 20,000 each on 31st December every year. The cash price of the machine is A 74,500 and vendors charge interest at 5% p.a. Depreciation is charged @ 20% p.a., on diminishing balance method. Calculate the amount of interest paid by buyer to the seller every year and also prepare important Ledger Accounts in the books of *A*. Ltd.

Solution

	A
Total Cash Price	74,500
Less : Down Payment	20,000
	54,500
Add : Interest on A 54,500 @ 5% for one year	2,725
	57,225
Less : First Hire Purchase Instalment	20,000
	37,225
Add : Interest on A 37,225 @ 5% for one year	1,861
	39,086
Less : Second Hire Purchase Instalment	20,000
	19,086
Add : Interest (*Bal. Fig. i.e.*, A 20,000 – 19,086)	914
	20,000
Less : Third Hire Purchase Instalment	20,000
	–

Note

1. It must be noted that the interest is calculated on the outstanding total cash price and not on the outstanding total instalments.

2. In the last year interest is the difference between the last instalment to be paid and cash price remaining unpaid.

In the Books of A Ltd.
Machine A/c

Dr. *Cr.*

Date	*Particulars*	*(A)*	*Date*	*Particulars*	*(A)*
2002			**2002**		
Jan. 1	To B Ltd.	74,500	Dec. 31	By Depreciation A/c	14.900
			Dec. 31	By Balance c/d	59,600
		74,500			74,500
2003			**2003**		
Jan. 1	To Balance b/d	59,600	Dec. 31	By Depreciation A/c	11,920
			Dec. 31	By Balance c/d	47,680
		59,600			59,600
2004			**2004**		
Jan. 1	To Balance b/d	47,680	Dec. 31	By Depreciation A/c	9,536
			Dec. 31	By Balance c/d	38,144
		47,680			47,680

B Ltd.

Dr. *Cr.*

Date	*Particulars*	*(A)*	*Date*	*Particulars*	*(A)*
2002			**2002**		
Jan. 1	To Bank A/c	20,000	Jan.1	By Machine A/c	74,500
Dec.31	To Bank A/c	20,000	Dec. 31	By Interest A/c	2,725
Dec.31	To Balance c/d	37,225			
		77,225			77,225
2003			**2003**		
Dec.31	To Bank A/c	20,000	Jan.1	By Balance b/d	37,225
Dec.31	To Balance c/d	19,086	Dec.31	By Interest A/c	1,861
		39,086			39,086
2004			**2004**		
Dec.31	To Bank A/c	20,000	Jan.1	By Balance b/d	19,086
			Dec.31	By Interest A/c	914
		20,000			20,000

Example 4

A Company purchased two machines of A 10,500 each on Hire Purchase System paying A 6,000 down and remainder in three equal instalments of A 5,000 each together with interest at 5% p.a. The company writes off Depreciation at 10% p.a., according to diminishing Balance Method.

The company could not pay the second instalment. The vendor left the machine with the company adjusting the value of the other against amount due taking the machine at 20% p.a., depreciation at Diminishing Balance Method. Prepare ledger accounts in the company's books.

Solution

Machines Account

Dr. *Cr.*

Particulars	*Amount*	*Particulars*	*Amount*
To Hire Vendor's A/c	21,000	By Depreciation A/c	2,100
		By Balance c/d	18,900
	21,000		21,000
To Balance c/d	18,900	By Depreciation A/c	1,890
		By Vendor's A/c	
		(Machine taken away)	6,720
		By P & L A/c (Loss)	1,785
		By Balance c/d	
		(Value of Machine left)	8,505
	18,900		18,900

Hire Vendor Account

Dr. *Cr.*

Particulars	*Amount*	*Particulars*	*Amount*
To Cash (down payment)	6,000	By Machines A/c	21,000
To Cash (1st Instalment)	5,750	By Interest A/c	750
To Balance c/d	10,000	[(A 21,000 – A 6,000 × 5/100]	
	21,750		21,750
To Machine (Taken away)	6,720	By Balance b/d	10,000
To Balance c/d	3,780	By Interest A/c [A 10,000 × 5/100]	500
	10,500		10,500

Working Notes

(*i*) Value of Machine left = A 10,500 × 90/100 × 90/100 = A 8,505

(*ii*) Value of Machine taken away by Hire Vendor = A 10,500 × 80/100×80/100 = A 6,720

Example 5

HV Ltd., sold three cars for a total cash price of A 9,00,000 on hire-purchase basis to Mr. *X* on 1st January, 2005. The terms of agreement provided for A 2,70,000 as cash down and the balance of the cash price in three equal instalments together with interest at 10% p.a. The instalments were payable at the end of each year. Mr. *X* paid the first instalment on time but failed to pay thereafter. On his failure to pay the second instalment, HV Ltd., repossessed two cars and valued them at 50% of the cash price. Mr. *X* charges 25% p.a., depreciation on written down value method.

Prepare necessary ledger accounts in the books of both parties.

Solution

In the Books of Mr. *X*

Cars Account

Dr. *Cr.*

Date	*Particulars*	*(A)*	*Date*	*Particulars*	*(A)*
2005			**2005**		
Jan.1	To HV Ltd.	9,00,000	Dec.31	By Depreciation A/c	2,25,000
				[A 9,00,000 × 25/100	
				By Balance c/d	6,75,000
		9,00,000			9,00,000
2006			**2006**		
Jan.1	To Balance b/d	6,75,000	Dec. 31	By Depreciation A/c	1,68,750
				[A 6,75,000 × 25/100]	
				By HV Ltd.	3,00,000
				(Cars taken away)	
				By Profit & Loss A/c	
				– Loss on default	37,500
				(*Bal. Fig.*)	
				By Balance c/d	1,68,750
		6,75,000			6,75,000

HV Ltd.

Dr. *Cr.*

Date	*Particulars*	*(A)*	*Date*	*Particulars*	*(A)*
2005			**2005**		
Jan.1	To Cash A/c		Jan. 1	By Cars A/c	9,00,000
	(Down Payment)	2,70,000	Dec. 31	By Interest A/c	63,000
Dec.31	To Cash A/c	2,73,000		10/100 [A 9,00,000	
	[2,10,000 + 63,000]			– 2,70,000]	
Dec.31	To Balance c/d	4,20,000			
		9,63,000			9,63,000
2006			**2006**		
Dec.31	To Cars A/c	3,00,000	Jan.1	By Balance b/d	4,20,000
	(Value of cars taken		Dec.31	By Interest A/c	
	away)			[10% of A 4,20,000]	42,000
	To Balance c/d	1,62,000			
		4,62,000			4,62,000

Hire Purchasers (Mr.*X*) will keep one car and will pay further A 1,62,000. New Contract will be signed for deciding the manner in which the amount will be paid.

Hire Vendor's Book : HV Ltd.
Mr X

Dr. *Cr.*

Date	*Particulars*	*(A)*	*Date*	*Particulars*	*(A)*
2005			**2005**		
Jan.1	To Hire Purchase Sales A/c	9,00,000	Jan.1	By Cash A/c	2,70,000
Dec.31	To Interest on Hire Purchase Sales A/c	63,000	Dec.31	By Cash A/c [2,10,000 + 63,000]	2,73,000
			Dec.31	By Balance c/d	4,20,000
		9,63,000			9,63,000
2006			**2006**		
Jan.1	To Balance b/d	4,20,000	Dec.31	By Goods Repossessed A/c (Value of Cars taken away)	3,00,000
Dec.31	To Interest A/c	42,000			
			Dec.31	By Balance c/d	1,62,000
		4,62,000			4,62,000

Working Notes

1. *Calculation of the value of two cars repossessed by the Vendor (HV Ltd.)* :

   Cash price of two cars = A 6,00,000

   Value of two cars repossessed = A 6,00,000 × 50/100 = A 3,00,000

2. *Calculation of the value of a car left with the buyer*

	A
Cost	3,00,000
Less : Depreciation @ 25% for 2005	75,000
Value on 01.1.2006	2,25,000
Less : Depreciation @ 25% for 2006	56,250
Value of car at the end of 2nd Year (*i.e.*, 31.12.2006)	1,68,750

Example 6

X purchased five trucks on 1st October, 2005. The Cash Price of each truck was A 5,50,000. *X* was to pay 20% of Cash Price at the time of delivery and 25% of Cash Price at the end of each of the subsequent four half-yearly periods beginning from 31st March, 2006.

On X failure to pay the instalment due on 30th September, 2006, it was agreed that *X* could keep three trucks, on the condition that value of two trucks would be adjusted against the amount due, the trucks being valued at cost less 25% depreciation.

Show the necessary ledger Accounts in the books of *X*, assuming that his books are closed on 31st March each year and he charges depreciation @ 15% on original cost of trucks.

Solution

In X's Books
Trucks Account

Dr. *Cr.*

Date	*Particulars*	*(A)*	*Date*	*Particulars*	*(A)*
1.10.05	To Hire Vendor A/c	27,50,000	31.3.06	By Depreciation A/c (Note-1)	2,06,250
				By Balance c/d	25,43,750
		27,50,000			27,50,000
01.4.06	To Balance c/d	25,43,750	30.9.06	By Depreciation A/c (Note-2)	82,500
			30.9.06	By Hire Vendor A/c (Note-3)	8,25,000
			30.9.06	By Profit & Loss A/c (Loss on Default) (Note-4)	1,10,000
			30.9.06	By Balance c/d	15,26,250
		25,43,750			25,43,750

Hire Vendor Account

Dr. *Cr.*

Date	*Particulars*	*(A)*	*Date*	*Particulars*	*(A)*
1.10.05	To Bank A/c	5,50,000	1.10.05	By Trucks A/c	27,50,000
1.03.06	To Bank A/c	6,87,500	31.3.06	By Interest A/c	2,20,000
1.03.06	To Balance c/d	17,32,500			
		29,70,000			29,70,000
30.09.06	To Trucks A/c	8,25,000	1.4.06	By Balance b/d	17,32,500
30.09.06	To Balance c/d	10,72,500	30.9.06	By Interest A/c	1,65,000
		18,97,500			18,97,500

Working Notes

1. *Depreciation on A 27,50,000 for 6 months @ 15% p.a.* A
   = A 27,50,000 × 6/12 × 15/100 = A 2,06,250
2. *Depreciation on two trucks taken away, for 6 months @ 15% p.a.*
   = A 11,00,000 × 6/12 × 15/100 = A 82,500
3. *Cash Price of two trucks* 11,00,000
   Less : Depreciation @ 25% p.a. for 1 year from
   Oct. 1, 2005 to 30th Sept., 2006 2,75,000
   Value of seized trucks 8,25,000

4.	*Cash price of two trucks*	11,00,000
	Less : Depreciation @ 15% p.a. for 1 year from October 1, 2005 to Sept. 30, 2006	1,65,000
	Written down value on Sept. 30, 2006	9,35,000
	Less : Value at which the trucks have been taken back by hire vendor	8,25,000
	Loss on default	1,10,000
5.	Total Interest = Hire Purchase Price – Cash Price = (A 6,87,500 × 4 + A 5,50,000 – A 27,50,000) =	5,50,000

Calculation of Interest

Instalment	*Ratio*	*Interest*	*A*
1	4	4/10 × 5,50,000	2,20,000
2	3	3/10 × 5,50,000	1,65,000
3	2	2/10 × 5,50,000	1,10,000
4	1	1/10 × 5,50,000	55,000

	A
Hire Purchase Price = (A 6,87,500 × 4 + A 5,50,000)	33,00,000
Less : Down Payment	5,50,000
Amount Outstanding on 1st Instalment	27,50,000
Less : Payment of first instalment	6,87,500
Amount outstanding on 2nd instalment	20,62,500
Less : Payment of 2nd instalment	6,87,500
Amount outstanding on 3rd installment	13,75,000
Less : Payment on 3rd instalment	6,87,500
Amount outstanding on 4th instalment	6,87,500

Ratio of outstanding Amount :	27,50,000	:	20,62,500	:	13,75,000	:	6,87,500
	4	:	3	:	2	:	1

Example 7

PQ and Co. purchased a truck on hire purchase system on 1st January, 2003. As per the terms of the agreement he is required to pay A 70,000 down; A 53,000 at the end of first year; A 49,000 at the end of the second year and A 55,000 at the end of the third year. Interest is charged @10% per annum. Accounts are closed on 31st December.

You are required to calculate the total cash price of the truck and interest paid with each instalment. Also prepare necessary ledger account in the books of hire-purchaser.

[*B.Com.* (*Hons.*) *Delhi University 2006*]

Solution

$$\text{Rate of Interest paid} \quad \frac{\text{Rate of Interest}}{100 \quad \text{Rate of Interest}} \quad \frac{10}{100 \quad 10} \quad \frac{1}{11}$$

Calculation of cash price	A
Down Payment	70,000
First Instalment	53,000
Second Instalment	49,000
Third Instalment	55,000
	2,27,000

Interest will be calculated first of all on 3rd instalment, then on second and after that on first.

Instalments	*Amount due at the time of Instalment*	*Interest included in Instalment*	*Cash price included in the Instalment (A)*
3rd	A 55,000	55,000 × 1/11 = A 5,000	50,000
2nd	[A 49,000 + A 50,000]	99,000 × 1/11 = A 9,000	40,000
1st	[A 53,000 + A 50,000 + 40,000]	1,43,000 × 1/11 = A 13,000	40,000
Down Payment	70,000	Nil	70,000
		Total Cash Price	2,00,000

In the Books of PQ and Co. Hire Vendor's Account

Date	*Particulars*	*Amount (A)*	*Date*	*Particulars*	*Amount (A)*
1.1.03	To Bank A/c	70,000	1.1.03	By Truck A/c	2,00,000
31.12.03	To Bank A/c	53,000	31.12.03	By Interest A/c	13,000
31.12.03	To Balance c/d	90,000			
		2,13,000			2,13,000
31.12.04	To Bank A/c	49,000	1.1.04	By Balance b/d	90,000
31.12.04	To Balance c/d	50,000	31.12.04	In Interest A/c	9,000
		99,000			99,000
31.12.05	To Bank A/c	55,000	1.1.05	By Balance b/d	50,000
			31.12.05	By Interest A/c	5,000
		55,000			55,000

Example 8

On 1st January 2001, Sunny purchased five cars, payment to be made A 1,87,500 down for each car and three instalments of A 1,87,00 each for each car at the end of each year. Rate of interest is charged at 5% p.a. on outstanding balance. Sunny depreciates the cars at 10% p.a. on written down value method. The cash price is A 7,00,000 for each car. Because of financial difficulties, Sunny could not pay the third instalment. The vendor repossessed 2 cars adjusting the value against the amount due. The repossession was done on the basis of depreciation @20% p.a. on written down value method.

You are asked to prepare Sunny's A/c in Hire Vendor's books and Cars' A/c and Hire Venfor's A/c in Sunny's books. Show all workings. [*B.Com.* (*Hons.*), *Delhi University, 2006*]

Solution

(*i*)	Cost price of 5 cars @ A 7,00,000 each	35,00,000
	Less : Down payment (A 1,87,500 × 5)	9,37,500
		25,62,500
	Add : Interest on first instalment @ 5% on A 25,62,500	1,28,125
		26,90,625
	Less : First instalment	9,37,500
		17,53,125
	Add : Interest on second instalment @5% on A 17,53,125	87,657
		18,40,782
	Less : Second instalment	9,37,500
		9,03,282
	Add : Interest (A 9,37,500 × A 9,03,282)	34,218
	Last instalment not paid	9,37,500
(*ii*)	Value of Cars Repossessed	A
	Cost price of 2 cars	14,00,000
	Less : Depreciation (20% on W.D.V.) I	2,80,000
		11,20,000
	Less : Depreciation II	2,24,000
		8,96,000
	Less : Depreciation III	1,79,200
		7,16,800
(*iii*)	Value of Cars Retained	A
	Cost price of 3 cars (A 7,00,000 × 3)	21,00,000
	Less : Depreciation I	2,10,000
		18,90,000
	Less : Depreciation II	1,89,000
		17,01,000
	Less : Depreciation III	1,70,100
		15,30,900

In the Books of Sunny
Cars on Hire Purchase Account

Date	*Particulars*	*Amount (A)*	*Date*	*Particulars*	*Amount (A)*
1.1.01	To Hire Vendor's A/c	35,00,000	31.12.01	By Depreciation A/c	3,50,000
				By Balance c/d	31,50,000
		35,00,000			35,00,000

1.1.02	To Balance b/d	31,50,000	31.12.02	By Depreciation A/c	3,15,000
				By Balance c/d	28,35,000
		31,50,000			31,50,000
1.1.03	To Balance b/d	28,35,000	31.12.03	By Depreciation A/c	2,83,500
				By Hire Vendor's A/c	7,16,800
				By Profit and Loss A/c (bal. fig.)	3,03,800
				By Balance c/d	15,30,900
		28,35,000			28,35,000

Hire Vendor's Account

Date	Particulars	Amount (A)	Date	Particulars	Amount (A)
1.1.01	To Bank A/c	9,37,500	1.1.01	By Cars on Hire Purchase A/c	35,00,000
31.12.01	To Bank A/c	9,37,500			
	To Balance c/d	17,53,125	31.12.01	By Interest A/c	1,28,125
		36,28,125			36,28,125
31.12.02	To Bank A/c	9,37,500	1.1.02	By Balance b/d	17,53,125
	To Balance c/d	9,03,282	31.12.02	By Interest A/c	87,657
		18,40,782			18,40,782
31.12.03	To Cars on Hire Purchase A/c	7,16,800	1.1.03	By Balance b/d	9,03,282
			31.12.01	By Interest A/c	34,218
	To Balance c/d	2,20,700			
		9,37,500			9,37,500

In the Books of Hire Vendor
Sunny's Account

Date	Particulars	Amount (A)	Date	Particulars	Amount (A)
1.1.01	To Sales A/c	35,00,000	1.1.01	By Bank A/c	9,37,500
31.12.01	To Interest A/c	1,28,125	31.12.01	By Bank A/c	9,37,500
				By Balance c/d	17,53,125
		36,28,125			36,28,125
1.1.02	To Balance b/d	17,53,125	31.12.02	By Bank A/c	9,37,500
31.12.02	To Interest A/c	87,657		By Balance c/d	9,03,282
		18,40,782			18,40,782
1.1.03	To Balance b/d	9,03,282	31.12.03	By Goods Repossessed A/c	7,16,800
31.12.03	To Interest A/c	34,218		By Balance c/d	2,20,700
		9,37,500			9,37,500

Example 9

BR Ltd. purchased three trucks costing A 1,00,000 each from Hindustan Auto Ltd. on 1.1.2004 on hire purchase system. The terms were :

Payment on delivery A 25,000 for each truck and balance of the principal amount in 3 equal instalments plus interest at 15% p.a. to be paid at the end of each year.

BR Ltd. writes off 25% depreciation each year on the diminishing balance method.

BR Ltd. paid the instalments due on 31.12.2004 and 31.12.2005 but could not pay the final instalment.

Hindustan Autho Ltd. repossessed two trucks adjusting values against the amount due.

The repossession was done on 31.12.2006 on the basis of 40% depreciation on the diminishing balance method. You are required to :

(*i*) Write up the ledger accounts in the books of BR Ltd. showing the transactions upto 31.12.06 and

(*ii*) Show the disclosure of the balances arising from the above in the balance sheet of BR Ltd. as on 31.12.06. [*B. Com. (Hons.), Delhi University 2007*]

Solution

In the Books of BR Ltd.

Truck Account

Date	*Particulars*	*Amount (A)*	*Date*	*Particulars*	*Amount (A)*
1.1.04	To Hindustan Auto Ltd. A/c	3,00,000	31.12.04	By Depreciation A/c (A 3,00,000 × 25/100)	75,000
				By Balance c/d	2,25,000
		3,00,000			3,00,000
1.1.05	To Balance b/d	2,25,000	31.12.05	By Depreciation A/c	56,250
				(A 2,25,000 × 25/100)	
				By Balance c/d	1,68,750
		2,25,000			2,25,000
1.1.06	To Balance b/d	1,68,750	31.12.750	By Depreciation A/c (A 1,68,750 × 25/100)	42,188
				By Hindustan Auto Ltd*$_2$ A/c	43,200
				By Profit and Loss A/c (bal. fig.)	41,175
				By Balance c/d*$_1$	42,187
		1,68,750			1,68,750

Hindustan Auto Ltd. Account

Date	*Particulars*	*Amount (A)*	*Date*	*Particulars*	*Amount (A)*
1.1.04	To Bank A/c	75,000	1.1.04	By Truck A/c	3,00,000
31.12.04	To Bank A/c*$_3$	1,08,750	31.12.04	By Interest A/c*$_3$	33,750

31.12.04	To Balance c/d	1,50,000			
		3,33,750			3,33,750
31.12.05	To Bank A/c*[3]	97,500	1.1.05	By Balance b/d	1,50,000
31.12.05	To Balance c/d	75,000	31.12.05	By Interest A/c*[3]	22,500
		1,72,500			1,72,500
31.12.06	To Truck A/c*[3]	43,200	1.1.2006	By Balance b/d	75,000
31.12.06	To Balance c/d (bal. fig.)	43,050	31.12.06	By Interest A/c	11,250
		86,250			86,250

Working Notes :

1. *Value of one truck retained*

	A
Cost Price of one truck	1,00,000
Less : Depreciation @ 25% (2004)	25,000
	75,000
Less : Depreciation @25% (2005)	18,750
	56,250
Less : Depreciation @ 25% (2006)	14,063
	42,187

2. *Value of two trucks repossessed*

	A
Cost price of two trucks	2,00,000
Less : Depreciation @ 40% (2004)	80,000
	1,20,000
Less : Depreciation @ 40% (2005)	48,000
	72,000
Less : Depreciation @ 40% (2006)	28,800
	43,200

3. *Calculation of Interest*

	A
Cost Price of 3 trucks	3,00,000
Less : Down Payment	75,000
	2,25,000
Add : Interest on first Instalment (15% 2,25,000)	33,750
	2,58,750
Less : First Instalment (A 75,000 + A 33,750)	1,08,750
	1,50,000
Add : Interest on Second Instalment (15% on A 1,50,000)	22,500
	1,72,500
Less : Second Instalment (A 75,000 + A 22,500)	97,500

	75,000
Add : Interest on Third Instalment (15% of A 75,000)	11,250
	86,250
Third Instalment (Not Paid) (A 75,000 + A 11,250)	86,250

Example 10

Ravi purchased a machine on hire purchase system from Moon and Sons. He paid A 100000 at the time of agreement and the remaining amount including interest was payable in four annual instalments of A 100000 each at the end of each year commencing from the date of agreement. Interest is charged @10% per annum.

You are required to prepare the Machinery Account and Moon and Sons account in the books of Ravi for four years if he provides depreciation on machinery @ 20 percent per annum on written down value basis.

[*I.C.W.A., Inter, Dec. 2010*]

Solution

Calculation of Interest and Cash Price

Instalment	*Amount of Instalment*	*Amount Payable at the time of Instalment*	*Interest*	*Amount Payable after Instalment*
IV	1,00,000	1,00,000	1,00,000 $\frac{10}{110}$ 9,091	90,909
III	1,00,000	1,00,000 + 90,909 = 1,90,909	1,90,909 $\frac{10}{110}$ 17,355	1,73,554
II	1,00,000	1,00,000 + 1,73,554 = 2,73,554	2,73,554 $\frac{10}{110}$ 24,869	2,48,685
I	1,00,000	1,00,000 + 2,48,685 = 3,48,685	3,48,685 $\frac{10}{110}$ 31,699	3,16,986

Total Interest = 9,091 + 17,355 + 24,869 + 31,699

= A 83,014

Hire Purchase Price = 1,00,000 + (1,00,000 × 4) = A 5,00,000

Cash Price = A 5,00,000 – A 83,104 = A 4,16,986

Ledger of Ravi

Machinery Account

Date	*Particulars*	*Amount (A)*	*Date*	*Particulars*	*Amount (A)*
I Year			1 Year		
Beginning	To Moon and Sons	4,16,986	End	By Depreciation	83,397
			End	Balance c/d	3,33,589
		4,16,986			4,16,986
II Year			II Year		
Beginning	To Balance b/d	3,33,589	End	By Depreciation	66,718

			End	By Balance c/d	2,66,871
		3,33,589			3,33,589
III Year			III Year		
Beginning	To Balance b/d	2,66,871	End	By Depreciation	53,374
			End	By Balance c/d	2,13,497
		2,66,871			2,66,871
IV Year			IV Year		
Beginning	To Balance b/d	2,13,497	End	By Depreciation	42,699
			End	By Balance c/d	1,70,798
		2,13,497			2,13,497

Moon and Son's Account

Date	*Particulars*	*Amount (A)*	*Date*	*Particulars*	*Amount (A)*
I Year			I Year		
Beginning	To Bank A/c	1,00,000	Beginning	By Machinery A/c	4,16,986
End	To Bank A/c	1,00,000	End	By Interest A/c	31,699
End	To Balance c/d	2,48,685			
		4,48,685			4,48,685
II Year			II Year		
End	To Bank A/c	1,00,000	Beginning	By Balance b/d	2,48,685
End	To Balance c/d	1,73,554	End	By Interest A/c	24,869
		2,73,554			2,73,554
III Year			III Year		
End	To Bank A/c	1,00,000	Beginning	By Balance b/d	1,73,554
End	To Balance c/d	90,909	End	By Interest A/c	17,355
		1,90,999			1,90,909
IV Year			IV Year		
End	To Bank A/c	1,00,000	Beginning	By Balance b/d	90,909
			End	By Interest A/c	9,091
		1,00,000			1,00,000

Example 11

A Ltd., sold 3 cars for a total cash sale price of A 6,00,000 on hire purchase basis to *B* on 01.01.2004. The terms of agreement provided for A 1,20,000 as down payment and the balance of cash price in three equal instalments together with interest at 12% p.a. The instalments were payable on the following dates :

First Instalment on 31.12.2004

Second Instalment on 31.12.2005

Third Instalment on 31.12.2006

B paid the two instalments on time but could not pay the third instalment on the due date. As a consequences the hire vendor repossessed the two cars and valued them at 60% of the cash price paid. *B* charges depreciation at 15% on diminishing balance method.

Prepare necessary ledger account in the books of *B*.

Solution

In the Books of B

Asset (Cars) Account

Dr. *Cr.*

Date	*Particulars*	*(A)*	*Date*	*Particulars*	*(A)*
1.01.04	To A Ltd.'s	6,00,000	31.12.04	By Depreciation A/c	90,000
				6,00,000 $\frac{15}{100}$	
				By Balance c/d	5,10,000
		6,00,000			6,00,000
01.1.05	To Balance b/d	5,10,000	31.12.05	By Depreciation A/c	76,500
				5,10,000 $\frac{15}{100}$	
				By Balance c/d	4,33,500
		5,10,000			5,10,000
1.1.06	To Balance b/d	4,33,500	31.12.06	By Depreciation A/c	65,025
				4,33,500 $\frac{15}{100}$	
				By A. Ltd.(Hire Vendor)	1,76,000
				By Profit & Loss A/c	69,650
				(Loss on Default)	
				By Balance c/d	1,22,825
		4,33,500			4,33,500

A Ltd.

Dr. *Cr.*

Date	*Particulars*	*(A)*	*Date*	*Particulars*	*(A)*
01.01.04	To Bank A/c	1,20,000	01.1.04	By Cars A/c	6,00,000
31.12.04	To Bank A/c		31.12.04	By Interest A/c	57,600
	(Ist Instalment)	2,17,600		$\frac{12}{100}$ 6,00,000 – 1,20,000	
	A 1,60,000 + A 57,600)				
31.12.04	To Balance c/d	3,20,000			
		6,57,600			6,57,600
31.12.05	To Bank A/c		01.01.05	By Balance b/d	3,20,000
	(2nd Instalment)	1,98,400	31.12.05	By Interest A/c	38,400
	[A 1,60,000 + 38,400]				

				$3{,}20{,}000 \times \frac{12}{100}$	
31.12.05	To Balance c/d	1,60,000			
		3,58,400			3,58,400
31.12.05	To Asset (Cars) A/c	1,76,000	01.01.06	By Balance b/d	1,60,000
	To Balance c/d	3,200	31.12.06	By Interest A/c	19,200
				$1{,}60{,}000 \times \frac{12}{100}$	
		1,79,200			1,79,200

Working Notes

(*i*) *Book value of Cars left and repossessed*

		1 *Left* A	2 *Repossessed* A
(*A*)	Cost	2,00,000	4,00,000
(*B*)	*Less* : Depreciation for 3 years @ 15% p.a. on dimishing Balance method	77,175	1,54,350
	Total Depreciation : [90,000 + 76,500 + 65,025 = A 2,31,525]	*i.e.*, $2{,}31{,}525 \times \frac{1}{3}$	*i.e.* $2{,}31{,}525 \times \frac{2}{3}$
		1,22,825	2,45,650

(*ii*) *Calculation of Cash Price paid for 2 Cars*

Cash Price paid for 3 cars till the date of default

= A 1,20,000 (Down) + A 1,60,000 (1st Inst.) + A 1,60,000 (2nd Inst.)

= A 4,40,000

Cash Price paid for 2 Cars = A $4{,}40{,}000 \times \frac{2}{3}$ = A 2,93,333

(*iii*) *Agreed value of 2 Cars Repossessed* = 60% of A 2,93,333

= A 1,76,000

(*iv*) *Loss on Default* = Agreed Value – Book Value

= A 1,76,000 – A 2,45,650

= A 69,650

Example 12

Deepak purchased 4 second hand cars on hire purchase, Cash Price A 52,500 each. The hire purchase price for all the four cars was A 2,40,000. The payment was to be made A 60,000 down and EMI of A 60,000 each. Deepak charged depreciation @ 10% p.a. Deepak paid the down payment and first instalment but could not pay the second instalment. The vendor, after negotiations, took back three cars. These cars were taken back after depreciating them @ 20% p.a. on written down value method. One car was left with the purchaser. The vendor spent A 3,600 on repairs and sold two of these cars for A 80,000. Show necessary ledger accounts in the book of both the parties. [*B.Com. (Hons.) Delhi University, 2011*]

Solution

Books of Deepak
Hire Vendor Account

Dr.			*Cr.*
	(A)		*(A)*
First Year		**First Year**	
Bank Account (beginning)	60,000	5 Cars on Hire-Purchase	
Bank Account (end)	60,000	Account (beginning))	2,10,000
Balance c/d (end)	1,05,000	Interest (end)	15,000
	2,25,000		2,25,000
Cars on Hire-Purchase		**Second Year**	
Account (end)	1,00,800	Balance b/d (beginning))	1,05,000
Balance c/d (end)	14,200	Interest (end)	10,000
	1,15,000		1,15,000

Cars on Hire-Purchase Account

Dr.			*Cr.*
	(A)		*(A)*
First Year		**First Year**	
(B) Sales Account (beginning))	2,10,000	Depreciation Account (end)	21,000
		Balance c/d (end)	1,89,000
	2,10,000		2,10,000
Second Year		**Second Year**	
Balance b/d (beginning))	1,89,000	Depreciation (end)	21,000
		Hire Vendor Account (end)	1,00,800
		Profit and Loss Account (end)	25,200
		(Balancing figure)	
		Balance c/d	42,000
	1,89,000		1,89,000

Books of Hire Vendor
Deepak Account

Dr.			*Cr.*
	(A)		*(A)*
First Year		**First Year**	
Sales Account (beginning))	2,10,000	Bank (beginning)	60,000
Interest Account (end)	15,000	Bank (end)	60,000
		Balance c/d	1,05,000
	2,25,000		2,25,000
Second Year		**Second Year**	
Balance b/d (beginning))	1,05,000	Goods Repossessed Account (end)	1,00,800
Interest Account (end)	10,000	Balance c/d	14,200
	1,15,000		1,15,000

Goods Repossessed Account

Dr. *Cr.*

	(A)		*(A)*
Deepak Account	1,00,800	Bank Account	80,000
Cash Account (Repairs)	3,600	Balance c/d	34,800
Profit and Loss A/c	10,400		
	1,14,800		1,14,800

Example 13

Dharma sold three machines costing A 1,00,000 each to Sharma on hire purchase basis on 01.01.2005. Sharma paid A 60,000 on the above date and agreed to pay the balance in five half yearly instalments of A 60,000 each starting from 30.6.2005. Sharma charges Depreciation @ 10% p.a. on Diminishing Balance method. Books are closed on 31st December every year.

Sharma could not pay the third instalment in time whereupon Dharma repossessed one Machine at an agreed value of cash price less 40%. Dharma sold the repossessed machine for A 45,000 after incurring A 2,000 on its repairs.

Show relevant accounts in the books of both the parties showing all your workings.

Solution

In the Books of Sharma (Hire Purchaser)

Machines on Hire Purchase Account

Dr. *Cr.*

Date	*Particulars*	*(A)*	*Date*	*Particulars*	*(A)*
1.01.05	To Dharma's A/c	3,00,000	31.12.05	By Depreciation A/c	30,000
				By Balance c/d	2,70,000
		3,00,000			3,00,000
1.1.06	To Balance b/d	2,70,000	30,06,06	By Depreciation A/c (on one machine for six months)	4,500
				By Dharma's A/c	60,000
				By Profit & Loss A/c	25,500
			31.12.06	By Depreciation A/c (on two machines) $\frac{10}{100}$ 2,00,00 – 20,000	18,000
				By Balance c/d	1,62,000
		2,70,000			2,70,000

Dharma' Account

Dr. Cr.

Date	Particulars	(A)	Date	Particulars	(A)
01.01.05	To Bank A/c	60,000	1.1.05	By Machines on HP A/c	3,00,000
30.6.05	To Bank A/c	60,000	30.6.05	By Interest A/c	20,000
31.12.05	To Bank A/c	60,000	31.12.05	By Interest A/c	16,000
	To Balance c/d	1,56,000			
		3,36,000			3,36,000
30.6.06	To Machine on HP A/c	60,000	01.1.06	By Balance b/d	1,56,000
30.6.06	To Balance c/d	1,08,000	30.6.06	By Interest A/c	12,000
		1,68,000			1,68,000

In the Books of Dharma (Hire Purchaser)
Sharma's Account

Dr. Cr.

Date	Particulars	(A)	Date	Particulars	(A)
01.01.05	To Sales A/c	3,00,000	1.1.05	By Bank A/c	60,000
30.6.05	To Interest A/c	20,000	30.6.05	By Bank A/c	60,000
31.12.05	To Interest A/c	16,000	31.12.05	By Bank A/c	60,000
			31.12.05	By Balance c/d	1,56,000
		3,36,000			3,36,000
01.1.06	To Balance b/d	1,56,000	30.6.06	By Goods Repossessed A/c	60,000
30.6.06	To Interest A/c	12,000		By Balance c/d	1,08,000
		1,68,000			1,68,000

Notes

1. *Calculation of Interest* :

	A
Total Hire Purchase price :	
Cash Down	60,000
Instalments (A 60,000 × 5)	3,00,000
	3,60,000
Cash Price (A 1,00,000 × 3)	3,00,000
Interest = Hire Purchase Price – Cash Price	
= A 3,60,000 – A 3,00,000 = A 60,000	60,000
Total Hire Purchase Price	3,60,000
Less : Down Payment	60,000
HPP outstanding after down payment	3,00,000
Less : First Instalment	60,000
HPP outstanding after 1st Instalment	2,40,000
Less : Second Instalment	60,000

HPP outstanding after 2nd Instalment	1,80,000
Less : Third Instalment	60,000
HPP outstanding after 3rd Instalment	1,20,000
Less : Fourth Instalment	60,000
HPP outstanding after 4th Instalment	60,000
Less : Fifth Instalment	60,000
	Nil

Hire Purchase Price Outstanding

= A 3,00,000; A 2,40,000; A 1,80,000; A 1,20,000; A 60,000

Ratio = 5 : 4 : 3 : 2 : 1

Interest on First Instalment $= \text{A } 60{,}000 \times \frac{5}{15} = \text{Rs.}20{,}000$

Interest on Second Instalment $= \text{A } 60{,}000 \times \frac{4}{15} = \text{Rs.}16{,}000$

Interest on Third Instalment $= \text{A } 60{,}000 \times \frac{3}{15} = \text{Rs.}12{,}000$

Interest on Fourth Instalment $= \text{A } 60{,}000 \times \frac{2}{15} = \text{Rs.}8{,}000$

Interest on Fifth Instalment $= \text{A } 60{,}000 \times \frac{1}{15} = \text{Rs.}4{,}000$

Note : In this question depreciation has been calculated on all the three machines on the date of default *i.e.,* on 30.6.2006. The reasons are :

(*i*) Depreciation is calculated on the remaining machines on 31st December every year.

(*ii*) In the diminishing balance method, the amount of depreciation will differ if charged on half yearly basis.

Example 14

X Transport Ltd., purchased from Manish Motors 3 Tempos costing A 4,00,000 each on hire-purchase basis on 01.1.2005. 25% of the cost was to be paid down and the balance in 3 equal annual instalments together with interest @ 9% at the end of each year. *X* Transport Ltd., paid the instalment due on 31st December, 2005, but could not pay thereafter. Manish Motors agreed to leave one tempo with the purchaser on 01.1.2007 adjusting the value of the other 2 Tempos against the amount due on that date. The Tempos recovered were valued on the basis of 30% depreciation annually on W.D.V.

X Transport Ltd., charges depreciation on Tempos @ 20% on diminishing balance method. M/s Manish Motors incur A 40,000 on repairs of Tempos repossessed and resell them at a profit of 5% on total cost. Write up necessary Ledger Accounts in the books of both parties giving effect to the above transactions.

Solution : Books of X Transport Ltd.

First, let us calculate value of Tempos taken away by the seller and value of Tempo left with the buyer.

1. *Value of Tempo left with the buyer*

No. of Tempos :	One
Cash Price : 1× A 4,00,000	A 4,00,000
Less : Depreciation @ 20% p.a. on diminishing Balance Method for one year (Ist Year 2005)	80,000
Value of Tempo left with the buyer at the end of the Ist Year	A 3,20,000
Less : Depreciation @ 20% p.a. (for 2006)	64,000
Value of the tempo left with the buyer at the end of IInd Year	2,56,000

2. *Value of Tempo taken away by the seller*

No. of Tempos :	Two
Cash Price (Cost)[A 4,00,000 × 2]	A 8,00,000
Depreciation 30% as per W.D.V. method for 2 years *i.e.,* A 2,40,000 + A 1,68,000 = A 4,08,000	4,08,000
Value of Tempos taken away at the end of 2nd year	3,92,000

Tempos (Asset) Account

Dr. *Cr.*

Date	*Particulars*	*(A)*	*Date*	*Particulars*	*(A)*
01.01.05	To Manish Motors [3 × A 4,00,000]	12,00,000	31.12.05	By Depreciation A/c 12,00,000 $\frac{20}{100}$	2,40,000
			31.12.05	By Balance c/d	9,60,000
		12,00,000			12,00,000
01.1.06	To Balance b/d	9,60,000	31,12,06	By Depreciation A/c 9,60,000 $\frac{20}{100}$	1,92,000
			31.12.06	Manish Motors (Value of 2 Tempos taken away-Note 2)	3,92,000
			31.12.06	By Profit & Loss A/c (Loss)	1,20,000*
			31.12.06	By Balance c/d (Value of one Tempo left) (Note-1)	2,56,000
		9,60,000			9,60,000

*(*i*) Book value of two Tempos on 31.12.06 = A 8,00,000 – 1,60,000 (Dep. First Year) – 1,28,000 (Dep. as per W.D.V., 2nd Year) = A 5,12,000

(*ii*) Value of Tempos taken (as per Note 2) = A 3,92,000

(*iii*) Loss due to default (*i* - *ii*) [5,12,000 – 3,92,000] = A 1,20,000

Manish Motor's Account

Dr. Cr.

Date	Particulars	(A)	Date	Particulars	(A)
01.01.05	To Bank A/c (Down Payment)	3,00,000	1.1.05	By Asset (Tempos)A/c	12,00,000
			31.12.05	By Interest A/c	
31.12.05	To Bank A/c [3,00,000 + 81,000]	3,81,000		9,00,000 $\frac{9}{100}$	81,000
31.12.05	To Balance c/d	6,00,000			
		12,81,000			12,81,000
31.12.06	To assets (Tempo) A/c- value of Tempo taken away	3,92,000	1.1.06	By Balance b/d	6,00,000
			31.12.06	By Interest A/c 6,00,000 × $\frac{9}{100}$	54,000
31.12.06	To Balance c/d	2,62,000			
		6,54,000			6,54,000

Books of Manish Motor's (Vendor)

X Transport Ltd.

Dr. Cr.

Date	Particulars	(A)	Date	Particulars	(A)
01.01.05	To Sales A/c	12,00,000	1.1.05	By Bank A/c (Down Payment)	3,00,000
31.12.05	To Interest	81,000	31.12.05	By Bank A/c	3,81,000
			31.12.05	By Balance c/d	6,00,000
		12,81,000			12,81,000
01.1.06	To Balance b/d	6,00,000	31.12.06	By Goods Repossessed A/c	3,92,000
31.12.96	To Interest A/c	54,000	31.12.06	By Balance c/d	2,62,000
		6,54,000			6,54,000

Goods Repossessed Account

Dr. Cr.

Particulars	(A)	Particulars	(A)
To X Transport Ltd.	3,92,000	By Bank A/c (Sales)	4,53,000
To Bank A/c (Repair)	40,000		
To Profit & Loss A/c – Profit on sale $\frac{5}{100}$ Rs. 3,92,000 + 10,000	21,600		
	4,53,600		4,53,600

Example 15

Pramod purchased four machines of A 14,000 each from Shiva under Hire Purchase system. The payment is to be made thus—A 15,000 cash down and three annual instalments of A 15,000 each. Pramod depreciates the machines at 10% p.a. on written down value method. On Pramod's failure to pay the second instalment Shiva took back three machines. The machines were taken back after depreciating them at 20% on written down value basis.

Shiva repaired the machines spending A 3,120 and resort them for A 35,000.

Open necessary accounts in the books of both the parties. Also show all your calculations neatly.

Solution

In the Books of Pramod

Machines Purchase on Hire Purchase Account

Dr. *Cr.*

Particulars	*(A)*	*Particulars*	*(A)*
I Year To Shiva's A/c	56,000	By Depreciation A/c	5,600
(4 × A 14,000)		By Balance c/d	50,400
	56,000		56,000
II Year To Balance b/d	50,400	By Depreciation A/c	5,040
		By Shiva's A/c (Note 3)	26,880
		By Profit & Loss A/c (*Bal. Fig.*)	7,140
		By Balance c/d (Note 2)	11,340
	50,400		50,400

Shiva's Account

Dr. *Cr.*

Particulars		*(A)*	*Particulars*	*(A)*
I Year	To Bank A/c (Down payment)	15,000	By Machines Purchased on Hire Purchase A/c	56,000
	To Bank A/c	15,000	By Interest (Note 1)	2,000
	To Balance c/d	28,000		
		58,000		58,000
II Year	To Machines Purchased on Hire Purchase A/c	26,880	By Balance b/d	28,000
			By Interest A/c (Note 1)	1,333
	To Balance c/d	2,453		
		29,333		29,333
			By Balance b/d	2,453

In the Books of Shiva Parmod's Account

Dr. *Cr.*

Particulars		*(A)*	*Particulars*	*(A)*
I Year	To Hire Sales A/c	56,000	By Bank A/c	15,000
	To Interest A/c	2,000	By Bank A/c	15,000
			By Balance c/d	28,000
		58,000		58,000
II Year	To Balance b/d	28,000	By Goods Repossessed	26,880
	To Interest	1,333	By Balance c/d	2,453
		29,333		29,333

Goods Repossessed Account

Dr. *Cr.*

Particulars	*(A)*	*Particulars*	*(A)*
To Parmod's A/c	26,880	By Bank A/c	35,000
To Cash A/c	3,120		
To Profit & Loss A/c (Profit) (*Bal. Fig.*)	5,000		
	35,000		35,000

Working Notes

1. *Calculation of Interest* *A*

Total hire purchase price of four machine (A 15,000 × 4)	= 60,000
Less : Total Cash price of four machines (A 14,000 × 4)	= 56,000
Total Interest	4,000

In the absence of rate of interest, the interest on each instalment should be calculated on the basis of ratio of outstanding amounts as calculated below :

Total Hire Purchase price	60,000
Less : Down Payment	15,000
	45,000
Less : First Instalment	15,000
	30,000
Less : Second Instalment	15,000
	15,000
Less : Third Instalment	15,000
	Nil

Outstanding Amount = A 45,000 : A 30,000 : A 15,000

Ratio = 3 : 2 : 1

Interest on First Instalment = *Rs.* 4,000 $\frac{3}{6}$ *Rs.* 2,000

Interest on Second Instalment = *Rs.* 4,000 $\frac{2}{6}$ *Rs.* 1,333

Interest on Third Instalment = Rs. 4,000 × $\frac{1}{6}$ = Rs. 666 (Not required)

2. *Calculation of the value of Machine Retained* *A*

Cost Price of one machine	14,000
Less : Depreciation for 1 Year	1,400
	12,600
Less : Depreciation for 2nd Year	1,260
	11,340

3. *Calculation of the value of machine returned*

Cash Price of three Machine (14,000 × 3) 42,000

Less : Depreciation for 1st Year (20% of 42,000)	8,400
	33,600
Less : Depreciation for 2nd Year (20% of A 33,600)	6,720
	26,880

Example 16

On April 1, 2002 Rahul Purchased five machines on hire purchase system from Varun Ltd. The cash Price of each machine was A 30,000. The terms of payment were :

(*a*) Down payment : A 30,000

(*b*) Six half yearly instalments of A 23,500 each payable on September 30 and March 31 each year.

Rahul wrote off depreciation @ 10% p.a. on diminishing balance method.

Rahul paid instalments due upto March 31, 2003; but due to financial crisis could not pay the instalment due on September 30, 2003. After negotiations, it was agreed that the vendor would repossess two machines for which Rahul would get credit for the amount paid towards the cost of the two machines less 25% thereof.

Varun Ltd., sold both the machines for A 23,800, after incurring A 700 on repairs.

You are asked to give :

(*i*) Varun Ltd., A/c, Machines A/c in the books of Rahul.

(*ii*) Rahul A/c and Goods Repossessed A/c in the books of Varun Ltd.

Solution

Calculation of Interest

Total Cash Price	=	A 1,50,000
Total Hire Purchase Price	=	30,000 + (23,500 × 6)
	=	A 1,71,000
Total Interest	=	A 1,71,000 – A 1,50,000
	=	A 21,000

Since the rate of interest has not been given, the amount of interest included in each instalment will be ascertained by dividing the total interest in the ratio of hire-purchase price outstanding in the beginning of each period. The ratio comes to 6 : 5 : 4 : 3 : 2 : 1

Instalments		*Interest*
1.	21,000 $\frac{6}{21}$	A 6,000
2.	21,000 $\frac{5}{21}$	A 5,000
3.	21,000 $\frac{4}{21}$	A 4,000
4.	21,000 $\frac{3}{21}$	A 3,000
5.	21,000 $\frac{2}{21}$	A 2,000
6.	21,000 $\frac{1}{21}$	A 1,000

Books of Rahul
Machines A/c

Dr. *Cr.*

Date	*Particulars*	*(A)*	*Date*	*Particulars*	*(A)*
2001			**2002**		
April 1	To Varun Ltd.	1,50,000	Mar.31	By Depreciation A/c	15,000
				By Balance c/d	1,35,000
		1,50,000			1,50,000
2002			**2003**		
April 1	To Balance b/d	1,35,000	Mar. 31	By Depreciation A/c	13,500
				1,35,000 $\frac{10}{100}$	
				By Balance c/d	1,21,500
		1,35,000			1,35,000
2003			**2003**		
April 1	To Balance b/d	1,21,500	Sep. 30	By Varun Ltd.	31,800
			Sep. 30	By P & L A/c (Loss on seizure of machines)	16,800
			Sep. 30	By Balance c/d	72,900
		1,21,500			1,21,500

Varun Ltd.

Dr. *Cr.*

Date	*Particulars*	*(A)*	*Date*	*Particulars*	*(A)*
2001			**2001**		
April 1	To Cash A/c (Down Payment)	30,000	April 1	By Machines A/c	1,50,000
			Sep. 30	By Interest A/c	6,000
Sep. 30	To Cash A/c	23,500			
2002			**2002**		
Mar. 31	To Cash A/c	23,500	Mar. 31	by Interest A/c	5,000
Mar. 31	To Balance c/d	84,000			
		1,61,000			1,61,000
2002			**2002**		
Sept. 30	To Cash A/c	23,500	April 1	By Balance b/d	84,000
			Sep. 30	By Interest A/c	4,000
2003					
Mar. 31	To Cash A/c	23,500	**2003**		
Mar. 31	To Balance c/d	44,000	Mar. 31	By Interest A/c	3,000
		91,000			91,000

2003			**2003**		
Sep. 30	To Machines A/c	31,800	April 1	By Balance b/d	44,000
	To Balance c/d	14,200	Sep. 30	By Interest	2,000
		46,000			46,000

Working Note

			A
	Loss on Machines seized by Vendor		
A.	*Cost price of two machines*		60,000
	Less : Depreciation		
	2001-02 : 15,000 $\frac{2}{5}$ =	6,000	
	2002-03 : 13,500 $\frac{2}{5}$ =	5,400	11,400
			48,600
B.	*Prices at which the machines were returned*		
	$\frac{2}{5}$ 30,000 + 23,500 × 4 − 18,000 Interest	= 42,400	
	Less : 25% of 42,400	10,600	31,800
C.	*Loss on Machines seized (A – B)*		16,800

Varun Ltd. (Hire Vendor)
Rahul's Account

Dr. *Cr.*

Date	*Particulars*	*(A)*	*Date*	*Particulars*	*(A)*
2001			**2001**		
April 1	To Sales A/c	1,50,000	April 1	By Cash A/c	30,000
Sep. 30	To Interest	6,000	Sep. 30	By Cash A/c	23,500
2002			**2002**		
Mar.31	To Interest	5,000	Mar. 31	By Cash A/c	23,500
			Mar. 31	By Balance c/d	84,000
		1,61,000			1,61,000
2002			**2002**		
April 1	To Balance b/d	84,000	Sep. 30	By Cash A/c	23,500
Sep. 30	To Interest A/c	4,000			
2003			**2003**		
Mar. 31	To Interest A/c	3,000	Mar. 31	By Cash A/c	23,500
			Mar. 31	By Balance c/d	44,000
		91,000			91,000
2003			**2003**		
April 1	To Balance b/d	44,000	Sep. 30	By Goods Rep. A/c	31,800
Sep. 30	To Interest A/c	2,000		By Balance c/d	14,200
		46,000			46,000

Goods Repossessed Account

Dr. *Cr.*

Particulars	*A*	*Particulars*	*A*
To Rahul's A/c	31,800	By Bank A/c	23,800
To Bank A/c (Repair)	700	By Profit & Loss A/c (loss)	8,700
	32,500		32,500

Example 17

On 01.1.97 Aditya purchased from S. Ltd., three machines costing A 2,00,000 each payable A 50,000 down and three annual instalments of A 60,000 each at the end of each year. The purchaser charges depreciation on machines @ 10% p.a., on written down value method.

Aditya could not pay second instalment and S. Ltd., took possession of two machines. Value of the two machines repossessed was to be determined after charging a depreciation at 25% p.a., under straight line method.

S. Ltd., paid A 10,000 for repairs on repossessed machines and sold them for A, 1,35,000 each.

Give S. Ltd., A/c and machinery A/c in the books of Aditya and Goods Repossessed A/c and Aditya's A/c in the books of S. Ltd.

Solution

Calculation of Interest

Total Hire Purchase Price	*A*
Down Payment (A 50,000 × 3)	1,50,000
Less : 3 Instalments of A 1,80,000 *i.e.,* (A 60,000 × 3)	5,40,000
	6,90,000
Add : Cash Price for three machines (A 2,00,000 × 3)	6,00,000
Total Interest	90,000

Interest would be calculated on the basis of outstanding amount, *i.e.,*	*A*
Total Hire Purchase Price	6,90,000
Less : Down Payment	1,50,000
	5,40,000
Less : First Instalment (A 60,000 × 3)	1,80,000
	3,60,000
Second Instalment	1,80,000
	1,80,000
Less : Third Instalment	1,80,000
	—

Outstanding Amount :	5,40,000	:	3,60,000	:	1,80,000
Ratio :	3	:	2	:	1

Thus, interest included in each instalment is calculated as under :

I Installment : $\text{Rs. } 90{,}000 \times \frac{3}{6} = \text{Rs. } 45{,}000$

II Instalment : $\text{Rs. } 90{,}000 \times \frac{2}{6} = \text{Rs. } 30{,}000$

III Instalment : $\text{Rs. } 90{,}000 \times \frac{1}{6} = \text{Rs. } 15{,}000$

Value of Machine Repossessed		Value of Machines Retained	
	A		A
Cost Price	4,00,000	Cost Price	2,00,000
Less : Depreciation	2,00,000	*Less* : Depreciation	
A (1,00,000 + 1,00,000)		for 1997 @ 10%	20,000
			1,80,000
		Less : Depreciation	
		for 1998 @ 10%	18,000
	2,00,000		1,62,000

In the Books of Aditya

Machinery Account

Dr. *Cr.*

Date	Particulars	(A)	Date	Particulars	(A)
01.1.97	To S. Ltd.	6,00,000	31.12.97	By Depreciation A/c	60,000
			31.12.97	By Balance c/d	5,40,000
		6,00,000			6,00,000
01.01.98	To Balance b/d	5,40,000	31.12.98	By Depreciation A/c	54,000
			31.12.98	By S. Ltd.	2,00,000
			31.12.98	By Profit & Loss A/c	1,24,000
				(Loss on Default)	
				By Balance c/d	1,62,000
		5,40,000			5,40,000

S. Ltd. Account

Dr. *Cr.*

Date	Particulars	(A)	Date	Particulars	(A)
01.01.97	To Bank A/c	1,50,000	01.01.97	By Machinery A/c	6,00,000
31.12.97	To Bank A/c	1,80,000		(Total Cash Price)	
31.12.97	To Balance c/d	3,15,000	31.12.97	By Interest A/c	45,000
		6,45,000			6,45,000
			01.01.98	By Balance b/d	3,15,000
31.12.98	To Machinery A/c	2,00,000	31.12.98	By Interest A/c	30,000
31.12.98	To Balance c/d	1,45,000			
		3,45,000			3,45,000

In the Books of S Ltd.

Aditya's Account

Dr. *Cr.*

Date	*Particulars*	*(A)*	*Date*	*Particulars*	*(A)*
01.01.97	To Hire Sales A/c	6,00,000	01.01.97	By Bank A/c	1,50,000
31.12.97	To Interest A/c	45,000	31.12.97	By Bank A/c	1,80,000
			31.12.97	By Balance c/d	3,15,000
		6,45,000			6,45,000
01.01.98	To Bank A/c	3,15,000	31.12,98	By Goods Rep. A/c	2,00,000
31.12.98	To Interest A/c	30,000	31.12.98	By Balance c/d	1,45,000
		3,45,000			3,45,000

Goods Repossessed Account

Dr. *Cr.*

Date	*Particulars*	*(A)*	*Date*	*Particulars*	*(A)*
31.12.98	To Aditya	2,00,000	31.12.98	By Bank A/c	1,35,000
	To bank A/c	10,000		By Profit & Loss A/c	75,000
				(Loss on Sale)	
		2,10,000			2,10,000

Example 18

Bombay Transport Ltd., purchased on 1st April, 2003 from Delhi Motors five trucks costing A 3,00,000 each on the hire purchase system. The payment was to be made as follows:

10% of cash price sown;

25% of cash price at the end of the four subsequent half years.

The payment due on 31st March, 2004 could not be made and hence the trucks were seized by the vendor. But, after negotiation, the hire purchaser was allowed to keep three trucks on the condition that the value of the other two trucks would be adjusted against the amount due, the trucks being valued at cost less 25% depreciation. Bombay Transport Ltd., closes its books on 31st March each year and the depreciation is charged at 15% per annum on the original cost.

The vendor spent A 60,000 on getting the trucks repaired and sold them for A 5,00,000.

Prepare necessary Ledger accounts in the books of both the parties.

Solution

Books of Bombay Transport Ltd. (Hire Purchaser)

Trucks Account

Dr. *Cr.*

Date	*Particulars*	*(A)*	*Date*	*Particulars*	*(A)*
2003			**2004**		
April 1	To Delhi Motors		Mar. 31	By Depreciation A/c	

	(Hire Vendor)	15,00,000		Rs. 15,00,000 × $\frac{15}{100}$	2,25,000
			Mar. 31	By Hire Vendor (Delhi Motors)	4,50,000
			Mar. 31	By Profit & Loss A/c (Loss on seizure of trucks)	60,000
			Mar. 31	By Balance c/d	7,65,000
		15,00,000			15,00,000

Delhi Motors (Hire Vendor) Account

Dr. *Cr.*

Date	*Particulars*	*(A)*	*Date*	*Particulars*	*(A)*
2003			**2003**		
Apr. 1	To Bank A/c	1,50,000	Apr. 1	By Trucks A/c	15,00,000
Oct. 30	To Bank A/c	3,75,000	Oct. 30	By Interest A/c	60,000
2004			**2004**		
Mar. 31	To Trucks A/c (Return)	4,50,000	Mar. 31	By Interest A/c	45,000
Mar. 31	To Balance c/d	6,30,000			
		16,05,000			16,05,000

Notes

Calculation of Interest

A. Total Cash Price = A 3,00,000 × 5 = A 15,00,000

B. Total Hire Purchase Price = 10% of Cash Price *i.e.,* A 1,50,000 + 25% Cash Price at the end of four subsequent half years *i.e.,* A 15,00,000 = A 16,50,000

C. Total Interest = A 16,50,000 – A 15,00,000 = A 1,50,000

Since the rate of interest has not been given, the amount of interest included in each instalment will be ascertained by dividing the total interest in the ratio of Hire Purchase price outstanding in the beginning of each period *i.e.,* of A 15,00,000; A 11,25,000; A 7,50,000 & A 3,75,000. The ratio comes to 4 : 3 : 2 : 1.

	Instalment	*Interest*
1	[Oct. 30, 2003] Rs. 1,50,000 $\frac{4}{10}$	A 60,000
2	[March 31, 2004] Rs. 1,50,000 × $\frac{3}{10}$	A 45,000
3.	[Oct. 30, 2004] Rs. 1,50,000 × $\frac{2}{10}$	A 30,000
4.	[March 31, 2005] Rs. 1,50,000 × $\frac{1}{10}$	A 15,000

Books of Delhi Motors (Hire Vendor)

Bombay Transport Ltd. Account

Dr. Cr.

Date	Particulars	(A)	Date	Particulars	(A)
2003			**2003**		
Apr. 1	To Sales A/c	15,00,000	Apr. 1	By Bank A/c	1,50,000
Oct. 30	To Interest A/c	60,000	Oct. 30	By Interest A/c	3,75,000
2004			**2004**		
Mar. 31	To Interest A/c	45,000	Mar. 31	By Goods Repossessed A/c	4,50,000
			Mar. 31	By Balance c/d	6,30,000
		16,05,000			16,05,000

Goods Repossessed Account

Dr. Cr.

Date	Particulars	(A)	Date	Particulars	(A)
2004			**2004**		
Mar. 31	To Bombay Transport Ltd.	4,50,000	Mar 31	By Sales (Cash)	5,00,000
	To Bank (expenses)	60,000		By Profit & Loss A/c	10,000 (Loss)
		5,10,000			5,10,000

Example 19

D Ltd., sold three machines costing A 10,000 each to *P* on hire purchase system on 01.1.2006. *P* paid A 6,000 on the above date to receive delivery of the machine and agreed to pay five half-yearly instalments of A 6,000 each.

P could not pay the third instalment in time whereupon *D* Ltd., repossessed one machine and *P* retained the other two machines. The value of the returned machine was agreed to be cash price less 40%. The purchaser charges depreciation @ 10% p.a., on reducing balance method.

D Ltd., sold the repossessed machine for A 4,500 on 31st December, 2007 after incurring repairs of A 200.

You are required to show :

1. *D.* Ltd., A/c and Machinery A/c in the books of hire-purchaser, and;
2. *P's* A/c and Goods Repossessed A/c in the books of *D.* Ltd.

Solution

Cash Price = A 10,000 × 3 = A 30,000

Hire Purchase Price = A 6,000 (Down) + (A 6,000 × 5) = 36,000

Interest = A 36,000 – A 30,000 = A 6,000

Calculation of Interest of Each Instalment

Half Yearly Instalment	Outstanding Amount (A)	Ratio	Interest A
1.	30,000	5	Rs. 6,000 × $\frac{5}{15}$ 2,000

2.	24,000	4	Rs. 6,000 × $\frac{4}{15}$ 1,600
3.	18,000	3	Rs. 6,000 × $\frac{3}{15}$ 1,200
4.	12,000	2	Rs. 6,000 × $\frac{2}{15}$ 800
5.	6,000	1	Rs. 6,000 × $\frac{1}{15}$ 400

Books of P (Hire Purchaser)
Machinery Account

Dr. *Cr.*

Date	*Particulars*	*(A)*	*Date*	*Particulars*	*(A)*
2006			**2006**		
Jan. 1	To D Ltd.	30,000	Dec. 31	By Depreciation A/c	3,000
				By Balance c/d	27,000
		30,000			30,000
2007			**2007**		
Jan. 1	To Balance b/d	27,000	June 30	By D Ltd. (Goods Repossessed)	6,000
				By Depreciation A/c (For 6 Months)	1,350
				By Profit & Loss A/c (*Bal. Fig*)	2,550
				By Balance c/d	17,100
		27,000			27,000
2007					
July 1	To Balance b/d	17,100			

D. Ltd. Account

Dr. *Cr.*

Date	*Particulars*	*(A)*	*Date*	*Particulars*	*(A)*
2006			**2006**		
Jan. 1	To Bank A/c	6,000	Jan. 1	By Machinery A/c	30,000
June 30	To Bank A/c	6,000	June 30	By Interest A/c	2,000
Dec. 31	To Bank A/c	6,000	Dec. 31	By Interest A/c	1,600
	To Balance c/d	15,600			
		33,600			33,600
2007			**2007**		
June 30	To Machinery A/c	6,000	Jan. 1	By Balance b/d	15,600
	To Balance c/d	10,800	June 30	By Interest A/c	1,200
		16,800			16,800
			2007		
			July 1	By Balance b/d	10,800

Books of D Ltd.

P 's Account

Dr. *Cr.*

Date	*Particulars*	*(A)*	*Date*	*Particulars*	*(A)*
2006			**2006**		
Jan. 1	To Sales A/c	30,000	Jan. 1	By Bank A/c	6,000
June 30	To Interest A/c	2,000	June 30	By Bank A/c	6,000
Dec. 31	To Interest A/c	1,600	Dec. 31	By Bank A/c	6,000
				By Balance c/d	15,600
		33,600			33,600
2007			**2007**		
Jan.1	To Balance b/d	15,600	June 30	By Goods Repossessed A/c	6,000
June 30	To Interest A/c	1,200		By Balance c/d	10,800
		16,800			16,800
2007					
July 1	To Balance b/d	10,800			

Goods Repossessed Account

Dr. *Cr.*

Date	*Particulars*	*(A)*	*Date*	*Particulars*	*(A)*
2007			**2007**		
June 30	To P	6,000	Dec. 31	By Cash A/c (Sales)	4,500
	To cash-Repairs	200		By Profit & Loss A/c (Loss on Goods Repossessed)	1,700
		6,200			6,200

Working Notes

*1	*Value of one returned machine*	*A*
	Cash Price	10,000
	Less : 40%	4,000
	Agreed Value	6,000
*2	*Balance Value of two machines*	*A*
	Cash Price of 2 machines	20,000
	Less : 10% Depreciation (2006)	2,000
	Book Value (01.1.2007)	18,000
	Less : 10% Depreciation for 6 months	900
		17,100

Example 20

X Ltd. purchased 2 machines costing A 80,000 each from Y Ltd. on 1st Jan., 2004 on the hire purchase system. The terms were :

Payment on delivery A 20,000 for each machine; Balance in 3 equal instalments together with interest at 10% p.a. to be paid at the end of each year.

X Ltd. writes off 25% depreciation each year on the diminishing balance method. X Ltd. paid the instalments due on 31.12.2004 and on 31.12.2005 but could not pay the final instalment. Y Ltd. repossessed one machine adjusting its value against the amount due. The repossession was done on the basis of 30% p.a. depreciation on the diminishing balance method. The vendor spent A 8,560 for the repairs and overhauling of the machine and sold it for A 40,000.

Pass journal entries in the books of Y Ltd. and prepare ledger accounts in the books of 'X' Ltd.

[*B.Com., (Hons.), Delhi University, 2008*]

Solution

Ledger of X Ltd.
Machines Account

Date	*Particulars*	*Amount (A)*	*Date*	*Particulars*	*Amount (A)*
2004			**2004**		
Jan. 1	To Y Ltd.	1,60,000	Dec. 31	By Depreciation A/c [A 1,60,000 × $^{25}/_{100}$]	40,000
				By Balance c/d	1,20,000
		1,60,000			1,60,000
2005			**2005**		
Jan. 1	To Balance b/d	1,20,000	Dec. 31	By Depreciation A/c [A 1,20,000 × $^{25}/_{100}$]	30,000
				By Balance c/d	90,000
		1,20,000			1,20,000
2006			**2006**		
Jan. 1	To Balance b/d	90,000	Dec. 31	By Depreciation A/c [A 90,000 × $^{25}/_{100}$]	22,500
				By Y Ltd. (Machine seized)*1	27,440
				By Profit and Loss A/c (Loss on machine seized)	6,310
				By Balance c/d (W.D.V. of one machine still in possession)	33,750
		90,000			90,000

Y Ltd.

Date	*Particulars*	*Amount (A)*	*Date*	*Particulars*	*Amount (A)*
2004			**2004**		
Jan. 1	To Bank A/c	40,000	Jan. 1	By Machines A/c	1,60,000
Dec. 31	To Bank A/c	52,000	Dec. 31	By Interest A/c	12,000

Date	Particulars	A	Date	Particulars	A
	A [40,000 + 12,000]			[10% of A 1,20,000]	
	To Balance c/d	80,000			
		1,72,000			1,72,000
2005			**2005**		
Dec. 31	To Bank A/c	48,000	Jan. 1	By Balance b/d	80,000
	A [40,000 + 8,000]		Dec. 31	By Interest A/c	8,000
	To Balance c/d	40,000		[10% of A 80,000]	
		88,000			88,000
2006			**2006**		
Dec. 31	To Machine A/c*	27,440	Jan. 1	By Balance b/d	40,000
	To Balance c/d	16,560		By Interest A/c	4,000
				[10% of A 40,000]	
		44,000			44,000

Working Notes

1. *Value of one Machine on repossession :*

	2004	*2005*	*2006*
	A	A	A
Cost/W.D.V. in the beginning	80,000	56,000	39,200
Depreciation for the year @ 30%	24,000	16,800	11,760
	56,000	39,200	27,440

In the Books of Y Ltd.
Journal Entries

Date	*Particulars*		*L.F.*	*Dr. Amount (A)*	*Cr. Amount (A)*
2004					
Jan. 1	X Ltd.	Dr.		1,60,000	
	To Hire Purchase Sales A/c				1,60,000
	(Being the goods sold on hire purchase)				
Jan. 1	Bank A/c	Dr.		40,000	
	To X. Ltd.				40,000
	(Being the receipt of down payment)				
Dec. 31	X Ltd.	Dr.		12,000	
	To Interest A/c				12,000
	(Being the interest charged @10% on A 1,20,000)				
Dec. 31	Bank A/c (A 40,000 + A 12,000)	Dr.		52,000	
	To X Ltd.				52,000
	(Being the first instalment received along with interest)				
Dec. 31	Interest A/c	Dr.		12,000	
	To Profit and Loss A/c				12,000
	(Being the transfer of interest)				

Date	Particulars		L.F.	Dr.	Cr.
2005					
Dec. 31	X Ltd.	Dr.		8,000	
	To Interest A/c				8,000
	(Being the interest charged @ 10% on A 80,000)				
Dec. 31	Bank A/c (A 40,000 + A 8,000)	Dr.		48,000	
	To X Ltd.				48,000
	(Being the second instalment received along with interest)				
Dec. 31	Interest A/c	Dr.		8,000	
	To Profit and Loss A/c				8,000
	(Being the transfer of interest)				
2006					
Dec. 31	X Ltd.	Dr.		4,000	
	To Interest A/c				4,000
	(Being the interest charged @ 10% on A 40,000)				
Dec. 31	Goods Repossessed A/c*	Dr.		27,440	
	To X Ltd.				27,440
	(Being one machine repossessed on default)				
Dec. 31	Goods Repossessed A/c	Dr.		8,560	
	To Bank A/c				8,560
	(Being expenses incurred on the repair and overhauling of the machine repossessed)				
	Bank A/c	Dr.		40,000	
	To Goods Repossessed A/c				40,000
	(Being repossessed machine sold)				
	Goods Repossessed A/c	Dr.		4,000	
	To profit and loss A/c				4,000
	(Being profit*2 on sale of goods repossessed)				

Goods Repossessed Account

Particulars	*(A)*	*Particulars*	*(A)*
To Y Ltd.	27,440	By Bank A/c	40,000
To Bank A/c (expenses)	8,560		
To Profit and Loss A/c (Profit and Sale)	4,000		
	40,000		40,000

Example 21

X Co. Ltd. purchased on 1.1.2008 from M/s R.V. Traders four machines having cash price A 80,000 each on hire purchase basis. The payment was to be made as follows :

10% of cash price down, and

25% of cash price at the end of each of the following four years.

X Co. Ltd. paid the first instalment but failed to pay the second instalment due on 31.12.2009. M/s R.V. Traders repossessed three machines leaving remaining one machine with the buyer. The value of three machines was taken at cost less depreciation @ 20% p.a. on reducing balance method. M/s X Co. Ltd. charges depreciation at 10% p.a. on reducing balance method on 31st Dec. of each year. M/s R.V. Traders spent A 42,000 on overhauling of the machines repossessed and sold two of the repossessed machines for A 1,20,000.

Prepare necessary Ledger Accounts in the books of both the parties.

[*B.Com.,* (*Hons.*) *Delhi University, 2010*]

Solution

Books of X Co. Ltd.
M/s R.V. Traders

Date	*Particulars*	*Amount (A)*	*Date*	*Particulars*	*Amount (A)*
1.1.08	To Bank A/c	32,000	1.1.08	By Machinery A/c	3,20,000
1.12.08	To Bank A/c	80,000	31.12.08	By Interest A/c*1	12,800
1.12.08	To Balance c/d	2,20,800			
		3,32,800			3,32,800
1.12.09	To Machinery A/c*2	1,53,600	1.1.09	By Balance b/d	2,20,800
1.12.09	To Balance c/d	76,800	31.12.09	By Interest A/c*1	9,600
		2,30,400			2,30,400

Machinery Account

Date	*Particulars*	*Amount (A)*	*Date*	*Particulars*	*Amount (A)*
1.1.08	To R.V. Traders	3,20,000	31.12.08	By Depreciation a/c	32,000
			31.12.08	By Balance c/d	2,88,000
		3,20,000			3,20,000
1.1.09	To Balance b/d	2,88,000	31.12.09	By Depreciation A/c	28,800
				By R.V. Traders	1,53,600
				By Profit and Loss A/c*1	40,800
				By Balance c/d*3	64,800
		2,88,000			2,88,000

Books of M/s R.V. Traders
X Co. Ltd. Account

Date	*Particulars*	*Amount (A)*	*Date*	*Particulars*	*Amount (A)*
1.1.08	To Hire Purchase A/c	3,20,000	1.1.08	By Bank A/c	32,000
1.12.08	To Interest A/c	12,800	31.12.08	By Bank A/c	80,000
			31.12.08	By Balance c/d	2,20,800
		3,32,800			3,32,800

1.1.09	To Balance b/d	2,20,800	31.12.09	By Goods Repossessed A/c*2	1,53,600
31.12.09	To Interest A/c	9,600	31.12.09	By Balance c/d	76,800
		2,30,400			2,30,400

Goods Repossessed Account

Date	*Particulars*	*Amount (A)*	*Date*	*Particulars*	*Amount (A)*
31.12.09	To R.V. Traders	1,53,600		By Bank A/c	1,20,000
	To Bank A/c	42,000		By Profit and Loss A/c*5 (Loss on Sale of goods repossessed)	10,400
				By Balance c/d*6	65,200
		1,95,600			1,95,600

Working Notes :

1. *Calculation of Interest :*

Total cash price of 4 machines = A 80,000 × 4 = A 3,20,000

Down payment (10% of Cash Price) = A 32,000

Four instalments (25% of Cash Price) = A 80,000 each

∴ Total Hire Purchase Price = A 32,000 + A 3,20,000 = A 3,52,000

∴ Total Interest = Hire Purchase Price – Cash Price

= A 3,52,000 – A 3,20,000 = A 32,000

Interest on each instalment is calculated as follows :

Hire Purchase Price outstanding at the beginning of each year :

A 3,20,000 (1st year); A 2,40,000 (2nd year); A 1,60,000 (3rd year); A 80,000 (4th year).

Ratio 4 : 3 : 2 : 1

1st year Interest = A 32,000 × $\frac{4}{10}$ = A 12,800;

2nd year Interest = A 32,000 × $\frac{3}{10}$ = A 9,600;

3rd year Interest = A 32,000 × $\frac{2}{10}$ = A 6,400;

4th year Interest = A 32,000 × $\frac{1}{10}$ = 3,200.

2. Value of Machinery Repossessed :

	A
Cost of machines (Rs. 80,000 × 3)	2,40,000
Less : Depreciation @20% 1st year (A 2,40,000 × $\frac{20}{100}$)	48,000
	1,92,000
Less : Depreciation @20% 2nd year (A 1,92,000 × $\frac{20}{100}$)	38,400
	1,53,600

3. Value of Machine left with the buyer :

Cost of machine	80,000
Less : Depreciation @ 10% 1st year	8,000
	72,000
Less : Depreciation @ 10% 2nd year	7,200
	64,800

4. Calculation of Loss on default :

Book Value of three machines on the date of default	
$[\frac{3}{4}$ (A 2,88,000 – A 28,800)$]$	1,94,400
Agreed Value of three machines taken away by the seller	1,53,600
Loss on default	40,800

5. Calculation of loss on sales of goods repossessed :

(*i*) Value of 3 machines repossessed A (1,53,600 + 42,000)	1,95,600
(*ii*) Value of 2 machines repossessed $\frac{1,95,600}{3}$ 2	1,30,400
Less : Sale of 2 machines repossessed	1,20,000
Loss on sale of 2 machines	10,400

6. Value of machines in stock = $\frac{1,95,600}{3}$ = A 65,200

Example 22

Bombay Okara Corporation Ltd., purchased on Jan. 1, 1997 from Delhi Motors five trucks costing A 50,000 each on the hire purchase system. The payment was to be made as follows : 10% of cash price down, 25% of cash price at the end of the four subsequent half years. The payment due on 31 December 1997 could not be made and hence the trucks were seized by the vendor. But, after negotiation, the hire purchaser was allowed to keep three trucks on the condition that the value of the other two trucks would be adjusted against the amount due, the trucks being valued at cost less 25% depreciation. Bombay Okara Corporation closes is books on 30 June each year and the depreciation is charged at 15% p.a. on trucks on the original cost. The vendor spent A 10,000 on getting the trucks thoroughly overhauled and sold them for A 90,000. Show the various accounts in the books of both the parties.

Solution

Before the solution is attempted, it is necessary to calculate the value of trucks taken away by the vendor and the value of the trucks left with the hire purchaser :

(*i*) *Value of the Trucks taken away*

No. of Trucks		2
Cost Price (2 × 50,000)	= A	1,00,000
Less : Depreciation @ 25%	= A	25,000
Value of Trucks at the time of repossession	A	75,000

(*ii*) *Value of the Trucks left with the Purchaser*

No. of Trucks		3
Cost Price (3 × 50,000)	= A	1,50,000
Less : Depreciation (normal) 15%	= A	22,500
	A	1,27,500

(*iii*) *Calculation of Interest*

Rate of interest is also not given; interest is calculated as under :

Total Interest = Hire Purchaser price – Cash Price

= 2,75,000 – 2,50,000 = A 25,000

Instalment	*Amount due before Instalment*	*Ratio*	*Interest*	*A*
1	2,50,000	4	$\frac{4}{10}$ ′ 25, 000	10,000
2	1,87,500	3	$\frac{3}{10}$ 25,000	7,500
3	1,25,000	2	$\frac{2}{10}$ 25,000	5,000
4	62,500	1	$\frac{1}{10}$ 25,000	2,500

Trucks on Hire Purchase Account

Dr. *Cr.*

Date	*Particulars*	*(A)*	*Date*	*Particulars*	*(A)*
1997			**1997**		
Jan. 1	Delhi Motors Account	2,50,000	June 30	Depreciation Account	18,750
				Balance c/d	2,31,250
		2,50,000			2,50,000
1997			**1997**		
July 1	Balance b/d	2,31,250	Dec. 31	Depreciation Account	18,750
				Delhi Motors Account	75,000
				Profit & Loss Account (*Bal. Fig.*)	10,000
				Balance c/d	1,27,500
		2,31,250			2,31,250
1998					
Jan. 1	Balance b/d	1,27,500			

Delhi Motors Account

Dr. *Cr.*

Date	*Particulars*	*(A)*	*Date*	*Particulars*	*(A)*
1997			**1997**		
Jan. 1	Cash Account (Down Payment)	25,000	Jan. 1	Trucks on Hire Purchase Account	2,50,000
	Cash Account	62,500	June 30	Interest on Hire Purchase Account	10,000
June 30	Balance c/d	1,72,500			
		2,60,000			2,60,000

1997			**1997**		
Dec. 31	Trucks on Hire Purchase Account	75,000	July 1	Balance b/d	1,72,500
	Balance c/d	1,05,000	Dec. 31	Interest on Hire Purchase Account	7,500
		1,80,000			1,80,000
			1998		
			Jan. 1	Balance b/d	1,05,000

Total Loss = A 10,000 *Plus* A 7,500 interest payable for the half year ended 31 December 1997 on A 17,500.

Books of Delhi Motors
Bombay Okara Corporation Account

Dr. *Cr.*

Date	*Particulars*	*(A)*	*Date*	*Particulars*	*(A)*
1997			**1997**		
Jan. 1	Hire Purchase Sales Account	2,50,000	Jan. 1	Cash Account	25,000
June 30	Interest on Hire Purchase Sales A/c	10,000	June 30	Cash Account	62,500
				Balance c/d	1,72,500
		2,60,000			2,60,000
1997			**1997**		
July 1	Balance b/d	1,72,500	Dec. 31	Goods Repossessed Account	75,000
Dec. 31	Interest on Hire Purchase Sales A/c	7,500		Balance c/d	1,05,000
		1,80,000			1,80,000
1998					
Jan. 1	Balance b/d	1,05,000			

Goods Repossessed A/c

Dr. *Cr.*

Date	*Particulars*	*(A)*	*Date*	*Particulars*	*(A)*
1997			**1997**		
Dec. 31	Bombay Okara Corporation account	75,000	Dec. 31	Cash Account (Sales)	90,000
	Cash Account (Repairs)	10,000			
	Profit & Loss Account	5,000			
		90,000			90,000

Example 23

On 01.1.2009 *X*, a television dealer, bought 5 television sets from Dolphia Television Co., on hire-purchase. The cash price of each set was A 20,000. It was agreed that A 25,000 should be paid immediately and the balance in three instalments of A 30,000 each at the end of each year. The Television Co., charges interest @ 10% p.a. The buyer depreciates television sets at 20% p.a., on the diminishing balance method.

X paid cash down and two instalments but failed to pay the last instalment. Consequently, the Television Co., repossessed three sets, leaving two sets with the buyer and adjusting the value of 3 sets against the amount due. The sets repossessed were valued on the basis of 30% depreciation p.a., on the written down value. The sets repossessed were sold by the Television Co., for A 30,000 after necessary repairs amounting to A 5,000. Open the necessary ledger accounts in the books of both the parties.

Solution

Calculation of Interest & Depreciation

Date of Payment	*Total Cash Price*	*Instalment* A	*Interest* A	*Cash Price* A	*Depreciation* A
Jan 1, 2009	(5 × A 20,000) 1,00,000				
(Down Payment)	25,000	25,000	–	25,000	–
	75,000				
Dec. 31, 2009	22,500	30,000	$75,000 \times \frac{10}{100}$ = 7,500	22,500	20,000
	52,500				
Dec. 31, 2010	24,750	30,000	$52,500 \times \frac{10}{100}$ = 5,250	24,750	16,000
	27,750				
Dec. 31, 2011	27,750	30,000	2,250	27,750	12,800
	—				

Books of X

Television Account

Dr. *Cr.*

Date	*Particulars*	*(A)*	*Date*	*Particulars*	*(A)*
2009			**2009**		
Jan. 1	To Dolphia Television Co. (5 × A 20,000)	1,00,000	Dec. 31	By Depreciation $1,00,000 \times \frac{20}{100}$	20,000
				By Balance c/d	80,000
		1,00,000			1,00,000
2010			**2010**		
Jan. 1	To Balance b/d	80,000	Dec. 31	By Depreciation $80,000 \times \frac{20}{100}$	16,000
				By Balance c/d	64,000

Date	Particulars	(A)	Date	Particulars	(A)
		80,000			80,000
2011			**2011**		
Jan. 1	To Balance b/d	64,000	Dec. 31	By Depreciation	
				64,000 $\frac{20}{100}$	12,800
				By Dolphia Television Co.–Goods repossessed	20,580
				By Profit & Loss A/c –Loss on default (*Bal.Fig.*)	10,140
				By Balance c/d	20,480
		64,000			64,000
2012					
Jan. 1	To Balance b/d	20,480			

Dolphia Television Co. (Vendor)

Dr. *Cr.*

Date	*Particulars*	*(A)*	*Date*	*Particulars*	*(A)*
2009			**2009**		
Jan. 1	To Bank	25,000	Jan. 1	By Television A/c	1,00,000
Dec. 31	To Bank	30,000	Dec. 31	By Interest	7,500
	To Balance c/d	52,500			
		1,07,500			1,07,500
2010			**2010**		
Dec. 31	To Bank	30,000	Jan. 1	By Balance b/d	52,500
	To Balance c/d	27,750	Dec. 31	By Interest	5,250
		57,750			57,750
2011			**2011**		
Dec. 31	To Television A/c – Goods repossessed	20,580	Jan. 1	By Balance b/d	27,750
			Dec. 31	By Interest	2,250
	To Balance c/d	9,420			
		30,000			30,000
			2012		
			Jan. 1	By Balance b/d	9,420

Notes

1. *Value of 3 Televisions repossessed* :

	A
Cash Price of 3 T.V Sets @ A 20,000	60,000
Less : Depreciation @ 30% p.a. on A 60,000	18,000

Balance as on 31.12.2009	42,000
Less : Depreciation @ 30% p.a. on A 42,000	12,600
Balance as on 31.12.2010	29,400
Less : Depreciation @ 30% p.a. on A 29,400	8,820
Balance as on 31.12.2011	20,580

2. *Value of 2 Televisions left with the buyer* :

	A
Cash Price of 2 T.V Sets @ A 20,000	40,000
Less : Depreciation @ 20% p.a. on A 40,000	8,000
Balance as on 31.12.2009	32,000
Less : Depreciation @ 20% p.a. on A 32,000	6,400
Balance as on 31.12.2010	25,600
Less : Depreciation @ 20% p.a. on A 25,600	5,120
Balance as on 31.12.2011	20,480

Books of Dolphia Television Co.

X's Account (Hire-purchaser)

Dr. *Cr.*

Date	*Particulars*	*(A)*	*Date*	*Particulars*	*(A)*
2009			**2009**		
Jan. 1	To Sales	1,00,000	Jan. 1	By Bank	25,000
Dec. 31	To Interest	7,500	Dec. 31	By Bank	30,000
				By Balance c/d	52,500
		1,07,500			1,07,500
2010			**2010**		
Jan. 1	To Balance b/d	52,500	Dec. 31	By Bank	30,000
Dec. 31	To Interest	5,250		By Balance c/d	27,750
		57,750			57,750
2011			**2011**		
Jan. 1	To Balance b/d	27,750	Dec. 31	By Goods Repossessed Account	20,580
Dec. 31	To Interest	2,250		By Balance c/d	9,420
		30,000			30,000

Goods Repossessed Account

Dr. *Cr.*

Particulars	*(A)*	*Particulars*	*(A)*
To X	20,580	By Bank —Sale	30,000
To Bank—Repairs	5,000		
To Profit & Loss A/c—Profit	4,420		
	30,000		30,000

Alternative Method

Television Account

Dr. *Cr.*

Date	Particulars	(A)	Date	Particulars	(A)
2009			**2009**		
Jan. 1	To Dolphia TV Co.	25,000	Dec. 31	By Depreciation	20,000
Dec. 31	To Dolphia TV Co.			By Balance c/d	27,500
	(30,000 – 7,500)	22,500			
		47,500			47,500
2010			**2010**		
Jan. 1	To Balance b/d	27,500	Dec. 31	By Depreciation	16,000
Dec. 31	To Dolphia TV Co.	24,750		By Balance c/d	36,250
	(30,000 – 5,250)				
		52,250			52,250
2011			**2011**		
Jan. 1	To Balance b/d	36,250	Dec. 31	By Depreciation	12,800
Dec. 31	To Dolphia TV Co.	9,420		By Profit & Loss A/c	12,390
	(Creating a liability			(Loss on default)	
	for the amount due now)			By Balance c/d	20,480
		45,670			45,670
2012					
Jan. 1	To Balance b/d	20,480			

Note : Loss on default A 12,390 includes A 2,250 for interest.

Dolphia Television Co. (Vendor)

Dr. *Cr.*

Date	Particulars	(A)	Date	Particulars	(A)
2009			**2009**		
Jan. 1	To Bank	25,000	Jan. 1	By Television A/c	25,000
Dec. 31	To Bank	30,000	Dec. 31	By Television A/c	22,500
				By Interest A/c	7,500
		55,000			55,000
2010			**2010**		
Dec. 31	To Bank	30,000	Dec. 31	By Television A/c	24,750
				By Interest A/c	5,250
		30,000			30,000
2011			**2011**		
Dec. 31	To Balance c/d	9,420	Dec. 31	By Television A/c—	9.420
				creating liability for	
				the amount due now	
		9,420			9,420
			2012		
			Jan. 1	By Balance b/d	9,420

Example 24

Mr. Y is a hire purchase trader and sells goods on hire purchase basis at cost plus 50%. From the following information, prepare Hire Purchase Trading Account to determine the profit for the year ending 31.3.2006 :

	A
Stock with costumers at HP price as at 1.4.2005	90,000
Stock at shop (at cost) as at 1.4.2005	1,80,000
Instalments due (customers paying) as at 1.4.2005	50,000
Goods repossessed (instalments due A 20,000) valued at	5,000
Cash received from customers	6,00,000
Stock at shop (excluding returned goods) at cost as at 31.3.2006	2,00,000
Instalments due but not received as at 31.3.2006	90,000
Stock with customers at HP price as at 31.3.2006	3,00,000

[*B.Com.* (*Hons.*), *Delhi University, 2006*]

Solution

Hire Purchase Trading Account

Particulars	(*A*)	*Particulars*	(*A*)
To Stock with the Customers A/c	90,000	By Stock Reserve A/c	
To Instalments Due A/c	50,000	[A 90,000 × 50/150] (Loading)	30,000
		By Goods repossessed A/c	5,000
To Goods sold on Hire Purchase A/c*2	8,70,000	By Cash A/c	6,00,000
To Stock Reserve A/c		By Goods sold on Hire Purchase A/c	
[A 3,00,000 × 50/150] (Loading)	1,00,000	[A 8,70,000 × 50/150] (Loading)	2,90,000
To Profit and Loss A/c	2,05,000	By Stock with Customers A/c	3,00,000
		By Instalment Due A/c	90,000
	13,15,000		13,15,000

Working Notes :

Stock at the Shop Account

Particulars	(*A*)	*Particulars*	(*A*)
To Balance c/d	1,80,000	By Stock with the Customers	
To Purchase A/c (*bal. fig.*)	6,00,000	A/c [A 8,70,000 – 2,90,000]	5,80,000
		By Balance c/d	2,00,000
	7,80,000		7,80,000

Stock with the Customers Account

Particulars	*(A)*	*Particulars*	*(A)*
To Balance b/d	90,000	By Instalment Due A/c	6,60,000
To Stock in the Shop A/c		By Balance c/d	3,00,000
(Goods sold on Hire Purchase)	8,70,000		
	9,60,000		9,60,000

Instalment Due Account

Particulars	*(A)*	*Particulars*	*(A)*
To Balance b/d	50,000	By Goods repossessed A/c	20,000
To Stock with Customer A/c	6,60,000	By Cash A/c	6,00,000
		By Balance c/d	90,000
	7,10,000		7,10,000

Example 25

Vikas of Delhi sells goods on hire-purchase basis. He add 50% to the cost of goods sold while selling goods at hire-purchase. From the information given below, prepare Hire-Purchase Trading A/c and all other relevant ledger accounts to show Profit or Loss :

January 1, 2005	A
Goods out on Hire-Purchase (at cost price)	80,000
Instalments due (customers paying)	3,000
Purchase during the year	6,04,000
Cash received during the year	9,06,000
Total amount of instalments that fell due during the year	9,27,000

One customer to whom goods were sold for A 15,000, paid only five instalments of A 1,000 each, on his failure to pay the monthly instalments of A 1,000 each due in November and December 2005, the goods were repossessed on 27th December, 2005 after legal proceedings.

[*B.Com. (Hons.), Delhi University, 2006*]

Solution

Hire Purchase Trading Account

Particulars	*(A)*	*Particulars*	*(A)*
To Balance b/d		By Cash A/c	9,06,000
– Stock with the Customers A/c (at H.P.P.)	1,20,000	By Goods sold on Hire Purchase A/c (Loading)	3,02,000
– Instalments due (Customers paying)	3,000	By Stock Reserve A/c (Loading in Op. Stock)	40,000
		By Goods repossessed A/c	10,000
To Goods Sold on Hire-Purchase A/c (HPP)*2	9,06,000	By Balance c/d (Cl. Balance) :	
		– Stock with Customers A/c (HPP)*2	91,000
To Stock Reserve A/c		– Instalment due A/c*3	22,000
(Loading in Closing Stock)	30,333		

To Profit transferred to Profit and Loss A/c	3,11,667		
	13,71,000		13,71,000

Working Notes :

Stock in Shop Account

Particulars	(*A*)	*Particulars*	(*A*)
To Balance b/d	–	By Stock with Customers A/c	6,04,000
To Purchases A/c	6,04,000		
	6,04,000		6,04,000

Stock with Customers Account

Particulars	(*A*)	*Particulars*	(*A*)
To Balance b/d [80,000 + 40,000]	1,20,000	By Instalment Due A/c	9,27,000
To Goods Sold on Hire-Purchase A/c [A 6,04,000[*1] + 50% of A 6,04,000]	9,06,000	By Goods Repossessed A/c	8,000
		By Balance c/d (*bal. fig.*)	91,000
	10,26,000		10,26,000

Instalment Due Account

Particulars	(*A*)	*Particulars*	(*A*)
To Balance b/d	3,000	By Cash A/c	9,06,000
To Stock with Customers A/c	9,27,000	By Goods Repossessed A/c	2,000
		By Balance c/d	22,000
	9,30,000		9,30,000

Note : In the absence of any information regarding revaluation, the value of the Goods Repossessed would not be changed.

Example 26

Mayur Electricals Ltd. sell TV sets and Music systems on hire purchase basis. From the following particulars prepare Hire Purchase Trading Account to find out the profit (show your workings clearly) :

	T.V. Sets	*Music Systems*
Cost	A 16,200	A 6,000
Cash Price	A 18,900	A 7,200
Down Payment	A 2,700	A 1,200
Monthly instalment	A 1,800	A 600
Number of instalments	10	12

During the year ended 31st December, 2008, the company sold 200 TV sets and 240 Music systems on hire purchase basis. 4 TV sets on which only 3 instalments each could be collected and 8 music systems on which only 5 instalments each could be collected were repossessed for non-payment of other instalments.

These were valued at 50% of their costs and after spending A 6,000 for their reconditioning, they were sold for A 84,000. Other instalments collected and due (customers still paying) were respectively as follows :

T.V. Sets	540 and 40
Music systems	800 and 60

[*B.Com., (Hons.), Delhi University, 2009*]

Solution

Working Notes :

1. *Cost and H.P. Price of goods sold on hire purchase :*

				Cost (A)
T.V. Sets	200 × A	16,200	=	32,40,000
Music Systems	240 × A	6,000	=	14,40,000
				46,80,000
				H.P. Price (Rs.)
T.V. Sets	200 × A	20,700*	=	41,40,000
Music Systems	240 × A	8,400**	=	20,16,000
				61,56,000

*A 2,700 + (A 1,800 × 10) = A 20,700

**A 1,200 + (A 600 × 12) = A 8,400

2. *Loading on goods sold on H.P.*

= A 61,56,000 – A 46,80,000 = A 14,76,000

3. *Cash collection on :*

T.V. Sets			
Down Payment	A 2,700 × 200	=	5,40,000
Instalments	A 1,800 × 540	=	9,72,000
On goods repossessed	A 1,800 × 4 × 3	=	21,600
			15,33,600
Music Systems			*A*
Down Payment	A 1,200 × 240	=	2,88,000
Instalments	A 600 × 800	=	4,80,000
On goods repossessed	A 600 × 8 × 5	=	24,000
			7,92,000

4. *Instalments not yet due on :*

	TV Sets		*Music Systems*
Total Number of Installments 196 × 10	1960	232 × 12	2784
(–) No. of Instalments Collected + Due (540 + 40)	580	(800 + 60)	860
	1380		1924
Amount due @ 1380 × 1800 = A 24,84,000		1,924 × 600 = A 11,54,400	

Total Amount due = A 24,84,000 + A 11,54,400 = A 36,38,400

5.(*i*) *Stock Reserve on T.V. Sets*

	A
Hire Purchase Price	20,700
Cost Price	16,200
Profit per set	4,500

$$\text{Stock Reserve} = \frac{4500}{20700} \times \text{A } 24,84,000 = \text{A } 5,40,000$$

(*ii*) *Stock Reserve on Music System*

	A
Hire Purchase Price	8,400
Less : Cost	6,000
Profit per set	2,400

$$\text{Stock Reserve} = \frac{2400}{8400} \times \text{A } 11,54,400 = \text{A } 3,29,829$$

Total Stock Reserve = A 5,40,000 + A 3,29,829 = A 8,69,829

6. *Value of goods repossessed*

	A
T.V. Set	
Cost of 4 sets	A 16,200 × 4 = 64,800
Music Systems	
Cost of 8 sets	A 6,000 × 8 = 48,000
	1,12,800

Valuation of Goods repossessed = 50% of A 1,12,800 = A 56,400

Hire Purchase Trading Account

Particulars	*(A)*	*Particulars*		*(A)*
To Goods sold on Hire Purchase A/c	61,56,000	By Goods Sold on Hire Purchase A/c		14,76,000
To Stock Reserve A/c (Loading)	8,69,829	(Loading)		
To Profit and Loss A/c	6,00,171	By Cash A/c :		
		T.V. Sets	15,33,600	
		Music Systems	7,92,000	23,25,600
		By Goods Repossessed A/c		56,400
		By Profit on Sale of Goods		
		Repossessed A/c		21,600*
		By Stock with Customers A/c		36,38,400
		By Instalments Due :		
		T.V. Sets : 40 × 1800		72,000
		Music System : 60 × 600		36,000
	76,26,000			76,26,000

*A 84,000 – A 56,400 – A 6,000 = A 21,600

Example 27

S Ltd. has a Hire-purchase department. Goods are sold on hire-purchase at cost plus 60%.

From the following particulars draft Hire-purchase trading account and compute profit or loss for the year ended 31st March, 2007 :

	(A)
Goods with customers on 1.4.2006 (instalments are not due)	3,20,000
Instalments due on 1.4.2006 (customers are paying)	20,000
Goods sold on hire-purchase during the year (i.e., from 1.4.2006 to 31.3.2007)	16,00,000
Cash received from customers	11,20,000
Goods re-possessed from customers valued at 40%	16,000
Unpaid instalments in respect of re-possessed goods	40,000
Goods with customers as on 31.3.2007 (at hire purchase price)	7,20,000

[*C.A. (May, 2007*]

Solution

In the Books of S. Ltd.
Hire Purchase Trading Account
for the year ended on 31st March, 2007

Particulars	*(A)*	*Particulars*	*(A)*
To Hire Purchase Stock	3,20,000	By Hire Purchase Stock Reserve (W.N. 1)	1,20,000
To Instalments due	20,000	By Bank A/c (Cash received)	11,20,000
To Goods sold on Hire Purchase	16,00,000	By Goods Repossessed A/c	16,000
To Hire Purchase Stock Reserve (W.N. 3)	2,70,000	By Goods sold on hire purchase (loading((W.N. 2)	6,00,000
To Profit and Loss A/c (*bal. fig.*)	4,26,000	By Hire purchase stock	7,20,000
		By Instalments due (W.N. 4)	60,000
	26,36,000		26,36,000

Working Notes :

			A
(*i*)	Opening H.P. Stock reserve	$3,20,000 \times \frac{60}{160}$	1,20,000
(*ii*)	Loading on goods sold on H.P.	$16,00,000 \times \frac{60}{160}$	6,00,000
(*iii*)	Closing H.P. Stock reserve	$7,20,000 \times \frac{60}{160}$	2,70,000
(*iv*)	Calculation of Instalments due at the end of the year.		
	Opening H.P. Stock + Opening Instalments due + H.P. Sales during the year (i.e., 3,20,000 + 20,000 + 16,00,000)		19,40,000
	Less : Cash received from customers	11,20,000	
	Instalments unpaid for repossessed goods	40,000	
	Closing balance of H.P. Stock	7,20,000	18,80,000
	Closing Instalments Due		60,000

Example 28

Wye sells goods on Hire-purchase at cost plus 50%. Prepare Hire Purchase Trading Account from the information given below :

	(A)
Stock with customers on hire-purchase price (opening)	1,62,000
Stock in hand at shop (opening)	3,24,000
Instalments overdue (opening)	1,35,000
Purchases during the year	10,80,000
Goods repossessed (instalments not due A 36,000)	9,000
Stock at shop excluding repossessed goods (closing)	3,60,000
Cash received during the year	10,35,000
Installments overdue (closing)	1,62,000

The vendor spent A 2,000 on goods repossessed and then sold it for A 15,000. [*C.A. November, 2008*]

Solution

Hire Purchase Trading Account

Particulars	(A)	*Particulars*	(A)
To Opening balance :		By Cash received (Instalments)	10,35,000
Hire Purchase Debtors	1,35,000	By Stock reserve (opening) (W.N. 2)	54,000
Hire Purchase Stock (Instalments overdue)	1,62,000	By Goods sold on hire purchase (loading) (W.N. 1)	5,22,000
To Goods sold on hire purchase (W.N. 1)	15,66,000	By Cash received (on sale of re-possessed goods)	15,000
To Cash	2,000	By Closing balance :	
To Stock reserve (closing) (W.N. 5)	2,10,000	Hire Purchase Stock (Inst. Overdue) (W.N. 4)	6,30,000
To Profit and loss account	3,43,000	Hire Purchase Debtors	1,62,000
	24,18,000		24,18,000

Working Notes **:**

(i) ***Memorandum Stock at Shop Account***

Particulars	(A)	*Particulars*	(A)
To Balance b/d	3,24,000	By Goods sold on hire purchase account (at cost)	10,44,000
To Purchase (at cost)	10,80,000	By Balance c/d	3,60,000
	14,04,000		14,04,000

Goods sold on hire purchase account (at invoice price) 10,44,000 × 150% = A 15,66,000

Loading = A 15,66,000 – A 10,44,000 A 5,22,000

2. Opening Stock reserve : $\frac{1,62,000}{150} \times 50$ = A 54,000

3. Hire Purchase Debtors Account

Particulars	*(A)*	*Particulars*	*(A)*
To Balance b/d	1,35,000	By Cash received	10,35,000
To Goods sold on hire purchase	15,66,000	By Hire purchase stock account (Bal. Fig.)	5,04,000
		By Balance c/d	1,62,000
	17,01,000		17,01,000

4. Hire Purchase Stock Account

Particulars	*(A)*	*Particulars*	*(A)*
To Balance b/d	1,62,000	By Goods repossessed (instalments not due)	36,000
To Hire Purchase Debtors A/c (W.N. 3)	5,04,000	By Balance c/d (Bal. Fig.)	6,30,000
	6,66,000		6,66,000

5. Closing stock reserve : $\frac{6,30,000}{150} \times 50$ = A 2,10,000.

Example 29

NR and Sons sells goods on hire purchases at cost plus 33 1/3 percent. Prepare hire purchase Trading Account from the following information :

		(A)
April 1, 2010	Stock with customers on hire purchase price	97,200
	Stock in hand at shop	1,94,400
	Instalments overdue	81,000
March 31, 2011	Purchase during the year	6,48,000
	Goods repossessed (Instalment not due A 21,600)	5,400
	Stock at shop (excluding repossessed)	2,16,000
	Cash received during the year	6,21,000
	Instalment overdue	97,200

[*I.C.W.A., Intermediate, June 2011*]

Solution

Hire Purchase Trading Account for the Year Ending 31 March, 2011

Date	*Particulars*	*Amount (A)*	*Date*	*Particulars*	*Amount (A)*
1.4.10	To stock with Customers at cost A 97200 × $\frac{100}{133\frac{1}{3}}$	72,900	31.3.11	By goods repossessed	5,400
	To installment over due	81,000		By Cash Received on due Installment	6,21,000

31.3.11	To goods sold on hire purchase at cost	6,26,400	By Installment overdue	97,200
	To profit and loss A/c	1,48,500	By stock with customers at cost price	
			A 273600 × $\frac{100}{133\frac{1}{3}}$	205,200
		928,800		9,28,800

Working Notes :

(*i*) *Goods sold on hire purchase*

	A
Stock at shop on 1.4.10 :	1,94,400
Add : Purchases during 2010-11 :	6,48,000
	8,42,400
Less : Stock at shop on 31.03.11	2,16,000
Goods sold on hire purchase :	6,26,400

(*ii*) Stock with customers on 31.3.2011

On 1.4.10 stock with customers at hire purchase :	97,200
On 1.4.10 installment overdue	81,000
2010-11 goods sold on hire purchase at H.P. Price 6, 26, 400 $\frac{133\frac{1}{3}}{100}$	8,35,200
	10,13,400
Less : Goods repossessed (Installment not due) :	21,600
Cash received :	6,21,000
Installment over due (31.3.11)	97,200
	7,39,800
Stock with customers at Hire Purchase Price on 31.3.11 (10,13,400 – 7,39,800)	2,73,600

Example 30

P sells goods at hire-purchase basis, the price being cost plus 50%. From the following calculate profit by preparing Ledger Accounts on Stock and Debtors system for the year ended 31st March, 2004 :

		(A)
1st April, 2003	Stock at the shop at cost	36,000
1st April, 2003	Stock out with H.P. customers at selling price	18,000
1st April, 2003	H.P. Debtors	10,000
31st March, 2004	Cash received from customers	1,20,000
31st March, 2004	Goods repossessed (A 4,000) valued at	1,200
31st March, 2004	H.P. Debtors at the end of the year	18,000
31st March, 2004	Stock at the shop at the end of the year, at cost	40,000
31st March, 2004	Stock out with H.P. customers at selling price	60,000
31st March, 2004	Purchases made during the year	1,20,000

[*B.Com.* (*Hons.*), *Delhi University, 2005*]

Solution

Stock at the Shop Account (at cost)

Particulars	*(A)*	*Particulars*	*(A)*
To Balance b/d	36,000	By Goods Sold on H.P. A/c	1,16,000
To Purchases A/c	1,20,000	By Balance c/d	40,000
	1,56,000		1,56,000

Hire Purchase Stock Account (HPP)
or
Stock out with H.P. Customers' Account

Particulars	*(A)*	*Particulars*	*(A)*
To Balance b/d	18,000	By Hire Purchase Debtors A/c	1,32,000
To Goods sold on H.P. A/c		(*Bal. Fig.*)	
(A 1,16,000 × $\frac{150}{100}$)	1,74,000	By Balance c/d	60,000
	1,92,000		1,92,000

Hire Purchase Debtors Account

Particulars	*(A)*	*Particulars*	*(A)*
To Balance b/d	10,000	By Cash	1,20,000
To H.P. Stock A/c	1,32,000	By Goods Repossessed	4,000
		By Balance c/d	18,000
	1,42,000		1,42,000

Hire Purchase Adjustment Account

Particulars	*(A)*	*Particulars*	*(A)*
To Goods Repossessed A/c		By Stock Reserve A/c	6,000
(Loss on repossession of goods)	2,800	(A 18,000 × $\frac{50}{150}$)	
To Stock Reserve A/c (A 60,000 × $\frac{50}{150}$)	20,000	By Goods sold on H.P. A/c (Loading)	58,000
To Profit and Loss A/c	41,200	(A 1,74,000 × $\frac{50}{150}$)	
	64,000		64,000

Example 31

Bharat Traders sell various items on Hire-purchase basis at cost plus 50%. Prepare Hire-Purchase Trading Account from the following particular and find out the profit for the year ended 31st March 1999:

1st April 1998 :	*(A)*
Stock out with customer	4,500

Stock at shop at cost	9,000
Instalments Due	2,500
31st March, 1999 :	
Cash received from customers	30,000
Goods Re-possessed (Instalments due A 1,000) valued at	250
Instalments due, customers still paying	4,500
Stock at shop at cost (excluding re-possessed goods)	10,000
Goods purchased during the year	30,000

[*B.Com. (Hons.)*, Delhi University, 2005]

Solution

(A) Calculation of Missing Figures

Stock at Shop Account

Particulars	*(A)*	*Particulars*	*(A)*
To Balance b/d	9,000	By Stock with Customers A/c	29,000
To Purchases	30,000	(Goods sold during the year) (*Bal. Fig.*)	
		By Balance c/d	10,000
	39,000		39,000

Stock with the Customer Account (Instalment Not Due Account)

Particulars	*(A)*	*Particulars*	*(A)*
To Balance b/d	4,500	By Instalment Due A/c	33,000
To Stock at Shop A/c	43,500	(Instalment due during the year)	
Goods sold during the year : A (29,000 + 50%)		By Balance c/d (missing figure)	15,000
	48,000		48,000

Instalment Due Account

Particulars	*(A)*	*Particulars*	*(A)*
To Balance b/d	2,500	By Cash A/c	30,000
To Stock with Customers A/c (*Bal. Fig.*)	33,000	By Goods Repossessed A/c	1,000
		By Balance c/d	4,500
	35,500		35,500

(B) Calculation of Profit or Loss. Missing figure is stock with customers = A 15,000. This figure will be utilised in preparing the Hire Purchase Trading A/c for calculating Profit or Loss.

Hire Purchase Trading Account
for the year ending 31st March, 1999

Particulars	(A)	Particulars	(A)
To Opening Balances :		By Cash A/c	30,000
Stock out with customer	4,500	By Good Repossessed A/c	250
Instalments due	2,500	By Good sold on Hire Purchase (Loading)	14,500
To Goods Sold on Hire Purchase	43,500		
To Stock Reserve (Loading in Closing Stock) ($\frac{1}{3}$ of A 15,000)	5,000	By Stock Reserve (Loading on Opening Stock) ($\frac{1}{3}$ of A 4,500)	1,500
To Profit and Loss A/c (Profit)	10,250	By closing balance :	
		Stock with customers	15,000
		Instalment Due	4,500
	65,750		65,750

Note : Profit on hire purchase can also be ascertained by preparing Hire Purchase Adjustment Account.

Hire Purchase Adjustment Account

Particulars	(A)	Particulars	(A)
To Stock Reserve (Loading on Closing Stock((15,000 × $\frac{1}{3}$)	5,000	By Goods sold on Hire Purchase (Loading)	14,500
To Loss on Goods Repossessed (A 1,000 – A 250)	750	By Stock Reserve (Loading on Opening Stock) (4,500 × $\frac{1}{3}$)	1,500
To Profit transferred to Profit and Loss Account (Profit)	10,250		
	16,000		16,000

Example 32

Deepak sells goods on hire purchase at cost + 60%. From the following particulars for the year ending on 31.12.2006, prepare :

(*i*) Hire Purchase Debtors Account;

(*ii*) Hire Purchase Stock Account;

(*iii*) Shop Stock Account; and

(*iv*) Hire Purchase Adjustment Account.

		(A)
1.1.2006	Stock with hire purchase customers at selling Price	12,000
1.1.2006	Stock at the shop at cost	5,000
1.1.2006	Instalments overdue	8,000

31.12.2006	Stock at the shop at cost (including goods repossessed A 400)	2,000
	Total instalments that fell due during the year	1,89,440
	Cash received from customers (including down payment of A 15,440)	1,75,440
	Goods repossessed (instalment due A 500)	400
	Purchases during the year	1,20,000
	Hire expenses	3,400

[*B.Com., (Hons.), Delhi University, 2007*]

Solution

Hire Purchase Debtors Account

Particulars	(*A*)	*Particulars*	(*A*)
To Balance b/d	8,000	By Cash A/c	1,75,440
To Hire Purchase Stock A/c	1,89,440	By Goods Repossessed	500
		By Balance c/d (*Bal. Fig.*)	21,500
	1,97,440		1,97,440

Hire Purchase Stock Account (at HPP)

Particulars	(*A*)	*Particulars*	(*A*)
To Balance b/d	12,000	By Hire Purchase Debtors A/c	1,89,440
To Goods sold on Hire Purchase A/c (A 1,23,400 × 160/100)	1,97,440	By Balance c/d (*Bal. Fig.*)	20,000
	2,09,440		2,09,440

Stock at Shop Account (at Cost)

Particulars	(*A*)	*Particulars*	(*A*)
To Balance b/d	5,000	By Goods sold on Hire Purchase A/c (*Bal. Fig.*)	1,23,400
To Purchases A/c	1,20,000	By Balance c/d A (2,000 – 400) (Excluding goods repossessed)	1,600
	1,25,000		1,25,000

Hire Purchase Adjustment Account

Particulars	(*A*)	*Particulars*	(*A*)
To Goods Repossessed A/c (Loss on repossession of goods : A 500 – 400)	100	By Stock Reserve A/c [A 12,000 × 60/160]	4,500
To Hire Expenses A/c	3,400	By Goods sold on Hire Purchase A/c (A 1,97,440 × 60/160)	74,040
To Stock Reserve A/c (A 20,000 × 60/160)	7,500		
To Profit and Loss A/c (Profit)	67,540		
	78,540		78,540

Example 33

Jain and Co. have a hire-purchase department. Goods are sold on hire-purchase at cost plus 33 1/3 %. From the following particulars prepare Shop Stock A/c, H.P. Debtors A/c, H.P. Stock A/c and H.P. Adjustment A/c :

	(A)
1.4.04	
Stock out with H.P. customers at S.P.	4,000
Stock at shop at cost	500
Instalments due	300
1.4.04 to 31.3.05	
Cash received from customers	8,000
Goods repossessed (instalments due A 2,000) valued at (this has been included at the end at A 500)	500
31.3.05	
Instalments due (customers paying)	500
Stock at shop at cost (including goods repossessed)	1,200
Stock out with H.P. customers at S.P.	4,600

Verify your results by preparing Hire Purchase Trading A/c.

[*B.Com.*, (*Hons.*), *Delhi University, 2008*]

Solution

Shop Stock Account

Particulars	(*A*)	*Particulars*	(*A*)
To Balance b/d	500	By Cost of Goods sold A/c*	8,100
To Purchases (*Bal. Fig.*)	8,300	[A 10,800 × $^{3}/_{4}$]	
		By Balance c/d A (1,200 – 500)	700
	8,800		8,800

*Balancing figure of Hire Purchase Stock A/c A 10,800.

Hire Purchase (H.P.) Debtors Account

Particulars	(*A*)	*Particulars*	(*A*)
To Balance b/d	300	By Cash	8,000
To H.P. Stock A/c (*Bal. Fig.*)	10,200	By Repossessed Stock	500
		By H.P. Adjustment A/c	1,500
		By Balance c/d	500
	10,500		10,500

Hire Purchase (H.P.) Stock Account

Particulars	(*A*)	*Particulars*	(*A*)
To Balance b/d	4,000	By Hire Purchase Debtors A/c	10,200
To Goods Sold on H.P. (*Bal. Fig.*)	10,800	By Balance c/d	4,600
	14,800		14,800

Hire Purchase (H.P.) Adjustment Account

Particulars	(A)	Particulars	(A)
To Stock Reserve (Closing Stock) [A. 4,600 × $^1/_4$]	1,150	By Stock Reserve (Opening Stock) [A 4,000 × $^1/_4$]	1,000
To H.P. Debtors A/c	1,500		
To Profit and Loss A/c (Profit)	1,050	By Goods sold on H.P. Stock [A 10,800 × $^1/_4$]	2,700
	3,700		3,700

Hire Purchase Trading Account

Particulars	(A)	Particulars	(A)
To H.P. Stock A/c	4,000	By Cash A/c	8,000
To Instalment Due	300	By Repossessed Stock	500
To Goods sold on H.P. A/c	10,800	By H.P. Stock A/c	4,600
To Stock Reserve*3 [A 4,600 × $^1/_4$]	1,150	By Instalment Due	500
		By Stock Reserve*4 [A 4,000 × $^1/_4$]	1,000
To Profit and Loss A/c (Profit)	1,050		
		By Goods sold on H.P. A/c*2 [A 10,800 × $^1/_4$]	2,700
	17,300		17,300

Working Notes :

*1 Goods are sold at a profit of $33^1/_3$% on cost. It means, if the cost is A 100, then profit is A 33.33 and Hire Purchase Price = A 100 + A 33.33 = A 133.33.
Therefore, loading on Hire Purchase Price = 33.33/133.33 = $^1/_4$.

*2. Loading on goods sold on Hire Purchase = $^1/_4$ of A 10,800 = A 2,700.

*3. Loading on Closing Balance of HIre Purchase Stock = $^1/_4$ of A 4,600 = A 1,150.

*4. Loading on Opening Balance of Hire Purchase Stock = $^1/_4$ of A 4,000 = A 1,000.

Example 34

X sells goods on hire-purchase basis also. He fixes hire-purchase price by adding 50% to the cost of goods to him. The following are the figure relating to the hire-purchase business for the year 2010 :

Balance on Hire-purchase Stock Account on 1st January, 2010	1,20,000
Balance on Hire-purchase Debtors Account on 1st January, 2010	3,000
Selling price of the goods sold on hire-purchase basis during the year	9,06,000
Cash received from customers	9,24,000
Total amount of instalments that fell due during the year 2010	9,27,000

One customer to whom goods had been sold for A 12,000 paid only three instalments of A 1,000 each. On his failure to pay the monthly instalment of A 1,000 due on 4th December 2010, the goods were repossessed on 27.12.2010 after legal notice. Prepare Hire-purchase Trading Account for the year ended 31.12.2010. Also verify your answer by preparing Hire-purchase Adjustment Account.

[*B.Com.* (*Hons.*), *Delhi University, 2011*]

Solution

Calculation of Missing Figures

H.D. Stock A/c (Instalment Not Due A/c)

Particulars	*(A)*	*Particulars*	*(A)*
To Balance b/d	1,20,000	By instalment due A/c	9,27,000
To Goods sold on H.P.	9,06,000	By Goods Repossessed	8,000
		By Balance c/d (*bal. fig*)	91,000
	10,26,000		10,26,000

Instalments Due A/c

Particulars	*(A)*	*Particulars*	*(A)*
To Balance b/d	3000	By Cash received	9,24,000
To H.P. Stock A/c	9,27,000	By Goods Repossessed	1,000
		By Balance c/d	5,000
	9,30,000		9,30,000

H.P. Trading Account

Particulars	*(A)*	*Particulars*	*(A)*
To Stock with H.P. customers	1,20,000	By Cash received	9,24,000
To Instalments Due	3000	By Goods Repossessed	9,000
To Goods sold on H.P.	9,06,000	By Stock Reserve	40,000
To Stock Reserve	30,333	By GSOHP (Loading)	3,02,000
To Profit Tr. to P&L	3,11,667	By Stock with HPC	91,000
		By Installment Due	5,000
	13,71,000		13,71,000

H.P. Adjustment A/c

Particulars	*(A)*	*Particulars*	*(A)*
To Stock Reserve	30,333	By St. Reserve	40,000
To Profit Tr. to P and L	3,11,667	By GSOHP (Loading)	3,02,000
	3,42,000		3,42,000

Example 35

Varun sells goods on hire purchase basis also. He fixes hire purchase price by adding 50% to the cost of goods sold. The following are the figures relating to his hire purchase business for the year 2009-2010.

	(A)
Balance of Hire Purchase Stock Account as on 1st April, 2009	84,000
Balance of Hire Purchase Debtors Account as on 1st April, 2009	2,100
Selling Price of goods sold on hire purchase basis during the year	6,34,200
Cash received from customers during the year	6,46,800
Total amount of installments that fell due during the year	6,48,900

One customer to whom goods had been sold for A 8,400 paid only 5 instalments of A 700 each. On his failure to pay the monthly instalment of A 700 due on 4th March, 2010 the goods were repossessed on 27th March, 2010 after due legal notice.

Prepare ledger accounts on Stock and Debtors Systems for the year ended 31st March, 2010.

[*I.C.W.A., Intermediate, June 2010*]

Solution

In the Books of Varun

Hire Purchase Stock Account

Particulars	(*A*)	*Particulars*	(*A*)
To Balance b/d	84,000	By Hire Purchase Debtor A/c	
To Goods Sold on Hire Purchase Account	6,34,200	– Instalments falling due	6,48,900
		By Goods Repossessed A/c – Six instalments on goods repossessed	4,200
		By Balance c/d	65,100
	7,18,200		7,18,200
To Balance b/d	65,100		

Hire Purchase Debtors Account

Particulars	(*A*)	*Particulars*	(*A*)
To Balance b/d	2,100	By Bank (Instalments received)	6,46,800
To Hire Purchase Stock A/c (Instalments falling due)	6,48,900	By Goods Repossessed A/c (Instalment due but not received)	700
		By Balance c/d	3,500
	6,51,000		6,51,000

Goods Sold on Hire Purchase Account

Particulars	(*A*)	*Particulars*	(*A*)
To Hire Purchase Adjustment Account – Loading	2,11,400	By Hire Purchase Stock Account	6,34,200
To Trading Account – Transfer	4,22,800		
	6,34,200		6,34,200

Hire Purchase Adjustment Account

Particulars	(*A*)	*Particulars*	(*A*)
To Hire Purchase Stock Reserve Account	21,700	By Hire Pur. Stock Res. A/c	28,000
To Profit and Loss Account (Transfer of Profit)	2,17,700	By Goods sold on Hire Purchase Account	2,11,400
	2,39,400		2,39,400

Hire Purchase Stock Reserve

Particulars	*(A)*	*Particulars*	*(A)*
To Hire Purchase – Adjustment Account–Transfer	28,000	By Balance b/d	28,000
To Balance c/d	21,700	By Hire Purchase Adjustment A/c	21,700
	49,700		49,700
		By Balance b/d	21,700

***Working Notes*:**

(*i*) Opening Balance of the Hire Purchase Stock Reserve

$$= \frac{50}{150} \times A\ 84{,}000 = A\ 28{,}000$$

(*ii*) Loading on goods sold on Hire Purchase

$$= \frac{50}{150} \times A\ 6{,}34{,}200 = A\ 2{,}11{,}400$$

(*iii*) Closing balance of Hire Purchase Stock Reserve

$$= \frac{50}{150} \times A\ 65{,}100 = A\ 21{,}700$$

LEASE

A business firm, while deciding to procure fixed assets, can use any of the following choices to use the asset :

(*i*) by purchasing the fixed asset whether with owned or loaned funds;
(*ii*) by purchasing fixed asset on instalment basis;
(*iii*) by purchasing on hire purchase basis;
(*iv*) by getting the asset on lease.

The business firm becomes the owner of the asset immediately in first two cases. It becomes the owner of the asset in the third case on payment of the last instalment. However, it does not become the owner in the fourth case. It merely gets the right to use the asset.

The lease is an agreement whereby the lessor transfer to the lessee, in return for rent, the right to use an asset for an agreed period of time. Lessor is a person, who under an arrangement, provides to another person, the lessee, the right to use an asset for an agreed period of time in return for rent. As per the agreement, the lessor remains the owner of the leased goods whereas lessee, for all practical purposes, is the user of the asset. However, the substance of the leasing agreement is that lessee for all practical purposes, uses the assets and acts like owner.

TYPES OF LEASE

The AS 19 titled 'Leases' issued by the Institute of Chartered Accountant of India mentions two types of leases :

1. Finance Lease
2. Operating Lease

FINANCE LEASE

A finance lease is that lease which transfers, substantially, all the risks and rewards incidental to the ownership of an asset. The title (ownership) of the asset may or may not be transferred. Generally, the finance lease is for a term equivalent to the useful economic life of the asset and is non-revocable.

The following are the features of finance lease.

(*i*) The lessor transfers the title to the lessee at the end of the lease period at the price agreed at the beginning of the lease.

(*ii*) The lessee has the option to buy the asset at the end of the lease period.

(*iii*) The lease cannot normally be cancelled.

(*iv*) The full cost of the asset will generally be repaid by the lessee to the lessor.

(*v*) Lessee is responsible for insurance and maintenance of the asset.

(*vi*) Lessee has the right of uninterrupted use of the asset till lease payments are made.

(*vii*) At the end of the lease term the lessor can take back the possession of the asset from the lessee or there can be a purchase/renewal option.

OPERATING LEASE

Operating lease is renewed a number of times during the economic life of an asset. Lease period is generally lower than the economic life of the asset. In operating lease, the risk and rewards incidental to the ownership of the asset remain with the lessor. Usually the asset is taken back by the lessor at the end of the lease and is again leased to another party or to the same party for another term. The rental payable under an operating lease is charged to the Profit and Loss Account.

Whether a lease is a finance lease or an operating lease depends on the substance of the transactions rather than its form. AS 19 identifies certain circumstances that would normally lead to a lease being classified as finance lease. The circumstances are :

(*a*) When the lease transfers ownership of the asset to the lessee by the end of the lease term.

(*b*) When the lessee has the option to purchase the asset at a price which is expected to be sufficiently lower than the fair value of the asset at the date, when such option is to be exercised.

(*c*) The lease term is for the major part of economic life of the asset even if title is not transferred.

(*d*) When at the inception of the lease the present value of the minimum lease payments amount to at least substantially the fair value of the leased asset; and

(*e*) When the leased asset is of a specialized nature and only the lessee can use it without the major modifications being made.

The AS 19 goes further to give indicators of the situations, which individually or in combination could lead to a lease being classified as a finance lease. Such situations include the following :

(*a*) If the lessee can cancel the lease, the lessor's losses associated with the cancellation are borne by the lessee;

(*b*) The lessee can continue the lease for a second period at a rent, which is substantially lower than the market rent.

Difference between Finance Lease and Operating Lease

The following are the differences between finance lease and operating lease.

Finance Lease	*Operating Lease*

1. In finance lease, the lease period is normally related to the useful life of the asset.	1. An operating lease is normally of a smaller duration and has no relation to the economic life of the asset.
2. The lessee has to bear the risk in a finance lease.	2. The lessee is protected against the risk of obsolescence in an operating lease.
3. A finance lease is normally non-revocable.	3. An operating lease can be revoked.
4. Lessee normally bears the expenses relating to the leased asset.	4. Under an operating lease, the cost of maintenance, repairs, taxes, insurance, etc. are borne by lessor.
5. In a Finance lease, the lease rentals would cover the leasor's original investment cost plus a reasonable return on the investment.	5. Under an Operating lease, the lease rentals are generally not sufficient to fully cover the cost of the asset.

ASSIGNMENT MATERIAL

Note : The Objective Type Questions (True/False, Multiple Choice Questions etc.) have been given in the Appendix at the end of the book.

SHORT-ANSWER THEORY QUESTIONS

1. Briefly explain Hire Purchase and Instalment System.
2. Explain briefly Hire Purchase System.
3. What is the meaning of the following terms?
   (*i*) Hire Vendor
   (*ii*) Hirer
   (*iii*) Hire Purchase Price
4. Distinguish between Hire Purchase System and Instalment System.
5. What are different methods of recording Hire Purchase transactions.
6. Explain full Cash Price of accounting for hire purchase transactions.
7. Explain accrual method of accounting for hire purchase transactions.
8. Distinguish between operating lease and financial lease. [*B.Com. (Hons.) Delhi University, 2006*]
9. Distinguish between hire purchase and instalment purchase system. [*B.Com. (Hons.) Delhi University, 2007, 2010, 2011*]
10. What is mean by good repossessed? How are they treated in books. [*B.Com. (Hons.) Delhi University, 2007*]

LONG-ANSWER THEORY QUESTIONS

1. What is hire purchase system? Who is hire purchaser and hire vendor?
2. Distinguish between Hire Purchase System and Instalment System.
3. Explain the procedure of calculating interest in hire purchase transactions.
4. Discuss fully cash price method of accounting for hire purchase. What journal entries are made in this method?
5. Explain accrual method of accounting for hire purchase. What journal entries are made in this method?
6. Explain the nature of Hire Purchasing Trading Account and Hire Purchase Adjustment Account.

PRACTICAL PROBLEMS

1. A purchased a truck on hire purchase system. The cash price of the truck was A 74,500. He paid A 20,000 on signing of the agreement and rest in three annual instalments of A 20,000 each. Calculate interest for each year. [***Ans.*** **:** Interest I A 2,750' II A 1,833; III A 917]

2. From the following particulars calculate :

   (*i*) Value of plant taken back by the vendor.

   (*ii*) Value of plant left with the purchaser.

   (*iii*) Profit or loss on plant taken back.

   (*iv*) Profit or loss on plant repossessed when sold by vendor.

   Particulars :

   (*i*) *X* purchased 3 plants from *Y* costing A 1,00,000 each.

   (*ii*) Purchaser charged depreciation @ 20% on dimishing balance method.

   (*iii*) 2 plants were seized by the vendor when second instalment was not paid at the end of second year and vendor valued the plants at cost less 30% depreciation annually charged at dimishing balance method.

   (*iv*) The vendor spent A 40,000 on overhauling the plants and sold for A 1,60,000.

3. *X* purchased a Truck on hire-purchase system. The total cash price of truck is A 31,960, payable A 8,000 down and three instalments of A 12,000, A 10,000 and A 4,000 payable at the end of the first, second and third year respectively. Interest is charged at 5% p.a. Charge depreciation at 10% on straight line method. Prepare ledger accounts in the books of *X*.

   [***Ans.*** **:** Interest : I-A 1,198; II-A 658; III-A 184.

4. Nice Roadways purchased from Harish Motors 3 tempos costing A 1,00,000 each on hire purchase basis on 1st April, 2006. 20% of the cost was to be paid down and balance in three equal annual instalments together with interest @ 9% at the end of each year. Nice Roadways paid the instalment due on 31st March, 2007, but could not pay instalments thereafter. Harish Motors agreed to leave one tempo with the purchaser on 31st march, 2008, adjusting the value of the other two tempos against the amount due on that date. The tempos recovered were valued on the basis of 30% depreciation annually. Nice Roadways charges depreciation on tempo @ 20% on diminishing balances method.

   Harish Motors incurred A 10,000 on repairs of tempos repossessed and resold them at a profit of 5% on total cost.

   Prepare the important ledger accounts in the books of both parties giving effect to the above mentioned transactions. [*CS(F) Dec. 2004*]

   [***Ans.*** **:** Profit on goods reposed A 4,500]

5. On 1st April, 2006, Turant Transport Ltd., acquired 3 trucks at the cash sale price of A 9,00,000 each on hire purchase from Hind Motors Ltd. The terms include cash down of A 5,40,000 and payment of the residue in two equal annual instalments together with interest at 9% per annum at the end of the year. First year dues were paid, but Turant Transport Ltd., could not pay the next instalment. Turant Transport Ltd., wrote off depreciation @ 20% annually on diminishing balance. Hind Motors Ltd., however, agreed to leave one truck with hire purchaser and adjust the value of two other trucks against the outstanding amount due. The trucks were valued on the basis of 30% annual depreciation on their written down value.

   Show important ledger accounts in the books of both parties assuming that the acquired trucks were sold on 30th April, 2008 for A 9,75,000 after incurring repair expenses of A 68,000. Both the companies close their books of account on 31st March every year. [*CS(F), Dec. 2005*]

   [***Ans.*** **:** Profit on goods repossed A 25,000].

6. A company purchased two machines of A 10,500 each on Hire Purchase System paying A 6,000 down and remainder in three equal installments of A 5,000 each together with interest at 5% p.a. The company writes off Depreciation at 10% p.a., according to Dinishing Balance method. The company could not pay the second instalment. The vendor left one machine with the company adjusting the value of the other against amount due taking the machine at 20% depreciation at Dinishing Balance method. Prepare ledger accounts in the company's books.

   [***Ans. :*** Balance in Hire Purchase A/c A 8,505].

7. Deepak purchased seven trucks on hire purchase on 1 July, 2006. The cash price of each truck was A 50,000. He was to pay 20% of the cash price at the time of delivery and balance in five half yearly instalments starting from 31.12.2006 with interest at 10% per annum.

   On Deepak's failure to pay the instalment due on 30th June, 2007, it was agreed that Deepak would return 3 trucks to the vendor and remaining 4 could be retained by him. The returning price of 3 trucks was A 40,500. Deepak charges depreciation @ 20% per annum.

   Vendor after spending A 1,000 on repairs sold away all the three Trucks for A 40,000.

   Show Trucks Account and Vendor's Account in the books of Deepak and Deepak's Account and Goods Repossessed Account in the books of the vendor assuming that their books are closed on June 30 every year.

   [***Ans. :*** Interest : I-A 14,000; II-A 11,200; Value of the Trucks Repossessed A 40,500; Value of Trucks Retained A 1,60,000; Loss on Repossession A 79,500; Balance in Deepak Account A 1,94,700]

8. *X* purchased a machine from *Y* for A 5,60,000 payment to be made A 1,50,000 down and three instalments of A 1,50,000 each at the end of each year. *X* depreciates asset at 10% p.a., on written down value method. Because of financial difficulties, *X* having paid down payment and first instalment at the end of first year, could not pay second instalment and the seller took possession of the asset. Prepare machine account and Vendor's account in the books of *X*. Also give purchaser's account in the books of *Y*. [***Ans. :*** Machine on hire purchase A/c (profit) A 1,60,267]

9. On 1 January, 1991 Ashok acquired a machinery on hire-purchase system from Real Aids Ltd., agreeing to pay four annual instalment of A 6,000 each payable at the end of each year. There is no down payment. Interest is charged @ 20% per annum and is included in the annual instalments. Because of financial difficulties, Ashok, after having paid the first and second instalments respectively, could not pay the third yearly instalment due on 31 December, 1993, whereupon the vendor repossessed the machinery. Ashok provides depreciation on the Machinery @ 10% per annum according to the written down value method. Show the machinery Account and the account of Real Aids Ltd., in the books of Ashok. All working should form part of your answer.

   [***Ans. :*** Profit in Machinery on Hire Purchase A/c A 324].

10. X company Ltd. purchased from Y Company Ltd. 3 Machines costing A 1,50,000 each on the hire-purchase system on 1.1.2007. Payment was to be as A 90,000 down and remainder in 3 equal annual instalments payable on 31.12.2007, 31.12.2008 and 31.12.2009 together with interest at 9%. X Company writes of depreciation at the rate of 20% on the reducing balance. X Company paid the instalment due at the end of first year, i.e. on 31.12.2007 but could not pay the next i.e., on 31.12.2008. Y Company agreed to leave one machine with the purchaser on 1.1.2009 adjusting the value of the other two machines against the amount due on 1.1.2009. The machines were valued on the basis of 30% depreciation annually on W.D.V. basis. Y Company spent A 15,000 on the repairs of the two repossessed machines and sold one machines for A 1,20,000 on 1.7.2009. Show Machine Account and Y Company's Account in the books of X Company Ltd. and Machines Repossessed Account in the books of Y Company Ltd. [*B. Com. (Hons.), Delhi University 2000*]

    [***Ans. :*** Profit on repossession A 39,000]

11. On 1 October, 2006, five trucks were purchased by Kartar on the hire purchase system. The cash price of each truck was A 5,50,000. The payment was to be made as follows :

- 10% of cash price at the time of delivery.
- 25% of cash price at the end of each one of the subsequent four half-years.

The payment due on 30 September, 2007 could not be made and, hence, trucks were seized by the hire vendor but after negotiations, Kartar was allowed to keep three trucks on the condition that the value of the other two trucks would be adjusted against the amount due, the trucks being valued at cost less 25% depreciation and Kartar would pay the balance in five half-yearly instalments together with interest @ 10% per annum. Both the parties close their books of account on 31 March every year. Kartar charges 15% depreciation on trucks on the original cost.

In October, 2007, the hire vendor spent A 60,000 on getting the seized trucks thoroughly overhauled and sold them for A 9,50,000.

Prepare for two accounting year ended 31 March, 2008 :

(*i*) Trucks Account in Kartar's ledger assuming that Kartar debited it with full cash price in the beginning of the contract; and

(*ii*) The personal account of Kartar and Goods Repossessed Account in hire vendor's ledger.

[*C.S.* (*Foundation*) *June 2001*]

[***Ans.*** **:** Profit in Repossessed A/C A 65,000.]

12. Delhi Corporation has a hire-purchase department. Goods are sold on hire-purchase at cost plus 25% From the following particulars, prepare the ledger accounts by stock and debtors method :

	(A)
Stock with hire-purchase customers at selling price on 1.4.2007	15,000
Instalments due (customers paying) on 1.4.2007	1,800
Sales on hire-purchase basis during the year ended 31.3.2008 at selling price	96,500
Cash received during the year	98,300
Goods repossessed (instalment due A 2,000) valued at	1,700
Instalments due (customers still paying) on 31.3.2008	1,100

[*C.S.* (*Foundation*)]

[***Ans.*** **:** Profit A 19,620]

13. XYZ Ltd. has a hire purchase department. Goods are sold on hire purchase at cost+40%. From the information given below, prepare Hire Purchase Trading Account in the books of XYZ Ltd. :

	(A)
1 July 2008 :	
Goods out on Hire Purchase (at H.P. Price)	21,000
During the year ended 30 June 2009 :	
Goods Sold on Hire Purchase (at H.P. Price)	1,05,000
Cash Received	70,000
Goods received back valued at (H.P. instalment unpaid A 2,800)	800
Goods with Hire Purchase Customers (at Hire Purchase Price)	45,500

[*I.C.W.A.* (*Inter*)]

[***Ans.*** **:** Profit A 21,000]

14. Amar and Company has a hire purchase department and goods are sold on hire purchase at cost plus 60%. From the following information, prepare Hire Purchase Trading Account to ascertain profit or loss made in the hire purchase department. Show your working clearly.

	(A)
1 January 2006	
Goods with H.P. Customers at H.P. Price	16,000
31 December 2006	
Goods sold on Hire Purchase during the year (at H.P. Prices)	80,000
Cash received during the year from customers	56,000
Goods received back from customers (Instalments due A 2,000), valued at	300
Goods with Hire Purchase Customers at H.P. Price	36,000

[*B.Com.* (*Hons.*) *Delhi University*]

[***Ans.*** **:** Profit A 20,800]

15. X had delivered goods to his customers on hire-purchase system at hire-purchase price A 92,000. He normally sells goods in the open market at retail price showing gross profit of 30% on that price. In order to sell goods at hire-purchase price, he adds 15% to retail price to cover enhanced risk. During the year, goods actually costing A 5,600 were returned by a customer who had paid nothing. Instalments received during the years A 36,800. Calculate :

    (*i*) Value of stock in the hands of customers.

    (*ii*) Profit to be transferred to Profit and Loss A/c on the basis of instalment received

[*B.Com.* (*Hons.*) *Delhi University 1999*]

[***Ans.*** **:** Profit A 14,400]

16. ABC Ltd. sells goods on Hire-purchase by adding 50% above cost. From the following particulars, prepare Hire-purchase Trading Account to reveal the profit for the year ended 31.3.2005:

		(A)
01.4.2004	Instalments due but not collected	10,000
01.4.2004	Stock at shop (at cost)	36,000
01.4.2004	Instalment not yet due	18,000
31.3.2005	Stock at shop	40,000
31.5.2005	Instalment due but not collected	18,000

Other details :

Total instalment became due	1,32,000
Goods purchased	1,20,000
Cash received from customers	1,21,000

Goods on which due instalments could not be collected were repossessed and valued at 30% below original cost. The vendor spent A 500 on getting goods overhauled and then sold for A 2800.

[*CA, May 2005*]

[***Ans.*** **:** Profit A 43,300]

17. Omega Corporation sells computers on hire purchase basis at cost plus 25%. Terms of sales are A 10,000 as down payment and 8 monthly instalments of A 5,000 for each computer. From the following particulars prepare Hire Purchase Trading Account for the year 2009 :

    As on 1 January, 2009 last instalment on 30 computers was outstanding as these were not due up to the end of the previous year.

    During 2009 the firm sold 240 computers. As on 31 December, 2009 the position of instalments outstanding were as under:

    Instalments due but not collected :

    2 instalments on 2 computers and last instalments on 6 computers.

    Instalments not yet due :

8 instalments on 50 computers, 6 instalments on 30 and last instalment on 20 computers. Two computers on which 6 instalments were due and one instalment not yet due on 31.12.09 had to be repossessed. Repossessed stock is valued at 50% of cost. All other instalments have been received.

[*C.A.* (*Inter*) *May 2000*]

[***Ans.*** **:** Profit A 18,00,000]

18. Neeta Limited commenced business on April 1,2008 The business is to sell VCPs and VCRs both for cash and on hire purchase basis. Information about terms is given below :

	VCPs (A)	*VCRs (A)*
Cash price	10,000	30,000
Cost	8,000	24,000
Cash down for Hire Purchase	2,000	6,000
Monthly Instalment	1,000	3,000
Number of Instalments	10	12

The company purchased goods costing A 1,00,00,000 in all and made cash sales totalling A 86,00,000. Stock in hand on 31 March 2009 was valued at A 12,00,000. Hire-purchase transaction were as follows:

	Number sold	*Instalments Collected*	*Instalments Due (customers paying)*
VCPs	20	110	10
VCRs	40	260	15

3 VCPs and 2 VCRs on which only 4 instalments were collected were repossessed and were valued at A 32,000. This is not included in the figure of stock mentioned above Prepare accounts showing the profit or loss made by the company by adopting Stock and Debtors system.

[*B.Com.* (*Hons.*) *Delhi University 1992*]

19. Videocon Ltd. sells washing machines for outright cash as well as on hire- purchase basis. The cost of a washing machine to the company is A 10,500. The company has fixed cash price of the machine at A 12,300 and hire-purchase price at A 13,500 payable as to A 1,500 down and the balance in 24 equal monthly instalments of A 500 each.

On 1 April 2006 the company had 26 washing machines lying in its showroom. On that date 3 instalments had fallen due, but not yet received and 675 instalments were yet to fall due in respect of machines lying with the hire- purchase customers.

During the year ended 31 March, 2007 the company sold 130 machines on cash basis and 80 machines on hire-purchase basis. After paying five monthly instalments, one customer failed to pay subsequent instalments and the company had to repossess the washing machine. After spending A 1,000 on it, the company resold it for A 11,500.

On 31 March, 2007 there were 21 washing machines in stock, 810 instalments were yet to fall due and 5 instalments had fallen due, but not yet received in respect of washing machines lying with the hire-purchase customers. Total selling expenses and office expenses including depreciation on fixed assets totalled A 1,60,000 for the year. You are required to prepare for the accounting year ended 31 March, 2007 :

(*i*) Hire-purchase Trading Account, and

(*ii*) Trading and Profit & Loss Account showing net profit earned by the company after making provision for Income-tax @ 35%

[*C.A.* (*Inter*) *November 2001*]

[***Ans.*** **:** Profit A 2,25,000]

20 The hire purchase department of L.G.Ltd. sells television sets and room coolers. This department was started in 2009. The relevant information for the year ended 31 December, 2009 is as follows :

	Television	*Room Cooler*
Cost	A 5,400	A 2,000
Cash price	A 6,300	A 2,400
Cash down payment	A 900	A 400
Monthly instalment	A 600	A 200
Number of instalments	10	12

During the year, 200 television sets and 240 room coolers were sold on hire purchase basis. Four television sets on which 3 instalments only could be collected and 8 room coolers on which 5 instalments had been collected were repossessed. These were valued at A 20,000; after reconditioning at a cost of A 2,000, they were sold outright for A 28,000. Other instalments collected and those due (customers still paying) were respectively as follows :

Television Sets	540	and	40
Room Coolers	800	and	60

Prepare accounts on stock and debtors system to reveal profit of the department. Show your working.

[*C.A.* (*Inter*)]

[***Ans. :*** Profit A 2,00,057]

CHAPTER 16

Branch Accounting

Learning Objectives

After studying this chapter, you should be able to :

1. *Know organizations requiring branches to operate the business.*
2. *Explain the nature of dependent branches.*
3. *Discuss the accounting treatment of branch transactions under*
   (i) *Debtor system and*
   (ii) *Stock and debtor system.*
   (iii) *Final account system*
   (iv) *Whole sale branch system*
4. *Explain nature of independent branches and accounts prepared in this case as well procedure of reconcilation and incorporation.*

Now-a-days, organizations have various options to exercise for the purpose of sale and distribution of their goods and products. These organizations aim to cover wide range of areas to reach to the maximum number of customers. In this objective, many organizations open branches in different areas with a view to avoid middlemen (whole sellers and retailers) to retain control over distribution, to keep the business secrets intact, to avoid chances of duplicate or similar product being mixed with the real one and to make customers quality conscious. The firm opening the branches is the main establishment known as head office and its subsidiary units within a city are known as Branches. Bata Shoe Co. is an example of branches in India.

From the accounting point of view, Branches can be divided into three categories–

1. Dependent Branches.
2. Independent/Autonomous Branches.
3. Foreign Branches.

DEPENDENT BRANCHES

Dependent branches are those which do not function independently like an ordinary business concern. They purely depend upon their head office. These branches get all instructions from the head office in connection with its operations or activities. Such branches sell only those goods which are supplied by the head office. The head office meets all branch expenses such as salaries, advertisement, rent etc. The branch manager is given petty cash on imprest system to meet incidental expenses. Branches send the amount direct to head office or pay into a local branch of a bank to the credit of head office account. Branches only keep some records *e.g.* stock register. However, Branches do not prepare accounts and do not maintain accounting records.

Accounting Treatment in the Books of Head Office

A head office may adopt any one of the following method of accounting to ascertain the result of branch operation.

1. Debtor System.
2. Stock and Debtor System.
3. Final Account System.
4. Wholesale Branch System.

1. DEBTOR SYSTEM

Under this method, the head office prepares a separate account of each branch on the basis of its location such as Delhi Branch, Mumbai Branch and so on. Alternatively, it may use code number for each branch on the basis of specific location for the sake of secrecy and confidential provision. In this method head office opens branch account, which is in the nature of Debtors Account. It debits the branch account with the goods sent and cash sent for expenses where as credits the branch account with the amount of cash received from branch, goods returned by branch and balances of various assets with the branch, if any. That is, why this system of accounting in known as Debtors System.

Journal Entries

The following journal entries are made to record various branch transactions in the books of head office.

(*i*) When goods are invoiced at cost

Branch A/c	Dr.
To goods sent to branch A/c	

(*ii*) When the goods are invoiced at selling price/loaded price

Branch A/c	Dr.
To Goods sent to branch the	(with total invoice price)
Goods sent to branch A/c	Dr.
To Branch A/c	(with the difference between selling price and cost price)

(*iii*) When goods are returned by branches to head office :

Goods sent to branch A/c	Dr.
To Branch A/c	

(*iv*) When goods are despatched at loaded price.

Good sent to branch A/c	Dr. (with loaded price)
To branch A/c	
Branch A/c	Dr.
To goods sent to branch A/c	(With difference between the invoice price and cost price of the goods)

(*v*) When the branch expenses are met by head office.

Branch A/c	Dr.
To Bank A/c	

(*vi*) Remittance from branches

Bank A/c	Dr.
To Branch A/c	

(*vii*) For transferring the balance of goods sent to branch account to Purchase/Trading A/c

Goods sent to branch A/c	Dr.
To Purchase A/c	
or	
To Trading A/c	

(*viii*) For recording closing balance of assets at the branch.
All assets (individually) A/c Dr.
To Branch A/c

(*ix*) For recording opening balance of assets at the branch.
Branch A/c Dr.
To All Assets (Individually)

(*x*) For recording opening liabilities
Opening liabilities (Individually) A/c Dr.
To Branch A/c

(*xi*) For recording closing liabilities :
Branch A/c Dr.
To Closing Liabilities (Individually)

(*xii*) For transferring profit :
Branch A/c Dr.
To P and L A/c

(*xiii*) For Transferring Loss
P/L A/c Dr.
To Branch A/c

Proforma of Branch Account and Branch Debtors Account are given below.

Proforma Branch Account

Dr. *Cr.*

Particulars	*Amount* *A*	*Particulars*	*Amount* *A*
Balance b/d (opening assets) (Balances of individual assets at the branch)	××	Balance b/d (opening liabilities)	××
Goods sent to branch A/c	××	Cash/Bank (remittances)	××
Cash/bank (exp)	××	Goods sent to branch (Return)	××
General P/L A/c	××	Balance c/d (closing	××
Balance c/d closing liabilities)	××	Balances of assets)	××

Branch Debtor Account

Dr. *Cr.*

Particulars	*Amount* *A*	*Particulars*	*Amount* *A*
Balance b/d (opening)	××	Cash/Bank	××
Credit Sale	××	(Collection from debtors)	
Bills Receivable Dishonored	××	Discount allowed	××
		Sales Return	××
		Bad Debts	××
		Bill Receivables	××
		Balance c/d (at the cost)	××

If goods are transferred to branch at loaded price.

In order to calculate profit at the branches, the followings adjustment entries will be made in the branch account.

(*i*) For adjustment of profit margin contained in the opening stock

Stock Reserve A/c Dr.

To Branch A/c

(*ii*) For Adjustment of profit margin in the goods sent to branch

Goods sent to branch A/c Dr.

To Branch A/c

Branch A/c (Impact of Loaded Item)

Dr. *Cr.*

Particulars	*Amount* A	*Particulars*	*Amount* A
Opening stock (Load)	××	Stock Reserve A/c	××
Goods sent to branch (loaded price)	××	(margin in opening stock)	
Stock Reserve A/c	××	Good sent to branch	××
(Profit margin)		(Margin in the goods sent to branch) Stock at the end (loading)	××

Example 1

Widespread Ltd. invoices goods to its branch at cost plus 20%. The branch sells goods for cash as well as on credit. The branch meets its expenses out of cash collected from its debtors and cash sales and remits the balance of cash to head office after withholding A 10,000 necessary for meeting immediate requirements of cash. On 31st March, 2005 the assets at the branch were as follow :

	A
Cash in Hand	10,000
Trade Debtors	3,84,000
Stock at invoice price	10,80,000
Furniture and Fittings	5,00,000

During the accounting year ended 31st March, 2006, the invoice price of goods despatched by the head office to the branch amounted to A 1,32,00,000. Out of the goods received by it, the branch sent back to head office goods invoiced at A 72,000. Other transactions at the branch during the year were as follows :

	A
Cash Sales	97,00,000
Credit sales	31,40,000
Cash collected by branch from credit customers	28,42,000
Cash discount allowed to debtors	58,000
Returns by customers	1,02,000
Bad debts written off	37,000
Expenses paid by branch	8,42,000

On 1st January, 2006 the branch purchased new furniture for A 1,00,000 for which payments were made by head office by means of a cheque.

On 31st March, 2006 branch expenses amounting A 6,000 were outstanding and cash in hand was again A 10,000. Furniture is subject to depreciation @16% p.a. on Diminishing Balances method.

Prepare Branch Account in the books of head office for the year ended 31st March, 2006.

Solution

Branch Account

Dr. *Cr.*

Particulars		*Amount* A	*Particulars*		*Amount* A
To Balance b/d			By Balance b/d		
Cash	10,000		Stock Reserve A/c		
Debtors	3,84,000		[A 10,80,000 × $^{20}/_{120}$]		1,80,000
Stock	10,80,000		By Goods sent to Branch		
Furniture	5,00,000	19,74,000	A/c (Loading)		
To Goods sent to Branch A/c		1,32,00,000	[A 1,32,00,000 × $^{20}/_{120}$]		22,00,000
To Goods sent to Branch A/c		12,000	By Branch Cash A/c :		
(Loading) [A 72,000 × $^{20}/_{12}$]			Cash Sales	97,00,000	
To Bank A/c (Furniture)		1,00,000	Cash Received	28,42,000	
To Stock Reserve A/c			from Debtors	1,25,42,000	
[$^{20}/_{120}$ × A 14,70,000]		2,45,000	*Less :* Expenses	8,42,000	1,17,00,000
To Outstanding Expenses		6,000	By Goods sent to Branch A/c		72,000
To Profit and Loss A/c (Profit)		10,96,000	By Balance c/d :		
			Stock (Note 1)	14,70,000	
			Debtors (Note 2)	4,85,000	
			Cash	10,000	
			Furniture (Note 3)	5,16,000	24,81,000
		1,66,33,000			1,66,33,000

Working Notes

1. In order to verify whether there was a Closing Stock at the branch, we should prepare Branch Stock Account as under :

Branch Stock Account

Dr. *Cr.*

Particulars	*Amount* A	*Particulars*	*Amount* A
To Balance b/d	10,80,000	By Goods sent to Branch A/c	72,000
To Goods Sent to Branch A/c	1,32,00,000	By Branch Cash A/c	97,00,000
To Branch Debtors A/c	1,02,000	By Branch Debtors A/c	31,40,000
		By Balance c/d (*Bal. Fig.*)	14,70,000
	1,43,82,000		1,43,82,000

Branch Debtors Account

Dr. *Cr.*

Particulars	*Amount* A	*Particulars*	*Amount* A
To Balance b/d	3,84,000	By Cash A/c	28,42,000
To Sales A/c	31,40,000	By Discount A/c	58,000
		By Bad Debts A/c	37,000
		By Sales Return A/c	1,02,000
		By Balance c/d	4,85,000
	35,24,000		35,24,000

		A
Furniture (31.3.2005)		5,00,000
Add : Purchases (1.1.2006)		1,00,000
6,00,000		
Less : Depreciation	A	
I A 5,00,000 × $^{16}/_{100}$	80,000	
II A 1,00,000 × $^{16}/_{100}$ × $^{3}/_{12}$	4,000	84,000
		5,16,000

Example 2

Modern Shoe Stores had an old established branch at Chandigarh. Goods are invoiced to the branch at 20% profit on sales, the branch having been instructed to send all cash daily to the head office. All expenses are paid by the head office except petty expenses which are met by the branch manager. From the following particulars, you are required to draw up branch account as it would appear in the books of the Head Office, *i.e.*, Modern Shoe Stores :

	A
Stock on January 1, 2006 (Invoice Price)	15,000
Sundry debts on Jan. 1,2006	9,000
Cash in hand on Jan. 1, 2006	400
Office furniture on Jan. 1,2006	1,200
Goods supplied by the Head Office (Invoice price)	80,000
Goods returned to Head Office	1,000
Goods Returned by Debtors	480
Cash received from Debtors	30,000
Cash Sales	50,000
Credit Sales	30,000
Discount Allowed	300
Expenses paid by the Head Office :	

Rent		1,200
Salary		2,400
Stationery and Printing	300	3,900
Petty expenses paid by the Branch Manager		280
Provide depreciation on furniture @10% p.a.		
Rent outstanding		500
Stock on 31.12.2006 (Invoice price)		14,000

Solution

In the Books of Modern Shoe Stores
Chandigarh Branch Account

Dr. *Cr.*

Particulars		*Amount* A	*Particulars*		*Amount* A
To Balance b/d			By Bank A/c		
Stock	15,000		Cash Sales	50,000	
Sundry Debtors	9,000		Cash Received from		
Furniture	1,200		Debtors	30,000	80,000
Petty Cash	400	25,600	By Goods Sent to Branch A/c		1,000
To Goods Sent to Branch A/c		80,000	(Returns from Branch)		
To Goods Sent to Branch A/c		200	By Goods Sent to Branch A/c		16,000
(Loading on goods returned)			(Loading) [A 80,000 × 20/100]		
[A 1,000 × 20/100]			By Balance c/d :		
To Bank A/c :			Stock	14,000	
Rent	1,200		Debtors (Note-1)	8,220	
Salary	2,400		Furniture (Note-2)	1,080	
Stationery and Printing	300	3,900	Petty cash (400-280)	120	23,420
To Stock Reserve A/c			By Stock Reserve A/c		
(Loading on closing stock)		2,800	(Load on opening stock)		3,000
[A 14,000 × 20/100]			[A 15,000 × 20/100]		
To Rent outstanding		500			
To Profit and Loss A/c (profit)		10,420			
		1,23,420			1,23,420

Working Notes

1. Debtors at the end are calculated as under :

Branch Debtors Account

Dr. *Cr.*

Particulars	*Amount* A	*Particulars*	*Amount* A
To Balance b/d	9,000	By Cash A/c	30,000
To Sales (Credit)	30,000	By Sales Return (2)	480
		By Discount A/c (3)	300
		by Balance c/d (*Bal. Fig.*)	8,220
	39,000		39,000

2. Depreciation on furniture is not debited as a separate item in the branch account. Instead furniture at the end is shown at the depreciated value.
3. Similarly, sales returns and discount are automatically incorporated when we write opening debtors and debtors at the end in the branch account.
4.

Goods Sent to Branch Account

Dr. *Cr.*

Particulars	*Amount* A	*Particulars*	*Amount* A
To Balance A/c (Load)	16,000	By Branch A/c	80,000
To Branch A/c		By Branch A/c (Load)	200
(Returns from Branch)	1,000		
To Purchases A/c	63,200		
(Balance Figure)			
	80,200		80,200

Example 3

A trader has its branch at Mumbai to which goods are invoiced at cost plus 20%. Prepare Branch Account in the books of the head office after taking into consideration the following information also.

	A
Opening stock at branch	72,000
Cash sales at branch	52,500
Credit sales at branch	1,23,000
Collections from branch debtors	1,13,700
Goods received from head office	90,000
Branch expenses :	
Paid by head office	9,000
Paid by branch	18,000
Expenses unpaid	4,200

Closing stock at branch	54,000
Closing balance of branch debtors	27,480
Goods sent from head office to branch remaining in transit on closing day.	10,800

Solution

Branch Account

Dr. *Cr.*

Particulars	*Amount* A	*Particulars*	*Amount* A
To Balance b/d		By Stock Reserve A/c	12,000
Branch Stock	72,000	[A 72,000 × 20/120]	
Branch Debtors	18,180	By Goods sent to Branch	
To Goods sent to Branch A/c		A/c [A 1,00,800 × 20/120]	16,800
[90,000 + 10,800]	1,00,800	By Cash A/c (Remittance)	1,48,200
To Cash/Bank A/c		By Balance c/d :	
(exp. paid by H.O.)	9,000	Branch Stock	64,800
To Balance c/d :		[A 54,000 + 10,800]	
Expenses outstanding	4,200	Branch Debtors	27,480
Branch Stock Reserve			
[64,800 × 20/120]	10,800		
To Profit and Loss A/c (Net Profit)	54,300		
	2,69,280		2,69,280

Working Notes

1. **Branch Debtors Account**

Dr. *Cr.*

Particulars	*Amount* A	*Particulars*	*Amount* A
To Balance b/d (*Bal. Fig.*)	18,180	By Cash A/c	1,13,700
To Sales A/c (Credit)	1,23,000	By Balance c/d	27,480
	1,41,180		1,41,180

2. **Branch Cash Account**

Dr. *Cr.*

Particulars	*Amount* A	*Particulars*	*Amount* A
To Balance b/d	Nil	By Expenses A/c	18,000
To Sales (Cash)	52,500	By H.O. A/c (*Bal. Fig.*)	1,48,200
To Debtors A/c	1,13,700	(Remittance)	
	1,66,200		1,66,200

Example 4

From the details given below relating to Patna branch for the year ending March 31, 2006, prepare Branch Account and Branch Debtors Account in the books of Head Office. Show your workings clearly. Goods are invoiced to give a profit of 20% on selling price : 10

		A
Stock on 1.4.2005		5,000
Debtors on 1.4.2005		2,000
Furniture on 1.4.2005		1,000
Petty cash on 1.4.2005		200
Insurance prepaid on 1.4.2005		50
Salaries due on 1.4.2005		1,000
Goods sent to branch		40,000
Cash sales		55,000
Total sales		70,000
Cash received from debtors		16,000
Goods returned by the branch		500
Goods returned by the debtors		200
Cash sent to the branch :	A	
Rent	3,600	
Salaries	10,200	
Petty cash	600	
Insurance (upto June 2006)	400	14,800
Petty cash expenses incurred by the branch		500
Stock on 31.3.2006		3,000
Depreciate furniture by 20%		

Solution

Patna Branch Account

Dr. *Cr.*

Particulars		*Amount* A	*Particulars*		*Amount* A
To Balance b/d			By Balance b/d :		
			Outstanding Salaries		1,000
Stock	5,000		By Stock Reserve [5,000 × 20/100]		1,000
Debtors	2,000		By Goods sent to Branch A/c [40,000 × 20/100]		8,000
Furniture	1,000				
Petty Cash	200		By Goods sent to Branch A/c		
Prepaid Insurance	50	8,250	(Returns to H.O.)		500
To Goods sent to Branch A/c		40,000	By Cash (Remittance) :		
			Cash Sales	55,000	

To Cash A/c (Expenses) :			Received from Debtors	16,000	71,000
Rent	3,600		By Balance c/d :		
Salaries	10,200		Stock	3,000	
Petty Cash	600		Debtors	800	
Insurance	400	14,800	Petty Cash		
To Stock Reserve			(200 + 600 – 500)	300	
(3,000 × 20/100)		600	Furniture (1,000 – 200)	800	
To Goods sent to Branch		100	Prepaid Insurance		
(Load) (500 × 20/100)			(1.4.06 to 30.6.06)	100	
To Profit and Loss A/c (Profit)		22,750	(400 × 1/4)		5,000
		86,500			86,500

Patna Branch Debtors' Account

Dr. *Cr.*

Particulars	*Amount* A	*Particulars*	*Amount* A
To Balance b/d	2,000	By Cash A/c	16,000
To Sales A/c (Credit)	15,000	By Sales Return A/c	200
[Total sales–Cash sales]		By Balance c/d	800
	17,000		17,000

Petty Cash Account

Dr. *Cr.*

Particulars	*Amount* A	*Particulars*	*Amount* A
To Balance b/d	200	By Petty Expenses	500
To H.O.	600	By Balance c/d	300
	800		800

Examples 5

From the following details relating to Agra branch for the year ending on 31.3.2006, prepare Branch Account in the books of Head Office :

Receipts	*A*	*Payments*	*A*
Opening Stock	25,000	Cash received from debtors	65,000
Opening Debtors	10,000	Cash paid by debtors directly	
Opening Furniture	6,000	to H.O.	5,000
Opening Petty Cash	1,000	Closing Stock	15,000
Opening Prepaid Insurance	300	Goods returned by branch	2,000
Opening Salaries Outstanding	4,000	Goods returned by debtors	1,000
Goods sent to branch	2,00,000	*Cash Sent to branch for*	
Cash Sales during the year	2,70,000	*expenses :*	

Total Sales	3,50,000	Rent (A 800 p.m.)	9,600
Petty Cash Expenses	2,200	Salary (A 4,000 p.m.)	48,000
Discount allowed to Debtors	500	Petty Cash	2,000
		Insurance (upto June 2006)	1,200

Goods costing A 2,500 were damaged in transit and a sum of A 2,000 was recovered from the insurance company in full settlement of the claim. Depreciate Furniture @10% p.a. The Branch Manager is entitled to a commission of 5% of profit at branch after charging such commission.

Solution

In the Books of Head Office
Agra Branch Account

Dr. *Cr.*

Date	*Particulars*	A	*Date*	*Particulars*	A
1.4.05	To Balance b/d :		1.4.05	By Balance b/d :	
	Stock	25,000	1.4.05	Outstanding Salaries	4,000
	Debtors	10,000	to	By Bank A/c :	
	Petty Cash	1,000	31.3.06	Cash Sales	2,70,000
	Furniture	6,000		Collection from Debtors	65,000
	Prepaid Insurance	300		Cash Paid by Debtors	
				directly to H.O.	5,000
1.4.05	To Goods sent to			Amount Received from	
to	Branch A/c	2,00,000		Insurance Company	2,000
31.3.06	To Bank A/c :			By goods sent to	
	Rent	9,600		Branch A/c	2,000
	Salary	48,000		(Returns to H.O.)	
	Petty Cash	2,000		By Balance c/d :	
	Insurance	1,200		Stock	15,000
31.3.06	To Balance c/d :			Debtors (Note-1)	18,500
	Outstanding Salaries	4,000		Petty Cash (Note-2)	800
		3,07,100		Furniture (6,000 – 600)	5,400
	To Branch Manager's			Prepaid Insurance	300
	Commission			(1,200 × 1/4)	
	5/105 [3,88,000				
	– 3,07,100]	3,852			
	To Net Profit t/f to				
	General				
	Profit and Loss A/c	77,048			
		3,88,000			3,88,000

Working Notes

1. Calculation of closing balance of Debtors

Memorandum Branch Debtors Account

Dr. *Cr.*

Particulars	*Amount* A	*Particulars*	*Amount* A
To Balance b/d	10,000	By Cash Received from	
To Sales (Credit)	80,000	Debtors by the Branch	65,000
[3,50,000 – 2,70,000]		By Cash received from	
		Debtors by the H.O.	5,000
		By Return Inward	1,000
		By Discount Allowed	500
		By Balance c/d (*Bal. Fig.*)	18,500
	90,000		90,000

2. Calculation of Closing Balance of Petty Cash

Memorandum Branch Petty Cash Account

Dr. *Cr.*

Particulars	*Amount* A	*Particulars*	*Amount* A
To Balance b/d	1,000	By Petty Expenses	2,200
To Remittance from H.O.	2,000	By Balance c/d	800
	3,000		3,000

3. Calculation of Outstanding Salaries

Memorandum Salaries Account

Dr. *Cr.*

Particulars	*Amount* A	*Particulars*	*Amount* A
To Bank A/c (4,000 + 44,000)	48,000	By Outstanding Salaries	4,000
To Outstanding Salaries		By Current Year's Salaries	
(*Balancing Figure*)	4,000	(4,000 × 12)	48,000
	52,000		52,000

Example 6

Pawan and Co. of Delhi has a branch at Jaipur. Goods are invoiced to the branch at cost plus 25%. The branch is instructed to deposit the receipts everyday in the head office account with the bank. All the expenses are paid through cheque by the head office except petty cash expenses which are paid by the Branch.

From the following information, you are required to prepare Branch Account in the books of head office :

	A
Stock at invoice price on 1.4.08	1,64,000
Stock at invoice price on 31.3.09	1,92,000

Debtors as on 1.4.08	63,400
Debtors as on 31.3.09	84,300
Furniture and fixtures as on 1.4.08	46,800
Cash sales	8,02,600
Credit sales	7,44,200
Goods invoiced to branch by head office	12,56,000
Expenses paid by head office	2,64,000
Petty expenses paid by the branch	20,900
Furniture acquired by the branch on 1.10.08 (payment was made by the branch from cash sales and collection from debtors)	5,000

Depreciation to be provided on branch furniture and fixtures @10% p.a. on WDV basis.

[*C.A. November, 2009*]

Solution

In the Books of Pawan and Co., Delhi (Head Office)
Jaipur Branch Account

Dr. *Cr.*

Particulars	*Amount* A	*Particulars*	*Amount* A
To Opening balances :		By Branch stock reserve	32,800
Branch stock A/c	1,64,000	By A/c (W.N. 4)	15,00,000
Branch debtors A/c	63,400	By Goods sent to branch A/c	2,51,200
Branch furniture A/c	46,800	(Loading)	
To Goods sent to branch	12,56,000	By Closing Balances :	
To Bank A/c (branch expenses)	2,64,000	Branch Stock A/c	1,92,000
To Branch stock reserve A/c	38,400	Branch debtors A/c	84,300
To Profit and loss A/c (*Bal. Fig.*)	2,74,570	Branch furniture A/c (W.N. 2)	46,870
	21,07,170		21,07,170

Working Notes

1. Depreciation on Furniture

	A
10% p.a. on A 46,800	4,680
10% p.a. for 6 months on A 5,000	250
	4,930

2. Closing balance of branch furniture as on 31.3.2009

	A
Branch furniture as on 1.4.2008	46,800
Add : Acquired during the year	5,000
	51,800
Less : Depreciation (W.N.1)	4,930
Branch furniture as on 31.3.2009	46,870

3. Collection from branch debtors

Receipts	A	*Payments*	A
To Balance b/d	63,400	By Bank A/c (*Bal. Fig.*)	7,23,300
To Sales	7,44,200	By Balance c/d	84,300
	8,07,600		8,07,600

4. Cash remitted by the branch to head office

   Cash sales + Collection from debtors – Petty expenses – Furniture acquired by branch.

   A 8,02,600 + A 7,23,300 – A 20,900 – A 5,000 = A 15,00,000.

Example 7

Johnson and Co. had a branch at Calcutta. Goods are invoiced to the branch at cost *plus* 25%. Branch is instructed to deposit cash everyday in the head office account with the bank. All expenses are paid by cheques by the head office except petty cash expenses which are paid by the branch manager. From the following particulars, prepare branch account in the books of head office :

	A
Stock on 1 April 2011	2,500
Stock on 31 March, 2012	3,000
Sundry debtors on 1 April, 2011	1,400
Sundry debtors on 31 March, 2012	1,800
Cash sales for the year	10,800
Credit sales for the year	7,000
Cash remitted to the head office	15,000
Furniture purchased by the branch manager	1,200
Goods invoiced from the head office	18,200
Expenses paid by the head office	1,640
Expenses paid by the branch	120

[*C.S.* (*Foundation*)]

Solution

Calcutta Branch Account

Dr. *Cr.*

Particulars		*Amount* A	*Particulars*		*Amount* A
Balance b/d			Stock Reserve Account		500
Stock	2,500		Goods Sent to Branch		
Debtors	1,400	3,900	Account (Load)		3,640
Goods Sent to Branch			Bank Account (Remittance)		15,000
Account		18,200	Balance c/d		
Bank Account (Expenses)		1,640	Stock	3,000	

		Debtors	1,800	
Stock Reserve Account	600	Furniture	1,200	
Profit and Loss Account	1,880	Cash	1,080	7,080
	26,220			26,220

Calcutta Branch Debtors Account

Dr. *Cr.*

Particulars	*Amount* A	*Particulars*	*Amount* A
To Balance b/d	1,400	Cash Account	6,600
Sales	7,000	Balance c/d	1,800
	8,400		8,400

Calcutta Branch Cash Account

Dr. *Cr.*

Particulars	*Amount* A	*Particulars*	*Amount* A
Sales	10,800	Remittance	15,000
Debtors	6,600	Furniture	1,200
		Petty Expenses	120
		Balance c/d	1,080
	17,400		17,400

Example 8

X Ltd. with its Head Office in Delhi, invoiced goods to its Chandigarh branch at 20% less than the catalogue price which is cost plus 50%, with instructions that cash sales were to be made at invoice price and credit sales at catalogue price. From the following particulars available from the branch, prepare Branch Account for the year ended 31st December, 2008 :

	A
Stock on 1.1.2008 at I.P.	48,000
Goods received from H.Q. at invoice price	5,28,000
Debtors on 1.1.2008	40,000
Cash sales	1,84,000
Credit sales	4,00,000
Cash received from customers	3,42,540
Discount allowed to customers	53,460
Branch Expenses	25,000
Remittance to Head Office	4,80,000
Debtors on 31.12.2008	44,000
Cash in hand on 31.12.2008	23,000
Closing Stock on 31.12.2008	60,000

It was reported that a part of stock at the branch was lost by fire during the year whose value is to be ascertained. It is decided to provide for discount on debtors @15%.

[*B.Com., (Hons.), Delhi University, 2009*]

Solution

Chandigarh Branch Account

Particulars		*(A)*	*Particulars*		*(A)*
To Balance b/d			By Cash A/c		
Stock	48,000		(Remittance to H.O.)		4,80,000
Debtors	40,000		By Stock Reserve A/c		8,000
Cash[*1]	1,460	89,460	[48,000 × 20/120]		
To Goods sent to Branch A/c		5,28,000	By Goods Sent to Branch A/c		88,000
To Provision for Discount on Debtors		6,600	[5,28,000 × 20/120]		
(15% of A 44,000)			By Balance c/d		
To Stock Reserve A/c			Stock	60,000	
[60,000 × 20/120]		10,000	Debtors	44,000	
To Profit and Loss A/c Profit		68,940	Cash	23,000	1,27,000
		7,03,000			7,03,000

Working Notes :

Chandigarh Branch Account

Particulars	*(A)*	*Particulars*	*(A)*
By Balance b/d (*Bal. Fig.*)[*1]	1,460	By H.O. A/c	4,80,000
To Sales A/c	1,84,000	By Branch Exp. A/c	25,000
To Debtors	3,42,540	By Balance c/d	23,000
	5,28,000		5,28,000

Example 9

X Co. Ltd. Mumbai invoices goods to its Delhi Branch at cost plus 25%. All expenses of the branch are met by Head Office and cash collected by the branch is sent to Head Office. From the following information, prepare Branch Account and Goods sent to Branch A/c in the books of Head Office :

	A
Branch Stock at invoice price on 1.1.09	20,000
Branch Debtors on 1.1.09	25,000
Branch Furniture on 1.1.09	40,000
Petty Cash on 1.1.09	3,000
Salary due for December, 2008	4,000
Goods sent to branch during the year (including goods in transit)	2,00,000
Goods returned by Branch to Head Office	5,000
Goods returned by customers to Branch	4,000

Loss of goods in transit at I.P. (not insured)		10,000
Cash Sales		70,000
Cash received from customers		90,000
Goods spoiled at I.P. (normal)		4,000
Bad Debts		1,000
Discount allowed		2,000
Petty expenses incurred by Branch		2,000
Cheque received from Head Office for :	A	
Salaries @ A 4,000 p.m.	48,000	
Rent	10,000	
Petty Cash	3,000	
Delivery Van	50,000	1,11,000
Branch Debtors on 31.12.09		30,000
Branch Stock on 31.12.09		?
Depreciate furniture and delivery van @ 10%.		

[*B.Com. (Hon.), Delhi University 2010*]

Solution

In the Books of Head Office
Branch Account

Particulars		*(A)*	*Particulars*		*(A)*
To Balance b/d :			By Balance b/d :		
Stock		20,000	Salary due		4,000
Debtors		25,000	By Goods Sent to Branch A/c		5,000
Furniture		40,000	(Goods returned by Branch)		
Petty Cash		3,000	By Goods Sent to Branch A/c		40,000
To Goods Sent to Branch A/c		2,00,000	[Loading : A $2,00,000 \times \frac{25}{125}$]		
To Bank A/c (Expenses) :			By Stock Reserve (Loading)		4,000
Salaries	48,000		[A $2,00,000 \times \frac{25}{125}$]		
Rent	10,000		By Bank A/c (Remittances) :		
Petty Cash	3,000		Cash Sales	70,000	
Delivery Van	50,000	1,11,000	Cash received from customers	90,000	1,60,000
To Goods Sent to Branch (Loading)		1,000	By Balance c/d :		
[A $5,000 \times \frac{25}{125}$]			Delivery Van		45,000
To Stock Reserve (Loading)		6,600	Debtors		30,000
[A $33,000 \times \frac{25}{125}$]			Stock[*1]		33,000

To Balance c/d :		Furniture [A 40,000 – A 4,000]	36,000
Outstanding Salary	4,000	Petty Cash	4,000
		[A 3,000 + A 3,000 – A 2,000]	
		By Net Loss transferred to	
		General Profit and Loss A/c	49,600
	4,10,600		4,10,600

Goods Sent to Branch Account

Particulars	(*A*)	*Particulars*	(*A*)
To Branch Stock A/c	5,000	By Branch Stock A/c	2,00,000
To Branch Adjustment A/c	39,000		
(Loading) (Net)			
[A 1,95,000 × $\frac{25}{125}$]			
To Purchases A/c	1,56,000		
	2,00,000		2,00,000

Working Notes :

Branch Stock Account (IP)

Particulars	(*A*)	*Particulars*	(*A*)
To Balance b/d	20,000	By Goods Sent to Branch A/c	5,000
To Goods Sent to Branch	2,00,000	(Return by branch)	
To Sales Return	4,000	By Loss of Goods in transit	10,000
		By Cash Sales	70,000
		By Branch Debtors A/c (Cr. Sales)	1,02,000
		By Branch Adjustment A/c	4,000
		(Normal loss)	
		By Balance c/d (*Bal. Fig.*)	33,000
	2,24,000		2,24,000

Branch Debtors Account

Particulars	(*A*)	*Particulars*	(*A*)
To Balance b/d	25,000	By Sales Return	4,000
To Credit Sales (*Bal. Fig.*)	1,02,000	By Cash A/c	90,000
		By Bad Debts	1,000
		By Discount Allowed	2,000
		By Balance c/d	30,000
	1,27,000		1,27,000

Example 10

A Head Office invoices goods to its Branch at 20% profit on sale. Major expenses are paid by Head Office and petty expenses are paid by the Branch. Prepare Branch A/c from the following particulars to ascertain profit or loss of the Branch :

Branch Stock on (1.1.2000)	15,000
Petty Cash (1.1.2000)	300
Debtors (1.1.2000)	8,500
Furniture (1.1.2000)	2,000
Cash Sales	56,000
Total Sales	88,000
Cash from debtors	28,500
Goods supplied to Branch	80,000
Discount allowed	250
Petty Expenses	360
Goods returned by Branch to H.O.	1,000
Salary o/s on 31.12.2000	400
Expenses of Branch paid by H.O. :	
(*i*) Rent	2,400
(*ii*) Salary	4,200
Furniture sent by H.O.	1,600
Stock with Branch on 31.12.2000	2,000
Sale of old furniture by Branch on 1.7.2000 (Book value of sold away furniture on the date of sale A 950)	900

Write off Furniture @10% per annum on the opening balance.

[*B.Com., (Hons.), Delhi University, 2005*]

Solution

In the Books of Head Office
Branch Account for the Year Ending 31 Dec. 2000

Particulars	(*A*)	*Particulars*		(*A*)
To Opening Balance of Assets :		By Stock Reserve (20/100 × 15,000)		3,000
Stock	15,000	By Bank A/c (Remittance) :		
Petty Cash	300	Cash Sales	56,000	
Debtors	8,500	Cash from debtors	28,500	
Furniture	2,000	Sale of Furniture[*2]	900	
To Goods supplied to Branch A/c	80,000		85,400	
To Bank A/c (Expenses)	6,600	*Less :* Petty Expenses	360	85,040
To Furniture (sent by Head Office)	1,600	By Goods Returned by Branch		1,000
To Goods Returned by Branch (Loading) (20/100 × 1,000)	200	By Goods Supplied to Branch A/c (Loading) (20/100 × 80,000)		16,000

To Stock Reserve (Closing) (Loading)		By Closing Balance of Assets :	
(2,000 × 20/100)	400	Stock	2,000
To Outstanding Salaries	400	Debtors*[1]	11,750
To Net Profit transferred to General		Furniture*[3]	2,500
Profit and Loss A/c	6,590	Petty Cash	300
	1,21,590		1,21,590

Working Notes :

Branch Debtors A/c*[1]

Particulars	*(A)*	*Particulars*	*(A)*
To Balance b/d	8,500	By Discount	250
To Sales (Credit)		By Cash A/c	28,500
(A 88,000 – A 56,000)	32,000	By Balance c/d	11,750
	40,500		40,500

*2 Sale proceeds of furniture A 900 also will be remitted to H.O.

*3 The balance of Furniture A/c on 31.12.2000 has been found as follows :

Furniture Account

Date	*Particulars*	*Amount (A)*	*Date*	*Particulars*	*Amount (A)*
1.1.2000	To Balance b/d	2,000	1.7.2000	By Bank A/c	900
	To Furniture Sent by H.O.	1,600		(Sale of Furniture)	
				By Dep. on Furniture sold for 6 months	
				(A 1000 × $\frac{10}{100}$ $\frac{1}{2}$)	50
				By Profit and Loss A/c	50
				(Loss on sale of Furniture)	
				By Depreciation A/c	100
				By Balance c/d	2,500
		3,600			3,600

(*a*) The furniture having book value of A 950 on 1.7.2000 was of the cost of A 1000 on 1.1.2000 = $\left(950 \times \frac{100}{95} = A\ 1,000\right)$

(*b*) Loss on Sale of Furniture = A 950 – A 900 = A 50.

Example 11

Head Office of a company invoices goods to its Chandigarh Branch at cost plus 20%. The Branch purchases goods from local parties also for which payments are made by the Head Office. All cash collected by the Branch is banked on the same day to the credit of the Head Office and all expenses are paid directly by the Head Office except for a petty cash account maintained by the Branch for which periodic transfers are made from the Head Office.

From the following particulars, show Branch Account as maintained by Head Office showing the profit for the year ended 31st March, 2003 :

	(A)
Imprest cash :	
on 1.4.2002	2,000
on 31.3.2003	1,850
Debtors on 1.4.2002	25,000
Stock on 1.4.2002	
(*i*) Transferred from H.O, at Invoice Price	24,000
(*ii*) Direct purchases made by Branch	16,000
Cash sales	45,000
Credit sales	1,30,000
Direct purchases made by Branch	45,000
Goods returned by customers	3,000
Goods sent to Branch from H.O. at invoice price	60,000
Cash transferred from H.O. to Branch for petty cash expenses	2,500
Bad debt	1,000
Discount allowed to customers	2,000
Cash received from customers	1,25,000
Branch Expenses	30,000
Stock on 31.3.2003 :	
(*i*) Transferred from H.O. at Invoice Price	18,000
(*ii*) Direct purchases made by Branch	12,000

[*B.Com.,* (*Hons.*), *Delhi University, 2005*]

Solution

Head Office Books
Chandigarh Branch Account

Particulars		(*A*)	*Particulars*		(*A*)
1.4.02			1.4.02		
To Balance b/d :			By Stock Reserve A/c		
Stock :			(Load on Opening Stock)		
Head Office Goods	24,000		$(\frac{20}{120} \times$ A 24,000)		4,000
Purchased Goods	16,000	40,000	31.3.03		
			By Bank (remittance received)		
Debtors		25,000	Cash Sales	45,000	
Imprest Cash		2,000	Collection from Debtors	1,25,000	1,70,000

Particulars			Particulars		
31.3.03					
To Bank (Payment for direct purchases)		45,000	By Goods sent to Branch A/c (Load on goods sent)		
To Goods sent to Branch A/c		60,000	$(\frac{20}{120} \times$ A 60,000)		10,000
To Bank A/c (remittance for) :			By Balance c/d :		
Petty Cash	2,500		Stock :		
Expenses	30,000	32,500	Head Office Goods	18,000	
To Stock Reserve A/c			Purchased Goods	12,000	30,000
(Load on Closing Stock)			Debtor*1		24,000
$(\frac{20}{120} \times$ A 18,000)		3,000	Imprest Cash		1,850
To Profit and Loss A/c (branch profit transferred)		32,350			
		2,39,850			2,39,850

Working Notes **:**

*1 Closing balance of debtor has been ascertained by preparing Debtors A/c as under :

Hire Purchase Trading Account

Particulars	*(A)*	*Particulars*	*(A)*
To Balance b/d	25,000	By Cash (collection)	1,25,000
To Credit Sales	1,30,000	By Returns Inward	3,000
		By Bad Debts	1,000
		By Discount	2,000
		By Balance c/d	24,000
	1,55,000		1,55,000

Example 12

Hari Traders invoices goods to its branch at Delhi at cost. Goods are generally sold by the branch at a profit of 10% of cost. From the following information, prepare Branch account to find out the profit/loss of the branch and also the necessary working notes.

Opening Balances :	*(A)*
Branch Stock	5,000
Branch Debtors	7,500
Branch Furniture	4,000
Branch Salary outstanding	2,500
Transactions during the year :	*(A)*
Goods sent to Branch	50,000
Goods received by Branch	47,500
Cash sent to Branch for Expenses	12,500

Actual branch expenses (including Branch Salary outstanding)	14,500
Cash Sales	25,000
Credit Sales	30,000
Cash received from debtors	27,500
Discount	3,000
Cash sent to branch for direct purchases from local market	10,000
Cost of direct purchases	12,500
Closing Balance :	
Branch Stock	?
Branch Debtors	?
Branch Cash	250

Cash remitted by the branch to H.O. A 2,750 was not received till close of the accounting period by H.O.

Provide 10% depreciation on Furniture.

[*B.Com.*, (*Hons.*), *Delhi University, Nov., 2011*]

Solution

Working Notes :

Branch Stock A/c

Particulars	(*A*)	*Particulars*	(*A*)
To Opening Balance	5000	By Sales :	
To Goods sent to Branch	50,000	Cash	25,000
To Direct purchases	12,500	Credit	30,000
To Profit in sales	5,000	By Stock in Transit (50,000 – 47,500)	2,500
$\left(\frac{10}{110} \text{ of } 25,000 + 30,000\right)$		By Balance c/d (*bal. fig.*)	15,000
	72,500		72,500

Branch Debtors A/c

Particulars	(*A*)	*Particulars*	(*A*)
To Balance b/d	7,500	By Cash	27,500
To Sales (Credit)	30,000	By Discount	3,000
		By Balance c/d (*bal. fig.*)	7,000
	37,500		37,500

Branch Cash A/c

Particulars	(*A*)	*Particulars*	(*A*)
To Cash for exp.	12,500	By Direct Purchases	12,500
To Cash from Debtors	27,500	By Cash in Transit	2,750

To Cash for Local Purchases	10,000	By Salary o/s (paid this year)	2,500
To Cash Sales	25,000	By Expenses (Remaining) (14,500 – 2,500)	12,000
		By Remittances (*bal. fig.*)	45,000
		By Balance c/d	250
	75,000		75,000

Branch A/c

Particulars		(A)	*Particulars*	(A)
To Balance b/d :			By Balance b/d	2,500
Stock	5000		By Remittances	45,000
Debtors	7500		By Balance c/d :	
Furniture	4000	16,500	Stock	15,000
To Goods sent to Branch		50,000	Stock in Transit	2,500
To Direct Purchases		12,500	Debtors	7,000
To Cash (exp.)		12,500	Cash	250
			Cash in Transit	2,750
			Furniture (4000 – 400)	3,600
			By Profit and Loss A/c (Loss)	12,900
		91,500		91,500

Example 13

Widespread Ltd. invoices goods to its branch at cost plus 20%. The branch sells goods for cash as well as on credit. The branch meets its expenses out of cash collected from its debtors and cash sales and remits the balance of cash to head office after withholding A 10,000 necessary for meeting immediate requirements of cash. On 31st march, 2010 the assets at the branch were as follows :

	(A)('000)
Cash in hand	10
Trade Debtors	384
Stock, at Invoice Price	1,080
Furniture and Fittings	500

During the accounting year ended 31st March, 2011 the invoice price of goods dispatched by the head office to the branch amounted to A 1 crore 32 lakhs. Out of the goods received by it, the branch sent back to head office goods invoiced at A 72,000. Other transactions at the branch during the year were as follows :

	(A)('000)
Cash Sales	9,700
Credit Sales	3,140
Cash collected by Branch from Credit Customers	2,842
Cash Discount allowed to Debtors	58
Returns by Customers	102
Bad Debts written off	37
Expenses paid by Branch	842

On 1st January, 2011 the branch purchased new furniture for A 1 lakh for which payment was made by head office through a cheque.

On 31st March, 2011 branch expenses amounting to A 6,000 were outstanding and cash in hand was again A 10,000. Furniture is subject to depreciation @ 16% per annum on diminishing balance method.

Prepare Branch Account in the books of head office for the year ended 31st March, 2011.

[*C.A., May, 2011*]

Solution

In the Head Office Books
Branch Account for the Year Ended 31st March, 2011

Particulars	*(A) ('000)*	*Particulars*	*(A) ('000)*
To Balance b/d		By balance b/d	
Cash in hand	10	Stock reserve A $1,080 \times \frac{1}{6}$	180
Trade debtors	384		
Stock	1,080	Goods sent to branch A/c	72
Furniture and fittings	500	(Returns to H.O.)	
To Goods sent to branch A/c	13,200	By Goods sent to branch A/c	2,188
To Bank A/c (payment for furniture)	100	(Loading on net goods sent to branch – $13,128 \times \frac{1}{6}$	
To Balance c/d	245	By Bank A/c	
stock reserve $1,470 \times \frac{1}{6}$		(Remittance from branch to H.O.)	11,700
To Outstanding expenses	6	By Balance c/d :	
To Profit and loss A/c (net profit)	1,096	Cash in hand	10
		Trade debtors	485
		Stock	1,470
		Furniture and fittings	516
	16,621		16,621

Working Notes :

1. *Invoice price and cost* — A

	A
Let cost be	100
So, invoice price	120
Loading	20

Loading : Invoice price = 20 : 120 = 1 : 6

2. *Invoice price of closing stock in branch*

Branch Stock Account

Particulars	*(A) ('000)*	*Particulars*	*(A) ('000)*
To Balance b/d	1,080	By Goods sent to Branch	72
To Goods sent to Branch	13,200	By Branch Cash	9,700

To Branch Debtors	102	By Branch Debtors	3,140
		By Balance c/d	1,470
	14,382		14,382

3. *Closing balance of branch debtors*

Branch Debtors Account

Particulars	*(A) ('000)*	*Particulars*	*(A) ('000)*
To Balance b/d	384	By Receipt from debtors	2,842
To Branch Stock	3,140	By Branch Expenses Discount	58
		By Branch Stock (Returns)	102
		By Branch Expenses (bad debts)	37
		By Balance b/d	485
	3,524		3,524

4. *Closing balance of furniture and fittings*

Branch Furniture and Fittings Account

Particulars	*(A) ('000)*	*Particulars*	*(A) ('000)*
To Balance b/d	500	By Depreciation (80 + 4)	84
To Bank	100	By Balance c/d	516
	600		600

5. *Remittance by branch to head office*

Branch Cash Account

Particulars	*(A) ('000)*	*Particulars*	*(A) ('000)*
To Balance b/d	10	By Branch Expenses	842
To Branch Stock	9,700	By Remittances to H.O.	11,700
To Branch Debtors	2,842	By Balance b/d	10
	12,552		12,552

2. STOCK AND DEBTOR SYSTEM

Profit and loss of a branch can be found out by preparing branch account but there is another method for this purpose. This method is known as Stock and Debtor System. This system helps the head office to have a more detailed account to control the working of branch. It is generally used when the goods are sent to the branch at proforma invoice price and the size of branch is large.

The main advantages of stock and debtor system are :

(*i*) The branch maintains a few central accounts to exercise greater control over the branch stock and other related expenses.

(*ii*) It helps to overcome the disadvantages in the debtor system and provides more details about the happenings at the branch.

Under Stock and Debtor System, following accounts are maintained.

1. **Branch Stock Account :** This account helps the head office in maintaining an effective control over the branch stock and tells about shortage and surplus in the branch stock. It is always prepared at invoice price which is invariably the loaded or inflated price, *i.e.* cost plus profit margin.
2. **Branch Debtor Account :** This account is maintained in the traditional manner to record the transactions between the branch and its credit customers.
3. **Branch Expense Account :** The purpose of maintaining this account is to compile all branch expenses at one place. This will include all types of expenses, *i.e.* cash based expenses and receivables based expenses.
4. **Branch Adjustment Account :** This account is nominal account in nature and is divided into two parts; the first part is used to ascertain gross profit and second part to determine the net profit. This is the account in which all expenses and losses are closed along with the margin *i.e.* difference between cost and selling price (load).
5. **Branch Profit and Loss Account :** This account is prepared to ascertain the net profit or net loss. It is not divided into two parts. The final result in the Branch profit and loss A/c is transferred to general profit and loss A/c.
6. **Stock Reserve Account :** When stock appears at the loaded price, it becomes necessary to open this account because stock cannot be shown at loaded price in the balance sheet.
7. **Goods Sent to Branch Account :** The purpose of this account is to ascertain the cost of the goods sent to branches so that the balancing figure can be transferred to either purchases account or trading account.
8. **Branch Asset Account :** A separate account for each asset at the branch such as cash, debtor, furniture, building etc. is maintained is the books of head office.

Pro-Forma of branch stock account is as follows :

Pro-Forma Branch Stock Account
(At Invoice Price)

Dr. *Cr.*

Particulars	*Amount* A	*Particulars*	*Amount* A
Balance b/d (opening stock)	××	Branch cash account (cash sales)	××
Goods sent to branch account	××	Branch debtor account (credit sales)	××
Branch debtors account (sales returns)	××	Goods sent to branch account (Returns to H.O.)	××
Goods sent to branch Account (transfer from another branch	××	Branch Adjustment A/c (Normal loss and Abnormal loss)	××
Branch adjustment Account (surplus)	××	Balance c/d (closing stock)	××
	××		××

Accounting Treatment Under Stock and Debtor System

The following journal entries are made under stock and debtor system to record the branch transactions in the books of the head office. All goods are transferred in this system at the loaded price.

1. When goods are supplied

   Branch stock A/c Dr.

   To goods sent to branch A/c

2. When goods are returned by the branch to head office
   Goods sent to branch A/c Dr.
   To Branch stock A/c
3. When sales are made
   – For cash sale
   Branch cash A/c Dr.
   To Branch stock A/c
   – For credit sale
   Branch debtors A/c Dr.
   To Branch stock A/c
4. For bad debts, discount allowed to debtors
   Branch profit and loss A/c Dr.
   To Branch debtors A/c
5. For returns of goods by the debtor to branch
   Branch stock A/c Dr.
   To Branch Debtor A/c
6. For depreciation in fixed asset
   Branch profit and loss A/c Dr.
   To Branch fixed asset A/c
7. For loading on loss, wastage of stock
   Branch Adjustment A/c Dr.
   To Branch stock A/c
8. For loading on goods returned to Head Office
   Branch Adjustment A/c Dr.
   To Goods sent to branch A/c
9. For loading on goods supplied by Head Office
   Goods sent to branch A/c Dr.
   To branch adjustment A/c
10. For cash sent by Head Office for Expenses
    Branch Cash A/c Dr.
    To Cash A/c
11. For expenses incurred by branch
    Branch expense A/c Dr.
    To Branch cash A/c
12. When cash in received from customers
    Branch cash A/c Dr.
    To Branch debtors A/c
13. For adjustment of excess price of stock
    – Opening stock
    Stock reserve A/c Dr.
    To Branch Adjustment A/c

– Closing Stock

Branch Adjustment A/c Dr.

To Stock Reserve A/c

14. For loading on goods sent to branch

Goods sent to branch A/c Dr.

To Branch Adjustment A/c

15. Transfer of profit or loss

– In case of profit

Branch profit and loss A/c Dr.

To General P/L A/c

– In case of loss

General P/L A/c Dr.

To Branch Adjustment A/c

16. For closing the goods sent to branch A/c

Goods sent to Branch A/c Dr.

To Purchase A/c

Treatment of Surplus/Shortage of Branch Stock

If there is surplus/shortage in branch stock, the loading part will be transferred to Branch Adjustment A/c and remaining part will be transferred to branch P/L A/c.

Treatment of Abnormal Loss

(*i*) The invoice value of abnormal loss will be transferred to credit side of branch stock A/c.

(*ii*) The load on such loss is then ascertained and the same will be debited to branch adjustment account and credited to abnormal loss A/c.

(*iii*) The balance of the abnormal loss account represents the cost price of the loss and it will be transferred to the second part of the branch adjustment account or Branch P/L A/c as the case may be.

Example 14

Onkar Corporation Ltd. has two branches–one at Jaipur and another at Lucknow. Goods are invoiced to branches at cost plus 50%. Branches remit all cash received to Head Office and all expenses are met by the H.O. From the following particulars, prepare the necessary accounts on the "Stock and Debtors System" to show the profit earned at the Jaipur Branch :

	(A)
Stock on January 1, 2011	9,300
Debtors on January 1, 2011	6,800
Goods sent to Branch (at cost)	34,000
Sales at Branch	
Cash	25,010
Credit	31,000
Cash collected from Debtors	30,400
Goods returned by Branch to H.O.	1,200

Goods transferred from Lucknow Branch to Jaipur Branch	1,500
Shortage of Stock	2,100
Shortage of Stock at Branch	450
Discount allowed to customers	200
Expenses at Branch	5,400

Solution

Invoice Price = Cost price + Reserve Price
= 100 + 50
= 150

Books of Onkar Corporation Ltd (H.O.)
Jaipur Branch Stock Account

Dr. *Cr.*

Particulars	*(A)*	*Particulars*	*(A)*
To Balance b/d (IP)	9,300	By Branch A/c (Cash Sales)	25,010
To Goods sent to Branch A/c (IP)	51,000	By Branch Debtors (Credit Sales)	31,000
To Goods sent to Branch A/c*$_1$ (IP)		By Goods sent to Branch A/c (IP)	1,200
(Goods from Lucknow Branch)	1,500	By Br. Adj. A/c I (Shortage)	150
		By Br. Adj. A/c II	300
		By Balance c/d	4,140
		(*Balancing Figure*)	
	61,800		61,800

Jaipur Branch Debtors A/c

Dr. *Cr.*

Particulars	*(A)*	*Particulars*	*(A)*
To Balance b/d	6,800	By Branch A/c	30,400
To Branch Stock A/c	31,000	(Cash collected by the	
(Credit Sales)		Branch from Debtors)	
		By Discount A/c	200
		By Balance c/d	7,200
	37,800		37,800

Jaipur Branch Adjustment A/c (I)

Dr. *Cr.*

Particulars	*(A)*	*Particulars*	*(A)*
To Goods sent to Branch		By Branch Stock Reserve A/c	3,100
A/c (load)	400	(1/3) (RP)	
To Branch Stock A/c (load)	150	By goods sent to Branch A/c	17,000
To Branch Stock Reserve A/c	1,380	(RP)	
(RP of Closing Stock		By Goods sent to Branch A/c	500

Gross Profit (Tr. to Branch P and L A/c)	18,670	(RP of goods for Lucknow)	
	20,600		20,600

Jaipur Branch P and L A/c
or Jaipur Branch Adjustment A/c (II)

Dr. *Cr.*

Particulars	*(A)*	*Particulars*	*(A)*
To Branch Stock A/c :		By Gross Profit	18,670
(CP of Goods Lost)	300		
To Discount A/c	200		
Expenses			
(Paid by Branch)	5,400		
Net Profit	12,770		
	18,670		18,670

Working Notes

1. Goods received from Lucknow Branch are treated as goods received from H.O. *i.e.*, goods are routed through the H.O.
2. Shortage of Stock of A 2,100 has not been charged to the Branch. It is H.O.'s Loss.

Example 15

Agra head office supplies goods to its branch at Alwar at invoice price which is cost plus 50%. All cash received by the branch is remitted to Agra and all branch expenses are paid by the head office. From the following particulars related to Alwar branch for the year 2011 prepare Branch Debtors Account, Branch Stock Account and Branch Adjustment Account in the Books of the Head Office so as to find out the gross profit and net profit made by the branch :

		A
Stock with Branch on 1.1.2011 (at invoice price)		66,000
Branch Debtors on 1.1.2011		22,000
Petty cash balance on 1.1.2011		500
Goods received from Head Office (at invoice price)		2,04,000
Goods returned to Head Office		6,000
Credit Sales		87,000
Sales Returns		3,000
Allowance to Customer on Selling Price (already adjusted while invoicing)		2,000
Cash received from debtors		93,000
Discount allowed to debtors		2,400
Expenses (cash paid by Head Office) :		
	A	
Rent	2,400	

Salaries	24,000	
Petty Cash	2,000	28,400
Cash Sales		1,06,000
Stock with Branch on 31.12.2011 (at Invoice Price)		69,000
Petty Cash Balance on 31.12.2011		100

Solution

Agra Head Office
Alwar Branch Debtors Account

Dr. *Cr.*

Particulars	(*A*)	*Particulars*	(*A*)
To Balance b/d	22,000	By Cash A/c	93,000
To Branch Stock A/c (Credit Sales)	87,000	By Branch Stock A/c (Sales Return)	3,000
		By Branch Adjustment A/c (Discount)	2,400
		By Balance c/d	10,600
	1,09,000		1,09,000

Alwar Branch Stock Account

Dr. *Cr.*

Particulars	(*A*)	*Particulars*	(*A*)
To Balance b/d	66,000	By Goods sent to Branch A/c (Returns to H.O.)	6,000
To Goods sent to Branch A/c	2,04,000	By Branch Cash A/c (Cash Sales)	1,06,000
To Branch Debtors A/c (Sales Return)	3,000	By Branch Debtors A/c (Credit Sales)	87,000
		By Branch Adjustment A/c (Allowance)	2,000
		By Shortage (*Bal. Fig.*)	3,000
		By Balance c/d	69,000
	2,73,000		2,73,000

Alwar Branch Adjustment Account

Dr. *Cr.*

Particulars	(*A*)	*Particulars*	(*A*)
To Stock Reserve A/c	23,000	By Stock Reserve A/c [A 66,000 × 50/150]	22,000
To Goods sent to Branch A/c [A 6,000 × 50/150]	2,000	By Goods sent to Branch A/c [A 2,04,000 × 50/150]	68,000
To Branch Stock A/c	2,000		

To Shortage (Load)		1,000			
To Gross Profit c/d		62,000			
		90,000			90,000
To Branch Expenses A/c			By Gross Profit b/d		62,000
Rent	2,400				
Salaries	24,000				
Petty Expenses	2,400	28,800			
To Branch Debtors A/c [Discount]		2,400			
To Shortage (Cost)		2,000			
To Net Profit		28,800			
		62,000			62,000

Note : If allowance is taken as sales promotion expenses, it will be debited to Branch Profit and Loss Account.

Alternative Solution

Alwar Branch Adjustment Account

Dr. *Cr.*

Particulars		*(A)*	*Particulars*		*(A)*
To Balance b/d :			By Stock Reserve A/c		
Stock	66,000		[A 66,000 × 50/150]		22,000
Debtors	22,000		By Goods sent to Branch		
Petty Cash	500	88,500	A/c [A 2,04,000 × 50/150]		68,000
To Goods sent to			By Goods sent to Branch		
Branch A/c		2,04,000	A/c (Return to H.O.)		6,000
To Goods sent to Branch		2,000	By Bank A/c [Remittance]		
(Load on Goods returned			Cash Sales	1,06,000	
to H.O.)			From Debtors	93,000	1,99,000
To Cash (Expenses) A/c			By Balance c/d :		
Rent	2,400		Stock	69,000	
Salaries	24,000		Debtors	10,600	
Petty Cash	2,000	28,400	Petty Cash	100	79,700
To Stock Reserve A/c					
[A 69,000 × 50/150]		23,000			
To Net Profit transferred to					
Profit and Loss A/c		28,800			
		3,74,700			3,74,700

Example 16

VS and Co. of Hyderabad have a branch at Warangal. All purchases are made by the head office and goods sent to branch are invoiced at selling price which is 20% above cost. All sales by the branch are on credit terms. Branch expenses are paid by the H.O. and all cash received by the branch is remitted to the H.O. All branch transactions are recorded in the H.O. books. The balances relating to the branch in the H.O., books on 1.1.2006 were as follows :

Particulars	(*A*)	*Particulars*	(*A*)
Branch Stock Account (Invoice Price) on 1st Jan.	36,000	Cash received from Debtors	3,10,000
Branch Debtors Account on 1st Jan.	25,750	Discount allowed to Debtors	5,750
Goods sent to branch at Invoice Price	3,24,600	Branch expenses paid by H.O.	30,000
Returns from branch to H.O., at invoice price	6,420	Branch Stock Account (Invoice Price) on 31st Dec.	48,180
		Branch Debtors on 31st Dec.	10,000

Required : Prepare in the H.O. books (a) Branch Stock Account, (*b*) Branch Debtors Account, (*c*) Branch Expenses Account and (*d*) Branch Adjustment Account.

Solution

Warangal Branch Stock Account

Dr. *Cr.*

Particulars	(*A*)	*Particulars*	(*A*)
To Balance b/d	36,000	By Goods sent to Branch A/c	6,420
To Goods sent to Branch A/c	3,24,600	By Branch Debtors A/c	3,00,000
		By Branch P and L A/c (Cost)	5,000
		By Branch Adjustment A/c [A 6,000 × 20/120)]	1,000
		By Balance c/d	48,180
	3,60,600		3,60,600

Warangal Branch Debtors Account

Dr. *Cr.*

Particulars	(*A*)	*Particulars*	(*A*)
To Balance b/d	25,750	By Cash A/c	3,10,000
To Branch Stock A/c [Credit sales]	3,0,000	By Discount allowed	5,750
		By Balance c/d	10,000
	3,25,750		3,25,750

Warangal Branch Expenses Account

Dr. *Cr.*

Particulars	(*A*)	*Particulars*	(*A*)
To Bank A/c	30,000	By Branch Profit and Loss A/c (Transfer)	35,750
To Discount Allowed	5,750		
	35,750		35,750

Warangal Branch Adjustment Account

Dr. *Cr.*

Particulars	(A)	*Particulars*	(A)
To Branch Stock A/c [A 48, 180 × 20/120]	8,030	By Branch Stock A/c [(A 3,24,600 – 6,420) × 20/120]	53,030
To Branch Stock A/c [A 6,000 × 20/120]	1,000	By Branch Stock A/c [A 36,000 × 20/120	6,000
To Gross Profit t/f to Branch Profit and Loss A/c	50,000		
	59,030		59,030

Warangal Branch Profit and Loss Account

Dr. *Cr.*

Particulars	(A)	*Particulars*	(A)
To Branch Expenses	35,750	By Branch Adjustment A/c (Gross Profit)	50,000
To Branch Stock A/c (Shortage)	5,000		
To Net Profit t/f to General Profit and Loss A/c	9,250		
	50,000		50,000

Example 17

Mumbai Soap Mills Ltd. has two branches at Kolkata and at Chennai. Goods are invoiced to branches at cost plus 50%. From the following particulars prepare the necessary accounts on Stock and Debtors system to reveal the profit earned at the branches :

	Kolkata A	*Chennai* A
Stock on 1.4.2002 at I.P.	9,300	15,600
Debtors on 1.4.2002	6,800	8,700
Goods invoiced to Branches (Cost Price)	34,000	36,000
Cash Sales	25,010	35,000
Credit Sales	31,000	30,100
Cash collected from Debtors	30,400	29,800
Goods returned by Debtors	1,200	1,500
Goods returned by Branch to Head Office	1,500	—
Goods transferred from Chennai to Kolkata	2,100	2,100
Surplus in Stock	—	300
Shortage in Stock	450	—
Discount allowed to customers	200	350
Expenses at Branches	5,400	6,700

Solution

Ledger Accounts
Branch Stock Account)

Dr. *Cr.*

Particulars	*Kolkata* *A*	*Chennai* *A*	*Particular*	*Kolkata* *A*	*Chennai* *A*
To Balance b/d :	9,300	15,600	By Bank/Cash Sales	25,010	35,000
To Goods sent to			By Branch Debtors A/c	31,000	30,100
Branch A/c			(Credit Sales)		
(Cost Price + 50%			By Goods sent to		
= Invoice Price)	51,000	54,000	Branch A/c	1,500	—
To Branch Debtors A/c			(Returns)		
(Returns)	1,200	1,500	By Goods sent to		
To Goods sent to			Branch-Goods		
Branch A/c	2,100	—	sent to Kolkata	—	2,100
(Goods Received			By Branch Adjustment		
from Chennai)			A/c-Shortage	450	
To Branch Adjustment			By Balance c/d	5,640	4,200
A/c-Surplus	—	300			
	63,600	71,400		63,600	71,400
To Balance b/d	5,640	4,200			

Branch Debtors Account

Dr. *Cr.*

Particulars	*Kolkata* *A*	*Chennai* *A*	*Particular*	*Kolkata* *A*	*Chennai* *A*
To Balance b/d	6,800	8,700	By Bank A/c	30,400	29,800
To Branch Stock A/c	31,100	30,100	By Branch Stock A/c	1,200	1,500
(Credit Sales)			(Returns)		
			By Branch Expenses A/c	200	350
			(Discount)		
			By Balance c/d	6,000	7,150
	37,800	38,800		37,800	38,800
To Balance b/d	6,000	7,150			

Branch Expenses Account

Dr. *Cr.*

Particulars	*Kolkata* A	*Chennai* A	*Particular*	*Kolkata* A	*Chennai* A
To Branch Debtors A/c (Discount)	200	350	By Branch Adjustment A/c - Transfer	5,600	7,050
To Bank A/c	5,400	6,700			
	5,600	7,050		5,600	7,050

Goods Sent to Branch Account

Dr. *Cr.*

Particulars	*Kolkata* A	*Chennai* A	*Particular*	*Kolkata* A	*Chennai* A
To Branch Stock A/c (Despatch to Kolkata Branch)	—	2,100	By Branch Stock A/c	51,000	54,000
To Branch Stock A/c (Returns)	1,500	—	By Branch Stock A/c from Chennai Branch	2,100	
To Branch Adjustment A/c (Loading)	17,200	17,300			
To Trading A/c (Transfer)	34,400	34,600			
	53,100	54,000		53,100	54,000

Branch Stock Reserve Account

Dr. *Cr.*

Particulars	*Kolkata* A	*Chennai* A	*Particular*	*Kolkata* A	*Chennai* A
To Branch Adjustment	3,100	5,200	By Balance b/d A [9,300 × 50/150 = 3,100] A [15,600 × 50/150 = 5,200]	3,100	5,200
To Balance c/d	1,880	1,400	By Branch Adjustment A/c [5,640 × 50/150 = 1,880] [4,200 × 50/150 = 1400]	1,880	1,400
			By Balance b/d	1,880	1,400

Branch Adjustment Account

Dr. Cr.

Particulars	Kolkata A	Chennai A	Particular	Kolkata A	Chennai A
To Branch Stock A/c [–Loading on shortage A 450 × 50/150]	150	—	By Branch Stock Reserve	3,100	5,200
To Branch Stock Reserve	1,880	1,400	By Goods sent to branch A/c – Loading	17,200	17,300
To Gross Profit c/d	18,270	21,200	By Branch Stock A/c [Loading on Surplus A 300 × 50/150]	—	100
	20,300	22,600		20,300	22,600
To Branch Stock A/c [Cost of shortage A 450 – A 150]	300	—	By Gross Profit b/d	18,270	21,200
To Branch Exp. A/c	5,600	7,050	By Branch Stock A/c [Cost of Surplus A 300 – A 100]	—	200
To Profit and Loss A/c (Net Profit)	12,370	14,350			
	18,270	21,400		18,270	21,400

Example 18

Lokesh Ltd. sent goods to its Ratlam Branch at cost plus 25%. From the following particulars prepare Branch Stock Account, Branch Adjustment Account and Branch Profit and Loss Account :

	(A)
Opening stock at branch (I.P.)	5,000
Goods sent to Branch	20,000
Loss-in-transit at invoice price	2,500
Theft at invoice price	1,000
Loss in weight (normal) at invoice price	500
Sales	25,500
Expenses	8,000
Closing stock at branch at cost	6,000
Claim received from insurance company for loss-in-transit by head Office	2,000

Solution

Branch Stock Account

Dr. Cr.

Particulars	(A)	Particulars	(A)
To Balance b/d	5,000	By Branch Bank/Debtors A/c (Sales)	25,500
To Goods Sent to Branch A/c	20,000	By Branch Adjustment A/c (Loading on loss-in-transit)	500
To Branch Adjustment A/c (excess over income price)	10,500		

		By Branch Profit and Loss A/c (Cost of Goods lost-in-transit)	2,000
		By Branch Adjustment A/c (Loading on goods) lost by theft)	200
		By Branch Profit and Loss A/c (Cost of Goods lost by theft)	800
		By Branch Adjustment A/c* [Loss in weight (normal)]	500
		By Balance c/d (Closing Stock)	6,000
	35,500		35,500

Working Notes

* This entry is necessary for reconciling Stock in money value.

Branch Adjustment Account

Dr. *Cr.*

Particulars		(*A*)	*Particulars*	(*A*)
To Branch Stock A/c :			By Stock Reserve (Opening Stock) (Load on Opening Stock) [A 5,000 × 25/125]	1,000
Loss in transit (Load)	500			
Loss by theft (Load)	200			
Normal Loss	500	1,200		
To Stock Reserve (Closing Stock) [A 6,000 × 25/125]		1,200	By Goods sent to branch A/c (Loading) [A 20,000 × 25/125]	4,000
To Branch Profit and Loss A/c (Gross Profit)		13,100	By Branch Stock A/c (Surplus)	10,500
		15,500		15,500

Branch Profit and Loss Account

Dr. *Cr.*

Particulars		(*A*)	*Particulars*	(*A*)
To Branch Stock A/c			By Branch Adjustment A/c (Gross Profit)	13,100
(Cost) loss-in-transit	2,000			
(Cost(loss-in-theft	800	2,800	By Bank A/c (Insurance claim)	2,000
To Branch Expenses A/c		8,000		
To Net Profit taken to General Profit and Loss A/c		4,300		
		15,100		15,100

Example 19

X Ltd. of Kolkata operates a branch at Chennai. Goods are sent to the branch at selling price, which is cost plus 50 per cent. Branch expenses are paid out of an impress account which is reimbursed by the H.O. All branch transactions are recorded in the books of the H.O. On January 1, 2003, stock in trade at Chennai, at selling price, amounted to 27,690 and debtors to A 5,480.

During the year 2003 the following transactions took place at the branch :

	(A)
Goods received from Kolkata, at selling price	93,720
Cash Sales	52,100
Credit Sales	43,190
Goods returned to H.O. at selling price	1,440
Cash received from debtors	39,860
Discount allowed to debtors	970
Bad debts	480
Expenses	14,380

On 31st December, 2003, stock in trade at Chennai at selling price, amounted to A 24,510.

You are required to prepare Branch Stock Account, Branch Debtors. Account, Branch Adjustment Account and Branch Profit and Loss Account for the year ending 31st December, 2003.

Solution

Branch Stock Account

Dr. *Cr.*

Particulars	*(A)*	*Particulars*	*(A)*
To Balance b/d	27,690	By Cash–Cash Sales	52,100
To Goods sent to Branch A/c	93,720	By Branch Debtors A/c	
		– Credit Sales	43,190
		By Goods sent to Branch A/c	
		– Returns	1,440
		By Shortage (*Bal. Fig.*)	170
		– Branch Adj. A/c	
		– Branch P and L A/c	
		By Balance c/d	24,150
	1,21,410		1,21,410

Branch Debtors Account

Dr. *Cr.*

Particulars	*(A)*	*Particulars*	*(A)*
To Balance b/d	5,480	By Cash A/c	39,860
To Branch Stock A/c		By Discount	970
–Credit Sales	43,190	By Bad Debts	480
		By Balance c/d	7,360
	48,670		48,670

Branch Adjustment Account

Dr. *Cr.*

Particulars	*(A)*	*Particulars*	*(A)*
To Stock Reserve A/c –Loading on Closing Stock (A 24,510 × 50/150)	8,170	By Stock Reserve A/c –Loading on Opening Stock (A 27,690 × 50/150)	9,230
To Loading on Goods Returned (A 1,440 × 50/150)	480	By Loading on Goods sent to Branch (A 93,720 × 50/150)	31,240
To Loading on Shortage of stock (170 × 50/150)	57		
To Gross Profit c/d	31,763		
	40,470		40,470

Branch Profit and Loss Account

Dr. *Cr.*

Particulars	*(A)*	*Particulars*	*(A)*
To Expenses	14,380	By Gross Profit b/d	31,763
To Shortage of Stock (Cost)	113		
To Discount	970		
To Bad Debts	480		
To Net Profit at Branch	15,820		
	31,763		31,763

Example 20

Mumbai Trader Ltd. sends goods to its Delhi branch at cost plus 25 per cent. From the following particulars you are required to prepare the Branch Stock Account. Branch Stock adjustment A/c in the head Office books; showing Gross Profit and Net Profit.

	(A)
Opening Stock at branch at invoice price	20,000
Goods sent to Branch at invoice price	1,00,000
Loss in transit at invoice price	10,000
Pilferage at invoice price	4,000
Sales	1,22,000
Expenses	22,000
Closing Stock at branch at invoice price	24,000
Recovered from insurance company against loss in transit	6,000

Solution

In the Books of Head Office
Branch Stock Account

Dr. *Cr.*

Particulars	*(A)*	*Particulars*	*(A)*
To Balance b/d	20,000	By Branch Cash A/c (Sales)	1,22,000
To Goods sent to Branch A/c	1,00,000	By Branch Adjustment A/c	

To Branch Adjustment A/c		(*i*) (Loading of abnormal loss)	
Surplus (*Balancing Figure*)	40,000	1/5 [10,000 + 4,000]	2,800
		By Branch Adjustment A/c	
		(*ii*) (Cost of abnormal loss)	
		[A 14,000 – A 2,800]	11,200
		By Closing Stock	24,000
	1,60,000		1,60,000

Branch Adjustment Account

Dr. *Cr.*

Particulars	(*A*)	*Particulars*	(*A*)
To Branch Stock (Loss)	2,800	By Goods sent to Branch	
To Stock Reserve (Closing)		A/c (1/5 of A 1,00,000)	20,000
[1/5 × A 24,000]	4,800	By Stock Reserve (Opening)	
To Gross Profit c/d	56,400	[A 20,000 × 1/5]	4,000
		By Branch Stock A/c (Surplus)	40,000
	64,000		64,000
To Branch Stock A/c		By Gross Profit b/d	56,400
(Cost of abnormal loss)	11,200	By Insurance Claim	6,000
To Branch Expenses A/c	22,000		
To Net Profit transferred			
to General P and L A/c	29,200		
	62,400		62,400

Example 21

Goods are sent by the H.O. to the Branch at selling price which is cost +25%. All expenses of the branch are paid by H.O. All cash collected by the branch (from customers and from cash sales) is deposited to the credit of H.O.

From the following particulars prepare Branch Stock A/c, Branch Debtors A/c, Branch Adjustment A/c and Branch P&L A/c in the books of H.O.

	(*A*)
Debtors on 1.1.2009	12,000
Debtors on 31.12.2009	14,000
Stock on 1.1.2009 (Invoice Price)	16,000
Stock on 31.12.2009 (I.P.)	17,000
Cash sales during the year	60,000
Credit sales (20% more than cash sales)	
Total amount deposited in the H.O. account during the year	1,27,000
Goods returned by Branch to H.O. (Invoice Price)	5,000
Expenses paid	10,000
Discount allowed to customers	2,000
Bad debts written off	1,000
(Abnormal) spoilage	2,000

[*B.Com. (Hons.), Delhi University, 2006*]

Solution

Branch Stock A/c

Dr. Particulars	(A)	Particulars		Cr. (A)
To Balance b/d	16,000	By Cash sales		60,000
To Goods sent to branch A/c (*Bal. Figure*)	1,40,000	By credit sales (60,000 + 12,000)		72,000
		By Goods sent to branch A/c (return)		5,000
		By Branch Adjustment		
		Abnormal loss	400	
		P&L	1600	2,000
		By Balance c/d		17,000
	1,56,000			1,56,000

Branch Debtors A/c

Dr. Particulars	(A)	Particulars	Cr. (A)
To Balance b/d	12,000	By Cash (1,27,000 – 60,000)	67,000
To Branch Stock A/c (Credit sales)	72,000	By Bad debts	1,000
		By Discount	2,000
		By Balance C/d	14,000
	84,000		84,000

Branch Adjustment A/c

Dr. Particulars	(A)	Particulars	Cr. (A)
To Branch Stock (Abnormal loss)	400	By Stock Reserve (20% of 16,000)	3,200
To Goods sent to branch (20% of 5,000)	1,000	By Goods sent to branch (20% of 1,40,000)	28,000
To Stock Reserve (20% of 17,000)	3,400		
To Gross profit	26,400		
	31,200		31,200

Branch Profits Loss A/c

Dr. Particulars	(A)	Particulars	Cr. (A)
To Expenses	10,000	By G/P b/d	26,400
To Debtors (discount)	2,000		

To Debtors (Bad debts)	1,000		
To Branch Stock (Abnormal loss)	1,600		
To General P and L A/c (Net Profit)	11,800		
	26,400		26,400

Example 22

Multichained Stores Ltd., Delhi has its branches at Lucknow and Madras. It charges goods to its branches at cost plus 25%. The following information is available of the transactions of the Lucknow branch for the year ended on 31st March, 2005 :

	A
Balance on 1.4.2004 :	
Stock	30,000
Debtors	10,000
Petty cash	50
Transactions during 2004-2005 (Lucknow Branch)	
– Goods sent to Lucknow Branch at invoice price	3,25,000
– Goods returned to Head Office at invoice price	10,000
– Cash sales	1,00,000
– Credit sales	1,57,000
– Goods pilfered (invoice price)	2,000
– Goods lost in fire (invoice price)	5,000
– Insurance company paid to H.O. for loss by fire at Lucknow	3,000
– Cash sent for petty expenses	34,000
– Bad debts at Branch	500
– Goods transferred to Madras Branch under H.O. advice	15,000
– Insurance charges paid by H.O.	500
– Goods returned by debtors	500
– Balance on 31.3.2005 :	
Petty cash	230
Debtors	14,000

Goods worth A 15,000 (excluded above) sent by Lucknow Branch to Madras were in transit on 31.3.2005. Show the following accounts in the books of Multichained Stores Ltd.:

(*a*) Lucknow Branch Stock Account;

(*b*) Lucknow Branch Debtors Account;

(*c*) Lucknow Branch Adjustment Account;

(*d*) Lucknow Branch Profit and Loss Account.

Solution

In the books of Multichained Stores Ltd.
Lucknow Branch Stock Account

Dr. Cr.

Particulars	(A)	Particulars	(A)
To Balance b/d	30,000	By Goods sent to Lucknow Branch A/c (Return)	10,000
To Goods sent to Lucknow Branch A/c [A 3,25,000 + 15,000 (Goods in transit)]	3,40,000	By Branch Cash A/c (Cash Sales)	1,00,000
To Lucknow Branch Debtors A/c (Return)	500	By Goods Pilfered A/c	2,000
		By Goods lost by fire A/c	5,000
		By Goods sent to Lucknow Branch A/c (Transfer)	15,000
		By Lucknow Branch Debtors A/c (Credit Sales)	1,57,000
		By Balance c/d (including goods in transit)	81,500
	3,70,500		3,70,500

Lucknow Branch Debtors Account

Dr. Cr.

Particulars	(A)	Particulars	(A)
To Balance b/d	10,000	By Bad Debts A/c	500
To Lucknow Branch Stock A/c	1,57,000	By Branch Cash A/c (*Bal. Fig.*) (Collection from debtors)	1,52,000
		By Lucknow Branch Stock A/c (Returns)	500
		By Balance c/d	14,000
	1,67,000		1,67,000

Lucknow Branch Adjustment Account

Dr. Cr.

Particulars	(A)	Particulars	(A)
To Goods Pilfered A/c [A 2,000 × $^{25}/_{125}$]	400	By Stock Reserve A/c [A 30,000 × $^{25}/_{125}$]	6,000
To Goods Lost by Fire A/c A 5,000 × $^{25}/_{125}$]	1,000	By Goods Sent to Branch A/c [Note 6]	63,000
To Stock Reserve A/c [A 81,500 × $^{25}/_{125}$]	16,300		
To Gross Profit Transfer to Branch Profit and Loss A/c	51,300		
	69,000		69,000

Lucknow Branch Profit and Loss Account

Dr. Cr.

Particulars	(A)	Particulars	(A)
To Goods Pilfered A/c (Cost) [2,000 – 400 (Loading)]	1,600	By Gross Profit b/d	51,300
To Branch Expenses A/c	34,820		
To General Profit and Loss A/c (Net Profit transfer to General Profit and Loss A/c) (Note-5) (*Bal. Fig.*)	14,880		
	51,300		51,300

Goods Sent to Lucknow Branch Account

Dr. Cr.

Particulars	(A)	Particulars	(A)
To Lucknow Branch Stock A/c (Returns)	10,000	By Lucknow Branch Stock A/c	3,40,000
To Lucknow Branch Stock A/c (Transfer)	15,000		
To Lucknow Branch Adjustment A/c (Note 6)	63,000		
To Purchase A/c (Transfer)	2,52,000		
	3,40,000		3,40,000

Working Notes

1. **Petty Cash Account**

Dr. Cr.

Particulars	(A)	Particulars	(A)
To Balance b/d	50	By Branch Expenses A/c (*Bal. Fig.*)	33,820
To Branch Cash A/c	34,000	By Balance c/d	230
	34,050		34,050

2. **Branch Expenses Account**

Dr. Cr.

Particulars	(A)	Particulars	(A)
To Bad Debts A/c	500	By Lucknow Branches Profit and Loss A/c	34,820
To Branch Cash A/c (Insurance charge)	500		
To Petty Cash A/c	33,820		
	34,820		34,820

3.

Branch Pilfered Account

Dr. *Cr.*

Particulars	(A)	*Particulars*	(A)
To Lucknow Branch Stock A/c	2,000	By Lucknow Branch Adjustment A/c (Loading) [2,000 × $^{25}/_{125}$]	400
		By Lucknow Branch Profit and Loss A/c (cost)	1,600
	2,000		2,000

4.

Goods Lost by Fire Account

Dr. *Cr.*

Particulars	(A)	*Particulars*	(A)
To Lucknow Branch Stock A/c	5,000	By Lucknow Branches Adjustment A/c (Loading) [5,000 × $^{25}/_{125}$]	1,000
		By Bank A/c (Claim received)	3,000
		By General Profit and Loss A/c (Note 5)	1,000
	5,000		5,000

5. For calculating true profit of the branch, any abnormal loss should be debited to General Profit and Loss Account. Here, A 1,000 has been charged to General Profit and Loss Account. However, if it charged to Branch Profit and Loss Account, the profit would be A 17,480.

6. **Net Goods Sent to Branch :** Goods sent to Branch = A 3,40,000 *less* goods returned by branch A 10,000 *less* goods transferred to Madras branch A 15,000 = A 3,15,000, Loading = $^{25}/_{125}$ × A 3,15,000 = A 63,000.

Example 23

Goods are supplied by Delhi Head Office to Patna Branch at Cost + 50%. From the following transactions for year 2005 find out the profit earned by branch by following Stock and Debtors system :

		(A)
Stock with Branch on 1.1.2005		60,000
Branch Debtors on 1.1.2005		12,000
Petty Cash on 1.1.2005		100
Goods Received from Head Office		1,86,000
Goods returned to Head Office		13,000
Credit Sales		86,000
Cash received from Debtors		98,000
Discount allowed		2,400
Cash sent by Head Office		
• For	2,400	
• For Salary	24,000	

• For Petty Cash	1,100	27,500
Cash Sales		1,04,000
Stock with Branch on 31.12.2005		54,000
Petty Cash On 31.12.2005		200

Solution

Patna Branch Stock Account

Dr. *Cr.*

Particulars	(*A*)	*Particulars*	(*A*)
To Balance b/d	60,000	By Goods Sent to Branch A/c	13,000
To Goods Sent to Branch A/c	1,86,000	By Branch Debtors A/c	86,000
To Branch Adjustment A/c (Surplus due to sale of goods at higher Price than invoice price (*Bal. Fig.*)	11,000	By Branch Cash A/c	1,04,000
		By Balance c/d	54,000
	2,57,000		2,57,000

Patna Branch Adjustment Account

Dr. *Cr.*

Particulars	(*A*)	*Particulars*	(*A*)
To Goods Sent to Branch A/c [A 13,000 × 50/150]	4,333	By Stock Reserve A/c [A 60,000 × 50/150]	20,000
To Stock Reserve A/c [A 54,000 × 50/150]	18,000	By Goods Sent to Branch A/c [A 1,86,000 × 50/150]	62,000
To Branch Profit and Loss A/c (*Bal. Fig.*)	70,667	By Patna Branch Stock A/c	11,000
	93,000		93,000

Branch Profit and Loss Account

Dr. *Cr.*

Particulars	(*A*)	*Particulars*	(*A*)
To Discount	2,400	By Patna Branch Adjustment A/c70,667	
To Expenses	26,400		
To Petty Expenses	1,000		
To Net Profit t/f to General Profit and Loss A/c	40,867		
	70,667		70,667

Example 24

Hari Bros. of Calcutta has a branch at Ranchi and in order to maintain strict control on stock, invoice goods to the branch at selling price which is cost plus $33\frac{1}{3}$%. From the following particulars, prepare Branch Stock Account and Branch Adjustment Accounts to show gross profit and net profit or loss made there :

	(A)
Stock on 1st January 2002 (Invoice Price)	15,000
Debtors on 1st January 2002	11,400
Goods invoiced to Branch during the year (Invoice Price)	67,000
Sales at the Branch :	
Cash	31,000
Credit	37,000
Cash received from Debtors	40,000
Bad Debts written off	250
Discount allowed to customers	300
Expenses at the Branch	6,700
Stock on 31st Dec. 2002 (Invoice Price)	13,400

Solution

Branch Stock Account

Dr. *Cr.*

Particulars	*(A)*	*Particulars*	*(A)*
To Balance b/d	15,000	By Branch Debtors A/c (Credit Sales)	37,000
To Goods sent to Branch A/c	67,000	By Branch Cash A/c (Cash Sales)	31,000
		By Shortage-in-Stock A/c (*Bal. Fig.*)	600
		By Balance c/d	13,400
	82,000		82,000

Branch Adjustment Account

Dr. Cr.

Particulars		*(A)*	*Particulars*	*(A)*
To Shortage (load) [600 × 1/4]		150	By Stock Reserve A/c [15,000 × 1/4]	3,750
To Stock Reserve A/c (Loading) [13,400 × 1/4]		3,350	By Goods sent to Branch A/c [67,000 × 1/4]	16,750
To Gross Profit c/d		17,000		
		20,500		20,500
To Branch Expenses		6,700	By Gross Profit b/d	17,000
To Branch Debtors A/c :				
Bad Debts	250			
Discount allowed	300	550		
To Shortage (cost)		450		
To Net Profit		9,300		
		17,000		17,000

Working Note

Suppose Cost = A 100

Loading = A $33\frac{1}{3}$ or $\frac{100}{3}$

Invoice Price = A 100 + A $33\frac{1}{3}=133\frac{1}{3}$ or $\frac{400}{3}$

$$\text{Loading on Invoice Price} = \frac{\text{Loading}}{\text{Invoice Price}} = \frac{\frac{100}{3}}{\frac{400}{3}}$$

$$= \frac{100}{3} \times = \frac{3}{400} = \frac{1}{4}$$

Example 25

Roma Industries, Mumbai invoices goods to its Delhi branch with instruction to make credit sales at catalogue price which is cost + 50% and cash sales at invoice price which is cost + 20%. The following information is made available :

Opening Balance :	
Branch Stock	18,000
Branch Debtor	7,000
Transactions during the year :	
Goods Received by Branch	2,30,000
Goods Returned by Branch	8,000
Credit Sales	2,00,000
Cash Sales	27,000
Goods Returned by Credit Customers to Branch	1,050
Goods Returned by Credit Customers Direct to HO	3,000
Goods Returned by Cash Customers Direct to HO	7,200
Closing Balance :	
Branch Stock	10,450
Branch Debtor	2,950
Branch Cash	25,000

Goods invoiced worth A 10,000 were still in transit. Cash customers who returned goods direct to HO settled accounts to the extent of A 6,000 only at accounting date. Prepare the necessary accounts in the books of Roma Industries according to stock and debtor system.

Solution

Cost = 100

Catalogue = 150

Invoice Price = 120 (20% less than 150)

Branch Stock Account

Dr. *Cr.*

Particulars	*(A)*	*Particulars*		*(A)*
Balance b/d	18,000	Goods Sent to Branch A/c		8,000
Goods Sent to Branch A/c (2,30,000 + 10,000)	2,40,000	Branch Debtor A/c		2,00,000
		Branch Cash A/c		27,000
Branch Debtor A/c	1,050	Branch Adjustment A/c (1,050 × 30/150)		210
Branch Adjustment A/c (Surplus on credit sales *i.e.*, [2,00,000 × 30/150]	40,000	Branch Adjustment A/c (loading on shortage)	7,232	
		Branch Profit and Loss A/c (cost of shortage)	36,158	43,390 (*b.f.*)
		Balance c/d : Physical stock		10,450
		Goods in transit		10,000
	2,99,050			2,99,050

Branch Debtor Account

Dr. *Cr.*

Particulars	*(A)*	*Particulars*	*(A)*
Balance b/d	7,000	Bank Stock A/c	1,050
Branch Stock A/c	2,00,000	Goods Sent to Branch a/c	3,000
		Branch Cash A/c (*Bal. Fig.*)	2,00,000
		Balance c/d	2,950
	2,07,000		2,07,000

Branch Cash Account

Dr. *Cr.*

Particulars	*(A)*	*Particulars*	*(A)*
Branch Stock A/c	27,000	Cash A/c (*Bal. Fig.*)	2,02,000
Branch Debtor A/c	2,00,000	Balance c/d	25,000
	2,27,000		2,27,000

Goods Sent to Branch Account

Dr. *Cr.*

Particulars	*(A)*	*Particulars*	*(A)*
Branch Stock A/c	8,000	Branch Stock A/c	2,40,000
Branch Adjustment A/c	40,000	Branch Adjustment A/c	1,333
Cash A/c	6,000	Branch Adjustment A/c	1,200
Creditor For Goods Returned A/c	1,200	Branch Adjustment A/c (loading and surplus on goods) returned debtors direct to H.O.)	1,000
Branch Debtor A/c	3,000		
Purchases A/c	1,85,333		
	2,43,533		2,43,533

Creditor for Goods Returned Account

Dr. *Cr.*

Particulars	*(A)*	*Particulars*	*(A)*
Balance b/d	1,200	Goods Sent to Branch A/c	1,200
	1,200		1,200

Branch Adjustment Account

Dr. *Cr.*

Particulars	*(A)*	*Particulars*		*(A)*
Goods Sent to Branch A/c (loading on goods returned to HO by Branch)	1,333	Stock Reserve A/c (loading on opening stock)		3,000
Goods Sent to Branch A/c (surplus and loading on goods returned by credit customers to HO 3,000 × 50/150)	1,000	Goods Sent to Branch A/c (loading on goods sent to branch)		40,000
Goods Sent to Branch A/c (loading on goods returned by cash customers to HO)	1,200	Branch Stock A/c : Excess of selling price over invoice price of goods sold on credit	40,000	
Branch Stock A/c (loading on shortage)	7,232	*Less :* Cancellation of surplus on goods returned by debtors [1,050 × 30/150]	210	39,790
Stock Reserve A/c (1,742 + 1,667) (loading on closing stock including stock in transit)	3,409			
Gross profit c/d	68,616			
	82,790			82,790
To Branch Stock A/c	36,158	Gross Profit b/d		68,616
To Profit and Loss A/c	32,458			
	68,616			68,616

Example 26

Concept and Co. with its Head Office at Mumbai has a branch at Nagpur. Goods are invoiced to the Branch at a cost plus $33\frac{1}{3}$%. The following information is given in respect of the branch for the year ended 31st March 2008.

	(A)
Good sent to Branch (Invoice price)	4,80,000
Stock at Branch on 1.4.2007 (Invoice price)	24,000
Cash sales	1,80,000
Return of goods by customers to the Branch	6,000
Branch expenses (paid in cash)	53,500
Branch debtors balance on 1.4.2007	30,000
Discount allowed	1,000

Bad debts	1,500
Collection from debtors	2,70,000
Branch debtors cheques returned dishonoured	5,000
Stock at Branch on 31.3.2008 (invoice price)	48,000
Branch debtors balance on 31.3.2008	36,500

Prepare, under the Stock and Debtors System, the following Ledger Accounts in the books of the Head Office :

(*i*) Nagpur Branch Stock Account

(*ii*) Nagpur Branch Debtors Account

(*iii*) Nagpur Branch Adjustment Account.

Also compute shortage of Stock at Branch, if any [*CAPE II, May 2006*]

Solution

In the Books of Head Office

Nagpur Branch Stock Account

Dr. Cr.

Date	Particulars	(A)	Date	Particulars	(A)
01.4.07	Balance b/d	24,000	31.3.08	Bank A/c	1,80,000
31.3.08	Goods sent to			Branch Debtors	2,80,000
	Branch A/c	4,80,000			
	Branch Debtors	6,000		Stock shortage :	
				Branch P and L A/c	1,500
				Branch Adjustment A/c	
				(Loading)	500
				Balance c/d	48,000
		5,10,000			5,10,000

Nagpur Branch Debtors Account

Dr. Cr.

Date	Particulars	(A)	Date	Particulars	(A)
01.4.07	Balance b/d	30,000	31.3.08	Bank A/c	2,70,000
31.3.08	Bank A/c			Branch Stock A/c	6,000
	(dishonour of cheques)	5,000			
	Branch Stock A/c	2,80,000		Bed debts	1,500
	(*Balancing Figure*)			Discount allowed	1,000
				Balance c/d	36,500
		3,15,000			3,15,000

Nagpur Branch Adjustment Account

Dr. Cr.

Particulars	(A)	Particulars	(A)
Branch Stock A/c (*Bal. Fig.*)	500	Stock Reserve A/c	
Stock Reserve (48,000 × 25%)	12,000	(24,000 × 25%)	6,000

Gross Profit c/d (1)	1,13,500	Goods sent to Branch A/c (4,80,000 × 25%)	1,20,000
	1,26,000		1,26,000
Branch Stock A/c	1,500	Gross Profit b/d	1,13,500
Branch Expenses (53,500 + 1500 + 1,000)	56,000		
Net Profit	56,000		
	1,13,500		1,13,500

Working Notes

Gross profit

Total sales (at invoice price)–Goods returned by customer (at invoice price) × $\frac{33.33}{100+33.33}$

[(A 1,80,000 + A 2,80,000) – A 6000] × $\frac{33.33}{133.33}$ = A 1,13,500.

Example 27

Red and Co. of Mumbai started a branch at Bangalore on 1.4.2006 to which goods were sent at 20% above cost. The branch makes both cash sales and credit sales. Branch expenses are met from branch cash and balance money remitted to H.O. The branch does not maintain double entry book of account and necessary accounts relating to branch are maintained in H.O. Following further details are given for the year ending on 31.3.2007.

Cost of goods sent to branch	1,00,000
Goods received by branch till 31.3.2007 at Invoice price	1,08,000
Credit sales for the year	1,16,000
Closing debtors on 31.3.2007	41,600
Bad debts written off during the year	400
Cash remitted to H.O.	86,000
Closing cash on hand at branch on 31.3.2007	4,000
Cash remitted by H.O. to branch during the year	6,000
Closing stock in hand at branch at invoice price	12,000
Expenses incurred at branch	24,000

Draw up the necessary Ledger Account like Branch Debtors Account, Branch Stock Account, Goods sent to Branch Account, Branch Cash Account, Branch Expenses Account and Branch Adjustment A/c for ascertaining gross profit and Branch Profit and Loss A/c for ascertaining Branch profit.

[CAPE II, May 2007]

Solution

Branch Debtors Account

Dr. *Cr.*

Particulars	*(A)*	*Particulars*	*(A)*
Branch Stock A/c	1,16,000	Branch Cash A/c (*Bal. Fig.*)	74,000
		Bad Debts (written off)	400
		Balance c/d	41,600
	1,16,000		1,16,000

Goods Sent to Branch A/c

Dr. *Cr.*

Particulars	(A)	*Particulars*	(A)
Branch Adjustment A/c $\left(1,00,000 \times \frac{20}{100}\right)$	20,000	Branch Stock A/c	1,20,000
Purchases/Trading A/c	1,00,000		
	1,20,000		1,20,000

Branch Cash A/c

Dr. *Cr.*

Particulars	(A)	*Particulars*	(A)
Branch Debtors A/c	74,000	Branch Expenses A/c	24,000
H.O. A/c (cash remittance)	6,000	H.O. (cash remittance)	86,000
Branch Stock A/c :		Balance c/d	4,000
Cash Sales (*Balancing Figure*)	34,000		
	1,14,000		1,14,000

Branch Stock A/c

Dr. Cr.

Particulars	(A)	*Particulars*	(A)
Goods sent to Branch A/c	1,20,000	Branch Debtors A/c	1,16,000
Branch Adjustment A/c	54,000	Branch Cash A/c (Sales)	34,000
(Excess profit over normal loading, balancing figure)		Goods in Transit (1,20,000 – 1,08,000)	12,000
		Balance c/d	12,000
	1,74,000		1,74,000

Branch Expenses A/c

Dr. *Cr.*

Particulars	(A)	*Particulars*	(A)
Branch Cash A/c	24,000	Branch P&L A/c	24,000

Branch Adjustment A/c

Dr. *Cr.*

Particulars	(A)	*Particulars*	(A)
Stock Reserve A/c (12,000 × $^1/_6$)	2,000	Goods sent to Branch A/c (1,20,000 × $^1/_6$)	20,000
Goods in transit Reserve A/c	2,000	Branch Stock A/c	54,000
Branch P&L A/c (*Bal. Fig.*)	70,000		
	74,000		74,000

Branch P&L A/c

Dr. *Cr.*

Particulars	(A)	*Particulars*	(A)
Branch Expenses A/c	24,000	Branch Adjustment A/c	70,000
Bad Debts	400		
Net Profit (transferred to General) P&L A/c	45,600		
	70,000		70,000

Example 28

Shyam Traders of Delhi, a firm of traders, has a branch at Hyderabad. In order to maintain strict control over stock, it invoice goods to the branch at the selling price including profit of 25% on selling price. From the following particulars, prepare the branch stock account, branch debtors account, branch adjustment account and branch profit and loss account :

	(A)
Branch stock on 1st April, 2007 (at invoice price)	3,00,000
Branch debtors on 1st April 2007	2,28,000
Goods invoiced to branch at invoice price during the year 2007-08	13,40,000
Sales at branch during the year :	
Cash	6,20,000
Credit	7,48,000
Cash received from branch debtors	8,00,000
Bad debts written off	5,000
Discount allowed to branch customers	6,000
Cash expenses at the branch	1,34,000
Branch stock on 31st March, 2008 (in invoice price)	2,68,000

[*CS(F) June 2006*]

Solution

Branch Stock A/c

Dr. *Cr.*

Particulars	(A)	*Particulars*	(A)
Balance b/d	3,00,000	Bank	6,20,000
Goods Sent to Branch A/c	13,40,000	Branch Debtors	7,48,000
		Branch Adjustment A/c	1,000
		Branch P&L A/c	3,000
		Balance c/d	2,68,000
	16,40,000		16,40,000

Branch Debtors Account

Dr. *Cr.*

Particulars	(A)	*Particulars*		(A)
Balance b/d	2,28,000	Bank		8,00,000
Branch Stock A/c	7,48,000	Branch P&L A/c :		
		– Bad Debts	5,000	
		– Discount allowed	6,000	11,000
		Balance c/d		1,65,000
	9,76,000			9,76,000

Branch Adjustment Account

Dr. *Cr.*

Particulars	(A)	*Particulars*	(A)
Branch Stock A/c (loading on shortage)	1,000	Branch Stock Reserve A/c (Opening)	75,000
Branch Stock Reserve A/c (closing)	67,000	Goods Sent to Branch A/c (loading)	3,35,000
Gross Profit (transferred to Branch Profit and Loss A/c)	3,42,000		
	4,10,000		4,10,000

Branch Profit and Loss A/c

Dr. *Cr.*

Particulars		(A)	*Particulars*	(A)
Branch Debtors :			Branch Adjustment A/c	
Bad Debts	5,000		(gross profit)	3,42,000
Discount allowed	6,000	11,000		
Bank (expenses)		1,34,000		
Branch Stock (cost of shortage)		3,000		
Profit and Loss A/c (profit at branch)		1,94,000		
		3,42,000		3,42,000

Example 29

Kushi of Delhi has a branch at Jaipur. She sends goods to the branch at a profit of 20% on sales. Following information is available of the transactions at Jaipur branch for the year ending 31st March, 2005:

	(A)
Stock at invoice price (on 1.4.04)	2,00,000
Debtors (on 1.4.04)	60,000
Debtors (on 31.3.05)	55,000

Petty cash (on 1.4.04)	750
Goods sent to branch at invoice price	21,00,000
Goods returned by branch to H.O.	75,000
Normal loss at invoice price	1,750
Goods lost by fire at invoice price	20,000
Goods pilfered at invoice price	15,000
Cash sales	5,25,000
Credit sales	9,00,000
Insurance company paid to H.O. for loss by fire at Jaipur	15,000
Bad debts	2,000
Cash sent for petty expenses	1,63,000
Goods transferred to Lucknow branch under instructions from H.O.	60,000
Insurance charges paid by H.O.	1,000
Goods returned by debtors to branch	2,500
Petty cash (on 31.3.05)	4,250

Prepare :

(*i*) Branch stock A/c

(*ii*) Branch debtors A/c

(*iii*) Branch adjustment A/c

(*iv*) Branch profit and loss A/c [*B.Com.*, (*Hons.*), *Delhi, University, 2006*]

Solution

In the Books of Head Office
Jaipur Branch Stock Account

Particulars	(*A*)	*Particulars*	(*A*)
To Balance b/d	2,00,000	By Goods sent to Branch A/c	75,000
To Goods sent to Branch A/c	21,00,000	By Branch Adjustment A/c (Normal loss)	1,750
To Jaipur Branch Debtors A/c	2,500	By Loss by fire	20,000
		By Goods pilfered	15,000
		By Jaipur Branch Cash A/c (cash sales)	5,25,000
		By Jaipur Branch Debtors A/c (credit sales)	9,00,000
		By Goods sent to Branch A/c (Transfer to Lucknow)	60,000
		By Balance c/d	7,05,750
	23,02,500		23,02,500

Jaipur Branch Debtors Account

Particulars	(*A*)	*Particulars*	(*A*)
To Balance b/d	60,000	By Cash A/c (bal. fig.)	9,00,500
To Jaipur Branch Stock A/c	9,00,000	By Bad Debts	2,000

		By Jaipur Branch Stock A/c	2,500
		By Balance c/d	55,000
	9,60,000		9,60,000

Jaipur Branch Adjustment Account

Particulars	(A)	Particulars	(A)
To Goods sent to Branch A/c	15,000	By Stock Reserve A/c	40,000
To Jaipur Branch Stock A/c	1,750	By Goods sent to Branch A/c	4,20,000
To Loss by fire (Loading)	4,000		
To Goods pilfered (Loading)	3,000		
To Goods Sent to Branch A/c	12,000		
To Stock Reserve A/c	1,41,150		
To Jaipur Branch Profit and Loss A/c (gross profit)	2,83,100		
	4,60,000		4,60,000

Jaipur Branch Profit and Loss Account

Particulars	(A)	Particulars	(A)
To Loss by Fire (Cost)	16,000	By Jaipur Branch Adjustment A/c (Gross Profit)	2,83,100
To Goods Pilfered (Cost)	12,000	By Insurance Company	15,000
To Bad Debts	2,000		
To Jaipur Branch Expenses A/c (Petty Expenses) A [750 + 1,63,000 – 4,250]	1,59,500		
To Insurance Charges	1,000		
To Profit and Loss A/c (Net Profit)	1,07,600		
	2,98,100		2,98,100

Example 30

Garima Stores of Delhi operates a retail branch at Chennai. The head office makes all the purchases and the branch is charged at cost price plus 50%. All cash received by the Chennai branch is remitted to Delhi. Branch expenses are paid by the branch out of an imprest account which is reimbursed by Delhi H.O. monthly.

The branch keeps a sales ledger and certain essential subsidiary books, but otherwise all branch transactions are recorded at Delhi. On 1.1.2006 stock in trade at the branch at selling price amounted to A 6,000 and debtor were A 4,000.

During the year ended 31.12.06 the following branch transactions were made :

	(A)
Goods received from Delhi at selling price	15,000
Cash sales	6,900
Goods returned to Delhi at selling price	300
Credit sales (less returns)	6,300
Authorised reductions in selling price of goods sold	150

Cash received from debtors	4,800
Debtors written off as irrecoverable	200
Cash discount allowed to debtors	150

A consignment of goods despatched to the branch on 28 Dec., 2006 with a selling price of A 180 was not received until 5.1.07 and had not been included in stock figure which at selling price was A 7,290.

The expenses relating to the branch for the year ended 31.12.06 amounted to A 1,800.

You are required to prepare Branch Stock A/c; Branch Debtors A/c, Branch Adjustment and P&L A/c maintained at Delhi under Stock and Debtors system. Any stock unaccounted for is to be regarded as normal wastage. [*B.Com.* (*Hons.*), *Delhi University, 2007*]

Solution

Chennai Branch Stock Account

Particulars		(*A*)	*Particulars*		(*A*)
To Balance b/d		6,000	By Branch Cash A/c (Cash Sales)		6,900
To Goods sent to Branch A/c :			By Goods sent to Branch A/c (Return)		300
Good received from H.O.	15,000		By Branch Debtors A/c (Cr. Sales)		6,300
Goods from H.O. in transit	180	15,180	By Branch Profit and Loss A/c (Reduction in S.P.)*		150
			By Branch Adjustment A/c (*Bal. Fig.*) (Normal Loss)		60
			By Balance c/d :		
			in hand	7,290	
			in transit	180	7,470
		21,180			21,180

Chennai Branch Debtors Account

Particulars	(*A*)	*Particulars*	(*A*)
To Balance b/d	4,000	By Branch Cash A/c	4,800
To Branch Stock A/c (Credit Sales)	6,300	By Bad Debts	200
		By Discount	150
		By Balance c/d (*Bal. Fig.*)	5,150
	10,300		10,300

Chennai Branch Adjustment Account

Particulars	(*A*)	*Particulars*	(*A*)
To Branch Stock A/c (Normal Shortage)	60	By Stock Reserve A/c [6,000 × 1/3]	2,000
To Stock Reserve A/c [(A 7,290 + 180) × 1/3]	2,490	By Goods sent to Branch A/c [(A 15,000 + 180 – 300) × 1/3]	4,960
To Gross Profit transferred to Branch Profit and Loss A/c (*bal. fig.*)	4,410		
	6,960		6,960

Chennai Branch Profit and Loss Account

Particulars		*(A)*	*Particulars*	*(A)*
To Chennai Branch Stock (Authorised reduction in S.P.)		150	By Branch Adjustment A/c (Gross Profit)	4,410
To Branch Expenses A/c		1,800		
To Branch Debtors A/c				
– Bad Debts	200			
– Discount	150	350		
To Net Profit transferred to General Profit and Loss A/c		2,110		
		4,410		4,410

*Authorised reduction in selling price is a sales promotion technique. Hence, it is indirect loss and would be debited to Profit and Loss Account.

Note : Trade discount is never transferred to Trading Account or Adjustment Account. In fact it is never considered for final accounts.

Example 31

X Ltd. of Delhi has a branch at Bhivani. Goods are invoiced to the branch at cost 25%. The branch does not maintain account books and all collections at the branch are remitted to Head Office. The expenses of the branch are reimbursed by the Head Office. From the following particulars prepare :

(*i*) Branch Stock Account;

(*ii*) Branch Debtors Account;

(*iii*) Branch Expenses Account;

(*iv*) Branch Adjustment Account to ascertain the profit at branch.

In the books of Head Office for the six months ending on 30 September, 2006.

	(A)
Opening Stock (at cost to H.O.)	55,000
Opening Debtors	15,000
Opening Furniture	12,000
Opening Petty Cash	500
Transactions for six months :	
Goods received from Head Office (at invoice price)	2,25,000
Cash Sales	1,95,000
Credit Sales	80,000
Goods returned to Head Office (at invoice price)	12,750
Normal loss (at invoice price)	1,000
Sales returns by credit customers to branch	500
Cash received from debtors	50,000
Bills receivable received from customers at branch	15,000
Bad Debts	400
Trade Discount to customers (already taken into account while invoicing)	12,000
Goods sent to branch on 27.9.2006 received by branch on 5.10.2006 (at. I.P.)	1,500

Cash sent to branch for expenses	10,500
Cash discount allowed to customers	800
Balance on 30.9.2006 :	
Stock-in-trade (at invoice price)	5,600
Debtors	?
Petty cash	500

Depreciation of furniture @ 40% p.a. Branch Manager is entitled to a commission of 5% of profit of branch after charging such commission. [*B.Com.*, (*Hons.*), *Delhi University, 2007*]

Solution

(*i*) Branch Stock Account

Particulars	(*A*)	*Particulars*	(*A*)
To Balance b/d (A 55,000 + A 13,750)	68,750	By Branch Cash A/c (Cash Sales)	1,95,000
To Goods sent to Branch A/c [A 2,25,000 + A 1,500 (Goods in transit)]	2,26,500	By Branch Debtors A/c (Credit Sales)	80,000
To Branch Debtors A/c (Return by customers to Branch)	500	By Goods sent to Branch A/c (Returns to H.O.)	12,750
		By Branch Adjustment A/c (Trade Discount)	12,000
To Branch Adjustment A/c (Surplus) (*Bal. Fig.*)	12,100	By Branch Adjustment A/c (Normal Loss)	1,000
		By Balance c/d A [5,600 + 1,500 (Goods in transit)]	7,100
	3,07,850		3,07,850

(*ii*) Branch Debtors Account

Particulars	(*A*)	*Particulars*	(*A*)
To Balance b/d	15,000	By Branch Stock A/c (Sales Return)	500
To Branch Stock A/c (Credit Sales)	80,000	By Branch Cash A/c	50,000
		By Bills Receivable	15,000
		By Bad Debts	400
		By Discount	800
		By Balance c/d (*bal. fig.*)	28,300
	95,000		95,000

(*iii*) Branch Expenses Account

Particulars	(*A*)	*Particulars*	(*A*)
To Bad Debts	400	By Branch Adjustment A/c	14,100
To Discount	800		
To Misc. Expenses	10,500		
To Dept. on Furniture (for six months)	2,400		
	14,100		14,100

(iv) Branch Adjustment Account

Particulars	(A)	Particulars	(A)
To Stock Reserve (closing) (A 7,100 × 25/125)	1,420	By Stock Reserve (Opening)	13,750
		By Goods from H.O. $\frac{25}{125}$ (A 2,26,500 – A 12,750)	42,750
To Normal Loss (Branch Stock)	1,000		
To Gross Profit c/d	66,180	By Branch Stock A/c	12,100
	68,600		68,600
To Branch Expenses A/c	14,100	By Gross Profit b/d	66,180
To Branch Stock A/c (Trade Discount)	12,000		
	26,100		
To Manager's Commission A/c $\frac{5}{105}$ × A 40,080[*1]	1,909		
To Net Profit transferred to Profit and Loss A/c	38,171		
	66,180		66,180

*1 A 66,180 – A 26,100 = A 40,080

Example 32

From the following figures for a year relating to the Delhi branch of a H.O. which invoices goods to its branch at cost plus 100%, prepare :

(i) Branch A/c;

(ii) Branch Stock Account;

(iii) Branch Debtors A/c; and

(iv) Branch Adjustment and Profit and Loss A/c.

Transactions during the year :	(A)
Goods invoiced to branch	1,00,000
Goods received by branch	1,10,000
Cash sent for expenses	25,000
Actual expenses at branch	28,000
Cash expenses at branch	27,000
Sales (at invoice price)	1,40,000
Cash received from debtors	1,25,000
Discount allowed to branch debtors	5,000
Goods returned by branch debtors direct to H.O.	20,000
Closing balances :	
Branch Stock	30,000
Branch Debtors	20,000

[*B.Com., (Hons.), Delhi University, 2008*]

Solution

(*i*) Branch Account

Particulars	(*A*)	Particulars	(*A*)
To Balance b/d :		By Stock Reserve	30,000
To Branch Stock	60,000	(Loading on Opening Stock)	
[See Branch Stock A/c]		By Goods-in-transit (Loading on	5,000
To Branch Debtors	30,000	opening Goods-in-transit)	
[See Branch Debtors A/c]			
To Goods-in-transit*1	10,000	By Cash remitted to H.O.*2	1,23,000
To Goods sent to Branch A/c	1,00,000	By Goods sent to Branch A/c	50,000
To Cash A/c (Cash for expenses)	25,000	(Loading on goods sent to branch)	
To Goods sent to Branch A/c	10,000	By Goods sent to Branch A/c	20,000
(Loading on goods returned by debtors to H.O.)		By Balance c/d :	
		Branch Stock	30,000
To Stock Reserve	15,000	Branch Debtors	20,000
(Loading on Closing Stock)			
To Balance c/d :			
Outstanding Expenses*3	1,000		
To Profit transferred to General			
Profit and Loss A/c (*bal. fig.*)	27,000		
	2,78,000		2,78,000

(*ii*) Branch Stock Account

Particulars	(*A*)	Particulars	(*A*)
To Balance b/d (Opening Stock)	60,000	By Sales A/c	1,40,000
(*Bal. Fig.*)		By Balance c/d	30,000
To Goods-in-transit*1	10,000		
To goods sent to Branch A/c	1,00,000		
	1,70,000		1,70,000

(*iii*) Branch Debtors Account

Particulars	(*A*)	Particulars	(*A*)
To Balance b/d (*bal. fig.*)	30,000	By Cash A/c	1,25,000
		By Discount Allowed	5,000
To Sales (credit)	1,40,000	By Goods Returned	20,000
		By Balance c/d	20,000
	1,70,000		1,70,000

(iv) Branch Adjustment and Profit and Loss Account

Particulars	*(A)*	*Particulars*	*(A)*
To Stock Reserve [A 30,000 × ½]	15,000	By Stock Reserve A/c [A 60,000 × ½]	30,000
To Goods sent to Branch A/c	10,000	By Goods sent to Branch A/c	50,000
(Goods returned by Branch debtors		[A 1,00,000 × ½]	
direct to H.O.) [A 20,000 × ½]		By Goods-in-transit	
To Gross Profit c/d (*bal. fig.*)	60,000	[Loading A 10,000 × ½]	5,000
	85,000		85,000
To Branch Expenses	28,000	By Gross Profit b/d	60,000
To Discount	5,000		
To Net Profit (*bal. fig.*)	27,000		
	60,000		60,000

Working Notes :

*1 *Calculation of Goods-in-transit :*

Since, goods received by branch A 1,10,000 are more than the goods sent to them by H.O. i.e., A 1,00,000 the difference A 10,000 is Goods-in-transit in the beginning of the year.

*2 *Calculation of Cash remitted to H.O. :*

Cash remitted to H.O. is cash received from debtors (A 1,25,000)

Less : extra spent on branch expenses (A 2,000) *i.e.,* A 1,23,000.

*3 *Calculation of Closing outstanding expenses :*

Since actual expenses at branch (A 28,000) are more than the expenses paid (A 27,000), the difference is outstanding expenses at the end of the year *i.e.,* A 1,000.

Example 33

Mayur Store Ltd. with their Head Office in Delhi, invoiced goods to its branch at Noida at 20% less than the list price which is cost plus 100% with instructions that cash sales were to be made at invoice price and credit sales at list price. From the following particulars, prepare Branch Stock Account, Branch Debtors Account, Branch Expenses Account, Branch Adjustment Account and Branch Profit and Loss Account for the year ended 31 December, 2008 :

	(A)
Branch Stock on 1.1.2008 at cost to Branch	40,000
Branch Debtors on 1.1.2008	30,000
Goods received from H.O. at invoice price	3,60,000
Cash sales	90,000
Credit sales	3,00,000
Cash received from Debtors	2,40,000
Goods in Transit	40,000
Branch Expenses	40,000
Bad Debts	2,000

Loss of Goods by fire at invoice price	2,400
Transfer of goods to Faridabad Branch at I.P.	6,000
Pilferage at I.P. (Normal)	1,000
Remittance to Head Office	3,30,000
Insurance claim admitted against loss by fire	1,200
Debtors on 31.12.2008	88,000
Stock on 31.12.2008 at invoice price	60,000

[*B.Com., (Hons.,) Delhi University, 2009*]

Solution

Branch Debtors' Account

Particulars	*(A)*	*Particulars*	*(A)*
To Balance b/d	30,000	By Branch Cash A/c	2,40,000
To Branch Stock A/c (Credit Sales)	3,00,000	By Branch Expenses A/c (Bad Debts)	2,000
		By Balance c/d	88,000
	3,30,000		3,30,000

Branch Expenses Account

Particulars	*(A)*	*Particulars*	*(A)*
To Bank A/c	40,000	By Branch Profit and Loss A/c	42,000
To Branch Debtors A/c (Bad Debts)	2,000		
	42,000		42,000

Noida Branch Stock Account

Particulars	*(A)*	*Particulars*	*(A)*
To Balance b/d	40,000	By Branch Cash A/c (Sales)	90,000
To Goods sent to Branch A/c		By Branch Debtors A/c	
(A 3,60,000 + A 40,000)	4,00,000	(Credit Sales)	3,00,000
To Branch Adjustment A/c		By Loss by fire :	
(Excess profit on Credit Sales)[*1]	60,000	Branch Adjustment A/c	900
		[2,400 × 60/160]	
		Branch Profit and Loss A/c	1,500
		[2,400 – 900]	
		By Faridabad Branch A/c (Transfer)	6,000
		By Branch Adjustment A/c	1,000
		(Normal Loss)	
		By Shortage (Balancing Figure)	

		Branch Adjustment A/c [600 × 60/160]		225
		Branch Profit and Loss A/c [600 – 225)		375
		By Balance c/d		
		In hand	60,000	
		In Transit	40,000	1,00,000
	5,00,000			5,00,000

Branch Adjustment Account

Particulars	*(A)*	*Particulars*	*(A)*
To Branch Stock A/c	900	By Stock Reserve A/c [40,000 × 60/160]	15,000
To Goods Sent to Branch A/c (Faridabad) [A 6,000 × 60/160]	2,250	By Goods sent to Branch A/c [4,00,000 × 60/160]	1,50,000
To Branch Debtors A/c	1,000	By Branch Stock A/c	60,000
To Branch Adjustment A/c	225		
To Stock Reserve A/c [1,00,000 × 60/160]	37,500		
To Gross Profit c/d	1,83,125		
	2,25,000		2,25,000

Branch Profit and Loss Account

Particulars	*(A)*	*Particulars*	*(A)*
To Branch Stock A/c	375	By Gross Profit b/d	1,83,125
To Branch Stock A/c	1,500	By Bank A/c (Insurance Claim)	1,200
To Branch Expenses A/c	42,000		
To Profit and Loss A/c	1,40,450		
	1,84,325		1,84,325

Working Notes :

*1 Cost = A 100

List Price = A 200

Invoice Price = A $200 - \frac{20}{100}$ 200 A 160

Loading on Invoice Price = $\frac{\text{Profit}}{\text{Invoice Price}}$ $\frac{60}{160}$

Surplus on Sale of goods on credit @ 20% $\frac{20}{100}$ 3, 00, 000 A 60, 000

Example 34

Linken Ltd. has its branches in Ambala and Ludhiana to whom goods are invoiced at cost plus 25%. The following information is available of the transactions at Ambala Branch for the year ending 31st March, 2009 :

	(A)
Balance at 1st April, 2008 :	
Stock at invoice price	20,000
Debtors	6,000
Petty Cash	475
Transactions during 2008-09	
Goods sent to branch at invoice price	2,40,000
Goods returned to H.O. at invoice price	7,500
Cash Sales	60,000
Credit Sales (Sold at cost + 50%)	90,000
Normal loss at invoice price	300
Goods pilfered at invoice price	1,500
Goods lost in fire at invoice price	3,000
Insurance Co. paid to H.O. for loss by fire at Ambala	2,000
Cash sent for petty expenses	16,000
Goods transferred to Ludhiana branch under instructions from H.O. at invoice price	6,000
Insurance charges paid by H.O.	1,000
Goods returned by debtors	500
Cash received from debtors	89,500

Balance on 31st March, 2009

Petty Cash A 425, Debtors A 5,500 Stock?

Prepare :

(*i*) Branch Stock Account;

(*ii*) Branch Adjustment Account;

(*iii*) Branch Profit and Loss Account;

(*iv*) Branch Debtors Account;

(*v*) Goods sent to Branch Account. [*B.Com.* (*Hons.*), *Delhi University, Nov., 2011*]

Solution

Branch Stock A/c

Particulars	(*A*)	*Particulars*	(*A*)
To Opening Stock	20,000	By Cash (Sales)	60,000
To Goods sent to Branch	2,40,000	By Debtors (credit sales)	90,000
To Branch debtors (returns)	500	By Goods Returned by Branch	7,500

To Branch Adjustment A/c (Surplus)	14,917	By Branch Adjustment A/c :	
$\frac{25}{150}$ 89,500		(Normal loss)	300
(90,000 – 500) = 89,500		Abnormal loss (900 + 3600)	4,500
		By Goods sent to Branch	6,000
		By Balance c/d (*bal. fig.*)	1,07,117
	2,75,417		2,75,417

Branch Adjustment A/c

Particulars	(*A*)	*Particulars*	(*A*)
To Branch Stock A/c :		By Branch Stock A/c :	
Goods returned $\frac{1}{5}$ 7,500	1500	Stock Reserve $\frac{1}{5}$ 20,000	4,000
Normal loss	300	By Goods sent to Branch	
Abnormal loss	900	$\frac{1}{5}$ 2,40,000	48,000
To Goods Transferred $\frac{1}{5}$ 6000	1200	By Surplus	14,917
To Stock Reserve $\frac{1}{5}$ 1,07,117	21,423		
To G/P	41,594		
	66,917		66,917

Branch Profit and Loss A/c

Particulars	(*A*)	*Particulars*	(*A*)
To Branch Stock (Abnormal loss)	3,600	By G/P	41,594
To Branch Petty Exp. (Petty Cash A/c)	16,050	By Insurance Co.	2,000
To Insurance Charges	1,000		
To Branch Debtors			
(Discount/Bad Debts)	500		
To Net Profit	22,444		
	43,594		43,594

Branch Debtors A/c

Particulars	(*A*)	*Particulars*	(*A*)
To Opening Balance	6,000	By Cash	89,500
To Branch Stock (Credit Sales)	90,000	By Branch Stock (Sales Returns)	500
		By Bad Debts (*Bal. Fig.*)	500

		By Balance c/d	5,500
	96,000		96,000

Petty Cash A/c

Particulars	*(A)*	*Particulars*	*(A)*
To Balance b/d	475	By Expenses (*Bal. Fig.*)	16,050
To Cash (Receipt)	16,000	By Balance c/d	425
	16,475		16,475

Goods Sent to Branch A/c

Particulars	*(A)*	*Particulars*	*(A)*
To Branch Stock A/c (Returns)	7,500	By Branch Stock	2,40,000
To Branch Stock	6,000	By Branch Adjustment A/c	1,500
To Branch Adjustment	48,000	By Branch Adjustment A/c	1,200
To Trading A/c	1,81,200		
	2,42,700		2,42,700

Example 35

Calcutta Head Office has its branch at Kanpur. Goods are invoiced to Branch at cost plus $33\frac{1}{3}$%. All expenses of the Branch are paid by the H.O. from the following particulars you are required to show Branch Stock A/c., Branch Adjustments A/c., Loss in Transit A/c., Pilferage A/c., and Branch P. & L. A/c. in the books of H.O.

	(A)
Opening stock at branch at cost to branch	60,000
Goods sent to branch at invoice price	1,30,000
Loss in transit at invoice price	20,000
Goods pilfered at Branch - (at invoice price)	6,000
Normal loss at invoice price	3,000
Sales (Credit)	2,20,000
Expenses of branch	35,000
Recovered from Insurance Co. against loss in transit	12,000
Closing stock at Branch at invoice price	80,500

[*I.C.W.A., Inter, Dec., 2010*]

Solution

In the Books of Calcutta Head Office
Branch Stock Account

Particulars	*(A)*	*Particulars*	*(A)*
To Balance b/d	60,000	By Sales	2,20,000
To Goods sent to Branch	1,30,000	By Loss in Transit	20,000

To Branch Adjustment A/c	1,39,500	By Pilferage	6,000
		By Br. Adjustment A/c (Normal Loss)	3,000
		By Balance c/f	80,500
	3,29,500		3,29,500

Branch Adjustment Account

Particulars	(A)	*Particulars*	(A)
To Branch Stock (Nornal Loss)	3,000	By Balance b/f (Branch Stock)	15,000
To Loss in transit (20000 × ¼)	5,000	(¼ × 60,000)	
To Pilferage (6,000 × ¼)	1,500	By Goods sent to Branch	32,500
To Gross profit (*bal. fig.*)	1,57,375	(¼ × 130000)	
To Balance Stock (80500 × ¼)	20,125	By Branch Stock	1,39,500
	1,87,000		1,87,000

Loss in Transit Account

Particulars	(A)	*Particulars*	(A)
To Branch Stock	20,000	By Branch Adjustment A/c	5,000
		By Bank (Ins. claim)	12,000
		By Branch P & L A/c	3,000
	20,000		20,000

Pilferage Account

Particulars	(A)	*Particulars*	(A)
To Branch Stock	6,000	By Branch Adjustment A/c	1,500
		By P & L A/c	4,500
	6,000		6,000

Branch Profit and Loss Account

Particulars	(A)	*Particulars*	(A)
To Expenses	35,000	By Branch Adjustment A/c	1,57,375
To Loss in Transit	3,000		
To Pilferage	4,500		
To Gen. P & L A/c	1,14,875		
	1,57,375		1,57,375

Note : Loading is $33\frac{1}{3}\%$ of cost i.e. 25% of Invoice Price.

Example 36

Red and Co. of Mumbai started a branch at Bangalore on 1.4.2010 to which goods were sent at 20% above cost. The branch makes both cash sales and credit sales. Branch expenses are met from branch cash and balance money remitted to H.O. The branch does not maintain double entry books of account and necessary accounts relating to branch are maintained in H.O. Following further details are given for the year ending on 31.3.2011 :

	(A)
Cost of goods sent to branch	1,00,000
Goods received by branch till 31.3.2011 at invoice price	1,08,000
Credit sales for the year	1,16,000
Closing debtors on 31.3.2011	41,600
Bad debts written off during the year	400
Cash remitted to H.O.	86,000
Closing cash on hand at branch on 31.3.2011	4,000
Cash remitted by H.O. to branch during the year	6,000
Closing stock in hand at branch at invoice price	12,000
Expenses incurred at branch	24,000

Draw up the necessary Ledger Accounts like Branch Debtors Account, Branch Stock Account, Goods sent to Branch Account, Branch Cash Account, Branch Expenses Account and Branch Adjustment A/c for ascertaining gross profit and Branch Profit and Loss A/c for ascertaining Branch profit. [*C.A., May, 2007*]

Solution

Branch Debtors A/c

Particulars	(A)	*Particulars*	(A)
To Branch Stock A/c	1,16,000	By Branch Cash A/c (*Bal. Fig.*)	74,000
		By Bad Debts (written off)	400
		By Balance c/d	41,600
	1,16,000		1,16,000

Goods Sent to Branch A/c

Particulars	(A)	*Particulars*	(A)
To Branch Adjustment A/c	20,000	By Branch Stock A/c	1,20,000
$1,00,000 \quad \frac{20}{100}$			
To Purchases / Trading A/c	1,00,000		
	1,20,000		1,20,000

Branch Cash A/c

Particulars	(A)	*Particulars*	(A)
To Branch Debtors A/c	74,000	By Branch Expenses A/c	24,000
To H.O. A/c (cash remittance)	6,000	By H.O. (cash remittance)	86,000
To Branch Stock A/c		By Balance c/d	4,000
– Cash Sales (*bal. fig.*)	34,000		
	1,14,000		1,14,000

Branch Stock A/c

Particulars	(A)	Particulars	(A)
To Goods sent to Branch A/c	1,20,000	By Branch Debtors A/c	1,16,000
To Branch Adjustment	54,000	By Branch Cash A/c (Sales)	34,000
(Excess profit over normal loading - *bal. fig.*)		By Goods in Transit (1,20,000 – 1,08,000)	12,000
		By Balance c/d	12,000
	1,74,000		1,74,000

Branch Expenses A/c

Particulars	(A)	Particulars	(A)
To Branch Cash A/c	24,000	By Branch P & L A/c	24,000

Branch Adjustment A/c

Particulars	(A)	Particulars	(A)
To Stock Reserve A/c	2,000	By Goods sent to Branch A/c	20,000
To Goods in transit Reserve A/c	2,000	By Branch Stock A/c	54,000
To Branch P&L A/c (*bal. fig.*)	70,000		–
	74,000		74,000

Branch P & L A/c

Particulars	(A)	Particulars	(A)
To Branch Expenses A/c	24,000	By Branch Adjustment A/c	70,000
To Bad Debts	400		
To Net Profit (transferred to General P & L A/c)	45,600		
	70,000		70,000

Working Notes :

1. Loading is 20% of cost i.e. 16.67% (1/6) of invoice value.
   Loading on closing stock = 1/6 of A 12,000 = A 2,000.
2. Loading on goods sent to branch = 1/6 of A 1,20,000 = A 20,000.
3. Loading on goods in transit = 1/6 of A 12,000 = A 2,000.

Example 37

Ram Limited of Chennai has a branch at Nagpur to which office, goods are invoiced at cost plus 25%. The branch makes sales both for cash and on credit. Branch expenses are paid direct from Head Office and the branch has to remit all cash received into the Head Office Bank Account at Nagpur.

From the following details, relating to the year 2011, prepare the accounts in Head Office Ledger and ascertain Branch Profit as per stock and debtors method. Branch does not maintain any books of accounts, but sends weekly returns to head office :

	(A)
Goods received from head office at invoice price	1,20,000
Returns to head office at invoice price	2,400
Stock at Nagpur branch on 1.1.2011 at invoice price	12,000
Sales during the year	
– Cash	40,000
– Credit	72,000
Debtors at Nagpur branch as on 1.1.2011	14,400
Cash received from debtors	64,000
Discounts allowed to debtors	1,200
Bad debts during the year	800
Sales returns at Nagpur branch	1,600
Salaries and wages at branch	12,000
Rent, rates and taxes at branch	3,600
Office expenses at Nagpur branch	1,200
Stock at branch on 31.12.2011 at invoice price	24,000

[*C.A., May, 2010*]

Solution

Nagpur Branch Stock Account

Particulars	(*A*)	*Particulars*	(*A*)
To Balance b/d	12,000	By Goods sent to Branch A/c (Returns)	2,400
To Goods sent to Branch A/c	1,20,000	By Bank A/c (Cash sales)	40,000
To Branch Debtors A/c (Returns)	1,600	By Branch Debtors A/c (credit sales)	72,000
To Branch Adjustment A/c		By Balance c/d	24,000
(Surplus over invoice price)	4,800		
	1,38,400		1,38,400

Nagpur Branch Adjustment Account

Particulars	(*A*)	*Particulars*	(*A*)
To Stock Reserve – 20% of A 24,000	4,800	By Stock reserve - 20% of A 12,000	2,400
(closing stock)		(Opening stock)	
To Branch Profit and Loss A/c	25,920	Goods sent to Branch A/c :	23,520
(Gross Profit)		20% of A 1,17,600	
		By Branch stock A/c	4,800
	30,720		30,720

Branch Profit & Loss Account

Particulars	(*A*)	*Particulars*	(*A*)
To Branch Expenses A/c	16,800	By Branch Adjustment A/c	25,920
		(Gross Profit)	
To Branch Debtors A/c (Discount)	1,200		
To Branch Debtors A/c (Bad Debts)	800		
To Net Profit			
(Transferred to Profit and Loss A/c)	7,120		
	25,920		25,920

Branch Expenses Account

Particulars	(*A*)	*Particulars*	(*A*)
To Bank A/c (rent, rates and taxes)	3,600	By Branch Profit and Loss A/c	16,800
To Bank A/c (salaries and wages)	12,000	(Transfer)	
To Bank A/c (office expenses)	1,200		
	16,800		16,800

Branch Debtors Account

Particulars	(*A*)	*Particulars*	(*A*)
To Balance b/d	14,400	By Bank A/c	64,000
To Branch Stock A/c	72,000	By Branch Profit and Loss A/c	2,000
		(Bad debts and discount)	
		By Branch Stock A/c (Sales returns)	1,600
		By Balance c/d (*bal. fig.*)	18,800
	86,400		86,400

Goods Sent to Branch Account

Particulars	(*A*)	*Particulars*	(*A*)
To Branch Stock A/c	2,400	By Branch Stock A/c	1,20,000
To Branch Adjustment A/c	23,520		
To Purchases A/c	94,080		
	1,20,000		1,20,000

Example 38

Neo Ltd., with headquarters at Mumbai, maintains a branch at Goa. Goods are invoiced at cost plus 25%. In respect of Goa branch, the following information pertaining to the year ended 31st March, 2011 are made available to you :

	(A)
Goods sent to Branch (at invoice price)	6,75,000
Goods returned by branch during the year (at invoice price)	24,000
Cash sales effected by branch	1,85,000
Discount allowed to customers	2,500
Amount received from branch debtors	3,25,000
Cheques of customers which got dishonored	8,000
Branch expenses met in cash	72,500
Sales return at Goa branch	10,000
Bad debts	5,500

	On 31 March, 2011	On 31 March, 2010
Branch Debtors	1,05,000	50,000
Stock at branch (at invoice price)	2,36,000	1,50,000

Adopting the Stock and debtors system, you are required to prepare the following Ledger accounts, as appearing in the books of the Head Office :

(*i*) Goa branch debtors account;

(*ii*) Goa branch adjustment account;

(*iii*) Goa branch profit and loss account. [*C.A., November, 2009*]

Solution

In the Books of Neo Ltd. (Head Office)
Goa Branch Debtors Account

Date	*Particulars*	*Amount (A)*	*Date*	*Particulars*	*Amount (A)*
1.4.10	To Balance b/d	50,000	31.3.11	By Bank (Collection from debtors)	3,25,000
31.3.11	To Bank A/c (Dishonour of cheques)	8,000		By Branch Stock (Goods returned by customers)	10,000
	To Branch Stock A/c (Credit sales)	3,90,000		By Bad Debts	5,500
				By Discount allowed	2,500
				By Balance c/d	1,05,000
		4,48,000			4,48,000

Goa Branch Adjustment Account

Date	*Particulars*	*Amount (A)*	*Date*	*Particulars*	*Amount (A)*
31.3.11	To Goods sent to Goa Branch A/c (goods returns to H.O.)	4,800	1.4.10	By Balance b/d (Opening stock reserve)	30,000

	To Branch P&L A/c (Profit on sale at invoice price) (*Bal. Fig.*)	1,13,000	31.3.11	Goods sent to Goa Branch A/c (Loading)	1,35,000
	To Balance c/d (Closing stock reserve)	47,200			
		1,65,000			1,65,000

Goa Branch Profit and Loss Account for the Year Ending 31 March, 2011

Particulars	*(A)*	*Particulars*	*(A)*
To Branch Expenses A/c	72,500	By Branch Adjustment A/c	1,13,000
To Branch Debtors - Discount	2,500		
Bad Debts	5,500		
To Net Profit (Transferred to General Profit and Loss A/c)	32,500		
	1,13,000		1,13,000

Working Note :

Goa Branch Stock Account

Date	*Particulars*	*Amount (A)*	*Date*	*Particulars*	*Amount (A)*
1.4.10	To Balance b/d	1,50,000	31.3.11	By Bank (Cash sales)	1,85,000
31.3.11	To Goods sent to Goa Branch	6,75,000		By Branch Debtors (Credit sales)	3,90,000
	To Branch Debtors (Goods Returned)	10,000		By Goods sent to Goa Branch (Goods returned to H.O.)	24,000
				By Balance c/d	2,36,000
		8,35,000			8,35,000

3. FINAL ACCOUNT SYSTEM

Under this system, the profit/loss of a branch is ascertained by preparing the trading and profit and loss account in the usual manner. But the trading and profit and loss account is not the part of the main accounting system and is prepared on memorandum basis. This system helps in ascertaining the profit of branch but fails to incorporate them in the books of HO. The trading and profit and loss account prepared in this system is known as Memorandum Trading and Profit and Loss Account and is prepared on the basis of cost of stocks (opening and closing) to HO as well as goods transferred to/from branch. If these figures are given at loaded price, they are converted to the cost to HO by removing the loading in them before ascertaining the results of branch with the help of the Memorandum trading and profit and loss account. In order to incorporate profit or loss made by branch as well as assets/liabilities, another account, branch account is opened in the books of Head Office. However, this branch account prepared under final account system is a personal account as compared to branch account prepared under debtor system which is a nominal account. But, the branch account is prepared on the same basis as it is prepared in the case of debtor system with the difference that entry for profit/loss (calculated with the help of the memorandum trading and profit and loss account) is done first and the final balance of branch account is derived as balancing figure. The final balance of branch account must be the same which is equal to final net assets (*i.e.*, assets at the end less liabilities at the end), to establish the accuracy of the accounts prepared.

A specimen of Branch Trading and Profit and Loss Account is displayed below :

Branch Trading and Profit and Loss Account for the Year Ending on...

Particulars		(*A*)	*Particulars*		(*A*)
To Opening Stock (at cost)		×××	By Sales		
To Goods sent	×××		Cash	×××	
Less : Returns to H.O.	×××	×××	Credit	×××	
To Direct Purchases		×××	*Less :* Returns from		
To Gross Profit c/d		×××	Branch Debtors	×××	×××
			By Abnormal Loss due to fire etc.		×××
			By Closing Stock :		
			Direct Purchases		×××
			Supplied by H.O.		×××
			In transit		×××
		×××			×××
To Branch Expenses		×××	By Gross Profit b/d		×××
To Abnormal Loss due to Fire etc.		×××	By Bank A/c/Insurance Co.		
To Net Profit t/f to General P&L A/c		×××	(Insurance Claim)		×××
		×××			×××

Example 39

On 31.3.2005, Kanpur Branch of Rajni Enterprises submits the following Trial Balance to its Head Office at Delhi : (*A in thousands*)

Dr. Balances	(*A*)	*Cr. Balances*	(*A*)
Furniture	900	Outstanding Expenses	150
Dep. on Furniture	100	Goods returned to H.O.	250
Salaries	1,250	Sales	18,000
Rent	500	Head Office A/c	4,000
Advertising	300		
Telephone charges	150		
Office expenses	50		
Stock (1.4.04)	3,000		
Goods received from H.O.	14,400		
Debtors	1,000		
Cash in hand	400		
Carriage inward	350		
	22,400		22,400

Stock on 31st March, 2005 was valued at A 31,00,000. On 29th march, 2005 the Head Office sent goods costing A 5,00,000 to its branch. Branch did not receive these goods before 1st April, 2005. The Head Office has charged the Branch with A 50,000 for services rendered by Head Office for which no entry has been made by the branch.

You are required to :

(*i*) Pass Journal entries in the book of Head Office to incorporate the whole of branch trial balance and to make necessary adjustments.

(*ii*) Prepare Trading and Profit and Loss A/c for the Branch in H.O. books.

[*B.Com.*, (*Hons.*), *Delhi University, 2006*]

Solution

In the Books of Head Office
Branch Trading and Profit and Loss Account
for the Year Ending 31st March, 2005

Particulars	*(A)*	*Particulars*	*(A)*
To Opening Stock	30,00,000	By Goods Returned to H.O.	2,50,000
To Goods Received from H.O.	1,44,00,000	By Sales A/c	1,80,00,000
To Carriage Inward	3,50,000	By Stock at the end	31,00,000
To Gross Profit c/d	36,00,000		
	2,13,50,000		2,13,50,000
To Depreciation on Furniture	1,00,000	By Gross Profit b/d	36,00,000
To Salaries	12,50,000		
To Rent	5,00,000		
To Advertising	3,00,000		
To Telephone Charges	1,50,000		
To Office Expenses	50,000		
To Head Office Expenses	50,000		
To Profit and Loss A/c	12,00,000		
	36,00,000		36,00,000

Head Office Journal (Incorporation of Journal Entries)

Date	*Particulars*		*Dr. Amount (A)*	*Cr. Amount (A)*
	Branch Trading A/c	Dr.	1,77,50,000	
	To Branch A/c			1,77,50,000
	[Being incorporation of Opening Stock (A 30,00,000), Goods received from Head Office (A 1,44,00,000) and Carriage inward (A 3,50,000)]			
	Branch A/c	Dr.	2,13,50,000	
	To Branch Trading A/c			2,13,50,000
	[Being incorporation of Goods returned to H.O. and sales at the branch and stock at the end, *i.e.*, 2,50,000 + 1,80,00,000 + 31,00,000]			
	Branch Trading A/c	Dr.	36,00,000	
	To Branch Profit and Loss A/c			36,00,000
	[Being Gross Profit at Branch]			

Branch Profit and Loss A/c	Dr.	24,00,000	
To Branch A/c			24,00,000
[Being incorporation of depreciation on furniture, salaries, rent, advertising and Head Office expenses (*i.e.*, 1,00,000 + 12,50,000 + 5,00,000 + 3,00,000 + 1,50,000 + 50,000 + 50,000)]			
Branch Profit and Loss A/c	Dr.	12,00,000	
To General Profit and Loss A/c			12,00,000
(Net Profit at the branch incorporated in the General Profit and Loss Account)			
Branch Furniture A/c	Dr.	9,00,000	
Branch Debtors A/c	Dr.	10,00,000	
Branch Cash A/c	Dr.	4,00,000	
Branch Stock A/c	Dr.	31,00,000	
To Branch A/c			54,00,000
(Incorporation of branch assets)			
Branch A/c	Dr.	1,50,000	
To Branch Outstanding Expenses A/c			1,50,000
(Incorporation of branch liability)			
Good-in-transit A/c	Dr.	5,00,000	
To Branch A/c			5,00,000
(Goods-in-transit incorporated)			
Branch A/c	Dr.	50,000	
To Head Office Profit and Loss A/c			50,000
(Head Office Expenses charged to branch)			

Example 40

Following is the information of the Jammu branch of Best Ltd., New Delhi for the year ending 31st March, 2010 from the following :

1. Goods are invoiced to the branch at cost plus 20%.
2. The sale price is cost plus 50%.
3. Other information :

	(A)
Stock as on 1.4.2009	2,20,000
Goods sent during the year	11,00,000
Sales during the year	12,00,000
Expenses incurred at the branch	45,000

Ascertain

(*i*) the profit earned by the branch during the year;

(*ii*) branch stock reserve in respect of unrealized profit. [*C.A., November, 2010*]

Solution

(*i*) Calculation of profit earned by the branch

In the Books of Jammu Branch
Trading Account

Particulars	*(A)*	*Particulars*	*(A)*
To Opening Stock	2,20,000	By Sales	12,00,000
To Goods sent by Head Office	11,00,000	By Closing Stock (Refer W.N.)	3,60,000
To Expenses	45,000		
To Gross Profit	1,95,000		
	15,60,000		15,60,000

(*ii*) Stock reserve in respect of unrealised profit

= A 3,60,000 × (20/120) = A 60,000

Working Notes :

Cost Price	100
Invoice Price	120
Sale Price	150

Calculation of closing stock at invoice price

	(A)	
Opening stock at invoice price	2,20,000	
Goods received during the year at invoice price	11,00,000	
	13,20,000	
Less : Cost of goods sold at invoice price	(9,60,000)	[12,00,000 × (120/150)]
Closing stock	3,60,000	

Note : It is assumed that all figures given in the questions is at invoice price.

Example 41

B.S. Ltd. operates a retail branch at Ranchi. All purchases are made by the Head Office at Kolkata, goods for the branch being delivered to it direct and charged out at selling price which is cost price *plus* 50%. All cash received by the branch is remitted to Kolkata. Branch expenses are paid by the branch out of an impreset amount which is reimbursed by Kolkata monthly. The branch keeps a sales ledger and certain essential subsidiary books; but otherwise all branch transactions are recorded in the books of the Kolkata office.

On 1 January 2008, stock in trade at the branch, at selling price, amounted to A 48,660 and debtors to A 6,440.

During the year ended 31 December 2008, the following transactions took place at the branch :

	(A)
Goods received by branch at selling price	1,21,800
Cash Sales	64,150
Credit Sales	51,280
Goods returned to Kolkata at selling price	1,560

Reduction in selling price authorised by H.O.	970
Cash received from Debtors	42,660
Debtors written off as irrecoverable	650
Cash discounts allowed	1,120

A consignment of goods despatched to branch in December 2008 at a selling price of A 1,200, was not received by the branch until January 6,2009 and had not been included in the stock figure. The expenses relating to the branch for the year ended 31 December 2008 amounted to A 17,290. On 31 December 2008, physical stock at branch, at selling price amounted to A 52,200.

You are required to write up the Branch Stock Account maintained in Kolkata books to prepare the Trading and Profit and Loss Account of the branch for the year ended 31 December 2008.

[*B.Com.*, (*Hons.*), *Delhi University*]

Solution

B.S. Ltd.
Ranchi Branch Trading and Profit and Loss Account for the Year Ending on 31 December 2008

Particulars		(*A*)	*Particulars*		(*A*)
Opening Stock (48,660–16,220)		32,440	Sales		
			– Cash	64,150	
			– Credit	51,280	1,15,430
Goods sent to Branch :			Stock at the end :		
Actually Received	1,21,800		With the branch	34,800	
Intransit	1,200		(52,200 – 17,400)		
	1,23,000		in transit	800	35,600
Less : Returns	1,560		(1,200 – 400)		
	1,21,440				
Less : Load	40,480	80,960			
Gross Profit c/d		37,630			
		1,51,030			1,51,030
Branch Expenses		17,290	Gross Profit c/d		37,630
Bad Debts		650			
Discount Allowed		1,120			
Profit and Loss Account		18,570			
		37,630			37,630

Ranchi Branch Stock Account

Particulars	(*A*)	*Particulars*	(*A*)
Balance b/d	48,660	Branch Bank A/c (Cash sales)	64,150
Goods sent to Branch		Branch Debtors A/c (Credit sales)	51,280
Account (1,21,800 + 1,200)	1,23,000	Branch Profit and Loss A/c	
		(Promotional Discount)	970
		Goods sent to Branch Account	

		(Return to H.O.)	1,560
		Branch Adjustment Account	
		(Load on shortages)	100
		Branch Profit and Loss Account	
		(Cost of Shortages)	200
		Balance c/d	
		Stock at Branch	52,200
		Stock in transit	1,200
	1,71,660		1,71,660

Ranchi Branch Debtors Account

Particulars	*(A)*	*Particulars*	*(A)*
Balance b/d	6,440	Bank (Cash Received)	42,660
Branch Stock Account (credit sales)	51,280	Bad Debts Account	650
		Discount Allowed Account	1,120
		Balance c/d	13,290
	57,720		57,720

Ranchi Branch Account (under Branch Final Account System)

Particulars	*(A)*	*Particulars*		*(A)*
Balance b/d :		Bank (Remittances) :		
Stock	32,440	Cash Sales	64,150	
Debtors	6,440	Collection from Debtors	42,660	1,06,810
Goods sent to Branch less		Balance c/d		48,890
Returns	80,960			
Bank (Expenses)	17,290			
Profit and loss account	18,570			
	1,55,700			1,55,700

Balance at the branch can be verified as :

Stock at the end	35,600
Debtors at the end	13,290
	48,890

Note : Reduction in selling price authorised by H.O. is a promotional discount. Hence it is treated as indirect expense and debited to Branch Profit and Loss Account.

4. WHOLE SALE BRANCH SYSTEM

Under whole sale Branch System, the Head Office of a business enterprise sends goods to the wholesalers and also to retailers and thus goods are sold by wholesalers as well as retail branches. The difference between the retail price and the whole sale price is that additional profit which the H.O. is likely to make by opening a branch. For example, assume that the H.O. has supplied goods (costing A 400) to whole salers at A 500 and to retail branches at A 525. So, the additional profit make by H.O. by opening the branch is

A 25. The total profit earned by H.O. through branch is A 125. The H.O. could earn A 100 by selling the goods on whole sale basis to other whole salers.

Under this system, the profit/loss of the branch is calculated by preparing the trading and profit and loss account on wholesale price basis. But the account is not the part of the main accounting system and is prepared on memorandum basis. Hence, like final account system (Cost price basis), this accounting system helps in ascertaining the profit of branch but fails to incorporate them in the books of H.O.

Under this system, the concept of branch profit is modified. Under the three systems discussed earlier, branch profit was recognised as the excess of selling price over the cost to H.O. of the goods supplied. But under this system, profit is divided into two parts as under :

1. Excess of wholesale price over the cost to H.O. This is recognised as profit of the H.O..
2. Excess of selling price over the wholesale price. This is recognised as profit of the branch.

The goods are supplied to the branch at wholesale price and the difference between wholesale price and cost price is the profit earned by the H.O. and this profit is shown in the books of H.O. The cost to the branch is assumed to be the wholesale price. The branch sells the goods at retail price and consequently, the profit of the branch is assumed to be the difference between the retail price and wholesale price. The logic for giving Branch, the credit for only profit equal to difference of retail price and wholesale price and not the total profit, lies in ascertaining the correct contribution made by the branch to the H.O. The H.O. always has the option of selling these goods on wholesale basis and the difference made by the branch is over and above that price and, hence, it should be given credit for that contribution only.

It should be kept in mind that Memorandum trading and profit and loss account is prepared on the basis of Wholesale price of the branch stock in the beginning, goods supplied by H.O., goods returned by branch and branch stock at the end of the year. If these figures are given on any other basis, they need to be converted to the wholesale price before ascertaining the profit of branch with the help of the Memorandum trading and profit and loss account. The profit/loss made by branch as well as the assets/liabilities are incorporated in the books of H.O. by opening the Branch Account in the books of H.O. as is done in case of final account system discussed earlier. However, the branch account made under the Wholesale Branch System, is a Personal Account as compared to branch account prepared under debtor system which is a Nominal account. However, the account is prepared on the same basis as is done in the case of Debtor System with the difference that loading is not removed in the branch account and entry for profit/loss (calculated with the help of the memorandum trading and profit and loss account) is done first and the final balance of branch account is derived as balancing figure. As excess of wholesale price over cost to H.O. of goods supplied (called loading) is taken as profit of the H.O., the loading on the opening and closing stock are removed in the H.O. Trading and Profit and Loss Account with the help of the following entries as it indicates unrealised portion of the loading on goods supplied :

(*i*) HO Trading and Profit and Loss A/c Dr.

To Stock Reserve A/c

(with loading on closing stock)

(*ii*) Stock Reserve A/c Dr.

To HO Trading and Profit and Loss A/c

(with loading on opening stock)

The final balance of branch account must be the same which is equal to final net assets (i.e., assets (inclusive of branch stock account at wholesale price basis) at the end less liabilities at the end) to establish the accuracy of the accounts prepared.

Specimen of different accounts prepared under Whole Sale Branch System are given below :

(a) Branch Stock Account (at Wholesale Price) Branch Trading Account

Particulars		(A)	*Particulars*		(A)
To Balance b/d (at Wholesale Price)		×××	By Sales (at Retail Price/list Price/Catalogue Price)		
To Goods sent to Branch (at wholesale price)	×××		Cash	×××	
Less : Returns to H.O.	×××	×××	Credit	×××	
To Gross Profit t/f to P&L A/c		×××	*Less* : Returns	×××	×××
			By Abnormal Loss (at wholesale Price)		×××
			By Balance c/d (at wholesale Price)		×××
		×××			×××

(b) Branch Profit and Loss Account

Particulars	(A)	*Particulars*	(A)
To Branch Expenses	×××	By Gross Profit b/d	×××
To Abnormal Loss (at wholesale price)	×××	By Claim from Insurance Co. (if any)	×××
To Net Profit t/f to H.O. P&L A/c	×××		
	×××		×××

(c) Branch Stock Reserve Account

Particulars	(A)	*Particulars*	(A)
To H.O. P&L A/c [T/F of Opening Stock reserve)	×××	By Balance b/d [Wholesale profit included in Opening Stock]	×××
To Balance c/d [Wholesale profit included Closing Stock]	×××	By H.O. P&L A/c [Wholesale profit included in Closing Stock]	×××
	×××		×××

(d) An Extract of H.O. Profit and Loss Account

Particulars	(A)	*Particulars*	(A)
To Stock Reserve A/c (Provision made for unrealised wholesale profit included in Closing Stock)	×××	By Branch Profit and Loss A/c (Net Profit)	×××
		By Stock Reserve A/c (Transfer of Provision for unrealised profit included in opening stock, now no longer required)	×××

Example 42

A Head Office invoices goods to its branch at 20% less than the list price. The list price is made up by adding 100% to cost price. Goods are sold to customers at list price both by Head Office and Branch. From the following particulars, prepare Trading and Profit and Loss Accounts for the year ended 31st March, 2010 to show profit made by Head Office and Branch on Wholesale Basis :

	Head Office (A)	Branch (A)
Opening Stock at Cost (at invoice price for branch)	60,000	24,000
Purchases	6,00,000	–
Goods sent to Branch at invoice price	–	1,44,000
Sales	9,00,000	1,20,000
Expenses	1,30,000	6,000

[*B.Com.*, (*Hons.*), *Delhi University, 2010*]

Solution

Trading and Profit and Loss A/c
for the year ending 31st March 2010

Particulars	H.O. (A)	Branch (A)	*Particulars*	H.O. (A)	Branch (A)
To Opening Stock	60,000	24,000	By Sales	9,00,000	1,20,000
To Purchases	6,00,000	–	By Goods Sent to Branch	1,44,000	–
To Goods Sent to Branch	–	1,44,000	By Closing Stock*	1,20,000	72,000
To Gross Profit c/d	5,04,000	24,000			
	11,64,000	1,92,000		11,64,000	1,92,000
To Expenses	1,30,000	6,000	By Gross Profit b/d	5,04,000	24,000
To Stock Reserve			By Stock Reserve		
[A 72,000 × 60/160]	27,000		[A 24,000 × 60/160]	9,000	
To Net Profit	3,56,000	18,000			
	5,13,000	24,000		5,13,000	24,000

Working Notes **:**

* Let Cost Price = A 100 List Price = A 200

∴ Invoice Price = 20% less than the list price, *i.e.*, A 200 – 20% of A 200 = A 160

(*i*) *Calculation of Closing Stock at Head Office :*

		(A)
Opening Stock		60,000
Add : Purchases		6,00,000
		6,60,000
Less : Cost of Goods Sold (9,00,000 × 100/200)	4,50,000	
Cost of Goods sent to Branch (1,44,000 × 100/160)	90,000	5,40,000
Closing Stock		1,20,000

(*ii*) *Calculation of Closing Stock at Branch :*

Opening Stock at Invoice Price	24,000
Add : Goods received from Head Office	1,44,000
	1,68,000
Less : Invoice Price of Goods sold [1,20,000 × 160/200]	96,000
Closing Stock	72,000

Example 43

A Ltd. has a retail branch at Kanpur. Goods are sold to consumers at cost plus 100%. The wholesale price is cost plus 80%. Goods are invoiced to Kanpur at wholesale price.

From the following particulars find out the profit made at head office and Kanpur branch for the year 2005-06.

	Head Office (A)	*Kanpur* (A)
Stock on 1.4.05	25,000	1,800
Purchases	1,50,000	–
Goods sent to branch at wholesale price	54,000	–
Sales	1,53,000	50,000
Expenses	8,000	2,000

Sales at Head Office are made only on wholesale basis and that at branch only to consumers. Stock at branch is valued at wholesale price.

[*B.Com., (Hons.), Delhi University 2007*]

Solution

Trading and Profit and Loss Account for the Year Ended 31 March, 2006

Particulars	H.O. (A)	Branch (A)	*Particulars*	H.O. (A)	Branch (A)
To Opening Stock	25,000	1,800	By Sales	1,53,000	50,000
To Purchases	1,50,000	–	By Goods sent to Branch	54,000	–
To Goods received from H.O.	–	54,000	By Closing Stock*1&*2	60,000	10,800
To Gross Profit c/d (*bal. fig.*)	92,000	5,000			
	2,67,000	60,800		2,67,000	60,800
To Expenses	8,000	2,000	By Gross Profit b/d	92,000	5,000
To Stock Reserve*3	4,800	–	By Stock Reserve*3	800	–
To Net Profit (*bal. fig.*)	80,000	3,000			
	92,800	5,000		92,800	5,000

Working Notes :

*1 *Calculation of Closing Stock at Head Office (H.O.)*

		A
Opening Stock		25,000
Add : Purchases		1,50,000
		1,75,000
Less		
(*i*) Cost of goods sent to Branch	: $\frac{100}{180} \times$ A 54,000 = 30,000	
(*ii*) Cost of goods sold to customer	: $\frac{100}{180} \times$ 1,53,000 = 85,000	1,15,000
	Closing Stock at the Head Office	60,000

* Let the Cost = A 100′ wholesale price will be = A 100 + A 80 = A 180

*2 *Calculation of Closing Stock at the Branch*

	(A)
Opening Stock at Invoice Price (*i.e.* Wholesale Price)	1,800
Add : Goods received from H.O.	54,000
	55,800
Less : Cost to Branch (Invoice Price) of goods sold by Branch (50,000 × 180/200*)	45,000
Closing Stock at the Branch	10,800

* Let the Cost = A 100; Cost of Branch = A 100 + A 80 = A 180;
Selling price for customer at Branch = A 100 + A 100 = A 200

*3. *Provision for unrealised Profit in Stock at Branch*

Opening Stock = $\frac{80}{180} \times 1,800$ = A 800

Closing Stock = $\frac{80}{180} \times 10,800$ = A 4,800

Example 44

A head office sends goods to its branch at cost *plus* 80%. Goods are sold to customers at cost *plus* 100%. From the following particulars ascertain the profits made at the Head Office :

	Head Office (*A*)	*Kanpur* (*A*)
Stock	20,000	–
Purchases	2,00,000	–
Goods sent to Branch (Invoice Price)	90,000	–
Sales	2,70,000	90,000

Note : Sales at the H.O. are made at wholesale basis.

[*B.Com.* (*Hons.*) *Delhi University*]

Solution

In the Books of H.O.
(H.O.) Trading Account

Particulars	(*A*)	*Particulars*	(*A*)
Stock	20,000	Sales	2,70,000
Purchases	2,00,000	Goods sent to Branch A/c	90,000
Gross Profit c/d	1,60,000	Stock at the end - at cost	20,000
		(See Working Notes)	
	3,80,000		3,80,000
Provision for unrealised		Gross Profit b/d	1,60,000
Profit on unsold stock at the branch	4,000		
General Profit and Loss Account	1,56,000		
	1,60,000		1,60,000

Branch Trading Account

Particulars	(A)	*Particulars*	(A)
Goods received from H.O.	90,000	Sales	90,000
Gross Profit	9,000	Stock at the end (at loaded price)	9,000
	99,000		99,000

Working Notes :

(*i*) *Calculation of stock at the end at the H.O.*

	A
Cost of goods available for sale (20,000 + 2,00,000)	2,20,000
Less : Cost of Sales and Goods sent to Branch	
(2,70,000 + 90,000) : $3,60,000 \frac{100}{180}$	2,00,000
Hence Stock at the end	20,000

(*ii*) *Calculation of stock at the end at Branch*

	(A)
Loaded price of goods available for sale	90,000
Less : Loaded price of goods sold : $90,000 \frac{180}{200}$	81,000
Stock at the end at loaded price	9,000

(*iii*) *Unrealised profit on closing stock at the Branch*

	(A)
Loaded price of the stock	9,000
Less : Cost of the stock $9,000 \frac{100}{180}$	5,000
	4,000

Example 45

Beta Ltd. having head office at Mumbai has a branch at Nagpur. The head office does wholesale trade only at cost plus 80%. The goods are sent to branch at the wholesale price *viz.*, cost plus 80%. The branch at Nagpur is wholly engaged in retail trade and the goods are sold at cost to H.O. plus 100%.

Following details are furnished for the year ended 31 March, 2007 :

	Head Office (A)	*Branch* (A)
Opening stock (as on 1.4.2006)	2,25,000	–
Purchases	25,50,000	–
Goods sent to branch (cost to H.O. plus 80%)	9,54,000	–
Sales	27,81,000	9,50,000
Office expenses	90,000	8,500
Selling expenses	72,000	6,300
Staff salary	65,000	12,000

You are required to prepare Trading and Profit and Loss Account of the head office and branch for the year ended 31 March, 2007. [*C.A., November, 2007*]

Solution

Trading and Profit and Loss A/c for the Year Ended 31 March 2007

Particulars	H.O. (*A*)	Branch (*A*)	*Particulars*	H.O. (*A*)	Branch (*A*)
To Opening Stock	2,25,000	–	By Sales	27,81,000	9,50,000
To Purchases	25,50,000	–	By Goods sent to branch	9,54,000	–
To Goods received from head office	–	9,54,000	By Closing stock (W.N. 1 and 2)	7,00,000	99,000
To Gross profit c/d	16,60,000	95,000			
	44,35,000	10,49,000		44,35,000	10,49,000
To Office expenses	90,000	8,500	By Gross profit b/d	16,60,000	95,000
To Selling expenses	72,000	6,300			
To Staff salaries	65,000	12,000			
To Branch Stock Reserve (W.N. 3)	44,000	–			
To Net Profit	13,89,000	68,200			
	16,60,000	95,000		16,60,000	95,000

***Working Notes* :**

1. *Calculation of closing stock of head office :*

	A
Opening Stock of head office	2,25,000
Goods purchased by head office	25,50,000
	27,75,000
Less : Cost of goods sold [37,35,000* × 100/180]	20,75,000
	7,00,000

2. *Calculation of closing stock of branch :*

	A
Goods received from head office [at invoice value]	9,54,000
Less : Invoice value of goods sold [9,50,000 × 180/200]	8,55,000
	99,000

3. *Calculation of unrealized profit in branch stock :*

Branch stock	A 99,000	
Profit included	80% of cost	
Hence, unrealized profit would be = A 99,000 × 80/180 =		A 44,000

INDEPENDENT BRANCHES

Independent branches are those branches which keep full system of accounting for their transactions. The H.O. allows such branches to make their own purchases, sales and other transactions. These branches are not required to send cash daily to the H.O. nor do they depend on the H.O. to meet their expenses requirements.

However, an independent branch does not mean that such a branch is independent and free from H.O. A branch is created by H.O. and therefore it has depend on H.O. in an organizational content. Truly speaking independent branch is independent only with regard to maintenance of accounts.

Branch Account in the Books of H.O. and Head Office Account in the Books of Branch

In case of independent branches, both branch as well as H.O. maintain their books. This leads to generation of trial balance in both the books. Since, the branch maintains its own trial balance, it can independently calculate its results as well as make its own balance sheet. The accounts are maintained in the usual manner and both H.O. and branch maintain an account for the other party *i.e.*, 'Branch Account' in the books of H.O. and 'Head Office Account' in the books of branch. Both accounts are personal in nature. The Branch Account in the books of the Head Office is debited by cash sent to branch, goods supplied, depreciation of branch fixed assets, charges made by the Head Office for rendering services and profit earned by the branch. The Branch Account is credited by cash received from the branch, goods returned to Head Office, payment by the branch for purchases of assets and the losses incurred at the branch. Similarly the branch will maintain Head Office Account which will have the same set of entries stated above but on the reverse sides. Generally the Balance of Branch Account (debit) in the books of Head Office should tally with the Balance of Head Office Account (credit) in the books of branch. But in exceptional cases there may be disagreement in these balances because of following reasons. That is, under independent branch system, the following cases/transaction need special attention.

1. Goods-in-Transit

It represents the goods supplied by the Head Office (or returned by the branch) a few days before the close of the accounting period but may remain undelivered because of transport delay or difficulties. After sending the goods, Head Office must have debited the account of branch in its books but there will be no corresponding credit to Head Office Account in the books of branch owing to non-receipt of the goods by the end of the accounting period. This introduces a 'difference' in the two reciprocal accounts namely Head Office Account and Branch Account. In order to reconcile the two accounts, the Head Office will make the following entry on the last day of the accounting period :

Goods-in-transit Account Dr.
　　To Branch Account

Normally this entry will be made in the books of Head Office which maintains the records of all the branches. In the combined Balance Sheet, Goods-in-Transit appears as an asset. In the next accounting year when the goods are actually delivered, the account is closed at the Head Office by making the following journal entry :

(*a*) If Head Office had supplied goods to branch Dr.
Branch Account
　　To Goods-in-Transit Account

(*b*) If Branch had returned the goods
Returns from (or Goods sent to) Branch Account Dr.
　　To Goods-in-Transit Account

2. Cash (or Remittances)-in-transit

Sometimes cash remitted by the Branch to the Head Office (or by the Head Office to the Branch) is in transit. Suppose a Branch sends the cash to the Head Office before the close of the accounting period, say 31 March, but it is received after 31 March. While remitting cash the branch will immediately debit the Head Office Account but the Head Office will not give credit to Branch until the cash is actually received by the Head Office. Thus the balances of the two accounts (*i.e.*, H.O. Account in the books of Branch and Branch Account in the books of H.O.) will not tally. In order to reconcile these two balances, the following adjustment entry will be made in the books of Head Office :

Goods-in-transit Account Dr.
　　To Branch Account

In the consolidated Balance Sheet, 'Cash-in-Transit' will appear as an asset.

On receipt of the remittances in the next accounting period, this is closed at the Head Office by making the following adjustment entry :

(*a*) If Branch had remitted Dr.
Cash Account
To Cash-in-Transit Account

(*b*) If Head Office had remitted :
Remittances-to Branch Account Dr.
To Cash-in-Transit Account

Besides the above reasons of disagreement in the balances of Head Office account and branch account in the respective books, there could be still some reasons for the difference in H.O. account and branch account. Such reasons are as follows :

(*a*) HO debtors having paid to branch directly.
(*b*) HO creditors paid by branch directly.
(*c*) Branch debtors having paid to HO directly.
(*d*) Branch creditors paid by HO directly.
(*e*) Branch income (*e.g.*, interest on loan advanced) received by HO directly.
(*f*) HO income received by branch directly.
(*g*) Goods abnormally lost-in-transit from HO to branch and branch declines to accept liability for the same etc.

3. Accounting for Fixed Assets

The account of fixed assets in the physical possession of and used by the branch, may or may not be kept at the branch. If the branch keeps its records, there is no difficulty and the usual entries are made. But where the accounts of fixed assets of the branch are maintained by the Head Office, the records for the purchases and depreciation are made as follows :

Transaction	*HO Books*	*Branch Books*
Payment for fixed asset made by the HO	Branch Assets A/c Dr. To Cash/Bank A/c	No Entry
Payment for fixed asset made by the branch	Branch Asset A/c Dr. To Branch A/c	HO A/c Dr. To Cash/Bank A/c
Payment for fixed assets to be made by the branch	Branch Asset A/c Dr. To Branch A/c	HO A/c Dr. To Creditors A/c
Depreciation on fixed assets	Branch A/c Dr. To Branch Asset A/c	Depreciation A/c Dr. To HO A/c

Where the accounts of fixed assets are maintained by the branch, the following entries are made.

Transaction	*HO Books*	*Branch Books*
Payment for fixed asset made by the HO	Branch Assets A/c Dr. To Cash Bank A/c	Fixed Assets A/c Dr. to HO A/c
Payment for fixed asset made by the branch	No Entry	Fixed Assets A/c Dr. to Cash/Bank A/c
Payment for fixed assets to be made by the branch	No Entry	Fixed Assets A/c Dr. to Creditors for Assets A/c
Depreciation on fixed assets	No Entry	Depreciation A/c Dr. to Fixed Assets A/c

4. HO Expenses Charged to Branch

The head Office sometimes pays expenses which are incurred for the sole benefit of the branch. The HO charges these expenses wholly to the Branch Account. For example, the rent of the branch building paid by HO would be charged fully to Branch Account. In addition to this, there can be expenses which are incurred for the benefit of both. Such expenses need to be allocated between HO and Branch in the ratio of benefit derived by both of them. For example, the salary is paid to the Accountant at HO who spends half of his time finalizing the accounts of the branch as well. In this case, half of accountant's salary will be charged to H.O. profit and loss account and the other half will be charged to Branch Account. The accounting entries needed to give effect in this case are as follows :

HO Books		*Branch Books*	
Branch A/c	Dr.	HO Expenses A/c	Dr.
To Respective Expenses A/c		To HO A/c	
(if the expenses has not been transferred to Income statement of HO)			
Or			
Branch A/c	Dr.		
To Trading and Profit and Loss A/c			
(if the expense has been transferred to the Income statement of HO)			

5. Inter Branch Transactions

When there are many branches operated by H.O., one branch may supply goods to another branch or receive cash from the other branch. These transactions among branches are known as inter branch transactions. The H.O. is within the knowledge of these branch transactions which take place under the instructions of the H.O. Such transactions may be recorded either directly by maintaining account of a branch in another branch's books or indirectly by all branches by making entries through the Head Office Account. Generally the latter procedure is adopted. For example, if goods amounting to A 50,000 are supplied by Delhi Branch to Mumbai Branch and the H.O. is in Lucknow, the following journal entries will be made under the 'direct' and 'indirect' records respectively :

When Directly Recorded by Branches

Delhi Branch Books			*Mumbai Branch Account*		
Mumbai Branch Account	Dr.	50,000	Goods sent to Branch Account	Dr.	50,000
To Goods sent to Branch A/c		50,000	To Delhi Branch A/c		50,000

When Branches Record Through Head Office Books

Delhi Branch Books		*Mumbai Branch Account*	
Head Office Account Dr. 50,000		Goods send to Branch A/c Dr. 50,000	
To Goods sent to Branch A/c	50,000	To Head Office A/c	50,000

In The Books of Lucknow Head Office

Mumbai Branch Account	Dr. 50,000	
To Delhi Branch Account		50,000

RECONCILIATION PROCEDURE

As stated earlier Head Office Account in the books of Branch and Branch Account in the books of H.O. need to be tallied before the accounts are consolidated in the books of H.O. The following steps are required to be taken for the reconciliation of transactions between the Head Office and the branch.

The first step towards reconciliation, is to calculate the amount to be reconciled. It is calculated as under:

(*i*) When the nature of balance (either Dr. or Cr.) of HO account and branch account is same, those balances are added to calculate the amount;

(*ii*) When the nature of balance of HO account and branch account is different (*i.e.,* one is Dr. and the other is Cr.), the difference of the amount of two accounts gives the amount to be reconciled.

When the disagreement in the two accounts is because of the transit items, it would mean record of transaction in one set of books only. It can be corrected by recording the aspect in the set of book where it is still not recorded. Hence, if HO has sent goods to branch and they are not received by it, the branch should record these goods in its books as goods-in-transit. The reason is that HO has already done its part of recording and the gap is there in the branch's books. The branch should record the following entry :

Goods-in-Transit/Cash-in-Transit* A/c Dr.

To HO A/c

*If cash is sent by HO and is not received by the branch.

Later on, when goods/cash is actually received by the branch in the next accounting period, the branch can pass the following entry :

Goods Sent to Branch A/c / Cash A/c Dr.

To Goods-in-Transit/Cash-in-Transit A/c

Similarly, if branch has sent cash to HO and it is not received by the HO, the HO should record this as cash-in-transit. The reason, as before, is that branch has already done its part of recording and the gap is there in the HO's books. The HO should record the following entry :

Cash-in-Transit/Goods-in-Transit* A/c Dr.

To Branch A/c

*If goods are returned by branch and are not received by the HO.

Later on, when goods/cash is actually received by the HO in the next accounting period, the HO can pass the following entry :

Goods Sent to Branch A/c/Cash A/c Dr.

To Goods-in-Transit/Cash-in-Transit A/c

Incorporation of Branch Results in the Books of Head Office

The method that will be adopted for incorporating the trading result of the branch with that of the head office would depend on whether it is desired to prepare separate Profit and Loss Account and Balance Sheet of the branch and the Head Office or consolidated statement of account of both branch and head office.

In incorporation of branch results the purpose is to combine the results of branch with that of HO as financial statement will be prepared as whole like Punjab National Bank may have several branches, but finally Balance Sheet is prepared only for one company i.e. HO Punjab National Bank.

The Branch result may be incorporated in the books of head office by adopting any of the following methods :

1. Separate Final Accounts Methods,
2. Consolidated Method.

1. **Separate Final Accounts Method :** The procedure to be followed under this method are as follows:

   (*i*) Prepare separate Trading and Profit and Loss Account and Balance Sheet of the Branch in the books of the respective branch.

   (*ii*) Transfer only the amount of net profit/loss as shown by Branch Profit and Loss Account to Head Office by passing the following journal entry.

   Profit and Loss A/c Dr.
   To Head Office A/c

   Note : *A reverse entry is passed in case of Net Loss.*

   (*iii*) Incorporate only the net profit of the branch in the books of Head Office by passing the following journal entry :

   Branch A/c Dr.
   To General P & L A/c

   Note : *A reverse entry is passed in case of Net Loss.*

   (*iv*) Prepare separate Trading and Profit and Loss Account and the Balance Sheet of the head office in its books.

The incorporation of branch results may be done into two parts :

(*a*) Incorporation of revenue accounts of branch and

(*b*) Incorporation of assets and liabilities of branch.

Incorporation of Revenue Accounts : This can be done in two different methods :

Method 1 : Under this method, Trading and Profit and Loss A/c of the branch is prepared by H.O. The entries to be passed are as follows :

1.	For items which will appear on the debit side of Trading A/c : Branch Trading A/c To Branch A/c	Dr.	×××	 ×××
2.	For items which will appear on the credit side of Trading A/c : Branch A/c To Branch Trading A/c	Dr.	×××	 ×××
3.	For Gross profit made by branch : Branch Trading A/c To Branch P and L A/c	Dr.	×××	 ×××
4.	For items which will appear on the debit side of P & L A/c : Branch P & L A/c To Branch A/c	Dr.	×××	 ×××
5.	For items which will appear on the credit side of Trading A/c : Branch A/c To Branch P & L A/c	Dr.	×××	 ×××
6.	For Net Profit made by the branch : Branch P & L A/c To General P & L A/c	Dr.	×××	 ×××

Method 2. Incorporation of Assets and Liabilities : The head office may or may not incorporate the Assets and Liabilities of the branch. If incorporated the following entries will be necessary :

1.	For Branch Assets :			
	Sundry Branch Asset A/c	Dr.	×××	
	To Branch A/c			×××
2.	For Branch Liabilities :			
	Branch A/c	Dr.	×××	
	To Sundry Branch Liability A/c			×××

After such incorporation of Assets and Liabilities, the Branch A/c (in which adjustment entries have already been posted) in HO books will be closed.

Note :

- At the commencement of the next accounting period, the entries passed for incorporation of Assets and Liabilities will be reversed, and then the Branch A/c will again be restored showing the opening balances of these items.
- If the Branch Assets and Liabilities are not incorporated, the Branch A/c in HO books will have closing balance equal to net assets of the branch.

While preparing a Balance Sheet of the HO, all the Assets and Liabilities of the HO and those of the branch will be taken into consideration.

If Branch sends its own profit and loss figure, then only assets and liability entries along with profit and Loss will be passed and final balance sheet is prepared.

2. Consolidated Method : The procedure to be followed are as follows :

(*i*) Prepare separate Trading and Profit and Loss Account of the Branch in the books of respective branch.

(*ii*) Transfer only the amount of net profit/loss, the assets and the liabilities of the branch to Head Office Account.

(*iii*) Incorporate the net profit/loss, the assets and the liabilities of the branch in the books of Head Office.

(*iv*) Prepare Trading and Profit and Loss Account after incorporating Branch net profit/loss and consolidated Balance Sheet in the books of Head Office.

Example 46

Goods worth A 50,000 sent by head office but the branch has received till the closing date goods for worth A 40,000 only. Give journal entry in the books of H.O. and branch for goods in transit.

[*C.A., November, 2008*]

Solution

Journal Entry in the Books of Head Office (No Entry)
Journal Entry in the Books of Branch

		(*A*)	(*A*)
Goods-on-transit account	Dr.	10,000	
To Head Office Account			10,000
(Being goods sent by head office is still in transit)			

Example 47

Alphas and Co., having head office in Mumbai has a branch in Nagpur. The branch at Nagpur is an independent branch maintaining separate books of account. On 31.3.2007, it was found that the goods dispatched by head office for A 2,00,000 was received by the branch only to the extent of A 1,50,000. The balance goods are in transit. What is the accounting entry to be passed by the branch for recording the goods in transit, in its books? [*C.A., May, 2007*]

Solution

Nagpur branch must include the inventory in its books as goods in transit.

The following journal entry must be made by the branch :

Goods in transit A/c	Dr.	50,000	
To Head Office A/c			50,000

[Being Goods sent by Head Office is still in transit on the closing date]

Example 48

A Kolkata firm whose accounting year ends on 31 December has two branches-one at Agra and other at Banaras. The branches keep a complete set of books. On 31 December, 2008, the Agra and the Banaras branch accounts in the Kolkata office books showed debit balances of A 30,450 and A 45,000 respectively before taking the following information into account :

(*a*) Goods valued A 2,000 were transferred from Agra to banaras under instructions from head office.

(*b*) The Agra branch collected A 2,500 from an Agra customer of the head office.

(*c*) The Banaras branch paid A 5,000 for certain goods purchased by the head office in Banaras.

(*d*) A 5,000 remitted by the Agra branch to Kolkata office on 29 December 2008 were received on 3 January following.

(*e*) The Banaras branch received on behalf of the head office A 1,500 as dividend from a Banaras company.

(*f*) For the year 2008 the Agra branch showed a net loss of A 1,250 and the Banaras branch a net profit of A 5,400.

Pass journal entries to record these matters in the head office books and write up the two branch accounts therein. [*B.Com.* (*Hons.*) *Delhi*]

Solution

Kolkata H.O.
Journal Entries

	Particulars	*L.F.*	*Dr. Amount (A)*	*Cr. Amount (A)*
(*a*)	Banaras Branch Account Dr.		2,000	
	To Agra Branch			2,000
	(Goods from Agra branch transferred to Banaras Branch)			
(*b*)	Agra Branch Account Dr.		2,500	
	To Sundry Debtors Account			2,500
	(Amount from debtors collected by the branch)			
(*c*)	Purchases Account Dr.		5,000	
	To Banaras Branch Account			5,000
	(Purchases of goods paid by Banaras branch)			

(*d*)	Cash-in-Transit Account	Dr.	5,000	
	To Agra Branch Account			5,000
	(Cash remitted by Agra Branch not received on 31 December)			
(*e*)	Banaras Branch Account	Dr.	1,500	
	To Dividends Account			1,500
	(Receipt of dividend by Branch on our behalf)			
(*f*)	Banaras Branch Account	Dr.	5,400	
	To Agra Branch Account			1,250
	To Profit and Loss Account			4,150
	(Profit at Banaras branch and loss at Agra branch transferred to general profit and loss account)			

Branch Accounts

Particulars	Agra (*A*)	Banaras (*A*)	*Particulars*	Agra (*A*)	Banaras (*A*)
Balance b/d	30,450	45,000	Banaras Branch Account	2,000	–
Agra Branch Account	–	2,000	Purchases Account	–	5,000
Sundry Debtors Account	2,500	–	Cash-in-Transit Account	5,000	–
Dividends Account	–	1,500	Banaras Branch (Loss)	1,250	–
Agra Branch Account	–	1,250	Balance c/d	24,700	48,900
Profit and Loss Account	–	4,150			
	32,950	53,900		32,950	53,900
Balance b/d	24,700	48,900			

Example 49

The following is the Trial Balance of Kolkata Branch as on 31 March, 2008 :

	Dr.	*Cr.*
Mumbai Head Office A/c	32,400	–
Stock on 1.4.2007	60,000	–
Purchases	1,78,000	–
Goods received from H.O.	90,000	–
Sales	–	3,80,000
Goods supplied to H.O.	–	60,000
Salaries	15,000	–
Debtors	37,000	–
Creditors	–	18,500
Rent	9,600	–
Office expenses	4,700	–
Cash and Bank balance	17,800	–
Furniture	14,000	–
	4,58,500	4,58,500

Closing stock was valued at Rs. 27,000. The Branch A/c in the books of Head Office stood at Rs. 4,600 (Debit Balance) on 31.3.08. On 28 March, 2008 the Head Office forwarded goods to the value of Rs. 25,000 to the branch where they were received on 3rd April 2008. Required in the books of H.O. :

(*i*) Branch Trading and Profit and Loss A/c.

(*ii*) Journal entries to incorporate the above Trial Balance; and

(*iii*) Kolkata Branch Account. [*B.Com., (Hons.), Delhi University, 2008*]

Solution

Branch Trading and Profit and Loss Account for the Year ended 31 March 2008

Particulars		*(A)*	*Particulars*		*(A)*
To Branch A/c			By Kolkata Branch A/c		
Stock	60,000		Sales	3,80,000	
Purchases	1,78,000		Goods Supplied to H.O.	60,000	
Goods from H.O.	90,000	3,28,000			
To Branch Profit and Loss A/c (Gross Profit)		1,39,000	Closing Stock	27,000	4,67,000
		4,67,000			4,67,000
To Branch A/c :			By Branch Trading A/c (Gross Profit)		1,39,000
Salaries	15,000				
Rent	9,600				
Office Expenses	4,700	29,300			
To General Profit and Loss A/c (Net Profit)		1,09,700			
		1,39,000			1,39,000

Journal Entries

Date	*Particulars*		*L.F.*	*Dr. Amount (A)*	*Cr. Amount (A)*
	Goods-in-transit A/c	Dr.		25,000	
	To Kolkata Branch A/c				25,000
	(Being adjustment of goods-in-transit)				
	Cash-in-transit A/c	Dr.		12,000	
	To Kolkata Branch A/c*				12,000
	(Being adjustment of remittance-in-transit)				
	Kolkata Branch Trading A/d	Dr.		3,28,000	
	To Kolkata Branch A.c				3,28,000
	[Stock Rs. 60,000 + Purchases Rs. 1,78,000 + Goods Received from H.O. Rs. 90,000]				
	(Being incorporation of debit items of Trading Account)				
	Kolkata Branch A/c	Dr.		4,67,000	
	To Kolkata Branch Trading A/c				4,67,000
	[Sales Rs. 3,80,000 + Goods supplied to H.O. Rs. 60,000 + Closing Stock Rs. 27,000]				

			Dr. (Rs.)	Cr. (Rs.)
	(Being incorporation of credit items of Trading Account)			
	Kolkata Branch Trading A/c	Dr.	1,39,000	
	To Kolkata Branch Profit and Loss A/c			1,39,000
	(Being transfer of Gross Profit to Profit and Loss Account)			
	Kolkata Branch Profit and Loss A/c	Dr.	29,300	
	To Kolkata Branch A/c			29,3000
	[Salaries Rs. 15,000 + Rent Rs. 9,600 + Office Expenses Rs. 4,700]			
	(Being the debit items of Profit and Loss Account Incorporated)			
	Kolkata Branch Profit and Loss A/c	Dr.	1,09,700	
	To General Profit and Loss A/c			1,09,700
	(Being transfer to branch profit to General Profit and Loss Account)			
	Kolkata Branch Debtors A/c	Dr.	37,000	
	Kolkata Branch Cash A/c	Dr.	17,800	
	Kolkata Branch Furniture A/c	Dr.	14,000	
	Kolkata Branch Stock A/c	Dr.	27,000	
	To Kolkata Branch A/c			95,800
	(Being incorporation of branch assets)			
	Kolkata Branch A/c	Dr.	18,500	
	To Kolkata Branch Creditors A/c			18,500
	(Being incorporation of branch creditors)			

Kolkata Branch Account

Particulars	*(A)*	*Particulars*	*(A)*
To Balance b/d	4,600	By Goods-in-transit	25,000
To Branch Trading A/c	4,67,000	By Cash-in-transit	12,000
To Branch Liabilities (creditors)	18,500	By Branch Trading A/c	3,28,000
		By Branch Profit and Loss A/c	29,300
		By Branch Assets A/c	95,800
	4,90,100		4,90,100

***Working Notes*:**

* While attempting a question on an Independent Branch, the students are advised to check whether the balance as shown by the Head Office Account in Branch books and the Branch Account in the Head Office books reconcile with each other or not. In the present question, there is a difference of A 37,000 [*i.e.,* Dr. Balance of Head Office A/c of A 32,400 (in the books of Branch) + Dr. Balance Branch A/c A 4,600 (in the books of Head Office)]. The difference is due to Goods-in-transit and Cash-in-transit. Goods-in-transit is A 25,000 (given). So, Cash-in-transit will be A 37,000 – A 25,000 = A 12,000.

Example 50

The H.O. of a business and its Branch keep their own books and each prepares Profit and Loss A/c. From the following balances appearing in the two sets of books as on 31.3.2002, prepare a Balance Sheet of the business as on 31.3.2002 and the Journal entries also (in both sets of books) to record the adjustments given after the two Trial Balances :

Particulars	Head Office		Branch	
	Dr. (A)	Cr. (A)	Dr. (A)	Dr. (A)
Capital	–	1,00,000	–	–
Fixed Assets	36,000	–	16,000	–
Stock	34,200	–	10,740	–
Debtors	7,820	–	4,840	–
Creditors	–	3,960	–	1,920
Cash	10,740	–	1,420	–
P & L A/c	–	14,660	–	3,060
Branch A/c	29,860	–	–	–
Head Office A/c	–	–	–	28,020
	1,18,620	1,18,620	33,000	33,000

Adjustments :

(*i*) On 31 March, 2002, the Branch had sent a cheque for A 1,000 to the H.O. but not received by the H.O. nor credited to Branch A/c till 3 April, 2002.

(*ii*) Goods valued at A 840 had been sent by the H.O. to the Branch and invoiced on 30 March, 2002 but were not received by the Branch till 11 April, 2002.

(*iii*) The profit shown by branch is to be transferred to the Head Office books.

(*iv*) Branch Assets and Liabilities are to be recorded in the books of Head Office.

[*B.Com., (Hons.), Delhi University, 2005*]

Solution

Important Note

While attempting a question on an independent Branch, the students are advised to check whether the balances as shown by the Head Office Account in Branch Books and the Branch Account in the Head Office Books reconcile with each other or not. In the present question, there is a difference of A 1,840. The difference is due to the causes (*i*) and (*ii*) as mentioned in the question.

Head Office Journal

	Particulars		L.F.	Dr. Amount (A)	Cr. Amount (A)
	Branch Fixed Assets A/c	Dr.		16,000	
	Branch Stock A/c	Dr.		10,740	
	Branch Debtors A/c	Dr.		4,840	
	Branch Cash A/c	Dr.		1,420	
	Cash in transit A/c (*i*)	Dr.		1,000	
	Goods in transit A/c (*ii*)	Dr.		840	
	To Branch A/c				34,840

	(Being the assets of the branch including the Goods and Cash in transit recorded in the books of Head Office)			
	Branch A/c Dr.		1,920	
	To Branch Creditors A/c			1,920
	(Being the Branch Creditors recorded in the books of the Head Office)			
	Branch A/c Dr.		3,060	
	To Profit and Loss A/c			3,060
	(Being Branch Profit and Loss A/c balance transferred to Head Office Profit and Loss A/c)			

Note : After the entries, balance in the Branch Account is Nil.

Branch Journal

Date	*Particulars*	*L.F.*	*Dr. Amount (A)*	*Cr. Amount (A)*
	Cash in Transit A/c Dr.		1,000	
	To Head Office A/c			1,000
	(Being cash in transit adjusted)			
	Profit and Loss A/c Dr.		3,060	
	To Head Office A/c			3,060
	(Being Profit and Loss A/c transferred to the Head Office)			

Head Office Balance Sheet as on 31.3.2002

Liabilities		*(A)*	*Assets*		*(A)*
Capital	1,00,000		Fixed Assets		
Add : H.O. Profit	14,660		H.O.	36,000	
Branch Profit	3,060	1,17,720	Branch	16,000	52,000
Creditors			Stock		
H.O.	3,960		H.O.	34,200	
Branch	1,920	5,880	Branch	10,740	
				44,940	
			Stock in transit	840	45,780
			Debtors		
			H.O.	7,820	
			Branch	4,840	12,660
			Cash		
			H.O.	10,740	
			Branch	1,420	
			In Transit	1,000	13,160
		1,23,600			1,23,600

Example 51

On 31 March, 2011 Kanpur Branch submits the following Trial Balance to its Head Office at Lucknow:

Debit Balances	A *in lacs*
Furniture and Equipment	18
Depreciation on furniture	2
Salaries	25
Rent	10
Advertising	6
Telephone, Postage and Stationery	3
Sundry Office Expenses	1
Stock on 1st April, 2010	60
Goods Received from Head Office	288
Debtors	20
Cash at bank and in hand	8
Carriage Inwards	7
	448
Credit Balances :	
Outstanding Expenses	3
Goods Returned to Head Office	5
Sales	360
Head Office	80
	448

Additional Information

Stock on 31 March, 2011 was valued at A 62 lacs. ON 29 March, 2011 the Head Office despatched goods closing A 10 lacs to its branch. Branch did not receive these goods before 1st April, 2011. Hence, the figure of goods received from Head Office does not include these goods. Also the head office has charged the branch A 1 lac for centralised services for which the branch has not passed the entry.

You are required to :

(*i*) Pass Journal Entries in the books of the branch to make the necessary adjustments.

(*ii*) Prepare Final Accounts of the branch including balance sheet, and

(*iii*) Pass Journal Entries in the books of the Head Office to incorporate the whole of the branch trial balance.

[*C.A., May, 2002*]

Solution

(*i*) Books of Branch
Journal Entries

(*A in Lacs*)

Particulars		*Dr. Amount (A)*	*Cr. Amount (A)*
Goods in Transit A/c	Dr.	10	
To Head Office A/c			10

(Goods dispatched by head office but not received by branch before 1st April, 2011)			
Expenses A/c	Dr.	1	
To Head Office A/c			1
(Amount charged by head office for centralised services)			

(*ii*) Trading and Profit and Loss Account of the Branch for the Year Ended 31 March, 2011

(A in Lacs)

Particulars		(*A*)	*Particulars*	(*A*)
To Opening Stock		60	By Sales	360
To Goods received from			By Closing Stock	62
Head Office	288			
Less : Returns	5	283		
To Carriage Inwards		7		
To Gross Profit c/d		72		
		422		422
To Salaries		25	By Gross Profit b/d	72
To Depreciation on Furniture		2		
To Rent		10		
To Advertising		6		
To Telephone, Postage and Stationery		3		
To Sundry Office Expenses		1		
To Head Office Expenses		1		
To Net Profit Transferred to Head Office A/c		24		
		72		72

Balance Sheet as on 31 March, 2011

Liabilities		A in lacs	*Assets*		*A in lacs*
Head Office	80		Furniture and Equipment	20	
Add : Goods in transit	10		*Less :* Depreciation	2	18
Head Office :			Stock in hand		62
Expenses	1		Goods in Transit		10
Net Profit	24		Debtors		20
		115	Cash at bank and in hand		8
Outstanding Expenses		3			
		118			118

(*iii*) Books of Head Office
Journal Entries

Particulars		*Dr. Amount (A)*	*Cr. Amount (A)*
Branch Trading Account	Dr.	355	
To Branch Account			355

Particulars		Dr.	Cr.
(The total of the following items in branch trial balance debited to branch trading account			
	A in lacs		
Opening Stock	60		
Goods received from Head Office	288		
Carriage Inwards	7)		
Branch Account	Dr.	427	
To Branch Trading Account			427
(Total sales, closing stock and goods returned to Head Office credited to branch trading account, individual amount being as follows :			
	A in lacs		
Sales	360		
Closing Stock	62		
Goods returned to Head Office	5)		
Branch Trading Account	Dr.	72	
To Branch Profit and Loss Account			72
(Gross profit earned by branch credited to Branch Profit and Loss Account)			
Branch Profit and Loss Account	Dr.	48	
To Branch Account			48
(Total of the following branch expenses debited to Branch Profit and Loss Account			
	A in lacs		
Salaries	25		
Rent	10		
Advertising	6		
Telephone, Postage and Stationery	3		
Sundry Office Expenses	1		
Head Office Expenses	1		
Depreciation on furniture and Equipment	2		
Branch Profit and Loss Account	Dr.	24	
To Profit and Loss Account			24
(Net profit at branch credited to (general) Profit and Loss A/c)			
Branch Furniture and Equipment	Dr.	18	
Branch Stock	Dr.	62	
Branch Debtors	Dr.	20	
Branch Cash at Bank and in Hand	Dr.	8	
Goods in Transit	Dr.	10	
To Branch			118
(Incorporation of different assets at the branch in H.O. books)]			

Branch	Dr.	3	
To Branch Outstanding Expenses			3
(Incorporation of Branch Outstanding Expenses in H.O. books)			

Example 52

A Limited Company has its Head Office in Delhi and a Branch in Mumbai where a separate-set of books is used. The following are the trial balances extracted on 31 December 2008 :

Head Office Trial Balance

	Dr.	*Cr.*
Share Capital (Authorised : 10,000 Equity Shares of A 100 each):	–	–
Issued : 8,000 Equity Shares	–	8,00,000
Profit and Loss Account 1.1.08	–	25,310
Interim Dividend paid 1.1.08	30,000	–
General Reserve	–	1,00,000
Current Assets	2,22,470	–
Fixed Assets	5,30,000	–
Debtors and Creditors	50,500	21,900
Profit for 2008	–	82,200
Cash Balance	62,730	–
Branch Current Account	1,33,710	–
	10,29,410	10,29,410

Branch Trial Balance

	A	A
Fixed Assets	95,000	–
Profit for 2008	–	31,700
Stock	50,460	–
Debtors and Creditors	19,100	10,400
Cash Balance	6,550	–
Head Office Current Account	–	1,29,010
	1,71,110	1,71,110

The difference between the balances of the Current Accounts in the two sets of books is accounted for as follows :

(*a*) Cash remitted by the Branch on 31 December 2008, but received by the Head Office on 1 January 2009 A 3,000.

(*b*) Stock stolen in transit from Head Office and charged to the Branch by the Head Office, but not credited to Head Office in the Branch books as the branch manager declined to admit the liability (not covered by insurance) A 1,700.

Give the Branch Current Account in the Head Office books after incorporating Branch Trial Balance through journal. Also prepare the Company's Balance Sheet as on 31 December 2008.

[*C.A. Inter*]

Solution

Delhi HO

As the Branch Current Account in the books of Head Office and Head Office Current Account in the books of Branch do not reconcile, the following Journal entries are required in the books of Head Office for the reconciliation :

Journal Entries

	Particulars		(A)	(A)
31.12.08				
(i)	Cash-in-Transit Account	Dr.	3,000	
	To Branch Current Account			3,000
	(Cash remitted by the Branch on 31 December 2008 but received at HO on 1 January, 2009)			
(ii)	Loss by theft Account	Dr.	1,700	
	To Branch Current Account			1,700
	(Stock lost in transit from Head Office to Branch)			

In order to incorporate, in the Head Office books, the given trial balance, which has been compiled after preparing the Branch Profit and Loss Account, the following Journal entries are necessary :

	Particulars		(A)	(A)
(i)	Branch Current Account	Dr.	31,700	
	To Profit and Loss Account			31,700
	(Profit at Branch for 2008)			
(ii)	Branch Fixed Assets Account	Dr.	95,000	
	Branch Stock Account	Dr.	50,460	
	Branch Debtors Account	Dr.	19,100	
	Branch Cash Account	Dr.	6,550	
	To Branch Current Account			1,71,110
	(Branch assets incorporated in the books of HO)			
(iii)	Branch Current Account	Dr.	10,400	
	To Branch Creditors Account			10,400
	(Branch creditors incorporated into Head Office books)			

Branch Current Account

Particulars	(A)	Particulars	(A)
Balance b/d	1,33,710	Cash-in-Transit	3,000
Profit and Loss Account	31,700	Loss by theft Account	1,700
Branch Creditors Account	10,400	Branch Sundry Assets Account	1,71,110
	1,75,810		1,75,810

(General) Profit and Loss Account

Particulars	*(A)*	*Particulars*		*(A)*
Loss by theft	1,700	Balance b/d		25,310
Interim dividend (2008)	30,000	Profit for 2008 :		
Balance c/d	1,07,510	At HO	82,200	
		At Branch	31,700	1,13,900
	1,39,210			1,39,210

Balance Sheet of the Company as at 31 December, 2008

Liabilities		*(A)*	*Assets*		*(A)*
Share Capital			**Fixed Assets**		
Authorised Capital :			H.O.	5,30,000	
10,000 Equity Shares of A 100 each		10,00,000	Branch	95,000	6,25,000
Issued and Subscribed Capital			*Current Assets :*		
8,000 Equity Shares of A 100 each fully paid		8,00,000	Stock :		
			HO	2,22,470	
			Branch	50,460	2,72,930
Reserves and Surplus :			*Debtors :*		
General Reserve		1,00,000	HO	50,500	
Profit and Loss Account		1,07,510	Branch	19,100	69,600
Current Liabilities			*Cash :*		
Creditors :			HO	62,730	
H.O.	21,900		Branch	6,550	
Branch	10,400	32,300	In transit	3,000	72,280
		10,39,810			10,39,810

Example 53

Show adjustment Journal entry in the books of Head Office at the end of April, 2011 for incorporation of inter-branch transactions assuming that only Head Office maintains different branch accounts in its books.

A. *Delhi Branch* :

1. Received goods from Mumbai – A 35,000 and A 15,000 from Kolkata.
2. Sent goods to Chennai – A 25,000, Kolkata – A 20,000.
3. Bill receivable received – A 20,000 from Chennai.
4. Acceptances sent to Mumbai – A 25,000, Kolkata – A 10,000.

B. *Mumbai Branch (apart from the above)* :

5. Received goods from Kolkata – A 15,000, Delhi – A 20,000.
6. Cash sent to Delhi – A 15,000, Kolkata – A 7,000.

C. *Chennai Branch (apart from the above)* :

7. Received goods from Kolkata – A 30,000.
8. Acceptances and cash sent to Kolkata – A 20,000 and A 10,000 respectively.

D. *Kolkata Branch (apart from the above)* :

9. Sent goods to *Chennai* – A 35,000.
10. Paid cash to Chennai – A 15,000.
11. Acceptances sent to Chennai – A 15,000. [*C.A., May, 2003*]

Solution

Journal Entry in the Books of Head Office

Date	*Particulars*		*Dr. Amount (A)*	*Cr. Amount (A)*
2011				
Apr. 30	Mumbai Branch Account	Dr.	3,000	
	Chennai Branch Account	Dr.	70,000	
	To Delhi Branch Account			15,000
	To Kolkata Branch Account			58,000
	(Being adjustment entry passed by head office in respect of inter-branch transactions for the month of April, 2011)			

Working Note :

Inter - Branch Transactions

	Delhi (*A*)	*Mumbai* (*A*)	*Chennai* (*A*)	*Kolkata* (*A*)
A. Delhi Branch				
1. Received goods	50,000 (Dr.)	35,000 (Cr.)		15,000 (Cr.)
2. Sent goods	45,000 (Cr.)		25,000 (Dr.)	20,000 (Dr.)
3. Received Bills receivable	20,000 (Dr.)		20,000 (Cr.)	
4. Sent acceptance	35,000 (Cr.)	25,000 (Dr.)		10,000 (Dr.)
B. Mumbai Branch				
5. Received goods	20,000 (Cr.)	35,000 (Dr.)		15,000 (Cr.)
6. Sent cash	15,000 (Dr.)	22,000 (Cr.)		7,000 (Dr.)
C. Chennai Branch				
7. Received goods			30,000 (Dr.)	30,000 (Cr.)
8. Sent cash and acceptances			30,000 (Cr.)	30,000 (Dr.)
D. Kolkata Branch				
9. Sent goods			35,000 (Dr.)	35,000 (Cr.)
10. Sent cash			15,000 (Dr.)	15,000 (Cr.)
11. Sent acceptances			15,000 (Dr.)	15,000 (Cr.)
	15,000 (Cr.)	3,000 (Dr.)	70,000 (Dr.)	58,000 (Cr.)

ASSIGNMENT MATERIAL

Note : The Objective Type Questions (True/False, Multiple Choice Questions, etc.) have been given in the Appendix at the end of the book.

SHORT ANSWER THEORY QUESTIONS

1. Write short notes on 'Stock and Debtors Method' under branch accounting.
[*B.Com., Delhi University, 2000*]
2. Explain features of branch account under debtor system.
3. What is the treatment of losses in branch adjustment account.
4. Why is stock and Debtor System of branch accounting is better than Debtor System.
5. What is the nature of branch account?
6. How do you treat loading in branch account.
7. What is the treatment of the following in branch accounting.
   (*i*) Surplus/shortage of branch stock.
   (*ii*) Abnormal loss.
8. What is final account system of branch accounting.
9. What is a whole sale branch system.
10. What is independent branch?
11. What is the nature of branch account and H.O. account under independent branch system.
12. How is goods-in-transit treated under branch accounting?
13. How is cash-in-transit treated under branch accounting?
14. Explain accounting for fixed assets under branch accounting.
15. Explain the nature and treatment of inter-branch transactions.
16. What are the methods of incorporating branch results in the books of Head Office.
17. What are the basic features of dependent branches? [*B.Com.,* (*Hons.*)*, Delhi University, 2011*]
18. Explain the procedure of incorporating the Branch Trial Balance in the books of Head Office.
[*B.Com.,* (*Hons.*)*, Delhi University, 2005*]
19. How will you deal with normal loss of stock, abnormal loss of stock, goods returned by branch, customers directly paying to Head Office and cash remitted by branch customers directly to Head Office under Debtor System. Make use of imaginary figures.
[*B.Com.,* (*Hons.*)*, Delhi University, 2005, 2007*]
20. Discuss the calculation of profit.
   (*a*) Under whole sale branch system with the help of an example.
   (*b*) Show the entries (including the entry for ending) in the books of Head Office to record the following transaction under : (*i*) debtors system; and (*ii*) stock and debtors system, assuming that goods are supplied to the branch at a profit of 20% on selling price.

   Goods returned by credit customers directly to the Head Office A 5,000.
   (*c*) What journal entries are passed in the books of the Head Office for incorporation of branch trial balance? [*B.Com.,* (*Hons.*)*, Delhi University, 2006, 2007*]
21. Discuss the nature of branch account maintained under debtor system of branch accounting.
[*B.Com.,* (*Hons.*)*, Delhi University, 2007*]
22. How will you deal with Abnormal Loss of Stock and Insurance Claim under :
   (*i*) Debtors method; and
   (*ii*) Stock and Debtors method of branch accounting. [*B.Com.,* (*Hons.*)*, Delhi University, 2007*]

LONG-ANSWER THEORY QUESTIONS

1. Explain fully debtor system of branch accounting.
2. Discuss stock and debtor system of branch accounting.
3. What journal entries are made under debtor system.
4. Give the specimen of branch account and branch debtors account with imaginary figures.
5. Discuss the advantages of stock and debtor system.
6. Explain the accounts which are opened under stock and debtor system.
7. How do you treat surplus and shortage of branch stock and abnormal loss.
8. Explain final account system of branch accounting. Give a specimen of Branch Trading and Profit and loss Account under final account system of branch accounting.
9. Explain fully whole sale branch system. What accounts are prepared under this system. Give their specimen also.
10. What are independent branches. Explain the treatment of goods in transit and cash in transit.
11. How is reconciliation done of branch transactions in case of independent branches.
12. Explain the following :
    (*a*) Goods-in-transit.
    (*b*) Cash-in-transit.
    (*c*) Accounting for fixed assets.
    (*d*) Inter-branch transactions.

PRACTICAL PROBLEMS

1. *X* Company has a branch a Delhi goods are invoiced form Head Office at cost plus $33\frac{1}{3}$%. Find out profit at the branch according to Debtors System.

	A
Opening Balances :	
Debtors	10,000
Petty Cash	1,000
Furniture	2,000
Stock (I.P.)	8,000
Cash sent by Head Office for Petty Expenses	2,000
Branch Expenses and Losses :	
Freight and Advertisement	5,600
Bad Debts	50
Depreciation on Furniture	80
Petty Expenses	1,500
Sales :	
Cash	50,000
Credit	36,000
Goods returned by Debtors	800
Goods returned by Branch to Head Office	2,000
Cash received from Debtors	20,000

Stock at the end at I.P.	7,800
Goods invoiced by Head Office during the year	88,000

[***Ans.*** **:** Profit A 13,320]

2. A trader has it branch at Calcutta to which the goods are invoiced at cost *plus* 20%. Prepare "Branch A/c" in H.O. books from the following :

	A
Opening stocks at branch	24,000
Cash sales at branch	17,500
Credit sales	41,000
Collections from Debtors	37,900
Goods received from H.O.	30,000
Branch Expenses :	
Paid by H.O.	3,000
Paid by Branch	6,000
Expenses unpaid	1,400
Closing stock at branch (in hand)	18,000
Closing balance of Debtors	9,160
Goods in transit from H.O.	3,600

[***Ans.*** **:** Profit A 18,100]

3. Twist's Stores Ltd., Bombay has a branch at Poona. Goods are invoiced to the branch at selling prices being cost *plus* 25%. The branch keeps its own Sales Ledger and deposits all cash received daily to the credit of the Head Office Account opened at the Bank of India, Poona. All expenses are paid by cheque from Bombay.

   From the following details, prepare a Branch Account in the Head Office Books and make the necessary adjustments therein to arrive at the actual branch profit or loss during the year 2011 :

Dr. *Cr.*

Expenditure	*Amount* *A*	*Income*	*Amount* *A*
Stock 1 Jan. 2011	75,000	Rent, Rates and Taxes	24,000
Stock 31 Dec. 2011	90,000	Sundry Expenses	4,800
Sundry Debtors 1 Jan., 2011	42,000	Cash Sales for the year	3,24,000
Sundry Debtors 31 Dec. 2011	54,000	Credit Sales	2,10,000
Goods Invoiced from H.O.	5,46,000	Cash Received from Ledger A/c	1,98,000
		Wages Paid	20,400
		Wages Still Owing	2,000

[***Ans.*** **:** Profit A 58,000]

4. A Head Office in Delhi has a branch in Chennai to which goods are invoiced by the Head Office at 20% profit on sale price. All cash received by the branch is daily remitted to Head Office. From the following particulars show how the Branch Account will appear in H.O. books. Also prepare necessary accounts. Entries are to be made at invoice price :

	A
Stock on January 1, 2011 (At Invoice Price)	62,500

Debtors on 1.1.2011		60,000
Goods Supplied by H.O.		2,00,000
Cash Sales		80,000
Cash Received from Customers		1,47,500
Goods Returned to H.O.		12,000
Cheques Received from H.O.		
Wages and Salaries	55,000	
Rent, Rates and Taxes	15,000	
Sundry Expenses	2,550	72,550
Stock on December 31, 2011 (Invoice Price)		75,000
Debtors on 31.12.2011		1,12,500
Liability for Petty Expenses		550

[***Ans.*** **:** Profit : A 66,500]

5. Rohit and Co. of Delhi has a branch at Kanpur. Goods are invoiced to the branch at cost *plus* 25%. The branch does not maintain account books and all collections at the branch are remitted to head office. The expenses of the branch are reimbursed by the head office. From the following particulars, prepare the branch account in the books of head office for the six months ending 30 September 2011 :

	A
Stock on 1.4.2011 (at cost to head office)	55,000
Debtors on 1.4.2011	15,000
Furniture on 1.4.2011	12,000
Petty cash on 1.4.2011	500
Transactions for six months :	
Goods received from head office (at invoice price)	2,25,000
Cash sales	1,95,000
Credit sales	80,000
Goods returned to head office (at invoice price)	12,750
Normal loss	1,000
Sales returns by customers to branch	500
Cash received from debtors	50,000
Bad debts	400
Trade discount to customers (already taken into account while invoicing)	12,000
Bills receivable received from customers at branch	15,000
Goods sent to Branch on 27.9.2011 received by Branch on 5.10.20111,500	
Cash sent to Branch for expenses	10,500
Cash discount allowed to customers	800
Balance on 30.9.2011	
Stock	5,600
Debtors	?
Petty Cash	500
Depreciate Furniture by 20% p.a.	

[***Ans.*** **:** Net Profit A 40,080]

6. Rajshree Textiles opened a branch on 1 January 2011. Goods are invoiced at selling price which was fixed by adding 25% to the cost. From the following particulars relating to 2011, ascertain the profit or loss made at the branch under the Stock and Debtors System :

	A
Goods sent to Branch (Invoice Price)	1,40,000
Cash Sales	50,000
Credit Sales	70,000
Cash received from Debtors	62,400
Discount allowed to Customers	1,600
Goods returned by Customers	2,000
Cash remitted to Branch for :	
Rent	1,200
Salaries	6,000
Sundry Expenses	800
Defective cloth found in the sales written off	200

[***Ans.*** : Gross Profit – A 23,600; Net Profit – A 13,840]

7. *XY* Limited with its head office in Calcutta invoiced goods to its branch at Mumbai at 20% less than the catalogue price which is cost *plus* 50% with instructions that cash sales were to be made at invoice price and credit sales at catalogue price *less* discount at 15 on prompt payments.

From the particulars available from the branch, prepare Branch Stock Account, Branch Adjustment Account and Branch Profit and Loss Account for the year ended 31 March 2011.

	A
Stock on 1 April 2011 (Invoice Price)	12,000
Debtors on 1 April 2011	10,000
Goods received from H.O. (Invoice Price)	1,32,000
Cash Sales	46,000
Credit Sales	1,00,000
Cash received from Debtors	85,635
Discount allowed to Debtors	13,365
Expenses at the Branch	6,000
Remittance to H.O.	1,20,000
Debtors on 31st March 2012	11,000
Cash in hand on 31 March 2012	5,635
Stock on 31st March 2012 (Invoice Price)	15,000

It was further reported that a part of the stock was lost by fire (not covered by insurance) during the year whose value is to be ascertained and a provision should be made for discount to be allowed to debtors as on 31 March 2012 on the basis of year's trend of prompt payments.

[***Ans.*** : Profit A 17,650]

8. Mr. *X* has its branches at Delhi and Hardwar to whom goods are invoiced at cost *plus* 25%. Following information is available of the transactions at Delhi Branch for the year ending 31st March 2012 :

	As. at 1.4.2011 A	As at 31.2.2012 A
Stock at its cost	40,000	?
Debtors	12,000	11,000
Petty Cash	150	250
Transactions during 2011-12		
Goods sent to branch		4,20,000
Gods returned to Head Office		15,000
Cash sales		1,05,000
Credit Sales		1,80,000
Normal Loss (at cost)		280
Goods pilfered (at invoice price)		3,000
Goods lost in fire (at invoice price)		4,000
Insurance company paid to Head Office for loss by fire at Delhi		3,000
Cash sent for petty expenses		32,000
Bad debts at Delhi Branch		400
Goods transferred to Hardware Branch under instructions from Head Office at Invoice price		12,000
Insurance charges paid by Head Office		200
Goods returned by debtors		500

Note : Goods transferred to Hardwar Branch (given above) were in transit on 31st March 2012.

Required : Prepare

(*i*) Branch stock account;

(*ii*) Branch Adjustment account;

(*iii*) Branch profit and loss account; and

(*iv*) Stock Reserve Account

[***Ans. :*** Profit A 21,520]

9. Goods are invoiced to branch at 20% less than the list price, which is cost plus 100%. From the following information, you are required to calculate branch gross profit as well as net profit :

(A)

Opening Stock	70,000	Branch Furniture purchased by Head Office	
10,000			
Opening Debtors	18,000	Cash Sales	70,000
Opening Petty Cash	500	Credit Sales	40,000
Goods received by Branch	1,20,000	Cash received from Branch Debtors	48,000
Goods sent to Branch	1,35,000	Bad Debts	3,000
Cash sent for petty expenses	1,000	Closing Petty Cash	300
Goods returned by Branch	12,000		

Provide 10% depreciation on furniture for full year. The cash sales are done at the invoice price whereas the credit sales are done at the list price.

[***Ans. :*** Profit A 41,050]

10. Omni Corporation Ltd. has two branches-one at Jaipur and another at Lucknow. Goods are invoiced to branches at cost plus 50%. Branches remit all cash received to head office and all expenses are paid by the head office. From the following particulars, prepare the necessary accounts on the 'stock and debtors system' to show the profit earned at Jaipur branch during the year ended 31st March, 2008.

	A
Stock on 1st April, 2007	93,000
Debtors on 1st April, 2007	68,000
Goods sent to branch, at cost	3,40,000
Sales at branch :	
Cash	2,50,100
Credit	3,10,000
Cash collected from debtors	3,04,000
Goods returned by branch to head office	12,000
Goods transferred from Lucknow branch to Jaipur branch	15,000
Shortage of stock at branch	4,500
Discount allowed to customers	2,000
Cash expenses at branch	54,000

[*CS(F) Dec. 2006*]

[***Ans. :*** Profit A 1,27,700]

11. A company sends goods to its branch at cost *plus* 25%. The following particulars are available in respect of the branch for the year ended 31 March, 2011 :

	A
Opening stock at branch at cost to the branch	80,000
Goods sent to branch at invoice price	12,00,000
Loss in transit at invoice price	15,000
Pilferage at invoice price	6,000
Sales 12,19,000	
Expenses	60,000
Closing stock at branch at cost to the branch	40,000
Recovery from insurance company against loss in transit	10,000

Prepare

(*i*) Branch Stock Account;

(*ii*) Goods Sent to Branch Account;

(*iii*) Branch Adjustment Account; and

(*iv*) Branch Profit and Loss Account, in the books of the head office.

[*C.S. (Foundation)*]

[***Ans. :*** Gross Profit A 2,43,800; Net Profit A 1,77,000]

12. **Branch Final Accounts System :** From the following particulars of Delhi Branch, prepare Branch Account and Branch Trading and Profit and Loss Account in the books of the H.O. :

	A
Stock (at cost to Branch) 1.1.2007	4,200
Stock (at cost to H.O.) 31.12.2007	24,000

Debtors 1.1.2007	–
Debtors 31.12.2007	16,000
Petty Cash 1.1.2007	–
Petty Cash 31.12.2007	1,000
Goods Received from H.O. (at cost to branch)	1,20,000
Goods Returned to H.O. (at cost to branch)	12,000
Cash Sales	60,000
Discount	400
Sales Returns	600
Bad Debts	1,000
Collections from Debtors	6,000
Petty Cash received from H.O.	3,000
Total Cash received from H.O.	66,000
General Expenses	5,000

Goods are received from H.O. at 20% above the cost to H.O.

The Branch Manager is paid a salary of A 1,260 on the closing date. However the expenditure is not included in the above particulars. [*B.Com.*, (*Hons.*), *Delhi University*]

[***Ans. :*** Branch Profit A 4240]

13. **Branch Final Accounts System :** Shri Nanak of Mumbai has a branch at Delhi. Goods are invoiced to the branch at cost *plus* 20 percent. The expenses of the branch are paid form Mumbai and the branch keeps a sales journal and the debtors journal only. From the information supplied by the branch, prepare Trading and Profit and Loss Account of the branch for the year ending 31 March, 2007 and show the account of the branch as it would appear in the books of Head Office :

	A
Opening Stock (at invoice price)	12,000
Closing Stock (at invoice price)	9,000
Credit Sales	20,500
Cash Sales	8,750
Receipts from Debtors	18,950
Sundry Debtors on 31 March, 2007	4,580
Goods received from Head Office	15,000
Goods-in-Transit from Head Office on March 31, 2007	1,800
Expenses paid by the Head Office for the branch	5,200

[*C.A. Inter*]

[***Ans. :*** Branch profit A 9050]

14. **Branch Final Accounts System :** The following information and particulars relate to New Delhi Branch for the year 2006-07 :

	31.3.06	*31.3.07*
Stock	50,000	75,000
Debtors	70,000	95,000
Petty Cash	250	120

Goods costing A 5,50,000 were sold by the Branch @ 25%, on cost; cash sales amounted to A 1,50,000 and the rest credit sales. Branch spent A 30,000 for salaries, A 12,000 for rent and A 8,000 for petty expenses. All expenses were remitted by H.O. Branch receives all goods from H.O. You are requested to show the New Delhi Branch Account in the books of Head Office for the year 2006-07 and prove your answer by preparing a Branch Trading and Branch Profit and Loss Account.

[*I.C.W.A.* (*Inter*) *December, 1997*]

[***Ans.*** **:** Branch profit A 87,500]

15. A business firm invoiced goods to its Delhi branch at cost. Head Office paid all the branch expenses from its bank account except petty cash expenses which were met by the Branch. All the cash collected by the branch was banked on the same day to the credit of the Head Office. The following is a summary of the transactions entered into at the branch during the year ended 31 December 2011:

	(A)		*(A)*
Stock January 1	7,000	Bad Debts	600
Debtors January 1	12,600	Goods returned by customers	500
Petty Cash, January 1	200	Salaries and Wages	6,200
Goods sent from H.O.	26,000	Rent and Rates	1,200
Goods returned to H.O.	1,000	Sundry Expenses	800
Cash Sales	17,500	Cash received from Sundry Debtors	28,500
Credit Sales	28,400	Stock, December 31	6,500
Allowances to customers	200	Debtors, 31 December	9,800
Discount to customers	1,400	Petty Cash, 31 December	100

Required : Prepare :

(*a*) Branch Account (Debtors Method),

(*b*) Memorandum Branch Trading and Profit and Loss Account to prove the results as disclosed by the Branch Account.

[*B.Com. (Hons.), Delhi University*]

[***Ans.*** **:** Branch profit 9,400]

16. **Wholesale Basis System :** A Ltd. has retail branch at Kanpur. Goods are sold to customers at cost *plus* 100%. The wholesale price is cost *plus* 80%. Goods are invoiced to Kanpur at wholesale price. From the following particulars find out the profit made at head office and Kanpur for the year 2008:

	Head Office *(A)*	*Branch* *(A)*
Stock on January 1, 2008	25,000	Nil
Purchases	1,50,000	Nil
Goods sent to branch (at invoice price)	54,000	–
Sales	1,53,000	50,000

Sales at head office are made on wholesale basis. Stock at branch is valued at invoice price.

[*C.A. Inter*]

[***Ans.*** **:** Branch gross profit A 5,400, H.O. profit A 88,000]

17. **Wholesale Basis System :** P.K. Co. Ltd. with their H.O. at Kolkata invoiced goods to their Mumbai Branch at invoice price. The invoice price is 20% *less* than the list price which is cost *plus* 100% with the instruction that sales are made at list price.

From the following particulars ascertain the profit earned by the H.O. at branch :

	Kolkata H.O. (A)	*Mumbai Branch (A)*
Opening Stock	40,000	32,000
Purchases	2,00,000	–
Goods Sent to Branch at Cost Price	62,500	–
Goods Received from H.O. at invoice price	–	96,000
Sales at list price	1,70,000	80,000
Trade Expenses	14,000	8,000

Stock at the H.O. are valued at cost price but those of branch are valued at invoice price.

[*B.Com., (Hons.), Delhi University)*

[***Ans. :*** Net profit,. Branch A 8,000; H.O. A 95000]

18. **Whole Sale Basis System :** A Head Office sends goods to its branch at cost + 80%. Goods are sold to customers at cost + 100%. However, sales at H.O. are made at wholesale price. From the following particulars, prepare Branch Account, HO Trading and Profit and Loss Account and Memorandum Trading and Profit and Loss Account (Branch) in the books of HO on wholesale basis :

	H.O.	*Branch*
Opening Stock	20,000	–
Purchases	2,00,000	–
Goods Sent to Branch (Invoice Price)	90,000	–
Goods Returned by Branch (Invoice Price)	–	9,000
Sales (all credit)	2,70,000	90,000
Cash Sent to Branch for expenses	5,000	–
Actual Expenses	10,000	4,000
Expenses Paid	10,000	6,000
Cash Received from Debtors	1,75,000	70,000
Bad Debts	–	2,000
Closing Debtors	1,00,000	20,000

[*B.Com., (Hons.), Delhi University*]

19. **Independent Branches :** Journalise the following transactions in the Branch Office and Head Office Books :

(*i*) Head Office has charged A 5,000 as depreciation on branch assets.

(*ii*) Goods worth A 25,000 have been supplied by the branch to another branch under the advice of the Head Office.

(*iii*) Branch has received A 15,000 from a customer of Head Office.

[*B.Com. (Hons.), Delhi University*]

20. **Independent Branches :** Give Journal Entries in the books of Branch A to rectify or adjust the following :

(*i*) Head Office expenses A 3,500 allocated to the Branch, but not recorded in the Branch Books.

(*ii*) Depreciation of branch assets, whose accounts are kept by the Head Office not provided earlier for A 1,500.

(*iii*) Branch paid A 2,000 as salary to H.O. Inspector, but the amount paid has been debited by the Branch to Salaries account.

(*iv*) H.O. collected A 10,000 directly from a customer on behalf of the Branch, but no intimation to this effect has been received by the Branch.

(*v*) A remittance of A 15,000 sent by the Branch has not yet been received by the Head Office.

(*vi*) Branch A incurred advertisement expenses of A 3,000 on behalf of Branch B.

[*C.A.(PE-II) Nov. 2004*]

21. **Independent Branches :** Head office passes adjustment entry at the end of each month to adjust the position arising out of inter-branch transactions during the month. From the following inter branch transactions in January 2011....., make the entry in the books of Head Office :

(*a*) *Mumbai Branch*

1. Received goods : A 6,000 from Kolkata Branch, A 4,000 from Patna Branch.
2. Sent goods : A 10,000 to Patna, A 8,000 to Kolkata.
3. Received B/R : A 6,000 from Patna.
4. Sent acceptances : A 4,000 to Kolkata, A 2,000 to Patna.

(*b*) *Madras Branch* (Apart from the above)

5. Received goods : A 10,000 from Kolkata, A 4,000 from Mumbai.
6. Cash sent : A 2,000 to Kolkata, A 6,000 to Mumbai.

(*c*) *Kolkata Branch* (Apart from the above)

7. Sent goods to Patna : A 6,000.
8. Paid B/P : A 4,000 to Patna; A 4,000 cash to Patna. [*C.A. (Inter)*]

22. **Independent Branches :** The following is the trial balance of Meerut Branch as on 31 December 2008 :

	Debit (*A*)	*Credit* (*A*)
Delhi Head Office	3,240	–
Stock 1.1.08	6,000	–
Purchases	97,800	–
Goods received from Head Office	19,000	–
Sales	–	1,38,000
Goods supplied to H.O.	–	6,000
Salaries	4,500	–
Debtors	3,700	–
Creditors	–	1,850
Rent	1,960	–
Office Expenses	1,470	–
Cast at Bank	1,780	–
Furniture	6,000	–
Depreciation on Furniture	400	–
	1,45,850	1,45,850

Stock at Branch on 31 December, 2008 was valued at A 7,700.

Meerut Branch in the H.O. Books on 31 December 2008 stood at A 460 (Debit). On 28 December 2008, the head office forwarded goods to the value of A 3,700 to the branch where they were received on 3 January 2009.

(*i*) Prepare Trading and Profit and Loss Account of Meerut Branch for the year ended 31 December 2008 and its Balance Sheet on that date.

(*ii*) Pass journal entries in the books of H.O. to incorporate the above-mentioned trial balance.

(*iii*) Show Meerut Branch Account as it would be closed in H.O. Ledger.

[*B.Com.* (*Hons.*) *Delhi*]

[***Ans.*** **:** Branch Profit A 20,570]

23. **Independent Branches :** From the following balances and additional informations, in the books of Head Office, you are required to prepare for ascertaining profit-loss at Branch :

(*i*) Branch Account

(*ii*) Branch Trading. Profit and Loss Account to ascertain the result of trading at Branch. Also give journal entries (without narration) to incorporate the above figures.

Balances as on 31st March, 2008

	(*A*)		(*A*)
Purchases	3,56,000	Bills Payable	7,000
Stock on 1.4.2007	1,20,000	Creditors	30,000
Salaries	20,000	Goods supplied to Head Office	1,20,000
Commission	10,000	Sales	7,60,000
Head Office Account	64,800		
Good received from Head Office	1,80,000		
Bills Receivable	4,000		
Debtors	70,000		
Rent and Expenses	28,600		
Plant	28,000		
Cash in hand and at Bank	35,600		
	9,17,000		9,17,000

Additional Informations :

1. The Branch Account in H.O. Books as on 31 March, 2008 stood at A 9,200 (Debit Balance).
2. On 25 March, 2008 the H.O. sent goods for A 45,000 to the branch, received on 2 April, 2008.
3. A cash remittance of A 29,000 by branch on 28 March was received by H.O. on 3 April, 2008.
4. Closing stock as on 31 March, 2008 valued at A 54,000. [*B.Com. (Hons.), Delhi University*]

24. **Independent Branches :** M/s. Shah and Co. commenced business on 1.4.2007 with Head Office at Mumbai and a Branch at Chennai. Purchases were made exclusively by the Head Office, where the goods were processed before sale. There was no loss or wastage in processing.

Only the processed goods received from Head Office were handled by the Branch. The goods were sent to branch at processed cost plus 10%.

All sales, whether by Head Office by the Branch, were at uniform gross profit of 25% on their respective cost. Following is the Trial Balance as on 31.3.2008.

	Head Office		Branch	
	Dr. A	Cr. A	Dr. A	Cr. A
Capital	–	3,10,000	–	–
Drawings	55,000	–	–	–
Purchases	19,69,500	–	–	–
Cost of processing	50,500	–	–	–
Sales	–	12,80,000	–	8,20,000
Goods sent to Branch	–	9,24,000	–	–
Administrative expenses	1,39,000	–	15,000	–
Selling expenses	50,000	–	6,200	–
Debtors	3,09,600	–	1,13,600	–
Branch Current account	3,89,800	–	–	–
Creditors	–	6,01,400	–	10,800
Bank Balance	1,52,000	–	77,500	–
Head Office Current account	–	–	–	2,61,500
Goods received from H.O.	–	–	8,80,000	–
	31,15,400	31,15,400	10,92,300	10,92,300

Following further information is provided :

(*i*) Goods sent by Head office to the Branch in March, 2008 of A 44,000 were not received by the Branch till 2.4.2008.

(*ii*) A remittance of A 84,300 sent by the Branch to Head Office was also similarly not received upto 31.3.2008.

(*iii*) Stock taking at the Branch disclosed a shortage of A 20,000 (at selling price to the branch).

(*iv*) Cost of unprocessed goods at Head Office on 31.3.2008 was A 1,00,000.

Prepare Trading and Profit and Loss account in columnar form and Balance Sheet of the business as a whole as at 31.3.2008. [*CA, PE II, Nov. 2005*]

[***Ans. :*** Profit, Branch A 1,26,800; H.O., A 1,28,091]

25. **Independent Branches :** A firm has its Head Office in Mumbai and an independent branch in Calcutta. The following were the balances as at the end of the year :

Liabilities	*H.O. (A)*	*Branch (A)*	*Assets*	*H.O. (A)*	*Branch (A)*
HO A/c	–	1,28,020	Fixed Assets	2,36,000	1,16,000
P & L A/c	14,660	3,060	Stock	35,200	20,740
Creditors	1,23,960	31,920	Debtors	17,820	24,840
Capital	3,00,000	–	Cash/Bank	19,740	1,420
			Branch A/c	1,29,860	–
	4,38,620	1,63,000		4,38,620	1,63,000

Information to be adjusted was as follows :

1. Branch had sent a cheque for A 1,000 to HO during the year but not received and recorded by HO till end of the year.

2. Depreciation of branch assets, of which accounts were maintained by the Head Office, not provided A 250.
3. It was agreed that Branch should be charged with A 300 for administrative service, rendered by the Head Office during the year.
4. Goods worth A 840 forwarded by HO to Branch during the year but not received and recorded by branch till end of the year.

Prepare Balance-Sheet of the firm for the whole business after passing journal entries for recording adjustments and profit in the books of Head Office and Branch. [*B.Com. (Hons.), Delhi University*]

26. **Independent Branches :** You are required to prepare the Trading and Profit and Loss Accounts and consolidated Balance Sheet of Eve. Ltd., in Kolkata and its branch at Delhi. Give journal entries for incorporation of Delhi Branch accounts in the Head Office and show the Branch account in Head Office books after incorporating therein the assets and liabilities.

The Trial Balance as on 31 December, 2008, is as under :

	Head Office		*Branch*	
	Dr. A	*Cr.* A	*Dr.* A	*Cr.* A
Manufacturing Expenses	30,000	10,000		–
Salaries	30,000	10,000		–
Wages	1,00,000	40,000		
Cash in hand	10,000	2,000		
Purchases	1,50,000	80,000		
Capital	–	–	2,00,000	–
Goods Received from H.O.	–	15,000	–	–
Rent	8,000	4,000	–	–
General Expenses	20,000	5,000	–	–
Sales	–	–	4,50,000	1,50,000
Goods sent to Branch	–	–	15,000	–
Purchase Returns	–	–	5,000	1,000
Opening Stock	50,000	30,000	–	–
Discounts earned	–	–	2,000	1,000
Machinery – H.O.	1,50,000	–	–	
Machinery – Branch	50,000	–	–	
Furniture – H.O.	7,000	–	–	
Furniture – Branch	3,000	–	–	
Debtors	40,000	15,00		
Creditors	–	–	30,000	5,000
H.O. Account	–	–	–	54,000
Branch Account	54,000	–	–	–
	7,02,000	2,11,000	7,02,000	2,11,000

Closing stock at Head Office was A 40,000 and at Branch A 30,000. Depreciation is to be provided on Machinery @ 20 per cent and Furniture @ 15 per cent. Rent Outstanding is A 500 (for Branch).

[*I.C.W.A. (Inter)*]

[***Ans. :*** Branch net loss A 22,950, H.O. profit A 92,950]

CHAPTER 17

Dissolution of Partnership Firm

Learning Objectives

After studying this chapter, you should be able to :

1. *Explain the meaning of dissolution.*
2. *Understand the reasons for dissolution of a firm.*
3. *Distinguish between dissolution of partnership and dissolution of partnership firm.*
4. *Discuss the settlements of accounts on dissolution.*
5. *Explain the procedure of realisation of assets and liabilities.*
6. *Discuss the settlement of the accounts of the partners.*
7. *Explain the procedure of settlement during insolvency of partners.*
8. *Know Garner Vs. Murray rule.*
9. *Differentiate between realization account and revaluation account.*
10. *Discuss the preparation of accounts under sale of a partnership firm to a limited company.*
11. *Explain piecemeal distribution and settlement of partners' Capital accounts in case of piecemeal distribution.*

A Partnerhsip Firm comes to an end when all partners, except one, become insolvent or the business of the firm becomes illegal or when partners agree unanimously to dissolve the firm. When the firm is dissolved, the accounts of the firm are settled. Assets are realized, liabilities are paid out and whatever is due to or from the Partners are settled. The process of settlement requires proper maintenance of Accounts books and records. This chapter aims to focus on accounting records and settlement amount the partners at the time of dissolution of the partnership firm.

MEANING OF DISSOLUTION

When a firm decides to close down its business, it is said to be dissolved. Dissolution means termination of a Partnership agreement. Indian Partnership Act 1932 makes a distinction between dissolution of partnership and dissolution of partnership firm. Dissolution of partnership means change in relationship between partners without affecting continuity of business. In this case the firm is reconstituted due to admission or retirement or death of a partner without dissolution of the firm.

Dissolution of partnership firm means complete breakdown of the partnership relationship among all the partners. This is winding up of business in partnership. As business is to be discontinued, it requires realisation of all the assets, payment of all the liabilities and settlement of partner's capital.

Reasons for Dissolution

The dissolution of the firm may be on account of any of the following reasons :

1. When all partners agree to dissolve the firm. (Section 40)

2. Compulsory dissolution (Section 41) – A firm is compulsorily dissolved if
   - All the partners except one are insolvent or all the partners are insolvent.
   - The business of the firm has become illegal.
3. On the happening of any one of the following incidents. (Section 42)
   - On the death of a partner.
   - On the insolvency of a partner.
   - On the fulfillment of the object for which the firm was formed.
   - On the expiry of the period for which the firm was formed.
4. **By notice (Section 43) :** When a partnership firm is not fixed and it is at will, any partner can give notice in writing to all other partners of his intention to dissolve the firm.
5. **By order of the court (Section 44) :** On a petition made by a partner to the court, it may dissolve a firm on the following grounds :
   - When a partner has become of unsound mind.
   - When a partner becomes permanently incapable in performing his duties as a partner.
   - When a partner becomes guilty of misconduct which is likely to affect the business.
   - When a partner frequently breaches the partnership agreement.
   - When a partner transfers his interest in the partnership.
   - When the court is satisfied that the firm cannot be carried on except at a loss.
   - When the court is satisfied that it is just and equitable to dissolve the firm.

Distinction between Dissolution of Partnership and Dissolution of Firm

The following are the differences between dissolution of partnership and dissolution of firm.

Dissolution of Partnership	*Dissolution of Partnership Firm*
1. It refers to a change in the existing relations /agreement among the partners.	1. It refers to the dissolution of partnership among all partners of the firm.
2. The firm continues its business.	2. The firm does not continue its business.
3. It does not require realization of asset and settlement of liabilities.	3. It involves realization of the assets and payment of liabilities of the firm.
4. A partnership is not dissolved by the order of the court.	4. Dissolution of partnership can be ordered by the court.
5. Dissolution of partnership does not necessarily mean the dissolution of firm.	5. Dissolution of partnership firm necessarily means the dissolution of partnership also.
6. It does not require final closure of books of accounts of the firm.	6. It requires final closure of the books of accounts of the firm.
7. It is voluntary.	7. It may be both voluntary and compulsory.

Firm Debts and Private Debts (Section 43)

Both a partnership firm and the partners may have separate debts. In this case the following sequential steps are followed :

(*i*) Debts of the firm will be paid first by property of the firm.

After this, if there is any surplus, that will be paid to each partner in their profit sharing ratio to be used further for payment of separate debts of the partners.

(*ii*) Private debts of the partners are first, paid by the private property of the partners.

After this, if there is any surplus, that will be used for payment of firm debts provided liabilities of the firm are more than the assets of the firm.

Settlement of Accounts on Dissolution

Section 48 of the Partnership Act 1932 specifies the mode of settlement of Accounts on the dissolution of a Partnership firm. These procedures are as follows :

1. Losses including deficiencies of Capital shall be paid first out of profits, next out of Capital and lastly, if necessary, by partners in their profit sharing ratio.
2. Amount realised from the assets of the firm and sum contributed by the partners shall be applied in the following order :
   - First, payment will be made to outside debt like Creditors, Bank Overdraft, Bills Payable etc.
   - Out of the remaining amount, the loans by Partners will be paid off.
   - There after the balance of Partners Capital Accounts will be returned.
   - If some amount remains, it will be distributed among the partners in their profit sharing ratio.

STEPS IN THE DISSOLUTION PROCESS OF A PARTNERSHIP FIRM

Step 1

In the process of dissolution of a Partnership firm, first a Balance Sheet as on the date of dissolution will be prepared. At the time of preparing the Balance Sheet on the date of dissolution, the effect of all transactions between the date of last Balance Sheet and the date of dissolution must be taken into consideration.

Step 2

A separate account will be opened which is called Realization Account.

Step 3

Next, all Non-Cash Assets are sold and converted into Cash. If the realized sale proceeds is more than the book value of the Assets, there is a gain from the sale. If it is less than the book value, it will be a loss. The amount realized on the sale of Assets will be transferred to Realization Account.

Step 4

Liabilities are discharged and Profit or Loss on dissolution will also be shown in Realization Account.

Step 5

The balance of Realisation Account is transferred to partner's Capital/Current Account in the agreed profit-sharing ratio before any cash is distributed among them.

Step 6

Next, transfer all the accumulated reserves, profits or loss to the partnership capital/current accounts in their agreed profit sharing ratio.

Step 7

Last step in the dissolution process is to distribute the available cash to creditors and partners.

Hence, the work that is to be done in dissolution process are as follows :

A. Realization of assets and settlement of liabilities.

B. Settlement of the accounts of the partners.

A. REALIZATION OF ASSETS AND SETTLEMENT OF LIABILITIES

A Realization Account is opened for disposing of all the Assets of the firm and making payment to all the Creditors. Realization is a nominal Account. The main objective of preparing this Account is to find out the profit or Loss on Realization of Assets and payment of liabilities. Journal entries in the Realization Account are made in the following manner :

1. **For closing the Asset Account :** Each asset account is closed by transferring it to Realization Account at its book value. The journal entry is :

Realization Account Dr.

To Sundry Assets Account (Individually)

Example : To Building Account

To Goodwill Account

To Plant Account

To Furniture Account

To Sundry Debtor Account etc.

Note

(*i*) The following items on the asset side of the Balance Sheet are not transferred to the Realization Account :

- Cash in hand.
- Cash at Bank.
- Debit balance of partner's current/Capital Accounts.
- Deferred Revenue expenditure. (Having no realizable value)
- Fictitious Assets like Preliminary Expenses. (Heaving no realisable value)
- Research and Development Expenses.
- Deferred Revenue Expenses.
- Advertisement Expenses etc.

(*ii*) Assets should be transferred to the Realization Account at gross figure (*i.e.* without deducting Provision or reserve).

2. For transfer of Provisions given on Assets side or Liabilities side of Balance Sheet to Realization Account.

Provision for Depreciation Account Dr.
Provision for Bad and Doubtful Debt Account Dr.
Provision for Discount on Debtors Account Dr.
Investment Fluctuation fund Account Dr.
Stock Reserve Account Dr.

Joint Life policy reserve Account Dr.

To realization account

Since provisions and reserves are not required when dissolution takes place, these should be closed by transfer to Realisation Account.

Note : Where Joint life policy appears on the asset side of the Balance Sheet at a value higher than its surrender value, Joint life policy reserve may be treated as a Provision and transferred to Realization Account as shown above. However if joint life policy appears on the asset side at its surrender value, Joint life policy reserve represents accumulated profits and should accordingly be transferred to Partner's Capital Accounts on the basis of profit sharing ratio.

3. For transfer of third parties liabilities to Realization Account.

Partner's wife Loan Account Dr.

Sundry Creditors Account Dr.

Bills Payable Account Dr.

Employees provident Account Dr.

Outside Loan Account (if any) Dr.

To Realization Account

Note : Loan from a partner will be excluded from the above entry.

4. For transfer of Discount on Creditors

Reserve for Discount on Creditors Account Dr.

To Realization Account

5. For sale of Assets to an outsider/Open Market

Bank/Cash Account (with the amount of sale) Dr.

To Realization Account

6. For Assets taken over by a partner at an agreed value.

Partners Capital/Current Account Dr.

To Realization Account

(at agreed value at which asset is to be taken over)

Note : The above entries are also passed if the firm's undisclosed goodwill or unrecorded assets are realised.

7. For payment to outside liabilities (both recorded and unrecorded if any)

Realization Account (Actual amount paid) Dr.

To Bank/Cash Account

8. For Payment to any creditor through surrender of Assets.

No entry

Note : If any asset has been taken over by any creditor in full or partial payment of the amount due to him, then the agreed value of the asset will be deducted from the amount due to the Creditors and payment will be nil in case of full settlement or payment will be restricted to the balance amount.

9. For payment of liabilities by any of the partner(s) :

If the liabilities have been taken by any of the partner(s), journal entries would be:

Realization Account (with the agreed amount) Dr.

To Partner's Current/Capital Accounts

10. For expenses on dissolution on Realization :

(*a*) Realization Account Dr.

To Bank Account/Cash Account

(*b*) If partner(s) (any one) bear the Realisation expenses :

Realization Account Dr.

To partner's current/Capital Account

(*c*) If Partners agree to do dissolution work for remuneration.

Realization Account (with the amount of remuneration) Dr.

To partner's Capital/Current Account

11. For transfer of profit on closing of Realization A/c

Realization Account Dr.

To Partner Current/Capital Accounts

Note : In the case of loss, reverse entry will be passed.

B. PROCEDURE FOR SETTLEMENT OF THE ACCOUNT OF THE PARTNERS

After closing the Realisation Account and transferring the balance to the Partner's Capital Accounts the next step is to settle the Accounts of the Partners. Since all the tangible asset and liabilities accounts have been transferred to Realisation Account, the Balance Sheet now has only the following Accounts.

Liabilities	*Amount A*	*Assets*	*Amount A*
Joint Life Policy Fund A/c		Preliminary Expenses	
Investment fluctuation fund A/c		Profit and Loss A/c (Dr.)	
General Reserve A/c		Partners Capital A/c (Dr.) (overdrawn)	
Partner loan A/c			
Partners current A/c		Partners Current A/c (Dr.) (overdrawn)	
Partner Capital A/c			
		Loan/Advance to Partners' A/c	

The following procedures are to be followed for settling the accounts of the partners.

Step 1

First, Capital Accounts of Partners are to be opened with the balance given in the Balance Sheet at the date of dissolution.

However, when Partners are maintaining fixed Capital, then, first a Current Account will be opened and the balance of Current Account (either debit or credit balance) will be transferred to the respective Capital Accounts of the Partners passing the following entries.

(For a credit Current Account balances)

Partner's Current Accounts Dr.

To Partner's Capital Accounts

For a debit Current Account balances, the entries will be

Partners Capital Accounts Dr.

To Partners Current Account

Step 2

If there is any reserve/joint life policy/Investment Fluctuations Fund or Profit and Loss Account (Cr.) balance in Balance Sheet, these should be transferred to the partner's Capitals Account in the profit sharing ratio. The journal entry will be

Reserve fund/Profit and Loss Account/Investment

Fluctuations Fund Account Dr.

Joint Life Policy Fund A/c Dr.

Workmen's Compensation Account Dr.

To Partners Capital Accounts

or

To Partner Current Account (if Partners are maintaining fixed Capital A/c)

Note : This entry is made, if joint life policy reserve is assumed as accumulated profits).

Step 3

If there are any accumulated losses or fictitious Assets in the Balance Sheet like Profit and Loss Account (Dr.) balance, Preliminary Expenses, advertisement expenses etc., they should be debited to partner's Capital Accounts or partners Current Account (if partners are maintaining fixed Capital method) in the profit sharing ratio.

The journal entries will be

Partner's Capital/Current Account Dr.

To Preliminary Expenses Account

To Advertisement Suspense Account

To Profit and Loss Account (Dr.)

Step 4

Finally, the Capital Accounts of the Partners are to be closed. The way this is to be done, depends on the solvency of the Partners. The following are the three cases to be considered in this regard. The Procedure of closing the partner's Capital Account will be different in each of the following cases.

Case 1 : Where all the Partners are solvent.

Case 2 : Where some of the Partners are solvent and others are insolvent.

Case 3 : Where all the Partners are insolvent.

Case 1 : Where all the Partners are Solvent

In this situation, the fallowing points are to be taken into account.

(*i*) If the Goodwill Account appears in the Balance Sheet, it will be treated like any Other Assets and the Account will be closed by transferring it to Realisation Account at book value.

(*ii*) If the **Goodwill** Account does not appear in the Balance Sheet, it is not transferred to Realisation Account and if some amount is realised on its sale, the same is credited to Realisation Account by making the following entries :

Bank Account Dr.

To Realisation Account

However, if Goodwill is purchased by any partner, then the Realization A/c would be credited by agreed amount and Partner's Capital A/c will be debited.

Partner's Capital Accounts Dr.

To Realisation Account.

(These entries are made whether Goodwill Account appears in the Balance Sheet or not)

(*iii*) The **unrecorded assets** will never be transferred to Realisation Account because the amount realised from its sale is in the nature of a gain and the Realisation Account is credited accordingly.

(*iv*) The **unrecorded liability** will never be transferred to Realisation Account, but payment will be made to unrecorded liability through Realisation Account.

(*v*) Where all the Partners are solvent, the loan from any partner is to be paid first. The journal entry will be

Partner's Loan Account Dr.

To Bank/Cash Account

(*vi*) If a partner has taken any loan from the firm, he is required to bring in the amount in Cash to the Business. The journal entries will be

Bank/Cash Account Dr.

To Partner's Loan Account

(*vii*) Thereafter, Partner's Capital Accounts are to be balanced.

(*viii*) The final payment is to be made to Partners through Cash/Bank Account.

(*ix*) At last there will be no balance in the Cash/Bank Account.

Case 2 : Where some of the Partners are Solvent and Others Insolvent

If, after all the adjustments in respect of the Realisation profit or loss and accumulated profit or loss etc., the Capital Accounts of a partner shows debit balance, then the partner is a debtor to the firm to that extent and has to bring necessary amount of Cash to make up for the debit balances (or deficiency) in his Capital Accounts. When he pays the Cash his Capital Accounts is closed. However, when a partner with the debit balance or deficiency in his Capital Accounts is unable to bring whole or part of the deficiency, he is said to be insolvent. In such a case, deficiency must be shared by all the solvent Partners. The important question is in what proportion/ratio?

The solvent Partners may share such deficiency in

(*i*) Either profit sharing ratio like other business loss or

(*ii*) In the ratio of last agreed Capitals (as has been decided in the case of Garner vs. Murray.

In this case (Garner vs. Murray) there were three Partners Garner, Murray and Wilkins. They shared their profits and losses equally. The Partnership was dissolved. Assets were realised and liabilities were paid off. There was a deficiency of £635 (realisation loss) and the Capital Accounts of Wilkins was showing a debit balance of £263. Nothing could be recovered from Wilkins. He was declared insolvent. There was no dispute among the Partners as regards sharing of Realisation loss. But they had a dispute regarding the basis of sharing loss due to insolvency of Wilkins. Then the matter went to the court. The decision was given by Mr. Justice Joyee in 1904. His decision was, "the solvent partners are only liable to make good their share of deficiency and that the remaining Assets should be divided among them in proportion to their Capitals."

Conclusion

(*i*) The loss on realisation (635 pounds) should be shared by all the Partners on the basis of profit sharing ratio which is equal in the present case *i.e.* solvent Partners, should bring Cash of 212 pounds (*i.e.* 635/3) each to make good their share of deficiency.

(*ii*) The debit balance of Wilkins 475 pounds (*i.e.* 212 pounds realisation loss + 265 pounds overdrawn) will be borne by Garner and Murray (solvent partners) in the ratio of their last agreed Capitals.

Notes

(*i*) Garner vs. Murray case decision/rule is applicable only when there is no agreement between/among the partners for sharing the deficiency in capital accounts of an insolvent partner.

(*ii*) The solvent partners should bring in Cash equal to their share of realization loss.

(*iii*) The loss due to insolvency of Partners should be shared by solvent partners in the ratio of their last agreed Capital.

(*iv*) Under fixed Capital method, last agreed Capital means fixed Capital given in the Balance Sheet.

(*v*) Under fluctuating Capital method, it means Capital after making adjustments for accumulated reserves, profits or losses, drawings, interest on Capitals, interest on drawings, and salary to Partners etc., up to the date of dissolution.

(*vi*) A Solvent Partner having debit balance in Capital Accounts will not share any loss due to insolvency of a partner.

Garner Vs. Murray rule is not applicable when :

1. Only one partner is solvent.
2. All partners are insolvent.
3. The partnership deed provides for a specific method to be followed in case of insolvency of a partner, and then the conditions given in the deed would prevail.

Fixed Capital

When the Partners are maintaining their Capitals in the Fixed Capital system, the following points should be considered.

(*i*) Insolvent partner's deficiency will be borne by the solvent Partners in the ratio of their Capitals appearing in the Balance Sheet. It means balances of profit or losses, reserves, loss on Realization etc. will not be taken into Account for calculating the Capital ratio.

(*ii*) If there are any undistributed profits appearing in the Balance Sheet such as credit balance of Profit and Loss Account, reserve fund, General Reserve A/c etc., they will have to be credited to Partner's Current Account.

(*iii*) Similarly, if there is any loss appearing in the Balance Sheet, the same will have to be debited to partner's Current Account.

(*iv*) Profit or Loss on Realisation must be transferred to Current Account.

(*v*) Share of Loss on Realisation brought in Cash by the solvent Partners should be credited to Current Account.

(*vi*) Current Accounts are closed by transferring their balances to the respective Capital Accounts.

Where the Capitals are Fluctuating

Where the Capitals are maintained on the fluctuating method, the true Capital (after adjustment) of each partner at the date of dissolution is determined. This means Capital after adjustment of the balances of reserve fund, debit or credit balance of Profit and Loss Account etc.

However, the loss or gain on Realisation is adjusted on the Capital Accounts of the Partners. Where there is a Loss on Realisation, each solvent partner will bring in Cash from their home.

Case 3 : When All the Partners are Insolvent

When the firm cannot meet the claims of its creditors in full because of insufficiency of firm's assets as well as private estates of the partners, all the partners are said to be insolvent. It is a case of insolvency of the firm. All the cash available will be paid to the creditors in proportion to their respective claims after the expenses on realisation have been paid. The realisation account should be prepared without transferring liabilities. The loss on realisation account will be debited to capital accounts of the partners in their profit sharing ratio. The available cash then should be used to pay the liabilities and the balance amount representing unpaid amount is transferred to a newly opened account called **Deficiency Account**. The capital accounts of the partners are closed by transferring the balances (**Debit or credit**) to the deficiency account.

Difference between Realisation Account and Revaluation Account

Realisation Account	*Revaluation Account*
1. It is prepared at the time of dissolution of the firm.	1. It is prepared at the time of dissolution of partnership when there is reconstitution of partnership through admission/retirement/death of a partner.
2. Since dissolution of firm implies winding up of business, assets are realised, liabilities are paid, and profit and loss on realisation is transferred to all partners in their profit sharing ratio through opening Realisation Account.	2. Since dissolution of partnership results in further continuation of business, assets and liabilities are revalued and profit (or loss) on revaluation is transferred to old partners in their old profit sharing ratio through opening Revaluation Account.
3. In realisation, all ledger accounts of all assets and liabilities are finally closed.	3. In revaluation, ledger accounts of all assets and liabilities are not finally closed.
4. In realisation, the objective is to ascertain profit or loss on realisation of all assets and liabilities.	4. In revaluation, the objective is to find out profit or loss on the revaluation of all assets and liabilities.
5. In realisation, it covers generally all assets and liabilities.	5. In revaluation, it covers only those assets and liabilities which are revalued.
6. In realisation, entries are made only with difference in book values and realised values *i.e.* realisation account is impacted only through this difference amount.	6. In revaluation account, revalued book values are always used for making journal entries.

Example 1

A, *B*, *C* and *D* were partners sharing profit and losses in the ratio of 3 : 3 : 2 : 2. Following was the Balance Sheet as on 31st March, 2008 :

Liabilities		Amount (A)	Assets		Amount (A)
Sundry Creditors		15,500	Sundry Debtors	16,000	
A's loan		10,000	*Less* : Provision for		
			Bad debts	500	15,500
Capital A/c :			Stock-in-Trade		10,000
A	20,000		Cash at Bank		2,000
B	15,000	35,000	Furniture and Fixture		4,000
			Trade Mark		7,000
			Capital A/c :		
			C	16,000	
			D	6,000	22,000
		60,500			60,500

On 1st April, 2008, the partnership firm was dissolved and *B* was appointed to realise the assets and pay off the liabilities. He was entitled to receive 5% commission on the amount finally paid to other partners as capital. He was to bear the expenses of realisation.

The assets realised were as follows ; Sundry Debtors A 11,000; Stock A 8,000; Furniture and Fixture A 1,000; Trade Mark A 4,000; Creditors were paid off in full; in addition to a contingent liability for bills receivable discounted, materialised to the extent of A 2,500. Also there was a joint life insurance policy for A 30,000. This was surrendered for A 3,000. Expenses of realisation amounted to A 500. *C* was insolvent, but A 3,700 were recovered from his estate.

You are required to show the following accounts of the book of partnership firm :

(*i*) Realisation Account,

(*ii*) Cash Account, and

(*iii*) Partner's Capital Account. [*CA Nov., 2003*]

Solution

Realisation Account

Dr. *Cr.*

Liabilities		Amount (A)	Assets		Amount (A)
Sundry Assets :			Provision for bad and		
Furniture and			doubtful debts		500
Fixture	4,000		Sundry Creditors		15,500
Trade Mark	7,000		Cash :		
Debtors	16,000		Furniture and Fixture	1,000	
Stock-in-Trade	10,000	37,000	Trade Mark	4,000	
			Debtors	11,000	

Realisation Account

Dr. Cr.

Particulars	Amount A	Particulars		Amount A
Cash (payment to creditors)	15,500	Stock-in-trade	8,000	
Cash (liability for bills discounted)	2,500	Surrender value of joint life policy	3,000	27,000
		Partner's Capital Accounts : (loss on realisation)		
		A	3,600	
		B	3,600	
		C	2,400	
		D	2,400	12,000
	55,000			55,000

Cash Account

Dr. Cr.

Particulars	Amount A	Particulars	Amount A
Balance b/d	2,000	Realisation A/c	15,500
Realisation A/c	27,000	Realisation A/c	2,500
C's Capital A/c	3,700	*A*'s Loan A/c	10,000
D's Capital A/c	8,400	*A*'s Capital A/c	7,619
		B's Capital A/c	5,481
	41,100		41,100

Partner's Capital Account

Dr. Cr.

	Amount A					Amount A			
Particulars	A	B	C	D	Particulars	A	B	C	D
Balance b/d	–	–	16,000	6,000	Balance b/d	20,000	15,000	–	–
Realisation A/c (Loss)	3,600	3,600	2,400	2,400	Cash A/c	–	–	3,700	8,400
C's Capital A/c (insolvency loss)	8,400	6,300	–	–	*A*'s Capital A/c (4/7)	–	–	8,400	–
					B's Capital	–	–	6,300	–
B's Capital A/c (Commission)	381	–	–	–	A's Capital A/c (commission)	–	381	–	–
Cash A/c	7,619	5,481	–	–					
	20,000	15,381	18,400	8,400		20,000	15,381	18,400	8,400

Working Notes

(*a*) Mr. *A*'s Loan is paid off in cash.

(*b*) There was a debit balance of A 8,400 in *D*'s Capital Account and although *D* is a solvent partner, he will not share deficiency arising from the insolvency of *C* but he must bring cash A 8,400.

(*c*) Deficiency in *C*'s Account is (A 16,000 + A 2,400 – A 3,700) A 14,700. *C* is insolvent and the deficiency in his account is borne by *A* and *B* in the ratio of 4 : 3 (capital ratio).

Borne by *A* = 4/7 × A 14,700 = A 8,400

Borne by B = 3/7 × A 14,700 = A 6,300

(*d*) '*B*' is entitled to get 5% commission on the amount finally paid to partner *A* only. The calculation is as follows : (A 20,000 – A 3,600 – A 8,400) A 8,000 × 5/105 = A 381.

Example 2

Asha, Rekha and Saroj sharing profits in the proportion of 1/6 : 1/3 : 1/2, agreed upon dissolution of their partnership on 31st December, 2008 on which date their Balance Sheet was as follows :

Liabilities		*Amount (A)*	*Assets*		*Amount (A)*
Capital account :			Sundry assets		37,500
Asha	30,000		Joint Life Policy		7,500
Rekha	22,500	52,500	Debtors	7,500	
Mrs. Asha's husband Loan		5,000	*Less :* Provision	375	7,125
Creditors	14,250		Stock (at Invoice price)		7,500
Less : Provision for			Investment		6,000
discount	375	13,875	Capital Account : Saroj		1,500
Joint Life Policy Fund		7,500	Cash in hand		7,625
Salary outstanding		1,500	Cash in bank		17,625
Investment fluctuation fund		3,000			
Reserve fund		7,500			
Stock Reserve		1,500			
		92,375			92,375

Additional Information

(*i*) Investments were taken over by Asha at A 4,500.

(*ii*) Creditors of A 7,500 were taken over by Rekha, who has agreed to settle the account with them at A 7,425 Remaining creditors were paid A 5,625.

(*iii*) Joint Life Policy was surrendered and Sundry assets realised A 52,500.

(*iv*) Stock and Debtors realised A 5,250 and A 6,750 respectively.

(*v*) A customer, whose account was written off as bad, now paid A 600, which is not included in A 7,500 above.

(*vi*) It was found that an investment not recorded in the books was worth A 2,250, half of which was handed over to an unrecorded liability of A 3,750 in settlement of his claim of A 1,875 and remaining half was sold in the market, which realised A 975.

(*vii*) The expenses of realisation amounted to A 825.

Prepare Realisation Account, Cash Account and Partner's Capital Accounts to close the books of firm. [*CA, Nov. 2004*]

Solution

Realisation Account

Dr. Particulars		Amount A	Particulars		*Cr.* Amount A
Sundry assets	37,500		Mrs. Asha's husband loan	5,000	
Joint life policy	7,500		Creditors	14,250	
Debtors	7,500		Outstanding Salaries	1,500	20,750
Stock	7,500				
Investments	6,000	66,000			
			Provision :		
Provisions for discount on creditors	375		Joint life policy fund	7,500	
Rekha's capital account (creditors)	7,425		Investment Fluctuation fund	3,000	
Cash/Bank account :					
Creditor	5,625		Stock Reserve	1,500	
Outstanding salaries	1,500		Provision for discount on debtors	375	12,375
Unrecorded liabilities (3,750 – 1,875)	1,875		Asha's capital account (Investment)		4,500
Mrs. Asha's Husband Loan	5,000				
Realisation Expenses	825	14,825	Cash/Bank account :		
Partner's capital account :			Joint life policy	7,500	
Asha	3,763		Sundry assets	52,500	
Rekha	7,525		Stock	5,250	
Saroj	11,287		Debtors	6,750	
		22,575	Unrecorded Investment	975	
			Bad debts recovered	600	73,575
		1,11,200			1,11,200

Partners' Capital Accounts

Capital Accounts

Dr.	Amount A				Amount A		*Cr.*
Particulars	Asha	Rekha	Saroj	Particulars	Asha	Rekha	Saroj
Balance b/d	–	–	1,500	Balance b/d	30,000	22,500	–
Realisation A/c (Investment)	4,500	–	–	Reserve fund	1,250	2,500	3,750
				Realisation A/c (Profit)	3,763	7,525	11,287
Cash A/c	30,513	39,950	13,537	Realisation A/c (Creditors)	–	7,425	–
	35,013	39,950	15,037		35,013	39,950	15,037

Cash/Bank Account

Dr. Particulars	Amount A	Particulars		Cr. Amount A
Balance b/d (7,625 + 17,625)	25,250	Realisation account (liabilities paid)		14,825
Realisation account (assets realised)	73,575	Partner's capital account		
		Asha	30,513	
		Rekha	39,950	
		Saroj	13,537	84,000
	98,825			98,825

Example 3

The following is the Balance Sheet of *A, B, C* and *D* as on 31st March 2009.

Liabilities		*Amount (A)*	*Assets*	*Amount (A)*
Creditors		20,000	Sundry Assets	30,000
B's Loan		5,000	Bank	1,000
Capitals :			P&L A/c	15,000
A	10,000		Drawings :	
B	6,000		B	2,000
C	6,000		C	2,000
D	3,000	25,000		
		50,000		50,000

They shared profits and losses in the ratio of 2 : 3 : 3 : 2 respectively. The position of partners on the date of dissolution was as follows :

	Private Estate	*Private Liabilities*
A	10,000	15,000
B	20,000	6,000
C	5,000	4,000
D	4,000	9,000

The assets realised A 26,000 only and expenses of dissolution came to A 1,000. Prepare necessary ledger accounts giving effect to the dissolution. [*B. Com., Delhi University, 2005, 2010*]

Solution

Realisation Account

Dr. Particulars	Amount A	Particulars	Cr. Amount A
To Sundry Assets A/c	30,000	By Creditors A/c	20,000
To Bank A/c (Creditors)	20,000	By Bank A/c	26,000

To Bank A/c (Expenses)	1,000	(Assets Realised)		
		By Loss transferred to :		
		A's Capital A/c	1,000	
		B's Capital A/c	1,500	
		C's Capital A/c	1,500	
		D's Capital A/c	1,000	5,000
	51,000			51,000

A's Capital Account

Dr. *Cr.*

Particulars	*Amount* A	*Particulars*	*Amount* A
To Profit and Loss A/c	3,000	By Balance b/d	10,000
To Realisation A/c (Loss)	1,000		
To *C*'s Capital A/c	1,000		
To *D*'s Capital A/c	1,000		
To Bank A/c	4,000		
	10,000		10,000

B's Capital Account

Dr. *Cr.*

Particulars	*Amount* A	*Particulars*	*Amount* A
To Profit and Loss A/c	4,500	By Balance b/d	6,000
To Drawings A/c	2,000	By Bank A/c	2,000
To Realisation A/c (Loss)	1,500		
	8,000		8,000

C's Capital Account

Dr. *Cr.*

Particulars	*Amount* A	*Particulars*	*Amount* A
To Profit and Loss A/c	4,500	By Balance b/d	6,000
To Drawings A/c	2,000	By Bank A/c	1,000
To Realisation A/c (Loss)	1,500	By A's Capital A/c	1,000
	8,000		8,000

D's Capital Account

Dr. *Cr.*

Particulars	*Amount* A	*Particulars*	*Amount* A
To Profit and Loss A/c	3,000	By Balance b/d	3,000
To Realisation A/c (Loss)	1,000	By A's Capital A/c	1,000
	4,000		4,000

Bank Account

Dr. *Cr.*

Particulars	*Amount* A	*Particulars*	*Amount* A
To Balance b/d	1,000	By Realisation A/c	20,000
To Realisation A/c	26,000	By Realisation A/c	1,000
To B's Capital A/c	2,000	By B's Loan A/c	5,000
To C's Capital A/c	1,000	By A's Capital A/c	4,000
	30,000		30,000

B's Loan Account

Dr. *Cr.*

Particulars	*Amount* A	*Particulars*	*Amount* A
To Bank A/c	5,000	By Balance b/d	5,000

Working Notes

1. *D* Cannot bring any amount. Therefore, his balance of deficiency is A 1,000 (see Capital A/c of *D*).
2. *C* can bring only A 1,000. Therefore, his balance of deficiency is A 1,000 (see Capital A/c of *C*).
3. Total deficiency of *C* and *D* is A 2,000 and this should be borne by *A* alone since *B*'s Capital A/c shows a debit balance of A 500 after transferring debit balance of Profit and Loss Account and Drawings A/c.
4. After debiting *A*'s capital A/c with deficiency of *C* and *D*, *A*'s Capital A/c shows a credit balance of A 4,000, which is paid to him.

Example 4

Following is the balance sheet of a firm as on 31 March, having three partners, Alfa, Beta and Gama sharing profits and losses equally.

Liabilities		*Amount* (*A*)	*Assets*	*Amount* (*A*)
Sundry Creditors		20,000	Cash	3,120
Loan (Secured by furniture)		10,000	Stock	15,630
Capital Accounts			Debtors	4,720
Alfa	8,000		Furniture	9,530
Beta	6,000		Profit and Loss Account	12,000
Gama	1,000	15,000		
		45,000		45,000

The firm was dissolved due to insolvency of all partners. Stock was sold for A 9,900 while furniture fetched A 5,000 A 4,100 were received from debtors. Realisation expenses totalled A 220. Nothing could be recovered from Beta and Gama but A 600 could be recovered from Alfa's private estate. Close the books of the firm. [*B. Com., Delhi University, 1999*]

Solution

Realisation Account

Dr. *Cr.*

Particulars	*Amount* A	*Particulars*	*Amount* A
Stock	15,630	Cash (Assets realised)	19,000
Debtors	4,720	Alfa's Capital Account	3,700
Furniture	9,530	Beta' Capital Account	3,700
Cash (Expenses)	220	Gama's Capital Account	3,700
	30,100		30,100

Loan Account

Dr. *Cr.*

Particulars	*Amount* A	*Particulars*	*Amount* A
Cash (to the extent of the realised value of stock)	5,000	Balance b/d	10,000
Sundry Creditors Account	5,000		
	10,000		10,000

Sundry Creditors Account

Dr. *Cr.*

Particulars	*Amount* A	*Particulars*	*Amount* A
Cash (to be paid on pro-rata basis)	17,500	Balance b/d	20,000
		Loan Account	5,000
Deficiency Account	7,500		
	25,000		25,000

Alfa's Capital Account

Dr. *Cr.*

Particulars	*Amount* A	*Particulars*	*Amount* A
Profit and Loss Account	4,000	Balance b/d	8,000
Realisation Account	3,700	Cash	600
Deficiency Account	900		
	8,600		8,600

Beta's Capital Account

Dr. Particulars	Amount A	Particulars	*Cr.* Amount A
Profit and Loss Account	4,000	Balance b/d	6,000
Realisation Account	3,700	Deficiency Account	1,700
	7,700		7,700

Gama's Capital Account

Dr. Particulars	Amount A	Particulars	*Cr.* Amount A
Profit and Loss Account	4,000	Balance b/d	1,000
Realisation Account	3,700	Deficiency Account	6,700
	7,700		7,700

Deficiency Account

Dr. Particulars	Amount A	Particulars	*Cr.* Amount A
Beta's Capital Account	1,700	Sundry Creditors Account	7,500
Gama's Capital Account	6,700	Alfa's Capital Account	900
	8,400		8,400

Cash Account

Dr. Particulars	Amount A	Particulars	*Cr.* Amount A
Balance b/d	3,120	Realisation Account	220
Realisation Account	19,000	Loan Account	5,000
Alfa's Capital Account	600	Sundry Creditors Account	17,500
	22,720		22,720

Working Note

(*i*) Loan account has been paid to the extent of A 5,000 (upto the realisation value of furniture) in full. The balance amount would rank as unsecured creditors and the same has been transferred to sundry creditors.

(*ii*) Total cash available for sundry creditors is A 17,500. It will be distributed *pro-rata* among the creditors so the loan account will further get 1/5 of A 17,500 that is A 3,500.

(*ii*) The available cash for creditors has been arrived at as follows :

		A
(*a*)	Balance in hand on the date of dissolution	3,120
(*b*)	Obtained from the sale of assets (9,900 + 5,000 + 4,100)	19,000
(*c*)	Recovered from Alfa's estate	600
	Total Cash available	22,720
	Less : Paid for expenses	220
		22,500
	Less : Paid for loan account to the extent of the realised value of furniture	5,000
		17,500

A 17,500 will be distributed among creditors of 20,000 and balance in the loan account A 5,000 in the ratio of 4 : 1. Thus creditors will get A 14,000 and loan will be further paid A 3,500 (1/5 of A 17,500).

Example 5

A, B and *C* are three partners in a firm with profit sharing ratio of 5 : 3 : 2. The Balance Sheet of the firm was as under on 31st March 2002 :

Balance Sheet

Liabilities	*Amount (A)*	*Assets*	*Amount (A)*
Creditors	40,000	Buildings	80,000
Bills payable	20,000	Furniture	10,000
Bank loan	20,000	Investments	30,000
Capitals :		P&L A/c	80,000
A	60,000		
B	40,000		
C	20,000		
	2,00,000		2,00,000

The bank loan was secured by charge on the building. Assets realised as under :

	A
Buildings	40,000
Furniture	4,000
Investments	14,000

B's private estate realised A 12,000 and his private liabilities are A 10,000. *C* was insolvent. *A* could just contribute 1/3 of what was finally due from him on his own account.

Show the ledger accounts closing the books of the firm.

Solution

Ledger Accounts
Realisation Account

Dr. *Cr.*

Particulars		A	*Particulars*		A
To Sundry Assets :			By Sundry liabilities :		
Buildings	80,000		Creditors	40,000	

Furniture	10,000		Bills payable	20,000	
Investments	30,000	1,20,000	Bank loan	20,000	80,000
To Bank–Bank loan		20,000	By Bank :		
To Bank–Creditors + Bills			Buildings	40,000	
payable		40,400	Furniture	4,000	
			Investments	14,000	58,000
			By *Loss* tr. to :		
			A's capital A/c – 5/10	21,200	
			B's capital A/c–3/10	12,720	
			C's capital A/c–2/10	8,480	42,400
		1,80,400			1,80,400

Bank Account

Dr. *Cr.*

Particulars	*Amount* *A*	*Particulars*	*Amount* *A*
To Realisation A/c–sale of assets	58,000	By Realisation A/c –Bank Loan	20,000
To *B*'s capital A/c–Excess of private assets over private liabilities (12,000 – 10,000)	2,000	By Realisation A/c –payment to creditors + B/P	40,400
To *A*'s capital a/c–contribution	400		
	60,400		60,400

***A's* Capital Account**

Dr. *Cr.*

Particulars	*Amount* *A*	*Particulars*	*Amount* *A*
To Profit and Loss A/c–5/10th Loss	40,000	By Balance b/d	60,000
To Realisation A/c–Loss	21,200	By Bank	400
		By Deficiency A/c	800
	61,200		61,200

***B's* Capital Account**

Dr. *Cr.*

Particulars	*Amount* *A*	*Particulars*	*Amount* *A*
To Profit and Loss A/c–3/10th Loss	24,000	By Balance b/d	40,000

To Realisation A/c–Loss	12,720	By Bank	2,000
To Deficiency A/c	5,280		
	42,000		42,000

C's Capital Account

Dr. *Cr.*

Particulars	*Amount* A	*Particulars*	*Amount* A
To Profit and Loss A/c –2/10th Loss	16,000	By Balance b/d	20,000
		By Deficiency A/c	4,480
To Realisation A/c–Loss	8,480		
	24,480		24,480

Deficiency Account

Dr. *Cr.*

Particulars	*Amount* A	*Particulars*	*Amount* A
To *A*'s Capital A/c	800	By *B*'s Capital A/c	5,280
To *C*'s Capital A/c	4,480		
	5,280		5,280

Notes

1. Bank loan will be paid off from the sale proceeds of Buildings.
2. The amount of contribution by *A* will be computed as follows :

Suppose the amount brought in by $A = x$

Cash balance before *A*'s contribution = A 40,000

∴ Payments to creditors + Bill payable = 40,000 + x

Loss on realisation = A 42,000 + x

∴ *A*'s share in loss on realisation = $(42,000 + x)/2$

$$x = \frac{1}{3}\left[40,000 + \left(\frac{42,000 + x}{2}\right) - 60,000\,(A\text{'s Capital balance})\right]$$

or $3x = 40,000 + 21,000 + x/2 - 60,000$

or $3x - x/2 = 40,000 + 21,000 - 60,000$

or $3x - x/2 = 1,000$

or $\frac{6x - x}{2} = 1,000$

or $6x - x = 2,000$

or $5x = 2,000$

or $x =$ A 400

Thus, *A* will contribute A 400 to the firm.

Example 6

A and B were partners on 31 March, 2002. Their Balance Sheet was as follows :

Liabilities	*(A)*	*Assets*		*(A)*
A's Capital	75,000	Fixed Assets	1,40,000	
B's Capital	35,000	*Less :* Provision for		
A's Loan	10,000	Depreciation	45,000	95,000
Creditors	26,800	Joint Life Policy		6,300
		Stock		27,000
		Debtors		15,000
		Cash		3,500
	1,46,800			1,46,800

On that date the partners dissolved the firm. Fixed Assets were sold to Jupiter Co. Ltd. for A 1,00,000 payable in the form of 10,000 shares of A 10 each. A took over joint life policy at an agreed valuation of A 5,000. Stock and debtors realised A 23,700. Realisation expenses were A 300.

A and B agreed to distribute shares in Jupiter Co. Ltd. between themselves in the ratio of their final claims, Creditors were paid at book value.

Show the necessary ledger accounts. [*B.Com. (Hons.) Delhi University, 2005*]

Solution

Particulars	*(A)*	*Particulars*		*(A)*
To Fixed Assets A/c	1,40,000	By Provision for Depreciation A/c		45,000
To Joint Life Policy A/c	6,300	By Creditors		26,800
To Stock A/c	27,000	By Jupiter Co. Ltd.		1,00,000
To Debtors A/c	15,000	By A's Capital A/c		
To Cash A/c (Creditors)	26,800	(Joint Life Policy)		5,000
To Bank A/c (Expenses)	300	By Bank A/c		
		(Stock and Debtors)		23,700
		By Loss on Realisation transferred to :		
		A's Capital A/c	7,450	
		B's Capital A/c	7,450	14,900
	2,15,400			2,15,400

Jupiter Co. Ltd. Account

Particulars	(A)	Particulars	(A)
To Realisation A/c (Purchase price)	1,00,000	By Shares in Jupiter Co. Ltd.	1,00,000
	1,00,000		1,00,000

A's Loan Account

Particulars	(A)	Particulars	(A)
To Bank A/c	100	By Balance b/d	10,000
To Shares in Jupiter Ltd.	9,900		
	10,000		10,000

Bank Account

Particulars	(A)	Particulars	(A)
To Cash A/c	3,500	By Realisation A/c (Exp.)	300
To Realisation A/c	23,700	By Realisation A/c (Crs.)	26,800
		By A's Loan (*Bal. Fig.*)	100
	27,200		27,200

A's Capital Account

Particulars	(A)	Particulars	(A)
To Realisation A/c (J.L.P.)	5,000	By Balance b/d	75,000
To Realisation A/c (Loss)	7,450		
To Shares in Jupiter Co. Ltd.	62,550		
	75,000		75,000

B's Capital Account

Particulars	(A)	Particulars	(A)
To Realisation A/c (Loss)	7,450	By Balance b/d	35,000
To Shares in Jupiter Co. Ltd.	27,550		
	35,000		35,000

Shares in Jupiter Co. Ltd.

Particulars	(A)	Particulars	(A)
To Jupiter Co. Ltd.	1,00,000	By A's Loan A/c	9,900
		By A's Capital A/c	62,550
		By B's Capital A/c	27,550
	1,00,000		1,00,000

Note

*1. A's Loan Account has to be paid before Capital Accounts of the partners. Hence, A 100, available after meeting the claims of creditors, shall be paid towards A's loan. The Balance in the loan account will have to be paid in equity shares received from Jupiter Co. Ltd.

*2. The remaining equity shares would be received by A and B in their final claims.

Example 7

The following Balance Sheet is presented to you :

Liabilities	*(A)*	*Assets*	*(A)*
Creditors	20,000	Sundry Assets	30,000
B's Loan	5,000	Cash	1,000
Capitals		Profit and Loss A/c	15,000
A	10,000	Drawings :	
B	6,000	B	2,000
C	6,000	C	2,000
D	3,000		
	50,000		50,000

The partners shared profits and losses as A $\frac{2}{10}$, B $\frac{3}{10}$, C $\frac{3}{10}$ and D $\frac{2}{10}$.

The position of partners was as follows :

	Private Estate	*Private Liability*
A	10,000	15,000
B	20,000	6,000
C	5,000	4,000
D	8,000	9,000

The Assets realised A 26,000 and expenses of realisation were A 1,000. Prepare Ledger Accounts giving effect to the dissolution. [*B.Com.* (*Hons.*) *Delhi University, 2005*]

Solution

Realisation A/c

Particulars	*(A)*	*Particulars*		*(A)*
To Sundry Assets	30,000	By Creditors		20,000
To Cash	1,000	By Cash–assets realised		26,000
To Cash (Creditors paid)	20,000	By Capital Accounts :		
		(Realisation Loss)		
		A	1,000	
		B	1,500	
		C	1,500	
		D	1,000	5,000
	51,000			51,000

Cash A/c

Particulars	*(A)*	*Particulars*	*(A)*
To Balance B/d	1,000	By Realisation A/c (Expenses)	1,000
To Realisation A/c (assets realised)	26,000	By Realisation A/c (Payment to creditors)	20,000

To B's Capital A/c	2,000	By B's Loan A/c	5,000
To C's Capital A/c	1,000	By A's Capital A/c	4,000
	30,000		30,000

A's Capital A/c

Particulars	*(A)*	*Particulars*	*(A)*
To Profit and Loss A/c – Loss	3,000	By Balance B/d	10,000
To Realisation A/c – Loss	1,000		
To D's Capital A/c	1,000		
To C's Capital A/c	1,000		
To Cash A/c (*Bal. Fig.*)	4,000		
	10,000		10,000

B's Capital A/c

Particulars	*(A)*	*Particulars*	*(A)*
To Profit and Loss A/c – Loss	4,500	By Balance B/d	6,000
To Drawings A/c	2,000	By Cash A/c (*Bal. Fig.*)	2,000
To Realisation A/c – Loss	1,500		
	8,000		8,000

C's Capital A/c

Particulars	*(A)*	*Particulars*	*(A)*
To Profit and Loss A/c – Loss	4,500	By Balance b/d	6,000
To Drawings A/c	2,000	By Cash A/c*4	1,000
To Realisation A/c – Loss	1,500	By A's Capital A/c	1,000
	8,000		8,000

D's Capital A/c

Particulars	*(A)*	*Particulars*	*(A)*
To Profit and Loss A/c – Loss	3,000	By Balance B/d	3,000
To Realisation A/c – Loss	1,000	By A's Capital A/c	1,000
	4,000		4,000

Working Notes :

*1 D cannot bring any amount. Therefore, his balance of deficiency is A 1,000 (See Capital A/c of D).

*2. C can bring only A 1,000. Therefore, his balance of deficiency is A 1000 (See Capital A/c of C).

*3. Total deficiency of C and D is A 2,000 and thus should be borne by A alone since B's Capital A/c shows a debit balance of A 500 after transferring Drawings and Debit balance of Profit and Loss Account.

*4. Out of C's personal property, only A 1,000 can be received as his private estate is A 5,000 but his private liability is A 4,000.

Example 8

Julie, Mili, Noorie and Seema were partners sharing profits and losses in the ratio of 3 : 3 : 2 : 2. Following is their Balance Sheet as on 31 March, 2006 :

Liabilities		(A)	*Assets*		(A)
Capital A/cs :			Capital A/cs :		
Julie	7,50,000		Noorie	4,80,000	
Mili	6,00,000	13,50,000	Seema	1,80,000	6,60,000
Creditors		6,65,000	Furniture		1,20,000
Julie's loan		3,00,000	Trade Marks		2,10,000
			Stock		3,00,000
			Debtors	4,80,000	
			(–) Provision	15,000	4,65,000
			Bank		60,000
			Profit and Loss Account		5,00,000
		23,15,000			23,15,000

The firm was dissolved on the above date and Mili was appointed to realise the assets and pay the liabilities. She was entitled to receive a commission of 5% on amounts finally paid to each partner(s) as capital. She was to bear the expenses of realisation. The assets realised as follows :

Debtors	A 4,50,000
Stock	A 2,50,000
Furniture	Nil
Trade Marks	A 3,65,000

Creditors were paid in full. In addition a contingent liability for bills discounted materialized to the extent of A 1,50,000. Also there was a Joint Life Policy for A 9,00,000. This was surrendered for A 1,80,000. Expenses of realisation amounted to A 1,50,000. Noorie was insolvent but A 1,60,000 was recovered from her estate.

Write up : Realisation Account, Bank Account and Capital Accounts, after considering commission payable to Mili as not a business expense. [*B.Com.*, (*Hons.*), *Delhi University, 2006*]

Solution

Realisation Account

Particulars	(A)	*Particulars*	(A)
To Furniture A/c	1,20,000	By Prov. for Doubtful Debts	15,000
To Trade Marks A/c	2,10,000	By Creditors A/c	6,65,000
To Stock A/c	3,00,000	By Bank A/c	
To Debtors A/c	4,80,000	[4,50,000 + 2,50,000 + 3,65,000]	10,65,000
To Bank A/c (Creditors)	6,65,000	By Bank A/c	
To Bank A/c (Bills Payable)	1,50,000	(Joint Life Policy)	1,80,000
	19,25,000		19,25,000

Julie's Capital Account

Particulars	(A)	*Particulars*	(A)
To Profit and Loss A/c	1,50,000	By Balance B/d	7,50,000
To Noorie's Capital Ac/	2,40,000	By Julie's Loan A/c	3,00,000
To Mili's Capital A/c (Commission)*1	17,142		
To Bank A/c	6,42,858		
	10,50,000		10,50,000

Mili's Capital Account

Particulars	(A)	*Particulars*	(A)
To Profit and Loss A/c	1,50,000	By Balance B/d	6,00,000
To Noorie's Capital A/c	1,80,000	By Julie's Capital A/c	17,142
To Bank A/c	2,87,142		
	6,17,142		6,17,142

Noorie's Capital Account

Particulars	(A)	*Particulars*	(A)
To Balance B/d	4,80,000	By Bank A/c	1,60,000
To Profit and Loss A/c	1,00,000	By Julie's Capital A/c	2,40,000
		By Mili's Capital A/c	1,80,000
	5,80,000		5,80,000

Seema's Capital Account

Particulars	(A)	*Particulars*	(A)
To Balance B/d	1,80,000	By Bank A/c	2,80,000
To Profit and Loss A/c	1,00,000		
	2,80,000		2,80,000

Bank Account

Particulars	(A)	*Particulars*	(A)
To Balance B/d	60,000	By Realisation A/c	6,65,000
To Realisation A/c	10,65,000	By Realisation A/c	1,50,000
To Realisation A/c	1,80,000	By Julie's Capital A/c	6,42,858
To Noorie's Capital A/c	1,60,000	By Mili's Capital A/c	2,87,142
To Seema's Capital A/c	2,80,000		
	17,45,000		17,45,000

Note : *1 Calculation of Commission : A [7,50,000 – 1,50,000 – 2,40,000] $\frac{5}{105}$ = A 17,142

Example 9

A, B, C and D are partners in a firm sharing profits and losses in the ratio of 4 : 3 : 2 : 1. The following is their Balance Sheet as at 31 March, 2006 :

Liabilities	*(A)*	*Assets*		*(A)*
Creditors	1,25,000	Cash in Hand		43,000
Reserve	10,000	Debtors	1,20,000	
Capital Accounts :		*Less :* Provision for bad debts	10,000	1,10,000
A	1,36,000	Other Assets		1,02,000
B	57,000	Capital Accounts :		
		C		42,000
		D		31,000
	3,28,000			3,28,000

On 31 March, 2006, the firm is dissolved. The partnership agreement provides that the deficiency of an insolvent partner will be borne by the solvent partners as per *Garner vs. Murray* rule.

A is to take over 60% of the book debts at A 56,000 and B is to take over 40% of the book debts at A 36,000. Other assets realised at a loss of 2% on net collection and creditors are paid at a discount of 20%. Realisation expenses amounted to A 5,000. D is insolvent and a dividend of 20% is realised from his estate.

Prepare necessary ledger accounts to close the books of the firm.

[*B.Com.,* (*Hons.*), *Delhi University, 2006*]

Solution

Realisation Account

Particulars	*(A)*	*Particulars*	*(A)*
To Debtors A/c	1,20,000	By Prov. for doubtful debts	10,000
To Other Assets A/c	1,02,000	By Creditors	1,25,000
To Bank A/c (Creditors)	1,00,000	By A's Capital A/c (Book debts)	56,000
To Bank A/c (Expenses)	5,000	By B's Capital A/c (book debts)	36,000
		By Bank A/c (Other Assets)	1,00,000
	3,27,000		3,27,000

Note : There is neither profit nor loss on Realisation.

A's Capital Account

Particulars	*(A)*	*Particulars*	*(A)*
To Realisation A/c	56,000	By Balance B/d	1,36,000
To D's Capital A/c*[1]	18,667	By Reserve	4,000
To Bank A/c (*Bal. Fig.*)	65,333		
	1,40,000		1,40,000

B's Capital Account

Particulars	*(A)*	*Particulars*	*(A)*
To Realisation A/c	36,000	By Balance B/d	57,000
To D's Capital A/c*[2]	5,333	By Reserve	3,000

To Bank A/c	18,667		
	60,000		60,000

C's Capital Account

Particulars	(A)	*Particulars*	(A)
To Balance B/d	42,000	By Reserve	2,000
		By Bank A/c	40,000
	42,000		42,000

D's Capital Account

Particulars	(A)	*Particulars*	(A)
To Balance B/d	31,000	By Reserve	1,000
		By Bank A/c	6,000
		By A's Capital A/c	18,667
		By B's Capital A/c	5,333
	31,000		31,000

Bank Account

Particulars	(A)	*Particulars*	(A)
To Cash A/c	43,000	By Realisation A/c	1,00,000
To Realisation A/c	1,00,000	By Realisation A/c	5,000
To C's Capital	40,000	By A's Capital A/c	65,333
To D's Capital	6,000	By B's Capital A/c	18,667
	1,89,000		1,89,000

Working Notes :

*1 Since C has a debit balance in his Capital Account on the date of Dissolution, he is not required to bear the deficiency in the Capital Account of D.

*2. D's deficiency is borne by A and B in their Capital Ratio (after all adjustments), *i.e.*, 84,000 : 24,000 or 7 : 2.

Example 10

A, B and C had the following Balance Sheet on 31.3.06.

Liabilities	(A)	*Assets*	(A)
Trade Creditors	40,000	Fixed Assets	40,000
Loan from Mrs. A		Debtors	24,000
(with a charge a stock)	15,000	Stock	20,000
Loan from A	10,000	Cash at bank	1,000
Capital A/cs :		Profit and Loss A/c	30,000
A	20,000		
B	20,000		
C	10,000		
	1,15,000		1,15,000

The firm was dissolved. Stock realised 50% and fixed assets and debtors realised A 30,000 in all. The private position of the partners was as under :

	Private Estate (*A*)	*Private Liabilities* (*A*)
A	10,000	15,000
B	8,000	6,000

C was able to pay 50 paise in the rupee of what was payable on his own account to the firm. The partners shared profits and losses in the ratio of 4 : 3 : 3 for A, B and C respectively. The loss on realisation is to be determined after considering the amount finally paid to the creditors. You are required to dose the books of the firm by preparing the necessary ledger accounts. [*B.Com.*(*Hons.*), *Delhi University, 1994, 2007]*

Solution

Realisation Account

Particulars		(*A*)	*Particulars*		(*A*)
To Sundry Assets (Transfer) :			By Trade Creditors		40,000
Fixed Assets	40,000		By Loan from Mrs. A		15,000
Debtors	24,000		By Bank A/c :		
Stock	20,000	84,000	Stock	10,000	
To Bank (Loan from Mrs. A)		10,000	Fixed Assets and Debtors	30,000	40,000
To Bank (Mrs. A's Loan and Creditors) (See Bank Account)		38,059	By Loss transferred to Capital A/cs :		
			A	14,823	
			B	11,118	
			C	11,118	37,059
		1,32,059			1,32,059

Bank Account

Particulars	(*A*)	*Particulars*	(*A*)
To Balance B/d	1,000	By Realisation A/c	10,000
To Realisation A/c	40,000	By Realisation A/c [Mrs. A's Loan and Creditors] (*Bal. Fig.*)	38,059
To B's Capital A/c (Surplus from private estate)	2,000		
To C's Capital A/c*[1]	5,059		
	48,059		48,059

Partners' Capital Accounts

Particulars	A (*A*)	B (*A*)	C (*A*)	*Particulars*	A (*A*)	B (*A*)	C (*A*)
To Realisation A/c (Loss)	14,823	11,118	11,118	By Balance B/d	20,000	20,000	10,000
To Profit and Loss A/c	12,000	9,000	9,000	By Loan A/c (Transfer)	10,000	–	–

Particulars	A	B	C	Particulars	A	B	C
To C's Capital A/c (Deficiency)*2	3,177	1,882	–	By Bank A/c	–	2,000	5,059
				By A's Capital A/c (Deficiency)	–	–	3,177
				By B's Capital A/c (Deficiency)	–	–	1,882
	30,000	22,000	20,118		30,000	22,000	20,118

Working Notes :

*1 The amount paid by C has been ascertained as follows :

Suppose the amount paid by C is x. Amount available for creditors and the balance of Mrs. A's loan will be = [(A 40,000 – A 10,000) + A 1,000 + A 2,000 + x]

= A 33,000 + x.

Loss on Realisation will be A 32,000 + x calculated as follows :

Realisation Account (Provisional)

Particulars	*(A)*	*Particulars*	*(A)*
To Sundry Assets (Transfer)	84,000	By Trade creditors (Transfer)	40,000
To Bank (Mrs. A's Loan)	10,000	By Loan from Mrs. A	15,000
To Bank (Balance of Liabilities paid)	33,000 + x	By Bank (Realised)	40,000
		By Loss on Realisation	32,000 + x
	1,27,000 + x		1,27,000 + x

C's share of loss will be 3/10 × (A 32,000 + x) = A 9,600 + 3/10 x.

C's Capital account will then appear as follows :

C's Capital A/c (Provisional)

Particulars	*(A)*	*Particulars*	*(A)*
To Profit and Loss A/c (Loss)	9,000	By Balance b/d	10,000
To Realisation A/c (Loss)	9,600 + 3/10x	By Balance c/d	8,6000+3/10x
	18,600+3/10x		18,600+3/10x

Since C has brought only half of what was due from him

Hence, $2x$ = A 8,600 + $3/10x$

or $2x - 3/10x$ = A 8,600

or $17/10x$ = A 8,600

or $x = \frac{8,600 \quad 10}{17}$ = A 5,059

*2 C's deficiency has been debited to the accounts of A and B to the extent of balance in their accounts.

Example 11

A, B, C and D were in partnership sharing profits and losses as 4 : 3 : 2 : 1. Their position on 30.6.2006 was as follows :

	(A)		(A)
Capital Accounts :		Sundry Assets	32,000
A	11,000	Loss to date	15,000
B	11,000	B's drawings	4,000
C	6,000	D's drawings	1,000
D	4,000		
Creditors	20,000		
	52,000		52,000

Credit purchases worth A 10,000 were omitted from the books. However, goods were included in stock. They decided to dissolve the firm on that date. The assets realised A 27,000, A and B are both insolvent. B's private assets amounted to A 8,000 and his private liabilities were A 7,000. D's private assets are A 6,000 and his private liabilities were A 1,000.

Show the relevant accounts, assuming that all the transactions are put through on that date and that B's estate realised A 4,000 and D's estate realised A 5,000. [*B. Com.*, (*Hons.*), *Delhi University, 2007*]

Solution

Realisation Account

Particulars	(A)	*Particulars*		(A)
To Sundry Assets	32,000	By Creditors		30,000
To Cash A/c	30,000	By Cash (assets realised)		27,000
		By Loss on Realisation transferred to Capital A/cs :		
		A	2,000	
		B	1,500	
		C	1,000	
		D	500	5,000
	62,000			62,000

Partners' Capital Accounts

Particulars	A (A)	B (A)	C (A)	D (A)	*Particulars*	A (A)	B (A)	C (A)	D (A)
To Creditors*[1]	4,000	3,000	2,000	1,000	By Balance B/d	11,000	11,000	6,000	4,000
To Drawings	–	4,000	–	1,000	By Cash*[2] (Amount) brought in by solvent partner's as per Garner *vs.* Murray Rule)	–	–	1,000	500
To Loss to date	6,000	4,500	3,000	1,500					
To Realisation A/c (Loss)	2,000	1,500	1,000	500					
To Balance C/d	–	–	1,000	500					
					By Balance B/d	1,000	2,000	–	–
	12,000	13,000	7,000	4,500		12,000	13,000	7,000	4,500

To Balance B/d	1,000	2,000	–	–	By Balance B/d	–	–	1,000	500
To A's Capital A/c	–	–	667	333	By C's Capital A/c (2/3)	667	1,333	–	–
To B's Capital A/c	–	–	1,333	667	By D's Capital A/c (1/3)	333	667	–	–
					By Cash A/c (Final Settlement)	–	–	1,000	500
	1,000	2,000	2,000	1,000		1,000	2,000	2,000	1,000

Cash Account

Particulars	*(A)*	*Particulars*	*(A)*
To Realisation A/c	27,000	By Realisation A/c (Creditors)	30,000
To C's Capital A/c	1,000		
To D's Capital A/c	500		
To C's Capital A/c	1,000		
To D's Capital A/c	500		
	30,000		30,000

***Working Notes* :**

*1 To find out capital ratio for distribution of insolvency loss error due to omission of credit purchases is rectified through Capital Accounts.

*2 C and D being solvent partners make cash contribution of A 1,000 and A 500 (their share of realisation loss) respectively in accordance with the decision in Garner *vs.* Murray Rule. They further contribute A 1,000 and A 500 respectively for final settlement of their accounts. The ratio of Capital of C and D for distribution of insolvency loss of A (A 1,000) and B (A 2000) is the capital ratio after cash contribution equal to their share of realisation loss. The ratio is 1,000 : 500 or 2 : 1.

*3. As the private assets of B realised A 4,000 and his private liabilities were A 7,000, he could not contribute anything from his personal account and, therefore, the debit balance of his account A 2,000 became insolvency loss. Similarly, the debit balance of A's Capital Account is treated as involvency loss, as no information was provided about his private assets and liabilities. On the other hand, both C and D are solvent and, therefore, they brought in cash to settle the final debit balances appearing in their accounts.

Example 12

A, B and C are partners in a firm sharing profits and losses in the ratio of 2 : 2 : 1. They decided to dissolve and appoint B to realise the assets and distribute the proceeds for which he is to receive as his remuneration 5% of the amounts ultimately paid to A and C but in lieu of this he is to bear all expenses of realisation. The Balance Sheet of the firm on the date of dissolution is as under :

Liabilities	*(A)*	*Assets*		*(A)*
Creditors	1,317	Debtors	4,229	
A's Capital	3,960	*Less :* Provision	211	4,018
B's Capital	2,970	Stock		1,872
		Cash		290
		Other assets		1,710
		C (overdrawn)		357
	8,247			8,247

B informs of the following realisation : Debtors A 3,462, Stock A 1,444, Goodwill A 50 and Other assets A 914.

Creditors which were not recorded in books are now paid A 100.

The expenses of realisation amount to A 310. C is able to contribute only A 100 beyond which he expresses his inability. Commission payable to B is to be treated as business expenses.

Close the books of the firm. [*B.Com.*, (*Hons.*), *Delhi University, 2008*]

Solution

Realisation Account

Particulars		(*A*)	*Particulars*		(*A*)
To Sundry Assets :			By Creditors		1,317
Debtors	4,229		By Provision for Doubtful Debts		211
Stock	1,872		By Cash A/c :		
Others	1,710	7,811	Debtors	3,462	
To Cash A/c (Creditors paid)		1,417	Stock	1,444	
[A 1,317 + A 100]			Goodwill	50	
To B's Capital A/c*[1]		140	Other Assets	914	5,870
(Commission)			By Loss to Capital A/cs :		
			A	788	
			B	788	
			C	394	1,970
		9,368			9,368

Cash Account

Particulars	(*A*)	*Particulars*	(*A*)
To Balance B/d	290	By Realisation A/c (creditors)	1,417
To Realisation A/c (Assets)	5,870	By A's Capital A/c*[1]	2,800
To C's Capital A/c	100	By B's Capital A/c	2,043
	6,260		5,260

Partners' Capital Accounts

Particulars	A	B	C	*Particulars*	A	B	C
To Balance b/d	–	–	357	By Balance B/d	3,960	2,970	–
To Realisation A/c	788	788	394	By Cash A/c	–	–	100
To C's Capital A/c*[2]	372	279	–	By Realisation A/c	–	140	–
To Cash A/c	2,800	2,043	–	(Commission)			
				By A's Capital A/c	–	–	372
				By B's Capital A/c	–	–	279
	3,960	3,110	751		3,960	3,110	751

Working Notes :

*1 *Calculation of Commission Payable to B :*

(*a*) B's Commission is 5% of amounts ultimately paid to A and C, therefore the actual expenses on Realisation are to be ignored.

Here ultimately nothing is being paid to C, hence B's commission is to be 5% of the amount finally paid to A.

Let B's commission be denoted by '*x*'.

We can find the realisation loss before taking into account B's commission. It is A 1,830 as shown in Realisation Account below.

Realisation Account

Particulars		(*A*)	*Particulars*		(*A*)
To Sundry Assets :			By Creditors		1,317
Debtors	4,229		By Provision for Doubtful Debts		211
Stock	1,872		By Cash A/c :		
Others	1,710	7,811	Debtors	3,462	
To Cash A/c		1,417	Stock	1,444	
(Creditors Paid)			Good will	50	
(A 1,317 + A 100)			Other Assets	914	5,870
			By Loss (before B's Commission)		1,830
			(*Bal. Fig.*)		
		9,228			9,228

∴ Loss after B's commission = A 1,830 + (*x*)

A's Share of this loss = 2/5 [A 1,830 + (*x*)] or A 732 + $\frac{2x}{5}$

B's Share of this loss = 2/5 [A 1,830 + (*x*)] or A 732 + $\frac{2x}{5}$

C's Share of this loss = 1/5 [A 1,830 + (*x*)] or A 366 + $\frac{x}{5}$

(*b*) Calculation of Loss because of C's insolvency (inability)

C's overdrawn balance	A 357
Add : C's Share of loss	A 366 + $\frac{x}{5}$
	= A 723 + $\frac{x}{5}$
Less : C's Contribution	A 100
	= A 623 + $\frac{x}{5}$

Loss borne by A and B in their Capital Ratio

i.e., A 3960 : A 2970

or 4 : 3 (as perGarner *vs.* Murray)

A's Share in this loss (deficiency = $\frac{4}{7}$ of C's insolvency (inability)

i.e., $\frac{4}{7}$ Rs. 623 $\frac{x}{5}$

Thus, amount finally paid to A is as under :

A's Capital = A 3,960

Less : Realisation loss = A 732 + $\frac{2x}{5}$

Less : C's Loss (deficiency) $\frac{4}{7}$ Rs. 623 $\frac{x}{5}$

∴ B's Commission *i.e.,* (*x*) is :

$$x \quad \frac{5}{100} \quad \text{Rs. } 3,960 \quad \text{Rs. } 732 \quad \frac{2x}{5} \quad \frac{4}{7} \quad \text{Rs. } 623 \quad \frac{x}{5}$$

$$\text{or} \quad x \quad \frac{1}{20} \quad \text{Rs. } 3,960 \quad \text{Rs. } 732 \quad \frac{2x}{5} \quad \frac{2,492}{7} \quad \frac{4x}{35}$$

$$\text{or} \quad x \quad \frac{1}{20} \quad \frac{\text{Rs. } 1,38,600 \quad \text{Rs. } 25,620 \quad 14x \quad 12,460 \quad 4x}{35}$$

$$\text{or} \quad 20x \quad \frac{\text{Rs. } 1,00,520 \quad 18x}{35}$$

or 700*x* = A 1,00,520 – 18*x*

or 718*x* = A 1,00,520

or '*x*' = A 140 (B's commission)

which is otherwise also 5% of A 2,800 finally paid to A.

*2 A's share in C's loss (deficiency)

$$= \frac{4}{7} \quad \text{Rs. } 623 \quad \frac{140}{5}$$

= A 372

B's share in C's loss (deficiency)

$$\frac{3}{7} \quad \text{Rs. } 623 \quad \frac{140}{5}$$

= A 279

Example 13

A, B and C were partners sharing profits and losses in the ratio of 3 : 2 : 1. On 31st December, 2008 their Balance Sheet was as follows :

Liabilities	(A)	*Assets*	(A)
Sundry Creditors	30,000	Cash at Bank	9,500
Bills Payable	5,000	Stock	15,500
A's Loan	6,000	Sundry Debtors	32,000
Reserve Fund	12,000	Furniture	5,000
Profit and Loss A/c	6,000	Plant	21,000
Capital Accounts :		A's Drawings	4,000
A	20,000	B's Drawings	1,000
B	15,000	C's Capital A/c	6,000
	94,000		94,000

The firm was dissolved on that date. Assets realised as follows :

Stock – A 12,200; Debtors – A 30,100 and Furniture realised – A 4,200. Plant was taken over by A at A 18,000. A contingent liability for bill discounted is settled at A 600. Realisation expenses amounted to A 600. C is insolvent and only A 1,900 could be recovered from his private estate.

Prepare necessary Ledger Accounts to close the books of the firm. Apply Garner *vs.* Murray.

[*B.Com.*, (*Hons., Delhi University, 2009*]

Solution

Realisation Account

Liabilities		(A)	*Assets*		(A)
To Stock A/c		15,500	By Creditors		30,000
To Sundry Debtors A/c		32,000	By Bills Payable		5,000
To Furniture A/c		5,000	By Bank A/c :		
To Plant A/c		21,000	Stock	12,200	
To Bank A/c :			Debtors	30,100	
S. Creditors	30,000		Furniture	4,200	46,500
Bills Payable	5,000		By A's Capital A/c (Plant)		18,000
Contingent Liability	600		By Loss (A 10,200)		
Expenses on Realisation	600	36,200	By Loss (A 10,200)		
			Transferred to :		
			A's Capital A/c	5,100	
			B's Capital A/c	3,400	
			C's Capital A/c	1,700	10,200
		1,09,700			1,09,700

A's Loan Account

Particulars	(A)	*Particulars*	(A)
To Bank A/c	6,000	By Balance b/d	6,000

C's Capital Account

Particulars	(A)	Particulars	(A)
To Balance b/d	6,000	By Reserve Fund	2,000
To Realisation A/c (Loss)	1,700	By Profit and Loss A/c	1,000
		By Bank A/c	1,900
		By A's Capital A/c*1	1,556
		By B's Capital A/c*1	1,244
	7,700		7,700

A's Capital Account

Particulars	(A)	Particulars	(A)
To Drawings A/c	4,000	By Balance b/d	20,000
To Realisation A/c	18,000	By Reserve Fund	6,000
To Realisation A/c (Loss)	5,100	By Profit and Loss A/c	3,000
To C's Capital A/c	1,556	By Bank A/c	5,100
To Bank A/c	5,444		
	34,100		34,100

B's Capital Account

Particulars	(A)	Particulars	(A)
To B's Drawing A/c	1,000	By Balance b/d	15,000
To Realisation A/c (Loss)	3,400	By Reserve Fund	4,000
To C's Capital A/c	1,244	By Profit and Loss A/c	2,000
To Bank A/c	18,756	By Bank A/c	3,400
	24,400		24,400

Bank Account

Particulars	(A)	Particulars	(A)
To Balance b/d	9,500	By Realisation A/c (creditors)	36,200
To Realisation A/c	46,500	By A's Loan A/c	6,000
To A's Capital A/c	5,100	By A's Capital A/c	5,444
To B's Capital A/c	3,400	By B's Capital A/c	18,756
To C's Capital A/c	1,900		
	66,400		66,400

Working Notes :

*1 Capital deficiency of C = A 2,800

Capital deficiency of C will be borne by A and C in the ratio of their Capital which stood before the date of dissolution *i.e.,* 5 : 4 calculated as follows :

	A (A)	B (A)
Balance b/d	20,000	15,000

	Reserve Fund	6,000	4,000
	Profit and Loss A/c	3,000	2,000
		29,000	21,000
Less :	Drawings	4,000	1,000
	Capital	25,000	20,000
	Capital Ratio 5 : 4		

Example 14

AB Ltd. was formed to acquire the business of A and B who share profits in the ratio of 3 : 2 respectively. The Balance Sheet of A and B as on 31 December, 2008 was as under :

Liabilities	*(A)*	*Assets*	*(A)*
Capital Accounts :		Land and Building	40,000
A	64,000	Machinery	20,000
B	40,000	Stock	24,000
Mrs. A's Loan	3,200	Debtors	23,200
Bills Payable	7,200	Bills Receivable	6,400
Sundry Creditors	21,600	Investments	4,800
		Cash at Bank	9,600
		Goodwill	8,000
	1,36,000		1,36,000

It was agreed by the company to take over the assets at book value with the exception of land and building, stock and goodwill which are taken over at A 45,000, A 20,000 and A 28,800 respectively. The investments were retained by the firm and sold for A 4,000. The firm discharged the loan of Mrs. A. The company took over the remaining liabilities. The purchase consideration was discharged by issuing 10,000 equity shares of A 10 each in AB Ltd. and the balance was paid in cash. Close the books of the firm assuming that shares are distributed amongst partners in their profit sharing ratio.

[*B.Com.,* (*Hons.*), *Delhi University, 2009*]

Solution

Realisation Account

Particulars	*(A)*	*Particulars*	*(A)*
To Land and Building	40,000	By Bills Payable A/c	7,200
To Machinery	20,000	By S. Creditors	21,600
To Stock	24,000	By AB Ltd.	
To Debtors	23,200	(Purchase consideration)*1	1,24,200
To Bills Receivable	6,400	By Bank A/c (Investment)	4,000
To Investments	4,800		
To Bank	9,600		
To Goodwill	8,000		
To Profit (A 21,000)			

Transferred to :				
A's Capital A/c	12,600			
B's Capital A/c	8,400	21,000		
		1,57,000		1,57,000

AB Ltd. Account

Particulars	(A)	Particulars	(A)
To Realisation A/c	1,24,200	By Shares in AB Ltd.	1,00,000
		By Bank A/c	24,200
	1,24,200		1,24,200

Shares in AB Ltd. Account

Particulars	(A)	Particulars	(A)
To AB Ltd.	1,00,000	By A's Capital A/c	60,000
		By B's Capital A/c	40,000
	1,00,000		1,00,000

Mrs. A's Loan Account

Particulars	(A)	Particulars	(A)
To Bank A/c	3,200	By Balance b/d	3,200
	3,200		3,200

Partners' Capital Accounts

Particulars	A	B	Particulars	A	B
To Share in AB Ltd.	60,000	40,000	By Balance b/d	64,000	40,000
To Bank A/c	16,600	8,400	By Realisation A/c	12,600	8,400
	76,600	48,400		76,600	48,400

Bank Account

Particulars	(A)	Particulars	(A)
To Balance b/d	9,600	By Realisation A/c	9,600
To AB Ltd.	24,200	By Mrs. A's Loan	3,200
To Realisation A/c	4,000	By A's Capital A/c	16,600
		By B's Capital A/c	8,400
	37,800		37,800

Working Notes :

*1 *Calculation of Purchase Consideration*

			(A)
Land and Building			45,000
Stock			20,000

Machinery		20,000
Debtors		23,200
Bills Receivable		6,400
Bank		9,600
Goodwill		28,800
		1,53,000
Less : Bills Payable	7,200	
Creditors	21,600	28,800
		1,24,200

Example 15

A, B and C shared profits and losses in the ratio of 5 : 3 : 2 respectively. On 31 March, 2009 their Balance Sheet was as follows :

Liabilities	*(A)*	*Assets*	*(A)*
A's Capital A/c	60,000	Furniture	22,000
B's Capital a/c	40,000	Stock	96,000
C's Capital A/c	20,000	Cash	2,000
Creditors	60,000	Profit and Loss A/c	80,000
Bank Loan	20,000		
	2,00,000		2,00,000

The bank had a charge on all the assets. Furniture realised A 6,000 and stock was sold for A 50,000. B's private estate realised A 12,000 and his private liabilities were A 10,000. C was unable to contribute anything. A paid one-third of what was due from him on his own account.

Prepare Realisation Account, Cash Account and Partners' Capital Accounts, passing all matters relating to realisation of assets and payment of liabilities through Realisation Account.

[*B.Com.*, (*Hons.*), *Delhi University, 2010*]

Solution

Working Notes :

Suppose A will contribute *x* amount.

Memorandum Realisation Account

Particulars		*(A)*	*Particulars*		*(A)*
To Sundry Assets :			By Creditors		60,000
Furniture	22,000		By Bank Loan		20,000
Stock	96,000	1,18,000	By Cash A/c (Assets Realised)		56,000
To Cash A/c (Bank Loan)		20,000	By Loss :		
To Cash A/c (Creditors)		40,000 + *x*	A	21,000 + 5*x*/10	
			B	12,600 + 3*x*/10	
			C	8,400 + 2*x*/10	42,000 + *x*
		1,78,000 + *x*			1,78,000 + *x*

Memorandum Cash Account

Particulars	(*A*)	*Particulars*	(*A*)
To Balance b/d	2,000	By Realisation A/c (Bank loan)	20,000
To Realisation A/c	56,000	By Realisation A/c (Creditors)	40,000 + x
To B's Capital A/c [12,000 – 10,000]	2,000		
To A's Capital A/c	x		
	60,000 + x		60,000 + x

Memorandum A's Capital Account

Particulars	(*A*)	*Particulars*	(*A*)
To Profit and Loss A/c (Loss)	40,000	By Balance b/d	60,000
To Realisation A/c (Loss)	21,000 + $5x/10$	By Balance c/d	1,000 + $x/2$
	61,000 + $5x/10$		61,000 + $x/2$

A will contribute $\frac{1}{3}$ of $1,000 \quad \frac{x}{2}$ $\qquad \therefore \qquad \frac{1,000}{3} \quad \frac{x}{6} \quad x$

$\Rightarrow \qquad 2,000 + x = 6x \qquad \Rightarrow \qquad 5x = A\ 2,000$

$\therefore \qquad x = A\ 400$

$\therefore$ Amount contributed by A = A 400

Realisation Account

Particulars		(*A*)	*Particulars*		(*A*)
To Sundry Assets :			By Creditors		60,000
Furniture	22,000		By Bank Loan		20,000
Stock	96,000	1,18,000	By Cash A/c :		
To Cash A/c (Bank Loan)		20,000	Furniture	6,000	
To Cash A/c (Creditors)		40,400	Stock	50,000	56,000
			By Loss transferred to :		
			A's Capital A/c	21,200	
			B's Capital A/c	12,720	
			C's Capital A/c	8,480	42,400
		1,78,400			1,78,400

Partners' Capital Accounts

Particulars	*A*	*B*	*C*	*Particulars*	*A*	*B*	*C*
To Realisation A/c (Loss)	21,200	12,720	8,480	By Balance B/d	60,000	40,000	20,000
To Profit and Loss A/c	40,000	24,000	16,000	By Cash	400	2,000	–
To Deficiency A/c	–	5,280	–	By Deficiency A/c	800	–	4,480
	61,200	42,000	24,480		61,200	42,000	24,480

Deficiency Account

Particulars	(A)	*Particulars*	(A)
To A's Capital A/c	800	By B's Capital A/c	5,280
To C's Capital A/c	4,480		
	5,280		5,280

Example 16

Bini, Mini and Tini are partners sharing profits and losses in the ratio of 4 : 3 : 2. Their Balance Sheet as on 31 March, 2011 stood as follows :

Liabilities	(A)	*Assets*		(A)
Creditors	20,000	Cash		2,000
Bank Overdraft (Secured against stock)	15,000	Debtors	18,000	
		Less : Provision	1,000	17,000
Loan (Secured against Machinery)	25,000	Stock		25,000
		Machinery		40,000
Capitals :		Profit and Loss A/c		9,000
Bini	20,000			
Mini	10,000			
Tini	3,000			
	93,000			93,000

The firm was dissolved. Stock was taken over by the Banker and it realised A 20,000. Bank paid back A 4,000 after recovering its overdraft and interest due thereon. Machinery was disposed off for A 24,000 and debtors realised A 14,000 only. Loan was fully paid off along with interest due A 1,000. There was an unrecorded asset valuing A 5,000 which was taken over by a creditor at A 2,000. Expenses amounted to A 300 which were paid by Bini. Tini became insolvent. Tini's private liabilities amounted A 1,000 while his private estate realised A 1,950.

Prepare necessary Ledger Accounts to close the books of the firm.

[*B.Com.*, (*Hons.*), *Delhi University, Nov. 2011*]

Solution

Realisation A/c

Particulars	(A)	*Particulars*	(A)
To Debtors	18,000	By Creditors	20,000
To Machinery	40,000	By Overdraft	15,000
To Stock	25,000	By Loan	25,000
To Cash (26,000 + 18,000)	44,000	By Provision	1,000
To Bini Capital	300	By Cash (24,000 + 14,000 + 4,000)	42,000
		By Loss :	
		Bini	10,800
		Mini	8,100
		Tini	5,400
	1,27,300		1,27,300

Capitals

Particulars	Bini (A)	Mini (A)	Tini (A)	Particulars	Bini (A)	Mini (A)	Tini (A)
To Profit and Loss A/c	4,000	3,000	2,000	By Balance	20,000	10,000	3,000
To Realisation	10,800	8,100	5,400	By Realisation	300	–	–
To Tini (16 : 7)	2,400	1,050	–	By Cash	10,800	8,100	–
To Cash	13,900	5,950	–	By Cash	–	–	950
				By Bini	–	–	2,400
				By Mini	–	–	1,050
	31,100	18,100	7,400		31,100	18,100	7,400

Cash A/c

Particulars	(A)	Particulars	(A)
To Balance	2,000	By Realisation	44,000
To Realisation :	42,000	By Capitals : Bini	13,900
To Tini	950	Mini	5,950
To Bini	10,800		
To Mini	8,100		
	63,850		63,850

Example 17

Exe, Wye and Zed have been carrying on business in partnership sharing profits and loesses in the ratio of 2 : 2 : 1. They decided to dissolve the firm on the basis of the following balance sheet as at 31 March, 2008.

Liabilities	(A)	Assets	(A)
Capital accounts :		Premises	65,000
Exe	40,000	Machinery	27,000
Wye	40,000	Car	26,000
Zed	20,000	Furniture	11,000
General reserve	35,500	Stock	15,000
Creditors	65,000	Debtors	45,000
Car loan from bank	22,000	Cash and bank balance	18,500
Loan to Zed	15,000		
	2,22,500		2,22,500

Following further information is submitted to you :

(*i*) Premises were taken over by Exe at book value *plus* 25%. The stamp duty amounting to 10% of takeover price was borne by Exe.

(*ii*) Car loan of A 22,000 was satisfied by giving total amount realised on sale of car. The shortfall of A 3,000 was met from firm's bank account.

(*iii*) All the debtors except debtors of A 2,500 which were proved bad, were taken over by Wye at 90% of book value.

(*iv*) Stock was taken over by one of the creditors against full and final settlement of his credit balance of A 17,500. All other creditors waived 4% of their total claim.

(*v*) Machinery was sold at 10% profit on sales price. Zed took over furniture at A 8,000.

(*vi*) General reserve was built up by appropriation of profits.

(*vii*) Realisation expenses amounted to A 1,500.

You are required to draw Realisation Account, Partners's Capital Accounts and Cash Account.

[*B.Com.* (*Hons.*) *Delhi University*]

Solution

Exe, Wye and Zed
Realisation Account

Particulars		(*A*)	*Particulars*	(*A*)
Premises		65,000	Creditors	65,000
Machinery		27,000	Loan from Bank	22,000
Car		26,000	Exe' Capital Account	81,250
Furniture		11,000	Wye' Capital Account	38,250
Stock		15,000	Bank Account (Machinery)	30,000
Debtors		45,000	Zed' Capital Account	8,000
Bank Account (Loan)		3,000		
Bank Account (Creditors)		45,600		
Bank Account (Expenses)		1,500		
Profit transferred to :				
Exe	2,160			
Wye	2,160			
Zed	1,080	5,400		
		2,44,500		2,44,500

Exe' Capital Account

Particulars	(*A*)	*Particulars*	(*A*)
Realisation Account	81,250	Balance b/d	40,000
		Realisation Account	2,160
		General Reserve	14,200
		Bank Account	24,890
	81,250		81,250

Wye' Capital Account

Particulars	(*A*)	*Particulars*	(*A*)
Realisation Account	38,250	Balance b/d	40,000
Bank Account	18,110	Realisation Account	2,160
		General Reserve	14,200
	56,360		56,360

Zed' Capital Account

Particulars	*(A)*	*Particulars*	*(A)*
Realisation Account	8,000	Balance b/d	20,000
Bank Account	20,180	Realisation Account	1,080
		General Reserve	7,100
	28,180		28,180

Cash and Bank Account

Particulars	*(A)*	*Particulars*	*(A)*
Balance b/d	18,500	Realisation Account (Loan)	3,000
Realisation Account	30,000	Realisation Account (Creditors)	45,600
Exe' Capital Account	24,890	Realisation Account (Expenses)	1,500
Loan to Zed	15,000	Why' Capital Account	18,110
		Zed' Capital Account	20,180
	88,390		88,390

Loan to Zed Account

Particulars	*(A)*	*Particulars*	*(A)*
Balance b/d	15,000	Bank Account	15,000

Working Notes **:**

(*i*) Premises were taken over by Exe at A 65,000 + 25% = A 81,250; stamp duty is always paid by the purchaser unless there is an agreement to the contrary.

(*ii*)	Total Debtors	A 45,000
	Less : Bad Debts	A 2,500
		42,500
	Taken over by Wye' at 95% of A 42,500 =	A 38,250
(*iii*)	Total Creditors	A 65,000
	Less : Paid in Stock	A 17,500
		47,500
	Less : 4% Rebate	1,900
	Net Payment	45,600
(*iv*)	Book value of Machinery =	A 27,000
	Profit on Sale	10%
	Sale Price : $27{,}000 \quad \frac{100}{90}$	A 30,000

Example 18

Neptune, Jupiter, Venus and Pluto had been carrying on business in partnership sharing profits and losses in the ratio of 3 : 2 : 1 : 1. They decide to dissolve the partnership on the basis of the following Balance Sheet as on 30 April, 2003 :

Liabilities	(A)	(A)	*Assets*	(A)	(A)
Capital Account :			Premises		1,20,000
Neptune	1,00,000		Furniture		40,000
Jupiter	60,000	1,60,000	Stock		1,00,000
General Reserve		56,000	Debtors		40,000
Capital Reserve		14,000	Cash		8,000
Sundry Creditors		20,000	Capital Overdrawn :		
Mortgage Loan		80,000	Venus	10,000	
			Plouto	12,000	22,000
		3,30,000			3,30,000

(*i*) The assets were realised as under :

	(A)
Debtors	24,000
Stock	60,000
Furniture	16,000
Premises	90,000

(*ii*) Expenses of dissolution amounted to A 4,000.

(*iii*) Further Creditors of A 12,000 had to be met.

(*iv*) General Reserve unlike Capital Reserve was built up by appropriation of profits.

You are required to draw up the Realisation Account, Partners' Capital Accounts and the Cash Account assuming that Venus became insolvent and nothing was realised from his private estate. Apply the principles laid down in Garner vs Murrary. [*C.A., November, 2003*]

Solution

Realisation Account

Particulars	(A)	*Particulars*		(A)
To Sundry assets A/c (transfer) :		By Sundry creditors A/c		20,000
Premises	1,20,000	By Cash A/c (Assets realised) :		
Furniture	40,000	Premises	90,000	
Stock	1,00,000	Furniture	16,000	
Sundry Debtors	40,000	Stock	60,000	
To Cash A/c (creditors paid)	32,000	Debtors	24,000	1,90,000
To Cash A/c (expenses)	4,000	By Loss transferred to Capital Accounts :		
		Neptune	54,000	
		Jupiter	36,000	
		Venus	18,000	
		Pluto	18,000	1,26,000
	3,36,000			3,36,000

Cash Account

Particulars		(A)	*Particulars*	(A)
To Balance b/d		8,000	By Realisation A/c (creditors)	32,000
To Realisation A/c (assets realised)		1,90,000	By Realisation A/c (expenses)	4,000
To Capital A/c			By Mortgage Loan	80,000
(realisation loss made good) :			By Neptune's Capital A/c	1,18,857
Neptune	54,000		By Jupiter's Capital A/c	73,143
Jupiter	36,000			
Pluto	18,000	1,08,000		
To Pluto's Capital A/c		2,000		
		3,08,000		3,08,000

Partners' Capital Accounts

Particulars	*Neptune* (A)	*Jupiter* (A)	*Venus* (A)	*Pluto* (A)	*Particulars*	*Neptune* (A)	*Jupiter* (A)	*Venus* (A)	*Pluto* (A)
To Balance b/d	–	–	10,000	12,000	By Balance b/d	1,00,000	60,000	–	–
To Realisation A/c (loss)	54,000	36,000	18,000	18,000	By General reserve A/c (3 : 2 : 1 : 1)	24,000	16,000	8,000	8,000
By Venus's Capital A/c (loss)	11,143	6,857	–	–	By Capital reserve A/c (3 : 2 : 1 : 1)	6,000	4,000	2,000	2,000
To Cash A/c	1,18,857	73,143	–	–	By Cash A/c (loss on realization)	54,000	36,000	–	18,000
					By Neptune's Capital A/c	–	–	11,143	–
					By Jupiter's Capital A/c	–	–	6,857	–
					By Cash A/c	–	–	–	2,000
	1,84,000	1,16,000	28,000	30,000		1,84,000	1,16,000	28,000	30,000

Example 19

X, Y and *Z* are partners of the firm *XYZ* and Co., sharing Profits and Losses in the ratio of 4 : 3 : 2. Following is the Balance Sheet of the firm as at 31 March, 2008 :

Balance Sheet as at 31 March, 2008

Liabilities	(A)	*Assets*	(A)
Partners' Capital :		Fixed Assets	5,00,000
X	4,00,000	Stock in trade	3,00,000
Y	3,00,000	Sundry debtors	5,00,000
Z	2,00,000	Cash in hand	10,000
General Reserve	90,000		
Sundry Creditors	3,20,000		
	13,10,000		13,10,000

Partners of the firm decided to dissolve the firm on the above said date. It was found that a credit purchase of A 20,000 in January, 2008 had not been recorded in the books of the firm.

Fixed assets realized A 5,20,000 and book debts A 4,40,000.

Stocks were valued at A 2,50,000 and it was taken over by partner Y.

Creditors allowed discount of 5% and the expenses of realization amounted to A 6,000.

You are required to prepare :

(*i*) Realisation account;

(*ii*) Partners capital account; and

(*iii*) Cash account. [C.A., November, 2008]

Solution

(*i*) Realisation Account

Particulars	*(A)*	*Particulars*	*(A)*
To Fixed assets	5,00,000	By Creditors	3,20,000
To Stock in trade	3,00,000	By Cash (5,20,000 + 4,40,000)	9,60,000
To Debtors	5,00,000	By Y (Stock taken over)	2,50,000
To Cash-Expenses	6,000	By Loss transferred to partners' capital accounts	
To Cash-Creditors (3,40,000 × 95%)	3,23,000	X	44,000
		Y	33,000
		Z	22,000
	16,29,000		16,29,000

(*ii*) Partners' Capital Account

Particulars	X (A)	Y (A)	Z (A)	*Particulars*	X (A)	Y (A)	Z (A)
To Realisation A/c	44,000	33,000	22,000	By Balance B/d	4,00,000	3,00,000	2,00,000
To Realisation A/c	–	2,50,000	–	By General reserve	40,000	30,000	20,000
To Cash	3,96,000	47,000	1,98,000				
	4,40,000	3,30,000	2,20,000		4,40,000	3,30,000	2,20,000

(*iii*) Cash Account

Particulars	(A)	*Particulars*	(A)
To Balance b/d	10,000	By Realisation A/c (Expenses)	6,000
To Realisation A/c (Fixed assets and book debts realized)	9,60,000	By Realisation A/c (Creditors)	3,23,000
		By X	3,96,000
		By Y	47,000
		By Z	1,98,000
	9,70,000		9,70,000

Example 20

P, Q and *R* are partners sharing profits and losses as to 2 : 2 : 1. Their Balance Sheet as on 31 March, 2011 is as follows :

Liabilities		*(A)*	*Assets*	*(A)*
Capital Accounts			Plants and Machinery	1,08,000
P	1,20,000		Fixtures	24,000
Q	48,000		Stock	60,000
R	24,000	1,92,000	Sundry debtors	48,000
Reserve Fund		60,000	Cash	60,000
Creditors		48,000		
		3,00,000		3,00,000

They decided to dissolve the business. The following are the amounts realized :

	(A)
Plant and Machinery	1,02,000
Fixtures	18,000
Stock	84,000
Sundry debtors	44,400

Creditors allowed a discount of 5% and realization expenses amounted to A 1,500. There was an unrecorded asset of A 6,000 which was taken over by Q at A 4,800. A bill for A 4,200 due for sales tax was received during the course of realization and this was also paid.

You are required to prepare :

(*i*) Realisation account.

(*ii*) Partners' capital accounts.

(*iii*) Cash account. [*C.A., November, 2009*]

Solution

Realisation Account

Particulars		*(A)*	*Particulars*		*(A)*
To Debtors		48,000	By Creditors		48,000
To Stock		60,000	By Cash A/c (Assets realized) :		
To Fixtures		24,000	Plant and Machinery	1,02,000	
To Plant and machinery		1,08,000	Fixtures	18,000	
To Cash A/c (Creditors)		45,600	Stock	84,000	
To Cash A/c (Sales tax)		4,200	Sundry Debtors	44,400	2,48,400
To Cash A/c (Realisation expenses)		1,500	Q (Unrecorded asset)		4,800
To Profit on Realisation					
P	3,960				
Q	3,960				
R	1,980	9,900			
		3,01,200			3,01,200

Partners' Capital Accounts

Particulars	P (A)	Q (A)	R (A)	Particulars	P (A)	Q (A)	R (A)
To Realisation A/c (unrecorded asset)		4,800		By Balance b/d	1,20,000	48,000	24,000
To Cash (*Bal. Fig.*)	1,47,960	71,160	37,980	By Reserve fund	24,000	24,000	12,000
				By Realisation A/c (Profit)	3,960	3,960	1,980
	1,47,960	75,960	37,980		1,47,960	75,960	37,980

Cash Account

Particulars	(A)	Particulars	(A)
To Balance b/d	60,000	By Realisation A/c (Creditors)	45,600
To Realisation A/c (Assets)	2,48,400	By Realisation A/c (Expenses)	1,500
		By Realisation A/c (Sales Tax)	4,200
		By P's Capital A/c	1,47,960
		By Q's Capital A/c	71,160
		By R's Capital A/c	37,980
	3,08,400		3,08,400

Example 21

A, B, C and *D* are sharing profits and losses in the ratio 5 : 5 : 4 : 2. Frauds committed by *C* during the year were found out and it was decided to dissolve the partnership on 31 March, 2010 when their Balance Sheet was as under :

Liabilities	(A)	*Assets*	(A)
Capital		Building	1,20,000
A	90,000	Stock	85,500
B	90,000	Investments	29,000
C	–	Debtors	42,000
D	35,000	Cash	14,500
General reserve	24,000	C	15,000
Trade creditors	47,000		
Bills payable	20,000		
	3,06,000		3,06,000

Following information is given to you :

(*i*) A cheque for A 4,300 received from debtor was not recorded in the books and was misappropriated by *C*.

(*ii*) Investments costing A 5,400 were sold by *C* at A 7,900 and the funds transferred to his personal account. This sale was omitted from the firm's books.

(*iii*) A creditor agreed to take over investments of the book value of A 5,400 at A 8,400. The rest of the creditors were paid off at a discount of 2%.

(*iv*) The other assets realized as follows :

Building	105% of book value
Stock	A 78,000
Investments	The rest of investments were sold at a profit or A 4,800
Debtors	The rest of the debtors were realized at a discount of 12%.

(*v*) The bills payable were settled at a discount of A 400.

(*vi*) The expenses of dissolution amounted to A 4,900.

(*vii*) It was found out that realization from *C*'s private assets would only be A 4,000.

Prepare the necessary Ledger Accounts. [*C.A., November, 2010*]

Solution

Realisation Account

Particulars		*(A)*	*Particulars*		*(A)*
To Building		1,20,000	By Trade Creditors		47,000
To Stock		85,500	By Bills Payable		20,000
To Investment		29,000	By Cash		
To Debtors		42,000	Building	1,26,000	
To Cash-creditors paid (W.N. 1)		37,828	Stock	78,000	
To Cash-expenses		4,900	Investments (W.N. 2)	23,000	
To Cash-bills payable (20,000-400)		19,600	Debtors (W.N. 3)	33,176	2,60,176
To Partners' Capital A/cs			By Debtors-unrecorded		4,300
A	171		By Investments-unrecorded		7,900
B	171				
C	137				
D	69	548			
		3,39,376			3,39,376

Cash Account

Particulars		*(A)*	*Particulars*	*(A)*
To Balance b/d		14,500	By Realisation-creditors paid	37,828
To Realisation - assets realised			By Realisation-bills payable	19,600
Building	1,26,000		By Realisation-expenses	4,900
Stock	78,000		By Capital account	
Investments	23,000		A	90,528
Debtors	33,176	2,60,176	B	90,528
To C's capital A/c		4,000	D	35,292
		2,78,676		2,78,676

Partners' Capital Accounts

Particulars	A (₹)	B (₹)	C (₹)	D (₹)	Particulars	A (₹)	B (₹)	C (₹)	D (₹)
To Balance b/d	–	–	15,000		By Balance b/d	90,000	90,000	–	35,000
To Debtors-misappropriation			4,300		By General reserve	7,500	7,500	6,000	3,000
To Investment-misappropriation			7,900		By Realisation profit	171	171	137	69
To C's capital A/c (W.N. 4)	7,143	7,143		2,777	By Cash A/c			4,000	
To Cash A/c	90,528	90,528		35,292	By A's Capital A/c			7,143	
					By B's Capital A/c			7,143	
					By D's Capital A/c			2,777	
	97,671	97,671	27,200	38,069		97,671	97,671	27,200	38,069

***Working Notes*:**

1. *Amount paid to creditors*

	(₹)
Book value	47,000
Less : Creditors taking over investments	(8,400)
	38,600
Less : Discount @ 2%	(772)
	37,828

2. *Amount received from sale of investments*

	(₹)
Book value	29,000
Less : Misappropriated by C	(5,400)
	23,600
Less : Taken over by a creditor	(5,400)
	18,200
Add : Profit on sale of investments	4,800
	23,000

3. *Amount received from debtors*

	(₹)
Book value	42,000
Less : Unrecorded receipt	(4,300)
	37,700
Less : Discount @ 12%	(4,524)
	33,176

4. *Deficiency of C*

	(A)
Balance of capital as on 31 March, 2010	15,000
Debtors-misappropriation	4,300
Investment-misappropriation	7,900
	27,200
Less : Realisation Profit	(137)
General reserve	(6,000)
Contribution from private assets	(4,000)
Net deficiency of capital	17,063

This deficiency of A 17,063 in *C*'s capital account will be shared by other partners *A, B* and *D* in their capital ratio of 90 : 90 : 35.

Accordingly,

A's share of deficiency = [17,063 × (90/215)] = A 7,143

B's share of deficiency = [17,063 × (90/215)] = A 7,143

D's share of deficiency = [17,063 × (35/215)] = A 2,777

Example 22

A, B and *C* who shared profits and losses equally, were in partnership for many years. As their business was declining, they decided to dissolve the partnership on 31 March. The closing balance sheet as on that date was as under :

Liabilities	(A)	*Assets*	(A)
Capital accounts :		Freehold property	4,00,000
A	2,19,000	*Less :* Mortgage	2,00,000
B	1,46,000		2,00,000
C	35,000	Machinery	1,00,000
Creditors	1,20,000	Closing stock	1,15,000
Bank overdraft	70,000	Debtors	1,75,000
	5,90,000		5,90,000

The plant and machinery and the stock were sold by auction and realised A 50,000 and A 21,500 respectively. The firm was able to obtain discount of A 3,000 and allowances of A 17,000 on settlement of creditors. The bank charged A 2,500 for bank charges and interest.

Debtors realised A 1,56,000. The freehold, property was taken over by *A* (subject to the existing mortgage) and was revalued at A 3,00,000. The legal costs and consultant's fees amounted to A 10,000 which were paid by the firm.

Prepare accounts showing the results of the dissolution, assuming that *C* was unable to contribute more than A 25,000 to his share of any deficiency of assets, and that the remaining amount due was shared by other partners equally. [*B.Com.,* (*Hons.*), *Delhi University*]

Solution

Realisation Account

Particulars	(A)	*Particulars*		(A)
Freehold Property	4,00,000	Creditors		1,20,000
Machinery	1,00,000	Mortgage Loan		2,00,000
Closing Stock	1,15,000	A' Capital Account		3,00,000
Debtors	1,75,000	Bank Account (Assets Realised) :		
A'Capital Account	2,00,000	Machinery	50,000	
Bank (Creditors)	1,00,000	Stock	21,500	
Bank (Bank Charges)	2,500	Debtors	1,56,000	2,27,500
Bank (Legal Charges etc.)	10,000	Loss transferred to :		
		A' Capital Account	85,000	
		B' Capital Account	85,000	
		C' Capital Account	85,000	2,55,000
	11,02,500			11,05,500

C' Capital Account

Particulars	(A)	*Particulars*	(A)
Realisation Account (Loss)	85,000	Balance b/d	35,000
		Bank	25,000
		A' Capital Account	12,500
		B' Capital Account	12,500
	85,000		85,000

A' Capital Account

Particulars	(A)	*Particulars*	(A)
Realisation Account	3,00,000	Balance b/d	2,19,000
C' Capital Account	12,500	Realisation Account	2,00,000
Realisation Account (Loss)	85,000		
Bank Account	21,500		
	4,19,000		4,19,000

B' Capital Account

Particulars	(A)	*Particulars*	(A)
Realisation Account (Loss)	85,000	Balance b/d	1,46,000
C' Capital Account	12,500		
Bank Account	48,500		
	1,46,000		1,46,000

Bank Account

Particulars	(A)	Particulars	(A)
Realisation Account	2,27,500	Balance b/d	70,000
C' Capital Account	25,000	Realisation Account	1,00,000
		Realisation Account	2,500
		Realisation Account	10,000
		A' Capital Account	21,500
		B' Capital Account	48,500
	2,52,500		2,52,500

Example 23

Robinson, Gulliver and Sindabad are partners to M/s. Adventure and Co. sharing profits and losses in the ratio of 2 : 1 : 1. On 31 March, their Balance Sheet was as under :

Liabilities		(A)	*Assets*		(A)
Creditors		40,000	Cash		5,000
Capitals :			Bank		30,000
Robinson	1,00,000		Debtors	70,000	
Gulliver	50,000		*Less :* Provision for doubtful		
Sindabad	35,000	1,85,000	debts	3,500	66,500
			Stock :		
			On ship	1,00,000	
			In godown	20,000	1,20,000
			Fixed assets		3,500
		2,25,000			2,25,000

On that day, there were three devastating incidents.

(*i*) A customer who owed A 60,000 became insolvent and nothing could be recovered from his estate.

(*ii*) The ship was caught in a storm and it sunk with the entire cargo. The stock was not insured.

(*iii*) The godown caught fire. The stock that could be saved was only worth A 3,000. This stock was also not insured.

The partners, therefore, decided to dissolve the firm. Fixed assets realised A 1,000; remaining debtors realised A 9,500; stock was sold for A 2,500. The creditors claiming payment totalled A 42,000. Robinson, Gulliver and Sindabad did not have any private assets. Realisation expenses amounted to A 500.

You are asked to pass journal entries to close the books of the firm. Also show realisation account, cash account, bank account and partners' capital accounts. [*B.Com.*, (*Hons.*), *Delhi University*]

Solution

Realisation Account

Particulars	(A)	*Particulars*	(A)
Debtors	70,000	Provision for Bad Debts	3,500
Stock :		Creditors	40,000

On Ship	1,00,000		Bank		13,000
In Godown	20,000	1,20,000	Loss transferred to :		
Fixed Assets		3,500	Robinson	89,750	
Bank (Creditors)		42,000	Gulliver	44,875	
Bank (Expenses)		500	Sindabad	44,875	1,79,500
		2,36,000			2,36,000

Robinson' Capital Account

Particulars	*(A)*	*Particulars*	*(A)*
Realisation Account	89,750	Balance b/d	1,00,000
Sindabad' Capital Account	6,583		
Bank Account	3,667		
	1,00,000		1,00,000

Gulliver' Capital Account

Particulars	*(A)*	*Particulars*	*(A)*
Realisation Account	44,875	Balance b/d	50,000
Sindabad' Capital Account	3,292		
Bank Account	1,833		
	50,000		52,000

Sindabad' Capital Account

Particulars	*(A)*	*Particulars*	*(A)*
Realisation Account	44,875	Balance b/d	35,000
		Robinson' Capital Account	6,583
		Gulliver' Capital Account	3,292
	44,875		44,875

Bank Account

Particulars	*(A)*	*Particulars*	*(A)*
Balance b/d	30,000	Realisation Account	42,000
Cash Account	5,000	Realisation Account	500
Realisation Account	13,000	Robinson' Capital Account	3,667
		Gulliver' Capital Account	1,833
	48,000		48,000

Example 24

Ram, Rahim, Rajesh and Rahbar are partners carrying business under partnership. Ram gets 1/4 share in profits. The other partners shared the balance equally. The following is their balance sheet as on 31 March.

Liabilities	(A)	*Assets*		(A)
Capital accounts :		Plant and machinery		67,500
Rajesh	65,000	Furniture and fixtures		28,000
Rahbar	35,000	Sundry debtors	50,000	
Reserves	1,00,000	*Less* : R.D.D.	15,850	34,150
Sundry creditors	40,000	Bills receivable		12,500
		Trademarks		7,000
		Stock		40,000
		Capital accounts:		
		Ram		30,000
		Rahim		14,850
		Cash in hand		6,000
	2,40,000			2,40,000

The partnership was dissolved on 31 March, on the following terms :

(*i*) On this day it was found that a liability for purchase of goods of A 20,000 had been omitted to be recorded and that the goods has been included in stock.

(*ii*) The assets realised as follows : Plant and machinery A 60,000; Furniture and fixtures A 18,000; Debtors A 21,000; Stock A 30,000.

(*iii*) the creditors including the unrecorded creditors were paid in full. There was a contingent liability in respect of bills discounted for A 3,500.

(*iv*) During the year there was an unrecorded asset purchased for A 10,000. Half of the assets was handed over to the vendor of the asset (also unrecorded) in full settlement of his claim. The remaining half was sold for A 4,000.

(*v*) The realisation expenses amounted to A 3,850.

(*vi*) Mr. Rahim is insolvent and can contribute only A 2,350.

(*vii*) The contingent liability did not materialise.

Prepare Realisation Account, Partners' Capital Accounts and Cash Account. Working should form part of the answer. [*B.Com.* (*Hons.*), *Delhi University*]

Solution

Realisation Account

Particulars	(A)	*Particulars*		(A)
Plant and Machinery	67,500	Reserve for Doubtful Debts		15,850
Furniture and Fixtures	28,000	Creditors (40,000 + 20,000)		60,000
Debtors	50,000	Cash (Assets Realised) :		
Bills Receivable	12,500	Plant and Machinery	60,000	
Trade Marks	7,000	Furniture and Fixtures	18,000	
Stock	40,000	Debtors	21,000	
Cash (Creditors)	60,000	Stock	30,000	
Cash (Expenses)	3,850	Unrecorded Asset	4,000	1,33,000

		Loss transferred to Capital A/c :	
		Ram' 15,000	
		Rahim' 15,000	
		Rajesh' 15,000	
		Rahbar' 15,000	60,000
	2,68,850		2,68,850

Rajesh' Capital Account

Particulars	*(A)*	*Particulars*	*(A)*
Creditors	5,000	Balance b/d	65,000
Realisation Account	15,000	Reserves	25,000
Rahim' Capital Account	4,553		
Cash Account	65,447		
	90,000		90,000

Rahbar' Capital Account

Particulars	*(A)*	*Particulars*	*(A)*
Creditors	5,000	Balance b/d	35,000
Realisation Account	15,000	Reserves	25,000
Rahim' Capital Account	2,947		
Cash Account	37,053		
	60,000		60,000

Ram' Capital Account

Particulars	*(A)*	*Particulars*	*(A)*
Balance b/d	30,000	Reserves	25,000
Creditors	5,000	Cash Account	25,000
Realisation Account	15,000		
	50,000		50,000

Rahim' Capital Account

Particulars	*(A)*	*Particulars*	*(A)*
Balance b/d	14,850	Reserves	25,000
Creditors	5,000	Cash	2,350
Realisation Account	15,000	Rajesh' Capital Account (17/28 × 7,500)	4,553
		Rahabar' Capital Account (11/28 × 7,500)	2,947
	34,850		34,850

Cash Account

Particulars	*(A)*	*Particulars*	*(A)*
Balance b/d	6,000	Realisation Account	60,000
Realisation Account	1,33,000	Realisation Account	3,850

Rahim' Capital Account	2,350	Rajesh' Capital Account	65,447
Ram' Capital Account	25,000	Rahabar' Capital Account	37,053
	1,66,350		1,66,350

Working Notes :

(*i*) Ram' Capital Account has a debit balance (even after transferring reserves) on the date of dissolution. He will not bear the deficiency in Rahim's Capital Account. Since he is solvent, he will bring in cash to make up his debit balance.

(*ii*) Rajesh' Capital balance on the date of dissolution is arrived at as follows :

	(*A*)
Capital as per Balance Sheet	65,000
Add : Reserves	25,000
	90,000
Less : Unrecorded Creditors	5,000
	85,000

Similarly Rahbar's Capital Account on the date of dissolution is calculated as under :

	(*A*)
Capital as per Balance Sheet	35,000
Add : Reserves	25,000
	60,000
Less : Unrecorded Creditors	5,000
	55,000

Thus their capitals, on the date of dissolution are : A 85,000 and A 55,000 respectively. Hence they will bear the deficiency of Rahim in the ratio of 85 : 55 or 17 : 11.

(*iii*) Total Profit = 1
Ram gets 1/4
Remaining Profit = 1 – 1/4 = 3/4
It is to be shared equally by other partners, i.e. 1/3 of 3/4 each
Rahim will get 1/3 of 3/4 = 3/12
Rajesh will get 1/3 of 3/4 = 3/12
Rahbar will get 1/3 of 3/4 = 3/12
Hence profit sharing ratio is : 1/4 : 3/12 : 3/12 : 3/12 or 3 : 3 : 3 : 3 or 1 : 1 : 1 : 1 or 1/4 for each partner.

Example 25

X, Y and *Z* were partners in a business sharing profits and losses equally. Their balance sheet as at 31 March 2005 was as follows :

Liabilities	(*A*)	*Assets*	(*A*)
X' Capital	1,60,000	Machinery	4,00,000
Z' Capital	1,00,000	Furniture	1,60,000
X' Loan	2,00,000	Stock	5,60,000
Creditors	10,00,000	Debtors	2,00,000
		Bank	10,000
		Y' Capital Overdrawn	1,30,000
	14,60,000		14,60,000

Due to adverse financial position of all the partners, the firm was dissolved on the above mentioned date. The assets were realised as follows :

	A
Machinery	1,40,000
Furniture	1,00,000
Stock	2,60,000
Debtors	1,10,000

Expenses on realisation amounted to A 10,000. All the partners were insolvent. While a sum of A 20,000 was received from Y's private assets, nothing could be recovered from the private estate of X and Z.

Prepare the realisation account, capital accounts of the partners, creditors account and deficiency account in the firm ledger. Also show the cash book. *[C.S. June, 2005]*

Solution

Realisation Account

Particulars	*(A)*	*Particulars*		*(A)*
Machinery	4,00,000	Bank (Assets Realised) :		
Furniture	1,60,000	Machinery	1,40,000	
Stock	5,60,000	Furniture	1,00,000	
Debtors	2,00,000	Stock	2,60,000	
Bank (Expenses)	10,000	Debtors	1,10,000	6,10,000
		Loss Transferred to :		
		X's Capital Account		2,40,000
		Y's Capital Account		2,40,000
		Z's Capital Account		2,40,000
	13,30,000			13,30,000

Creditors Account

Particulars	*(A)*	*Particulars*	*(A)*
Bank Account	6,30,000	Balance b/d	10,00,000
Deficiency Account	3,70,000		
	10,00,000		10,00,000

X's Loan Account

Particulars	*(A)*	*Particulars*	*(A)*
Deficiency Account	20,000	Balance b/d	20,000

X's Capital Account

Particulars	*(A)*	*Particulars*	*(A)*
Realisation Account	2,40,000	Balance b/d	1,60,000
		Deficiency Account	80,000
	2,40,000		2,40,000

Y's Capital Account

Particulars	(A)	*Particulars*	(A)
Balance b/d	1,30,000	Bank Account	20,000
Realisation Account	2,40,000	Deficiency Account	3,50,000
	3,70,000		3,70,000

Z's Capital Account

Particulars	(A)	*Particulars*	(A)
Realisation Account	2,40,000	Balance b/d	1,00,000
		Deficiency Account	1,40,000
	2,40,000		2,40,000

Deficiency Account

Particulars	(A)	*Particulars*	(A)
X's Capital Account	80,000	Creditors Account	3,70,000
Y's Capital Account	3,50,000	X's Loan Account	2,00,000
Z's Capital Account	1,40,000		
	5,70,000		5,70,000

Bank Account

Particulars	(A)	*Particulars*	(A)
Balance b/d	10,000	Realisation Account	10,000
Realisation Account	6,10,000	Creditors Account	6,30,000
Y's Capital Account	20,000		
	6,40,000		6,40,000

Notes :

(*i*) Since the firm does not have enough cash (including A 20,000) from the private estate of Y, to pay the creditors in full, the firm is insolvent including all partners. Hence Realisation Account will be prepared with the assets accounts only.

(*ii*) The available amount A 6,40,000 (i.e. A 6,10,000 from the sale of assets, A 20,000 from the estate of Y and A 10,000 cash in bank has been distributed in the following order :

(*i*)	Realisation expenses	10,000
(*ii*)	Sundry creditors	6,30,000
		6,40,000

SALE OF PARTNERSHIP FIRM TO A LIMITED COMPANY

A partnership firm, after dissolution, may be converted into a limited liability company or may be sold to an existing limited liability company. In these situations, dissolution of the old firm takes place and it is also known as sale of a partnership firm to a limited company. The price payable by the company for assets and liabilities taken over is known as 'Purchase Consideration.' The purchase consideration (or price) can be computed in any one of the following ways, if lump sum considerations is not given in the examination problem :

(*i*) **Net Asset Method :** The value of net assets taken over by the purchasing company is the amount payable. It is computed as follows :

Agreed value of Individual Assets Taken Over	xxx
Less : Agreed Value of Individual Liabilities Taken Over	xxx
Value of Net Assets Taken Over (Purchase Consideration)	xxx

It is known as Net Asset Method of calculation of purchase consideration.

(*ii*) **Net Payment Method :** Sometimes, the agreed values of assets and liabilities, not taken over are not given in the problem. The problem specifies the payments made by the company in cash/shares/debentures etc. To arrive at purchase consideration all payments made by the company to the firm (irrespective the purpose and form of payment) are added together. It is done as under :

Cash Paid	xxx
Issue Price of Equity Shares	xxx
Issue Price of Preference Shares	xxx
Issue Price of Debentures	xxx
Total Payments being the amount of purchase consideration	xxx

It is known as 'Payment Method' of purchase consideration. The journal entries passed to deal with purchase consideration are as under :

For purchase Consideration Due :		
Purchasing Company A/c	Dr.	(With the amount of purchase consideration)
To Realisation A/c		
For Purchase Consideration Received		
Cash/Bank A/c	Dr.	(With various payments received showing securities at their issue price)
Equity Shares in Purchasing Company A/c	Dr.	
Preference Shares in Purchasing Company A/c	Dr.	
Debentures in Purchasing Company A/c	Dr.	
To Purchasing Company A/c		

It should be noted that the same accounting procedure is adopted to close the books and settlement of accounts as followed for simple dissolution, discussed earlier in this chapter, with some exceptions because there are some special features in this type of dissolution of the partnership firm. When the company takes over the business of the firm, it takes over all assets and liabilities.

Realisation account is opened in this case also. The accounting procedure followed in dissolution of partnership firm and its sale to a limited company is as follows :

1. Open a Realisation Account.
2. Transfer all assets and outside liabilities accounts, (whether or not taken over by the purchasing company) to the Realisation Account at their respective book values.
3. Cash and Bank Balances would be transferred to Realisation Account only and only when taken over by the purchasing company, otherwise not.
4. The disposal of assets not taken over by the purchasing company would be recorded through Realisation Account as is done in simple dissolution.

5. The payment to outside liabilities not taken over by the purchasing company would be paid through Realisation Account as explained.
6. The price paid by the purchasing company is the purchase consideration; and is known as the sale price. The agreed purchase consideration is recorded by Debiting the Purchasing Company's Account and Crediting the Realisation Account.

Accounting of Unrealisable Assets

Sometimes the purchasing company does not take over the assets of a partnership firm. If such assets, not taken over by the company, cannot be sold, the partners may agree among themselves as to how these assets are to be divided. In the absence of any agreement, the unrealisable assets should be divided among the partners in their profit sharing ratio. This way, assets account existing in the books of the firm will stand closed.

Distribution of Shares and Debentures among Partners

In sale of a partnership firm to a limited company, there is always a question of deciding the basis of distributing the shares and debentures among the partners if partners do not have any agreement on this matter. If purchase consideration comprises of cash only, no such problem arises. There are many views available in accounting pronouncements regarding distribution of shares and debentures among the partners as mentioned below :

(*i*) The shares and debentures should be distributed among the partners in the ratio of their final claims, i.e. capital ratios of partners after taking into account profit or loss on realisation; other accumulated profits such as credit balance in the profit and loss account, reserve fund; losses (debit balance in the profit and loss account).

(*ii*) Distribution should be done in the profit sharing ratio.

(*iii*) Shares and debentures received from the limited company should be independently valued in order to find out their intrinsic worth as well as their yield value and the profit and loss on such valuation (of shares and debentures) is transferred to partners' capital accounts. The shares and debentures will then be distributed among the partners in proportion to their capitals as adjusted by profit or loss on realisation as well as such valuation of shares. Other things remaining the same, the shares, debentures etc., are assumed to be worth their book value.

(*iv*) The equity shares can be allotted to the partners in their profit sharing ratio. Preference shares and debentures can be allotted for their excess capital i.e., the capital in excess of their profit sharing ratio. Such a division it is claimed would preserve the main rights of the partners, namely (*a*) sharing of profits and losses and (*b*) interest on capitals.

Among the above four methods, generally the first method i.e. distribution of shares, debentures etc. on the basis of final claims appears to be more appropriate.

It should be noted that shares and debentures are hot issued in parts or fraction; the nearest whole number of shares or debentures is allotted to a partner. Also, agreed value of shares and debentures is considered, not the nominal value of shares and debentures.

Example 26

A, *B* and *C* share profit and losses in the ratio 3 : 2 : 1 after allowing interest on capital @ 9% p.a. Their capitals on 31 December, 2000 were : *A* A 50,000, *B* A 30,000 and *C* A 20,000. On 1 January, 2001 the business was converted into a limited company and was valued at A 1,30,000. Suggest a scheme of capitalisation, whereby the mutual interest of partners may remain intact as far as possible. [*C.A. Foundation*]

Solution

The total capital being A 1,00,000 and the value placed on the business being A 1,30,000, there is goodwill of A 30,000 to be shared by the partners in the ratio of 3 : 2 : 1 or *A* A 15,000, *B* A 10,000 and *C* A 5,000. The capital will now be : *A* A 65,000, *B* A 40,000 and *C* A 25,000.

Example 27

On 31.3.2008, the balance sheet of *A* and *B* sharing profits as 2 : 1 was as follows :

Liabilities		*(A)*	*Assets*		*(A)*
Capital Accounts :			Fixed Assets		75,000
A	50,000		Stock		35,000
B	40,000	90,000	Debtors	70,000	
Current Accounts :			*Less* : Provision	5,000	65,000
A	20,000		Bank		15,000
Less : *B*	10,000	10,000			
B's Loan		30,000			
Creditors		55,000			
Reserve		5,000			
		1,90,000			1,90,000

The firm was dissolved on the above date. Following additional information was made available :

1. Fixed assets included two motor cars having book value of A 8,000 and A 6,000 respectively.
2. X Ltd. acquired fixed assets (other than motor cars) and stock at price of A 1,60,000.
3. The purchase consideration was to be satisfied by a cash payment of A 56,000, the allotment of 8,000 equity shares of A 10 each at 10% discount and the allotment of 200, 12% preference shares of A 100 each.
4. *A* agreed to take over one car at a valuation of A 12,000 and *B* took the other car at A 8,000.
5. *B* was to be allotted preference shares to the value of his loan and the remaining preference shares were allotted to *A*.
6. The equity shares were distributed between *A* and *B* in proportion to their capital and the balance was settled in cash.
7. Debtors realised A 61,000 and creditors were settled at A 51,000.

Prepare Realisation Account, Current Accounts and Capital Accounts.

[*B.Com.*, (*Hons.*), *Delhi University*]

Solution

Payment of purchase consideration of A 1,60,000 is as under :

Bank	56,000	
Equity shares	72,000	(8,000 × 9)
Preference shares (*bal. fig.*)	32,000	(200 × 160)
	1,60,000	

Realisation Account

Particulars	*(A)*	*Particulars*	*(A)*
Fixed Asset	75,000	Provision on Debtors	5,000
Stock	35,000	Creditors	55,000
Debtors	70,000	X Ltd.	1,60,000
Bank (Creditors)	51,000	Bank (Debtors)	61,000
Profit to :		A's Current A/c	12,000

A's Current A/c	46,667	B's Current A/c	8,000
B's Current A/c	23,333		
	3,01,000		3,01,000

Current Accounts

Particulars	A (A)	B (A)	Particulars	A (A)	B (A)
Balance b/d		10,000	Balance b/d	20,000	–
Realisation A/c	12,000	8,000	Reserve	3,333	1,667
(Assets taken over)			Realisation A/c (Profit)	46,667	23,333
Capital A/c (balancing figure)	58,000	7,000			
	70,000	25,000		70,000	25,000

Capital Account

Particulars	A (A)	B (A)	Particulars	A (A)	B (A)
12% Preference shares in X Ltd.	2,000	–	Balance b/d	50,000	40,000
Equity shares in X Ltd.	40,000	32,000	Current A/c	58,000	7000
Cash A/c (*bal. fig.*)	66,000	15,000			
	1,08,000	47,000		1,08,000	47,000

X Ltd.

Particulars	(A)	Particulars	(A)
Realisation A/c	1,60,000	Bank	56,000
		Preference shares in X Ltd.	32,000
		Equity shares in X Ltd.	72,000
	1,60,000		1,60,000

Bank Account

Particulars	(A)	Particulars	(A)
Balance b/d	15,000	Realisation (Creditors)	51,000
X Ltd.	56,000	A's Capital	66,000
Realisation (Debtors)	61,000	B's Capital	15,000
	1,32,000		1,32,000

Preference Shares in X Ltd. Account

Particulars	(A)	Particulars	(A)
X Ltd.	32,000	B's Load A/c	30,000
(200 × 160)		A's Capital A/c	2,000
	32,000		32,000

Equity Shares in X Ltd. Account

Particulars	(*A*)	*Particulars*	(*A*)
X Ltd.	72,000	A's Capital A/c	40,00
(8,000 × 9)		B's Capital A/c	32,000
	72,000		72,000

Alternatively, the purchase consideration may be calculated on the basis of payment if the question states that preference shares are issued at 60% premium.

		(*A*)	
Net payment	Bank	– 56,000	
	Preference shares	– 32,000	
	Equity shares	– 72,000	1,60,000

If the question states, that fixed assets (other than cash) are valued at A 1,20,000 and stock at A 40,000 the purchase consideration by net Assets method will be follows :

Fixed Assets (Other than car)	1,20,000	
Stock	40,000	1,60,000

Example 28

Khanak and Nitya were carrying on business. Their Balance Sheet as on 31 March, 2011 was as follows:

Liabilities	(*A*)	*Assets*	(*A*)
Creditors	65,500	Plant and Machinery	1,82,000
Bank Overdraft	30,000	Furniture	15,000
Bills Payable	12,500	Leasehold Premises	34,500
Capitals :		Joint Life Policy	9,500
Khanak	1,50,000	Stock	54,000
Nitya	1,48,000	Book Debts	73,000
		Profit and Loss A/c	26,000
		Drawings :	
		Khanak	9,000
		Nitya	3,000
	4,06,000		4,06,000

The business was carried on till 30 September, 2011. The partners withdrew in amounts half the amount of profits made during the period of six months (April-September, 2011) after depreciating leasehold premises and plant and machinery by 10% p.a. and furniture by 5% p.a. Meanwhile, creditors were reduced by A 10,000. On 30 September, 2011, stock was valued at A 63,400. Bills payable and bank overdraft were reduced by A 2,300 and A 15,000 respectively. Book debts were valued at A 65,000, the Joint Life Policy was realised for A 9,500 and the amount was utilized to reduce the bank overdraft. Other items remained as on 31 March, 2011.

On 30 September, 2011 the firm sold the business to Jalaj Ltd. Goodwill was estimated at A 1,08,000 and other assets were valued on the basis of Balance Sheet as on 30 September, 2011. The purchase consideration was paid in fully paid equity shares of A 10 each.

Prepare relevant Ledger Accounts in the books of partnership firm.

[*B.Com., (Hons.), Delhi University, Nov. 2011*]

Solution

Balance Sheet as on 30 September 2011

Liabilities	(*A*)	*Assets*		(*A*)
Creditors (65,500 – 10,000)	55,500	Stock		63,400
Bank Overdraft (30,000 – 15,000 – 9,500)	5,500	Plant and Machinery	1,82,000	
Bills Payable (12,500 – 2,300)	10,200	Dep.	9,100	1,72,900
Capitals (B/F)	2,77,500	Furniture	15,000	
		Dep	375	14,625
		Lease hold premises	34,500	
		Dep	1,725	32,775
		Book Debts		65,000
	3,48,700			3,48,700

Statement of Profit for 6 Months Ending 30 Sept. 2011

	(*A*)
Capital on 30 Sept. 2011	2,77,500
Capital on 31 March 2011 (1,50,000 + 1,48,000 – 9,000 – 3,000 – 26,000)	2,60,000
Profit retained	17,500
Profit with drawn	17,500
Net Profit	35,000

Purchase Consideration

	(*A*)
Net Assets	2,77,500
+ Goodwill	1,08,000
	3,85,500

Realisation A/c

Liabilities	(*A*)	*Assets*	(*A*)
To Premises	32,775	By Creditors	55,500
To Plant and Machinery	1,72,900	By Bank overdraft	5,500
To Furniture	14,625	By Bills Payablea	10,200
To Stock	63,400	By Jalaj Ltd.	3,85,500
To Book Debits	65,000		
To Profit :			
Khanak	54,000		
Nitya	54,000		
	4,46,700		4,56,700

Capitals

Particulars	*Kanak* (*A*)	*Nitya* (*A*)	*Particulars*	*Kanak* (*A*)	*Nitya* (*A*)
Profit and Loss	13,000	13,000	Balance	1,50,000	1,48,000
Drawings	9,000	3,000	Profit	17,500	17,500
Drawings	8,750	8,750	Realisation	54,000	54,000
Shares in J Ltd.	1,90,750	1,94,750			
	2,21,500	2,19,500		2,21,500	2,19,500

Example 29

Rajesh and Sushil who were sharing profits in proportion of 5 : 3 decided to convert their partnership into a limited company under the name of R.S. Enterprises Limited. Their Balance Sheet as at 31 March, 2006 was as follows :

Liabilities	*(A)*	*Assets*	*(A)*
Capital Accounts :		Equipments	7,20,000
Rajesh	8,80,000	Vans	3,20,000
Sushil	6,00,000	Trade Marks	80,000
General Reserve	2,40,000	Stock	6,80,000
Loan from Rajesh	1,60,000	Bills Receivable	4,80,000
Overdraft	3,20,000	Debtors	1,20,000
Creditors	2,00,000		
	24,00,000		24,00,000

Various terms and conditions of conversion agreed upon by and between the partners were as under:

(*a*) Goodwill of the firm to be valued on the basis of purchase of two years average of profits of the previous three years which A 2,80,000; A 3,00,000 and A 2,84,000 after transferring a sum of A 80,000 to general reserve each year.

(*b*) Equipments are to be taken at A 8,00,000.

(*c*) 12% Debentures in R.S. Enterprises Limited to be issued to discharge loan from Rajesh.

(*d*) Stock was valued at A 6,88,000.

(*e*) Partners to be issued 40,000 equity shares of A 50 each fully paid and balance in cash.

(*f*) Partners decided to distribute equity shares in R.S. Enterprises in their profit sharing ratio.

You are required to :

(*a*) Calculate purchase consideration.

(*b*) Prepare :

(*i*) Realisation Account.

(*ii*) Partners' Capital Account.

(*iii*) Bank Account. [*B.Com.* (*Hons.*), *Delhi University, 2006*]

Solution

1. Calculation of the Value of goodwill :

(*a*) Total profits of the previous three years

= A 2,80,000 + A 3,00,000 + A 2,84,000 + A 2,40,000

(Amount transferred to General Reserve)

= A 11,04,000

(*b*) Average Profit $\frac{\text{Rs. } 11,04,000}{3}$ Rs. 3, 68, 000

(*c*) Goodwill = Average Profit × 2

= A 3,68,000 × 2 = A 7,36,000

2. Calculation of Purchase Consideration :

	(A)	*(A)*
Goodwill*[1]		7,36,000
Equipment		8,00,000
Stock		6,88,000

Vans		3,20,000
Trade Marks		80,000
Bills Receivable		4,80,000
Debtors		1,20,000
		32,24,000
Less : Creditors	2,00,000	
Overdraft	3,20,000	5,20,000
		27,04,000

Mode of Payment for Purchase Consideration

	(*A*)
Equity Shares	20,00,000
12% Debentures	1,60,000
Bank	5,44,000
	27,04,000

Realisation Account

Particulars		(*A*)	*Particulars*	(*A*)
To Equipment A/c		7,20,000	By Overdraft A/c	3,20,000
To Vans A/c		3,20,000	By Creditors A/c	2,00,000
To Trade Marks A/c		80,000	By R.S. Enterprises Ltd.	
To Stock A/c		6,80,000	(Purchase consideration)	27,04,000
To Bills Receivable A/c		4,80,000		
To Debtors A/c		1,20,000		
To Profit Transferred to :				
Rajesh's Cap. A/c	5,15,000			
Sushil's Cap. A/c	3,09,000	8,24,000		
		32,24,000		32,24,000

Rajesh's Capital Account

Particulars	(*A*)	*Particulars*	(*A*)
To Equity Share of R.S. Enterprise Ltd.	12,50,000	By Balance b/d	8,80,000
To Bank A/c	2,95,000	By General Reserve	1,50,000
		By Realisation A/c (Profit)	5,15,000
	15,45,000		15,45,000

Sushil's Capital Account

Particulars	(*A*)	*Particulars*	(*A*)
To Equity Share of		By Balance b/d	6,00,000
R.S. Enterprise Ltd.	7,50,000	By General Reserve	90,000
To Bank A/c	2,49,000	By Realisation A/c (Profit)	3,09,000
	9,99,000		9,99,000

Loan from Rajesh's Account

Particulars	(A)	*Particulars*	(A)
To 12% Debentures in R.S. Enterprises Ltd.	1,60,000	By Balance b/d	1,60,000

R.S. Enterprises Ltd.

Particulars	(A)	*Particulars*	(A)
To Realisation A/c	27,04,000	By Equity Shares in R.S. Enterprises Ltd.	20,00,000
		By 12% Debentures in R.S. Enterprises Ltd.	1,60,000
		By Bank A/c	5,44,000
	27,04,000		27,04,000

Bank Account

Particulars	(A)	*Particulars*	(A)
To R.S. Enterprises Ltd.	5,44,000	By Rajesh's Capital A/c	2,49,000
		By Sushil's Capital A/c	2,95,000
	5,44,000		5,44,000

Example 30

S and *T* were carrying on business as equal partner. Their Balance Sheet as on 31 March, 2008 stood as follows :

Liabilities		(A)	*Assets*	(A)
Capital accounts :			Stock	2,70,000
S	6,40,000		Debtors	3,65,000
T	6,60,000	13,00,000	Furniture	75,000
Creditors		3,27,500	Joint life policy	47,500
Bank overdraft		1,50,000	Plant	1,72,500
Bills payable		62,500	Building	9,10,000
		18,40,000		18,40,000

The operations of the business were carried on till 30 September, 2008. *S* and *T* both withdrew in equal amounts half the amount of profits made during the current period of 6 months after 10% per annum had been written off on building and plant and 5% per annum written off on furniture. During the current period of 6 months, creditors were reduced by A 50,000, Bills payable by A 11,500 and Bank overdraft by A 75,000. The Joint Life policy was surrendered for A 47,500 on 30 September, 2008. Stock was valued at A 3,17,000 and debtors at A 3,25,000 on 30 September, 2008. The other items remained the same as on 31 march, 2008.

On 30 September, 2008 the firm sold its business to ST Ltd. The value of goodwill was estimated at A 5,40,000 and the remaining assets were valued on the basis of the Balance Sheet as on 30 September, 2008. The ST Ltd. paid the purchase consideration in equity shares of A 10 each. You are required to prepare to Realisation Account and Capital Accounts of the partners. [*C.A., November, 2008*]

Solution

Realisation Account

Particulars		(A)	Particulars	(A)
To Sundry Assets :			By Creditors	2,77,500
Stock		3,17,000	By Bills Payable	51,000
Debtors		3,25,000	By Bank Overdraft	75,000
Plant		1,63,875	By Shares in ST Ltd. (W.N. 3)	18,80,000
Building		8,64,500		
Furniture		73,125		
To Profit :				
S	2,70,000			
T	2,70,000	5,40,000		
		22,83,500		22,83,500

Partners' Capital Accounts

Date	Particulars	S	T	Date	Particulars	S	T
2008			2008				
April 1	To Cash–Drawings (W.N. 2)	20,000	20,000	April 1	By Balance b/d	6,40,000	6,60,000
Sep. 30	To Shares in St Ltd.	9,30,000	9,50,00	Sep. 30	Profit (W.N. 2)	40,000	40,000
					By Realisation A/c (Profit)	2,70,000	2,70,000
		9,50,000	9,70,000			9,50,000	9,70,000

Working Notes **:**

1. *Ascertainment of total capital :*

Balance Sheet as at 30 September, 2008

Liabilities	(A)	*Assets*		(A)
Sundry creditors	2,77,500	Building	9,10,000	
Bills payable	51,000	*Less :* Depreciation	45,500	8,64,500
Bank overdraft	75,000	Plant	1,72,500	
Total capital (*bal. fig.*)	13,40,000	*Less :* Depreciation	8,625	1,63,875
		Furniture	75,000	
		Less : Depreciation	1,875	73,125
		Stock		3,17,000
		Debtors		3,25,000
	17,43,500		17,43,500	

2. *Profit earned during six months to 30 September, 2008*

	(A)	(A)
Total capital (of *S* and *T*) on 30 September, 2008 (W.N. 1)		13,40,000
Capital on 1 April, 2008		

S	6,40,000	
T	6,60,000	13,00,000
Net increase (after drawings)		40,000

Since drawings are half of profits therefore, actual profit earned is A 40,000 × 2 = A 80,000 (shared equally by partners *S* and *T*).

Half of the profits, has been withdrawn by both the partners equally i.e. drawings A 40,000 (A 80,000 × ½) withdrawn by *S* and *T* in 1 : 1 (*i.e.* A 20,000 each).

3. *Purchase consideration*

	(A)
Total assets (W.N. 1)	17,43,500
Add : Goodwill	5,40,000
	22,83,500
Less : Liabilities (2,77,500 + 51,000 + 75,000)	4,03,500
Purchase consideration	18,80,000

Note : The above solution is given on the basis that reduction in bank overdraft is after surrender of Joint life policy.

Example 31

XYZ and *Co.* is a partners firm consisting of Mr. *X*, Mr. *Y* and Mr. *Z* who share profits and losses in the ratio of 2 : 2 : 1 and *ABC Ltd.* is a company doing similar business.

Following is the Balance Sheet of the firm and that of the company as at 31.3.2009 :

Liabilities	*XYZ & Co.* (A)	*ABC Ltd.* (A)	*Assets*	*XYZ* (A)	*ABC Ltd.* (A)
Equity share capital :			Plant and machinery	5,00,000	16,00,000
Equity shares of A 10 each		20,00,000	Furniture and fixture	50,000	2,25,000
Partners capital :			Stock in trade	2,00,000	8,50,000
X	2,00,000		Sundry debtors	2,00,000	8,25,000
Y	3,00,000		Cash at bank	10,000	4,00,000
Z	1,00,000		Cash in hand	40,000	1,00,000
General reserve	1,00,000	7,00,000			
Sundry creditors	3,00,000	13,00,000			
	10,00,000	40,00,000		10,00,000	40,00,000

It was decided that the firm *XYZ & Co.* be dissolved and all the assets (except cash in hand and cash at bank) and all the liabilities of the firm be taken over by *ABC* Ltd. by issuing 50,000 shares of A 10 each at a premium of A 2 per share.

Partners of *XYZ & Co.* agreed to divide the shares issued by *ABC* Ltd. in the profit sharing ratio and bring necessary cash for settlement of their capital.

The creditors of *XYZ & Co.* includes A 1,00,000 payable to *ABC Ltd.* An unrecorded liability of A 25,000 of *XYZ & Co.* must also be taken over by *ABC Ltd.*

Prepare :

(*i*) Realisation account, Partners' capital accounts and cash in hand/bank account in the books of *XYZ & Co.*

(*ii*) Pass journal entries in the books of *ABC* Ltd. for acquisition of *XYZ & Co.* and draw the balance sheet after the takeover. [*C.A., November, 2009*]

Solution

In the Books of XYZ & Co.
Realisation Account

	(*A*)		(*A*)
To Plant and Machinery	5,00,000	By Sundry Creditors	3,00,000
To Furniture and Fixture	50,00	By ABC Ltd. (Refer W.N.)	6,00,000
To Stock in Trade	2,00,000	By Partners' Capital Accounts (loss) :	
To Sundry Debtors	2,00,000	X's Capital A/c	20,000
		Y's Capital A/c	20,000
		Z's Capital A/c	10,000
	9,50,000		9,50,000

Partners' Capital Accounts

Particulars	*X* (*A*)	*Y* (*A*)	*Z* (*A*)	*Particulars*	*X* (*A*)	*Y* (*A*)	*Z* (*A*)
To Realisation A/c	20,000	20,000	10,000	By Balance b/d	2,00,000	3,00,000	1,00,000
To Shares in ABC Ltd.	2,40,000	2,40,000	1,20,000	By General Reserve	40,000	40,000	20,000
To Cash A/c	–	80,000	–	By Cash A/c	20,000	–	10,000
	2,60,000	3,40,000	1,30,000		2,60,000	3,40,000	1,30,000

Cash and Bank Account

Particulars	*Cash* (*A*)	*Bank* (*A*)	*Particulars*	*Cash* (*A*)	*Bank* (*A*)
To Balance b/d	40,000	10,000	By Cash A/c (Contra)*		10,000
To Bank A/c (Contra)*	10,000		By Y	80,000	
To X	20,000				
To Z	10,000				
	80,000	10,000		80,000	10,000

*It is assumed that cash at bank has been withdrawn to pay A 80,000 to partner Y. However, payment to Y of A 80,000 can also be made by cash A 70,000 & by cheque A 10,000.

In the Books of ABC Ltd.
Journal Entries

S. No.	*Particulars*		*Dr. Amount* (*A*)	*Cr. Amount* (*A*)
1.	Business Purchases Account	Dr.	6,00,000	
	To XYZ & Co.			6,00,000

	(Being business of XYZ & Co. purchased and payment due)			
2.	Plant and Machinery Account	Dr.	5,00,000	
	Furniture and Fixture Account	Dr.	50,000	
	Stock in Trade Account	Dr.	2,00,000	
	Sundry Debtors Account	Dr.	2,00,000	
	To Sundry Creditors Account			3,00,000
	To Unrecorded Liability Account			25,000
	To Business Purchases Account			6,00,000
	To Capital Reserve Account (*Bal. Fig.*)			25,000
	(Being taken over of all assets and liabilities)			
3.	XYZ & Co.	Dr.	6,00,000	
	To Equity Share Capital Account			5,00,000
	To Securities Premium Account			1,00,000
	(Being purchases consideration discharged in the form of shares of A 10 each issued at a premium of A 2 each)			
4.	Sundry Creditors Account	Dr.	1,00,000	
	To Sundry Debtors Account			1,00,000
	(Being mutual owings eliminated)			

Balance Sheet of ABC Ltd. (After take over of XYZ & Co.)
as at 31.3.2009

Liabilities	*(A)*	*Assets*	*(A)*
Share Capital : 2,50,000, Equity shares of A 10 each fully paid up (out of which 50,000 shares has been issued for consideration other than cash)	25,00,000	Plant and Machinery (5,00,000 + 16,00,000)	21,00,000
		Furniture and fixture (50,000 + 2,25,000)	2,75,000
Securities Premium	1,00,000	Stock in trade (2,00,000 + 8,50,000)	10,50,000
Capital Reserve	25,000	Sundry Debtors (2,00,000 + 8,25,000 – 1,00,000)	9,25,000
General Reserve	7,00,000	Cash at Bank	4,00,000
Sundry Creditors (3,00,000 + 13,00,000 – 1,00,000)	15,00,000	Cash in hand	1,00,000
Unrecorded Liability	25,000		
	48,50,000		48,50,000

Working Notes :

Computation of purchases consideration :

50,000, Equity shares of A 12, (10 + 2) each = A 6,00,000

Equity shares distributed among partners :

Partner X	=	20,000 shares @ A 12	= A 2,40,000
Partner Y	=	20,000 shares @ A 12	= A 2,40,000
Partner Z	=	10,000 shares @ A 12	= A 1,20,000
			A 6,00,000

Example 32

A, *B* and *C* share profit of a partnership business as 3 : 2 : 1 respectively. Their balance sheet as at December 31, 2008 was as follows :

Liabilities	*(A)*	*Assets*		*(A)*
Capital Accounts :		Goodwill		10,000
A	70,000	Land		20,000
B	80,000	Building		1,10,000
C	10,000	Machinery		50,000
General Reserve	18,000	Motor		28,000
Investment Fluctuation Fund	4,000	Furniture		12,000
C's Loan	33,000	Investment		18,000
Mrs. A's Loan	15,000	Loose Tools		7,000
Creditors	76,000	Bills Receivable		20,000
Outstanding Expenses	20,000	Debtors	40,000	
Bills Payable	14,000	*Less :* provision	2,000	38,000
Bank Overdraft	60,000	Cash		1,000
		C's Current Account		56,000
		Profit and Loss Account		12,000
	4,00,000			4,00,000

The partners decided to convert their firm into a joint stock company. For this purpose M.N. Ltd. was incorporated with an authorized capital of A 10,00,000 divided into equity shares of A 100 each and the business of the firm was sold to the company as at the date of the balance sheet given above on the following terms :

- Motor, furniture, investments, loose tools, debtors and cash are not to be taken over by the company.
- Liabilities for bills payable and bank overdraft are to be taken over by the company.
- The purchase consideration is settled at A 1,95,500 payable as to A 75,500 in cash and the balance in company's fully paid shares of A 100 each.

The remaining assets and liabilities of the firm are directly disposed of by the firm as per the details given below :

Investments are taken over by *A* for A 13,000, Debtors realise in all A 20,000, motor, furniture and loose tools were sold for A 24,000, A 4,000 and A 1,000 respectively. A agrees to pay his wife's loan and creditors were paid A 74,000 in final settlement of their claim. Outstanding liability for expenses is met fully. The realisation expenses amounted to A 500.

The equity shares received from the purchasing company are divided amongst the partners in their profit sharing ratio.

You are required to pass journal entries in the books of the partnership firm. *[CA–Inter]*

Solution

Date	*Particulars*		*L.F.*	*Dr. Amount (A)*	*Cr. Amount (A)*
	Realisation A/c	Dr.		3,33,000	
	To Goodwill A/c				10,000

Particulars		L.F.	Dr.	Cr.
To Land A/c				20,000
To Building A/c				1,10,000
To Machinery A/c				50,000
To Motor A/c				28,000
To Furniture A/c				12,000
To Investment A/c				18,000
To Loose Tools A/c				7,000
To Stock A/c				18,000
To Bills Receivable A/c				20,000
To Debtors A/c				40,000
(for transfer of assets except cash)				
Provision on Debtors A/c	Dr.		2,000	
Investment Fluctuation Fund A/c	Dr.		4,000	
Creditors A/c	Dr.		76,000	
Outstanding Expenses A/c	Dr.		20,000	
Bills Payable A/c	Dr.		14,000	
Bank Dues draft A/c	Dr.		60,000	
To Realisation A/c				1,76,000
(for transfer of liabilities and provision on assets)				
Cash A/c	Dr.		49,000	
A's Capital A/c	Dr.		13,000	
To Ralisation A/c				62,000
(for assets realised in cash and investments taken over by A)				
Realisation A/c	Dr.		94,000	
To Cash A/c				94,000
(For payment of creditors and outstanding expenses)				
Realisation A/c	Dr.		500	
To Cash A/c				500
(For payment of realisation expenses)				
M.N. Ltd.	Dr.		1,95,500	
To Realisation A/c				1,95,500
(For purchase consideration due)				
Realisation A/c	Dr.		6,000	
To A's Capital A/c				3,000
To B's Capital A/c				2,000
To C's Capital A/c				1,000
(For transfer of realisation profit)				
General Reserve A/c	Dr.		18,000	
To Profit and Loss A/c				12,000

Particulars		L.F.	Dr.	Cr.
To A's Capital A/c				3,000
To B's Capital A/c				2,000
To C's Capital A/c				1,000
(For transfer of general reserve and accumulated loss)				
Mrs. A's Loan A/c	Dr.		15,000	
C's Loan A/c	Dr.		33,000	
To A's Capital A/c				15,000
To C's Capital A/c				33,000
(For transfer of loan to capital accounts)				
C's Capital A/c	Dr.		56,000	
To C's Current A/c				56,000
(For transfer of current account to capital account)				
Cash A/c	Dr.		75,500	
Equity shares in M.N. Ltd.	Dr.		1,20,000	
To M.N. Ltd. A/c				1,95,500
(For purchase consideration received)				
A's Capital A/c	Dr.		60,000	
B's Capital A/c	Dr.		40,000	
C's Capital A/c	Dr.		20,000	
To Equity shares in M.N. Ltd.				1,20,000
(For distribution of shares)				
Cash A/c	Dr.		31,000	
To C's Capital A/c				31,000
(For Cash brought by C)				
A's Capital A/c	Dr.		18,000	
B's Capital A/c	Dr.		44,000	
To Cash A/c				62,000
(For payment made to A & B)				

Example 33

X and *Y* carrying on business in partnership sharing Profit and Losses equally, wished to dissolve the firm and sell the business to *X* Limited Company on 31.3.2008, when the firm's position was as follows :

Liabilities	(*A*)	*Assets*	(*A*)
X's Capital	1,50,000	Land and Building	1,00,000
Y's Capital	1,00,000	Furniture	40,000
Sundry Creditors	60,000	Stock	1,00,000
		Debtors	66,000
		Cash	4,000
	3,10,000		3,10,000

The arrangement with *X* Limited Company was as follows :

(*i*) Land and Building was purchased at 20% more than the book value.

(*ii*) Furniture and stock were purchased at book values less 15%.

(*iii*) The goodwill of the firm was valued at A 40,000.

(*iv*) The firm's debtors, cash and creditors were not to be taken over, but the company agreed to collect the book debts of the firm and discharge the creditors of the firm as an agent, for which services, the company was to be paid 5% on all collections from the firm's debtors and 3% on cash paid to firm's creditors.

(*v*) The purchase price was to be discharged by the company in fully paid equity shares of A 10 each at a premium of A 2 per share.

The company collected all the amounts from debtors. The creditors were paid off less by A 1,000 allowed by them as discount. The company paid the balance due to vendors in cash.

Prepare the Realisation account, the capital accounts of the partners and the cash account In the books of partnership firm. [*CA PE II Nov. 2006*]

Solution

Realisation Account

Particulars		*(A)*	*Particulars*		*(A)*
Land & Building		1,00,000	Sundry Creditors		60,000
Furniture		40,000	X Ltd. Co. Purchase consideration (1)		2,79,000
Stock		1,00,000	X Ltd. Company		
			Sundry Debtors	66,000	
Debtors		66,000	*Less :* Commission		
			5% on 66,000	3,300	62,700
X Ltd. Co.–Sundry Creditors		59,000			
X Ltd. Co. Commission 3% on 59,000		1,770			
Profits transferred to					
A's Capital A/c	17,465				
B's Capital A/c	17,465	34,930			
		4,01,700			4,01,700

Capital Accounts

Particulars	*A (A)*	*B (A)*	*Particulars*	*A (A)*	*B (A)*
Shares in X Ltd. Co. (2)	1,63,980	1,15,020	Balance b/d	1,50,000	1,00,000
Cash - Final Payment	3,485	2,445	Realisation A/c – Profit	17,465	17,465
	1,67,465	1,17,465		1,67,465	1,17,465

Cash Account

Balance b/d	4,000	A's Capital A/c - Final payment	3,485
X Ltd. Co. (Amount realized from Debtors less amount paid to creditors) - (3)	1,930	B's Capital A/c - Final payment	2,445
	5,930		5,930

Working Notes :

1. *Calculation of Purchase consideration :*

	A
Land and Building	1,20,000
Furniture	34,000
Stock	85,000
Goodwill	40,000
	2,79,000

2. The shares received from the company have been distributed between the two partners *A* and *B* in the ratio of their final claims *i.e.,* 1,67,465 : 1,17,468.

   No of shares received from the company $\frac{2,79,000}{12}$ 23, 250

   A gets $\frac{23,250 \quad 1,67,465}{2,84,930}$ 13, 665 shares valued at 13,665 × 12 = A 1,63,980. B gets the remaining 9,585 shares, valued at A 1,15,020 (9,585 × 12)

3. Calculation of net amount received from X Ltd. on account of amount realized from debtors, fees amount paid to creditors.

	(A)
Amount realized from Debtors	66,000
Less : Commission for realization from debtors (5% on 66,000)	3,300
	62,700
Less : Amount paid to creditors	59,000
	3,700
Less : Commission for cash paid to creditors (3% on 59,000)	1,770
Net amount received	1,930

4. In the above situation, shares received from *X* Ltd. company have been distributed between two partners *A* and *B* in the ratio of their final claims. Alternatively, shares received from *X* Ltd. can be distributed among the partners in their profit sharing ratio *i.e.* A 2,79,000 × ½ = A 1,39,500 each. In that case, firm will pay cash amounting A 27,965 to *A* and will receive cash A 22,035 from *B*.

Example 34

Ram, Rahim and Robert are partners of the firm 'RR Traders' for the past 5 years. The partners decided to dissolve the firm consequent to insolvency of partner Robert in October, 2008. The Balance Sheet of the firm as on 31.10.2008 is furnished below. They share profits and losses equally :

Liabilities	(A)	*Assets*	(A)
Capital Accounts :		Land and Building	5,00,000
Ram	4,50,000	Plant and Machinery	2,00,000
Rahim	4,50,000	Furniture and Fittings	50,000

Robert	2,00,000	Stock in Trade	3,00,000
General Reserve	2,10,000	Debtors	5,00,000
Creditors	2,90,000	Cash at Hand/Bank	50,000
	16,00,000		16,00,000

The partners Ram and Rahim decided to form a new firm 'RR Enterprises' and takeover all the assets and liabilities of the firm at values given below :

	A
Land and Building	3,50,000
Plant and machinery	1,50,000
Furniture and Fittings	20,000
Stock in trade	2,00,000

Debtors include A 3,00,000 due from SK and Co. owned by Robert. (Nothing is recoverable from the said concern).

Other debtors can be recovered fully.

Prepare :

(*i*) Realisation account, Partners' capital accounts in the books of RR Traders; and

(*ii*) The Balance Sheet of RR Enterprises (immediately after commencement). [*CA PE II, May 2003*]

Solution

In the Books of RR Traders
Realisation Account

Particulars	*(A)*	*Particulars*		*(A)*
Sundry Assets :		Creditors		2,90,000
Land and building	5,00,000	RR Enterprises (1)		9,70,000
Plant and machinery	2,00,000	Loss transferred to partner's		
Furniture and fittings	50,000	capital accounts		
Stock	3,00,000	Ram	1,10,000	
Debtors	2,00,000	Rahim	1,10,000	
Cash at hand/bank	50,000	Robert	1,10,000	
RR Enterprises (liability taken over)	2,90,000			3,30,000
	15,90,000			15,90,000

Partners' Capital Accounts

Particulars	Ram	Rahim	Robert	*Particulars*	Ram	Rahim	Robert
Sundry Debtors			3,00,000	Balance b/d	4,50,000	4,50,000	2,00,000
Realisation Account	1,10,000	1,10,000	1,10,000	General Reserve	70,000	70,000	70,000
Robert's (deficiency borne by solvent partners)	70,000	70,000	–	Cash	1,10,000*	1,10,000*	–
				Ram and Rahim (deficiency borne by solvent partners)			

Balance c/d	4,50,000	4,50,000	–		–	–	1,40,000
	6,30,000	6,30,000	4,10,000		6,30,000	6,30,000	4,10,000

Solvent partners bring cash to the extent of loss arising upon realization of assets of the firm as per Garner *v.* Murray Rule.

Balance Sheet of RR Enterprises as on 31.10.2008
(immediately after commencement)

Liabilities	*(A)*	*Assets*	*(A)*
Capital Accounts		Land and building	3,50,000
Ram	4,50,000	Plant and machinery	1,50,000
Rahim	4,50,000	Furniture and fittings	20,000
Creditors	2,90,000	Stock in trade	2,00,000
		Debtors	2,00,000
		Cash at hand/bank (2)	2,70,000
	11,90,000		11,90,000

***Working Notes* :**

1. *Agreed value of assets taken over by RR Enterprises*

	A
Land and building	3,50,000
Plant and machinery	1,50,000
Furniture and fittings	20,000
Stock in trade	2,00,000
Debtors (5,00,000 – 3,00,000)	2,00,000
Cash at hand/bank	50,000
	9,70,000

2. Cash in hand/bank balance of RR Enterprises as on 31.10.2008

	A
Opening Balance	50,000
Add : Ram's and Rahim's contribution (A 1,10,000 + A 1,10,000)	2,20,000
	2,70,000

Example 35

A, B and *C* carried on business in partnership, sharing Profit and Losses in the ratio of 1 : 2 : 3. They decided to form a private limited company, *AB* (P) Ltd. and *C* is not interested to take over the shares in *AB* (P) Ltd. The authorized share capital of the company is A 12,00,000 divided into 12,000 ordinary shares of A 100 each.

The company was incorporated and took over goodwill as valued and certain assets of the partnership firm on 31.3.2008. The Balance Sheet of the partnership firm on that date was as follows :

Liabilities	*(A)*	*Assets*	*(A)*
Capital Accounts :		Fixed Assets :	
A	1,00,000	Machinery	1,20,000
B	2,00,000	Land	1,74,000
C	3,00,000	Motorcycles	30,000

Current Accounts :			Furniture and Fittings	11,000
A		39,420	Current Assets :	
B		60,580	Stock	2,35,000
A's Loan A/c	28,000		Debtors	43,000
(+) Interest accrued	2,000	30,000	Cash in hand	87,000
Current Liability :			C's overdrawn	1,00,000
Creditors		70,000		
		8,00,000		8,00,000

C, who retired was presented by the other partners (*A* and *B*) with one motorcycle valued in the books of the firm A 9,000. The remaining motorcycles were sold in the open market for A 13,000. *C* also received certain furniture for which he was charged A 2,000. The debtors which were all considered good, were taken over by *C* for A 40,000. *A* and *B* were charged in their profit sharing ratio for the book value of Motorcycle presented by them to *C*.

It was agreed that *C* who is not willing to take the shares in *AB* (P) Ltd. was discharged first by providing necessary cash. *A* and *B* should bring cash, if necessary.

AB(P) Ltd. took over the remaining furniture and fittings at a price of A 13,000, the machinery for A 1,25,000, the stock at an agreed value of A 2,00,000 and the land at its book value. The value of the goodwill of the partnership firm was agreed at A 88,000. The creditors of the firm were settled by the firm for A 70,000. A's loan account together with interest accrued was transferred to his capital account.

The purchase consideration was discharged by the company by the issue of equal number of fully paid up equity shares at par to *A* and *B*.

Prepare Realisation A/c, Capital A/cs of the partners and Cash A/c. Also draw the Balance Sheet of AB(P) Ltd. [*CAPE II, May, 2007*]

Solution

Realization Account

Particulars	*(A)*	*Particulars*	*(A)*
Machinery	1,20,000	Creditors	70,000
Land	1,74,000	AB (P) Ltd. Purchase consideration (Working Note)	6,00,000
Motor Cycles	30,000	A's Capital A/c	3,000
Furniture and Fittings	11,000	B's Capital A/c	6,000
Stock	2,35,000	C's Capital A/c (2,000 + 40,000)	42,000
Debtors	43,000	Cash A/c (Sale of Motor Cycle)	13,000
Cash (payment to creditors)	70,000		
Profit transferred to			
A's Capital A/c	8,500		
B's Capital A/c	17,000		
C's Capital A/c	25,500		
	7,34,000		7,34,000

Partners' Capital Accounts

Particulars	A	B	C	*Particulars*	A	B	C
Current A/c	–	–	1,00,000	Balance b/d	1,00,000	2,00,000	3,00,000
Realisation A/c (Assets taken over)	3,000	6,000	42,000	Current A/c	39,420	60,580	–
Equity shares in AB (P) Ltd.	3,00,000	3,00,000	–	A's Loan A/c	30,000	–	–
Cash A/c	–	–	1,83,500	Realization A/c (Profit)	8,500	17,000	25,500
				Cash A/c	1,25,080	28,420	
	3,03,000	3,06,000	3,25,500		3,03,000	3,06,000	3,25,500

Cash Account

Particulars	(A)	*Particulars*	(A)
Balance b/d	87,000	Realisation A/c	70,000
Realisation A/c	13,000	C's Capital A/c	1,83,500
A's Capital A/c	1,25,080		
B's Capital A/c	28,420		
	2,53,500		2,53,500

Balance Sheet of AB (P) Ltd.

Liabilities	(A)	*Assets*	(A)
Authorized Share Capital :		*Fixed Assets :*	
12,000 Equity Shares of A 100 each	12,00,000	Goodwill	88,000
Issued, Subscribed and Paid up :		Land	1,74,000
6,000 equity shares of A 100 each fully paid up (shares were issued for consideration otherwise than for cash)	6,00,000	Machinery	1,25,000
		Furniture and Fittings	13,000
		Current Assets :	
		Stock	2,00,000
	6,00,000		6,00,000

Working Notes :

Calculation of Purchase Consideration

Assets taken over by AB (P) Ltd.	
Machinery	1,25,000
Furniture and Fittings	13,000
Land	1,74,000
Stock	2,00,000
Goodwill	88,000
Purchase Consideration	6,00,000

Purchase consideration is discharged by the issue of equal number of equity shares of A 100 each (3,000 shares) at par to A and B.

PIECEMEAL DISTRIBUTION

So far, the earlier discussion on dissolution of partnership has assumed that all assets are realised and settlement is done on the same date. However, in reality, assets are not realised on a single day but gradually involving many days. This is known as gradual realisation and piecemeal distribution. There are two choices before a firm with regard to gradual realisation of assets.

1. Distributing cash only after final realisation : In this case, amounts finally due to all parties including partners are easily determined and settlement is done accordingly.
2. Distributing cash as and when it is realised known as Piecemeal Distribution of Cash. In this case, cash is utilized for settlement as and when it is available for distribution. Cash realised is distributed in the following sequence.
    1. First, realisation expenses should be paid.
    2. Second, payments to outside or external liabilities should be made other than partners' loans or capitals. When cash is gradually collected, the external liabilities are paid *prorata.*
    3. Third, once all liabilities due to outsiders are paid in full, the amount due to a partner as loan has to be paid. Where loans are due to more than one partner, the payment, if not sufficient, has to be made *pro rata* i.e., rateably.
    4. Fourth, when firm's creditors and loans of the partners have been paid in full, any balance of cash remaining will be applied in paying the partners the amounts owing to them, i.e., the sum total of their capitals and current accounts, as far as possible.

At the fourth stage, difficulties may be faced. The capital contributions of partners may not be equal or in profit-sharing ratio and the problem is how to ensure that none of the partners is paid more than what is properly due to him. Whatever procedure or method of distributing cash, realised on piecemeal basis, is followed, it should ensure that at the end (when all realisations have been made), the loss on realisation or final deficiency or deficit balances should be in the profit sharing ratio.

Settlement of Capital Accounts of Partners

The capital accounts of the partners after adjustment for drawings, accumulated losses, reserves, accumulated profits, current account balances are settled by following any one of the two methods.

1. Proportionate Capital Method.
2. Maximum Loss Method.

1. PROPORTIONATE CAPITAL METHOD

As stated earlier, the gradual realisation of cash should be distributed among the partners in such a way as to ensure that unpaid balance of capital of each partner are in the profit sharing ratio. No difficulty would arise when the capitals of the partners are in the profit sharing ratio because if the payments are made in the profit sharing ratio, the amount finally unpaid would also be in the profit sharing ratio. But where the capitals are not in the profit sharing ratio, the distribution of cash either in the profit sharing ratio or capital ratio would leave the unpaid balances different from the profit sharing ratio.

Example 36

From the following information show surplus capital of partners :

Particulars	*A*	*B*	*C*
Actual Capital	20,000	15,000	5,000
Profit sharing ratio	2	2	1
Actual Capital	20,000	15,000	5,000

Profit Ratio	2	2	1
Capital per unit	10,000	7,500	5,000
Proportionate Capital (takin minimum capital per unit of A 5,000 as base)	10,000	10,000	5000
Surplus Capital (Actual - Proportionate)	10,000	5,000	–

It means first A 15,000 is not shared by C. Out of A 15,000, *A* and *B* get A 10,000 and A 5,000 respectively. If cash available is less than A 15,000 then surplus of *A* in comparison of *B* is determined as under :

Particulars	*B*	*C*
Actual Capital	20,000	15,000
Profit Ratio	2	2
Capital per unit	10,000	7,500
Proportionate Capital (taking minimum capital per unit A 7,500 as base)	15,000	15,000
Surplus Capital	5,000	–

It means *B* will not share in first A 5,000.

Thus, distribution on the basis of proportionate capital should be as follows :

(*i*) Initial A 5,000 to A only.

(*ii*) Next A 10,000 (A 15,000 – A 5,000) to *A* and *B* in ratio 2 : 2.

(*iii*) Balance of cash to *A, B* and *C* in the ratio 2 : 2 : 1.

2. MAXIMUM LOSS METHOD

Under maximum loss method the outside liabilities are paid first and after that loans from partners are paid. The surplus amount is distributed to meet claims on account of partners' capitals. Under this method total unpaid capital of the partners is determined and cash available for distribution is subtracted from it. The balance left is treated as maximum loss which is shared by partners in their profit sharing ratio. If it results in a debit balance in partner's capital account, it is transferred to remaining partners in accordance with Garner *vs.* Murray Rule. This process is repeated till all capital accounts show positive balances. Now, each partner is given cash equal to the balance shown by his account. At the time of each realisation, this process is repeated to determine distribution of cash at every stage. At the time of final realisation, the partner with debit balance brings cash provided he is solvent and total cash available (including contribution by partners with debit balances) is distributed to settle the accounts of partners with credit balances.

Assets taken over by a Partner

Sometimes, an asset or liability is taken over by a partner. In that case, proportionate capital should be adjusted for asset or liability taken over by the partner. Under maximum loss method, the value of asset taken over is subtracted from amount due and then, the usual procedure is followed. In proportionate capital method, it is simple to adjust the value of asset taken away by partner(s) provided the partner taking over the asset has his share in that realisation more than the value of asset taken over.

Example 37

A, B and *C* are partners sharing profits and losses in the ratio of 5 : 3 : 2. Their capitals were A 9,600, A 6,000 and A 8,400 respectively.

After paying creditors, the liabilities and assets of the firm were :

Liabilities	*(A)*	*Assets*	*(A)*
Liability for interest on loans from :		Investments	1,000
Spouses of partners	2,000	Furniture	2,000
Partners	1,000	Machinery	1,200
		Stock	4,000

The assets realised in full in the order in which they are listed above. *B* is insolvent.

You are required to prepare a statement showing the distribution of cash as and when available, applying maximum possible loss procedure. [*B.Com.,* (*Hons.*), *Delhi University, 2007*]

Solution

Statement of Distribution of Cash

	Realisation (A)	*Interest on loans from partners' spouses (A)*	*Interest on loans from partners (A)*	*Interest on Partners'* A *(A)*	B *(A)*	C *(A)*	*Total (A)*
Balances due (1)		2,000	1,000	9,600	6,000	8,400	24,000
(i) Sale of investments	1,000	(1,000)	–				
		1,000	1,000				
(ii) Sale of furniture	2,000	(1,000)	(1,000)				
		–	–				
(iii) Sale of machinery	1,200						
Maximum possible loss	22,800						
(total of capitals A 24,000 less cash available A 1,200) allocated to partners in the profit sharing ratio i.e. 5 : 3 : 2				(11,400)	(6,840)	(4,560)	(22,800)
Amounts at credit				(1,800)	(840)	3,840	1,200
Deficiency of *A* and *B* written off against *C*				1,800	840	(2,640)	–
Amount paid (2)				–	–	1,200	1,200
Balances in capital accounts (1–2) = (3)				9,600	6,000	7,200	22,800
(iv) Sale of stock	4,000						
Maximum possible loss	18,800						
(A 22,800 – A 4,000) Allocated to partners in the ratio 5 : 3 : 2				(9,400)	(5,640)	(3,760)	(18,800)
Amounts at credit and cash paid (4)				200	360	3,440	(4,000)
Balances in capital accounts left unpaid – Loss (3 – 4) = 5				9,400	5,640	3,760	18,800

Example 38

Ram, Shyam and Mohan are in partnership sharing profits and losses in the ratio 3 : 2 : 1 respectively. They decided to dissolve the business on 1.1.2008 on which date their balance sheet was as follows :

Liabilities		*(A)*	*Assets*	*(A)*
Capital Accounts			Land and Building	30,810
Ram	38,700		Motor Car	5,160
Shyam	10,680		Investment	1,080
Mohan	11,100	60,480	Stock	19,530
Loan A/c : Mohan		3,000	Debtors	11,280
Creditors		10,320	Cash	5,940
		73,800		73,800

The assets are realised piecemeal as follows and it was agreed that cash should be distributed as and when realised :

15.1.2008	10,380	(Cash)
20.2.2008	27,900	(Cash)
23.3.2008	3,600	(Cash)
15.4.2008	1,260	(Investments taken over by Mohan)
27.4.2008	19,200	(Cash)

Dissolution expenses were originally provided for an estimated amount of A 2,700 but the actual amount spent on 29.3.2008 was A 1,920. The creditors were settled for A 10,080.

You are required to prepare a statement showing distribution of cash amongst the partners by proportionate capital method. [*B.Com.(Hons.), Delhi University, 2002, 2008*]

Solution

Calculation of Surplus Capital on 1.1.2008

Particulars	*Ram*	*Shyam*	*Mohan*
Actual Capital	38,700	10,680	11,100
Profit-sharing ratio	3	2	1
Actual capital per unit of profit	12,900	5,340	11,100
Proportionate capital, taking Shyam's capital as base	16,020	10,680	5,340
Surplus capital of Ram and Mohan	22,680	–	5,760
Proportionate capital of Ram and Mohan taking Mohan's capital as base	33,300	–	11,100
Surplus capital of Ram over Mohan (38,700 – 33,300)	5,400	–	–

First A 5,400 to Ram only

Next (22,680 – 5,400 + 5,760) A 23,040 to Ram and Mohan in the ratio 3 : 1

Statement Showing Distribution of Cash

Date	*Particulars*		*Creditors*	*Loan of Mohan*	*Capital*		
					Ram	*Shyam*	*Mohan*
1.1.2008	Balance b/d		10,320	3,000	38,700	10,680	11,100
	Cash available	5,940					
	Prov. for expenses	2,700					
		3,240					
	Paid to creditors	3,240	3,240				
			7,080				
15.1.2008	Cash available	10,380					
	Payment to creditors	6,840	6,840				
	(10,080 – 3,240)	3,540	240				
	Discount received		240				
	Payment of Mohan's loan	3,000		3,000			
	Cash available for partners	540					
	Paid to Ram	540			540		
					38,160	10,680	11,100
20.2.2008	Cash available	27,900					
	Paid to Ram (5,400–540)	4,860			4,860		
	Paid to Ram and Mohan	23,040			17,280		5,760
					16,020	10,680	5,340
23.3.2008	Cash available	3,600					
	Paid to all partners (3 : 2 : 1)	3,600			1,800	1,200	600
					14,220	9,480	4,740
29.3.2008	Cash available being excess provision for expenses	780					
	Paid to partners	780			390	260	130
					13,830	9,220	4,610
15.4.2008	Investments taken over by Mohan at						1,260
					13,830	9,220	3,350
27.4.2008	Cash available	19,200			3,780	2,520	
	Paid to Ram and Shyam*	6,300					
	(1,260 × 3 and 1,260 × 2)	12,900					
	Paid to all partners (3 : 2 : 1)	12,900			6,450	4,300	2,150
					3,600	2,400	1,200

Calculation of Surplus Capital on 27.4.2008

	Ram	*Shyam*	*Mohan*
Actual Capital	13,830	9,220	3,350
Profit Ratio	3	2	1
Actual Capital per unit	4,610	4,610	3,350

Proportionate capital, taking Mohan as base	10,050	6,700	3,350
Surplus Capital	3,780	2,520	

Example 39

A, B and *C* were in partnership sharing profits and losses in the proportions of 1/2, 1/3 and 1/6 respectively. The partnership was dissolved on 30 June, 2008 when the position was as follows :

Liabilities	*(A)*	*Assets*	*(A)*
Capitals :		Cash Hand	28,000
A	1,40,000	Sundry Debtors	2,94,000
B	70,000	Stock-in-Trade	1,12,000
C	14,000		
Creditors	2,10,000		
	4,34,000		4,34,000

There was a bill for A 10,000 due on 30 November, 2002 under discount. It was agreed that net realisation should be distributed in their due order (at the end of each month) but as safely as possible. The realisations and expenses were as under :

	Stock and Debtors	*Expenses*
31.7.2008	84,000	7,000
31.8.2008	1,26,000	5,400
39.9.2008	70,000	4,900
31.10.2008	77,000	3,500
30.11.2008	35,500	3,500

The stock was completely disposed of and the amounts due from debtors were realised, the balance being irrecoverable. The acceptor of the bill under discount met the bill on the due date.

Draw up a detailed statement showing the monthly distribution of cash realised, using proportionate capital method. [*B.Com.* (*Hons.*), Delhi - 2001]

Solution

Detailed Statement Showing the Monthly Distribution of Cash

			Capitals		
		Creditors	*A*	*B*	*C*
Amount Due		2,10,000	1,40,000	70,000	14,000
Cash in Hand	28,000				
Less : Contingent Liability	10,000				
Paid to Creditors		18,000			
Balance Due		1,92,000	1,40,000	70,000	14,000
Net Realization on 31.7.2008	77,000				
Paid to Creditors	77,000	77,000			
Balance Due		1,15,000	1,40,000	70,000	14,000
Net Realization on 31.8.2008	1,20,600				
Paid to creditors	1,15,000	1,15,000			

		A	B	C
Balance paid to A	5,600	5,600		
Balance Due		1,34,400	70,000	14,000
Net Realization on 30.9.2008	65,100			
Paid to A	29,400	29,400		
To A and B in 3 : 2	35,700	21,420	14,280	
Balance Due		83,580	55,720	14,000
Net Realization on 31.10.2008	73,500			
To A and B in 3 : 2	69,300	41,580	27,720	
To A, B and C in 3 : 2 : 1	4,200	2,100	1,400	700
Balance Due		39,900	26,600	13,300
Net Realization on 30.11.2008	32,000			
Bill realized	10,000			
	42,000			
To A, B and C in 3 : 2 : 1	42,000	21,000	14,000	7,000
Balance unpaid being deficiency		18,900	12,600	6,300

Working Notes **:**

Calculation of surplus capital

	A	*B*	*C*
Capital	1,40,000	70,000	14,000
Capital in profit sharing of 3 : 2 : 1 taking C's Capital as the base	42,000	28,000	14,000
Surplus	98,000	42,000	–
Per unit capital of *A* and *B* in their profit ratio 3 : 2	32,667	21,000	–
Proportionate capital taking *B*'s capital as the base	63,000	42,000	–
Surplus Capital	35,000	–	–

Hence first A 35,000 will be given to *A*, next A 1,05,000 to *A* and *B* in the ratio 3 : 2 and after that the money will be shared by *A*, *B* and *C* in the ratio of 3 : 2 : 1.

Example 40

A partnership firm was dissolved on 30 June. Its balance sheet on the date of dissolution was as follows:

Liabilities		*(A)*	*Assets*	*(A)*
Capitals :			Cash	5,400
Ram	38,000		Sundry Assets	94,600
Shyam	24,000			
Mohan	18,000	80,000		
Loan Account – Shyam		5,000		
Sundry Creditors		15,000		
		1,00,000		1,00,000

The assets were realised in installments and payment was made on the proportionate capital basis. Creditors were paid A 14,500 in full settlement of their account. Expenses of realisation were estimated to be A 2,700 but actual amount spent on this account was A 2,000. This amount was paid on 15 September. Draw up a memorandum of distribution of cash, which was released as follows :

On 5 July,	A 12,600
On 30 August,	A 30,000
On 15 September	A 40,000

The partners shared profits and losses in the ratio of 2 : 2 : 1. Give working notes.

[*B.Com. (Hons.), Delhi University, 1990*]

Solution

Ram, Shyam and Mohan
Statement Showing Distribution of Gradual Realisation

		Creditors (A)	*Shyam's Loan (A)*	*Capitals* Ram (A)	Shyam (A)	Mohan (A)
Opening Balance		**15,000**	**5,000**	**38,000**	**24,000**	**18,000**
Cash in hand	5,400					
Less : Provision for Realisation expenses	2,700					
Paid to Creditors	2,700	2,700	–	–	–	–
Opening Balance		**12,300**	**5,000**	**38,000**	**24,000**	**18,000**
5 July						
Realisation	12,600					
Paid to creditors	11,800	11,800				
Paid to Shyam's Loan	800		800	–	–	–
		500				
Less : Discount written off		500				
30 August		×				
Opening Balance			**4,200**	**38,000**	**24,000**	**18,000**
Realisation	30,000					
Paid to Shyam's Loan	4,200		4,200			
	25,800					
Paid to Ram : 16,320				16,320		
(2,000 + 12,000 + 2,320)					2,320	7,160
Paid to Shyam (2,320)						
Paid to Mohan (6,000 + 1,160)			–	21,680	21,680	10,840
15 September						
Opening Balance				**21,680**	**21,680**	**10,840**
Realisation	40,000					
Surplus from Provision for expenses	700					
	47,000					

Paid to Partners in the ratio of 2 : 2 : 1			16,280	16,280	8,140
Unpaid Amounts			5,400	5,400	2,700
Capital claims			38,000	24,000	18,000
Capitals in the profit sharing ratio (taking B's capitals as base, being the minimum capital per unit of profit) 2 : 2 : 1			24,000	24,000	12,000
Surplus Claims			14,000	–	6,000
Surplus capital between A and C in profit Sharing ratio 2 : 1 (taking C's capital as base)			12,000	–	6,000
Ultimate surplus capital to be paid first			2,000	–	–

Ram and Mohan have been paid from the second realisation A 14,000 and A 6,000 respectively in the first instance thus making their capitals, along with Shyam, in proportion to profit sharing ratio of 2 : 2 : 1. The balance of second realisation i.e. A 5,800 (30,000 - 4,200 - 14,000 - 6,000) has been further distributed in the ratio of 2 : 2 : 1 e.g. Ram 2,320, Shyam A 2,320 and Mohan A 1,160. So Ram gets from the second realisation A 16,320 (2,000 + 12,000 + 2,320); Shyam gets only A 2,320 and Mohan A 7,160 (6,000 + 1,160).

The final realisation is A 40,000. But actual expenses on realisation are A 2,000 as against the provision of A 2,700. Thus a surplus of A 700 is also available for partners. So the total amount of third realisation for partners is A 40,700 (40,000 + 700). Ram gets A 16,280; Shyam gets A 16,280 and Mohan gets A 8,140.

Example 41

A, B and *C* were in partnership sharing profit and losses in the ratio of 3 : 2 : 1. They dissolved the firm on 31.12.2008, On which date their balance sheet appeared as follows :

Liabilities		*(A)*	*Assets*	*(A)*
Creditors		40,000	Cash	10,000
Loan from A		10,000	Debtors	80,000
General Reserve		12,000	Stock	27,000
Capital Accounts :	A	20,000		
	B	25,000		
	C	10,000		
		1,17,000		1,17,000

The realisation and expenses were as under :

Date	*Debtors*	*Stock*	*Expenses*
Jan., 2009	12,000	6,000	1,000
Feb., 2009	22,000	1,000	1,500
Mar., 2009	6,000	10,000	1,200
April, 2009	18,000	5,000	900
May, 2009	15,500	3,000	1,500

It was agreed that available cash and net realisation should be distributed at the end of each month.

It was decided in May, 2009 that *C* would take the remaining debtors at A 2,500.

Prepare a statement by proportionate Capital method showing the distribution of cash. Also show realisation account. [*B.Com.* (*Hons.*), *Delhi University 2001*]

Solution

Statement Showing the Distribution of Cash

Date	*Particulars*		*Creditors*	*Loan from A*	*A*	*B*	*C*
1.1.2009			40,000	10,000	26,000	29,000	12,000
31.1.2009	(10,000 + 12,000 + 6,000 – 1,000)	27,000	–27,000				
28.2.2009	(22,000 + 1,000 – 1,500)	21,500	13,000				
	Paid to creditors	13,000	–13,000				
	Paid loan from A	8,500	–	–8,500			
31.3.2009	(6,000 + 10,000 – 1,200)	14,800		1,500			
	Paid loan from A	–1,500		–1,500			
		13,300		–			
	Paid to B	–5,000			–	–5,000	–
	Paid to B and C in 2 : 1	8,300			–	–5,533	–2,767
					26,000	18,467	9,233
30.4.2009	(18,000 + 5,000 – 900)	22,100					
	Paid to B and C in 2 : 1	1,700		–		–1,134	–566
		20,400					
	Paid to A, B and C in 3 : 2 : 1				–10,200	–6,800	–3,400
					15,800	10,533	5,267
31.5.2009	(15,500 + 3,000 – 1,500) =	17,000					
	Add : Debtors takeover	2,500					
		19,500					
	Less : Debtors to C	2,500			–	–	–2,500
		17,000					
	A 12,500 to A and B in 3 : 2 (2,500 × 5/1)				–7,500	–5,000	–
	and A 4,500 to A, B and C in 3 : 2 : 1				–2,250	–1,500	–750
	Unpaid Balance (Realisation Loss)				6,050	4,033	2,017

Calculation of Surplus Capital

	A	*B*	*C*
Actual Capital	26,000	29,000	12,000
Profit/Loss Ratio	3	2	1
Capital per unit of profit	8,667	14,500	12,000
Proportionate Capital (taking A's Capital as base)	26,000	17,333	8,667
Surplus Capital	–	11,667	3,333
Proportionate Surplus (taking C's surplus as base)		6,667	3,333
Surplus of B as compared to C	–	5,000	–

Thus, distribution of cash among partners is as follows :

First A 5,000 to B only.

Next (11,667 – 5,000 + 3,333) to B and C in 2 : 1

Balance to A, B and C in 3 : 2 : 1.

Realisation Account

31.12.2008	Debtors A/c	80,000	31.12.2008	Creditors	40,000
	Stock A/c	27,000	31.1.2009	Cash A/c (assets realised)	18,000
31.1.2009	Cash A/c (expenses)	1,000	28.2.2009	Cash A/c (assets realised)	23,000
	Cash A/c (creditors)	27,000	31.3.2009	Cash A/c (assets realised)	16,000
28.2.2009	Cash A/c (expenses)	1,500	30.4.2009	Cash A/c (assets realised)	23,000
	Cash A/c (creditors)	13,000	31.5.2009	Cash A/c (assets realised)	18,500
31.3.2009	Cash A/c (expenses)	1,200		C's Capital	2,500
30.4.2009	Cash A/c (expenses)	900		(Debtors taken over)	
31.5.2009	Cash A/c (expenses)	1,500		Capital A/cs : (realisation loss)	
				A 6,050	
				B 4,033	
				C 2,017	12,100
		1,53,100			1,53,100

In case the share of the partner in that realisation is less than the value of asset, the asset is given to the partner concerned but it disturbs the earlier calculation of surplus capital. Therefore, surplus capital of partners is determined again in such a case.

Example 42

A, *B* and *C* were partners sharing in the ratio of 4 : 3 : 1. Their Balance Sheet as on 31 March 2011 was as follows :

Liabilities	(A)	*Assets*	(A)
Creditors	26,250	Buildings	60,000
Bank loan (secured)	8,750	Plant	20,000
Loan from *A*	10,000	Stock	55,000
Capital Accounts :		Debtors	60,000
A	70,000		
B	30,000		
C	50,000		
	1,95,000		1,95,000

They decided to dissolve the firm. The assets were realised gradually and the net amount were distributed immediately as given below :

	(A)		(A)
2011 May 20	22,000	Expenses paid	2,000
July 30	16,800	Expenses paid	1,800
September 20	38,000	Expenses paid	3,000
November 15	45,000	Expenses paid	5,000
December 31	72,00	Expenses paid	7,000

Required : Show the piece-meal distributions of cash and the loss to be borne by the partners.
[*B.Com.* (*Hons.*), *Delhi University, 1998*]

Solution

Statement Showing the Distribution of Cash
(According to Maximum Loss Method)

	Particulars	*Bank Loan (Secured)*	*Creditors*	*Loan from A*	*A*	*B*	*C*
A.	Balance due	8,750	26,250	10,000	70,000	30,000	50,000
B.	Net cash pay on May 20	(8,750)	(11,250)	–	–	–	–
C.	Balance due (*A* – *B*)		15,000	10,000	70,000	30,000	50,000
D.	Net cash paid on July 30		(15,000)	–	–	–	–
E.	Balance due			10,000	70,000	30,000	50,000
F.	A 10,000 paid to *A* (loan Repayment) on September 20			(10,000)	–	–	–
G.	Balance outstanding (*E* – *F*)				70,000	30,000	50,000
	Cash available for distribution A 35,000 – A 10,000 = 25,000						
	Less : Maximum Possible loss A (70,000 + 30,000 + 50,000 – 25,000) = A 1,25,000 in the ratio 4 : 3 : 1				(62,500)	(46,875)	(15,625)
	Balance				7,500	(16,875)	34,375
	Deficiency of *B* charged to *A* and *C* in the ratio 7 : 5				(9,844)	16,875	(7,031)
					2,344	–	27,344
	Deficiency of *A* charged to *C*				2,344		2,344
H.	Net Cash paid to *C* on September 20				–	–	25,000
L.	Balance outstanding				70,000	30,000	25,000
	Less : Maximum loss A [(70,000 + 30,000 + 25,000) – 40,000] = A 85,000 in the ratio 4 : 3 : 1				(42,500)	(31,875)	(10,625)
	Balance				27,500	(1,875)	14,375
	Deficiency of *B* charged to *A* and *C* in ratio of 7 : 5				(1,094)	1,875	(781)
J.	Net Cash paid on November 15				26,406	–	13,594
K.	Balance outstanding				43,594	30,000	11,406
L.	*Less :* Maximum loss A (44,000 + 30,000 + 11,000) – 65,000 = A 20,000 in the ratio 4 : 3 : 1				(10,000)	(7,500)	(2,500)
M.	Cash paid on December 31				33,594	22,500	8,906
N.	Unpaid balance (*K* – *M*)				10,000	7,500	2,500

Example 43

A, *B* and *C* are in partnership. The following is their Balance Sheet as on March 31, 2003 on which date they dissolve partnership. They share profit in the ratio of 5 : 3 : 2.

Liabilities	(*A*)	*Assets*	(*A*)
Creditors	40,000	Premises	40,000
A's Loan	10,000	Machinery	30,000
Capitals		Furniture	13,700

A	50,000	Stock	40,800
B	15,000	Debtors	35,500
C	45,000		
	1,60,000		1,60,000

It was agreed to repay the amounts due to the partners as and when the assets were realised. The Assets realised as under :

	(A)
1 May, 2003	30,000
1 July, 2003	73,000
1 September, 2003	47,000

Prepare a statement showing how the distribution should be made among the partners and write up Partners Capital Accounts. [*B.Com.* (*Hons.*), *Delhi University 2005*]

Solution

Statement Showing Distribution of Cash

Particulars	*Sundry Creditors* (A)	*A's Loan* (A)	*A's Capital* (A)	*B's Capital* (A)	*C's Capital* (A)
Amount Due	40,000	10,000	50,000	15,000	45,000
1st Ralisation (1.3.03) : A 30,000 A 30,000 paid to creditors	30,000				
	10,000				
2nd Realisation (1.7.03) : A 73,000 A 10,000 paid to sundry creditors	10,000				
A 10,000 paid to A for Loan	–	10,000			
Balance now available A 53,000 (i.e. A 73,000 – 10,000 – 10,000)					
Maximum Loss = A 1,10,000 – A 53,000 = A 57,000 divided in the ratio of 5 : 3 : 2			28,500	17,100	11,400
Amount at Credit			21,500	(–) 2,100	33,600
B's Deficiency transferred to *A* and *C* in the ratio of 50 : 45			1,105	(+) 2,100	995
			20,395	–	32,605
Balance left in Capital Accounts (A)			29,605	15,000	12,395
Third Realisation (1.9.03) : A 47,000 Maximum Loss : A 57,000 – A 47,000 = 10,000 divided in the ratio of 5 : 3 : 1 paid to partner (B)			5,000	3,000	2,000
			24,605	12,000	10,395
Balance in Capital Accounts left unpaid being Loss (*A* – *B*)			5,000	3,000	2,000

Example 44

A, B and *C* were in partnership sharing profits and losses in the ratio of 2 : 1 : 1 respectively. On 31 March, 2005 they decided to dissolve the partnership when their Balance Sheet stood as follows :

Balance Sheet as on 31 March, 2005

Liabilities	*(A)*	*Assets*	*(A)*
Trade Creditors	5,000	Premises	40,000
Loan (on mortgage of premises)	30,000	Furniture	10,000
Loan from A	15,000	Stock	70,000
General Reserve	10,000	Sundry Debtors	50,000
A's Capital	50,000	Cash	3,000
B's Capital	40,000		
C's Capital	23,000		
	1,73,000		1,73,000

The assets were realised in piecemeal as follows :

April, 2005 : Premises : A 35,000; Sundry debtors : A 6,000 and Stock : A 9000.

May, 2005 : Sundry debtors : A 7,500 and Stock : A 8,500.

June, 2005 : Sundry debtors : A 20,000 and Stock : A 23,000.

July, 2005 : Sundry debtors : A 15,000; Stock : A 25,000 and Furniture : A 8,000.

The remaining stock was taken over by B at the end of July, 2005 at an agreed amount of A 3,000. The trade creditors were settled for A 4,000. The partners distributed cash at the end of every month beginning 30th April, 2005.

You are required to show the distribution of cash in the form of a statement applying the 'maximum loss method'. Show your working notes clearly. [*B.Com. (Hons.) Delhi University, 2006*]

Solution

Calculation of Surplus Capital

Particulars		*A A*	*B A*	*C A*
Balance of Capital Account on 31.3.05		50,000	40,000	23,000
Add : Share in General Reserve (Profit Sharing Ratio 2 : 1 : 1)		5,000	2,500	2,500
Adjusted Capital	(*a*)	55,000	42,500	25,500
Profit Sharing Ratio		2	1	1
Adjusted Capital ÷ Profit Sharing Ratio		27,500	42,500	25,500
Proportionate Capitals on the basis of C's Capital	(*b*)	51,000	25,500	25,500
Surplus Capital (*a* – *b*)		4,000	17,000	
Profit Sharing Ratio		2	1	
Surplus Capital ÷ Profit Sharing Ratio		2,000	17,000	
Revised proportionate capitals on the basis of A's Surplus Capital		4,000	2,000	
Absolute Surplus Capital over revised proportionate Capital		—	15,000	

Thus after paying the creditors and A's loan, B will receive A 15,000. Then A and B will receive cash in the ratio of 2 : 1 respectively till A has received A 4,000 and B has received A 2,000 more. At this stage, the capital of A, B and C will be in their profit sharing ratio. Hence, therefore, cash will be distributed among A, B and C in the profit sharing ratio.

		Creditors A	A's Loan A	A's Capital A	B's Capital A	C's Capital A
April 30, Amount Payable		4,000	15,000	55,000	42,500	25,500
Cash Available :						
Cash in hand	3,000					
Premises (A 35,000 – 30,000)	5,000					
Sundry Debtors	6,000					
Stock	9,000					
	23,000					
Payment made		4,000	15,000	Nil	4,000	Nil
Balance Due		Nil	Nil	55,000	38,500	25,500
May 31 Cash Available						
Sundry Debtors	7,500					
Stock	8,500					
	16,000					
					11,000	
Payment made				3,333	1,667	
Balance Due				51,667	25,833	25,500
June 30, Cash Available						
Sundry Debtors	20,000					
Stock	23,000			667	333	
	43,000			21,000	10,500	10,500
				30,000	15,000	15,000
July 31, Amount Available						
Sundry Debtors	15,000					
Stock	25,000					
Furniture	8,000					
Stock taken by B	3,000					
	51,000					
Payment made : Stock						3,000
Cash				25,500	9,750	12,750
Balance left being loss				4,500	2,250	2,250

Example 45

The partnership firm presented you with the following Balance Sheet drawn as on 31.3.2006.

Liabilities		*(A)*	*Assets*	*(A)*
Sundry Creditors		37,000	Cash in Hand	3,000
Capital A/cs :		10,000	Sundry Debtors	34,000
A	40,000		Stock in trade	39,000
B	30,000		Plant & Machinery	51,000

C	27,000	97,000	Current A/cs :		
			B	4,000	
			C	3,000	7,000
		1,34,000			1,34,000

Partner shared profit and losses in the ratio of 4 : 3 : 3. Due to differences among the partners, it was decided to wind up the firm, realise the assets and distribute cash among the partners at the end of each month.

The following realisations were made :

(*i*) May : A 15,000 from debtors and A 20,000 by sale of stock. Expenses on realisation were A 500.

(*ii*) June : Balance of debtors realised A 10,000. Balance of stock fetched A 24,000.

(*iii*) August : Part of machinery was sold for A 18,000. Expenses incidental to sale were A 600.

(*iv*) Sept : Part of machinery valued in the books at A 5,000 was taken by B, in part discharge at an agreed value of A 10,000. Balance of Machinery was sold for A 30,000.

Partners decided to keep a minimum cash balance of A 2,000 in the first three months and A 1,000 thereafter. Show the statement of distribution of cash among partners under Proportionate Capital Method.

[*B.Com. (Hons.) Delhi University, 2007*]

Solution

Statement showing the distribution of Proceeds of Realisation
(According to Proportionate Capital Method)

Particulars	*Amount Available* A	*Creditors* A	*Capitals* A A	B A	C A
Amount Due		37,000	40,000	26,000	24,000
Cash in hand	3,000				
Less : Provision for Realisation expenses*2	2,000				
	1,000				
Less : Paid to the creditors	1,000	1,000	—	—	—
Balance Due		36,000	40,000	26,000	24,000
Realisation of May 2006 (A 15,000 + 20,000 – 500]	34,500	—	—	—	—
Less : Paid to Creditors	34,500	34,500	—	—	—
Balance Due	—	1,500	40,000	26,000	24,000
Realisation of June 2006 [A 10,000 + 24,000]	34,000				
Less : Paid to Creditors	1,500	1,500	—	—	—
	32,500				
Less : Paid to A (Absolute Surplus)*1	5,333	—	5,333	—	—
	27,167				
Less : Paid to A and B in the ratio of 4 : 3	4,667	—	2,667	2,000	—
	22,500				
Less : Paid to A, B and C in the ratio of 4 : 3 : 3	22,500	—	9,000	6,750	6,750
Balance Due			23,000	17,250	17,250
Realisation of August 2006					

[A 18,000 – 600]	17,400				
Add : Excess provision of Realisation Expenses	1,000				
	18,400				
Less : Paid to Partners in the ratio of 4 : 3 : 3	18,400		7,360	5,520	5,520
Balance Due			15,640	11,730	11,730
Realisation of September 2006	30,000				
Add : Machinery taken over by B	10,000				
Add : Excess (Balance) Provision for Realisation expenses	1,000				
	41,000				
Less : Paid to Partners in the ratio of 4 : 3 : 3	41,000		16,400	12,300*	12,300
Excess Payment (being profit on Realisation)			760	570	570

*The payment of A 12,300 to B including A 10,000 in machinery and A 2,300 in cash

Working Notes

*1 Calculation of Absolute Surplus Capital

Particulars	*A* *A*	*B* *A*	*C* *A*
A. Actual Capital (After adjustment of Current A/c)	40,000	26,000	24,000
B. Profit Sharing Ratio	4	3	3
C. Actual Capital ÷ Profit Sharing Ratio	10,000	8,667	8,000
D. Proportional Capital taking C's Capital (being the least) as Base Capital	32,000	24,000	24,000
E. Surplus Capital of A & B (A – D)	8,000	2,000	—
F. E/B	2,000	667	
G. Revised Base Capital (Being the lessor)		667	
H. Relative Capital (G × B)	2,667	2,000	
Absolute Surplus Capital [E – H]	5,333	Nil	Nil

Statement showing Priority of Distribution

First A 2,000 should be kept for Realisation expenses.

Next A 37,000 to be paid to the Creditors.

Next A 5,333 to be paid to A (Absolute Surplus)

Next (A 2,667 + A 2,000) *i.e.,* A 4,667 to be paid to A and B in the ratio of 4 : 3.

Balance to be paid to A, B and C in the profit sharing ratio.

*2 Minimum Cash balance of A 2,000 in first three months and A 1,000 thereafter is considered as provision for realisation expenses.

Example 46

A, B and C were partners sharing profit and losses in the ratio of 4 : 3 : 1. Their Balance Sheet as on 31st March, 2009 was as follows :

Liabilities	(A)	*Assets*	(A)
A's Capital A/c	1,05,000	Building	90,000
B's Capital A/c	45,000	Machinery	30,000
C's Capital A/c	75,000	Stock	82,500
Bank Loan (Secured)	13,500	Debtors	90,000
Creditors	39,000		
A's Loan	15,000		
	2,92,500		2,92,500

They decided to dissolve the business. The assets were realised gradually and the net amounts were distributed immediately as follows :

2009	(A)	*Assets*	(A)
May 30	33,000	Expenses paid	3,000
July 30	25,200	Expenses paid	2,200
Sept. 30	57,000	Expenses paid	4,500
Nov. 30	68,000	Expenses paid	8,000
Dec. 31	1,08,000	Expenses paid	10,000

Show the distribution of cash amount partners using maximum possible loss method.

[*B. Com. (Hons.), Delhi University, 2010*]

Solution

Statement of Distribution of Cash

		Bank Loan A	*Creditors* A	*A's Loan* A	*A's Capital* A	*B's Capital* A	*C's Capital* A
Balance as per Balance Sheet		13,500	39,000	15,000	1,05,000	45,000	75,000
30.5.2009							
Net Cash Realised [33,000 – 3,000] =	30,000						
Paid to Bank Loan & Creditors	30,000	13,500	16,500	—	—	—	—
Balance Due		—	22,500	15,000	1,05,000	45,000	75,000
3.7.2009							
Net Cash Realised [25,200 – 2,200] =	23,000						
Paid to Crs. & A's Loan	23,000		22,500	500			
Balance Due			—	14,500	1,05,000	45,000	75,000
30.9.2009							
Net Cash Realised [57,000 – 4,500 =	52,500						
Paid A's Loan	14,500						
Cash Available	38,000			14,500			
Minimum Loss [2,25,000* – 38,000] = 1,87,000 distributed among A, B and C in the ratio of 4 : 3 : 1					(93,500)	(70,125)	(23,375)
				—	11,500	(25,125)	51,625

B's deficiency borne by A & C in their Capital Ratio (7 : 5)				(14,655)	25,125	(10,470)
				(3,155)	—	41,155
A's deficiency to be borne by C				3,155		(3,155)
Amounted Paid to C				—	—	38,000
Balance Due				1,05,000	45,000	37,000
30.11.2009 Net Cash Realised [A 68,000 – 8,000] = 60,000 Maximum Loss [1,87,000 – 60,000] = 1,27,000 distributed among partners in the ratio of 4 : 3 : 1				(63,500)	(47,625)	(15,875)
				41,500	(2,625)	21,125
B's deficiency to be borne by A & C in Capital Ratio, i.e., 7 : 5				(1,532)	2,625	(1,093)
Amt. paid to A & C				**39,968**	—	**20,032**
Balance Due				65,032	45,000	16,968
1.12.2009 Net Cash Realised [1,08,000 – 10,000] = 98,000 Maximum Loss [1,27,000 – 98,000] = 29,000 distributed among partners in the ratio of 4 : 3 : 1				(14,500)	(10,875)	(3,625)
Paid to A, B & C				50,532	34,125	13,343
Balance unpaid or **Final Loss** (Balance Due – Amount Paid)				14,500	10,875	3,625

* A 1,05,000 (A's Capital) + A 45,000 (B's Capital) + A 75,000 (C's Capital) = A 2,25,000

Example 47

Amar, Akbar and Antony are in partnership. The following is their Balance Sheet as at March 31, 2010 on which date they dissolved their partnership. They shared profit in the ratio of 5 : 3 : 2.

Liabilities	*(A)*	*Assets*	*(A)*
Creditors	80,000	Plant and Machinery	60,000
Loan A/c Amar	20,000	Premises	80,000
Capital A/cs Amar	1,00,000	Stock	60,000
Akbar	30,000	Debtors	1,20,000
Antony	90,000		
	3,20,000		3,20,000

It was agreed to repay the amounts due to the partners as and when the assets were realised, *viz.,*

	(A)
April 15, 2010	60,000
May 1, 2010	1,46,000
May 31, 2010	94,000

Prepare a statement showing how the distribution should be made under maximum loss method and write up the cash account and partner's capital accounts. [*C.A. May, 2010*]

Solution

(*a*) Statement of Distribution of Cash by 'Maximum Loss Method'.

		Creditors *A*	*Amar's Loan* *A*	*Amar* *A*	*Akbar* *A*	*Antony* *A*
Balance due		80,000	20,000	1,00,000	30,000	90,000
15th April 2010 realised	60,000					
Paid to creditors		60,000	—	—	—	—
Balance due		20,000	20,000	1,00,000	30,000	90,000
1st May 2010 realised	1,46,000					
Paid to Creditors	20,000	20,000	—	—	—	—
Paid to Amar's Loan	20,000	—	20,000	—	—	—
Balance due (1)		Nil	Nil	1,00,000	30,000	90,000
Balance	1,06,000					
Maximum Loss (1,00,000 + 30,000 + 90,000 – 1,06,000) = 1,14,000 shared in Profit & Loss ratio 5 : 3 : 2				57,000	34,200	22,800
				43,000	(4,200)	67,200
Akbar's deficiency shared by Amar & Antony in Capital ratio 100 : 90				(2,210)	4,200	(1,990)
Cash paid (2)				40,790	—	65,210
Balance due (3) [1 – 2]				59,210	30,000	24,790
31st May 2010 realised A 94,000						
Maximum Loss [59,210 + 30,000 + 24,790 – 94,000] = A 20,000 shared in 5 : 3 : 2				10,000	6,000	4,000
Cash paid (4)				49,210	24,000	20,790
Balance/Loss* on realisation (3–4)				10,000	6,000	4,000

Cash Account

	(*A*)		(*A*)
To Realization Account	60,000	By Creditors Account	60,000
To Realization Account	1,46,000	By Creditors Account	20,000
To Realization Account	94,000	By Amar's Loan Account	20,000
		By Amar's Capital Account	40,790
		By Antony's Capital Account	65,210
		By Amar's Capital Account	49,210
		By Akbar's Capital Account	24,000
		By Antony's Capital Account	20,790
	3,00,000		3,00,000

Partner's Capital Accounts

Liabilities	*(A)*	*(A)*	*(A)*	*Assets*	*(A)*	*(A)*	*(A)*
To Cash	40,790	–	65,210	By Balance b/d	1,00,000	30,000	90,000
To Cash	49,210	24,000	20,790				
To Balance c/d							
Realization loss*	10,000	6,000	4,000				
	1,00,000	30,000	90,000		1,00,000	30,000	90,000

* If no further realization takes place, then Amar, Akbar and Antony will bear loss on realization A 10,000, A 6,000 and A 4,000 respectively.

ASSIGNMENT MATERIAL

Note *:* The Objective Type Questions (True/False, Multiple Choice Questions etc.) have been given in the Appendix at the end of the book.

SHORT-ANSWER THEORY QUESTIONS

1. Briefly explain Hire Purchase and Instalment System.
2. Explain briefly Hire Purchase System.
3. What is the meaning of the following terms?
   (*i*) Hire Vendor
   (*ii*) Hirer
   (*iii*) Hire Purchase Price
4. Distinguish between Hire Purchase System and Instalment System.
5. What are different methods of recording Hire Purchase transactions.
6. Explain full Cash Price of accounting for hire purchase transactions.
7. Explain accrual method of accounting for hire purchase transactions.
8. (*a*) What is Garner Vs. Murray Rule? Explain with the help of imaginary figures.
   (*b*) Explain the Maximum Loss method of Piecemeal distribution.
   (*c*) Explain the Proportionate Capitals method of piece-meal distribution.
   [*B.Com (Hons.), Delhi University, 2005*]
9. What is gradual distribution of cash. [*B.Com (Hons.), Delhi University, 2009*]
10. Explain the rule of Garner Vs. Murray. [*B.Com (Hons.), Delhi University, 2010*]
11. Explain the maximum loss method of piece-meal distribution.
    [*B.Com (Hons.), Delhi University, 2007*]
12. Explain Net Asset Method and Net Payment Method under sale of partnership firm to a limited company.
13. How are shares and debentures distributed among partners in case of sale of partnership firm to a limited company.
14. What is a piecemeal distribution? When is it necessary?
15. How are partner's capital accounts settled under piecemeal distribution.

16. Explain the following :
    (*i*) Proportionate Capital Method.
    (*ii*) Maximum Loss Method.
17. *A, B* and *C* are partners; *A* became insolvent on 15.4.2010. The capital account balance of partner B is on the debit side. Partner *B* is solvent. Should partner *B* bear the loss arising on account of the insolvency of partner *A*? [*C.A., May, 2010*]

Ans. According to Garner Vs. Murray Rule, if a solvent partner is having a debit balance in his capital account, then he cannot be called upon to bear the loss on account of the insolvency of the other partner. Hence, 'B' needs not bear the loss due to insolvency of partner 'A'.

LONG ANSWER THEORY QUESTIONS

1. What are the situations under which dissolution can take place?
2. How are accounts settled on dissolution of firm?
3. Explain the journal entries recorded for realisation of assets and liabilities.
4. Discuss the procedures followed for settling the accounts of the partners.
5. How are partners capital accounts settled under the following situations :
    (*i*) Where all the partners are solvent.
    (*ii*) Where some of the partners are solvent and others are insolvent.
    (*iii*) Where all the partners are insolvent.

PRACTICAL PROBLEMS

SIMPLE DISSOLUTION

1. The following is the Balance Sheet of *A* and *B* as on 31 December, 2011 :

Balance Sheet As On 31 December, 2011

Dr. *Cr.*

Liabilities	Amount (A)	Assets		Amount (A)
Trade Creditors	45,000	Cash at Bank		12,000
Bills Payable	12,000	Sundry Debtors	22,000	
Mrs. *A*'s Loan	10,000	*Less* : Provision	2,000	20,000
Bank Overdraft (against stock)	15,000	Stock		25,000
		Buildings		55,300
Reserve Fund	15,000	Furniture		14,700
Capitals :				
A	15,000			
B	15,000			
	1,27,000			1,27,000

The firm was dissolved on the above date with the following arrangements :

1. Assets were realised as follows : Debtors 80% of the book value; Building A 79,000; Furniture A 14,400.
2. Stock was taken over by the bank and it realised A 20,000. Bank paid back A 4,000 after receiving its overdraft and interest due there on.
3. Trade Creditors and Bills Payable were due on average basis one month after 31 December, but were paid immediately on 31 December, at 2% discount per annum.
4. A agreed to bear all realisation expenses. For this service A was paid A 395. Actual expenses amounted to A 1,200.

Show the ledger accounts recording the dissolution in the books of the firm.

[***Ans. :*** Profit on Realisation – A 14,700; Payment to *A* – A 29,045; Payment to *B* – A 29,850; Total of Bank Account A 1,27,000]

2. *X, Y, Z* were sharing profits in the ratio of 3 : 1 : 1 respectively. They decided to dissolve their firm on 31st march, 2011 when their position was as follows :

Dr. *Cr.*

Liabilities		*Amount (A)*	*Assets*		*Amount (A)*
Capitals :			Machinery		51,000
X	82,500		Furniture		3,000
Y	30,000		Stock		23,400
Z	21,000	1,33,500	Debtors	72,600	
Loan		4,500	Less :		
Sundry creditors		18,000	Provisions for		
			bad debts	3,600	69,000
			Cash in hand		9,600
		1,56,000			1,56,000

(*i*) *X* agreed to takeover furniture at A 2,400, debtors amounting to A 60,000 at A 51,600 and also the creditors at their book value.

(*ii*) *Y* agreed to takeover stock at A 21,000 and a part of the machinery at A 21,600 (being book value less 10%).

(*iii*) *Z* agreed to take over the remaining machinery at 90% of the book value less A 300 as allowance. He also assumed the responsibility for payment of loan together with accrued interest A 90 (not recorded in the books).

(*iv*) Dissolution expenses amounted to A 810.

(*v*) The remaining debtors were sold to a debt-collecting agency at 50% of book value.

Prepare the important ledger accounts to close the books of account.

[*CS*(*F*) *June 2006*]

[***Ans. :*** Loss or realisation *X* A 12,240; *Y* 4080; *Z* 4080 cash A/c total A 35,070]

3. *A, B* and *C* sharing profits in the proportion of 3 : 2 : 1 agreed to dissolution of their partnership on 31 December 2011 on which date their Balance Sheet was as under:

Liabilities	*Amount* (*A*)	*Assets*		*Amount* (*A*)
Capital Accounts		Machinery		40,500
A	40,000	Stock-in-trade		7,550
B	20,000	Investments		20,830
Mrs. *A*'s Loan	10,000	Joint Life Policy		14,000
Life Policy Fund	14,000	Debtors	9,300	
Creditors	18,500	*Less* : Reserve	600	8,700
Investment Fluctuation		Current Account-*C*		11,500
Fund	6,000	Cash at Bank		5,420
	1,08,500			1,08,500

The Life Policy is surrendered for A 12,000. The investments are taken over by *A* for A 17,500. A agreed to discharge his wife's loan. *B* takes over all the stock at A 7,000 and debtors amounting to A 5,000 at A 4,000. Machinery is sold for A 55,000. The remaining debtors realise 50% of book value. The expenses of realisation amount to A 600. It is found that an investment not recorded in the books is worth A 3,000. The same is taken over by one of the creditors at this value. Prepare necessary accounts.

[***Ans.*** Profit on Realisation – A 28,470; Final Payments : *A* – A 46,735; *B* – A 18,490; Contribution by *C* – A 6,755].

4. Anu, Nimmi and Sonu sharing profits in the ratio of 4 : 3 : 2 decided to dissolve their firms on 31st March, 2011, on which date their balance sheet was as under :

Liabilities		*Amount* (*A*)	*Assets*		*Amount* (*A*)
Capital Accounts :			Fixed Assets :		1,00,000
Anu		82,000	Joint Life Policy		
Nimmi		60,000	(at Surrender value)		20,000
Reserve Fund		18,000	Debtors	20,000	
Joint Life Policy Reserve		20,000	*Less* : Provision	1,000	19,000
Creditors	38,000		Stock at Invoice Price	20,000	
Less : Provision for					
Discount	1,000	37,000	*Less* : Provision for Load	4,000	16,000
Salary Payable		4,000	Investments (face value A 20,000)		16,000
Investment Fluctuation Fund		1,000			
			Sonu - Overdrawn		4,000
			Bank		47,000
		2,22,000			2,22,000

Investments were taken over by Anu at cost price. Creditors of A 20,000 were taken over by Nimmi at A 19,000. Remaining creditors were paid A 15,000. Joint life policy was surrendered. Fixed assets realised A 1,38,000 while stock and debtors fetched A 30,000. One customer (not included in Debtors above) whose account was written off as bad now paid A 2,000. There was one unrecorded asset of A 6,000, half of which was handed over to settle half of the unrecorded liability of A 14,000 and the balance of the unrecorded liability was paid in cash. The remaining half of the unrecorded asset was sold in the market for A 2,000.

Prepare necessary accounts to close the books of the firm.

[***Ans.*** **:** Profit on realisation A 54,000; Bank A/c total A 2,39,000]

5. *A*, *B* and *C* were partners in a firm and shared profits in the ratio of 3 : 2 : 1. On 31.12.2011 their balance sheet was as follows :

Balance Sheet As On 31 December, 2011

Dr. Liabilities	Amount (A)	Assets	*Cr.* Amount (A)
Creditors	65,000	Cash	22,500
Bills Payable	20,000	Debtors	52,300
Provident Fund	12,000	Stock	36,000
Investment Fluctuation Fund	6,000	Investment	15,000
Commission Received in Advance	8,000	Plant	91,200
Capital Accounts :		Profit and Loss A/c	54,000
A	80,000		
B	50,000		
C	30,000		
	2,71,000		2,71,000

On this date, the firm was dissolved. A was appointed to realise the assets. A was to receive 5% commission on the sale of assets (except cash) and was to bear all expenses of realisation.

A realised the assets as follows :

Debtors A 30,000; Stock A 26,000; Investments 75% of book value, Plant A 42,720. Expenses of realisation paid by the firm amounted to A 4,100.

Commission received in advance was returned to the customers after deducing A 3,000.

Firm had to pay A 7,200 for outstanding salary not provided for earlier. Compensation paid to employees amounted to A 9,800. This liability was not provided for in the above balance sheet A 25,000 had to be paid for provident fund. Prepare a Realisation Account, Capital Accounts and Cash Account.

[***Ans.*** **:** Loss on realisation A 1,11,000; cash A/c total A 1,38,600]

6. The following the Balance Sheet of *A* and *B* on 31st December, 2011 :

Balance Sheet As On 31 December, 2011

Dr. Liabilities	Amount (A)	Assets	*Cr.* Amount (A)
Sundry Creditors	30,000	Cash in hand	500
Bills Payable	8,000	Cash at Bank	8,000
Mrs. *A*'s Loan	5,000	Stock in Trade	5,000
Mrs. *B*'s Loan	10,000	Investments	10,000

General Reserve	10,000	Debtors	20,000	
Investment Fluctuation Fund	1,000	*Less* : Provision	2,000	18,000
A's Capital	10,000	Plant		20,000
B's Capital	10,000	Building		15,000
		Goodwill		4,000
		Profit and loss A/c		3,500
	84,000			84,000

The firm was dissolved on 31st December, 2011 on the following term :

(*a*) *A* promised to pay of Mrs. *A*'s loan and took away stock-in-trade at A 4,000.

(*b*) *B* took away half of the investment at 10% discount.

(*c*) Debtors realised A 19,000.

(*d*) Creditors and Bills Payable were due on an average basis one month after 31st December, but they were paid immediately on 31st December at 6% discount p.a.

(*e*) Plant realised A 25,000, building A 40,000, goodwill A 6,000 and remaining investment at A 4,500.

(*f*) There was an old typewriter in the firm which had been written off completely from the books. It is now estimated to realise A 300. It was taken away by *B* at this estimated price.

(*g*) Realisation expenses amounted to A 1,000.

You are required to give necessary ledger accounts.

[***Ans.*** **:** Profit on realisation A 15,745 to *A* and *B* each; Cash A/c total A 1,03,000]

7. *P*, *Q* and *R* are partners sharing profits and losses equally. On 31.3.2011 their balance sheet stood as follows :

Dr. *Cr.*

Liabilities	*Amount* (*A*)	*Assets*	*Amount* (*A*)
Bills payable	16,000	Cash in Bank	15,000
Creditors	1,19,000	Debtors	1,25,000
Loan from *Q*	25,000	Stock	2,90,000
General reserve	30,000	Furniture	40,000
		Machinery	1,20,000
P's Current Account	15,000	Current account : *R*	30,000
Q,'s Current Account	15,000		
Capital account :			
P	2,00,000		
Q	1,00,000		
R	1,00,000		
	6,20,000		6,20,000

The firm was dissolved on the above-mentioned date. *P* agreed to pay creditors at par. *Q* took over the entire furniture for A 36,000. The remaining assets were sold for A 5,53,000. Bills payable were retired for a discount of A 100 received for payment before the due dates of maturity. Expenses of dissolution amounted to A 1,200. Prepare important ledger accounts and cash book. The current accounts and the capital accounts may be prepared in columnar form. [*CS(F) June 2001*]

[***Ans.*** **:** Profit on realisation A 12,900; Bank A/c total A 5,68,000]

8. A, B and C sharing profit in the ratio of 3 : 1 : 1 decided to dissolve their firm on 31 December ....., their position was as follows :

Liabilities		(A)	*Assets*		(A)
Creditors		6,000	Cash at Bank		3,500
Loan		1,500	Debtors	24,200	
Capitals :			*Less* : Reserve	1,200	23,000
A	27,500		Stock		8,300
B	11,000		Furniture		1,200
C	10,000	48,500	Sundry Assets		20,000
		56,000			56,000

It is agreed that :

(*i*) A is to take over all the furniture at A 1,000 and debtors amounting to A 20,200 at A 18000. A also agrees to pay the creditors.

(*ii*) B is to take over all the stock at book value and some of the sundry assets at A 7,200 (being book value less 10%).

(*iii*) C is to take over the remaining sundry assets at 90% of the book value and assume responsibility for the discharge of the loan.

(*iv*) The remaining debtors were taken by a Debt-Collecting Agency at 80% of the book value.

(*v*) The expenses of dissolution amounted to A 200. Prepare Realisation Account, Bank Account and Capital Accounts of the Partners. [*B.Com. (Hons.) Delhi University*]

[***Ans.*** **:** Loss on Realisation A 4,200]

9. Appollo, Binaca and Colgate, the three partners give you the following Balance Sheet as on December 31, ...;

Liabilities		(A)	*Assets*	(A)
Appollo's Loan		15,000	Plant & Machinery	30,000
Reserve Fund		27,000	Furniture	12,000
Capital Accounts :			Stock	12,000
Appollo	26,000		Debtors	18,000
Binaca	10,000	36,000	Joint Life Policy	15,000
Sundry Creditors		17,000	Patents & Trade Marks	12,000
Loan on Hypothecation of Stock		7,000	Cash at Bank	13,000
			Capital Account Colgate	2,000
Joint Life Policy Reserve		12,000		
		1,14,000		1,14,000

The partners shared profits and losses in the ratio 5 : 3 : 2. The firm was dissolved and you are given the following information :

(*i*) Colgate had taken a loan from insurance company for A 6,000 on the security of the Joint Life Policy. The policy was surrendered and the company paid a sum of A 10,000 after deducting A 6,000 for Colgate's loan and A 5000 interest thereon.

(*ii*) One of the creditors took some patents whose book value was A 10,000 at A 8,000. The balance to the creditors was paid in cash.

(*iii*) The firm had a typewriter which was depreciated to its full cost. One of the credits agreed to take it at an agreed value of A 5,000.

(*iv*) The remaining assets were realised as under :

	(A)
Plant	15,000
Furniture	5,000
Stock	10,000
Debtors	17,000
Patents	40% of book value

(*v*) The liabilities were paid and a total discount of A 450 was allowed by the creditors.

(*vi*) Appollo was entitled to 2% commission on assets realised in cash except joint life policy.

(*vii*) The expenses of realisation amounted to A 2,284. Prepare the necessary accounts to close the book of the firm. [*B.Com. (Hons.) Delhi University*]

[**Ans. :** Loss on realisation A 12,000]

10. Arun, Dawood and Shakeel are partners of M/s. Richman Corporation sharing profits and losses at 20%, 40% and 40% respectively. Their summarised balance sheet on 31.12.2007, when they decided to dissolve the firm, was as follows :

Liabilities	(*A*)	*Assets*	(*A*)
Capital accounts	5,00,000	Cash and Bank balance	50,000
Current accounts	50,000	Sundry debtors	3,00,000
Provision for depreciation :		Stock	1,75,000
Depreciation on machinery	50,000	Machinery	4,00,000
General reserve	1,35,000	Goodwill	1,00,000
Provision for doubtful debts	75,000	Deferred revenue expenses	50,000
Sundry creditors	2,65,000		
	10,75,000		10,75,000

Additional Information :

(*i*) Capital and current accounts are in proportion of profit sharing ratio.

(*ii*) Debtors realised 2/3 of its gross value while stock and machinery realised A 1,10,000 and A 2,00,000 respectively. Investments written off in the past were taken over by Arun for A 2,30,000.

(*iii*) Suppliers allowed discounts of A 15,000 in full settlement.

(*iv*) Realisation expenses of A 25,000 were paid by Dawood and Shakeel in ratio of their capital accounts.

(*v*) An old machinery fully written off was sold for A 21,000 while an extra payments of A 1,000 is made to bank for a discounted bill being dishonoured.

Prepare :

(1) Realisation Account, (2) Cash and bank Account and (3) Capital accounts.

[*B.Com. (Hons.) Delhi University*]

Ans. : Loss on realisation A 1,00,000

11. The following is the trial balance of the firm of P, Q and R, on 31 March :

	Dr. (A)	Cr. (A)
Freehold Property (Mumbai)	45,000	—
Leasehold Property (Kolkata)	15,000	—
Leasehold Property (Chennai)	12,000	—

Investments	6,000	—
Office Furniture	1,000	—
Stock (Mumbai)	18,000	—
Stock (Kolkata)	16,000	—
Stock Chennai	14,000	—
Sundry debtors	12,500	—
Sundry creditors	—	18,500
Capita : P	—	50,000
Q	—	45,000
R	—	30,000
Cash at bank	4,000	—
	1,43,500	1,43,500

They agreed to dissolve the firm with immediate effect, on the following terms :

(*a*) The freehold property was sold and realised A 1,00,000; the investments realised A 7,500, debtors A 11,500 and office furniture A 600.

(*b*) P retired from the business.

(*c*) Q took over the Kolkata business and the assets in connection therewith at book values; the goodwill thereof being valued at A 10,000.

(*d*) R took over the Chennai business and the corresponding assets at book values; goodwill for this purpose being valued at A 5,000.

(*e*) The expenses of realisation amounted to A 1,200. Creditors were paid A 17,000 in full settlement.

(*f*) The Mumbai stock was taken over by Q and R equally at book value.

(*g*) The partners shared profit in the proportion of 4 : 3 : 3.

Pass entries necessary to close the book, assuming that each partner finally settled his account with the firm. Open also the necessary accounts to show the working. [*B.Com. (Hons.) Delhi University*]

Ans. : Profit on realisation A 70,400.

12. P, Q and R are partners sharing profits and losses equally. On 31 March 2007, their balance sheet stood as follows :

Liabilities	(*A*)	*Assets*	(*A*)
Bill payable	16,000	Cash at Bank	15,000
Creditors	1,19,000	Debtors	1,25,000
Loan from Q	25,000	Stock	2,90,000
General reserve	30,000	Furniture	40,000
P's current account	15,000	Machinery	1,20,000
Q's current account	15,000	R's current account	30,000
P's capital account	2,00,000		
Q's capital account	1,00,000		
R's capital account	1,00,000		
	6,20,000		6,20,000

The firm was dissolved on the above-mentioned date. P agreed to pay creditors at par. Q took over the entire furniture for A 36,000. The remaining assets were sold for A 5,53,000. Bills payable were retired for a discount of A 100 received for payment before the due dates of maturity. Expenses of dissolution amounted to A 1,200.

Prepare important ledger accounts and cash book. The current accounts and the capital accounts may be prepared in columnar form. [*CS (Foundation) June 2001*]

Ans. : Profit on realisation A 12,900.

INSOLVENCY OF PARTNER

13. A, B, C and D were partners sharing profits and losses in the ratio of 3 : 3 : 2 : 2 respectively. The following is their balance sheet as at 31st March 2011 :

Balance Sheet as at 31.3.2011

Liabilities		*Amount (A)*	*Assets*		*Amount (A)*
Creditors		31,000	Cash in Hand		4,000
A's Loan		20,000	Debtors	32,000	
Capital Accounts :			*Less :* Provisions	1,000	31,000
A	40,000		Stock		20,000
B	30,000	70,000	Furniture		8,000
			Scooter		14,000
			Capital Accounts :		
			C	12,000	
			D	32,000	44,000
		1,21,000			1,21,000

It was decided to dissolve the firm with effect from 31st march, 2011, *B* was appointed to liquidate the assets and pay the creditors. He was to bear the expenses of realization, which amounted to A 500.

B was also entitled to receive 5% commission on the amounts payable to *A* (including for his loan, but excluding the cash brought by *A* towards his share of loss on realization) after charging such commission. *A* has agreed to bear this commission wholly himself.

The assets realized A 54,000.

Creditors were paid in full

In addition, a sum of A 5,000 was also paid to staff on retrenchment in full settlement of their claims. *D* was insolvent and the partners accepted A 7,400 from his estate in full settlement.

Applying the rule in Garner *v.* Murry, prepare the necessary ledger accounts.

[***Ans. :*** Loss on realisation A 24,000; Cash A/c total 96,000]

14. *A, B* and *C* were partners. Their profit sharing ratio was 4 : 2 : 3. They dissolved their business on which date Balance Sheet of the firm was as follows :

Balance Sheet

Liabilities	*Amount (A)*	*Assets*	*Amount (A)*
A's Capital	68,000	Buildings	60,000
B's Capital	46,000	Furniture	27,700
C's Capital	3,000	Stock and Debtors	50,400
A's Loan	2,000	Cash	13,100
Creditors	15,100		
Reserve Fund	17,100		
	1,51,200		1,51,200

Assets realised A 1,00,200. Realisation expenses A 600. *C* became insolvent and only A 1,024 received from him. Prepare Realisation Account, Cash Account and Partners' Capital Accounts following the rule of *Garner vs. Murray's* case. [***Ans. :*** Loss on Realisation – A 38,500]

15. The following is the Balance Sheet of Anil, Amit and Asif as on 31 December, 2011.

Balance Sheet As On 31 December, 2011

Liabilities		*Amount (A)*	*Assets*	*Amount (A)*
Creditors		25,000	Cash	9,000
Reserve Fund		18,000	Stock	25,000
Capitals :			Plant and Machinery	30,000
Anil	30,000		Sundry Debtors	15,000
Amit	20,000		Bills Receivable	5,000
		50,000	Asif's Capital	9,000
		93,000		93,000

Asif is insolvent and his estate could pay only A 3,000. It is decided to wind up the partnership. The assets realised as follows :

Sundry Debtors	10,000
Stock	20,000
Plant and Machinery	15,000
Bills Receivable	3,000

The expenses came to A 1,000. It was also found that there was a liability for A 2,000 for damages which had to be paid.

Give Ledger Accounts to close the Books of Account.

[***Ans. :*** Loss on Realisation – A 30,000; Deficiency in Asif's Capital Account has been divided in the ratio of 18 : 13 by solvent partners]

16. *A, B, C* and *D* are partners in a firm sharing profits and losses in the ratio of 4 : 1 : 2 : 3. The following is their balance sheet as at 31.3.2011 :

Balance Sheet as at 31.3.2011

Liabilities	*Amount (A)*	*Assets*		*Amount (A)*
Sundry Creditors	3,00,000	Sundry Debtors		3,50,000
Capital A/c :		*Less :* Provision for Bad Debts		50,000
A	7,00,000			3,00,000
D	3,00,000			
		Stock		2,00,000
		Cash in hand		1,40,000
		Other Assets		3,10,000
		Capital A/c :		
		B	2,00,000	
		C	1,50,000	3,50,000
	13,00,000			13,00,000

The firm is dissolved on the following terms :

(*i*) *A* is to take over sundry debtors at 80% of book value.

(*ii*) *D* is to take over stock at 95% of the book value.

(*iii*) *C* is to discharge sundry creditors.

(*iv*) Other assets realise A 3,00,000 and expenses of realisation come to A 30,000.

(*v*) *B* is found insolvent and A 21,900 is realised from his Estate.

Prepare Realisation Account, Capital Accounts of the partners and the Cash Account. Strictly apply the decision in *Garner v. Murray* case.

[***Ans. :*** Loss on realisation A 70,000; cash A/c total A 5,10,000].

17. *A, B* and *C* were carrying on business in partnership sharing profits and losses in the ration of 3 : 2 : 1. They decided to dissolve the firm on 31 December on which date their Balance Sheet stood as follows :

Balance Sheet As On 31 December, 2011

Liabilities		*Amount (A)*	*Assets*	*Amount (A)*
Creditors		94,000	Land and Building	1,14,000
A's Loan Account		20,000	Stock	1,00,000
Capital Accounts :			Debtors	1,00,000
A	1,80,000		Cash	6,000
B	20,000		Profit and Loss Account	3,000
C	20,000	2,20,000	*B*'s Current Account	4,000
A's Current Account		3,000	*C*'s Current Account	10,000
		3,37,000		3,37,000

Land and Building were sold for A 80,000, Stock and Debtors realised A 60,000 and A 84,000 respectively. The Goodwill was sold for A 1,200. The expenses of realisation amounted to A 2,400. *C* is insolvent and a final dividend of 50 paise in a rupee is received from his estate in full settlement. Prepare the necessary accounts closing the books of the firm applying the ruling given in *Garner vs. Murray.*

[***Ans.*** Loss on Realisation – A 91,200]

18. Following was the balance sheet of a firm as at 31st March, 2011 :

Balance Sheet As On 31 December, 2011

Liabilities	*Amount (A)*	*Assets*	*Amount (A)*
Creditors	2,04,800	Bank balance	11,000
P's loan account	60,000	Debtors	1,92,120
Q's loan account	24,000	Stock	1,28,000
P's current account	42,400	Machinery	57,200
Q's current account	5,000	Land	1,68,000
Capital accounts :		*R*'s current account	19,880
P	1,20,000		
Q	80,000		
R	40,000		
	5,76,200		5,76,200

It was decided to dissolve the firm on that date. The assets (with the exception of bank balance) realised A 4,53, 600. The firm had to pay A 3,000 for an outstanding bill not recorded in the books. *R* became insolvent and A 2,000 were realised from his estate. Prepare necessary ledger accounts in the books of the firm when—

(*i*) Partners' capitals were fixed; and

(*ii*) *Garner v. Murray* Rule was followed. *[CS(F) Dec. 2006]*

[***Ans. :*** Loss on realisation A 94,720; Bank A/c total A 5,29,747].

19. Ram, Shyam and Mohan were partners sharing profits and losses in the ratio of 5 : 3 : 2 respectively. Their balance sheet as on 31st March, 2011 was as follows :

Liabilities		*Amount (A)*	*Assets*		*Amount (A)*
Sundry creditors		2,30,000	Furniture and fixtures		60,000
General reserves		1,00,000	Stock		2,60,000
Capital accounts :			Debtors	4,00,000	
Ram	2,00,000		*Less :*		
Shyam	1,60,000		Provision for bad debts	20,000	3,80,000
Mohan	30,000	3,90,000	Cash		20,000
		7,20,000			7,20,000

The firm was dissolved as on the above mentioned date. Assets realised as follows furniture and fixtures : A 20,000; Stock : A 2,00,000 and Debtors : A 2,40,000. Sundry creditors to the extent of A 1,000 were paid in full. The total payment to sundry creditors was A 2,09,000. It was found that there was a liability of A 61,000 for damages which had also to be paid.

Winding up expenses amounted to A 20,000 Mohan because insolvent and he could pay only 20 paise in a rupee.

Prepare ledger accounts to close the books of the firm following *Garner v. Murray* Rule.

[*CS(F) June 2004*]

[***Ans. :*** Loss on realisation A 3,00,000; Cash A/c total A 7,22,000]

20. The Balance Sheet *A, B* and *C* who are sharing profits and losses in the ratio of 2 : 2 : 1, was as follows on 31st March 2011, the date of dissolution :

Balance Sheet

Liabilities		*Amount (A)*	*Assets*	*Amount (A)*
Sundry Creditors		1,20,000	Cash	1,000
Bank Loan (with a charge on stock)		50,000	Stock	60,000
Capitals :			Other Assets	1,09,000
A	30,000		Goodwill	30,000
B	20,000	50,000	Capital – *C*	20,000
		2,20,000		2,20,000

Stock realised A 52,000 and other assets were sold for A 90,000. Expenses on realisation amounted to A 3,000. Assuming that all the partners are insolvent, prepare the necessary ledger accounts to close the books of the firm. [***Ans. :*** Loss on realisation A 60,000 Cash A/c total A 1,43,000]

21. The following is the balance sheet of a firm on 31 March 2011.

Balance Sheet As On 31 December, 2011

Liabilities		*Amount (A)*	*Assets*	*Amount (A)*
Creditors		1,02,400	Bank	5,500
Loans :			Debtors	96,060
P	30,000		Stock	64,000
Q	12,000	42,000	Machinery	28,600
Current Accounts :			Land	84,000
P	21,200		*R*'s Current Account	9,940
Q	2,500	23,700		
Capital Accounts :				
P	60,000			
Q	40,000			
R	20,000	1,20,000		
		2,88,100		2,88,100

Owing to heavy losses, the firm was dissolved. The assets, except bank balance, realised A 2,26,880. The firm has to pay A 1,500 for an outstanding bill not recorded in the books. *R* becomes insolvent and A 1,000 is realised from his private estate. Prepare the necessary accounts to close the books of the firm. [*B.Com., Delhi University, 1998*]

[***Ans. :*** Loss on realisation to *P, Q, R* A 15,760 each. Bank A/c total A 2,33,380]

22. *A, B* and *C* are partners in a firm sharing profits and losses in the ratio of 2 : 2 : 1. They decided to dissolve and appoint *B* to realise the assets and distribute the proceeds for which he is to receive as his remuneration 5% of the amounts ultimately paid to *A* and *C* but in lieu of this he is to bear all expenses of realisation. The balance sheet of the firm on the date of dissolution is as under :

Liabilities	Amount (A)	Assets		Amount (A)
Creditors	1,317	Debtors	4,229	
A's Capital	3,960	*Less :* Provision	211	4,018
B's Capital	2,970	Stock		1,872
		Cash		290
		Other assets		1,710
		C (overdrawn)		357
	8,247			8247

B informs of the following realisation :

Debtors A 3,462, Stock A 1,444, Goodwill A 50 and Other assets A 914.

Creditors which were not recorded in books are now paid A 100.

The expenses of realisation amount to A 310. *C* is able to contribute only A 100 beyond which he expresses his inability. Commission payable to *B* is to be treated as business expenses. Close the books of the firm. [***Ans. :*** Loss on realisation A 1970 Cash A/c total A 6260]

23. A, B and C are carrying on business and sharing profits and losses in the ratio of 2 : 2 : 1. They dissolved their firm as on March 31, ... on which date their Balance Sheet was as follows :

Liabilities		(A)	Assets		(A)
Sundry Creditors		20,000	Cash		4,500
Profit and Loss Account		10,000	Stock		16,000
J.P.L. Reserve		8,000	Debtors	10,000	
Mrs. A's Loan		3,000	*Less :* Provision	500	9,500
Advance from C		1,000	Joint Life Policy		11,000
A	15,000		Premises		26,000
B	14,000		A's drawing		1,000
C	2,000	31,000	C's drawings		5,000
		73,000			73,000

Note : A Bill of A 800 received from P is under discount.

The assets except cash and joint life policy were sold to a company for A 45,500 cash. The policy was surrendered and a sum of A 10,800 was received. P proved insolvent and a sum A 500 was received from his estate. Sundry creditors were paid A 19,500 in full settlement. Realisation expenses amounted to A 3,000. C was declared insolvent. His private estate was worth A 5,000 and his personal liabilities amounted to A 4,900. An unrecorded asset worth A 2,550 was given as a gift to the manager of the firm on behalf of the firm for service rendered by him. Prepare Realisation Account and Partner's Capital Accounts. [*B. Com. (Hons.) Delhi University*]

Ans. : Loss on realisation A 1,000]

24. Ram, Shyam and Mohan were partners sharing profits and losses in the ratio of 5 : 3 respectively. The balance sheet as on 31 March 2004 was as follows :

Liabilities	(A)	Assets	(A)
Sundry creditors	2,30,000	Furniture and Fixtures	60,000
General reserves	1,00,000	Stock	2,60,000

Capital Accounts :			Debtors	4,00,000	
Ram	2,00,000		*Less :* Provision or bad debts.	20,000	3,80,000
Shyam	1,60,000		Cash		20,000
Mohan	30,000	3,90,000			
		7,20,000			7,20,000

The firm was dissolved as on the above mentioned date. Assets realised as follows: Furniture, and fixtures : A 20,000; Stock A 2,00,000 and Debtors : A 2,40,000.

Sundry creditors to the extent of A 1,000 were paid in full. The total payment to sundry creditors was A 2,09,000. It was found that there was a liability of A 61,000 for damages which had also to be paid.

Winding up expenses amounted to A 20,000. Mohan became insolvent and he could pay only 20 paise in a rupee.

Prepare ledger accounts to close the books of the firm following Garner Vs. Murray rule.

[C.S. (Foundation) June 2004]

Ans. : Loss on realisation A 3,00,000

SALE TO A LIMITED COMPANY

25. A, B and C were partners sharing profit and losses in the ratio 2 : 2 : 1. Their balance sheet on the date of dissolution was as follows :

Liabilities		*(A)*	*Assets*	*(A)*
Capital Account : A	5,000		Plant and Machinery	8,000
B	3,000		Motor Car	2,000
C	2,000	10,000	Stock	2,800
Current Accounts : A	500		Debtors	6,000
B	1,500	2,000	Cash	150
Loan		1,000	C's current A'c	450
Creditors		4,000		
Bank overdraft		2,400		
		19,400		19,400

X. Ltd. agreed to take over assets with the exception of debtors, cash and motor car for A 13,000. X Ltd . agreed to discharge purchase consideration by issuing A 3,000 6% preference shares at par, 100 equity shares of A 50 each at a premium of A 40 per share and the balance in cash.

Debtors realised A 4,200 and creditors were settled at A 3,900. B agreed to take over motor car at A 1,400. A agreed to discharge loan account. Equity shares were distributed in capital ratio and preference share were distributed in profit sharing ratio.

Prepare necessary ledger accounts. [CA. Inter]

Ans. : Loss on realisation A 100.

26. A, R and M were carrying on business in partnership sharing profits and losses in the ratio of 5 :

4 : 3 respectively. The trial balance of the firm as on 31.3.2008 was as the following :

	(A)	(A)
Plant	1,05,000	—
Stock	60,200	—
Sundry Debtors	85,000	—
Sundry Creditors	—	1,05,200
Capital A/cs :		
A	—	70,000
R	—	50,000
M	—	30,000
Drawings A/cs :		
A	30,000	—
R	25,000	—
M	20,000	—
Depreciation on Plant and Machinery	—	35,000
Trading Profit for the year	—	1,29,800
Cash at Bank	94,800	—
	4,20,000	4,20,000

Additional Information

Interest on Capital accounts at 10% on the amount standing to the credit of partners capital accounts at the beginning of the year was not provided before preparing the above trial balance

On 31.3.2008 they formed a Private Ltd. Company, ARM (P) Ltd. to take over the partnership business.

You are further informed as under :

(*i*) Plant and Machinery is to be transferred at A 80,000.

(*ii*) Equity shares of A 10 each of the company are to be issued to the partners at par in such numbers as to ensure that by reason of their shareholdings alone, they will have the same rights of sharing profits and losses as they had in the partnership. Balance, if any in their capital accounts, will be settled by giving 7½% preference Shares at par.

(*iii*) Before transferring the business, the partners withdrew by cash from partnership the following amounts over and above the drawings as shown in the trial balance : A–A 20,000; R–A 10,600; M–A 14,200.

(*iv*) All assets and liabilities except plant and machinery and the bank balance are to be transferred at value in the books of the partnership as at 31.3.2008.

You are required to prepare :

(*a*) Profit and Loss Adjustment for the year ending 31.3.2008.

(*b*) Capital Accounts showing all the adjustments required to dissolve the partnership.

[*CA (PE-II) November, 2002*]

Ans. : Profit on realisation A 10,000

27. X, Y and Z decide to dissolve their partnership firm on 31st March, 2008 when their balance sheet

stands as under :

Liabilities		(A)	*Assets*	(A)
Creditors		34,000	Cash at Bank	25,000
Capital accounts :			Debtors	62,000
X	1,20,000		Stock	37,000
Y	90,000		Tools	8,000
Z	60,000	2,70,000	Motor car	12,000
			Furniture	60,000
			Machinery	1,00,000
		3,04,000		3,04,000

Y and Z agree to form a new partnership to carry on the business and it is agreed that they will acquire from the old firm the following assets at amounts shown against them :

	(A)
Stock	40,000
Tools	5,000
Motor car	25,000
Furniture	78,000
Machinery	84,000
Goodwill	60,000

The partnership agreement of X, Y and Z provides that trading profits or losses will be divided among X, Y and Z in the ratio of 3 : 2 : 1 respectively and that capital profits or losses will be divided in proportion of their capitals.

Debtors realise A 59,000 and discount amounting to A 720 are secured on payments due to creditors.

Prepare the necessary accounts of X, Y and Z giving effect to these transactions and also prepare the opening balance sheet of Y and Z who bring the necessary cash in the ratio of 3:2 respectively to pay to X.

[*CS (F) Dec. 2003*]

Ans. : Profit on realisation A 72,720

28. A, B and C share profits and losses in the ratio of 5 : 3 : 2. Their firm was dissolved due to misconduct of B and their balance sheet on that date was as under :

Balance Sheet as at 31.3.2008

Liabilities		(A)	*Assets*	(A)
Capital Accounts :			Land and Building	2,00,000
A	3,00,000		Plant	2,00,000
B	2,00,000		Sundry Debtors	50,000
C	1,00,000	6,00,000	Stock	1,50,000
Current Accounts :			Bills Receivable	50,000
A	50,000		Cash	1,00,000
B	30,000	80,000	Current Account :	
Sundry Creditors		40,000	C	50,000
Bills Payable		80,000		

	8,00,000		8,00,000

The whole business of the firm was sold to X Company Limited, on that day on the following terms :

(*i*) X Company Limited will issue the following securities in consideration for transfer of business : 10,000 equity shares @ A 15 each; 15,000 preference shares @ A 15 each; and 20,000 debentures @ A 14.725 each.

(*ii*) The agreed value of assets and liabilities of partnership firm are as follows :

Land & Building A 3,00,000; Plants : A 1,50,000; Sundry Debtors : A 47,500; Stock : A 1,40,000; Bills Receivable : A 50,000; Sundry Creditors : s. 38,000 and Bills Payable : A 80,000.

C was admitted to the partnership firm on 1.4.2005 and paid goodwill premium for her share of A30,000 based on 5 years purchase of super profit method. A and B were sharing profits in equal ratio before C's admission. It is mutually decided that preference shares will be distributed in profit sharing ratio and debentures and cash will be shared equally by all the partners.

Prepare the necessary accounts to close the books of the firm. [*B.Com. (Hons.) Delhi University*]

Ans. : Profit on realisation A 39,500

PIECEMEAL DISTRIBUTION

29. Leela, Sweta and Shyama are in partnership. They share profits in the ratio of 5 : 3 : 2. The following is their balance sheet as at 31st March, 2006 on which date they dissolved partnership.

Liabilities		*(A)*	*Assets*	*(A)*
Creditors		2,00,000	Premises	2,00,00
Loan Account : Leela		50,000	Plant and Machinery	1,50,000
Capital accounts :			Furniture	68,500
Leela	2,50,000		Stock	2,04,000
Sweta	75,000		Debtors	1,77,500
Shyama	2,25,000	5,50,000		
		8,00,000		8,00,000

It was agreed to repay the amounts due to the partners as and when the assets were realized, *viz* :

	(A)
1st May, 2008	1,50,000
1st July, 2008	3,65,000
1st September, 2008	2,35,000

Prepare a statement showing the distribution of cash using maximum loss method and write up the cash account. [*B.Com. (Hons.) Delhi, CS June 2007*]

Ans. : Unpaid amount Leela : A 25,000; Sweta : A 15,000; Shyama : A 10,000

30. The firm if LMS was dissolved on 31 March at which date its balance sheet stood as follows :

Liabilities	*(A)*	*Assets*	*(A)*
Creditors	2,00,000	Fixed Assets	45,00,000
Bank Loan	5,00,000	Cash and Bank	2,00,000
L's Loan	10,00,000		
Capitals :			
L	15,00,000		
M	10,00,000		
S	5,00,000		

	47,00,000		47,00,000

Partners share profits equally. A firm of chartered accountants is retained to realise the assets and distribute the cash after discharge of liabilities. Their fees which are to include all expenses is fixed at A 1,00,000. No loss is expected on realisation since fixed assets include valuable land and building. Realisations are :

S.No.	A
1.	5,00,000
2.	15,00,000
3.	15,00,000
4.	30,00,000
5.	30,00,000

The chartered accountants firm decided to pay off partners in Higher Relative Capital Method. Prepare a statement showing distribution of cash with necessary workings.

[CA (Inter) November 1995]

31. A, B and C sharing profits in the ratio of 3 : 2 : 1 decided to dissolved the partnership firm on 31.12.2008. Their balance sheet on that date was as follows :

Liabilities		*(A)*	*Assets*		*(A)*
Capital Accounts			Cash		10,000
A	49,000		Other Assets		90,000
B	21,000		Drawings		
C	10,000	80,000	A	10,000	
Reserve		12,000	B	10,000	
Secured loan		18,000	C	5,000	25,000
Bills Payable		10,000			
Creditors		5,000			
		1,25,000			1,25,000

Additional Information

(*i*) Realisation Expenses : Estimated A 4,000, Actual A 5,000.

(*ii*) Assets Realised : 15.1.2009 : A 20,000; 31.1.2009 : A 4,000; 10.2.2009 A 27,000; and 19.2.2009 A 26,000.

Prepare a statement showing distribution of cash by applying :

(*a*) Proportionate Capital Method

(*b*) Maximum Loss Method *[B.Com.(Hons.), Delhi University]*

Appendix

OBJECTIVE TYPE QUESTIONS

Note : The Objective Type Questions have been selected from B.Com. (Hons.)/B. Com. examination of University of Delhi and C.A., I.C.W.A. examinations.

SECTION I : TRUE/FALSE QUESTIONS

State whether the following statements are True and False :

1. An expenditure intended to benefit the current period is a revenue expenditure.
2. Receipts and payments account is a summary of all capital receipts and payments.
3. Expenditure which results in the acquisition of a permanent asset of ending benefit to the business is a capital expenditure.
4. Sale of office furniture should be credited to sales account.
5. Errors of principle will affect the Trial Balance.
6. The balance in the Petty Cash Book represents expense.
7. Goodwill is not a fictitious asset.
8. Profit and Loss Account shows the financial position of the concern.
9. Capital = Net Assets
10. Patent rights is in the nature of nominal account.
11. Land is also depreciable asset.
12. Amount written off from the cost of fixed assets is capital expenditure.
13. Rectification of mistake is necessary to tally the Trial Balance.
14. Capital is all assets less fictitious assets.
15. Wages paid for erection of machinery are debited to Profit & Loss Account.
16. Subsidiary books are also called books of original entry.
17. Cash Purchase are recorded in the cash book in the name of the supplier.
18. A tallied trial balance means that the books of accounts contain no errors.
19. Expenditure incurred to keep the machine in working condition is a capital expenditure.
20. A Joint venture business has a definite life.
21. Expenses incurred to keep the machine in working condition is a capital expenditure.
22. Accrual concept implies accounting on cash basis.

23. Depreciation cannot be provided in case of loss in a financial year.
24. Prudence is a concept to recognise unrealised profits and not losses.
25. The receipts and payments accountant records receipts and payments of revenue nature only.
26. Provision for depreciation in accounts reduces the amount available for dividends.
27. Legal expenses incurred in an action for infringement of its trade mark is a capital expenditure.
28. Goodwill is a fictitious asset.
29. Revenue should be recognised only when cash is received.
30. First In First Out (FIFO) method of inventory valuation is most suitable under inflationary conditions.
31. All assets and liabilities not taken over by the vendee company are transferred to capital accounts of the partners.
32. The Hire Vendor has to refund the amount of instalments received on repossession of goods in the case of default by the buyer.
33. Under debtors system, branch account is debited with losses like bad debts, discount allowed and depreciation.
34. No method of depreciation accurately calculates the charge to be made in respect of the asset.
35. An expenditure which is unreasonably large is capital expenditure.
36. A business entity can keep its account on accrual basis of accounting.
37. Legal Fees paid to acquire a property is capital expenditure.
38. Higher depreciation will not affect cash profit of the business.
39. Receipts and Payments Account highlights total income and expenditure.
40. Deferred revenue expenditure is current year's revenue expenditure to be paid in later years.
41. All capital expenditures associated with a particular asset are added to the cost of the asset.
42. The depreciation process does not set aside any cash for the replacement of an asset.
43. The terms depreciation, depletion and amortization mean the same thing.
44. The depreciation is an appropriation of profit when sinking fund is maintained.
45. Under written down value method, the asset gets reduced to zero.
46. Depreciation cannot be provided in case of loss in a financial year.
47. Providing depreciation in the accounts reduces the amount of profit available for dividend.
48. M/s Ram & Co. did not provide any depreciation on Plant and Machinery, as its market value is much higher than the cost price.
49. There exists difference between the written down the value method and diminishing balance method of depreciation.
50. The expressions–depreciation is to be charged at 10% and 10% p.a. on furniture and fittings–carry the same meaning.
51. Higher depreciation will not affect cash profit of the business.
52. There is no difference between the written down value method and diminishing balance method of depreciation.
53. Land is also depreciable asset.

54. Depreciation is a cash expenditure like other normal expenses.
55. Depreciation is a process of allocation of the cost of fixed asset.
56. Large amounts spent on any item are always capital expenditure.
57. Repairs to a second hand mother car before it is put to use are capitalised.
58. Embezzlement of cash by an employee is a capital loss.
59. The construction of temporary huts for labour by a builder in connection with the construction of a college building constitutes capital expenditure.
60. Compensation paid to employees under voluntary retirement scheme is a capital expenditure.
61. Balance sheet is an account.
62. Depreciation given in the trial balance is transferred to profit and loss account.
63. Income Tax is deducted from the capital in the final accounts of a sole trader.
64. Premium paid on life insurance policy is treated as business expense.
65. The withdrawals of goods by the proprietor are deducted from the purchases at the sale price.
66. The debts written off as bad, if recovered subsequently, are credited to debtors account.
67. Good will is a fictitious asset.
68. When closing stock is given in the trial balance, it is shown in the balance sheet only.
69. Manufacturing account is prepared to calculate gross profit.
70. A withdrawal of cash from the business by the proprietor should be charged to profit and loss account as an expense.
71. Profit and Loss Account shows the financial position of the concern.
72. Fixed Assets are stated in the Balance Sheet at their market value.
73. A Profit and Loss Account is a point statement whereas a Balance Sheet is period statement.
74. Contingent liability is an ascertained liability but its amount and due date are indeterminate.
75. The provision of discount on Debtors is calculated before deducing the provision for doubtful debts from Debtors.
76. Profit and loss account shows the financial position of the concern.
77. The provision for discount on debtors in calculated after deducting the provision for doubtful debts from Debtors.
78. Provision for Bad debts is debited to Sundry Debtors Account.
79. Freight paid on purchases of goods is added to the amount of purchases.
80. The debit balance in the Profit and Loss Account is surplus.
81. Capital is all assets less fictitious assets.
82. Debit Balance of Profit and Loss Account is a real Asset.
83. Under the 'Liquidity Approach', assets which are most liquid are presented at the bottom of the Balance Sheet.
84. Deferred revenue expenditure is current year' revenue expenditure to be paid in later years.
85. An expenditure intended to benefit the current period is a revenue expenditure.
86. Discount on bills receivable received as an advance is debited to consignment account.

87. Consignee is responsible for loss of goods-in-transit.
88. Unsold goods with consignee must be included in the ending inventory of the consignor.
89. Abnormal loss is credited to consignment account.
90. Consignment transaction is similar to goods sold on sale or return basis
91. The relationship between the consignor and the consignee is that of a principal and Agent.
92. In consignment, the goods are dispatched on the basis the goods will be sold on behalf of, at the expense of and at the risk of the consignee.
93. Account Sales is the statement sent by the consignor to the consignee.
94. *Del credere* commission is normally calculated on total sales.
95. If the consignee is not authorised to get the *del credere* commission, then he is liable for all losses on account of non-recovery of debts.
96. Loss of stock is said to be normal loss when such loss is not due to inherent characteristics of the commodities.
97. Consignee has no right in the profit on goods sent on consignment.
98. In a consignment transaction ownership of the goods remains with the consignor.
99. The party to whom goods are sent is called 'Consignee'.
100. Overriding commission is paid only on credit sales.
101. Joint venture is a particular partnership.
102. Persons participating in a joint venture are called partners.
103. A joint venture has a limited life.
104. Joint bank account is prepared to record the expenses on joint venture.
105. When a co-venture takes goods at the completion of the venture, purchases account is debited when records are being maintained separately.
106. A joint venture is also known as joint trade.
107. Joint bank account is opened when no separate books are kept.
108. A joint venture business has a definite life.
109. Joint venture is a very short duration business mainly confined to single deal entered into by two or more persons jointly.
110. A joint venture is partnership under partnership Act.
111. A joint venture business does not have a definite life.
112. Receipts and Payments Account is a summary of all capital receipts and payments.
113. The receipts and payments account records receipts and payments of revenue nature only.
114. If there appears a sports fund, the expenses incurred on sports activities will be taken into income and expenditure account.
115. Receipts and Payments Account highlights total income and expenditure account.
116. Scholarship granted to students out of funds provided by Government will be debited to Income and Expenditure Account.
117. Income and Expenditure Account is a real account.

118. Entrance fees when capitalised are shown in the Liabilities side of the balance sheet.
119. Subscriptions in advance in the current accounting period are treated as assets of the Non-For-Profit organisation.
120. In case there is a Prize Fund, any income received or accrued from this fund would be added to Prize Fund Account.
121. Receipts from the sale of an old asset is treated as an ordinary income.
122. Trial balance is an account.
123. The trial balance is prepared primarily to check the arithmetical accuracy of the double entry.
124. Errors of principle are not disclosed by the trial balance.
125. Trial balance is prepared after preparing the Profit and Loss Account but before the preparation of the balance sheet.
126. Trial balance is prepared on a particular date.
127. Errors of recording in the books of original entry will affect the trial balance
128. Compensating error is disclosed by the trial balance.
129. A trial balance will agree if the balance of an account is not listed at all in the trial balance.
130. Goodwill is a current asset.
131. The error of principle is caused due to incorrect allocation of expenses.
132. Accommodation bill is used without a trade transaction and is for mutual benefit.
133. Cash received from Kishor will be debited to his account.
134. Balances on personal accounts are carried forward to the next year.
135. Single Entry System does not recognize two effects of a transaction.
136. Joint Venture is a permanent partnership.
137. Wages paid for installation should be debited to wages account.
138. Subsidiary books are also called books of original entry.
139. Cash book is both a subsidiary book and ledger account.
140. The double column cash book records cash as well as bank transactions.
141. A contra entry is made in the cash book when the owner introduces additional capital.
142. Cash discount is given on credit sales.
143. Trade discount is allowed for prompt payments by the customers.
144. A business enterprise would record purchase of furniture in the purchases day book.
145. A builder would record sale of building in journal proper.
146. Cash book is called a journalised ledger.
147. Imprest system permits the petty cashier to retain certain sum every day.
148. Sales returns are always recorded in the journal proper.
149. A credit note is issued by the seller to the buyer.
150. Opening entry need not be posted.
151. Cash purchases are recorded in the cash book in the name of the supplier.

152. Payment received from a customer is recorded in the sales account.
153. Loan taken for 5 years is a current liability.
154. Error of Principle affects the Trial Balance.
155. P&L A/c is for a period of time.
156. Consignee is the owner of consignment stock.
157. Joint Venture is a Temporary partnership.
158. Income received is an asset.
159. Goodwill is fictitious asset.
160. If the consignee gets del-credere commission, loss of bad debt is borne by him.
161. The profit and loss account shows the profitability of a business enterprise and is dated as of particular date, such as March 31, 2012.
162. All of the steps in the accounting cycle are performed only at the end of the accounting period.
163. A transaction must be journalized in the journal before it can be posted to the ledger accounts.
164. The left side of any account is the credit side.
165. Revenues, liabilities, and Capital accounts are increased by debits.
166. The Dividends account is increased by debits.
167. If the trial balance has equal debit and credit totals, it cannot contain any errors.
168. Every adjusting entry affects at least one income statement account and one balance sheet account.
169. All calender years are also fiscal years, but not all fiscal years are calendar years.
170. The accumulated depreciation account is an asset account that shows the amount of depreciation for the current year only.
171. The Unearned Delivery Fees account is a revenue account.
172. If all of the adjusting entries are not made, the financial statements are incorrect.
173. At the end of the accounting period, three trial balances are prepared.
174. The amounts in the Adjustments columns are always added to the amounts in the Trial Balance Columns to determine the amounts in the Adjusted Trial Balance columns.
175. If a net loss occurs, it appears in the Income Statement credit column.
176. After the closing process is complete, no balance can exist in any revenue, Dividends or Income Summary account.
177. The post-closing trial balance may contain revenue and expense accounts.
178. All accounting systems currently in use are computerized.
179. The business entity concept assumes that each business has an existence separate from all parties except its owners.
180. When the substance of a transaction differs from its legal form, the accountant should record the economic substance.
181. The matching principle is fundamental to the accrual basis of accounting.
182. Exceptions to the realization principle include the installment basis of revenue recognition for sales revenue and the completed-contract method for long-term construction projects.

183. Immaterial items do not have to be recorded at all.
184. Depreciation is the process of valuation of an asset to arrive at its market value.
185. The cost of land includes its purchase price and other related costs, including the cost of removing an old unusable building that is on the land.
186. A business entity can keep its accounts on accrual basis of accounting.
187. Legal Fees paid to acquire a property is capital expenditure.
188. Higher depreciation will not affect cash profit of the business.
189. Receipts and Payments Account highlights total income and expenditure.
190. Deferred revenue expenditure is current year's revenue expenditure to be paid in later years.
191. Expenses incurred to keep the machine in working condition is a capital expenditure.
192. Accrual concept implies accounting on cash basis.
193. Depreciation cannot be provided in case of loss in a financial year.
194. Prudence is a concept to recognise unrealised profits and not losses.
195. The receipts and payments account records receipts and payments of revenue nature only.
196. Heavy expenditure incurred on advertisement at the time of introducing a new product is Revenue expenditure.
197. Expenses incurred to keep the machine in working condition is a capital expenditure.
198. Depreciation cannot be provided in case of loss, in a financial year.
199. Legal fees paid to acquire a property is Capital Expenditure.
200. Cash Account may have credit balance also.
201. Interest is calculated on the hire-purchase price at the given rate of interest.
202. Periodic inventory gives a continuous balance of stock in hand.
203. The issue of shares at a discount must be authorised by a special resolution of the company.
204. At the end of the accounting period the balance of "Goods sent to Branch account" is transferred to trading account.
205. Operating or Finance lease comes under provision of AS-13.
206. For life business premium income is to be recognized on receipt basis.
207. A Banking company cannot grant any loans on securities of its own shares.
208. A change in the accounting policy should be made when the statute so requires.
209. In consignment sales, revenue should be recognised when the goods are sold to third party.
210. As per AS-10 when a fixed asset is revalued, other assets should not be revalued.
211. Outstanding rent, if shown in the Trial Balance, it would appear in the debit side of the trial balance.
212. Bonus shares can be issued out of Capital Redemption Reserve even before the redemption of Preference Shares.
213. Preference shares may be redeemed from the securities premium.
214. Life membership fee may be capitalized and shown in Balance Sheet in liabilities side.
215. R and S divided profit in the ratio of 3 : 2. T is admitted for 1/5 the share in the business. The new profit sharing ratio will be 3 : 2 : 1.

216. As per AS-2 inventory is valued at the lower of net realizable value and current replacement cost.
217. The contract of insurance is a contract of guarantee.
218. The three forms of business organizations are single proprietorship, partnership, and trust.
219. The three types of business activity are service, merchandising, and manufacturing.
220. The income statement shows the profitability of the company and is dated as of a particular date, such as December 31, 2012.
221. The statement of retained earnings shows both the net income for the period and the beginning and ending balances of retained earnings.
222. The balance sheet contains the same major headings as appear in the accounting equation.
223. All off the steps in the accounting cycle are performed only at the end of the accounting period.
224. A transaction must be journalized in the journal before it can be posted to the ledger accounts.
225. The left side of any account is the credit side.
226. Revenues, liabilities, and Capital Stock accounts are increased by debits.
227. The Dividends account is increased by debits.
228. If the trial balance has equal debit and credit totals, it cannot contain any errors.
229. Every adjusting entry affects at least one income statement account and one balance sheet account.
230. All calendar years are also fiscal years, but not all fiscal years are calendar years.
231. The accumulated depreciation account is an asset account that shows the amount of depreciation for the current year only.
232. The Unearned Delivery Fees account is a revenue account.
233. If all of the adjusting entries are not made, the financial statements are incorrect.
234. At the end of the accounting period, three trial balances are prepared.
235. The amounts in the Adjustments columns are always added to the amounts in the Trial Balance columns to determine the amounts in the Adjusted Trial Balance columns.
236. If a net loss occurs, it appears in the Income Statement credit column and Statement of Retained Earnings debit column.
237. After the closing process is complete, no balance can exist in any revenue, expense, Dividends, or Income Summary account.
238. The post-closing trial balance may contain revenue and expense accounts.
239. All accounting systems currently in use are computerized.
240. The business entity concept assumes that each business has an existence separate from all parties except its owners.
241. When the substance of a transaction differs from its legal form, the accountant should record the economic substance.
242. The matching principle is fundamental to the accrual basis of accounting.
243. Exceptions to the realization principle include the installment basis of revenue recognition for sales revenue and the completed-contract method for long-term construction projects.
244. Immaterial items do not have to be recorded at all.
245. The conceptual framework project of IASB resulted in identifying two primary qualitative

characteristics that accounting information should possess–relevance and reliability.

246. Overstated ending inventory results in an overstatement of cost of goods sold and an understatement of gross margin and net income.

247. In a period of rising prices, FIFO results in the lowest cost of goods sold.

248. Under LCM, inventory is written down to market value when the market value is less than the cost, and inventory is written up to market value when the market value is greater than the cost.

249. Under perpetual procedure, cost of goods sold is determined as a result of the closing entries made at the end of the period.

250. The cost of land includes its purchase price and other related costs, including the cost of removing an old unusable building that is on the land.

251. Depreciation is the process of valuation of an asset to arrive at its market value.

252. The purpose of depreciation accounting is to provide the cash required to replace plant assets.

253. Expenditures made on plant assets that increase the quality of services are debited to the Accumulated Depreciation account.

254. Plant asset subsidiary ledgers are used to increase control over plant assets.

255. When a plant asset is still being used after it has been fully depreciated, depreciation can be taken in excess of its cost.

256. In an exchange of dissimilar assets, the new asset is recorded at the fair market value of the asset received or the fair market value of the asset given up plus cash paid, whichever is more clearly evident.

257. In calculating depletion, the residual value of acquired land containing an ore deposit is included in total costs subject to depletion.

258. All recorded intangible assets are subject to amortization.

SECTION I : ANSWER TO TRUE/FALSE QUESTIONS

1.	True	15.	False	29.	False	43.	False	57.	True	71.	False
2.	False	16.	True	30.	False	44.	False	58.	True	72.	False
3.	True	17.	False	31.	False	45.	False	59.	True	73.	False
4.	False	18.	False	32.	False	46.	False	60.	False	74.	False
5.	False	19.	False	33.	False	47.	True	61.	False	75.	False
6.	False	20.	True	34.	True	48.	False	62.	True	76.	False
7.	False	21.	False	35.	False	49.	False	63.	True	77.	True
8.	False	22.	False	36.	True	50.	False	64.	False	78.	False
9.	True	23.	False	37.	True	51.	True	65.	False	79.	True
10.	False	24.	False	38.	True	52.	True	66.	False	80.	False
11.	False	25.	False	39.	False	53.	False	67.	False	81.	False
12.	False	26.	True	40.	False	54.	False	68.	True	82.	False
13.	False	27.	False	41.	True	55.	True	69.	False	83.	False
14.	False	28.	False	42.	True	56.	False	70.	False	84.	False

85. True
86. False
87. False
88. True
89. True
90. False
91. True
92. False
93. False
94. True
95. False
96. False
97. True
98. True
99. True
100. False
101. True
102. False
103. True
104. False
105. False
106. True
107. False
108. True
109. True
110. False
111. False
112. False
113. False
114. False
115. False
116. False
117. False
118. True
119. False
120. True
121. False
122. False
123. False
124. True
125. False
126. True
127. False
128. False
129. False
130. False
131. False
132. True
133. False
134. True
135. True
136. False
137. False
138. True
139. True
140. False
141. False
142. False
143. False
144. False
145. False
146. True
147. False
148. False
149. True
150. False
151. False
152. False
153. False
154. False
155. True
156. False
157. True
158. False
159. False
160. True
161. False
162. False
163. True
164. False
165. False
166. True
167. True
168. True
169. True
170. False
171. False
172. False
173. True
174. False
175. True
176. True
177. False
178. False
179. False
180. True
181. True
182. False
183. False
184. False
185. True
186. True
187. True
188. True
189. False
190. False
191. False
192. False
193. False
194. False
195. False
196. False
197. False
198. False
199. True
200. False
201. False
202. False
203. False
204. True
205. False
206. False
207. True
208. True
209. True
210. True
211. False
212. False
213. False
214. True
215. False
216. False
217. False
218. False
219. True
220. False
221. True
222. True
223. False
224. True
225. False
226. False
227. True
228. False
229. True
230. True
231. False
232. False
233. True
234. True
235. False
236. True
237. True
238. False
239. False
240. False
241. True
242. True
243. False
244. False
245. False
246. False
247. True
248. False
249. False
250. True
251. False
252. False
253. False
254. True
255. False
256. True
257. False
258. True

SECTION II : MULTIPLE CHOICE QUESTIONS

Select the best answer for each of the following multiple choice questions.

1. The economic resources that a business owns and expects to be useful to the enterprise are called.

   (*a*) Assets
   (*b*) Liabilities
   (*c*) Owner's equity
   (*d*) Receivables

2. A business has assets of Rs. 1,40,000 and liabilities of Rs. 60.000. How much is its owner's equity?

   (*a*) $0
   (*b*) $80,000
   (*c*) $140,000
   (*d*) $200,000

3. The purchase of office supplies (or any other asset) on account will
   (*a*) Increase an asset and increase a liability
   (*b*) Increase an asset and increase owner's equity
   (*c*) Increase one asset and decrease another asset
   (*d*) Increase an asset and decrease a liability
4. The performance of service for a customer or client and immediate receipt of cash will
   (*a*) Increase on asset and decrease another asset
   (*b*) Increase an asset and increase owner's equity
   (*c*) Decrease an asset and decrease a liability
   (*d*) Increase an asset and increase a liability
5. The payment of an account payable (or any other liability) will
   (*a*) Increase one asset and decrease another asset
   (*b*) Decrease an asset and decrease owner's equity
   (*c*) Decrease an asset and decrease a liability
   (*d*) Increase an asset and increase a liability
6. The business document that reports assets, liabilities, and owner's equity is called the
   (*a*) Financial statement
   (*b*) Balance sheet
   (*c*) Income statement
   (*d*) Statement of owner's equity
7. The financial statement that are dated for a time period (rather than a specific time) are the
   (*a*) Balance sheet and income statement
   (*b*) Balance sheet and statement of owner's equity
   (*c*) Income statement and statement of owner's equity
   (*d*) All financial statements are dated for a time period.
8. An account has two sides called the
   (*a*) Debit and credit
   (*b*) Asset and liability
   (*c*) Revenue and expense
   (*d*) Journal and ledger
9. Increases in liabilities are recorded by
   (*a*) Debits
   (*c*) Credits
10. Why do accountants record transactions in the journal?
    (*a*) To ensure that all transactions are posted to the ledger
    (*b*) To ensure that total debits equal total credits
    (*c*) To have a chronological record of all transactions
    (*d*) To help prepare the financial statements.
11. Posting is the process of transferring information from the
    (*a*) Journal to the trial balance
    (*b*) Ledger to the trial balance

(*c*) Ledger to the financial statements

(*d*) Journal to the ledger

12. The purchase of land for cash is recorded by a

(*a*) Debit to Cash and a credit to Land

(*b*) Debit to Cash and a debit to Land

(*c*) Debit to Land and a debit to Land

(*d*) Credit to Cash and a credit to Land

13. The purpose of the trial balance is to

(*a*) Indicate whether total debits equal total credits

(*b*) Ensure that all transactions have been recorded

(*c*) Speed the collection of cash receipts from customers.

(*d*) Increase assets and owner's equity

14. What is the normal balance of the Accounts Receivable, Office Supplies, and Rent Expense accounts?

(*a*) Debit (*b*) Credit

15. A business has Cash of Rs. 3,000, Notes Payable of 2,500. Accounts Payable of Rs. 4,300, Service Revenue of Rs. 7,000, and Rent Expense of Rs. 1,8000. Based on these data, how much are its total liabilities?

(*a*) Rs. 5,500 (*c*) 9,800

(*b*) Rs. 6,800 (*d*) Rs. 13,800

16. The earning of revenue that is no received in cash is recorded by a

(*a*) Debit to Cash and a credit to Revenue

(*b*) Debit to Accounts Receivable and a credit to Revenue

(*c*) Debit to Accounts Payable and a credit to Revenue

(*d*) Debit to Revenue and a credit to Accounts Receivable

17. The account credited for a receipt of cash on account is

(*a*) Cash (*c*) Service Revenue

(*b*) Accounts Payable (*d*) Accounts Receivable

18. Accrual-basis accounting

(*a*) Results in higher income than cash-basis accounting

(*b*) Leads to the reporting of more complete information than does cash-basis accounting

(*c*) Is not acceptable under GAAP

(*d*) Omits adjusting entries at the end of the period

19. Under the revenue principle, revenue is recorded

(*a*) At the earliest acceptable time

(*b*) At the latest acceptable time

(*c*) After it has been earned, but not before

(*d*) At the end of the accounting period

20. The matching principle provides guidance in accounting for
    (*a*) Expenses
    (*b*) Owner's equity
    (*c*) Assets
    (*d*) Liabilities

21. Adjusting entries
    (*a*) Assign revenues to the period in which they are earned
    (*b*) Help to properly measure the period's net income or net loss
    (*c*) Bring asset and liability accounts to correct balances
    (*d*) All of the above.

22. A law firm began November with office supplies of Rs. 160. During the month, the firm purchased supplies of Rs. 290. At November 30 supplies on hand total Rs. 210. Supplies expense for the period is
    (*a*) Rs. 210
    (*b*) Rs. 240
    (*c*) Rs. 290
    (*d*) Rs. 450

23. A building that cost Rs. 120,000 has accumulated depreciation of Rs. 50,000. The book value of the building is
    (*a*) Rs. 50,000
    (*b*) Rs. 70,000
    (*c*) Rs. 120,000
    (*d*) Rs. 170,000

24. The adjusting entry to accrue salary expense
    (*a*) Debits Salary Expense and credits Cash
    (*b*) Debits Salary Payable and credits Salary Expense
    (*c*) Debits Salary Payable and credits Cash
    (*d*) Debits Salary Expense and credits Salary Payable

25. A business received cash of Rs. 3,000 in advance for revenue that will be earned later. The cash receipt entry debited Cash and credited Unearned Revenue for Rs. 3,000. At the end of the period, Rs. 1,100 is still unearned. The adjusting entry for this situation will
    (*a*) Debit Unearned Revenue and credit Revenue for Rs. 1,900
    (*b*) Debit Unearned Revenue and credit Revenue for Rs. 1,100
    (*c*) Debit Revenue and credit Unearned Revenue for Rs. 1,900
    (*d*) Debit Revenue and credit Unearned Revenue for Rs. 1,100

26. The links between the financial statements are
    (*a*) Net income from the income statement to the statement of owner's equity
    (*b*) Ending capital from the statement of owner's equity to the balance sheet
    (*c*) Both of the above
    (*d*) None of the above

27. Accumulated Depreciation is reported on the
    (*a*) Balance Sheet
    (*b*) Income statement
    (*c*) Statement of owner's equity
    (*d*) Both a and b

28. The focal point of the accounting cycle is the

(*a*) Financial statements (*c*) Adjusted trial balance

(*b*) Trial balance (*d*) Work sheet

29. Which of the following accounts is not closed?

(*a*) Supplies Expense (*c*) Interest Revenue

(*b*) Prepaid Insurance (*d*) Owner Withdrawals

30. The closing entry for Salary Expense, with a balance of Rs. 322,000 is

(*a*)	Salary Expense	322,000	
	Income Summary		322,000
(*b*)	Salary Expense	322,000	
	Salary outstanding		322,000
(*c*)	Income Summary	322,000	
	Salary Expense		322,000
(*d*)	Salary Outstanding	322,000	
	Salary Expense		322,000

31. The purpose of the postclosing trial balance is to

(*a*) Provide the account balances for preparation of the balance sheet

(*b*) Ensure that the ledger is in balance for the start of the next period

(*c*) Aid the journalizing and posting of the closing entries

(*d*) Ensure that the ledger is in balance for completion of the work sheet

32. Which of the following accounts will appear on the postclosing trial balance?

(*a*) Building

(*b*) Depreciation Expense–Building

(*c*) Service Revenue

(*d*) Owner Withdrawals

33. The classification of assets and liabilities as current or long-term depends on

(*a*) Their order of listing in the general ledger

(*b*) Whether they appear on the balance sheet or the income statement

(*c*) The relative liquidity of the item

(*d*) The format of the balance sheet–account format or report format

34. Posting a Rs. 300 debit as a credit causes an error.

(*a*) That is evenly divisible by 9

(*b*) That is evenly divisible by 2

(*c*) In the journal

(*d*) Known as a transposition

35. The major expense of a merchandising business is

(*a*) Cost of goods sold (*c*) Rent

(*b*) Depreciation (*d*) Interest

36. Sales total Rs. 440,000, cost of goods sold is Rs. 210,000, and operating expenses are Rs. 1,60,000. How much is gross margin?

    (*a*) Rs. 440,000
    (*b*) Rs. 230,000
    (*c*) Rs. 210,000
    (*d*) Rs. 70,000

37. A purchase discount results from

    (*a*) Returning goods to the seller
    (*b*) Receiving a purchase allowance from the seller
    (*c*) Buying a large enough quantity of merchandise to get the discount
    (*d*) Paying within the discount period

38. Which one of the following pairs includes items that are the most similar?

    (*a*) Purchase discounts and purchase returns
    (*b*) Cost of goods sold and inventory
    (*c*) Net sales and sales discounts
    (*d*) Sales returns and sales allowances

39. Which of the following is *not* an account?

    (*a*) Sales revenue
    (*b*) Net sales
    (*c*) Inventory
    (*d*) Supplies expense

40. Cost of goods sold is computed by adding beginning inventory and net purchases and subtracting X. What is X?

    (*a*) Net sales
    (*b*) Sales discounts
    (*c*) Ending inventory
    (*d*) Net purchases

41. Which account causes the main difference between a merchandiser's adjusting and closing process and that of a service business?

    (*a*) Advertising Expense
    (*b*) Interest Revenue
    (*c*) Inventory
    (*d*) Accounts Receivable

42. The major item on a merchandiser's income statement that a service business does not have is

    (*a*) Cost of goods sold
    (*b*) Inventory
    (*c*) Net purchases
    (*d*) Net Sales

43. The closing entry for Sales Discounts is

    (*a*) Sales Discounts
    Income Summary
    (*b*) Sales Discounts
    Sales Revenue
    (*c*) Income Summary
    Sales Discounts
    (*d*) Not used because Sales Discounts is a permanent account, which is not closed.

44. Which of the following is *not* a correct form of the accounting equation?

    (*a*) Assets = Equalities
    (*b*) Assets = Liabilities + Stockholders' Equity
    (*c*) Assets – Liabilities = Stockholders' Equity

(*d*) Assets + Stockholders' Equity = Liabilities.

45. When the proprietors invest cash in the business, what is the effect?
(*a*) Liabilities increase and stockholders' equity increases
(*b*) Both assets and liabilities increase
(*c*) Both assets and stockholders' equity increase.
(*d*) None of the above.

46. The underlying assumptions of accounting include all the following except :
(*a*) Business entity
(*b*) Going concern
(*c*) Matching
(*d*) Money measurement and periodicity

47. The concept that requires all companies to use the same accounting practices and reporting practices through time is :
(*a*) Substance over form
(*b*) Consistency
(*c*) Articulation
(*d*) None of the above

48. Which of the following statements is false regarding the revenue recognition principle?
(*a*) Revenue must be substantially earned before it is recognized.
(*b*) The accountant usually recognizes revenue before the seller acquires the right to receive payment from the buyer.
(*c*) Some small companies use the cash basis of accounting.
(*d*) Under the installment basis, the gross margin recognized in a period is equal to the amount of cash received from installment sales times the gross margin percentage for the year of sale.

49. Accounting conventions include all of the following except.
(*a*) Periodicity
(*b*) Cost-benefit
(*c*) Materiality
(*d*) Conservation

50. Which of the following does *not* describe accounting?
(*a*) Language of business
(*b*) Is an end rather than a means to an end
(*c*) Useful for decision making
(*d*) Used by business, government, nonprofit organizations and individuals.

51. Purposes of an accounting system include all of the following *except :*
(*a*) Interpret and record the effects of business transactions.
(*b*) Classify the effects of transactions to facilitate the preparation of reports
(*c*) Summarize and communicate information to decision makers.
(*d*) Dictate the specific types of business transactions that the enterprise may engage in.

52. External users of financial accounting information include all the following *except :*
(*a*) Investors
(*b*) Labor unions
(*c*) Line managers
(*d*) General public

53. Financial accounting information is characterized by all of the following *except* :
    (*a*) It is historical in nature
    (*b*) It sometimes results from inexact and approximate measures.
    (*c*) It is factual, so it does not require judgment to prepare
    (*d*) It is enhanced by management's explanation.
54. According to the rules of debit and credit for balance sheet accounts :
    (*a*) Increases in asset, liability, and owners' equity accounts are recorded by debits.
    (*b*) Decreases in asset and liability accounts are recorded by credits.
    (*c*) Increases in asset and owners' equity accounts are recorded by debits.
    (*d*) Decreases in liability and owners' equity accounts are recorded by debits.
55. Which of the following is provided by a trial balance in which total debits equal total credits?
    (*a*) Proof that no transaction was completely omitted from the ledger during the posting process.
    (*b*) Proof that the correct debit or credit balance has been computed for each account.
    (*c*) Proof that the ledger is in balance.
    (*d*) Proof that transactions have been correctly analyzed and recorded in the proper accounts.
56. Which of the following explains the debit and credit rules relating to the recording of revenue and expenses?
    (*a*) Expenses appear on the left side of the balance sheet and are recorded by debits; revenue appears on the right side of the balance sheet and is recorded by credits.
    (*b*) Expenses appear on the left side of the income statement and are recorded by debits; revenue appears on the right side of the income statement and is recorded by credits.
    (*c*) The effects of revenue and expenses on owners' equity.
    (*d*) The realization principle and the matching principle.
57. The purpose of adjusting entries is to :
    (*a*) Adjust the Retained Earnings account for the revenue, expense, and dividends recorded during the accounting period.
    (*b*) Adjust daily the balances in asset, liability, revenue, and expense accounts for the effects of business transactions.
    (*c*) Apply the realization principle and the matching principle to transactions affecting two or more accounting periods.
    (*d*) Prepare revenue and expense accounts for recording the transactions of the next accounting period.
58. Which of the following financial statements is generally prepared first?
    (*a*) Income statement
    (*b*) Balance sheet
    (*c*) Statement of retained earnings
    (*d*) Statement of each flows.
59. Which of the following accounts would *never* be reported in the income statement as an expense?
    (*a*) Depreciation expense
    (*b*) Income taxes expense
    (*c*) Interest expense
    (*d*) Dividends expense

60. 'Brand Value' for a business is :
    (*a*) Capital
    (*b*) Asset
    (*c*) Profit
    (*d*) Liability

61. Sale of goods has :
    (*a*) Only Revenue effect
    (*b*) Only Expense effect
    (*c*) Both Revenue Effect and Expense Effect
    (*d*) None of the above

62. Error of omission means :
    (*a*) That errors are compensating each other
    (*b*) That any entry is totally missed
    (*c*) That there is a wrong entry in the books of accounts
    (*d*) That a transaction is recorded twice

63. Cash sales at exhibition hall are :
    (*a*) Recorded in Journal Proper
    (*b*) Recorded in Cash Book
    (*c*) Recorded in Sales Book
    (*d*) Not recorded

64. In case of an 'Unpresented Cheque' :
    (*a*) Bank Balance in Cash Book is more than Bank Passbook
    (*b*) Bank Balance in Cash Book is less than Bank Passbook
    (*c*) Either (a) or (b)
    (*d*) No effect in both the books

65. A Bill of Exchange is :
    (*a*) Drawn on a specific banker
    (*b*) Drawn by seller and accepted by banker
    (*c*) An unconditional undertaking signed by the maker
    (*d*) An unconditional order signed by the maker

66. Joint Venture Account is a
    (*a*) Nominal Account
    (*b*) Real Account
    (*c*) Artificial Personal Account
    (*d*) Representative Personal Account

67. The Abnormal Loss on Consignment is credited to :
    (*a*) Profit and Loss Account
    (*b*) Consignee's Account
    (*c*) Consignment Account
    (*d*) Insurance Company Account

68. A Capital Reserve is built out of
    (*a*) Recurring profits
    (*b*) Non-recurring profits
    (*c*) Revenue
    (*d*) Reserve Fund

69. Till the discounted bill is paid by the acceptor, it remains
    (*a*) A contingent liability
    (*b*) A liability
    (*c*) An expense
    (*d*) An asset

70. *Del Credere* Commission is allowed to cover the risk of
    (*a*) Theft (*c*) Fire
    (*b*) Bad Debts (*d*) Damage of goods in transit
71. The amount of yearly depreciation under diminishing balance method
    (*a*) Remains constant over the years (*b*) Decreases year after year
    (*c*) Increases year after year (*d*) Fluctuates
72. The credit purchases of fixed assets are recorded in
    (*a*) Purchase Book (*c*) Journal Proper
    (*b*) Cash Book (*d*) Sales Return Book
73. Expenses paid but not accrued means
    (*a*) Cash expenses (*c*) Outstanding expenses
    (*b*) Prepaid expenses (*d*) Capital expenses
74. When goods are purchased for the joint venture, the account to be debited is
    (*a*) Purchases account (*c*) Venturer's Capital account
    (*b*) Joint Venture account (*d*) Consignee's account
75. The total of discount column on the debit side of the Cash Boo, is posted to the
    (*a*) Credit of the discount allowed account (*b*) Debit of the discount received account
    (*c*) Credit of the discount received account (*d*) Debit of the discount allowed account
76. Goods purchased from Mr. Ajay for Rs. 10,000 passed through the Sales Book. The rectification will result in
    (*a*) Increase in gross profit (*c*) No effect on gross profit
    (*b*) Decrease in gross profit (*d*) Either A or B
77. Which of the following is not a negotiable instrument?
    (*a*) Bearer Cheque (*c*) Bill of Exchange
    (*b*) Promissory Note (*d*) Crossed Cheque
78. Transfer to Capital Redemption Reserve is not allowed from
    (*a*) General Reserve (*c*) Reserve Fund
    (*b*) Profit prior to incorporation (*d*) None of the above
79. Goodwill in case of joint stock company is shown under asset side under the heading
    (*a*) Fixed Assets (*c*) Current Assets
    (*b*) Investments (*d*) None of the above
80. Survey expenses for marine insurance claims must be
    (*a*) Added to claim (*c*) Added to Administrative
    (*b*) Added to legal charges (*d*) None of the above
81. A non-performing asset is
    (*a*) Money at call and short notices (*b*) An asset that ceases to generate income
    (*c*) Cash balance in till (*d*) None of the above

82. An amount spent for inauguration of new factory building is
 (*a*) Revenue Expenditure
 (*b*) Capital Expenditure
 (*c*) Prepaid Expenditure
 (*d*) None of the above

83. A profit on sale of furniture of a club will be taken to
 (*a*) Cash account
 (*b*) Receipt and Payment Account
 (*c*) Income and Expenditure Account
 (*d*) Profit and Loss Account

84. When interest on own debentures becomes due it will be credited to
 (*a*) Profit and Loss Account
 (*b*) Own Debentures Account
 (*c*) Debentures Interest Account
 (*d*) Interest on own Debentures Account

85. Profit prior to incorporation is transferred to
 (*a*) General Reserve
 (*b*) Capital Reserve
 (*c*) Profit and Loss Account
 (*d*) Development Reserve

86. Under instalment system of purchase, interest suspense account is debited with
 (*a*) The difference between instalment price and cash price.
 (*b*) Amount of interest included in each instalment.
 (*c*) Instalment price and discounted cash price.
 (*d*) Difference between Cash Price and Depreciated Value.

87. Free Reserves include
 (*a*) Securities Premium
 (*b*) Revaluation Reserve
 (*c*) Capital Reserve
 (*d*) All of the above

88. In the absence of an agreement amongst the partners, loan given by a partner to the firm will be at an interest at the rate of
 (*a*) 5%
 (*b*) 6%
 (*c*) 8%
 (*d*) 10%

89. Depreciation accounting is a process of
 (*a*) Apportionment
 (*b*) Valuation
 (*c*) Allocation
 (*d*) Appropriation

90. Which of the following is a Capital Expenditure
 (*a*) Freight and cartage on purchase of new machine.
 (*b*) Legal expenses in connection with defending a title to firm's property.
 (*c*) Expenditure on painting of factory shed.
 (*d*) Wages paid to machine operator.

91. AS-6 is related to :
 (*a*) Valuation of Inventories.
 (*b*) Accounting for Construction Contracts.
 (*c*) Cash Flow Statements
 (*d*) Depreciation accounting.

92. As per Section 17 of Banking Companies Act, an Indian Banking company prior to declaration of divident must transfer to reserve fund the following percentage of profit

(*a*) 10% (*c*) 25%

(*b*) 20% (*d*) 30%

93. Financial data is recorded by means of a system known as:

(*a*) Management accounting (*b*) Auditing

(*c*) Double-entry bookkeeping (*d*) Generaly Accepted Accounting Principles

94. Which of the following is a key indicator of performance for investors?

(*a*) Number of Shares issued by a company (*b*) Number of directors

(*c*) Ratio of customers to suppliers (*d*) Earnings per share

95. Once an accounting policy is adopted by a company, it:

(*a*) Must never be changed

(*b*) Must be changed on an annual basis

(*c*) Can be changed if another policy is more appropriate

(*d*) Can only be changed with the government's approval

96. If a company is said to be a 'going concern', which one of the following statements is certain about that company?

(*a*) It is about to go out of business

(*b*) It is assumed to be able to continue in business for the foreseeable future.

(*c*) It is a company that people are concerned about

(*d*) It is profitable and has more assets than liabilities

97. The 'accruals' concept means that, when calculating a company's profit or loss:

(*a*) All relevant transactions, whether or not cash transfers are involved, are included

(*b*) Any money owed by customers at the end of the period is ignored.

(*c*) Any invoices received but not paid in the period are ignored

(*d*) Only cash paid and received in a period is included.

98. Which one of the following is not a major category of financial information?

(*a*) Capital (*b*) Assets

(*c*) Income (*d*) Wages

99. Which of the following formulae would be used to establish the value of Capital at a specific moment in time?

(*a*) Assets + Liabilities (*b*) Assets – Liabilities

(*c*) Income – Expenditure (*d*) Assets – Expenditure

100. The first stage of the bookkeeping process is made in :

(*a*) The balance sheet (*b*) The bank statement

(*c*) A book of prime entry (*d*) The general ledger

101. The second stage of the bookkeeping process is made in :

(*a*) The ledger (*b*) A book of prime entry

(*c*) The profit and loss account (*d*) The balance sheet

102. Which one of the following is the closest definition to a 'financial year'?
   (*a*) A period of any length which ends on 31 December
   (*b*) A 12-month period ending on the last day of any month
   (*c*) A 12-month period ending on any day
   (*d*) A 12-month period ending on 31 December

103. If a business buys a machine for A10,000 with a cheque, what effect would that transaction have?
   (*a*) Only an increase in assets–nothing else
   (*b*) An increase in an asset and a decrease in another asset
   (*c*) An increase in an asset and an increase in a liability
   (*d*) An increase in an asset and a decrease in a liability.

104. A sale of goods where no invoice was issued would be first recorded in which one of the following :
   (*a*) Sales ledger (*b*) Sales journal
   (*c*) Purchase journal (*d*) Cash book

105. Accounts with more debit entries than credit entries are referred to as having 'debit balances': Which one of the following accounts is unlikely to have a 'debit balance'.
   (*a*) Sales account in the general ledger (*b*) Debtor's account in the sales ledger
   (*c*) Machinery account in the general ledger (*d*) Wages payable account in the general ledger

106. The 'personal ledgers' of a business are :
   (*a*) General and sales ledgers (*b*) Cash book and sales journal
   (*c*) General and purchase ledgers (*d*) Sales and purchase ledgers

107. Which one of the following assets would be classified as a *fixed* asset?
   (*a*) Stock of unsold goods (*b*) Motor lorry
   (*c*) Amounts owed by debtors (*d*) Bank balance

108. A financial period :
   (*a*) Always ends on 31 December (*b*) Always ends on 31 March
   (*c*) Is always twelve months long (*d*) Can start or end at any time.

109. A business has paid A 6,000 for electricity by the ends of its financial period but owes a fuerher A 1,000 for electricity used within that period. It did not owe anything for electricity at the start of the period. What relevant figure would be shown in that company's profit and loss account and balance sheet?
   (*a*) Profit and loss account expenses include A 7,000 and the balance sheet shows A 1,000 as a current liability.
   (*b*) Profit and loss account expenses include A 6,000 and the balance sheet shows A 1,000 as a current liability
   (*c*) Profit and loss account expenses include A 7,000 but there are no relevant entries in the balance sheet
   (*d*) Profit and loss account expenses include A 6,000 but there are no relevant entries in the balance sheet.

110. Straight line depreciation is calculated :

(*a*) By using the formula : $\frac{\text{Cost of the asset + Estimated value at end of asset's life}}{\text{Estimated life in years.}}$

(*b*) By applying the same % each year to the net book value of the asset

(*c*) By using the formula :

$$\frac{\text{Cost of the asset – Estimated value at end of asset's life}}{\text{Estimated life in years.}}$$

(*d*) By the directors deciding each year what the asset's value is at the balance sheet date, with the year's depreciation being the estimated fall in value since the previous year's valuation.

111. A theoretical stock valuation such as FIFO (First In First Out) would be used when :

(*a*) Stock has deteriorated to a point where it is unsaleable

(*b*) Stock is difficult or impossible to value by relating the stock to a price shown on a purchase invoice

(*c*) Stock has been bought just after the balance sheet date

(*d*) It is assumed that the most recent stock purchased is sold before older stock.

112. In a balance sheet, stock is unually valued :

(*a*) At average selling prices during the financial period

(*b*) At the selling prices on the date of the balance sheet

(*c*) At the higher of cost and net realizable value

(*d*) At the lower of cost and net realizable value.

113. The asset of 'debtors' included in the 'current assets' total in a balance sheet should contain :

(*a*) Good debts only

(*b*) All sales ledger balances

(*c*) All sales ledger balances less bad debts written off

(*d*) Bad and doubtful debts.

114. Which of the following might be shown in a partnership's profit and loss account, but not a sole trader's?

(*a*) Wages
(*b*) Interest charged on drawings
(*c*) Provision for depreciation
(*d*) Bank overdraft interest

115. Which of the following might be shown in a limited company's profit and loss account, but not a partnership's?

(*a*) Retained profits for the period
(*b*) Provision for doubtful debts
(*c*) Bad debts written off
(*d*) Provision for depreciation

116. If a company issues convertible loan stock, what is it normally convertible into at a later date?

(*a*) Cash
(*b*) Debentures
(*c*) Shares
(*d*) Reserves

117. Which one of the following would never be seen as the heading of a profit and loss account?

(*a*) Profit and loss account for the year ending 31 December 2012

(*b*) Profit and loss account for the year ending 29 December 2012 (*c*) Profit and loss account for the 52 weeks ending 29 December 2012

(*d*) Profit and loss account as at 31 December 2012

118. Revenue should be recognized only :

(*a*) When the product has been manufactured

(*b*) When sample products have been requested by a customer

(*c*) When the product has been delivered to the customer

(*d*) When the customer has accepted liability for paying for the product.

119. 'PBIT' is an acronym for :

(*a*) Profit before interest (*b*) Profit before income tax

(*c*) Profit before income and tax (*d*) Profit before interest and tax

120. Which one of the following statements is correct?

(*a*) A balance sheet shows the current value of a company

(*b*) A balance sheet shows the stock market value of a company

(*c*) A balance sheet shows the value as recorded in the books of a company

(*d*) A balance sheet shows the income and expenditure of a company.

121. Goodwill can only be shown in the balance sheet of the company if :

(*a*) If has been sold

(*b*) If has been generated internally

(*c*) It has been purchased

(*d*) It has an estiamted useful life of over twenty years.

122. Which one of the following is a tangible fixed asset?

(*a*) Goodwil (*b*) Leasehold property

(*c*) Brand names (*d*) Patents

SECTION II : ANSWER TO MULTIPLE CHOICE QUESTIONS

1. (*a*)	12. (*c*)	23. (*b*)	34. (*b*)	45. (*c*)	56. (*c*)
2. (*b*)	13. (*a*)	24. (*d*)	35. (*a*)	46. (*c*)	57. (*c*)
3. (*a*)	14. (*a*)	25. (*a*)	36. (*b*)	47. (*d*)	58. (*a*)
4. (*b*)	15. (*b*)	26. (*c*)	37. (*d*)	48. (*b*)	59. (*d*)
5. (*c*)	16. (*b*)	27. (*a*)	38. (*d*)	49. (*a*)	60. (*b*)
6. (*b*)	17. (*d*)	28. (*a*)	39. (*b*)	50. (*b*)	61. (*c*)
7. (*c*)	18. (*b*)	29. (*b*)	40. (*c*)	51. (*d*)	62. (*b*)
8. (*a*)	19. (*c*)	30. (*c*)	41. (*c*)	52. (*c*)	63. (*d*)
9. (*b*)	20. (*a*)	31. (*b*)	42. (*a*)	53. (*c*)	64. (*b*)
10. (*c*)	21. (*d*)	32. (*a*)	43. (*c*)	54. (*d*)	65. (*d*)
11. (*d*)	22. (*b*)	33. (*c*)	44. (*d*)	55. (*c*)	66. (*a*)

67.	(*c*)	77.	(*d*)	87.	(*a*)	96.	(*b*)	105.	(*a*)	114.	(*b*)
68.	(*b*)	78.	(*b*)	88.	(*b*)	97.	(*a*)	106.	(*d*)	115.	(*a*)
69.	(*a*)	79.	(*a*)	89.	(*c*)	98.	(*d*)	107.	(*b*)	116.	(*c*)
70.	(*b*)	80.	(*a*)	90.	(*a*)	99.	(*b*)	108.	(*d*)	117.	(*d*)
71.	(*b*)	81.	(*b*)	91.	(*d*)	100.	(*c*)	109.	(*a*)	118.	(*d*)
72.	(*c*)	82.	(*a*)	92.	(*b*)	101.	(*a*)	110.	(*c*)	119.	(*d*)
73.	(*b*)	83.	(*c*)	93.	(*c*)	102.	(*c*)	111.	(*b*)	120.	(*c*)
74.	(*b*)	84.	(*d*)	94.	(*d*)	103.	(*b*)	112.	(*d*)	121.	(*c*)
75.	(*d*)	85.	(*b*)	95.	(*c*)	104.	(*d*)	113.	(*a*)	122.	(*b*)
76.	(*b*)	86.	(*a*)								

SECTION III : FILL IN THE BLANKS QUESTION

Fill in the blanks

1. The ____________ balance in the bank column of the Cash Book indicates bank overdraft.
2. Expenditure is called ____________ expenditure, if the benefits from it extend to more than one year.
3. The ____________ discount is never entered in the books of accounts.
4. The burden of noting charges is ultimately borne by the ____________ of the bill.
5. Prepaid expenses appear on the ____________ side of the Balance Sheet.
6. Debtor is a person who ____________ money to the business.
7. Every debit has a ____________ credit.
8. Cash account never has ____________ balance.
9. Goodwill can be better explained as ____________ asset.
10. If the two sided of the trial balance tally, it is indication of the fact that the books of accounts are ____________ accurate.
11. As per AS-6 when there is a change in the method of providing depreciation, the differential amount of depreciation would have ____________ effect.
12. As per AS-6 when there is a change in the estimated useful life of the asset the, differential would be calculated ____________.
13. Profit on revaluation of assets on the admission of a new partner is to be credited to the old partners in their ____________ profit sharing ratio.
14. Amalgamation Adjustments Accounts is opened in the books of the transferee company to incorporate ____________.
15. When a new partner enters in the partnership firm and the partners decide to maintain the General Reserve in the books of the firm at its original value, the amount of general reserve is ____________ to the old partners and ____________ to all partners.
16. A company cannot redeem preference shares unless they are ____________ paid up.
17. Unclaimed dividend is shown under ____________ head in the Balance Sheet of a banking company.
18. Tax deducted at source, from interest on investment is shown under ____________ in Schedule VI.
19. Selling Commission is apportioned among departments in the ratio of ____________ of each department.

20. By products should be valued as lower of cost and net __________ value.
21. When minimum rent is more than Royalty the amount payable to landlord is the __________.
22. Where hire vendor reckons the profit on the basis of instalments received, the method is known as __________.
23. Excess of hire purchase price over __________ is treated as hire purchase charges.
24. Excess of minimum rent over royalties is termed as __________ .
25. Balance of preliminary expenses account is shown in Company's Balance Sheet under the head of __________ on assets side.
26. The "Average Clause" is applicable when the actual loss is __________ than the sum assured.
27. Turnover ratios are also known as __________ ratios.

SECTION III : ANSWER TO FILL IN THE BLANKS QUESTIONS

1. Credit
2. Deferred Revenue
3. Trade
4. Drawee/Acceptor
5. Asset
6. Owes
7. Corresponding
8. Credit
9. Intangible
10. Arithmetically
11. Retrospective
12. Prospective
13. Old
14. Statutory Reserve
15. Credited, Debited
16. Fully
17. Current Liabilities
18. Current Liabilities
19. Sales
20. Realisable
21. Short Working
22. Cash received basis profit
23. Cash price
24. Short Working
25. Miscellaneous expenditure
26. More
27. Velocity